# Lecture Notes in Computer Science 8796

Commenced Publication in 1973
Founding and Former Series Editors:
Gerhard Goos, Juris Hartmanis, and Jan van Leeuwen

Peter Mika   Tania Tudorache
Abraham Bernstein   Chris Welty
Craig Knoblock   Denny Vrandečić
Paul Groth   Natasha Noy
Krzysztof Janowicz   Carole Goble (Eds.)

# The Semantic Web – ISWC 2014

13th International Semantic Web Conference
Riva del Garda, Italy, October 19-23, 2014
Proceedings, Part I

 Springer

Volume Editors

*Peter Mika*, Yahoo Labs, Barcelona, Spain
E-mail: pmika@yahoo-inc.com

*Tania Tudorache*, Stanford University, CA, USA
E-mail: tudorache@stanford.edu

*Abraham Bernstein*, University of Zurich, Switzerland
E-mail: bernstein@ifi.uzh.ch

*Chris Welty*, IBM Research, Yorktown Heights, NY, USA
E-mail: welty@us.ibm.com

*Craig Knoblock*, University of Southern California, Los Angeles, CA, USA
E-mail: knoblock@isi.edu

*Denny Vrandečić, Natasha Noy*, Google, USA
E-mail: vrandecic@google.com; natashafn@acm.org

*Paul Groth*, VU University Amsterdam, The Netherlands
E-mail: p.t.groth@vu.nl

*Krzysztof Janowicz*, University of California, Santa Barbara, CA, USA
E-mail: jano@geog.ucsb.edu

*Carole Goble*, The University of Manchester, UK
E-mail: carole.goble@manchester.ac.uk

ISSN 0302-9743                           e-ISSN 1611-3349
ISBN 978-3-319-11963-2                   e-ISBN 978-3-319-11964-9
DOI 10.1007/978-3-319-11964-9
Springer Cham Heidelberg New York Dordrecht London

Library of Congress Control Number: 2014949616

LNCS Sublibrary: SL 3 – Information Systems and Application,
incl. Internet/Web and HCI

*Typesetting:* Camera-ready by author, data conversion by Scientific Publishing Services, Chennai, India

Printed on acid-free paper

Springer is part of Springer Science+Business Media (www.springer.com)

# Preface

The Semantic Web is now a maturing field with a significant and growing adoption of semantic technologies in a variety of commercial, public sector, and scientific fields. Linked Data is pervasive: from enabling government transparency, to helping integrate data in life sciences and enterprises, to publishing data about museums, and integrating bibliographic data. Significantly, major companies, such as Google, Yahoo, Microsoft, and Facebook, have created their own "knowledge graphs" that power semantic searches and enable smarter processing and delivery of data: The use of these knowledge graphs is now the norm rather than the exception. The schema.org effort led by the major search companies illustrates the industry interest and support of the Semantic Web. Commercial players such as IBM, Siemens, BestBuy, and Walmart are seeing the value of semantic technologies and are regular presenters at Semantic Web conferences. The papers and the research topics covered in these proceedings follow directly from the requirements of this large adoption, and contribute greatly to the continuing success of the field.

The International Semantic Web Conference is the premier forum for Semantic Web research, where cutting-edge scientific results and technological innovations are presented, where problems and solutions are discussed, and where the future of this vision is being developed. It brings together specialists in fields such as artificial intelligence, databases, social networks, distributed computing, Web engineering, information systems, human–computer interaction, natural language processing, and the social sciences for tutorials, workshops, presentations, keynotes, and ample time for detailed discussions.

This volume contains the main proceedings of the 13th International Semantic Web Conference (ISWC 2014), which was held in Riva del Garda, Trentino, Italy, in October 2014. We received tremendous response to our calls for papers from a truly international community of researchers and practitioners. Indeed, several tracks of the conference received a record number of submissions this year. The careful nature of the review process, and the breadth and scope of the papers finally selected for inclusion in this volume, speak to the quality of the conference and to the contributions made by researchers whose work is presented in these proceedings. As such, we were all honored and proud that we were invited to serve the community in the stewardship of this edition of ISWC.

The proceedings include papers from four different tracks: the Research Track, the Semantic Web In-Use Track, the newly added Replication, Benchmark, Data and Software (RBDS) Track, and a selection of Doctoral Consortium papers. For the first time since we started publishing the LNCS proceedings, the papers are organized by their topic rather than by their track and correspond closely to the sessions in the conference schedule. The topics of the accepted papers reflect the broad coverage of the Semantic Web research and application: Linked Data, its quality, link discovery, and application in the life sciences; data integration, search and query answering, SPARQL, ontology-based data access and query rewriting and reasoning; natural language processing and information extraction; user interaction and personalization, and social media; ontology alignment and modularization; and sensors and streams.

Creating the program for ISWC 2014 would not have been possible without the tireless and fantastic work of the Senior Program Committees (SPC), the Program Committees (PC), as well as of the many sub-reviewers in the different tracks, several of whom volunteered to provide high-quality emergency reviews. To acknowledge this work, the Research Track and the Semantic Web In-Use Track each offered a best reviewer award. The decision on the awards was taken with the input of the SPC members, of the fellow reviewers from the PC, of the authors, and also using objective measures about the reviews provided by EasyChair, the conference management system.

The Research Track of the conference attracted 180 submissions, 38 of which were accepted, resulting in a 21% acceptance rate. Each paper received at least three, and sometimes as many as five, reviews from members of the PC. After the first round of reviews, authors had the opportunity to submit a rebuttal, leading to further discussions among the reviewers, a metareview and a recommendation from a member of the SPC. The SPC held a 10-hour virtual meeting in order to select the final set of accepted papers, paying special attention to papers that were borderline or had at least one recommendation for acceptance. In many cases, additional last-minute reviews were sought out to better inform the SPC's decision.

The best paper nominations for the Research Track reflect the broad range of topics that were submitted to this track:

Best paper nominations:

- AGDISTIS - "Graph-Based Disambiguation of Named Entities Using Linked Data" by Ricardo Usbeck, Axel-Cyrille Ngonga Ngomo, Michael Röder, Daniel Gerber, Sandro Athaide Coelho, Sören Auer and Andreas Both
- "Expressive and Scalable Query-based Faceted Search over SPARQL Endpoints" by Sébastien Ferré
- "Explass: Exploring Associations Between Entities via Top-K Ontological Patterns and Facets" by Gong Cheng, Yanan Zhang and Yuzhong Qu
- "Querying Factorized Probabilistic Triple Databases" by Denis Krompaß, Maximilian Nickel and Volker Tresp

Best student paper nominations:

- "OBDA: Query Rewriting or Materialization? In Practice, Both!" by Juan F. Sequeda, Marcelo Arenas and Daniel P. Miranker
- "SYRql: A Dataflow Language for Large Scale Processing of RDF Data" by Fadi Maali, Padmashree Ravindra, Kemafor Anyanwu and Stefan Decker
- "Pushing the Boundaries of Tractable Ontology Reasoning" by David Carral, Cristina Feier, Bernardo Cuenca Grau, Pascal Hitzler and Ian Horrocks

The Semantic Web In-Use Track received 46 submissions. Fifteen papers were accepted – a 33% acceptance rate. The papers demonstrated how semantic technologies are applied in a variety of domains, including: biomedicine and drug discovery, smart cities, sensor streams, multimedia, visualization, link generation, and ontology development. The application papers demonstrated how semantic technologies are applied in diverse ways, starting from using linked data in mobile environments to employing fully fledged artificial intelligence methods in real-time use cases. At least three members of the In-Use PC provided reviews for each paper. After the first round of reviews, authors had the opportunity to submit a rebuttal, leading to further discussions among the reviewers, a metareview and a recommendation from a member of the SPC.

The best paper nominations for the Semantic Web In-Use Track are:

- "Web Browser Personalization with the Client Side Triplestore" by Hitoshi Uchida, Ralph Swick and Andrei Sambra
- "Semantic Traffic Diagnosis with STAR-CITY: Architecture and Lessons Learned from Deployment in Dublin, Bologna, Miami and Rio", by Freddy Lecue, Robert Tucker, Simone Tallevi-Diotallevi, Rahul Nair, Yiannis Gkoufas, Giuseppe Liguori, Mauro Borioni, Alexandre Rademaker and Luciano Barbosa
- "Adapting Semantic Sensor Networks for Smart Building Analytics" by Joern Ploennigs, Anika Schumann and Freddy Lecue

This year we introduced the Replication, Benchmark, Data and Software (RBDS) track that provides an outlet for papers of these four categories. It extended and transformed last year's evaluations and experiments track to incorporate new categories of contributions. The four types of papers had very clearly specified scope and reviewing criteria that were described in the Call for Papers: (1) Replication papers focus on replicating a previously published approach in order to shed light on some important, possibly overlooked aspect; (2) benchmark papers make available to the community a new class of resources, metrics or software that can be used to measure the performance of systems in some dimension; (3) data papers introduce an important data set to the community; and (4) software framework papers advance science by sharing with the community software that can easily be extended or adapted to support scientific study and experimentation. The RBDS track received 39 submissions (18 benchmark studies, eight data papers, eight software framework papers, and four replication studies), and accepted 16 papers (five benchmark studies, five data papers, four software framework papers, and two replication studies), corresponding to an acceptance rate of 41%. Each paper was reviewed by at least three members of the PC and discussed thoroughly. The papers address a range of areas, such as linked stream data, federated query processing, tag recommendation, entity summarization, and mobile semantic web.

The Doctoral Consortium is a key event at the ISWC conference. PhD students in the Semantic Web field get an opportunity to present their thesis proposals and to interact with leading academic and industrial scientists in the field, who act as their mentors. The Doctoral Consortium received 41 submissions, a record number compared to previous years. Each paper received two reviews, one from an SPC member, and one from a co-chair. Out of 41 submissions, six were selected to be both included in these proceedings and for presentation at the Doctoral Consortium, while an additional 11 were selected for presentation. The Doctoral Consortium day is organized as a highly interactive event, in which students present their proposals and receive extensive feedback and comments from mentors as well as from their peers.

A unique aspect of the ISWC conference is the Semantic Web Challenge, now in its 12th year, with the goal of demonstrating practical progress toward achieving the vision of the Semantic Web. The overall objective of the challenge is to apply Semantic Web techniques in building online end-user applications that integrate, combine, and deduce information needed to assist users in performing tasks. Organized this year by Andreas Harth and Sean Bechhofer, the competition enables practitioners and scientists to showcase leading-edge real-world applications of Semantic Web technology. The Semantic Web Challenge is advised by a board of experts working at universities and in industry. The advisory board also acts as a jury and awards the best applications at the conference.

The keynote talks given by leading scientists or practitioners in their field further enriched the ISWC program. Prabhakar Raghavan, Vice-President of Engineering at Google, discussed "Web Search – From the Noun to the Verb." Paolo Traverso, Director of the Center for Information Technology at Fondazione Bruno Kessler, talked about "To Be or to Do?: The Semantics for Smart Cities and Communities." Yolanda Gil, Associate Director of the Intelligent Systems Division at ISI University of South California, discussed the "Semantic Challenges in Getting Work Done" addressing the application of semantics to scientific tasks. The industry track featured a plenary keynote on "The Semantic Web in an Age of Open Data" by Sir Nigel Shadbolt, Chairman and Co-Founder of the UK's Open Data Institute and Professor of Artificial Intelligence at the University of Southampton.

As in previous ISWC editions, the conference included an extensive tutorial and workshop program. Johanna Völker and Lora Aroyo, the chairs of this track, created a stellar and diverse collection of eight tutorials and 23 workshops, where the only problem that the participants faced was which of the many exciting workshops and tutorials to attend. This year, we hosted for the first time the Developers' Workshop, a dedicated event for software developers discussing implementations, methods, techniques, and solutions to practical problems of Semantic Web and Linked Data. The main topic of the Developers' Workshop was "Semantic Web in a Browser."

We would like to thank Matthew Horridge, Marco Rospocher, and Jacco van Ossenbruggen for organizing a lively poster and demo session. This year, the track got a record 156 submissions, a 50% increase compared with previous years. Moreover, 71 posters and 50 demos were introduced in a "minute madness session," where each presenter got 45 seconds to provide a teaser for their poster or demo. Axel Polleres, Alexander Castro, and Richard Benjamins coordinated an exciting Industry Track with presentations both from younger companies focusing on semantic technologies and from large enterprises, such as British Telecom, IBM, Oracle, and Siemens, just to name a few. With a record number of 39 submissions (seven of which were selected for full presentations and 23 for short lightning talks) in the industry track this year, the mix of presentations demonstrated the success and maturity of semantic technologies in a variety of industry- and business-relevant domains. The extended abstracts for posters, demos, and industry talks will be published in separate companion volumes in the CEUR workshop proceedings series.

We are indebted to Krzysztof Janowicz, our proceedings chair, who provided invaluable support in compiling the volume that you now hold in your hands (or see on your screen) and who put in many hours of additional work to create a completely new structure for these proceedings based on the topic rather than the tracks, as in previous years. Many thanks to Oscar Corcho and Miriam Fernandez, the student coordinators, for securing and managing the distribution of student travel grants and thus helping students who might not have otherwise attended the conference to come to Riva. Roberta Cuel, Jens Lehmann, and Vincenzo Maltese were tireless in their work as sponsorship chairs, knocking on every conceivable virtual "door" and ensuring an unprecedented level of sponsorship this year. We are especially grateful to all the sponsors for their generosity.

As has been the case in the past, ISWC 2014 also contributed to the Linked Data cloud by providing semantically annotated data about many aspects of the conference. This contribution would not have been possible without the efforts of Li Ding and Jie Bao, our metadata chairs.

Mauro Dragoni, our publicity chair, tirelessly tweeted, sent old-fashioned announcements on the mailing lists, and updated the website, creating more lively "buzz" than ISWC has had before.

Our very special thanks go to the local organization team, led by Luciano Serafini and Chiara Ghidini. They did a fantastic job of handling local arrangements, thinking of every potential complication way before it arose, often doing things when members of the Organizing Committee were only beginning to think about asking for them. Many thanks to the Rivatour Agency for providing great service for local arrangements.

Finally, we would like to thank all members of the ISWC Organizing Committee not only for handling their tracks superbly, but also for their wider contribution to the collaborative decision-making process in organizing the conference.

October 2014

Peter Mika
Tania Tudorache
Abraham Bernstein
Chris Welty
Craig Knoblock
Denny Vrandečić
Paul Groth
Natasha Noy
Krzysztof Janowicz
Carole Goble

# Conference Organization

## Organizing Committee

### General Chair

Carole Goble                 University of Manchester, UK

### Local Chairs

| | |
|---|---|
| Chiara Ghidini | Fondazione Bruno Kessler, Italy |
| Luciano Serafini | Fondazione Bruno Kessler, Italy |

### Program Committee Chairs

| | |
|---|---|
| Peter Mika | Yahoo Labs, Spain |
| Tania Tudorache | Stanford University, USA |
| Abraham Bernstein | University of Zurich, Switzerland |
| Chris Welty | IBM Research, USA |
| Craig Knoblock | University of Southern California, USA |
| Denny Vrandečić | Google, USA |

### Research Track Chairs

| | |
|---|---|
| Peter Mika | Yahoo Labs, Spain |
| Tania Tudorache | Stanford University, USA |

### In-Use Track Chairs

| | |
|---|---|
| Craig Knoblock | University of Southern California, USA |
| Denny Vrandečić | Google, USA |

### Industry Track Chairs

| | |
|---|---|
| Richard Benjamins | Telefonica, Spain |
| Alexander G. Castro | LinkingData I/O LLC, USA |
| Axel Polleres | Vienna University of Economics and Business, Austria |

### Replication, Benchmark, Data and Software Track Chairs

| | |
|---|---|
| Abraham Bernstein | University of Zurich, Switzerland |
| Chris Welty | IBM Research, USA |

## Workshops and Tutorials Chairs

| | |
|---|---|
| Lora Aroyo | VU University Amsterdam, The Netherlands |
| Johanna Völker | University of Mannheim, Germany |

## Posters and Demos Chairs

| | |
|---|---|
| Matthew Horridge | Stanford University, USA |
| Marco Rospocher | Fondazione Bruno Kessler, Italy |
| Jacco van Ossenbruggen | Centrum voor Wiskunde en Informatica, The Netherlands |

## Doctoral Consortium Chairs

| | |
|---|---|
| Paul Groth | VU University Amsterdam, The Netherlands |
| Natasha Noy | Google, USA |

## Proceedings Chair

| | |
|---|---|
| Krzysztof Janowicz | University of California, Santa Barbara, USA |

## Semantic Web Challenge Chairs

| | |
|---|---|
| Sean Bechhofer | The University of Manchester, UK |
| Andreas Harth | Karlsruhe Institute of Technology, Germany |

## Sponsorship Chairs

| | |
|---|---|
| Roberta Cuel | University of Trento, Italy |
| Jens Lehmann | University of Leipzig, Germany |
| Vincenzo Maltese | DISI - University of Trento, Italy |

## Publicity Chairs

| | |
|---|---|
| Mauro Dragoni | Fondazione Bruno Kessler, Italy |

## Metadata Chairs

| | |
|---|---|
| Jie Bao | Memect, USA |
| Li Ding | Memect, USA |

## Student Coordinators

| | |
|---|---|
| Oscar Corcho | Universidad Politécnica de Madrid, Spain |
| Miriam Fernandez | KMI, Open University, UK |

## Senior Program Committee – Research

| | |
|---|---|
| Harith Alani | The Open University, UK |
| Lora Aroyo | VU University Amsterdam, The Netherlands |
| Sören Auer | Bonn Universität, Germany |
| Philipp Cimiano | Bielefeld University, Germany |
| Oscar Corcho | Universidad Politécnica de Madrid, Spain |
| Philippe Cudré-Mauroux | University of Fribourg, Switzerland |
| Claudio Gutierrez | Chile University, Chile |
| Jeff Heflin | Lehigh University, USA |
| Ian Horrocks | University of Oxford, UK |
| Lalana Kagal | MIT, USA |
| David Karger | MIT, USA |
| Spyros Kotoulas | IBM Research, Ireland |
| Diana Maynard | University of Sheffield, UK |
| Natasha Noy | Google, USA |
| Jeff Pan | University of Aberdeen, UK |
| Terry Payne | University of Liverpool, UK |
| Marta Sabou | MODUL University Vienna, Austria |
| Uli Sattler | The University of Manchester, UK |
| Steffen Staab | University of Koblenz-Landau, Germany |
| Hideaki Takeda | National Institute of Informatics, Japan |

## Program Committee – Research

| | |
|---|---|
| Karl Aberer | Paolo Bouquet |
| Sudhir Agarwal | Loris Bozzato |
| Faisal Alkhateeb | John Breslin |
| Pramod Anantharam | Christopher Brewster |
| Sofia Angeletou | Paul Buitelaar |
| Kemafor Anyanwu | Gregoire Burel |
| Marcelo Arenas | Andrea Calì |
| Manuel Atencia | Diego Calvanese |
| Medha Atre | Amparo E. Cano |
| Isabelle Augenstein | Iván Cantador |
| Nathalie Aussenac-Gilles | Soumen Chakrabarti |
| Jie Bao | Pierre-Antoine Champin |
| Payam Barnaghi | Gong Cheng |
| Sean Bechhofer | Key-Sun Choi |
| Klaus Berberich | Smitashree Choudhury |
| Christian Bizer | Michael Compton |
| Roi Blanco | Isabel Cruz |
| Eva Blomqvist | Bernardo Cuenca Grau |
| Kalina Bontcheva | Claudia D'Amato |

Yves Raimond
Ganesh Ramakrishnan
Maya Ramanath
Chantal Reynaud
Riccardo Rosati
Marco Rospocher
Matthew Rowe
Sebastian Rudolph
Harald Sack
Satya Sahoo
Hassan Saif
Manuel Salvadores
Francois Scharffe
Ansgar Scherp
Stefan Schlobach
Daniel Schwabe
Juan F. Sequeda
Amit Sheth
Michael Sintek
Milan Stankovic
Markus Strohmaier
Rudi Studer
Gerd Stumme
Jing Sun

Vojtěch Svátek
Valentina Tamma
Kerry Taylor
Krishnaprasad Thirunarayan
Ioan Toma
Nicolas Torzec
Thanh Tran
Raphaël Troncy
Giovanni Tummarello
Anni-Yasmin Turhan
Jacopo Urbani
Victoria Uren
Jacco van Ossenbruggen
Maria-Esther Vidal
Johanna Völker
Haofen Wang
Kewen Wang
Zhichun Wang
Yong Yu
Fouad Zablith
Qingpeng Zhang
Antoine Zimmermann

## Additional Reviewers – Research

Nitish Aggarwal
Muhammad Intizar Ali
Carlos Buil Aranda
Mihael Arcan
Estefanía Serral Asensio
Andrew Bate
Wouter Beek
Konstantina Bereta
David Berry
Nicola Bertolin
Leopoldo Bertossi
Dimitris Bilidas
Stefano Bortoli
Adrian Brasoveanu
Volha Bryl
Jean-Paul Calbimonte
Diego Calvanese

Delroy Cameron
Michele Catasta
Sam Coppens
Julien Corman
Jérôme David
Jana Eggink
Jae-Hong Eom
Ju Fan
Jean-Philippe Fauconnier
Daniel Fleischhacker
Andre Freitas
Riccardo Frosini
Irini Fundulaki
Stella Giannakopoulou
Jangwon Gim
Kalpa Gunaratna
Andreas Harth

Julia Hoxha
Gao Huan
Armen Inants
Ernesto Jimenez-Ruiz
Zoi Kaoudi
Patrick Kapahnke
Mario Karlovcec
Robin Keskisärkkä
Taehong Kim
Magnus Knuth
Haridimos Kondylakis
Aljaz Kosmerlj
Egor V. Kostylev
Adila A. Krisnadhi
Sarasi Lalithsena
Christoph Lange
Sungin Lee
Zhixing Li
Juanzi Li
Nuno Lopes
Yongtao Ma
Andre de Oliveira Melo
Albert Meroño-Peñuela
Ankush Meshram
Hyun Namgoong
Radim Nedbal
Hai Nguyen
Quoc Viet Hung Nguyen
Vinh Nguyen
Inna Novalija
Andrea Giovanni Nuzzolese
Francesco Osborne
Matteo Palmonari
Bianca Pereira
Jorge Pérez
Catia Pesquita
Robert Piro
Camille Pradel

Freddy Priyatna
Jay Pujara
Jean-Eudes Ranvier
David Ratcliffe
Martin Rezk
Laurens Rietveld
Petar Ristoski
Giuseppe Rizzo
Víctor Rodríguez-Doncel
Yannis Roussakis
Tong Ruan
Brigitte Safar
Andreas Schwarte
Kunal Sengupta
Chao Shao
Philipp Singer

Panayiotis Smeros
Kostas Stefanidis
Andreas Steigmiller
Nenad Stojanovic
Aynaz Taheri
Vahid Taslimitehrani
Veronika Thost
Alberto Tonon
Trung-Kien Tran
Tran Quoc Trung
Jung-Ho Um
Joerg Waitelonis
Simon Walk
Zhigang Wang
Zhe Wang
Guohui Xiao
Nasser Zalmout
Eva Zangerle
Dmitriy Zheleznyakov
Zhiqiang Zhuang

# Senior Program Committee – Semantic Web In-Use

| | |
|---|---|
| Yolanda Gil | University of South California, USA |
| Paul Groth | VU University Amsterdam, The Netherlands |
| Peter Haase | fluid Operations, Germany |
| Siegfried Handschuh | Digital Enterprise Research Institute (DERI), Ireland |
| Andreas Harth | Karlsruhe Institute of Technology, Germany |
| Krzysztof Janowicz | University of California, Santa Barbara, USA |
| Natasha Noy | Google, USA |
| Matthew Rowe | Lancaster University, UK |
| Uli Sattler | University of Manchester, UK |

# Program Committee – Semantic Web In-Use

| | |
|---|---|
| Dean Allemang | Pavel Klinov |
| Phil Archer | Matthias Klusch |
| Isabelle Augenstein | Christoph Lange |
| Sean Bechhofer | Yuan-Fang Li |
| Christian Bizer | Thorsten Liebig |
| Sebastian Blohm | Antonis Loizou |
| Dan Brickley | Markus Luczak-Roesch |
| Iván Cantador | Pablo Mendes |
| Vinay Chaudhri | Hannes Mühleisen |
| Michelle Cheatham | Lyndon Nixon |
| Paolo Ciccarese | Daniel Oberle |
| Michael Compton | Massimo Paolucci |
| Oscar Corcho | Carlos Pedrinaci |
| Mathieu D'Aquin | Héctor Pérez-Urbina |
| Brian Davis | Edoardo Pignotti |
| Mike Dean | Yves Raimond |
| Leigh Dodds | Marco Rospocher |
| Basil Ell | Manuel Salvadores |
| Fabian Floeck | Miel Vander Sande |
| Alasdair Gray | Marc Schaaf |
| Tudor Groza | Michael Schmidt |
| Giancarlo Guizzardi | Oshani Seneviratne |
| Armin Haller | Juan F. Sequeda |
| Sebastian Hellmann | Evren Sirin |
| Martin Hepp | William Smith |
| Matthew Horridge | Milan Stankovic |
| Wei Hu | Thomas Steiner |
| Prateek Jain | Nenad Stojanovic |
| Anja Jentzsch | Pedro Szekely |
| Benedikt Kämpgen | Ramine Tinati |

Nicolas Torzec
Giovanni Tummarello
Jacco van Ossenbruggen
Ruben Verborgh
Holger Wache
Jesse Jiaxin Wang
Kewen Wang

Zhe Wu
Fouad Zablith
Amrapali Zaveri
Qingpeng Zhang
Amal Zouaq

## Additional Reviewers – Semantic Web In-Use

Ana Sasa Bastinos
Anila Sahar Butt
Charles Vardeman II

Gwendolin Wilke
Zhe Wang

## Program Committee – Replication, Benchmark, Data and Software

Sören Auer
Jie Bao
Cosmin Basca
Chris Biemann
Philipp Cimiano
Oscar Corcho
Philippe Cudré-Mauroux
Richard Cyganiak
Claudia D'Amato
Victor de Boer
Gianluca Demartini
Jérôme Euzenat
Javier D. Fernández
Alfio Gliozzo
Martin Grund

Siegfried Handschuh
Matthew Horridge
Jens Lehmann
Alejandro Llaves
Axel Polleres
Marta Sabou
Thomas Scharrenbach
Heiner Stuckenschmidt
Jamie Taylor
Jürgen Umbrich
Gerhard Weikum
Stuart Wrigley
Josiane Xavier Parreira

## Additional Reviewers – Replication, Benchmark, Data and Software

Judie Attard
Mihaela Bornea
Yu Chen
Souripriya Das
Sarthak Dash
Michael Glass
Tatiana Lesnikova

Michael Luggen
Christian Meilicke
Niels Ockeloen
Matthew Perry
Roman Prokofyev
Stephan Radeck-Arneth
Eugen Ruppert

Joerg Schoenfisch
Claus Stadler
Wei Tai
Alberto Tonon
Joerg Unbehauen

Han Wang
Marcin Wylot
Seid Muhie Yimam

## Program Committee – Doctoral Consortium

Harith Alani
Lora Aroyo
Abraham Bernstein
Oscar Corcho
Philippe Cudré-Mauroux
Fabien Gandon
Paul Groth
Pascal Hitzler

Lalana Kagal
Diana Maynard
Enrico Motta
Natasha Noy
Terry Payne
Guus Schreiber
Elena Simperl

# Sponsors

**Student Travel Award Sponsor**
Semantic Web Science Association (SWSA)
National Science Foundation (NSF)

**Invited Speakers Sponsor**
*Artificial Intelligence Journal*

**Semantic Web Challenge Sponsor**
Elsevier

**Platinum**
Yahoo! Labs
Elsevier

**Gold**
Telefonica
Parlance project
Google
IBM Research
Microsoft Research
LinkedUp project
The Open PHACTS Foundation
Systap
Semantic Valley

**Silver**
OpenLink software
Poolparty
fluid Operations
News Reader project
Synerscope
Okkam
SICRaS
Bpeng
Centro Ricerche GPI
Expert System
Informatica Trentina s.p.a.
Institute of Cognitive Sciences
 and Technologies - CNR

**Doctoral Consortium Sponsor**
iMinds

**Video Sponsor**
Videolectures

**Organizing Institution/Foundation**
Fondazione Bruno Kessler
Semantic Web Science Association

# Keynote Talk (Abstracts)

# Web Search - From the Noun to the Verb (Keynote Talk)

Prabhakar Raghavan

Vice President Engineering
Google, USA

**Abstract.** This talk examines the evolution of web search experiences over 20 years, and their impact on the underlying architecture. Early web search represented the adaptation of methods from classic Information Retrieval to the Web. Around the turn of this century, the focus shifted to triaging the need behind a query - whether it was Navigational, Informational or Transactional; engines began to customize their experiences depending on the need. The next change arose from the recognition that most queries embodied noun phrases, leading to the construction of knowledge representations from which queries could extract and deliver information regarding the noun in the query. Most recently, three trends represent the next step beyond these "noun engines": (1) "Queryless engines" have begun surfacing information meeting a user's need based on the user's context, without explicit querying; (2) Search engines have actively begun assisting the user's task at hand - the verb underlying the noun query; (3) increasing use of speech recognition is changing the distribution of queries.

# "To Be or to DO?": The Semantics for Smart Cities and Communities (Keynote Talk)

Paolo Traverso

Director
Center for Information Technology
Fondazione Bruno Kessler, Italy

**Abstract.** The major challenge for so-called smart cities and communities is to provide people with value added services that improve their quality of life. Massive individual and territorial data sets – (open) public and private data, as well as their semantics which allows us to transform data into knowledge about the city and the community, are key enablers to the development of such solutions. Something more however is needed. A "smart" community needs "to do things" in a city, and the people need to act within their own community. For instance, not only do we need to know where we can find a parking spot, which cultural event is happening tonight, or when the next bus will arrive, but we also need to actually pay for parking our car, buy a bus ticket, or reserve a seat in the theater. All these activities (paying, booking, buying, etc.) need semantics in the same way as data does, and such a semantics should describe all the steps needed to perform such activities. Moreover, such a semantics should allow us to define and deploy solutions that are general and abstract enough to be "portable" across the details of the different ways in which activities can be implemented, e.g., by different providers, or for different customers, or for different cities. At the same time, in order to actually "do things", we need a semantics that links general and abstract activities to the possibly different and specific ICT systems that implement them. In my talk, I will present some of the main problems for realizing the concept of smart city and community, and the need for semantics for both understanding data and "doing things". I will discuss some alternative approaches, some lessons learned from applications we have been working with in this field, and the still many related open research challenges.

# Semantic Challenges in Getting Work Done (Keynote Talk)

Yolanda Gil

Associate Director
Information Sciences Institute and Department of Computer Science
University of Southern California, USA

**Abstract.** In the new millennium, work involves an increasing amount of tasks that are knowledge-rich and collaborative. We are investigating how semantics can help on both fronts. Our focus is scientific work, in particular data analysis, where tremendous potential resides in combining the knowledge and resources of a highly fragmented science community. We capture task knowledge in semantic workflows, and use skeletal plan refinement algorithms to assist users when they specify high-level tasks. But the formulation of workflows is in itself a collaborative activity, a kind of meta-workflow composed of tasks such as finding the data needed or designing a new algorithm to handle the data available. We are investigating "organic data science", a new approach to collaboration that allows scientists to formulate and resolve scientific tasks through an open framework that facilitates ad-hoc participation. With a design based on social computing principles, our approach makes scientific processes transparent and incorporates semantic representations of tasks and their properties. The semantic challenges involved in this work are numerous and have great potential to transform the Web to help us do work in more productive and unanticipated ways.

# The Semantic Web in an Age of Open Data (Keynote Talk)

Nigel Shadbolt

Professor of Artificial Intelligence
The University of Southampton
and
Chairman of the Open Data Institute

**Abstract.** The last five years have seen increasing amounts of open data being published on the Web. In particular, governments have made data available across a wide range of sectors: spending, crime and justice, education, health, transport, geospatial, environmental and much more. The data has been published in a variety of formats and has been reused with varying degrees of success. Commercial organisations have begun to exploit this resource and in some cases elected to release their own open data. Only a relatively small amount of the data published has been linked data. However, the methods and techniques of the semantic web could significantly enhance the value and utility of open data. What are the obstacles and challenges that prevent the routine publication of these resources as semantically enriched open data? What can be done to improve the situation? Where are the examples of the successful publication and exploitation of semantically enriched content? What lessons should we draw for the future?

# Table of Contents – Part I

## Large-Scale RDF Processing and Dataset Availability

## Linked Data

## Linked Data and Data Quality

## Mobile Reasoning and SPARQL Updates

# Natural Language Processing and Information Extraction

# OBDA and Query Rewriting

# Table of Contents – Part II

# Reasoning

# Semantic Infrastructures and Streams

# Sensors

## Social Media

## SPARQL Extensions

## User Interaction and Personalization

## Doctoral Consortium

# CAMO: Integration of Linked Open Data for Multimedia Metadata Enrichment

Wei Hu[1], Cunxin Jia[1], Lei Wan[2], Liang He[2], Lixia Zhou[2], and Yuzhong Qu[1]

[1] State Key Laboratory for Novel Software Technology, Nanjing University, China
{whu, yzqu}@nju.edu.cn, jiacunxin@smail.nju.edu.cn
[2] Samsung Electronics (China) R&D Center, China
{l.wan,jaimely.he,lixia.zhou}@samsung.com

**Abstract.** Metadata is a vital factor for effective management, organization and retrieval of multimedia content. In this paper, we introduce CAMO, a new system developed jointly with Samsung to enrich multimedia metadata by integrating Linked Open Data (LOD). Large-scale, heterogeneous LOD sources, e.g., DBpedia, LinkMDB and MusicBrainz, are integrated using ontology matching and instance linkage techniques. A mobile app for Android devices is built on top of the LOD to improve multimedia content browsing. An empirical evaluation is conducted to demonstrate the effectiveness and accuracy of the system in the multimedia domain.

**Keywords:** Linked Data, multimedia, semantic data integration.

## 1 Introduction

Multimedia metadata and semantic annotation are vital to improve services on multimedia content [21]. The search, browsing and management of multimedia content become very difficult if no or only limited metadata and annotations are provided. Driven by the Linking Open Data Initiative, plenty of open datasets are published and interlinked, in order to enable users to make use of such rich source of information [22].

Looking at the existing multimedia metadata models and standards, they do not provide formal semantics and typically focus on a single media type. For example, EXIF is widely used for image description, but it is incompatible with MPEG-7 [21]. In real world, different media types often coexist in a multimedia presentation, where for example a movie may have a theme music and a poster. We believe that a unified, well-defined ontology (with its mappings to others) is needed in many multimedia application scenarios to gain interoperability. Additionally, metadata from diverse data sources can denote the same multimedia content. Linking and integrating these heterogeneous datasets are challenging, especially when meeting legacy data reserved in relational databases (RDBs) or on the Deep Web. Thus, accurate methods are desired to (semi-)automatically link the overlapping parts of the datasets. The integrated metadata can provide benefits to many multimedia applications like mobile devices, whose market is expected to rise to $9.5 billion by 2014 [7].

P. Mika et al. (Eds.) ISWC 2014, Part I, LNCS 8796, pp. 1–16, 2014.

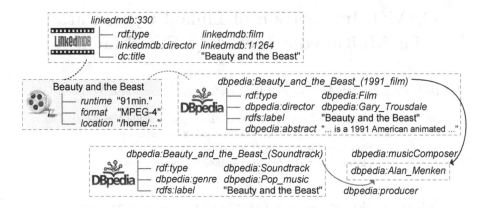

**Fig. 1.** An example of integrating LOD for multimedia metadata enrichment

*A motivating example.* Fig. 1 illustrates a real-world example about the movie *Beauty and the Beast*. The original video already has a few low-level metadata like runtime and location. By integrating LOD, e.g., LinkedMDB [10] and DBpedia [17], the description of this movie would be enriched significantly. However, LinkedMDB and DBpedia use different but related ontologies for movie description, thus creating mappings between their classes and properties is important for integrating the descriptions into the movie metadata. Additionally, DBpedia and LinkedMDB refer to the same movie by using different instances, e.g., dbpedia:Beauty_and_the_Beast_(1991_film) and linkedmdb:330 in this example. But it may not be sufficient and accurate to only match their titles/labels, where for example a music dbpedia:Beauty_and_the_Beast_(Soundtrack) with exactly the same label should not be linked.  □

In this paper, we describe CAMO, a system developed jointly with Samsung for enriching multimedia metadata via integrating LOD. CAMO achieves this by using our ontology matching and instance linkage techniques and adapting them to the multimedia domain. The technical contributions of this paper are threefold: (i) CAMO selects the DBpedia ontology as the mediation model and matches with other ontologies; (ii) CAMO links the instances in DBpedia with other sources and aggregates their descriptions; (iii) CAMO incorporates RDBs with DBpedia to cope with legacy data. We hope that our methods and system can provide reusable experience for applications consuming Linked Data.

We develop a mobile app for browsing and searching multimedia content on Android devices. We perform a user-centered evaluation of CAMO to measure how well it compares with existing apps, in particular with Last.fm, IMDb and Wikipedia mobile apps. We also conduct an experiment on the accuracy of the ontology matching and instance linkage in the multimedia domain. The results demonstrate the advantages of integrating LOD into multimedia metadata for improving the quality of multimedia content services. More information about CAMO is available at http://ws.nju.edu.cn/camo/.

The remainder of this paper is structured as follows. Section 2 outlines the system architecture of CAMO and the used LOD sources. In Section 3 and 4, we present the methods to match ontologies and link instances with DBpedia, respectively. Section 5 describes the approach for incorporating legacy RDBs. Evaluation is reported in Section 6 and related work is discussed in Section 7. Finally, we conclude this paper and summarize the lessons learned.

# 2   System Architecture

The architecture of CAMO is illustrated in Fig. 2, which follows a widely-used Client-Server paradigm providing the system with high bandwidth, processing and storage on a large amount of data. For the server side, we choose the DBpedia 3.6 ontology as the mediation and use the Global-as-View solution of data integration, because it is efficient for query rewriting and the used LOD sources are relatively stable. Various LOD sources are all integrated with DBpedia by the ontology matching and instance linkage techniques. The used LOD sources are chosen in terms of popularity. Due to the unstable availability of SPARQL endpoints [4], we currently materialize the original data from their dump files.

**DBpedia.** DBpedia [17] is a crowd-sourced community effort to extract structured, multi-lingual information from Wikipedia and make this information available on the Web. The reason to choose the DBpedia ontology is that it is generic enough to encapsulate various kinds of multimedia domains and can be matched with a large number of ontologies [14]. Besides the ontology, the instances itself are also comprehensive. This is another reason for choosing it rather than other ontologies such as M3O [21].

**DBTune.** DBTune[1] is a non-commercial site, which hosts a number of servers providing access to music-related structured data in a Linked Data fashion. We choose three datasets, namely Jamendo, Magnatune and BBC John Peel session, from DBTune because they already provide links to DBpedia. Note that our approaches are also ready for integrating other datasets.

**LinkedMDB.** The LinkedMDB project [10] aims at publishing an open Semantic Web database for movies, including a large quantity of links to several datasets on the LOD cloud and references to related webpages.

**DBTropes.** DBTropes[2] transforms numerous movies, books and other pages to RDF with the Skipinions ontology.

**MusicBrainz.** MusicBrainz[3] is an open music encyclopedia that collects music metadata and makes it available to the public. Different from other sources providing data in RDF, the MusicBrainz Database is built on RDB (although the LinkedBrainz project[4] helps MusicBrainz transform to Linked Data). We will present how to integrate it in Section 5.

---

[1] http://dbtune.org/
[2] http://dbtropes.org/
[3] http://musicbrainz.org/
[4] http://linkedbrainz.org/

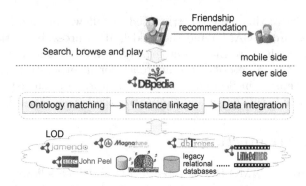

**Fig. 2.** System architecture of CAMO

For the client side, we build the client on Android-based mobile devices[5] and integrate it with a multimedia player. General users can search and browse multimedia content with the enriched metadata, and the metadata is displayed in an integrated view. Additionally, we provide several value-added functionalities, e.g., a Horn-rule based friendship recommendation based on users' favorites and play histories. The recommendation rules are customizable in terms of application requirements, and we implement a rule-based inference engine by ourselves. We omit the details of this rule-based recommendation engine in this paper.

## 3    Matching Ontologies with DBpedia

Different LOD sources have different preferences on ontologies, some of which prefer to develop their own ontologies from scratch to meet their requirements rather than reuse existing ones. Among the LOD sources integrated in CAMO, LinkedMDB and DBTropes define their own ontologies. Meanwhile, other LOD sources reuse some famous ontologies as their conceptual models. For example, the Music Ontology [19] is chosen as the underlying ontology by Jamendo, Magnatune and BBC John Peel. Whichever ontology a data source uses, in order to query and browse the distributed multimedia metadata, a necessary phase is to match ontologies for resolving the heterogeneity between them.

To match ontologies with DBpedia, we use Falcon-AO [12], which is an automatic ontology matching system. The methodological steps of matching ontologies with DBpedia are depicted in Fig. 3, where the output is a set of mappings between the classes or properties in two ontologies. The strength of Falcon-AO is that it leverages various powerful matchers, not only the linguistic matchers like V-Doc but also the structural matcher GMO. S-Match [9] is an alternative system for this purpose. We extend Falcon-AO with domain knowledge to support synonym identification in the multimedia domain, e.g., `track` and `song`.

Before the matching step, an optional partitioning step is involved to cope with large ontologies. We propose a divide-and-conquer approach for generating block

---

[5] Also because Samsung is a leading company in Android-based mobile devices.

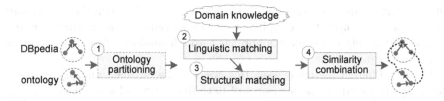

**Fig. 3.** Methodological steps of matching ontologies with DBpedia

mappings between large ontologies, which has two main advantages: (i) it avoids the matching algorithms suffering from the lack of memory; and (ii) it decreases the running time without much loss of accuracy, since it is likely that large portions of one or both ontologies have no matched counterparts. Specifically, all the classes and properties of an ontology are firstly partitioned into a set of small blocks based on the structural proximity (e.g., the distance between classes in the hierarchy, the overlapping between the domains of properties). Then, the blocks are matched using some prefound mappings between classes or properties; only the block pairs with high similarity are further matched with the linguistic and structural matchers.

Linguistic features are widely used for matching ontologies. We employ two linguistic matchers, V-Doc and I-Sub, to calculate the linguistic similarity. V-Doc is a TF-IDF based matcher, representing each class or property as a virtual document (a bag of weighted words). Local descriptions $LD()$ and neighboring information are both considered in V-Doc. For a literal, its description is a collection of words derived from the lexical form; for a named class or property, it is a collection of words extracted from the local name of its URI, `rdfs:label`(s), `rdfs:comment`(s) and other annotations; and for a blank node, it is a collection of words extracted from the information originated from the forward neighbors. To incorporate the descriptions of neighbors in virtual documents, we use three neighboring operations to cover different kinds of neighbors: subject neighbors $SN()$, predicate neighbors $PN()$ and object neighbors $ON()$. Also, synonyms are replaced to refine the documents. Let $e$ be a named class or property. The virtual document of $e$, denoted by $VD(e)$, is defined as follows:

$$VD(e) = LD(e)$$
$$+ \gamma_s * \sum_{e' \in SN(e)} LD(e') + \gamma_p * \sum_{e' \in PN(e)} LD(e') + \gamma_o * \sum_{e' \in ON(e)} LD(e'), (1)$$

where $\gamma_s, \gamma_p, \gamma_o$ are in $[0, 1]$. The measure in V-Doc to determine if two classes or properties are similar is the cosine similarity of their virtual documents.

I-Sub [24] is an improved string matcher considering not only the commonalities between the descriptions of classes or properties but also their differences.

V-Doc and I-Sub are combined linearly. We find that setting the weightings to 0.8 and 0.2 for V-Doc and I-Sub respectively achieves a good accuracy.

Another popular type of matchers is structure-based. A graph-based matcher GMO is employed in Falcon-AO. GMO transforms each ontology into a directed bipartite graph and measures the structural similarity between the two graphs. GMO accepts as input the mappings that are prefound by the linguistic matchers, and iteratively yields more mappings through similarity propagation on the graphs as output.

To meet different matching scenarios, we design a flexible similarity combination strategy based on the measures of both linguistic and structural comparability. The linguistic comparability is assumed to be more reliable, specifically, if the linguistic comparability is high enough, indicating the matching is almost done, there is no need to run the structural matcher any longer. Nevertheless, when the two linguistic matchers fail to find enough candidates, the structural matcher becomes the primary choice.

# 4   Linking Instances with DBpedia

Matching ontologies with DBpedia enables it to query and browse multimedia metadata from the global view. However, overlaps among the LOD sources at the instance level are inevitable, due to the distributed nature of the Semantic Web. Hence, instance linkage is helpful to merge all the descriptions in different sources that refer to the same multimedia content. Complementary information from distributed sources helps understand the content more comprehensively.

As of today, a portion of instances among LOD sources have been explicitly interlinked with `owl:sameAs`, however, there still exist plenty of instances that potentially denote the same real-world objects without being linked yet. Linking them manually is an uphill work. Therefore, we propose an automatic method to learn instance links between DBpedia and other LOD sources based on a set of important properties for characterizing instances (referred to as discriminative properties) [11]. The methodological steps are depicted in Fig. 4.

The first step is to construct a training set automatically. Five vocabulary elements, i.e., `owl:sameAs`, `skos:exactMatch`, inverse functional property (IFP), functional property (FP) and (max-)cardinality, are considered, which are widely used to infer the equivalence relation in many instance linkage systems [13]. We implement the Floyd-Warshall algorithm to obtain the transitive closure of the equivalence relation between instances, which contribute "positive examples" to the training set. As reported in [11], an instance only links to a small number of others, so finding positive examples is computationally cheap at large scale.

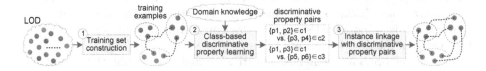

**Fig. 4.** Methodological steps of linking instances with DBpedia

The instances, which do not hold the equivalence relation, are useful to learn non-discriminative properties as well. However, the number of instances explicitly claimed as different using the vocabulary elements like `owl:differentFrom` is small, which is inadequate for a reasonable-sized training set. Therefore, we approximately regard instance pairs that cannot infer the equivalence relation as denoting different real-world objects. However, this way generates tremendous "negative examples" and most of them are totally orthogonal. Hence, a tailoring strategy is introduced to eliminate superfluous negative examples. Besides, this approximation may involve wrong negative examples to some extent, because positive examples include false negatives. But considering the significant difference between the sizes of positive and negative examples, the number of wrong negatives is typically rare.

Discriminative properties are important to link instances, which are learned with a class-based way from the training set. We extract the descriptions of the instances in the training set and pairwise compare them with V-Doc. The discriminability of a property pair is measured by information gain, which computes the change in information entropy from the original state of the training set to a state that uses the properties to identify instance links. The information gain measure is widely used for classification. The discriminability of a property pair is refined w.r.t. different classes due to the different preferences of data publishers on the use of properties, and domain knowledge is used for reasoning types. Let $\mathbf{D}$ be the training set (including both positive and negative examples) satisfying that the types of the instances in each instance pair are $c_i$ and $c_j$, respectively. For a property pair $(p_i, p_j)$, we select all instance pairs $(u_i, u_j)$ in $\mathbf{D}$, denoted by $\mathbf{D}_{(p_i,p_j)}$, where $u_i$ involves $p_i$, and $u_j$ involves $p_j$. The discriminability of $(p_i, p_j)$ in $\mathbf{D}$ w.r.t. $(c_i, c_j)$ is measured by the information gain $IG()$ as follows:

$$IG(p_i, p_j) = H(\mathbf{D}) - H(\mathbf{D}_{(p_i,p_j)}),\tag{2}$$

where $H(\mathbf{D})$ measures the information entropy of $\mathbf{D}$, while $H(\mathbf{D}_{(p_i,p_j)})$ measures the information entropy using $(p_i, p_j)$ to classify instance pairs in $\mathbf{D}$.

With discriminative properties, the instance linkage phase can be conducted online. Given two instances to be linked, the first step is to retrieve the types of them. Then, the most discriminative properties w.r.t. the types are queried out (this can be treated as a blocking step). Finally, a link is generated if the linear aggregation of the similarity of the values from the discriminative properties is greater than a pre-fixed threshold.

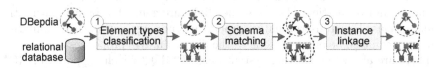

**Fig. 5.** Methodological steps of integrating RDBs with DBpedia

The descriptions of linked instances in different sources are integrated and displayed in a structured and compressed way. Firstly, the linked instances are grouped and all their descriptions are retrieved. Then, the properties with the same value are clustered together. For the properties matched in the ontology matching phase, their values are merged if matched, and we preferentially show the properties and values in DBpedia. But the descriptions can also be enriched by other data sources. Additionally, with the provenance information for each value, users are capable of determining which source is more trustworthy when encountering inconsistency.

## 5   Integrating Legacy Relational Databases

Despite the amount of multimedia-related sources in the LOD cloud is considerable, there are still a great deal of legacy data stored in RDBs, such as from the multimedia content providers in Samsung for years, as well as MusicBrainz. Moreover, some data sources (e.g., LinkedMDB and LinkedBrainz) in LOD are published as Linked Data from their relational versions. To address legacy multimedia metadata using the relational model, we propose a lightweight method to integrate RDBs with DBpedia [15]. Fig. 5 shows the methodological steps.

Due to the differences in data models, in the first step an element classifier takes as input an ontology and a relational schema, and classifies the elements in them into different categories. Tables in a relational schema are categorized in two types in terms of their primary keys and foreign keys: entity table and relationship table. An entity table is used to represent a class of instances, and can match a class in the ontology intuitively. A relationship table, which connects entity tables to reveal their relationships, can match an object property in the ontology. Columns in an entity table can be regarded as non-foreign keys and foreign keys. Non-foreign keys can match datatype properties, while foreign keys can match object properties. This step is also called reverse engineering.

The next step is to match the elements in each category by reusing the V-Doc matcher. As mentioned before, V-Doc is a linguistic matcher considering both local descriptions and neighboring information. The virtual documents of the elements in the relational schema and the ontology are built and compared with the cosine similarity measure. The elements holding the similarity greater than a pre-defined threshold are considered as element mappings, which are expressed using the W3C R2RML language.

Instances in the RDB are linked using a similar way to that for LOD. The tables and columns matched in the previous schema matching step are treated as classes and properties. Then, instance links are generated by comparing the values of class-based discriminative properties and aggregating their similarity. This step can also be online as long as the discriminative properties are learned.

There are also some existing systems, e.g., D2RQ,[6] which support SPARQL queries against non-RDF databases; however, they are not well suitable for

---

[6] http://d2rq.org/

integrating heterogeneous data sources. Additionally, D2R is an alternative system that requires user-defined mappings to match with RDBs.

# 6  Evaluation

CAMO is a system to integrate LOD for multimedia metadata enrichment. To evaluate its effectiveness and accuracy, we conduct two kinds of experiments: (i) the usability and effectiveness of the mobile app of CAMO are compared with several popular apps in a user-centered way, and (ii) the integration accuracy is evaluated in the multimedia domain using the well-known precision and recall.

The mobile app is deployed on a Samsung Galaxy S3 with 4.8 inch screen, 1GB RAM and Android OS 4.0, and the data are stored on a server with two Xeon E7440 2.4GHz CPUs and 4GB memory for JVM, using Apache Jena and PostgreSQL. The integration approaches also run on the server. The user interface of CAMO is shown in Fig. 6, where the integrated metadata for the movie *Beauty and the Beast* is displayed with the provenance.

**Fig. 6.** User interface of CAMO on a mobile phone

## 6.1  Evaluation on Usability and Effectiveness

*Experimental Methodology.* We choose three mobile apps in the Google Play app store for comparison: Last.fm, IMDb and Wikipedia, whose underlying datasets are very similar to those integrated in CAMO (see Section 2). We introduce the three apps briefly as follows:

- Last.fm provides a mobile app that has the capability to learn about users' favorite artists, find nearby concerts and share music tastes with the Last.fm library. Last.fm uses the FOAF ontology for user profiles and MusicBrainz for music metadata.
- IMDb is a database of movie, TV and celebrity information. There are more than two million movie and TV titles in IMDb. The IMDb Android app has the features like search, rating and browsing.
- The Wikipedia Android app is open-sourced and developed mainly by Java-Script. Users of supported mobile devices are automatically redirected to the mobile version of Wikipedia.

We design six testing tasks of three groups: music, movie and cross-domain, which are listed in Table 1. Users are asked to use the four mobile apps afore-mentioned to complete a randomly designated task of each group. The tasks in the music group are performed on Last.fm and CAMO, while the tasks in the movie group are assigned to compare IMDb and CAMO. Cross-domain tasks regarding both music and movie are accomplished by Wikipedia and CAMO. The cross-domain tasks may also be done by the collaboration of Last.fm and IMDb, but it is burdensome for users, so we leave this out of consideration. The tasks are chosen due to their high popularity among university students.

**Table 1.** Tasks for usability and effectiveness assessment

| Domain | Task description |
|---|---|
| Music | $T1$. $X$ is a *Lady Gaga*'s song whose name is started with letter "P". Please find the album of $X$. |
| | $T2$. $X$ is a *Coldplay*'s song whose name is started with letter "Y". Please find the writer of $X$. |
| Movie | $T3$. $X$ is the producer of *The Godfather*. Please find $X$'s name and any two films for which $X$ won the Academy Award. |
| | $T4$. $X$ is the music composer of *The Terminator*. Please find $X$'s name and any two films of which $X$ was also the music composer. |
| Cross-domain | $T5$. $X$ is the director of *Michael Jackson*'s movie *Michael Jackson's That Is It*, and $Y$ is the album of *Michael Jackson*'s song *Beat It*. Please find the names of $X$ and $Y$, respectively. |
| | $T6$. $X$ is the distributor of *Will Smith*'s movie *The Pursuit of Happiness*, and $Y$ is an *Will Smith*'s album named "Born to Reign". Please find $X$'s name and the release date of $Y$. |

We invite 50 users to participate in the evaluation. 10 of them are graduate students in our group and have adequate knowledge of the Semantic Web and LOD; another 22 users are undergraduate students randomly picked up in our university; the rest 18 users are software engineers in Samsung. The users with different backgrounds reflect diversity.

Before starting a task, the users are asked to score the familiarity and difficulty about the task. The time limit for each task is 5 minutes. When finishing the task, a user is required to fill a System Usability Scale (SUS) questionnaire and a post-task questionnaire. SUS is a reliable and low-cost way to assess system usability. The post-task questionnaire is shown in Table 2. These questions are designed to evaluate the quality, diversity and coverage of the underlying metadata for the four mobile apps.

**Table 2.** Post-task questionnaire

| Question description | Score (1–5) |
|---|---|
| Q1. The app has an accurate description about content. | 1 for strongly disagree, and 5 for strongly agree. |
| Q2. The app has a comprehensive coverage about content. | |
| Q3. The app helps me easily find content that I am interested in. | |
| Q4. The app provides few redundant and irrelevant information. | |
| Q5. The app often shows me some unexpected facts in browsing. | |

**Table 3.** Scores of SUS

| CAMO | 87.88 |
|---|---|
| Last.fm | 79.81 |
| IMDb | **89.62** |
| Wikipedia | 84.04 |

**Table 4.** Scores of post-task questionnaire

| | Music | | Movie | | Cross-domain | |
|---|---|---|---|---|---|---|
| | CAMO | Last.fm | CAMO | IMDb | CAMO | Wikipedia |
| Q1. | **4.92** | 4.53 | **5.00** | 4.92 | **5.00** | **5.00** |
| Q2. | **4.69** | 2.38 | **4.46** | 4.38 | 4.62 | **4.69** |
| Q3. | **4.69** | 2.92 | **4.62** | 3.46 | **4.77** | 3.23 |
| Q4. | **4.31** | 4.23 | **4.38** | 3.77 | **4.54** | 3.31 |
| Q5. | **3.61** | 2.54 | 3.54 | **4.00** | 3.85 | **4.15** |

*Results and discussions.* Table 3 lists the average SUS scores of CAMO, Last. fm, IMDb and Wikipedia respectively: 87.88 ($SD = 8.28, median = 90$), 79.81 ($SD = 5.44, median = 80$), 89.62 ($SD = 5.67, median = 90$) and 84.04 ($SD = 4.95, median = 85$). Repeated measures ANOVA indicates that the differences are statistically significant ($p < 0.01$). LSD post-hoc tests ($p < 0.05$) indicate that IMDb and CAMO are more usable than Wikipedia, and Wikipedia is more usable than Last.fm. Although SUS is not an absolute and overall criterion, this result reflects that CAMO is user-friendly in a sense. Besides, all the users are very familiar with the tasks and think them easy.

The result of post-task questionnaire is shown in Table 4. Due to the high-quality multimedia metadata, the scores of all the apps in Q1 are close to each other. Last.fm gets the lowest score in Q1 and Q2 because it gives only limited information about artists. Additionally, 35 users (70%) tell that they are very confused when clicking a song leads to browse the artist of the song rather than the song itself. The competitive performance of CAMO in Q1 and Q2 reflects the advantages of integrating multimedia metadata from multiple sources.

CAMO outperforms the other apps in Q3 and repeated measures ANOVA reveals that the difference is statistically significant ($p < 0.01$). 42 users (84%) think that they can find information that they want from CAMO without much effort. Although all the four apps are capable of keyword search, some features of CAMO makes it more prone to locate content. The first feature is browsing between content via links, which is not implemented in Last.fm. In contrast to Wikipedia, CAMO organizes and displays multimedia metadata in a structured way. Moreover, the properties in CAMO are more plentiful than those of IMDb.

By taking benefits from the structured nature of RDF data, CAMO achieves a higher score in $Q4$. CAMO performs better than Last.fm in $Q5$ but not as well as IMDb and Wikipedia. 28 users (56%) tell that IMDb contains a large amount of interesting, user-generated content like movie reviews and ratings, which are not considered in the current version of CAMO.

We also analyze the result of questionnaire according to the typology of the users. Generally, we see that different users have different focuses. The software engineers are more interested in the usability and performance of the apps, while the students pay more attention to the content quality. Also, the students with different background hold diverse opinions. Taking $Q2$ for example, 12 students (10 graduate students and 2 undergraduates) having Semantic Web knowledge approve that CAMO has a better coverage of integrated data than the others. On the contrary, the rest 20 students neglect this advantage more or less.

## 6.2   Evaluation on Integration Accuracy

We also carry out two experiments to test the integration accuracy of CAMO: one for ontology matching, while the other for instance linkage. In our previous works [11,12,15], we verify the underlying methods of CAMO systematically on a number of widely-used benchmarks from OAEI, and the results demonstrate the effectiveness of these methods. In this evaluation, we particularly focus on assessing them in the multimedia domain. Due to the lack of "golden standard", the generated results are judged manually by two software engineers in Samsung from a practical viewpoint. It is worth mentioning that the evaluation process is time-consuming, error-inevitable and even subjective sometimes. Still, we believe the evaluation is important to make progress in real use.

CAMO discovers 78 mappings between DBpedia and the other ontologies within about 4 minutes, including 18 mappings between DBpedia and the MusicBrainz relational schema. The precision and recall are in Fig. 7(a), where for LinkedMDB and DBTropes, only the classes and properties instantiated in the RDF data are matched because of the unavailability of their ontologies, but this causes the complete semantics loss and narrows the searching space. As compared with the accuracy of BLOOMS [14] on matching DBepdia with the Music Ontology (precision = 0.39, recall = 0.62), CAMO achieves a better accuracy (precision = 0.83, recall = 0.89). Note that this comparison is for reference only, because the results are judged by different people. It is also shown that CAMO finds a bulk of correct mappings between DBpedia and MusicBrainz. We also receives feedback from the judges that a small amount of mappings holding the subclass relationship should be involved to support query reformulation.

For instance linkage, CAMO spends nearly a whole day to generate more than 60 thousand links, where a half of them come from the owl:sameAs links

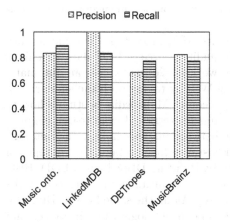 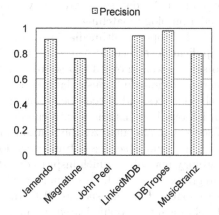

(a) Precision & recall of matching ontologies/relational schema with DBpedia

(b) Precision of sampled instance links between DBpedia and others

**Fig. 7.** Integration accuracy of CAMO

that already exist in the LOD sources. Notice that the instance linkage phase is done online for the actual system. Since there are too many instance links to evaluate the recall, only the precision is measured on 100 sample links between DBpedia and each LOD source at present. The result is shown in Fig. 7(b). As compared to the precision of the system [10] on linking DBpedia with Linked-MDB (precision = 0.98), CAMO gets a slightly worse result (precision = 0.94). The reason may be that the result in [10] is made by carefully adjusting the threshold, while CAMO has to balance the threshold for the whole multimedia domain. We estimate that the recalls of the two systems are close, because they find a similar number of links. It is also observed that the most discriminative properties for DBpedia are `rdfs:label` and `dbpedia:releaseDate`.

# 7   Related Work

Roughly speaking, a semantic data integration process consists of three phases: ontology matching, instance linkage and data fusion [3]. A number of works have been proposed to address the issues in each phase [6,5,3], which exploit many kinds of features in ontologies and instances. Recent works also apply machine learning and crowdsourcing to complex data integration tasks [13]. We discuss the semantic data integration works relevant to the multimedia domain.

The survey in [22] investigates the techniques to generate, expose, discover, and consume Linked Data in the context of multimedia metadata, and discusses representative applications and open issues with the goal of bringing the fields of multimedia and Linked Data together. BLOOMS [14] is a system to generate schema-level links between LOD datasets based on the idea of bootstrapping information already in the LOD cloud. It conducts a comprehensive evaluation on many LOD datasets, and our system achieves comparable accuracy in multi-media ontology matching.

To link open multimedia data, the LinkedMDB project [10] is a movie data triplification project and supplies a high quality source of RDF data that links to several well-known LOD sources. The work in [20] introduces an automatic method to interlink music datasets on the Web by taking both the similarity of web resources and of their neighbors into account. Multipedia [8] studies how to enrich ontology instances with candidate images retrieved from search engines. The work in [23] analyzes the relationship between instance linkage and ontology matching and describes a framework for instance linkage taking advantages of ontology matching, which inspires our study. By using DBpedia and LOD, BBC integrates data and links documents to build more meaningful navigation paths across BBC domains, such as BBC Music [16]. Along the same lines as BBC, we develop a set of sophisticated methods to match ontologies, link instances and integrate legacy RDBs in the multimedia domain.

Tabulator [2] and Sig.ma [25] are two representative "desktop" browsers for Linked Data, which provide integrated data views for general users. As mobile devices penetrate everyone's life, more and more mobile apps emerge to exploit Linked Data. DBpedia Mobile [1] is a location-aware client, which supports users to discover, search and publish Linked Data using mobile devices. dbrec [18] is a music recommender system built on top of DBpedia. Additionally, LinkedTV, seevl.fm, wayOU, Who's Who and many others in AI Mashup Challenges give us valuable experiences for developing CAMO.

# 8    Conclusion and Lessons Learned

In this paper, we describe how LOD is integrated for multimedia metadata enrichment. We develop CAMO, a system that leverages ontology matching and instance linkage techniques for data integration and supports users to browse and search multimedia content on mobile devices. We perform an empirical test to evaluate how CAMO competes with three relevant mobile apps. At the time of writing this paper, we are working on combining the proposed approaches with Samsung Hub to make it better to find and browse multimedia content from a simple, seamless app. During the development and use of CAMO, three specific lessons are learned, and we would like to share them with the community:

**Ontology matters.** The first lesson learned concerns the importance of ontology. Ontologies stay at the heart of semantic data integration, and in our architecture the global ontology gives a conceptual view over the schematically heterogeneous source schemas. To support high-level query reformulation, a trade-off exists between the ontology's expressiveness and ease of use. Furthermore, the global ontology must cover a wide range of application domains. We use DBpedia in the system, but we want to extend it compatible with existing multimedia metadata models and standards.

**Data integration quality.** Another lesson learned is about the quality of LOD and the accuracy of integration. The LOD cloud is far from perfect to build applications using it directly. The situation becomes even worse when integrating legacy RDBs. The ambiguous semantics and incorrect/missing data affect the accuracy of integration. Furthermore, all ontology matching and instance linkage techniques have strengths and weaknesses. So, we have to resort to domain experts to establish some links manually. However, human interaction is expensive and often difficult to perform at large scale. Machine learning is a possible way to leverage human computation for improving the accuracy and adaptability of data integration. Additionally, semantic query reformation may require complex mappings, which is not well supported in the current system.

**Mobile app design.** As is often the case with mobile devices, a limited screen size makes it difficult to efficiently present information and help users view the information. Therefore, a concise and aggregated description of multimedia content is very important. Although we merge the values of matched properties, the method is somehow straightforward without considering inconsistency, and the ranking scheme of properties and values still needs to be studied. Also, user feedback indicates that a user-friendly interface and content are vital to attract users' interests. In the current version of CAMO, we do not expand into NLP, but integrating user-generated content should be considered in the future.

**Acknowledgments.** This work is supported by the National Natural Science Foundation of China (Nos. 61370019, 61223003 and 61321491), the Natural Science Foundation of Jiangsu Province (No. BK2011189), and the Samsung Electronics. We are greatly thankful to our students and the software engineers in Samsung for participating in the evaluation.

# References

1. Becker, C., Bizer, C.: Exploring the Geospatial Semantic Web with DBpedia Mobile. Journal of Web Semantics 7(4), 278–286 (2009)
2. Berners-Lee, T., Hollenbach, J., Lu, K., Presbrey, J., Pru d'ommeaux, E., Schraefel, M.C.: Tabulator Redux: Browsing and Writing Linked Data. In: WWW Workshop on LDOW (2008)
3. Bleiholder, J., Naumann, F.: Data Fusion. ACM Computing Survey 41(1), 1–41 (2008)
4. Buil-Aranda, C., Hogan, A., Umbrich, J., Vandenbussche, P.-Y.: SPARQL Web-Querying Infrastructure: Ready for Action? In: Alani, H., et al. (eds.) ISWC 2013, Part II. LNCS, vol. 8219, pp. 277–293. Springer, Heidelberg (2013)
5. Elmagarmid, A.K., Ipeirotis, P.G., Verykios, V.S.: Duplicate Record Detection: A Survey. IEEE Transactions on Knowledge and Data Engineering 19(1), 1–16 (2007)
6. Euzenat, J., Shvaiko, P.: Ontology Matching, 2nd edn. Springer (2013)
7. Fernando, N., Loke, S.W., Rahayu, W.: Mobile Cloud Computing: A Survey. Future Generation Computer Systems 29(1), 84–106 (2013)
8. García-Silva, A., Jakob, M., Mendes, P.N., Bizer, C.: Multipedia: Enriching DBpedia with Multipedia Information. In: K-CAP 2011, pp. 137–144 (2011)

9. Giunchiglia, F., Shvaiko, P., Yatskevich, M.: S-Match: An Algorithm and an Implementation of Semantic Matching. In: Bussler, C.J., Davies, J., Fensel, D., Studer, R. (eds.) ESWS 2004. LNCS, vol. 3053, pp. 61–75. Springer, Heidelberg (2004)
10. Hassanzadeh, O., Consens, M.: Linked Movie Data Base. In: WWW Workshop on LDOW (2009)
11. Hu, W., Chen, J., Qu, Y.: A Self-Training Approach for Resolving Object Coreference on the Semantic Web. In: WWW 2011, pp. 87–96 (2011)
12. Hu, W., Qu, Y., Cheng, G.: Matching Large Ontologies: A Divide-and-Conquer Approach. Data and Knowledge Engineering 67(1), 140–160 (2008)
13. Isele, R., Bizer, C.: Active Learning of Expressive Linkage Rules Using Genetic Programming. Journal of Web Semantics 23, 2–15 (2013)
14. Jain, P., Hitzler, P., Sheth, A.P., Verma, K., Yeh, P.Z.: Ontology Alignment for Linked Open Data. In: Patel-Schneider, P.F., Pan, Y., Hitzler, P., Mika, P., Zhang, L., Pan, J.Z., Horrocks, I., Glimm, B. (eds.) ISWC 2010, Part I. LNCS, vol. 6496, pp. 402–417. Springer, Heidelberg (2010)
15. Jia, C., Hu, W., Bai, W., Qu, Y.: SMap: Semantically Mapping Relational Database Schemas to OWL Ontologies. Journal of Computer Research and Development 49(10), 2241–2250 (2012)
16. Kobilarov, G., Scott, T., Raimond, Y., Oliver, S., Sizemore, C., Smethurst, M., Bizer, C., Lee, R.: Media Meets Semantic Web – How the BBC Uses DBpedia and Linked Data to Make Connections. In: Aroyo, L., et al. (eds.) ESWC 2009. LNCS, vol. 5554, pp. 723–737. Springer, Heidelberg (2009)
17. Lehmann, J., Isele, R., Jakob, M., Jentzsch, A., Kontokostas, D., Mendes, P.N., Hellmann, S., Morsey, M., van Kleef, P., Auer, S., Bizer, C.: DBpedia – A Large-scale, Multilingual Knowledge Based Extracted from Wikipedia. Semantic Web Journal (2014)
18. Passant, A.: dbrec — Music Recommendations Using DBpedia. In: Patel-Schneider, P.F., Pan, Y., Hitzler, P., Mika, P., Zhang, L., Pan, J.Z., Horrocks, I., Glimm, B. (eds.) ISWC 2010, Part II. LNCS, vol. 6497, pp. 209–224. Springer, Heidelberg (2010)
19. Raimond, Y., Abdallah, S., Sandler, M., Giasson, F.: The Music Ontology. In: International Conference on Music Information Retrieval, pp. 417–422 (2007)
20. Raimond, Y., Sutton, C., Sandler, M.: Automatic Interlinking of Music Datasets on the Semantic Web. In: WWW Workshop on LDOW (2008)
21. Saathoff, C., Scherp, A.: M3O: The Multimedia Metadata Ontology. In: SAMT Workshop on SeMuDaTe (2009)
22. Schandl, B., Haslhofer, B., Bürger, T., Langegger, A., Halb, W.: Linked Data and Multimedia: The State of Affairs. Multimedia Tools and Applications 59(2), 523–556 (2012)
23. Scharffe, F., Euzenat, J.: Linked Data Meets Ontology Matching – Enhancing Data Linking through Ontology Alignments. In: International Conference on Knowledge Engineering and Ontology Development, pp. 279–284 (2011)
24. Stoilos, G., Stamou, G., Kollias, S.: A String Metric for Ontology Alignment. In: Gil, Y., Motta, E., Benjamins, V.R., Musen, M.A. (eds.) ISWC 2005. LNCS, vol. 3729, pp. 624–637. Springer, Heidelberg (2005)
25. Tummarello, G., Cyganiak, R., Catasta, M., Danielczyk, S., Delbru, R., Decker, S.: Sig.ma: Live Views on the Web of Data. Journal of Web Semantics 8(4), 355–364 (2010)

# HELIOS – Execution Optimization for Link Discovery

Axel-Cyrille Ngonga Ngomo

Department of Computer Science
University of Leipzig
Johannisgasse 26, 04103 Leipzig
ngonga@informatik.uni-leipzig.de
http://limes.sf.net

**Abstract.** Links between knowledge bases build the backbone of the Linked Data Web. In previous works, the combination of the results of time-efficient algorithms through set-theoretical operators has been shown to be very time-efficient for Link Discovery. However, the further optimization of such link specifications has not been paid much attention to. We address the issue of further optimizing the runtime of link specifications by presenting HELIOS, a runtime optimizer for Link Discovery. HELIOS comprises both a rewriter and an execution planner for link specifications. The rewriter is a sequence of fixed-point iterators for algebraic rules. The planner relies on time-efficient evaluation functions to generate execution plans for link specifications. We evaluate HELIOS on 17 specifications created by human experts and 2180 specifications generated automatically. Our evaluation shows that HELIOS is up to 300 times faster than a canonical planner. Moreover, HELIOS' improvements are statistically significant.

## 1 Introduction

Link Discovery (LD) plays a central role in the realization of the Linked Data paradigm. Several frameworks such as LIMES [9] and SILK [5] have been developed to address the time-efficient discovery of links. These frameworks take a *link specification* (short: LS, also called linkage rule [5]) as input. Each LS is converted internally into a sequence of operations which is then executed. While relying on time-efficient algorithms (e.g., PPJoin+ [17] and $\mathcal{HR}^3$ [7]) for single operations has been shown to be very time-efficient [9], the optimization of the execution of whole LS within this paradigm has been payed little attention to.

In this paper, we address this problem by presenting HELIOS, the (to the best of our knowledge) first execution optimizer for LD. HELIOS aims to reduce the costs necessary to execute a LS. To achieve this goal, our approach relies on two main components: a *rewriter* and a *planner*. The rewriter relies on algebraic operations to transform an input specification into an equivalent specification deemed less time-consuming to execute. The planner maps specifications to *execution plans*, which are sequences of operations from which a mapping results. HELIOS' planner relies on time-efficient evaluation functions to generate possible plans, approximate their runtime and return the one that is likely to be most time-efficient.[1] Our contributions are:

---

[1] HELIOS was implemented in the LIMES framework. All information to the tool can be found at http://limes.sf.net. A graphical user interface for the tool can be accessed via the SAIM interface at http://aksw.org/projects/SAIM

P. Mika et al. (Eds.) ISWC 2014, Part I, LNCS 8796, pp. 17–32, 2014.
© Springer International Publishing Switzerland 2014

1. We present a novel generic representation of LS as bi-partite trees.
2. We introduce a novel approach to rewriting LS efficiently.
3. We explicate a novel planning algorithm for LS.
4. We evaluate HELIOS on 2097 LS (17 manually and 2080 automatically generated) and show that it outperforms the state of the art by up to two orders of magnitude.

The rest of this paper is structured as follows: First, we present a formal specification of LS and execution plans for LS. Then, we present HELIOS and its two main components. Then, we evaluate HELIOS against the state of the art. Finally, we give a brief overview of related work and conclude.

## 2  Formal Specification

In the following, we present a graph grammar for LS. We employ this grammar to define a *normal form* (NF) for LS that will build the basis for the rewriter and planner of HELIOS. Thereafter, we present execution plans for LS, which formalize the sequence of operations carried out by execution engines to generate links out of specifications. As example, we use the RDF graphs shown in Table 1, for which the perfect LD results is $\{(\text{ex1:P1, ex2:P1}), (\text{ex1:P2, ex2:P2}), (\text{ex1:P3, ex2:P3}), (\text{ex1:P4}, \text{ex2:P4})\}$.

### 2.1  Normal Form for Link Specifications

Formally, most LD tools aim to discover the set $\{(s,t) \in S \times T : R(s,t)\}$ provided an input relation $R$ (e.g., owl:sameAs), a set $S$ of source resources (for example descriptions of persons) and a set $T$ of target resources. To achieve this goal, declarative LD frameworks rely on LS, which describe the conditions under which $R(s,t)$ can be assumed to hold for a pair $(s,t) \in S \times T$. Several grammars have been used for describing LS in previous works [7,5,10]. In general, these grammars assume that LS consist of two types of atomic components: *similarity measures $m$*, which allow comparing property values of input resources and *operators op*, which can be used to combine these similarities to more complex specifications.

**Table 1.** Examplary graphs

| Persons1 graph | Persons2 graph |
|---|---|
| ex1:P1 ex:label "Anna"@en . | ex2:P1 ex:label "Ana"@en . |
| ex1:P1 ex:age "12"^^xsd:integer . | ex2:P1 ex:age "12"^^xsd:integer . |
| ex1:P1 a ex:Person . | ex2:P1 a ex:Person . |
| ex1:P2 ex:label "Jack"@en . | ex2:P2 ex:label "Jack"@en . |
| ex1:P2 ex:age "15"^^xsd:integer . | ex2:P2 ex:age "14"^^xsd:integer . |
| ex1:P2 a ex:Person . | ex2:P2 a ex:Person . |
| ex1:P3 ex:label "John"@en . | ex2:P3 ex:label "Joe"@en . |
| ex1:P3 ex:age "16"^^xsd:integer . | ex2:P3 ex:age "16"^^xsd:integer . |
| ex1:P3 a ex:Person . | ex2:P3 a ex:Person . |
| ex1:P4 ex:label "John"@en . | ex2:P4 ex:label "John"@en . |
| ex1:P4 ex:age "19"^^xsd:integer . | ex2:P4 ex:age "19"^^xsd:integer . |
| ex1:P4 a ex:Person . | ex2:P4 a ex:Person . |

Without loss of generality, a similarity measure $m$ can be defined as a function $m :$
$S \times T \to [0, 1]$. We use *mappings* $M \subseteq S \times T \times [0, 1]$ to store the results of the
application of a similarity function to $S \times T$ or subsets thereof. We also store the results
of whole link specifications in mappings. The set of all mappings is denoted by $\mathcal{M}$.
We call a measure *atomic* iff it relies on exactly one similarity measure $\sigma$ (e.g., the
edit similarity, dubbed edit)[2] to compute the similarity of a pair $(s, t) \in S \times T$
with respect to the (list of) properties $p_s$ of $s$ and $p_t$ of $t$ and write $m = \sigma(p_s, p_t)$. A
similarity measure $m$ is either an atomic similarity measure or the combination of two
similarity measures via a *metric operator* such as max, min or linear combinations.
For example, edit($s$.label, $t$.label) is an atomic measure while max(edit($s$.label,
$t$.label), edit($s$.age, $t$.age)) is a complex similarity measure.

We define a *filter* as any function which maps a mapping $M$ to another mapping $M'$.
*Similarity filters* $f(m, \theta)$ return $f(m, \theta, M) = \{(s, t, r')|\exists r : (s, t, r) \in M \wedge m(s, t) \geq$
$\theta \wedge r' = \min\{m(s, t), r\}\}$. *Threshold filters* $i(\theta)$ return $i(\theta, M) = \{(s, t, r) \in M :$
$r \geq \theta\}$. Note that $i(0, M) = M$ and that we sometimes omit $M$ from similarity filters
for the sake of legibility.

We call a specification *atomic* when it consists of exactly one filtering function.
For example, applying the atomic specification $f$(edit(ex:label, ex:label), 1) to
our input data leads to the mapping $\{$(ex1:P3, ex2:P4, 1), (ex1:P2, ex2:P2, 1),
(ex1:P4, ex2:P4, 1)$\}$. A complex specification can be obtained by combining two
specifications $L_1$ and $L_2$ by (1) a *mapping operator* (that allows merging the mappings
which result from $L_1$ and $L_2$) and (2) a subsequent filter that allows postprocessing the
results of the merging.[3] In the following, we limit ourselves to the operators based on
$\cup$, $\cap$ and $\backslash$ (set difference), as they are sufficient to describe any operator based on set
operators. We extend these operators to mappings as follows:

- $M_1 \cap M_2 = \{(s, t, r) : \exists a, b \, (s, t, a) \in M_1 \wedge (s, t, b) \in M_2 \wedge r = \min(a, b)\}$.
- $M_1 \cup M_2 = \{(s, t, r) : (\neg \exists (s, t, a) \in M_1 \wedge (s, t, r) \in M_2) \vee (\neg \exists (s, t, b) \in$
  $M_2 \wedge (s, t, r) \in M_1) \vee (\exists (s, t, a) \in M_1 \wedge \exists (s, t, b) \in M_2 \wedge r = \max(a, b))\}$.
- $M_1 \backslash M_2 = \{(s, t, r) \in M_1 : \neg \exists (s, t, a) \in M_2\}$.

For example, if $M_1 = \{$(ex1:P1, ex2:P2, 1), (ex1:P1, ex2:P3, 1)$\}$ and $M_2 =$
$\{$(ex1:P1, ex2:P2, 0.5)$\}$ then $M_1 \cup M_2 = M_1$, $M_1 \cap M_2 = M_2$ and $M_1 \backslash M_2 =$
$\{$(ex1:P1, ex2:P3, 1)$\}$.

Based on this grammar, we can regard all LS as *bi-partite directed trees*
$L = (V(L), E(L))$ which abide by the following restrictions:

1. The vertices of $L$ can be either *filter nodes* $f \in F$ or *operator nodes* $op \in OP$, i.e.,
   $V(L) = F \cup OP$. The leaves and the root of $L$ are always filter nodes. The leaves
   are filters that run on $S \times T$.
2. Edges in $L$ can only exist between filters and operators, i.e., $E(L) \subseteq (F \times OP) \cup$
   $(OP \times F)$.

---

[2] We define the edit similarity of two strings $s$ and $t$ as $(1 + lev(s, t))^{-1}$, where $lev$ stands for
the Levenshtein distance.

[3] We rely on binary operators throughout this paper because n-ary set operators can always be
mapped to a sequence of binary operators.

An example of a LS is shown in Figure 1. We call this representation of LS their NF. In the rest of this paper, we deal exclusively with finite specifications, i.e., specifications such that their NF contains a finite number of nodes. We call the number of filter nodes of a specification $L$ the *size* of $L$ and denote it $|L|$. For example, the size of the specification in Figure 1 is 3. We dub the direct child of $L$'s root the *operator of L*. For example, the operator of the specification in Figure 1 is $\cap$. We call a LS $L'$ a *sub-specification* of $L$ (denoted $L' \subseteq L$) if $L'$'s NF is a sub-tree of $L$'s NF that abides by the definition of a specification (i.e., if the root of $L'$'s NF is a filter node and the NF of $L'$ contains all children of $L'$ in $L$). For example, $f(\texttt{edit}(label, label), 0.3)$ is a sub-specification of our example. We call a $L'$ a *direct sub-specification* of $L$ (denoted $L' \subset_1 L$) if $L'$ is a sub-specification of $L$ whose root node a grandchild of the $L$'s root. For example, $f(\texttt{edit}(label, label), 0.3)$ is a direct sub-specification of the LS shown in Figure 1. Finally, we transliterate LS by writing $f(m, \theta, op(L_1, L_2))$ where $f(m, \theta)$ is $L$'s root, $op$ is $L$'s operator, $L_1 \subset_1 L$ and $L_2 \subset_1 L$.

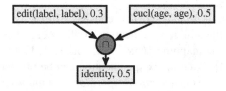

**Fig. 1.** A LS for linking the datasets Person1 and Person2. The filter nodes are rectangles while the operator nodes are circles. $\texttt{eucl}(s.age, t.age) = (1 + |s.age - t.age|)^{-1}$. This LS can be transliterated $i(\cap(f(\texttt{edit}(label, label), 0.3), f(\texttt{eucl}(age, age), 0.5)), 0.5)$.

## 2.2 Execution Plans

We define an execution plan $P$ as a sequence of *processing steps* $p_1, ..., p_n$ of which each is drawn from the set $\mathcal{A} \times \aleph \times \mathcal{T} \times \mathcal{M} \times \mathcal{M}$, where:

1. $\mathcal{A}$ is the set of all *actions* that can be carried out. This set models all the processing operations that can be carried out when executing a plan. These are:
   (a) $\texttt{run}$, which runs the computation of filters $f(m, \theta)$ where $m$ is an atomic measure. This action can make use of time-efficient algorithms such as $\mathcal{HR}^3$.
   (b) $\texttt{filter}$, which runs filters $f(m, \theta)$ where $m$ is a complex measure.
   (c) $\texttt{filterout}$, which runs the negation of $f(m, \theta)$.
   (d) Mapping operations such as $\texttt{union}$, $\texttt{intersection}$ and $\texttt{minus}$ (mapping difference) and
   (e) $\texttt{return}$, which terminates the execution and returns the final mapping.
   The result of each action (and therewith of each processing step) is a mapping.
2. $\aleph$ is the set of all complex measures as described above united with the $\emptyset$-measure, which is used by actions that do not require measures (e.g., $\texttt{return}$).
3. $\mathcal{T}$ is the set of all possible thresholds (generally $[0, 1]$) united with the $\emptyset$-threshold for actions that do not require any threshold (e.g., $\texttt{union}$) and
4. $\mathcal{M}$ is the set of all possible mappings, i.e., the powerset of $S \times T \times [0, 1]$.

We call the plan $P$ atomic if it consists of exactly one processing step. An *execution planner EP* is a function which maps a LS to an execution plan $P$. The *canonical planner $EP_0$* is the planner that runs specification in *postorder*, i.e., by traversing the NF of LS in the order left-right-root. The approach currently implemented by LIMES [9] is equivalent to $EP_0$. For example, the plan generated by $EP_0$ for Figure 1 is shown in the left column of Table 2. For the sake of brevity and better legibility, we will use abbreviated versions of plans that do not contain $\emptyset$ symbols. The abbreviated version of the plan generated by $EP_0$ for the specification in Figure 1 is shown in the right column of Table 2. We call two plans *equivalent* when they return the same results for all possible $S$ and $T$. We call a planner *complete* when it always returns plans that are equivalent to those generated by $EP_0$.

**Table 2.** Plans for the specification shown in Figure 1

| Canonical Plan | Abbreviated Canonical Plan |
|---|---|
| $M_1$=(run,edit(label,label),0.3,$\emptyset$,$\emptyset$) | $M_1$=(run,edit(label,label),0.3) |
| $M_2$=(run,eucl(age,age),0.5,$\emptyset$,$\emptyset$) | $M_2$=(run,eucl(age,age),0.5) |
| $M_3$=(intersection,$\emptyset$,$\emptyset$,$M_1$,$M_2$) | $M_3$=(intersection,$M_1$,$M_2$) |
| $M_4$=(return,$\emptyset$,$\emptyset$,$M_3$,$\emptyset$) | $M_4$=(return,$M_3$) |

| Alternative Plan1 (abbreviated) | Alternative Plan2 (abbreviated) |
|---|---|
| $M_1$=(run,edit(label,label),0.3) | $M_1$=(run,eucl(age,age),0.5) |
| $M_2$=(filter,eucl(age,age),0.5,$M_1$) | $M_2$=(filter,edit(label,label),0.3,$M_1$) |
| $M_3$=(return,$M_2$) | $M_3$=(return,$M_2$) |

The insight behind our paper is that equivalent plans can differ significantly with respect to their runtime. For example, the canonical plan shown in Table 2 would lead to 32 similarity computations (16 for edit and 16 for euclidean) and one mapping intersection, which can be computed by using 16 lookups. If we assume that each operation requires 1ms, the total runtime of this plan would be 48ms. The alternative plan 1 shown in Table 2 is equivalent to the plans in Table 2 but only runs 16 computations of edit (leading to $M_1$ of size 6) and 6 computations of euclidean on the data contained in $M_1$. The total runtime of this plan would thus be 22ms. Detecting such *runtime-efficient* and *complete plans* is the goal of HELIOS.

## 3  HELIOS

HELIOS is an optimizer for LS which consists of two main components: a rewriter (denoted RW) and a planner (denoted HP). Each LS $L$ to be processed is first forwarded to RW, which applies several algebraic transformation rules to transform $L$ into an equivalent LS $L'$ that promises to be more efficient to execute. The aim of HP is then to derive a *complete plan $P$* for $L'$. This plan is finally sent to the execution engine, which runs the plan and returns a final mapping. In the following, we present each of these components.[4] Throughout the formalization, we use $\rightarrow$ for logical implications and $\Rightarrow$ to denote rules.

---

[4] Due to space restrictions, some of the details and proofs pertaining to the rewriter and planner are omitted. Please consult http://limes.sf.net for more details.

## 3.1   The HELIOS Rewriter

RW implements an iterative rule-based approach to rewriting. Each iteration consists of three main steps that are carried out from leaves towards the root of the input specification. In the first step, sub-graphs of the input specification $L$ are replaced with equivalent sub-graphs which are likely to be more efficient to run. In a second step, dependency between nodes in $L$ are determined and propagated. The third step consists of removing portions of $L$ which do not affect the final results of $L$'s execution. These three steps are iterated until a fixpoint is reached.

**Step 1: Rewriting**   Given a LS $L$, RW begins by rewriting the specification using algebraic rules dubbed *leaf generation rules*.

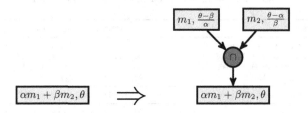

**Fig. 2.** Leaf generation rule for linear combinations

The leaf generation rules ($\mathcal{LR}$) make use of relations between metric operators and specification operators to transform leaf nodes with complex measures into graphs whose leaves contain exclusively atomic measures. For example, the rule shown in Figure 2 transforms a filter that relies on the linear combinations of 2 measures into a LS with three filters whose leaves only contain atomic measures as described in [9]. While it might seem absurd to alter the original filter in this manner, the idea here is that we can now run specialized algorithms for $m_1$ and $m_2$, then compute the intersection $M$ of the resulting mapping and finally simply check each of the $(s, t)$ with $\exists r : (s, t, r) \in M$ for whether it abides by the linear combination in the root filter. This approach is usually more time-efficient than checking each $(s, t) \in S \times T$ for whether it abides by the linear combination in the original specification. Similar rules can be devised for min (see Figure 3), max and the different average functions used in LD frameworks. After $L$ has been rewritten by the rules in $\mathcal{LR}$, each of its leaves is a filter with atomic measures.

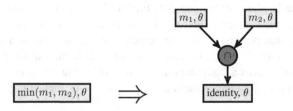

**Fig. 3.** Rule for minimum. In the corresponding rule for maximum, the mapping union is used.

**Step 2: Dependency Detection and Propagation.** The idea behind the use of *dependencies* is to detect and eliminate redundant portions of the specification. Consequently, $RW$ implements two types of dependency-based rules: *dependency detection rules* and *dependency propagation rules*. Formally, we say that $L_1$ *depends* on $L_2$ (denoted $depends(L_1, L_2)$) if the mapping resulting from $L_1$ is a subset of the mapping resulting from $L_2$ for all possible $S$ and $T$. RW generates dependencies between leaves (which now only contain atomic measures) by making use of

$$L_1 = f(m, \theta_1) \wedge L_2 = f(m, \theta_2) \wedge \theta_1 \geq \theta_2 \Rightarrow depends(L_1, L_2). \qquad (1)$$

Moreover, RW makes use of dependencies have been shown to apply between several similarity and distance measures that are commonly used in literature. For example, the authors of [17] show that for two non-empty strings $x$ and $y$, $\text{jaccard}(x, y) \geq \theta \rightarrow$ $\text{overlap}(x, y) \geq \frac{\theta}{1+\theta}(|x| + |y|)$. Given that $|x| \geq 1$ and $|y| \geq 1$, we can infer that

$$\text{jaccard}(x, y) \geq \theta \rightarrow \text{overlap}(x, y) \geq \frac{2\theta}{1+\theta}. \qquad (2)$$

Thus, if $L_1 = f(\text{jaccard}(p_s, p_t), \theta_1)$ and $L_2 = f(\text{overlap}(p_s, p_t), \theta_2)$ with $\theta_2 \leq \frac{2\theta_1}{1+\theta_1}$, then $depends(L_1, L_2)$ holds. Currently, RW implements dependencies between the $\text{overlap}$, $\text{trigrams}$ and the $\text{jaccard}$ similarities discussed in [17].

Leaf-level dependencies can be propagated towards the root of the specification based on the following rules:

$p_1$: $L = i(\theta, op(L_1, L_2)) \wedge L_1 = f(m, \theta_1, op_1(L_{11}, L_{12})) \wedge L_2 = f(m, \theta_2, op_2(L_{21}, L_{22})) \wedge \theta_1 \geq \theta \wedge \theta_2 \geq \theta) \Rightarrow L := i(0, op(L_1, L_2))$ (if the threshold of the father of any operator is smaller than that of all its children and the father node is an identity filter, then the threshold of the father can be set to 0).

$p_2$: $depends(L_1, L') \wedge depends(L_2, L') \wedge L = f(m, \theta, \cap(L_1, L_2)) \Rightarrow depends(L, L')$ (if all children of a conjunction depend on $L'$ then the father of this conjunction depends on $L'$).

$p_3$: $L = f(m, 0, \cup(L_1, L_2)) \wedge (depends(L', L_1) \vee depends(L', L_2)) \Rightarrow depends(L', L)$ (if $L'$ depends on one child of a disjunction and the father of the disjunction has the threshold 0 then $L'$ depends on the father of the disjunction).

**Step 3: Reduction.** Given two specifications $L_1 \subset_1 L$ and $L_2 \subset_1 L$ with *depends* $(L_1, L_2)$, we can now *reduce* the size of $L = filter(m, \theta, op(L_1, L_2))$ by using the following rules:

$r_1$: $L' = filter(m, \theta, \cap(L_1, L_2)) \wedge depends(L_1, L_2) \Rightarrow L' := filter(m, \theta, L_1))$,
$r_2$: $L' = filter(m, \theta, \cup(L_1, L_2)) \wedge depends(L_1, L_2) \Rightarrow L' := filter(m, \theta, L_2))$,
$r_3$: $L' = filter(m, \theta, \backslash(L_1, L_2)) \wedge depends(L_1, L_2) \Rightarrow L' := \emptyset$ where := stands for overwriting.

An example that elucidates the ideas behind $\mathcal{DR}$ is given in Figure 4. Set operators applied to one mapping are assumed to not alter the mapping.

The leaf generation terminates after at most as many iterations as the total number of atomic specifications used across all leaves of the input LS $L$. Consequently, this step has a complexity of $O(|L'|)$ where $L' = \mathcal{LR}(L)$. The generation of dependencies requires $O(|L'|^2)$ node comparisons. Each time a reduction rule is applied, the size of the $L'$ decreases, leading to reduction rules being applicable at most $|L'|$ times. The complexity of the reduction is thus also $O(|L'|)$. In the worst case of a left- or right-linear specification, the propagation of dependencies can reach the complexity $O(|L'|^2)$. All three steps of each iteration thus have a complexity of at most $O(|L'|^2)$ and the specification is at least one node smaller after each iteration. Consequently, the worst-case complexity of the rewriter is $O(|L'|^3)$.

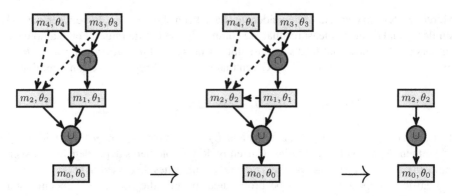

**Fig. 4.** Example of propagation of dependencies. The dashed arrows represent dependencies. The dependencies from the left figure are first (using rule $p_1$). Then, the reduction rule $r_2$ is carried out, leading to the specification on the right.

## 3.2   The HELIOS Planner

The goal of the HELIOS planner HP is to convert a given LS into a plan. Previous work on query optimization for databases have shown that finding the optimal plan for a given query is exponential in complexity [15]. The complexity of finding the perfect plan for a LS is clearly similar to that of finding a play for a given query. To circumvent the complexity problem, we rely on the following optimality assumption: Given $L_1 \subset_1 L$ and $L_2 \subset_1 L$ with $L = f(m, \theta, op(L_1, L_2))$, a good plan for $L$ can be derived from plans for $L_1$ and $L_2$. In the following, we begin by explaining core values that HP needs to evaluate a plan. In particular, we explain how HP evaluates atomic and complex plans. Thereafter, we present the algorithm behind HP and analyze its complexity.

**Plan Evaluation.** HP uses two values to characterize any plan $P$: (1) the approximate runtime of $P$ (denoted $\gamma(P)$) and (2) the selectivity of $P$ (dubbed $s(P)$), which encodes the size of the mapping returned by $P$ as percentage of $|S \times T|$.

*Computing $\gamma(P)$ and $s(P)$ for atomic LS:* Several approaches can be envisaged to achieve this goal. In our implementation of HP, we used approximations based on sampling. The basic assumption behind our feature choice was that LD frameworks are usually agnostic of $S$ and $T$ before the beginning of the LD. Thus, we opted for approximating the runtime of atomic plans $P$ by using $|S|$ and $|T|$ as parameters. We chose these values because they be computed in linear time.[5] To approximate $\gamma(P)$ for atomic plans, we generated source and target datasets of sizes $1000, 2000, \ldots, 10000$ by sampling data from the English labels of DBpedia 3.8. We then stored the runtime of the measures implemented by our framework for different thresholds $\theta$ between 0.5 and 1.[6] The runtime of the $i^{th}$ experiment was stored in the row $y_i$ of a column vector $Y$. The corresponding experimental parameters $(1, |S|, |T|, \theta)$ were stored in the row $r_i$ of a four-column matrix $R$. Note that the first entry of all $r_i$ is 1 to ensure that we can learn possible constant factors. We finally computed the vector $\Gamma = (\gamma_0, \gamma_1, \gamma_2, \gamma_3)^T$ such that

$$\gamma(P) = \gamma_0 + \gamma_1 |S| + \gamma_2 |T| + \gamma_3 \theta. \tag{3}$$

To achieve this goal, we used the following exact solution to linear regression: $\Gamma = (R^T R)^{-1} R^T Y$. The computation of $s(P)$ was carried out similarly with the sole difference that the entries $y_i$ for the computation of $s(P)$ were $\frac{|M_i|}{|S| \times |T|}$, where $M_i$ is the size of the mapping returned by the $i^{th}$ experiment. Figure 5 shows a sample of the results achieved by different algorithms in our experiments. The plan returned for the atomic $LSf(m, \theta)$ is $(\text{run}, \text{m}, \theta)$.

*Computing $\gamma(P)$ and $s(P)$ for complex LS:* The computation of the costs associated with atomic `filter`, `filterout` and operators was computed analogously to the computation of runtimes for atomic LS. For filters, the feature was the size of the input mapping. For non-atomic plans $P$, we computed $\gamma(P)$ by summing up the $\gamma(p_i)$ for all the steps $p_i$ included in the plan. The selectivity of operators was computed based on the selectivity of the mappings that served as input for the operators. To achieve this goal, we assumed that the selectivity of a plan $P$ to be the probability that a pair $(s, t)$ is returned after the execution of $P$. Moreover, we assumed the input mappings $M_1$ (selectivity: $s_1$) resp. $M_2$ (selectivity: $s_2$) to be the results of independent computations. Based on these assumptions, we derived the following selectivities for $op(M_1, M_2)$:

- $op = \cap \to s(op) = s_1 s_2$.
- $op = \cup \to s(op) = 1 - (1 - s_1)(1 - s_2)$.
- $op = \backslash \to s(op) = s_1(1 - s_2)$.

**The HP Algorithm.** The core of the approach implemented by HP is shown in Algorithm 1. For atomic specifications $f(m, \theta)$, HP simply returns $(\text{run}, \text{m}, \theta)$ (GETBESTPLAN method in Algorithm 1). If different algorithms which allow running $m$ efficiently are available, HP chooses the implementation that leads to the smallest runtime $\gamma(P)$. Note that the selectivity of all algorithms that allow running $m$ is exactly the same given that they must return the same mapping. If the specification $L = (m, \theta, op(L_1, L_2))$ is not atomic, HP's core approach is akin to a divide-and-conquer approach. It first devises a plan for $L_1$ and $L_2$ and then computes the costs of different possible plans for $op$. For $\cap$ for example, the following three plans are equivalent:

---

[5] Other values can be used for this purpose but our results suggest that using $|S|$ and $|T|$ is sufficient in most cases.

[6] We used the same hardware as during the evaluation.

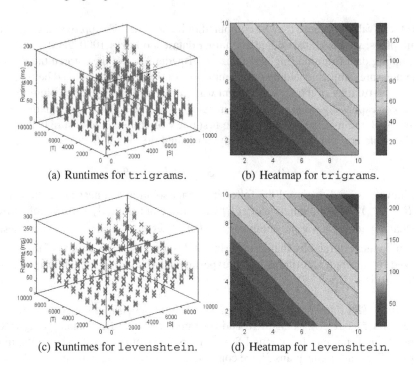

(a) Runtimes for `trigrams`.

(b) Heatmap for `trigrams`.

(c) Runtimes for `levenshtein`.

(d) Heatmap for `levenshtein`.

**Fig. 5.** Runtimes achieved by PPJoin+ (`trigrams`) and EDJoin (`levenshtein`) for $\theta = 0.5$. The x-axis of the heatmap show $|S|$ in thousands, while the y-axis shows $|T|$ in thousands. The color bars show the runtime in ms.

1. **Canonical plan.** This plan simply consists of merging (via the CONCATENATE method in Algorithm 1) the results of the best plans for $L_1$ and $L_2$. Consequently, the plan consists of (1) running the best plan for $L_1$ (i.e., $Q_1$ in Algorithm 1), (2) running the best plan for $L_2$(i.e., $Q_2$ in Algorithm 1), then (3) running the intersection action over the results of $Q_1$ and $Q_2$ and finally (4) running filter over the result of the intersection action.
2. **Filter-right plan.** This plan uses $f(m_2, \theta_2)$ as a filter over the results of $Q_1$. Consequently, the plan consists of (1) running the best plan for $L_1$, then (2) running the filter action with measure $m_2$ and threshold $\theta_2$ over the results of $Q_1$ and finally (3) running filter with measure $m$ and threshold $\theta$ over the previous result.
3. **Filter-left plan.** Analogous to the filter-right plan with $L_1$ and $L_2$ reversed.

Similar approaches can be derived for the operators $\cup$ and $\setminus$ as shown in Algorithm 1. HP now returns the least costly plan as result (GETLEASTCOSTLY method in Algorithm 1). This plan is finally forwarded to the execution engine which runs the plan and returns the resulting mapping.

Given that the alternative plans generated by HP are equivalent and that HP always chooses one of this plan, our algorithm is guaranteed to be complete. Moreover, HP approximates the runtime of at most 3 different plans per operator and at most $k$ different plans for each leaf of the input specification (where $k$ is the maximal number of algorithms that implements a measure $m$ in our framework). Consequently, the runtime complexity of HP is $O(\max\{k, 3\} \times |L|)$.

---

**Algorithm 1.** The PLAN method

---

**if** $L$ is atomic **then**
    $P = $ GETBESTPLAN$(L)$;
**else**
    **if** $L = f(m, \theta, op(L_1))$ **then**
        $P := $ GETBESTPLAN$(L_1)$
    **else**
        $Q_1 := $ PLAN$(L_1)$
        $Q_2 := $ PLAN$(L_2)$
        **if** $L = f(m, \theta, \cap(L_1, L_2))$ **then**
            $P_0 := $ CONCATENATE(intersection, $Q_1, Q_2$)
            $P_1 := $ CONCATENATE(filter$(m_1, \theta_1), Q_2$)
            $P_2 := $ CONCATENATE(filter$(m_2, \theta_2), Q_1$)
            $P := $ GETLEASTCOSTLY$(P_0, P_1, P_2)$
        **else if** $L = f(m, \theta, \cup(L_1, L_2))$ **then**
            $P_0 := $ CONCATENATE(union, $Q_1, Q_2$)
            $P_1 := $ CONCATENATE(union, filter$(m_2, \theta_2, S \times T), Q_2$)
            $P_2 := $ CONCATENATE(union, filter$(m_1, \theta_1, S \times T), Q_1$)
            $P := $ GETLEASTCOSTLY$(P_0, P_1, P_2)$
        **else if** $L = f(m, \theta, \backslash(L_1, L_2))$ **then**
            $P_0 := $ CONCATENATE(minus, $Q_1, Q_2$)
            $P_1 := $ CONCATENATE(filterout$(m_2, \theta_2), Q_2$)
            $P := $ GETLEASTCOSTLY$(P_0, P_1)$
        **end if**
    **end if**
    $a_0 = filter(m, \theta)$
    $P = $ CONCATENATE$(a_0, P)$
**end if**
**return** P

---

# 4 Evaluation

## 4.1 Experimental Setup

The aim of our evaluation was to measure the runtime improvement of HELIOS the overall runtime of LS. We thus compared the runtimes of $EP_0$ (i.e., LIMES), RW (i.e., RW + $EP_0$), HP and HELIOS (i.e., RW +HP) in our experiments. We chose LIMES because it has been shown to be very time-efficient in previous work [9]. We considered manually created and automatically generated LS. All experiments were carried out on server running Ubuntu 12.04. In each experiment, we used a single kernel of a 2.0GHz AMD Opteron processor with 10GB RAM.

The manually created LS were selected from the LATC repository.[7] We selected 17 LS which relied on SPARQL endpoints that were alive or on data dumps that were available during the course of the experiments. The specifications linked 18 different datasets and had sizes between 1 and 3. The small sizes were due to humans tending to generate small and non-redundant specifications.

---

[7] https://github.com/LATC/24-7-platform/tree/master/link-specifications

The automatic specifications were generated during a single run of specification learning algorithm EAGLE [8] on four different benchmark datasets described in Table 4.[8] The mutation and crossover rates were set to 0.6 while the number of inquiries per iteration was set to 10. The population size was set to 10. The sizes of the specifications generated by EAGLE varied between 1 and 11. We compared 1000 LS on the OAEI 2010 Restaurant and the DBLP-ACM dataset each, 80 specifications on the DBLP-Scholar dataset and 100 specifications on LGD-LGD. We chose to use benchmark datasets to ensure that the specifications used in the experiments were of high-quality w.r.t. the F-measure they led to. Each specification was executed 10 times. No caching was allowed. We report the smallest runtimes over all runs for all configurations to account for possible hardware and I/O influences.[9]

## 4.2    Results on Manual Specifications

The results of our experiments on manual specifications are shown in Table 3 and allow deriving two main insights: First, HELIOS can improve the runtime of atomic specifications (which made up 62.5% of the manual LS). This result is of tremendous importance as it suggests that the overhead generated by HELIOS is mostly insignificant, even for specifications which lead to small runtimes (e.g., DBP-DataGov requires 8ms). Moreover, our experiments reveal that HELIOS achieves a significant improvement of the overall runtime of specifications with sizes larger than 1 (37.5% of the manual LS). In the best case, HELIOS is 49.5 times faster than $EP_0$ and can reduce the runtime of the LS LDG-DBP (A) from 52.7s to 1.1s by using a filter-left plan. Here, we see that the gain in runtime generated by HELIOS grows with $|S| \times |T|$. This was to be expected as a good plan has more effect when large datasets are to be processed. Overall, HELIOS outperforms LIMES' canonical planner on all non-atomic specifications. On average, HELIOS is 4.3 times faster than the canonical planner on LS of size 3.

## 4.3    Results on Automatic Specifications

Overall, our results on automatic specifications show clearly that HELIOS outperforms the state of the art significantly. In Table 4, we show the average runtime of $EP_0$, RW, HP and HELIOS on four different datasets of growing sizes. The overall runtime of HELIOS is clearly superior to that of $EP_0$ on all datasets. As expected, the gain obtained by using HELIOS grows with the size of $|S| \times |T|$. In particular, the results on the very small Restaurant dataset support the results achieved on the manual specifications. While HP alone does not lead to a significant improvement, HELIOS leads to an improvement of the overall runtime by 6.35%. This improvement is mostly due to RW eliminating filters and therewith altering the plans generated by HP. These alterations allow for shorter and more time-efficient plans.

---

[8] The Restaurant data is available at `http://oaei.ontologymatching.org/2010/` DBLP-ACM and DBLP-Scholar are at `http://dbs.uni-leipzig.de/en/` `research/projects/object_matching/` `fever/benchmark_datasets_for_entity_resolution`

[9] All evaluation results can be found at `https://github.com/AKSW/LIMES`

**Table 3.** Comparison of runtimes on manual specifications. The top portion of the table shows runtimes of specifications of size 1 while the bottom part shows runtimes on specifications of size 3. EVT stands for Eventseer, DF for DogFood, (P) stands for person, (A) stands for airports, (U) stands for universities, (E) stands for events. The best runtimes are in bold.

| Source - Target | $|S| \times |T|$ | $EP_0$ (ms) | $RW$ (ms) | $HP$ (ms) | HELIOS (ms) | Gain (ms) |
|---|---|---|---|---|---|---|
| DBP - Datagov | $1.7 \times 10^3$ | **8** | **8** | **8** | **8** | 0 |
| RKB - DBP | $2.2 \times 10^3$ | **1** | **1** | **1** | **1** | 0 |
| Epo - DBP | $73.0 \times 10^3$ | 54 | **53** | 54 | **53** | 1 |
| Rail - DBP | $133.2 \times 10^3$ | 269 | **268** | **268** | **268** | 1 |
| Stad - Rmon | $341.9 \times 10^3$ | 25 | 23 | 15 | **14** | 11 |
| EVT - DF (E) | $531.0 \times 10^3$ | **893** | 906 | 909 | 905 | -12 |
| Climb - Rail | $1.9 \times 10^6$ | 41 | **40** | **40** | **40** | 1 |
| DBLP - DataSW | $92.2 \times 10^6$ | 59 | 59 | 58 | 54 | 5 |
| EVT - DF (P) | $148.4 \times 10^6$ | 2,477 | 2,482 | 2,503 | **2,434** | 43 |
| EVT - DBLP | $161.0 \times 10^6$ | 9,654 | **9,575** | 9,613 | 9,612 | 42 |
| DBP - OpenEI | $10.9 \times 10^3$ | **2** | **2** | **2** | **2** | 0 |
| DBP - GSpecies | $94.2 \times 10^3$ | 120 | **119** | 120 | **119** | 1 |
| Climb - DBP | $312.4 \times 10^3$ | **55** | **55** | **55** | **55** | 0 |
| DBP - LGD (E) | $34.1 \times 10^6$ | 2,259 | 2,133 | **1,206** | 1,209 | 1,050 |
| Climb - LGD | $215.0 \times 10^6$ | 24,249 | 24,835 | **3,497** | 3,521 | 20,728 |
| DBP - LGD (A) | $383.8 \times 10^6$ | 52,663 | 59,635 | 1,066 | **1,064** | 51,599 |
| LGD - LGD | $509.3 \times 10^9$ | 46,604 | 38,560 | 32,831 | **22,497** | 24,107 |

On the larger DBLP-ACM dataset, HELIOS achieve a runtime that is up to 185.8 times smaller than that of $EP_0$ (e.g., for $f(\cap(f(\texttt{jaccard}(\text{authors, authors}), 0.93)$, $f(\texttt{edit}(\text{venue, venue}), 0.93)),0.53))$. Yet, given that the runtime approximations are generic, HELIOS sometimes generated plans that led to poorer runtimes. In the worst case, a plan generated by HELIOS was 6.5 times slower than the plan generated by $EP_0$ (e.g., for $f(\cap(f(\texttt{edit}(\text{authors, authors}), 0.59), f(\texttt{cosine}(\text{venue,venue}),0.73)),0.4))$. On average, HELIOS is 38.82% faster than $EP_0$. Similar results can be derived from DBLP-Scholar, where HELIOS is 29.61% faster despite having run on only 80 specifications. On our largest dataset, the time gain is even larger with HELIOS being 46.94% faster. Note that this improvement is very relevant for end users, as it translates to approximately 1h of runtime gain for each iteration of our experiments. Here, the best

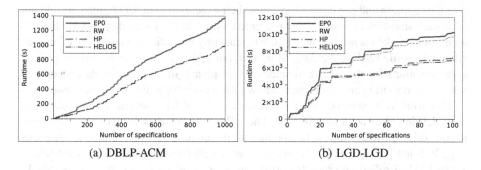

(a) DBLP-ACM          (b) LGD-LGD

**Fig. 6.** Cumulative runtimes on DBLP-ACM and LGD-LGD

**Table 4.** Summary of the results on on automatically generated specifications. $|L|$ shows for the average size $\pm$ standard deviation of the specifications in the experiment. $F_1$ shows the F-measure achieved by EAGLE on the dataset. The runtimes in four rightmost columns are the average runtimes in seconds.

|  | $|S| \times |T|$ | $|L|$ | $F_1$ | $EP_0$ | RW | HP | HELIOS |
|---|---|---|---|---|---|---|---|
| Restaurants | $72.3 \times 10^3$ | 4.44±1.79 | 0.89 | 0.15 | 0.15 | 0.15 | **0.14** |
| DBLP-ACM | $6.0 \times 10^6$ | 6.61±1.32 | 0.99 | 1.38 | 1.37 | 1.00 | **0.99** |
| DBLP-Scholar | $168.1 \times 10^6$ | 6.42±1.47 | 0.91 | 17.44 | 17.41 | 13.54 | **13.46** |
| LGD-LGD | $5.8 \times 10^9$ | 3.54±2.15 | 0.98 | 102.33 | 97.40 | 72.19 | **69.64** |

plan generated by HELIOS is 314.02 times faster than $EP_0$. Moreover, we can clearly see the effect of RW with average runtime improvement of 5.1% (see Figure 6).

We regard our overall results as very satisfactory given that the algorithms underlying $EP_0$ are in and of themselves already optimized towards runtime. Still, by combining them carefully, HELIOS can still cut down the overall runtime of learning algorithms and even of manually created link specifications. To ensure that our improvements are not simply due to chance, we compared the distribution of the cumulative runtimes of $EP_0$ and RW, HP and HELIOS as well $EP_0$ and HELIOS by using a Wilcoxon paired signed rank test at a significance level of 95%. On all datasets, all tests return significant results, which shows that the RW, HP and HELIOS lead to statistically significant runtime improvements.

## 5  Related Work

The task we address shares some similarities with the task of query optimization in databases [15]. A large spectrum of approaches have been devised to achieve this goal including System R's dynamic programming query optimization [13], cost-based optimizers and heuristic optimizers [6] and approaches based on genetic programming [1]. HELIOS is most tightly related to heuristic optimizers as it relies on an optimality assumption to discover plans in polynomial time. Overviews of existing approaches can be found in [2,15]. The main difference between the task at hand and query optimization for databases are as follows: First, databases can store elaborate statistics on the data they contain and use these to optimize their execution plan. LD frameworks do not have such statistics available when presented with a novel LS as they usually have to access remote data sources. Thus, HELIOS must rely on statistics that can be computed efficiently while reading the data. Moreover, our approach also has to rely on generic approximations for the costs and selectivity of plans. Still, we reuse the concepts of selectivity, rewriting and planning as known from query optimization in databases.

This work is a contribution to the research area of LD. Several frameworks have been developed to achieve this goal. The LIMES framework [9], in which HELIOS is embedded, provides time-efficient algorithms for running specific atomic measures (e.g., PPJoin+ [17] and $\mathcal{H}\mathcal{R}^3$ [7]) and combines them by using set operators and filters. While LIMES relied on graph traversal until now, most other systems rely on blocking. For example, SILK [5] relies on MultiBlock to execute LS efficiently. Multiblock allows mapping a whole link specification in a space that can be segmented to overlapping blocks. The similarity computations are then carried out within the blocks only. A similar approach is followed by the KnoFuss system [10]. Other time-efficient systems include [16] which present a lossy but time-efficient approach for the efficient processing of LS. Zhishi.links on the other hand relies on a pre-indexing of the resources to improve its runtime [11]. CODI uses a sampling-based approache to compute anchor alignments to reduce the its runtime [4]. Other systems descriptions can be found in the results of the Ontology Alignment Evaluation Initiative [3].[10] The idea of optimizing the runtime of schema matching has also been considered in literature [14]. For example, [12] presents an approach based on rewriting. Still, to the best of our knowledge, HELIOS is the first optimizer for link discovery that combines rewriting and planning to improve runtimes.

## 6 Conclusion and Future Work

We presented HELIOS, the (to the best of our knowledge) first execution optimizer for LS. We evaluated our approach in manually created and automatically generated LS. Our evaluation shows that HELIOS outperforms the canonical execution planner implemented in LIMES by up to two orders of magnitude. Our approach was intended to be generic. Thus, we used generic evaluation functions that allowed to detect plans that should generally work. Our results suggest that using more dataset-specific features should lead to even better runtimes and higher improvements. We thus regard HELIOS as the first step in a larger agenda towards creating a new generation of self-configuring and self-adapting LD frameworks. During the development of HELIOS, we noticed interesting differences in the behaviour of LD algorithms for different languages. For example, the $\Gamma$ vector for the different measures differs noticeably for French, English and German. We will investigate the consequences of these differences in future work. Moreover, we will investigate more elaborate features for approximating the selectivity and runtime of different algorithms.

**Acknowledgement.** This work was partially financed the EU FP7 project GeoKnow (GA: 318159) and the DFG project LinkingLOD.

## References

1. Bennett, K., Ferris, M.C., Ioannidis, Y.E.: A genetic algorithm for database query optimization. In: Proceedings of the Fourth International Conference on Genetic Algorithms, pp. 400–407 (1991)
2. Chaudhuri, S.: An overview of query optimization in relational systems. In: Proceedings of the Seventeenth ACM SIGACT-SIGMOD-SIGART Symposium on Principles of Database Systems, PODS 1998, pp. 34–43. ACM (1998)
3. Euzenat, J., Ferrara, A., Robert van Hage, W., Hollink, L., Meilicke, C., Nikolov, A., Ritze, D., Scharffe, F., Shvaiko, P., Stuckenschmidt, H., Sváb-Zamazal, O., Trojahn dos Santos, C.: Results of the ontology alignment evaluation initiative 2011. In: OM (2011)

---

[10] http://ontologymatching.org

4. Huber, J., Sztyler, T., Nößner, J., Meilicke, C.: Codi: Combinatorial optimization for data integration: results for oaei 2011. In: OM (2011)
5. Isele, R., Jentzsch, A., Bizer, C.: Efficient Multidimensional Blocking for Link Discovery without losing Recall. In: WebDB (2011)
6. Kanne, C.-C., Moerkotte, G.: Histograms reloaded: the merits of bucket diversity. In: Proceedings of the 2010 ACM SIGMOD International Conference on Management of Data, SIGMOD 2010, pp. 663–674. ACM (2010)
7. Ngonga Ngomo, A.-C.: Link discovery with guaranteed reduction ratio in affine spaces with minkowski measures. In: Cudré-Mauroux, P., et al. (eds.) ISWC 2012, Part I. LNCS, vol. 7649, pp. 378–393. Springer, Heidelberg (2012)
8. Ngonga Ngomo, A.-C., Lyko, K.: EAGLE: Efficient active learning of link specifications using genetic programming. In: Simperl, E., Cimiano, P., Polleres, A., Corcho, O., Presutti, V. (eds.) ESWC 2012. LNCS, vol. 7295, pp. 149–163. Springer, Heidelberg (2012)
9. Ngonga Ngomo, A.-C.: On link discovery using a hybrid approach. Journal on Data Semantics 1, 203–217 (2012)
10. Nikolov, A., d'Aquin, M., Motta, E.: Unsupervised learning of link discovery configuration. In: Simperl, E., Cimiano, P., Polleres, A., Corcho, O., Presutti, V. (eds.) ESWC 2012. LNCS, vol. 7295, pp. 119–133. Springer, Heidelberg (2012)
11. Niu, X., Rong, S., Zhang, Y., Wang, H.: Zhishi.links results for oaei 2011. In: OM (2011)
12. Peukert, E., Berthold, H., Rahm, E.: Rewrite techniques for performance optimization of schema matching processes. In: EDBT, pp. 453–464 (2010)
13. Griffiths Selinger, P., Astrahan, M.M., Chamberlin, D.D., Lorie, R.A., Price, T.G.: Access path selection in a relational database management system. In: Proceedings of the 1979 ACM SIGMOD International Conference on Management of Data, SIGMOD 1979, pp. 23–34. ACM, New York (1979)
14. Shvaiko, P., Euzenat, J.: Ontology matching: State of the art and future challenges. IEEE Trans. Knowl. Data Eng. 25(1), 158–176 (2013)
15. Silberschatz, A., Korth, H., Sudarshan, S.: Database Systems Concepts, 5th edn. McGraw-Hill, Inc., New York (2006)
16. Song, D., Heflin, J.: Automatically generating data linkages using a domain-independent candidate selection approach. In: Aroyo, L., Welty, C., Alani, H., Taylor, J., Bernstein, A., Kagal, L., Noy, N., Blomqvist, E. (eds.) ISWC 2011, Part I. LNCS, vol. 7031, pp. 649–664. Springer, Heidelberg (2011)
17. Xiao, C., Wang, W., Lin, X., Yu, J.X.: Efficient similarity joins for near duplicate detection. In: WWW, pp. 131–140 (2008)

# SAKey: Scalable Almost Key Discovery in RDF Data

Danai Symeonidou[1], Vincent Armant[2], Nathalie Pernelle[1], and Fatiha Saïs[1]

[1] Laboratoire de Recherche en Informatique, University Paris Sud, France
[2] Insight Center for Data Analytics, University College Cork, Ireland
{danai.symeonidou,nathalie.pernelle,fatiha.sais}@lri.fr,
{vincent.armant}@insight-centre.org

**Abstract.** Exploiting identity links among RDF resources allows applications to efficiently integrate data. Keys can be very useful to discover these identity links. A set of properties is considered as a key when its values uniquely identify resources. However, these keys are usually not available. The approaches that attempt to automatically discover keys can easily be overwhelmed by the size of the data and require clean data. We present SAKey, an approach that discovers keys in RDF data in an efficient way. To prune the search space, SAKey exploits characteristics of the data that are dynamically detected during the process. Furthermore, our approach can discover keys in datasets where erroneous data or duplicates exist (i.e., almost keys). The approach has been evaluated on different synthetic and real datasets. The results show both the relevance of almost keys and the efficiency of discovering them.

**Keywords:** Keys, Identity Links, Data Linking, RDF, OWL2.

## 1 Introduction

Over the last years, the Web of Data has received a tremendous increase, containing a huge number of RDF triples. Integrating data described in different RDF datasets and creating semantic links among them, has become one of the most important goals of RDF applications. These links express semantic correspondences between ontology entities, or semantic links between data such as *owl:sameAs* links. By comparing the number of resources published on the Web with the number of *owl:sameAs* links, the observation is that the goal of building a Web of data is not accomplished yet.

Even if many approaches have been already proposed to automatically discover *owl:sameAs* links (see [5] for a survey), only some are knowledge-based. In [16,1], this knowledge can be expressive and specific linking rules can be learnt from samples of data. [13,10] exploit key constraints, declared by a domain expert, as knowledge for data linking. A key expresses a set of properties whose values uniquely identify every resource of a dataset. Keys can be used as logical rules to clean or link data when a high precision is needed, or to construct more

P. Mika et al. (Eds.) ISWC 2014, Part I, LNCS 8796, pp. 33–49, 2014.

complex similarity functions [13,7,16]. Nevertheless, in most of the datasets published on the Web, the keys are not available and it can be difficult, even for an expert, to determine them.

Key discovery approaches have been proposed recently in the setting of the Semantic Web [3,11]. [3] discovers *pseudo keys*, keys that do not follow the OWL2 semantics [12] of a key. This type of keys appears to be useful when a local completeness of data is known. [11] discovers OWL2 keys in clean data, when no errors or duplicates exist. However, this approach cannot handle the huge amount of data found on the Web.

Data published on the Web are usually created automatically, thus may contain erroneous information or duplicates. When these data are exploited to discover keys, relevant keys can be lost. For example, let us consider a "dirty" dataset where two different people share the same social security number (SSN). In this case, SSN will not be considered as a key, since there exist two people sharing the same SSN. Allowing some exceptions can prevent the system from losing keys. Furthermore, the number of keys discovered in a dataset can be few. Even if a set of properties is not a key, it can lead to generate many correct links. For example, in most of the cases the telephone number of a restaurant is a key. Nevertheless, there can be two different restaurants located in the same place sharing phone numbers. In this case, even if this property is not a key, it can be useful in the linking process.

In this paper we present SAKey, an approach that exploits RDF datasets to discover *almost keys* that follow the OWL2 semantics. An almost key represents a set of properties that is not a key due to few exceptions (i.e., resources that do not respect the key constraint). The set of almost keys is derived from the set of *non keys* found in the data. SAKey can scale on large datasets by applying a number of filtering and pruning techniques that reduce the requirements of time and space. More precisely, our contributions are as follows:

1. the use of a heuristic to discover keys in erroneous data
2. an algorithm for the efficient discovery of non keys
3. an algorithm for the efficient derivation of almost keys from non keys

The paper is organized as follows. Section 2 discusses the related works on key discovery and Section 3 presents the data and ontology model. Sections 4 and 5 are the main part of the paper, presenting almost keys and their discovery using SAKey. Section 6 presents our experiments before Section 7 concludes.

## 2   Related Work

The problem of discovering Functional Dependencies (FD) and keys has been intensively studied in the relational databases field. The key discovery problem can be viewed as a sub-problem of Functional Dependency discovery. Indeed, a FD states that the value of one attribute is uniquely determined by the values of some other attributes. To capture the inherent uncertainty, due to data heterogeneity and data incompleteness, some approaches discover approximate keys and FDs instead of exact keys and FDs only. In [17], the authors propose a way of retrieving non composite probabilistic FDs from a set of datasets. Two strategies are proposed: the first merges the data before discovering FDs, while the second merges the FDs obtained from each dataset. TANE [8] discovers approximate FDs, i.e., FDs that almost hold. Each approximate FD is associated to an error measure which is the minimal fraction of tuples to remove for the FD to hold in the dataset. For the key discovery problem, in relational context, Gordian method [14] allows discovering exact composite keys from relational data represented in a prefix-tree. To avoid scanning all the data, this method discovers first the maximal non keys and use them to derive the minimal keys. In [6], the authors propose DUCC, a hybrid approach for the discovery of minimal keys that exploits both the monotonic characteristic of keys and the anti-monotonic characteristic of non keys to prune the search space. To improve the efficiency of the approach, DUCC uses parallelization techniques to test different sets of attributes simultaneously.

In the setting of Semantic Web where data can be incomplete and may contain multivalued properties, KD2R [11] aims at deriving exact composite keys from a set of non keys discovered on RDF datasets. KD2R, extends [14] to be able to exploit ontologies and consider incomplete data and multivalued properties. Nevertheless, even if KD2R [11] is able to discover composite OWL2 keys, it can be overwhelmed by large datasets and requires clean data. In [3], the authors have developed an approach based on TANE [8], to discover pseudo-keys (approximate keys) for which a set of few instances may have the same values for the properties of a key. The two approaches [11] and [3] differ on the semantics of the discovered keys in case of identity link computation. Indeed, the first considers the OWL2 [12] semantics, where in the case of multivalued properties, to infer an identity link between two instances, it suffices that these instances share at least one value for each property involved in the key, while in [3], the two instances have to share all the values for each property involved in the key, i.e., local completeness is assumed for all the properties (see [2] for a detailed comparison). In [15], to develop a data linking blocking method, discriminating data type properties (i.e., approximate keys) are discovered from a dataset. These properties are chosen using unsupervised learning techniques and keys of specific size are explored only if there is no smaller key with a high discriminative power. More precisely, the aim of [15] is to find the best approximate keys to construct blocks of instances and not to discover the complete set of valid minimal keys that can be used to link data.

Considering the efficiency aspect, different strategies and heuristics can be used to optimize either time complexity or space complexity. In both relational or Semantic Web settings, approaches can exploit monotonicity property of keys and the anti-monotonicity property of non keys to optimize the data exploration.

## 3  Data Model

RDF (Resource Description Framework) is a data model proposed by W3C used to describe statements about web resources. These statements are usually represented as triples $<subject, property, object>$. In this paper, we use a logical notation and represent a statement as $property(subject, object)$.

An RDF dataset D can be associated to an ontology which represents the vocabulary that is used to describe the RDF resources. In our work, we consider RDF datasets that conform to OWL2 ontologies. The ontology $O$ is presented as a tuple $(\mathcal{C}, \mathcal{P}, \mathcal{A})$ where $\mathcal{C}$ is a set of classes[1], $\mathcal{P}$ is a set of properties and $\mathcal{A}$ is a set of axioms.

In OWL2[2], it is possible to declare that a set of properties is a key for a given class. More precisely, hasKey($CE(ope_1, \ldots, ope_m)$ $(dpe_1, \ldots, dpe_n)$) states that each instance of the class expression $CE$ is uniquely identified by the object property expressions $ope_i$ and the data property expressions $dpe_j$. This means that there is no couple of distinct instances of $CE$ that share values for all the object property expressions $ope_i$ and all the data type property expressions $dpe_j$[3] involved. The semantics of the construct $owl:hasKey$ are defined in [12].

## 4   Preliminaries

### 4.1   Keys with Exceptions

RDF datasets may contain erroneous data and duplicates. Thus, discovering keys in RDF datasets without taking into account these data characteristics may lead to lose keys. Furthermore, there exist sets of properties that even if they are not keys, due to a small number of shared values, they can be useful for data linking or data cleaning. These sets of properties are particularly needed when a class has no keys.

In this paper, we define a new notion of keys with exceptions called $n$-almost keys. A set of properties is a $n$-almost key if there exist at most $n$ instances that share values for this set of properties.

To illustrate our approach, we now introduce an example. Fig. 1 contains descriptions of films. Each film can be described by its name, the release date, the language in which it is filmed, the actors and the directors involved.

One can notice that the property $d1:hasActor$ is not a key for the class $Film$ since there exists at least one actor that plays in several films. Indeed, "G. Clooney" plays in films $f2$, $f3$ and $f4$ while "M. Daemon" in $f1$, $f2$ and $f3$. Thus, there exist in total four films sharing actors. Considering each film that shares actors with other films as an exception, there exist 4 exceptions for the property $d1:hasActor$. We consider the property $d1:hasActor$ as a 4-almost key since it contains at most 4 exceptions.

Formally, the set of exceptions $E_P$ corresponds to the set of instances that share values with at least one instance, for a given set of properties $P$.

---

[1] $c(i)$ will be used to denote that $i$ is an instance of the class $c$ where $c \in \mathcal{C}$.

[2] http://www.w3.org/TR/owl2-overview

[3] We consider only the class expressions that represent atomic OWL classes. An *object property expression* is either an *object property* or an inverse *object property*. The only allowed *data type property expression* is a *data type property*.

Dataset D1:
**d1:Film(f1)**, d1:hasActor(f1," B.Pitt"), d1:hasActor(f1," J.Roberts"),
d1:director(f1," S.Soderbergh"), d1:releaseDate(f1," 3/4/01"), d1:name(f1," Ocean's 11"),
**d1:Film(f2)**, d1:hasActor(f2," G.Clooney"), d1:hasActor(f2," B.Pitt"),
d1:hasActor(f2," J.Roberts"), d1:director(f2," S.Soderbergh"), d1:director(f2," P.Greengrass"),
d1:director(f2," R.Howard"), d1:releaseDate(f2," 2/5/04"), d1:name(f2," Ocean's 12")
**d1:Film(f3)**, d1:hasActor(f3," G.Clooney"), d1:hasActor(f3," B.Pitt")
d1:director(f3," S.Soderbergh"), d1:director(f3," P.Greengrass"), d1:director(f3," R.Howard"),
d1:releaseDate(f3," 30/6/07"), d1:name(f3," Ocean's 13"),
**d1:Film(f4)**, d1:hasActor(f4," G.Clooney"), d1:hasActor(f4," N.Krause"),
d1:director(f4," A.Payne"), d1:releaseDate(f4," 15/9/11"), d1:name(f4," The descendants"),
d1:language(f4," english")
**d1:Film(f5)**,d1:hasActor(f5," F.Potente"), d1:director(f5," P.Greengrass"),
d1:releaseDate(f5," 2002"), d1:name(f5," The bourne Identity"), d1:language(f5," english")
**d1:Film(f6)**,d1:director(f6," R.Howard"), d1:releaseDate(f6," 2/5/04"),
d1:name(f6," Ocean's twelve")

**Fig. 1.** Example of RDF data

**Definition 1. (Exception set).** *Let c be a class (c $\in$ C) and P be a set of properties (P $\subseteq$ P). The exception set $E_P$ is defined as:*

$$E_P = \{X \mid \exists Y (X \neq Y) \wedge c(X) \wedge c(Y) \wedge ( \bigwedge_{p \in P} \exists U p(X,U) \wedge p(Y,U))\}$$

For example, in D1 of Fig. 1 we have: $E_{\{d1:hasActor\}} = \{f1, f2, f3, f4\}$, $E_{\{d1:hasActor, d1:director\}} = \{f1, f2, f3\}$.
Using the exception set $E_P$, we give the following definition of a $n$-almost key.

**Definition 2. ($n$-almost key).** *Let c be a class (c $\in$ C), P be a set of properties (P $\subseteq$ P) and n an integer. P is a n-almost key for c if $|E_P| \leq n$.*

This means that a set of properties is considered as a $n$-almost key, if there exist from 1 to $n$ exceptions in the dataset. For example, in D1 $\{d1:hasActor, d1:director\}$ is a 3-almost key and also a $n$-almost key for each $n \geq 3$. By definition, if a set of properties $P$ is a $n$-almost key, every superset of $P$ is also a $n$-almost key. We are interested in discovering only minimal $n$-almost keys, i.e., $n$-almost keys that do not contain subsets of properties that are $n$-almost keys for a fixed $n$.

### 4.2   Discovery of $n$-Almost Keys from $n$-non Keys

To check if a set of properties is a $n$-almost key for a class $c$ in a dataset D, a naive approach would scan all the instances of a class $c$ to verify if at most $n$ instances share values for these properties. Even when a class is described by few properties, the number of candidate $n$-almost keys can be huge. For example, if we consider a class $c$ that is described by 60 properties and we aim to discover all the $n$-almost keys that are composed of at most 5 properties, the number of candidate $n$-almost keys that should be checked will be more than 6 millions. An efficient way to obtain $n$-almost keys, as already proposed in [14,11], is to discover first all the sets of properties that are not $n$-almost keys and use them to derive the $n$-almost keys. Indeed, to show that a set of properties is not a $n$-almost key, it is sufficient to find only $(n+1)$ instances that share values for this set. We call the sets that are not $n$-almost keys, $n$-*non keys*.

**Definition 3. ($n$-non key).** *Let $c$ be a class ($c \in C$), $P$ be a set of properties ($P \subseteq \mathcal{P}$) and $n$ an integer. $P$ is a $n$-non key for $c$ if $|E_P| \geq n$.*

For example, the set of properties $\{d1{:}hasActor, d1{:}director\}$ is a 3-non key (i.e., there exist at least 3 films sharing actors and directors). Note that, every subset of $P$ is also a $n$-non key since the dataset also contains $n$ exceptions for this subset. We are interested in discovering only maximal $n$-non keys, i.e., $n$-non keys that are not subsets of other $n$-non keys for a fixed $n$.

## 5   The SAKey Approach

The SAKey approach is composed of three main steps: (1) the preprocessing steps that allow avoiding useless computations (2) the discovery of maximal $(n+1)$-non keys (see Algorithm 1) and finally (3) the derivation of $n$-almost keys from the set of $(n+1)$-non keys (see Algorithm 2).

### 5.1   Preprocessing Steps

Initially we represent the data in a structure called *initial map*. In this map, every set corresponds to a group of instances that share one value for a given property. Table 1 shows the initial map of the dataset D1 presented in Fig. 1. For example, the set $\{f2, f3, f4\}$ of $d1{:}hasActor$ represents the films that "G.Clooney" has played in.

**Table 1.** Initial map of D1

| d1:hasActor | {{f1, f2, f3}, {f2, f3, f4}, {f1, f2}, {f4}, {f5}, {f6}} |
|---|---|
| d1:director | {{f1,f2,f3}, {f2, f3, f5}, {f2, f3, f6}, {f4}} |
| d1:releaseDate | {{f1}, {f2, f6}, {f3}, {f4}, {f5}} |
| d1:language | {{f4, f5}} |
| d1:name | {{f1}, {f2}, {f3}, {f4}, {f5}, {f6}} |

**Data Filtering.** To improve the scalability of our approach, we introduce two techniques to filter the data of the initial map.

*1. Singleton Sets Filtering.* Sets of size 1 represent instances that do not share values with other instances for a given property. These sets cannot lead to the discovery of a $n$-non key, since $n$-non keys are based on instances that share values among them. Thus, only sets of instances with size bigger than 1 are kept. Such sets are called *v-exception sets*.

**Definition 4. (v-exception set $E_p^v$).** *A set of instances $\{i_1, \ldots, i_k\}$ of the class $c$ is a $E_p^v$ for the property $p \in \mathcal{P}$ and the value $v$ iff $\{p(i_1, v), \ldots, p(i_k, v)\} \subseteq D$ and $|\{i_1, \ldots, i_k\}| > 1$.*

We denote by $\mathfrak{E}_p$ the *collection* of all the v-exception sets of the property $p$.

$$\mathfrak{E}_p = \{E_p^v\}$$

For example, in D1, the set $\{f1, f2, f3\}$ is a v-exception set of the property d1:*director*.

Given a property $p$, if all the sets of $p$ are of size 1 (i.e., $\mathfrak{E}_p = \emptyset$), this property is a 1-almost key (key with no exceptions). Thus, singleton sets filtering allows the discovery of single keys (i.e., keys composed from only one property). In D1, we observe that the property d1:*name* is an 1-almost key.

**2. v-exception Sets Filtering.** Comparing the $n$-non keys that can be found by two v-exception sets $E_p^{v_i}$ and $E_p^{v_j}$, where $E_p^{v_i} \subseteq E_p^{v_j}$, we can ensure that the set of $n$-non keys that can be found using $E_p^{v_i}$, can also be found using $E_p^{v_j}$. To compute all the maximal $n$-non keys of a dataset, only the maximal v-exception sets are necessary. Thus, all the non maximal v-exception sets are removed. For example, the v-exception set $E_{d1:hasActor}^{``J.\ Roberts''}$ $\{f1, f2\}$ in the property d1:*hasActor* represents the set of films in which the actress "*J. Roberts*" has played. Since there exists another actor having participated in more than these two films (i.e., "*B, Pitt*" in films $f1$, $f2$ and $f3$), the v-exception set $\{f1, f2\}$ can be suppressed without affecting the discovery of $n$-non keys.

Table 2 presents the data after applying the two filtering techniques on the data of table 1. This structure is called *final map*.

**Table 2.** Final map of D1

| | |
|---|---|
| d1:*hasActor* | $\{\{f1, f2, f3\}, \{f2, f3, f4\}\}$ |
| d1:*director* | $\{\{f1, f2, f3\}, \{f2, f3, f5\}, \{f2, f3, f6\}\}$ |
| d1:*releaseDate* | $\{\{f2, f6\}\}$ |
| d1:*language* | $\{\{f4, f5\}\}$ |

**Elimination of Irrelevant Sets of Properties.** When the properties are numerous, the number of candidate $n$-non keys is huge. However, in some cases, some combinations of properties are irrelevant. For example, in the DBpedia dataset, the properties *depth* and *mountainRange* are never used to describe the same instances of the class *NaturalPlace*. Indeed, *depth* is used to describe natural places that are lakes while *mountainRange* natural places that are mountains. Therefore, *depth* and *mountainRange* cannot participate together in a $n$-non key. In general, if two properties have less than $n$ instances in common, these two properties will never participate together to a $n$-non key. We denote by *potential n-non key* a set of properties sharing two by two, at least $n$ instances.

**Definition 5. (Potential $n$-non key).** *A set of properties $pnk_n = \{p_1, ..., p_m\}$ is a* potential $n$-non key *for a class c iff:*

$$\forall \{p_i, p_j\} \in (pnk_n \times pnk_n) \mid I(p_i) \cap I(p_j)| \geq n$$

*where $I(p)$ is the set of instances that are subject of p.*

To discover all the maximal $n$-non keys in a given dataset it suffices to find the $n$-non keys contained in the set of maximal potential $n$-non keys $(PNK)$. For this purpose, we build a graph where each node represents a property and each edge between two nodes denotes the existence of at least $n$ shared instances between these properties. The maximal potential $n$-non keys correspond to the maximal cliques of this graph. The problem of finding all maximal cliques of a graph is NP-Complete [9]. Thus, we approximate the maximal cliques using a greedy algorithm inspired by the min-fill elimination order [4].

In D1, $PNK = \{\{d1:hasActor, d1:director, d1:releaseDate\},\{d1:language\}\}$ corresponds to the set of maximal potential $n$-non keys when $n{=}2$. By construction, all the subsets of properties that are not included in these maximal potential $n$-non keys are not $n$-non keys.

## 5.2   $n$-Non Key Discovery

We first present the basic principles of the $n$-non key discovery. Then, we introduce the pruning techniques that are used by the $n$NonKeyFinder algorithm. Finally, we present the algorithm and give an illustrative example.

**Basic Principles.** Let us consider the property $d1:hasActor$. Since this property contains at least 3 exceptions, it is considered as a 3-non key. Intuitively, the set of properties $\{d1:hasActor, d1:director\}$ is a 3-non key iff there exist at least 3 distinct films, such that each of them share the same actor and director with another film. In our framework, the sets of films sharing the same actor is represented by the collection of v-exception sets $\mathfrak{E}_{hasActor}$, while the sets of films sharing the same director is represented by the collection of v-exception sets $\mathfrak{E}_{director}$. Intersecting each set of films of $\mathfrak{E}_{hasActor}$ with each set of films of $\mathfrak{E}_{director}$ builds a new collection in which each set of films has the same actor and the same director. More formally, we introduce the *intersect operator* $\otimes$ that intersects collections of exception sets only keeping sets greater than one.

**Definition 6. (Intersect operator $\otimes$).** *Given two collections of v-exception sets $\mathfrak{E}_p$ and $\mathfrak{E}_{p'}$, we define the intersect $\otimes$ as follow:*

$$\mathfrak{E}_{p_i} \otimes \mathfrak{E}_{p_j} = \{E^v_{p_i} \cap E^v_{p_j} \mid E^v_{p_i} \in \mathfrak{E}_{p_i}, E^v_{p_j} \in \mathfrak{E}_{p_j}, and \ |E^v_{p_i} \cap E^v_{p_j}| > 1\}$$

Given a set properties $P$, the set of exceptions $E_P$ can be computed by applying the intersect operator to all the collections $\mathfrak{E}_p$ such that $p \in P$.

$$E_P = \bigcup_{p \in P} \otimes \ \mathfrak{E}_p$$

For example, for the set of properties $P = \{d1:hasActor, \ d1:hasDirector\}$, $\mathfrak{E}_P{=}\{\{f_1, f_2, f_3\}, \{f_2, f_3\}\}$ while $E_P = \{f_1, f_2, f_3\}$

**Pruning Strategies.** Computing the intersection of all the collections of v-exception sets represents the worst case scenario of finding maximal $n$-non keys within a potential $n$-non key. We have defined several strategies to avoid useless computations. We illustrate the pruning strategies in Fig. 2 where each level corresponds to the collection $\mathfrak{C}_p$ of a property $p$ and the edges express the intersections that should be computed in the worst case scenario. Thanks to the prunings, only the intersections appearing as highlighted edges are computed.

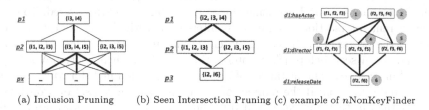

(a) Inclusion Pruning        (b) Seen Intersection Pruning    (c) example of $n$NonKeyFinder

Fig. 2. $n$NonKeyFinder prunings and execution

**1. Antimonotonic Pruning.** This strategy exploits the anti-monotonic characteristic of a $n$-non key, i.e., if a set of properties is a $n$-non key, all its subsets are by definition $n$-non keys. Thus, no subset of an already discovered $n$-non key will be explored.

**2. Inclusion Pruning.** In Fig. 2(a), the v-exception set of $p_1$ is included in one of the v-exception sets of the property $p_2$. This means that the biggest intersection between $p_1$ and $p_2$ is $\{i_3, i_4\}$. Thus, the other intersections of these two properties will not be computed and only the subpath starting from the v-exception set $\{i_3, i_4, i_5\}$ of $p_2$ will be explored (bold edges in Fig. 2(a)). Given a set of properties $P = \{p_1, \ldots, p_{j-1}, p_j, \ldots, p_n\}$, when the intersection of $p_1, \ldots, p_{j-1}$ is included in any v-exception set of $p_j$ only this subpath is explored.

**3. Seen Intersection Pruning.** In Fig. 2(b), we observe that starting from the v-exception set of the property $p_1$, the intersection between $\{i_2, i_3, i_4\}$ and $\{i_1, i_2, i_3\}$ or $\{i_2, i_3, i_5\}$ will be in both cases $\{i_2, i_3\}$. Thus, the discovery using the one or the other v-exception set of $p_2$ will lead to the same $n$-almost keys. More generally, when a new intersection is included in an already computed intersection, this exploration stops.

**$n$NonkeyFinder Algorithm.** To discover the maximal $n$-non keys, the v-exception sets of the final map are explored in a depth-first way. Since the condition for a set of properties $P$ to be a $n$-non key is $E_P \geq n$ the exploration stops as soon as $n$ exceptions are found.

The algorithm takes as input a property $p_i$, $curInter$ the current intersection, $curNKey$ the set of already explored properties, $seenInter$ the set of already computed intersections, $nonKeySet$ the set of discovered $n$-non keys, $E$ the set of exceptions $E_P$ for each explored set of properties $P$, $n$ the defined number of exceptions and $PNK$ the set of maximal potential $n$-non keys.

The first call of $n$NonKeyFinder is: $n$NonKeyFinder$(p_i, I, \emptyset, \emptyset, \emptyset, \emptyset, n, PNK)$ where $p_i$ is the first property that belongs to at least one potential $n$-non key and $curInter$ the complete set of instances $I$. To ensure that a set of properties should be explored, the function *uncheckedNonKeys* returns the potential $n$-non keys that (1) contain this set of properties and (2) are not included in an already discovered $n$-non key in the *nonKeySet*. If the result is not empty, this set of properties is explored. In Line 3, the Inclusion pruning is applied i.e., if the *curInter* is included in one of the v-exception sets of the property $p_i$, the *selected*$\mathfrak{E}_p$ will contain only the *curInter*. Otherwise, all the v-exception sets of the property $p_i$ are selected. For each selected v-exception set of the property $p_i$, all the maximal $n$-non keys using this v-exception set are discovered. To do so, the current intersection (*curInter*) is intersected with the selected v-exception sets of the property $p_i$. If the new intersection (*newInter*) is bigger than 1 and has not been seen before (Seen intersection pruning), then $p_i \cup curNonKey$ is stored in *nvNkey*. The instances of *newInter* are added in $E$ for *nvNkey* using the update function. If the number of exceptions for a given set of properties is bigger than $n$, then this set is added to the *nonKeySet*. The algorithm is called with the next property $p_{i+1}$ (Line 16). When the exploration of an intersection (*newInter*) is done, this intersection is added to *SeenInter*. Once, all the $n$-non keys for the property $p_i$ have been found, nNonKeyFinder is called for the property $p_{i+1}$ with *curInter* and *curNKey* (Line 19), forgetting the property $p_i$ in order to explore all the possible combinations of properties.

Table 3 shows the execution of nNonKeyFinder for the example presented in Fig. 2(c) where $PNK = \{\{d1{:}hasActor, d1{:}director, d1{:}releaseDate\}\}$. We represent the properties in Table 3 by $p_1, p_2, p_3$ respectively.

---

**Algorithm 1.** nNonKeyFinder

**Input:** $p_i, curInter, curNKey, seenInter, nonKeySet, E, n$
**Output:** $nonKeySet$: set of the non keys
1  $uncheckedNonKeys \leftarrow unchecked(\{pi\} \cup curNKey, nonKeySet, PNK)$
2  **if** $uncheckedNonKeys \neq \emptyset$ //PNK and Antimonotonic Pruning **then**
3     **if** $(curInter \subseteq E_{p_i}^v$ s.t. $E_{p_i}^v \in \mathfrak{E}_{p_i})$ //Inclusion Pruning **then**
4        ⌞ $selected\mathfrak{E}_{p_i} \leftarrow \{\{curInter\}\}$
5     **else**
6        ⌞ $selected\mathfrak{E}_{p_i} \leftarrow \mathfrak{E}_{p_i}$
7     **for each** $E_{p_i}^v \in selected\mathfrak{E}_{p_i}$ **do**
8        $newInter \leftarrow E_{p_i}^v \cap curInter$
9        **if** $(|newInter| > 1)$ **then**
10          **if** $(newInter \nsubseteq k$ s.t. $k \in seenInter)$ //Seen Intersection Pruning **then**
11             $nvNKey \leftarrow \{p_i\} \cup curNKey$
12             $update(E, nvNKey, newInter)$
13             **if** $(|E_{nvNkey}| > n)$ **then**
14                ⌞ $nonKeySet \leftarrow nonKeySet \cup \{nvNKey\}$
15             **if** $((i+1) < \#\ properties)$ **then**
16                ⌞ nNonKeyFinder$(p_{i+1}, newInter, nvNKey, seenInter, nonKeySet, E, n)$
17       ⌞ $seenInter \leftarrow seenInter \cup \{newInter\}$
18 **if** $((i+1) < \#\ properties)$ **then**
19 ⌞ nNonKeyFinder$(p_{i+1}, curInter, curNKey, seenInter, nonKeySet, E, n)$

---

**Table 3.** $n$NonKeyFinder execution on the example of Fig. 2(c)

| $p_i$ | $selected\,\mathfrak{E}_p$ | $E_p^v$ | $curInter$ | $curNkey$ | $seenInter$ | $nonKeySet$ | $E$ |
|---|---|---|---|---|---|---|---|
| $p_1$ | $\{1,2\}$ | 1 | $\{f1,\ldots,f6\}$ | $\{\}$ | $\{\}$ | $\{\{p_1\}\}$ | $\{(p_1):(f_1,f_2,f_3)\}$ |
| $p_2$ | $\{3\}$ | 3 | $\{f1,f2,f3\}$ | $\{p_1\}$ | $\{\}$ | $\{\{p_1\},\{p_1,p_2\}\}$ | $\{(p_1):(f_1,f_2,f_3)$ $(p_1,p_2):(f_1,f_2,f_3)\}$ |
| $p_3$ | $\{6\}$ | 6 | $\{f1,f2,f3\}$ | $\{p_1,p_2\}$ | $\{\}$ | $\{\{p_1\},\{p_1,p_2\}\}$ | $\{(p_1):(f_1,f_2,f_3)$ $(p_1,p_2):(f_1,f_2,f_3)\}$ |
| $p_3$ | $\{6\}$ | 6 | $\{f1,f2,f3\}$ | $\{p_1\}$ | $\{\{f_1,f_2,f_3\}\}$ | $\{\{p_1\},\{p_1,p_2\}\}$ | $\{(p_1):(f_1,f_2,f_3)$ $(p_1,p_2):(f_1,f_2,f_3)\}$ |
| $p_1$ | $\{1,2\}$ | 2 | $\{f1,\ldots,f6\}$ | $\{\}$ | $\{\{f_1,f_2,f_3\}\}$ | $\{\{p_1\},\{p_1,p_2\}\}$ | $\{(p_1):(f_1,f_2,f_3)$ $(p_1,p_2):(f_1,f_2,f_3)\}$ |
| ... | ... | ... | ... | ... | ... | ... | ... |
| $p_3$ | $\{6\}$ | 6 | $\{f2,f3,f6\}$ | $\{p_2\}$ | $\{\{f_1,f_2,f_3\}$ $\{f_2,f_3,f_4\}\}$ | $\{\{p_1\},\{p_1,p_2\},$ $\{p_2,p_3\}\}$ | $\{(p_1):(f_1,f_2,f_3)$ $(p_1,p_2):(f_1,f_2,f_3)\}$ $(p_2,p_3):(f_2,f_6)\}$ |

## 5.3 Key Derivation

In this section we introduce the computation of minimal $n$-almost keys using maximal $(n+1)$-non keys. A set of properties is a $n$-almost key, if it is not equal or included to any maximal $(n+1)$-non key. Indeed, when all the $(n+1)$-non keys are discovered, all the sets not found as $(n+1)$-non keys will have at most n exceptions ($n$-almost keys).

Both [14] and [11] derive the set of keys by iterating two steps: (1) computing the Cartesian product of complement sets of the discovered non keys and (2) selecting only the minimal sets. Deriving keys using this algorithm is very time consuming when the number of properties is big. To avoid useless computations, we propose a new algorithm that derives fast minimal $n$-almost keys, called key-Derivation. In this algorithm, the properties are ordered by their frequencies in the complement sets. At each iteration, the most frequent property is selected and all the $n$-almost keys involving this property are discovered recursively. For each selected property $p$, we combine $p$ with the properties of the selected complement sets that do not contain $p$. Indeed, only complement sets that do not contain this property can lead to the construction of minimal $n$-almost keys. When all the $n$-almost keys containing $p$ are discovered, this property is eliminated from every complement set. When at least one complement set is empty, all the $n$-almost keys have been discovered. If every property has a different frequency in the complement sets, all the $n$-almost keys found are minimal $n$-almost keys. In the case where two properties have the same frequency, additional heuristics should be taken into account to avoid computations of non minimal $n$-almost keys.

Let us illustrate the key derivation algorithm throughout and example. Let $\mathcal{P}= \{p_1, p_2, p_3, p_4, p_5\}$ be the set of properties and $\{\{p_1, p_2, p_3\}, \{p_1, p_2, p_4\}, \{p_2, p_5\}, \{p_3, p_5\}\}$ the set of maximal $n$-non keys. In this example, the complement sets of $n$-non keys are $\{\{p_1, p_2, p_4\}, \{p_1, p_3, p_4\}, \{p_3, p_5\}, \{p_4, p_5\}\}$. The properties of this example are explored in the following order: $\{p_4, p_1, p_3, p_5, p_2\}$. Starting from the most frequent property, $p_4$, we calculate all the $n$-almost keys containing this property. The selected complement set that does not contain this property is $\{p_3, p_5\}$. The property $p_4$ is combined with every property of this set. The set of $n$-almost keys is now $\{\{p_3, p_4\}, \{p_4, p_5\}\}$. The next property to be explored is $p_1$. The selected complement sets are $\{p_5\}$ and $\{p_3, p_5\}$. To avoid the discovery of non-minimal $n$-almost keys, we order the properties of the selected complement sets, according to their frequency (i.e., $\{p_5, p_3\}$). To discover $n$-almost keys containing $p_1$ and $p_5$, we only consider the selected complement sets that do not contain $p_5$. In this case, no complement set is selected and the key $\{p_1, p_5\}$ is added to the $n$-almost keys. $p_5$ is locally suppressed for $p_1$. Since there is an empty complement set, all the $n$-almost keys containing $p_1$ are found and $p_1$ is removed from the complement sets. Following these steps, the set of minimal $n$-almost keys in the end will be $\{\{p_1, p_5\}, \{p_2, p_3, p_5\}, \{p_3, p_4\}, \{p_4, p_5\}\}$.

---

**Algorithm 2.** keyDerivation

---

    **Input**: *compSets*: set of complement sets
    **Output**: *KeySet*: set of $n$-almost keys
1  $KeySet \leftarrow \emptyset$
2  $orderedProperties = $ getOrderedProperties(compSets)
3  **for** *each* $p_i \in orderedProperties$ **do**
4       $selectedCompSets \leftarrow$ selectSets($p_i$, *compSets*)
5       **if** $(selectedCompSets == \emptyset)$ **then**
6          $KeySet = KeySet \cup \{\{p_i\}\}$
7       **else**
8          $KeySet = KeySet \cup \{p_i \times$ keyDerivation($selectedCompSets$)$\}$
9       $compSets = $ remove($compSets$, $p_i$)
10      **if** ( $\exists\, set \in compSet\ s.t.\ set == \emptyset$ ) **then**
11         break

12 **return** $KeySet$

---

# 6   Experiments

We evaluated SAKey using 3 groups of experiments. In the first group, we demonstrate the scalability of SAKey thanks to its filtering and pruning techniques. In the second group we compare SAKey with KD2R, the only approach that discovers composite OWL2 keys. The two approaches are compared in two steps. First, we compare the runtimes of their non key discovery algorithms and second, the runtimes of their key derivation algorithms. Finally, we show how $n$-almost keys can improve the quality of data linking. The experiments are executed on 3 different datasets, DBpedia[4], YAGO[5] and OAEI 2013[6].

The execution time of each experiment corresponds to the average time of 10 repetitions. In all experiments, the data are stored in a dictionary-encoded map,

---

[4] http://wiki.dbpedia.org/Downloads39
[5] http://www.mpi-inf.mpg.de/yago-naga/yago/downloads.html
[6] http://oaei.ontologymatching.org/2013

where each distinct string appearing in a triple is represented by an integer. The experiments have been executed on a single machine with 12GB RAM, processor 2x2.4Ghz, 6-Core Intel Xeon and runs Mac OS X 10.8.

## 6.1  Scalability of SAKey

SAKey has been executed in every class of DBpedia. Here, we present the scalability on the classes *DB:NaturalPlace*, *DB:BodyOfWater* and *DB:Lake* of DBpedia (see Fig. 3(b) for more details) when $n = 1$. We first compare the size of data before and after the filtering steps (see Table 4), and then we run SAKey on the filtered data with and without applying the prunings (see Table 5).

**Data Filtering Experiment.** As shown in Table 4, thanks to the filtering steps, the complete set of $n$-non keys can be discovered using only a part of the data. We observe that in all the three datasets more than 88% of the sets of instances of the initial map are filtered applying both the singleton filtering and the v-exception set filtering. Note that more than 50% of the properties are suppressed since they are single 1-almost keys (singleton filtering).

**Table 4.** Data filtering results on different DBpedia classes

| class | # Initial sets | # Final sets | # Singleton sets | # $E_p^v$ filtered | Suppressed Prop. |
|---|---|---|---|---|---|
| *DB:Lake* | 57964 | 4856(8.3%) | 50807 | 2301 | 78 (54%) |
| *DB:BodyOfWater* | 139944 | 14833(10.5%) | 120949 | 4162 | 120 (60%) |
| *DB:NaturalPlace* | 206323 | 22584(11%) | 177278 | 6461 | 131 (60%) |

**Prunings of SAKey.** To validate the importance of our pruning techniques, we run nNonKeyFinder on different datasets with and without prunings. In Table 5, we show that the number of calls of nNonKeyFinder decreases significantly using the prunings. Indeed, in the class *DB:Lake* the number of calls decreases to half. Subsequently, the runtime of SAKey is significantly improved. For example, in the class *DB:NaturalPlace* the time decreases by 23%.

**Table 5.** Pruning results of SAKey on different DBpedia classes

| class | without prunings | | with prunings | |
|---|---|---|---|---|
| | Calls | Runtime | Calls | Runtime |
| *DB:Lake* | 52337 | 13s | 25289 (48%) | 9s |
| *DB:BodyOfWater* | 443263 | 4min28s | 153348 (34%) | 40s |
| *DB:NaturalPlace* | 1286558 | 5min29s | 257056 (20%) | 1min15s |

To evaluate the scalability of SAKey when $n$ increases, nNonKeyFinder has been executed with different $n$ values. This experiment has shown that nNonKeyFinder is not strongly affected by the increase of $n$. Indeed, allowing 300 exceptions ($n=300$) for the class *DB:NaturalPlace*, the execution time increases only by 2 seconds.

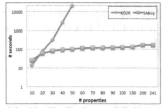

| class | # triples | # instances | # prop. | KD2R Runtime | SAKey Runtime |
|---|---|---|---|---|---|
| *DB:Lake* | 409016 | 9438 | 111 | outOfMem. | 8s |
| *DB:BodyOfWater* | 1068428 | 34000 | 200 | outOfMem. | 37s |
| *DB:NaturalPlace* | 1604348 | 49913 | 243 | outOfMem. | 1min10s |
| *YA:Building* | 114783 | 54384 | 17 | 26s | 9s |
| *YA:SportsSeason* | 83944 | 17839 | 35 | 2min | 9s |
| *DB:Website* | 8506 | 2870 | 66 | 13min | 1s |
| *DB:Mountain* | 115796 | 12912 | 124 | 191min | 11s |

(a) *n*NonKeyFinder on *DB:NaturalPlace*      (b) *n*NonKeyFinder in different classes

**Fig. 3.** *n*NonKeyFinder runtime for DBpedia and YAGO classes

## 6.2  KD2R vs. SAKey: Scalability Results

In this section, we compare SAKey with KD2R in two steps. The first experiment compares the efficiency of SAKey against KD2R in the non key discovery process. Given the same set of non keys, the second experiment compares the key discovery approach of KD2R against the one of SAKey. Note that, to obtain the same results from both KD2R and SAKey, the value of $n$ is set to 1.

*n*-**non key Discovery.** In Fig. 3(a), we compare the runtimes of the non key discovery of both KD2R and SAKey for the class *DB:NaturalPlace*. Starting from the 10 most frequent properties, properties are added until the whole set of properties is explored. We observe that KD2R is not resistant to the number of properties and its runtime increases exponentially. For example, when the 50 most frequent properties are selected, KD2R takes more than five hours to discover the non keys while SAKey takes only two minutes. Moreover, we notice that SAKey is linear in the beginning and almost constant after a certain size of properties. This happens since the class *DB:NaturalPlace* contains many single keys and unlike KD2R, SAKey is able to discover them directly using the singleton sets pruning. In Fig. 3(b), we observe that SAKey is orders of magnitude faster than KD2R in classes of DBpedia and YAGO. Moreover, KD2R runs out of memory in classes containing many properties and triples.

*n*-**almost key Derivation.** We compare the runtimes of the key derivation of KD2R and SAKey on several sets of non keys. In Fig. 4(a), we present how the time evolves when the number of non keys of the class *DB:BodyOfWater* increases. SAKey scales almost linearly to the number of non keys while the time of KD2R increases significantly. For example, when the number of non keys is 180, KD2R needs more than 1 day to compute the set of minimal keys while SAKey less than 1 minute. Additionally, to show the efficiency of SAKey over KD2R, we compare their runtimes on several datasets (see Fig. 4(b)). In every case, SAKey outperforms KD2R since it discovers fast the set of minimal keys.

In the biggest class of DBpedia, *DB:Person* (more than 8 million triples, 9 hundred thousand instances and 508 properties), SAKey takes 19 hours to compute the *n*-non keys while KD2R cannot even be applied.

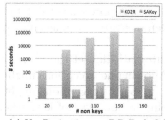

| Class | # non keys | # keys | KD2R | SAKey |
|---|---|---|---|---|
| $DB{:}Website$ | 9 | 44 | 1s | 1s |
| $YA{:}Building$ | 15 | 34 | 1s | 1s |
| $YA{:}SportsSeason$ | 22 | 175 | 2s | 1s |
| $DB{:}Lake$ | 50 | 480 | 1min10s | 1s |
| $DB{:}Mountain$ | 49 | 821 | 8min | 1s |
| $DB{:}BodyOfWater$ | 220 | 3846 | > 1 day | 66s |
| $DB{:}NaturalPlace$ | 302 | 7011 | > 2 days | 5min |

(a) KeyDerivation on $DB{:}BodyOfWater$       (b) KeyDerivation on different classes

**Fig. 4.** KeyDerivation runtime for DBpedia and YAGO classes

## 6.3 Data Linking with $n$-Almost Keys

Here, we evaluate the quality of identity links that can be found using $n$-almost keys. We have exploited one of the datasets provided by the OAEI'13. The benchmark contains one original file and five test cases. The second file is taken from the first test case. Both files contain DBpedia descriptions of persons and locations (1744 triples, 430 instances, 11 properties). Table 6 shows the results when $n$ varies from 0 to 18. In Table 6(a), strict equality is used to compare literal values while in Table 6(b), the Jaro-Winkler similarity measure is used. The recall, precision and F-measure of our linking results has been computed using the gold-standard provided by OAEI'13.

**Table 6.** Data Linking in OAEI 2013

| # exceptions | Recall | Precision | F-Measure |
|---|---|---|---|
| 0, 1, 2 | 25.6% | 100% | 41% |
| 3, 4 | 47.6% | 98.1% | 64.2% |
| 5, 6 | 47.9% | 96.3% | 63.9% |
| 7, ..., 17 | 48.1% | 96.3% | 64.1% |
| 18 | 49.3% | 82.8% | 61.8% |

(a) Data Linking using strict equality

| # exceptions | Recall | Precision | F-Measure |
|---|---|---|---|
| 0, 1, 2 | 64.4% | 92.3% | 75.8% |
| 3, 4 | 73.7% | 90.8% | 81.3% |
| 5, 6 | 73.7% | 90.8% | 81.3% |
| 7, ..., 17 | 73.7% | 90.8% | 81.3% |
| 18 | 74.4% | 82.4% | 78.2% |

(b) Data Linking using similarity measures

In both tables, we observe that the quality of the data linking improves when few exceptions are allowed. As expected, when simple similarity measures are used, the recall increases while the precision decreases, but overall, better F-measure results are obtained. As shown in [11],using keys to construct complex similarity functions to link data, such as [13], can increase even more the recall. Therefore, linking results can be improved when $n$-almost keys are exploited by sophisticated data linking tools.

## 7 Conclusion

In this paper, we present SAKey, an approach for discovering keys on large RDF data under the presence of errors and duplicates. To avoid losing keys when data are "dirty", we discover $n$-almost keys, keys that are almost valid in a dataset. Our system is able to scale when data are large, in contrast to the state-of the art that discovers composite OWL2 keys. Our extensive experiments show that

SAKey can run on millions of triples. The scalability of the approach is validated on different datasets. Moreover, the experiments demonstrate the relevance of the discovered keys.

In our future work, we plan to define a way to automatically set the value of $n$, in order to ensure the quality of a $n$-almost key. Allowing no exceptions might be very strict in RDF data while allowing a huge number of exceptions might end up to many false negatives. We also aim to define a new type of keys, the conditional keys which are keys valid in a subset of the data.

SAKey is available for download at https://www.lri.fr/sakey.

**Acknowledgments.** This work is supported by the ANR project Qualinca (QUALINCA-ANR-2012-CORD-012-02).

# References

1. Arasu, A., Ré, C., Suciu, D.: Large-scale deduplication with constraints using dedupalog. In: ICDE, pp. 952–963 (2009)
2. Atencia, M., Chein, M., Croitoru, M., Jerome David, M.L., Pernelle, N., Saïs, F., Scharffe, F., Symeonidou, D.: Defining key semantics for the rdf datasets: Experiments and evaluations. In: ICCS (2014)
3. Atencia, M., David, J., Scharffe, F.: Keys and pseudo-keys detection for web datasets cleansing and interlinking. In: ten Teije, A., Völker, J., Handschuh, S., Stuckenschmidt, H., d'Acquin, M., Nikolov, A., Aussenac-Gilles, N., Hernandez, N. (eds.) EKAW 2012. LNCS, vol. 7603, pp. 144–153. Springer, Heidelberg (2012)
4. Dechter, R.: Constraint Processing. Morgan Kaufmann Publishers Inc., San Francisco (2003)
5. Ferrara, A., Nikolov, A., Scharffe, F.: Data linking for the semantic web. Int. J. Semantic Web Inf. Syst. 7(3), 46–76 (2011)
6. Heise, A., Jorge-Arnulfo, Q.-R., Abedjan, Z., Jentzsch, A., Naumann, F.: Scalable discovery of unique column combinations. VLDB 7(4), 301–312 (2013)
7. Hu, W., Chen, J., Qu, Y.: A self-training approach for resolving object coreference on the semantic web. In: WWW, pp. 87–96 (2011)
8. Huhtala, Y., Kärkkäinen, J., Porkka, P., Toivonen, H.: Tane: An efficient algorithm for discovering functional and approximate dependencies. The Computer Journal 42(2), 100–111 (1999)
9. Karp, R.M.: Reducibility among combinatorial problems. In: Miller, R.E., Thatcher, J.W. (eds.) Complexity of Computer Computations. The IBM Research Symposia Series, pp. 85–103 (1972)
10. Nikolov, A., Motta, E.: Data linking: Capturing and utilising implicit schema-level relations. In: Proceedings of Linked Data on the Web workshop at WWW (2010)
11. Pernelle, N., Saïs, F., Symeonidou, D.: An automatic key discovery approach for data linking. J. Web Sem. 23, 16–30 (2013)
12. Recommendation, W.: Owl2 web ontology language: Direct semantics. In: Motik, B., Patel-Schneider, P.F., Grau, B.C. (eds.), W3C (October 27, 2009), http://www.w3.org/TR/owl2-direct-semantics
13. Saïs, F., Pernelle, N., Rousset, M.C.: Combining a logical and a numerical method for data reconciliation. Journal on Data Semantics 12, 66–94 (2009)

14. Sismanis, Y., Brown, P., Haas, P.J., Reinwald, B.: Gordian: efficient and scalable discovery of composite keys. In: VLDB, pp. 691–702 (2006)
15. Song, D., Heflin, J.: Automatically generating data linkages using a domain-independent candidate selection approach. In: Aroyo, L., Welty, C., Alani, H., Taylor, J., Bernstein, A., Kagal, L., Noy, N., Blomqvist, E. (eds.) ISWC 2011, Part I. LNCS, vol. 7031, pp. 649–664. Springer, Heidelberg (2011)
16. Volz, J., Bizer, C., Gaedke, M., Kobilarov, G.: Discovering and maintaining links on the web of data. In: Bernstein, A., Karger, D.R., Heath, T., Feigenbaum, L., Maynard, D., Motta, E., Thirunarayan, K. (eds.) ISWC 2009. LNCS, vol. 5823, pp. 650–665. Springer, Heidelberg (2009)
17. Wang, D.Z., Dong, X.L., Sarma, A.D., Franklin, M.J., Halevy, A.Y.: Functional dependency generation and applications in pay-as-you-go data integration systems. In: WebDB (2009)

# Introducing Wikidata to the Linked Data Web

Fredo Erxleben[1], Michael Günther[1], Markus Krötzsch[1],
Julian Mendez[1], and Denny Vrandečić[2]

[1] Technische Universität Dresden, Germany
[2] Google, San Francisco, USA

**Abstract.** Wikidata is the central data management platform of Wikipedia. By the efforts of thousands of volunteers, the project has produced a large, open knowledge base with many interesting applications. The data is highly interlinked and connected to many other datasets, but it is also very rich, complex, and not available in RDF. To address this issue, we introduce new RDF exports that connect Wikidata to the Linked Data Web. We explain the data model of Wikidata and discuss its encoding in RDF. Moreover, we introduce several partial exports that provide more selective or simplified views on the data. This includes a class hierarchy and several other types of ontological axioms that we extract from the site. All datasets we discuss here are freely available online and updated regularly.

## 1 Introduction

Wikidata is the community-created knowledge base of Wikipedia, and the central data management platform for Wikipedia and most of its sister projects [21]. Since its public launch in late 2012, the site has gathered data on more than 15 million entities, including over 34 million statements, and over 80 million labels and descriptions in more than 350 languages. This is the work of well over 40 thousand registered users who have actively contributed so far. Their ceaseless efforts continue to make Wikidata more and more comprehensive and accurate.

One reason for this strong community participation is the tight integration with Wikipedia: as of today, almost every Wikipedia page in every language incorporates content from Wikidata. Primarily, this concerns the links to other languages shown on the left of every page, but Wikipedia editors also make increasing use of the possibility to integrate Wikidata content into articles using special syntax. Upcoming improvements in Wikidata's query capabilities will add more powerful options for doing this, which is expected to further increase the participation of the Wikipedia communities in Wikidata.

A result of these efforts is a knowledge base that is a valuable resource for practitioners and researchers alike. Like Wikipedia, it spans a wide body of general and specialised knowledge that is relevant in many application areas. All of the data is freshly curated by the Wikimedia community, and thus new and original. Naturally, the data is also completely free and open. More than any other factor, however, it is the richness of the data that makes Wikidata unique. Many statements come with provenance information or include additional context data, such as temporal validity; data is strongly connected to external datasets in many domains; and all of the data is multi-lingual by design. Moreover, the data is highly dynamic and based on complex community processes that are interesting in their own right.

P. Mika et al. (Eds.) ISWC 2014, Part I, LNCS 8796, pp. 50–65, 2014.
© Springer International Publishing Switzerland 2014

The relevance of Wikidata for researchers in semantic technologies, linked open data, and Web science thus hardly needs to be argued for. Already the success of DBpedia [2] and Yago(2) [11] testifies to the utility of Wikipedia-related data in these areas. Other related projects include Cyc [14] and Freebase [3]. Each of these projects differs from Wikidata in important aspects [21], and in particular the content of Wikidata is not covered by any of them. Even the most similar datasets, Freebase and DBpedia, contain completely different data. For example, less than 10% of Wikidata items are mapped to objects in Freebase, and even their data is mostly different. Indeed, these differences are already obvious when considering the vocabulary used in each project: DBpedia, e.g., has over 18,000 properties while Wikidata has little more than 1,000, including many that do not correspond to properties in DBpedia. Nevertheless, the success of such projects hints at the potential of Wikidata.

In spite of all this, Wikidata has hardly been used in the semantic web community so far. The simple reason is that, until recently, the data was not available in RDF. To change this, we have developed RDF encodings for Wikidata, implemented a tool for creating file exports, and set up a site where the results are published. Regular RDF dumps of the data can now be found at http://tools.wmflabs.org/wikidata-exports/rdf/. This paper describes the design underlying these exports and introduces the new datasets:

- In Section 2, we introduce the data model of Wikidata, which governs the structure of the content that we want to export.
- In Section 3, we present the RDF encoding of this content. This includes URI schemes, our handling of multilingual content, and our use of external vocabularies.
- The rich information in Wikidata also leads to relatively complex RDF encodings. Therefore, in Section 4, we discuss alternative and simplified RDF encodings, which we provide for applications that do not require access to all aspects of the data.
- Wikidata also contains interesting schema information which can be expressed naturally using RDFS and OWL. In Section 5, we present several forms of terminological information that we obtain from Wikidata, and for which we provide exports as well.
- The content of Wikidata is strongly connected to external datasets, but rarely uses URIs to do so. To fully integrate Wikidata with the linked data Web, we translate many references to external databases into URIs, as explained in Section 6.
- In Section 7, we present the actual export files and provide some statistics about their current content.

Besides the actual file exports, we also provide all source code that has been used for creating them. Our implementation is part of *Wikidata Toolkit*,[1] a Java library for working with Wikidata content that we develop.

## 2   The Data Model of Wikidata

Like Wikipedia, Wikidata is organised in pages, and this is also how the data is structured. Every subject on which Wikidata has structured data is called an *entity*, and every entity has a page. The system distinguishes two types of entities so far: *items* and

---

[1] https://www.mediawiki.org/wiki/Wikidata_Toolkit

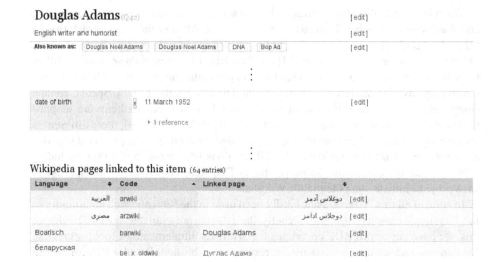

**Fig. 1.** Excerpt of a typical Wikidata item page with terms, statements, and site links

*properties.* In the familiar terms of semantic technologies, items represent individuals and classes, and Wikidata properties resemble RDF properties. Virtually every Wikipedia article in any language has an associated item that represents the subject of this article.

Every item has a page where users can view and enter the data. For example, the item page for the English writer Douglas Adams can be seen at https://www.wikidata.org/wiki/Q42; an excerpt is shown in Fig. 1. The title of this page is "Q42" rather than "Douglas Adams" since Wikidata is a multi-lingual site. Therefore, items are not identified by a label in a specific language, but by an opaque item identifier, which is assigned automatically when creating the item and which cannot be changed later on. Item identifiers always start with "Q" followed by a number. Every item page contains the following main parts:

- the *label* (e.g., "Douglas Adams"),
- a short *description* (e.g., "English writer and humorist"),
- a list of *aliases* (e.g., "Douglas Noël Adams"),
- a list of *statements* (the richest part of the data, explicated below),
- the list of *site links* (links to pages about the item on Wikipedia and other projects).

The first three pieces of data (label, descriptions, aliases) are collectively known as *terms*. They are mainly used to find and to display items. An item can have terms in every language supported by Wikidata. What is displayed on the pages depends on the language setting of the user.

Site links can be given for any of the 286 language editions of Wikipedia, and for several sister projects, such as Wikivoyage and Wikimedia Commons. Site links are functional (at most one link per site) and inverse functional (injective; at most one item for any site link). As opposed to the former system of Wikipedia language links, site links should only be used for articles that are exactly about the item, not about a broader,

**Table 1.** Wikidata datatypes and their current member fields and field types

| Datatype | Member fields |
|---|---|
| Item | item id (IRI) |
| String | string |
| URL | URL (IRI) |
| Commons Media | article title (string) |
| Time | point in time (dateTime), timezone offset (int), preferred calendar (IRI), precision (byte), before tolerance (int), after tolerance (int) |
| Globe coordinates | latitude (decimal), longitude (decimal), globe (IRI), precision (decimal) |
| Quantity | value (decimal), lower bound (decimal), upper bound (decimal) |

narrower, or otherwise related topic. Some items do not have any site links, e.g., the item "female" (Q6581072) which is used as a possible value for the sex of persons.

## 2.1 Properties and Datatypes

Figure 1 shows a simple example statement, which closely resembles an RDF triple with subject *Douglas Adams* (Q42), property *date of birth*, and value 11 March 1952. Properties, like items, are described on pages and use opaque identifiers starting with "P." For example, *date of birth* is actually P569. Properties do have terms (labels etc.), but no statements or site links.[2]

In addition, Wikidata properties also have a *datatype* that determines the kind of values they accept. The datatype of *date of birth* is *time*. Table 1 (left) shows the list of all available datatypes. Most types are self explaining. *Commons media* is a special type for referring to media files on the Wikimedia Commons media repository used by all Wikipedias. Datatypes determine the structure of the values accepted by properties. A single property value may correspond to a single RDF resource (as for type *item*) or to a single RDF literal (as for type *string*); or it may be a complex value that requires several elements to be described, as for *time*, *globe coordinates*, and *quantity*. Table 1 (right) shows the essential components of each value, as they would appear in RDF.

Many of the member fields should be clear. For *time*, we store an additional time-zone offset (in minutes) and a reference to the calendar model that is preferred for display (e.g., Julian calendar, Q1985786); our RDF exports always specify dates in (proleptic) Gregorian calendar. The remaining members of *time* allow to indicate the precision to express uncertain values such as "September 1547" or "3rd century." The details are beyond the scope of this paper. For the most common types of imprecision (precision to day, month, year) we use specific XML Schema datatypes (`xsd:date`, `xsd:gYearMonth`, `xsd:gYear`) to encode this information directly in the literal that specifies a time point.

For *globe coordinates*, the only unusual member field is *globe*, which gives the celestial body that the coordinates refer to (e.g., Earth, Q2). The remaining members for *globe* and *quantity* are again means of specifying imprecision. Finally, we remark that it is planned to extend quantities with units of measurement in 2014, which will then become another member.

---

[2] As of August 2014, support for statements on property pages is under development.

**Fig. 2.** Part of a complex statement about the wife of Douglas Adams as displayed in Wikidata

## 2.2 Complex Statements and References

The full data model of Wikidata statements is slightly more complex than Fig. 1 might suggest. On the one hand, statements can be enriched with so-called *qualifiers*, which provide additional context information for the claim. On the other hand, every statement can include one or more *references*, which support the claim. A statement where both aspects are given is shown in Fig. 2. The main property-value pair in this statement is "spouse: Jane Belson" (P26: Q14623681), but there is additional context information.

The qualifiers in Fig. 2 are "start date: 25 November 1991" and "end date: 11 May 2011," which state that Adams has been married to Belson from 1991 till his death in 2011. As before, we are using properties *start date* (P580) and *end date* (P582) of suitable types (time). These property-value pairs refer to the main part of the statement, not to the item on the page (Adams). In RDF, we will need auxiliary nodes that the qualifiers can refer to – the same is true for the references.

Qualifiers are used in several ways in Wikidata. Specifying the validity time of a claim is the most common usage today, so Fig. 2 is fairly typical. However, Wikidata uses many other kinds of annotations that provide contextual information on a statement. Examples include the *taxon author* (P405, essential context for biological taxon names) and the *asteroid taxonomy* (P1016, to contextualise the spectral classification of asteroids). In some cases, qualifiers provide additional arguments of a relationship that has more than two participants. For example, the property *website account on* (P553) specifies a website (such as Twitter, Q918), but is usually used with a qualifier P554 that specifies the account name used by the item on that site. Arguably this is a ternary relationship, but the boundary between context annotation and *n*-ary relation is fuzzy. For example, *Star Trek: The Next Generation* (Q16290) has *cast member* (P161) *Brent Spiner* (Q311453) with two values for qualifier *character role* (P453): *Data* (Q22983) and *Lore* (Q2609295). Note that the same property can be used in multiple qualifiers on the same statement.

The first part of the (single) reference in Fig. 2 is displayed below the qualifiers. Each reference is simply a list of property-value pairs. Wikidata does not provide a more restricted schema for references since the requirements for expressing references are very diverse. References can be classical citations, but also references to websites and datasets, each of which may or may not be represented by an item in Wikidata. In spite of this diversity, references are surprisingly uniform across Wikidata: as of April 2013, there are 23,225,184 pointers to references in Wikidata statements, but only 124,068 different references. This might be unexpected since Wikidata does not support the re-use of references, i.e., the system really stores 23,225,184 lists of property-value pairs which just happen to be the same in many cases. The reason for this uniformity are community processes (stating how references are to be structured), but also systematic imports that used one source for many statements.

We have used property-value pairs are used in many places: as main parts of claims, as qualifiers, and in references. In each of these cases, Wikidata supports two special "values" for *none* and *some*. *None* is used to say that the given property has no value as in "Elizabeth I of England had no spouse." Similar to negation in OWL, this allows us to state a simple form of negative information to distinguish it from the (frequent) case that information is simply incomplete. This also allows us to add references for negative claims. *Some* is used when we know that a property has a value, but cannot provide further details, as in "Pope Linus had a date of birth, but it is unknown to us." This is similar to the use of blank nodes in RDF and to *someValuesFrom* restrictions in OWL. Formally speaking, neither *none* nor *some* are values that belong to a particular datatype. Nevertheless, both of these special "values" can be used in all places where normal property values are allowed, hence we will usually not mention them explicitly.

### 2.3   Order and Ranking

All data in Wikidata is ordered – aliases, statements, property-value pairs in a reference, etc. However, representing order is difficult in RDF, since triples in an RDF graph are naturally unordered. Fortunately, the ordering information is only used for presentation, and is not considered meaningful for query answering in Wikidata. It is neither possible nor planned to have queries that can retrieve data based on, e.g., statement order. Hence, we ignore this information in our exports, although this means that the RDF export does not really capture all aspects of the data faithfully.

Even if we do not wish to use statement order in query answering, it can still be necessary to distinguish some statements from the rest. For example, Wikidata contains a lot of historic data with suitable qualifiers, such as the population numbers of cities at different times. Such data has many applications, but a simple query for the population of a city should not return a long list of numbers. To simplify basic filtering of data, Wikidata statements can be given one of three *ranks*: normal (used by default), preferred (used to single out values that are preferred over normal ones), and deprecated (to mark wrong or otherwise unsuitable information that is to be kept in the system for some practical reason). Ranks can be used to reduce the complexity of the dataset to include only the most relevant statements; this is also useful for generating RDF exports.

## 3   Representing Wikidata Content in RDF

We can now present our primary mapping of Wikidata content to RDF (and, occa-sionally, OWL). We further discuss this encoding and present simplified approaches

**Table 2.** Example RDF serialization of terms (top) and sitelinks (bottom) in Turtle

```
<http://www.wikidata.org/entity/Q80>
  a <http://www.wikidata.org/ontology#Item> ;
  <http://www.w3.org/2000/01/rdf-schema#label> "Tim Berners-Lee"@en ;
  <http://schema.org/description> "izumitelj World Wide Weba"@hr ;
  <http://www.w3.org/2004/02/skos/core#altLabel> "TimBL"@pt-br .

<http://es.wikipedia.org/wiki/Tim_Berners-Lee>
  a <http://www.wikidata.org/ontology#Article> ;
  <http://schema.org/about> <http://www.wikidata.org/entity/Q80> ;
  <http://schema.org/inLanguage> "es" .
```

in Section 4. Wikidata uses a uniform scheme for URIs of all entities, i.e., items and properties:

http://www.wikidata.org/entity/<*id*>

is the URI for an entity with identifier <*id*>, such as Q42 or P184. These URIs follow linked data standards [1]. They implement content negotiation and redirect to the most suitable data, which might be an RDF document with basic information about the entity, or the HTML page of the entity on Wikidata. Page URLs are of the form http://www.wikidata.org/wiki/Q42 for items and of the form http://www.wikidata.org/wiki/Property:P184 for properties. In addition, there are specific URLs to obtain the data in several formats, such as http://www.wikidata.org/wiki/Special:EntityData/Q42.nt (RDF in NTriples format) or http://www.wikidata.org/wiki/Special:EntityData/Q42.json (JSON). The RDF information provided by the live export of the site is currently limited to term data; while this already satisfies linked data standards as a basic "useful" piece of information, it is intended to provide all of the data that is found in the dumps there in the future.

In addition to the URIs of Wikidata entities, we also use URIs from an ontology that captures general concepts of the Wikidata data model explained earlier. The base URI of this ontology is http://www.wikidata.org/ontology#, and its current version used for the exports is included in the export directory.

### 3.1 Exporting Terms and Site Links

We start by describing the RDF export of terms and site links. Labels, descriptions, and aliases can be given in any of the more than 350 languages supported by Wikidata. For exporting this data in RDF, we need to use language tags that follow the BCP 47 standard.[3] We use the tags of the IANA language tag registry[4] whenever possible, although the official tag does not always agree with the identifier used in Wikipedia and Wikidata. For example, als.wikipedia.org is the Alemannic edition of Wikipedia, which has IANA code "gsw" rather than "als" (Tosk Albanian). We translate such exceptions accordingly. Finally, some languages supported by Wikidata do not have their own IANA

---

[3] http://tools.ietf.org/html/bcp47
[4] http://www.iana.org/assignments/language-subtag-registry/

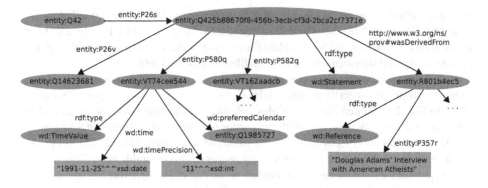

**Fig. 3.** Partial RDF graph for the statement in Fig. 2

tag, and we coin a suitable custom tag following the rules of BCP 47. For example, Basa Banyumasan is represented by the tag "jv-x-bms" as an extension to Javanese (jv).

Wikidata terms are then exported as RDF string literals with language tags. We use standard vocabularies for each type of data: RDFS label for labels, schema.org description for descriptions, and SKOS altLabel for aliases. Table 2 (top) shows examples for each. Whenever we use third-party vocabularies, we include an OWL declaration to clarify the type of the property, e.g., DatatypeProperty for description and altLabel.

For 286 languages used in Wikidata, there are also corresponding Wikipedia editions, which might be pointed to in site links. This means that Wikidata contains terms in languages that are not found in any Wikipedia. There are several reasons for this fact. First, Wikipedia editions are only created for languages that have a sufficient community of editors to maintain such a project. This is the reason why languages such as Herero and Afar do not currently have a Wikipedia. Secondly, Wikipedia editions generally try to combine closely related languages. For example, there is only one Portuguese Wikipedia, while Wikidata distinguished Brazilian Portuguese as a separate language that may use different labels. Thirdly, Wikidata may provide terms for the same language in different scripts, such as Kazakh in Arab, Cyrillic, and Latin scripts.

Site links are exported using the schema.org property about to associate a Wikipedia page URL with its Wikidata item, and the schema.org property inLanguage to define the BCP 47 language code of a Wikipedia page. Table 2 (bottom) gives an example.

## 3.2  Representing Statements and References in RDF

We will now present our approach for modelling Wikidata statements in RDF. A discussion of this modelling and possible alternatives follows in Section 4. The result of modelling the statement of Fig. 2 is displayed in Fig. 3. Qualified names are used for abbreviating URIs, where entity: represents http://www.wikidata.org/entity/, wd: represents http://www.wikidata.org/ontology#, and rdf: and xsd: are as usual. We will explain the parts of this graph step by step.

As discussed in Section 2.2, Wikidata statements are not just triples but can have additional quantifiers and references. The natural approach of representing such data in

RDF is to introduce an auxiliary individual that represents the statement itself, denoted by entity:Q42Sb88670f8-456b-3ecb-cf3d-2bca2cf7371e in Fig. 3 (the lengthy identifier is based on a UUID defined by Wikidata for every statement). We can then relate items to statements, and statements to values, qualifier values, and references.

A consequence of this approach is that Wikidata properties do not directly correspond to properties in RDF. A direct relationship as expressed by property "spouse" (P26) in Fig. 2 is broken into two triples, relating item to statement and statement to value, respectively. We use two RDF properties to capture this: entity:P26s to link to the statement and entity:P26v to link to the value (which is entity:Q14623681 in Fig. 3). As discussed in Section 4, using two distinct properties is preferable here.

For qualifiers cannot be annotated further, so we can relate them directly to the statement, without introducing additional resources. To distinguish statement qualifiers from the main value, we create another RDF property by appending q to the Wikidata property URI. The qualifiers in Fig. 3 use properties entity:P582q and entity:P580q, respectively. The underlying Wikidata properties are of type *time* in both cases. To express all member fields of this complex datatype shown in Table 1, we introduce additional RDF individuals to represent these values. Figure 3 shows the triples for the value displayed as "25 November 1991" in Fig. 2. The value entity:Q1985727 for the preferred calendar model is the Wikidata item for the proleptic Gregorian calendar.

Values of types *time*, *globe coordinates*, and *quantity* are represented in this fashion, using additional individuals that are named with hash-based URIs. Every such complex value is represented only once in RDF, even if it is used many times throughout the data. Values of datatype *string* are represented by RDF string literals; values of the remaining datatypes *item*, *URL*, and *Commons media* are represented by RDF resources.

References are also represented using dedicated individuals with hash-based names. To relate statements to references, we use the property wasDerivedFrom from the W3C PROV Ontology [13]. Property-value pairs in references are again encoded directly, using yet another variant of properties using with postfix r. Like complex values, references are shared among statements, which saves millions of triples in the RDF dumps.

Finally, the special values *none* and *some* are represented using OWL axioms that state that a property has a value (owl:someValuesFrom) or that this is not the case (owl:complementOf). This use of negation does not usually make the ontology inconsistent, since it refers to the level of statements or references. In particular, it is not contradictory if one statement claims that a property has no value while another gives a value. This might even be desirable to capture conflicting claims of different references.

## 4   Alternative Ways of Expressing Statements in RDF

The RDF exports discussed in Section 3 are faithful representations of all information of Wikidata that is relevant for query answering. In the case of statements, however, RDF leads to a rather complex representation where information is distributed across many triples. In this section, we discuss the design of our main exports, possible alternatives, and a simplified RDF export format that we provide alongside our main exports.

## 4.1   Design Principles for Mapping Statements to RDF

We start by explaining the design principles that have guided our RDF encoding of statements in Section 3.2. Our solution makes use of *reification*, the process of encoding complex structures in RDF by introducing new individuals to represent them. We reify statements, complex values, and references. Our main design principles are as follows:

1. Reification: all major structures of the Wikidata data model correspond to resources
2. OWL compatibility: our RDF data can also be read as OWL
3. Strong property typing: all properties used in RDF have a specific range and domain
4. URIs for auxiliary resources: we never use blank nodes for objects of the data model
5. Vocabulary re-use: we make use of third-party vocabularies where suitable

Reification is widely acknowledged as the standard solution of representing complex structures in RDF. The Semantic Web Best Practices group recommends a similar encoding for capturing *n*-ary relations, which is closely related to our task [17], and the W3C standard OWL 2 uses reification to support the annotation of axioms [18]. Such general uses of reification should not be confused with the specific reification vocabulary that RDF provides for triples [6]. This approach has been discussed controversially since it is rather inefficient (using four triples to represent one reified triple), and since it lacks a formal semantics (to relate reified and original triple). The crucial difference to our approach is that there is no "non-reified" RDF structure that we start from: we do not reify RDF triples but Wikidata objects. These objects exist as conceptual entities in the domain that we model. Wikidata statements can even be argued to be the primary subjects that Wikidata collects information about. In this sense, representing Wikidata objects by RDF individuals is not a technical workaround but a modelling goal. We will discuss other approaches that achieve a similar goal later in this section.

OWL compatibility is motivated by our general goal to support the widest range of consumers possible. While OWL can be used on any RDF graph (OWL Full), reasoning on large ontologies is more practical using one of the lightweight profiles of OWL 2, which impose the stricter requirements of OWL DL. Applications of reasoning in the context of Wikidata are conceivable, given that there is already a fair amount of schema information (see Section 5). In addition, we already use various OWL features to encode Wikidata content, and it would be unfortunate if our exports would not be valid OWL.

Strong property typing is simply good modelling practice, following the general guideline of using one URI for one thing. Moreover, it is a prerequisite for obtaining valid OWL DL, where object properties and data properties are strictly separate.

Our use of URIs for resources also follows best practices. Blank nodes add a certain amount of complexity to processing, and their use in OWL DL is subject to some restrictions. The downside of our choice is that we need to coin URIs for complex values and references, which do not have any identifier in the system. This makes it technically difficult to provide useful linked data for the hash-based URIs of these objects. It would be a considerable overhead for Wikidata to keep a global reverse lookup of all such objects that are currently used on some page (recall that references and values are also shared, and thus do not refer to any entity in their URIs). Nevertheless, using blank nodes instead would hardly improve the situation.

Vocabulary re-use is generally encouraged on the semantic web. A special choice that we made for our exports is to use only one vocabulary for each piece of data, even if several would be available. For example, RDFS label is used for labels, but SKOS prefLabel and schema.org name would be just as suitable. The Wikidata linked data service actually provides label data in each of these, since LOD consumers may expect labels to be given in a specific form.[5]

## 4.2 Alternatives to Reification

We now discuss alternative options for modelling statements without (explicit) reification. One of the oldest approaches for avoiding reification is to move from triples to *quads* (quadrupels), where the fourth component can be used to attach context information [9]. In relation to RDF, this has first been suggested by Sean B. Palmer in 2001,[6] but very similar ideas have already been proposed in 1993 for the knowledge representation system Loom [15]. Closely related to our work is the use of quads in YAGO2 to model temporal and spatial context information for statements extracted from Wikipedia [11].

RDF 1.1 introduces N-Quads as an official W3C recommendation [7]. While syntactically similar to earlier proposals, the underlying concept there are so-called RDF *datasets*, and the fourth component of quads is interpreted as the identifier for a *named graph*. RDF 1.1 specifies named graphs to have a "minimal semantics" meaning that entailment is not defined for named graphs. It is left to the application to decide which named graphs are to be considered when computing query results or inferences. The SPARQL query language also provides facilities for interacting with named graphs.

Proposals for the semantics of named graphs have been made [8], but did not find their ways into standards. This topic is more closely related to the general discussion of context modelling in semantic web and AI. Notable works in the area include C-OWL [5], Distributed Description Logic [4], TRIPLE [19], and a context-aware semantics proposed by Guha et al. [10]. In spite of these works, there is no standard approach of reasoning over contextualized data today.

We could have used named graphs instead of reification for representing statements. We would still introduce a URI for each statement and use it as the name for a graph that contains the single main triple of the statement. Everything else would remain unchanged. Complex values and references would be reified as before, since named graphs cannot simplify this encoding any further. The main advantage of this approach would be that it keeps the main property-value assignment of each statement in one triple, avoiding the need for joins in query answering. The main disadvantage is that we loose OWL compatibility, and that essential parts of the modelled data are encoded as annotations on graph names, for which no current standard provides any semantics. Nevertheless, there is no harm in providing another variant of the export to those who prefer this view, and we intend to do so in the future (contributions of interested parties are welcome).

---

[5] It would obviously be preferable if vocabulary providers could agree on a single label property.
[6] Discussion with Bijan Parsia and Aaron Swartz:
http://chatlogs.planetrdf.com/rdfig/2001-08-10.txt; resulting email:
http://lists.w3.org/Archives/Public/www-rdf-logic/2001Aug/0007.html

Most recently, Nguyen et al. proposed *singleton properties* as yet another approach of annotating RDF statements [16]. Roughly speaking, they combine the fourth component of quads with the predicate URI, to obtain a new property URI that they require to be globally unique. This approach would work for our setting, but, again, the semantic relationship between triples with singleton properties and their annotations are not captured by standard semantics.

### 4.3  Exporting Statements as Triples

Whether we use reification or named graphs, we cannot avoid to use relatively complex RDF graphs if we want to capture the rich structure of Wikidata statements. Yet, it is sometimes desirable to have a simpler view of the data. We therefore provide several secondary data dumps that are not faithful but still meaningful.

The complexity of serialising statements is caused by qualifiers and references. References provide additional information that could be ignored when interpreting statements. In contrast, omitting qualifiers may change the meaning of the statement substantially. Many qualifiers, such as *start date* and *end date*, restrict the validity of a claim to a particular context, and one would obtain wrong or misleading claims when ignoring this information.

To obtain simpler RDF exports, we thus focus on statements without qualifiers and ignore all references. In this situation, we can represent many statements by single RDF triples. This leads to a different RDF graph structure, and we therefore use new RDF properties which use the postfix c. In addition, many complex values can be reduced to their most important member, so that no additional individuals are required. For example, the statement in Fig. 1 can be represented by a single triple

entity:Q42  entity:P569c  "1952-03-11"^^xsd:date .

We thus obtain an export of *simple statements* which can be combined with the (faithful) exports of terms and site links.

## 5   Extracting Schema Information from Wikidata

While most of the content of Wikidata is naturally focussed on instances, there is also an interesting and growing amount of schematic information that we provide exports for. On the one hand, this includes an elaborate class hierarchy that is used to classify Wikidata items; on the other hand, we extract an OWL ontology that captures a variety of constraints on the use of properties in Wikidata.

Classification information can be obtained from the Wikidata properties *instance of* (P31) and *subclass of* (P279). The names of these properties suggest a close relationship to rdf:type and rdfs:subClassOf, and it can be seen from the community discussions that these RDF(S) properties have indeed been an important role model for P31 and P279. To extract this information, we apply the approach for exporting simplified statements of Section 4.3. In particular, we ignore statements with qualifiers. This is hardly a restriction for *subclass of*, but there are many cases where *instance of* is used with a temporal annotation to express that an item has not always been a member of a certain class.

In addition, the Wikidata community has started to formulate *constraints* for the use of properties. For example, a constraint on property *mother* (P25) specifies that all of its

**Table 3.** Property constraints in Wikidata and their number of occurrences as of April 2014

| Constraint name | Description | Uses |
|---|---|---|
| Single value | Property is functional | 305 |
| Unique value | Property is inverse functional | 290 |
| Symmetric | Property is symmetric | 11 |
| Inverse | Specifies the inverse of a property | 25 |
| Format | Values must match a given formatting pattern | 282 |
| One of | Values must come from a given list of values | 60 |
| Existing file | Values must be files on Wikimedia Commons | 23 |
| Value type | Values must have some *instance of* or *subclass of* relation | 262 |
| Range | Values must be numbers or times in a certain closed interval | 53 |
| Target required claim | Values must be items that satisfy further claims | 100 |
| Item | Items with this property must also satisfy further claims | 436 |
| Type | Items with this property must have some *instance of* or *subclass of* relation | 389 |
| Multi value | Items with this property must use it with two or more values | 2 |
| Conflicts with | Items with this property must not satisfy certain other claims | 8 |

values must be instances of *person* (Q215627). This information is used to detect errors in the data, but also to clarify the intended use of properties.

Constraints are not part of the data model of Wikidata, and are in fact completely ignored by the system. Rather, the Wikidata community developed its own way of encoding constraints on the *talk pages* of Wikidata properties. These pages are normal wiki pages, similar to articles on Wikipedia, where constraints are defined by suitable formatting commands. Constraint violation reports are generated and uploaded to Wikidata by scripts. Table 3 gives an overview of the current constraints with the names used in Wikidata, together with a short explanation of their meaning. Constraints that require something to "satisfy further claims" usually require statements to be given for one or more properties, optionally with specific values. The most general constraints of this kind are *Item* and *Target required claim*.

Many constraints can be expressed in terms of OWL axioms. In contrast to OWL ontologies, constraints are not used for inferring new information (or even inconsistencies) but to detect possible errors. Nevertheless, the schematic information expressed in constraints is still meaningful and the corresponding OWL ontology makes sense as a high-level description of the data. Thus, we extract constraints and provide a dedicated export of the resulting OWL axioms.

The axioms we extract refer to the RDF encoding of Section 3, and only to the the main property of a statement. Currently, the constraints are not applied for qualifiers or references in Wikidata. Clearly, some constraints are difficult or impossible to express in OWL. *Format* can be expressed using a regular expression datatype facet on xsd:string, but few OWL systems support this. *Existing file* expresses a requirement that is not really part of the semantic model we work in. Most other constraints correspond to OWL axioms in a rather direct way. Interestingly, however, neither *Symmetric* nor *Inverse* can be expressed in OWL. While OWL supports symmetric and inverse properties, these apply only to single triples and cannot entail structures like in Fig. 3.

**Table 4.** Overview of dump files of 20th April 2014

| File topic | File size | Triples | | Content |
|---|---|---|---|---|
| instances | 16 M | 6,169,821 | 6,169,821 | rdf:type relations |
| taxonomy | 336 K | 82,076 | 40,192 | rdfs:subclassOf relations |
| | | | 41,868 | OWL classes |
| simple-statements | 300 M | 55,925,337 | 34,146,472 | simplified statements |
| statements | 1.8 G | 148,513,453 | 34,282,659 | statements |
| terms | 579 M | 106,374,085 | 47,401,512 | labels |
| | | | 8,734,890 | aliases |
| | | | 35,143,663 | descriptions |
| properties | 616 K | 52,667 | 1,005 | properties |
| sitelinks | 618 M | 126,658,004 | 37,316,300 | site links |

# 6   Connecting Wikidata to the Linked Data Web

A key characteristic of linked open data is the interconnection of datasets [1]. Wikidata, too, makes many connections to external datasets from many domains, ranging from international authority files, such as ISSN or VIAF, to highly specialised databases such as HURDAT, the database of North Atlantic hurricanes. However, not all of these data sources provide RDF exports or even URIs for their data, and those that do often consider RDF as a secondary service that is provided as one of many export services.

As a consequence, most databases use identifiers that are not URIs, and (at best) provide some scheme of computing URIs from these ids. For example, the Freebase identifier /m/05r5c (Piano) corresponds to the URI http://rdf.freebase.com/ns/m.05r5c, where one has to replace "/" by "." to obtain the local name. Naturally, Wikidata tends to store the identifier, not the URI. The former is usually more concise and readable, but also required in many applications where the identifier plays a role.

Thus, when exporting Wikidata content to RDF, we do not immediately obtain any links to external datasets. To address this problem, we have manually inspected Wikidata properties of type string, and searched for suitable URIs that can be used instead. If possible, we have exported the data using URIs instead of strings. The URI is exported like a Wikidata property value; we never use owl:sameAs to relate external URIs to Wikidata, since this would often not be justified. In some cases, related URIs are available from third parties, but there is no official URI that is endorsed by the owner of the identifier. For example, there are no URIs for *SMILES* ids as used in chemistry, but ChemSpider[7] serves relevant RDF for these identifiers. We have not exported such URIs so far, but we consider to include them in addition the string ids in the future.

Overall, we have found 17 widely used Wikidata properties for which we generate direct links to other RDF datasets. Linked semantic datasets and knowledge bases include Freebase (P646), the Gene Ontology (P686), ChemSpider (661), PubChem (662), several types of entities found in MusicBrainz (P434–P436, P966, P982, P1004), the Virtual International Authority File VIAF (P214) as well as several other national authority files. In total, this allowed for the creation of 2.5 million links to external databases.

---

[7] http://chemspider.com/

Importantly, our main goal is to generate RDF exports that faithfully represent the original data using the language of RDF and linked data properly. We do not aspire to discover links to external datasets that are not already stated explicitly in the data. In particular, we restrict to target datasets for which Wikidata has a property. In some cases, suitable properties might be introduced in the future; in other cases, it might be more suitable for third-party datasets to link to Wikidata.

## 7 RDF Exports

We provide exports in the form of several bz2-compressed N-Triples files that allow users to get access to part of the data without having to donwload all of it. Exports are created once a month, and historic files will remain available. Links to all exports are found at http://tools.wmflabs.org/wikidata-exports/rdf/.

The main RDF export as described in Section 3 is found in four files: *terms* (labels, descriptions, aliases), *statements*, and *sitelinks* contain parts of the item data; *properties* contains all property data (terms and datatypes). In addition, we provide an export of *simple statements* as discussed in Section 4.3, and an export of the class hierarchy (*taxonomy*) and of corresponding rdf:type relations (*instances*) as discussed in Section 5.

The export results for the Wikidata content dump of 20 April 2014 are shown in Table 4, together with some statistics on their size and number of content objects. In total these files cover 15,093,996 items and 1,005 properties. The exported taxonomy turned out to be very interesting since it was built with the semantics of rdfs:subClassOf in mind. This is completely different from Wikipedia's hierarchy of *categories*, which is based on broader/narrower relations [20], as in *Humans* → *Culture* → *Food and drink* → *Meals* → *Breakfast* → *Bed and breakfast* → *Bed and breakfasts in the United States*. Yago(2) reorganizes Wikipedia categories using WordNet [11], and DBpedia integrates Yago's class hierarchy. Yet, many of the over 150,000 classes in DBpedia are still based on English Wikipedia categories, as in *AmericanAcademicsOfJapaneseDescent*. In contrast, Wikidata provides a completely new dataset, which, while certainly far from perfect, is a promising starting point for future research and applications.

## 8 Conclusions

Wikidata, its content, and the underlying software are under continued development, the outcome of which is hard to foresee. Given the important role that Wikidata plays for Wikipedia, one can be certain that the project will continue to grow in size and quality. Many exciting possibilities of using this data remain to be explored.

Wikidata has had its origins in the Semantic Web community [12], and continues to be inspired by the research and development in this field. With this paper, the results of these efforts are finally available as machine-readable exports. It remains for the community of researchers and practitioners in semantic technologies and linked data to show the added value this can bring.

**Acknowledgements.** This work has been funded by the DFG in project DIAMOND (Emmy Noether grant KR 4381/1-1).

# References

1. Bizer, C., Heath, T., Berners-Lee, T.: Linked data: The story so far. Int. J. Semantic Web and Information Systems 5(3), 1–22 (2009)
2. Bizer, C., Lehmann, J., Kobilarov, G., Auer, S., Becker, C., Cyganiak, R., Hellmann, S.: DBpedia – A crystallization point for the Web of Data. J. Web Semantics 7(3), 154–165 (2009)
3. Bollacker, K., Evans, C., Paritosh, P., Sturge, T., Taylor, J.: Freebase: A collaboratively created graph database for structuring human knowledge. In: Proc. 2008 ACM SIGMOD Int. Conf. on Management of Data, pp. 1247–1250. ACM (2008)
4. Borgida, A., Serafini, L.: Distributed description logics: Assimilating information from peer sources. J. Data Semantics 1, 153–184 (2003)
5. Bouquet, P., Giunchiglia, F., van Harmelen, F., Serafini, L., Stuckenschmidt, H.: C-OWL: Contextualizing ontologies. In: Fensel, D., Sycara, K., Mylopoulos, J. (eds.) ISWC 2003. LNCS, vol. 2870, pp. 164–179. Springer, Heidelberg (2003)
6. Brickley, D., Guha, R. (eds.): RDF Schema 1.1. W3C Recommendation (February 25, 2014), http://www.w3.org/TR/rdf-schema/
7. Carothers, G. (ed.): RDF 1.1 N-Quads: A line-based syntax for RDF datasets. W3C Recommendation (February 25, 2014), http://www.w3.org/TR/n-quads/
8. Carroll, J.J., Bizer, C., Hayes, P.J., Stickler, P.: Named graphs. J. Web Semantics 3(4), 247–267 (2005)
9. Cyganiak, R., Harth, A., Hogan, A.: N-Quads: Extending N-Triples with Context. Public Draft (2012), http://sw.deri.org/2008/07/n-quads/
10. Guha, R.V., McCool, R., Fikes, R.: Contexts for the semantic web. In: McIlraith, S.A., Plexousakis, D., van Harmelen, F. (eds.) ISWC 2004. LNCS, vol. 3298, pp. 32–46. Springer, Heidelberg (2004)
11. Hoffart, J., Suchanek, F.M., Berberich, K., Weikum, G.: YAGO2: A spatially and temporally enhanced knowledge base from Wikipedia. Artif. Intell., Special Issue on Artificial Intelligence, Wikipedia and Semi-Structured Resources 194, 28–61 (2013)
12. Krötzsch, M., Vrandečić, D., Völkel, M., Haller, H., Studer, R.: Semantic Wikipedia. J. Web Semantics 5(4), 251–261 (2007)
13. Lebo, T., Sahoo, S., McGuinness, D. (eds.): PROV-O: The PROV Ontology. W3C Recommendation (April 30, 2013), http://www.w3.org/TR/prov-o
14. Lenat, D., Guha, R.V.: Building Large Knowledge-Based Systems: Representation and Inference in the Cyc Project. Addison-Wesley (1990)
15. MacGregor, R.M.: Representing reified relations in Loom. J. Experimental and Theoretical Artificial Intelligence 5, 179–183 (1993)
16. Nguyen, V., Bodenreider, O., Sheth, A.P.: Don't like RDF reification?: making statements about statements using singleton property. In: WWW 2014, pp. 759–770 (2014)
17. Noy, N., Rector, A. (eds.): Defining N-ary Relations on the Semantic Web. W3C Working Group Note (April 12, 2006), http://www.w3.org/TR/swbp-n-aryRelations/
18. OWL Working Group, W.: OWL 2 Web Ontology Language: Document Overview. W3C Recommendation (October 27, 2009), http://www.w3.org/TR/owl2-overview/
19. Sintek, M., Decker, S.: TRIPLE – a query, inference, and transformation language for the Semantic Web. In: Horrocks, I., Hendler, J. (eds.) ISWC 2002. LNCS, vol. 2342, pp. 364–378. Springer, Heidelberg (2002)
20. Voss, J.: Collaborative thesaurus tagging the Wikipedia way. CoRR abs/cs/0604036 (2006)
21. Vrandečić, D., Krötzsch, M.: Wikidata: A free collaborative knowledge base. Comm. ACM (to appear, 2014)

# Web-Scale Extension of RDF Knowledge Bases
# from Templated Websites

Lorenz Bühmann[1,*], Ricardo Usbeck[1,2,*], Axel-Cyrille Ngonga Ngomo[1],
Muhammad Saleem[1], Andreas Both[2], Valter Crescenzi[3],
Paolo Merialdo[3], and Disheng Qiu[3]

[1] Universität Leipzig, IFI/AKSW
{lastname}@informatik.uni-leipzig.de
[2] Unister GmbH, Leipzig
{firstname.lastname}@unister.de
[3] Università Roma Tre
{lastname}@dia.uniroma3.it

**Abstract.** Only a small fraction of the information on the Web is represented as
Linked Data. This lack of coverage is partly due to the paradigms followed so far
to extract Linked Data. While converting structured data to RDF is well supported
by tools, most approaches to extract RDF from semi-structured data rely on extraction methods based on ad-hoc solutions. In this paper, we present a holistic
and open-source framework for the extraction of RDF from templated websites.
We discuss the architecture of the framework and the initial implementation of
each of its components. In particular, we present a novel wrapper induction technique that does not require any human supervision to detect wrappers for web
sites. Our framework also includes a consistency layer with which the data extracted by the wrappers can be checked for logical consistency. We evaluate the
initial version of REX on three different datasets. Our results clearly show the
potential of using templated Web pages to extend the Linked Data Cloud. Moreover, our results indicate the weaknesses of our current implementations and how
they can be extended.

## 1 Introduction

The Linked Open Data (LOD) Cloud has grown from 12 datasets (also called knowledge bases) to over 2000 knowledge bases in less than 10 years.[1] This steady growth of
the LOD Cloud promises to continue as very large datasets such as Linked TCGA [20]
with 20.4 billion triples are added to it. However, the LOD Cloud still contains only a
fraction of the knowledge available on the Web [13]. This lack of coverage is mainly
due to the way the data available on the LOD Cloud is extracted. Most commonly, the
data in the LOD Cloud originates from one of two types of sources: structured data
(especially databases such as Drugbank,[2] Diseasome,[3] etc.) and semi-structured data

---

* Both authors contributed equally to this work.
[1] http://stats.lod2.eu/
[2] http://www.drugbank.ca
[3] http://diseasome.eu

sources (for example data extracted from the Wikipedia[4] infoboxes). While generating RDF triples from structured data (especially databases) is well supported by tools such as Triplify [3], D2R [4] and SPARQLMap [21] , devising automatic means to generate RDF from semi-structured data is a more challenging problem. Currently, this challenge is addressed by ad-hoc or manual (e.g., community-driven) solutions. For example, the well-known DBpedia [2] provides a mapping Wiki[5] where users can explicate how the content of infoboxes is to be transformed into RDF. On the one hand, manual approaches offer the advantage of leading to high-precision data; on the other hand, they suffer of a limited recall because of the small number of web sources from which the data is extracted. For example, DBpedia only contains a fraction of the movies that were published over the last years because it was extracted exclusively from Wikipedia. Moreover, the same knowledge base only contains a fraction of the cast of some of the movies it describes.

The main aim of this paper is to address the challenge of extracting RDF from semi-structured data. We introduce REX, an open-source framework for the extraction of RDF from templated websites (e.g., Wikipedia, IMDB, ESPN, etc.). REX addresses the extraction of RDF from templated websites by providing a modular and extensible architecture for learning XPath wrappers and extracting consistent RDF data from these web pages. Our framework is thus complementary to RDF extraction frameworks for structured and unstructured data. While REX targets the extraction of RDF from templated websites in its current version, the architecture of the framework is generic and allows for creating versions of the tool that can extract RDF from other sources on websites, for example from unstructured data or from the billions of tables available on the Web. Our framework has the following features:

1. *Extensibility*, i.e., our framework is open-source, available under the MIT license and can thus be extended and used by any third party;
2. *Use of standards*, i.e., REX relies internally on widely used libraries and on W3C Standards such as RDF, SPARQL and OWL;
3. *Modularity*, i.e., each of the modules can be replaced by another implementation;
4. *Scalability*, i.e., the current algorithms can be used on large amounts of data;
5. *Low costs*, i.e., REX requires no human supervision;
6. *Accuracy*, i.e., the current implementation achieves satisfactory F-measures and
7. *Consistency*, i.e., REX implements means to generate triples which abide by the ontology of the source knowledge base providing the training data.

In addition to being novel in itself, REX introduces a *novel wrapper induction technique* for extracting structured data from templated Web sites. This induction approach makes use of the large amount of data available in the LOD Cloud as training data. By these means, REX circumvents the problem of high annotation costs faced by several of the previous wrapper induction approaches [16,11] while keeping the high accuracy of supervised wrapper induction methods. By post-processing the output of website wrappers, our system can generate novel triples. To ensure that these novel triples are consistent, REX provides a consistency check module which computes and uses the

---

[4] http://wikipedia.org
[5] http://mappings.dbpedia.org

axioms which underlie the input knowledge base $K$. Only those triples which do not break the consistency rules are returned by REX. The contributions of this paper are consequently as follows:

1. We introduce a novel framework for the extraction of RDF from templated web-sites.
2. We present a novel wrapper induction approach for the extraction of subject-object pairs from the Web.
3. We integrate state-of-the-art disambiguation and schema induction techniques to retrieve high-quality RDF.
4. We evaluate the first version of REX on three datasets and present both the strengths and weaknesses of our approach.
5. Overall, we present the (to the best of our knowledge) first web-scale, low-cost, accurate and consistent framework that allows extracting RDF from structured web-sites.

The rest of this paper is organized as follows. In Section 2, we introduce the notation that underlies this paper and the problems that we tackle. Section 3 presents the architecture of REX in more detail as well as the current implementation of each of its components. In particular, we illustrate our approach to generate examples from a knowledge base $K$ and we show our algorithm to learn web wrappers from such examples. Subsequently, we give an overview of AGDISTIS [22] which we use to address the problem of URI disambiguation. Finally, we describe our current solution to ensuring the validity of the data generated by REX. In Section 4 we present the results of REX on 3 datasets, each containing at least 10,000 pages. We discuss related work in Section 5, and we conclude the paper in Section 6. More information on REX can be found at http://aksw.org/Projects/REX including inks to the source code repository (incl. examples), to the documentation and to a tutorial of the framework.

## 2  Notation and Problem Statement

In this section, we present the concepts and notation to understand the concept behind REX. We denote RDF triples as $< s, p, o >$ where $(s, p, o) \in R \times P \times (R \cup L)$. We call $R$ the set of resources, $P$ the set of properties and $L$ the set of literals. We call $A = R \cup P \cup L$ the set of all atoms. We regard knowledge bases $K$ as sets of triples. We denote the set of all pairs $(s, o)$ such that $< s, p, o > \in K$ with $pairs(p, K)$. We define the in-degree $in(a)$ of an atom $a$ in $K$ as the number of distinct $x$ such that there is a predicate $q$ with $< x, q, a > \in K$. Conversely, the out-degree $out(a)$ of $a$ is defined as the number of distinct atoms $y$ that are such that there exists a predicate $q'$ with $< a, q', y > \in K$. We assume the existence of a labeling function $label$, which maps each element of $A$ to a sequence of words from a dictionary $D$. Formally, $label :$ $A \to 2^D$. For example, the value of $label(r)$ can be defined as the set of x with $<r,$ rdfs:label, $x> \in K$ if r is a resource and as the lexical form of r if r is a literal.

Based on this formalisation, we can define the problem that REX addresses as follows: Given (1) a predicate $p$ that is contained in a knowledge base $K$ and (2) a set of unlabeled web pages $W = \{w_1, w_2, \dots, w_{|W|}\}$, extract a set of triples $< s_i, p, o_i >$ from the websites of $W$. Several tasks have to be addressed and solved to achieve this goal within the paradigm that we adopt:

*Problem 1:* We first require an approach for extracting pairs of resource labels out of unlabelled pages $w_i$. We tackle this problem by means of a wrapper induction algorithm (see Section 3.4). We assume that we are given (1) a set $E \subseteq \{(s, o) : < s, p, o > \in K\}$ of positive examples for a predicate $p$ from the Linked Data Web and (2) a set of web pages $W$ without any labeling. Our aim is to generate high-quality wrappers, expressed as pairs of XPath expressions over these unlabeled web pages $W$, that extract a pair of values from each page.

*Problem 2:* Once the pairs of values have been extracted from web pages, we need to ground them in the knowledge base $K$. In this context, grounding means that for each value extracted by our solution to Problem 1 we have to either (1) find a matching resource or (2) generate a novel resource or literal for this particular value. We address this challenge by using a URI disambiguation approach that combines breadth-first search and graph algorithms to determine a resource that matches a given string. If no URI is found, our approach generates a new resource URI (see Section 3.5).

*Problem 3:* Once new knowledge has been generated, it is central to ensure that the knowledge base $K$ to which it is added remains consistent. To this end, we need to ensure that we do not add any statements to $K$ that go against its underlying axioms. The problem here is that these axioms are not always explicated in knowledge bases in the LOD Cloud. We thus devise an approach to generate such axioms from instance data (see Section 3.5). To achieve this goal, we use a statistical analysis of the use of predicates across the knowledge base $K$. Moreover, we provide means to use RDFS inference to generate new knowledge from new resources generated by our solution to Problem 2.

# 3   The REX Framework

In the following, we present REX, an integrated solution to the three problems presented above. We begin by giving an overview of its architecture. Then, we present each of its components. As running example, we use the extraction of movie directors from web pages.

## 3.1   Overview

Figure 1 gives an overview of REX. All modules are interfaces, for which we provide at least one implementation. Hence, REX can be ran out of the box. Given a predicate $p$ and a knowledge base $K$, REX provides a domain identification interface, which allows for detecting Web domains which pertain to this predicate. For example, the predicate `dbo:actor` leads to the domain `http://imdb.com` being retrieved. From this domain, a set $W$ of web pages can be retrieved by using a *crawler*. The results of the crawling are stored in a solution for unstructured data, for example an index. REX then generates a set of examples using an instantiation of the *example generator* interface. The goal here is to generate a sample $E$ of all elements of $pairs(p, K)$ that allows learning high-quality pairs of XPath expressions. The examples are given to a *wrapper inducer*, which learns pairs of XPath expressions for extracting the pairs of values in $E$ from the elements of $W$. These pairs are then applied to all pages of $W$. The extraction results, i.e., pairs of strings, are passed on to a *URI generator*, which implements a graph-based disambiguation approach for finding or generating URIs for the strings contained in the extraction results. The resulting set $C$ of candidate triples are finally forwarded to an *validation engine*, which learns axioms from $K$ and applies these to $C$ to derive a set of triples that are consistent with $K$. In the following, we detail our current implementation of each of these components.

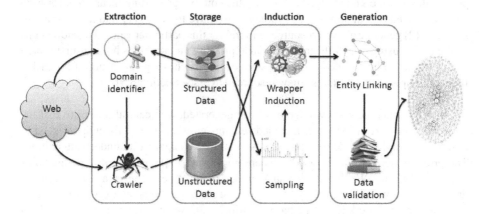

**Fig. 1.** Architecture of REX

## 3.2   Extraction Layer

REX's data extraction layer consists of two main components: The *domain identification module* is the first component of the layer and takes a set of triples $(s, p, o)$ as examples and returns a ranked list of Web domains. Our current implementation simply uses the Google interface to search for websites that contain the label of all $s$, $p$ and $o$. The top-10 domains for each triple are selected and their rank is averaged over all triples. The resulting ranking is returned. For our example dbo:actor, we get http://imdb.com as top-ranked domain. The second component consists of a *crawler interface* which allows to gather the web pages that are part of the detected domain and collect them in a storage solution for unstructured data. Currently, we rely on crawler4j[6] for crawling and Apache Lucene[7] for storing the results of the crawling.

## 3.3   Storage Layer

The storage layer encapsulates the storage solutions for structured data (i.e., the knowledge base $K$) and the unstructured data (i.e., the output of the extraction layer). We assume that the structured data can be access via SPARQL. The unstructured data

---

[6] https://code.google.com/p/crawler4j/
[7] http://lucene.apache.org/

storage is expected to return data when presented with a pair $(s, o)$ of resources, which is commonly a positive or negative example for the pairs that abide by $p$. As stated above, we rely on a Lucene index that can access the labels of resources and simply search through its index for pages that contain both a label for $s$ and a label for $o$.

## 3.4  Induction Layer

The induction layer uses the data in the storage layer to compute wrappers for the website crawled in the first step. To this end, it contains two types of modules: The *example generation* module implements sampling algorithms that are used to retrieve examples of relevant pairs $(s, o)$ such that $(s, p, o) \in K$. These examples are used to feed the *wrapper induction* module, which learns the wrappers that are finally used to extract data from web pages. Hereafter, we present the implementations of these modules.

**Generation of Examples.** Given a knowledge base $K$, the generation of all examples $E$ for a predicate $p$ can be retrieved by computing all triples $< s, p, o >$ from $K$. However, using all triples might lead to poor scalability, especially if $K$ is very large. To ensure the scalability of our approach, we thus aimed to ensure that we can provide REX with only a sample of $E$ and thus reduce its learning runtime without diminishing its accuracy. Our first intuition was that it is more likely to find resources that stand for well-known real-world entities on the Web. Thus, by selecting the most prominent examples from the knowledge $K$, we should be able to improve the probability of finding web pages that contain both the subject and the object of our examples. This intuition can be regarded as prominence-driven, as it tries to maximize the number of annotated pages used for learning. We implemented this intuition to generating a sample of $E$ by implementing a first version of the example generator that ranks the examples $(s, o)$ in $E$ in descending order by how prominent they are in the knowledge base. The score $scr$ for ranking the examples was computed by summing up the in- and out-degree of $s$ and $o$: $scr(s, o) = in(s) + in(o) + out(s) + out(o)$. We call this example selection *prominence-based.*

The main drawback of this first intuition is that it introduces a skew in the sampling as we only consider a subset of entities with a particular distribution across the pages in $W$. For example, actors in IMDB have different templates depending on how popular they are. Learning only from popular actors would then lead to learning how to extract values only from web pages obeying to particular type of HTML template. While this problem can be by choosing a large number of examples, we revised our sampling approach to still use the ranking but to sample evenly across the whole list of ranked resources. To this end, given a number $n$ of required pairs, we return the first $n$ pairs $(s, o)$ from the ranked list computed above whose index $idx$ abides by $idx(s, o) \equiv 0 \left( mod \left\lfloor \frac{|E|}{n} \right\rfloor \right)$. We call this second implementation of the example generator interface the *uniform* approach .

**Wrapper Generation.** Detecting rules to extract the subject-object pairs related to a property $p$ is the most difficult step when aiming to extract RDF from templated website. Here, we present our current implementation of the wrapper induction module interface of REX, which aims to extract subject-object pairs for $p$ from a set of pages $W$ that belong to the same website and share a common template. We assume that an *example generator* provides the input set $E$ containing a subset of the pairs that can be extracted from the pages in $W$. Formally, let $Q$ denote the set of pages that contain a pair in $E$: $Q = \{w : w \in W, (s,o) \in E \wedge (label(s), label(o)) \in w\}$, where $(label(s), label(o)) \in w$ denotes that at least one of the labels of $s$ and at least one of the labels of $o$ occur in the page $w$. We use the pairs in $E$ to gain the positive annotations for the pages in $Q$. These annotations are needed to automatically infer a set of wrappers, i.e., a set of extraction rule pairs that extract the target subject-object pairs.

To avoid the extraction of incorrect values, our approach includes a technique to evaluate the output wrapper coverage, i.e., the number of pages in $W$ for which the wrappers inferred from $Q$ correctly extract the target subject-object pairs.

Listing 1 reports the pseudo-code of our algorithm to generate the wrappers that extract subject-object pairs related to a property $p$ from a set of pages: it takes as input the set of pages $W$ and the set of examples $E$. To abstract the extraction rules generative process in our implementation, we assume that there exists, as a parameter of the algorithm, a class of all the creatable extraction rules $\mathcal{R}$. It corresponds to the set of XPath expressions that we can generate over the pages in $W$.

As a first step (line 2), the algorithm computes the set of pages $Q$ (we assume $Q \neq \emptyset$). Then, it picks up a small set of sample pages $I$ from $Q$.[8] From the pages in $I$ two initial sets of extraction rules, $R_s$ and $R_o$, are generated (lines 4-5), as follows. First, we analyze the DOM tree of the pages to locate nodes that are part of the template. We use these nodes as roots of XPath expressions that match with the input pair. To discover the template nodes, we compute the occurrences of the textual leaf nodes in the pages. Following the intuition developed in [1], we consider template nodes the document root, the nodes with an *id* attribute, and the text leaves that occur exactly once with same value and same root-to-leaf sequence of tags in a significant percentage (80%) of pages. The rationale is that it is very unlikely that a node occurs exactly once in several pages with the same root-to-leaf path by chance; rather, it is likely repeated in every page since it comes from a piece of the underlying HTML template.

Template nodes are then used as *pivot nodes* to generate XPath expressions that match with nodes containing a textual leaf that equals the subject (object) of the input pair. Given a pivot node $l$, an XPath expression for the textual node $t$ is computed by appending three expressions: $(i)$ an expression that matches with the pivot node $t$, $(ii)$ the path from $t$ to the first ancestor node, $n_{lt}$, shared by $t$ and $l$, $(iii)$ the path from $n_{lt}$ to $l$ (which descends from the shared ancestor node to the target textual node). To avoid an excessive proliferation of rules, we bound the length of the XPath expressions, i.e., the number of XPath steps.[9]

The above step produces several extraction rules that correctly work on the pages in $I$. However some of these rules could not work on a larger set of pages. For example, consider a set of pages such as those shown in Figure 2(a). Assuming that the leaf nodes 'Director:' and 'Ratings:' appear once with the same root-to-leaf path in most

---

[8] In our implementation $k = |I| = 10$.

[9] We observed that producing rules longer than 8 steps do not produce any benefit.

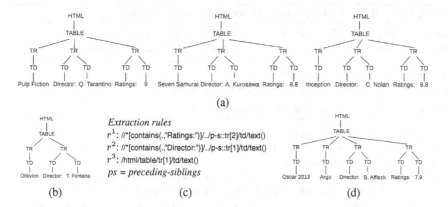

**Fig. 2.** (a) DOM trees of three pages (in a fictional set $I$), (b) a page in $Q$ (with a template that differs from those of the pages in $I$), (c) some rules to extract the movie title, and (d) a page in $W$ (with a template that differs from those of the pages in $Q$).

of the pages in $I$, they would be considered as template nodes. Figure 2(c) reports an example of the XPath expressions pivoted in these nodes, and generated to extract the movie title. Notice, however, that rule $r^1$ does not extract the movie title on pages like that depicted in Figure 2(b), i.e., pages without user ratings. To improve the accuracy of the rules generated from pages in $I$, we evaluate the generated rules over $Q$, and select those that extract the largest number of annotations (line 6). In our example, the extraction rules $r^2$ and $r^3$ would be selected, while $r^1$ would be discarded, as the former rules work also on the page of Figure 2(b), while the latter does not.

The selected rules are those better working for the pages in $Q$, that are the pages containing pairs of $K$. Although it is likely that these rules also work for the whole collection of input pages, it might also be the case that $W$ contains pages obeying to a slightly different template not observed within $Q$. For example, consider the page in Figure 2(d): since the movie has been awarded 3 Oscars, the corresponding page has small structural differences, and neither $r^1$ nor $r^3$ correctly extract the title.

To overcome this issue, we leverage the redundancy of equivalent rules generated in the above steps. Targeting only resources from pages for which the extraction is likely to work correctly, we return the pairs (lines 7-8) on which all the distinct yet equivalent rules return the same value. Again from our example, observe that rules $r^2$ and $r^3$ extract different values from the page in Figure 2(d) (*Argo* and *Oscar 2013*, respectively), therefore, none of the values extracted from that page would be added in the final output. All these rules are used later (lines 9-13) to check that they extract the same value (line 10) from a web page.

### 3.5 Generation Layer

Now that data has been extracted from the websites, REX is ready to generate RDF out of them. To achieve this goal, two steps needs to be carried out. First, the strings retrieved have to be mapped to RDF resources or literals. This is carried out by the *URI disambiguation* modules. The resulting triples then need to be checked for whether

---

**Listing 1.** ALFREX: Extract Subject-Object Pairs from a Website

**Input:** knowledge base $K$, a predicate $p$, a set of examples $E = \{(s,o)|(s,p,o) \in K\}$
**Input:** a set of pages $W = \{w_1, \ldots, w_{|W|}\}$ containing data related to the predicate $p$

---

**Parameter:** a class of extraction rules $\mathcal{R}$ over $W$
**Parameter:** $k$, the number of sample pages for generating the rules

---

**Output:** set $T$ of pairs of strings extracted from pages $W$

---

```
1:  T := ∅; // output pairs of strings
2:  Q := {w ∈ W : (label(s), label(o)) ∈ w, (s, o) ∈ E};
3:  I := a set of k random pages from Q;
4:  R_s := {r, r ∈ R, w ∈ I, (label(s), label(o)) ∈ w, r(w) = label(s)};
5:  R_o := {r, r ∈ R, w ∈ I, (label(s), label(o)) ∈ w, r(w) = label(o)};
6:  (r_s, r_o) := argmax_{r_s∈R_s,r_o∈R_o}  |{w, w ∈ Q, (label(s), label(o)) ∈ w, r_s(q) = 
       label(s) and r_o(q) = label(o)}|;
7:  {r_s^1, r_s^2, ..., r_s^n} ← {r, r ∈ R_s, r(Q) = r_s(Q)};
8:  {r_o^1, r_o^2, ..., r_o^m} ← {r, r ∈ R_o, r(Q) = r_o(Q)};
9:  for q ∈ W do
10:     if (r_s^1(q) = ... = r_s^n(q) and r_o^1(q) = ... = r_o^m(q)) then
11:         T ← T ∪ {(r_s^1(q), r_o^1(q))};
12:     end if
13: end for
14: return T;
```

---

they go against the ontology of the knowledge base or other consistency rules. This functionality is implemented in the *data validation* modules.

**URI Disambiguation.** URI disambiguation is not a trivial task, as several resources can share the same label in a knowledge base. For example, "Brad Pitt" can be mapped to the resource :Brad_Pitt (the movie star) or :Brad_Pitt_(boxer), an Australian boxer. We address this problem by using *AGDISTIS*, a framework for URI disambiguation [22]. In our current implementation, we chose to simply integrate the AGDISTIS framework using DBpedia 3.8. We chose this framework because it outperforms the state-of-the-art frameworks AIDA [15] and DBpedia Spotlight [18] by 20% w.r.t. its accuracy. Especially on short RSS feeds containing only two resource labels, the approach achieves 3% to 11% higher accuracy. More details on AGDISTIS as well as a thorough evaluation against popular frameworks such as DBpedia Spotlight and AIDA can be found in [22]. Note that if no resources in $K$ has a URI which matches $s$ or $o$, we generate a new cool URI[10] for this string.

**Data Validation.** Sequentially applying the steps before results in a set of triples $< s, p, o >$ that might not be contained in $K$. As we assume that we start from a consistent knowledge base $K$ and the whole triple generation process until here is carried out automatically, we need to ensure that $K$ remains consistent after adding $< s, p, o >$

---

[10] http://www.w3.org/TR/cooluris

to $K$. To this end, REX provides a data validation interface whose first implementation was based on the DL-Learner.[11] Depending on the size of $K$, using a standard OWL reasoner for consistency checks can be intractable. Thus, our current implementation applies the following set of rules based on the schema of $K$ and add a triple $< s_1, p, o_1 >$ only if it holds that:

1. If a class $C$ is the domain of $p$, there exists no type $D$ of $s_1$ such that $C$ and $D$ are disjoint.
2. If a class $C$ is the range of $p$, there exists no type $D$ of $o_1$ such that $C$ and $D$ are disjoint.
3. If $p$ is declared to be functional, there exists no triple $< s_1, p, o_2 >$ in $K$ such that $o_1 \neq o_2$.
4. If $p$ is declared to be inverse functional, there exists no triple $< s_2, p, o_1 >$ in $K$ such that $s_1 \neq s_2$.
5. If $p$ is declared to be asymmetric, there exists no triple $< o_1, p, s_1 >$ in $K$.
6. If $p$ is declared to be irreflexive, it holds that $s_1 \neq o_1$.

Note that this approach is sound but of course incomplete. Although an increasing number of RDF knowledge bases are published, many of those consist primarily of instance data and lack sophisticated schemata. To support the application of the above defined rules, we follow the work in [6,7], which provides a lightweight and efficient schema creation approach that scales to large knowledge bases.

# 4 Evaluation

The goal of the evaluation was to provide a detailed study of the behavior of the current REX modules with the aim of (1) ensuring that our framework can be used even in its current version and (2) detecting current weaknesses of our framework to trigger future developments. In the following, we begin by presenting the data and hardware we used for our experiments. Thereafter, we present and discuss the results of our experiments. Detailed results can be found at the project website.

## 4.1 Experimental Setup

We generated our experimental data by crawling three websites, i.e.,

1. imdb.com where we extracted dbo:starring, dbo:starring$^{-1}$ and dbo:director;
2. goodreads.com, from which we extracted dbo:author and dbo:author$^{-1}$;
3. espnfc.com with the target relations dbo:team and dbo:team$^{-1}$.

We chose these websites because they represent three different categories of templated websites. imdb.com widely follows a uniform template for all pages in the same subdomain. Thus, we expected the wrapper learning to work well here. goodreads.com

---
[11] http://dl-learner.org

represents an average case of templated websites. While template are most widely used and followed, missing values and misused fields are more common here than in our first dataset. The third dataset, espnfc.com, was chosen as worst-case scenario. The dataset contains several blank pages, a large variety of templates used in manifold different fashions. Consequently, defining a set of golden XPaths is a tedious task, even for trained experts. Thus, we expected the results on this dataset to be typical for the worst-case behavior of our approach. We randomly sampled 10,000 HTML pages per subdomain for our experiments and manually built reference XPath expressions to evaluate the precision and recall of the generated extraction rules. The precision, recall and F-measure reported below were computed by comparing the output of REX with the output of the reference XPath expressions. All extraction runtime experiments were carried out on single nodes of an Amazon EC2.small instance.

## 4.2  Results

**Effect of Number of Examples and Sampling Strategy on F-Measure.** The results of our experiments on altering the number of examples used for learning are shown in Figures 3a-3h. Due to space limitations, we show the average results over all the pairs extraction by our wrapper induction approach for each of the domains. The results achieved using the prominence-based sampling show the expected trend: on pages that use a consistent template (such as the director pages in imdb.com), our approach requires as few as around 70 pages for $|Q|$. Once this value is reached, REX can compute high-quality extraction rules and achieves an F-measure of 0.97 (see Figures 3a). For pages that change template based on the prominence of the entities they describe (like the actors' pages, see Figure 3b), our approach requires more training data to achieve a high F-measure. The increase of F-measure is clearly due to an increase in precision, pointing to REX being able to better choose across different alternative XPaths when provided with more information. The results of goodreads.com support our conjecture. With more training data, we get an increase in precision to up to 1 while the recall drops, leading to an overall F-measure of 0.89 for 40k examples. In our worst-case scenario, we achieve an overall F-measure close to 0.6. The lower value is clearly due to the inconsistent use of templates across the different pages in the subdomains.

**Table 1.** Average evaluation results using all available pairs as training data

|              | P    | R    | F-measure | # pages |
|--------------|------|------|-----------|---------|
| dbo:director | 0.82 | 1.00 | 0.89      | 216     |
| dbo:starring | 0.86 | 1.00 | 0.90      | 316     |
| dbo:author   | 0.94 | 0.85 | 0.86      | 217     |
| dbo:team     | 0.32 | 0.43 | 0.35      | 656     |

The results based on the uniform sampling strategy reveal another trait of REX. As expected, the coverage achieved using uniform sampling is clearly smaller in all cases. The results achieved with all the training data available clearly show the importance of sampling (see Table 1). While one could conjecture that using all data for training would

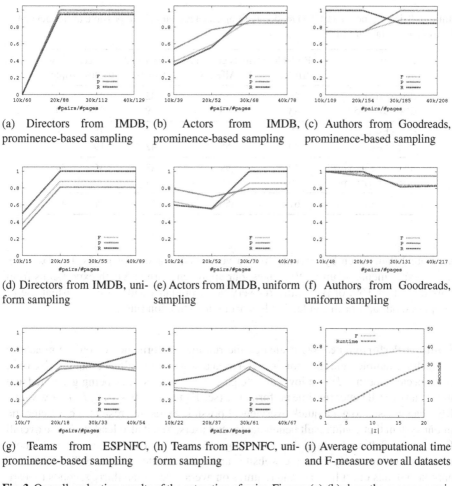

(a) Directors from IMDB, prominence-based sampling

(b) Actors from IMDB, prominence-based sampling

(c) Authors from Goodreads, prominence-based sampling

(d) Directors from IMDB, uniform sampling

(e) Actors from IMDB, uniform sampling

(f) Authors from Goodreads, uniform sampling

(g) Teams from ESPNFC, prominence-based sampling

(h) Teams from ESPNFC, uniform sampling

(i) Average computational time and F-measure over all datasets

**Fig. 3.** Overall evaluation results of the extraction of pairs. Figures (a)-(h) show the average precision, recall and F-measure achieved the generated XPaths for the prominence-based and uniform sampling. The x-axis shows the number of examples and the number of sample pages retrieved in the format $|E|/|Q|$. Figure (i) shows the average computational time and the corresponding F-measures for different sizes of $|I|$.

be beneficial for our approach, the F-measures achieved by using all the data suggest that sampling can be beneficial for the extraction, especially when the web pages do not follow a rigid template (e.g., in esnpfc.com) or when the data in the knowledge base is noisy. Overall, our results suggest that our approach is accurate, also for pages where entities with different prominence are assigned variable templates as in imdb.com actors. If multiple occurrences of the same value are present in the same page (as in the case of books, actors and directors), our algorithm is able to detect the most stable one. Moreover, our approach seems robust against noisy labels, even when there are many false positive in the page (e.g., book author pages that include many links to different books by the same author). An important feature of our approach is that it can obtain

**Table 2.** Triples generated by 100 randomly sampled pages, number of possible triples generated by using gold standard rules

| Property | #Possible triples | #Triples generated by AlfREX | #Consistent triples | #Correct triples | #New triples |
|---|---|---|---|---|---|
| dbo:author$^{-1}$ | 54 | 32 | 32 | 22 | 22 |
| dbo:author | 83 | 83 | 69 | 54 | 54 |
| dbo:team$^{-1}$ | 2 | 1 | 1 | 0 | 0 |
| dbo:team | 30 | 55 | 42 | 19 | 13 |
| dbo:starring$^{-1}$ | 40 | 99 | 83 | 35 | 34 |
| dbo:starring | 70 | 70 | 44 | 33 | 32 |
| dbo:director | 61 | 56 | 52 | 41 | 41 |

accurate XPaths even by learning from a very small fraction of pages. For example, in our experiments on up to 40k pages, our approach learned XPath expressions from only 0.5% to 1.16% of $|W|$. Still, for very noisy domains with an inconsistent use of templates, our approach can lead to less accurate extraction rules.

**Runtime Performance.** We evaluated the runtime performance of our approach by using 40k examples and the prominence-based distribution while altering the size of $I$. As expected, setting $|I|$ to a low value (e.g., 1) leads to less rules being generated and thus to an overall better runtime performance (see Figure 3i). By setting $I$ to a low value, REX can be used to get a quick overview of possible extraction results, a characteristic of our system that could result beneficial for end users. Yet, it also leads to worse overall F-measures. Setting $I$ to a higher value (e.g., 15) leads to a more thorough (i.e., more time-demanding) analysis of the websites and thus to better results. Still overall, our approach scales quasi linearly and requires on average less than thirty seconds to learn wrappers out of existing data even for $|I| = 20$.

**Quality of RDF Output.** To check the quality of the RDF we generated, we manually checked the triples extracted from each property of our three domains. Each triple was checked by at least two annotators, which reached a significant Kohen's kappa score of 0.88 overall. On goodreads.com we achieved a precision of 75.24%. While we achieve a precision of 78.85% when extraction directors from *imdb.com* and of 75% on starring, the extraction of starring$^{-1}$ proves more tedious (precision = 42.17%). As expected, the data extracted from *espnfc.com* has a low precision of 44.19%. The results on starring$^{-1}$ are due to the fact that several actors can star in a movie while assuming other roles. Thus, our extraction framework often overgenerates triples and produces false positives (e.g., directors are often included). The results on *espnfc.com* are clearly due to the templates not being used correctly. Still, our results clearly show the potential of our approach, as 60.68% of the triples we extracted are both correct and novel.

## 5 Related Work

To the best of our knowledge, no open-source framework covers the complete functionality of the REX framework. REX relies internally on URI disambiguation and data validation based on automatically extracted axioms [6]. These are both areas of research with a wide of body of publications. Especially, several approaches to URI disambiguation based on graphs [15,22] and statistical information from text [18] have been developed recently. The extraction of axioms from knowledge based using statistical information [6,7] as also flourished over the last years. The main idea underlying these approaches is to use instance knowledge from knowledge bases without expressive schemas to compute the axioms which underlie the said knowledge bases. We refer the reader to the publications above for an overview of these two research areas.

REX is mainly related to wrapper induction. Early approaches to learning web wrappers were mostly supervised (see, e.g., [16,11]). These systems were provided with annotated pages out of which they infer extraction rules that allow extracting data from other unlabeled pages with the same structure as the annotated pages). For example [16] presents *Tresher*, a system that allows non-technical end-users to teach their browser how to extract data from the Web. Supervised approaches were yet deemed costly due to the human labor necessary to annotate the input web pages. Unsupervised wrapper induction methods have thus been explored [8,1] to reduce the annotation costs. However, the absence of a supervision often lead these systems to produce wrappers of accuracy not suitable for production level usage. Novel approaches thus aim to minimize the annotation costs while keeping a high precision. For example, the approach presented in [10] relies on the availability of a knowledge base in the form of dictionaries and regular expressions to automatically obtain training data. Recently, [9] describes a supervised framework that is able to profit from crowd-provided training data. The learning algorithm controls the cost of the crowd sourcing campaign w.r.t. quality of the output wrapper. However, these novel approaches do not target the generated of RDF data.

Linked Data has been used to learn wrappers to extract RDF from the Web in recent years. For example, [12] exploits Linked Data as a training data to find instances of given classes such as universities and extract the attributes of these instances while relying on the supervised wrapper induction approach presented in [14]. However, they require a manual exploration of the Linked Data sources to generate their training data, which leads to a considerable amount of manual effort. The DEIMOS project [19] is similar to REX, as it aims at bringing to the Semantic Web the data that are published through the rest of the Web. However, it focuses on the pages behind web forms. OntoSyphon [17] operates in an "ontology-driven" manner: taking any ontology as input, OntoSyphon uses the ontology to specify web searches that identify possible semantic instances, relations, and taxonomic information, in an unsupervised manner. However, the approach makes use of extraction patterns that work for textual documents rather than structured web pages. To the best of our knowledge, none of the existing approaches covers all steps that are required to extract consistent RDF from the Web. Especially, only [19] is able to generate RDF but does not check it for consistency. In contrast, REX is the first approach that is scalable, low-cost, accurate and can generate consistent RDF.

## 6  Conclusions

In this paper we presented the first framework for the consistent extraction of RDF from templates Web pages. REX is available as open source[12] Java implementation in an easily extendable fashion. Our framework uses the LOD Cloud as source for training data that are used to learn web wrappers. The output of these wrappers is used to generate RDF by the means of a URI disambiguation step as well as a data validation step. We studied several sampling strategies and how they affect the F-measure achieved. Our overall results show that although we can extract subject-object pairs with a high accuracy from well-templated websites, a lot of work still needs to be done in the area of grounding these strings into an existing ontology. One solution to this problem might be to use more context information during the disambiguation step. Moreover, more sophisticated approaches can be used for crawling websites offering structured navigation paths towards target pages [5]. By these means, we should be able to eradicate some of the sources of error in our extraction process. Our approach can be further improved by combining it with crowdsourcing-based approaches for wrapper induction such as ALFRED [9] or by learning more expressive wrappers. We thus regard this framework as a basis for populating the Web of Data using Web pages by professional end-users.

**Acknowledgments.** Parts of this work were supported by the ESF and the Free State of Saxony. We thank M. Speicher & M. Röder.

## References

1. Arasu, A., Garcia-Molina, H.: Extracting structured data from web pages. In: SIGMOD, pp. 337–348 (2003)
2. Auer, S., Bizer, C., Kobilarov, G., Lehmann, J., Cyganiak, R., Ives, Z.G.: DBpedia: A nucleus for a web of open data. In: Aberer, K., et al. (eds.) ISWC/ASWC 2007. LNCS, vol. 4825, pp. 722–735. Springer, Heidelberg (2007)
3. Auer, S., Dietzold, S., Lehmann, J., Hellmann, S., Aumueller, D.: Triplify: light-weight linked data publication from relational databases. In: WWW, pp. 621–630 (2009)
4. Bizer, C., Seaborne, A.: D2rq - treating non-rdf databases as virtual rdf graphs. In: ISWC 2004 (posters) (November 2004)
5. Blanco, L., Crescenzi, V., Merialdo, P.: Efficiently locating collections of web pages to wrap. In: Cordeiro, J., Pedrosa, V., Encarnação, B., Filipe, J. (eds.) WEBIST, pp. 247–254. IN-STICC Press (2005)
6. Bühmann, L., Lehmann, J.: Universal OWL axiom enrichment for large knowledge bases. In: ten Teije, A., Völker, J., Handschuh, S., Stuckenschmidt, H., d'Acquin, M., Nikolov, A., Aussenac-Gilles, N., Hernandez, N. (eds.) EKAW 2012. LNCS, vol. 7603, pp. 57–71. Springer, Heidelberg (2012)
7. Bühmann, L., Lehmann, J.: Pattern based knowledge base enrichment. In: Alani, H., et al. (eds.) ISWC 2013, Part I. LNCS, vol. 8218, pp. 33–48. Springer, Heidelberg (2013)
8. Crescenzi, V., Merialdo, P.: Wrapper inference for ambiguous web pages. Applied Artificial Intelligence 22(1&2), 21–52 (2008)

---

[12] http://rex.aksw.org

9. Crescenzi, V., Merialdo, P., Qiu, D.: A framework for learning web wrappers from the crowd. In: Proceedings of the 22nd International Conference on World Wide Web, WWW 2013, Republic and Canton of Geneva, Switzerland, pp. 261–272. International World Wide Web Conferences Steering Committee (2013)

10. Dalvi, N., Kumar, R., Soliman, M.: Automatic wrappers for large scale web extraction. Proc. VLDB Endow. 4(4), 219–230 (2011)

11. Flesca, S., Manco, G., Masciari, E., Rende, E., Tagarelli, A.: Web wrapper induction: a brief survey. AI Communications 17(2), 57–61 (2004)

12. Gentile, A.L., Zhang, Z., Augenstein, I., Ciravegna, F.: Unsupervised wrapper induction using linked data. In: Proceedings of the Seventh International Conference on Knowledge Capture, K-CAP 2013, pp. 41–48. ACM, New York (2013)

13. Gerber, D., Hellmann, S., Bühmann, L., Soru, T., Usbeck, R., Ngonga Ngomo, A.-C.: Real-time RDF extraction from unstructured data streams. In: Alani, H., et al. (eds.) ISWC 2013, Part I. LNCS, vol. 8218, pp. 135–150. Springer, Heidelberg (2013)

14. Hao, Q., Cai, R., Pang, Y., Zhang, L.: From one tree to a forest: a unified solution for structured web data extraction. In: Proceedings of the 34th International ACM SIGIR Conference on Research and Development in Information Retrieval, SIGIR 2011, pp. 775–784. ACM, New York (2011)

15. Hoffart, J., Yosef, M.A., Bordino, I., Fürstenau, H., Pinkal, M., Spaniol, M., Taneva, B., Thater, S., Weikum, G.: Robust Disambiguation of Named Entities in Text. In: Conference on Empirical Methods in Natural Language Processing, EMNLP 2011, Edinburgh, Scotland, pp. 782–792 (2011)

16. Hogue, A., Karger, D.: Thresher: automating the unwrapping of semantic content from the world wide web. In: Proceedings of the 14th International Conference on World Wide Web, WWW 2005, pp. 86–95. ACM, New York (2005)

17. McDowell, L., Cafarella, M.J.: Ontology-driven, unsupervised instance population. J. Web Sem. 6(3), 218–236 (2008)

18. Mendes, P.N., Jakob, M., Garcia-Silva, A., Bizer, C.: Dbpedia spotlight: Shedding light on the web of documents. In: Proceedings of the 7th International Conference on Semantic Systems (I-Semantics) (2011)

19. Parundekar, R., Knoblock, C.A., Ambite, J.L.: Linking the deep web to the linked dataweb. In: AAAI Spring Symposium: Linked Data Meets Artificial Intelligence. AAAI (2010)

20. Saleem, M., Padmanabhuni, S.S., Ngonga Ngomo, A.-C., Almeida, J.S., Decker, S., Deus, H.F.: Linked cancer genome atlas database. In: Proceedings of I-Semantics (2013)

21. Unbehauen, J., Stadler, C., Auer, S.: Accessing relational data on the web with sparqlmap. In: Takeda, H., Qu, Y., Mizoguchi, R., Kitamura, Y. (eds.) JIST 2012. LNCS, vol. 7774, pp. 65–80. Springer, Heidelberg (2013)

22. Usbeck, R., Ngomo, A.-C.N., Röder, M., Gerber, D., Coelho, S.A., Auer, S., Both, A.: AGDISTIS - graph-based disambiguation of named entities using linked data. In: Mika, P., et al. (eds.) ISWC 2014. LNCS, vol. 8796, pp. 449–463. Springer, Heidelberg (2014)

# EPCIS Event-Based Traceability
# in Pharmaceutical Supply Chains via Automated
# Generation of Linked Pedigrees

Monika Solanki and Christopher Brewster

Aston Business School
Aston University, UK
{m.solanki,c.a.brewster}@aston.ac.uk

**Abstract.** In this paper we show how event processing over semantically annotated streams of events can be exploited, for implementing tracing and tracking of products in supply chains through the automated generation of linked pedigrees. In our abstraction, events are encoded as spatially and temporally oriented named graphs, while linked pedigrees as RDF datasets are their specific compositions. We propose an algorithm that operates over streams of RDF annotated EPCIS events to generate linked pedigrees. We exemplify our approach using the pharmaceuticals supply chain and show how counterfeit detection is an implicit part of our pedigree generation. Our evaluation results show that for fast moving supply chains, smaller window sizes on event streams provide significantly higher efficiency in the generation of pedigrees as well as enable early counterfeit detection.

## 1    Introduction

Recent advances in sensor technology has resulted in wide scale deployment of RFID enabled devices in supply chains. Timely processing of RFID data facilitates efficient analysis of product movement, shipment delays, inventory shrinkage and out-of-stock situation in end-to-end supply chain processes [1]. The scanning of RFID tags in production and storage facilities generates unprecedented volumes of events as data streams, when trading partners exchange and handle products from inception through to the end-of-life phase.

In this paper we present a methodology for the automated generation of event-based traceability/visibility information, referred to as "linked pedigrees". We propose a pedigree generation algorithm based on complex processing of real time streams of RFID data in supply chains. Our streams comprise of events annotated using RDF/OWL vocabularies. Annotating streams using standardised vocabularies ensures interoperability between supply chain systems and expands the scope to exploit ontology based reasoning over continuously evolving knowledge. We represent supply chain events as streams of RDF encoded linked data, while complex event patterns are declaratively specified through extended SPARQL queries. In contrast to existing approaches [6, 8, 9] where an element

P. Mika et al. (Eds.) ISWC 2014, Part I, LNCS 8796, pp. 82–97, 2014.

in a stream is a triple, our streams comprise of events where each event is represented as a named graph [5]. A linked pedigree is considered as a composition of named graphs, represented as an RDF dataset[1].

Our exemplifying scenario is an abstraction of the pharmaceutical supply chain. Counterfeiting has increasingly become one of the major problems prevalent in these chains. The WHO estimates that between five and eight percent of the worldwide trade in pharmaceuticals is counterfeit [11]. Many industry experts believe this to be a conservative estimate. Increased visibility of supply chain knowledge, enabled through exchange of event-based traceability data or pedigrees is anticipated to play a key role in addressing the problem.

In the fall of 2013, the U.S. House of Representatives and Senate passed the Drug Quality and Security Act (DQSA)[2]. The track-and-trace provisions, themselves known as *The Drug Supply Chain Security Act* (DSCSA)[3] within the DQSA outlines critical steps to build an electronic, interoperable system to identify and trace certain prescription drugs as they are distributed in the United States. In readiness for its implementation in the healthcare sector from 2015 onwards, the GS1 Healthcare US Secure Supply Chain Task Force has developed guidelines[4] to identify and serialise pharmaceutical products, in order to trace their movement through the U.S. pharmaceutical supply chains. The guidelines are based around the implementation of EPCIS[5] (Electronic Product Code Information Services) as a standard for event oriented, pedigree track and trace. In accordance to these guidelines, the algorithm proposed in this paper utilises EEM[6] (EPCIS Event Model) [14] - an OWL DL ontology for EPCIS, CBVVocab[7] an OWL DL ontology for the Core Business Vocabulary[8], as the specifications for encoding the event data streams and OntoPedigree[9] a content ontology design pattern for generating the linked pedigrees. To the best of our knowledge, stream processing of events annotated with semantics enriched metadata for the generation of traceability/visibility data has so far not been explored for EPCIS events within the Semantic Web or supply chain communities.

The paper is structured as follows: Section 2 presents our motivating scenario from the pharmaceuticals supply chain. Section 3 discusses background and related work. Section 4 presents the preliminaries needed for events and pedigrees that we use in Section 5 for generating our pedigree composition algorithm. Section 6 highlights our evaluation requirements, illustrates the execution environment and discusses evaluation results. Section 7 presents conclusions.

---

[1] http://www.w3.org/TR/rdf11-datasets/
[2] http://www.gpo.gov/fdsys/pkg/BILLS-113hr3204enr/pdf/
   BILLS-113hr3204enr.pdf
[3] http://www.fda.gov/Drugs/DrugSafety/DrugIntegrityandSupplyChainSecurity/
   DrugSupplyChainSecurityAct/
[4] www.gs1us.org/RxGuideline
[5] http://www.gs1.org/gsmp/kc/epcglobal/epcis
[6] http://purl.org/eem#
[7] http://purl.org/cbv#
[8] http://www.gs1.org/gsmp/kc/epcglobal/cbv
[9] http://purl.org/pedigree#

## 2   Motivating Scenario

We outline the scenario of a pharmaceutical supply chain, where trading partners exchange product track and trace data using linked pedigrees. Figure 1 illustrates the flow of data for four of the key partners in the chain. The *Manufacturer* commissions[10], i.e, assigns an EPC (Electronic Product Code) to the items, cases and pallets. The items are packed in cases, cases are loaded onto pallets and pallets are shipped. At the *Warehouse*, the pallets are received and the cases are unloaded. The cases are then shipped to the various *Distribution centers*. From the Distribution centers the cases are sent to retail *Dispenser* outlets, where they are received and unpacked. Finally, the items are stacked on shelves for dispensing, thereby reaching their end-of-life in the product lifecycle.

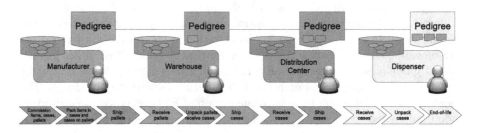

**Fig. 1.** Trading partners in a pharmaceutical supply chain and the flow of information

As the serialised items, cases and pallets move through the various phases of the supply chain at a trading partner's premises, EPCIS events are generated and recorded at several RFID reader nodes. Figure 2 illustrates the phases at a manufacturer's packaging setup and the event streams that can be possibly generated in these phases. For example, events are generated when `Case001` is tagged, i.e, commissioned and read by `Reader011`, when it is packed and read by `Reader013` and finally when the case is made a part of shipment `SSCC001` which is read by `Reader015`. When the pallets with the cases are shipped from the manufacturer's premises to the warehouse, pedigrees encapsulating the minimum set of EPCIS events are published at an IRI based on a predefined IRI scheme. At the warehouse, when the shipment is received, the IRI of the pedigree is dereferenced to retrieve the manufacturer's pedigree. When the warehouse ships the cases to the distribution center, it incorporates the IRI of the manufacturer's pedigree in its own pedigree definition. As the product moves, pedigrees are generated with receiving pedigrees being dereferenced and incorporated, till the product reaches its end-of-life stage.

Given this scenario, for a fast moving supply chain with high volumes (approx. 100,000 per day, cf. Section 6) of commissioned items, we evaluate the algorithm proposed in this paper against the time taken for pedigree generation and counterfeit detection. We experiment with varying sizes of event streams,

---

[10] Associating the serial number with the physical product.

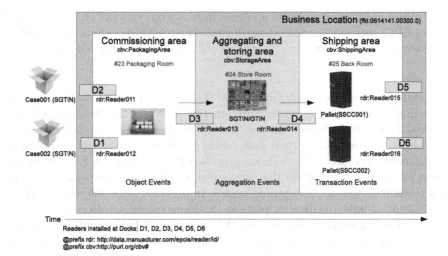

**Fig. 2.** EPCIS Read points and events at the Manufacturer's packaging setup

items, cases and pallets. In particular we would like to ascertain the trade offs between the time taken in generating a large number of pedigrees, each corresponding to a small number of commissioned items against generating a small number of pedigrees for large number of commissioned items, aggregated cases and pallets.

## 3 Background and Related Work

An Electronic Product Code (EPC)[11] is a universal identifier that gives a unique, serialised identity to a physical object. EPCIS is a ratified EPCglobal[12] standard that provides a set of specifications for the syntactic capture and informal semantic interpretation of EPC based product information. As the EPC tagged object moves through the supply chain, RFID readers record and transmit the tagged data as "events". In this paper we are particularly concerned with three types of EPCIS events:

- *ObjectEvent* represents an event that occurred as a result of some action on one or more entities denoted by EPCs, e.g., *"This list of objects was observed entering warehouse #12 at 12:01AM, during Receiving"*.
- *AggregationEvent* represents an event that happened to one or more EPC-denoted entities that are physically aggregated (constrained to be in the same place at the same time, as when cases are aggregated to a pallet), e.g., *"This list of objects was just Palletized with this Pallet ID at Palletizer #27 at 12:32PM"*.

---

[11] http://www.gs1.org/gsmp/kc/epcglobal/tds/
    tds_1_6-RatifiedStd-20110922.pdf
[12] http://www.gs1.org/epcglobal

- *TransactionEvent* represents an event in which one or more entities denoted by EPCs become associated or disassociated with one or more identified business transactions, e.g., *"Order #123 was fulfilled with objects x, y and z"*.

A Pedigree is an (electronic) audit trail that records the chain of custody and ownership of a drug as it moves through the supply chain. Each stakeholder involved in the manufacture or distribution of the drug adds visibility-based data about the product at their end, to the pedigree. Recently the concept of "Event-based Pedigree"[13] have been proposed that utilises the EPCIS specification for capturing events in the supply chain and generating pedigrees based on a relevant subset of the captured events. In previous work [13] we introduced the concept of linked pedigrees, proposed a decentralised architecture and presented a communication protocol for the exchange of linked pedigrees among supply chain partners. In this paper we build upon that work and propose an automated pedigree generation algorithm using streams of EPCIS event data.

Several approaches [16, 17] have been proposed that utilise Complex Event Processing (CEP) for RFID events. In [16], an event composition language, declarative rules and a graph based event processing model are presented. In [17] the authors synthesise behavioural profiles of business processes for query optimisation, based on external process models that define potential sequences of events. Formal modelling of RFID events and roles for the pharmaceuticals supply chain has been proposed in [10], but the focus there is on addressing security threats and counterfeits rather than generating pedigrees for traceability. In contrast, the approach proposed in this paper addresses counterfeit detection implicitly while generating pedigrees.

RFID platforms built around EPCIS have also been made available by major IT vendors such as Oracle's Pedigree and Serialization Manager[14], Frequentz's IRIS Information Repository and Intelligence Server[15], Microsoft's BizTalk RFID[16] and SAP's Auto-ID Infrastructure[17]. In all the above frameworks, event descriptions are not interoperable, they cannot be shared and combined with background knowledge about the objects being tracked and traced. Further, none of these platforms provide any support for semantic descriptions of EPCIS events or generation of pedigrees as linked data nor do they provide any explicit mechanism for counterfeit detection. However our proposed approach could complement these implementations very well by providing a scalable data sharing model and framework for exchanging pedigrees using open standards.

---

[13] http://www.gs1.org/docs/healthcare/
Healthcare_Traceability_Pedigree_Background.pdf

[14] http://www.oracle.com/us/products/applications/life-sciences/
pedigree-serialization/index.html

[15] Originally IBM's InfoSphere Traceability Server,
http://frequentz.com/traceability-server/

[16] http://msdn.microsoft.com/en-us/biztalk/dd409102

[17] https://help.sap.com/aii

Within the Semantic Web Community [7], Several frameworks for CEP and querying over RDF streams such as C-SPARQL [6], CQELS [8], EP-SPARQL [2] and INSTANS [9] have been proposed. Social media and smart cities have proved to be important use cases for the application of these frameworks, however there have been no applications in the business and supply chain sector. While most approaches assume streams to comprise of a sequence of time-stamped RDF triples, our streams are sequences of time-stamped RDF graphs. Some other approaches for streaming data sources such as [3,4] have also been proposed. A rule based approach to CEP of event streams that are semantically annotated is presented in [15].

## 4  Preliminaries

### 4.1  EPCIS Events

For the generation of pedigrees we are interested in the three types of EP-CIS events outlined in Section 3. The set of predefined[18] EPCIS event types $E_{types} = \{O_e, A_e, T_e\}$, where $O_e$ is an Object event, $A_e$ is an Aggregation event and $T_e$ is a Transaction event. The set of predefined EPCIS business step types $B_{steps} = \{com, pck, shp\}$ represent the business steps of "commissioning", "packing" and "shipping" respectively as defined in the Core Business Vocabulary and correspondingly in our CBVVocab ontology.

An EPCIS event $E$ as defined in this paper, is a 6-tuple $\langle I_e, t_o, t_r, e_t, b_s, R_e \rangle$ where,

- $I_e \in I$ is the IRI for the event.
- $t_o$ is the time at which the event occurred.
- $t_r$ is the time at which the event was recorded, henceforth referred to as the *timestamp* of the event.
- $e_t \in E_{types}$ is the type of event.
- $b_s \in B_{steps}$ is the business step.
- $R_e$ is a non empty set of EPCs associated with the event.

An EPCIS event named graph, $E_g$, is a pair $(I_n \in I, G_e \in G)$, where $I_n$ is the name (as well as the IRI) of the event graph and $G_e$ is the RDF event graph. Additionally, we define functions eventGraph $(E_g)$ and eventIRI (eventGraph $(E_g)$) that return the event graph and the event IRI respectively for the EPCIS event represented by $E_g$. Further, we define a function, eventOccurrenceTime (eventGraph $(E_g)$) that returns the time of occurrence $t_o$ of the event represented in $G_e$.

An EPCIS stream $(G_s)$ is an ordered sequence of RDF triples $\langle (I_n, \text{eventRecordedAt}, t_r) : [t_o] \rangle$ published at an IRI $I_s \in I$, and ordered by $t_o$. The set of triples in $G_s$ are valid at timestamp $t_r$.

We use the notations and definitions defined above in the pedigree generation algorithm proposed in Section 5.

---

[18] Also referred to as an enum.

## 4.2 Provenance Based Linked Pedigrees

In [13] we proposed a content ontology design pattern, "OntoPedigree"[19], for the modelling of traceability knowledge as linked pedigrees. As provenance of information in supply chains is of critical importance, in this paper we extend the pedigree definition to include provenance.

As pat of the core supply chain knowledge, a linked pedigree includes IRIs for products, transaction and consignment. For provenance, we exploit the PROV-O[20] ontology. In particular, we define provenance assertions for the service and the organisation that created the pedigree as well as for the events and other information artifacts used in the creation of the pedigree. It is worth noting that our event ontology EEM has also been mapped to PROV-O[21]. This implies that we can trace the provenance associated with any event encapsulated within a pedigree. This capability has proved immensely useful in associating authorities with counterfeits (cf. Section 6) when they are detected.

Figure 3 illustrates the graphical representation of OntoPedigree augmented with provenance information. In particular we link pedigrees to the creating authority through the prov:wasAttributedTo property. Pedigrees are created by every partner in the supply chain. Apart from the pedigree initiated and created by the first partner, all other linked pedigrees include IRIs to the pedigree datasets for the stakeholders in the immediate upstream or downstream of the supply chain. Pedigrees received from external partners are related via the ped:hasReceivedPedigree property which is defined as a subproperty of prov:wasDerivedFrom and the time of pedigree generation is captured via the prov:generatedAt property.

## 5 Incremental Linked Pedigree Generation Algorithms

### 5.1 Extracting Events from EPCIS Streams

Central to the generation of linked pedigrees from streaming EPCIS events is the notion of "windows" that allow the extraction of an event graph from the streams for further processing. We extract events from EPCIS event streams using windows in two steps: In the first step, the window is selected based on the time interval. In the second step, the filtering of the event IRIs for inclusion in the pedigree is carried out based on the business steps that generated the event graphs.

The following SPARQL queries corresponding to the window selection criteria identified above are defined.The prefix eem corresponds to the EEM ontology.

**Window Selection: Time Interval ($Q_t$)**

In this step all event IRIs within a time interval of X hrs (tumbling windows) are selected from the event stream serialised in the TRIG[22] format. As TRIG is

[19] http://purl.org/pedigree#
[20] http://www.w3.org/TR/prov-o/
[21] http://fispace.aston.ac.uk/ontologies/eem_prov#
[22] http://www.w3.org/TR/trig/

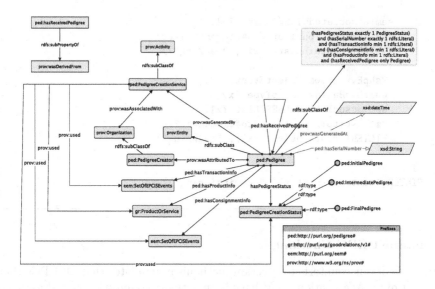

**Fig. 3.** Graphical Representation of Provenance based OntoPedigree

currently not supported by any of the stream processing frameworks, we perform this step as part of our implementation using customised functions.

```
SELECT DISTINCT ?g ?eventGraphIRI ?time WHERE{
  GRAPH ?g {
  ?eventGraphIRI eem:eventRecordedAt ?time ;
  BIND(now() AS ?t1)
  FILTER(fun:extractHours(?t1, ?time) <= X) }}
```

## Window Selection: Business Step ($Q_{bs}$)

Event based consignment information to be included in a pedigree consists of events corresponding to (a) the commissioning of the items, cases and pallets, (b) aggregation of the items in the cases (c) loading of cases on the pallets and shipping. The following SPARQL query, extracts the events corresponding to these business step from each event graph.

```
SELECT DISTINCT ?objEvt ?aggEvt ?shpEvt WHERE
{
  ?objEvt a eem:ObjectEvent;
    eem:hasBusinessStepType ?x;
    eem:associatedWithEPCList ?y.
    ?y  <http://purl.org/co#element> ?epc1.
    {
        ?aggEvt a eem:AggregationEvent;
        eem:hasAggregationURI ?au;
        eem:hasBusinessStepType ?x1;
```

```
        eem:associatedWithEPCList ?y1.
        ?y1 <http://purl.org/co#element> ?epc1.
        FILTER( contains(str(?x1), "packing"))
        {
         ?shpEvt a eem:ObjectEvent;
         eem:hasBusinessStepType ?x2;
         eem:associatedWithEPCList ?z1.
         ?z1 <http://purl.org/co#element> ?au.
         FILTER( contains(str(?x2), "shipping"))
        }
    }
   FILTER (contains(str(?x), "commissioning"))
}
```

### Counterfeit EPC Checking

The basis of our counterfeit detection mechanism mandates that all EPCs that are part of an Aggregation event have been actually commissioned and asserted as part of an Object event. This implies that if the business step is "packing" for an Aggregation event, we further check if the EPCs included in the event have indeed been commissioned as part of an Object event with business step "commissioning".

We experimented with various forms of aggregates and joins in our SPARQL queries to efficiently retrieve and compare the EPCs in the commissioning and aggregation events at the query level itself, however this proved to be highly inefficient and time-intensive. Simple queries for individually retrieving the EPCs and running the counterfeit checks within our implementation gave us a much better performance for counterfeit detection. We reproduce only one of the queries here due to space constraints.

```
SELECT ?epc1  WHERE{
    ?event1IRI a eem:ObjectEvent;
    eem:hasBusinessStepType ?x1;
    eem:associatedWithEPCList ?y1.
    ?y1 <http://purl.org/co#element> ?epc1.
    FILTER( (contains(str(?x1), "commissioning")))}
```

### 5.2 Pedigree Generation Algorithm: Commissioning-Packing-Shipping

In accordance to the scenario presented in Section 2, Algorithm 1 generates the pedigrees. It instantiates the pedigree graph, applies various checks as per the SPARQL queries defined above, retrieves and integrates external datasets, before finally publishing the linked pedigrees. The steps in the algorithm have been illustrated in a self explanatory way within the pseudo code itself for brevity.

# 6  Evaluation

## 6.1  Evaluation Requirements

Our evaluation for the pharmaceutical scenario outlined in Section 2 focuses on two critical timing requirements for pedigree generation in the pharmaceutical supply chain:

- **The time taken to detect counterfeit products in varying volumes of shipments:** This is important as counterfeits have to be detected either before or along with the pedigree generation. We consider the case where counterfeits may be introduced as additional items or as replacement of existing items, when items are being packed into cases. The items have EPCs assigned and tagged to them, although they have not been commissioned at the manufacturing unit.
- **The time taken for pedigree generation:** This time is crucial as pedigree generation for a specific shipment must be initiated as soon as a shipping event for the shipment is recorded. The pedigree must be published imminently when the shipment is dispatched. Given this requirement, we evaluate the time taken for the execution of the various queries in the algorithm for varying number of commissioning, aggregation and shipping events, as well as the overall time taken to generate the pedigrees.

## 6.2  EPCIS Event Volumes

In order to estimate the volume and velocity of events generated in pharmaceutical event streams, we referred to grey literature and interviewed people closely involved in the pharmaceutical sector and EPCIS experts. We referred to a survey [12] that studied the cost benefit analysis of introducing EPCIS event based pedigrees in the pharmaceutical supply chain. As per the survey, the average volume (number) of pallets, cases and items per month being shipped out of a typical manufacturing unit is 290, 5800 and 580,000 respectively. Interviews with experts corroborated the facts, however they also stated that for some large scale units, the number of items shipped could be as high as 100,000 per day.

Assuming an average rate of production as 6 days per week and 10 hours per day, we ran a simulation that replicated the volume and velocity of event generation. We generated the commissioning events based on the number of items ranging from 24,000 to 102,000 per day or approximately 40 to 170 per minute[23]. As the number of items packed per case and the number of cases loaded per pallet could vary across manufacturing units, we generated aggregation and shipping events, considering aggregated items ranging from 100 to 500 (increments of 100) per case and number of cases per pallet ranging from 20 to 100 (increments

---

[23] Since the number of pallets and cases commissioned is significantly lower than that of the items, as a close approximation we assume that commissioning of the items subsumes the commissioning of the cases and pallets and therefore do not consider these events separately.

---

**Algorithm 1.** Pedigree generation: Commissioning-Packing-Shipping

---

// Input is the event graph stream and output is the linked pedigree
**Data:** $I_s$
**Result:** $G_p$
// Set up the pedigree graph
1 Instantiate the pedigree provenance graph, $G_{pp}$
2 Insert triple $(I_p, \text{prov:wasGeneratedAt}, t_p)$ in $G_{pp}$
3 Instantiate the pedigree default graph, $G_{pd}$
4 Insert triple $(I_p, \text{hasStatus}, \text{ped:Initial})$ in $G_{pd}$
5 Insert triple $(I_p, \text{hasSerialNumber}, n_p)$ in $G_{pd}$
6 **while** $I_s$ *has events* **do**

   // extracts the event graphs based on the window length for time
      interval.
7   Execute $Q_t$ on the incoming stream $I_s$ to get the event IRI result set $R_e$
8   **for** $E_g \in R_e$ **do**
9      Execute counterfeit EPC checking queries on $R_e$ to get counterfeit EPC
         result set, $R_c$
10     **if** *($R_c$ is non-empty)* **then**
11        | Send notification for counterfeit EPC
12     **else**
13        Retrieve event graph, eventGraph($E_g$)
14        Transform $E_g$ to N-Triples representation
15        Execute $Q_{bs}$ on $E_g$ using a RDF stream processor
16        Extract event URIs for commissioning, aggregation and shipping
            events in $R_{com}$, $R_{agg}$, $R_{shp}$ respectively
17        **for** $I_a$ *rdf:type* $A_e \in R_{agg}$ **do**
18           | Insert triple $(I_p, \text{eem:hasConsignmentInfo}, I_a)$ in $G_{pd}$
19        **end for**
20        **for** $I_e$ *rdf:type* $O_e \in R_{com}$ **do**
21           Retrieve product master IRI, $I_m$ for EPCs in $I_e$
22           Insert triple $(I_p, \text{eem:hasProductInfo}, I_m)$ in $G_{pd}$
23           Insert triple $(I_p, \text{eem:hasConsignmentInfo}, I_e)$ in $G_{pd}$
24        **end for**
25        **for** $I_s$ *rdf:type* $T_e \in R_{shp}$ **do**
26           | Insert triple $(I_p, \text{eem:hasTransactionInfo}, I_e)$ in $G_{pd}$
27        **end for**
28     **end if**
29   **end for**
30   Merge graphs $G_{pp}$ and $G_{pd}$
31   Publish $G_p$ at IRI $I_p$
32 **end while**

---

of 20). We experimented with tumbling window sizes of 3, 5, 7 and 10 hours respectively. For the window size of 10 hours and rate of 120 and 170 items per minute in the stream, the number of commissioning, aggregation and shipping events are highlighted in Table 1 giving an indication of the overall volume of events we considered. Based on the rate of counterfeits as highlighted in Section 1, we introduce 8% of the total items as counterfeits in order to estimate the time taken for detection. The event dataset dumps used for the various runs of the algorithm as part of our simulation have been made available[24].

**Table 1.** Number of commissioning, aggregation and shipping events for a window size of 10 hours and item commissioning rate of 120 and 170 per minute

| | | | 100-500 per case | 20-100 per pallet |
|---|---|---|---|---|
| Window size (hrs) | Items/min. event stream velocity | Commissioned events | Aggregation events (increments of 100) | Shipping events for each of the aggregates (increments of 20) |
| 10 | 120 | 72000 | 720/360/240/180/144 | 36/18/12/9/7 |
| | | | | 18/9/6/5/4 |
| | | | | 12/6/4/3/3 |
| | | | | 18/9/6/5/4 |
| | | | | 7/4/3/2/2 |
| | 170 | 102000 | 1020/510/340/255/204 | 51/26/17/13/11 |
| | | | | 26/13/9/7/5 |
| | | | | 17/9/7/5/4 |
| | | | | 13/7/5/4/3 |
| | | | | 10/5/4/3/2 |

## 6.3 Pedigree Generation Framework

Figure 4 illustrates the workflow and execution environment of our EPCIS stream processing framework. We have developed a library, LinkedEPCIS[25] for encoding EPCIS events as linked data. RFID tag data, read by readers is converted into a stream of linked EPCIS event named graphs using the library, which is deployed on the edge server or as part of a custom app. EPCIS event streams are accessed by the Linked Pedigree server that deploys various components for facilitating the generation of linked pedigrees from event IRIs.

As our event streams are named graphs, we natively generated the streams in TRIG. However currently none of the stream processing engine support the TRIG format. We therefore implemented an event extractor component that extracts the event graphs from the stream based on predefined window sizes, computed using the rate of event generation identified above.

---

[24] http://fispace.aston.ac.uk/pharma/eventDatasets
[25] https://github.com/nimonika/LinkedEPCIS

As part of our machinery, we incorporate an enhanced version of an existing semantic stream processing engine, INSTANS [9] for continuously executing queries over our event streams. As INSTANS accepts event streams in NTriples, we convert the extracted event stream into the N-Triples serialisation before piping it with INSTANS, where the queries are executed. The results are event graph IRIs, that are passed to the pedigree generator which compiles the pedigrees. The pedigree generator integrates the pedigrees with any external datasets such as location based information, product master data or any other information the trading partner may consider useful. The pedigrees are persistently stored for history based analysis and are also published at IRIs that can be accessed by invoking the REST services published on the Linked Pedigree server.

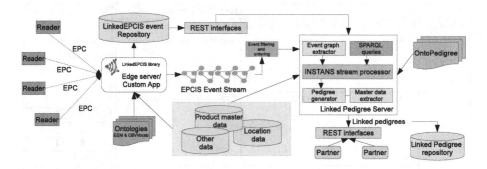

**Fig. 4.** Generating linked pedigrees from EPCIS event streams

## 6.4   Evaluation Results

We carried out an extensive and exhaustive evaluation of the pedigree generation algorithm. For the four window sizes and varying number of commissioning, aggregation and shipping events, we ran a total of 400 iterations of the algorithm. The evaluations were made on Mac OSX 10.9.2, 1.7GHz Intel core i5, 4GB 1333 MHz DDR3. Figures 5 and 6 illustrate some of the key findings of our experiments. We observed that the time taken for the generation of pedigrees was most influenced by and increased with the number of commissioning events. Surprisingly, varying the number of items per case (100-500 with increments of 100) or the number of cases per pallet (20-100 with increments of 20) for the same number of commissioning events had little influence. The time taken for the detection of counterfeits did increase with the number of commissioning events, however the increase was not as significant as that observed with the pedigree generation time. The formulation of the SPARQL queries did have an influence on the time taken to detect counterfeits as noted in Section 1. For high numbers of commissioned items, we consistently ran out of memory when we tried to run a combined query for retrieving the EPCs from the commissioning and aggregation events. However splitting the query and checking for counterfeits within the implementation resolved the problem. Further, as the EEM ontology

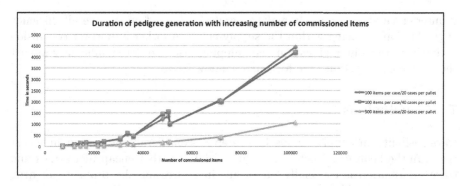

**Fig. 5.** Pedigree generation duration for increasing number of commissioning events

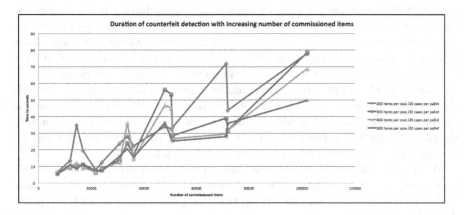

**Fig. 6.** Counterfeit detection duration for increasing number of commissioning events

and the OntoPedigree pattern heavily exploit the PROV-O vocabulary, when a counterfeit was detected, we were able to trace it back to the agent responsible for the generation of the pedigree using the `prov:wasAttributedTo` relationship. This feature of Semantic Web/Linked data technologies for counterfeit detection in pedigree generation, immediately gives us a significant advantage compared to the various commercial efforts reviewed in Section 3. Update queries took comparatively little time as compared to querying, so we do not report those results here.

The results of our experiments provide noteworthy insights into improving the performance of the supply chain and optimising the process of pedigree generation in real time. In Section 2, we set out to establish the trade off between generating a large number of pedigrees, each corresponding to a small number of commissioned items against a small number of pedigrees for large number of commissioned items, aggregated cases and pallets. Based on our observation we can conclude that using smaller window sizes of 3 - 5 hrs for generating pedigrees, yields less number of commissioning events which can not only significantly reduce the running time of the algorithm, but it can also enable quicker detection of counterfeits and consequently make a significant impact on the overall efficiency of tracking and tracing within the supply chain. Another important conclusion is that variations in aggregation and shipping loads do not significantly impact the pedigree generation time for small window sizes.

# 7 Conclusions

Data visibility in supply chains has received considerable attention in recent years. In the healthcare sector, visibility of datasets that encapsulate track and trace information is especially important in addressing the problems of drug counterfeiting. In this paper we have shown how Semantic Web standards, ontologies and linked data can be utilised to represent and process real time streams of supply chain knowledge, thereby significantly contributing to the vision. We have presented an algorithm that illustrates how linked pedigrees can be automatically harnessed from streaming EPCIS event datasets. Our algorithm, besides generating the pedigrees, also checks an important constraint of EPC mismatch, which can play a major role in identifying counterfeit drugs illegally introduced in the supply chain. Provenance, which is a critical aspect of supply chain knowledge is an integral part of our framework. We have performed an exhaustive evaluation of the algorithm using various combinations of commissioning, aggregation and shipping events. Our results provide very useful insights in improving the overall efficiency of the supply chain.

Much work still needs to be done. We are extending our algorithms to automatically assert aggregation and containment relationships using stream reasoning techniques, and persistently update the knowledge base with the newly derived relationships.

**Acknowledgements.** The research described in this paper has been partially supported by the EU FP7 FI PPP projects, SmartAgriFood (http://smartagrifood.eu) and FISpace http://www.fispace.eu/. The authors would like to thank Mikko Rinne from the INSTANS team for the extensive support with their stream processing engine.

# References

1. Alexander Ilic, F.M., Andersen, T.: EPCIS-based Supply Chain Visualization Tool. Auto-ID Labs White Paper WP-BIZAPP-045 (2009)
2. Anicic, D., et al.: EP-SPARQL: A Unified Language for Event Processing and Stream Reasoning. In: Proceedings of the 20th International Conference on World Wide Web, WWW 2011. ACM (2011)
3. Bolles, A., Grawunder, M., Jacobi, J.: Streaming SPARQL - Extending SPARQL to Process Data Streams. In: Bechhofer, S., Hauswirth, M., Hoffmann, J., Koubarakis, M. (eds.) ESWC 2008. LNCS, vol. 5021, pp. 448–462. Springer, Heidelberg (2008)

4. Calbimonte, J.-P., Corcho, O., Gray, A.J.G.: Enabling ontology-based access to streaming data sources. In: Patel-Schneider, P.F., Pan, Y., Hitzler, P., Mika, P., Zhang, L., Pan, J.Z., Horrocks, I., Glimm, B. (eds.) ISWC 2010, Part I. LNCS, vol. 6496, pp. 96–111. Springer, Heidelberg (2010)
5. Carroll, J.J., Bizer, C., Hayes, P., Stickler, P.: Named graphs, provenance and trust. In: Proceedings of the 14th International Conference on World Wide Web, WWW 2005. ACM (2005)
6. Francesco, D., et al.: C-SPARQL: a Continuous Query Language for RDF Data Streams. Int. J. Semantic Computing (2010)
7. Della Valle, E., et al.: It's a Streaming World! Reasoning upon Rapidly Changing Information. IEEE Intelligent Systems (2009)
8. Le-Phuoc, D., Dao-Tran, M., Xavier Parreira, J., Hauswirth, M.: A native and adaptive approach for unified processing of linked streams and linked data. In: Aroyo, L., Welty, C., Alani, H., Taylor, J., Bernstein, A., Kagal, L., Noy, N., Blomqvist, E. (eds.) ISWC 2011, Part I. LNCS, vol. 7031, pp. 370–388. Springer, Heidelberg (2011)
9. Rinne, M., Abdullah, H., Törmä, S., Nuutila, E.: Processing Heterogeneous RDF Events with Standing SPARQL Update Rules. In: Meersman, R., et al. (eds.) OTM 2012, Part II. LNCS, vol. 7566, pp. 797–806. Springer, Heidelberg (2012)
10. Schapranow, M.-P., et al.: A Formal Model for Enabling RFID in Pharmaceutical Supply Chains. In: Hawaii International Conference on System Sciences. IEEE Computer Society (2011)
11. Schuster, E.W., Koh, R.: Auto-ID Labs, Massachusetts Institute of Technology Cambridge, MA
12. Sinha, A.: Systems engineering perspective of e-pedigree system. Master's thesis, Systems Design and Management (SDM). MIT (2009)
13. Solanki, M., Brewster, C.: Consuming Linked data in Supply Chains: Enabling data visibility via Linked Pedigrees. In: Fourth International Workshop on Consuming Linked Data (COLD 2013) at ISWC. CEUR-WS.org proceedings, vol. 1034 (2013)
14. Solanki, M., Brewster, C.: Representing Supply Chain Events on the Web of Data. In: Workshop on Detection, Representation, and Exploitation of Events in the Semantic Web (DeRiVE) at ISWC. CEUR-WS.org proceedings (2013)
15. Teymourian, K., Rohde, M., Paschke, A.: Fusion of background knowledge and streams of events. In: Proceedings of the 6th ACM International Conference on Distributed Event-Based Systems, DEBS 2012. ACM (2012)
16. Wang, F., Liu, S., Liu, P.: Complex RFID event processing. The VLDB Journal (2009)
17. Weidlich, M., Ziekow, H., Mendling, J.: Optimising Complex Event Queries over Business Processes Using Behavioural Profiles. In: Muehlen, M.z., Su, J. (eds.) BPM 2010 Workshops. LNBIP, vol. 66, pp. 743–754. Springer, Heidelberg (2011)

# Scientific Lenses to Support Multiple Views over Linked Chemistry Data

Colin Batchelor[1], Christian Y.A. Brenninkmeijer[2], Christine Chichester[3], Mark Davies[4], Daniela Digles[5], Ian Dunlop[2], Chris T. Evelo[6], Anna Gaulton[4], Carole Goble[2], Alasdair J.G. Gray[7], Paul Groth[8], Lee Harland[9], Karen Karapetyan[1], Antonis Loizou[8], John P. Overington[4], Steve Pettifer[2], Jon Steele[1], Robert Stevens[2], Valery Tkachenko[1], Andra Waagmeester[6], Antony Williams[1], and Egon L. Willighagen[6]

[1] Royal Society of Chemistry, UK
[2] School of Computer Science, University of Manchester, Manchester, UK
[3] Swiss Institute for Bioinformatics, Switzerland
[4] European Molecular Biology Laboratory European Bioinformatics Institute, Hinxton, UK
[5] University of Vienna, Department of Pharmaceutical Chemistry, Vienna, Austria
[6] Maastricht University, Maastricht, The Netherlands
[7] Heriot-Watt University, Edinburgh, UK
[8] VU University of Amsterdam, The Netherlands
[9] Connected Discovery, UK

**Abstract.** When are two entries about a small molecule in different datasets the same? If they have the same drug name, chemical structure, or some other criteria? The choice depends upon the application to which the data will be put. However, existing Linked Data approaches provide a single global view over the data with no way of varying the notion of equivalence to be applied.

In this paper, we present an approach to enable applications to choose the equivalence criteria to apply between datasets. Thus, supporting multiple dynamic views over the Linked Data. For chemical data, we show that multiple sets of links can be automatically generated according to different equivalence criteria and published with semantic descriptions capturing their context and interpretation. This approach has been applied within a large scale public-private data integration platform for drug discovery. To cater for different use cases, the platform allows the application of different *lenses* which vary the equivalence rules to be applied based on the context and interpretation of the links.

## 1 Introduction

Links between datasets are generally defined by the data providers using the `owl:sameAs` predicate [1]. However, Halpin *et al.* [2] have shown that `owl:sameAs` is widely misused to capture different degrees of equivalence, i.e. its practical use is not limited to the case where two resources are truly identical (implying logical equivalence) but instead capture some application scenario where the

P. Mika et al. (Eds.) ISWC 2014, Part I, LNCS 8796, pp. 98–113, 2014.

two distinct data entries can be treated as being *operationally equivalent*. This is because datasets frequently capture alternative views of the world at different levels of granularity. For example, in the case of chemical datasets used for drug discovery the focus can be on the molecular structure (e.g. ChemSpider [3]) or the drug (e.g. DrugBank [4]), which are not necessarily the same thing. This can lead to multiple ways to equate the entries in these datasets, e.g. for some applications the fact that the entries share the same drug name is enough to consider them operationally equivalent whereas for other applications a stricter criteria may be required such as having the same chemical structure or being one of the many variations possible for the compound. This means that the data can be linked in a variety of ways to satisfy different application needs depending upon the perspective of the user for a particular task.

We argue that the application using the Linked Data should decide upon the operational equivalence to apply between entries in different datasets by using a suitable *scientific lens* [5] — a set of rules that modifies the links between datasets according to some notion of operational equivalence. For the chemical example, distinct sets of links should be created for each of the different equivalence interpretations. To enable the lenses approach, the *meaning* of the link between two resources needs to be published together with the mapping. We call this the context of the link.

The work presented in this paper has been conducted as part of the Open PHACTS project [6]; a public-private partnership that has built and deployed a large scale drug discovery information space supporting several applications[1]. The Open PHACTS Discovery Platform [7] provides a domain specific Linked Data API [8] through which drug discovery data can be retrieved. The development of the platform was guided by research questions provided by drug discovery researchers both in academia and industry [9]. A requirement for the platform drawn from these research questions was to provide a mechanism through which different notions of equivalence between data sources could be supported.

This paper presents

- an approach to capturing the meaning of links which is compatible with existing published Linked Data (Section 3) and demonstrates that these can be automatically generated for chemical datasets (Section 4);
- chemical lenses that change the links between entities in different datasets based on the chemical alignments that are deemed to represent equivalent concepts under different assumptions (Section 5);
- an evaluation of the use of the chemistry lenses within the Open PHACTS Discovery Platform (Section 7).

## 2  Multiple Identifiers, But Are They the Same?

Scientific data is messy. It is stored in multiple datasets, each of which has been created with its own focus. For example information about drugs can be

---

[1] http://www.openphactsfoundation.org/apps.html accessed July 2014.

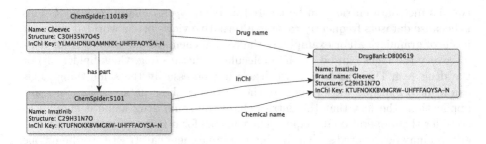

**Fig. 1.** Example showing the different links for relating the ChemSpider entries for imatinib and gleevec to the DrugBank record for gleevec. The equivalence encoded by each link has been provided. It also provides an equivalence relationship between the two ChemSpider records.

retrieved from DrugBank [4] while data about the chemical substances that compose the drug are available from ChEMBL [10] and ChemSpider [3]. The entries in these datasets do not align neatly, or in the ways that the scientists who need an integrated view of the data expect. The datasets use their own identifier schemes and do not always follow best practice for representing their data, e.g. representing the chemical structure with full details of charges and stereochemistry [11,12]. The challenge is identifying when two entries should be considered equivalent to meet specific scientific needs, particularly when these needs change on a per use case basis.

Consider the entries for the drug gleevec–the chemical substance imatinib mesylate– shown in Figure 1. The ChemSpider entry (**ChemSpider:110189**[2]) has the name field set to gleevec and the chemical structure for imatinib mesylate. The entry on the right is from DrugBank (**DrugBank:DB00619**[3]). It has its chemical name set to imatinib, the drug name field shows gleevec and the chemical structure is that of imatinib. Note that imatinib mesylate is a salt-form of imatinib, shown by the **has_part** relationship between the two ChemSpider records. Are the ChemSpider and DrugBank records for gleevec the "same"? For a scientist interested in the biological and medical effects of gleevec they would be, but not for a scientist interested in the physicochemical properties of imatinib mesylate.

Many datasets contain links to other related datasets. For example, UniProt [13] includes links to several related datasets. However, the nature of these links are not captured; in the case of the RDF export of UniProt they are all stated as **rdfs:seeAlso**. This is to avoid making inaccurate claims about the links, but reduces the knowledge conveyed. At the other extreme, the datasets in the Linked Data Cloud widely use the predicate **owl:sameAs** [1]; typically they do not intend the strict semantics of **owl:sameAs** [2].

For users and applications to interpret and reuse links between datasets, they need to understand what notion of equivalence is being expressed by the link.

---

[2] http://www.chemspider.com/110189 accessed July 2014.

[3] http://www.drugbank.ca/drugs/DB00619 accessed July 2014.

They need to distinguish between (i) two entries that capture different aspects of the same real-world concept, e.g. the ChemSpider and ChEMBL entries for imatinib mesylate, (ii) two entries that are highly related, e.g. the ChemSpider and DrugBank records for gleevec, and (iii) an entry that is a relevant reference but not the same real-world concept, e.g. the protein target that gleevec interacts with in the body. It is therefore hard to automatically reuse such links due to the differing natures of the datasets and meaning of the link. As such, existing links need to be used with caution in many application domains, particularly in science. To overcome this, we argue that the context of the links, i.e. the setting in which the operational equivalence between the data entries holds true, should be captured in the metadata of the link.

## 3   Describing Datasets and Their Links

The power of Linked Data comes from the links that relate the entities represented by the data resources. In many integration scenarios, including that of the Open PHACTS Discovery Platform, these links represent an equivalence relationship, i.e. stating that the two linked entities can be considered "the same". For example, consider the co-reference links available through the sameas.org service[4].

To enable the reuse of the links between datasets, the link consumer – a human user or an application – needs to understand what have been linked and in which context. That is, the consumer needs to know which datasets, and in particular which version of a dataset, has been linked, and what were the reasons for claiming the mapping relationship, e.g. the entities can be considered an exact match as they share the same chemical structure. (The notion of exact match is defined in SKOS [14].)

We use the approach of a VoID linkset to capture the context of the links [15]. A VoID linkset contains a collection of link triples that relate the entries in a pair of datasets through a single mapping relationship. The linked datasets are themselves described using VoID. For the purposes of the Open PHACTS Discovery Platform, we have defined a checklist of properties that must be provided, e.g. the license and version number, and those that are optional to provide, e.g. the location of a SPARQL endpoint containing the data [16].

As shown by the example in Figure 1, there can be many reasons to equate entries across datasets. The VoID linkset metadata captures details of the datasets linked, i.e. the context, and the link relationship. However, the link predicate tends to be a generic mapping relationship such as `owl:sameAs` or one from SKOS which does not convey the *reason why* the entries are equivalent, i.e. the *justification* for the equivalence relationship.

One approach to capture the equivalence relationship conveyed by a link between two data entries is to define a domain specific predicate. For example, one could define a mapping predicate that states that two linked chemical entries are considered operationally equivalent because they have the same drug

---

[4] `http://sameas.org/` accessed July 2014.

name. This new mapping predicate could be declared as a sub-property of the skos:exactMatch predicate. This would allow standard inferencing rules to be applied. However there is a major social barrier to such an approach – gaining consensus on the required linking predicates. Additionally, there is the burden of updating the existing links in the datasets to use these new link predicates; a human intensive task. Such an approach is unlikely to gain traction.

An alternative is to continue using existing link predicates such as owl:sameAs and those in SKOS, and annotate the linkset descriptions with additional contextual data that captures the equivalence criteria used to generate the links. This enables the use of the existing links unchanged. Thus, lowering the barrier to uptake as the annotations can be retrofitted to the existing links.

We term this additional metadata the *justification* for the linkset; the notion captured is the scientific interpretation of the operational equivalence applied by the linkset. For example, the linkset relating ChemSpider and DrugBank because they have the same InChI representation of the chemical[5] would express the justification in the linkset VoID header with the triples

```
:Chemspider-Drugbank_Linkset void:linkPredicate skos:exactMatch ;
            bdb:linksetJustification cheminf:CHEMINF_000059 .
:cheminf:CHEMINF_000059 rdfs:label "InChIKey" .
```

where :Chemspider-Drugbank_Linkset is the resource that describes the linkset, the link predicate is declared to be skos:exactMatch using the VoID predicate, and the justification is specified using the BridgeDb vocabulary (namespace bdb[6]) with the value for InChI Key taken from the Chemical Information Ontology (namespace cheminf[7]). The set of supported justifications within the Open PHACTS Discovery Platform can be found in [16]; the subset relating to chemistry data are included in Tables 1 and 2. A key advantage of this approach is that it extends rather than changes the existing data, i.e. the metadata can be added later on with minimal effort.

# 4   Linked Chemistry Data

There are a large number of datasets (openly) available that contain information about chemicals. However, differences in scientific or technical approaches to molecular structure representation mean that data sources will not always be in agreement in the chemical structure for a given substance. Various efforts are ongoing to link entries for the same chemical between databases, for example, to link metabolites [18,19].

---

[5] InChI is a standardised string representation for chemical compounds, the hash value of which is called the InChI Key [17].

[6] http://vocabularies.bridgedb.org/ops to appear soon.

[7] http://semanticscience.org/resource/ accessed May 2014.

**Table 1.** Predicates used to capture the justification of chemical linksets and the operational equivalence that is interpreted. `sio`: Semantic Science Integrated Ontology, `cheminf`: Chemical Information Ontology, and `chebi`: Chemical Entities of Biological Interest Ontology.

| Term | Justification |
|------|---------------|
| Chemical entity `sio:SIO_010004` | The concepts linked represent the same chemical entity. |
| InChI Key `cheminf:CHEMINF_000059` | The concepts linked have the same InChI Key. |
| Has part `chebi:has_part` | Used to indicate the relationship between part and whole. |
| Is tautomer of `chebi:is_tautomer_of` | Used to denote that the related chemical entities are tautomers. |

## 4.1   Chemistry Registration Service

It is common for compounds in separate datasets to be represented differently and this can lead to various challenges when comparing and interlinking chemical data. To ensure data quality for the representation of chemical compounds, the Open PHACTS Discovery Platform provides a Chemical Registration Service [20], which reads a standard chemical structure information file (SD File) [21] and performs validation and standardization of the representations of the compound. The validation step checks the chemical representation for chemistry issues such as hypervalency, charge imbalance, absence of stereochemistry, etc. The standardization step uses a series of rules, based on those of the US Food and Drug Administration's Substance Registration System [22], to standardize the chemical representations.

The Chemical Registration Service identifies the *chemical counterparts* of each molecule—these are representations of the substance stripped of their stereo bonds, salts and charge. These counterparts provide a resource for relating representations across datasets. Previously, ChEBI [23] had the richest set of relationships between molecular structures, including parthood relations, relations between enantiomers (opposite stereo forms) and relations between tautomers (rapidly interconverting forms of a molecule such as the ring and chain forms of glucose) [24], and of course the subclass relation relating a more-completely specified structure to a less-completely specified structure (in terms of, for example, stereochemistry or isotopic composition). However, ChEBI does not distinguish between different subclass relations, indicate which of the forms of a tautomer are in the majority under physiological conditions, or indeed relate structures to structures that have been normalized according to the Open PHACTS rules. Thus we have for the moment, after discussion with ChEBI about adding more relationships, extended CHEMINF with the concepts and relationships given in Table 2. The ChEBI team will consider them for future inclusion in their

**Table 2.** Additional predicates for representing chemical equivalences. The `cheminf` namespace refers to `http://semanticscience.org/resource/`.

| Term | Description |
|---|---|
| has uncharged counterpart `cheminf:CHEMINF_000460` | Connects a molecule to molecule with identical heavy-atom connectivity which is neutral. It is not a subclass relation. |
| has component with uncharged counterpart `cheminf:CHEMINF_000480` | Connects a molecular substance, say a mixture containing ions, with a neutral form of one of the ions. |
| has stereoundefined parent `cheminf:CHEMINF_000456` | Subclass relation between a class that has stereochemistry defined and an otherwise identical class that does not. |
| has isotopically unspecified parent `cheminf:CHEMINF_000459` | Subclass relation between a class that has isotopes specified, for example D2O or 14C-urea, and an otherwise identical class that does not, for example water or urea. |
| has major tautomer at pH 7.4 `cheminf:CHEMINF_000486` | $A$ exists in an equilibrium with $B$ at pH 7.4 and physiological temperature and $B$ is the dominant isomer. |
| has OPS normalized counterpart `cheminf:CHEMINF_000458` | This connects a molecule to its normalized counterpart according to the OPS specification. |

ontology [25]. These predicates can be used in addition to those in Table 1 as the justification property of the linkset descriptions to capture the equivalence condition applied. For example, the relationship between the two ChemSpider records in Figure 1 would use the justification `chebi:has_part`.

## 4.2   Generating Linked Chemistry Data

From the input SD file the Chemical Registration Service generates an RDF representation of the data, with each distinct chemical structure having its own Open PHACTS identifier (URI). Various properties are computed including its InChI representation [26] and properties that can be derived from the canonical structure, e.g. SMILES strings and various physicochemical properties such as molecular weight. Based on the InChI representation, the Chemical Registration Service is able to collapse and aggregate the source dataset representations, and thus generate linksets from the Chemical Registration Service data to each of these datasets, e.g. ChEBI, ChEMBL and DrugBank. Note that mol V2000 is used for the internal representation for chemicals [27].

The generation of linksets has been implemented as part of the data processing pipeline of the Chemical Registration Service. Each dataset and linkset has a metadata description conforming to the specification in [16]. The metadata

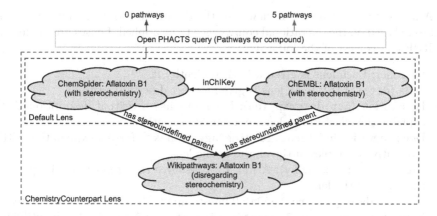

**Fig. 2.** A graphical depiction of the Aflatoxin B1 example. The blue dashed box encompasses the linksets activated under the Default lens while the red dashed box encompasses the additional linksets activated under the ChemistryCounterpart lens. The top of the figure states the number of pathways discovered under each lens when querying for Aflatoxin B1 with details of its stereochemistry.

description captures the *context* of the linkset, i.e. which specific version of a dataset has been loaded into the Chemical Registration Service on which date, as well as the *justification* for the links, i.e. the equivalence criterion used to generate the linkset.

## 5   Chemistry Lenses

Users of data integration systems such as the Open PHACTS Discovery Platform expect answers to their queries despite discrepancies in the underlying data that make aligning the data difficult. For example, consider the Wikipathways [28] entry WP699[8] representing the cellular pathway for the human metabolism of aflatoxin B1. When mappings are based on entries sharing the same InChI, the pathway is not returned when searching for pathways containing the compound aflatoxin B1 as represented by the ChemSpider entry `ChemSpider:162470`[9], represented by the blue box in Figure 2. This is due to one, or more, of the underlying data sources not containing details of the stereochemistry – it is common for datasets to not include details of the stereochemistry as it is simply unknown in many cases. However, the users expect that the pathway would be returned for the call since they loosen their notion of equivalence to include stereoisomers, corresponding to the red box in Figure 2. We propose the use of lenses to enable such functionality, i.e. to vary the equivalence criteria applied for a given query by applying a different lens.

---

[8] http://www.wikipathways.org/instance/WP699 accessed May 2014.
[9] http://www.chemspider.com/162470 accessed July 2014.

A *lens* defines a conceptual view over the data that varies the links between datasets based on the operational equivalence to be applied. Lenses are modelled in RDF and consist of the following:

- Identifier: Each lens is given a URI to identify it.
- Title (`dct:title`): Each lens is given a short descriptive title.
- Description (`dct:description`): Each lens has a textual description that explains the effect of the lens to a domain scientist.
- Documentation link (`dcat:landingPage`): A link to further explanation with illustrative examples of the effects of the lens.
- Creator (`pav:createdBy`): A link to a resource that represents the person that created the lens.
- Creation date (`pav:createdOn`): Timestamp of when the lens was created.
- Equivalence rules (`bdb:linksetJustification`): A set of URIs identifying the justifications that hold under the lens.

At present, we capture minimal provenance information (creator and creation date), using properties from the PAV ontology [29]. We have found it necessary to provide detailed documentation of the effects of each of the lenses deployed on the Open PHACTS Discovery Platform. This documentation demonstrates the effects of the lens using examples to show the changes in the results returned.

Within the Open PHACTS consortium, we are testing two lenses. The first encapsulates a set of default expected behaviours. This lens equates chemicals that have the same InChI representation or where the datasets equate their identifiers. This lens provides the primary linking between chemical compounds and matches the behaviour of existing integration strategies and in particular that of the Open PHACTS Discovery Platform prior to the introduction of lenses.

The second lens, called the ChemistryCounterpart lens exploits the full set of relationships generated by the Chemical Registration Service, i.e. the justifications captured in Tables 1 and 2. It is very permissive in its notion of equivalence, relating all entries that are variations of charge, isotopes, stereochemistry, salt forms, tautomers, and compounds in a mixture.

Additional lenses that only activate one of these variations, e.g. a stereochemistry lens, could easily be added from a technical perspective – the infrastructure and data exist to provide the lens. However, considerable effort is required to explain the behaviour of a given lens to the scientific users of the system.

For the cellular pathway example, the users of the Open PHACTS API benefit from the use of lenses. Under the default lens, no pathways are returned due to the datasets containing different stereoisomers. Using the ChemistryCounterpart lens, five pathways are returned including the Wikipathways one.

## 6   Identity Mapping with Lenses

The lenses functionality is provided within the Open PHACTS Discovery Platform by the Identity Mapping Service (IMS). The IMS provides a lookup service to return "equivalent" URIs for a given URI. The notion of equivalence can be

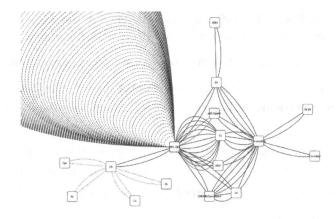

**Fig. 3.** Visualisation showing the interlinking of the 16 chemistry datasets. Blue edges depict InChI equivalences, red edges depict the same chemical entity equivalences, and grey depict the ChEBI and CHEMINF equivalences from Tables 1 and 2. Solid lines are `skos:exactMatch` links, dashed lines are `skos:closeMatch` links and dotted lines are `skos:relatedMatch` links.

varied by supplying the URI for the lens to be applied. The IMS implementation is an extended version of the BridgeDb framework that maps database identifiers [30]. The IMS implementation supports cross-references over Linked Data sources, i.e. supporting the use of URIs to represent entries in datasets and loading mapping data from VoID linksets. The source code is available from `https://github.com/openphacts/IdentityMappingService` and the service is accessible through the Open PHACTS API, `https://dev.openphacts.org/`.

## 6.1   Interconnected Data

The linked chemistry data consists of 130 linksets containing 13,970,556 links that connect the Chemical Registration Service to each of its source datasets, generating a hub of data shown in Figure 3. To answer the queries behind the Open PHACTS API methods we require links directly between the various source datasets[10]. These can be computed by the IMS using custom inference chains. However, this process needs to consider the justifications associated with the linksets.

Based on the justification of linksets, we can compute inferred linksets. For example, we can generate a linkset between datasets $A$ and $C$ through some intermediary dataset $B$ if there is a linkset between $A$ and $B$ and one between $B$ and $C$ such that both linksets have the same justification. Definition 1 formally gives the rule for computing inferred linksets based on their justification. We denote a linkset between datasets $A$ and $B$ with the link predicate $p$ and justification $j$ as $A \xrightarrow[p]{j} B$. Note that we do not require that the linksets have

---

[10] In order that these queries run efficiently, the links are materialised in the IMS.

the same link predicate when inferring linksets. The resulting inferred linkset is given the weaker of the two link predicates with a hierarchy of

$$\texttt{owl:sameAs} \preceq \texttt{skos:exactMatch} \preceq \texttt{skos:closeMatch} \preceq \texttt{rdfs:seeAlso}.$$

Thus, if $p$ was the link predicate `owl:sameAs` and $r$ the link predicate `rdfs:seeAlso`, the computed linkset $A \xrightarrow[r]{j} C$ would have the link predicate `rdfs:seeAlso`.

**Definition 1 (Inferring linksets based on justifications).** *Given datasets $A$, $B$, and $C$, linksets $A \xrightarrow[p]{j} B$ and $B \xrightarrow[r]{j} C$ both with the justification $j$ and link predicates $p$ and $r$ respectively then we can generate the linkset*

- $A \xrightarrow[r]{j} C$ *if $p \preceq r$;*
- $A \xrightarrow[p]{j} C$ *if $r \prec p$.*

By iteratively applying the rule given in Definition 1 it is possible to compute chains of linksets that use the same justification. This can be seen as materialising the network of 'follow-your-nose' links in the data for a given equivalence type. It is possible to enter an infinite cycle while computing these links; thus the IMS implementation prevents a dataset being revisited in a chain. As part of the provenance of the computed linkset, the linksets that are used to compute it are tracked and reported in the resulting VoID description of the linkset.

By inferring the network of links over the Open PHACTS datasets, the deployed IMS contains 51,168,586 links from 40,802 linksets. Note that the link materialisation is independent of the lenses applied. The materialisation mechanism computes every possible inferred linkset based on the justification and link predicate.

## 6.2   Lens Implementation

The IMS responds to a request for equivalent URIs by performing a lookup in its internal database. Since the network of interlinks is pre-computed, the implementation of lenses is straightforward. The API call is extended with a new parameter to pass in the lens URI. This URI is used to retrieve the justifications that are enabled by the lens. The equivalent URI lookup query has additional conditions added which ensure that only links with enabled justifications are returned.

A lookup for data through the Open PHACTS Discovery Platform must provide the URI of the entity of interest. However, the user does not need to know the equivalent URIs in all of the datasets used by the Discovery Platform. This is handled by the IMS which is called by the workflow that fulfils the API call. We have previously shown that this adds a small overhead to the execution time of a method call, but that a user will not perceive this [31]. We believe the advantage of enabling the user to select their operational equivalence conditions outweighs this small performance hit.

# 7    Evaluation

The effects of the chemistry lenses on the answers returned by the Open PHACTS
Discovery Platform were analysed by two pharmacology researchers. The researchers used a set of 22 chemicals which were chosen for the different chemical
features they exhibit[11], viz. stereochemistry (15), tautomers (10), isotopes (3),
charge (2), salts (3). One compound acted as a control as it did not contain any
of the above features. Note that a single chemical may exhibit multiple features
unless it is in the control group. This resulted in an extensive number of relationships that were systematically compared to verify their correctness by the
pharmacology researchers. (A very labourious task.)

For each chemical, identified using its ChemSpider URI[12], the evaluator executed the `mapUri` API call[13], which returns the set of equivalent URIs for the
given seed value under the supplied lens. The calls were made first using the Default lens, which matches the behaviour of earlier releases of the Open PHACTS
Discovery Platform, and then with the ChemistryCounterpart lens.

The results of each call were analysed. First the images of the chemicals returned by the call were visually inspected against the associated image of the
seed chemical. This visual inspection was used to determine that the returned
substances were related to the seed substance, e.g. as a charge neutral parent
chemical. Next, the result set was inspected to ensure that each of the relevant
parent chemicals were returned when the ChemistryCounterpart lens was invoked, i.e. if a chemical exhibits stereochemistry and is a salt we would expect
that the stereo parent as well as the salt base and the base chemical would be
returned. The lenses were found to work as expected.

The linkset data and the lens enabled IMS have been deployed in the Open
PHACTS Discovery Platform. The Linked Data API of the platform has been
extended to enable the lens parameter to be passed in; if no URI is supplied then
the Default lens is applied. The Open PHACTS Discovery Platform receives over
2 million hits a month providing further assurance of the correctness of the lenses
and the underlying linksets.

# 8    Related Work

Data integration has been widely studied both in the relational database and
the semantic web communities [32]. Integration systems expose a single view
of the world to users and require the work of a domain expert to interrelate
the datasets to be integrated. Dataspaces [33] aim to lower the up-front cost
by starting with rough relationships that can be refined automatically through

---

[11] Values in brackets indicates the number of chemicals that exhibit that property.

[12] ChemSpider chemicals are indexed using the InChI code set to the standard settings
with the exception of the reconnected layer, so distinguish the various forms that a
substance can take.

[13] https://beta.openphacts.org/1.3/mapUri accessed July 2014. To create a free
API access key and read documentation see https://dev.openphacts.org/

user feedback. The Open PHACTS Discovery Platform takes a similar approach; integration is achieved through queries and the relationships between datasets are captured in our global-as-view queries. However, we enable multiple views over the data by varying the active equivalence relationships for the instance URIs through the use of lenses.

Lenses rely on the availability of multiple links between datasets which provide different equivalence relationships. Several tools have been developed for generating links between datasets [34]. Since 2009 there has been an instance matching track[14] in the annual ontology matching competition[15] to compare such tools. The most recent results are available from [35]. These are general purpose link generators that look for similarities between resources in two datasets. In general, they generate one set of links based on the matching algorithms applied and a threshold value for closeness. The Chemical Registration Service exploits domain knowledge, viz. properties of the chemicals, to generate multiple linksets, each based on different equivalence criteria. Other efforts are ongoing to link entries for the same chemical between databases, for example, to link metabolites [18,19,36], but these are focused on linking database entries and do not consider the need to support multiple linkages for different use cases. We are investigating similar approaches for proteins and other entities of interest.

There are two approaches in the literature for managing the multiple URI problem. The first approach recognises that the same logical resource can be given multiple URIs, e.g. when a dataset is served by multiple mirrors, or that some entities may be unambiguously identified. Services such as the Identifiers.org [37] which addresses the multiple data mirrors problem and the Entity Name System [38] which addresses the disambiguation problem provide a URI for the concept that can be used unambiguously. However, this is not the problem addressed by the lenses proposed in this paper. The second approach are co-reference services that provide links between entities in different datasets. This is the problem addressed by the lenses. Co-reference services such as sameas.org[16] [39] provide a service by which equivalent URIs can be obtained. sameas.org harvests `owl:sameAs` links from publicly available datasets on a wide range of topics. These existing co-reference services do not consider under what conditions the equivalence holds. The data loaded into the IMS is curated and comes with a justification for the equivalence. We believe that these third party co-reference services are an underutilized but key part of developing practical semantic web applications.

## 9   Conclusions

In this paper, we have shown the importance of understanding the nature of how links between datasets are created in order to effectively answer scientific

---

[14] http://www.instancematching.org/oaei/imei2013/results.html accessed May 2014.

[15] http://oaei.ontologymatching.org/ accessed May 2014.

[16] http://www.sameas.org accessed May 2014.

questions. We describe a process for generating such domain specific links and techniques for applying them. Our approach is deployed on a live system that has been used as the basis for a variety of drug discovery applications[17]. Moreover, expert users have verified the validity of the results of our system. Lenses have practical benefits in allowing users to vary how the data is exposed under integration.

While the technical implementation of lenses is relatively straightforward and indeed the overall concept of a lens is easy to grasp, the effects of applying a lens requires considerable training and educating of the users. To this end, we are endeavouring to supply suitable user-oriented documentation for each lens deployed in the Open PHACTS Discovery Platform.

Given the broad capabilities of the scientific lenses approach, we are still discussing which set of lenses will be included in future versions of the platform. The division of the chemical features between the Default lens and other lenses remains to be decided. There is some interest in including the tautomers in the default and dividing the other chemical features (stereochemistry, salt forms, *etc.*) into their own specific lenses rather than one lens which contains all features. This may simplify the results returned, but increases the choice presented to applications and users.

Finally, we are looking at expanding our lenses approach to the other types of datasets needed for drug discovery, viz. proteins, splice variants, cross-species relationships. We are also looking at how lenses can be used to vary the quality associated with the links, e.g. curated versus non-curated links.

**Acknowledgements.** The research has received support from the Innovative Medicines Initiative Joint Undertaking under grant agreement number 115191, resources of which are composed of financial contribution from the European Union's Seventh Framework Programme (FP7/2007- 2013) and EFPIA companies in kind contribution.

# References

1. Heath, T., Bizer, C.: Linked Data: Evolving the Web into a Global Data Space. Morgan & Claypool (2011)
2. Halpin, H., Hayes, P.J., McCusker, J.P., McGuinness, D.L., Thompson, H.S.: When owl:sameAs Isn't the Same: An Analysis of Identity in Linked Data. In: Patel-Schneider, P.F., Pan, Y., Hitzler, P., Mika, P., Zhang, L., Pan, J.Z., Horrocks, I., Glimm, B. (eds.) ISWC 2010, Part I. LNCS, vol. 6496, pp. 305–320. Springer, Heidelberg (2010)
3. Pence, H.E., Williams, A.J.: ChemSpider: an online chemical information resource. Journal of Chemical Education 87(11), 10–11 (2010)
4. Knox, C., Law, V., Jewison, T., Liu, P., Ly, S., Frolkis, A., Pon, A., Banco, K., Mak, C., Neveu, V., Djoumbou, Y., Eisner, R., Guo, A.C., Wishart, D.S.: Drug-Bank 3.0: a comprehensive resource for 'omics' research on drugs. Nucleic Acids Research 39(Database issue), D1035–D1041 (2011)

---

[17] http://www.openphactsfoundation.org/apps.html accessed July 2014.

5. Brenninkmeijer, C.Y.A., Evelo, C., Goble, C., Gray, A.J.G., Groth, P., Pettifer, S., Stevens, R., Williams, A.J., Willighagen, E.L.: Scientific Lenses over Linked Data: An approach to support task specific views of the data. A vision. In: Proc. Linked Science, Boston, MA, USA. CEUR-WS.org (2012)
6. Williams, A.J., Harland, L., Groth, P., Pettifer, S., Chichester, C., Willighagen, E.L., Evelo, C.T., Blomberg, N., Ecker, G., Goble, C., Mons, B.: Open PHACTS: semantic interoperability for drug discovery. Drug Discovery Today 17(21-22), 1188–1198 (2012)
7. Gray, A.J.G., Groth, P., Loizou, A., Askjaer, S., Brenninkmeijer, C.Y.A., Burger, K., Chichester, C., Evelo, C.T., Goble, C.A., Harland, L., Pettifer, S., Thompson, M., Waagmeester, A., Williams, A.J.: Applying linked data approaches to pharmacology: Architectural decisions and implementation. Semantic Web 5(2), 101–113 (2014)
8. Groth, P., Loizou, A., Gray, A.J.G., Goble, C., Harland, L., Pettifer, S.: API-centric Linked Data Integration: The Open PHACTS Discovery Platform Case Study. Journal of Web Semantics (2014)
9. Azzaoui, K., Jacoby, E., Senger, S., Rodríguez, E.C., Loza, M., Zdrazil, B., Pinto, M., Williams, A.J., de la Torre, V., Mestres, J., Pastor, M., Taboureau, O., Rarey, M., Chichester, C., Pettifer, S., Blomberg, N., Harland, L., Williams-Jones, B., Ecker, G.F.: Scientific competency questions as the basis for semantically enriched open pharmacological space development. Drug Discovery Today 18(17-18), 843–852 (2013)
10. Bento, A.P., Gaulton, A., Hersey, A., Bellis, L.J., Chambers, J., Davies, M., Krüger, F.A., Light, Y., Mak, L., McGlinchey, S., Nowotka, M., Papadatos, G., Santos, R., Overington, J.P.: The ChEMBL bioactivity database: an update. Nucleic Acids Research 42(Database issue), D1083–D1090 (2014)
11. Williams, A.J., Ekins, S.: A quality alert and call for improved curation of public chemistry databases. Drug Discovery Today 16(17-18), 747–750 (2011)
12. Williams, A.J., Ekins, S., Tkachenko, V.: Towards a gold standard: regarding quality in public domain chemistry databases and approaches to improving the situation. Drug Discovery Today 17(13-14), 685–701 (2012)
13. The UniProt Consortium: Update on activities at the Universal Protein Resource (UniProt) in 2013. Nucleic Acids Research 41(Database issue), D43–D47 (2013)
14. Miles, A., Bechhofer, S.: SKOS Simple Knowledge Organization System Reference. Recommendation, W3C (2009), http://www.w3.org/TR/skos-reference
15. Alexander, K., Cyganiak, R., Hausenblas, M., Zhao, J.: Describing Linked Datasets with the VoID Vocabulary. Note, W3C (2011)
16. Gray, A.J.G.: Dataset descriptions for the Open Pharmacological Space. Working draft, Open PHACTS (2013)
17. Heller, S., McNaught, A., Stein, S., Tchekhovskoi, D., Pletnev, I.: InChI-the world-wide chemical structure identifier standard. J. of Cheminformatics 5(1), 1–9 (2013)
18. Wohlgemuth, G., Haldiya, P.K., Willighagen, E., Kind, T., Fiehn, O.: The chemical translation service a web-based tool to improve standardization of metabolomic reports. Bioinformatics 26(20), 2647 (2010)
19. Haraldsdóttir, H.S., Thiele, I., Fleming, R.M.: Comparative evaluation of open source software for mapping between metabolite identifiers in metabolic network reconstructions: application to recon 2. Journal of Cheminformatics 6(1), 2 (2014)
20. Karapetyan, K., Tkachenko, V., Batchelor, C., Sharpe, D., Williams, A.J.: RSC chemical validation and standardization platform: A potential path to quality-conscious databases. In: 245th American Chemical Society National Meeting and Exposition, New Orleans, LA, USA (2013)

21. Dalby, A., Nourse, J.G., Hounshell, W.D., Gushurst, A.K.I., Grier, D.L., Leland, B.A., Laufer, J.: Description of several chemical structure file formats used by computer programs developed at molecular design limited. Journal of Chemical Information and Modeling 32(3), 244 (1992)
22. US Food and Drug Administration: Food and Drug Administration Substance Registration System Standard Operating Procedure. 5c edn. (2007), http://www.fda.gov/downloads/ForIndustry/DataStandards/SubstanceRegistrationSystem-UniqueIngredientIdentifierUNII/ucm127743.pdf
23. Degtyarenko, K., de Matos, P., Ennis, M., Hastings, J., Zbinden, M., McNaught, A., Alcántara, R., Darsow, M., Guedj, M., Ashburner, M.: ChEBI: a database and ontology for chemical entities of biological interest. Nucleic Acids Research 36, D344–D350 (2008)
24. Sayle, R.A.: So you think you understand tautomerism? Journal of Computer-Aided Molecular Design 24, 485–496 (2010)
25. Hastings, J.: Personal communication
26. McNaught, A.: The IUPAC international chemical identifier: InChI. Chemistry International 28(6) (2006)
27. Dalby, A., Nourse, J.G., Hounshell, W.D., Gushurst, A.K.I., Grier, D.L., Leland, B.A., Laufer, J.: Description of several chemical structure file formats used by computer programs developed at molecular design limited. Journal of Chemical Information and Computer Sciences 32(3), 244–255 (1992)
28. Pico, A.R., Kelder, T., van Iersel, M.P., Hanspers, K., Conklin, B.R., Evelo, C.: WikiPathways: pathway editing for the people. PLoS Biol. 6(7), e184 (2008)
29. Ciccarese, P., Soiland-Reyes, S., Belhajjame, K., Gray, A.J.G., Goble, C., Clark, T.: PAV ontology: Provenance, Authoring and Versioning. Journal of Biomedical Semantics 4(37) (2013)
30. van Iersel, M.P., Pico, A.R., Kelder, T., Gao, J., Ho, I., Hanspers, K., Conklin, B.R., Evelo, C.T.: The BridgeDb framework: standardized access to gene, protein and metabolite identifier mapping services. BMC Bioinformatics 11(5) (2010)
31. Brenninkmeijer, C.Y.A., Goble, C., Gray, A.J.G., Groth, P., Loizou, A., Pettifer, S.: Including Co-referent URIs in a SPARQL Query. In: 4th International Workshop on Consuming Linked Data, Sydney, Australia (2013)
32. Doan, A., Halevy, A., Ives, Z.: Principles of Data Integration. Elsevier (2012)
33. Halevy, A.Y., Franklin, M.J., Maier, D.: Principles of dataspace systems. In: PODS 2006, Chicago (IL, USA), pp. 1–9. ACM (2006)
34. Shvaiko, P., Euzenat, J.: Ontology Matching: State of the Art and Future Challenges. IEEE Trans. Knowl. Data Eng. 25(1), 158–176 (2013)
35. Cuenca Grau, B., Dragisic, Z., Eckert, K., Euzenat, J., Ferrara, A., Granada, R., Ivanova, V., Jiménez-Ruiz, E., Kempf, A.O., Lambrix, P., Nikolov, A., Paulheim, H., Ritze, D., Scharffe, F., Shvaiko, P., Trojahn, C., Zamazal, O.: Results of the Ontology Alignment Evaluation Initiative 2013. In: Ontology Matching (2013)
36. Galgonek, J., Vondrasek, J.: On InChI and evaluating the quality of cross-reference links. Journal of Cheminformatics 6(1), 15+ (2014)
37. Juty, N., Le Novère, N., Laibe, C.: Identifiers.org and MIRIAM Registry: community resources to provide persistent identification. Nucleic Acids Research 40(Database issue), D580–D586 (2012)
38. Bouquet, P., Stoermer, H., Bazzanella, B.: An Entity Name System (ENS) for the Semantic Web. In: Bechhofer, S., Hauswirth, M., Hoffmann, J., Koubarakis, M. (eds.) ESWC 2008. LNCS, vol. 5021, pp. 258–272. Springer, Heidelberg (2008)
39. Glaser, H., Jaffri, A., Millard, I.: Managing Co-reference on the Semantic Web. In: WWW 2009 Work. Linked Data Web, Madrid, Spain (2009)

# Linked Biomedical Dataspace: Lessons Learned Integrating Data for Drug Discovery

Ali Hasnain[1], Maulik R. Kamdar[1], Panagiotis Hasapis[2], Dimitris Zeginis[3,4],
Claude N. Warren Jr.[5], Helena F. Deus[6], Dimitrios Ntalaperas[2],
Konstantinos Tarabanis[3,4], Muntazir Mehdi[1], and Stefan Decker[1]

[1] Insight Center for Data Analytics, National University of Ireland, Galway
{ali.hasnain,maulik.kamdar,muntazir.mehdi,
stefan.decker}@insight-centre.org
[2] UBITECH Research, 429 Messogion Avenue, Athens, Greece
{phasapis,dntalaperas}@ubitech.eu
[3] Centre for Research and Technology Hellas, Thessaloniki, Greece
[4] Information Systems Lab, University of Macedonia, Thessaloniki, Greece
{zeginis,kat}@uom.gr
[5] Xenei.com
claude@xenei.com
[6] Foundation Medicine Inc. Cambridge, MA
hdeus@foundationmedicine.com

**Abstract.** The increase in the volume and heterogeneity of biomedical data sources has motivated researchers to embrace Linked Data (LD) technologies to solve the ensuing integration challenges and enhance information discovery. As an integral part of the EU GRANATUM project, a Linked Biomedical Dataspace (LBDS) was developed to semantically interlink data from multiple sources and augment the design of *in silico* experiments for cancer chemoprevention drug discovery. The different components of the LBDS facilitate both the bioinformaticians and the biomedical researchers to publish, link, query and visually explore the heterogeneous datasets. We have extensively evaluated the usability of the entire platform. In this paper, we showcase three different workflows depicting real-world scenarios on the use of LBDS by the domain users to intuitively retrieve meaningful information from the integrated sources. We report the important lessons that we learned through the challenges encountered and our accumulated experience during the collaborative processes which would make it easier for LD practitioners to create such dataspaces in other domains. We also provide a concise set of generic recommendations to develop LD platforms useful for drug discovery.

**Keywords:** Linked Data, Drug Discovery, SPARQL Federation, Visualization, Biomedical Research.

## 1 Introduction

Drug discovery entails the effective integration of data and knowledge from multiple disparate sources, the intuitive retrieval of vital information and the active involvement of domain scientists at all stages [33]. Biomedical data, encompassing a diverse range of spatial (gene $\Rightarrow$ organism) and temporal (cell division $\Rightarrow$ human

P. Mika et al. (Eds.) ISWC 2014, Part I, LNCS 8796, pp. 114–130, 2014.

lifespan) scales, is organized in separate datasets, each originally published to address a specific research problem. As a result, there are a large number of voluminous datasets available with varying representations, models, formats and semantics. Consequently, retrieving meaningful information for drug discovery-related queries, like *'List of molecules, with 5 Hydrogen bond donors, Molecular Weight <400 and effective against DNA Methyltransferase targets, referenced in any publications'*, becomes time-consuming and tedious as the scientist has to manually search and assemble results from several portals.

The advent of Linked Data (LD) technologies to solve the integrative challenges has opened exciting new avenues for scientific research in drug discovery [13]. These technologies not only facilitate the integration of various voluminous and heterogeneous data sources (i.e. experimental data, libraries, databases) but also provide an aggregated view of the biomedical data in a machine-readable and semantically-enriched way that enables re-use. However, domain users need to traverse a steep technical learning curve to use these technologies for addressing their research problems. Hence, the adoption of LD technologies by the actual beneficiaries of the integrated data sources is yet to be achieved.

An approach that facilitates the adoption of LD by the domain users was proposed by us, under the European FP7-funded GRANATUM project[1]. The project was conceived to semantically interlink knowledge and data for the design and execution of *in silico* experiments in the domain of cancer chemoprevention drug discovery. A Linked Biomedical Dataspace (LBDS) was developed as an integral part[2] of the GRANATUM project to offer a single-point, integrated access to multiple, diverse biomedical data sources for non-technical, domain users. We also provide a rich suite of tools to enable users publish, access and visualize their experimental datasets in conjunction with the LBDS. Our main motivation was to enable cancer researchers to retrieve information pertaining to their research questions. Previously, the domain experts have extensively evaluated the accuracy of our integration and the usability of our platform for information discovery [42,15,18]. During the development of the components we learnt important lessons by tackling the complex challenges associated with the complexity of biomedical data integration and discovery, and believe that our gained insights would be useful for LD practitioners.

The rest of this paper is structured as follows: Section 2 describes the related research carried out in this area. In Section 3, we provide a brief overview of the LBDS and its different components. In congruence with the domain experts, we outlined a set of questions (Table 1) which should be satisfactorily answered by the components. Section 4 showcases the use of different components to solve three research tasks associated with information discovery in cancer chemoprevention. Section 5 describes the evolution of our LBDS, summarizes the results of previous evaluations and compares our design decisions against some of the popular LD platforms developed for drug discovery. Finally, we report on the important lessons that we learned through the collective experience and challenges encountered, during the collaborative processes.

---

[1] www.granatum.org

[2] http://goo.gl/xo3KJB

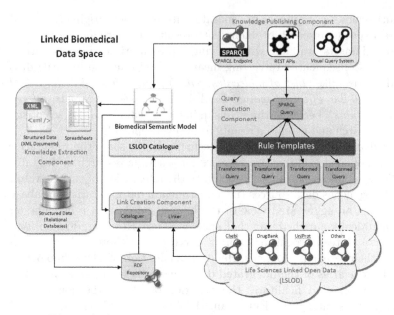

**Fig. 1.** Architecture of the Linked Biomedical Dataspace

## 2 Related Work

Initiatives, notably Bio2RDF [4] and Neurocommons [27], have been carried out for publishing biomedical resources using semantic web technologies. The Linking Open Drug Data (LODD) task force under the W3C Health Care and Life Sciences Interest Group (HCLS IG) has provided best practices and recommendations for transforming and exposing publicly available data about drugs in a LD representation [30]. Architectures like SQUIN [14] and FedX [32] could be configured for distributed querying across these data sources. Some projects have applied LD technologies for integrating and exploring biomedical data sources. OpenPHACTS [41], a pharmacological space, uses a bottom-up data-warehousing approach. DistilBio[3] was developed as a proprietary, graph-based, visual search platform for the life sciences. Health-e-child [5] employs knowledge resources and OLAP-based data normalization tools to build multi-dimensional semantic spaces from biomedical data collections. Linked2Safety [2], aims to accelerate clinical practice and medical research. Finally, Linked TCGA [29] enables evidence-based personalized prognosis for cancer.

## 3 Linked Biomedical Dataspace

The Linked Biomedical Dataspace (LBDS) enables the semantically-enriched representation, exposure, interconnection, querying and browsing of biomedical data and knowledge in a standardized and homogenized way. We envision the

---

[3] http://distilbio.com/

LBDS to comprise of four distinct components, namely: *i)* Knowledge Extraction (KEC), *ii)* Link Creation (LCC), *iii)* Query Execution (QEC), *iv)* Knowledge Publishing (KPC) (Fig. 1). A Biomedical Semantic Model is proposed as a common reference model and vocabulary for the synchronization of the four components. For LBDS, data is integrated from multiple sources including experimental datasets provided by the biomedical scientists and public repositories.

### 3.1   Biomedical Semantic Model

The role of the Biomedical Semantic Model is to unify the diverse and heterogeneous data sources scattered across the Life Sciences Linked Open Data (LSLOD) Cloud consistently. When the same concept (e.g. Molecule) is referred in two sources using different terms, the semantic model ensures that those terms are mapped appropriately (coreference). Furthermore, the semantic model is used for the creation of new links between entities in different data sources, the assembly of SPARQL queries and data browsing. A specific Cancer Chemoprevention semantic model (CanCO) was created for application in the cancer domain. The methodology for the CanCO development follows a "meet-in-the-middle" approach where the concepts emerged both in a bottom-up (i.e. analyze the domain) and a top-down (i.e. analyze ontologies/vocabularies) fashion [42].

### 3.2   Knowledge Extraction Component

Biomedical datasets are available in various formats like domain-specific CSV, XML (eXtended Markup Language) files or heterogeneous, structured databases. Representation using RDF allows standardized access and interlinking of data. The Knowledge Extraction Component (KEC) supports two main features :-

**Extracting Knowledge from Dataset files:** Specialized scripts were developed to transform the large datasets semi-automatically by using mapping rules, established in a simple declarative language. Any developer can easily map the structure of batch-produced XML or CSV files to concepts and properties derived from CanCO (Query Elements - *Qe*). Google RDF Refine[4] is also made available for the semantic enrichment of smaller files by domain users.

**Extracting Knowledge from Relational Database:** We have followed the D2RQ approach to expose any relational database as a virtual RDF graph and to make it available through a SPARQL endpoint [6]. The assignment of tables and columns into ontology terms, as well as the translation of SPARQL to SQL queries, is being handled via mappings expressed in the D2R language.

### 3.3   Link Creation Component

To assemble powerful queries traversing several SPARQL endpoints[5], it is first necessary to link the underlying data sources. A 'Cataloguer' explores and catalogues the schema used to represent data in more than 60 public LSLOD

---

[4] http://refine.deri.ie/

[5] http://srvgal78.deri.ie/RoadMapEvaluation/#Sparql_Endpoints

**Table 1.** Questionnaire

| | |
|---|---|
| Q1 | What is the scope of Linked Biomedical Dataspace (LBDS)? |
| Q2 | What are the different types of relevant data sources integrated in the LBDS? |
| Q3 | How would you confirm uninterrupted data availability from integrated sources? |
| Q4 | How would you deal with bad quality Linked Data sources? |
| Q5 | What should be the link types, granularity, format, size and structure of the catalogue? |
| Q6 | What are the available linking and aligning strategies, approaches and tools? |
| Q7 | How can the domain users intuitively search information from the LBDS? |
| Q8 | How could the retrieved information be presented in a human-readable, domain-specific format? |
| Q9 | How are the limitations of the LBDS, in terms of the availability, scalability and interoperability across different platforms addressed? |
| Q10 | What is the role of domain experts during the development of LBDS? |
| Q11 | What are the possible uses of the LBDS demonstrated in real scenarios? |
| Q12 | Should external links to Linked Data sources be locally materialized to enhance query responses? |
| Q13 | How would the LBDS address emerging user needs? |

SPARQL endpoints, and a 'Linker' links the catalogued concepts and properties to CanCO $Qe^6$. The Linker creates links using the following strategies: *i)* Naïve Matching/Syntactic Matching/Label Matching, *ii)* Named Entity Matching and *iii)* Manual and Domain-specific unique identifier Matching [15].

### 3.4  Query Execution Component

The core component of our LBDS is a federated graph query engine, which reasons over the previously catalogued links - {Concept_A subClassOf Qe}, {Concept_A void:uriRegexPattern stringPattern} and {sparqlEndpoint void:class Concept_A}, to transform a simple query {?s a Qe} to a SPARQL construct {{?s a Concept_A} UNION {?s a Concept_B}} and execute the federated alternatives against the specific sparqlEndpoint. This ensures semantic interoperability as the formulated queries use the same semantic model and information retrieval is independent of the underlying schemas. An *ad hoc* module recursively monitors the latency of the SPARQL endpoints to 'smartly' determine which endpoints are available for querying. The query engine also provides a permission-based access to the RDFized experimental datasets.

### 3.5  Knowledge Publishing Component

The QEC is exposed as a SPARQL endpoint and as REST web services by the Knowledge Publishing Component (KPC). The KPC also provides a Visual Query System - ReVeaLD[7] (Real-time Visual Explorer and Aggregator of Linked Data) for facilitating non-technical biomedical users to intuitively formulate advanced SPARQL queries by interacting with a visual concept map representation of CanCO [18]. Results are aggregated from the LBDS and presented in a data browser with 'Smart Icons', which render domain-specific visualizations using a set of $Qe$-based Graphic Rules, and refer to additional information available on portals like ChemSpider [25] and PubChem [21].

---

[6] http://srvgal78.deri.ie/arc/roadmap.php
[7] http://srvgal78.deri.ie:8080/explorer

# 4    Workflows

Our interactions with the domain experts during the development of the LBDS, allowed us to establish a set of questions (Table 1) which the components should satisfactorily address. As such, the identification of practices for addressing these is a necessary step to enable future practitioners to conceptualize dataspaces in other domains. We segregated three separate workflows where we present how the different components can be used in sequence to solve specific research problems. We attempt to address the previous questions through these workflows. The users of our LBDS fall into two categories: a bioinformatician - a computer scientist with a biology background, who is responsible for data management, and a biomedical researcher who has no knowledge of computer science and uses the LBDS to query and explore the data (**Q1**). Workflow 4.1 is relevant only for the bioinformatician whereas 4.2 and 4.3 involves both users.

## 4.1    Discovering and Cataloguing Relevant Sources from LSLOD

LBDS enables querying multiple, heterogeneous, distributed data sources through a single interface to address domain-specific problems. Two approaches are considered by a bioinformatician: "*a priori* integration", that uses the same vocabularies and ontologies, and "*a posteriori* integration", a methodology that defines mapping rules between different schemas, enabling the modification of the topology of queried graphs and the integration of data sources using alternative vocabularies. The steps taken for "*a posteriori* integration" are :-

1. There are multiple datasets in the LSLOD describing the concept `Molecule` - Bio2RDF KEGG `<kegg#Compound>`, DrugBank `<drugbank:Drug>`, ChEBI `<chebi#Compound>` and BioPAX `<biopax-level3.owl#SmallMolecule>` (**Q2**).
2. LSLOD SPARQL endpoints and the contained concepts and properties are catalogued. Sample instances and associated labels are also catalogued and linked to the corresponding concept using `void:exampleResource` predicate. Regular Expressions are used to identify the source of the instance (**Q5**).
3. Instances are assigned to new concepts through inference by identifying and creating a link that two concepts are similar (e.g. `owl:sameAs`, `rdfs:subClassOf`). Based on the nature of the data, the most appropriate linking process is decided using the aforementioned strategies (**Q5,Q6**).
4. SPARQL algebra rewrites the query at QEC to retrieve all `Molecules`.

**Listing 1.** SPARQL Algebra to rewrite query at QEC

```
CONSTRUCT (bgp (triple ?molecule a gr:Molecule)) UNION (
    SERVICE (<kegg/sparql>,<kegg/sparql>
        bgp(triple ?molecule rdf:type <kegg#Compound>))
    SERVICE (<chebi/sparql>,<chebi/sparql>
        bgp(triple ?molecule rdf:type <chebi#Compound>)))
```

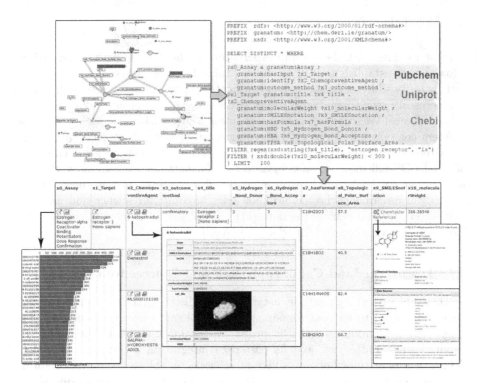

**Fig. 2.** Using ReVeaLD to retrieve and visualize information on small molecules, identified for favorable binding activity towards Estrogen receptors

## 4.2 Retrieving Molecules, Which Interact with Estrogen Receptors

One of the primary objectives[8] of the GRANATUM project was to identify molecules having a favorable binding affinity with Estrogen receptors-$\alpha$ and $\beta$ for the prognosis of breast cancer drug therapy [36]. PubChem is a vast public repository cataloguing the potency of small molecules towards various biological targets, as determined by bioactivity assays (BioAssays) [21]. The central idea is to retrieve favorable agents (with `Molecular Weight`<300) targeting the Estrogen receptors from the PubChem BioAssays, and provide additional biological information of the resources (**Q1**). The steps taken were as follows :-

1. The bioinformatician realizes that the PubChem data source exposed as a SPARQL endpoint under Bio2RDF Release 1 experiences frequent query timeouts, making it unfeasible for integration. The datasets are downloaded through an FTP server[9] in CSV and XML formats. (**Q2**).
2. After discussing with the domain experts, the CanCO model is incremented by adding a new concept `AssayResult`, relationships {`Assay hasResult AssayResult`} and {`AssayResult mentionMolecule Molecule`}, and

---

[8] http://goo.gl/2OJePz
[9] ftp://ftp.ncbi.nih.gov/pubchem

AssayResult-associated properties outcomeMeasure ($EC_{50}$, $IC_{50}$, *Potency*), outcomeType (Active or Inactive) and outcomeValue. (**Q10,Q13**)

3. The PubChem datasets are transformed using KEC and the extended CanCO model, and stored locally to ensure uninterrupted data availability. (**Q3**)
4. The advanced SPARQL query can be formulated by the biomedical researcher by clicking the concepts Assay, Chemopreventive Agent (CMA) and Target using ReVeaLD's concept map visualization, and setting a numerical filter (<300) on the CMA:Molecular Weight and a text filter (~estrogen receptor) on the Target:title properties (**Q7**). Additional biological properties of the CMAs could be retrieved by clicking the UI inputs.
5. ReVeaLD's data browser replaces the RDF URIs with associated titles from the extracted dictionary. Entity information and domain-specific visualizations are accessed through 'Smart Icons' (Fig. 2) (**Q8**). Corrupt visualizations, due to deprecated structure file locations or unsupported libraries, are presented as text by default, making ReVeaLD interoperable (**Q9**).
6. ReVeaLD could transfer SMILES identifiers [39] of retrieved molecules to the ChemSpider REST API[10] to obtain information on patents and vendors, and to virtual screening platforms like LISIs [19] for *in silico* analysis (**Q11**).

### 4.3   Combining Knowledge Extracted from Publications with LD

It is necessary to identify the adverse events associated with potential molecules (as discovered in assays and clinical trials) before selecting them. There is a huge wealth of knowledge stored in scientific publications, outlining the results of molecules tested previously. PubMed, an online search engine, is used by biomedical researchers globally. It comprises of citations for biomedical literature extracted from MEDLINE, Life Sciences Journals and books. Information in PubMed (publication metadata and open-access papers) is well-structured and maintained; however, the full potential of integrating this information with non-LD and LSLOD entities is yet to be realized (**Q1**). The steps taken are :-

1. The bioinformatician retrieves the XML files, regarding publication data, through PubMed Utilities (**Q2**). The KEC converts these files to RDF triples by using the $Qe$ Target, Molecule and Publication concepts, and stores them locally to enhance query performance (**Q12**).
2. Databases of diseases and molecules, maintained by domain users, are identified and exposed as RDF Virtual Graphs using D2RQ [6]. The LCC creates links between the two aforementioned data sources. Only data sources of good granularity are selected as potential repositories to scan for links (**Q4**).
3. The QEC could perform queries upon an interlinked data sources as a single data graph. The biomedical researcher can select the Publication concept in ReVeaLD and request the SMILES information of the molecules, excluding those associated with adverse events harmful to human subjects (**Q7,Q11**).

---

[10] http://www.chemspider.com/AboutServices.aspx

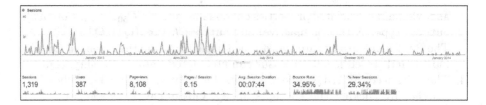

**Fig. 3.** Usage Statistics of ReVeaLD logged using Google Analytics

## 5    Evolution and Evaluation

Since the launch of LBDS in October 2012, the bioinformaticians and biomedical researchers, associated with the project, have used the components to link newer datasets and mine the LBDS (Section 3). We exposed a database, providing structural information on interesting molecules, using D2R, and converted the PubChem BioAssay XML datasets to RDF for secure access. Our discussions with the domain experts led to the inclusion of an auto-complete search input in ReVeaLD to allow single entity search, and the use of SMILES identifiers for *in silico* analysis. SPARQL endpoints under the Bio2RDF Release 2 were integrated later in May 2013 due to better uptime. To aid the non-technical users we created a screencast[11] outlining the different steps (Workflow II, III), which was made available on the project website and has been downloaded by ~175 users[12] by October 2013. Google Analytics tracking showed that ReVeaLD was accessed by 387 distinct users from 29 countries, up to February 2014 (Fig. 3), for querying and extending the CanCO semantic model. CanCO underwent 15 different changes, 9 of them were merged with the main model, whereas 6 are available as independent extensions on the GRANATUM platform.

As the LBDS evolved, we evaluated the different components separately. The expressivity, completeness, correctness, usability and simplicity of CanCO semantic model in the context of cancer chemoprevention domain was evaluated using an application-based and a human assessment methodology [42]. The links generated by LCC were evaluated both empirically and comparatively, as well as validated by the domain experts [15]. The usability and user experience of ReVeaLD was evaluated using the HCI-based 'Tracking Real-time User Experience (TRUE)' methodology [18]. Functional (http://goo.gl/m67o03) and non-functional (http://goo.gl/dEZuUE) requirements were evaluated later using questionnaires. Summarizing our results: *i)* CanCO fully covers the needs of the domain and facilitates easy usage, *ii)* existing linking strategies could not be used for LSLOD, and *iii)* a domain-specific model improves the intuitiveness of semantic search. A preliminary evaluation shows QEC to be the only federated query engine that ensures privacy and supports all SPARQL features [28].

We carried out an empirical comparative evaluation with some of the popular LD platforms, introduced in Section 2, enabling drug discovery (Table 2). In most

---

[11] http://www.granatum.org/pub/bscw.cgi/d82084/3%20ReVeaLD.mp4
[12] http://goo.gl/hvKkQf

**Table 2.** Comparative Evaluation against Popular Linked Data Platforms

| | GRANATUM | OpenPHACTS | Linked2Safety | DistilBio | Linked TCGA | Health-e-Child |
|---|---|---|---|---|---|---|
| Domain-specific model | ✓ | ✗ | ✓ | ✗ | ✓ | ✗ |
| Knowledge and Data Extraction | ✓ | ✗ | ✗ | ✗ | ✗ | ✗ |
| Query Federation | ✓ | ✗ | ✓ | ✗ | ✓ | ✗ |
| Data warehousing | ✓ | ✓ | ✗ | ✓ | ✗ | ✓ |
| Intuitive Querying | ✓ | ✓ | ✗ | ✓ | ✓ | ✓ |
| Domain-specific Visualization | ✓ | ✗ | ✗ | ✗ | ✓ | ✓ |
| Linked Open Data | ✓ | ✓ | ✓ | ✓ | ✓ | ✓ |
| Commercial Data | ✗ | ✓ | ✗ | ✓ | ✗ | ✓ |

cases, these initiatives are not yet user-driven or scalable and some approaches are too generic, whereas drug discovery is domain-specific [33]. OpenPHACTS [41], DistilBio and Health-e-child [5] platforms transform and store information from multiple providers (including commercial and private [13]) in semantic interoperable formats. Adoption by the actual users is impeded due to their use of a comprehensive ontology instead of a domain-specific model and they have emphasized the need for community-driven annotation and personalization. Linked2Safety [2] and Linked TCGA [29] are pursuing the domain-specific query federation approach towards data integration. However, the scalability of these platforms for integrating newer data sources is yet to be evaluated. Linked TCGA and Health-e-child also provide domain-specific visualizations [17].

## 6 Lessons Learned

While reviewing the state-of-the-art technologies and developing the LBDS components to address the questions (Table 1), we learned numerous lessons which may be useful for LD practitioners to develop such dataspaces in other domains.

*Q1. What is the scope of Linked Biomedical Dataspace?*
The scope of the LBDS in general, and the semantic model in particular [37], should be determined initially before its conceptualization. The scope definition includes: *i)* the identification of the actual beneficiaries (end-users), *ii)* the identification of the potential use cases, and *iii)* the definition of the functional and non-functional requirements [42]. A well-defined scope will drive the whole design and development of the LBDS and facilitate subsequent decisions, like the selection of relevant resources i.e. models, ontologies, non-ontological resources, and the identification of the core $Qe$. The identification of the re-usable sections and the method of integration in the semantic model is also important [38].

*Q2. What are the different types of relevant data sources integrated in the LBDS?*
Due to the large number of data sources available dispersed across the web, it is crucial to determine the relevance of these sources with respect to the target domain before integration in the LBDS. The possible source types include ontologies (e.g. Gene Ontology - GO [3]), existing datasets from LSLOD (e.g. DrugBank, PubChem, PubMed), data dumps, SPARQL endpoints, user-provided data (e.g. Excel files, experimental data). A starting point of investigation could be the BioPortal [40], Bio2RDF [4] and Neurocommons [27].

*Q3. How would you confirm uninterrupted data availability from integrated sources?*

The latency and functionality of public SPARQL endpoints affects the quality of the retrieved query results and the domain users may not be able to get information from an important data source (e.g. PubChem). Most endpoints aggregate all the SPARQL results and push back to the client in bulk, instead of buffering them, making it difficult to determine if the endpoint has timed out or is still collecting the results. Moreover, databases like ZINC [16] are very useful for structure-based virtual screening, but are not available as SPARQL endpoints or RDF Dumps. Data warehousing approaches could be used, but the maintenance, storage and continuous updating is rate-limiting and may necessitate manual intervention [10]. Specialized applications like SPARQLES could be used to recursively monitor the availability of public SPARQL endpoints to determine query federation and make the data publishers conscious [8] .

*Q4. How can one manage Linked Data sources that are of bad quality?*

Curated data sources in LSLOD suffer from lack of accuracy, incompleteness, temporal inconsistency or coverage. We found issues like: *i)* Different namespaces used by the same provider, e.g. `<http://bio2rdf.org/kegg_vocabulary:xGene>`, `<http://bio2rdf.org/ns/biopax#pathway>`, `<http://bio2rdf.org/ns/ns/bind#interactionPart>`, and `<http://bio2rdf.org/ns/ns/ns/pubchem#Molecular_Formula>`, *ii)* URL-encoded labels, e.g. `pdb:1%2C1%2C5%2C5tetrafluorophosphopentylphosphonicAcidAdenylateEster`, *iii)* non-dereferenceable URIs, e.g. `kegg_vocabulary:bpm+BURPS1710b_1815+BURPS1710b_A0336`, and *iv)* Alpha-numeric URIs, for which no labels were defined, e.g. `so:0000436` [15]. Possible solutions include using partial snapshots of the endpoints (not whole RDF dumps) or mechanisms to assess the quality of LD repositories during link creation.

*Q5. What should be the link types, granularity, format, size and structure of the catalogue?*

As different data catalogues exist to serve distinct purposes, one should decide how well the chosen catalogue fulfills the requirements. When data linking is a key requirement it is prudent to compile a catalogue from scratch. Existing vocabularies e.g. VoID [1], DCAT[13], Dublin Core (DC)[14], and FOAF[15] can be used to describe data in the catalogue. The selection of a vocabulary depends upon the purpose of the catalogue and the granularity under consideration. For example, the PROV Namespace[16] can be used when the user wants to record the provenance information in the catalogue. The overall structure of the catalogue and its format is an important design factor. If Query Transformation Rules are to be derived from the catalogue, it should be conceived to suit considered

---

[13] `http://www.w3.org/TR/2012/WD-vocab-dcat-20120405/`
[14] `http://dublincore.org/documents/dcmi-terms/`
[15] `http://xmlns.com/foaf/spec/`
[16] `http://www.w3.org/ns/prov#`

linking approaches. *Qe* in the catalogue could be linked using link types with completely different semantics (e.g. `rdfs:subClassOf`, `owl:sameAs`).

*Q6. What are the available linking and aligning strategies, approaches and tools?*
Linking and aligning the semantic model with other models and ontologies plays a pivotal role in ensuring semantic interoperability and addressing data heterogeneity. However alignment of ontologies is generally suited when the data has been structured as a hierarchy which is not always the case [11]. Vocabularies e.g. WordNet [23], and Unified Medical Language System (UMLS) [7] can be used to achieve automated similarity and relatedness scores. As these vocabularies and available linking tools e.g. SILK and LIMES are very generic for LSLOD, limited success is obtained (non-specific, unrealistic and redundant links) [15].

Instance Alignment i.e. identifying the same entity referenced using different URIs, is currently very difficult to achieve at run-time and query results often contain duplicates. There is no set of common properties and unique identifiers may be encoded using different nomenclatures. For example, *Aspirin* (Drug-Bank), also referred as *Acetylsalicylic Acid* (ChEBI), is an interesting compound for *in silico* studies of colorectal cancer [31]. However, there is a marked difference in their InChi and SMILES representations (`smilesStringIsomeric` versus `smilesStringCanonical`). Molecular Weights and Formulas could not be used, as stereo-isomers have similar values for these attributes but are drastically different from a biological perspective (e.g. *D-Glucose* and *L-Glucose*). Approaches like [24] could be delved into deeper and tested for LSLOD.

*Q7. How can the domain users intuitively search information from the LBDS?*
Semantic search applications allow the formulation of highly expressive queries but SPARQL is the least usable *modus operandi* for biomedical users who may not have technical knowledge of LD Technologies. Even for a skilled LD practitioner it is difficult to assemble federated queries. An interface, which effectively lowers the barrier between Usability (*Natural*) and Expressivity (*Formal*), should be developed [20]. Such an interface evolves through 5 distinct stages - SPARQL, VQS, Single entity search, Keyword search and Google-like NL-queries. Instead of using standard ontologies a semantic model devised by the domain experts increases the intuitiveness as users are familiar with the *Qe* [42]. Concept maps augment translation of any knowledge graph, to solve a domain-specific problem, into a formal representation [22]. ReVeaLD allows visual interaction through a concept map, but still shows an extreme reliance on the CanCO *Qe*, e.g. compulsory selection of the `Drug` concept to retrieve information on *Aspirin* [18]. Primarily, an exhaustive dictionary summarizing all types of 'biological entities' should be compiled using machine-learning term extraction [34] and the gap could then be bridged further by proposed methodologies [12,20].

*Q8. How could the retrieved information be presented in a human-readable, domain-specific format?*
Although RDF representations are more suitable for semantic reasoning, RDF URIs are confusing for the biomedical researcher. Fresnel Vocabulary [26] could be used to provide a more human-readable representation. Most biomedical data

sources expose REST APIs which provide structural information on any entity (i.e. 3D structures, pathway maps, etc.) and native web technologies makes it relatively easy to develop and integrate visualization libraries. ReVeaLD searches for specific triple patterns (Graphic Rules) to provide a domain-specific outlook e.g. `drugbank:targets/844 drugbank:pdbIdPage <http://www.pdb.org/pdb/explore/explore.do?structureId=1IVO>` [18]. However, many entities in the LSLOD do not have values for the predicates `rdfs:label` and `dc:title`, or the required triple patterns (`drugbank:pdbIdPage`) for the Graphic Rules.

*Q9. How are the limitations of the LBDS, in terms of the availability, scalability and interoperability across different platforms addressed?*
The scalability of our LBDS is directly impacted by: *i)* Number of desirable SPARQL endpoints to be queried by the QEC (current threshold is 105 endpoints), *ii)* The size and complexity of the datasets to be RDFized, and limitations of the existing tools of KEC, and *iii)* Visualization of a larger number of results (>10000) and computing facets for data navigation. A rule-based reasoning-enabled QEC for *Qe*-specific queries (i.e. DrugBank and ChEBI for `Molecule`) may alleviate this but the processing time would differ between the *Qe* i.e. retrieving information on `Molecules` is more taxing than `Assays`. The reliance of ReVeaLD on the configuration of the client system (graphics card, system RAM and browser version) affects the interoperability across different platforms [18]. Some technologies, like WebGL, are only supported by modern browsers, necessitating backward compatibility. Libraries like Modernizr[17] could be used to detect which browser-based features are supported in real-time.

*Q10. What is the role of domain experts during the development of LBDS?*
Domain experts should be actively involved throughout all stages of the development, especially during conceptualization of the semantic model, since they would be the final users. The existing methodologies for building ontologies and semantic models lack interaction with the domain experts which results in a well-construed ontology that may be not be useful for the end-users [42]. We found the collaborative decision-making between the computer scientists and domain experts essential for: *i)* Model development, by identifying the scope, relevant data sources and core *Qe, ii)* Validation of the links generated by LCC, *iii)* Prototyping of ReVeaLD [18] and *iv)* Evaluation of the LBDS. However, domain experts need a stronger motivation for active participation. We obtained their input and feedback through brainstorming, interviews and questionnaires.

*Q11. What are the possible uses of the LBDS demonstrated in real scenarios?*
The main application of the LBDS would be to significantly reduce the time and costs of current drug discovery techniques. The LBDS enables domain scientists to strategically and informatively isolate ~100 biological compounds of biological 'relevance' from >300,000 compounds (Workflows II, III). These compounds can be virtually screened using *in silico* methods like Protein-Ligand Docking [35], to obtain around 10 potential compounds for *in vivo* analysis. LBDS could also

---

[17] http://modernizr.com/

be used for the discovery of biological interactions (protein-protein or gene-drug interactions) by integrating '-omics' datasets with GO or PubChem.

*Q12. Should external links to Linked Data sources be locally materialized to enhance query responses?*
RDF entities existing in repositories are subject to changes, data unavailability or are badly-curated. As interfaces request data from a federated query engine, which executes queries to remote repositories, the user experience or semantic reasoning by agents is disrupted in such situations. A potential solution can be the partial materialization of RDF triples from remote resources to local repositories [9]. The query engine could first try to resolve a query locally and if it is not possible, the query can be forwarded to external repositories. The selection of triples to be cached, as well as the refresh mechanisms is subject to a lot of parameters that could be solved by weighted-equations.

*Q13. How would the LBDS address emerging user needs?*
Even if the model seems to fully represent an area of interest (e.g. cancer chemoprevention) at the time of its creation, new needs might emerge in the future (e.g. new *Qe*) for end-users. The LBDS has to provide a maintenance mechanism that satisfies these demands. An incrementation tool was integrated with ReVeaLD to enable users to extend or merge the semantic model by adding new *Qe*. A naive versioning is enabled for domain users to maintain and share different modifications of their extensions.

## 7    Recommendations

We summarize a set of generic recommendations that initiatives developing LD platforms for drug discovery might find useful.

1. End-users (i.e. domain experts) should be involved at all stages (from conceptualization to evaluation) of the LBDS development.
2. Developers must use a domain-specific semantic model for the homogenisation of the data sources and the integration of the LBDS components.
3. Quality and availability of the RDF data sources should be taken into consideration when discovering datasets.
4. SPARQL endpoints must be monitored constantly for availability and interoperability, and feedback should be used to inform data publishers.
5. Caching mechanisms must be incorporated at the data sources and QEC.
6. Data publishers must ensure that the RDF URIs are HTTP-dereferenceable.
7. User-driven tools for data extraction and annotation must be provided.
8. Retrieved information from the LBDS should be made more human-readable and personalized to meet the needs of the domain.
9. Concept maps must be used for knowledge visualization, to enable preliminary users to interpret and formulate domain problems.
10. HCI-based (Human-computer interaction) evaluations of semantic web applications must be carried out to enhance user experience and usability.

# 8   Conclusion

In this paper, we present the important lessons learned during the collaborative development of a Linked Biomedical Dataspace (LBDS) for supplementing drug discovery. We provided a brief overview of the different components and the state-of-the-art technologies which could be integrated to publish, interlink, access and visualize LD. We emphasize the collaborative involvement of domain users in all the decision-making processes of the LBDS development. Three workflows showcase how the LBDS can be exploited by bioinformaticians and biomedical researchers for cancer chemoprevention drug discovery. We compare the main features of our LBDS against some of the popular LD platforms available for drug discovery. Our experiences and the challenges encountered have helped us outline the important lessons and summarize generic recommendations for LD practitioners to create such dataspaces in other domains.

**Acknowledgments.** This research has been supported in part by the EU FP7 GRANATUM project, ref. FP7-ICT-2009-6-270139, Science Foundation Ireland under Grant Number SFI/12/RC/2289 and SFI/08/CE/I1380 (Lion 2). The authors would like to acknowledge the members of the GRANATUM Consortium, for providing essential inputs during the development stages of the different components of the LBDS.

# References

1. Alexander, K., Cyganiak, R., et al.: Describing linked datasets. In: LDOW (2009)
2. Antoniades, A., Georgousopoulos, C., Forgo, N., et al.: Linked2Safety: A secure linked data medical information space for semantically-interconnecting EHRs advancing patients' safety in medical research. In: 12th International Conference on Bioinformatics & Bioengineering (BIBE), pp. 517–522. IEEE (2012)
3. Ashburner, M., Ball, C.A., Blake, J.A., Botstein, D., Butler, H., et al.: Gene Ontology: tool for the unification of biology. Nature Genetics 25(1), 25–29 (2000)
4. Belleau, F., Nolin, M.A., et al.: Bio2RDF: towards a mashup to build bioinformatics knowledge systems. Journal of Biomedical Informatics 41(5), 706–716 (2008)
5. Berlanga, R., et al.: Exploring and linking biomedical resources through multidimensional semantic spaces. BMC Bioinformatics 13(suppl. 1), S6 (2012)
6. Bizer, C., Seaborne, A.: D2RQ-treating non-RDF databases as virtual RDF graphs. In: Proceedings of the 3rd International Semantic Web Conference (ISWC) (2004)
7. Bodenreider, O.: The unified medical language system (UMLS): integrating biomedical terminology. Nucleic Acids Research 32(suppl. 1), D267–D270 (2004)
8. Buil-Aranda, C., Hogan, A., Umbrich, J., Vandenbussche, P.-Y.: SPARQL Web-Querying Infrastructure: Ready for Action? In: Alani, H., et al. (eds.) ISWC 2013, Part II. LNCS, vol. 8219, pp. 277–293. Springer, Heidelberg (2013)
9. Castillo, R., Leser, U.: Selecting materialized views for RDF data. In: Daniel, F., Facca, F.M. (eds.) ICWE 2010. LNCS, vol. 6385, pp. 126–137. Springer, Heidelberg (2010)
10. Cheung, K.H., Frost, H.R., Marshall, M.S., et al.: A journey to semantic web query federation in the life sciences. BMC Bioinformatics 10(suppl. 10), S10 (2009)

11. Euzenat, J., Meilicke, C., Stuckenschmidt, H., Shvaiko, P., Trojahn, C.: Ontology alignment evaluation initiative: Six years of experience. In: Spaccapietra, S. (ed.) Journal on Data Semantics XV. LNCS, vol. 6720, pp. 158–192. Springer, Heidelberg (2011)
12. Freitas, A., Curry, E., et al.: Querying linked data using semantic relatedness: a vocabulary independent approach. IEEE Internet Computing, 24–33 (2012)
13. Goble, C., et al.: Incorporating commercial and private data into an open linked data platform for drug discovery. In: Alani, H., et al. (eds.) ISWC 2013, Part II. LNCS, vol. 8219, pp. 65–80. Springer, Heidelberg (2013)
14. Hartig, O., Bizer, C., Freytag, J.C.: Executing sparql queries over the web of linked data. In: Bernstein, A., Karger, D.R., Heath, T., Feigenbaum, L., Maynard, D., Motta, E., Thirunarayan, K. (eds.) ISWC 2009. LNCS, vol. 5823, pp. 293–309. Springer, Heidelberg (2009)
15. Hasnain, A., Fox, R., Decker, S., Deus, H.F.: Cataloguing and linking life sciences LOD Cloud. In: 1st International Workshop on Ontology Engineering in a Data-driven World at EKAW 2012 (2012)
16. Irwin, J.J., Shoichet, B.K.: ZINC-a free database of commercially available compounds for virtual screening. Journal of Chemical Information and Modeling 45(1), 177–182 (2005)
17. Kamdar, M.R., Iqbal, A., Saleem, M., Deus, H.F., Decker, S.: GenomeSnip: Fragmenting the Genomic Wheel to augment discovery in cancer research. In: Conference on Semantics in Healthcare and Life Sciences (CSHALS). ISCB (2014)
18. Kamdar, M.R., Zeginis, D., Hasnain, A., Decker, S., Deus, H.F.: ReVeaLD: A user-driven domain-specific interactive search platform for biomedical research. Journal of Biomedical Informatics 47, 112–130 (2014)
19. Kannas, C., Achilleos, K., Antoniou, Z., Nicolaou, C., Pattichis, C., et al.: A workflow system for virtual screening in cancer chemoprevention. In: 12th International Conference on Bioinformatics & Bioengineering (BIBE), pp. 439–446. IEEE (2012)
20. Kaufmann, E., Bernstein, A.: Evaluating the usability of natural language query languages and interfaces to Semantic Web knowledge bases. Web Semantics: Science, Services and Agents on the World Wide Web 8(4), 377–393 (2010)
21. Li, Q., Cheng, T., Wang, Y., Bryant, S.H.: PubChem as a public resource for drug discovery. Drug Discovery Today 15(23), 1052–1057 (2010)
22. Markham, K.M., et al.: The concept map as a research and evaluation tool: Further evidence of validity. Journal of Research in Science Teaching 31(1), 91–101 (1994)
23. Miller, G.A., Beckwith, R., Fellbaum, C., et al.: Introduction to WordNet: An online lexical database. International Journal of Lexicography 3(4), 235–244 (1990)
24. Nikolov, A., Uren, V., Motta, E., de Roeck, A.: Overcoming schema heterogeneity between linked semantic repositories to improve coreference resolution. In: Gómez-Pérez, A., Yu, Y., Ding, Y. (eds.) ASWC 2009. LNCS, vol. 5926, pp. 332–346. Springer, Heidelberg (2009)
25. Pence, H.E., Williams, A.: ChemSpider: an online chemical information resource. Journal of Chemical Education 87(11), 1123–1124 (2010)
26. Pietriga, E., Bizer, C., Karger, D.R., Lee, R.: Fresnel: A browser-independent presentation vocabulary for RDF. In: Cruz, I., Decker, S., Allemang, D., Preist, C., Schwabe, D., Mika, P., Uschold, M., Aroyo, L.M. (eds.) ISWC 2006. LNCS, vol. 4273, pp. 158–171. Springer, Heidelberg (2006)
27. Ruttenberg, A., Rees, J.A., et al.: Life sciences on the semantic web: the Neurocommons and beyond. Briefings in Bioinformatics 10(2), 193–204 (2009)
28. Saleem, M., Khan, Y., Hasnain, A., Ermilov, I., et al.: A fine-grained evaluation of SPARQL endpoint federation systems. Semantic Web Journal (2014)

29. Saleem, M., et al.: Big linked cancer data: Integrating linked TCGA and PubMed. In: Web Semantics: Science, Services and Agents on the World Wide Web (2014)
30. Samwald, M., Jentzsch, A., et al.: Linked open drug data for pharmaceutical research and development. Journal of Cheminformatics 3(1), 19 (2011)
31. Sandler, R.S., Halabi, S., Baron, J.A., Budinger, S., Paskett, E., et al.: A randomized trial of aspirin to prevent colorectal adenomas in patients with previous colorectal cancer. New England Journal of Medicine 348(10), 883–890 (2003)
32. Schwarte, A., Haase, P., Hose, K., Schenkel, R., Schmidt, M.: FedX: Optimization techniques for federated query processing on linked data. In: Aroyo, L., Welty, C., Alani, H., Taylor, J., Bernstein, A., Kagal, L., Noy, N., Blomqvist, E. (eds.) ISWC 2011, Part I. LNCS, vol. 7031, pp. 601–616. Springer, Heidelberg (2011)
33. Searls, D.B.: Data integration: challenges for drug discovery. Nature Reviews Drug Discovery 4(1), 45–58 (2005)
34. Shi, L., Campagne, F.: Building a protein name dictionary from full text: a machine learning term extraction approach. BMC Bioinformatics 6(1), 88 (2005)
35. Sousa, S.F., et al.: Protein-ligand docking: current status and future challenges. Proteins: Structure, Function, and Bioinformatics 65(1), 15–26 (2006)
36. Speirs, V., Parkes, A.T., et al.: Coexpression of Estrogen Receptor $\alpha$ and $\beta$ Poor Prognostic factors in Human Breast Cancer? Cancer Research 59(3), 525–528 (1999)
37. Uschold, M., Gruninger, M.: Ontologies: Principles, methods and applications. The Knowledge Engineering Review 11(2), 93–136 (1996)
38. Visser, P.R., Jones, D.M., Bench-Capon, T., Shave, M.: An analysis of ontology mismatches; heterogeneity versus interoperability. In: AAAI 1997 Spring Symposium on Ontological Engineering, Stanford CA., USA, pp. 164–172 (1997)
39. Weininger, D.: SMILES, a chemical language and information system. Journal of Chemical Information and Computer Sciences 28(1), 31–36 (1988)
40. Whetzel, P.L., Noy, N.F., et al.: Bioportal: enhanced functionality via new web services from the national center for biomedical ontology to access and use ontologies in software applications. Nucleic Acids Research 39(suppl. 2), W541–W545 (2011)
41. Williams, A.J., Harland, L., Groth, P., Pettifer, S., et al.: Open PHACTS: semantic interoperability for drug discovery. Drug Discovery Today 17(21), 1188–1198 (2012)
42. Zeginis, D., et al.: A collaborative methodology for developing a semantic model for interlinking Cancer Chemoprevention linked-data sources. Semantic Web (2013)

# Drug-Target Interaction Prediction Using Semantic Similarity and Edge Partitioning

Guillermo Palma[1], Maria-Esther Vidal[1], and Louiqa Raschid[2]

[1] Universidad Simón Bolívar, Venezuela
[2] University of Maryland, USA
gpalma,mvidal@ldc.usb.ve, louiqa@umiacs.umd.edu

**Abstract.** The ability to integrate a wealth of human-curated knowledge from scientific datasets and ontologies can benefit drug-target interaction prediction. The hypothesis is that similar drugs interact with the same targets, and similar targets interact with the same drugs. The similarities between drugs reflect a chemical semantic space, while similarities between targets reflect a genomic semantic space. In this paper, we present a novel method that combines a data mining framework for link prediction, semantic knowledge (similarities) from ontologies or semantic spaces, and an algorithmic approach to partition the edges of a heterogeneous graph that includes drug-target interaction edges, and drug-drug and target-target similarity edges. Our semantics based edge partitioning approach, semEP, has the advantages of edge based community detection which allows a node to participate in more than one cluster or community. The semEP problem is to create a minimal partitioning of the edges such that the cluster density of each subset of edges is maximal. We use semantic knowledge (similarities) to specify edge constraints, i.e., specific drug-target interaction edges that should not participate in the same cluster. Using a well-known dataset of drug-target interactions, we demonstrate the benefits of using semEP predictions to improve the performance of a range of state-of-the-art machine learning based prediction methods. Validation of the novel best predicted interactions of semEP against the STITCH interaction resource reflect both accurate and diverse predictions.

**Keywords:** Drug-target interaction prediction, vertex coloring graph, community detection, graph partitioning.

## 1 Introduction

Linked Open Data has important applications across the biomedical enterprise where there is a nexus created by the availability of publicly accessible richly curated scientific collections and the extensive use of ontologies and thesauri. This ability to seamlessly integrate a wealth of human-curated knowledge can benefit many applications including drug-target interaction prediction and drug-drug similarity ranking. Consider that drugs are molecules that participate in some biomolecular reaction associated with a disease related genomic target (protein).

P. Mika et al. (Eds.) ISWC 2014, Part I, LNCS 8796, pp. 131–146, 2014.

The ability to predict new drug-target interactions can have applications in drug re-purposing to find new targets for drugs. A related application is drug-drug side effect prediction, e.g., to construct the SIDER [16] side effect resource, or to populate ADEpedia [14], a knowledge base of adverse drug events (ADEs) for drug safety surveillance.

Beyond drug-target interaction prediction, drug-drug similarity rankings are an important component of the comprehensive evidence that is used to make clinical or policy recommendations. Consider the following example relevant to a group of monoclonal antibodies (mab) drugs: On November 3, 2010, The New York Times reported that Genentech began offering secret rebates to ophthalmologists in an apparent inducement to get them to prescribe Ranibizumab rather than the less expensive Bevacizumab. Several studies have shown no superior effect of Ranibizumab over Bevacizumab for the treatment of macular degeneration, an aging-related eye condition. Subsequently, on April 8, 2014, the Washington Post highlighted the results from analyzing a BIGDATA Medicare collection revealing that one of the largest Medicare billers, an ophthalmologist in West Palm Beach, Fla., earned $20 million in 2012; a large fraction of his earnings came from injecting patients with Lucentis (Ranibizumab) instead of Avastin (Bevacizumab).

Figures 1(a) and (b) show a schematic overview of drug-target interaction networks; drugs are circles and targets are squares. For interaction prediction, or to determine functionally equivalent drugs, one must exploit drug-drug and target-target similarities; the hypothesis is that similar drugs interact with the same targets, and similar targets interact with the same drugs. The similarities between drugs reflect a chemical semantic space, while similarities between targets reflect a genomic semantic space [8,21]. Within these semantic spaces, pairs of drugs or pairs of targets may have multiple semantics-based similarity scores. For example, drugs can have similarities based on chemical structure or shared side-effects, while gene targets may share sequence based or protein-protein interaction based similarity [21]; this is illustrated by the multiple edge types.

For the purpose of this paper we focus on drug-target interaction edges. However, our method can be applied to a variety of Linked Data collections and ontologies as will be seen in the next section.

There are many approaches for link prediction or similarity ranking, e.g., drug-target interaction networks [29] or citation graphs [20]. The importance of structured knowledge and collective classification for drug-target prediction was discussed in [11]. Structured knowledge include *triads*; in Figure 1(b), the interaction edge $(d_i, t_x)$, the similarity between targets $t_x$ and $t_y$, and the potential interaction edge $(d_i, t_y)$ form a triad. Similarly, in Figure 1(a), the two interaction edges $(d_i, t_x)$ and $(d_j, t_y)$, the corresponding drug-drug similarity between $d_i$ and $d_j$, and the target-target similarity between $t_x$ and $t_y$, form a *tetrad*. Further, collective classification would support the simultaneous reasoning over the edges $(d_i, t_x)$, $(d_i, t_y)$, $(d_i, t_z)$, etc., in Figure 1(b), and their corresponding similarities.

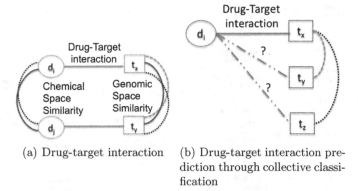

(a) Drug-target interaction     (b) Drug-target interaction prediction through collective classi-
fication

**Fig. 1.** (a) Drug-Target Interaction Network. Drugs are circles and diseases are rectangles. (b) An Example of Collective Classification of Potential Interactions.

We present semEP, an unsupervised semantics based edge partitioning method;
semEP combines a data mining framework for link prediction, semantic knowledge (similarities) from ontologies or semantic spaces, and an algorithmic
approach to partition the edges of a heterogeneous graph. For this paper, we
consider a graph that includes drug-target interaction edges, and drug-drug and
target-target similarities. The semEP problem is to create a minimal partitioning of the edges such that the cluster density of each subset of edges is maximal.
An advantage of semEP edge clustering is that it allows a node to participate in
more than one cluster or community; this is a natural match with the semantics
of drugs that have multiple functions, and thus interact with different targets.
We do not limit semEP to triad or tetrad clusters and we consider clusters of
varying shape and size. Further, semEP can use semantic knowledge on similarities to specify edge constraints, i.e., specific pairs of drug-target interaction
edges that should not occur in the same cluster.

Using a well-known dataset of drug-target interactions [3,8], we demonstrate
the benefits of using semEP predictions to improve the performance of all the
state-of-the-art machine learning based prediction methods [8]. We also validate
the best novel predictions of all the methods (where the interactions are not in
the test dataset) against the STITCH drug-target interaction resource [17]. The
good performance of semEP reflects its ability to exploit structured semantic
knowledge to make accurate and diverse predictions.

This paper is organized as follows: Section 2 provides a motivating example
of Linked Data and ontological knowledge and Section 3 describes the semEP
edge partitioning problem. Section 4 summarizes related research. Experimental
results are reported in Section 5 and Section 6 concludes.

## 2   Semantics of Annotations and Ontological Relatedness

In this paper, we focus on a specific link prediction use case – the problem of predicting drug-target or drug-disease interaction edges. However, as motivation, we

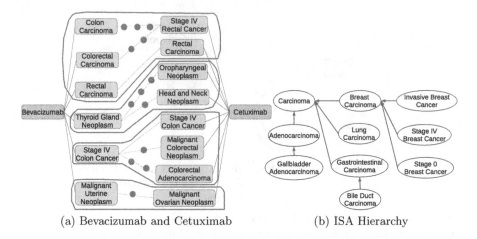

(a) Bevacizumab and Cetuximab          (b) ISA Hierarchy

**Fig. 2.** (a) Drugs Bevacizumab and Cetuximab (green rectangles), Disease Annotations (orange rectangles) and NCI Thesaurus Terms (red ovals). Four communities are highlighted in blue. (b) Fragment of an ISA Hierarchy in the NCIt. The red lines indicate ISA relationships

consider the more general problem of drug-drug similarity ranking. Bevacizumab and Cetuximab are exemplars of monoclonal antibodies that are anti-neoplastic agents used in cancer treatment. We consider the similarity of Bevacizumab and Cetuximab using their neighborhood graph of shared annotations of disease terms. Figure 2(a) represents (partial) disease annotations associated with each drug; the disease terms are mapped to terms in the NCI Thesaurus (NCIt). Each path between a pair of diseases, e.g., Colon Carcinoma and Stage IV Rectal Cancer, is identified with red circles representing intermediate NCIt terms.

A simple shared annotation pattern would include the identical term, e.g., Rectal Carcinoma. Ontological relatedness indicates that non-identical terms such as Colon Carcinoma and Stage IV Rectal Cancer are also related to each other. Combining shared annotation and ontological relatedness, we may determine that (Colon Carcinoma, Colorectal Carcinoma, Rectal Carcinoma, Stage IV Rectal Cancer), together, form a shared community of ontologically related disease terms. Further, (Malignant Colorectal Neoplasm, Stage IV Colon Cancer, Colorectal Adenocarcinoma) appear to form a (possibly overlapping) community, while (Thyroid Gland Neoplasm, Oropharyngeal Neoplasm, Head and Neck Neoplasm) and (Malignant Uterine Neoplasm, Malignant Ovarian Neoplasm) form additional distinct communities.

Figure 2(b) shows a fragment of the NCIt ISA hierarchy. Carcinoma can be specialized to various organs, e.g., Lung Carcinoma; to specific types of disease, e.g., Adenocarcinoma; to disease stages, e.g., Stage IV Breast Cancer; or to combinations, e.g., Stage III Colorectal Adenocarcinoma (not shown).

# 3  Semantics Based Edge Partitioning Problem (semEP)

## 3.1  From Structured Knowledge to Link Prediction for Drug Target Interaction Networks

Let $D = \{d_1, d_2, \cdots, d_m\}$ be a drug set and let $T = \{t_1, t_2, \cdots, t_n\}$ be a target set. Let $S_d$ be a drug similarity matrix where the $(i,j)$-th element denoted $s_d(d_i, d_j)$ is a similarity score (potentially there are multiple scores) between drugs $d_i$ and $d_j$. Let $S_t$ be a target similarity matrix where the $(i,j)$-th element denoted $s_t(t_i, t_j)$ is a similarity score between targets $t_i$ and $t_j$.

Let $Y$ be a binary matrix of **true labels** of drug-target interactions. $Y_{i,j} = 1$ if drug $d_i$ interacts with target $t_j$; $Y_{i,j} = 0$ otherwise.

The objective is to produce a score matrix $F$ where the $(i,j)$-th element denoted $F_{i,j}$ is the score or probability that the drug $d_i$ interacts with target $t_j$.

The hypothesis underlying most solutions is that similar drugs interact with the same targets, and similar targets interact with the same drugs. While this appears to be straightforward, there are many challenges. First, there is no single approach to determine the similarities between drugs or between targets; indeed there are many similarities based on different semantics [21]. Referring to the Linked Data example in the previous section, the NCIt can be used to define a semantic space for drugs and for targets (diseases), while taxonomic metrics can be used to determine similarity scores using the NCIt structure.

A bigger challenge is that the bipartite drug-target interaction network expresses multi-relational or graph structured knowledge. A drug $d_i$ may be complex in its functional behavior and may have multiple targets. Hence, a drug $d_j$ that is similar to $d_i$ based on chemical structure but not on side-effect similarity, may only share some of the targets of $d_i$.

A state-of-the-art solution for the drug-target interaction prediction problem is presented in [11] where they propose a drug-target prediction framework based on Probabilistic Soft Logic (PSL) [5]. The PSL based solution reasons collectively over interactions using structured rules that capture the multi-relational nature of the network, e.g., the triads and tetrads of Figure 1(a) and (b). Finding the most promising candidates for triad and tetrad based learning is an expensive problem that requires significant tuning [11] and the PSL based program was thus limited to triads and tetrads.

In contrast, semEP can make predictions using larger complex clusters. We can also exploit the drug-drug or target-target similarities to control the shape of the clusters. Figure 3 illustrates a drug-target interaction network on the left, with three drugs DB01100 (Pimozide), DB01244 (Bepridil), and DB00836 (Loperamide), and eight targets. Drugs DB01100 (Pimozide) and DB01244 (Bepridil) share 6 interactions. A node partition may place these two drugs into one community and place DB00836 (Loperamide) in a second community.

Since semEP is an edge partitioning, it can instead consider more complex communities with an overlap of nodes. The broken (dotted) edges in Figure 3 (left) connect each target to its *least similar* target. A visual inspection of these edges reveals that a split of the targets, with 782, 784, and 785 appearing in one community, while 774, 776, 778, 779, and 8912 are placed in a second community, has the property that no target is placed in a community together with its least similar target. To capture such properties, semEP will consider *edge constraints* as follows: Consider the scenario where targets 784 and 779 have a mutual least-similar-target relationship. Then semEP will guarantee an edge constraint for this pair, i.e., no edge incident to 784 will be placed in the same cluster together with an edge incident to target 779.

Thus, semEP combines the benefit of edge partitioning that allows node overlap in the clusters, and the edge constraints that prohibit (some) pairs of edges to be placed in the same cluster. This accommodates both the semantics of nodes with complex function (node overlap in multiple clusters), and the semantics of separating the edges incident to the least similar pairs of nodes (edge constraints).

Figure 3 (b) shows the two edge communities created by semEP on the right. Community 1 includes drugs DB01100 (Pimozide), DB01244 (Bepridil), and five targets. Community 2 includes those two drugs as well as DB00836 (Loperamide), and has three targets. We note that these communities, with 6 and 7 nodes, respectively, are more complex compared to triads. The predicted drug-target interaction(s) based on these two communities are shown as broken edge(s) in the edge communities on the right. We note that through the use of structured knowledge (edge constraints), edge partitioning and node overlap, semEP predicts an interaction between DB00836 (Loperamide) and target 784.

We summarize the objectives of semEP as follows:

- An edge partitioning that allows the overlap of nodes in multiple clusters; this matches the semantics of complex function associated with nodes.
- Create clusters with high cluster density to improve prediction accuracy.
- Exploit semantic knowledge about the least similar pairs of nodes to identify edge constraints; they will be used to prohibit the placement of incident edges, of the least similar nodes, in the same cluster.
- Balance these competing objectives by creating a minimal number of clusters, each of which has maximal cluster density.

## 3.2   Problem Definition: semEP

The semantics based edge partition problem (semEP) is the minimal partitioning $P$ of the edges of a graph $BG$ such that the aggregate cluster density over all subsets of edges (clusters) $p \in P$ is maximized. We note that a partitioning $P$ of edges may result in the overlap of nodes across different clusters.

**Definition 1 (Cluster (Similarity) Density).** *Consider a labeled bipartite graph $BG=(D \cup T, WE)$. Nodes in $D$ represent a set of drugs and nodes in $T$ represent a set of targets. $WE$ is a set of drug-target interactions, i.e., there is an edge $e = (d,t) \in WE$ iff $Y_{d,t} = 1$. Let $p$ be a subset of interactions of $WE$. Let $D_p \subseteq D$ be the drug set incident on the edges $(d,t) \in p$, and let $T_p \subseteq T$ be the target set incident on the edges $(d,t) \in p$. Let $s_d(i,j)$ represent*

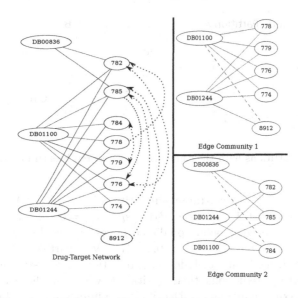

**Fig. 3.** Using Structured Knowledge for semEP. (a) A drug-target interaction network of three drugs DB01100 (Pimozide), DB01244 (Bepridil) and DB00836 (Loperamide), and eight targets. (b) Two edge communities created by semEP. Community 1 includes drugs DB01100 (Pimozide) and DB01244 (Bepridil) and five targets. Community 2 includes all three drugs and has three targets.

*the similarity score between a pair of drugs $i$ and $j \in D_p$. Let $s_t(i,j)$ represent the similarity score between a pair of targets $i$ and $j \in D_t$. Under the condition that $|Dp| > 0 \wedge |Tp| > 0$, the cluster (similarity) density of p cDensity(p) =*
$$\frac{1 + \frac{2*\sum_{i,j \in Dp}[i \neq j]s_d(i,j)}{|Dp|(|Dp|-1)} + \frac{2*\sum_{i,j \in Tp}[i \neq j]s_t(i,j)}{|Tp|(|Tp|-1)}}{3}.$$ *If $|Dp| = 0$, or if $|Tp| = 0$, then we replace the respective fraction by the value 0.*

To explain, the three terms in the numerator correspond to (1) the average score of the interaction edges in $p$, (2) the average drug-drug similarity score between all pairs of drugs in $p$, and (3) the average target-target similarity score between all pairs of targets in $p$, respectively. We note that the score for interactions is given by $Y_{d,t}$ and is an unweighted score of 1.0 for this special case of drug-target interactions. The cluster (similarity) cDensity penalizes singleton clusters or clusters with a singleton drug or target node.

**Definition 2 (The Semantics Based Edge Partition Problem (semEP)).** *Given a labeled bipartite graph $BG=(D \cup T, WE)$ described as before, semEP identifies a (minimal) partition P of WE such that the aggregate cluster density over all subsets $p \in P$ semEP(P) = $\frac{\sum_{p \in P}(cDensity(p))}{|P|}$ is maximal.*

Recall that a solution to semEP corresponds to a partition of the edges where the number of clusters is minimized while the overall cDensity is maximized. We illustrate the impact of these two objectives on drug-target interaction prediction accuracy using the two edge partitions A and B in Figure 4. Consider the

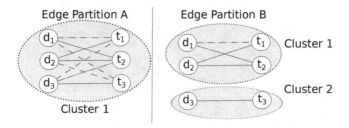

**Fig. 4.** Two partitions with the same cDensity and red broken predicted edges

following drug-drug and target-target similarity scores: $s_d(d_1, d_3) = s_d(d_2, d_3) = s_t(t_1, t_3) = s_t(t_2, t_3) = 0.1$, and $s_d(d_1, d_2) = s_t(t_1, t_2) = 0.4$. Positive interaction edges are black solid edges while predicted edges are red broken edges. Both partitions have the same cDensity of 0.47. However, partition A includes four prediction edges while B only includes one prediction edge. Assuming that these are all true positive predictions, then partition A, which satisfies the two semEP objectives of maximum aggregate cDensity and minimal number of clusters, has the same precision and greater recall, compared to partition B.

**Definition 3 (Edge Constraint).** *Given nodes i and j, let Inc(i) and Inc(j) correspond to the sets of incident edges to i and j, respectively. Given a real number $\theta_d$ or $\theta_t$ in the range $[0 : 1]$ and a similarity score $s_d(i, j) < \theta_d$ or $s_t(i, j) < \theta_t$, then there exists an edge constraint EdgeConstraint(i, j, Inc(i), Inc(j), θ).*

**Property 1 (Edge Constraint).** *Let P be a solution to the semEP. For a given edge constraint EdgeConstraint(i, j, Inc(i), Inc(j), θ) to hold, there can be no cluster p in P such that $e_i \in Inc(i)$ and $e_j \in Inc(j)$ occur in p.*

We map semEP to the Vertex Coloring Graph (VCG) problem. The Vertex Coloring Graph problem assigns a color to every vertex in a graph such that adjacent vertices are colored with different colors and the number of colors is minimized. Each cluster (component) p in the partition P produced by semEP corresponds to a color in the VCG problem. This will ensure that a minimal number of colors will guarantee a minimal partitioning P.

**Definition 4 (Mapping of the Vertex Coloring Problem to the Semantics Based Edge Partition Problem).** *Consider a labeled bipartite graph $BG=(D \cup T, WE)$ and a vertex coloring graph $G=(V, F)$. For each edge or interaction l in WE there is a node $v_i$ in V. Further, there is an edge $l = (v_i, v_j)$ in F, iff there are nodes i and j such that $v_i \in Inc(i)$, $v_j \in Inc(j)$, and Edge-Constraint(i, j, Inc(i),Inc(j), θ)[1] holds. Let P be the (minimal) partition of WE to maximize semEP(P). Let M be a mapping from V to SC, where SC is a set of colors, two vertices from G share the same color if they are in the same partition component p of P and the value cDensity(p) is maximized. The Vertex*

---

[1] There are thresholds $\theta_d$ and $\theta_t$ for drugs and targets, respectively.

*Coloring Problem for BG is to identify M such that the number of colors used in the coloring of the graph G, namely nc(G), is minimized. Given the set Used-Colors of colors in SC that are used in the coloring of the graph, the number of colors corresponds to* $nc(G) = \sum_{cl \in UsedColors}(1 - cDensity(cl))$, *where cDensity(cl) represents the density of the labels of edges from component p in P, from BG, that are colored with the color cl.*

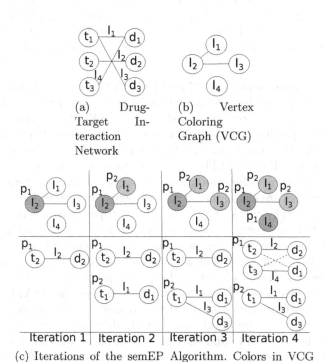

(a) Drug-Target Interaction Network

(b) Vertex Coloring Graph (VCG)

Iteration 1 | Iteration 2 | Iteration 3 | Iteration 4

(c) Iterations of the semEP Algorithm. Colors in VCG correspond to clusters in the interaction network.

**Fig. 5.** Example Iterations of semEP

**Example Iterations of semEP:** Consider the drug-target interaction network of Figure 5(a) with four interactions and the following similar scores: $s_t(t_1, t_2) = 0.1$, $s_t(t_1, t_3) = 0.9$, $s_t(t_2, t_3) = 0.8$, $s_d(d_1, d_2) = 0.75$, $s_d(d_1, d_3) = 0.8$, and $s_d(d_2, d_3) = 0.75$. Consider thresholds $\theta_d = \theta_t = 0.6$ below which pairs of drug or pairs of targets are used to specify edge constraints. Figure 5(b) is the Vertex Coloring Graph (VCG) for the interaction network of Figure 5(a). For example the edge $(I_1, I_2)$ is in VCG because the similarity score $s_t(t_1, t_2)$ of targets $t_1$ and $t_2$ are below the threshold $\theta_t = 0.6$. Figure 5(c) shows the iterations of *semEP*; in each iteration, the figure on the top assigns a color to a node of the VCG while the figure at the bottom places an edge in a cluster. In the first iteration, semEP chooses vertex $I_2$ of the VCG since it has the greatest degree, and assigns color

$p_1$. Simultaneously, the interaction $I$ is placed in the cluster $p_1$. In the second iteration, vertices $I_1$ and $I_3$ have the greatest degree; semEP breaks the tie in favor of $I_1$. Vertex $I_1$ is assigned the color $p_2$ and this creates a new cluster $p_2$ with interaction $I_1$. In the third iteration, the vertex $I_3$ is assigned the feasible color $p_2$; this adds the interaction $T_3$ to cluster $p_2$. In the last iteration, vertex $I_4$ can be colored with $p_1$ or $p_2$; semEP chooses $p_1$ and interaction $I_4$ is placed in cluster $p_1$. The cluster $p_1$ has a cDensity $1 = (1.0 + 0.8 + 0.75)/3 = 0.85$, and cluster $p_2$ has cDensity $= (1.0 + 0.0 + 0.8)/3 = 0.6$; thus, the aggregate cDdensity is $(0.85 + 0.6)/2 = 0.73$. If $I_4$ had instead been placed in $p_2$, the aggregate cDensity would have been lower and $= (0.33 + 0.9)/2 = 0.62$. Figure 5(c) shows the two predicted edges (broken edges) in the fourth iteration.

**An Efficient Implementation of semEP:** VCG is NP-hard [15], and many approximate algorithms have been proposed to solve this problem [23]. semEP extends the well-known approximate algorithm DSATUR [4] to solve VCG to obtain the edge partitions. DSATUR is a greedy iterative algorithm that colors each vertex of the graph once by following a heuristic to choose the colors. Given a graph $G=(V,E)$, DSATUR orders vertices in $V$ dynamically based on the number of different colors assigned to the adjacent vertices of each vertex in $V$, i.e., the vertices are chosen based on the degree of saturation on the partial coloring of the graph built so far. Only colored adjacent nodes are considered. Intuitively, selecting a vertex with the maximum degree of saturation allows one to first color the vertex (vertices) with more restrictions; this is one for which there is a smaller set of colors. Ties are broken based on the vertex degree of the adjacent nodes. As a result of casting the semEP problem to VCG, semEP iteratively adds an edge or interaction to a cluster following the DSATUR heuristic to create clusters that maximize the cluster density. semEP assigns a score to an edge $e$ in *WE* according to the number of edges whose adjacent terms are dissimilar to the terms of $e$, and that have been already assigned to a cluster. Then, edges are chosen in terms of this score (descendant order). Intuitively, selecting an edge with the maximum score, allows semEP to place first the edges with more restrictions; this is one for which there is a smaller set of potential clusters. The selected edge is assigned to the cluster that maximized cDensity. Time complexity of DSATUR is $O(|V|^3)$, thus semEP is $O(|WE|^3)$.

## 4   Related Work

We briefly compare with research in graph data mining, link prediction, clustering, community detection and ranking. Graph data mining [7] covers a broad range of methods dealing with the identification of (sub)structures and patterns in graphs; state-of-the-art approaches include spectral graph clustering [26], RankClus [24], and GNetMine [13]. Spectral graph clustering relies on an unnormalized Laplacian graph representation of a homogeneous network to cluster the graph based on information encoded in its eigenvectors [26]. RankClus [24] and GNetMine [13] interleave link analysis-based ranking with clustering to place highly ranked entities in highly ranked clusters. These approaches focus on the use of graph properties to partition the graph.

The problem of dealing with multiple types of similarity scores has been modeled as follows: Perform *simultaneous clustering* with multiple heterogeneous networks over an identical set of nodes; the complexity has been shown to be as hard as the *k densest subgraphs* problem [18]. JointCluster [19] is a simultaneous clustering or partition of the nodes such that nodes within each set or cluster in the partition are well connected in each graph, and the total cost of inter-cluster edges (edges with endpoints in different clusters) is low. Khuller et al. presented one of the earliest solutions to a related *K-Center* problem [2].

There has been significant work on community detection [1,9,20,22]; multiple approaches have been identified as follows: [9]: *i*) topology-based techniques that consider network structure; *ii*) topic-based approaches that rely on textual information within nodes; *iii*) hybrid solutions that combine topology- and topic-based approaches. The majority of existing techniques focus on partitioning nodes rather than edge partitioning. Similar to semEP, Ahn et al. [1] introduce a partition density function based on the similarity of nodes; they detect communities that maximize partition density using optimization methods. This may produce a large number of communities, unlike semEP that produces a minimal number. Ereteo et al. [10] tackle the problem of a semantic social network and propose a topology- and topic-based algorithm, SemTagP, to detect communities from the RDF representation of social networks. Osborne et al. [20] present Temporal Semantic Topic-Based Clustering (TST); it uses similarity between research trajectories and a Fuzzy C-Means algorithm.

Ding et al. [8] provides a comprehensive survey of similarity-based machine learning approaches for drug-target interaction prediction. Several machine learning techniques have been evaluated [11,21,28,29]. Approaches presented by Zheng et al. [29] and Perlman et al. [21] consider feature engineering over multiple similarity features. A PSL based solution [11] directly considers multi-relational structured knowledge and learns from multiple similarity metrics.

# 5    Evaluation of semEP and State-of-the-Art Methods

## 5.1    Dataset and Evaluation Protocol

**Dataset:** A well known dataset of over 900 drugs, almost 1,000 targets, and over 5,000 interactions [3] has been used by Ding et al. to compare several state-of-the-art machine learning based interaction prediction methods [8]. This dataset provides a drug-drug chemical similarity score based on the hashed fingerprints from the SMILES resource, and a target-target similarity score based on the normalized Smith-Waterman sequence similarity score. The targets belong to the following four groups: Nuclear receptors, Gprotein-coupled receptors (GPCRs), Ion channels and Enzymes. Dataset statistics are reported in Table 1.

A 10-fold cross validation will randomly select 90% of positive and negative interactions as *training data*, and will use the remaining 10% of elements as *test data*, for each of the four groups of targets in the dataset.

**Table 1.** Statistics for the Drug-Target Interaction Dataset [3]

| Statistics | Nuclear receptor | GPCR | Ion channel | Enzyme |
|---|---|---|---|---|
| Number of drugs | 54 | 223 | 210 | 445 |
| Number of targets | 26 | 95 | 204 | 664 |
| Number of drug target interactions | 90 | 635 | 1,476 | 2,926 |
| Average interaction count per target | 3.46 | 6.68 | 7.23 | 4.4 |
| Average interaction count per drug | 1.66 | 2.84 | 7.02 | 6.57 |
| Graph Density[2] | 0.028 | 0.013 | 0.017 | 0.005 |

**semEP Prediction:** Recall that Y is a binary matrix where $Y_{i,j} = 1$ if drug $d_i$ interacts with target $t_j$ and $F_{i,j}$ is the score or probability of the prediction. Since semEP is not a machine learning method, it works as follows: We represent the training data from $Y$ as a bipartite graph and apply edge partitioning. Table 2 shows the values of the thresholds $\theta_d$ and $\theta_t$ used to specify edge constraints in Definition 1. For a selected cluster $p$, all missing interactions are assigned to be positive interactions in $Y$. The $F_{i,j}$ score assigned to the interactions in $p$ is the normalized graph density $= \frac{|I|}{|D_p|*|T_p|}$, where $|I|$, $|D_p|$ and $|T_p|$ are the cardinalities of the interactions, drugs and targets in $p$, respectively. We label this density as the interaction prediction density or $iDensity$.

**Table 2.** Score threshold $\theta_d$ and $\theta_t$ for edge constraints in Definition 1

| Threshold | Nuclear receptor | GPCR | Ion channel | Enzyme |
|---|---|---|---|---|
| $\theta_d$ | 0.3421 | 0.2759 | 0.2619 | 0.2333 |
| $\theta_t$ | 0.1832 | 0.1416 | 0.1355 | 0.0209 |

**State-of-the-Art Methods:** We used the code and results from multiple machine learning based prediction methods that are available as supplemental material to the research reported in [8]. Due to space limitations, we simply label and name all the methods as follows: i) BLM: Bipartite Local Method [6]; ii) LapRLS: Laplacian Regularized Least Squares [27]; iii) GIP: Gaussian Interaction Profile [25]; iv) KBMF2K: Kernelized Bayesian Matrix Factorization with twin Kernels [12]; and v) NBI: Network-Based Inference [6].

## 5.2   Results

First, we demonstrate the benefits of using semEP predictions to improve the performance of the prediction methods in [8]. We then validate the best *novel* predictions of all the methods against the STITCH drug-target interaction resource [17].

**Using semEP to Improve Performance:** To measure the impact of semEP predictions on the performance of the methods, we enhance the (initial) interaction prediction matrix $Y$ of each method, over the hold-out test data, with the best predicted interactions of semEP. The best predictions of semEP are those with an $iDensity$ prediction score equal or greater than a 0.5 threshold.

---

[2] Graph Density is defined as $\frac{2\times\#Edges}{\#Nodes\times(\#Nodes-1)}$.

Further, we limit the added predictions to be no more than 30% of the positive interactions in the holdout set. We label this matrix $Y_{semEP}$. We also create a control binary matrix $Y_{cntrl}$ which enhances the initial predictions of each method, $Y$ with $K$ interactions, where $K$ corresponds to the cardinality of the added predictions in $Y_{semEP}$. The entries in $Y_{i,j} = 0$ are randomly chosen (K times) without replacement, following a uniform distribution, to create $Y_{cntrl}$.

We use the metrics Area Under the Curve (AUC) for precision, and Area Under the Precision-Recall curve (AUPR) for the trade-off between precision and recall. Table 3 reports on the AUC and AUPR of each machine learning method $Y$, the performance when using semEP predictions, $Y_{semEP}$, and the control predictions $Y_{cntrl}$, for each of the four target groups.

The AUC for the methods are generally high, representing the robust performance of these methods. Despite this high baseline, $Y_{semEP}$ is able to improve the performance for all of the methods, for all of the target groups. We also observe that the performance of $Y_{cntrl}$ degrades for all of the methods, for all of the target groups.

The impact of $Y_{semEP}$ is noteworthy when considering the AUPR; these values are somewhat low in general, for all methods, reflecting the sparse training data. Again, we observe a major improvement of AUPR, for all of the methods, for all of the target groups. In addition, there is a sharp decrease of performance of $Y_{cntrl}$ for all of the methods / target groups.

**Table 3.** 10-fold cross validation AUC and AUPR for methods in [8]. $Y$ is the state-of-the-art method; $Y_{semEP}$ is the semEP enhancement; $Y_{cntrl}$ is the random control.

| | AUC | | | | | | | | | | | |
|---|---|---|---|---|---|---|---|---|---|---|---|---|
| **Method** | **Nuclear receptor** | | | **GPCR** | | | **Ion channel** | | | **Enzyme** | | |
| | $Y$ | $Y_{semEP}$ | $Y_{cntrl}$ | $Y$ | $Y_{semEP}$ | $Y_{cntrl}$ | $Y$ | $Y_{semEP}$ | $Y_{cntrl}$ | $Y$ | $Y_{semEP}$ | $Y_{cntrl}$ |
| BLM | 0.724 | 0.778 | 0.665 | 0.888 | 0.911 | 0.798 | 0.920 | 0.929 | 0.879 | 0.929 | 0.935 | 0.838 |
| NBI | 0.690 | 0.825 | 0.670 | 0.833 | 0.900 | 0.769 | 0.925 | 0.947 | 0.888 | 0.895 | 0.915 | 0.810 |
| GIP | 0.861 | 0.895 | 0.803 | 0.943 | 0.958 | 0.843 | 0.975 | 0.981 | 0.932 | 0.968 | 0.973 | 0.874 |
| LapRLS | 0.848 | 0.877 | 0.799 | 0.941 | 0.956 | 0.844 | 0.967 | 0.972 | 0.925 | 0.962 | 0.966 | 0.868 |
| KBMF2K | 0.876 | 0.914 | 0.822 | 0.939 | 0.960 | 0.845 | 0.981 | 0.985 | 0.936 | 0.967 | 0.971 | 0.869 |
| | **AUPR** | | | | | | | | | | | |
| **Method** | **Nuclear receptor** | | | **GPCR** | | | **Ion channel** | | | **Enzyme** | | |
| | $Y$ | $Y_{semEP}$ | $Y_{cntrl}$ | $Y$ | $Y_{semEP}$ | $Y_{cntrl}$ | $Y$ | $Y_{semEP}$ | $Y_{cntrl}$ | $Y$ | $Y_{semEP}$ | $Y_{cntrl}$ |
| BLM | 0.242 | 0.369 | 0.238 | 0.472 | 0.481 | 0.327 | 0.599 | 0.622 | 0.542 | 0.499 | 0.537 | 0.373 |
| NBI | 0.465 | 0.682 | 0.342 | 0.615 | 0.719 | 0.467 | 0.829 | 0.854 | 0.744 | 0.786 | 0.818 | 0.616 |
| GIP | 0.657 | 0.749 | 0.520 | 0.705 | 0.764 | 0.563 | 0.888 | 0.897 | 0.813 | 0.869 | 0.878 | 0.700 |
| LapRLS | 0.577 | 0.676 | 0.468 | 0.630 | 0.704 | 0.517 | 0.800 | 0.818 | 0.733 | 0.830 | 0.838 | 0.663 |
| KBMF2K | 0.557 | 0.725 | 0.475 | 0.673 | 0.760 | 0.544 | 0.879 | 0.891 | 0.810 | 0.796 | 0.822 | 0.656 |

To further explore the benefit of the semEP predictions, Table 4 compares the overlap of the Top 10 positive predictions in $Y_{semEP}$ and the Top 10 positive predictions of each method in $Y$. The overlap (equal count) is remarkably low, across all methods, and across all target groups. These results suggest that the interactions predicted by semEP are both *accurate and diverse*, compared to the range of state-of-the-art machine learning based prediction methods. The diversity explains the major impact on AUPR by $Y_{semEP}$ and the potential for semEP to exploit structured knowledge in the relevant semantic space(s).

**Table 4.** Overlap of Top 10 predictions of semEP and each of the methods in [8]. Entries highlighted in bold are cases where predictions are all different.

|  | Nuclear receptor | | GPCR | | Ion channel | | Enzyme | |
|--------|-------|-----------|-------|-----------|-------|-----------|-------|-----------|
| Method | Equal | Different | Equal | Different | Equal | Different | Equal | Different |
| BLM    | 1 | 9  | 0 | 10 | 0 | 10 | 0 | 10 |
| NBI    | 0 | 10 | 1 | 9  | 0 | 10 | 0 | 10 |
| GIP    | 2 | 8  | 1 | 9  | 0 | 10 | 3 | 7  |
| LapRLS | 4 | 6  | 1 | 9  | 0 | 10 | 2 | 8  |
| KBMF2K | 4 | 6  | 0 | 10 | 0 | 10 | 0 | 10 |

**Validation Using STITCH:** We validated the Top 5 *novel* predicted interactions of all methods; novel interactions are those with $Y_{i,j} = 0$ in the hold-out test dataset. The validation was performed against the latest online version of the STITCH [17] drug target interaction portal[3]. Table 5 reports on the number of validated novel predictions. We observe that as before, semEP is able to identify validated novel interactions across all target groups and it identifies the highest number of validated novel interactions for the target groups of GPCRs and Enzymes. We note that the graphs of GPCRs and Enzymes are sparser than the other two graphs (see Graph Density in Table 1). This provides few opportunities for learning in the training data. Nevertheless, semEP can exploit structured knowledge, edge partitioning and node overlap, to make accurate and diverse predictions, even in this sparse learning environment.

**Table 5.** Top 5 novel interactions manually validated with STITCH. Entries highlighted in bold correspond to the largest number of novel validations.

| Method | Nuclear receptor | GPCR | Ion channel | Enzyme |
|--------|------------------|------|-------------|--------|
| semEP  | 4 | **5** | 1 | **4** |
| BLM    | 2 | 1 | 0 | 0 |
| NBI    | 1 | 1 | 1 | 2 |
| GIP    | 3 | 3 | 1 | 1 |
| LapRLS | **5** | 3 | 2 | 2 |
| KBMF2K | 3 | 4 | 2 | 2 |

# 6   Conclusions and Future Work

We defined the semEP problem to create a minimal partitioning of drug-target interaction edges such that the cluster density of each subset of interaction edges is maximal. We map the semEP problem to the Vertex Coloring Graph problem using *Edge Constraints*. semEP combines the benefits of edge partitioning and edge constraints (incident to the least similar drug-drug or target-target pairs) to identify communities. We conducted an extensive evaluation of semEP on a well-known dataset of drug-target interactions. The results suggest that semEP exploits structured knowledge from semantically annotated data, and is clearly able to predict novel interactions and enhance the performance of sophisticated machine learning methods.

---

[3] http://stitch.embl.de/

In future work, we will explore the use of semEP to identify interesting clusters, and combine / compare with the structure learning of the PSL-based method [11]. We will also apply semEP to other domains, e.g., citation graphs, to identify topical and to predict future relationships between researchers.

**Acknowledgement.** This research has been partially supported by NSF grant 1147144 and DID-USB. We thank Shobeir Fakhraei and Shanfeng Zhu for providing access to the datasets and algorithms that were evaluated in this paper and Shobeir for valuable feedback.

# References

1. Ahn, Y.-Y., Bagrow, J.P., Lehmann, S.: Link communities reveal multiscale complexity in networks. Nature 466(7307), 761–764 (2010)
2. Bhatia, R., Guha, S., Khuller, S., Sussmann, Y.: Facility location with dynamic distance functions. Journal of Combinatorial Optimization 2(3), 199–217 (1998)
3. Bleakley, K., Yamanishi, Y.: Supervised prediction of drug–target interactions using bipartite local models. Bioinformatics 25(18), 2397–2403 (2009)
4. Brélaz, D.: New methods to color vertices of a graph. Commun. ACM 22(4), 251–256 (1979)
5. Broecheler, M., Mihalkova, L., Getoor, L.: Probabilistic similarity logic. In: Conference on Uncertainty in Artificial Intelligence (2010)
6. Cheng, F., Liu, C., Jiang, J., Lu, W., Li, W., Liu, G., Zhou, W., Huang, J., Tang, Y.: Prediction of drug-target interactions and drug repositioning via network-based inference. PLoS Computational Biology 8(5), e1002503 (2012)
7. Cook, D.J., Holder, L.B.: Mining graph data. Wiley-Blackwell (2007)
8. Ding, H., Takigawa, I., Mamitsuka, H., Zhu, S.: Similarity-based machine learning methods for predicting drug-target interactions: A brief review. Briefings in Bioinformatics (2013)
9. Ding, Y.: Community detection: Topological vs. topical. Journal of Infometrics 5(4), 498–514 (2011)
10. Erétéo, G., Gandon, F., Buffa, M.: Semtagp: semantic community detection in folksonomies. In: 2011 IEEE/WIC/ACM International Conference on Web Intelligence and Intelligent Agent Technology (WI-IAT), vol. 1, pp. 324–331. IEEE (2011)
11. Fakhraei, S., Huang, B., Raschid, L., Getoor, L.: Network-based drug-target interaction prediction with probabilistic soft logic. In: IEEE/ACM Transactions on Computational Biology and Bioinformatics (2014)
12. Gönen, M.: Predicting drug–target interactions from chemical and genomic kernels using bayesian matrix factorization. Bioinformatics 28(18), 2304–2310 (2012)
13. Ji, M., Sun, Y., Danilevsky, M., Han, J., Gao, J.: Graph regularized transductive classification on heterogeneous information networks. In: Balcázar, J.L., Bonchi, F., Gionis, A., Sebag, M. (eds.) ECML PKDD 2010, Part I. LNCS, vol. 6321, pp. 570–586. Springer, Heidelberg (2010)
14. Jiang, G., Solbrig, H.R., Chute, C.G.: Adepedia: a scalable and standardized knowledge base of adverse drug events using semantic web technology. In: AMIA Annual Symposium Proceedings (2011)
15. Karp, R.: Reducibility among combinatorial problems. In: Miller, R., Thatcher, J. (eds.) Complexity of Computer Computations, pp. 85–103. Plenum Press (1972)

16. Kuhn, M., Campillos, M., Letunic, I., Jensen, L.J., Bork, P.: A side effect resource to capture phenotypic effects of drugs. Molecular Systems Biology 6(1) (2010)

17. Kuhn, M., Szklarczyk, D., Franceschini, A., von Mering, C., Jensen, L.J., Bork, P.: Stitch 3: zooming in on protein–chemical interactions. Nucleic Acids Research 40(D1), D876–D880 (2012)

18. Li, Z., Narayanan, M., Vetta, A.: The complexity of the simultaneous cluster problem. Journal of Graph Algorithms and Applications (2014)

19. Narayanan, M., Vetta, A., Schadt, E.E., Zhu, J.: Simultaneous clustering of multiple gene expression and physical interaction datasets. PLoS Computational Biology 6(4) (2010)

20. Osborne, F., Scavo, G., Motta, E.: Identifying diachronic topic-based research communities by clustering shared research trajectories. In: Presutti, V., d'Amato, C., Gandon, F., d'Aquin, M., Staab, S., Tordai, A. (eds.) ESWC 2014. LNCS, vol. 8465, pp. 114–129. Springer, Heidelberg (2014)

21. Perlman, L., Gottlieb, A., Atias, N., Ruppin, E., Sharan, R.: Combining drug and gene similarity measures for drug-target elucidation. Journal of Computational Biology 18(2), 133–145 (2011)

22. Porter, M.A., Onnela, J.-P., Mucha, P.J.: Communities in networks. Notices of the AMS 56(9), 1082–1097 (2009)

23. Segundo, P.S.: A new dsatur-based algorithm for exact vertex coloring. Computers & OR 39(7), 1724–1733 (2012)

24. Sun, Y., Han, J., Zhao, P., Yin, Z., Cheng, H., Wu, T.: Rankclus: integrating clustering with ranking for heterogeneous information network analysis. In: Proceedings of the 12th EDBT. ACM (2009)

25. van Laarhoven, T., Nabuurs, S.B., Marchiori, E.: Gaussian interaction profile kernels for predicting drug–target interaction. Bioinformatics 27(21) (2011)

26. Von Luxburg, U.: A tutorial on spectral clustering. Statistics and Computing 17(4), 395–416 (2007)

27. Xia, Z., Wu, L.-Y., Zhou, X., Wong, S.T.: Semi-supervised drug-protein interaction prediction from heterogeneous biological spaces. BMC Systems Biology 4(suppl. 2), S6 (2010)

28. Yamanishi, Y., Araki, M., Gutteridge, A., Honda, W., Minoru Kanehisa, M.: Prediction of drug-target interaction networks from the integration of chemical and genomic spaces. Bioinformatics 24(13), i232–i240 (2008)

29. Zheng, X., Ding, H., Mamitsuka, H., Zhu, S.: Collaborative matrix factorization with multiple similarities for predicting drug-target interactions. In: KDD, pp. 1025–1033 (2013)

# SYRql: A Dataflow Language for Large Scale Processing of RDF Data

Fadi Maali[1], Padmashree Ravindra[2], Kemafor Anyanwu[2], and Stefan Decker[1]

[1] Insight Centre for Data Analytics, National University of Ireland Galway
{fadi.maali,stefan.decker}@insight-centre.org
[2] Department of Computer Science, North Carolina State University, Raleigh, NC
{pravind2,kogan}@ncsu.edu

**Abstract.** The recent big data movement resulted in a surge of activity on layering declarative languages on top of distributed computation platforms. In the Semantic Web realm, this surge of analytics languages was not reflected despite the significant growth in the available RDF data. Consequently, when analysing large RDF datasets, users are left with two main options: using SPARQL or using an existing non-RDF-specific big data language, both with its own limitations. The pure declarative nature of SPARQL and the high cost of evaluation can be limiting in some scenarios. On the other hand, existing big data languages are designed mainly for tabular data and, therefore, applying them to RDF data results in verbose, unreadable, and sometimes inefficient scripts. In this paper, we introduce *SYRql*, a dataflow language designed to process RDF data at a large scale. SYRql blends concepts from both SPARQL and existing big data languages. We formally define a closed algebra that underlies SYRql and discuss its properties and some unique optimisation opportunities this algebra provides. Furthermore, we describe an implementation that translates SYRql scripts into a series of MapReduce jobs and compare the performance to other big data processing languages.

## 1 Introduction

Declarative query languages have been a corner stone of data management since the early days of relational databases. The initial proposal of relational algebra and relational calculus by Codd [8] was shortly followed by other languages such as SEQUEL [7] (predecessor of SQL) and QUEL [34]. Declarative languages simplified programming and reduced the cost of creation, maintenance, and modification of software. They also helped bringing the non-professional user into effective communication with a database. Database languages design continued to be an active area of research and innovation. In 2008, the Claremont Report on Database Research identified declarative programming as one of the main research opportunities in the data management field [2].

There is, indeed, a large number of examples of publications describing design and implementation of query languages that embed queries in general purpose programming languages [19,37,30], for semi-strucutred data [25,1], for Semantic

P. Mika et al. (Eds.) ISWC 2014, Part I, LNCS 8796, pp. 147–163, 2014.

Web data [12,3], for graphs [6,17] and for network analysis [10,27,26] to name a few. Furthermore, the recent big data movement resulted in a surge of activity on layering declarative languages on top of distributed computation platforms. Examples include PIG Latin from Yahoo [20], DryadLINQ from Microsoft [39], Jaql from IBM [4], HiveQL [35] from Facebook and Meteor/Sopremo [13]. This paper focuses on declarative languages for large Semantic Web data represented in RDF.

In fact, there has been a significant growth in the available RDF data and distributed systems have been utilised to support larg-scale processing of the RDF data [36,15,16]. Nevertheless, the surge of analytics languages was not reflected in the Semantic Web realm. To analyse large RDF datasets, users are left mainly with two options: using SPARQL [12] or using an existing non-RDF-specific big data language.

SPARQL is a graph pattern matching language that provides rich capabilities for slicing and dicing RDF data. The latest version, SPARQL 1.1, supports also aggregation and nested queries. Nevertheless, the pure declarative nature of SPARQL obligates a user to express their needs in a single query. This can be unnatural for some programmers and challenging for complex needs [18,11]. Furthermore, SPARQL evaluation is known to be costly [22,29].

The other alternative of using an existing big data language such as Pig Latin or HiveQL has also its own limitations. These languages were designed for tabular data mainly, and, consequently, using them with RDF data commonly results in verbose, unreadable, and sometimes inefficient scripts. For instance, listings 1.1 and 1.2 show a basic SPARQL graph pattern and an equivalent Pig Latin script, respectively. Listing 1.2 has double the number of lines compared to listing 1.1 and is, arguably, harder to read and understand.

**Listing 1.1.** SPARQL basic pattern

```
?prod a :ProductType .
?r :reviewFor ?prod .
?r :reviewer ?rev
```

**Listing 1.2.** Corresponding Pig Latin script

```
rdf = LOAD 'data' USING PigStorage(' ') AS (S,P,O);
SPLIT rdf INTO reviewers IF P = ':reviewer',
          reviews IF P = ':reviewFor',
          prods IF P = 'a' and O = 'ProductType';
tmp1 = JOIN prods BY S, reviews BY O;
tmp2 = JOIN tmp BY reviews::S, reviewers BY S;
```

In this paper we present SYRql, a declarative dataflow language that focuses on the analysis of large-scale RDF data. Similar to other big data processing languages, SYRql defines a small set of basic operators that are amenable to parallelisation and supports extensibility via user-defined custom code. On the other hand, SYRql adopts a graph-based data model and supports pattern matching as in SPARQL.

SYRql could not be based on SPARQL Algebra [22] as this algebra is not fully composable. The current SPARQL algebra transitions from graphs (i.e. the initial inputs) to sets of bindings (which are basically tables resulting from pattern matching). Subsequently, further operators such as Join, Filter, and Union are applied on sets of bindings. In other words, the flow is partly "hard-coded" in the SPARQL algebra and a user cannot, for instance, apply a pattern matching on the results of another pattern matching or "join" two graphs. In a dataflow language, the dataflow is guided by the user and cannot be limited to the way SPARQL imposes. We, therefore, define a new algebra that underpins the SYRql language. In particular, this paper provides the following contributions:

- We define the syntax and semantics of a compositional RDF algebra (sections 2.2). The algebra achieves composability by always pairing graphs and bindings together. We relate the defined algebra to SPARQL algebra (section 2.3) and report some of its unique properties that can be useful for optimising evaluation (section 2.4).
- We describe SYRql, a dataflow language based on the defined algebra (section 3.1). An open source implementation of SYRql that translates scripts into a series of MapReduce jobs is also described (section 3.2).
- We present a translation of an existing SPARQL benchmark into a number of popular big data languages (namely Jaql, HiveQL, and Pig Latin). The performance of equivalent SYRql scripts is compared with the other big data languages (section 4). The comparable results that SYRql implementation showed are encouraging giving its recency relative to the compared languages. Nevertheless, a number of improvements are still needed to ensure a good competitiveness of SYRql.

## 2   RDF Algebra

The goal of this algebra is to define operators similar to those defined in SPARQL algebra but that are fully composable. To achieve such composability, the algebra operators input and output are always a pair of a graph and a corresponding table. We next provide the formal definitions and description.

### 2.1   Preliminaries

We use $\mathbb{N}$ to denote the set of all natural numbers. We assume the existence of two disjoint infinite sets: $\mathcal{U}$ (URIs) and $\mathcal{L}$ (literals). The set of all terms is denoted by $\mathcal{T}$ (i.e. $\mathcal{T} = \mathcal{U} \bigcup \mathcal{L}$). We also assume that both $\mathcal{U}$ and $\mathcal{L}$ are disjoint from $\mathbb{N}$. An RDF triple[1] is a triple $(s, p, o) \in \mathcal{U} \times \mathcal{U} \times \mathcal{T}$. In this triple, $s$ is the subject, $p$ is the predicate and $o$ is the object. An RDF graph is a set of RDF triples. We use $\mathcal{G}$ to refer to the set of all RDF graphs. Furthermore, we assume the existence of the symbol '?' such that $? \notin \mathcal{T}$ and define a triple pattern as any triple in $(\mathcal{T} \bigcup \{?\}) \times (\mathcal{T} \bigcup \{?\}) \times (\mathcal{T} \bigcup \{?\})$.

**Definition 1.** *A binding is a sequence of RDF terms (URIs or literals).*

Bindings are used to represent results of some operator over RDF graphs. Notice that our notion of binding is similar to that of SPARQL. However, in SPARQL a binding is a function that maps variable names to values. Our definition of binding obviates the need for variable names by using an ordered

---

[1] We only consider *ground* RDF graphs and therefore we do not consider blank nodes.

sequence. A common way to represent a set of bindings is by using a table. We use subscript to access binding elements based on their position in the sequence (i.e. The *ith* element of a binding $S$ is $S_i$). The length of a binding $S$ is denoted as $|S|$ and the empty binding is denoted as () (notice that $|()| = 0$).

The concatenation of two bindings $S = (a_1, a_2, ..., a_n)$ and $T = (b_1, b_2, ..., b_m)$ is the binding $(a_1, a_2, ..., a_n, b_1, b_2, ..., b_m)$. We denote concatenation by a dot (i.e. $S \cdot T$).

## 2.2    RDF Algebra Expressions

**Syntax.** An RDF expression $e$ is defined inductively as follows:

1. **Atomic:** if $g$ is an RDF graph (i.e. $g \in \mathcal{G}$) then $g$ is an RDF expression.
2. **Projection:** if $e$ is an RDF expression and $(a_1, ..., a_n)$ is a sequence of natural numbers, then $(e|_{(a_1,...,a_n)})$ is an RDF expression. For example $(e|_{(4,2)})$ is a projection RDF expression.
3. **Extending bindings:** if $e$ is an RDF expression, $h$ is an n-ary function that takes $n$ RDF terms and produces an RDF term (i.e. $h : \mathcal{T}^n \to \mathcal{T}$) and $a_1, ..., a_n$ is a sequence of natural numbers then
   $(e \oplus_{(a_1,...,a_n)} h)$ is also an RDF expression.
4. **Extending graphs:** if $e$ is an RDF expression, $a_1, a_2, a_3$ are three natural numbers or RDF terms (i.e. $a_1, a_2, a_3 \in \mathcal{T} \bigcup \mathbb{N}$) then
   $(e \oplus (a_1, a_2, a_3))$ is also an RDF expression.
5. **Triple pattern matching:** If $e$ is an RDF expression and $t$ is a triple pattern then $(e[t])$ is also an RDF expression.
6. **Filtering:** if $e$ is an RDF expression, $a, b \in \mathbb{N}$ and $u, v \in T$ then the following are valid RDF expressions:
   $(e[\, a \, \theta \, b\,])$, $(e[\, a \, \theta \, u\,])$ and $(e[\, u \, \theta \, v\,])$
   Where $\theta$ is $=$, $\neq$, $<$ or $\leq$. For example, $(e[\, 1 \leq 2\,])$ and $(e[\, 1 = \text{"label"}\,])$ are two filtering RDF Expressions.
7. **Cross product:** if $e_1$ and $e_2$ are RDF expressions, then so is $(e_1 \times e_2)$.
8. **Aggregation:** we define aggregate functions that take a set of terms and return a single value[2]. Therefore, the signature of an aggregate function is $f : 2^T \to \mathbb{N}$. If $e$ is an RDF expression, $a$ and $b$ are two natural numbers and $f$ is an aggregate function then $(e \langle a, f, b \rangle)$ is an RDF expression.

**Semantics.** We now define the semantics of the previous expressions. For each expression $e$ the value of it is denoted as $[\![e]\!]$. The value is always a set of pairs of a graph and a binding. The graph and binding components of $[\![e]\!]$ are, respectively, denoted as $[\![e]\!].g$ and $[\![e]\!].b$. To depict the values in this paper, we denote each pair by drawing a graph and a table close to each other. The table represents a binding and uses the order of elements in the binding as columns headers. The set of pairs that constitute an expression value are surrounded by curly brackets.

---

[2] For simplicity of the presentation here, we restrict aggregate functions to those that take a set of single values and return an integer. Generalising this is straightforward.

In the figures, sub-figure *(a)* is the input while sub-figure *(b)* shows the result of applying an operator to the input (see figure 1 for an example).

1. **Atomic:** $[\![g]\!] = \{(g, ())\}$
   The value of an atomic expression gives an empty binding.
2. **Projection:** $[\![(e|_{(a_1,...,a_n)})]\!] = \{(g, S) \,|\, (g, S') \in [\![e]\!], S = (S'_{a_1}, ..., S'_{a_n})\}$

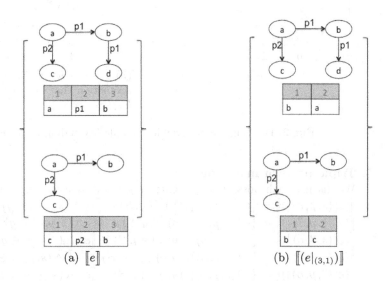

(a) $[\![e]\!]$        (b) $[\![(e|_{(3,1)})]\!]$

**Fig. 1.** Projection example

Projection allows choosing a sub-sequence of the bindings while leaves the graph component in each pair unaffected. Figure 1 provides an example of a projection expression value.

3. **Extending bindings:**

$$[\![(e \oplus_{(a_1,...,a_n)} h)]\!] = \{(g, S \cdot (h(S_{a_1}, ..., S_{a_n}))) \,|\, (g, S) \in [\![e]\!]\}$$

These expressions allow extending the binding with a new value that is calculated based on existing values in the binding. See Figure 2 for an example. Notice that $h$ can be viewed as a Skolem function arising from the quantification $\forall S_{a_1} \forall S_{a_2} ... \forall S_{a_n} \exists c : c = h(S_{a_1}, ..., S_{a_n})$

4. **Extending graphs:** We use the convention that $S_a = a$ for some binding $S$ and a term $a \in \mathcal{T}$. Notice that $\mathcal{T}$ and $\mathbb{N}$ are disjoint and therefore the previous convention does not cause any ambiguity.
   $$[\![(e \oplus (a_1, a_2, a_3))]\!] = \{(g \bigcup \{(S_{a_1}, S_{a_2}, S_{a_3})\}, S) \,|\, (g, S) \in [\![e]\!]\}$$
   These expressions are similar to the extending bindings expressions defined before but they allow extending the graph. An example evaluation of such expression can be seen in Figure 3.

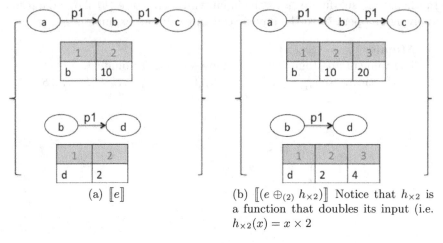

(a) $[\![e]\!]$      (b) $[\![(e \oplus_{(2)} h_{\times 2})]\!]$ Notice that $h_{\times 2}$ is a function that doubles its input (i.e. $h_{\times 2}(x) = x \times 2$

**Fig. 2.** Defining a new variable example (extending bindings)

5. **Triple pattern matching:**

We discuss each possible triple pattern separately assuming $s, p, o \in \mathcal{T}$

$$[\![(e[\,(s,p,o)\,])]\!] = \{(\,\{(s,p,o)\}, (\,)\,) \mid \exists(g,S) \in [\![e]\!] \wedge (s,p,o) \in g\}$$
$$[\![(e[\,(s,p,?)\,])]\!] = \{(\,\{(s,p,o)\}, (o)\, \mid \exists(g,S) \in [\![e]\!] \wedge (s,p,o) \in g\}$$
$$[\![(e[\,(s,?,o)\,])]\!] = \{(\,\{(s,p,o)\}, (p)\,) \mid \exists(g,S) \in [\![e]\!] \wedge (s,p,o) \in g\}$$
$$[\![(e[\,(s,?,?)\,])]\!] = \{(\,\{(s,p,o)\}, (p,o)\,) \mid \exists(g,S) \in [\![e]\!] \wedge (s,p,o) \in g\}$$
$$[\![(e[\,(?,p,o)\,])]\!] = \{(\,\{(s,p,o)\}, (s)\,) \mid \exists(g,S) \in [\![e]\!] \wedge (s,p,o) \in g\}$$
$$[\![(e[\,(?,p,?)\,])]\!] = \{(\,\{(s,p,o)\}, (s,o)\,) \mid \exists(g,S) \in [\![e]\!] \wedge (s,p,o) \in g\}$$
$$[\![(e[\,(?,?,o)\,])]\!] = \{(\,\{(s,p,o)\}, (s,p)\,) \mid \exists(g,S) \in [\![e]\!] \wedge (s,p,o) \in g\}$$
$$[\![(e[\,(?,?,?)\,])]\!] = \{(\,\{(s,p,o)\}, (s,p,o)\,) \mid \exists(g,S) \in [\![e]\!] \wedge (s,p,o) \in g\}$$

Triple pattern matching expressions filter graphs to only triples matching the provided pattern and introduces the corresponding bindings. A key difference from SPARQL pattern evaluation is retaining the matching triples in addition to the bindings. Figure 4 shows an example. Notice that a triple pattern matching expression yields a graph with only one triple and eliminates previous bindings. Notice also that one can still apply further pattern matching on the results, something that is not possible in SPARQL.

6. **Filtering:**

$$[\![(e[\,a\,\theta\,b\,])]\!] = \{(g,S) \in [\![e]\!] \mid S_a\,\theta\,S_b\}$$
$$[\![(e[\,a\,\theta\,u\,])]\!] = \{(g,S) \in [\![e]\!] \mid S_a\,\theta\,u\}$$
$$[\![(e[\,u\,\theta\,v\,])]\!] = \begin{cases} [\![e]\!] & \text{if } u\,\theta\,v \\ \phi & \text{Otherwise} \end{cases}$$

7. **Cross product:**

$$[\![(e_1 \times e_2)]\!] = \{(g_1 \cup g_2, S\,.\,T) \mid (g_1,S) \in [\![e_1]\!] \wedge (g_2,T) \in [\![e_2]\!]\}$$

See figure 5 for an example.

8. **Aggregation:**

the expression $(e\,\langle a, f, b\rangle)$ groups by the $a^{th}$ element in the binding, then

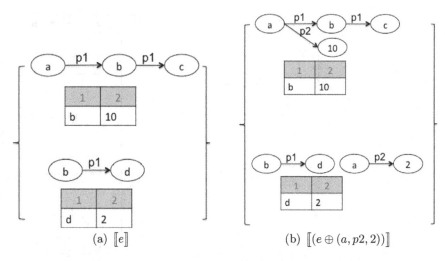

(a) $\llbracket e \rrbracket$                    (b) $\llbracket (e \oplus (a, p2, 2)) \rrbracket$

**Fig. 3.** Defining a new triple (extending graphs)

apply the aggregate function $f$ on the values of the $b^{th}$ element in each group. $\llbracket (e \langle a, f, b \rangle) \rrbracket = \{(\phi, \{k, f(\{S_b \mid \exists (g, S) \in \llbracket e \rrbracket \wedge S_a = k\})\})\}$
See Figure 6 for an example and notice that the resulting RDF graphs are empty (absence of graph in the figure indicates empty graph component).

## 2.3 Relationship to SPARQL

**Lemma 1.** *RDF Algebra expressions can express SPARQL 1.1 basic graph patterns with filters, aggregations and assignments.*

*Proof.* SPARQL filters, aggregation and assignments can be directly mapped to "filtering", "aggregation" and "extending bindings" expressions in RDF Algebra. SPARQL individual triple patterns can be expressed by "triple pattern matching" expressions. Basic graph patterns in SPARQL imply a join on common variables among individual triple patterns. These expressions can be expressed by a sequence of "cross products" and filtering "expressions" in the same way that natural join is defined in relational algebra.                    □

We provide next a couple of example SPARQL queries along with their equivalent RDF Algebra expressions:

- The SPARQL query: `SELECT ?s ?v WHERE { ?s :p ?o . ?o :p2 ?v }`
  evaluated on the RDF graph $g$ is equivalent to the expression:
  $((((g[(?, : p, ?)]) \times (g[(?, : p2, ?)]))[2 = 3])|_{(1,4)})$
- The SPARQL query:
  `SELECT ?s ?z WHERE { ?s :p ?o . ?o :p2 ?v BIND(?v * 1.1) AS ?z }`
  evaluated on the RDF graph $g$ is equivalent to the expression:
  $((\ ((((g[(?, : p, ?)]) \times (g[(?, : p2, ?)]))\ )[2 = 3])\ \oplus_{(4)}\ \times_{1.1}\ )|_{(1,5)})$
  Where $\times_{1.1}(x) = x \times 1.1$

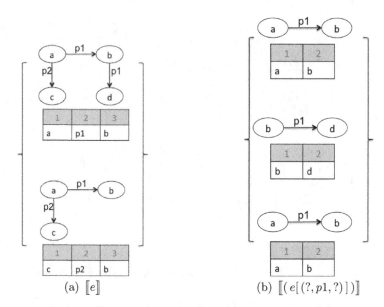

(a) $\llbracket e \rrbracket$                          (b) $\llbracket (e[(?, p1, ?)]) \rrbracket$

**Fig. 4.** Triple pattern matching example

## 2.4 Algebraic Properties

Algebraic laws are important for query optimisation. RDF Algebra shares some operators with SPARQL algebra and therefore related properties and laws defined in SPARQL algebra carry along. We focus here on triple patterns properties that are unique to our algebra. First, we define a partial ordering relationship between triple patterns.

**Definition 2.** $\forall x, y \in \mathcal{T} \bigcup \{?\} : x \preceq y$ *iff one of the following holds:*

- *Both x and y are ?.*
- *x and y are equal RDF terms (i.e. $x, y \in \mathcal{T} \wedge x = y$).*
- *x is a term and y is ? (i.e. $x \in \mathcal{T} \wedge y =?$).*

We generalise $\preceq$ to triple patterns.

**Definition 3.** *For two triple patterns $(x_1, x_2, x_3)$ and $(y_1, y_2, y_3)$ we say that $(x_1, x_2, x_3) \preceq (y_1, y_2, y_3)$ iff $x_1 \preceq y_1$, $x_2 \preceq y_2$, and $x_3 \preceq y_3$.*

The defined partial ordering relationship between triple patterns ($\preceq$) can be thought of as a "more specific" relationship. The following list contains a number of algebraic properties that use this relationship. We also highlight potential optimisation opportunities of each of these algebraic property.

1. $\llbracket ((e[t_1])[t_2]) \rrbracket . g = \llbracket (e[t_1]) \rrbracket . g$ if $t_1 \preceq t_2$
   Applying a less specific triple pattern does not change the resulting graph. It can nevertheless change the binding. For example,
   $\llbracket ((e[(?, : p, : o)])[(?, ?, : o)]) \rrbracket . g = \llbracket (e[(?, : p, : o)]) \rrbracket . g$

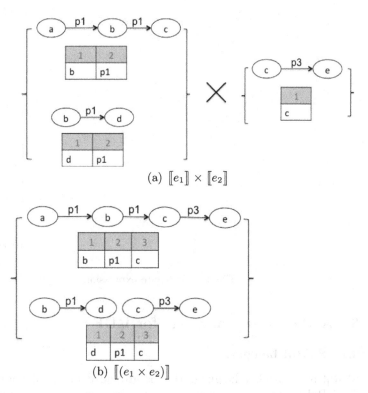

(a) $\llbracket e_1 \rrbracket \times \llbracket e_2 \rrbracket$

(b) $\llbracket (e_1 \times e_2) \rrbracket$

**Fig. 5.** Cross product example

2. $\llbracket (e[t_1]) \rrbracket = \llbracket ((e[t_2])[t_1]) \rrbracket$ if $t_1 \preceq t_2$
   Therefore to calculate the results of matching expression $e$ to the pattern $t_1$ one can instead try matching $t_1$ against the results of matching $t_2$ against $e$. This can be advantageous if the $e[t_2]$ is "cached".
3. $\llbracket ((e_1 \times e_2)[t]) \rrbracket = \llbracket (((e_1[t]) \times (e_2[t]))[t]) \rrbracket$
   More generally $\llbracket ((e_1 \times e_2)[t]) \rrbracket = \llbracket (((e_1[t_1]) \times (e_2[t_2]))[t]) \rrbracket$ for all $t_1, t_2$ such that $t \preceq t_1$ and $t \preceq t_2$. This can cut down the cost of a cross product between two expressions by substituting them with further matched expressions.

The list above is not comprehensive by any means. Further study of other algebraic properties of triple patterns is one of our current research focus. We believe that studying this "triple algebra" can yield fruitful results that can further be applied in tasks like caching RDF query results, views management and query results re-use.

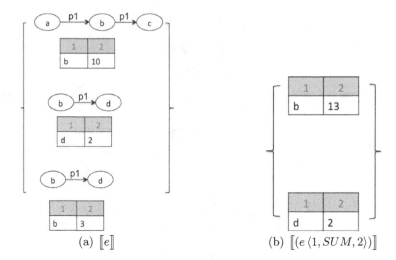

(a) $\llbracket e \rrbracket$         (b) $\llbracket (e \langle 1, SUM, 2 \rangle) \rrbracket$

**Fig. 6.** Aggregate expression example

# 3  A Data flow Language for RDF

## 3.1  SYRql Language

SYRql is a dataflow language that is grounded in the algebra defined before. A SYRql script is a sequence of statements and each statement is either an assignment or an expression. The core set of operators in SYRql are those defined by the algebra in sections 2.2.

The syntax of SYRql borrows the use of "− >" syntax to explicitly show the data flow. According to the designers of Jaql, the "− >" syntax, inspired by the Unix pipes, makes scripts easier to read and debug [4]. It allows eliminating the need for defining variables (as in PIG) or for a WITH clause (as in SQL) in each computational step. It is worth mentioning that Meteor [13] language dropped the pipe notation of Jaql to support operators with multiple inputs and outputs. In SYRql, operators with multiple inputs or outputs are not common and therefore we decided to adopt the pipe syntax. However, SYRql does support multi-input operators such as multi-way joins.

Pattern matching in SYRql uses identical syntax to basic graph patterns of SPARQL. SPARQL syntax for patterns is intuitive, concise and well-known to many users in the Semantic Web field. We hope that this facilitates learning SYRql for many users.

Listing 1.3 shows an example SYRql script that performs pattern matching, filtering, and aggregation. Notably, line 10 in the script provides an example of composability that is not directly available in SPARQL. In line 10, a pattern matching is applied to the results of another pattern matching. We believe that such capabilities are useful for complicated scripts, specifically for exploratory tasks, and for reusing previous scripts as well as previously computed results.

Further description and examples of the SYRql language is available online[3].
The BNF grammar defining the syntax can also be found on SYRql website.

**Listing 1.3.** Example SYRql script

```
1   $rdf = load ('hdfs :// master :9001/ bsbm20k ');
2
3   $janReviewers = $rdf -> pattern ('?review rev:reviewer ?reviewer .
4                                     ?review dc:date ?date .
5                                     ?reviewer bsbm:country ?cntry .')
6               -> filter (?date >= '2008-01-01' && ?date < '2008-02-01');
7
8   $janReviewers -> group by ?cntry into janReviewersCount:count(?review );
9
10  $irelandJanReviewers = $janReviewers -> pattern ('?rev bsbm:country :IE ');
```

## 3.2 SYRql Implementation

The current implementation[4] translates SYRql scripts into a series of MapReduce [9] jobs. We use Java and Apache Hadoop 2 API[5] in our implementation.

**Data Representation:** JSON[6] is used for internal representation of the data.
Particularly, we use JSON arrays for bindings and JSON-LD [31] to represent
graphs. JSON-LD is a recent W3C recommended serialisation of RDF. It has
attracted good adoption so far and this can be expected to grow. Consequently,
by using JSON-LD a large amount of RDF data can be directly processed using
SYRql. Furthermore, existing works such as NTGA [24] have demonstrated the
benefit of manipulating RDF graphs as "groups of triples" that share the same
subject. In this work, we utilize JSON-LD's ability to represent star subgraphs as
single JSON objects, thus eliminating the need for joins when evaluating star-join
queries. This particular way of encoding RDF in JSON-LD is referred to as the
flattened document form[7] and it is the format used in SYRql implementation.
Moreover, we provide a MapReduce implementation that converts RDF data
serialised as N-Triple format[8] into flattened JSON-LD.

**Parsing, Compiling and Evaluation:** We use ANTLR[9] to parse SYRql
scripts and build the abstract syntax tree. Each node in the tree represents
an expression and the children of the node are its inputs. For triple matching
expressions, triple patterns are grouped by subject to utilise the data stored as
star-structured subgraphs, thus reducing the number of required joins. The tree
is then translated into a directed acyclic graph (DAG) of MapReduce jobs. Sequences of expressions that can be evaluated together are grouped into a single
MapReduce job. Finally, the graph is topologically sorted and the MapReduce

---

[3] https://gitlab.insight-centre.org/Maali/syrql-jsonld-imp/wikis/home
[4] https://gitlab.insight-centre.org/Maali/syrql-jsonld-imp
[5] http://hadoop.apache.org/
[6] http://json.org
[7] http://www.w3.org/TR/json-ld/#flattened-document-form
[8] http://www.w3.org/TR/2014/REC-n-triples-20140225/
[9] http://www.antlr.org/

jobs are scheduled to execute on the cluster. It is worth mentioning that for join expressions we implemented the optimised repartition join [14].

# 4   Evaluation

We conducted a performance evaluation of SYRql. Our goal of this evaluation is two-fold:

- Compare performance of SYRql to other popular alternatives, namely Jaql, Pig Latin, and HiveQL. Our thesis is that SYRql's features and syntax can improve user productivity when processing RDF data and help generating scripts that are easier to understand and debug. Therefore, we want to measure the loss in performance, if any, that an early adopter of the language might have to tolerate.
- In the same spirit of Pig Mix[10] that is developed as part of Pig, we want this benchmark to measure performance on a regular basis so that the effects of individual code changes on performance could be understood.

We based our benchmark on the Berlin SPARQL Benchmark (BSBM) [5] that defines an e-commerce use case. Specifically, we translated a number of queries in the BSBM Business Intelligence usecase (BSBM BI)[11] into equivalent programs in a number of popular big data languages. In particular, we provide programs in the following languages:

**Jaql.** A scripting language designed for Javascript Object Notation (JSON).
**Pig Latin.** A dataflow language that provides high-level data manipulation constructs that are similar to relational algebra operators.
**HiveQL.** A declarative language that uses a syntax similar to SQL.

The programs were written by the authors of this paper who have intermediate to high expertise in those languages. We believe that they reflect what an interested user would write given a reasonable amount of time. We evaluated four queries from BSBM BI that cover all core operators i.e., filters, patterns, joins and aggregation. We plan to evaluate other benchmark queries as part of the near future work.

## 4.1   Setup

**Environment:** The experiments were conducted on VCL[12], an on-demand computing and service-oriented technology that provides remote access to virtualised resources. Nodes in the clusters had minimum specifications of single or duo core Intel X86 machines with 2.33 GHz processor speed, 4G memory and running

---

[10] https://cwiki.apache.org/confluence/display/PIG/PigMix
[11] http://wifo5-03.informatik.uni-mannheim.de/bizer/berlinsparqlbenchmark/
spec/BusinessIntelligenceUseCase/index.html
[12] https://vcl.ncsu.edu/

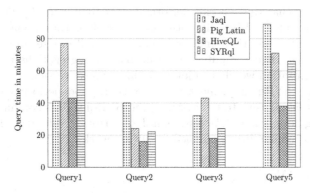

**Fig. 7.** Query processing times

Red Hat Linux. We used a 10-node cluster and the following software versions: Apache Hadoop 2.3.0, Jaql 0.5.1, Pig 0.12.1, and Hive 0.12.0.

**Dataset and Queries:** We generated BSBM data for 400K products in N-triple format. The size of the data was about 35GB containing approximately 140 million triples. As mentioned before, the queries are the scripts corresponding to BSBM BI queries.

### 4.2  Results and Discussion

Figure 7 shows corresponding response time for each of the scripts. Jaql and SYRql required pre-processing of the data to convert the N-Triple RDF data into JSON-LD. The conversion, which took 40 minutes, is only needed once and then the data can be used by all the queries. In general, our SYRql implementation shows encouraging results. It is comparable to the times that Jaql and Pig Latin showed. However, Hive outperformed all the other four systems significantly. The superior performance of Hive was also reported in [33].

Both SYRql and Jaql can evaluate triple patterns that share the same subject together due to their underlying data model and their use of JSON-LD. Pig, on the other hand, evaluates each triple pattern individually and then joins the results. We believe that this is the main reason for the better performance that Jaql and SYRql generally achieved in comparison to Pig despite the maturity and the larger developers community that Pig enjoys.

Examining the generated MapReduce jobs, it was observed that Jaql and SYRql generated similar sequences of jobs. However, SYRql computes results for both graphs and bindings as specified in the underlying algebra. This results in more computation to be done. Nevertheless, separating bindings and graphs helped speeding up some operators through reading and processing less data. For example, filters operate only on the bindings and do not need to process the graphs. Similarly, joins are calculated based on the bindings and then joining the corresponding graphs is a simple union of the matched graphs (see the semantics of the cross product operator in Section 2.2).

We speculate that the superior performance of Hive is mostly due to its efficient join performance. Hive join optimisations such as conversion to map-joins can be applicable when the joining relations are small in size. Additionally, for grouping queries, Hive computes map-side partial aggregations using a Combiner, an optimisation we plan to integrate in our next version.

In summary, SYRql implementation showed a good performance that will hopefully encourage users to try it. Moreover, SYRql scripts contained 50% less lines than Pig scripts and 42% less than Jaql scripts. Evaluating the language ease-of-use and readability is planned for future work.

## 5   Related Work

A large number of declarative languages were introduced recently as part of the big data movement. These languages vary in their programming paradigm, and in their underlying data model. Pig Latin [20] is a dataflow language with a tabular data model that also supports nesting. Jaql [4] is a declarative scripting languages that blends in a number of constructs from functional programming languages and uses JSON for its data model. HiveQL [35] adopts a declarative syntax similar to SQL and its underlying data model is a set of tables. Other examples of languages include Impala[13], Cascalog[14], Meteor [13] and DryadLINQ [39]. [33] presented a performance as well as a language comparison of HiveQL, Pig Latin and Jaql. [28] also compared a number of big data languages but focuses on their compilation into a series of MapReduce jobs.

In the semantic web field, SPARQL is the W3C recommended querying language for RDF. A number of extensions to SPARQL were proposed in the literature to support search for semantic associations [3], and to add nested regular expressions [23] for instances. However, these extensions do not change the pure declarative nature of SPARQL. There are also a number of non-declarative languages that can be integrated in common programming languages to provide support for RDF data manipulation [21,32]. In the more general context of graph processing languages, [38] provides a good survey.

## 6   Conclusions and Future Work

RDF Algebra, a fully composable algebra that is similar to SPARQL algebra, was presented in this paper. The composabilty of RDF Algebra is obtained by pairing graphs and bindings together. A number of unique algebraic properties were presented. Further study of these properties is at the top of our research agenda. We believe that this is a fruitful direction that can have impact in a number of related research problems.

Based on RDF Algebra, we presented SYRql, a dataflow language for large scale processing of RDF data. An implementation of SYRql on top of MapReduce platform was described. This paper also reported some initial results on a

---

[13] https://github.com/cloudera/impala
[14] http://cascalog.org/

performance comparison between SYRql implementation and other existing big data languages. Our future work includes refining SYRql syntax and improving its performance. In particular, we plan to provide an implementation that runs SYRql scripts on top of Apache Spark[15] and to use binary representation of the JSON-LD RDF data instead of the textual one currently used.

**Acknowledgements.** This publication has emanated from research supported in part by a research grant from Science Foundation Ireland (SFI) under Grant Number SFI/12/RC/2289. Fadi Maali is funded by the Irish Research Council, Embark Postgraduate Scholarship Scheme. We thank Aidan Hogan, Marcel Karnstedt and Richard Cyganiak for valuable discussions.

# References

1. Abiteboul, S., Quass, D., McHugh, J., Widom, J., Wiener, J.L.: The lorel query language for semistructured data. International Journal on Digital Libraries (1997)
2. Agrawal, R., et al.: The Claremont Report on Database Research. SIGMOD Rec. (2008)
3. Anyanwu, K., Sheth, A.: P-queries: enabling querying for semantic associations on the semantic web. In: WWW (2003)
4. Beyer, K.S., Ercegovac, V., Gemulla, R., Balmin, A., Eltabakh, M.Y., Kanne, C.-C., Özcan, F., Shekita, E.J.: Jaql: A Scripting Language for Large Scale Semistructured Data Analysis. In: PVLDB (2011)
5. Bizer, C., Schultz, A.: The Berlin SPARQL Benchmark. In: IJSWIS (2009)
6. Buneman, P., Fernandez, M., Suciu, D.: UnQL: A Query Language and Algebra for Semistructured Data Based on Structural Recursion. In: VLDB (2000)
7. Chamberlin, D.D., Boyce, R.F.: SEQUEL: A Structured English Query Language. In: SIGFIDET (1974)
8. Codd, E.F.: A Data Base Sublanguage Founded on the Relational Calculus. In: SIGFIDET (1971)
9. Dean, J., Ghemawat, S.: MapReduce: Simplified Data Processing on Large Clusters. In: OSDI (2004)
10. Dries, A., Nijssen, S., De Raedt, L.: A Query Language for Analyzing Networks. In: CIKM (2009)
11. Hagedorn, S., Sattler, K.-U.: Efficient Parallel Processing of Analytical Queries on Linked Data. In: Meersman, R., Panetto, H., Dillon, T., Eder, J., Bellahsene, Z., Ritter, N., De Leenheer, P., Dou, D. (eds.) ODBASE 2013. LNCS, vol. 8185, pp. 452–469. Springer, Heidelberg (2013)
12. Harris, S., Seaborne, A.: SPARQL 1.1 Query Language. W3C Recommendation (March 21, 2013), http://www.w3.org/TR/sparql11-query/
13. Heise, A., Rheinländer, A., Leich, M., Leser, U., Naumann, F.: Meteor/Sopremo: An Extensible Query Language and Operator Model. In: BigData (2012)
14. Holmes, A.: Hadoop In Practice, ch. 4. Manning Publications Co. (2012)
15. Huang, J., Abadi, D.J., Ren, K.: Scalable SPARQL Querying of Large RDF Graphs. In: PVLDB (2011)

---

[15] https://spark.apache.org/

16. Li, R., Yang, D., Hu, H., Xie, J., Fu, L.: Scalable RDF Graph Querying Using Cloud Computing. J. Web Eng. (2013)
17. Liu, Y.A., Stoller, S.D.: Querying Complex Graphs. In: Van Hentenryck, P. (ed.) PADL 2006. LNCS, vol. 3819, pp. 199–214. Springer, Heidelberg (2005)
18. Maali, F., Decker, S.: Towards an RDF Analytics Language: Learning from Successful Experiences. In: COLD (2013)
19. Meijer, E., Beckman, B., Bierman, G.: LINQ: Reconciling Object, Relations and XML in the.NET Framework. In: SIGMOD (2006)
20. Olston, C., Reed, B., Srivastava, U., Kumar, R., Tomkins, A.: Pig Latin: a Not-so-foreign Language for Data Processing. In: SIGMOD (2008)
21. Oren, E., Delbru, R., Gerke, S., Haller, A., Decker, S.: Activerdf: Object-oriented semantic web programming. In: WWW (2007)
22. Pérez, J., Arenas, M., Gutierrez, C.: Semantics and Complexity of SPARQL. In: Cruz, I., Decker, S., Allemang, D., Preist, C., Schwabe, D., Mika, P., Uschold, M., Aroyo, L.M. (eds.) ISWC 2006. LNCS, vol. 4273, pp. 30–43. Springer, Heidelberg (2006)
23. Pérez, J., Arenas, M., Gutierrez, C.: nSPARQL: A navigational language for RDF. In: Sheth, A.P., Staab, S., Dean, M., Paolucci, M., Maynard, D., Finin, T., Thirunarayan, K. (eds.) ISWC 2008. LNCS, vol. 5318, pp. 66–81. Springer, Heidelberg (2008)
24. Ravindra, P., Kim, H., Anyanwu, K.: An Intermediate Algebra for Optimizing RDF Graph Pattern Matching on MapReduce. In: Antoniou, G., Grobelnik, M., Simperl, E., Parsia, B., Plexousakis, D., De Leenheer, P., Pan, J. (eds.) ESWC 2011, Part II. LNCS, vol. 6644, pp. 46–61. Springer, Heidelberg (2011)
25. Robie, J., Chamberlin, D., Dyck, M., Snelson, J.: Xquery 3.0: An XML query language (2014), http://www.w3.org/TR/xquery-30/
26. Ronen, R., Shmueli, O.: SoQL: A Language for Querying and Creating Data in Social Networks. In: ICDE (2009)
27. Martın, M.S., Gutierrez, C., Wood, P.T.: SNQL: A social networks query and transformation language. In: AMW (2011)
28. Sauer, C., Haerder, T.: Compilation of query languages into mapreduce. In: Datenbank-Spektrum (2013)
29. Schmidt, M., Meier, M., Lausen, G.: Foundations of sparql query optimization. In: ICDT (2010)
30. Spiewak, D., Zhao, T.: ScalaQL: Language-integrated database queries for scala. In: van den Brand, M., Gašević, D., Gray, J. (eds.) SLE 2009. LNCS, vol. 5969, pp. 154–163. Springer, Heidelberg (2010)
31. Sporny, M., Longley, D., Kellogg, G., Lanthaler, M., Lindström, N.: JSON-LD 1.0. W3C Recommendation (January 16, 2014)
32. Staab, S.: Liteq: Language integrated types, extensions and queries for rdf graphs. In: Interoperation in Complex Information Ecosystems (2013)
33. Stewart, R.J., Trinder, P.W., Loidl, H.-W.: Comparing High Level MapReduce Query Languages. In: Temam, O., Yew, P.-C., Zang, B. (eds.) APPT 2011. LNCS, vol. 6965, pp. 58–72. Springer, Heidelberg (2011)
34. Stonebraker, M., Held, G., Wong, E., Kreps, P.: The Design and Implementation of INGRES. ACM Trans. Database Syst. (1976)

35. Thusoo, A., Sarma, J.S., Jain, N., Shao, Z., Chakka, P., Zhang, N., Anthony, S., Liu, H., Murthy, R.: Hive - a Petabyte Scale Data Warehouse Using Hadoop. In: ICDE (2010)
36. Urbani, J., Kotoulas, S., Oren, E., van Harmelen, F.: Scalable Distributed Reasoning Using MapReduce. In: Bernstein, A., Karger, D.R., Heath, T., Feigenbaum, L., Maynard, D., Motta, E., Thirunarayan, K. (eds.) ISWC 2009. LNCS, vol. 5823, pp. 634–649. Springer, Heidelberg (2009)
37. Wong, L.: Kleisli, a functional query system. Journal of Functional Programming (2000)
38. Wood, P.T.: Query Languages for Graph Databases. In: SIGMOD (2012)
39. Yu, Y., Isard, M., Fetterly, D., Budiu, M., Erlingsson, Ú., Gunda, P.K., Currey, J.: DryadLINQ: A System for General-purpose Distributed Data-parallel Computing Using a High-level Language. In: OSDI (2008)

# Sempala: Interactive SPARQL Query Processing on Hadoop

Alexander Schätzle, Martin Przyjaciel-Zablocki,
Antony Neu, and Georg Lausen

Department of Computer Science, University of Freiburg
Georges-Köhler-Allee 051, 79110 Freiburg, Germany
{schaetzle,zablocki,neua,lausen}@informatik.uni-freiburg.de

**Abstract.** Driven by initiatives like Schema.org, the amount of semantically annotated data is expected to grow steadily towards massive scale, requiring cluster-based solutions to query it. At the same time, Hadoop has become dominant in the area of Big Data processing with large infrastructures being already deployed and used in manifold application fields. For Hadoop-based applications, a common data pool (HDFS) provides many synergy benefits, making it very attractive to use these infrastructures for semantic data processing as well. Indeed, existing SPARQL-on-Hadoop (MapReduce) approaches have already demonstrated very good scalability, however, query runtimes are rather slow due to the underlying batch processing framework. While this is acceptable for data-intensive queries, it is not satisfactory for the majority of SPARQL queries that are typically much more selective requiring only small subsets of the data. In this paper, we present *Sempala*, a SPARQL-over-SQL-on-Hadoop approach designed with selective queries in mind. Our evaluation shows performance improvements by an order of magnitude compared to existing approaches, paving the way for interactive-time SPARQL query processing on Hadoop.

## 1  Introduction

In recent years, the *Semantic Web* has made its way from academia and research into real-world applications (e.g. Google Knowledge Graph) driven by initiatives like *Freebase* and *Schema.org*. With the agreement of leading search engine providers to support the Schema.org ontology, one can expect the amount of semantically annotated data to grow steadily at web-scale, making it infeasible to store and process this data on a single machine [12].

At the same time, new technologies and systems have been developed in the last few years to store and process *Big Data*. In some sense, RDF can also be seen as an instance of Big Data since RDF datasets can have a very diverse structure and require expensive operations for evaluation. In this area, the *Hadoop* ecosystem has become a de-facto standard due to its high degree of parallelism, robustness, reliability and scalability while running on heterogeneous commodity hardware. Though Hadoop is not developed with regard to the Semantic Web,

P. Mika et al. (Eds.) ISWC 2014, Part I, LNCS 8796, pp. 164–179, 2014.

we advocate its adaptation for Semantic Web purposes for two main reasons: (1) The expected growth of semantic data requires solutions that scale out as witnessed by the annual Semantic Web Challenge[1]. (2) Industry has settled on Hadoop (or Hadoop-style) architectures for their Big Data needs. This means there exists a tremendous momentum to address existing shortcomings, leading to (among others) scalable, interactive SQL-on-Hadoop as a recent trend.

In our view, using a dedicated infrastructure for semantic data processing solely would abandon all potential synergy benefits of a common data pool among various applications. Therefore, we believe that following the trend to reuse existing Big Data infrastructures is superior to a specialized infrastructure in terms of cost-benefit ratio. Consequently, there has been a lot of work done on processing RDF and SPARQL, the core components of the Semantic Web stack, based on Hadoop (MapReduce), e.g. [14,22,23,25,28]. These approaches scale very well but exhibit pretty high runtimes (several minutes to hours) due to the underlying batch processing framework. This is acceptable for ETL like workloads and *unselective* queries, both in terms of input and output size. However, the majority of SPARQL queries exhibit an explorative ad-hoc style, i.e. they are typically much more *selective*. There is currently an evolution of user expectations, demanding for *interactive* query runtimes regardless of data size, i.e. in the order of seconds to a few minutes. This is especially true for selective queries where runtimes in the order of several minutes or even more are not satisfying. This trend can be clearly observed in the SQL-on-Hadoop field where we currently see several new systems for interactive SQL query processing coming up, e.g. Stinger initiative for Hive, Shark, Presto, Phoenix, Impala, etc. They all have in common that they store their data in HDFS, the distributed file system of Hadoop, while not using MapReduce as the underlying processing framework.

Following this trend, we introduce *Sempala*, a SPARQL-over-SQL approach to provide interactive-time SPARQL query processing on Hadoop. We store RDF data in a columnar layout on HDFS and use Impala, a massive parallel processing (MPP) SQL query engine for Hadoop, as the execution layer on top of it. To the best of our knowledge, this is the first attempt to run SPARQL queries on Hadoop using a combination of columnar storage and an MPP SQL query engine. Just as Impala is meant to be a supplement to Hive [27], we see our approach as a supplement to existing SPARQL-on-Hadoop solutions for queries where interactive runtimes can be expected.

Our major contributions are as follows: (1) We present a space-efficient, unified RDF data layout for Impala using Parquet, a novel columnar storage format for Hadoop. (2) Moreover, we provide a query compiler from SPARQL into the SQL dialect of Impala based on our data layout. The prototype of Sempala is available for download[2]. (3) Finally, we give a comprehensive evaluation to demonstrate the performance improvements by an order of magnitude on average compared to existing SPARQL-on-Hadoop approaches, paving the way for interactive-time SPARQL query processing on Hadoop.

---

[1] See http://challenge.semanticweb.org/

[2] See http://dbis.informatik.uni-freiburg.de/Sempala for download.

## 2   Impala and Parquet

*Impala* [1] is an open-source MPP SQL query engine for Hadoop inspired by Google *Dremel* [16] and developed by *Cloudera*, one of the biggest Hadoop distribution vendors. It is seamlessly integrated into the Hadoop ecosystem, i.e. it can run queries directly on data stored in HDFS without requiring any data movement or transformation. Moreover, it is designed from the beginning to be compatible with Apache Hive [27], the standard SQL warehouse for Hadoop. For this purpose, it also uses the Hive Metastore to store table definitions etc. so that Impala can query tables created with Hive and vice versa. The main difference to Hive is that Impala does not use MapReduce as the underlying execution layer but instead deploys an MPP distributed query engine. The architecture of Impala and its integration into Hadoop is illustrated in Fig. 1 with Sempala being an application on top of it. The Impala daemon is collocated with every HDFS DataNode such that data can be accessed locally. One arbitrary node acts as the coordinator for a given query, distributes the workload among all nodes and receives the partial results to construct the final output. Impala is a relatively young project with its first non-beta version released at the beginning of 2013 and new features and performance enhancements being constantly added. At the time of writing this paper, Impala still lacks the support for on-disk joins, i.e. joins are only done in-memory. The support for external joins is scheduled for the second half of 2014.

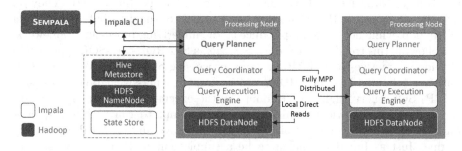

**Fig. 1.** Impala architecture and integration into the Hadoop stack

*Parquet* [2] is a general purpose columnar storage format for Hadoop inspired by Google *Protocol Buffers* [16] and primarily developed by *Twitter* and *Cloudera*. Though not developed solely for Impala, it is the storage format of choice regarding performance and efficiency for Impala. A big advantage of a columnar format compared to a row-oriented format is that all values of a column are stored consecutively on disk allowing better compression and encoding as all data in a column is of the same type. Parquet comes with built-in support for bit packing, run-length and dictionary encoding as well as compression algorithms like Snappy. In addition, also nested data structures can be stored where so-called *repetition* and *definition levels* are used to decompose a nested schema into a list of flat columns and to reconstruct a record such that only those columns are accessed that are requested. This way, Parquet is very efficient in storing wide schemes with hundreds of columns while accessing only a few of them in a request. In contrast, a row-oriented format would have to read the entire row and select the requested columns later on. It is worth mentioning that NULL values are not stored explicitly in Parquet as they can be determined by the definition levels. We utilize both, the efficient support of wide tables and compact representation of NULL values, in our data layout for RDF (cf. Sect. 3.1).

## 3   Sempala

In the following, we describe the architecture of Sempala consisting of two main components as illustrated in Fig. 2. The *RDF Loader* converts an RDF dataset into the data layout used by Sempala, which we describe in Sect. 3.1. The *Query Compiler*, described in Sect. 3.2, rewrites a given SPARQL query into the SQL dialect of Impala based on our data layout.

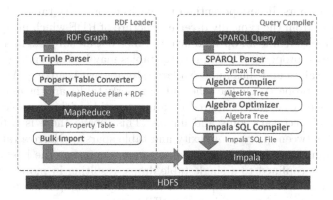

**Fig. 2.** Overview of Sempala architecture

## 3.1   RDF Data Layout for Impala

For the following remarks, consider the small example RDF graph about articles and corresponding authors using a simplified RDF notation in Fig. 3. It is a common approach by many RDF engines to store RDF data in a relational DBMS back-end, e.g. [30]. These solutions typically use a giant so-called *triples table* with three columns, containing one row for each RDF statement, i.e. $triples(sub, prop, obj)$. While being flexible and simple in its representation, it is not an efficient approach for large-scale datasets as queries typically cause several self-joins over this table. In [29] the author describes the usage of so-called *property tables* for query speed-up in Jena2. In general, a property table has a schema $propTable(sub, prop_1, ..., prop_n)$ where the columns (properties) are either determined by a clustering algorithm or by the class of the subject.

The idea is to store all properties in one table that tend to be defined together, e.g. an article can have properties *title, pages, author* and *cite* in our example. The biggest advantage of property tables compared to a triples table is that they can reduce the number of subject-subject self-joins that result from *star-shaped* patterns in a SPARQL query, e.g. {*?s title ?t . ?s author ?a . ?s pages ?p*}. This is particularly relevant for selective SPARQL queries as they often contain such patterns. Hence, the efficient support of star-shaped patterns is also an important design goal for Sempala.

**Fig. 3.** Simplified RDF graph about articles and corresponding authors

In [3] the authors discuss potential drawbacks of property tables. The biggest problem arises from the typically diverse structure of RDF which makes it virtually impossible to define an optimal layout. Since not all subjects in a cluster or class will use all properties, wide property tables may be very sparse containing many NULL values and thus impose a large storage overhead, e.g. Article2 does not have a *cite* property. On the other side, property tables are the more effective the more property columns required by a query reside within a table, reducing the number of necessary joins and unions. This means there is a fundamental trade-off between query complexity and table sparsity. Narrow tables where property columns are highly correlated are more dense but the likelihood that a query can be confined to a single table drops, resulting in more complicated queries. Wide tables, indeed, require less joins simplifying query complexity but they are more sparse, i.e. contain many NULL values.

The authors in [3] argue that a poorly-selected property table layout can significantly slowdown query performance and propose a *vertical partitioned* schema having a two-column table for every RDF property instead, e.g. *author(sub, obj)*. However, in their evaluation they used a row-oriented RDBMS (Postgres) as back-end to store property tables, which is clearly not the best of choice for wide tables. In the following, we explain how we leverage the properties of Parquet to overcome the aforementioned trade-off and drawbacks in Sempala.

In contrast to a row-oriented RDBMS, the column-oriented format of Parquet is designed for very wide tables (in the order of hundreds of columns) where only a few of them are accessed by a request. Therefore, we use a single *unified property table* consisting of all RDF properties used in a dataset to reduce the number of joins required by a query. In fact, star patterns can be answered entirely without the need for a join. Furthermore, we do not need any kind of clustering algorithm that is likely to produce suboptimal schemes for an arbitrary RDF dataset. It also eases query translation and plan generation as all queries use a single table, thus leaving more leeway for query optimization in general and the Impala query optimizer in particular. Of course, this table will be typically sparse as an RDF dataset can use many properties and most subjects will only use a small subset of these properties. But since NULL values are not stored explicitly in Parquet (cf. Sect. 2), sparse columns cause little to no storage overhead.

Nevertheless, our unified approach also comes at a cost. While it is straight-forward to store properties with a maximum cardinality of one, multi-valued properties (cf. e.g. *author* property in Fig. 3) cannot be easily expressed in a flat schema. As Parquet supports nested data structures, we could use a repeated field to store multiple values of a property. Unfortunately, Impala does currently not support nested data (version 1.$x$). To represent multi-valued properties in a flat table, we use the following strategy: For each value of a multi-valued prop-erty we store a duplicate of the corresponding row containing all other column values. That means for a subject having $n$ multi-valued properties, each consist-ing of $m$ values, we would store $n \times m$ rows in our table. For example, the unified property table for the RDF graph in Fig. 3 is depicted in Table 1.

**Table 1.** Unified Property Table for RDF graph in Fig. 3

| subject | author:string | title:string | pages:int | cite:string | erdoesNr:int |
|---------|---------------|--------------|-----------|-------------|--------------|
| Article1 | Paul_Erdoes | "Title 1" | 12 | Article2 | |
| Article1 | Alice | "Title 1" | 12 | Article2 | |
| Article2 | Paul_Erdoes | "Title 2" | 8 | | |
| Paul_Erdoes | | | | | 0 |
| Alice | | | | | 1 |

At first glance, this representation seems to impose a large storage overhead if many multi-valued properties exist. In fact, this effect is strongly mitigated by the built-in run-length encoding of Parquet. As all duplicates are stored in consecutive rows in the table, they are represented by a pair $(value, count)$. As a consequence of this multi-value treatment, we have to use DISTINCT in our (sub)queries where we access the table such that we do not produce a lot of duplicate results. As we only do this when accessing the table, the query semantics is not affected but it causes an additional overhead. With the support for nested data as column values, e.g. lists, scheduled for Impala version 2.0, we could refine this strategy to avoid duplicate rows in future versions of Sempala.

As URIs and literals in RDF tend to be rather long strings, it is also a common approach to use a dictionary encoding for compaction which is an already built-in feature of Parquet. In addition, we also store a triples table along with the unified property table as triple patterns with an unbound property in a SPARQL query, e.g. $\{s\ ?p\ o\}$, cannot be easily answered using a property table. It would not make sense to use a vertical partitioning in this case as the table is only used for those parts of a query where the property is not specified anyway.

We implemented the conversion from RDF in N-Triples format into our unified property table layout using MapReduce such that it can also scale with the dataset size. In an initial preprocessing job we identify all properties used in the dataset together with their types (data types of the objects). In a second job we then apply the actual conversion and parse the object values into the corresponding data types of Impala, if possible. For all other types, we store them as strings. We tested our data layout on an RDF dataset with 100 million triples and compared it with the standard triples table and vertical partitioning described in [3], all stored with Parquet (except for the original RDF). For performance comparison, we defined a set of carefully chosen SPARQL queries consisting of *basic graph patterns* in various shapes (star and chain) as these patterns are the core of every SPARQL query. Table 2 summarizes the results. We see that the unified property table achieves an excellent compression ratio - the compressed size is actually smaller than the compressed original RDF - while having the best query performance both in arithmetic and geometric mean.

**Table 2.** Pre-evaluation results on an RDF dataset with 100 million triples

|                      | Original RDF | Triples Table | Vertical Partitioning | Unified Property Table |
|----------------------|--------------|---------------|-----------------------|------------------------|
| **size**             | Text         | Parquet       | Parquet               | Parquet                |
| (uncompressed)       | 10.5 GB      | 9.7 GB        | 8.6 GB                | 14.2 GB                |
| (snappy compressed)  | 2.1 GB       | 2.0 GB        | 2.3 GB                | 1.8 GB                 |
| (ratio)              | 0.2          | 0.2           | 0.27                  | 0.13                   |
| **runtimes**         |              |               |                       |                        |
| (arithmetic mean)    |              | 17.9 s        | 7.3 s                 | 5.1 s                  |
| (geometric mean)     |              | 7.2 s         | 4.3 s                 | 2.7 s                  |

## 3.2 Query Compiler

The *Query Compiler* of Sempala is based on the algebraic representation of SPARQL expressions defined by the official W3C recommendation [21]. We use *Jena ARQ* to parse a SPARQL query into the corresponding algebra tree. Next, some basic algebraic optimizations, e.g. filter pushing, are applied. However, SPARQL query optimization was not a core aspect when developing Sempala, hence there is still much room for improvement in this field. Finally, the tree is traversed from bottom up to generate the equivalent Impala SQL expressions based on our unified property table layout described in Sect. 3.1. Due to space limitations, we focus on the most relevant key points in the following.

Every SPARQL query defines a graph pattern to be matched against an RDF graph. The smallest pattern is called a *triple pattern* which is simply an RDF triple where subject, property and object can be a variable. A set of triple patterns concatenated by AND (.) is called a *basic graph pattern* (BGP). BGPs are the core of any SPARQL query as they are the leaf nodes in the algebra tree. Consider, for example, the BGP

$$p = \{?s\ title\ ?t\ .\ ?s\ cite\ ?c\ .\ ?c\ author\ Paul\_Erdoes\}.$$

Applied to the RDF graph in Fig. 3, it would yield a single result

$$(?s \rightarrow Article1, ?t \rightarrow "Title\ 1", ?c \rightarrow Article2).$$

For the translation of a BGP into an Impala SQL expression, we can exploit the fact that all properties of a subject are stored in the same row in the unified property table. Thus, we do not need an extra subquery for every triple pattern but instead can use a single subquery for all triple patterns that have the same subject, regardless of whether it is a variable or a fixed value. We call a set of triple patterns in a BGP having the same subject a *triple group*. A BGP can thus be decomposed into a disjoint set of triple groups, called a *join group*. Considering BGP $p$, its join group consists of two distinct triple groups, $tg_1 = \{?s\ title\ ?t\ .\ ?s\ cite\ ?c\}$ and $tg_2 = \{?c\ author\ Paul\_Erdoes\}$. The algorithm to decompose a BGP into its corresponding join group is depicted in Algorithm 1. For the sake of clarity, it is slightly simplified in a way that it ignores the case when the property in a triple pattern is a variable. As already mentioned in Sect. 3.1, such patterns can be answered using the triples table.

---

**Algorithm 1.** computeJoinGroup(BGP)

---

    **input**  :  BGP : $Set\langle TriplePattern : (subject, property, object)\rangle$
    **output**:  JoinGroup : $Map\langle key : String \rightarrow TripleGroup : Set\langle TriplePattern\rangle\rangle$

1   $JoinGroup \leftarrow$ new Map()
2   **foreach** $triple : TriplePattern \in BGP$ **do**
3       **if** $JoinGroup.containsKey(triple.subject)$ **then** // add triple to exisiting TripleGroup
4        |  $JoinGroup.getByKey(triple.subject).add(triple)$
5       **else** // add a new TripleGroup for that triple
6        |  $JoinGroup.add(triple.subject \rightarrow$ new TripleGroup$(triple))$
7        |
8   **end**
9   **return** $JoinGroup$

---

Every triple group is answered by a subquery that does not contain a join. The basic idea is that, at first, variables occurring in a triple group define the columns to be selected by the query. At second, fixed values are used as conditions in the WHERE clause. The names of the variables are also used to rename the output columns such that an outer query can easily refer to it. This strategy is depicted in Algorithm 2 using a simplified relational algebra style notation. Again, we omit the special case of a property being a variable. For every variable in a triple pattern, we have to add the corresponding column (identified by the property) to the list of projected columns (lines 4, 7). Additionally, if the object is a variable, we also have to add a test for not NULL to the list of conditions (line 8) because NULL values indicate that the property was not set for this subject. This is not necessary for variables on subject position as the subject column does not contain NULL values. For example, the subquery $sq_1$ for $tg_1$ is

```
SELECT DISTINCT subject AS s, title AS t, cite AS c FROM propTable
WHERE  title IS NOT NULL AND cite IS NOT NULL
```

and the subquery $sq_2$ for $tg_2$ is

```
SELECT DISTINCT subject AS c FROM propTable WHERE author = 'Paul_Erdoes'
```

Finally, if a join group consists of more than one triple group, we have to combine the results of all corresponding subqueries using a sequence of joins. The join attributes are determined by the shared variables in the triple groups which correspond to the projected columns in respective subqueries. Since we rename the columns according to variable names, we essentially have to compute

---

**Algorithm 2.** TripleGroup2SQL(TripleGroup)

---

  **input**  :  TripleGroup : $Set\langle TriplePattern : (subject, property, object)\rangle$
  **output**: SQL query (written in relational algebra style for the sake of clarity)

1  $projection \leftarrow \emptyset, conditions \leftarrow \emptyset$
2  **foreach** $triple : TriplePattern \in TripleGroup$ **do**
3       **if** $isVariable(triple.subject)$ **then**
4           $projection$.add($subject \rightarrow triple.subject$)
5       **else** $conditions$.add($subject = triple.subject$) ; // subject is a fixed value
6       **if** $isVariable(triple.object)$ **then**
7           $projection$.add($triple.property \rightarrow triple.object$)
8           $conditions$.add($triple.property$ not null)
9       **else** $conditions$.add($triple.property = triple.object$) ; // object is a fixed value
10 **end**
11 **return** $\pi_{projection}(\sigma_{conditions}(propTable))$

---

the natural join between all subqueries. To avoid unnecessary cross products, we order the triple groups by the number of shared variables, assuming that joins are more selective the more attributes they have. This strategy is depicted in Algorithm 3. For example, the final query for $p$ is

SELECT q1.s, q1.t, q2.c FROM $(sq_1)$ q1 JOIN $(sq_2)$ q2 ON (q1.c = q2.c)

---

**Algorithm 3.** JoinGroup2SQL(JoinGroup)

---

  **input**  :  JoinGroup : $Map\langle key : String \rightarrow TripleGroup : Set\langle TriplePattern\rangle\rangle$
  **output**: SQL query (written in relational algebra style for the sake of clarity)

1  $JoinGroup \leftarrow JoinGroup$.orderBySharedVariables()
2  $query \leftarrow$ TripleGroupToSQL($JoinGroup$.getFirst())
3  $JoinGroup$.removeFirst()
4  **foreach** $group : TripleGroup \in JoinGroup$ **do**
5       $query \leftarrow query \bowtie$ TripleGroup2SQL($group$)
6  **end**
7  **return** $query$

---

In general, this strategy does not guarantee an optimal join order. However, after creating the unified property table, we utilize the built-in analytic features of Impala to compute table and column statistics that are used to optimize join order. In our tests, the automatic optimization showed almost the same performance as a manually optimized join order.

A FILTER expression in SPARQL can be mapped to the equivalent conditions in Impala SQL where we essentially have to adapt the SPARQL syntax to the syntax of SQL. These conditions can then be added to the WHERE clause of the corresponding (sub)query. The OPTIONAL pattern is realized by a left outer join in Impala SQL. If it contains an additional filter in the optional pattern (right-hand side), e.g. {?s title ?t OPTIONAL{?s pages ?p FILTER(?p > 10)}}, these conditions are added to the ON clause of the left outer join, according to the W3C specification. UNION, OFFSET, LIMIT, ORDER BY and DISTINCT can be realized using their equivalent clauses in the SQL dialect of Impala.

Finally, a translated query is executed with Impala where the results are not materialized locally but stored in a separate results table in HDFS. This way, we can even query them later one with Impala, if necessary.

**Example.** A complete example of how a a SPARQL query is translated to Impala SQL is illustrated in Fig. 4. The SPARQL query (1) asks for page numbers, authors and optionally their Erdős numbers (if smaller than three) of all articles, ordered by number of pages in descending order. The corresponding algebra tree is illustrated in (2) and the final Impala SQL query is given in (3). This query is then executed with Impala.

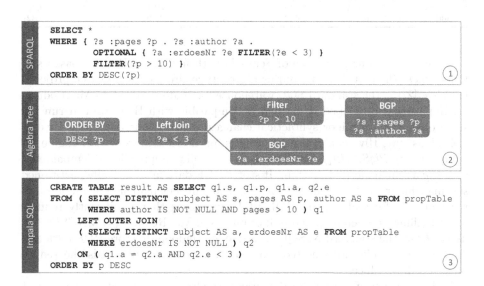

**Fig. 4.** Sempala Query Compiler workflow from SPARQL to SQL

# 4 Evaluation

The evaluation was performed on a small cluster of ten machines, each equipped with a six core Xeon E5-2420 CPU, $2\times2$ TB disks and 32 GB RAM having the Hadoop distribution of Cloudera in version 4.5 and Impala in version 1.2.3 installed. The machines were connected via Gigabit network. This is actually a rather low-end configuration as Cloudera recommends 256 GB RAM and 12 disks or more for Impala nodes which is also a typical configuration in an Hadoop production cluster. We used two well-known SPARQL benchmarks for our evaluation, Lehigh University Benchmark (LUBM) [10] with datasets from 1000 to 3000 universities and Berlin SPARQL Benchmark V3.1 (BSBM) [6] with datasets from one to three million products. For LUBM, we used *WebPie* [28] to pre-compute the transitive closure as Sempala does not support OWL reasoning. The load times and store sizes for Sempala are listed in Table 3. We can see that – although we store both, property and triples table – the actual store size is significantly smaller than the size of the original RDF graph. This is achieved by Parquets built-in support for run-length and dictionary encoding in combination with Snappy compression that perform great for storing RDF in a column-oriented format.

**Table 3.** Load times and store sizes for Sempala (sizes in GB)

|      |       | RDF triples | RDF size | Load time | Prop. Tab. | Triples Tab. | Ratio |
|------|-------|-------------|----------|-----------|------------|--------------|-------|
| LUBM | 1000  | 205 million | 34.1     | 40 min    | 2.4        | 2.4          | 0.14  |
|      | 2000  | 410 million | 68.5     | 76 min    | 4.8        | 5.7          | 0.15  |
|      | 3000  | 615 million | 102.9    | 113 min   | 7.2        | 9.8          | 0.16  |
| BSBM | 1000K | 350 million | 85.9     | 70 min    | 11.1       | 14.9         | 0.30  |
|      | 2000K | 700 million | 172.5    | 92 min    | 22.1       | 29.8         | 0.30  |
|      | 3000K | 1050 million| 259.3    | 138 min   | 38.9       | 44.6         | 0.32  |

We compared our prototype of Sempala with four other Hadoop based systems, where three of them are our own prototypes from other research projects. (1) *Hive* [27] is the standard SQL warehouse for Hadoop based on MapReduce. As Impala was developed to be highly compatible with Hive, we can run the same queries (with minor syntactical changes) on the same data with Hive as well. This way, Hive could also be seen as an alternative execution engine for Sempala. (2) *PigSPARQL* [25,26] follows a similar approach as Sempala but uses *Pig* as the underlying system. It stores RDF data in a vertically partitioned schema similar to [3]. (3) *MapMerge* [22] is an efficient map-side merge join implementation for scalable SPARQL BGP processing that significantly reduces data shuffling between map and reduce phases in MapReduce. (4) *MAPSIN* [24] uses *HBase*, the standard NoSQL database for Hadoop, to store RDF data and applies a map-side index nested loop join that completely avoids the reduce phase of MapReduce.

LUBM consists of 14 predefined queries taken from an university domain, most of them rather selective returning a limited number of results. This is the kind of workload where Sempala can play its full strength. The performance comparison for LUBM 3000 is illustrated in Fig. 5 on a log scale while absolute runtimes are given in Table 4. We can clearly observe that Sempala outperforms all other systems by up to an order of magnitude on average (geometric mean). Q1, Q3, Q4, Q5, Q10, Q11 are the most selective queries returning only a few results and can be answered by Sempala within ten seconds or less. All these queries define a star-shaped pattern which can be answered very efficiently with the unified property table of Sempala. In addition, runtimes remain almost constant when scaling the dataset size. Q6 and Q14 have the slowest runtimes as they are the most unselective queries returning all students and undergraduate students, respectively. For this queries, the runtime is dominated by storing millions of results back to HDFS. This is evidenced by the fact that if we just count the number of results, runtimes again drop below ten seconds. Q2, Q7, Q8, Q9 and Q12 are more challenging with Q2 and Q9 defining the most complex patterns. Also for this queries, runtimes of Sempala are significantly faster than for all other systems, remaining way below one minute.

For BSBM, we used the query templates defined in the Explore use case that imitate consumers looking for products in an e-commerce domain. We had to omit Q9 and Q12 as we do currently not support CONSTRUCT and DE-SCRIBE queries. For each dataset size we generated 20 instances of every query

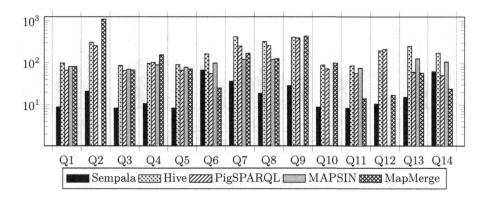

**Fig. 5.** Performance comparison for LUBM 3000 (log scale)

**Table 4.** LUBM query runtimes (in s), GM: geometric mean, n/a: not applicable

| LUBM Query | 1 | 2 | 3 | 4 | 5 | 6 | 7 | 8 | 9 | 10 | 11 | 12 | 13 | 14 | GM |
|---|---|---|---|---|---|---|---|---|---|---|---|---|---|---|---|
| Sempala | 7 | 11 | 6 | 8 | 6 | 28 | 17 | 10 | 14 | 7 | 6 | 8 | 9 | 24 | 10 |
| Hive | 77 | 253 | 75 | 89 | 82 | 133 | 310 | 243 | 312 | 77 | 74 | 165 | 217 | 125 | 137 |
| PigSPARQL | 44 | 144 | 48 | 56 | 40 | 35 | 129 | 140 | 207 | 45 | 40 | 119 | 39 | 39 | 66 |
| MapMerge | 36 | 405 | 31 | 63 | 33 | 15 | 71 | 58 | 179 | 43 | 13 | 15 | 28 | 16 | 41 |
| MAPSIN | 32 | n/a | 30 | 35 | 33 | 45 | 60 | 60 | n/a | n/a | 32 | n/a | 42 | 42 | 40 |
| Sempala | 7 | 15 | 7 | 9 | 7 | 47 | 27 | 14 | 21 | 7 | 7 | 9 | 12 | 43 | 13 |
| Hive | 80 | 298 | 89 | 97 | 85 | 153 | 353 | 284 | 371 | 82 | 80 | 180 | 237 | 145 | 154 |
| PigSPARQL | 65 | 196 | 55 | 78 | 55 | 50 | 195 | 195 | 309 | 60 | 50 | 158 | 50 | 49 | 89 |
| MapMerge | 61 | 750 | 52 | 117 | 56 | 18 | 120 | 93 | 311 | 75 | 13 | 16 | 46 | 18 | 62 |
| MAPSIN | 52 | n/a | 47 | 60 | 52 | 67 | 93 | 92 | n/a | n/a | 51 | n/a | 81 | 78 | 65 |
| Sempala | 8 | 21 | 8 | 10 | 8 | 66 | 36 | 18 | 28 | 8 | 8 | 10 | 15 | 61 | 16 |
| Hive | 98 | 305 | 85 | 96 | 85 | 162 | 417 | 320 | 407 | 87 | 84 | 192 | 245 | 170 | 165 |
| PigSPARQL | 66 | 255 | 65 | 102 | 66 | 55 | 251 | 256 | 391 | 71 | 56 | 208 | 60 | 50 | 107 |
| MapMerge | 81 | 1099 | 67 | 153 | 71 | 25 | 167 | 124 | 432 | 98 | 14 | 17 | 57 | 24 | 80 |
| MAPSIN | 81 | n/a | 70 | 89 | 78 | 98 | 120 | 119 | n/a | n/a | 74 | n/a | 125 | 105 | 94 |

template using the BSBM test driver, summing up to a total of 200 queries per dataset. In Table 5 we report the average query execution time (aQET) per query. MapMerge and MAPSIN could not be used for BSBM evaluation as they only support SPARQL BGPs. Again, Sempala outperforms Hive and also PigSPARQL by an order of magnitude on average while runtimes for Q1, Q3, Q4, Q6 and Q10 remain almost constant around ten seconds for all dataset sizes. For Q7, a memory error occurred due to the reason that Impala in version 1.2.3 does only support in-memory joins and whenever an Impala node exceeds its memory resources, the whole query execution is cancelled. So the resources of an individual Impala node can be a bottleneck for scalability as adding more nodes to the cluster would not solve this issue. The support for on-disk joins in Impala is announced for a version beyond 2.0 in the second half of 2014. In the interim, we can fall back on Hive without additional effort if a memory intensive query fails on Impala.

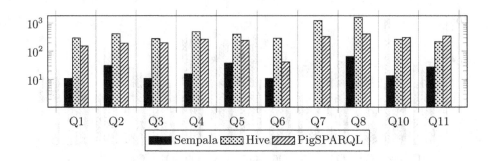

**Fig. 6.** Performance comparison for BSBM 3000K (log scale)

**Table 5.** BSBM query runtimes (in s), GM: geometric mean

| BSBM Query | 1 | 2 | 3 | 4 | 5 | 6 | 7 | 8 | 10 | 11 | GM |
|---|---|---|---|---|---|---|---|---|---|---|---|
| **1000K** Sempala | 8 | 16 | 8 | 12 | 17 | 8 | 28 | 36 | 11 | 14 | 14 |
| Hive | 164 | 219 | 148 | 292 | 233 | 139 | 631 | 818 | 169 | 114 | 234 |
| PigSPARQL | 127 | 169 | 161 | 189 | 200 | 35 | 235 | 278 | 226 | 131 | 157 |
| **2000K** Sempala | 11 | 23 | 11 | 16 | 27 | 8 | 37 | 48 | 12 | 18 | 18 |
| Hive | 202 | 307 | 188 | 336 | 309 | 188 | 828 | 1169 | 211 | 170 | 309 |
| PigSPARQL | 144 | 184 | 180 | 226 | 224 | 36 | 278 | 358 | 259 | 235 | 187 |
| **3000K** Sempala | 11 | 30 | 11 | 16 | 37 | 10 | MEM | 63 | 13 | 27 | 19 |
| Hive | 294 | 414 | 277 | 490 | 399 | 285 | 1203 | 1554 | 265 | 216 | 427 |
| PigSPARQL | 151 | 191 | 198 | 265 | 240 | 41 | 330 | 409 | 307 | 343 | 215 |

Overall, the evaluation clearly demonstrates that combining existing technologies for Big Data processing can be an efficient solution for querying semantic data. In that sense, Sempala is a significant step towards interactive-time SPARQL query processing on Hadoop.

## 5   Related Work

*RDF-3X* [18] is considered to be one of the fastest single machine RDF systems but its performance degrades for queries with unbound objects and low selectivity factor [14]. Furthermore, with continuously increasing dataset sizes it becomes more and more challenging to store and process RDF datasets on a single machine only [12], raising the need for distributed solutions.

The authors in [13,17] were among the first to use Hadoop for RDF storage and retrieval. They presented systems based on MapReduce for SPARQL BGP processing, omitting more complex SPARQL language elements. *HadoopDB* [4] is a hybrid of MapReduce and DBMS where MapReduce is the communication layer above multiple single node DBMS aiming to combine the speed of a SQL database with the scalability of MapReduce. The authors in [12] adopted this hybrid approach for RDF data using RDF-3X instead of a SQL database. An RDF graph is partitioned into subgraphs, each of them stored on a single node running an instance of RDF-3X. Furthermore, each node also stores the *n*-hop neighborhood of his subgraph such that queries within an $n$-hop distance can be answered locally. However, the initial graph partitioning is done on a single machine which strongly limits scalability and query performance drops significantly when a query cannot be answered within the $n$-hop neighborhood. So there is a fundamental trade-off between query performance and scalability as the size of locally replicated data growth exponentially with $n$. *HadoopRDF* [14] is a MapReduce based RDF system that stores data directly in HDFS and rebalances automatically when cluster size changes but join processing is done in the reduce phase only, thus there is always a costly data shuffling phase involved [24]. There is a large body of work on join optimization in MapReduce, e.g. [5,7,22,24]. However, they still suffer from overall MapReduce batch processing overhead what makes interactive runtimes virtually impossible to achieve on MapReduce.

There are several approaches which store RDF data in HBase, a NoSQL database based on HDFS. *Jena-HBase* [15] provides a combination of the Semantic Web framework Jena and HBase to overcome the lack of scalability of single machine RDF-stores. However, they do not provide a distributed query engine, thus scalability and query performance for large RDF data is still an issue. The *MAPSIN* join proposed in [24] utilizes HBase to avoid costly shuffle phases by processing joins in the map phase with a focus on selective star pattern queries. The authors of *RDFChain* [8] refined this idea to support chained queries more efficiently. $H_2RDF+$ [20] also stores RDF data in HBase and processes joins locally or distributed depending on join complexity estimation. However, like most RDF systems for Hadoop, also MAPSIN, RDFChain and $H_2RDF$ do solely support join-only queries, i.e. SPARQL BGPs. In contrast, Sempala supports the full range of single graph operators from the SPARQL 1.0 spec.

Instead of implementing a SPARQL processing engine directly in MapReduce, *PigSPARQL* [26] translates SPARQL queries to Pig Latin, a high-level languages for data processing on MapReduce. As with Sempala, it supports all SPARQL 1.0 operators and benefits from further developments of Pig as illustrated in a revised work [25]. However, based on MapReduce execution, it cannot provide interactive query runtimes.

Beyond general-purpose platforms like Hadoop, *Virtuoso Cluster Edition* [9], *Clustered TDB* [19] and *4store* [11] are specialized distributed RDF stores. However, they require a dedicated infrastructure and pose additional installation and management overhead whereas our approach builds upon the idea to use existing platforms that are open-source, well-known and widely used. Moreover, as we do not require any changes to Hadoop, Sempala runs on any existing Hadoop cluster or cloud service (Impala is also supported by Amazon Elastic MapReduce).

# 6  Conclusion

In recent years, the Hadoop ecosystem has become a de-facto standard for distributed storage and processing of Big Data. A core idea of Hadoop is to have a common data pool while providing various applications on top of it. This makes it also an attractive choice to store and query semantic data at web-scale. However, while existing approaches for SPARQL-on-Hadoop have proven very good scalability, they fail to provide interactive query runtimes.

In this paper, we presented Sempala, a SPARQL query processor for Hadoop based on Impala. Combining a state-of-the-art columnar file format to store RDF data in HDFS with a massive parallel processing engine integrated seamlessly into the Hadoop stack provides an elegant and at the same time efficient approach to query large volumes of RDF data. Our comprehensive evaluation demonstrated that Sempala is a big step towards interactive-time SPARQL query processing on Hadoop. For future work, we plan to refine our RDF data layout of Sempala by incorporating nested data structures that will be introduced in Impala 2.0 and to add support for features beyond SPARQL 1.0 such as subqueries and aggregations.

# References

1. Cloudera Impala, http://impala.io/
2. Parquet, http://parquet.io/
3. Abadi, D.J., Marcus, A., Madden, S.R., Hollenbach, K.: Scalable Semantic Web Data Management Using Vertical Partitioning. In: VLDB, pp. 411–422 (2007)
4. Abouzeid, A., Bajda-Pawlikowski, K., Abadi, D.J., Rasin, A., Silberschatz, A.: HadoopDB: An Architectural Hybrid of MapReduce and DBMS Technologies for Analytical Workloads. PVLDB 2(1), 922–933 (2009)
5. Afrati, F.N., Ullman, J.D.: Optimizing Multiway Joins in a Map-Reduce Environment. IEEE Trans. Knowl. Data Eng. 23(9), 1282–1298 (2011)
6. Bizer, C., Schultz, A.: The Berlin SPARQL Benchmark. International Journal on Semantic Web and Information Systems (IJSWIS) 5(2), 1–24 (2009)
7. Blanas, S., Patel, J.M., Ercegovac, V., Rao, J., Shekita, E.J., Tian, Y.: A Comparison of Join Algorithms for Log Processing in MapReduce. In: SIGMOD (2010)
8. Choi, P., Jung, J., Lee, K.-H.: RDFChain: Chain Centric Storage for Scalable Join Processing of RDF Graphs using MapReduce and HBase. In: ISWC (Posters & Demos), pp. 249–252 (2013)
9. Erling, O., Mikhailov, I.: Towards web scale RDF. In: Proc. SSWS (2008)
10. Guo, Y., Pan, Z., Heflin, J.: LUBM: A Benchmark for OWL Knowledge Base Systems. Web Semantics 3(2), 158 (2005)
11. Harris, S., Lamb, N., Shadbolt, N.: 4store: The Design and Implementation of a Clustered RDF Store. In: SSWS, pp. 94–109 (2009)
12. Huang, J., Abadi, D.J., Ren, K.: Scalable SPARQL Querying of Large RDF Graphs. PVLDB 4(11), 1123–1134 (2011)
13. Husain, M.F., Doshi, P., Khan, L., Thuraisingham, B.M.: Storage and Retrieval of Large RDF Graph Using Hadoop and MapReduce. In: CloudCom, pp. 680–686 (2009)
14. Husain, M.F., McGlothlin, J.P., Masud, M.M., Khan, L.R., Thuraisingham, B.M.: Heuristics-Based Query Processing for Large RDF Graphs Using Cloud Computing. IEEE TKDE 23(9) (2011)
15. Khadilkar, V., Kantarcioglu, M., Thuraisingham, B.M., Castagna, P.: Jena-HBase: A Distributed, Scalable and Efficient RDF Triple Store. In: ISWC (Posters & Demos) (2012)

16. Melnik, S., Gubarev, A., Long, J.J., Romer, G., Shivakumar, S., Tolton, M., Vassilakis, T.: Dremel: Interactive Analysis of Web-Scale Datasets. Proc. VLDB Endow. 3(1-2), 330–339 (2010)
17. Myung, J., Yeon, J., Lee, S.-g.: SPARQL Basic Graph Pattern Processing with Iterative MapReduce. In: MDAC, pp. 1–6 (2010)
18. Neumann, T., Weikum, G.: RDF-3X: a RISC-style engine for RDF. PVLDB 1(1), 647–659 (2008)
19. Owens, A., Seaborne, A., Gibbins, N.: Clustered TDB: A Clustered Triple Store for Jena. In: WWW (2009)
20. Papailiou, N., Konstantinou, I., Tsoumakos, D., Karras, P., Koziris, N.: H2RDF+: High-performance Distributed Joins over Large-scale RDF Graphs. In: BigData Conference, pp. 255–263 (2013)
21. Prud'hommeaux, E., Seaborne, A.: SPARQL Query Language for RDF. W3C Recom (2008), http://www.w3.org/TR/rdf-sparql-query/
22. Przyjaciel-Zablocki, M., Schätzle, A., Skaley, E., Hornung, T., Lausen, G.: Map-Side Merge Joins for Scalable SPARQL BGP Processing. In: CloudCom, pp. 631–638 (2013)
23. Rohloff, K., Schantz, R.E.: High-Performance, Massively Scalable Distributed Systems using the MapReduce Software Framework: The SHARD Triple-Store. In: PSI EtA, Reno, Nevada, pp. 4:1–4:4 (2010)
24. Schätzle, A., Przyjaciel-Zablocki, M., Dorner, C., Hornung, T., Lausen, G.: Cascading Map-Side Joins over HBase for Scalable Join Processing. In: SSWS+HPCSW, p. 59 (2012)
25. Schätzle, A., Przyjaciel-Zablocki, M., Hornung, T., Lausen, G.: PigSPARQL: A SPARQL Query Processing Baseline for Big Data. In: ISWC (Posters & Demos), pp. 241–244 (2013)
26. Schätzle, A., Przyjaciel-Zablocki, M., Lausen, G.: PigSPARQL: Mapping SPARQL to Pig Latin. In: SWIM, Athens, Greece, pp. 4:1–4:4 (2011)
27. Thusoo, A., Sarma, J.S., Jain, N., Shao, Z., Chakka, P., Anthony, S., Liu, H., Wyckoff, P., Murthy, R.: Hive: A Warehousing Solution over a Map-Reduce Framework. Proc. VLDB Endow. 2(2), 1626–1629 (2009)
28. Urbani, J., Kotoulas, S., Maassen, J., van Harmelen, F., Bal, H.: WebPIE: A Webscale Parallel Inference Engine using MapReduce. J. Web Sem. 10, 59–75 (2012)
29. Wilkinson, K.: Jena Property Table Implementation. In: SSWS, pp. 35–46 (2006)
30. Wilkinson, K., Sayers, C., Kuno, H.A., Reynolds, D.: Efficient RDF Storage and Retrieval in Jena2. In: SWDB, pp. 131–150 (2003)

# Querying Datasets on the Web
# with High Availability

Ruben Verborgh[1], Olaf Hartig[2], Ben De Meester[1], Gerald Haesendonck[1],
Laurens De Vocht[1], Miel Vander Sande[1], Richard Cyganiak[3], Pieter Colpaert[1],
Erik Mannens[1], and Rik Van de Walle[1]

[1] Ghent University – iMinds, Belgium
{firstname.lastname}@ugent.be
[2] University of Waterloo, Canada
ohartig@uwaterloo.ca
[3] Digital Enterprise Research Institute, NUI Galway, Ireland
richard@cyganiak.de

**Abstract.** As the Web of Data is growing at an ever increasing speed,
the lack of reliable query solutions for live public data becomes apparent.
SPARQL implementations have matured and deliver impressive performance for public SPARQL endpoints, yet poor availability—especially
under high loads—prevents their use in real-world applications. We propose to tackle this availability problem by defining triple pattern fragments, a specific kind of Linked Data Fragments that enable low-cost
publication of queryable data by moving intelligence from the server to
the client. This paper formalizes the Linked Data Fragments concept,
introduces a client-side SPARQL query processing algorithm that uses
a dynamic iterator pipeline, and verifies servers' availability under load.
The results indicate that, at the cost of lower performance, query techniques with triple pattern fragments lead to high availability, thereby
allowing for reliable applications on top of public, queryable Linked Data.

**Keywords:** Linked Data, Linked Data Fragments, querying, availability,
scalability, SPARQL.

## 1 Introduction

The past few years, the performance of SPARQL endpoints has increased steadily.
In spite of all this progress, reliable queryable access to public Linked Data
datasets largely remains impossible due to the low availability percentages of
public SPARQL endpoints. As of end-2013, the average SPARQL endpoint is down
for more than 1.5 days *each month* [4]. This means we cannot build reliable
applications on top of queryable public data. No matter how fast SPARQL implementations become, if their availability does not increase, no one will take the
risk of depending on public data providers to provide querying for their applications. Availability, not performance, is currently the main threat to the success
of the Semantic Web as a viable technology for today's challenges.

P. Mika et al. (Eds.) ISWC 2014, Part I, LNCS 8796, pp. 180–196, 2014.
© Springer International Publishing Switzerland 2014

To circumvent the availability issue, consumers who want to query public data typically download a data dump and host their own private SPARQL endpoint. While this seems to solve the issue, it has the following drawbacks:

- Hosting an endpoint requires (possibly expensive) infrastructural support and involves (often manual) set-up and maintenance.
- The data in the endpoint is not guaranteed to be up-to-date.
- Each dataset required by any of the desired queries must be fully loaded into the endpoint, even if only a small part of that dataset is actually needed.

Furthermore, querying a local machine can hardly be considered *Web* querying, as everything happens offline. Making the Semantic Web vision scalable by downloading and querying all data locally seems an unsatisfactory paradox.

In order to advance towards a solution for high-availability Web querying, *Linked Data Fragments (LDFs)* [27] were proposed as a framework to analyze all possible ways of publishing parts of a Linked Data dataset, ranging from SPARQL endpoints with highly specific results to data dumps that contain the entire dataset. In particular, this framework allows to define specific types of fragments that can be generated with minimal effort by servers, while still enabling efficient client-side querying. One such type are *triple pattern fragments* (formerly called *basic* Linked Data Fragments [27]), which offer triple-pattern-based access to a dataset.

In this paper, we show that client-side query processing using triple pattern fragments allows live querying with high availability and scalability of public datasets. This result demonstrates that this enables reliable query execution on the Web of Data, with minimal server-side cost. First, the next section discusses related work on querying RDF-based datasets on the Web. We then provide a formalization of Linked Data Fragments in Section 3, followed by a client-side, iterator-based query execution algorithm in Section 4. Section 5 contains the availability evaluation and discussion. We conclude the paper in Section 6.

## 2  Related Work

On the current Web, several HTTP interfaces that provide access to triple-based data are available. We will discuss public SPARQL endpoints, Linked Data publishing, and other HTTP interfaces for triples, as well as their querying methods.

### 2.1  Public SPARQL Endpoints

The SPARQL language [12] is the W3C standard to query a collection of RDF triples [16]. Many triple stores, such as Virtuoso [5] and Jena TDB [11], offer a SPARQL interface. Even though current SPARQL interfaces offer high performance [3, 19, 22], individual queries can consume a significant amount of server processor time and memory. In fact, it has been shown that the evaluation problem for SPARQL is PSPACE-complete [21]. Like any high-performance database server, SPARQL servers with high demand are generally expensive to host, which is further complicated for public servers because of unpredictable loads.

The current de-facto way for providing queryable access to triples on the Web is the SPARQL protocol [6]: clients send SPARQL queries through a specific HTTP interface; the server executes these queries and responds with their results. This contrasts with the majority of machine-to-machine HTTP interactions on the Web, where the server implements a rigidly structured API through which clients access the data. Such APIs purposely limit the kind of queries a client can ask, as it allows those servers to place a bound on the computation time needed for each API request [27]. With SPARQL endpoints, clients can demand the execution of arbitrarily complicated queries[1] [6]. Furthermore, since each client requests unique, highly specific queries, regular HTTP caching mechanisms are ineffective, since they can only optimize repeated identical requests.

These factors contribute to the low availability of public SPARQL endpoints, which is documented extensively [4]. It is important to note that this low availability is *not* the result of poor performance: as indicated by multiple benchmarks [3, 19, 22], many SPARQL implementations deliver very high performance. Instead, it is the consequence of the architectural decision of the current SPARQL protocol, which demands the server responds to highly complex requests [27]. This makes providing reliable public SPARQL endpoints an exceptionally difficult challenge, incomparable to hosting any other public HTTP server.

## 2.2   Linked Data

Perhaps the most well-known alternative interface to RDF triples is described by the Linked Data principles [2] which, not coincidentally, align with the Web's architectural constraints [8]. The principles require servers to publish documents ("subject pages") with triples about specific entities, which a client can access through their entity-specific URI, a practice which is called *dereferencing*. Each of these Linked Data documents contains triples that mention URIs of other entities, which can be dereferenced in turn. Serving such documents is like serving HTML files, which does not require much processor time or memory, so hosting them at low cost is straightforward. Several Linked Data querying techniques [14] aim to use dereferencing to solve SPARQL queries over the Web of Data. This process happens client-side, so the availability of servers is not impacted.

The Linked Data publishing and querying strategy has two main drawbacks. First, query execution times are high, and many queries cannot be solved (efficiently). For example, it is nearly impossible to directly answer the following seemingly simple query for any given dataset:

```
SELECT ?person WHERE { ?person a <http://xmlns.com/foaf/0.1/Person> }
```

A client could try to fetch the URL http://xmlns.com/foaf/0.1/Person but, because of the Web's unidirectional linking structure, the document at that URL cannot possibly link to all instances of foaf:Person. In fact, it does not link to any, so the query execution yields an empty result.

---

[1] Many endpoints allow to only expose a subset of all SPARQL queries, for instance, by limiting the allowed execution time. However, even under those circumstances, the availability of public SPARQL endpoints remains low [4].

Second, documents about an entity are looked up through dereferencing, and the URI of an entity only points to the single document on the server that hosts the domain of that URI. For example, the URI http://dbpedia.org/resource/ Barack_Obama leads to triples about Barack Obama on the DBpedia server, not to the triples hosted on other sources that also have data about Barack Obama, such as the BBC or the New York Times. And even though DBpedia could link to those sources, this is entirely up to the server's discretion. While anybody can reuse the DBpedia URI to add triples about an entity, it is highly unlikely that those triples are considered by Linked Data querying. This contrasts with SPARQL endpoints, which can provide data about resources with *any* URI.

### 2.3    Other HTTP Interfaces to RDF Triples

Finally, several other HTTP interfaces for triples have been designed. Strictly speaking, the most trivial HTTP interface is a data dump, which is a single-file representation of a (part of a) dataset. As discussed in Section 1, this allows consumers to set up a private query endpoint. Typical HTTP APIs offer more granular access, albeit still far less flexible than SPARQL endpoints.

The Linked Data Platform [23] is a read/write HTTP interface for Linked Data, scheduled to become a W3C recommendation. It details several concepts that extend beyond the Linked Data principles, such as containers and write access. However, the API has been designed primarily for consistent read/write access to Linked Data resources, not to enable reliable and/or efficient query execution. Another read/write interface is the SPARQL Graph Store Protocol [20], which describes HTTP operations to manage RDF graphs through SPARQL queries.

Additionally, several other fine-grained HTTP interfaces for triples have been proposed, such as the Linked Data API [17] and Restpark [18]. Some of them aim to bridge the gap between the SPARQL protocol and the REST architectural style underlying the Web [28]. However, none of these proposals are widely used at the moment and no query engines for them are implemented to date.

## 3    Linked Data Fragments

### 3.1    Concept and Context

What all of the above interfaces have in common is that, in one sense or another, they publish certain *fragments* of a Linked Data dataset. A SPARQL endpoint response, a Linked Data document, and a data dump each offer specific parts of all triples of a given collection. Rather than presenting them as fully distinct approaches, we uniformly call the result of each request to such interfaces a *Linked Data Fragment (LDF)* [25, 27]. As Fig. 1 shows, each kind of fragment mainly differs in its specificity. Depending on this, the workload to compute answers to queries is divided differently between clients and servers. The key to efficient and reliable Web querying is to find fragments that strike an optimal balance between client and server effort. Before we examine particular options, let us define formally what LDFs are.

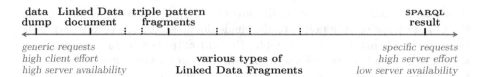

Fig. 1. All HTTP triple interfaces offer Linked Data Fragments of a dataset. They differ in the specificity of the data they contain, and thus the effort needed to create them.

## 3.2  Formal Definitions

As a basis for our formalization, we use the following concepts of the RDF data model [16] and the SPARQL query language [12]. We write $\mathcal{U}$, $\mathcal{B}$, $\mathcal{L}$, and $\mathcal{V}$ to denote the sets of all URIs, blank nodes, literals, and variables, respectively. Then, $\mathcal{T} = (\mathcal{U} \cup \mathcal{B}) \times \mathcal{U} \times (\mathcal{U} \cup \mathcal{B} \cup \mathcal{L})$ is the (infinite) set of all RDF *triples*. Any tuple $tp \in (\mathcal{U} \cup \mathcal{V}) \times (\mathcal{U} \cup \mathcal{V}) \times (\mathcal{U} \cup \mathcal{L} \cup \mathcal{V})$ is a *triple pattern*. Any finite set of such triple patterns is a *basic graph pattern* (BGP). Any more complex SPARQL *graph pattern*, typically denoted by $P$, combines triple patterns (or BGPs) using specific operators [12,21]. The standard (set-based) query semantics for SPARQL defines the *query result* of such a graph pattern $P$ over a set of RDF triples $G \subseteq \mathcal{T}$ as a set that we denote by $[\![P]\!]_G$ and that consists of partial mappings $\mu : \mathcal{V} \to (\mathcal{U} \cup \mathcal{B} \cup \mathcal{L})$, which are called *solution mappings*. An RDF triple $t$ is a *matching triple* for a triple pattern $tp$ if there exists a solution mapping $\mu$ such that $t = \mu[tp]$, where $\mu[tp]$ denotes the triple (pattern) that we obtain by replacing the variables in $tp$ according to $\mu$.

For the sake of a more straightforward formalization, in this paper, we assume without loss of generality that every dataset $G$ published via some kind of fragments on the Web is a finite set of blank-node-free RDF triples; i.e., $G \subseteq \mathcal{T}^*$ where $\mathcal{T}^* = \mathcal{U} \times \mathcal{U} \times (\mathcal{U} \cup \mathcal{L})$. Each fragment of such a dataset contains triples that somehow belong together; they have been selected based on some condition, which we abstract through the notion of a selector:

**Definition 1 (selector).** *A selector is a partial function* $s : 2^{\mathcal{T}} \to \{\mathsf{true}, \mathsf{false}\}$.

A more concrete type of this abstract notion are triple pattern selectors, which select triples that match a certain triple pattern:

**Definition 2 (triple pattern selector).** *Given a triple pattern* $tp$, *the* triple pattern selector *for* $tp$ *is the selector* $\mathsf{s}_{tp}$ *that, for any singleton set* $\{t\} \subseteq 2^{\mathcal{T}}$, *is defined by*

$$\mathsf{s}_{tp}(\{t\}) = \begin{cases} \mathsf{true} & \text{if } t \text{ is a matching triple for } tp, \\ \mathsf{false} & \text{else.} \end{cases}$$

When publishing data on the Web, we should equip its representations with hypermedia controls [1,8,9]. We encounter them on a daily basis when browsing HTML pages; they are usually present as hyperlinks or forms. What all these controls have in common is that, given some (possibly empty) input, they result in our browser performing a request for a specific URL.

**Definition 3 (control).** *A control is a function that maps from some set to* $\mathcal{U}$.

In particular, we are interested in controls whose domain is a set of selectors, as they allow to create URLs that correspond to data matching those selectors.

By now, we have introduced all elements necessary to define fragments of an RDF-based dataset.

**Definition 4 (Linked Data Fragment).** *Let $G \subseteq \mathcal{T}^*$ be a finite set of blank-node-free RDF triples. A Linked Data Fragment (LDF) of $G$ is a tuple $f = \langle u, s, \Gamma, M, C \rangle$ with the following five elements:*

- *$u$ is a URI (which is the "authoritative" source from which $f$ can be retrieved);*
- *$s$ is a selector;*
- *$\Gamma$ is a set consisting of all subsets of $G$ that match selector $s$, that is, for every $G' \subseteq G$ it holds that $G' \in \Gamma$ if and only if $G' \in \mathrm{dom}(s)$ and $s(G') = \mathsf{true}$;*
- *$M$ is a finite set of (additional) RDF triples, including triples that represent metadata for $f$; and*
- *$C$ is a finite set of controls.*

Any source of RDF-based data on the Web can be described as an LDF by specifying the corresponding values for $u$, $s$, $\Gamma$, $M$, and $C$. For example, the result of a SPARQL CONSTRUCT query is an LDF where the selector is the query, the metadata set is empty, and the control set contains a SPARQL endpoint URL [6].

Informally, we distinguish different types of LDFs, each of which represents LDFs that have the same type of selector and the same kind of conditions on their metadata $M$ and on their controls $C$. Section 3.3 will show a specific LDF type.

Some LDFs can be quite large; for instance, a data dump typically contains millions of triples. Downloading such a large fragment can be undesired in certain situations, for instance, if we just want to inspect part of the data in the fragment, or if we are only interested in a fragment's metadata but not its actual data. Therefore, a server that hosts LDFs can segment them into smaller pages. Formally, we capture such a page as follows:

**Definition 5 (LDF page).** *Let $f = \langle u, s, \Gamma, M, C \rangle$ be an LDF of some finite set of blank-node-free RDF triples. A page partitioning of $f$ is a finite, nonempty set $\Phi$ consisting of so-called pages of $f$ such that the following properties hold:*

1. *Each page $\phi \in \Phi$ is a tuple $\phi = \langle u', u_f, s_f, \Gamma', M', C' \rangle$ with the following six elements: (i) $u'$ is a URI from which page $\phi$ can be retrieved with $u' \neq u$, (ii) $u_f = u$, (iii) $s_f = s$, (iv) $\Gamma' \subseteq \Gamma$, (v) $M' \supseteq M$, and (vi) $C' \supseteq C$.*
2. *For every pair of two distinct pages $\phi_i = \langle u'_i, u_f, s_f, \Gamma'_i, M'_i, C'_i \rangle \in \Phi$ and $\phi_j = \langle u'_j, u_f, s_f, \Gamma'_j, M'_j, C'_j \rangle \in \Phi$ it holds that $u'_i \neq u'_j$ and $\Gamma'_i \cap \Gamma'_j = \emptyset$.*
3. *$\Gamma = \bigcup_{\langle u', u_f, s_f, \Gamma', M', C' \rangle \in \Phi} \Gamma'$.*
4. *There exists a strict total order $\prec$ on $\Phi$ such that, for every pair of two pages $\phi_i = \langle u'_i, u_f, s_f, \Gamma'_i, M'_i, C'_i \rangle \in \Phi$ and $\phi_j = \langle u'_j, u_f, s_f, \Gamma'_j, M'_j, C'_j \rangle \in \Phi$ with $\phi_j$ being the direct successor of $\phi_i$ (i.e., $\phi_i \prec \phi_j$ and $\neg \exists \phi_k \in \Phi : \phi_i \prec \phi_k \prec \phi_j$), there exists a control $c \in C'_i$ with $u'_j \in \mathrm{img}(c)$.*

Note in particular that each page contains *all* metadata and controls of the corresponding fragment, in addition to the controls that allow to navigate from one page to the next. If paging is available, servers should automatically redirect clients from the fragment to its first page, to avoid sending overly large chunks.

The collection of all LDFs of a certain dataset provided by a server is captured formally as follows:

**Definition 6 (LDF collection).** *Let $G \subseteq \mathcal{T}^*$ be a finite set of blank-node-free RDF triples, and let c be a control. The c-specific LDF collection over G is a set F of LDFs such that, for each LDF $f \in F$ with $f = \langle u, s, \Gamma, M, C \rangle$, the following three properties hold: 1. f is an LDF of G;    2. $s \in \mathrm{dom}(c)$;    3. $c(s) = u$.*

Finally, we define a query semantics for evaluating SPARQL queries over a dataset that is published as a collection of LDFs.

**Definition 7 (query semantics).** *Let $G \subseteq \mathcal{T}^*$ be a finite set of blank-node-free RDF triples, and let F be some LDF collection over G. The evaluation of a SPARQL graph pattern P over F, denoted by $[\![P]\!]_F$, is defined by $[\![P]\!]_F = [\![P]\!]_G$.*

## 3.3   Triple Pattern Fragments

The current HTTP interfaces for RDF, as discussed in Section 2 and summarized in Fig. 1, have limitations for query evaluation over live data with high availability. To facilitate querying on the client side, clients should be able to access those fragments that correspond to important parts of the query. To maximize availability on the server side, servers should only offer those fragments they can generate with minimal effort. In other words, we have to search for a compromise along the axis in Fig. 1. Offering triple-pattern-based access to datasets seems an interesting compromise because *a)* graph patterns, the main building blocks for SPARQL queries, consist of triple patterns, so they are important query parts for clients; and *b)* servers can select triples corresponding to a certain triple pattern at low processing cost [7]. For this reason, we introduced a triple-pattern-based HTTP interface for data access [26, 27], which we formalize as follows.

**Definition 8 (triple pattern fragment and collection).** *Given a control c, a c-specific LDF collection F is called a* triple pattern fragment collection *if, for any possible triple pattern tp, there exists an LDF $\langle u, s, \Gamma, M, C \rangle \in F$, referred to as a* triple pattern fragment, *such that the following three properties hold:*

1. *s is the triple pattern selector for triple pattern tp (as per Definition 2).*
2. *There exists a (metadata) RDF triple $\langle u, \mathtt{void{:}triples}, cnt \rangle \in M$ with cnt representing an estimate of the cardinality of $\Gamma$, that is, cnt is an integer that has the following two properties:*
   (a) *If $[\![tp]\!]_G = \emptyset$, then $cnt = 0$.*
   (b) *If $[\![tp]\!]_G \neq \emptyset$, then $cnt > 0$ and $\mathrm{abs}(|[\![tp]\!]_G| - cnt) \leq \epsilon$ for some F-specific threshold $\epsilon$.*
3. *$c \in C$.*

Since the selector s of a triple pattern fragment $f = \langle u, s, \Gamma, M, C \rangle$ is a triple pattern selector, all elements of $\Gamma$ are singleton sets: $|G'| = 1$ for all $G' \in \Gamma$. Large fragments would usually be paged as in Definition 5; so while a single page would not contain all matching triples of the fragment, it would contain the *cnt* estimate metadata for the entire fragment, together with the collection's control.

Furthermore, any triple pattern fragment collection over some set of RDF triples $G$ consists of the *complete* set of triple pattern fragments of $G$, which in practice means the server can provide any of them when requested, i.e., it does not need to have materialized versions for all of them. Each of these fragments includes the collection-specific hypermedia control (e.g., using the Hydra Core Vocabulary [26]), making triple pattern fragment collections hypermedia-driven REST APIs [9]. Consequently, by discovering an arbitrary fragment of a collection, a client can directly reach and retrieve *all* fragments of the collection. In particular, this includes all fragments with a selector for one of the triple patterns of a given SPARQL graph pattern. Therefore, clients can compute a complete query result for such a pattern over the collection after obtaining *any* of its fragments. In the following section, we discuss an efficient approach for performing this.

# 4 SPARQL Queries over Triple Pattern Fragments

## 4.1 High-Level Algorithm

Triple pattern fragments offer triple-pattern-based access to a dataset on the Web. If a client wants to evaluate a SPARQL query over this dataset, it should thus transform this query into a sequence of triple pattern queries. To optimize the performance of the execution, the number of HTTP requests should be minimized, and they should execute in parallel to the extent possible. Reducing the number of expensive operations is possible by selecting a suitable order in which query parts are evaluated. Therefore, database systems use a *query planner* to create an optimized order, based on statistical information about the data [10]. Since such information is usually not available for data on the Web, query planners have to resort to heuristics [13]. To mitigate this, triple pattern fragments contain metadata, i.e., the number of triples matching a certain pattern.

We previously introduced a recursive algorithm to efficiently evaluate basic graph patterns (BGPs) over a triple pattern collection [27], since BGPs form the main building blocks of SPARQL queries. We summarize the algorithm here:

1. For each triple pattern $tp_i$ in the BGP $B = \{tp_1, \ldots, tp_n\}$, fetch the first page $\phi_1^i$ of the LDF $f_i$ for $tp_i$, which contains an estimate $cnt_i$ of the total number of matches for $tp_i$. Choose $\epsilon$ such that $cnt_\epsilon = \min(\{cnt_1, \ldots, cnt_n\})$.
2. Fetch all remaining pages of $f_\epsilon$. For each triple $t$ in the LDF, generate the solution mapping $\mu_t$ such that $\mu_t[tp_\epsilon] = t$. Then compose the subpattern $B_t = \{tp \mid tp = \mu_t[tp_j] \wedge tp_j \in B\} \setminus \{t\}$. If $B_t \neq \emptyset$, find mappings $\Omega_{B_t}$ by calling the algorithm for $B_t$. Else, $\Omega_{B_t} = \{\mu_\emptyset\}$ with $\mu_\emptyset$ the empty mapping.
3. Return all solution mappings $\mu \in \{\mu_t \cup \mu' \mid \mu' \in \Omega_{B_t}\}$.

By recursively fetching those fragments with the lowest number of matches, and applying their mappings to the graph pattern, we narrow down the number of HTTP requests that are subsequently needed.

While this algorithm finds all matches for the BGP in the collection, its recursive calling structure returns all results at once, i.e., we have to wait for the first result until all other results have been computed. Furthermore, adding support for additional SPARQL operators to such a monolithic algorithm is impractical.

## 4.2 Dynamic Iterator Pipelines

A common approach to implement query execution in database systems is through *iterators* that are typically arranged in a tree or a *pipeline*, based on which query results are computed recursively [10]. Such a pipelined approach has also been studied for Linked Data query processing [13,15]. In order to enable *incremental* results and allow the straightforward addition of SPARQL operators, we implement a triple pattern fragments client using iterators.

The previous algorithm, however, cannot be implemented by a *static* iterator pipeline. For instance, consider a query for architects born in European capitals:

```
SELECT ?person ?city WHERE {
    ?person a dbpedia-owl:Architect.              # tp₁
    ?person dbpprop:birthPlace ?city.             # tp₂
    ?city dc:subject dbpedia:Capitals_in_Europe.  # tp₃
} LIMIT 100
```

Suppose the pipeline begins by finding `?city` mappings for $tp_3$. It then needs to choose whether it will next consider $tp_1$ or $tp_2$. The optimal choice, however, differs depending on the value of `?city`:

- For `dbpedia:Paris`, there are ±1,900 matches for $tp_2$, and ±1,200 matches for $tp_1$, so there will be less HTTP requests if we continue with $tp_1$.
- For `dbpedia:Vilnius`, there are 164 matches for $tp_2$, and ±1,200 matches for $tp_1$, so there will be less HTTP requests if we continue with $tp_2$.

With a static pipeline, we would have to choose the pipeline structure in advance and subsequently reuse it.

In order to generate an optimized pipeline for each (sub-)query, we propose a divide-and-conquer strategy in which a query is decomposed *dynamically* into subqueries depending on partial solution mappings. The main function of an iterator is `next()`, which either returns a mapping or `nil` if no mappings are left.

We first introduce a trivial *start iterator*, which outputs the empty mapping $\mu_0$ on the first call to `next()`, and `nil` on all subsequent calls.

Next, we implement a previously defined *triple pattern iterator* [15] for triple pattern fragments. This iterator $I_{tp}$ is initialized with a predecessor iterator $I_p$, a triple pattern $tp$, and a page $\phi_0$ of an arbitrary triple pattern fragment of a collection $F$. The iterator then extends mappings from its predecessor by reading triples from the LDF corresponding to triple pattern $tp$. The URL of this LDF is retrieved through the collection control in the start page $\phi_0$. Each call to $I_{tp}$.`next()` results in mappings for $tp$ in $F$, depending on the predecessor's mappings.

To solve BGPs of SPARQL queries, we introduce a triple pattern fragment *BGP iterator*. Such a *BGP iterator* is initialized with a predecessor $I_p$, a BGP $B = \{tp_1, \ldots, tp_n\}$, and an arbitrary triple pattern fragment page $\phi_0$ of a collection $F$. For an empty pattern ($n = 0$), a BGP iterator is equal to a start iterator. For a pattern length $n = 1$, it is constructed by creating a triple pattern iterator for $(I_p, tp_1, \phi_0)$. For $n \geq 2$, a BGP iterator uses Algorithm 1.

BGP iterators evaluate a BGP by recursively decomposing it into smaller iterators. For each triple pattern in the BGP mapped by each result of $I_p$, the iterator

**Data:** (predecessor $I_p$, BGP $B = \{tp_1, \ldots, tp_n\}$ with $n \geq 2$, start page $\phi_0$)

```
1  I ← nil; c ← the triple pattern control in the control set C_0 of φ_0;
2  Function BasicGraphPatternIterator.next()
3  |  μ ← nil;
4  |  while μ = nil do
5  |  |  while I = nil do
6  |  |  |  μ_p ← I_p.next();
7  |  |  |  return nil if μ_p = nil;
8  |  |  |  Φ ← {φ_1^i | φ_1^i = HTTP GET first fragment page using URL c(μ_p[tp_i])};
9  |  |  |  ε ← i such that cnt_{φ_1^i} = min({cnt_{φ_1^1}, …, cnt_{φ_1^n}});
10 |  |  |  I_ε ← TriplePatternIterator(StartIterator(), μ_p[tp_ε], φ_1^ε);
11 |  |  |  I ← BasicGraphPatternIterator(I_ε, {μ[tp] | tp ∈ B \ {tp_ε}}, φ_1^ε);
12 |  |  μ ← I.next();
13 |  return μ ∪ μ_p;
```

**Algorithm 1.** For all mappings $\mu_p$ of a predecessor $I_p$, a BGP iterator for a pattern $B = \{tp_1, \ldots, tp_n\}$ creates a triple pattern iterator $I_\epsilon$ for the least frequent pattern $tp_\epsilon$, passed to a BGP iterator for the remainder of $P$.

fetches the first page of the corresponding LDF. This page contains the *cnt* metadata, which tells us how many matches the dataset has for each triple pattern. The pattern is then decomposed by evaluating it using *a)* a triple pattern iterator for the triple pattern with the smallest number of matches, and *b)* a new BGP iterator for the remainder of the pattern. This results in a *dynamic* pipeline for *each* of the mappings of its predecessor, as visualized in Fig. 2. Each pipeline is optimized *locally* for a specific mapping, reducing the number of requests.

To evaluate a SPARQL query over a triple pattern fragment collection, we proceed as follows. For each BGP of the query, a BGP iterator is created. Dedicated iterators are necessary for other SPARQL constructs such as UNION and OPTIONAL, but their implementation need not be LDF-specific; they can reuse the triple pattern fragment BGP iterators. The predecessor of the first iterator is a start iterator. We continuously pull solution mappings from the last iterator in the pipeline and output them as solutions of the query, until the last iterator responds with nil. This pull-based process is able to deliver results incrementally.

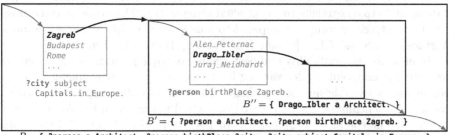

**Fig. 2.** A BGP iterator decomposes a BGP $B = \{tp_1, \ldots, tp_n\}$ into a triple pattern iterator for an optimal $tp_i$ and, for each resulting solution mapping $\mu$ of $tp_i$, creates a BGP iterator for the remaining pattern $B' = \{tp \mid tp = \mu[tp_j] \wedge tp_j \in B\} \setminus \{\mu[tp_i]\}$

As most time of an LDF client is spent waiting on HTTP requests, the process can be sped up by buffering the individual iterators. A major advantage of our dynamic pipelines is that, because each element of a BGP iterator uses its own separate sub-pipeline, multiple pipelines can run in parallel. E.g., given the context of Fig. 2, the pipelines for Zagreb, Budapest, and Rome can run in parallel, and so can those for the Alen_Peternac, Drago_Ibler, and Juraj_Neidhardt. This results in more concurrent HTTP requests and thus a lower average waiting time per request. Since triple pattern fragment APIs are deliberately designed to allow high throughput, clients are not bound by crawler politeness rules [14].

## 5    Evaluation

The goal of the evaluation is to compare the availability–performance relationship of triple-pattern-based query execution to query execution over other LDFs, SPARQL endpoints in particular. *Performance* in this case refers to the query response time (i.e., time until the client reports a first solution of the query result) and total execution time. We measure *availability* of a server as the fraction of cases in which the client receives a response within a specified amount of time after sending a request. For this evaluation, we use a timeout of 60 seconds.

Since overloaded servers are a major cause of unavailability, we also monitor processor, memory, and bandwidth usage of servers. The assumption is that servers with high resource usage will be more prone to low availability, i.e., a temporal inability to process responses in a reasonable time.

### 5.1    Experimental Setup

We implemented the triple pattern fragments query execution approach of Section 4 as an open-source LDF client for SPARQL queries. This client is written in JavaScript, so it can be used either as a standalone application, or as a library for browser and server applications. While we also implemented an LDF client as an adapter for the popular Java framework Jena [11], it was not included in the comparison, because it uses the existing Jena ARQ querying infrastructure instead of our algorithm. The used LDF server is an open-source Java server with the compressed HDT format [7] as back-end. We provide all source code of the implementations, as well as the full benchmark configuration, at https://github.com/LinkedDataFragments/. The triple pattern fragments client/server setup is compared to four SPARQL endpoint infrastructures: Virtuoso (6.1.8 and 7.1.1) [5] and Jena Fuseki [11] (TDB 1.0.1 and HDT 1.1.1).

To measure the availability and performance of triple pattern fragment servers and SPARQL endpoints under varying loads, we set up an environment with one server and a variable number of clients. In order to obtain repeatable experiments, the benchmarks were executed on virtual machines on the Amazon AWS platform. The complete setup consists of 1 server (4 virtual CPUs, 7.5 GB RAM), 1 HTTP cache (8 virtual CPUs, 15 GB RAM) and 60 client machines (4 virtual CPUs, 7.5 GB RAM), capable of running 4 single-threaded clients each. We purposely chose a modest server machine to show the impact for low-budget scenarios. The HTTP cache acts as a proxy server between servers and clients and was chosen for its bandwidth capabilities (which Amazon associates with specific CPU/RAM combinations). It caches HTTP requests for a maximum of 5 minutes.

To date, no SPARQL availability benchmark exists; however, several performance benchmarks exist. We chose the Berlin SPARQL Benchmark (BSBM) [3] because of its wide-spread use, with a dataset size of 100 million triples. To mimic the variability of real-world scenarios, each client executes different BSBM query workloads based on its own random seed. As existing work on Linked Data querying focuses exclusively on BGP queries [14], this paper is the first to use a SPARQL benchmark on a Linked Data publishing method with a non-SPARQL HTTP interface. We do *not* aim for best performance with triple pattern fragments; instead, we strive to improve the availability/performance balance.

For our experiments, we have extended BSBM with support for parsing streaming Turtle results, and added the possibility to measure the *response time* (reception of first solution) in addition to the *total query execution time* (reception of all solutions). Some of the BSBM queries use the ORDER BY operator, which has to be implemented in a blocking way; i.e., the first solution can only be sent after all solutions have been computed. Therefore, (only) for measurements of the response time, we use variants of these queries without ORDER BY, assuming the user application prefers streaming results and performs sorting itself.

After every 1-second interval during the evaluation, we measure on the server, cache, and client the current value of several properties, including CPU usage of each core, memory usage, and network IO. These measurements are obtained using PerfMon, while distributed testing happens using JMeter.[2]

## 5.2   Results and Discussion

Figs. 3.1 to 3.10 summarize the main measurements of the evaluation. All $x$-axes use a logarithmic scale, because we varied the number of clients exponentially.

Fig. 3.1 shows that the performance of SPARQL endpoints significantly decreases with the number of clients. Even though a triple pattern fragments setup executes SPARQL queries with lower performance, the performance decrease with a higher number of clients is significantly lower. Because of caching effects, triple pattern fragments querying starts performing slightly better with a high number of clients ($n > 100$). The per-core processor usage of the SPARQL endpoints grows rapidly (Fig. 3.5) and quickly reaches the maximum; in practice, this means the endpoint spends all CPU time processing queries while newly incoming requests are queued. The triple pattern fragments server consumes only limited CPU, because each individual request is simple to answer, and due to their finer granularity, the cache can answer several requests (Fig. 3.4).

At the client side, the opposite happens (Fig. 3.7): clients of SPARQL endpoints hardly use CPU, whereas triple pattern fragments clients do use between 20% and 100% CPU. This percentage decreases with higher numbers of clients, because the networking time dominates. Memory consumption remains fairly constant and low (Fig. 3.8). On the server (Fig. 3.6), memory usage remains constantly high; however, each considered implementation could be configured to use less memory.

---

[2] http://jmeter.apache.org/ and http://jmeter-plugins.org/wiki/PerfMonAgent/

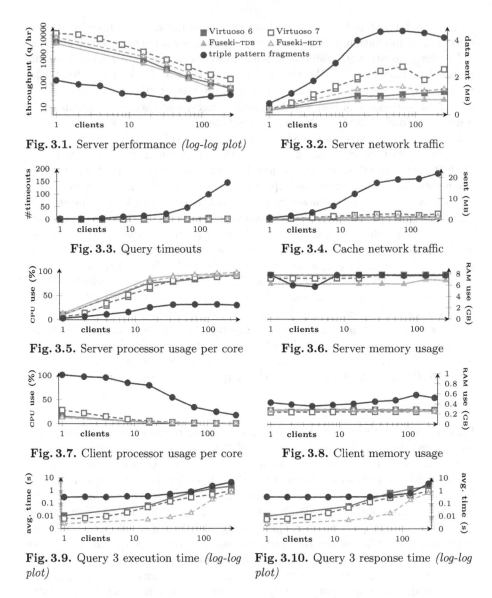

**Fig. 3.1.** Server performance *(log-log plot)*

**Fig. 3.2.** Server network traffic

**Fig. 3.3.** Query timeouts

**Fig. 3.4.** Cache network traffic

**Fig. 3.5.** Server processor usage per core

**Fig. 3.6.** Server memory usage

**Fig. 3.7.** Client processor usage per core

**Fig. 3.8.** Client memory usage

**Fig. 3.9.** Query 3 execution time *(log-log plot)*

**Fig. 3.10.** Query 3 response time *(log-log plot)*

Fig. 3.2 shows the outbound network traffic on the server with an increasing number of clients. This traffic is substantially higher with triple pattern fragment servers, because clients need to ask for several responses to evaluate a single query. The cache ensures that responses to identical requests are reused; Fig. 3.4 indeed shows that caching is far more effective with triple pattern fragments.

Some of the BSBM queries execute slowly on triple pattern fragments clients, especially those queries that strongly depend on operators such as FILTER, which in a triple-pattern-based interface can only be evaluated on the client. The execution times of these queries exceed the timeout limit of 60s (Fig. 3.3).

Therefore, we separately study BSBM query template 3 (finding products that satisfy 2 numerical inequalities and an OPTIONAL clause), which is one of the templates whose queries cause few timeouts. Note how its execution time (Fig. 3.9) for triple pattern fragments starts high, but only increases very gradually, whereas the execution time on SPARQL endpoints rises very rapidly. Furthermore, the response times increase more slowly with increased load (Fig. 3.10). Only on the triple pattern fragments server, CPU usage remains low for this query at all times.

These results indicate that triple pattern fragments query execution succeeds in reducing server usage, at the cost of increased query times. Triple pattern fragments servers cope better with increasing numbers of clients than SPARQL endpoints. Furthermore, querying benefits strongly from regular HTTP caching, which can be added at any point in the network. This is all the more remarkable since, to allow comparisons with other work, these results were obtained with an *existing* SPARQL benchmark that focuses on performance, not availability. Even though certain queries make it difficult for an LDF client to find *all* results within the timeout window (especially with blocking operators such as ORDER BY), the *first* results to all queries arrive before the timeout period. In the future, the development of an availability-focused SPARQL benchmark could stimulate availability improvements of the considered systems. The full results of our experiments are published as LDFs at http://data.linkeddatafragments.org/.

# 6    Conclusions

Publishers of Linked Data strive to host their data reliably at minimal cost. Applications, on the other hand, need to query data in the most flexible way. The three well-known RDF interfaces on the Web—SPARQL endpoints, Linked Data documents, and data dumps—are just a fraction of all possible ways to transfer Linked Data from a server to a client. Since SPARQL endpoints offer the most flexibility, they are not coincidentally the most expensive to host with high availability. The *Linked Data Fragments* framework captures the search for alternative HTTP interfaces to RDF data, trying to balance the server's desire for maximum reliability and the client's need for maximum flexibility.

In this paper, we have shown that triple pattern fragments, which additionally contain count metadata and hypermedia controls, can reduce the load on servers to less than 30% of the load on SPARQL endpoints. This happens by shifting the query-specific tasks to clients, at the cost of slower query execution. Instead of sending one complex query, clients use a dynamic iterator pipeline to combine the results of several simpler queries, thereby also vastly improving the effectiveness of HTTP caching. This captures the spirit of *Web* querying: clients browse pages and iteratively extract bits of information to find complex answers. The goal of triple pattern fragments is to provide those bits that are helpful for clients to evaluate queries, yet inexpensive to generate by servers.

Triple pattern fragments are definitely not the final answer to querying RDF datasets on the Web. In fact, there will probably never be such a final answer. By definition, each API on the Web that publishes RDF triples (which, through

JSON-LD [24], can include those APIs that publish JSON) offers its own kind of LDFs. The challenge for future clients is to find answers to queries through all kinds of *different* fragments along the axis of LDFs. The results indicate the potential of this querying strategy, as we have shown they allow executing complex queries of common SPARQL benchmarks over live data on the Web with high availability. Whereas the Linked Data principles emphasize *hyperlinks* between data documents [2], triple pattern fragments add *forms* that let clients control what data they request. Those forms allow custom access, but at the same time limit the possible kind of queries in order to save on server processing resources.

Especially in cases where there are limited financial resources to publish data, triple pattern fragments could make a significant difference: data can be hosted at low cost, in a way that allows live querying, with high availability. In addition to our own open source implementations of LDF servers, two third-party implementations are available. The Belgian Crossroads Bank for Enterprises recently published their data as triple pattern fragments (http://data.kbodata.be/) using their own open-source server. The open-source data management system The DataTank (http://thedatatank.com/) now also supports triple pattern fragments. This lowers the entry barrier for publishers even further. Implementers of clients and servers can follow the triple pattern fragments specification [26].

Improving the performance is possible if clients can query more specific fragments. In particular, support for certain FILTER expressions would speed up several queries, as triple pattern fragments only allow for exact matches. Interesting future work is therefore to define new classes of LDFs that support such features, where we always need to keep in mind that minimizing the server's processing cost for each fragment is the key to maximizing its availability. Part of this work includes the *description* of such fragments, so a client can dynamically discover what fragment types a server offers, and thus how it can execute a query in an optimal way. For instance, if a server supports (a subset of) SPARQL, clients need to ask fewer queries than when only triple patterns are supported. This trade-off between server cost/availability and client performance will continue to exist.

Finally, LDF querying shows us that we perhaps need to re-evaluate the way we develop applications on top of Linked Data. The dominant paradigm so far has been: *"ask a complex question to a server; wait; act on the results"*, where the "waiting" part can be long if the server has low availability. As the response times of the evaluation indicate, new applications might prefer not to wait, evolving towards a real-time, distributed paradigm: *"ask simple questions to many servers, acting on results as they arrive"*. A major benefit of clients that solve queries by fetching fragments of Linked Data, in addition to incrementally updating results, is that they can support distributed querying by asking fragments from different servers. In other words, limiting the HTTP interfaces of RDF servers does not only lead to higher availability, it encourages clients to solve complex queries themselves—and for that, they have the entire Web of Data at their disposal.

# References

1. Amundsen, M.: Hypermedia types. In: REST: From Research to Practice, pp. 93–116. Springer (2011)
2. Bizer, C., Heath, T., Berners-Lee, T.: Linked Data – the story so far. International Journal on Semantic Web and Information Systems 5(3), 1–22 (2009)
3. Bizer, C., Schultz, A.: The Berlin SPARQL benchmark. International Journal on Semantic Web and Information Systems 5(2), 1–24 (2009)
4. Buil-Aranda, C., Hogan, A.: SPARQL Web-querying infrastructure: Ready for action? In: Proceedings of the 12th International Semantic Web Conference (November 2013)
5. Erling, O., Mikhailov, I.: Virtuoso: RDF support in a native RDBMS. In: Semantic Web Information Management, pp. 501–519. Springer (2010)
6. Feigenbaum, L., Williams, G.T., Clark, K.G., Torres, E.: SPARQL 1.1 protocol Recommendation, W3C (March 2013), http://www.w3.org/TR/sparql11-protocol/
7. Fernández, J.D., Martínez-Prieto, M.A., Gutirrez, C., Polleres, A., Arias, M.: Binary RDF representation for publication and exchange (HDT). Journal of Web Semantics 19, 22–41 (2013)
8. Fielding, R.T.: Architectural Styles and the Design of Network-based Software Architectures. Ph.D. thesis, University of California (2000)
9. Fielding, R.T.: REST APIS must be hypertext-driven (October 2008), http://roy.gbiv.com/untangled/2008/rest-apis-must-be-hypertext-driven
10. Graefe, G.: Query evaluation techniques for large databases. ACM Computing Surveys 25(2), 73–169 (June 1993)
11. Grobe, M.: RDF, Jena, SPARQL and the Semantic Web. In: Proceedings of the 37th Annual ACM SIGUCCS Fall Conference: Communication and Collaboration (2009), doi:10.1145/1629501.1629525
12. Harris, S., Seaborne, A.: SPARQL 1.1 query language. Recommendation, W3C (March 2013), http://www.w3.org/TR/sparql11-query/
13. Hartig, O.: Zero-knowledge query planning for an iterator implementation of link traversal based query execution. In: Antoniou, G., Grobelnik, M., Simperl, E., Parsia, B., Plexousakis, D., De Leenheer, P., Pan, J. (eds.) ESWC 2011, Part I. LNCS, vol. 6643, pp. 154–169. Springer, Heidelberg (2011)
14. Hartig, O.: An overview on execution strategies for Linked Data queries. Datenbank-Spektrum 13(2), 89–99 (2013)
15. Hartig, O., Bizer, C., Freytag, J.-C.: Executing SPARQL Queries over the Web of Linked Data. In: Bernstein, A., Karger, D.R., Heath, T., Feigenbaum, L., Maynard, D., Motta, E., Thirunarayan, K. (eds.) ISWC 2009. LNCS, vol. 5823, pp. 293–309. Springer, Heidelberg (2009)
16. Klyne, G., Carrol, J.J.: Resource Description Framework (RDF): Concepts and abstract syntax. Rec., W3C (February 2004), http://www.w3.org/TR/rdf-concepts/
17. Linked Data API, https://code.google.com/p/linked-data-api/
18. Matteis, L.: Restpark: Minimal RESTful API for retrieving RDF triples (2013), http://lmatteis.github.io/restpark/restpark.pdf
19. Morsey, M., Lehmann, J.: DBpedia SPARQL benchmark performance assessment with real queries on real data. In: Proceedings of the 9th International Semantic Web Conference (2011)
20. Ogbuji, C.: SPARQL 1.1 Graph Store HTTP Protocol. Recommendation, W3C (March 2013), http://www.w3.org/TR/sparql11-http-rdf-update/

21. Pérez, J., Arenas, M., Gutierrez, C.: Semantics and complexity of SPARQL. ACM Transactions on Database Systems 34(3), 16:1–16:45 (2009)
22. Schmidt, M., Hornung, T., Meier, M., Pinkel, C., Lausen, G.: SP²Bench: A SPARQL performance benchmark. In: Semantic Web Information Management (2010)
23. Speicher, S., Arwe, J., Malhotra, A.: Linked Data Platform 1.0. Candidate recommendation, W3C (June 2014), http://www.w3.org/TR/2014/CR-ldp-20140619/
24. Sporny, M., Longley, D., Kellogg, G., Lanthaler, M., Lindström, N.: JSONLD 1.0. Recommendation, W3C (January 2014), http://www.w3.org/TR/json-ld/
25. Verborgh, R.: Linked Data Fragments. Unofficial draft, Hydra WTHREEC Community Group, http://www.hydra-cg.com/spec/latest/linked-data-fragments/
26. Verborgh, R.: Triple Pattern Fragments. Unofficial draft, Hydra W3C Community Group, http://www.hydra-cg.com/spec/latest/triple-pattern-fragments/
27. Verborgh, R., Vander Sande, M., Colpaert, P., Coppens, S., Mannens, E., Van de Walle, R.: Web-scale querying through Linked Data Fragments. In: Proceedings of the 7th Workshop on Linked Data on the Web (2014)
28. Wilde, E., Hausenblas, M.: RESTful SPARQL? You name it! – Aligning SPARQL with REST and resource orientation. In: Proceedings of the 4 Workshop on Emerging Web Services Technology, pp. 39–43. ACM (2009)

# Diversified Stress Testing
# of RDF Data Management Systems

Güneş Aluç, Olaf Hartig, M. Tamer Özsu, and Khuzaima Daudjee

David R. Cheriton School of Computer Science, Waterloo, ON, Canada
{galuc,ohartig,tamer.ozsu,kdaudjee}@uwaterloo.ca

**Abstract.** The Resource Description Framework (RDF) is a standard for conceptually describing data on the Web, and SPARQL is the query language for RDF. As RDF data continue to be published across heterogeneous domains and integrated at Web-scale such as in the Linked Open Data (LOD) cloud, RDF data management systems are being exposed to queries that are far more diverse and workloads that are far more varied. The first contribution of our work is an in-depth experimental analysis that shows existing SPARQL benchmarks are not suitable for testing systems for diverse queries and varied workloads. To address these shortcomings, our second contribution is the Waterloo SPARQL Diversity Test Suite (WatDiv) that provides stress testing tools for RDF data management systems. Using WatDiv, we have been able to reveal issues with existing systems that went unnoticed in evaluations using earlier benchmarks. Specifically, our experiments with five popular RDF data management systems show that they cannot deliver good performance uniformly across workloads. For some queries, there can be as much as five orders of magnitude difference between the query execution time of the fastest and the slowest system while the fastest system on one query may unexpectedly time out on another query. By performing a detailed analysis, we pinpoint these problems to specific types of queries and workloads.

**Keywords:** RDF, SPARQL, systems, benchmarking, workload diversity.

## 1 Introduction

With the proliferation of very large, heterogeneous RDF datasets such as those in the Linked Open Data (LOD) cloud [6], there is increasing demand for high-performance RDF data management systems. A number of such systems have been developed; however, as queries executed on these systems become increasingly more diverse [4], [10], [16], these systems have started to display unpredictable behaviour, even to the extent that on some queries they time out (cf., Fig. 4). This behaviour is not captured by existing benchmarks. The problem is that data that are handled by these RDF data management systems have become far more heterogeneous [10], and web applications that are supported by these systems have become far more varied [4], [16], but existing benchmarks do not have the corresponding variability in their datasets and workloads. Consequently, problems go undetected in evaluations using existing benchmarks until systems are actually deployed. To address these shortcomings, we have designed the Waterloo SPARQL Diversity Test Suite (WatDiv) that offers stress testing tools to reveal a much wider range of problems with RDF data management systems.

P. Mika et al. (Eds.) ISWC 2014, Part I, LNCS 8796, pp. 197–212, 2014.

Our contributions with WatDiv and the work leading up to its design can be summarized in three steps. First, we introduce two classes of query features, namely, structural (cf., Section 2.1) and data-driven features (cf., Section 2.2) that should be used to evaluate the variability of the datasets and workloads in a SPARQL benchmark. More specifically, with these features we differentiate as much as possible those types of queries that may result in unpredictable system behaviour and are indicators of potential flaws in physical design. For example, in a previous work, we illustrate that the choice of physical design in an RDF system is very sensitive to the types of joins that the system can efficiently support [2]. Hence, we introduce a feature called "join vertex type". Likewise, we note that a system's performance depends on the characteristics of the data as much as the query itself. Consequently, we introduce additional features that capture multiple notions of selectivity and result cardinality.

Second, we have performed an in-depth analysis on existing SPARQL benchmarks using the two classes of query features that we introduce. Our experimental evaluation demonstrates that no single benchmark (including those that are based on actual query logs) is sufficiently varied to test whether a system has consistently good performance across diverse workloads (cf., Section 3). Furthermore, these benchmarks do not provide the tools to localize problems to specific types of queries if needed. For example, it would be useful if one could diagnose that the system under test has problems with queries that have a particular join vertex type, and drill down the evaluation if necessary. These are exactly the type of evaluations that we aim to facilitate with WatDiv.

Third and last, we use WatDiv to experimentally evaluate five popular RDF data management systems (cf., Section 5). Our discussion consists of two parts. First, we demonstrate that evaluations using a diverse workload can help reveal problems about systems that existing benchmarks cannot identify. Second, we show that by analyzing results across one or more structural and data-driven features, it is possible to diagnose and reason about specific problems—a feature not supported by any other benchmark.

## 2   Preliminaries

This section defines query features based on which we shall discuss the diversity of SPARQL benchmark workloads. These features can be categorized into two classes: (i) structural features and (ii) data-driven features. We assume the reader is familiar with the RDF data model [21] and the SPARQL query language [14].

We define these features over a basic fragment of SPARQL, namely, basic graph patterns (BGPs) with filter expressions. For the sake of brevity, we denote queries in this fragment by a pair $\bar{B} = \langle B, F \rangle$, hereafter, referred to as a *constrained BGP* (*CBGP*), where $B$ is a finite set of triple patterns (i.e., a BGP) and $F$ is a finite set of SPARQL filter expressions. Hence, by using the algebraic syntax for SPARQL [3], a CBGP $\bar{B} = \langle B, F \rangle$ with $F = \{f_1, \ldots, f_n\}$ is equivalent to a SPARQL graph pattern $P$ of the form $\big((\ldots(B \text{ FILTER } f_1)\ldots) \text{ FILTER } f_n\big)$ (if $F = \emptyset$, then $P$ is the BGP $B$). Consequently, the *evaluation* of $\bar{B}$ over an RDF graph $G$, denoted by $[\![\bar{B}]\!]_G$, is the bag (multiset) of solution mappings $[\![P]\!]_G$ as defined by the standard SPARQL query semantics [3], [14].

While a discussion of a more expressive fragment of SPARQL is certainly possible, for our purposes, this is not necessary: the objective of our benchmark is stress testing,

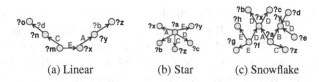

(a) Linear                (b) Star                (c) Snowflake

**Fig. 1.** Possible query structures

with an emphasis on revealing issues with the physical design of RDF data management systems. To this end, we try to generate test queries that are as diverse as possible within this basic fragment of SPARQL and deliberately avoid testing of complex functionality such as filters, unions, aggregation and optional graph patterns.

## 2.1 Structural Features

Every BGP (as used by a CBGP) combines a set of triple patterns into one of numerous query structures such as those in Fig. 1a–1c. As a basis for comparing the structural diversity of different sets of CBGPs we introduce four features.

**Triple Pattern Count:** This feature refers to the number of triple patterns in (the BGP of) a CBGP. Triple pattern count allows one to broadly distinguish between simple and structurally complex queries. Ideally, we would like an RDF system to execute simple queries extremely fast while scaling well with increasing number of triple patterns. In fact, DBpedia query logs [17] reveal that while in general most queries contain only a few triple patterns, users may issue (albeit infrequently) queries having more than 50 triple patterns.

**Join Vertex Count:** This feature represents the number of RDF terms (i.e., URIs, literals, and blank nodes) and variables that are the subject or object of multiple triple patterns in a CBGP. Hereafter, we refer to these terms and variables as *join vertices* of the CBGP. Formally, if $\mathcal{T}$ and $\mathcal{V}$ denote the set of all RDF terms and the set of all variables, respectively, an element $x \in (\mathcal{T} \cup \mathcal{V})$ is a *join vertex* of CBGP $\bar{B} = \langle B, F \rangle$ if there exist two distinct triple patterns $tp = \langle s, p, o \rangle$ and $tp' = \langle s', p', o' \rangle$ such that (i) $tp \in B$ and $tp' \in B$, (ii) $x \in \{s, o\}$, and (iii) $x \in \{s', o'\}$.

**Join Vertex Degree:** For each join vertex $x$ of a CBGP $\bar{B} = \langle B, F \rangle$, the *degree* of $x$ is the number of triple patterns in $B$ whose subject or object is $x$. Hereafter, for any such triple pattern $\langle s, p, o \rangle \in B$ with $x \in \{s, o\}$ we say that the triple pattern is *incident* on $x$.

Join vertex count and join vertex degree offer a finer distinction of structural complexity than the triple pattern count. For example, the two queries in Fig. 1a and Fig. 1b have the same number of triple patterns but they differ in their join vertex count and join vertex degrees. That is, Fig. 1a is a long linear-shaped query with multiple (4) low-degree (2) join vertices, whereas Fig. 1b is a star-shaped query with a single high-degree (5) join vertex. A system may show completely different performance for these two queries and a benchmark should capture such blind spots if any.

**Join Vertex Types:** The data representation and indexing schemes employed by RDF systems can result in completely different behaviour on different types of joins [2], and a benchmark should include a sufficiently large sample of queries for each join type. Consequently, we distinguish the following three (mutually non-exclusive) types of join vertices: A join vertex $x$ of a CBGP $\bar{B} = \langle B, F \rangle$ is of *type SS⁺* if $x = s$ for every triple pattern $\langle s, p, o \rangle \in B$ that is incident on $x$; similarly, $x$ is of *type OO⁺* if $x = o$ for every $\langle s, p, o \rangle \in B$ that is incident on $x$; and $x$ is of *type SO⁺* if $x = s$ and $x = o'$ for two triple patterns $\langle s, p, o \rangle \in B$ and $\langle s', p', o' \rangle \in B$ (both of which are incident on $x$, respectively). For example, the join vertices $?a$, $?x$ and $?y$ in Fig. 1c have types SS⁺, SO⁺ and OO⁺, respectively.

## 2.2  Data-Driven Features

The structural query features (discussed above) are often not sufficient. More specifically, a system's choice of a query (execution) plan depends on the characteristics of the data as much as the query itself. For example, systems rely heavily on selectivity and cardinality estimations for query plan optimization [23]. Consider the following example: A system chooses to break down a BGP $B = \{tp_A, tp_B, tp_C\}$ into its triple patterns and to execute them in a specific order, namely, $tp_A$, $tp_B$ and then $tp_C$. The system picks this particular query plan because the subset of triples that match $tp_A$ is smaller. Furthermore, it estimates the intermediate result cardinalities to be sufficiently low and decides to use in-memory data structures and algorithms. To enumerate different plan choices, we consider the following test cases:

- queries have a diverse mix of result cardinalities;
- a single or few triple patterns are very selective, while the remaining ones are not;
- all of the triple patterns in a query are almost equally selective (hence, there is a higher probability that the optimizer picks a sub-optimal query plan due to estimation errors); etc.

Next, we define result cardinality and notions of selectivity, and explain how we use them in our evaluations to distinguish among such different test cases.

**Result Cardinality:** This feature represents the number of solutions in the result of evaluating a CBGP $\bar{B} = \langle B, F \rangle$ over an RDF graph $G$. Recall that this result, denoted by $[\![\bar{B}]\!]_G$, is a bag (multiset) of solution mappings (cf. Sec. 2.1). Consequently, if $\Omega$ denotes the set underlying the bag $[\![\bar{B}]\!]_G$ and $\mathrm{card}_{[\![\bar{B}]\!]_G}$ denotes the function that maps each solution mapping $\mu \in \Omega$ to its cardinality in the bag [3], we define the result cardinality of $\bar{B}$ over $G$ by

$$\mathrm{CARD}(\bar{B}, G) = \sum_{\mu \in \Omega} \mathrm{card}_{[\![\bar{B}]\!]_G}(\mu). \tag{1}$$

**Filtered Triple Pattern Selectivity (f-TP Selectivity):** Given some CBGP $\bar{B} = \langle B, F \rangle$ and a BGP $B^*$ such that $B^* \subseteq B$, we write $\lambda^F(B^*)$ to denote the CBGP $\bar{B}' = \langle B', F' \rangle$ with $B' = B^*$ and $F' = \{f \in F \mid \mathrm{vars}(f) \subseteq \mathrm{vars}(B^*)\}$, where $\mathrm{vars}(\cdot)$ denotes the variables in a filter expression or a BGP. Then, for any triple pattern $tp \in B$ in a CBGP $\bar{B} = \langle B, F \rangle$, the *f-TP selectivity* of $tp$ over an RDF graph $G$, denoted by $\mathrm{SEL}_G^F(tp)$, is the ratio of distinct solution mappings in $[\![\lambda^F(\{tp\})]\!]_G$ to the number of triples in $G$. Formally, if $\Omega$ denotes the set underlying the (bag) query result $[\![\lambda^F(\{tp\})]\!]_G$, then

$$\mathrm{SEL}_G^F(tp) = |\Omega|/|G|. \tag{2}$$

In our evaluations, we use three related measures. We use the result cardinality of a CBGP as it is defined, and we compute the *mean* and *standard deviation* of the f-TP selectivities of the triple patterns in the CBGP. The latter is especially important in distinguishing queries whose triple patterns are almost equally selective from queries with varying f-TP selectivities.

While result cardinality and f-TP selectivity are useful features, they are not entirely sufficient. More specifically, once a system picks a particular query plan and starts executing it, it is often the case that there are intermediate solution mappings which do not make it to the final result. What this means is that *all* triple patterns of a CBGP contribute to its overall "selectiveness", or stated differently, in every join step, some intermediate solution mappings are being pruned. Contrast this to another possible case in which the overall "selectiveness" of a CBGP can be attributed to a single triple pattern in that CBGP. In that case, a system could use runtime optimization techniques such as sideways-information passing [18] to *early-prune* most of the intermediate results, which may not be possible in the original example (for a more detailed discussion refer to [2]). From a testing point of view, it is important to include both cases. In fact, in Section 5.5, we shall revisit this example and experimentally show that systems behave differently on these two cases. To capture these constraints, we study two more features, namely BGP-restricted and join-restricted f-TP selectivity. The former is concerned with how much a filtered triple pattern contributes to the overall "selectiveness" of the query, whereas the latter is concerned with how much a filtered triple pattern contributes to the overall "selectiveness" of the join(s) that it participates in. Just as we do with f-TP selectivity, for our evaluations, we compute the mean and standard deviation of these two features.

**BGP-Restricted f-TP Selectivity:** For any triple pattern $tp \in B$ in a CBGP $\bar{B} = \langle B, F \rangle$, the $\bar{B}$-*restricted f-TP selectivity* of $tp$ over an RDF graph $G$, which is denoted by $\text{SEL}_G^F(tp \mid \bar{B})$, is the fraction of distinct solution mappings in $[\![\lambda^F(\{tp\})]\!]_G$ that are *compatible* (as per standard SPARQL semantics [3]) with a solution mapping in the query result $[\![\bar{B}]\!]_G$. Formally, if $\Omega$ and $\Omega'$ denote the sets underlying the (bag) query results $[\![\lambda^F(\{tp\})]\!]_G$ and $[\![\bar{B}]\!]_G$, respectively, then

$$\text{SEL}_G^F(tp \mid \bar{B}) = \frac{\left| \{\, \mu \in \Omega \mid \exists \mu' \in \Omega' : \mu \text{ and } \mu' \text{ are compatible} \,\} \right|}{|\Omega|}. \tag{3}$$

**Join-Restricted f-TP Selectivity:** Given a CBGP $\bar{B} = \langle B, F \rangle$, a join vertex $x$ of $\bar{B}$, and a triple pattern $tp \in B$ that is incident on $x$, the $x$-*restricted f-TP selectivity* of $tp$ over an RDF graph $G$, denoted by $\text{SEL}_G^F(tp \mid x)$, is the fraction of distinct solution mappings in $[\![\lambda^F(\{tp\})]\!]_G$ that are compatible with a solution mapping in the (join) query result $[\![\lambda^F(B^x)]\!]_G$ with $B^x \subseteq B$ being the subset of all the triple patterns in $B$ that are incident on $x$ (i.e, $B^x = \{tp \in B \mid tp \text{ is incident on } x\}$). Hence, if $\Omega$ and $\Omega'$ denote the sets underlying $[\![\lambda^F(\{tp\})]\!]_G$ and $[\![\lambda^F(B^x)]\!]_G$, respectively, then

$$\text{SEL}_G^F(tp \mid x) = \frac{\left| \{\, \mu \in \Omega \mid \exists \mu' \in \Omega' : \mu \text{ and } \mu' \text{ are compatible} \,\} \right|}{|\Omega|}. \tag{4}$$

# 3  Evaluation of Existing SPARQL Benchmarks

Even though existing SPARQL benchmarks [7], [12], [17], [20] offer valuable testing capabilities, we demonstrate in this section that they are not suitable for stress testing RDF systems. We consider the following 4 benchmarks:

- The *Lehigh University Benchmark* (LUBM) [12] was originally designed for testing the inferencing capabilities of Semantic Web repositories.
- The *Berlin SPARQL Benchmark* (BSBM) [7] contains multiple use cases such as (i) explore, (ii) update, and (iii) business intelligence use cases. Furthermore, it goes into testing how well RDF systems support different (and important) SPARQL features, namely, aggregation, union, and optional graph patterns.
- *SP²Bench* [20] tests various SPARQL features such as union and optional graph patterns.
- The *DBpedia SPARQL Benchmark* [17] (DBSB) uses queries that have been generated by mining actual query logs over the DBpedia dataset [5]. Thus, it contains a more "diverse set of queries" [17].

We assess the diversity of existing benchmarks using the structural and data-driven features presented in Section 2. In our evaluations of benchmarks, we only consider SELECT queries. For BSBM, we focused on the explore use case and generated 100 queries per query template. We observed this to be a sufficiently large sample to understand the general properties of BSBM. For DBSB, we analyzed a sample of 12500 queries that were drawn uniformly at random from the subset of SELECT queries in the query logs (the other two benchmarks have a fixed number of queries). For WatDiv, we generate the same number of queries (12500). Recall that the query features in Section 2 are defined over CBGPs. For this reason, when analyzing existing benchmarks (with respect to these features), we first translate each complex non-CBGP query into a CBGP by replacing OPT and UNION operators with AND. Hereafter, we refer to these CBGPs (including those for which translation was not necessary) as the queries of the benchmark. To compute the statistics reported in this section, for each benchmark, we generated a benchmark-specific dataset of 1 million triples, and executed all of the queries in the benchmark.

## 3.1  Evaluation Using Structural Features

Consider Fig. 2a, which compares queries in each benchmark with respect to their triple pattern count (x-axis).[1] Benchmarks are stacked along the y-axis. For each benchmark, the presence of a point indicates that the benchmark contains at least one query with the corresponding number of triple patterns indicated by the x-axis value. Fig. 2a–2c and Fig. 3a– 3f should be read similarly. The actual *distribution* of queries with respect to these features are available in the online version of this paper.[2]

---

[1] For the time being ignore WatDiv in these figures. The results about WatDiv are not important for this section. We discuss WatDiv in Section 4.

[2] https://cs.uwaterloo.ca/~galuc/watdiv/paper/

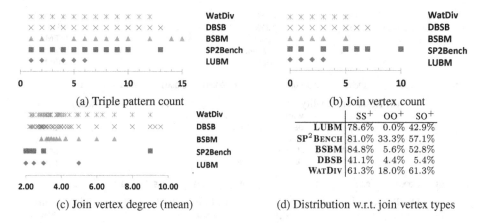

**Fig. 2.** Analysis w.r.t. structural features: in Fig. 2a–2c, each point indicates the presence of a query with the corresponding x-axis value for a given feature

While most benchmarks contain large queries with more than 10 triple patterns (Fig. 2a)[3], LUBM contains only small queries—not exceeding 6 triple patterns in cardinality. Furthermore, LUBM's join vertex count is also lower than the other benchmarks (Fig. 2b). This is reasonable as LUBM is intended for semantic inferencing. In fact, the true complexity of an LUBM query lies in its semantics, not in its structure. For this reason, the suitability of LUBM for performance evaluation is limited if the system under test does not support inferencing.

By considering mean join vertex degrees (Fig. 2c), we observe that DBSB is more diverse than any of the synthetic benchmarks (i.e., LUBM, BSBM, $SP^2$Bench). LUBM contains fairly simple queries (cf., Fig. 2a), which explains why the mean join vertex degree is also low for most of these queries. $SP^2$Bench contains (i) linear queries that are long, or (ii) star queries that are large and centered around a single join vertex, but not much in between; hence, the join-vertex degree values are concentrated at the two ends of the x-axis in Fig. 2c. BSBM contains queries that are a little bit more diverse in their join vertex degrees, but it does not test the two extremes as $SP^2$Bench does.

In Fig. 2d, we compare and contrast benchmarks with respect to the types of join vertices present in each of the queries. This comparison reveals three problems: LUBM does not contain any query with an $OO^+$join; BSBM contains some, but their percentage is significantly low. In DBSB, queries with both $OO^+$and $SO^+$joins have a low percentage. Consequently, these three benchmarks may be biased towards particular physical designs that are more effective for $SS^+$(or $SO^+$) joins, which limits the suitability of these benchmarks for stress tests.

## 3.2 Evaluation Using Data-Driven Features

Regarding result cardinality, the following observations can be made. BSBM contains only low-cardinality queries, $SP^2$Bench contains almost only high-cardinality queries,

---

[3] Some DBSB queries have as many as 50 triple patterns, but for clarity of presentation we are not displaying them.

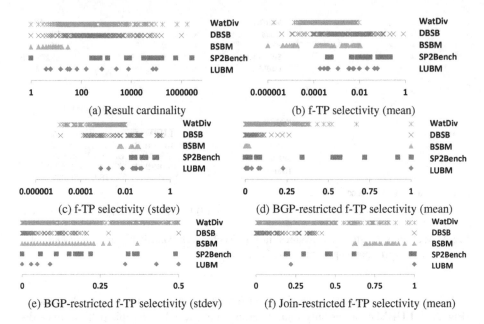

**Fig. 3.** Analysis w.r.t. data-driven features at 1 million triples: each point indicates the presence of a query with the corresponding x-axis value for a given feature

and LUBM contains only medium-cardinality queries (cf., Fig. 3a), which reveals another limitation of what each of these three benchmarks can test individually.

Fig. 3b–3c show another issue with existing benchmarks. Although benchmarks are fairly diverse with respect to f-TP selectivity (i.e., especially DBSB and BSBM), the standard deviation of f-TP selectivities of filtered triple patterns (within any single query) is generally high. As explained in Section 2.2, this implies that these benchmarks are missing the test case in which the triple patterns are more or less equally selective.

As depicted in Fig. 3d, among the four benchmarks, only SP$^2$Bench has a diverse selection of queries regarding mean BGP-restricted f-TP. LUBM, BSBM and DBSB have queries in which either the mean value is 1.0, indicating that each triple pattern in separation does not contribute to the selectiveness of the query, or the mean is extremely low, indicating the opposite. For BSBM, the contrast is even extreme. Fig. 3e highlights an even further problem with DBSB and BSBM. For these two benchmarks, the variation in BGP-restricted f-TP lies mostly in the lower end of the spectrum, which indicates that these benchmarks cannot be used to test with queries in which triple patterns contribute unevenly to the pruning of intermediate results (cf., Section 2.2).

Finally, consider Fig. 3f, which compares benchmark queries using join-restricted f-TP (mean). One can observe two important limitations. First, both LUBM and SP$^2$Bench queries sparsely cover the spectrum of possible values. Second, although BSBM and DBSB are much more diverse, they cover completely different ends of the spectrum. A system can generate completely different query plans for these two scenarios, and therefore, stress testing should use workloads that include both scenarios.

### 3.3 Summary of Findings

In summary, the best known benchmarks (including DBSB, which is based on actual query logs), individually, are not sufficiently diverse to test the strengths and weaknesses of different physical design choices employed by RDF systems. Aggregating results from multiple benchmarks is not a good solution to the diversity problem either. First, the underlying datasets have completely different characteristics; therefore, we may get queries with completely disjoint distributions across the structural and data-driven features. For example, even though it may appear, based on Fig. 3f, that DBSB and BSBM complement each other (i.e., they cover the opposite ends of the set of possible x-axis values), Fig. 3a suggests that it is not quite so. The problem is that these two benchmarks do not complement each other on *all* possible features. Hence, in an aggregated (hypothetical) benchmark, we would still be missing queries with *high* cardinality and *high* join-restricted f-TP selectivity values. Second, scalability is an issue. It is not clear (i) how we can generate more queries given that some of the above-mentioned benchmarks have a fixed number of queries, or (ii) how results from multiple benchmarks should be combined given that each benchmark has its own scalability restrictions. Our benchmark is designed to address these issues.

## 4   Waterloo SPARQL Diversity Test Suite (WatDiv)

WatDiv consists of multiple tools[4] that enable diversified stress testing of RDF data management systems:

- The *data generator* generates scalable datasets at user-specified scale factors—a common feature of benchmarks. A more interesting feature is that data are generated according to the WatDiv schema[5] with customizable value distributions.
- The *query template generator* traverses the WatDiv schema and generates a diverse set of query templates (which is the first step in generating a workload for the stress tests). Users can specify the number of query templates to be generated as well as certain restrictions on the query templates such as the maximum number of triple patterns or whether predicates in triple patterns should be bound.
- Given a set of query templates, the *query generator* instantiates these templates with actual RDF terms from the dataset (which is the second and last step in generating a workload for the stress tests). The number of queries to be instantiated per query template can be specified by users.
- Given a WatDiv dataset and test workload, for each query in the workload, the *feature extractor* computes the structural and data-driven features discussed in Section 2. For this to work, the tool needs to point to a third party RDF data management system that is already installed on the system.

**Dataset Description:** What distinguishes WatDiv datasets from existing RDF benchmarks is the diversity of the structuredness: some entities in WatDiv are well-structured,

---

[4] http://db.uwaterloo.ca/watdiv/
[5] http://db.uwaterloo.ca/watdiv/watdiv-data-model.txt

meaning that they contain few optional attributes, while some others are less well-structured [10]. We discuss in Section 4 that this enables the generation of test queries that are far more diverse in their data-driven features.

Three properties contribute to the diversity of WatDiv. First, instances of the same entity type (i.e., class) do not necessarily have the same properties. Consider the different types of entities used in WatDiv.[6] *Product* instances may be associated with different *Product Categories* (e.g., Book, Movie, Classical Music Concert, etc.), but depending on the category a product belongs to, it will have a different set of properties. For example, products that belong to the category "Classical Music Concert" have the properties *opus, movement, composer* and *performer* (in addition to the properties that are common to every product), whereas products that belong to the category "Book" have the properties *isbn, bookEdition* and *numberOfPages*.

Second, even within a single product category, not all instances share the same set of properties. For example, while *isbn* is a mandatory property for books, *bookEdition* ($Pr = 0.5$) and *numberOfPages* ($Pr = 0.25$) are optional properties, where $Pr$ indicates the probability that an instance will be generated with that property. Users are able to modify the WatDiv schema, hence these probabilities.

Third, a group of attributes can be correlated, which means that either all or none of the correlated attributes in that group will be present in any instance of the entity type. For example, *opus* and *movement* are two correlated properties for "Classical Music Concert" products (cf. <pgroup> construct in the WatDiv dataset schema).

**Test Queries:** The benchmark queries are generated in two steps. First, a set of query templates are created by performing a random walk over the graph representation of the schema of the dataset (i.e., query template generator). In this regard, we use the following (internal) representation: every entity type in the schema corresponds to a graph vertex, relationships among entity types (i.e., which correspond to RDF predicates in the instantiated dataset) are represented using graph edges, and each vertex is annotated with the set of properties of that entity type. This produces a set of BGPs with a maximum $n$ triple patterns, where $n$ was set to 15 in our experiments. Note that we generate BGPs with triple patterns that have unbound subjects and objects, whereas their predicates are bound. Then, $k$ uniformly randomly selected subjects/objects are replaced with WatDiv-specific placeholders (i.e., placeholders are enclosed within percentage [%] signs in the benchmark). In the second step, placeholders in each query template are instantiated with RDF terms from the WatDiv dataset (i.e., query generator). To this end, the WatDiv tools maintain, for each placeholder, a set of values that are applicable to that placeholder, and during the instantiation step, a value is drawn uniformly at random. For the study in this paper, we generated 12500 test queries from a total of 125 query templates (i.e., the same number of queries we sampled in DBSB). These queries are available online.[7]

**Discussion:** In Fig. 2a–2d and Fig. 3a–3f, we characterize the aforementioned 12500 WatDiv test queries. With respect to most of the structural query features, WatDiv has comparable characteristics to DBSB and it is far more diverse than LUBM, SP²Bench

---

and BSBM (cf., Fig. 2a–2c). For example, the mean join vertex degree values are densely distributed between 2.0 and 10.0, indicating a rich mix of queries. Furthermore, with respect to join vertex types, WatDiv has a much more balanced distribution than DBSB: a significant 18.0% of queries in the WatDiv workload have $OO^+$-type join vertices, compared to only 4.4% in DBSB, and 61.3% versus 5.4% for queries with $SO^+$ joins.

With respect to most of the data-driven features, WatDiv is far more diverse, often filling in the gaps that are not supported by existing benchmarks (cf., Fig. 3d, 3e and 3f). For example, while DBSB and BSBM cover only the opposite ends of the spectrum of mean join-restricted f-TP selectivity values, WatDiv covers the full spectrum (cf., Fig. 3f). With respect to mean f-TP selectivity (hence, also standard deviation), WatDiv covers a lower range of values than DBSB and other benchmarks (cf., Fig. 3b–3c). This is because in DBSB there are unselective queries that return the whole dataset, that is, the subjects, predicates and objects in a triple pattern are all unbound. In contrast, recall from Section 4 that for our evaluation we generated queries in which the predicates in a triple pattern are bound (enabling this feature in WatDiv is a configuration option). Therefore, for this feature WatDiv complements the other benchmarks. Overall, due to the comprehensiveness of WatDiv, it has enabled us to reveal performance issues about existing RDF systems that were missed in studies that used the other four benchmarks.

## 5  Evaluation of RDF Systems

We used WatDiv to evaluate a number of existing RDF data management systems. In this section, we report our experimental results and discuss various issues with existing systems.

### 5.1  Systems Under Test

RDF systems can be classified broadly into two categories in terms of their data representations: (i) tabular and (ii) graph-based. For tabular implementations, one option is to represent data in a single large table. While earlier triplestores followed this approach [8,9], it has been demonstrated that maintaining redundant copies with different sort orders and indexes can be much more effective [19]. Consequently, in our evaluations we include the popular prototype RDF-3x [19] (v0.3.7) that follows the latter approach. It has also been argued that grouping data can significantly improve performance for some workloads [22]. Hence, a second option is to group data by RDF predicates, where data are explicitly partitioned into multiple tables (one table per predicate) and the tables are stored in a column-store [1]. We test the effectiveness of this approach on MonetDB [15] (v1.7), which is a state-of-the-art column-store. A third option is to natively represent RDF graph structure, for which we use the prototype system gStore [24] (v0.2). We also test three industrial systems, namely, Virtuoso Open Source (VOS) [11] (v6.1.8 and v7.1.0) and 4Store [13] (v1.1.5). Both VOS and 4Store group and index data primarily based on RDF predicates. Furthermore, VOS 6.1 is a row-store and VOS 7.1 is a column-store.

## 5.2   Experimental Setup

In our experiments, we use a commodity machine with AMD Phenom II ×4 955 3.20 GHz processor, 16 GB of main memory and a Seagate 3.$AA$ hard disk drive with 100 GB of free space at the time of experimentation. The operating system on the machine is Ubuntu 12.04 LTS.

In this paper, our objective is to understand how well state-of-the-art RDF systems perform on a diverse SPARQL workload; however, we do *not* intend to test the scalability of these systems given more computational nodes and/or CPUs. Therefore, we restrict each system to use single-threading. WatDiv is equally suitable for scalability experiments, but these results are not included in this paper.

In our stress-tests we use two versions of the WatDiv dataset, one generated at scale-factor 100 and the other at 1000, which correspond to approximately 10 million and 100 million triples, respectively. Recall from Section 4 that we use 12500 queries generated from 125 query templates.

We evaluate the systems using a warm cache. Therefore, we generate two workloads: a warmup workload and a test workload, both containing the same 12500 queries. On each system, first the warmup workload and then the test workload is executed. To achieve higher confidence, we repeat the experiments 5 times. Furthermore, to reduce the effects of query interactions within the test workload, every time, the sequence of queries in the test workload is randomized (the warmup experimental run is just another randomized test run). This way, for each query in a test sequence, we measure and record its execution time as well as various structural and data-driven features about that query. For practical reasons, whenever query execution exceeds 60 seconds, we automatically timeout, proceed with the next query in the sequence, and ignore that query in the consecutive runs for that system.

## 5.3   Results

The experimental results are summarized in Fig. 4a–4d. The complete results with error margins are available in the aforementioned online version of the paper. Fig. 4a displays, for each system, the total execution time (averaged over the five randomized sequences) of the test workload. Fig. 4b depicts, for each system, the percentage of queries in the workload that particular system is the fastest (timeouts are ignored) or up to 10 times slower than the fastest system, and so on. Fig. 4c–4d display for each query in the workload (x-axis), the query execution time (in milliseconds) of the fastest as well as the slowest system for that query (which may be different systems for different queries). For presentation purposes, queries are sorted according to their maximum execution times. Note that for some queries, the maximum execution time is capped at 60 seconds, which marks the timeout threshold.

gStore ran into errors during the execution of some of the queries: we do not consider these cases in our discussions. Consequently, the percentages for gStore in Fig. 4b do not add up to 100%. Furthermore, gStore timed out on the queries on the larger dataset, hence, we excluded it from Fig. 4b.

## 5.4   Observations

Regarding Fig. 4a, we make two observations. First, VOS (and to some extent RDF-3x) perform much better than the other three systems on the larger dataset. Second,

| | RDF-3x | VOS [6.1] | VOS [7.1] | MonetDB | 4Store | gStore |
|---|---|---|---|---|---|---|
| 10M triples | 58,312 | **41,612** | 51,268 | 48,329 | 94,289 | n/a |
| 100M triples | 97,409 | 75,224 | **74,997** | 139,015 | 260,045 | n/a |

(a) Total workload execution time (in seconds) for the systems under test

| | 10M triples | | | | | | 100M triples | | | | | |
|---|---|---|---|---|---|---|---|---|---|---|---|---|
| | RDF-3x | VOS [6.1] | VOS [7.1] | MonetDB | 4Store | gStore | RDF-3x | VOS [6.1] | VOS [7.1] | MonetDB | 4Store | gStore |
| fastest | 11.4% | 6.5% | 18.7% | 31.7% | 0.8% | 30.9% | 20.9% | 0.0% | 22.6% | 56.5% | 0.0% | n/a |
| 1–10× | 77.2% | 67.5% | 63.4% | 65.0% | 49.6% | 35.8% | 60.9% | 59.1% | 54.8% | 31.3% | 53.0% | n/a |
| 10–100× | 6.5% | 23.6% | 13.0% | 1.6% | 41.5% | 2.4% | 13.9% | 40.0% | 20.0% | 2.6% | 21.7% | n/a |
| 100–1K× | 3.3% | 1.6% | 4.1% | 0.0% | 0.8% | 0.0% | 3.5% | 0.9% | 1.7% | 6.1% | 15.7% | n/a |
| 1K–10K× | 1.6% | 0.8% | 0.8% | 1.6% | 7.3% | 0.0% | 0.0% | 0.0% | 0.9% | 3.5% | 7.0% | n/a |
| 10K–100K× | 0.0% | 0.0% | 0.0% | 0.0% | 0.0% | 0.0% | 0.0% | 0.0% | 0.9% | 3.5% | 7.0% | n/a |

(b) Performance breakdown (10M and 100M triples)

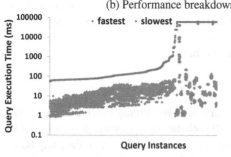

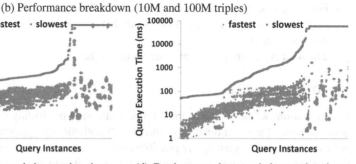

(c) Gap between the recorded execution times of the fastest and slowest systems at 10M triples (per query instance)

(d) Gap between the recorded execution times of the fastest and slowest systems at 100M triples (per query instance)

**Fig. 4.** WatDiv Results: Robustness of Existing Systems

although VOS has the lowest total execution time for the whole workload (Fig. 4a), it is the fastest system in not more than 23 percent of the queries (Fig. 4b). This highlights an interesting trade-off between robustness across a diverse set of queries versus speed within a specific type of workload.

Note that no single system is the absolute winner in all of the queries (cf., Fig. 4b. Furthermore, note that each system performs poorly (i.e., a few orders of magnitude worse than the fastest system) in a significant percentage of queries in the workload.

The results in Fig. 4c–4d highlight two more issues. First, for most queries, there can be 2 orders of magnitude difference between the fastest and slowest system, and in the worst case, this gap can be as large as 5 orders of magnitude (note that this gap exists even when query execution times are grouped by query template). Second, the worst case gap widens from the smaller to the larger dataset.

In summary:

- No single system is a sole winner across all queries;
- No single system is the sole loser across all queries, either;

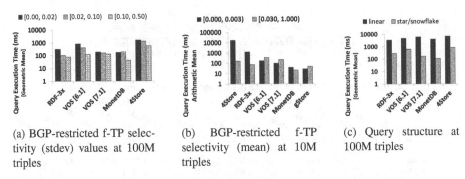

(a) BGP-restricted f-TP selectivity (stdev) values at 100M triples

(b) BGP-restricted f-TP selectivity (mean) at 10M triples

(c) Query structure at 100M triples

**Fig. 5.** Detailed evaluation: results are analyzed across various combinations of features

- For some queries, there can be as much as 5 orders of magnitude difference in the performance (i.e., query execution time) between the best and the worst system for that query; and
- The winner in one query may timeout in another.

### 5.5  Detailed Analysis

In this section, we provide a more detailed evaluation by drilling down into particular query features (and combinations thereof). Hypothetically speaking, it is possible to perform such analyses using any possible combination of features (including any additional feature not covered by our study). However, due to space limitations, we focus on a few special cases where the results stand out, and while doing so, we demonstrate how WatDiv can be used for stress testing.

As our first exercise, we quantify an observation that we made in Section 2.2. That is, we want to test whether systems behave differently for queries in which all (or most) triple patterns contribute almost equally to the overall "selectiveness" of the query (Case-A) versus the case in which the overall "selectiveness" of the query can be attributed to a single (or few) triple patterns (Case-B). To distinguish between these two cases, we rely on the standard deviation of BGP-restricted f-TP selectivity, where a low (resp., high) standard deviation implies Case-A (resp., Case-B). For this exercise, we take into account only the queries with result cardinality $\leq 2000$ (i.e., selective queries). We divide the spectrum of standard deviation values into three intervals such that we have an equal number of queries in each interval (approximately 3300 queries per interval). Fig. 5a depicts, for each system, the geometric mean of the query execution times of all queries in each of the three intervals. We note that, for all four systems, the (mean) query execution times decrease as the standard deviation of BGP-restricted f-TP selectivity increases. These results indicate that, while systems have integrated techniques to early-prune intermediate results [18], these techniques do not seem to be effective for Case-A.

Next, we demonstrate a case in which different systems show varied behavior on a particular type of workload. In this exercise, we consider only the queries with a single join vertex and result cardinality $\leq 2000$. Then, based on the mean of BGP-restricted f-TP selectivity, we devised two types of workloads: one in which queries have very low mean BGP-restricted f-TP selectivity, and the other in which the mean is high (each interval contains approximately 2200 queries). The former workload captures those queries in which due to data distributions, the query itself becomes much more selective than the individual triple patterns participating in the query. Fig. 5b illustrates an interesting trend: while the five systems behave similarly to some extent for the latter workload, they have completely differing performance in the former one. An investigation that may reveal a reason for this observation is beyond the scope of this paper.

Last, we test whether systems are biased towards a particular query structure (i.e., linear vs. star/snowflake). To this end, we select two sets of queries: (i) those queries with mean join vertex degree $\leq 3.0$ and join vertex count $\geq 3$ (representing linear queries), and (ii) those with mean join vertex degree $\geq 5.0$ and join vertex count $\leq 2$ (representing star or snowflake queries). The results in Fig. 5c demonstrate that all of the four systems are indeed biased against linear queries, highlighting a room for improvement.

## 6 Conclusions

In this paper, we discuss WatDiv. First, we introduce a set of query features that can be used for assessing the diversity of the data and workloads in a SPARQL benchmark. We explain why these features are important and how they relate to special test cases that need to be included in a stress testing tool. Then, we discuss our experimental evaluation of existing SPARQL benchmarks with a specific emphasis on identifying test cases that are not handled by these benchmarks, which led us to the development of WatDiv. Our experimental evaluation of existing RDF data management systems with WatDiv demonstrate that these systems are not sufficiently robust across a diverse set of queries. Then, we use WatDiv to drill down into specific combinations of query features to reveal problems that only this type of stress testing could reveal. Specifically, we illustrate cases where all of the evaluated systems show bias against a particular type of workload, or where a particular system has some advantage over the others for a specific type of workload. We believe that evaluations that involve stress testing as demonstrated in this paper are crucial to build more robust RDF data management systems. For future work, we consider extending WatDiv to support provenance and temporal data.

## References

1. Abadi, D.J., Marcus, A., Madden, S.R., Hollenbach, K.: SW-Store: a vertically partitioned DBMS for semantic web data management. VLDB J. 18, 385–406 (2009)
2. Aluç, G., Özsu, M.T., Daudjee, K.: Workload matters: Why RDF databases need a new design. Proc. VLDB 7(10), 837–840 (2014)
3. Arenas, M., Gutierrez, C., Pérez, J.: On the semantics of SPARQL. In: Semantic Web Inf. Man., pp. 281–307 (2009)
4. Arias, M., Fernández, J.D., Martínez-Prieto, M.A., de la Fuente, P.: An empirical study of real-world SPARQL queries. CoRR abs/1103.5043 (2011)

5. Auer, S., Bizer, C., Kobilarov, G., Lehmann, J., Cyganiak, R., Ives, Z.G.: DBpedia: A nucleus for a web of open data. In: Aberer, K., et al. (eds.) ASWC 2007 and ISWC 2007. LNCS, vol. 4825, pp. 722–735. Springer, Heidelberg (2007)
6. Bizer, C., Heath, T., Berners-Lee, T.: Linked data - the story so far. Int. J. Semantic Web Inf. Syst. 5(3), 1–22 (2009)
7. Bizer, C., Schultz, A.: The Berlin SPARQL benchmark. Int. J. Semantic Web Inf. Syst. 5(2), 1–24 (2009)
8. Broekstra, J., Kampman, A., van Harmelen, F.: Sesame: A generic architecture for storing and querying RDF and RDF Schema. In: Proc. 1st Int. Semantic Web Conference, pp. 54–68 (2002)
9. Carroll, J.J., Dickinson, I., Dollin, C., Reynolds, D., Seaborne, A., Wilkinson, K.: Jena: implementing the semantic web recommendations. In: Proc. 13th Int. World Wide Web Conf. - Alternate Track Papers & Posters, pp. 74–83 (2004)
10. Duan, S., Kementsietsidis, A., Srinivas, K., Udrea, O.: Apples and oranges: a comparison of RDF benchmarks and real RDF datasets. In: SIGMOD Conference, pp. 145–156 (2011)
11. Erling, O.: Virtuoso, a hybrid RDBMS/graph column store. IEEE Data Eng. Bull. 35(1), 3–8 (2012)
12. Guo, Y., Pan, Z., Heflin, J.: LUBM: A benchmark for OWL knowledge base systems. J. Web Semantics 3(2-3), 158–182 (2005)
13. Harris, S., Lamb, N., Shadbolt, N.: 4store: The design and implementation of a clustered RDF store. In: Proc. 5th Int. Workshop on Scalable Semantic Web Knowledge Base Systems, pp. 81–96 (2009)
14. Harris, S., Seaborne, A., Prud'hommeaux, E.: SPARQL 1.1 query language. W3C Recommendation (March 2013)
15. Idreos, S., Groffen, F., Nes, N., Manegold, S., Mullender, K.S., Kersten, M.L.: MonetDB: Two decades of research in column-oriented database architectures. IEEE Data Eng. Bull. 35(1), 40–45 (2012)
16. Kirchberg, M., Ko, R.K.L., Lee, B.S.: From linked data to relevant data – time is the essence. CoRR abs/1103.5046 (2011)
17. Morsey, M., Lehmann, J., Auer, S., Ngonga Ngomo, A.-C.: DBpedia SPARQL benchmark – performance assessment with real queries on real data. In: Aroyo, L., Welty, C., Alani, H., Taylor, J., Bernstein, A., Kagal, L., Noy, N., Blomqvist, E. (eds.) ISWC 2011, Part I. LNCS, vol. 7031, pp. 454–469. Springer, Heidelberg (2011)
18. Neumann, T., Weikum, G.: Scalable join processing on very large RDF graphs. In: Proc. ACM SIGMOD Int. Conf. on Management of Data, pp. 627–640 (2009)
19. Neumann, T., Weikum, G.: The RDF-3X engine for scalable management of RDF data. VLDB J. 19(1), 91–113 (2010)
20. Schmidt, M., Hornung, T., Meier, M., Pinkel, C., Lausen, G.: Sp$^2$bench: A sparql performance benchmark. In: Semantic Web Inf, pp. 371–393 (2009)
21. Schreiber, G., Raimond, Y.: RDF 1.1 primer. W3C Note (February 2014)
22. Sidirourgos, L., Goncalves, R., Kersten, M., Nes, N., Manegold, S.: Column-store support for RDF data management: not all swans are white. Proc. VLDB 1(2), 1553–1563 (2008)
23. Stocker, M., Seaborne, A., Bernstein, A., Kiefer, C., Reynolds, D.: Sparql basic graph pattern optimization using selectivity estimation. In: Proc. 17th Int. World Wide Web Conf., pp. 595–604 (2008)
24. Zou, L., Mo, J., Zhao, D., Chen, L., Özsu, M.T.: gStore: Answering SPARQL queries via subgraph matching. Proc. VLDB 4(1), 482–493 (2011)

# LOD Laundromat: A Uniform Way of Publishing Other People's Dirty Data

Wouter Beek, Laurens Rietveld, Hamid R. Bazoobandi,
Jan Wielemaker, and Stefan Schlobach

Dept. of Computer Science, VU University Amsterdam, NL
{w.g.j.beek,laurens.rietveld,h.bazoubandi,
j.wielemaker,k.s.schlobach}@vu.nl

**Abstract.** It is widely accepted that *proper* data publishing is difficult. The majority of Linked Open Data (LOD) does not meet even a core set of data publishing guidelines. Moreover, datasets that are *clean* at creation, can get *stains* over time. As a result, the LOD cloud now contains a high level of *dirty* data that is difficult for humans to clean and for machines to process.

Existing solutions for cleaning data (standards, guidelines, tools) are targeted towards human data creators, who can (and do) choose not to use them. This paper presents the LOD Laundromat which removes stains from data without any human intervention. This fully automated approach is able to make very large amounts of LOD more easily available for further processing *right now*.

LOD Laundromat is not a new dataset, but rather a uniform point of entry to a collection of cleaned siblings of existing datasets. It provides researchers and application developers a wealth of data that is guaranteed to conform to a specified set of best practices, thereby greatly improving the chance of data actually being (re)used.

**Keywords:** Data Publishing, Data Cleaning, Data Reuse, Standards Conformance.

## 1   Introduction

Uptake of Linked Open Data (LOD) has seen a tremendous growth over the last decade. Due to the inherently heterogeneous nature of interlinked datasets that come from very different sources, LOD is not only a fertile environment for innovative data (re)use, but also for mistakes and incompatibilities [4,5]. Such stains in datasets not only degrade a dataset's own quality, but also the quality of other datasets that link to it (e.g., via owl:sameAs). There is thus an incentive that goes beyond that of the original dataset creators to clean stains in LOD.

Existing solutions for cleaning Semantic Web (SW) data (standards, guidelines, tools) are targeted towards human data creators, who can (and do) choose not to use them. Therefore, despite these efforts, much of LOD is still difficult to use today, mostly because of mistakes for which solutions exist. We believe

P. Mika et al. (Eds.) ISWC 2014, Part I, LNCS 8796, pp. 213–228, 2014.

that this poses an unnecessary impediment to the (re)use of LOD for academic and commercial purposes.

This paper presents the LOD Laundromat, which takes *immediate* action by targeting the *data* directly, not its maintainers. By cleaning stains in LOD without any human intervention, LOD Laundromat is able to make very large amounts of LOD more easily available for further processing *right now*. The collection of cleaned datasets that LOD Laundromat produces are standards- and guidelines-compliant siblings of existing, idiosyncratic datasets.

The data-oriented approach of LOD Laundromat is complementary to existing efforts, since it is preferable that someday the original dataset is cleaned by its own maintainers. However, we believe that until that day, our complementary approach is necessary to make LOD succeed while the momentum is still there. LOD Laundromat is unlike any of the existing initiatives towards realizing standards-compliant LOD in each of the following three ways:

1. The **scale** on which clean data is made available: LOD Laundromat comprises thousands of data files, and billions of triples.
2. The **speed** at which data is cleaned and made available: LOD Laundromat cleans about a billion triples a day and makes them immediately available online.
3. The **level of automation.** LOD Laundromat automates the entire data processing pipeline, from dataset discovery to serialization in a standards-compliant canonical format that enables easy reuse.

Besides making LOD standards-compliant, LOD Laundromat implements existing standards in such a way that the resultant data documents are specifically geared towards easy reuse by further tooling. This includes simplifying certain aspects of LOD that often cause problems in practice, such as blank nodes, and significantly reducing the complexity for post-processors to parse the data, e.g., through a syntax that is regular expression-friendly.

The LOD Laundromat is available at `http://lodlaundromat.org`. The collection of datasets that it comprises is continuously being extended. Anyone can add new seed points to the LOD Laundry Basket by using a Web form or HTTP GET request. The fully automated LOD Washing Machine takes seed points from the LOD Laundry Basket and cleans them. Cleaned datasets are disseminated in the LOD Wardrobe. Human data consumers are able to navigate a large collection of high-quality datasets. Machine processors are able to easily load very large amounts of real-world data, by selecting clean data documents via a SPARQL query. For illustrative purposes, various visualizations about the cleaned data are available as well.

This paper is organized as follows: section 2 gives an overview of related work. Section 3 specifies the requirements we pose for clean and useful data, and briefly explores alternative approaches, towards collecting large amounts of Linked Data. Section 4 details the major operationalization decisions that allow the data cleaning process to be fully automated. Section 5 elaborates on the way in which LOD Laundromat makes data available for further processing. Section 6 concludes and mentions future work.

## 2    Related Work

In this section we firstly discuss standards and best practices with respect to Linked Data publishing. Secondly, we discuss existing Linked Data collections and crawlers. Finally, we discuss available Linked Data catalogs, together with their advantages and disadvantages.

### 2.1    Standards

The VoID standard[1] is a vocabulary to formally describe datasets. It supports general metadata (e.g., the homepage of a dataset), access metadata (e.g., which protocols are available), possible links with other datasets, as well as structural metadata. Structural metadata includes exemplary resources and statistics (e.g., the number of triples, properties and classes).

Bio2RDF [2] presents a collection of dataset metrics which extends the structural metadata of the VoID description, and provides more detail (e.g. the number of unique objects linked from each predicate).

While such standards are useful from both the data publisher and the data consumer perspective, uptake of VoID is lacking.[2] Additionally, from a data consumer perspective, the issue of findability through fully automated means is not resolved.

A number of observations and statistics related to Linked Data publishing best practices are presented in [5,3] and by the W3C Linked Data best practices working group[3]. The former have analyzed over a billion triples from 4 million crawled RDF/XML documents. This analysis shows that on average 15.7% of the RDF nodes are blank nodes. Furthermore, their analysis shows that most Linked Data is not fully standards-compliant, corroborating the need for sanitizing Linked Data. However, note that this study is purely observational, and the accessed data is not made available in a cleaned form.

### 2.2    Data Crawlers

Sindice [8] presents itself as a Semantic Web indexer. The main question Sindice tries to address, is how and where to find statements about certain resources. It does so by crawling Linked Data resources, including RDF, RDFa and Microformats, although large RDF datasets are imported on a per-instance and manual opt-in basis. Sindice maintains a large cache of this data, and provides access via a user interface and API. Public access to the raw data crawler by Sindice is not available, nor is access via SPARQL, restricting the usefulness of Sindice for

---

[1] http://www.w3.org/TR/void/

[2] A overview of VoID descriptions that can be found by automated means, is given by the SPARQL Endpoint Status service: http://sparqles.okfn.org/

[3] http://www.w3.org/TR/ld-bp/

Semantic Web and Big Data research. Built on top of Sindice, Sig.ma [10] is an explorative interactive tool, which enables Linked Data discovery. Similar to Sindice, Sig.ma provides an extensive user interface, as well as API access. Even though this service can be quite useful for data exploration, like with Sindice, the actual raw data is not accessible for further processing.

Contrary to Sig.ma and Sindice, data from the Billion Triple Challenge[4] (BTC) 2012 are publicly available and are – as a consequence – often used in Big Data research. The BTC dataset is crawled from the LOD cloud[5], and consists of 1.4 billion triples. It includes large RDF datasets, as well as data in RDFa and Microformats. However, this dataset is not a complete crawl of the Linked Open Data cloud (nor does it aim to be), as datasets from several catalogs are missing from the BTC. Additionally, the latest version of this dataset dates back to 2012.

Freebase [1] publishes 1.9 billion triples, taken from manual user input and existing RDF and Microformat datasets. Access to Freebase is possible via an API, via a (non-SPARQL) structured query language, and as a complete dump of N-Triples. However, these dumps include many non-conformant, syntactically incorrect triples. To give a concrete example, the data file that is the derefer- ence of the Freebase concept 'Monkey'[6] visually appears to contain hundreds of triples, but a state-of-the-art standards-conformant parser such as Raptor[7] only extracts 30 triples. Additionally, knowing *which* datasets are included in Freebase, and finding these particular datasets, is not trivial.

Similarly, LODCache[8], provided by OpenLink, takes a similar crawling ap- proach as Freebase does, but does not make a data dump available, making actual re-use of the data difficult. However, LODCache does have a SPARQL endpoint, as well as features such as entity URI and label lookup.

The Open Data Communities service[9] is the UK Department for Commu- nities and Local Government's official Linked Open Data site. These datasets are published as data dumps, and are accessible via SPARQL and API calls. Although this service supports a broad selection of protocols for accessing the data, the number of datasets is limited and restricted to a particular domain.

Finally, DyLDO [6] is a long-term experiment to monitor the dynamics of a core set of 80 thousand Linked Data documents on a weekly basis. Each week's crawl is published as an N-Quads file. This work provides interesting insight in how Linked Data evolves over time. However, it is not possible to easily select the triples from a *single* dataset, and not all datasets belonging to the LOD cloud are included. Another form of incompleteness stems from the fact that the crawl is based on URI dereferences, not guaranteeing that a dataset is included in its entirety (see section 3).

---

[4] http://km.aifb.kit.edu/projects/btc-2012/
[5] http://lod-cloud.net/
[6] http://rdf.freebase.com/ns/m.08pbxl
[7] Tested with version 2.0.9, http://librdf.org/raptor/rapper.html
[8] http://lod.openlinksw.com/
[9] http://opendatacommunities.org/

## 2.3   Portals

Several Linked Data portals exist, attempting the improve the findability of Linked Datasets. The Datahub[10] lists a large set of RDF datasets and SPARQL endpoints, including the famous collection of datasets that is called the LOD cloud. Datasets that are missing from the BTC collection are present in the Datahub catalog, and the other way round. This catalog is updated manually, and there is no direct connection to the data: all metadata comes from user input. This increases the risk of stale dataset descriptions[11] and missing or incorrect metadata. vocab.cc [9] builds on top of the BTC dataset. At the time of writing, it provides a list of 422 vocabularies. Access to these vocabularies is possible via SPARQL and an API. This service increases the ease of finding and re-using existing vocabularies. It has the same incompleteness properties that the BTC has, and does not (intend to) include instance data.

# 3   Context

Due to the points mentioned above, the poor data quality on the LOD cloud poses great challenges to Big Data and SW researchers, as well as to the developers of Web-scale applications and services. In practice, this means that LOD is less effectively (re)used than it should and could be. We first enumerate the requirements that we pose on clean datasets in order to be easily (re)usable (section 3.1). We then compare three approaches towards collecting LOD, and evaluate each with respect to the completeness of their results (section 3.2).

## 3.1   Requirements

Besides the obvious requirements of being syntactically correct and standards-compliant, we also pose additional requirements for how SW datasets should be serialized and disseminated. We enumerate these additional requirements, and briefly explain why they result in data that is more useful for Big Data researchers and LOD developers in practice.

**Easy grammar.** We want LOD to be disseminated in such a way that it is easy to handle by subsequent processors. These subsequent processors are often non-RDF tools, such as Pig [7], grep, sed, and the like. Such easy post-processing is guaranteed by adherence to a uniform data format that can be safely parsed in an unambiguous way, e.g., by being able to extract triples and terms with one simple regular expression.

**Speed.** We want to allow tools to process LOD in a speedy way. Parsing of data documents may be slow due to the use of inefficient serialization formats (e.g., RDF/XML, RDFa), the occurrence of large numbers of duplicate triples, or the presence of syntax errors that necessitate a parser to come up with fallback options.

---

[10] http://datahub.io/

[11] For example, DBpedia links to version 3.5.1 instead of 3.9: http://datahub.io/dataset/dbpedia (12 May 2014).

**Quantity.** We want to make available a large number of data documents (tens of thousands) and triples (billions), to cover a large parts of the LOD cloud.

**Combine.** We want to make it easy to combine data documents, e.g., splitting a single document into multiple ones, or appending multiple documents into a single one. This is important for load job balancing in large-scale processing, since the distribution of triples across data documents is otherwise very uneven.

**Streaming.** We want to support streamed processing of triples, in such a way that the streamed processor does not have to perform additional bookkeeping on the processed data, e.g., having to check for statements that were already observed earlier.

**Completeness.** The data must be a complete representation of the input dataset, to the extent at which the original dataset is standards-compliant.

### 3.2  Dataset Completeness

The first problem that we come across when collecting large amounts of LOD, is that it is difficult to claim completeness while collecting LOD. Since there are alternative approaches towards collecting large volumes of LOD, we give an overview of the incompleteness issues that arise for each of those alternatives. At the moment, three options exist for collecting large volumes of LOD:

1. Crawling resources
2. Querying endpoints
3. Downloading datadumps

**Resource Crawlers** use the dereferenceability of IRIs in order to find LOD. This approach has the following deficiencies:

1. Datasets that do not contain dereferenceable IRIs are ignored. In [4], 7.2% of the crawled IRIs were not dereferenceable.
2. For IRIs that can be dereferenced, back-links are often not included [5] As a consequence of this, even datasets that contain dereferenceable IRIs exclusively can still have parts that cannot be reached by a crawler.
3. Even for datasets that have only dereferenceable IRIs that include back-links, the crawler can never be certain that the entire dataset has been crawled.

**Querying Endpoints** provides another way of collecting large volumes of LOD. The disadvantages of this approach are:

1. Datasets that do not have a query endpoint are ignored. While hundreds of SPARQL endpoints are known to exist today, there are at least thousands of Linked Datasets.
2. Datasets that have a custom API and/or that require an API key in order to pose questions, are not generally accessible and require either appropriation to a specific API or the creation of an account in order to receive a custom key.

3. For practical reasons, otherwise standards-compliant SPARQL endpoints put restrictions on either the number of triples that can be retrieved or the number of rows that can be involved in a sort operation that is required for paginated retrieval.[12] This results in incomplete datasets retrieval.
4. Existing LOD observatories show that SPARQL endpoint availability is quite low.[13] This may be a result of the fact that keeping a SPARQL endpoint up and running requires considerably more resources than hosting a Web document.

**Downloading Data Dumps** is the third approach to collecting large volumes of LOD. Its disadvantages are:

1. Datasets that are not available as datadump are ignored.
2. Datasets that have only part of their documents available for download are incomplete.

With the LOD Laundromat we want to clean existing datasets, not create a new dataset that is a collection of parts coming from different datasets (like BTC, for instance). In addition to that, we find that most datasets for which a SPARQL endpoint exists, we are also able to find a datadump version. We therefore believe that downloading datadumps is the best approach towards collecting large amounts of data documents for cleaning.

# 4   LOD Washing Machine

In the previous section we have describe the requirements that we believe Linked Datasets should conform to in order to be more useful in practice. We also explained why we have chosen to download datadumps in order to guarantee the best completeness guarantees. Here, we will make the aforementioned requirements concrete in such a way that they can be automatically applied to dirty Linked Datasets. The part of the LOD Laundromat that performs automated data cleaning is called the LOD Washing Machine.[14]

*Step A: Collect URLs that denote dataset dumps.* Before we start laundrying data, we need some dirty data to fill our LOD Laundry Basket with. The LOD Washing Machine does not completely automate the search for the initial seed points for collecting LOD. The reasons for this are that, firstly, catalogs that collect metadata descriptions must be accessed by website-specific APIs, Secondly, standards-compliant metadata descriptions are stored at multiple locations, and cannot always be found by Web search operations that can be automated. Thirdly, metadata descriptions of datasets, whether standards-compliant

---

[12] E.g., Virtuoso, an often used triple store, by default limits both the result set size and the number of rows within a sort operation.
[13] http://sparqles.okfn.org/
[14] Code available at https://github.com/LODLaundry/LOD-Washing-Machine

or catalog-specific, are often outdated (e.g., pointing to an old server) or incomplete. Finally, many datasets are not described anywhere, and require someone to know the server location at which the data is currently stored.

Due to these reasons, the LOD Washing Machine relies on catalog-specific scripts that collect such seed URLs for washing. An example of this is the CKAN API[15], which provides access to the datasets described in the Datahub, including the datasets that are in the original LOD cloud. This means that URLs that are not included in a LOD catalog or portal are less likely to be washed by the LOD Washing Machine. In addition, we have added several seed points by hand, for datasets that we know reside at specific server locations. Anyone can queue washing jobs by adding such seed URLs to the LOD Laundry Basket via the LOD Laundromat Website.

Some URL strings – e.g., values for the "URL" property in a catalog – do not parse according to the RFC 3986 grammar.[16] Some URL strings are parsed as IRIs but not as URLs, mostly because of unescaped spaces. Some URL strings parse per RFC 3986, but have no IANA-registered scheme[17], or the `file` scheme which is host-specific and cannot be used for downloading. The LOD Washing Machine uses only URLs that parse per RFC 3986 (after IRI-to-URL conversion) and that have an IANA-registered scheme that is not host-specific.

*Step B: Connect to the hosting server.* When processing the list of URLs from the previous step, we must be careful with URLs that contain the same authority part, since they are likely to reside at the same server. Since some servers do not accept multiple (near) simultaneous requests from the same IP, we must avoid parallel processing of such URLs. The LOD Washing Machine therefore groups URLs with the same authority, and makes sure they get processed in sequence, not in parallel. This is implemented by handling URLs with the same authority in a single thread.

At the level of TCP/IP, not all URL authorities denote a running server or host. Some running servers do not react to requests (neither reject nor accept), and some actively reject establishing a connection. Some connections that are established are broken off during communication.

*Step C: Communicate with the hosting server.* Once a connection has been established over TCP/IP, the LOD Washing Machine sends an HTTP request with SSL verification (for secure HTTP) and an accept header that includes a preference for LOD content types. This includes standardized content types and content types that occur in practice.

Some requests are unsuccessful, receiving either a server, existence, or permission error. Some requests are unsuccessful due to redirection loops.

*Step E: Unpack archived data.* Many Linked Datasets are contained in archives. The LOD Washing Machine supports the archive filters and formats that are

---

[15] http://ckan.org/

[16] http://tools.ietf.org/html/rfc3986

[17] http://www.iana.org/assignments/uri-schemes/uri-schemes.xhtml

supported by library libarchive[18]. The LOD Washing Machine accesses archives in a stream and opens additional streams for every archive entry it contains. Since archive entries can themselves be archives, this procedure is nested, resulting in a tree of streams. The root node of the tree is the stream of the original archive file, the leaf nodes are streams of non-archived files, and the other non-leaf nodes are streams of intermediate archived files.

Some archives cannot be read by libarchive, which throws an exception. We have not been able to open these archives with any of the standard unarchiving tools on Linux. Consequently, the LOD Washing Machine gives up on such archived files, but does report the exception that was thrown.

*Step F: Guess serialization format.* In order to parse the contents of the textual data that resides in the leaf nodes of the stream tree, we need to know the grammar of that data. The LOD Washing Machine uses content types to denote the grammar that is used for parsing, as content types are often included in the header of an HTTP responses.

There are various ways in which the content type of a streamed file can be assessed. The most reliable way is to parse the whole file using each of the RDF serialization parsers, and take the one that emits the least syntax errors and/or reads the most valid RDF triples. A theoretical example of why one needs to parse the whole file, not just a first segment of it, can be given with the difference between the Turtle and TriG formats. This difference may only become apparent in the last triple that appears in the file, by the occurrence of curly brackets (indicating a named graph).

Unfortunately, parsing every dataset with every parser is inefficient (CPU) and requires either local storage of the whole file (disk space) or multiple downloads of the same file (bandwidth).

In addition, we make the observation that the standardized RDF serialization formats occur in two families: XML-like (RDF/XML, RDFa) and Turtle-like (Turtle, TriG, N-Triples, N-Quads). The distinction between these two families can be reliably made by only looking at an initial segment of the file.

In order to keep the hardware footprint low, the LOD Washing Machine tries to guess the content type of a file based on a parse of only a first chunk of that file, in combination with the extension of the file (if any) and the content type header in the HTTP response message (if any). Using a look-ahead function on the stream, the LOD Washing Machine can use the first bytes on that stream in order to guess its content type, without consuming those bytes so that no redownload is necessary. The number of bytes available in the look-ahead is the same as the stream chunk size that is used for in-memory streaming anyway.

As explained above, this method may result in within-family mistakes, e.g., guessing Turtle for TriG or guessing N-Triples for N-Quads. In order to reduce the number of within-family mistakes, we use the content type and file extension. If these denote serialization formats that belong within the guessed family, we use that format. Otherwise, we use the most generic serialization format within the guessed family.

---

[18] https://code.google.com/p/libarchive/

This approach ensures that the LOD Washing Machine uses a fully streamed pipeline and relatively few hardware resources.

*Step G: Syntax errors while parsing RDF serializations.* The LOD Washing Machine parses the whole file using standards-conforming grammars. For this it uses the parsers from the SemWeb library [11]. This library passes the RDF 1.1 test cases, and is actively used in SW research and applications. Using this library, the LOD Washing Machine is able to recognize different kinds of syntax errors, and recover from them during parsing.

We enumerate some of the most common syntax errors the LOD Laundromat is able to identify:

- Bad encoding sequences (e.g., non-UTF-8).
- Undefined IRI prefixes.
- Missing end-of-statement characters between triples (i.e., 'triples' with more than three terms).
- Non-escaped, illegal characters inside IRIs.
- Multi-line literals in serialization formats that do not support them (e.g., multi-line literals that are only legal in Turtle, also occur in N-Triples and N-Quads).
- Missing or non-matching end tags (e.g., RDF/XML).
- End-of-file occurs within the last triple (probably indicating a mistake that was made while splitting files).
- IRIs that no not occur in between angular brackets (Turtle-family).

The LOD Washing Machine reports each syntax error it comes across. For data documents that contain syntax errors, there is no formal guarantee that a one-to-one mapping between the original document and a cleaned sibling document exists. This is an inherent characteristic of dirty data, and the application of heuristics in order to clean as many stains as possible. In the absence of a formal model describing all the syntactic mistakes that can be made, recovery from arbitrary syntax errors is more of an art than a science. We illustrate this with respect to the following example:

```
ex:a1  ex:a2  $""  ex:b1  ex:b2  ex:b3  .
               ex:c1  ex:c2  ex:c3  .
               ...
               ex:z1  ex:z2  ex:z3  .
        """ .
```

A standards-compliant RDF parser will not be able to parse this piece of syntax, and will give a syntax error. A common technique for RDF parsers is to look for the next end-of-triple statement (i.e., the dot at the end of the first line), and resume parsing from there. This results in parsing the collection of triples starting with $\langle rdf:c1, rdf:c2, ex:c3 \rangle$ and ending with $\langle rdf:z1, rdf:z2, ex:z3 \rangle$. The triple quotes at the end of the code sample will result in a second syntax error.

However, using other heuristics may produce very different results. For instance, by using minimum error distance, the syntax error can also be recovered by replacing the dollar sign with a double quote sign. This results in a single triple with a unusually long, but standards-compliant, literal term.

*Step H: De-duplicate RDF statements.* The LOD Washing Machine loads the parsed triples into a memory-based triple store. By loading the triples into a triple store, it performs deduplication of interpreted RDF statements. Deduplication cannot be performed without interpretation, i.e., on the syntax level, because the same RDF statement can be written in different ways. Syntactically, the same triple can look differently due to the use of character escaping, the use of extra white spaces and/or newlines and interspersed comments, the use of different/no named prefixes for IRIs, abbreviation mechanisms in serialization formats that support them (e.g., RDF/XML, Turtle). Another source of the many-to-one mapping between syntax and semantics occurs for RDF datatypes / XML Schema 1.1 datatypes, for which multiple lexical expressions can map onto the same value.[19] For example, the lexical expressions 0.1 and 0.10000000009 map to the same value according to data type `xsd:float`, but to different values according to data type `xsd:decimal`.

While reading RDF statements into the triple store, the contents of different data documents are stored in separate transactions, allowing the concurrent loading of data in multiple threads. Each transaction represents an RDF graph or set of triples, thereby automatically deduplicating triples within the same file.

*Step I: Save RDF in a uniform serialization format.* Once the triples are parsed using an RDF parser, and the resulting RDF statements are loaded into memory without duplicates, we can use a generator of our choice to serialize the cleaned data. We want our generator to be compliant with existing standards, and we want to support further processing of the data, as discussed in section 3.1. The LOD Washing Machine produces data in a canonical format that enforces a one-to-one mapping between data triples and file lines. This means that the end-of-line character can be reliably used in subsequent processing, such as pattern matching (e.g., regular expressions) and parsing. This also means that data documents can be easily split without running the risk of splitting in-between triples. Furthermore, the number of triples in a graph can be easily and reliably determined by counting the number of lines in a file describing that graph. Secondly, the LOD Washing Machine leaves out any header information. This, again, makes it easy to split existing data documents into smaller parts, since the first part of the file is not treated specially due to serialization-specifc header declarations (e.g., RDF/XML, RDFa) and namespace definitions (e.g., RDF/XML, Turtle). Thirdly, the LOD Washing Machine replaces all occurrences of blank nodes with well-known IRIs[20], in line with the RDF 1.1 specification[21]. Effectively, this means that blank nodes are interpreted as Skolem constants, not

---

[19] http://www.w3.org/TR/xmlschema11-2/

[20] https://tools.ietf.org/html/rfc5785

[21] http://www.w3.org/TR/2014/REC-rdf11-concepts-20140225/
    #section-skolemization

as existentially quantified variables. The Skolem constant is an IRI that is based on the URL that was used to stream the RDF data from, thereby making it a universally unique name at the moment of processing.[22] This makes it easy to append and split data documents, without the need to standardize apart blank nodes that originate from different graphs.

From the existing serialization formats, N-Triples and N-Quads come closest to these requirements. Since the tracking of named graphs is out of scope for our initial version of the LOD laundry (see section 6), we use a canonical form of N-Triples that excludes superfluous white space (only one space between the RDF terms in a triple and one space before the end-of-triple character), superfluous newlines (only one newline after the end-of-triple character), and comments (none at all). Newlines that occur in multi-line literals, supported by some serialization formats, are escaped according to the N-Triples 1.1 specification. Also, simple literals are not written, always adding the XML Schema string datatype explicitly.

*Step J: VoID closure.* After having stored the data to a canonical format, we make use of the fact that the valid triples are still stored in memory, by perform a quick query on the memory store. In this query we derive any triples that describe Linked Datasets. Specifically, we look for occurrences of predicates in the VoID namespace. We store these triples in a publicly accessible metadata graph that can be queried using SPARQL. For each dataset that is described in VoID triples, we follow links to datadumps (if present), and add them to the LOD Laundry Basket, and clean those datadumps by using the LOD Washing Machine as well. Since a dataset may describe a dataset that describes another dataset, this process is recursive.

*Step K: Consolidate and disseminate datasets for further processing.* Since we want to incentivise the dataset creators to improve their adherence to guidelines, we keep track of all the mistakes that were discussed in this section. The mistakes (if any) are asserted together with some basic statistics, e.g. number of triples, number of bytes processed, in the publicly queryable metadata graph. For syntax errors we include the line and column number at which the error occurred, relative to the original file. This makes it easy for the dataset maintainers to improve their data and turn out cleaner in a next wash, since the metadata descriptions are automatically updated at future executions of the LOD Washing Machine.

## 5   The LOD Laundromat Web Service

When the LOD Washing Machine has cleaned a data document, it is ironed and folded, and made available on a publicly accessible Website that provides

---

[22] When a new file is disseminated at the same URL at a later point in time, the same Skolem constant may be used to denote a different blank node. Using skolemization, this becomes an instance of the generic problem that IRIs can denote different things at different times, as the data document is updated.

additional support for data consumers. We now describe the components that make up this Website, and lift out the support features that make LOD Laundromat a good source for finding large volumes of high-quality Linked Data.

## 5.1  LOD Wardrobe

The LOD Wardrobe (Figure 1) is where the cleaned datasets are disseminated for human data consumers. The data documents are listed in a table that can be sorted according to various criteria (e.g., cleaning data, number of triples). For every data document, a row in the table includes links to both the old (dirty) and new (cleaned) data files, as well as a button that brings up a pop-up box with all the metadata for that data document. Furthermore, it is easy to filter the table based on a search string, and multiple rows from the table can be selected for downloading at the same time.

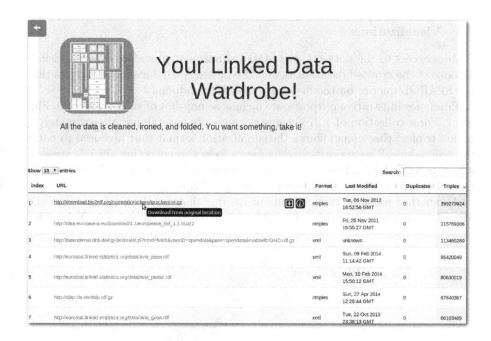

**Fig. 1.** The LOD Wardrobe is available at `http://lodlaundromat.org/wardrobe`

## 5.2  SPARQL Endpoint

All the metadata that is collected during the cleaning process, is stored in an RDF graph that is publicly accessible via the SPARQL endpoint `http://lodlaundromat.org/sparql`. For human data consumers, we provide the feature-rich SPARQL editor Yasgui.[23] For machine consumption, the

---

[23] `http://yasgui.laurensrietveld.nl/`

SPARQL endpoint can be queried algorithmically. For instance, a SPARQL query can return URLs for downloading all clean data documents with over one million syntactically correct triples. In this way, LOD Laundromat provides a very simple interface for running Big Data experiments. The metadata that is stored by the LOD Washing Machine includes information such as the number of triples in a dataset:

- the number of removed duplicates,
- the original serialization format,
- any VoID descriptions that were found,
- various kinds of syntax errors,
- and more.

The metadata that the LOD Wardrobe publishes is continuously updated whenever new cleaned laundry comes in.

## 5.3  Visualizations

Besides access to the datasets, the LOD Laundromat provides real-time visualizations of the crawled datasets as well. These are small JavaScript widgets that use SPARQL queries on the metadata SPARQL endpoint.

Purely for illustrative purposes, we include a snapshot of such a widget in Figure 2. For a collection of 1.276 cleaned documents (containing approximately 2 billion triples) this widget shows the serialization format that was used to parse the original file. The majority of documents from this collection, 59.2%, are serialized as RDF/XML. Turtle and RDFa amount to 29.5% and 6.7% respectively. Only 4.4% of all documents are serialized as N-Triples.

As another example of the kinds of queries that can be performed on the SPARQL endpoint, we take the HTTP `Content-Length` header. Values for

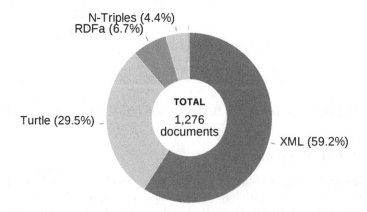

**Fig. 2.**    RDF serialization formats for a collection of RDF documents. Illustrative example of a visualization widget at `http://lodlaundromat.org/visualizations`.

this header are often set incorrectly. Ideally, a properly set `Content-Length` header would allow data consumers to retrieve data more efficiently, e.g., by load-balancing data depending on the expected size of the response. However, our results show that 32% of the documents return an invalid content length value, thereby showing that in practice it is difficult to reliably make use of this property.

### 5.4  LOD Laundry Basket

In order to extend our collection of datasets over time, users can add seed URLs to the LOD Laundry Basket. Seed points can be either URLs that point to VoID descriptions, or to data dumps directly. Seed locations can be added via a Web form or via a direct HTTP GET request.

## 6  Conclusion

Existing research shows that many LOD does not comply with existing standards. To deal with this issue, we have presented LOD Laundromat, a uniform way of publishing other peoples dirty data. Using LOD Laundromat, we publish standards- and guidelines-compliant datasets that are siblings of existing, idiosyncratic datasets. LOD Laundromat implements a Linked Data cleaner that *continuously* crawls for additional datasets; the amount of data that we publish (over ten billion triples at the time of writing) already surpasses that of existing data collections, such as the Billion Triple Challenge. In addition, the LOD Laundromat publishes metadata for every cleaned document on a publicly accessible Web site, and through machine-accessible Web services. Because anybody can drop their dirty data in the LOD Laundry Basket, the coverage of the LOD Laundromat will increase over time. All datasets are published in a very simple canonical form of N-Triples, which makes it easy for post-processing tools to parse, possibly in streamed form. By using the LOD Laundromat, data consumers do not have to worry about different serialization formats, syntax errors, encoding issues, or triple duplicates. In doing so, LOD Laundromat can act as an enabler for Big Data and SW research, as well as a provider of data for Web-scale applications.

Although the LOD Laundromat offers many advantages for data consumers today, we aim to further increase the level of support. Fistly, the metadata we collect does not yet make use of existing vocabularies, like DCAT[24], VoID, and Prov-O[25]. Secondly, LOD Laundromat currently disseminates datasets in the N-Triples serialization format, in which it is not possible to represent multiple graphs. Even though the use of multiple graphs within the same data document is not very common today, the few datasets for which this is used would be better supported by the N-Quads format. This also requires the scope of the triple deduplication phase to be narrowed down to graphs. Thirdly, not all Linked

---

[24] http://www.w3.org/TR/vocab-dcat/
[25] http://www.w3.org/TR/prov-o/

Data is Open. Some data may be licensed under conditions that do not allow free data reuse. However, restricting licenses are difficult to detect by automated means, since very few datasets contain explicit licensing conditions. Still, in those cases in which a dataset does explicitly mention a license, and this license is not defined open by the Open Data Commons[26], we would like the LOD Washing Machine to skip it. Finially, we may choose to store multiple versions of the collection of cleaned datasets as different 'snapshots'. Such snapshots may, for instance, improve the reproducibility of LOD experiments.

# References

1. Bollacker, K., Evans, C., Paritosh, P., Sturge, T., Taylor, J.: Freebase: a Collaboratively Created Graph Database for Structuring Human Knowledge. In: Proceedings of the 2008 ACM SIGMOD International Conference on Management of Data, pp. 1247–1250. ACM (2008)
2. Callahan, A., Cruz-Toledo, J., Ansell, P., Dumontier, M.: Bio2RDF Release 2: Improved Coverage, Interoperability and Provenance of Life Science Linked Data. In: Cimiano, P., Corcho, O., Presutti, V., Hollink, L., Rudolph, S. (eds.) ESWC 2013. LNCS, vol. 7882, pp. 200–212. Springer, Heidelberg (2013)
3. Ermilov, I., Martin, M., Lehmann, J., Auer, S.: Linked Open Data Statistics: Collection and Exploitation. In: Klinov, P., Mouromtsev, D. (eds.) KESW 2013. Communications in Computer and Information Science, vol. 394, pp. 242–249. Springer, Heidelberg (2013)
4. Hogan, A., Harth, A., Passant, A., Decker, S., Polleres, A.: Weaving the pedantic web. In: Linked Data on the Web Workshop (2010)
5. Hogan, A., Umbrich, J., Harth, A., Cyganiak, R., Polleres, A., Decker, S.: An Empirical Survey of Linked Data Conformance. Web Semantics: Science, Services and Agents on the World Wide Web 14, 14–44 (2012)
6. Käfer, T., Abdelrahman, A., Umbrich, J., O'Byrne, P., Hogan, A.: Observing Linked Data Dynamics. In: Cimiano, P., Corcho, O., Presutti, V., Hollink, L., Rudolph, S. (eds.) ESWC 2013. LNCS, vol. 7882, pp. 213–227. Springer, Heidelberg (2013)
7. Olston, C., Reed, B., Srivastava, U., Kumar, R., Tomkins, A.: Pig latin: A not-so-foreign language for data processing. In: Proceedings of the 2008 ACM SIGMOD International Conference on Management of Data, pp. 1099–1110. ACM (2008)
8. Oren, E., Delbru, R., Catasta, M., Cyganiak, R., Stenzhorn, H., Tummarello, G.: Sindice.com: a Document-Oriented Lookup Index for Open Linked Data. International Journal of Metadata, Semantics and Ontologies 3(1), 37–52 (2008)
9. Stadtmüller, S., Harth, A., Grobelnik, M.: Accessing Information about Linked Data Vocabularies with vocab.cc. In: Semantic Web and Web Science, pp. 391–396. Springer (2013)
10. Tummarello, G., Cyganiak, R., Catasta, M., Danielczyk, S., Delbru, R., Decker, S.: Sigma: Live Views on the Web of Data. Web Semantics: Science, Services and Agents on the World Wide Web 8(4), 355–364 (2010)
11. Wielemaker, J.: SWI-Prolog Semantic Web Library 3.0, http://prolog.cs.vu.nl/download/doc/semweb.pdf

---

[26] An overview of machine-readable licence descriptions for data can be found at http://licenses.opendefinition.org/licenses/groups/all.json

# Dutch Ships and Sailors Linked Data

Victor de Boer[1], Matthias van Rossum[2], Jurjen Leinenga[3], and Rik Hoekstra[3]

[1] Netherlands Institute for Sound and Vision, Hilversum, The Netherlands
Dept. of Computer Science, VU University Amsterdam, The Netherlands
v.de.boer@vu.nl
[2] Dept. of History, VU University Amsterdam, The Netherlands
m.van.rossum@vu.nl
[3] Huygens ING Institute for Dutch History, Den Haag, The Netherlands
leinenga@xs4all.nl, rik.hoekstra@huygens.knaw.nl

**Abstract.** We present the Dutch Ships and Sailors Linked Data Cloud. This heterogeneous dataset brings together four curated datasets on Dutch Maritime history as five-star linked data. The individual datasets use separate datamodels, designed in close collaboration with maritime historical researchers. The individual models are mapped to a common interoperability layer, allowing for analysis of the data on the general level. We present the datasets, modeling decisions, internal links and links to external data sources. We show ways of accessing the data and present a number of examples of how the dataset can be used for historical research. The Dutch Ships and Sailors Linked Data Cloud is a potential hub dataset for digital history research and a prime example of the benefits of Linked Data for this field.

**Keywords:** Digital History, Maritime Data, Heterogeneous Data Cloud.

## 1 Introduction

As (digital) humanities researchers seek more (international and cross-domain) collaboration, integrating humanities datasets becomes more important to those researchers. One subdomain where this is very much prevalent is in (social) historical research. Often historical researchers collect data from historical archives for their specific research questions. However, these datasets are often not presented in sharable formats to other researchers. If they are shared at all, the datasets are published in a multitude of formats. To further the digital history agenda, it has been recognized that representing and sharing data is key [4,10]. Using Linked Data principles and practices, we can integrate generic data with smaller datasets that have been created with a specific historical research goal. Linked Data allows us to publish these datasets using the modeling principles of the original datasets, while -through the use of (schema) links- still achieving a level of integration. In this paper, we present the Dutch Ships and Sailors (DSS) data cloud. This Linked Data cloud brings together four Dutch maritime historical datasets, each with its own datamodel. The data is available as five-star linked data making sharing and reuse possible. The data is integrated at

P. Mika et al. (Eds.) ISWC 2014, Part I, LNCS 8796, pp. 229–244, 2014.

a meta-level through common vocabularies and linked to generic external data sources allowing for new types of queries and analysis.

As a sea-faring nation, a large portion of Dutch history is found on the water. The maritime industry has been central to regional and global economic, social and cultural exchange. It is also one of the best historically documented sectors of human activity. Many aspects of it have been recorded by shipping companies, governments, newspapers and other institutions. In the past few decades, much of the data in the preserved historical source material has been digitized. Among the most interesting data are those on shipping movement and crew members (cf. [15]). However, much of the digitized historical source material is still scattered across many databases and archives while still referring to common places, ships, persons and events. By linking the different available databases, the data can complement and amplify each other, and new research possibilities open up. The DSS datacloud bring together the rich maritime historical data preserved in four of these different databases. Two of these databases have been used extensively in historical research and by presenting them in this interoperable format, future reuse is likely to be easier.

The presented dataset is significant to the digital history community since it brings together seminal datasets on maritime history in a re-usable and integrated way. The complexity of the original data is retained and not 'dumbed down' to a specific data model for online presentation. At the same time, multiple enrichments have been performed and additional enrichments are possible at a later stage. The four datasets together integrated can serve as a pivot data cloud for international maritime historical datasets as well as for other (Dutch) historical datasets. The work here is also significant to the broader Linked Data community since it presents a prime example of how collaboration between historians and computer scientists can lead to high-quality digital history datasets that are actually trusted and used by the historians. Digital humanities is a rapidly growing field in which it is recognized that Linked Data presents interesting opportunities. Furthermore, this datacloud presents the results of a method where individual datasets are converted to RDF, maintaining their own datamodel but are integrated through RDF(S) links into a datacloud. This methodology can be re-used in other multi-part datasets.

## 2    General Approach

We here describe the general conversion pipeline and modeling principles. Section 3 describes the specific datamodels and conversion steps.

### 2.1    Conversion and Modeling Pipeline

The conversion and modeling pipeline is based on previous work described in [6] where more details about the methodology and tools can be found. We here give a brief overview. In a first step of the generic pipeline, we have data available in some XML format. For datasets, not available as XML, we use simple syntactic export functions[1]. The output of the pipeline is linked RDF, corresponding to a specific datamodel. The pipeline is built on the ClioPatria semantic server (http://cliopatria.swi-prolog.org). ClioPatria is an RDF triple store that through a web interface provides feedback on the (intermediary) produced RDF, which is crucial for the interactivity of the conversion and modeling. We start by ingesting the XML into ClioPatria, which converts the XML tree into a raw RDF graph, assigning blank nodes to each node in the tree.

**Graph Restructuring.** The ClioPatria XMLRDF[2] package is a tool for restructuring an RDF graph using *graph rewrite rules*. In the second step, the crude RDF is rewritten to RDF adhering to a data model format, using handwritten rules which are interpreted by the XMLRDF tool. These rules are constructed in an iterative interactive process[3]. In this step, some blank nodes from the rough RDF graph are assigned URIs and resources and triples can be copied, merged, replaced or deleted. Depending on the datamodel, some literal values are consolidated to RDF resources. For each dataset, we also generated an RDFS schema which lists the produced classes and properties and relates them to the more generic DSS schema (see Section 3.5). ClioPatria provides support for this by presenting the user with a schema template based on the RDF data loaded.

**Linking.** We establish links to external resources. This can be done using either the XMLRDF tool, for example when in dataset A there is an explicit reference to a unique identifier in dataset B. When linking requires more complex techniques, we employ the ClioPatria package Amalgame[4]. Amalgame is an iterative alignment platform that allows a user to mix-and-match multiple label- and structure-matching algorithms as well as filtering operations into an alignment workflow. The tool is used to establish identity or other semantic relations (e.g. broader/narrower) between concepts and instances.

## 2.2   Generic Modeling Decisions

**Resources and URI Schema.** RDF Resources can be either blank nodes or receive a URI. In general, we only use blank nodes to group properties. An example is given in Section 3.1, where statistics about specific crew membership are grouped. Any resource that is considered to be a meaningful 'thing' is assigned a URI. This includes resources that might be linked to from outside of the dataset. URIs are typically created from an identifier metadata field (such as the original database record ID). Within the DSS cloud, we have defined five namespaces: http://purl.org/collections/nl/dss/ for DSS generic data and   http://purl.org/collections/nl/dss/gzmvoc/,   http://purl.org/

---

[1] For example, for MS Excel files, we use the built-in export function.
[2] http://semanticweb.cs.vu.nl/xmlrdf/
[3] The XMLRDF scripts used for the DSS datacloud are found online at https://github.com/biktorrr/dss/tree/master/script
[4] http://semanticweb.cs.vu.nl/amalgame/

232    V. de Boer et al.

collections/nl/dss/mdb/, http://purl.org/collections/nl/dss/das/ and
http://purl.org/collections/nl/dss/vocopv/ for the four datasets. In this
paper we abbreviate URIs with the respective CURIEs[5] dss:, gzmvoc:, mdb:,
das: and vocopv:. We use PURL URIs that redirect to a ClioPatria instance,
this allows for persistence of the URIs even beyond the life expectancy of the
project or any specific institute.

**Linked Data for Multilayered Enrichment.** In some cases, new resources
are created, where in the original metadata, there are only literal values. We do
this specifically to group properties about things that are separately identifiable
and that might reoccur in the datasets. Specifically, we do this for *persons,
places, ships, ship types* and *ranks.* In most cases, the original literal values are
retained and a new resource is created in a separate named graph with its own
provenance information. An example of this is shown in Figure 2. By not 'hard
coding' the enrichment but separating the enriched data from the original data,
we can benefit from the latter, while still always being able to go back to the
original data. This corresponds to an important requirement as put forward by
the historical researchers.

Another important modeling decision that is partly specific to the domain is
that for most types of resources, we assume that they are unique, even though
they have a number of metadata fields in common. For example, two records
(say from 1850 and 1851) might both refer to a person "Piet Janssen" who
sailed on the ship "Alberdina". We do not assume that these are the same
person, and therefore assign them separate URIs. This was an explicit modeling
decision taken in collaboration with the historians, since many Dutch names are
common and often fathers and sons with the same first and last name sailed on
the same ships. Therefore, in the basic data, we assume that all persons and ships
are unique and assigned separate URIs. At a later stage, automatic or manual
methods can be used to establish identity links. In Section 3.2, we describe this
effort for one of the datasets.

**Mapping Properties and Classes to DSS Interoperability Layer.** We
model the datasets using separate datamodels with their own properties and
classes and do not use common classes or properties directly in the individual datasets. Rather we use subproperty and subclass relations to map our
classes and properties to common ones (either in the DSS domain or to external schemas). This way we can retain the specificity of the dataset and the
intended semantics of the model and still allow for reasoning and querying at the
interoperability level (DSS). For example, the notion of a ship name is slightly
different amongst the datasets even though they use the same field name. In some
cases, some normalization process has taken place in the original archive data
and in other cases it has not. These (sometimes subtle) differences are regarded
as crucial by the historians and they need to be maintained in the converted
datasets to ensure trust and usage. This example is shown in Figures 2 and 3.

---
[5] http://www.w3.org/TR/2007/WD-curie-20070307/

The DSS schema itself is mapped to often-used schema's. Other than RDF(S) these are: SKOS[6] to describe concepts schemes (ranks, ship types,...); FOAF[7] to describe person information; and Dublin Core terms[8] to describe record information (description, identifier,...). ClioPatria as well as many other triple stores supports RDFS entailment in its SPARQL interface and can therefore exploit these mappings.

### 2.3   The Role of Provenance and Named Graphs

Provenance plays an important role in historical research and specifically in archival research. The origin and history of archival data is crucial to estimate the scientific value of data [13]. This holds even truer for digital data, where in many cases its provenance is unknown or lost. For Linked Data, the provenance of resources can be modeled using the PROV-O ontology[7]. In the DSS cloud we model the provenance on the named graph level. Each named graph is a separate set of triples that come from one source. This can be either (a table in) an original data source, or the result of an enrichment or linking process. In the DSS cloud, each RDF named graph has a URI that is defined also as a prov:Entity. This URI is the subject and object for the provenance triples, including those listing the different conversion activities and the human and software agents involved in the conversion. We also refer to the original data sources and their web URIs as far as they are present. All the provenance triples are stored in a separate named graph[9].

Next to provenance information, for automatically derived data we list the content confidence[12]. This provenance information allows for SPARQL queries that include or exclude triples from specific named graphs because they are the result of an operation of a software agent or because they have a too low content confidence value. For a total of four link sets we performed a structured manual evaluation of random samples by the domain expert. For these named graphs we assign confidence levels based on the evaluation results.

## 3   The Datasets

In this section we describe the individual datasets. The first two are modeled and converted in close collaboration with the historical researchers responsible for the source datasets and we describe them in more detail. The third and fourth datasets are conversions of previously published historical datasets and are described less elaborately. They were converted with the help of the historians. We also list the main statistics in Section 3.6 as well as describe the interoperability layer and links. Figure 1 gives an overview of the entire DSS data cloud and the internal and external links.

---

[6] http://www.w3.org/2004/02/skos/
[7] http://xmlns.com/foaf/0.1/
[8] http://dublincore.org/documents/dcmi-terms
[9] http://www.dutchshipsandsailors.nl/data/browse/list_graph?graph= http://purl.org/collections/nl/dss/dss_provenance.ttl

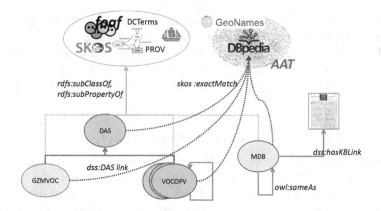

**Fig. 1.** The Dutch Ships and Sailors Linked Data cloud. The individual datasets are represented by ovals in the bottom half of the image. Internal links are represented by arrows. External links are represented by dotted arrows.


## 3.1  GZMVOC

**Original Data.** The "Generale Zeemonsterrollen VOC" (GZMVOC) (*en:* "General sea muster rolls VOC") is a dataset describing the crews of all ships of the Dutch East India Company (VOC)[10] from 1691–1791. The data was gathered by a Dutch social historian Matthias van Rossum (co-author of this paper) in the course of his research on labor situations for European and Asiatic crews on Dutch VOC ships. The data is based on archival records from the VOC itself and lists data of all ships that sailed between Europe and Asia. The data consists of the size of the crew as well as its composition (number of European and Asiatic sailors, soldiers and passengers). In a number of occasions the location of the ship on the moment of counting -the month of June of each year- as well as data on the name and type of ship. Where possible, details on the Asiatic crew members are listed, including wages, job descriptions, place of origin, categorization and hierarchical structure. For ships with a mixed European and Asiatic crew, often data about the captain and offices is listed. In this dataset, references to the Dutch Asiatic Shipping (DAS) dataset are present through numerical IDs (see Section 3.4). The original data was presented as a Microsoft Excel file, which we exported to XML.

**Data Model and Conversion.** An initial RDFS datamodel for GZMVOC was derived from the structure of the Excel sheet as well as documentation provided. After that, the model was corrected and refined in close collaboration with van Rossum. The primary citizens of this dataset are records (countings) which are the subjects of locations, registration numbers, etc. Counts of Asiatic and European crews are grouped using blank nodes, rather than linking numbers

---

[10] http://en.wikipedia.org/wiki/Dutch_East_India_Company

directly to individual records. Each record is connected to a ship resource, which groups information assumed to be persistent beyond the counting such as the ship name and type. For the captain, a resource is also created, with name and birthplace information. Several literal values are consolidated to resources, including ship types, ranks and places, to allow for later linking. The original triples with literals are always retained.

After ingestion and conversion to raw RDF. A total of 10 XMLRDF rules were created to restructure the graph to match the datamodel. The results were verified by van Rossum by inspecting a number of resources by hand. In total 110,986 triples are stored in the GZMVOC main data named graph `gzmvoc:gzmvoc_data.ttl`[11] (see Table 3.6 for all graphs and statistics). A further 591 triples make up the consolidated places and 166 triples make up a small vocabulary of ship types and ranks. This is the smallest dataset in the DSS datacloud. The figure below shows a small sample of the RDF graph for GZMVOC.

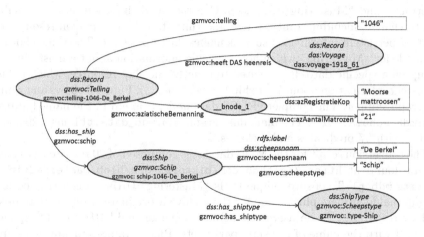

**Fig. 2.** Small sample of the RDF graph for GZMVOC showing a counting, a linked ship and detailed counting information connected to a blank node. Resources are represented using ovals, with the URI at the bottom line under italicized superclasses above, properties are represented by arrows, with property URIs next to them and their superproperties italicized. Literals are represented using boxes.

**Links.** The referenced identifiers of the DAS dataset are used to establish RDF links to resources in that dataset using a simple lookup script. There are two types of properties linking GZMVOC and DAS: one representing outgoing journeys (`gzmvoc:has_das_link_heen`) and one representing homebound journeys (`gzmvoc:has_das_link_terug`). Those link triples are stored in a separate named graph, to enable listing separate provenance information. A total of 5,303 link triples are stored.

---

[11] `mdb:mdb_data.ttl`

## 3.2  MDB

**Original Data.** The "Noordelijke Monsterollen Databases" (MDB) (*en:* "Northern muster rolls databases") is a dataset describing mustering information found in mustering archives in the three northern Dutch provinces (Groningen, Friesland, Drenthe)[12] in the period 1803–1937. The original Noordelijke Monsterollen Databases (MDB) was provided as a SQL dump file by the original maker of the data, historian Jurjen Leinenga (also co-author of this paper). The database consists of two tables, one with records of ship muster rolls and one with records of person-contracts, related to those muster rolls. The SQL dump was loaded into a MySQL database and exported to XML. This resulted in two XML files, one for the ship records and one for the person records.

**Data Model and Conversion.** The datamodel was developed interactively in collaboration with the historian, based on the original SQL data model and extensive written documentation. In this model, the two main classes are a "Person Contract", and "Mustering". A Person Contract holds information that is subject to change, including ranks, wages and time stamps. The Person resource is used for persistent information such as names, birth place etc. The same choices are made for "Mustering" which holds specific information about a mustering of a ship on a specific date. It is related to exactly one ship resource, which holds persistent information about that ship (name, type, ...). Figure 3 shows an example graph snippet. The complete RDFS datamodel is found in the named graph `mdb:mdb_schema.ttl`[13]. The main data graph `mdb:mdb_data.ttl` has 1,296,641 triples, with 27 predicates and 8 classes.

The conversion script for the MDB dataset is composed of 20 rewrite rules and can be found at `https://github.com/biktorrr/dss/blob/master/script/rewrite_mdb.pl`. To ensure unique URIs "Mustering" URIs are constructed using internal identifiers plus a code for the archive it originates from (this archive is also a resource in the dataset itself). For ship, person and URIs, we add expand this URI with the name of the ship, person etc. Places, ranks and shiptypes are consolidated to place resources.

**Internal Links.** In the MDB dataset many ships occur multiple times, however it is initially unknown which ships are which. We therefore assume that all ships are unique and only at a later state attempt to identify recurring ships. For this enrichment, multiple algorithms were designed and implemented. A sample of the results was evaluated by Jur Leinenga and a subset with an acceptable precision was found (0.95). More details about the linking are found in [14]. The links are stored in a separate named graph (`mdb:mdb_ship_sameas.ttl`) with appropriate provenance and content confidence metadata. A total of 33,435 sameAs links are established.

---

[12] `http://en.wikipedia.org/wiki/Provinces_of_the_Netherlands`

[13] For brevity, we shorten graph URIs with CURIEs. The expanded URIs are dereferenceable.

**External Links.** One of the more interesting external links are those from DSS records to digital historical newspaper articles from the Dutch Royal Library (KB)[14]. The linking algorithm uses a number of features such as ship names, captain names, time constraints and automatically derived indicator phrases for maritime events (such as "left port", "sailing for" etc.) to establish likely links between MDB records and KB articles. Multiple versions of the algorithm were developed, focusing either more on precision or on recall. For each version, random samples of the results were evaluated manually by Jurjen Leinenga. More details about the linking can be found in [1]). In the end, it was decided that the results of a high-precision version (precision here is 0.90) of the algorithm were consolidated and added to the datacloud as a separate named graph (`mdb:mdb_2_kb.ttl`) with appropriate provenance and content confidence metadata. Links are manifested as RDF links between MDB musterings and external KB paragraph URIs. Figure 3 shows such a link. Note that the KB as of yet does not provide RDF after dereferencing, rather an XML snippet with the text of the newspaper article is returned. In total 179,120 `dss:has_kb_link` triples are stored.

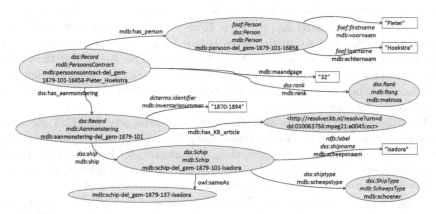

**Fig. 3.** Small sample of the RDF graph for MDB showing a person-contract and linked person; the counting (mustering) and a linked ship. Also shown are an internal owl:sameAs and an external link to a KB newspaper resource. For a number of properties, we list the DSS-superproperties in italics.

### 3.3   VOCOPV

The original dataset "VOC Opvarenden" [17] is the result of a manual digitization of the personnel data of the VOC in the 18th Century. The original data consists of three separate parts (*en:* 'voyagers', 'salary books' and 'beneficiaries') and was downloaded as a CSV file from DANS Easy website[15]. It was converted to an XML version using a simple python script.

---

[14] http://kranten.delpher.nl
[15] https://easy.dans.knaw.nl/ui/datasets/id/easy-dataset:33602

The XML version was then converted to RDF with an XMLRDF rewriting script. The model was developed in a collaboration between the authors, based on the original data model, expert knowledge and documentation available. There are three main classes: "Voyager"; "Salary Book", which links to ships and "Beneficiary". Links are present between instances of each of these classes. The complete RDFS datamodel is found in the named graph vocopv:vocopv_schema.ttl. With more than 22 Million triples, this is the largest dataset in the DSS cloud.

The original VOC Opvarenden dataset uses explicit references to DAS voyages. These were used to generate explicit links between VOC Opvarenden and DAS. We use three different RDF properties, which correspond to the original metadata fields. All links are stored in a separate named graph (vocopv:vocopv_2_das.ttl.gz). In total 1,128,416 links are established.

## 3.4   DAS

The Dutch Asiatic Shipping (DAS) dataset contains data regarding outward and homeward voyages of more than 4,700 ships that sailed under the flag of the (VOC) between 1595 and 1795. The dataset is a conversion of a previously digitized DAS dataset hosted at Huygens ING [3] at http://resources.huygens.knaw.nl/das/index_html_en. Between 1595 and 1795 the Dutch East India Company (VOC) and its predecessors before 1602 equipped more than 4,700 ships to sail from the shores of the Netherlands bound for Asia. More than 3,400 ships made the return voyage home. The reference work Dutch-Asiatic Shipping has classified these voyages on which Dutch trade between Europe and Asia was founded in a systematic survey.

The original Dutch Asiatic Shipping data was downloaded as a CSV file. That data was converted to an XML version using a simple python script (available on Github). The XML version was then converted to RDF with an XMLRDF rewriting script. The model was developed in a collaboration between the authors and is based on the original data model, expert knowledge and documentation available. Here the main class is "Voyage" detailing a specific voyage of a VOC ship either from the Netherlands to Asia or back. The complete RDFS datamodel is found in the named graph das:das_schema.ttl. The main data graph das:das_data.ttl has 149,357 triples, with 21 predicates and 6 classes.

## 3.5   Generic DSS Data

As was described in Section 2.2, places, ship types and ranks were consolidated to resources so that they can be linked to internal or external data sources. For a number of ranks and ship types, a manually constructed SKOS thesaurus was created by the historians. In a DSS schema (dss:dss_schema.ttl), manually defined 7 classes that are common to the four datasets (Ship, Chamber, Sailor etc.) as well as three DSS specific properties (eg. ship name), found in dss:dss_schema.ttl. The other properties and classes in the interoperability layer are from SKOS, FOAF or DCTERMS. We use rdfs:subPropertyOf and rdfs:subClassOf triples to relate the properties and classes to this layer.

**Identity Links.** Although *GeoNames*[16] does not provide historical place information, it still is a very usable source of information, providing lat/long coordinates, hierarchical information and place names in other languages. It is a much linked-to data source on the Web of Data, thereby increasing the reusability of the DSS data. Place names from all four datasets are aligned with the GeoNames dataset, but only for the subset of Dutch places[17]. For this, we used the Amalgame toolkit using simple label matching algorithms. The links are stored in a separate named graph (`dss:al_all_place_2_geonames.ttl`). We used `skos:exactMatch` properties to link DSS place names to GeoNames resources. In total 2,510 links are established. These place names are spread over the four datasets. *The Getty Art and Architecture Thesaurus (AAT)*[18] lists many concepts that are relevant for our dataset, for example ship types and ranks. We use a version of the AAT that has Dutch language labels making it possible to semi-automatically link DSS ranks and ship types to AAT. The mappings were based on matching labels and performed by Amalgame. The links are stored in the named graph (`mdb:ranks_and_shiptypes_1.ttl`) A total of 75 concepts were matched. We finally link ranks and ship types to *DBPedia*[19] again using the Amalgame alignment tool. A total of 123 links are established and stored in `dss:dbpedia_links.ttl`

### 3.6 Statistics

In Table 3.6, we list the named graphs that make up the DSS datacloud. For each named graph we list the URI, the number of triples and the dataset it belongs to[20]. A number of linked external data sources are also loaded to allow for single access-point SPARQL querying.

## 4 Accessing the Data

**Web Interface.** The data is accessible through two live ClioPatria triple store instances. A 'stable version' is published at http://dutchshipsandsailors.nl/data with a development version online at http://semanticweb.cs.vu.nl/dss. The stable version is especially interesting since it is hosted and maintained at the Huygens ING institute for historical research as part of their digital history infrastructure, rather than through a university server. This ensures stability and sustainability of the dataset beyond the research project. The ClioPatria web interface allows for browsing the data. The graphs can be browsed or downloaded

---

[16] http://www.geonames.org
[17] We are planning on expanding the links and adding those as separate named graphs to the data. Initial experiments linking to Indonesian locations have been performed.
[18] http://www.getty.edu/research/tools/vocabularies/aat/
[19] http://dbpedia.org/
[20] A live version of these statistics can be seen at
http://www.dutchshipsandsailors.nl/data/browse/list_graphs

| RDF Graph | Triples | Dataset |
|---|---|---|
| vocopv:vocopv_opv.ttl.gz | 19,104,514 | VOC Opvarenden |
| vocopv:vocopv_sol.ttl.gz | 2,231,367 | VOC Opvarenden |
| mdb:mdb_data.ttl.gz | 1,296,641 | MDB |
| vocopv:vocopv_2_das.ttl.gz | 1,128,416 | VOC Opvarenden |
| vocopv:vocopv_beg.ttl.gz | 636,333 | VOC Opvarenden |
| http://sws.geonames.org/geonames-NL.ttl | 309,678 | External |
| http://e-culture.multimedian.nl/ns/rkd/aatned/aatned.rdf | 264,968 | External |
| mdb:mdb_2_kb.ttl | 179,120 | MDB |
| das:das_data.ttl | 149,357 | DAS |
| gzmvoc:gzmvoc_data.ttl | 110,986 | GZMVOC |
| http://sws.geonames.org/geonames_nl_as_skos.ttl | 42,811 | External |
| mdb:mdb_ship_sameas.ttl | 33,435 | MDB |
| vocopv:vocopv_gen_thes.ttl | 12,851 | VOC Opvarenden |
| das:das_thes_gen.ttl | 7,034 | DAS |
| dss:dbpedia_links.ttl | 5,449 | External |
| gzmvoc:gzmvoc_2_das.ttl | 5,303 | GZMVOC |
| http://sws.geonames.org/ontology_v2.2.1.rdf | 2,895 | External |
| dss:al_all_place_2_geonames.ttl | 2,528 | DSS (all) |
| mdb:mdb_thes_places.ttl | 2,273 | MDB |
| gzmvoc:gzmvoc_thes_gen_places.ttl | 591 | GZMVOC |
| mdb:mdb_thes_rangen.ttl | 585 | MDB |
| vocopv:vocopv_schema.ttl | 337 | VOC Opvarenden |
| dss:dss_provenance.ttl | 273 | DSS (all) |
| mdb:ranks_and_shiptypes_1.ttl | 245 | MDB |
| gzmvoc:gzmvoc_schema.ttl | 232 | GZMVOC |
| mdb:mdb_thes_generated.ttl | 196 | MDB |
| file:///data/cliopatria/ClioPatria/rdf/base/rdfs.rdfs | 190 | External |
| gzmvoc:gzmvoc_thes_gen.ttl | 166 | GZMVOC |
| mdb:mdb_schema.ttl | 149 | MDB |
| das:das_schema.ttl | 98 | DAS |
| dss:dss_schema.ttl | 59 | DSS (all) |
| http://e-culture.multimedian.nl/ns/rkd/aatned/aatned.rdfs | 27 | External |
| Total no. triples: | 25,529,107 | |

and basic statistics are provided[21]. Local views of resources are also provided[22]. A search functionality, which includes autocompletion, is available. The provenance can be visualized using the PROV-O-Viz tool[23], which is integrated with the triple store at http://dutchshipsandsailors.nl/data/provoviz.

**SPARQL Endpoint.** A SPARQL 1.1 compliant endpoint is provided at http://dutchshipasandsailors.nl/data/sparql/, with a number of interactive interfaces provided, such as the YASGUI interface at http://dutchshipasandsailors.nl/data/dss/yasgui/. A number of editable example SPARQL queries are also presented at http://www.dutchshipsandsailors.nl/data/dss_queries.

**Linked Data.** The PURL URIs redirect to the specific resources on the stable server which will respond through content negotiation. In the case of an RDF value for the HTTP accept header the server returns RDF triples concerning the resource. In the current setup the *symmetric concise bounded description* of

---

[21] http://www.dutchshipsandsailors.nl/data/browse/list_graphs
[22] For example http://www.dutchshipsandsailors.nl/data/browse/list_resource?
r=http://purl.org/collections/nl/dss/vocopv/opvarenden-344716
[23] http://provoviz.org/

a resource is returned, which is made up by all triples that have that resource either as a subject or as an object. This conforms to the Linked Data principles [2]. ClioPatria can respond with RDF in XML, ntriples, turtle or JSON-LD serialization. In the case of a HTML request, the HTML local view is returned

**Raw Data.** Finally, the raw RDF data is available i) through the web interface, where individual graphs can be downloaded as RDF/Turtle or RDF/XML; ii) through a public repository at `https://www.github.com/biktorrr/dss`; iii) as archived humanities datasets at the EASY online archiving system of Data Archiving and Networking Services (DANS)[24]. Here the four datasets as well as the interoperability layer are available as RDF/XML files with persistent identifiers. Here they are ensured sustainability beyond the life expectancy of the live versions.

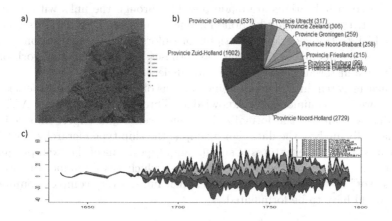

**Fig. 4.** Three visualizations of VOC data made possible through GeoNames links a) shows a plot of birth places on a map; b) shows aggregation by provinces of sailors in one year (1750) and c) shows a stream plot of the sailors per province over all the years for which we have data. These visualizations are made through a simple SPARQL query on the datacloud and visualizing the results using R.

## 5    Digital History Examples

In this section, we present three example uses developed in collaboration with the historians associated with the project. For the sake of brevity, we omit the complete SPARQL queries used in these use cases here, but they are reproduced on the semantic server at `http://dutchshipsandsailors.nl/data/dss_queries`.

Because many dataset-specific properties are mapped to DSS properties, we can use RDFS reasoning to search for resources across the different datasets. It is not hard to define a search query that retrieves all ships with the ship name "Johanna" or that have some person with the rank of Captain that has

---

[24] `https://easy.dans.knaw.nl/ui/home`

"Veldman" as a last name. This allows for search and comparison between the datasets and for example to research correlations between variables (rank and wages?) using data from more than one dataset.

Analysis of the types of persons that sailed on the VOC ships can give insight into the socio-economic realities of the 18th Century. The datasets lists the birthplaces of many of those embarked on (VOC) ships. Through the links with GeoNames, we can get more information about those places of origin. One of these uses is to use the GeoNames geo-coordinates to plot information on a map. Figure 4a) shows such a plot. We can also use the GeoNames geographical hierarchy to -for example- analyze the provinces of origin of the voyagers, giving insight at an aggregated level. We used the SPARQL package for the statistical analysis tool R to provide a quantitative analysis and visualizations of the results[25]. Figure 4b)shows the birth provinces of sailors for one year (1750) and Figure 4c) shows a stream plot of the birth provinces of sailors over multiple years. These visualizations are made possible through the links with an external dataset, they can easily be done for one or multiple DSS datasets and give an insight into the geographical origins of sailors. These visualizations can be used to detect anomalies, formulate hypotheses and to make the work of the quantitative historian more effective and efficient.

In their research, historians combine analysis of data with their expert knowledge as well as common-sense knowledge. Through the link with AAT and DBPedia, we can use the formalized common sense and expert knowledge to automatically analyze the data. For example, the ship type hierarchy from AAT can be used to analyze features of specific ship types. One of the example queries lists persons that embarked on coastal ships (which has a number of subtypes such as "kof" or "tjalk"). Without the explicit links, a very complex conjunctive query would have to be formulated.

# 6   Related Work

This work builds on previous research that resulted in the Amsterdam Museum Linked Dataset as well as the Verrijkt Koninkrijk Linked dataset[6,5]. The latter effort also was done in close collaboration with historians, using specific digital history research goals. In this case, multiple datasets are combined into one datacloud, which makes new types of analysis possible. Some tools and methods are re-used for this paper. Our work has a similar relation to other efforts that attempt to link historical data to the Web of data [8,16]. In fact there are multiple examples of datasets that are the result of collaborations between computer scientists and historians[11]. However, in most cases, this concerns a single dataset, published using a single metadata model. In our approach, we work with historians from different backgrounds, who are responsible for their own data and datamodel. This results in a datacloud of multiple datasets rather than one monolithic dataset. In the related cultural heritage domain, publishing of metadata as linked data is gaining ground. Examples include Europeana [9]

---

[25] http://cran.r-project.org/web/packages/SPARQL/

which uses the Linked Data architecture to provide access to Europe's cultural heritage metadata from multiple collection metadata providers.

## 7    Conclusions and Future work

We presented the Dutch Ships and Sailors Linked Data cloud, developed in collaboration with the historical researchers responsible for those datasets. We make four separate and important maritime digital history datasets available as linked data to researchers and the public. Beyond these four datasets, this paper shows how Linked Data principles and technologies serve to integrate different datasets in a flexible way. In the case of these relatively "small" datasets, close collaboration between data experts and the converting party ensures that the richness of the original data is not lost, and interoperability is gained up to a level where it can be used for further historical research. It is an example of how Linked Data can benefit humanities research -more specifically digital history. The datacloud can serve as a hub dataset for international maritime historical datasets as well as for other (Dutch) historical datasets. We identified a total of 25 maritime historical datasets that can be added to the datacloud[26]. Links to more datasets are currently being established. For example, part of the Dutch historical census data made available through the CEDAR project[10] is already partly linked available in the development version. This presents opportunities for even more elaborate types of analysis beyond the maritime context.

We are also experimenting with more user-friendly interfaces for specific types of historical research questions. For the MDB dataset, we will make the digital scans available and link these to the MDB records, deepening the provenance information. This enables tracing results of (SPARQL) queries back to the original data even more than is currently possible, ensuring further trust and usability in the historical research context.

**Acknowlegdgements.**    This    work    was    supported    by    CLARIN-NL (http://www.clarin.nl) under project name DSS. We would like to thank Robin Ponstein and Andrea Bravo Balado.

## References

1. Bravo Balado, A.: Information extraction on newspaper archives for historical research. a dutch maritime history case study. M.Sc. thesis VU University Amsterdam, (forthcoming, 2014)
2. Berners-Lee, T.: Linked data - design issues (2006),
   http://www.w3.org/DesignIssues/LinkedData.html
3. Bruijn, J.R., Gaastra, F.S., Schffer, I.: Dutch-asiatic shipping in the 17th and 18th centuries, i, ii and iii. Rijks Geschiedkundige Publication Grote Serie 165, 166, 167. Martinus Nijhoff, Den Haag (1987, 1979)

---

[26] A list can be found at http://dutchshipsandsailors.nl

4. al., D.J.C.e.: Interchange: The promise of digital history. Special Issue, Journal of American History 95(2) (2008)
5. de Boer, V., van Doornik, J., Buitinck, L., Marx, M., Veken, T., Ribbens, K.: Linking the kingdom: Enriched access to a historiographical text. In: Proceedings of KCAP 2013, Banff, Canada, June 23-26 (2013)
6. de Boer, V., Wielemaker, J., van Gent, J., Hildebrand, M., Isaac, A., van Ossenbruggen, J., Schreiber, G.: Supporting linked data production for cultural heritage institutes: The amsterdam museum case study. In: Simperl, E., Cimiano, P., Polleres, A., Corcho, O., Presutti, V. (eds.) ESWC 2012. LNCS, vol. 7295, pp. 733–747. Springer, Heidelberg (2012)
7. Groth, P., Moreau, L.: PROV-Overview. An Overview of the PROV Family of Documents. W3C Working Group Note NOTE-prov-overview-20130430, World Wide Web Consortium (April 2013)
8. Hyvönen, E., Lindquist, T., Törnroos, J., Mäkelä, E.: History on the semantic web as linked data – an event gazetteer and timeline for the world war i. In: Proc. of CIDOC 2012 - Enriching Cultural Heritage, Helsinki, Finland (June 2012)
9. Isaac, A., Haslhofer, B.: Linked open data - data.europeana.eu. Semantic Web 4(3), 291–297 (2013)
10. Meroño-Peñuela, A., Ashkpour, A., Rietveld, L., Hoekstra, R.: Linked humanities data: The next frontier? a case-study in historical census data. In: Proceedings of the 2nd International Workshop on Linked Science 2012, vol. 951 (2012)
11. Meroño-Peñuela, A., Ashkpour, A., van Erp, M., Mandemakers, Breure, L., Scharnhorst, A., Schlobach, S., van Harmelen, F.: Semantic technologies for historical research: A survey. Semantic Web Journal (2012) (to appear)
12. De Nies, T., Coppens, S., Mannens, E., Van de Walle, R.: Modeling uncertain provenance and provenance of uncertainty in w3c prov. In: Proceedings of WWW 2013, pp. 167–168.
13. Ockeloen, N., Fokkens, A., Braake, S.t., Vossen, P., Boer, V.d., Schreiber, G.: Biographynet: Managing provenance at multiple levels and from different perspectives. In: Proceedings of the Workshop on Linked Science (LiSC) at ISWC 2013, Sydney, Australia (October 2013)
14. Ponstein, R.: Reconciling dutch ships and sailors. M.Sc. thesis VU University Amsterdam (forthcoming, 2014)
15. van Rossum, M.: De intra-aziatische vaart. schepen, de aziatische zeeman en ondergang van de voc. Tijdschrift voor Sociale en Economische Geschiedenis 8(3), 32–69 (2011)
16. van Erp, M., Oomen, J., Segers, R., van de Akker, C., Aroyo, L., Jacobs, G., Legne, S., van der Meij, L., van Ossenbruggen, J.R., Schreiber, G.: Automatic Heritage Metadata Enrichment With Historic Events. In: Proc. of Int. Conference for Culture and Heritage On-line-Museums and the Web 2011, Archimuse (April 2011)
17. van Velzen, A.J.M., Gaastra, F.S.: Thematische collectie: Voc opvarenden; voc sea voyagers. urn:nbn:nl:ui:13-v73-sq8 (2000–2010)

# Adoption of the Linked Data Best Practices in Different Topical Domains

Max Schmachtenberg, Christian Bizer, and Heiko Paulheim

University of Mannheim
Research Group Data and Web Science, Germany
{max,chris,heiko}@informatik.uni-mannheim.de

**Abstract.** The central idea of Linked Data is that data publishers support applications in discovering and integrating data by complying to a set of best practices in the areas of linking, vocabulary usage, and metadata provision. In 2011, the *State of the LOD Cloud* report analyzed the adoption of these best practices by linked datasets within different topical domains. The report was based on information that was provided by the dataset publishers themselves via the *datahub.io* Linked Data catalog. In this paper, we revisit and update the findings of the 2011 *State of the LOD Cloud* report based on a crawl of the Web of Linked Data conducted in April 2014. We analyze how the adoption of the different best practices has changed and present an overview of the linkage relationships between datasets in the form of an updated LOD cloud diagram, this time not based on information from dataset providers, but on data that can actually be retrieved by a Linked Data crawler. Among others, we find that the number of linked datasets has approximately doubled between 2011 and 2014, that there is increased agreement on common vocabularies for describing certain types of entities, and that provenance and license metadata is still rarely provided by the data sources.

**Keywords:** Linked Open Data, Web of Linked Data, Best Practices.

## 1 Introduction

The Web of Linked Data [3,7] has grown from a dozen datasets in 2007 into a large data space containing hundreds of datasets today. In order to enable Linked Data applications to discover datasets as well as to ease the integration of data from multiple sources, Linked Data publishers should comply with a set of best practices [4]. These best practices can be grouped into three areas:

*Linking*: By setting RDF links, data providers connect their datasets into a single global data graph which can be navigated by applications and enables the discovery of additional data by following RDF links.

*Vocabulary Usage*: The best practices advise publishers to use terms from widely-used vocabularies in order to ease the interpretation of their data. If data providers use their own vocabularies, the terms of such proprietary vocabularies

P. Mika et al. (Eds.) ISWC 2014, Part I, LNCS 8796, pp. 245–260, 2014.

should be *dereferencable* into their RDF schema or OWL definitions. The definitions of proprietary vocabulary terms should contain RDF links pointing at terms from widely-used vocabularies in order to ease their interpretation.

*Metadata Provision*: Linked Data should be as self-descriptive as possible, and thus include metadata. An important form of metadata is *provenance* metadata describing the origin of datasets and enabling applications to assess their quality. The best practices also advise to provide *licensing* metadata and *dataset-level metadata*, e.g., in the form of a VoID file[1]. If datasets are accessible via additional access methods, such as a SPARQL endpoint or data dumps, then the VoID file should contain information about these access methods.

The adoption of the Linked Data best practices by datasets belonging to different topical domains was analyzed in the *State of the LOD Cloud* report [7] in 2011. The report is based on information provided by the data publishers themselves via the `datahub.io` Linked Data catalog[2]. In this paper, we revisit and update the findings of the *State of the LOD Cloud* report from 2011 based on a crawl of the Web of Linked Data conducted in April 2014. The paper is structured as follows: Section 2 describes the crawling strategy that was used to gather the data that forms the basis of our analysis. Section 3 explains the categorization of the data by topical domain. Sections 4, 5, and 6 discuss the adoption of best practices in the areas of linking, vocabulary usage, and metadata provision. Section 7 gives an overview of related work. The paper closes with a wrap-up of our findings.

## 2    Crawl of the Linked Data Web

To evaluate the conformance to the best practices, we have crawled a snapshot of the Linked Data Web. For this, we used *LDSpider*, a framework for crawling Linked Data [6]. We seeded LDSpider with 560 thousand seed URIs originating from three sources: 1. We included all URIs of example resources from datasets contained in the *lod-cloud* group in the `datahub.io` dataset catalog as well as example URIs from other datasets in the catalog marked with Linked Data related tags; 2. We included a sample of the URIs contained in the Billion Triple Challenge 2012 dataset[3]; 3. We collected URIs from datasets advertised on the `public-lod@w3.org` mailing list since 2011. With those seeds, we performed crawls during April 2014 to retrieve entities from every dataset using a breadth-first crawling strategy. Altogether, we crawled 900,129 documents describing 8,038,396 resources. The crawled data is provided for download on the website accompanying this paper[4] so that all results presented in the following can be verified.

For grouping the retrieved resources into datasets, we generally assume that all data originating from one pay-level domain (PLD) belongs to a single dataset.

---

[1] http://www.w3.org/TR/void/

[2] http://datahub.io/group/lodcloud

[3] http://km.aifb.kit.edu/projects/btc-2012/

[4] http://data.dws.informatik.uni-mannheim.de/lodcloud/2014/ISWC-RDB/

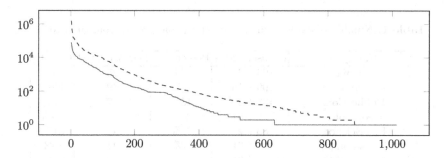

**Fig. 1.** Distribution of the number of resources (- - -) and documents (———) per dataset contained in the crawl (log scale)

If the *datahub.io* catalog lists multiple datasets for a single PLD, we apply an exception to the general rule and use the dataset definitions from the catalog. Altogether, the crawled data belongs to 1014 different datasets. Figure 1 shows the distribution of the number of resources and documents per dataset contained in the crawl.

Our crawler did respect crawling restrictions expressed by the data sources via `robots.txt` files. Altogether, we discovered 77 linked datasets which do not allow crawling and did not retrieve data from these sources.

## 3    Categorization by Topical Domain

Since the adoption of the Linked Data best practices might vary depending on the topical domain of the datasets, we classify the datasets into the following topical categories: *media, government, publications, life sciences, geographic, cross-domain, user-generated content*, and *social networking*. This categorization schema is the same as the one used by the 2011 *State of the LOD Cloud* report with the only difference that we added the category *social networking* as we discovered a large number of datasets providing data about people and their social ties. For datasets that are contained in the *datahub.io* dataset catalog, we adopt the topical categorization form the catalog. We manually assigned categories to the newly discovered datasets after inspecting them. In the following, we define the categories and refer to some prominent datasets from each category. Afterwards, we compare the overall number of datasets per category with the findings of the 2011 *State of the LOD Cloud* report.

The *media* category contains datasets providing information about films, music, TV and radio programmes, as well as print media. Prominent datasets within this category are the *dbtune.org* music datasets, the *New York Times* dataset, and the *BBC radio and television program* datasets. The *government* category contains Linked Data published by federal or local governments, including a lot of statistical datasets. Prominent examples include the `data.gov.uk` and `opendatacommunities.org` datasets. The category *publications* holds library datasets, information about scientific publications and conferences, reading

**Table 1.** Number of datasets in each category and growth compared to 2011

| Category | Datasets 2014 | Percentage | Datasets 2011 | Growth |
|---|---|---|---|---|
| Media | 24 (-2) | 2% | 25 | -4% |
| Government | 199 (-16) | 18% | 49 | 306% |
| Publications | 138 (-42) | 13% | 87 | 59% |
| Geographic | 27 (-6) | 2% | 31 | -13% |
| Life Sciences | 85 (-2) | 8% | 41 | 107% |
| Cross-domain | 47 (-6) | 4% | 41 | 15% |
| User-generated Content | 51 (-3) | 5% | 20 | 155% |
| Social Networking | 520 (-0) | 48% | - | - |
| Total | 1091 (-77) | | 294 | 271% |

lists from universities, and citation databases. Well known datasets include the German National Library dataset, the L3S DBLP dataset, and the Open Library dataset. The category *geographic* contains datasets like geonames.org and linkedgeodata.org comprising information about geographic entities, geopolitical divisions, and points of interest. The *life sciences* category comprises biological and biochemical information, drug-related data, and information about species and their habitats. The *cross-domain* category includes general knowledge bases such as DBpedia or UMBEL, linguistic resources such as WordNet or Lexvo, as well as product data. The the category *user-generated content* contains data from portals that collect content generated by larger user communities. Examples include metadata about blogposts published as Linked Data by wordpress.com, data about open source software projects published by apache.org, scientific workflows published by myexperiment.org, and reviews published by goodreads.com or revyu.com. The category *social networking* contains people profiles as well as data describing the social ties amongst people. We include into this category individual FOAF profiles, as well as data about the interconnections amongst users of the distributed microblogging platform StatusNet. The distinction between the categories *user-generated content* and *social networking* is that the datasets in the former category focus on the actual content while datasets in the later focus on user profiles and social ties. The 2011 *State of the LOD Cloud* report did not contain *social networking* as a separate category since the report did not count individual FOAF profiles as separate datasets and since StatusNet servers did not export Linked Data in 2011.

Table 1 gives an overview of the number of datasets in each category as well as the growth per category compared to the 2011 report. A list with the exact assignments of each dataset to a category is found on the accompanying website. The numbers in brackets in the second column refer to the number of datasets that do not allow crawling. The by far largest category is *social networking* with 520 datasets (48% of all datasets). The second largest category is *government* with 199 datasets (18%), followed by *publications* with 138 datasets (13%). Compared to the 2011 *State of the LOD Cloud* report, we observe a larger number of datasets in all categories except *geographic* and *media* data. The category

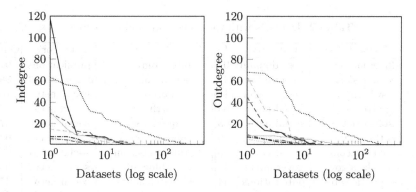

**Fig. 2.** Degree distributions for datesets belonging to the categories crossdo-main(——), user-generated content(- - -), social networking(·········), publications(- - - -), media(      ), life sciences(- - - -), government(——) and geographic(- - - -·).

*government* shows the largest growth, followed by the categories *user-generated content* and *life sciences*. Excluding the new category *social networking*, the overall number of Linked Datasets has approximately doubled from 2011 (294 datasets) to 2014 (571 datasets). Including the new category, we observe an overall growth of 271% (from 294 to 1091 datasets).

## 4    Adoption of the Linking Best Practices

The linking best practice encourages publishers to set RDF links between datasets in order to enable the discovery of additional data and to support the integration of data from multiple sources. For analyzing the linkage between datasets, we aggregate all RDF links by dataset, meaning that we consider two datasets to be linked if there exists at least one RDF link between resources belonging to the datasets.

### 4.1    Degree Distributions

In total, 56% of all datasets in our crawl set RDF links pointing to at least one other dataset. The remaining 44% are either only the target of RDF links from other datasets or are isolated. Figure 2 shows the distribution of the in- and outdegrees for each category. We see that the in- and outdegrees vary widely with a small number of datasets in each category being highly linked, while the majority of the datasets is only sparsely linked. Overall, datasets from the category *social networking* show the highest degree values. The categories *cross-domain*, *user-generated content*, and *geographic* show an imbalance between in- and outdegrees, with *user-generated content* having larger out- than indegrees, and *cross-domain* and to a lesser extent *geographic* having larger in- than out-degrees (measured as area under the curve).

**Table 2.** Datasets with the highest in- and outdegrees

| Dataset | Category | In | Dataset | Category | Out |
|---|---|---|---|---|---|
| dbpedia.org | cross-domain | 207 | bibsonomy.org | publications | 91 |
| geonames.org | geographic | 141 | semanlink.net | user-gen. cnt. | 88 |
| w3.org | cross-domain | 117 | deri.org | social netw. | 70 |
| quitter.se | social netw. | 64 | harth.org | social netw. | 68 |
| status.net | social netw. | 63 | quitter.se | social netw. | 67 |
| postblue.info | social netw. | 56 | semanticweb.org | user-gen. cnt. | 64 |
| skilledtest.com | social netw. | 55 | skilledtests.com | social netw. | 60 |
| reference.data.gov.uk | government | 45 | postblue.info | social netw. | 59 |
| data.semanticweb.org | publications | 44 | status.net | social netw. | 47 |
| fragdev.com | social netw. | 41 | w3.org | crossdomain | 45 |
| lexvo.org | cross-domain | 37 | data.semanticweb.org | publications | 45 |

Looking at the top ten datasets by in- and outdegree in Table 2, we see that datasets from categories *social networking*, *user-generated content*, and *publications* are among the top ten with respect to outdegree. While datasets with a high indegree are `dbpedia.org` (cross-domain), `geonames.org` (geographic), `w3.org` (cross-domain), `reference.data.gov.uk` (government) as well as several datasets from the category *social networking*.

### 4.2  Overall Graph Structure

Analyzing the overall graph structure, we find one large weakly connected component which consists of 71.99% of all datasets. In addition, there are three small components, one consisting of three and two consisting of two datasets. Within the large weakly connected component, there exists one large strongly connected component consisting of 36.29% of all datasets.

Figure 3 shows the overall graph structure using the same *LOD cloud* visualization as the 2011 report. The size of the circles reflects the indegree of the corresponding dataset. A zoom-able version of Figure 3 is available on the accompanying website. Note that we have aggregated all individual FOAF profiles into a single circle. Compared to the *LOD cloud* visualization from the 2011 report which was centered around `dbpedia.org` as central linking point, Figure 3 shows a much more decentralized graph with multiple high-degree nodes: The `geonames.org` and `dbpedia.org` datasets are linked by a large number of datasets belonging to different topical categories. In addition, the `statistics.data.gov.uk` and `reference.data.gov.uk` are highly linked from within the *government* category. In the category *publications*, the `Library of Congress Subject Headings (LCSH)` and the `German National Library (DNB)` datasets are highly linked. We can also see in Figure 3 that the category *social networking* is the most densely interlinked.

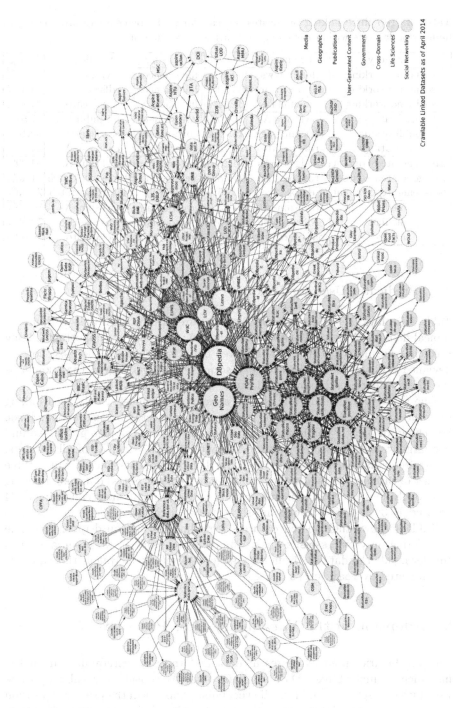

**Fig. 3.** Overall graph structure and categorization of the datasets by topical domain. The size of the circles reflects their indegree. A zoom-able version of the diagram is available on the accompanying website.

**Table 3.** Top three linking predicates per category. The percentages are relative to number of datasets within the category which set outgoing links.

| Category | Predicate | Usage | Category | Predicate | Usage |
|---|---|---|---|---|---|
| social networking | foaf:knows | 60.27% | life sciences | owl:sameAs | 52.17% |
| social networking | foaf:based_near | 35.69% | life sciences | rdfs:seeAlso | 43.48% |
| social networking | sioc:follows | 34.34% | life sciences | dct:creator | 21.74% |
| publications | owl:sameAs | 32.20% | government | dct:publisher | 47.57% |
| publications | dct:language | 25.42% | government | dct:spatial | 30.10% |
| publications | rdfs:seeAlso | 23.73% | government | owl:sameAs | 24.27% |
| user-generated content | owl:sameAs | 53.13% | geographic | owl:sameAs | 64.29% |
| user-generated content | rdfs:seeAlso | 21.88% | geographic | skos:exactMatch | 21.43% |
| user-generated content | dct:source | 18.75% | geographic | skos:closeMatch | 21.43% |
| media | owl:sameAs | 81.25% | crossdomain | owl:sameAs | 80.00% |
| media | rdfs:seeAlso | 18.75% | crossdomain | rdfs:seeAlso | 52.00% |
| media | foaf:based_near | 18.75% | crossdomain | dct:creator | 20.00% |

### 4.3 Predicates Used for Linking

Table 3 displays the top three predicates that are used by RDF links within each topical domain. A first observation is that owl:sameAs is an important linking predicate within most categories, followed by rdfs:seeAlso. The most notable deviance is observed for the category *social networking*, where foaf:knows is the most widely used linking predicate.

Due to the outstanding role of owl:sameAs as the most widely used linking predicate, we take a closer look at the datasets connected by owl:sameAs links. Searching for weakly connected components in the owl:sameAs graph, we find one large weakly connected component containing 297 (29.3%) of all datasets. Apart from that, there are only eight further components, out of which three consist of three datasets and the remaining five consist of two datasets. Looking at strongly connected components, we find one large component consisting of 74 datasets (7.3%), one with four and six with two datasets.

Table 4 shows the top ten datasets regarding in- and outdegree, this time considering only owl:sameAs links. Compared to Table 2, we observe a much smaller number of datasets from the category *social networking* as this category is dominated by foaf:knows links.

## 5    Adoption of the Vocabulary Best Practices

The vocabularies used to represent data and their interpretability are a key ingredient to make Linked Data *semantic* data. We consider a vocabulary to be *used* by a dataset if a term from the vocabulary appears in the predicate position of a triple from the dataset or at the object position of a rdf:type triple from the dataset.

**Table 4.** Top 10 datasets regarding in- and outdegree for `owl:sameAs` links by category

| Dataset | Category | In | Dataset | Category | Out |
|---|---|---|---|---|---|
| dbpedia.org | crossdomain | 89 | bibsonomy.org | publications | 91 |
| geonames.org | geographic | 29 | data.semanticweb.org | publications | 31 |
| data.semanticweb.org | publications | 24 | myopenlink.net | user-gen. cnt. | 25 |
| l3s.de | publications | 24 | dbpedia.org | crossdomain | 23 |
| semanticweb.org | user-gen. cnt. | 18 | semanticweb.org | user-gen. cnt. | 18 |
| nytimes.com | media | 11 | revyu.com | user-gen. cnt. | 16 |
| dbtune.org | social networking | 11 | advogato.org | social networking | 16 |
| kit.edu | social networking | 9 | el.dbpedia.org | crossdomain | 13 |
| revyu.com | user-gen. cnt. | 8 | nl.dbpedia.org | crossdomain | 11 |
| w3.org | crossdomain | 8 | harth.org | social networking | 11 |
| it.dbpedia.org | crossdomain | 8 | | | |

**Table 5.** Vocabularies used by more than 5% of all datasets

| Prefix | Occurrence | Quota | Prefix | Occurrence | Quota |
|---|---|---|---|---|---|
| rdf | 996 | 98.22% | void | 137 | 13.51% |
| rdfs | 736 | 72.58% | bio | 125 | 12.32% |
| foaf | 701 | 69.13% | cube | 114 | 11.24% |
| dcterm | 568 | 56.01% | rss | 99 | 9.76% |
| owl | 370 | 36.49% | odc | 86 | 8.48% |
| wgs84 | 254 | 25.05% | w3con | 77 | 7.60% |
| sioc | 179 | 17.65% | doap | 65 | 6.41% |
| admin | 157 | 15.48% | bibo | 62 | 6.11% |
| skos | 143 | 14.11% | dcat | 59 | 5.82% |

## 5.1   Usage of Well-Known Vocabularies

Table 5 lists the vocabularies that are used by more than five percent of all datasets[5]. The vocabularies *RDF*, *FOAF*, *RDFS*, *DCTerms*, and *OWL* are the top vocabularies used by many datasets from across all topical categories. Compared to the 2011 report, we can state that there is a trend towards the adoption of well-known vocabularies by more datasets. For instance, while the *FOAF* vocabulary was used by 27.46% of all datasets in 2011, it is used by 69.1% of all datasets in 2014. The same is true for the Dublin Core vocabulary which is used today by 56.01% of the datasets and was used by only 31.19% in 2011.

The extent to which well-known vocabularies are used within the different topical categories reveals some differences. In the category *social networking*, there is a high quota of datasets using *FOAF* (85.96%), followed by the Dublin Core and the *WGS84* vocabulary used by 40% and 37% of all datasets. The *admin* vocabulary, which is used by some FOAF generators, finds comparatively wide adoption. In the category *publications*, *DCTerms* is widely used at a quota of 83%. Furthermore, the *bibo* ontology is used by 41.67% of the datasets

---

[5] Prefixes are taken from http://prefix.cc

belonging to this category. The vocabularies *SKOS, resourcelist*, which is used
to create reading lists, and *SIOC* also find some adoption. In the category *cross-
domain*, several vocabularies are used by 10-40% of all datasets: The *dbpedia.org*,
*georss.org, opengis.net, bibo*, the *prov* vocabulary, the *skos* vocabulary, and *void*,
showing that a wide variety of topics is covered in this category. In the category
*government*, vocabularies for representing statistical data (*cube* with 61.75% and
*sdmx* with 26.22%) are found frequently. Vocabularies for expressing metadata,
like the *void* vocabulary, the sparql-service-description vocabulary, *prov* and *prv*
are also find some use. Within the category *geographic*, 66.67% of all datasets use
the *WGS84* vocabulary for encoding geographic coordinates. Other well adopted
vocabularies are *skos* or the geonames ontology. In the category *user-generated
content*, many datasets use the *FOAF* vocabulary together with the *SIOC* vocabulary (50%) as well as the *RSS* and the *admin* vocabulary (both around
17%). The *DOAP* vocabulary is used by 12.5% of the datasets.

Please note that the *schema.org* vocabulary promoted by Google, Yahoo and
Microsoft is not listed in Table 5 as we found this vocabulary to be hardly used
in the Linked Data context[6]. In contrast, the vocabulary is very widely used
together with the Microdata syntax for annotating HTML pages [2].

## 5.2   Usage of Proprietary Vocabularies

Widely-used vocabularies often do not provide all terms that are needed to
publish the complete content of a dataset on the Web. Thus, data providers
often define proprietary terms that are used in addition to terms from widely
deployed vocabularies. We have also analyzed to which extent datasets from different categories make use of proprietary vocabularies. We consider a vocabulary
to be proprietary if it is used only by a single dataset. Out of the 638 different
vocabularies that we encountered in our crawl, 375 vocabularies (58.77%) are
proprietary according to our definition, while 263 (41.22%) are non-proprietary.
In total, 234 datasets (23.08%) use proprietary vocabularies, while nearly all
datasets also use non-proprietary vocabularies. These numbers show that the
adoption of the best practice to use common vocabularies is improving compared to the *State of the LOD Cloud* report from 2011 which found 64.41% of
all datasets to use proprietary terms. Table 6 further details the usage of proprietary vocabularies by topical category. The second column of the table shows
the number of proprietary vocabularies used by datasets from each category.
The third column contains the number of datasets in each category that use
proprietary vocabularies.

## 5.3   Dereferencability of Proprietary Vocabulary Terms

In order to enable applications to retrieve the definition of vocabulary terms,
the URIs identifying vocabulary terms should be made dereferencable. To assess

---

[6] One data source that uses the *schema.org* type system in addition to its own type
system in order to increase interoperability is *dbpedia.org*.

**Table 6.** Proprietary vocabularies with dereferencability per category and quota of vocabularies linking to others

| Category | Different prop. vocabs. used (% of all prop. vocab.) | # of datasets using prop. vocab. (% of all datasets) | Dereferencability | | | #of vocabs linking (quota) |
|---|---|---|---|---|---|---|
| | | | full | partial | none | |
| Social networking | 126 (33.60%) | 81 (15.57%) | 19.47% | 8.8% | 77.78% | 20 (15.87%) |
| Publications | 59 (15.73%) | 33 (34.38%) | 22.03% | 8.47% | 69.49% | 15 (25.42%) |
| Government | 47 (12.53%) | 34 (18.58%) | 21.28% | 12.77% | 65.96% | 16 (34.04%) |
| Cross-domain | 56 (14.93%) | 17 (41.46%) | 26.79% | 10.71% | 62.50% | 14 (25.00%) |
| Geographic | 13 (3.47%) | 8 (38.10%) | 15.38% | 7.69% | 76.92% | 2 (15.38%) |
| Life sciences | 36 (9.60%) | 27 (32.53%) | 27.78% | 5.56% | 66.67% | 4 (11.11%) |
| Media | 12 (3.20%) | 12 (54.55%) | 0.00% | 16.67% | 83.33% | 2 (16.67%) |
| User-gen. cnt. | 26 (6.93%) | 22 (45.83%) | 11.54% | 11.54% | 76.92% | 6 (23.08%) |
| Total | 375 (58.77%) | 234 (23.08%) | 19.47% | 8.80% | 71.73% | 79 (21.07%) |

**Table 7.** Predicates used to link terms between different vocabularies

| Term | % of vocabularies | Term | % of vocabularies |
|---|---|---|---|
| rdfs:range | 9.87% | rdfs:seeAlso | 1.60% |
| rdfs:subClassOf | 8.80% | owl:equivalentClass | 1.60% |
| rdfs:subPropertyOf | 6.93% | owl:inverseOf | 1.33% |
| rdfs:domain | 5.60% | swivt:type | 1.07% |
| rdfs:isDefinedBy | 3.73% | owl:equivalentProperty | 0.80% |

whether a vocabulary is dereferencable, we requested the definitions of all used terms from the vocabulary via HTTP GET requests. The resulting corpus of vocabulary definitions is provided for download on the accompanying website. We define the dereferencability quota of a vocabulary as the number of dereferencable terms divided by the number of all terms of the vocabulary. In total, 19.47% of all proprietary vocabularies are fully dereferencable (i.e., their quota is 1.0). On the other hand, 71.73% of all proprietary vocabularies are not dereferencable at all. The remaining 8.8% of all proprietary vocabularies are partially dereferencable, meaning that for some terms, but not for all, a definition could be retrieved. Possible causes for partial dereferencability are *namespace squatting*, i.e. accidentally or incidentally using terms not defined in a vocabulary, and vocabularies having changed without proper marking of old terms as deprecated. Columns 4, 5 and 6 in Table 6 show the percentage of fully, partially and not dereferencable proprietary vocabularies per topical category.

## 5.4   RDF Links to Terms from Other Vocabularies

Vocabulary terms should be related to corresponding terms within other vocabularies in order to enable applications to understand as much data as possible. Table 7 contains the different predicates that are used to link terms between

**Table 8.** Provenance vocabulary usage and license vocabulary usage by category

| Category | Any prov vocab | | Dublin Core | Admin | Prv/Prov | Any license vocab |
|---|---|---|---|---|---|---|
| social networking | 169 | (32.5%) | 57.39% | 57.39% | 1.18% | 5.38% |
| publications | 39 | (40.63%) | 94.87% | 5.13% | 2.56% | 4.17% |
| government | 76 | (41.54%) | 100.00% | 0.00% | 1.32% | 30.05% |
| life sciences | 20 | (24.10%) | 100.00% | 0.00% | 0.5% | 3.61% |
| cross-domain | 7 | (17.07%) | 100.00% | 14.29% | 0.00% | 9.76% |
| geographic | 3 | (14.29%) | 100.00% | 0.00% | 33.34% | 0.00% |
| user-gen. content | 9 | (18.75%) | 88.89% | 66.67% | 0.00% | 10.42% |
| media | 4 | (18.18%) | 100% | 0.00% | 0.00% | 5.41% |
| Total | 372 | (36.69%) | 29.09% | 11.05% | 0.79% | 9.96% |

vocabularies together with the percentage of all vocabularies using each predicate for linking. We see that 9.87% of all vocabularies use the rdfs:range predicate to link to other vocabularies (for instance defining the range of a term to be foaf:Person). The table also shows that only a very small fraction of the vocabularies provides equivalence links to terms from other vocabularies.

## 6    Adoption of the Metadata Best Practices

The Linked Data best practices propose that every dataset should provide provenance and licensing information, dataset-level metadata, and information about additional access methods.

### 6.1    Providing Provenance Information

For our evaluation, we have collected a list of vocabularies that are designed for the representation of provenance information. Information about such vocabularies came from the W3C Provenance Working Group, the LOV vocabulary catalog, as well as our own experience, adding up to a total of 26 vocabularies. Using those vocabularies, we searched for provenance information in our corpus. We followed the approach sugested in [5] and searched for triples using predicates from those vocabularies and containing a document URI as subject.

As shown in Table 8, 36.69% of all datasets use some provenance vocabulary, which is a slight decrease compared to the *State of the LOD Cloud* report from 2011, which reports 36.63% of all datasets to provide provenance information. 29.09% of all datasets use Dublin Core Terms, 11.05% use MetaVocab, while W3C *PRV* and *PROV* are used by only 0.79% of the datasets. The provision of provenance information is widely adopted in the *publications* and *government* domains, while *media* and *geographic* datasets show less adoption. For *government* data, there is also a remarkable increase compared to the *State of the LOD Cloud* document from 2011, which reports only 20.41% for this topical domain.

## 6.2  Providing Licensing Information

With the help of machine-readable licensing information, Linked Data applications can assess whether they may use data for their purpose at hand. To evaluate whether a dataset provides license information, we again followed the approach proposed in [5] and searched for triples which have the document as their subject and a predicate containing the string *'licen'*. To this list, we added all predicates containing the string *'rights'* as well as the waiver vocabulary, which leads to a total of 47 terms.

In total, 9.96% of all datasets provide licensing information in RDF. This number is lower than the 17.84% reported in the *State of the LOD Cloud* report from 2011, but still higher than the 3.4% reported in [5]. The most important predicates for indicating the license are dc/dct:license (7.39%), cc:license (2.07%) and dc/dct:rights (1.68%). As shown in the last column of Table 8, the provision of licensing information varies widely across topical domains. More than a third of all *government* datasets provide licensing information, while none of the *geographic* datasets provides licensing information. A main cause for the low overall number is the category *social networking* which contains 48% of all datasets and in which only 5.38% of the dataset offer licensing information.

## 6.3  Providing Dataset Level Metadata

Dataset-level metadata can be provided using the VoID vocabulary, either as inline statements in the dataset or in a separate VoID file. In the latter case, that file has to be linked from the data via backlinks or be provided at a well-known location which is created by appending /.well-known/void to the host part of a URI. As reported in [8], the latter condition is often too strict for data providers due to missing root-level access to the servers. Thus, we follow the approach proposed in [8] of relaxing the search for VoID files at well-known locations, appending /.well-known/void to any portion of the URI.

In general, dataset-level metadata is still rarely provided by datasets within all topical domains. Some trends towards emerging best practices and de facto standards can be observed: Dataset-level metadata is rather linked to than provided at well-known locations and the Dublin Core vocabulary is becoming the de-facto standard for providing dataset-level provenance information. In total, 149 datasets (14.69%) use the VoID vocabulary. Out of these datasets, 42 (4.14%) use a backlinking mechanism. Columns 2 to 5 of Table 9 show the VoID adoption by topical category.

Compared to the 2011 report, the overall percentage of datasets publishing dataset-level metadata using VoiD has decreased from 32.20% to 14.69%, with the categories *government, geographic,* and *life sciences* being exceptions in which the adoption has slightly grown. Again, the category *social networking* is a main cause for the low overall number.

**Table 9.** Percentage of datasets using the VoID vocabulary and percentage of datasets offering alternative access methods

| Category | VoID | Link | Well-known | Inline | Alt. access | SPARQL | Dump |
|---|---|---|---|---|---|---|---|
| social networking | 5 (0.96%) | 0.19% | 0.77% | 0.00% | 4 (0.77%) | 0.77% | 0.19% |
| publications | 13 (13.54%) | 6.25% | 3.13% | 7.29% | 13 (13.54%) | 12.50% | 4.17% |
| life sciences | 30 (36.14%) | 28.92% | 2.41% | 4.82% | 20 (24.10%) | 24.10% | 15.66% |
| government | 72 (42.08%) | 2.73% | 2.73% | 36.61% | 63 (34.43%) | 31.15% | 31.15% |
| user-gen. content | 6 (11.76%) | 11.76% | 0.00% | 0.00% | 3 (6.25%) | 6.25% | 2.08% |
| geographic | 6 (38.10%) | 14.29% | 9.52% | 14.29% | 5 (23.81%) | 14.29% | 19.05% |
| cross-domain | 5 (12.20%) | 7.32% | 2.44% | 4.88% | 4 (9.76%) | 4.88% | 4.88% |
| media | 2 (9.09%) | 0.00% | 0.00% | 9.09% | 1 (4.55%) | 0.00% | 4.55% |
| Total | 149 (14.69%) | 4.14% | 1.28% | 9.27% | 113 (11.14%) | 9.96% | 8.19% |

## 6.4   Providing Alternative Access Methods

According to the 2011 *State of the LOD Cloud* report, many datasets provide additional access methods, such as SPARQL endpoints (68.14%) and dumps (39.66%). In our analysis, the numbers are much lower as shown in columns 6 to 8 of Table 9. Apart from the *government*, *life sciences* and *geographic* domains, almost no information on alternative access methods are found. The deviation can be explained by the fact that we only look at those alternative access methods that can be discovered via VoID descriptions linked from the datasets or provided at well-known URLs. As reported in [8], the actual number of existing SPARQL endpoints may be higher, as many endpoints cannot be discovered from the data. This is a severe problem for automatic agents navigating the Linked Data graph, as they are not capable of discovering alternative access methods. While the numbers for alternative access methods are low, one has to keep in mind that such methods do not always make sense. For example, the large number of small FOAF files in the *social networking* category are mostly datasets contained in exactly one file. In these cases, it does not make sense to provide a data dump, because the file itself *is* a data dump. Likewise, the use of a SPARQL endpoint for a dataset consisting of only a few dozen triples would not justify the provision effort.

## 7   Related Work

An effort that is closely related to the work presented in this paper is the *LOD-Stats* project[7] which has retrieved and analyzed Linked Data from the Web until February 2014 [1]. The *LODStats* website provides statistics about the overall number of discovered linked datasets as well as the adoption of different vocabularies. What distinguishes *LODStats* from the work presented in this paper is that they do not categorize datasets by topical domain and do not analyze the

---

[7] http://stats.lod2.eu/

overall graph structure, as well as the conformance with the best practices in the areas of vocabulary dereferencability and metadata provision. Their results concerning the overall number of accessible datasets (they found 928 datasets) and the adoption of well-known vocabularies are inline with the findings of this paper.

A comprehensive empirical survey of Linked Data conformance is presented by Hogan et al. [5]. Their survey is based on a large-scale Linked Data crawl from May 2010 as well as a series of smaller snapshots taken between March and November 2010. The work presented in this paper can be seen as an update of the results presented by Hogan et al. as we use a crawl from March 2014. Another major difference is that Hogan et al. do not categorize datasets by topical domain and thus can not analyze the differences in the adoption of the best practices in different domains. The article by Hogan et al. contains a detailed and comprehensive discussion of earlier work on analyzing the adoption of the Linked Data practices as well as work in the wider area of characterizing the Semantic Web/Linked Data, its link structure as well as the semantics of its content. The discussion covers related work from the time span of 2005 to 2012. For space reasons, we can not repeat this excellent review of related work here. The general difference between the works discussed by Hogan et al. and our work is that our analysis is more up-to-date and that we distinguish the datasets by topical domain.

## 8   Conclusion

This paper revisited and updated the finding of the *State of the LOD Cloud* report [7] from 2011 based on a Linked Data crawl gathered in April 2014. Our analysis shows that the overall number of Linked Datasets on the Web has grown significantly since 2011. Looking only at the topical categories covered in the original report, the number of datasets has approximately doubled since 2011. Also taking the category *social networking* into account, the number of datasets has grown by 271%.

Concerning the linkage of the datasets, our analysis shows that there is still a relatively small number of datasets that set RDF links pointing at many other datasets, while many datasets only links to a few other datasets. Compared to the 2011 *LOD cloud*, which was centered around dbpedia.org as central linking hub, we have discovered a more decentralized graph structure with geonames.org and dbpedia.org being linked from many datasets besides of the existence of further category-specific linking hubs. Concerning the types of RDF links that connect datasets, we have found the predicates owl:sameAs, rdfs:seeAlso and foaf:knows to be most widely used.

We have observed a trend towards the adoption of well-known vocabularies by more datasets, the most prominent one being FOAF, which is used by more than two thirds of all linked datasets, independent of their respective topical domain. In parallel, the usage of proprietary vocabularies has decreased from 64.41% in 2011 to 23.08% of all datasets in 2014.

While provenance information is provided for roughly a third of all datasets, only 10% of all datasets provide machine-readable licensing information. A positive exception concerning licensing information is the *government* domain in which licensing information is provided by 30% of all dataset. Compared to the 2011 report, the percentage of datasets providing provenance metadata is approximately the same, while the percentage of datasets providing machine-readable licensing information has dropped from 17% to 10%. The similar negative trend is also found for the percentage of datasets publishing dataset-level metadata using VoID. In 2011, 32.20% of all datasets published VoID while in 2014 only 14.69% provide such metadata. The categories *government, geographic*, and *life sciences* are exceptions to this trend and the adoption has slightly grown in these domains.

**Acknowledgements.** The work presented in the paper was supported by the research project *PlanetData* (Ref.No. 257641), funded by the European Communitys Seventh Framework Programme.

# References

1. Auer, S., Demter, J., Martin, M., Lehmann, J.: LODStats – an extensible framework for high-performance dataset analytics. In: ten Teije, A., Völker, J., Handschuh, S., Stuckenschmidt, H., d'Acquin, M., Nikolov, A., Aussenac-Gilles, N., Hernandez, N. (eds.) EKAW 2012. LNCS, vol. 7603, pp. 353–362. Springer, Heidelberg (2012)
2. Bizer, C., Eckert, K., Meusel, R., Mühleisen, H., Schuhmacher, M., Völker, J.: Deployment of rDFa, microdata, and microformats on the web – A quantitative analysis. In: Alani, H., Kagal, L., Fokoue, A., Groth, P., Biemann, C., Parreira, J.X., Aroyo, L., Noy, N., Welty, C., Janowicz, K. (eds.) ISWC 2013, Part II. LNCS, vol. 8219, pp. 17–32. Springer, Heidelberg (2013)
3. Bizer, C., Heath, T., Berners-Lee, T.: Linked data-the story so far. International Journal on Semantic Web and Information Systems 5(3), 1–22 (2009)
4. Heath, T., Bizer, C.: Linked data: Evolving the web into a global data space. Synthesis Lectures on the Semantic Web: Theory and Technology 1(1), 1–136 (2011)
5. Hogan, A., Umbrich, J., Harth, A., Cyganiak, R., Polleres, A., Decker, S.: An empirical survey of linked data conformance. J. Web Sem. 14, 14–44 (2012)
6. Isele, R., Umbrich, J., Bizer, C., Harth, A.: LDSpider: An open-source crawling framework for the web of linked data. In: Proceedings of the ISWC 2010 Posters and Demonstrations Track (2010)
7. Jentzsch, A., Cyganiak, R., Bizer, C.: State of the lod cloud (September 2011), http://lod-cloud.net/state/
8. Paulheim, H., Hertling, S.: Discoverability of SPARQL endpoints in linked open data. In: Proceedings of the Posters and Demos Track of ISWC 2013 (2013)

# Analyzing Schema.org

Peter F. Patel-Schneider

Nuance Communications, Sunnyvale, California, U.S.A.
pfpschneider@gmail.com

**Abstract.** Schema.org is a way to add machine-understandable information to web pages that is processed by the major search engines to improve search performance. The definition of schema.org is provided as a set of web pages plus a partial mapping into RDF triples with unusual properties, and is incomplete in a number of places. This analysis of and formal semantics for schema.org provides a complete basis for a plausible version of what schema.org should be.

Schema.org[1] "provides a collection of schemas, i.e., html tags, that webmasters can use to [mark up] their pages in ways recognized by major search providers."[2] The major search engine providers, including Bing, Google, Yahoo!, and Yandex use schema.org markup to improve the display of search results and schema.org has been designed by and is controlled by these organizations. This makes schema.org markup an important kind of machine-understandable data in the web. Not only are there many web pages with schema.org information, but this information is used in important ways.

Aside from being a collection of schemas, schema.org is a language for representing information on the Web, different from other languages used for this purpose, such as RDF [1,2], OWL [3,4], and the language underlying Freebase [5]. Using this language, the schema.org schemas are organized into a simple taxonomy by generalization relationships and other ontolological aspects of schema.org information are specified.

The publicly available definition of schema.org is, however, incomplete and contradictory. It is only provided as English text on various web pages in *schema.org*, plus mappings of the collection of schemas[3] into RDF (*http://schema.org/docs/full_md.html*) and OWL (*http://schema.org/docs/schemaorg.owl*). The RDF mapping centrally uses non-RDFS properties, such as *http://schema.org/domainIncludes*, so it is not possible to determine the meaning of schema.org constructs from the RDF mapping. The OWL mapping is somewhat better, as domains and ranges employ OWL unions, but the mapping is only a translation of part of what defines schema.org. The lack of a complete definition of schema.org limits the possibility of extracting the correct information from web pages that have schema.org markup.

This paper provides a full basis for schema.org as it should be, filling in the holes in the available descriptions of schema.org and fixing up discrepancies. The paper provides both a pre-theoretic analysis of schema.org and an abstract syntax and formal model-theoretic semantics for schema.org. This paper does not, however, draw on

---

[1] Throughout this paper schema.org refers to the general idea and *schema.org* refers to the collection of documents available at the *https://schema.org* web site.

[2] From *https://schema.org*, as of 1 April 2014.

[3] See *http://schema.org/docs/datamodel.html*

P. Mika et al. (Eds.) ISWC 2014, Part I, LNCS 8796, pp. 261–276, 2014.

the use of schema.org on web pages. Researchers can use the basis provided here to further investigate the properties of schema.org and schema.org markup. Providers of schema.org data can use this basis to reliably determine the meaning of the schema.org data they create. Developers can use this basis to build software that uses schema.org markup as information in a way that is compatible with the description of schema.org.

## Description of Schema.org at *schema.org*

The description of schema.org in this section of the paper is taken from information on the web pages in *schema.org*, as of 1 April 2014. It ignores most of the surface syntax aspects of schema.org, concentrating on the underlying concepts and their intent.

Schema.org information is about items, e.g., the movie Avatar. Items can have types, e.g., the type identified by the URL *http://schema.org/Movie*. Items can have associated property-value pairs, e.g., the property identified by *http://schema.org/director* with value *"James Cameron"*. The value in a property value pair can be text, i.e., a Unicode string; a literal, e.g., a number or date; a URL, which identifies an item; or another item. There is no requirement that properties have only a single value for an item. Items can have associated URLs, e.g., *http://www.avatarmovie.com/index.html* and *http://en.wikipedia.org/wiki/Avatar_(2009_film)*, each of which identifies the item.

Schema.org provides a collection of types, via pages in *schema.org*, organized in a multi-parent generalization hierarchy. Each type is identified by the URL of the page that provides its definition. Each type has a set of parents, i.e., more-general types. Each type, except for datatypes, has a set of allowable properties for the type.

The types that are more specific than *http://schema.org/Enumeration* are enumeration types that also specify a set of URLs identifying all the items that are instances of the type. Datatypes are the types more specific than *http://schema.org/Datatype* and implicitly provide a set of non-item data values for them and a mapping from text to these values.

Schema.org also provides a collection of properties, again from *schema.org*, which may be also organized in a multi-parent generalization hierarchy.[4] Each property is identified by the URL of the page that provides its definition. Each property may have one or more types as domains, and can be used on items belonging to any of these types. Each property has one or more types as ranges, and values for the property belong to one or more of these types. However, property values can always be provided as just text.

There is a description of an extension mechanisms for schema.org, which only permits very simple extensions. It appears that the extension mechanism exists only to further subdivide existing schema.org properties, classes, and enumeration items and that these extensions are ignored within schema.org.

The translations of the type and property definitions of schema.org into RDF and OWL abide by the above description, except that there is no translation for the property hierarchy. These translations provide no extra information beyond what is given here.

---

[4] At the time of writing of this paper there was no general notation of the property hierarchy. While this paper was in review, the property hierarchy was officially announced (*http://lists.w3.org/Archives/Public/public-vocabs/2014Jun/0095.html*)

# Analysis of *schema.org* as a Description of Schema.org

There are quite a number of aspects of schema.org and schema.org markup that are left unspecified in *schema.org*, are unclear, or raise issues. This section describes these aspects and provides extra assumptions that will be used in the account for schema.org presented here. The extra assumptions have been made in a way that is congruent with the information on *schema.org*, that make sense in an environment where there are large central consumers of large amounts of data, and that generate a reasonable representation formalism. (In several places, the comments in *schema.org* do not match the actual class or property, for example, instances of *http://schema.org/StructuredValue* are not strings, but this sort of mismatch is not the subject of this paper.)

It is unclear whether types and properties can also be items. However, items work quite differently from types and properties, and having arbitrary web pages being able to modify the types and properties of schema.org leads to difficulties, such as not being able to determine when a property is valid for an item until after all item information has been processed, so this account treats types and properties as being different from items. In particular, in this account different URLs that identify the same item do not identify the same type or the same property. Data values also act differently from items, so this account treats them as being disjoint from types, properties, and items. The identifiers of types and properties are different in schema.org, as URLs for types have initial capitals and URLs for properties do not, so it is fairly obvious that types are disjoint from properties.

Schema.org uses URLs as identifiers. URLs can be used to retrieve web pages, and this aspect of URLs is a main basis of schema.org. URLs officially can include fragment ids, and such URLs then identify parts of web pages. Although fragment identifiers are not currently used for any types and properties in *schema.org*, there is nothing technical preventing their use, and so they will be allowed in the account herein for types, properties, and items.

It is unclear whether schema.org types and properties must be identified by URLs in *schema.org*, but all current schema.org types and properties are so identified. This account does not formally make the assumption that types and properties must be identified by URLs in *schema.org*, but some of the pragmatic analysis does make the assumption that type and property definitions change infrequently, as is the case for types and properties identified by URLs in *schema.org*.

The mechanisms for working with datatypes are underspecified in *schema.org*. This account adds in a formal mechanism for determining the set of values for a datatype and a formal method for determining the data value corresponding to a text string for the datatype.

The name of the most general datatype in schema.org is *http://schema.org/Datatype*. This is an unfortunate name—*http://schema.org/Literal* would be much better—but the schema.org name will be used in this account. The name of the datatype for floating point numbers in schema.org is *http://schema.org/Float*. *http://schema.org/Float* and *http://schema.org/Integer* both have generalization *http://schema.org/Number*. This can lead to problems because floating point numbers are imprecise whereas integers are precise. This account, however, does not address the issue.

It is unclear whether the instances of an enumeration have to be items, or can also be data values. This account assumes that the instances of an enumeration are given as URLs, as is the case for all examples currently in schema.org, and thus that instances of an enumeration are items, not data values.

Some examples in *schema.org* only make sense if different but similar URLs identify different items. This is particularly the case for URLs that make up enumerations. This account assumes that different URLs in an enumeration identify different items, but does not otherwise assume that different URLs in the same namespace, e.g., different Wikipedia URLs, or in the same document identify different items. This extra assumption would be easy to add.

The domains of a property are specified both as part of types and as part of properties in *schema.org*. In all the examples there is no divergence between the two specifications, but the possibility of divergence is not ruled out. This account treats the specification in the type as the actual specification, as that seems to make more sense for disjunctive domains.

Because several properties indicate that they are subproperties of other properties, this account incorporates a multi-parent property hierarchy. There are some additions to the account herein that have to be made to support the property hierarchy.

Both domains and ranges of properties are disjunctive. This is different from most other representation formalisms, such as description logics [6] and RDF [2]. The stated rationale for this decision is that it reduces the need for general types that exist only to be domains or ranges. However, disjunctive domains and ranges mean that additions to a collection of schema.org information can be non-monotonic. The disjunctive nature of domains and ranges is fully explored in this account, including how it interacts with the property hierarchy.

Several aspects of the predominant syntaxes for schema.org markup obscure the workings of schema.org. This account transforms these aspects of surface syntax into a different abstract syntax.

Several types and properties are used as part of the foundations of schema.org in *schema.org*. Nearly all uses of these types and properties as general types or properties undermines the foundations of schema.org, so their use is disallowed in this account. The extension mechanism for schema.org is of very limited utility and appears to not have any effect on the processing of schema.org markup, so it is ignored in this account.

## Description of Schema.org as It Should Be

This section contains a pre-theoretic description of schema.org and schema.org content as it should be, consonant with the discussion in the previous section. This description is designed to say how schema.org could work in a way that can be easily turned into a formal definition of schema.org, as is done in the following section of this paper.

Throughout this account, a URL is a uniform resource locator, optionally including a fragment part. The document (fragment) at that URL is (the appropriate fragment of) the document obtained by the usual web mechanisms for retrieving a document given a URL. URLs will be generally written as CURIES [7], with the prefixes *s* expanding to *http://schema.org/* and *w* expanding to *http://en.wikipedia.org/wiki/*, and the prefixes *rdf*, *rdfs*, and *owl* expanding to their usual expansions. The constituents of schema.org information are types, properties, data values, and items.

There is a collection of types, in a multi-parent generalization taxonomy, with two roots, *s:Thing* and *s:Datatype*. Each type is identified by a unique URL. The document (fragment) at that URL defines the type, listing:

1. some types that are more general than it (its parents), and
2. for non-datatypes, its properties (see below).

Parents and properties, and information about instances where appropriate, are the only information about a type obtainable from its defining document (fragment).

Each type has as a generalization (not necessarily directly specified in its defining document) either *s:Thing* or *s:Datatype*, but not both.

The types with strict generalization *s:Datatype* are datatypes. All the data values belonging to the datatype are described in the datatype's defining document (fragment), as is a way of transforming text strings into these data values. The datatypes are *s:Boolean*, *s:Date*, *s:DateTime*, *s:Number*, *s:Float*, *s:Integer*, *s:Text* (Unicode strings), *s:URL*, and *s:Time*. The details of these datatypes do not matter for this account, except for *s:Text*, and are not described here.

The type *s:Enumeration* has *s:Thing* as a parent.[5] Those types with strict generalization *s:Enumeration* are enumeration types. All those items with the enumeration type as a direct type are listed in the type's defining document (fragment). Different URLs identify different items in an enumeration.

The type *s:Thing* has properties *s:description* and *s:name*.[6]

There is a collection of properties, disjoint from types, in a multiple-parent generalization taxonomy with multiple roots. Each property is identified by a unique URL. The document (fragment) at that URL defines the property, providing:

1. types that its values belong to (its ranges), and
2. some properties that are more general than it (its parents).

Ranges and parents are the only information about a property obtainable from its defining document (fragment).

For each parent of the property for each range of the property the parent must have a range that is the same as or a generalization of the range. This condition on property ranges means that the validity of a property value can be checked by looking only at the range types of the property itself.

The properties *s:description* and *s:name* both have range *s:Text*.

Data values belong to one or more datatypes, and are disjoint from types and properties. Data values are written as a combination of a URL identifying a datatype and a text string. The mapping in the datatype turns the text string into a value of the datatype. Every data value belongs to *s:Datatype*. If a data value belongs to a datatype then it belongs to the parents of the datatype.

---

[5] Enumeration actually has a different supertype on *schema.org* but this account removes the unneeded supertype.

[6] There are several other properties for *s:Thing* on *schema.org*, but these do not play a role in this account and are ignored here.

Items are things in the world, including information things, and are disjoint from types, properties, and data values. Items belong to (one or more) non-datatype types. Items have zero or more URLs identifying them. Items are associated with (other) items and data values via properties. Every item belongs to *s:Thing*. If an item belongs to a type then it belongs to the parents of the type.

If an item or data value is associated with an item via a property then the item or data value is also associated with the item via each parent of the property. For each item or data value associated with an item via a property,

1. one of the item's types has the property as one of its properties, and
2. the item or data value belongs to one of the ranges of the property.

The documents (document fragments) at the URLs identifying an item provide information about the item, including types for the item as well as items and data values associated with the item via properties.

Bare text can be used as if it was the value for any property. If the property does not have *s:Text* or *s:Datatype* as one of its ranges, but does have one or more datatypes as a range that have a data value that can be written as the bare text then the actual value for the property is one of these data values. If the property does not have *s:Text* or *s:Datatype* as one of its ranges, and does not have any suitable datatypes as a range, but does have one or more non-datatypes as a range, then the actual value for the property is some item that has a type that is one of these ranges and this item has the text as a value of its *s:description* property. (The property *s:description* is used instead of *s:name*, as the text might not truly be a name for the value.) Otherwise the actual value for the property is the bare text itself.

Any surface syntax must provide ways to write all possible data values (as long as they are not too big). Any surface syntax must have ways to provide items with any number of types, including none, and values for any property of any of the provided types or their generalizations or *s:Thing*, including allowing multiple values for a property. Any surface syntax must provide ways for writing items with no identifying URLs. Any surface syntax must specially process syntax that would otherwise produce values for *s:additionalType*, turning the values into types; and *s:url* and *s:sameAs*, turning the values into identifying URLs.

The following URLs are not used to identify types or properties: *s:Class, s:Property, s:domainIncludes, s:rangeIncludes, rdfs:subClassOf, rdfs:subPropertyOf, rdfs:domain, rdfs:range, rdfs:type, rdfs:Class, rdf:Property,* and *owl:Class.* If they are used in a surface syntax to provide information about an item they and their values must be ignored. The following URLs are not used to identify properties: *s:additionalType, s:url,* and *s:sameAs.*

## Formal Definition for Schema.org

This definition for schema.org defines an abstract syntax for schema.org, abstracting away from the details of the various surface syntaxes, and a model-theoretic semantics, that provides a formal meaning for schema.org. It conforms to the pre-theoretic description above.

**Abstract Syntax**

Surface syntaxes for schema.org are transformed into an abstract syntax, in a process not fully described here. The abstract syntax plays a similar role as triples do for RDF [2], but is more complicated, as it makes distinctions between definitions and information about items. The abstract syntax removes artifacts of the surface syntaxes that make a formal account difficult, but transforming schema.org surface syntaxes into this abstract syntax is simple.

The gathering of information from Web documents is performed when building the abstract syntax. Constructs in the abstract syntax that start with a URL (or set of URLs) may be constructed from the document at the URL (or documents at one or more of the URLs), although they need not be.

**Definition 1.** *A* URL *in this document is a URL with optional fragment identifier, as defined in the W3C Working Draft on URLs [8]. A* text string *is a sequence of Unicode characters [9]. A* literal *is a pair consisting of a URL, the* datatype identifier *of the literal, and a text string.*

One part of schema.org information consists of definitions—of regular types, of enumerated types, of datatypes, and of properties.

**Definition 2.** *A* (regular) type definition *is a triple, $\langle U, S, P \rangle$, where $U$ is a URL, the identifier of the type; $S$ is a set of URLs, the supertypes of the type; and $P$ is another set of URLs, the properties of the type.*

For example, the type definition for movies could be[7]

  ⟨ *s:Movie*, { *s:CreativeWork* },
    { *s:actor, s:director, s:producer, s:duration, s:musicBy,*
      *s:productionCompany, s:trailer s:author, s:copyrightYear* } ⟩

indicating that movie is a subtype of creative work and has eight locally-specified properties.

The type of actions that update a collection would be

  ⟨ *s:UpdateAction*, { *s:Action* }, { *s:collection* } ⟩

indicating that update actions are actions and have only one locally-specified property.

**Definition 3.** *An* enumerated type definition *is a quadruple, $\langle U, S, P, E \rangle$, where $U$, $S$, and $P$ are as in a regular type definition, and $E$ is yet another set of URLs, the direct instances of the enumerated type.*

For example, the enumerated type definition for book formats would be

  ⟨ *s:BookFormatType*, { *s:Enumeration* }, {},
    { *s:EBook, s:Hardcover, s:Paperback* } ⟩

indicating that there are three different book formats.

---

[7] This definition of movies ignores the legacy properties for movies in *schema.org*, and adds in some properties from *s:CreativeWork* for illustrative purposes.

**Definition 4.** *A datatype definition is a quadruple, $\langle U, S, W, I \rangle$, where $U$ and $S$ are as in a regular type definition, $W$ is a set of values for the datatype, and $I$ is a partial mapping from text strings into $W$.*

For example, the datatype for URLs would be

$$\langle \text{ s:URL}, \{\text{s:Text}\}, \text{U}, id^U \rangle$$

where $U$ is the set of Unicode strings that are valid URLs and $id^U$ is the string identity function restricted to valid URLs, indicating that URL values are those text strings that are valid URLs.

It is a bit unusual to include formal datatype definitions in an abstract syntax. It would be more usual to pull these out into some sort of side definition. However, this way of defining datatypes puts all aspects of the definition in one place, as is done for other type and property definitions.

**Definition 5.** *A property definition is a triple, $\langle U, S, R \rangle$, where $U$ is a URL, the identifier of the property; $S$ is a set of URLs, the superproperties of the property; and $R$ is a non-empty set of URLs, the ranges of the property.*

For example, the *s:collection* property (used in update actions), a subproperty of the *s:object* property with range *s:Thing*, would be written as the first of the following property definitions:

$\langle$ s:collection, {s:object}, {s:Thing} $\rangle$,
$\langle$ s:actor, {}, {s:Person} $\rangle$,
$\langle$ s:director, {}, {s:Person} $\rangle$,
$\langle$ s:copyrightYear, {}, {s:Number} $\rangle$,
$\langle$ s:author, {}, {s:Organization, s:Person} $\rangle$.

**Definition 6.** *A type definition is either a regular type definition, an enumerated type definition, or a datatype definition. A definition is either a type definition or a property definition A definition is said to be a definition for its identifier.*

Type and property definitions define separate generalization partial orders on types and properties, building up from the supertypes and superproperties of type definitions and property definitions.

**Definition 7.** *A type (property) definition, $D$, is a child of another, $D'$, if $D'$ is one of the supertypes (superproperties) of $D$. A type (property) definition, $D$, is a descendant of another, $D'$, in a set of definitions, if there is a chain of child relationships from $D$ to $D'$, in the set of definitions.*

**Definition 8.** *A URL, $U$, is a type (property) descendant of another, $U'$, in a set of definitions, written $U < U'$, if $U$ is the identifier of a type (property) definition that is a descendant of a type (property) definition that is identified by $U'$.*

The other part of schema.org information consists of information about items, providing types and property values for items. Note that this information is not called definitions, as there is no requirement that different items in the abstract syntax provide information about different resources.

**Definition 9.** *A property value pair, $\langle U, V \rangle$, consists of $U$, a URL identifying the property, and $V$, a text string or a literal or a URL or an item, indicating the value.*

**Definition 10.** *An item is a triple, $\langle N, T, PV \rangle$, where $N$ is a (possibly empty) set of URLs, identifiers of the item; $T$ is a (possibly empty) set of URLs, identifiers of types of the item; and $PV$ is a (possibly empty) set of property value pairs.*

For example, an item for a particular movie could be

   ⟨ { *http://www.avatarmovie.com/index.html, w:Avatar_(2009_film)* },

    { *s:Movie* },

    { ⟨*s:name, "Avatar"*⟩ ,

     ⟨*s:director,* ⟨ {}, { *s:Person* }, { ⟨*s:name, "James Cameron"*⟩ } ⟩ ⟩ ,

     ⟨*s:actor, "Sam Worthington"*⟩ ,

     ⟨*s:actor, w:Sigourney_Weaver*⟩ }

    ⟨*s:year, "2009"*⟩ ,

    ⟨*s:author, "James Cameron"*⟩ ⟩

This item has two identifiers and six property-value pairs, one providing a text value for a name of the movie, one providing an in-line item for a director of the movie, one providing a text value for an actor in the movie, one providing a URL identifying an actor in the movie, one providing a text value for a copyright year of the movie, and another providing a text value for an author of the movie.

A collection of definitions and items is a knowledge base, the overall way of collecting schema.org information together. There are many side conditions on schema.org knowledge bases to provide an overall structure of the generalization hierarchies for types and properties, to account for the built-in types and properties, and to ensure that literals are well behaved.

**Definition 11.** *A schema.org knowledge base is a triple, $\langle T, P, I \rangle$, where $D$ is a set of type definitions, $P$ is a set of property definitions, and $I$ is a set of items that satisfies the following conditions:*

1. *Each URL is the identifier of at most one definition in $T$, and similarly for $P$. There is at most one definition for any URL in $T$ and $P$.*
2. *The descendant relationship for types (properties) in $T$ $(P)$ is a strict partial order.*
3. *$T$ contains the following regular type definitions:*
   ⟨ *s:Thing, {}, { s:description, s:name }* ⟩,
   ⟨ *s:Datatype, {}, {}* ⟩, *and*
   ⟨ *s:Enumeration, { s:Thing }, {}* ⟩.
4. *$T$ contains the following datatype definition, where $S$ is the set of text strings and id is the identity mapping on text strings:*
   ⟨ *s:Text, { s:Datatype }, S, id* ⟩
5. *$P$ contains the following property definitions:*
   ⟨ *s:description, {}, { s:Text }* ⟩ *and* ⟨ *s:name, {}, { s:Text }* ⟩.
6. *For each literal $\langle U, V \rangle$ in the knowledge base there is a datatype definition $\langle U, S, W, I \rangle$ in $T$ such that $I$ is defined on $V$.*

7. *T has a datatype definition for U iff U < s:Datatype in T.*
8. *T has an enumerated type definition for U iff U < s:Enumeration in T.*
9. *T has a regular type definition for U iff U is s:Datatype or s:Thing or U < s:Thing but not U < s:Enumeration in T.*

There is nothing about web document retrieval in the abstract syntax (nor in the formal semantics immediately following). The *intent* should be clear, however—that type and property definitions come from the document (fragment) obtained by dereferencing the URL identifying the type or property and that item information often comes from the document (fragment) obtained by dereferencing a URL identifying the item.[8]

Building a schema.org knowledge base then generally starts with a collection of web documents that have schema.org markup about items. However, first the pages in *schema.org* that define types and properties are parsed to produce type and property definitions for the knowledge base. The document (fragments) accessible from URLs identifying items encountered during this parsing are added to the initial collection of web documents. Then this collection of documents is parsed to produce items for the knowledge base.

URLs for items that are encountered during the parsing may be used to direct that the web document (fragment) at that URL also be parsed to produce items for the knowledge base. Whether this "follow your nose" behavior is actually performed during the construction of a particular knowledge base depends on many factors that are outside the purview of this account.

**Model-theoretic Semantics**

The semantics for schema.org here is built up in the standard way from interpretations, which provide formal meanings for all URLs as identifying types or properties, and items and URLs as identifying resources. Items are mapped into sets of resources, not resources, as the resource corresponding to an item is indeterminate unless there is a URL that identifies the item. A single URL can independently identify a type, a property, and a resource, but these do not have any formal connection between them.

**Definition 12.** *An* interpretation *is a sextuple,* $\langle I_R, I_V, I_T, I_P, I_U, I_I \rangle$, *where* $I_R$ *is a set of resources;* $I_V$ *is a set of data values, disjoint from* $I_R$; *and*

$$I_T : U \to 2^{I_R} \cup 2^{I_V}$$
$$I_P : U \to 2^{I_R \times (I_R \cup I_V)}$$
$$I_U : U \to I_R$$
$$I_I : I \to 2^{I_R}$$
$$I_T(\text{s:Thing}) = I_R$$
$$I_T(\text{s:Datatype}) = I_V$$

*where U is the set of URLs with optional fragments and I is the set of items.*

---

[8] Note that types and properties have a unique identifier whereas items may have multiple identifiers, or none.

$I_T$ maps types into their extensions, a set of resources or a set of data values. $I_P$ maps properties into their extensions, sets of pairs whose first element is a resource and whose second element is a resource or a data value. $I_I$ maps items into their extensions, a set of resources. $I_U$ maps URLs into their extensions as item identifiers, a resource;

Although the mappings above are infinite, in any knowledge base the only part of the mappings that are relevant are for the URLs and items that occur in the knowledge base (or query, in entailment and querying situations).

**Definition 13.** *An interpretation, $\langle I_R, I_V, I_T, I_P, I_U, I_I \rangle$, satisfies a knowledge base, $\langle K_T, K_P, K_I \rangle$ iff*

1. *for $\langle U, \{S_1, ..., S_n\}, P \rangle$ a regular type definition in $K_T$, $I_T(U) \subseteq I_T(S_i)$;*
2. *for $\langle U, \{S1, ..., Sn\}, P, \{E1, ...Em\} \rangle$ an enumerated type definition in $K_T$,*
   (a) *$I_T(U) \subseteq I_T(S_i)$,*
   (b) *$I_T(U) = \{I_U(e) \mid e \in E\}$, and*
   (c) *$\forall e_i \neq e_j \in E \quad I_U(e_i) \neq I_U(e_j)$,*
   *where $E = \cup \{E' \mid \langle U', S', P', E' \rangle \in K_T \wedge (U' = U \vee U' < U)\}$;*
3. *for $\langle U, \{S_1, ..., S_n\}, W, I \rangle$ a datatype definition in $K_T$,*
   (a) *$I_T(U) \subseteq I_T(S_i)$ and*
   (b) *$I_T(U) = W$;*
4. *for $\langle U, \{S1, ..., Sn\}, R \rangle$ a property definition in $K_P$, $\quad I_P(U) \subseteq I_P(S_i)$;*
5. *for $I = \langle \{U_1, ..., U_n\}, \{T_1, ..., T_m\}, \{\langle P_1, V_1 \rangle, ..., \langle P_l, V_l \rangle\} \rangle$, an item in $K_I$,*
   (a) *$I_I(I) = \{I_U(U_1)\}$, for $1 \leq i \leq n$,*
   (b) *$I_I(I) \subseteq I_T(T_i), 1 \leq i \leq m$,*
   (c) *for $x \in I_I(I)$, for $1 \leq i \leq l$, there exists $\langle P_i, S, R\} \rangle$ a property definition and there exists $y$ such that $\langle x, y \rangle \in I_P(P_i)$ and*
      - *if $V_i$ is an item then $y \in I_I(V_i)$*
      - *if $V_i$ is a URL then $y = I_U(V_i)$*
      - *if $V_i$ is a literal $\langle D, T \rangle$ then there exists $\langle D, S, W, ID \rangle$ a datatype definition and $y = I_D(T)$*
      - *if $V_i$ is a text string then*
        - *if s:Text $\in R$ or s:Datatype $\in R$ then $y = V_i$*
        - *otherwise if there exists $\langle D, S, W, I \rangle$ a datatype with $D$ in $R$ and $V_i$ mapped by $I$ then $y = I_T(V_i)$ for some one of these datatypes*
        - *otherwise if there exists $\langle T, S, P \rangle$ a type with $T$ in $R$ then $y \in I_T(T)$ for some one of these types, and $\langle y, V_i \rangle \in I_P($s:description$)$*
        - *otherwise $y = V_i$;*
6. *for each $U$, for each $\langle x, y \rangle \in I_P(U)$,*
   (a) *there exists $\langle T, S, P \rangle$ a type definition or $\langle T, S, P, E \rangle$ an enumerated type definition in $K_T$ such that $U \in P$ and $x \in I_T(U)$, and*
   (b) *there exists $\langle U, S, R \rangle$ a property definition in $K_P$ such that either $R = \{\}$ or there exists $R' \in R$ with $y \in I_T(R')$.*

From this basis the standard notions of entailment and inference and simple querying can be defined in the usual way.

The first clause in the satisfaction definition above provides the basis for the type generalization hierarchy, saying that the extension of a regular type is a subset of the extensions of each of its parent types. This is repeated for enumerated types and datatypes in the first part of the second and third clauses. Because regular and enumerated types are all descendants of *s:Thing*, their extensions are are subsets of the set of resources.

The second part of the second clause states that the extension of an enumeration is just the set of all the items that are stated to belong to it and its subtypes. The third part of the second clause states that all these items are different.

The third clause states that the extension of a datatype is its set of values. Because datatypes are all descendants of *s:Datatype*, their extensions must be subsets of the set of data values.

The fourth clause enforces the property generalization hierarchy.

The fifth clause handles all the parts of item syntax. The first part of this clause says that the extension of an item is the same as the extension of its identifiers, if any. Note that if there are no identifiers for an item, then the extension of the item need not be a singleton set. The second part says that the extension of an item is in the extension of the extensions of its types. The third part provides meaning for the property-value pairs in the item. There must be a property relationship from the item to a value that for item values is in the extension of the item, for URL values is the extension of the URL as an item identifier, and for literals is the correct data value. For values that are text there is a determination of what the most suitable ranges are with text datatypes the most suitable, other compatible datatypes next, and other types least suitable. Then one of these types is chosen and a data value or item is chosen to belong to this type.

So the movie item above would be a resource that is the same as the extensions of *http://www.avatarmovie.com/index.html* and *w:Avatar_(2009_film)* and is in the extension of *s:Movie*. This resource would be related to the string *"Avatar"* via (the property extension of) *s:name*, because *s:name* has *s:Text* as its sole range; to a resource in the extension of *s:Person* that has name *"James Cameron"* via *s:director*, to a resource in the extension of *s:Person* that has description *"Sam Worthington"* via *s:actor*, because *s:director* has *s:Person* as its sole range; to the extension of *w:Sigourney_Weaver* via *s:actor*, to the number 2009 via *s:copyrightYear*, because the supplied text is compatible with the *s:Number* datatype; and via *s:author* to a resource that is either in the extension of *s:Organization* or *s:Person* and that has description *"James Cameron"*, because *s:author* has ranges *s:Organization* and *s:Person*, and no datatype ranges.

The sixth clause enforces domain and range restrictions. The first part says that for each property, for each relationship between an item and a value in that property, there is a regular or enumerated type that has that property and contains the item. The second part similarly says that if the the definition of the property states ranges, then the value belongs to one of the ranges. Because parent properties have to have a range that is an ancestor of this range, this also satisfies the range restriction for each ancestor property.

## Discussion

The above formal semantics is quite dense, particularly the definition of satisfaction. However, there is nothing particularly sophisticated going on, it is just that there are quite a few bits of schema.org markup to take into account.

The formal semantics is actually more standard than the formal semantics of RDF [10], as there are no resources for types and properties. It is easy to see that nothing about items can affect the relationships within and between types and properties (except that, as usual, inconsistencies in the information about items cause the semantics to collapse). If two URLs identify the same item, it is not necessarily the case that the two URLs define the same type or define the same property. This stands in stark contrast to RDF, but means that the only source of information for a type or property is its definition (which would come from the appropriate *schema.org* page). Thus consumers of schema.org information do not need to process any items to understand types and properties.

If two items share an identifying URL, then their extension is the same. If an item does not have a URL, but has a type that is an enumeration, then the item is one of finite, enumerated instances of the enumeration. This provides a weak form of disjunction for schema.org. The distinctness of the extensions of the URLs in an enumeration provides inequality for arbitrary resources in schema.org

As schema.org has weak disjunction and inequality for resources, its expressive power is considerably above that of RDFS, even though there is a translation provided from schema.org types and properties into RDFS.

Schema.org can, however, be translated into OWL, but the translation is not into a simple variant of OWL. For some parts of schema.org it is easy to see the translation. The special types *s:Thing* and *s:Datatype* are translated into *owl:Thing* and *owl:Literal*, respectively. All other non-datatype types become OWL classes. Supertypes where the parent type is a regular type translate into subtype axioms.

Property ranges for a property translate into a disjunctive property range axiom. However, a property can have both regular types and datatypes as ranges. A property with such a range cannot be categorized as either an object property or a data property, and so cannot be translated into OWL 2 DL. However, OWL 2 Full [11] permits uncategorized properties. Superproperties for properties then translate into subproperty axioms.

For some parts, the translation needs to take into account more than just one part of the knowledge base. Domains for a property are constructed by taking all the types that mention the property and producing a disjunctive property domain for the property from them. Enumerations are constructed by finding all the item URLs belonging to the enumeration type and its subtypes and constructing an axiom stating that the enumeration type is equivalent to the object one-of containing all these objects. This construction handles the supertype relationship where the supertype is an enumeration type. As well, a different individuals axiom is added stating that all the distinct URLs belonging to the enumeration type and its subtypes are different.

The translation for datatypes requires the construction of a datatype map that has the same effect as the datatype definitions. The datatypes in schema.org fit within what can be done for OWL datatypes, so this is possible. Supertypes for datatypes are either true, because the datatype's value spaces are in the correct relationship, or false. The first case can be ignored, as it has no effect. The second case can be translated into an inconsistent OWL assertion, as it produces an inconsistency.

The translation for items is a bit tricky, to allow for items that do not have any associated URLs. Anonymous individuals are employed in the translation to avoid the need for extra URLs, for each item there is generated a different anonymous individual.

For each identifier of the item, there is a same-as assertion between the anonymous individual and the identifier. For each type of the item, there is a class assertion stating that the anonymous individual belongs to the type.

Property value pairs are treated as follows.

1. If the value is a URL, then it identifies an item, and the URL is used directly as the value of a property assertion from the anonymous individual to the value via the property.
2. If the value is a literal, then the corresponding OWL literal is used instead in the property assertion.
3. If the value is an item, then the item is translated, and the anonymous individual for the item is used instead.
4. If the value is text, the situation is more complex. First then the ranges for the property are determined.
   (a) If *s:Text* or *s:Datatype* is one of the ranges then a string literal is constructed from the text and used as the value as above.
   (b) If there is a range that is a datatype with the text in the domain of its literal-to-value mapping, then those datatypes with the text in the domain of their literal-to-value mappings are used to construct one or more literals. The anonymous individual is then asserted to belong to a data some-value-from with the property to a data one-of constructed from these literals.
   (c) If there are no suitable datatype ranges then if there are any non-datatype ranges then the translation of the property-value pair is a property assertion from the anonymous individual via the property to a fresh anonymous individual. This fresh anonymous individual is asserted to belong to the disjunction of the non-datatype ranges and is also asserted to have the text as the value of the *s:description*.

The correctness of this mapping is not hard to verify, but a full proof of the correctness would be long and tedious and so is omitted here.

The translation into OWL does not determine how hard or easy reasoning is in schema.org because reasoning in OWL Full is undecidable. There are no inverse properties in schema.org, so not making the division between object and data properties does not appreciably affect reasoning. As this is the only part of the mapping that is not in OWL 2 DL, the mapping into OWL shows that the reasoning in schema.org is decidable.

It is easy to show that reasoning here is in PSpace, as reasoners need not introduce new types, properties, or items. Showing the precise complexity of reasoning is more difficult, as enumerations and the disjunctive nature of domain and range includes need to be addressed. For example, if this account of schema.org were modified to use the underlying semantics of RDF and lift the restrictions on the use of certain URLs the set cover problem could be encoded, introducing a new source of hardness to reasoning.

The intent of schema.org appears to be that all the types and properties defined in schema.org will remain in the *schema.org* namespace and thus under the control of the owners of *schema.org* and will change only infrequently. Other web pages will not be allowed to make changes or additions to these types and properties. This limits the effect of the non-monotonic nature of the disjunctive domains and ranges of schema.org.

The model-theoretic account here is a standard one, based on inference instead of constraints. If an item has a value for a property, then the item is inferred to belong to one of the domains of the property. The constraint reading [12] would instead require that the item be stated to belong to a domain for the property before a value could be provided. There are benefits to the constraint account, as it is closer to the database situation, but it is less flexible [13].

It is possible to get the effect of the constraint approach in a surface syntax. A surface syntax can have constructs that require that property-value pairs for an item be only for items that mention a type or subtype of one of the domains of the property. In this way most benefits of both approaches can be obtained.

## Conclusion

This paper has provided an analysis of what schema.org should be, leading up to a complete formal treatment of schema.org including an abstract syntax and a model-theoretic semantics. It fills in voids in the publicly-available description of schema.org, including whether types and properties and items are disjoint, whether enumerations are distinct, whether properties can have generalizations, and how to handle text values. This may not exactly correspond to intent of the schema.org members, but it is consistent with the available information about schema.org, and uses only a reasonable set of additional assumptions.

This paper shows that even the unusual parts of schema.org can be translated into OWL. Although schema.org cannot be translated into OWL 2 DL, because schema.org properties cannot be categorized into object and data properties, the extensions are cosmetic, and schema.org reasoning is no harder than reasoning in OWL 2 DL. Determining just how hard schema.org reasoning is remains as further work.

Schema.org does not provide local ranges for properties, such as saying that the author of a movie is a person even though in general authors can be either people or organizations. This lack of expressive power limits what can be said about property values and is especially problematic as quite a few roles in *schema.org* could benefit from local ranges (e.g., a season of a TV series should be a TV season, but can only be a general season, as Radio Series also have seasons). Adding this feature to schema.org would usefully improve its expressive power.

The account of schema.org here should provide a starting point for further formal analysis of schema.org and a firm foundation for systems that consume schema.org information. Web pages that contain schema.org information can be checked against this account to provide a formal account of what the information conveys, thus reducing the possibility of mismatches between providers and consumers of schema.org information.

The obvious next step is to gather large amounts of schema.org information to see how schema.org is used in practice. This usage should then be analyzed to see how well the various aspects of schema.org are used and how the account here helps to better provide meaning for actual information that uses schema.org.

# References

1. Schreiber, G., Raimond, Y.: RDF 1.1 primer. W3C Working Group Note (February 25, 2014), http://www.w3.org/TR/rdf11-primer/
2. Cyganiak, R., Wood, D., Lanthaler, M.: RDF 1.1 concepts and abstract syntax. W3C Recommendation (February 25, 2014), http://www.w3.org/TR/rdf-concepts/
3. W3C OWL Working Group: OWL 2 Web Ontology Language: Document overview. W3C Recommendation (December 11, 2012), http://www.w3.org/TR/owl2-overview
4. Motik, B., Patel-Schneider, P.F., Parsia, B.: OWL 2 web ontology language: Structural specification and functional-style syntax. W3C Recommendation (December 11, 2012), http://www.w3.org/TR/owl2-syntax/
5. Bollacker, K., Tufts, P., Pierce, T., Cook, R.: A platform for scalable, collaborative, structured information integration. In: Sixth International Workshop on Information Integration on the Web. AAAI Press (July 2007)
6. Baader, F., Calvanese, D., McGuinness, D.L., Nardi, D., Patel-Schneider, P.F.: The Description Logic Handbook: Theory, implementation, and applications, 2nd edn. Cambridge University Press (2007)
7. Birbeck, M., McCarron, S.: CURIE syntax 1.0: A syntax for expressing compact URIs. W3C Working Group Note (2007), http://www.w3.org/TR/curie/
8. Arvidsson, E., Smith, M.: URL. W3C Working Draft (May 24, 2012), http://www.w3.org/TR/URL/
9. The Unicode Consortium: The unicode standard (2013), http://www.unicode.org/versions/latest/
10. Hayes, P., Patel-Schneider, P.F.: RDF 1.1 semantics. W3C Recommendation (February 25, 2014), http://www.w3.org/TR/rdf11-mt/
11. Schneider, M.: OWL 2 web ontology language: RDF-based semantics (2second edition). W3C Recommendation (December 11, 2012), http://www.w3.org/TR/owl-rdf-based-semantics/
12. de Bruijn, J., Polleres, A., Lara, R., Fensel, D.: OWL DL vs. OWL Flight: Conceptual modeling and reasoning for the semantic web. In: Proceedings of the 14th World Wide Web Conference, Japan (May 2005)
13. Patel-Schneider, P.F., Horrocks, I.: Position paper: A comparison of two modelling paradigms in the semantic web. In: Proceedings of the 15th International Conference on the World Wide Web (WWW2006). ACM Press, New York (May 2006)

# The WebDataCommons Microdata, RDFa and Microformat Dataset Series

Robert Meusel, Petar Petrovski, and Christian Bizer

University of Mannheim, Germany
Research Group Data and Web Science
{robert,petar,chris}@informatik.uni-mannheim.de

**Abstract.** In order to support web applications to understand the content of HTML pages an increasing number of websites have started to annotate structured data within their pages using markup formats such as Microdata, RDFa, Microformats. The annotations are used by Google, Yahoo!, Yandex, Bing and Facebook to enrich search results and to display entity descriptions within their applications. In this paper, we present a series of publicly accessible Microdata, RDFa, Microformats datasets that we have extracted from three large web corpora dating from 2010, 2012 and 2013. Altogether, the datasets consist of almost 30 billion RDF quads. The most recent of the datasets contains amongst other data over 211 million product descriptions, 54 million reviews and 125 million postal addresses originating from thousands of websites. The availability of the datasets lays the foundation for further research on integrating and cleansing the data as well as for exploring its utility within different application contexts. As the dataset series covers four years, it can also be used to analyze the evolution of the adoption of the markup formats.

**Keywords:** Microdata, RDFa, Microformats, Dataset, Web Science.

## 1   Introduction

A large number of websites have started to use markup standards to annotate information about products, reviews, blog posts, people, organizations, events, and cooking recipes within their HTML pages. The most prevalent of these standards are Microformats,[1] which use style definitions to annotate HTML text with terms from a fixed set of vocabularies; RDFa [1], which is used to embed any kind of RDF data into HTML pages, and Microdata [7], a recent format developed in the context of HTML5.

The embedded data is crawled together with the HTML pages by search engines such as Google, Yahoo!, Yandex, and Bing, which use the data to enrich search results and to display entity descriptions within their applications [6,3]. Since 2011, those four search engine companies have been collaborating on the

---

[1] http://microformats.org/

P. Mika et al. (Eds.) ISWC 2014, Part I, LNCS 8796, pp. 277–292, 2014.

*Schema.org* initiative,[2] which offers a single vocabulary for describing entities that is understood by applications from all four companies [5]. So far, only the big search engine companies had access to large quantities of Microdata, RDFa, and Microformats data as they were the only ones possessing large web crawls. However, the situation has changed with the advent of the *Common Crawl Foundation*.[3] Common Crawl is a non-profit foundation that crawls the Web and regularly publishes the resulting web corpora for public usage.

We have extracted all Microdata, RDFa, and Microformats data from the Common Crawl corpora gathered in 2010, 2012 and 2013 and provide the extracted data for public download. Table 1 gives an overview of the Common Crawl corpora as well as the overall quantity of the extracted data. The second and third column show the number of HTML pages and pay-level domains (PLDs) covered by the different crawls. The forth and fifth column contain the percentages of all pages and PLDs that use at least one of the three markup formats. Column six shows the overall number of RDF quads that we have extracted from each corpus, while column seven contains the compressed size of the resulting datasets. The 2013 Common Crawl corpus, for instance, consists of 2.2 billion HTML pages originating from over 12 million PLDs. 26.33% of these pages and 13.87% of the PLDs use at least one markup format, resulting in an extracted dataset containing 17 billion RDF quads.

**Table 1.** Overview of the Common Crawl corpora and the overall quantity of the extracted data

| Dataset | Crawl Size | | Extracted Data | | | |
|---|---|---|---|---|---|---|
| | # HTML Pages | # PLDs | % HTML Pages | % PLDs | # RDF Quads | Compressed Size |
| 2010 | 2 565 741 671 | - | 5.76% | - | 5 193 767 058 | 332 GB |
| 2012 | 3 005 629 093 | 40 600 000 | 12.29% | 5.63% | 7 350 953 995 | 101 GB |
| 2013 | 2 224 829 946 | 12 831 509 | 26.33% | 13.87% | 17 241 313 916 | 40 GB |

This paper is structured as follows: first, we give an overview of the Common Crawl initiative and the web corpora that it provides to the public. Afterwards, we explain the methodology that was used to extract the data from the corpora and describe the data format that we use to offer the data for public download. In order to give an impression of the content of the extracted data, we discuss the distribution of the different markup formats within the 2013 dataset in Section 5. Afterwards, we analyze the topical domains as well as the richness of the annotations in Section 6 for RDFa, Section 7 for Microdata, and Section 8 for Microformats. In [2], we have presented a similar analysis of the 2012 dataset. In order to illustrate the evolution of the adoption of the different formats, we compare our findings from the 2012 and 2013 datasets wherever this reveals interesting trends. Section 9 discusses related work, while Section 10 concludes the paper by discussing the challenges that need to be addressed for using the data within applications.

---

[2] http://schema.org
[3] http://commoncrawl.org

## 2    The Common Crawl

Our dataset series was extracted from three web corpora published by the Common Crawl Foundation. The first corpus contains pages that have been crawled between 2009 and 2010. The second corpus was gathered in the first half of 2012. The crawler that was used to gather both corpora employed a breath-first selection strategy and was seeded with a large number of URLs from former crawls. The seed URLs were ordered according to their PageRank. Since the end of 2012 the Common Crawl Foundation releases two crawls per year. Each crawl consists of around two billion pages. For the recent crawls the foundation uses seed lists provided by the search engine company blekko.[4] The new seed lists should improve the quality of the crawl by avoiding "webspam, porn and the influence of excessive SEO" [8]. In addition to using an external seed list, the Common Crawl Foundation has also shifted their crawling infrastructure to a modified version of Apache Nutch to gather the pages contained in the seed list instead of using their own crawling framework.[5] All Common Crawl corpora are provided as (W)ARC files[6] and are available as free download from Amazon S3.[7]

## 3    Methodology

In order to extract RDFa, Microdata, and Microformats data from the corpora, we developed a parsing framework which can be executed on Amazon EC2[8] and supports parallel processing of multiple (W)ARC files. The framework relies on the *Anything To Triples* parser library (Any23)[9] to extract Microdata, RDFa, and Microformats data from the corpora. For processing the Common Crawl corpora on Amazon EC2 we used 100 AWS EC2 *c1.xlarge* machines. Altogether, extracting the HTML-embedded data from the 2013 corpus required a total machine rental fee of US\$ 263.06 using Amazon spot instances.[10]

We used Apache Pig[11] running on Amazon Elastic MapReduce to calculate most of the statistics presented in this paper as well as to generate the vector representation used for the co-occurrence analysis.[12] As the three crawls cover different HTML pages and as the number of crawled pages per PLD differs

---

[4] http://blekko.com/
[5] The code which was used for the crawl can be downloaded at
https://github.com/Aloisius and the original distribution of Nutch at
https://nutch.apache.org/
[6] The WARC file format is proposed by the Internet Archive foundation as successor to the ARC file format – http://archive-access.sourceforge.net/warc/.
[7] http://aws.amazon.com/datasets/41740
[8] http://aws.amazon.com/de/ec2/
[9] http://any23.apache.org/
[10] Additional information about the extraction framework can be found at
http://webdatacommons.org/framework
[11] http://pig.apache.org/
[12] All used scripts can also be downloaded from the websites of the Web Data Commons project.

widely, we aggregate the data by PLD, especially for analyzing the deployment of the different markup languages and comparing the deployment between the different datasets. To determine the PLD of each page, we use the Public Suffix List.[13] Hence, a PLD not always equals a second-level domain, but country-specific domains such as "co.uk" or mass hosting domains like *blogspot.com* are considered as top-level domains in our analysis.

## 4    Dataset Format and Download

The extracted data is represented as RDF quads (encoded as N-Quads[14]), with the forth element being used to represent the provenance of each triple. This means in addition to subject, predicate, and object, each quad includes the URL of the HTML page from which it was extracted. The extracted data is provided for download in the various sub-datasets. Each sub-dataset includes the information extracted for one markup language from one crawl, e.g. all quads representing information embedded in web pages from the 2013 crawl using Microdata form a sub-dataset. All datasets are provided for public download on the Web Data Commons website.[15] In addition to the datasets, the website also provides detailed background data for the analysis presented in this paper, such as the lists of all websites using specific formats or vocabulary terms.

## 5    Distribution by Format

Table 2 gives an overview of the distribution of the different markup formats within the 2013 dataset. For each format, the table contains the number of PLDs and the number of URLs using the format. For Microformats, the numbers are reported separately for each sub-format. Column 5 and 6 contain the number of quads and the compressed file size of the extracted datasets. The largest number of quads, namely 8.7 billion, were generated from Microdata annotations, followed by the Microformat hcard with 4.9 billion and RDFa with over 2.6 billion quads. Regarding the number of websites annotating information using the different markup languages, we find 995 thousand websites using hcard, followed by 471 thousand using RDFa and 463 thousand using Microdata.

In order to give an impression about the number of entities that are described in the data as well as the richness of the entity descriptions, we group all quads that have the same subject URI into a *record*. Column four of Table 2 contains the overall number of records contained in each dataset. We see, for instance, that the Microdata dataset describes 1.9 billion entities. Each entity description (record) consists of an average of 4.48 quads.

---

[13] http://publicsuffix.org/list/
[14] http://sw.deri.org/2008/07/n-quads/
[15] http://webdatacommons.org/structureddata/

**Table 2.** Number of websites (PLDs) and webpages (URLs) containing RDFa, Microdata, and Microformats annotations, as well as number of records and quads within the 2013 dataset

|  | # PLDs | # URLs | # Records | # Quads | File Size |
|---|---|---|---|---|---|
| RDFa | 471 406 | 296 005 115 | 436 100 210 | 2 636 964 693 | 66 GB |
| Microdata | 463 539 | 276 348 609 | 1 964 777 851 | 8 795 074 538 | 189 GB |
| Microformats (geo) | 23 044 | 14 436 467 | 56 611 312 | 222 780 517 | 4 GB |
| Microformats (hcalendar) | 20 981 | 3 683 002 | 41 683 362 | 212 675 776 | 2 GB |
| Microformats (hcard) | 995 258 | 113 402 968 | 1 643 288 889 | 4 884 918 863 | 60 GB |
| Microformats (hlisting) | 2 854 | 528 387 | 19 204 882 | 65 494 465 | 890 MB |
| Microformats (hrecipe) | 3 539 | 814 793 | 7 094 914 | 34 062 142 | 890 MB |
| Microformats (hresume) | 262 | 52 675 | 81 924 | 231 573 | 4 MB |
| Microformats (hreview) | 12 880 | 3 504 643 | 33 027 023 | 145 692 102 | 4 GB |
| Microformats (species) | 109 | 22 419 | 121 200 | 373 033 | 6 MB |
| Microformats (xfn) | 195 663 | 18 467 168 | 62 571 191 | 243 046 214 | 2 GB |

# 6  RDFa Data

The 2013 RDFa dataset includes data from over 471 thousand websites, which are 26% of all websites containing structured data in the crawl. The largest amount of RDF statements was extracted from *tripadvisor.com* with 78 million quads, followed by *yahoo.com* with over 28 million quads and *hotels.com* with more than 17 million quads.

**Class/Property Frequency Distribution:** The corpus contains over 646 thousand different classes and over 27 thousand different RDFa properties. Figure 1(a) shows the class and property distribution using a log-scale for the y-axis, which reports the number of websites making use of a class or property. The x-axis draws the classes and properties ordered descending by the number of websites using them. Similar to our observations for the 2012 dataset [2], both distributions are long-tailed and only a small number of classes and properties are used by a large number of websites. Altogether, we find 949 classes and 2 069 properties that are used by at least two different websites. The majority of the terms are only used by a single website. Manually inspecting some of these terms reveals a large number of typos in spelling terms from more widely used vocabularies. On the other hand, there exists also a large number of proprietary vocabularies which are used only by a single website.

**Frequent Classes:** Table 3 lists the most frequently used RDFa classes ordered by the number of websites deploying them. The table also includes the total number of records of each class included in the 2013 dataset. For comparison, we also state the total as well as the percental number of websites deploying the classes in 2012.[16] Table 3 shows that the *Facebook* ecosystem has a strong presence in the most frequently used classes, i.e. nine out of 30 classes belong to the Open Graph Protocol (OGP). Although the total number of websites using

---

[16] The namespaces of the classes are abbreviated with the corresponding prefix from the `http://prefix.cc/list`. Classes with an *og*-namespace prefix belong to the OGP and are within the HTML pages not maintained with a namespace, but as literals instead.

the classes *og:"article"* and *og:"website"* is smaller in the 2013 dataset than in the 2012 dataset, the percental usage is higher. This is due to the smaller number of PLDs covered in the 2013 crawl (see Table 1). Looking at the total number of records of each class (column 3 in Table 3), we see that the dataset contains 13 million *og:"product"* records, 15 million *gd:Organization* records, as well as 22 million *sioc:UserAccount* records.

**Table 3.** Most frequently used RDFa classes within the 2013 dataset sorted by the number of websites (PLDs) using the class, including the total number of records in 2013 as well as the number of websites using the class in 2012

| | | 2013 | | | 2012 | | |
|---|---|---|---|---|---|---|---|
| | | Records | PLDs | | Records | PLDs | |
| | Class | # (in k) | # | % | # (in k) | # | % |
| 1 | og:"article" | 82 882 535 | 167 544 | 40.14 | 35 438 354 | 183 046 | 35.24 |
| 2 | og:"website" | 24 951 292 | 71 590 | 17.15 | 9 197 072 | 56 573 | 10.89 |
| 3 | foaf:Image | 143 179 835 | 46 505 | 11.14 | 12 618 426 | 44 644 | 8.60 |
| 4 | foaf:Document | 31 601 886 | 45 542 | 10.91 | 3 709 728 | 49 252 | 9.48 |
| 5 | gd:Breadcrumb | 53 156 451 | 39 561 | 9.48 | 52 521 380 | 9 054 | 1.74 |
| 6 | og:"blog" | 6 364 724 | 29 629 | 7.10 | 2 365 037 | 58 971 | 11.35 |
| 7 | sioc:Item | 30 863 230 | 29 521 | 7.07 | 3 325 019 | 33 141 | 6.38 |
| 8 | og:"product" | 13 199 034 | 13 813 | 3.31 | 7 517 484 | 19 107 | 3.68 |
| 9 | sioc:UserAccount | 22 195 639 | 12 632 | 3.03 | 2 067 204 | 19 331 | 3.72 |
| 10 | skos:Concept | 24 011 250 | 11 873 | 2.84 | 5 197 930 | 13 477 | 2.59 |
| 11 | gd:Review-aggregate | 16 626 171 | 5 266 | 1.26 | 7 419 398 | 6 236 | 1.20 |
| 12 | sioc:Post | 26 571 378 | 4 958 | 1.19 | 1 079 844 | 6 994 | 1.35 |
| 13 | gd:Rating | 979 322 | 3 603 | 0.86 | 1 567 226 | 4 139 | 0.80 |
| 14 | og:"company" | 1 834 688 | 3 105 | 0.74 | 2 483 995 | 6 758 | 1.30 |
| 15 | sioctypes:BlogPost | 653 322 | 2 703 | 0.65 | 159 553 | 3 936 | 0.76 |
| 16 | sioctypes:Comment | 25 831 008 | 2 639 | 0.63 | 903 696 | 3 339 | 0.64 |
| 17 | vcard:Address | 55 425 | 2 225 | 0.53 | 746 673 | 3 167 | 0.61 |
| 18 | gr:Offering | 498 333 | 2 199 | 0.53 | 371 864 | 1 342 | 0.26 |
| 19 | gr:BusinessEnttiy | 394 556 | 2 155 | 0.52 | 119 394 | 3 155 | 0.61 |
| 20 | og:"activity" | 1 049 085 | 2 037 | 0.49 | 913 007 | 3 303 | 0.64 |
| 21 | gr:UnitPriceSpecification | 429 409 | 1 681 | 0.40 | 450 220 | 1 562 | 0.30 |
| 22 | gr:SomeItems | 235 785 | 1 429 | 0.34 | 148 689 | 670 | 0.13 |
| 23 | og:"profile" | 940 016 | 1 276 | 0.31 | 573 848 | 394 | 0.08 |
| 24 | gd:Organization | 15 693 269 | 1 232 | 0.30 | 7 324 570 | 2 502 | 0.48 |
| 25 | gd:Review | 1 415 844 | 1 221 | 0.29 | 1 085 | 1 321 | 0.25 |
| 26 | og:"band" | 106 524 | 1 168 | 0.28 | 468 385 | 1 988 | 0.38 |
| 27 | og:"game" | 679 546 | 1 123 | 0.27 | 936 482 | 1 336 | 0.26 |
| 28 | gr:TypeAndQuantityNode | 187 865 | 1 121 | 0.27 | 122 137 | 530 | 0.10 |
| 29 | gr:QuantitativeValue | 192 560 | 1 032 | 0.25 | 282 325 | 1 077 | 0.21 |
| 30 | foaf:Person | 1 338 823 | 851 | 0.20 | 128 475 | 1 209 | 0.23 |

**Facebook Data:** In the following we will have a brief look at the OGP data and state properties included in the dataset for the OGP classes. The OGP is developed and promoted by *Facebook* in order to enable the integration of external content into the social networking platform. In contrast to other RDFa vocabularies, OGP allows the usage of literals instead of URIs to identify classes. Table 4 shows the properties that are most frequently used together with the top five OGP classes. Similar to our findings for the 2012 dataset [2], the top 15 most frequently used properties are rather generic, whereas there is a small shift in the usage of namespaces as the *ogm* namespace is used more frequently.

**Table 4.** Absolute and relative number of quads of the top properties co-occurring with all five of the most frequently used OGP classes, ordered by usage frequency with og: "article"

| Property | og: "article" # | % | og: "website" # | % | og: "blog" # | % | og: "product" # | % | og: "company" # | % |
|---|---|---|---|---|---|---|---|---|---|---|
| ogo:type | 116 898 | 69.77 | 32 034 | 44.75 | 15 534 | 52.43 | 9 909 | 71.74 | 1 096 | 35.30 |
| ogo:title | 115 867 | 69.16 | 31 737 | 44.33 | 15 024 | 50.71 | 9 845 | 71.27 | 985 | 31.72 |
| ogo:url | 115 508 | 68.94 | 31 416 | 43.88 | 15 224 | 51.38 | 9 662 | 69.95 | 965 | 31.08 |
| ogo:site_name | 109 888 | 65.59 | 27 088 | 37.84 | 15 365 | 51.86 | 9 709 | 70.29 | 963 | 31.01 |
| ogo:image | 92 874 | 55.43 | 23 567 | 32.92 | 9 716 | 32.79 | 9 793 | 70.90 | 921 | 29.66 |
| ogo:description | 80 209 | 47.87 | 25 258 | 35.28 | 10 931 | 36.89 | 9 157 | 66.29 | 729 | 23.49 |
| ogm:type | 49 631 | 29.62 | 39 347 | 54.96 | 14 122 | 47.66 | 3 785 | 27.40 | 2 017 | 64.96 |
| ogm:title | 49 152 | 29.34 | 38 292 | 53.49 | 13 982 | 47.19 | 3 697 | 26.76 | 1 978 | 63.70 |
| ogm:url | 48 769 | 29.11 | 37 784 | 52.78 | 13 931 | 47.02 | 3 578 | 25.90 | 1 904 | 61.32 |
| ogm:site_name | 46 865 | 27.97 | 31 234 | 43.63 | 13 880 | 46.85 | 3 241 | 23.46 | 1 847 | 59.49 |
| ogm:description | 42 068 | 25.11 | 28 499 | 39.81 | 11 501 | 38.82 | 3 020 | 21.86 | 1 667 | 53.70 |
| ogm:image | 36 923 | 22.04 | 26 300 | 36.74 | 9 983 | 33.69 | 3 540 | 25.63 | 1 863 | 60.00 |
| fb_2008:fbmlapp_id | 27 865 | 16.63 | 11 550 | 16.13 | 10 769 | 36.35 | 2 275 | 16.47 | 812 | 26.16 |
| ogo:locale | 24 200 | 14.44 | 14 809 | 20.69 | 4 731 | 15.97 | 126 | 0.91 | 103 | 3.32 |
| fb_2008:fbmladmins | 22 773 | 13.59 | 11 097 | 15.50 | 10 076 | 34.01 | 2 796 | 20.24 | 1 351 | 43.52 |

# 7 Microdata

The 2013 Microdata dataset contains data from over 463 thousand different websites, which are 26% of all websites containing structured data. Compared to the 6.1% of all websites using Microdata in 2012 [2], the adoption has grown by more than factor four in just one year. The largest amounts of Microdata statements were extracted from *citysearch.com* with 797 million quads, *ebay.com* with 153 million quads and *hp.com* with 65 million quads.

**Class/Property Frequency Distribution:** The dataset contains over 15 thousand different classes and over 170 thousand different properties that are used by Microdata annotations. Figure 1(b) shows the class and property distribution using a log-scale in the same manner as Figure 1(a). Altogether, the Microdata dataset contains 1 200 classes and 12 506 properties that are used by at least two different websites. Similar to the observations made for the RDFa deployment, classes and properties in the long tail include large numbers of typos as well as website-specific terms.

**Frequent Classes:** Table 5 shows the most frequently used Microdata classes ordered by the number of PLDs deploying them. The second column shows the absolute number of records of each class. The most popular classes belong to the topical domains product data (Product, Offer, Review, Rating), blogs (Article, Blog, BlogPosting), navigational information (Breadcrumb), people (Person), organizations (LocalBusiness, Organization) and addresses (PostalAddress, Address). Due to the growing adoption of Microdata, we discuss some of the major topical domains of the data in more detail in the following.

**Postal Addresses:** The dataset contains 124 million *schema:PostalAddress* records originating from over 52 thousand websites. On average each address is described by 3.96 property values. Table 6(a) shows that more than 90% of the

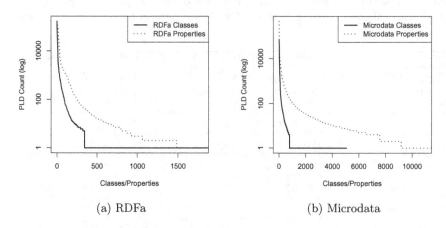

(a) RDFa                                    (b) Microdata

**Fig. 1.** Class and Property distribution by PLD count within the 2013 dataset

records contain the properties *schema:addressLocality* and *schema:addressRegion*. Table 7(a) shows the top ten websites ordered by number of address records that we have extracted from the sites.

**Local Business:** The dataset contains over 76 million records of type *schema: LocalBusiness* coming from 35 403 websites. On average *schema:LocalBusiness* records contain 5.22 properties. As shown in Table 6(b), over 80% of all records contain four out of the top five properties. This means, that for a large proportion of records we can expect information about the address of the business, the name, as well as the URL. When comparing the websites using the *schema:LocalBusiness* class (cf. Table 7(b)) with the ones using the class *schema: PostalAddress* we see *citysearch.com* at the first position in both lists. The website is a local business search engine, providing information about companies within different cities. A remarkable observation for local businesses is that more than 6% of the records contain several values for the property "name".

**Product Data:** The 2013 dataset contains 202 million product records originating from almost 71 thousand different websites. This makes product data the second largest topical domain in the dataset. Table 7(c) shows the top ten PLDs offering product data ordered by the number of records. Product descriptions are markup with two different classes: *schema:Product* (80%) and *dv:Product* (20%). On average each product is described by 4.56 properties. Table 6(c) shows that the properties "name", "offers", and "image" are provided for almost 50% of all product records. Only around 17% of the records contain a "description" property. Only 15% of all records use of the property "productId" which might help to identify product records from different websites that refer to the same product. Petrovski *et al.* [12] have examined the content of product name properties of electronic products. Their analysis shows that there is quite some variation in the names that are used by different websites to refer to the same product and that many e-shops include different product features for marketing reasons

**Table 5.** Most frequently used Microdata classes within the 2013 dataset, sorted by the number of websites using the class, including the total number of records in 2013 as well as the number of websites using the class in 2012

| | Class | 2013 Records # (in k) | PLDs # | % | 2012 Records # (in k) | PLDs # | % |
|---|---|---|---|---|---|---|---|
| 1 | schema:WebPage | 33 806 314 | 69 712 | 15.04 | 5 927 825 | 6 678 | 4.76 |
| 2 | schema:Article | 53 456 896 | 65 930 | 14.22 | 5 012 240 | 15 718 | 11.20 |
| 3 | schema:Blog | 2 281 401 | 64 709 | 13.96 | 1 421 909 | 2 084 | 1.49 |
| 4 | schema:Product | 178 334 394 | 56 388 | 12.16 | 19 386 194 | 16 612 | 11.84 |
| 5 | schema:PostalAddress | 125 780 525 | 52 446 | 11.31 | 9 513 985 | 19 592 | 13.96 |
| 6 | dv:Breadcrumb | 223 814 124 | 44 187 | 9.53 | 75 537 788 | 21 729 | 15.49 |
| 7 | schema:AggregateRating | 47 467 552 | 36 823 | 7.94 | 4 446 934 | 7 029 | 5.01 |
| 8 | schema:Offer | 154 407 699 | 35 635 | 7.69 | 13 725 226 | 8 456 | 6.03 |
| 9 | schema:LocalBusiness | 76 317 387 | 35 264 | 7.61 | 7 467 891 | 16 383 | 11.68 |
| 10 | schema:BlogPosting | 5 505 020 | 32 056 | 6.92 | 12 143 573 | 25 235 | 17.98 |
| 11 | schema:Organization | 91 321 833 | 24 255 | 5.23 | 3 060 174 | 7 011 | 5.00 |
| 12 | schema:Person | 143 648 178 | 21 107 | 4.55 | 5 912 833 | 5 237 | 3.73 |
| 13 | schema:ImageObject | 32 712 837 | 16 084 | 3.47 | 5 404 | 283 | 0.20 |
| 14 | dv:Product | 19 990 466 | 13 844 | 2.99 | 6 235 638 | 6 770 | 4.82 |
| 15 | schema:Review | 35 213 270 | 13 137 | 2.83 | 3 114 092 | 2 585 | 1.84 |
| 16 | dv:Review-aggregate | 5 462 245 | 13 075 | 2.82 | 2 994 221 | 8 517 | 6.07 |
| 17 | dv:Organization | 4 951 153 | 9 582 | 2.07 | 2 311 548 | 5 853 | 4.17 |
| 18 | dv:Offer | 7 722 086 | 9 298 | 2.01 | 4 201 002 | 1 957 | 1.39 |
| 19 | dv:Address | 1 629 193 | 8 866 | 1.91 | 1 277 451 | 5 559 | 3.96 |
| 20 | dv:Rating | 5 878 816 | 8 360 | 1.80 | 2 063 366 | 1 532 | 1.09 |
| 21 | schema:Event | 10 551 937 | 8 258 | 1.78 | 1 018 398 | 4 102 | 2.92 |
| 22 | schema:Place | 38 519 652 | 7 653 | 1.65 | 1 819 200 | 4 131 | 2.94 |
| 23 | dv:Review | 1 868 702 | 6 432 | 1.39 | 1 019 152 | 2 816 | 2.01 |
| 24 | schema:Recipe | 1 523 363 | 6 019 | 1.30 | 379 433 | 718 | 0.51 |
| 25 | schema:GeoCoordinates | 72 961 757 | 5 888 | 1.27 | 1 045 302 | 4 677 | 3.33 |
| 26 | schema:ProfilePage | 116 065 | 4 833 | 1.04 | 86 572 | 30 | 0.02 |
| 27 | schema:AutoDealer | 49 706 | 4 563 | 0.98 | 31 615 | 280 | 0.20 |
| 28 | schema:VideoObject | 7 124 628 | 4 530 | 0.98 | 31 452 643 | 764 | 0.54 |
| 29 | dv:Person | 23 386 913 | 3 993 | 0.86 | 2 609 898 | 5 237 | 3.73 |
| 30 | schema:Thing | 1 214 435 | 3 724 | 0.80 | 141 641 | 587 | 0.42 |

into the product names. Both findings illustrate the difficulties that an application will need to face that tries to build an integrated product catalog based on Microdata product records. Petrovski *et al.* approach this problem by first extracting product features from the product names and descriptions and then using these features for identity resolution, reaching an F1-measure of 82% [12].

**Job Postings:** As a result of a collaboration with the United States Office of Science and Technology Policy, *schema.org* started to provide vocabulary terms for describing job postings in the end of 2011 [4]. Our dataset contains 21 million records of class *schema:JobPosting* originating from over two thousand websites. *schema:JobPosting* records contain, on average, 5.93 properties and the class *schema:JobPosting* thus belongs to the classes with the highest average number of properties used. Table 6(d) shows the most frequent properties of *schema:JobPosting* records. 1% of the records contain more than one "name" property value. Table 7(d) shows the top ten PLDs by record count providing data for job postings.[17]

---
[17] A complete list of websites that embed Microdata can be found at
http://www.webdatacommons.org/structureddata/2013-11/stats/
stats.html#html-microdata

**Table 6.** Most frequently used properties for selected classes. For space reasons, the *schema*-namespace prefix is shortened to *s* and class names are shortened according the respective heading.

(a) PostalAdress (PA) Records

| Property | Records # (in k) | % |
|---|---|---|
| s:PA/addressLocality | 122 008 | 98.07 |
| s:PA/addressRegion | 114 072 | 91.69 |
| s:PA/streetAddress | 81 719 | 65.69 |
| s:PA/postalCode | 25 447 | 20.45 |
| s:PA/addressCountry | 11 010 | 8.85 |
| s:PA/telephone | 2 790 | 2.21 |
| s:PA/url | 1 422 | 1.13 |
| s:PA/AddressLocality | 1 262 | 1.00 |
| s:PA/AddressRegion | 1 248 | 0.99 |
| s:PA/name | 615 | 0.49 |

(b) LocalBusiness (LB) Records

| Property | Records # (in k) | % |
|---|---|---|
| s:LB/name | 80 832 | 106.13 |
| s:LB/address | 70 427 | 92.47 |
| s:LB/url | 64 139 | 84.21 |
| s:LB/geo | 63 450 | 83.31 |
| s:LB/telephone | 9 165 | 12.03 |
| s:LB/description | 8 310 | 10.89 |
| s:LB/image | 8 115 | 10.63 |
| s:LB/aggregateRating | 4 320 | 5.66 |
| s:LB/review | 3 807 | 4.99 |
| s:LB/openingHours | 1 957 | 2.56 |

(c) Product (P) Records

| Property | Records # (in k) | % |
|---|---|---|
| s:P/name | 115 326 | 57.07 |
| s:P/offers | 112 826 | 55.83 |
| s:P/image | 96 193 | 47.60 |
| s:P/url | 59 848 | 29.62 |
| s:P/description | 34 334 | 16.99 |
| s:P/productID | 30 820 | 15.11 |
| s:P/aggregateRating | 24 832 | 12.17 |
| s:P/image | 24 082 | 11.81 |
| s:P/brand | 23 077 | 11.31 |
| s:P/sku | 14 637 | 7.18 |

(d) JobPosting (JP) Records

| Property | Records # (in k) | % |
|---|---|---|
| s:JP/title | 21 548 | 101.77 |
| s:JP/hiringOrganization | 20 539 | 97.01 |
| s:JP/jobLocation | 19 101 | 90.22 |
| s:JP/description | 14 877 | 70.27 |
| s:JP/url | 8 633 | 40.77 |
| s:JP/name | 8 283 | 39.12 |
| s:JP/datePosted | 5 578 | 26.35 |
| s:JP/image | 2 782 | 13.14 |
| s:JP/skills | 1 298 | 6.13 |
| s:JP/address | 606 | 2.86 |

## 7.1 New Microdata Adopters

In the following, we will analyze the websites that newly adopted Microdata in 2013. We use the list of websites extracted by Meusel *et al.* [9] from the 2012 crawl and calculate the overlap with the crawled websites in 2013. We then identify every website which is included in the 2012 and 2013 crawl and has adopted RDFa, Microdata, or Microformats in 2013 but did not adopt it in 2012. This results in a list of 490 778 websites out of which 169 134 make use of Microdata.

Table 8 gives an overview of the classes that are used by at least 1% of new adopters. Again, classes of the *Schema.org* vocabulary dominate, however despite its deprecation in 2011 the *data-vocabulary* vocabulary is still being used by the new adopters in 2013. Similar to the overall distribution of Microdata classes, websites newly adopting Microdata cover a broad range of different topics with a slight focus on product related data.

As an example, we calculated a co-occurrence matrix for classes and properties on websites newly adopting *schema:Product* and compare the co-occurring properties with the analysis of all *schema:Product* websites from the 2013 and 2012 datasets. Table 9 shows the top 20 most co-occurring properties on websites newly adopting Microdata. The table also shows in column six and eight the difference between the new adopters and the complete datasets from 2013 and 2012. Product records appearing on websites newly adopting Microdata are more likely described by the top six properties than in the overall dataset of

**Table 7.** Top ten PLDs ordered by number of Microdata records

(a) PostalAdress Records

| Website | Records # (in k) | % |
|---|---|---|
| citysearch.com | 61 623 | 49.53 |
| peoplefinders.com | 19 089 | 15.34 |
| stubhub.com | 4 921 | 3.96 |
| seatgeek.com | 4 205 | 3.38 |
| viagogo.com | 2 760 | 2.22 |
| apartmentguide.com | 2 299 | 1.85 |
| monster.com | 2 257 | 1.81 |
| avvo.com | 1 534 | 1.23 |
| zillow.com | 1 453 | 1.17 |
| radaris.com | 1 248 | 1.00 |

(b) LocalBusiness Records

| Website | Records # (in k) | % |
|---|---|---|
| citysearch.com | 64 297 | 84.42 |
| yell.com | 3 429 | 4.50 |
| bbb.org | 857 | 1.13 |
| partypop.com | 682 | 0.90 |
| justia.com | 343 | 0.45 |
| vcahospitals.com | 281 | 0.37 |
| leisurepro.com | 218 | 0.29 |
| travelpod.com | 215 | 0.28 |
| vacationroost.com | 196 | 0.26 |
| nakedapartments.com | 183 | 0.24 |

(c) Product Records

| Website | Records # (in k) | % |
|---|---|---|
| ebay.com | 18 362 | 9.09 |
| fotolia.com | 16 319 | 8.08 |
| aliexpress.com | 9 747 | 4.82 |
| ebay.co.uk | 8 600 | 4.26 |
| competitivecyclist.com | 5 549 | 2.75 |
| swatch.com | 5 199 | 2.57 |
| ebay.ca | 5 141 | 2.54 |
| crateandbarrel.com | 4 303 | 2.13 |
| hp.com | 4 018 | 1.99 |
| bentgate.com | 3 776 | 1.87 |

(d) JobPosting Records

| Website | Records # (in k) | % |
|---|---|---|
| snagajob.com | 5 899 | 27.86 |
| indeed.com | 4 176 | 19.72 |
| startuphire.com | 2 704 | 12.77 |
| monster.com | 2 418 | 11.42 |
| simplyhired.com | 1 847 | 8.73 |
| glassdoor.com | 1 492 | 7.05 |
| itjobswatch.co.uk | 522 | 2.47 |
| spherion.com | 109 | 0.52 |
| glassdoor.ca | 91 | 0.43 |
| glassdoor.com.au | 91 | 0.43 |

2013 and 2012. Further, this subset includes less rating information, but the records are more likely to contain information about the *manufacturer* and the *itemConditions*.

# 8 Microformats Data

Microformats are used on approximately 1.1 million websites within the 2013 crawl. This makes Microformats the most widely adapted markup format being used by over 62.7% of all sites using any markup languages.

**Frequent Classes:** Table 10 gives an overview of the most frequently used Microformats classes. The third column shows the absolute number of records of a certain class in the 2013 dataset. Column four shows the absolute number of PLDs from which the records originate. The last two columns show the percentage of PLDs making use of a certain Microformats classes in the 2013 and 2012 datasets. The most popular Microformat class is *hcard:VCard*. The dataset includes over 787 million records of this class originating from almost one million different sites. The second most frequent used class is *hCard:Organization*. The 2013 dataset contains over 126 million records of this class. Both classes belong to the *hCard* vocabulary. The second most frequently used Microformats vocabulary is *geo* with 75 million records of type *geo:Location* spread over 23 thousand sites. Besides the over 37 million *hCalendar:Vevents* records and 19 million *hReview:Review* records, the dataset also offers over one million recipes originating

**Table 8.** Microdata classes used by at least 1% of websites which newly annotate data using Microdata in 2013, ordered by the number of websites using them

| | Class | PLDs # | % | | Class | PLDs # | % |
|---|---|---|---|---|---|---|---|
| 1 | s:Product | 28 198 | 16.67 | 15 | dv:Offer | 4 512 | 2.67 |
| 2 | s:WebPage | 27 672 | 16.36 | 16 | s:Review | 4 498 | 2.66 |
| 3 | s:Article | 23 908 | 14.14 | 17 | http:/schema.orgStore | 4 213 | 2.49 |
| 4 | s:PostalAddress | 22 731 | 13.44 | 18 | dv:Organization | 4 086 | 2.42 |
| 5 | s:Offer | 19 185 | 11.34 | 19 | s:Event | 3 969 | 2.35 |
| 6 | dv:Breadcrumb | 16 972 | 10.03 | 20 | dv:Address | 3 596 | 2.13 |
| 7 | s:LocalBusiness | 14 515 | 8.58 | 21 | s:Place | 3 417 | 2.02 |
| 8 | s:AggregateRating | 14 140 | 8.36 | 22 | dv:Rating | 2 770 | 1.64 |
| 9 | s:Organization | 11 123 | 6.58 | 23 | s:ImageObject | 2 690 | 1.59 |
| 10 | s:Blog | 9 780 | 5.78 | 24 | s:Rating | 2 503 | 1.48 |
| 11 | s:Person | 7 350 | 4.35 | 25 | s:GeoCoordinates | 2 387 | 1.41 |
| 12 | s:BlogPosting | 7 083 | 4.19 | 26 | s:VideoObject | 1 865 | 1.10 |
| 13 | dv:Product | 6 548 | 3.87 | 27 | dv:Review | 1 685 | 1.00 |
| 14 | dv:Review-aggregate | 4 782 | 2.83 | | | | |

from 3 530 different sites. The top PLDs from which the data originates are *epicurious.com, grouprecipes.com* and *chefkoch.de.* Comparing the percentage of PLDs using Microformats annotations between the 2012 and 2013 datasets, the deployment of Microformats does not grow significantly but appears stable.

## 9   Related Work

In this section we review other public Microdata, RDFa, and Microformats datasets and refer to related work analyzing the deployment of these standards.

The only other public large-scale source of Microdata, RDFa, and Microformats data – that we are aware of – is the Sindice search engine.[18] Sindice collects data from the Web and allows the data to be searched using keyword as well as SPARQL queries. The Sindice index includes not only data gathered from HTML pages but also data extracted from WebAPIs as well as data from the Linked Data Cloud. The data is mixed by Sindice within their index which makes it difficult to get a pure HTML-extracted dataset. Also note that Sindice only crawls HTML pages from websites that offer a site map. According to the latest Sindice statistics from September 2013, their corpus contains 3.36 million different classes for which they could find at least six records within their data sources.[19] The index includes around 700 million records of class *hCard:VCard*, 68 million records of class *hCard:Organization*, 28 million records of class *og:article* and over 10 million records of class *schema:Product.* Unfortunately, according to recent Sindice blog posts, there are no plans to keep the SPARQL endpoint alive as well as to update their large datasets.[20] As Sindice is restricted to websites offering sitemaps, it does not cover as many websites as our datasets. On the other hand, Sindice covers websites in a more complete

---

[18] http://sindice.com
[19] http://sindice.com/stats/direct/basic-class-stats
[20] https://groups.google.com/forum/#!topic/sindice-dev/ASzK-hKzNFA

**Table 9.** Top properties that are used to describe *schema:Product* records on websites newly annotating data using Microdata in 2013, all websites from 2013 and all websites from 2012 as well as the difference between the new websites and the all websites of 2012 and 2013. Outstanding differences are marked in bold.

| | Property | New PLDs # | % | PLDs'13 % | Change in % | PLDs'12 % | Change in % |
|---|---|---|---|---|---|---|---|
| 1 | s:Product/name | 25 679 | 91.07 | 89.62 | 1.62 | 86.34 | 5.48 |
| 2 | s:Product/description | 19 977 | 70.85 | 67.45 | 5.03 | 61.99 | 14.29 |
| 3 | s:Product/image | 19 037 | 67.51 | 61.93 | **9.02** | 48.72 | **38.58** |
| 4 | s:Product/offers | 18 179 | 64.47 | 58.68 | **9.86** | 45.42 | **41.94** |
| 5 | s:Offer/price | 16 829 | 59.68 | 54.55 | **9.41** | 41.50 | **43.81** |
| 6 | s:Offer/availability | 11 977 | 42.47 | 37.40 | **13.58** | 10.29 | **312.63** |
| 7 | s:AggregateRating | 7 809 | 27.69 | 30.25 | −8.45 | 25.93 | 6.79 |
| 8 | s:Product/aggregateRating | 7 664 | 27.18 | 29.26 | −7.12 | 11.87 | **128.96** |
| 9 | s:AggregateRating/ratingValue | 7 469 | 26.49 | 28.95 | −8.50 | 24.02 | 10.28 |
| 10 | s:Offer/priceCurrency | 6 934 | 24.59 | 24.28 | 1.29 | 9.63 | **155.31** |
| 11 | s:Product/url | 5 897 | 20.91 | 21.17 | −1.20 | 12.90 | 62.11 |
| 12 | s:Product/manufacturer | 5 671 | 20.11 | 14.85 | **35.44** | 1.98 | **915.47** |
| 13 | s:AggregateRating/reviewCount | 5 662 | 20.08 | 20.94 | −4.11 | 8.06 | **149.11** |
| 14 | s:Product/productID | 3 983 | 14.13 | 13.11 | 7.76 | 10.52 | 34.24 |
| 15 | s:AggregateRating/bestRating | 3 089 | 10.95 | 13.87 | −21.01 | 16.10 | −31.97 |
| 16 | s:Product/brand | 2 959 | 10.49 | 10.43 | 0.65 | 11.94 | −12.09 |
| 17 | s:Offer/itemCondition | 2 659 | 9.43 | 6.86 | **37.43** | 2.16 | **337.56** |
| 18 | s:AggregateRating/ratingCount | 2 651 | 9.40 | 12.37 | −24.01 | 16.21 | −41.99 |
| 19 | dv:Breadcrumb/url | 2 131 | 7.56 | 7.73 | −2.26 | 10.64 | −28.99 |
| 20 | dv:Breadcrumb/title | 2 124 | 7.53 | 7.67 | −1.82 | 10.63 | −29.15 |

fashion compared to our datasets which can only contain data from HTML pages included in the Common Crawl.

The big search engine companies Google, Yahoo!, Microsoft and Yandex extract Microdata, RDFa, and Microformats data from their Web crawls but, for economic reasons, do not provide public access to the resulting datasets. Although they have published a number of studies about the deployment of the markup languages: Mika and Potter analyze the adoption of the languages based on Web crawls from the Bing search engine dating from 2011 and 2012 [10,11]. Guha presented an updated analysis of the deployment of Microdata with a special focus on the *Schema.org* vocabulary at the LDOW 2014 workshop [5].

# 10   Conclusion

This paper has presented a series of publicly accessible Microdata, RDFa, Microformats datasets that we have extracted from three large Web corpora dating from 2010, 2012 and 2013. The extracted datasets show that all three markup standards are used by hundreds of thousands of websites. Comparing the 2012 and 2013 datasets reveals that the number of websites using Microdata has grown by more than factor four in just one year. Altogether, the extracted datasets consist of almost 30 billion RDF quads and contain large quantities of product, review, address, blog post, people, organization, event, and cooking recipe data. As far as we know, the WebDataCommons datasets are the largest publicly accessible datasets of this kind.

We believe that the data will be useful for various applications such as building product catalogs, address databases or event and cooking websites. The data also

**Table 10.** Most frequently used Microformats classes within the 2013 dataset sorted by the number of websites using the class, including the total number of records in 2013 as well as the number of websites using the class in 2012

| | | 2013 | | | 2012 | | |
| | | Records | PLDs | | Records | PLDs | |
| | Class | # (in k) | # | % | # (in k) | # | % |
|---|---|---|---|---|---|---|---|
| 1 | hCard:VCard | 787 859 | 994 829 | 89.14 | 525 300 858 | 1 511 467 | 84.03 |
| 2 | hCard:Organization | 126 356 | 119 049 | 10.67 | 62 880 238 | 195 493 | 10.87 |
| 3 | geo:Location | 75 945 | 23 044 | 2.06 | 13 206 248 | 48 415 | 2.69 |
| 4 | hCalendar:vcalendar | 4 173 | 20 981 | 1.88 | 3 883 524 | 37 620 | 2.09 |
| 5 | hCalendar:Vevent | 37 989 | 17 633 | 1.58 | 28 737 655 | 36 349 | 2.02 |
| 6 | hReview:Review | 19 734 | 12 880 | 1.15 | 27 781 420 | 20 781 | 1.16 |
| 7 | hRecipe:Recipe | 1 009 | 3 530 | 0.32 | 1 260 116 | 3 281 | 0.22 |
| 8 | hListing:Lister | 9 016 | 2 584 | 0.23 | 9 992 047 | 4 030 | 0.22 |
| 9 | hListing:Listing | 9 016 | 2 584 | 0.23 | 9 992 047 | 4 030 | 0.18 |
| 10 | hRecipe:Ingredient | 6 825 | 2 524 | 0.23 | 8 405 151 | 2 658 | 0.16 |
| 11 | hListing:Item | 1 656 | 1 793 | 0.16 | 5 236 418 | 2 957 | 0.15 |
| 12 | hRecipe:Duration | 344 | 1 044 | 0.09 | 341 601 | 1 323 | 0.07 |
| 13 | hRecipe:Nutrition | 399 | 446 | 0.04 | 1 688 412 | 818 | 0.05 |
| 14 | species:species | 37 | 109 | 0.01 | 82 610 | 91 | 0.01 |
| 15 | species:Genus | 21 | 74 | 0.01 | 40 589 | 61 | 0.00 |
| 16 | species:Family | 20 | 72 | 0.01 | 40 651 | 60 | 0.00 |
| 17 | species:Kingdom | 19 | 72 | 0.01 | 40 833 | 59 | 0.00 |
| 18 | species:Order | 20 | 70 | 0.01 | 40 462 | 59 | 0.00 |

constitutes a valuable source of evaluation data for testing methods from various research areas. For evaluation purposes, the amount of data contained in the datasets should be large and representative enough. For commercial purposes, it has to be kept in mind that the Common Crawl only contains a subset of the pages from each website. Thus, the extracted datasets can also only contain a subset of the Microdata, RDFa, Microformats annotations offered by each website and should thus rather be used to identity seeds for more complete directed crawls. Before Microdata, RDFa, Microformats data can be used in application settings, several challenges need to be addressed:

**Information Extraction:** Most entities are only marked up with a relatively small number of properties and these properties tend to be rather generic, such as name or description properties, leading to rather flat records. It is thus often necessary to apply further information extraction methods to the property values in order to reach more fine grained data structures that allow the application of more sophisticated data integration and cleansing methods [12].

**Identity Resolution:** The data hardly contains entity identifiers, such as ISBN EAN numbers, which would make it easy to identity records from different websites that described the same entity. Instead, applications that want to deduplicate data from multiple websites need to match the entity descriptions published by the sites. An example of how such an identity resolution heuristic is applied to Microdata product records is given in [12].

**Data Quality Assessment:** As the Web is an open and unrestricted information environment, web data might be outdated or simply wrong. Thus, before data is used in an application context its quality should be assessed based on its content as well as its provenance. An interesting identity resolution and data quality assessment challenge is for instance given by the Microdata address data: Which of the provided addresses is the current address of a company? How to determine this address given that many yellow pages websites copy from each other and simple voting thus does not work?

We believe that the adoption of the Microdata, RDFa, Microformats standards by hundreds of thousands of websites provides a huge potential for using Web data within various applications. On the other hand, it also raises tough challenges concerning the integration and cleansing of the data. By providing the WebDataCommons dataset series, we hope to contribute to addressing these challenges and to lift the potential of the data.

**Acknowledgement.** The extraction of the datasets from the Common Crawl was in part supported by the FP7-ICT projects PlanetData (GA 247641), and LOD2 (GA 257943) and by an Amazon Web Services in Education Grant award. We would like to thank the Common Crawl foundation for publishing the web crawls. We also thank the Any23 team for their great parsing framework as well as Hannes Mühleisen for his initial work on the Web Data Commons extraction framework.

# References

1. Ben Adida and Mark Birbeck. RDFa primer - bridging the human and data webs - W3C recommendation (2008), http://www.w3.org/TR/xhtml-rdfa-primer/
2. Bizer, C., Eckert, K., Meusel, R., Mühleisen, H., Schuhmacher, M., Völker, J.: Deployment of rdfa, microdata, and microformats on the web a quantitative analysis. In: Alani, H., et al. (eds.) ISWC 2013, Part II. LNCS, vol. 8219, pp. 17–32. Springer, Heidelberg (2013)
3. Goel, K., Guha, R.V., Hansson, O.: Introducing rich snippets (2009), http://googlewebmastercentral.blogspot.de/2009/05/introducing-rich-snippets.html
4. Guha, R.V.: Schema.org support for job postings (2011), http://blog.schema.org/2011/11/schemaorg-support-for-job-postings.html
5. Guha, R.V.: Schema.org update (April 2014), http://events.linkeddata.org/ldow2014/slides/ldow2014_keynote_guha_schema_org.pdf
6. Haas, K., Mika, P., Tarjan, P., Blanco, R.: Enhanced results for web search. In: Proceedings of the 34th International ACM SIGIR Conference on Research and Development in Information Retrieval, SIGIR 2011, pp. 725–734. ACM, New York (2011)
7. Hickson, I.: HTML Microdata, Working Draft (2011), http://www.w3.org/TR/microdata/
8. Lindahl, G.: Blekko donates search data to common crawl (December 2012), http://blog.blekko.com/2012/12/17/common-crawl-donation/
9. Meusel, R., Vigna, S., Lehmberg, O., Bizer, C.: Graph structure in the web - revisited: a trick of the heavy tail. In: Proceedings of the Companion Publication of the 23rd International Conference on World Wide Web Companion, International World Wide Web Conferences Steering, pp. 427–432 (2014)

10. Mika, P.: Microformats and RDFa deployment across the Web (2011),
    http://tripletalk.wordpress.com/2011/01/25/
    rdfa-deployment-across-the-web/
11. Mika, P., Potter, T.: Metadata statistics for a large web corpus. In: LDOW 2012:
    Linked Data on the Web, CEUR Workshop Proceedings, vol. 937, CEUR-ws.org
    (2012)
12. Petrovski, P., Bryl, V., Bizer, C.: Integrating product data from websites offer-
    ing microdata markup. In: 4th Workshop on Data Extraction and Object Search,
    DEOS 2014 (2014)

# On Publishing Chinese Linked Open Schema

Haofen Wang[1], Tianxing Wu[2], Guilin Qi[2], and Tong Ruan[1]

[1] East China University of Science and Technology, Shanghai, 200237, China
{whfcarter,ruantong}@ecust.edu.cn
[2] Southeast University, China
{wutianxing,gqi}@seu.edu.cn

**Abstract.** Linking Open Data (LOD) is the largest community effort
for semantic data publishing which converts the Web from a Web of
document to a Web of interlinked knowledge. While the state of the art
LOD contains billion of triples describing millions of entities, it has only
a limited number of schema information and is lack of schema-level axioms. To close the gap between the lightweight LOD and the expressive
ontologies, we contribute to the complementary part of the LOD, that is,
Linking Open Schema (LOS). In this paper, we introduce Zhishi.schema,
the first effort to publish Chinese linked open schema. We collect navigational categories as well as dynamic tags from more than 50 various most
popular social Web sites in China. We then propose a two-stage method
to capture equivalence, subsumption and relate relationships between
the collected categories and tags, which results in an integrated concept
taxonomy and a large semantic network. Experimental results show the
high quality of Zhishi.schema. Compared with category systems of DB-
pedia, Yago, BabelNet, and Freebase, Zhishi.schema has wide coverage
of categories and contains the largest number of subsumptions between
categories. When substituting Zhishi.schema for the original category
system of Zhishi.me, we not only filter out incorrect category subsumptions but also add more finer-grained categories.

**Keywords:** Linking Open Data, Linking Open Schema, Integrated
Category Taxonomy, Large Semantic Network.

## 1 Introduction

With the development of Semantic Web, a growing amount of structured (RDF)
data has been published on the Web. Linked Data [3] initiates the effort to
connect distributed data across the Web. Linking Open Data (LOD)[1] is the
largest community for semantic data publishing and interlinking. It converts the
Web from a Web of document to a Web of knowledge. There have been over 200
datasets within the LOD project. Among these datasets, DBpedia [4], Yago [9],
and Freebase [5] serve as hubs to connect others. More recently, Zhishi.me [11]
has been developed as the first effort of Chinese LOD. It extracted RDF triples
from three largest Chinese encyclopedia Web sites, namely Baidu Baike, Hudong

---

[1] http://linkeddata.org/

P. Mika et al. (Eds.) ISWC 2014, Part I, LNCS 8796, pp. 293–308, 2014.

Baike, and Chinese Wikipedia. It also creates `owl:sameAs` links between two resources from different sources if these resources refer to the same entity.

While LOD contains billions of triples describing millions of entities, the number of schemas in LOD is limited. Yago defines explicit schema to describe concept subsumptions as well as domains and ranges of properties. Freebase has a very shallow taxonomy with domains and types. If we consider the schemas having labels in Chinese, the number is even smaller. Moreover, the qualities of schemas within these datasets are not always satisfactory. The DBpedia community creates the DBpedia Ontology project[2] which lets users define mapping rules to generate high-quality schema from ill-defined raw RDF data.

On the other hand, there exist some works to publish schema-level knowledge. Schema.org[3] provides a shared collection of schemas that webmasters can use to markup HTML pages in ways recognized by major search providers. However, it is manually created and does not have a Chinese version. BabelNet [10] is a multilingual encyclopedic dictionary, with lexicographic and encyclopedic coverage of terms in 50 languages. It is also a semantic network which connects concepts and named entities, made up of more than 9 million entries. Probase [12] is a universal probabilistic taxonomy which contains 2.7 million concepts harnessed automatically from a corpus of 1.68 billion Web pages. While it is the largest taxonomy, the usage of Probase is restricted in Microsoft. Meanwhile, the development of social media provides us a chance to create schema-level knowledge from folksonomies. A recent survey paper [8] compares different approaches of discovering semantics of tags. The main focus of these approaches is to capture the hierarchical semantic structure of folksonomies.

In this paper, we contribute to Linking Open Schema (LOS). LOS aims at adding more expressive ontological axioms between concepts. Links in LOS are created between concepts from different sources and are not limited to equivalence relations. More precisely, we introduce Zhishi.schema, the first effort to publish Chinese linked open schema. We collect navigational categories as well as dynamic tags from more than 50 most popular social Web sites in China. We then propose a two-stage method to capture equivalence, subsumption and relate relationships between the collected categories and tags. Compared with approaches to build a taxonomy from the tag space, Zhishi.schema additionally extracts `equal` and `relate` relations to form a large semantic network. Different from Probase, we publish Zhishi.schema as open data for public access. BabelNet is the closest work to ours. But it collects data from a small number of sources including WordNet, Open Multilingual WordNet, Wikipedia, OmegaWiki, Wiktionary, and Wikidata while Zhishi.schema extracts semantic relations between categories from a large number of popular Chinese social Web sites.

The rest of the paper is organized as follows. Section 2 gives an overview of our approach. Section 3 describes the technical details. Section 4 shows the experimental results of Zhishi.schema in terms of data size, quality, and coverage.

---

[2] http://wiki.dbpedia.org/Ontology
[3] https://schema.org/

Section 5 introduces Web access to Zhishi.schema and finally we conclude the paper in Section 6.

## 2 Overview

In this section, we start with a brief introduction of the problem, then list several challenges, and finally provide the overall process.

### 2.1 Problem Definition

**Input:** Given a set of Chinese social media Web sites $WS = \{ws_1, ws_2, \ldots, ws_n\}$, for each Web site $ws$, it might contain a set of categories $C_{ws} = \{c_1, c_2, \ldots, c_n\}$ as well as a set of tags $T_{ws} = \{t_1, t_2, \ldots, t_m\}$. These categories are organized in a hierarchical way. In a *category hierarchy*, a category might be associated with zero or several parent categories as well as child categories. We call $c_i$ a *static category* as it is relatively stable and predefined by the Web site. The tags are organized in a flat manner. We call $t_j$ a *dynamic category* because it is created on the fly by Web users. In fact, a tag can be treated as a single node category with no parents or children.

**Output:** We aim at building a Chinese linked open schema called *Zhishi.schema* composed of categories from the input Web sites. Zhishi.schema contains three types of semantic relations, namely `relate`, `subclassOf`, and `equal`. More precisely, two categories (no matter static or dynamic) are related if their meanings are close. One category is a subclass of another if and only if the former is a child of the latter. Two categories are equal if and only if they refer to the same meaning. The `relate` relation is the weakest semantic relation among the three types. All these semantic relations are asymmetric just like `owl:sameAs` in LOD. That is to say, $c_1$ `sr` $c_2$ is not identical to $c_2$ `sr` $c_1$ where $c_1, c_2$ are two categories, and `sr` $\in \{$relate, subclassOf, equal$\}$. The `subclassOf` relations form an integrated concept taxonomy while the other two kinds of semantic relations build a large semantic network.

### 2.2 Challenges

As categories come from various sources, extracting semantic relations between categories is not a trivial task. In particular, we have the following challenges.

- *Incorrect hierarchy of static categories.* A category and its parents from the hierarchy of a Web site might dissatisfy the `subclassOf` relation. For instance, "Athlete" is defined as a parent category of "Athlete Type". Clearly, it indicates an incorrect subsumption relation. Therefore, the quality cannot be ensured if we directly treat the existing hierarchy of static categories as a part of the local site schema without any refinement.

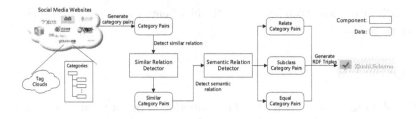

**Fig. 1.** The Workflow of Our Approach

- *Ambiguity of categories in different contexts.* If the label of a category refers to more than one meaning, the category becomes ambiguous. In another word, we cannot distinguish two categories sharing the common label if contexts are not taken into account. For example, "Apple" can be a kind of fruit or the Apple company. We cannot determine its exact meaning until it has a parent category labeled by "IT company". So it is quite important to consider context information when revealing the meaning of a category.
- *Lack of representation for categories* Unlike documents, categories do not have plenty of textual information to describe them. When detecting semantic relations between categories, current text mining techniques cannot be directly applied until we find a way to enrich the representation of categories.

### 2.3 Workflow

We now provide a workflow to explain the whole process and its components. As shown in Figure 1, we have two main components, namely *Similar Relation Detector (SimRD)* and *Semantic Relation Detector (SemRD)*.

The input of Similar Relation Detector is category pairs generated from different Web sites. *SimRD* tries to filter out dissimilar pairs and feeds similar category pairs as the input of Semantic Relation Detector. Then *SemRD* identifies the semantic relation type (i.e. `relate`, `subclassOf`, or `equal`) of each similar category pair. These semantic relations are converted into RDF triples for building Zhishi.schema. Our approach is a two-stage method. In the first stage, we design "cheap" features to represent each category and use lightweight learning algorithms to find out similar pairs. This leads to a significant reduction of the number of category pairs and a much cleaner input for the second stage. We then represent categories with more sophisticated features and treat semantic relation detection as a multi-class classification problem to solve. The details of *SimRD* and *SemRD* will be introduced in the next section.

## 3 Approach

### 3.1 Similar Relation Detection

**Category Representation.** The simplest way to represent a category $c$ is using its category label $l(c)$. However, it is insufficient if the labels of two categories do not have any overlapped words or share very few words. For example, "NYC" and "New York City" are synonyms, but their labels are totally different.

Inspired by Explicit Semantic Analysis (ESA) [7], we map a category into several concepts in a knowledge base, and then use these concepts to represent the category. The benefits are three-folds. First, the category representation is enriched from its label into a set of concepts. Second, the dimension of concepts is usually much lower than that of text features so that we avoid curse of dimensionality and enable efficient processing. Third, the concepts are higher-quality than texts with less ambiguities.

Here, Baidu Zhidao[4], the largest Chinese community QA site, is chosen to serve as the knowledge base. When submitting $l(c)$ as a keyword to Baidu Zhidao, we collect first 10 pages containing relevant questions. From these questions, their associated categories are obtained. These categories form the related concept set of $c$, denoted as $\text{RCS}(c) = \{rc_1, rc_2, \ldots, rc_n\}$ where $rc_i$ is the $i$-th related concept. We can further use them to define the related concept vector $\text{RCV}(c)$ in form of $< rc_1(c), rc_2(c), \ldots, rc_n(c) >$ where $rc_i(c)$ stands for the occurrence of the related concept $rc_i$. The occurrence is the number of questions belonging to $rc_i$. It reflects the importance or popularity of $rc_i$. These two representations can help discover similar category pairs if two categories share a large portion of related concepts but vary a lot on their labels.

The key to the success of ESA lies on the coverage of the knowledge base and the quality of concept mapping. We tried every category from a collection of Web sites (see Section 4.1 for details), only 1.2% categories do not have any related concepts. Then we use Baidu Zhidao's own categories to test the mapping quality. For 14 root categories, 10 are the most occurred related concepts of themselves, and 4 are ranked second. For all categories (2118 in all), more than half are ranked in top three. Only 17% (366 categories) do not contain themselves in their related concept vectors. The above two tests show Baidu Baike has a wide coverage to return related concepts for most categories, and therefore suitable to be a knowledge base for concept mapping.

The label representation $l(c)$ and two variants of the related concept representation (i.e. $\text{RCS}(c)$ and $\text{RCV}(c)$) are called *local representations* of $c$. Besides, static categories are organized in a hierarchical way. Thus, a category $c$ might have ancestors and descendants which can be treated as *neighbors* of the category. If we aggregate related concepts of these neighbors to $\text{RCS}(c)$ and $\text{RCV}(c)$, we get *enriched representations* of $c$, denoted as $\text{RCS}^+(c)$ and $\text{RCV}^+(c)$ respectively. $\text{RCS}^+(c)$ only adds related concepts of $c$'s neighbors which are not related concepts of $c$. $\text{RCV}^+(c)$ not only counts the occurrence of the newly added related concepts, but also increases the occurrences of existing ones if they are related concepts of some neighbor of $c$. Compared with the local representations, the enriched ones further capture context information to represent the category, and thus can help disambiguate its meaning.

---

[4] http://zhidao.baidu.com/

**Category Similarity Measures.** We apply some widely-used similarity measures to the above category representations.

- *Similarity based on category label.* This measure is actually string matching based on longest common substring (LCS)[5]. The similarity between categories $c_1$ and $c_2$ is defined as:

$$\text{CLsim}(c_1, c_2) = \frac{\text{LCS}(l(c_1), l(c_2))}{|l(c_1)|} \qquad (1)$$

  Where $|l(c)|$ is the string length of $c$'s label, and $\text{LCS}(l(c_1), l(c_2))$ is the longest common substring between $l(c_1)$ and $l(c_2)$.
- *Similarity based on related concept set.* This measure is actually the Jaccard similarity[6] between two sets. The similarity is defined as follows.

$$\text{RCSsim}(c_1, c_2) = \frac{|\text{RCS}(c_1) \cap \text{RCS}(c_2)|}{|\text{RCS}(c_1)|} \qquad (2)$$

- *Similarity based on related concept vector.* This measure is based on cosine similarity[7] between two vectors, which is defined as:

$$\text{RCVsim}(c_1, c_2) = \frac{\sum_{rc \in \text{RCS}(c_1) \cap \text{RCS}(c_2)} rc(c_1) \cdot rc(c_2)}{\sum_{rc \in \text{RCS}(c_1)} rc(c_1)^2} \qquad (3)$$

While the label-based string measure captures the linguistic similarity between two categories, the related concept based measures capture structural similarities between these categories. Thus, we consider all these three similarity measures to estimate the relatedness of a category pair. We treat these similarity measures as features and apply a machine learning algorithm to predicting whether the two categories are similar or not.

$$P_{sim}(c_1, c_2) = m(\text{CLsim}(c_1, c_2), \text{RCSsim}(c_1, c_2), \text{RCVsim}(c_1, c_2)) \qquad (4)$$

Where $m$ stands for some learning model and $P_{sim}(c_1, c_2)$ is the prediction probability. If $P_{sim}(c_1, c_2)$ is greater than a threshold, the two categories are considered to be similar. Analogously, we define $\text{RCSsim}^+(c_1, c_2)$ and $\text{RCVsim}^+(c_1, c_2)$ when the enriched representations are used. $P_{sim}^+(c_1, c_2)$ is further defined when $\text{RCSsim}^+(c_1, c_2)$, $\text{RCVsim}^+(c_1, c_2)$, and $\text{CLsim}(c_1, c_2)$ are used as features.

In fact, similar relation detection is a binary classification problem. We choose three most popular classification models for $m$. They are J48 Decision Tree, Logistic Regression, and Multi-Layer Perceptron. For all the three models, we use the implementations in Weka[8] with default parameter values to perform experiments. For $P_{sim}^+(c_1, c_2)$, we need to decide which neighbors should be used

---

[5] http://en.wikipedia.org/wiki/Longest_common_substring_problem
[6] http://en.wikipedia.org/wiki/Jaccard_similarity
[7] http://en.wikipedia.org/wiki/Cosine_similarity
[8] http://sourceforge.net/projects/weka/

for the enriched representations of $c_1$ and $c_2$. Here, we only consider the parents and children of a category in some hierarchy as its neighbors. This is because high-level ancestors and low-level descendants cannot represent the context of a category in a discriminative way. Also, the average depth of a category hierarchy is usually of a small value (See Table 1 in Section 4 for details). Moreover, some improper categories are placed as the parents or children of a category in some hierarchy for the purpose of Web site navigation only. To reduce the noise, we filter out neighbors if the probabilities of being similar with the category are low. More details and more experimental results will be discussed in Section 4.2.

## 3.2   Semantic Relation Detection

**Textual Context Based Category Representation.** Semantic relations are finer-grained similar relations. The above mentioned category representations are insufficient especially for tags to detect semantic relations. Thus, we leverage contextual words co-occurred with a category $c$ frequently to represent the category. We call it the *textual context representation* of $c$, denoted as $\mathrm{TC}(c)$.

A category $c$ might be associated with several pages in a Web site. We could use the contents of these pages for $\mathrm{TC}(c)$. However, the numbers of pages associated with different categories vary a lot. Moreover, pages from different sites differ in terms of content length and wording styles. For example, a tweet is much shorter than a news page and contains more informal language expressions.

Instead, we use text snippets returned by a search engine to represent a category. More precisely, we submit $l(c)$ as a keyword to the largest Chinese search engine Baidu[9] and return a list of relevant Web pages in form of snippets. Each snippet contains the page title, a small fraction of the page content with surrounding words of $l(c)$, and the link to the page. The snippets of top 20 search results are selected for further processing. After word segmentation and stopword removal, a set of terms are obtained to represent $c$ as a "virtual" document. In our implementation, we use Ansj[10] as the Chinese word segmenter with a widely used stopword list in Chinese. We further adopt TF-IDF (short for Term Frequency-Inverse Term Frequency) [1] for term weighting. As a result, $\mathrm{TC}(c)$ is a $n$-dimension vector $< w_1(c), w_2(c), \ldots, w_n(c) >$ where the weight of the $i$-th term $\mathrm{TC}(c)_i$ is $w_i(c)$ and $n$ is the number of all terms of all categories. If a term $w$ does not co-occur with $l(c)$, the corresponding value in $\mathrm{TC}(c)$ is zero.

**Category Similarity Measures.** We additionally define $\mathrm{TCsim}(c_1, c_2)$ to measure the *similarity based on textual context*:

$$\mathrm{TCsim}(c_1, c_2) = \frac{\sum\limits_{i=1}^{n} \mathrm{TC}(c_1)_i \cdot \mathrm{TC}(c_2)_i}{\sum\limits_{i=1}^{n} \mathrm{TC}(c_1)_i^2} \tag{5}$$

---

[9] http://www.baidu.com

[10] https://github.com/ansjsun/ansj_seg

We add this similarity measure as a new feature to a learning model for predicting the probability a certain kind of semantic relation holds. Since the prediction accuracy of $P^+_{sim}(c_1, c_2)$ is higher that that of $P_{sim}(c_1, c_2)$ for detecting similar relations no matter which learning model is used, we combine $TCsim(c_1, c_2)$ with $CLsim(c_1, c_2)$, $RCSsim^+(c_1, c_2)$, and $RCVsim^+(c_1, c_2)$ as follows.

$$P_{sem}(c_1, c_2) = m(CLsim(c_1, c_2), RCSsim^+(c_1, c_2), \\ RCVsim^+(c_1, c_2), TCsim(c_1, c_2)) \tag{6}$$

Semantic relation detection is treated as a three-class classification problem where class labels are "relate", "subclassOf", and "equal". We use Support Vector Machine (SVM) for $m$ with the Radial Basis Function (known as RBF) kernel implemented in Weka. In addition to the learning-based approach, we also propose a heuristic-based method as a baseline to detect semantic relations. For a similar category pair $(c_1, c_2)$, if $l(c_1)$ is the same as $l(c_2)$, we create an `equal` relation. If $l(c_1)$ is the suffix of $l(c_2)$, a `subclassOf` relation is generated to indicate $c_2$ is a child category of $c_1$. After applying these two heuristic rules, the remaining similar category pairs are considered to have `relate` relations.

## 4  Experiments

### 4.1  Data Statistics

We select 51 popular social media Web sites in China. The data was crawled in December, 2013. The detailed statistics of each site are shown in Table 1. From the table, we list the site name, its URL, the site type, the category number, the tag number, and the average depth of the category taxonomy. If some site does not contain any category or tag, we use / to indicate the value of that column is missing. Since the semantics of tags are less stable than those of static categories. We do not take all tags from these sites to build Zhishi.schema. Instead, we only selected popular tags during last December. In total, we collected 408,069 labels in which 328,288 are categories and 79,781 are tags.

### 4.2  Accuracy Evaluation

We first carry out experiments on small labeled datasets to determine the optimal combination of category representations and the learning algorithms. The trained model having the best performance is then used to detect semantic relations on the whole dataset. Finally, an evaluation theme is introduced along with quality assessment results on Zhishi.schema.

**Training on Small Labeled Datasets.** Classification is supervised learning, which requires labeled data for training. The classification performance depends on whether the labeled data is adequate and whether training data and test data have the similar distributions. In order to ease the burden of manual labeling and

**Table 1.** Statistics for 51 Popular Social Media Web Sites in China

| Site | URL | Type | #Category | #Tag | Avg Depth |
|---|---|---|---|---|---|
| 360 Mobile Phone Assistant | http://sj.360.cn/ | App Market | 49 | / | 1.69 |
| 91 Mobile Phone Assistant | http://zs.91.com/ | App Market | 76 | / | 1.55 |
| Amazon | http://www.amazon.cn/ | E-commerce | 3,311 | / | 3.65 |
| Android Market | http://apk.hiapk.com/ | App Market | 279 | / | 2.56 |
| Apple App Store | http://www.apple.com/cn/ | App Markets | 90 | / | 1.69 |
| Baidu Baike | http://baike.baidu.com/ | Wiki | 10,445 | / | 2.67 |
| Baidu Tieba | http://tieba.baidu.com/ | BBS | 214 | / | 1.57 |
| Baidu Wenku | http://wenku.baidu.com/ | Document Sharing | 299 | / | 1.87 |
| Baidu Zhidao | http://zhidao.baidu.com/ | Q&A | 2,118 | / | 3.24 |
| BaiXing | http://www.baixing.com/ | Classified | 55,179 | / | 4.08 |
| DangDang | http://www.dangdang.com/ | E-commerce | 6,847 | / | 2.59 |
| DianDian | http://www.diandian.com/ | Light Blog | / | 14,294 | / |
| DingDing Map | http://www.ddmap.com/ | Customer Review | 34,142 | / | 2.64 |
| Docin | http://www.docin.com/ | Document Sharing | 734 | / | 1.60 |
| Douban | http://www.douban.com/ | Social Network | 13,172 | / | 4.04 |
| FanTong | http://www.fantong.com/ | Customer Review | 3,842 | / | 2.61 |
| XianGuo | http://xianguo.com/ | RSS | 38 | / | 1.62 |
| GanJi | http://www.ganji.com/ | Classified | 25,274 | / | 3.81 |
| Guang | http://guang.com/ | Social E-commerce | 299 | / | 2.61 |
| Hudong Baike | http://www.baike.com/ | Wiki | 23,995 | / | 5.49 |
| JiangNanQingYuan | http://www.88999.com/ | Dating | 153 | / | 2.02 |
| ShiJiJiaYuan | http://www.jiayuan.com/ | Dating | 82 | / | 1.83 |
| 360buy | http://www.jd.com/ | E-commerce | 31,140 | / | 3.59 |
| KaiXing | http://www.kaixin001.com/ | Social Network | 125 | / | 2.45 |
| Lvping | http://www.lvping.com/ | Online Travel | 4,0475 | / | 3.57 |
| MeiLiShuo | http://www.meilishuo.com/ | Social E-commerce | 316 | / | 2.57 |
| Mop | http://www.mop.com/ | BBS | 25 | / | 1.57 |
| PPS | http://www.pps.tv/ | Video Sharing | 814 | / | 1.67 |
| QieKe | http://www.qieke.com/ | LBS | 6,224 | / | 3.51 |
| QiongYou | http://www.qyer.com/ | Online Travel | 107 | 7,400 | 1.68 |
| RenHe | http://www.renhe.cn/ | Business Social Network | 250 | / | 2.55 |
| RenRen | http://www.renren.com/ | Social Network | 119 | / | 1.98 |
| RenRen Game | http://wan.renren.com/ | Social Gaming | 43 | / | 1.70 |
| RenRen XiaoZhan | http://zhan.renren.com/ | Light Blog | / | 7,038 | / |
| RuoLin | http://www.wealink.com/ | Business Social Network | 62 | / | 1.56 |
| Sina iAsk | http://iask.sina.com.cn/ | Q&A | 5,247 | / | 3.24 |
| Sina Blog | http://blog.sina.com.cn/ | Blog | 27 | 16,190 | 1.56 |
| Sina Game | http://games.sina.com.cn/ | Social Gaming | 54 | / | 1.67 |
| Sina GongXiang | http://ishare.sina.com.cn/ | Document Sharing | 234 | / | 1.57 |
| Sina Micro Blog | http://weibo.com/ | Microblogging | 184 | / | 2.66 |
| TaoBao | http://www.taobao.com/ | E-commerce | 1,845 | / | 3.34 |
| Tencent Blog | http://blog.qq.com/ | Blog | 24 | / | 1.65 |
| Tencent Micro Blog | http://t.qq.com/ | Microblogging | 16 | / | 1.00 |
| TianYa | http://www.tianya.cn/ | BBS | 1,769 | / | 3.18 |
| Tudou | http://www.tudou.com/ | Video Sharing | 755 | / | 1.64 |
| TuiTa | http://www.tuita.com/ | Light Blog | / | 5,122 | / |
| Netease Blog | http://blog.163.com/ | Blog | 20 | / | 1.60 |
| Netease Micro Blog | http://t.163.com/ | Microblogging | / | 29,737 | / |
| Netease Reader | http://yuedu.163.com/ | RSS | 46 | / | 1.83 |
| Chinese Wikipedia | http://zh.wikipedia.org/ | Wiki | 56,985 | / | 3.71 |
| Youku | http://www.youku.com/ | Video Sharing | 744 | / | 1.62 |

to avoid distribution bias, we propose an effective method to create labeled data. To detect similar category pairs, the training data has two labels: "similar" as positive and "dissimilar" as negative. A category pair $(c_1, c_2)$ is considered as a positive candidate if the arithmetic mean of $\mathrm{CLsim}(c_1, c_2)$, $\mathrm{RCSsim}(c_1, c_2)$, and $\mathrm{RCVsim}(c_1, c_2)$ is above 0.5. Otherwise, the category pair is possibly negative. We randomly select positive and negative candidates in a uniform way from all the collected Web sites for further user verification. To build a labeled dataset for semantic relation detection, we evenly sample similar category pairs from all these sites and apply the heuristic-based method to generate possible labels. These labels are manually verified and revised accordingly.

We apply 5-fold cross validation to train models in all experiments. Note that K-fold cross validation is widely used in statistics to overcome the over-fitting problem. *Precision, recall,* and *F-measure* are used for effectiveness study. Precision is the fraction of retrieved category pairs that are relevant while recall is the fraction of relevant category pairs that are retrieved. For similar relation

**Table 2.** Effectiveness Comparison between Local and Enriched Representations

| Method | Precision | | Recall | | F-Measure | |
|---|---|---|---|---|---|---|
| J48 Decision Tree | 0.777 | **0.80** | 0.754 | **0.882** | 0.765 | **0.839** |
| Logistic Regression | 0.767 | **0.778** | 0.736 | **0.864** | 0.751 | **0.819** |
| Multi-Layer Perceptron | 0.749 | **0.783** | 0.781 | **0.922** | 0.765 | **0.847** |

detection, similar category pairs are relevant. For semantic relation detection, a category pair having a certain type of semantic relation is relevant. The F-measure (also known as $F_1$ score) is the harmonic mean of precision and recall.

- *Evaluating similar relation detection.* The dataset contains 1,986 category pairs in which 398 pairs are labeled as "similar" and 1,588 pairs are labeled as "dissimilar". We list the precision, recall, and F-Measure of different learning models using local representations trained on the labeled dataset on the left side in Table 2. From the table, we can see that the Multi-Layer Perceptron model performs best. In the case of enriched representation, we remove neighbors of a category if the prediction probabilities of being similar with the category are below 0.1. The prediction probability is given by the best model using local representations (i.e., Multi-Layer Perceptron). After filtering, 76.14% static categories have one or more parents while only 10.18% have children. The right side of Table 2 shows the evaluation results of using enriched representations. All three learning models achieve significant improvements when enriched category representations are used. Still, Multi-Layer Perceptron has the best accuracy performance. Thus, this model is used to find similar category pairs in all Web sites.
- *Evaluating semantic relation detection.* The training data has 800 similar category pairs. Among them, 500 are labeled as "relate", 240 are labeled as "subclassOf", and 60 are labeled as "equal". We compare three approaches (i.e. heuristic-based, learning-based, and their combination) in our effectiveness study. The combined approach first accepts `equal` relations and `subclassOf` relations found by the heuristic rules. For the remaining similar category pairs, it uses the learning-based approach for classification. Table 3 shows the evaluation results of three approaches for all kinds of semantic relations. From the table, we can see that the heuristic-based method performs better than the learning-based one when dealing with `equal` and `subclassOf` relations. This is because the heuristic-based one uses "hard" rules, which achieves very high precisions. The learning-based approach gets more promising results for `relate` relation detection since the heuristic-based one simply treats all remaining category pairs as `relate`, which brings more false positive examples. The combined one outperforms both approaches.

**Accuracy of Three Semantic Relations in Zhishi.schema.** Zhishi.schema contains 1,560,725 `subclassOf` relations, 22,672 `equal` relations and 229,167 `relate` relations. Since there are no ground truths available, we have to verify these relations manually. Due to the large number of semantic relations, it is impossible to evaluate all of them by hand. Therefore, we design an evaluation

**Table 3.** Heuristic-based vs. Learning-based Approach

| Relation | Method | Precision | Recall | F-Measure |
|---|---|---|---|---|
| | Heuristic-based | 0.794 | 0.981 | 0.787 |
| relate | Learning-based | 0.861 | 0.938 | 0.898 |
| | **Combination** | **0.894** | **0.947** | **0.914** |
| | Heuristic-based | 0.927 | 0.543 | 0.685 |
| subclassOf | Learning-based | 0.695 | 0.489 | 0.574 |
| | **Combination** | **0.854** | **0.606** | **0.709** |
| | Heuristic-based | 0.958 | 0.857 | 0.905 |
| equal | Learning-based | 0.909 | 0.657 | 0.763 |
| | **Combination** | **0.912** | **0.939** | **0.925** |

theme including a *sampling* strategy and a *labeling* process. Sampling aims to extract a subset of relations (called *samples*) which can represent the distribution of the whole result set. Then we can perform manual labeling to evaluate the correctness of samples. The accuracy assessment on samples are used to approximate the correctness of Zhishi.schema.

*Sampling.* For a kind of semantic relation sr, we study the relation distribution w.r.t. Web sites. A relation is of the form $c_1$ sr $c_2$ where $c_1$ and $c_2$ are categories. If $c_1$ or $c_2$ comes from a Web site, the Web site is treated as a *source* of the relation. A relation can have at most two sources. After iterating all relations of the same type, we can get the number of sources along with the relations in each source. For each source, we randomly select $k$ relations. If $k$ is greater than the total number of relations in the source, we take all of them for evaluation.

*Labeling.* We use the similar labeling process as that used in Yago. Four students participant in the labeling process. We provide them three choices namely *agree, disagree* and *unknown* to label each sample. After they label all the samples, we can compute the average accuracy. Finally, the Wilson interval [6] at $\alpha$ = 5% is used to generalize our findings on the subset to the whole Zhishi.schema.

When applying the above evaluation theme, we get encouraging results.

- 50 Web sites contains equal relations. We randomly select 10 relations from each site and 487 samples are returned. After labeling, the average number of agree votes is 440, and the precision achieves 90.03% ± 2.63%.
- 45 sources have relate relations. We get 450 samples with $k = 10$. The average number of agree votes is 404, and the precision is 89.44% ± 2.80%.
- Compared with the flat structure of equal or relate relations, subclassOf relations form a hierarchical acyclic graph (*HAG*). The root depth is 1 and the maximal depth is 16. Since a category may have one or more parents, we can traverse to the category from the roots via different paths. These paths might have different lengths so that each category could exist at multiple depths of HAG. On average, the depth of each category is 3.479. In order for comprehensive evaluation, we need to cover every source at each depth of HAG. When sampling at a depth ranging from 2 to 16, $k$ is set to 5. As a result, we get 2,922 subclassOf relations for manual labeling. The average number of agree votes is 2,456, and the final precision is 84.01% ± 1.33%.

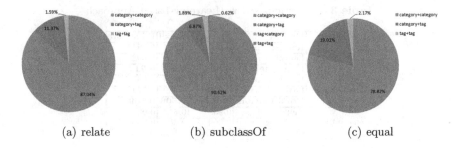

(a) relate                    (b) subclassOf                    (c) equal

**Fig. 2.** Category Pair Pattern Distribution in Three Types of Semantic Relations

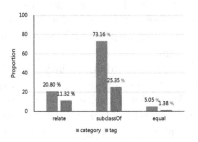

**Fig. 3.** Relation Proportions        **Fig. 4.** Subclass Distribution

## 4.3   Data Distribution of Zhishi.schema

Category pairs can be grouped into three patterns, namely `category+category`, `category+tag`, and `tag+tag`. For `subclassOf` relation, we divide `category+tag` into two sub-patterns. `tag+category` indicates a tag is a sub concept of a category while `category+tag` means a category is a sub concept of a tag. Figure 2 shows the category pair pattern distribution in all three types of semantic relations. From the figure, we can see `category+category` contributes to the largest proportion (more than 75%) of relations for any kind of semantic relation. In contract, less than 5 percent come from `tag+tag`. The huge gap can be explained by the semantic stability of categories and the ambiguity nature of tags.

As shown in Figure 3, 73.16% categories (25.35% tags) appear in `subclassOf` relations, 20.80% (11.32% respectively) contribute to `relate` relations, and 5.05% (1.38% respectively) for `equal` relations. The high proportion of `subclassOf` relations among categories (tags) enables Zhishi.schema to form a large concept taxonomy. The ratio of `equal` relations is pretty low because it is the most strict semantic relation and thus similar category pairs seldom satisfy such relation.

We also check the number of `subclassOf` relations already defined in some category hierarchies. As shown in Figure 4, the proportion of existing subsumptions is 16.52%. Another 23.63% `subclassOf` relations can be inferred from category hierarchies via intermediate paths. Notice that 59.85% new `subclassOf` relations are discovered, which shows the value of Zhishi.schema.

**Table 4.** Overlap between Zhishi.schema and Other Datasets

|  | Zhishi.schema | DBpedia | Yago | BabelNet | Freebase |
|---|---|---|---|---|---|
| Category Number | 408,069 | 142,139 | 49,407 | 619,226 | 2,035 |
| Overlap with Zhishi.schema | / | 82,586 | 24,036 | 23,193 | 567 |
| Subclass Number | **1,560,725** | 3 | 256,538 | 55,486 | 1,092 |
| Subclass Overlap with Zhishi.schema | / | 2 | 34,354 | 2,762 | 79 |

### 4.4    Comparison With Other Datasets

**Overlap of Categories and Subsumptions.** We compare Zhishi.schema with other well-known datasets namely DBpedia[11], Yago[12], BabelNet[13] and Freebase[14] in terms of categories and subclasses. Table 4 shows the category and subclass information of each dataset. It also lists the category overlap and subclass overlap between Zhishi.schema and the other datasets. As for the category number, Zhishi.schema is larger than DBpedia, Yago and Freebase. It also contains half of the categories from DBpedia and Yago. In BabelNet, a category corresponds to a synset. Since many synsets contain Chinese labels, BabelNet has the largest number of categories. Regarding subclassOf relations, Zhishi.schema has the largest number (six times larger than the second largest one – Yago). You may find that there are only 3 subclassOf relations in DBpedia. Ontological subsumptions are only defined in the DBpedia ontology while the ontology does not contain a Chinese version. So we leverage the multilingual nature of Wikipedia and finally get three subclassOf relations with both sides having the Chinese correspondences. When looking at the subclass overlap, we find only small overlaps between Zhishi.schema and the other datasets. Thus, combining Zhishi.schema with these datasets could form a larger linked open schema.

**Overlap of Equivalence Relations with BabelNet.** Zhishi.schema contains 22,672 equal relations where 4,380 of them represent the same meaning with different labels. BabelNet is the largest multilingual semantic network in the world. For each conept in BabelNet, it is organized in form of a synset in which there are synonyms representing the same concept in different labels or languages. Therefore, we would like to check how many extracted equal relations are covered by BabelNet. Here, we do not count a equal relation when categories in a pair have the same string. In this way, we get 1,270 equal relations covered by BabelNet. Due to the small overlaps of both subclassOf and equal relations, Zhishi.schema and BabelNet can complement with each other.

**Refining Zhishi.me Category System.** Since Zhishi.schema includes all three Chinese encyclopedia sites (used for Zhishi.me), the resulting concept taxonomy comprises categories and category subsumptions in these three sites. Hence, we can compare Zhishi.schema with Zhishi.me[15] to see how many

---

[11] http://dbpedia.org/About
[12] http://www.mpi-inf.mpg.de/yago-naga/yago/
[13] http://babelnet.org/
[14] https://www.freebase.com/
[15] http://zhishi.me/

incorrect `subclassOf` relations are filtered out and how many new `subclassOf` relations are discovered. We have developed two variants of Zhishi.schema: basic refined Zhishi.me category system (*Basic*) and enriched Zhishi.me category system (*Enriched*). Basic is obtained by collecting categories in Zhishi.me and `subclassOf` relations between these categories from Zhishi.schema. It only considers `subclassOf` relations in form of $c_1$ `subclassOf` $c_2$ where $c_1$ and $c_2$ belong to categories in Zhishi.me and $c_1$ is the direct child of $c_2$. Enriched further considers `subclassOf` relation paths with one or more intermediate categories from other sites in Zhishi.schema. The original Zhisih.me category system contains 251,160 `subclassOf` relations. Basic removes 211,386 `subclassOf` relations and adds 29,177 ones. Enriched additionally increases 69,776 `subclassOf` relations.

# 5    Web Access to Zhishi.schema

Besides the application of Zhishi.schema to refine the existing category system of Zhishi.me, we also provide online Web access for Zhishi.schema. Moreover, we allow users to download the data dump to build their own applications.

## 5.1    Linked Data

According to the Linked Data principles[16], Zhishi.schema creates URIs for all categories and provides sufficient information when someone looks up a URI by the HTTP protocol. Since Zhishi.schema contains categories from different sites, we design a URI pattern to indicate where a category comes from and whether it is static or dynamic. The pattern `http://zhishi.schema/[site]/[category type]/[label]` comprises of fours parts. `http://zhishi.schema/` is the namespace. The second part tells the provenance of the category. If it is a tag, the third part is `dynamic`. Otherwise, it is `static`. The last part is the category label.

When publishing Zhishi.schema, we follow the best practice recipes [2] and try to reuse existing RDF vocabularies which have clear semantics and are widely used. Particularly, we use `skos:related` for `relate` relations, `rdfs:subClassOf` for `subclassOf` relations, and `owl:equivalentClass` for `equal` relations. When Semantic Web agents that accept "application/rdf+xml" content type access our server, resource descriptions in the RDF format will be returned.

## 5.2    Lookup Service

We provide a lookup service for users to access Zhishi.schema. The service is available at `http://los.linkingopenschema.info/LookUp.jsp`. Given a query, all categories whose labels exactly match the query are returned. If two categories are `equal`, they are automatically merged as an integrated view for browsing.

If a user searches for "Water Purifier", as shown in Figure 5, we return a page integrating two equivalent categories from two e-commerce Web sites

---

[16] http://www.w3.org/DesignIssues/LinkedData.html

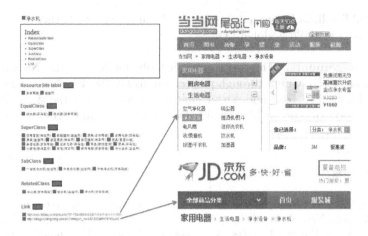

**Fig. 5.** An Example Page of Integrated Categories

(i.e. 360buy and DangDang). From the page, we can see provenances of two categories, other equivalent categories with different labels, their parent categories, child categories, related categories, and links to their original pages in Web sites. These information are organized in the `Resource Site Label,` `EqualClass,` `SuperClass,` `SubClass,` `RelatedClass` and `Link` sections respectively.

We can click on any parent category or child category to switch to another page view. Such an interaction stands for navigation in the integrated concept taxonomy of Zhishi.schema. A click on one related category or an equivalent category corresponds to traversal on the semantic network of Zhishi.schema.

### 5.3 SPARQL Endpoint

We also provide a SPARQL endpoint for querying Zhishi.Schema. Professional users can submit customized queries at `http://los.linkingopenschema.info/SPARQL.jsp`. We use AllegroGraph RDFStore[17] as the backend triple store.

## 6 Conclusions and Future Work

In this paper, we introduced Zhishi.schema, the first effort of publishing Chinese linked open schema. It contains an integrated concept taxonomy. It also comprises a large semantic network composed of `equal` relations and `relate` relations. Thus, Zhishi.schema can be a good start point to serve as the Chinese version of schema.org. Moreover, since Zhishi.schema reuses RDF and OWL vocabularies, it can be imported into any ontology editor for further refinement.

As for future work, we will apply our approach to social media Web sites in other languages especially in English. The resulting dataset can be further linked with Zhishi.schema to form a multilingual linked open schema. We also

---

[17] `http://www.franz.com/agraph/allegrograph/`

plan to publish links between categories in Zhishi.schema and other data sources in LOD so as to build a global LOS.

**Acknowledgements.** This work was partially funded by the National Science Foundation of China through project No: 61272378. We thank Jianhao Li, Shaowei Ling, Wen Rui, and Yishu Fang for helping label the data. We also thank Chengyuan Xue for his valuable feedback and detailed comments during the proofreading process.

# References

1. Baeza-Yates, R., Ribeiro-Neto, B., et al.: Modern information retrieval, vol. 463. ACM Press, New York (1999)
2. Berrueta, D., Phipps, J., Miles, A., Baker, T., Swick, R.: Best practice recipes for publishing rdf vocabularies. Working draft, W3C (2008)
3. Bizer, C., Heath, T., Berners-Lee, T.: Linked data-the story so far. International Journal on Semantic Web and Information Systems 5(3), 1–22 (2009)
4. Bizer, C., Lehmann, J., Kobilarov, G., Auer, S., Becker, C., Cyganiak, R., Hellmann, S.: Dbpedia-a crystallization point for the web of data. Web Semantics: Science, Services and Agents on the World Wide Web 7(3), 154–165 (2009)
5. Bollacker, K., Evans, C., Paritosh, P., Sturge, T., Taylor, J.: Freebase: a collaboratively created graph database for structuring human knowledge. In: Proceedings of the 2008 ACM SIGMOD International Conference on Management of Data, pp. 1247–1250. ACM (2008)
6. Brown, L.D., Cai, T.T., DasGupta, A.: Interval estimation for a binomial proportion. Statistical Science, 101–117 (2001)
7. Gabrilovich, E., Markovitch, S.: Computing semantic relatedness using wikipedia-based explicit semantic analysis. In: IJCAI, vol. 7, pp. 1606–1611 (2007)
8. Garcia-Silva, A., Corcho, O., Alani, H., Gomez-Perez, A.: Review of the state of the art: Discovering and associating semantics to tags in folksonomies. The Knowledge Engineering Review 27(01), 57–85 (2012)
9. Hoffart, J., Suchanek, F.M., Berberich, K., Weikum, G.: Yago2: A spatially and temporally enhanced knowledge base from wikipedia. Artificial Intelligence 194, 28–61 (2013)
10. Navigli, R., Ponzetto, S.P.: Babelnet: Building a very large multilingual semantic network. In: Proceedings of the 48th Annual Meeting of the Association for Computational Linguistics, pp. 216–225. Association for Computational Linguistics (2010)
11. Niu, X., Sun, X., Wang, H., Rong, S., Qi, G., Yu, Y.: Zhishi.me - weaving chinese linking open data. In: International Semantic Web Conference, vol. (2), pp. 205–220 (2011)
12. Wu, W., Li, H., Wang, H., Zhu, K.Q.: Probase: A probabilistic taxonomy for text understanding. In: Proceedings of the 2012 ACM SIGMOD International Conference on Management of Data, pp. 481–492. ACM (2012)

# Discovery and Visual Analysis
# of Linked Data for Humans

Vedran Sabol[1,2], Gerwald Tschinkel[1], Eduardo Veas[1], Patrick Hoefler[1],
Belgin Mutlu[1], and Michael Granitzer[3]

[1] Know-Center
{vsabol,gtschinkel,eveas,phoefler,bmutlu}@know-center.at
[2] Graz University of Technology
[3] University of Passau
Michael.Granitzer@uni-passau.de

**Abstract.** Linked Data has grown to become one of the largest available knowledge bases. Unfortunately, this wealth of data remains inaccessible to those without in-depth knowledge of semantic technologies. We describe a toolchain enabling users without semantic technology background to explore and visually analyse Linked Data. We demonstrate its applicability in scenarios involving data from the Linked Open Data Cloud, and research data extracted from scientific publications. Our focus is on the Web-based front-end consisting of querying and visualisation tools. The performed usability evaluations unveil mainly positive results confirming that the Query Wizard simplifies searching, refining and transforming Linked Data and, in particular, that people using the Visualisation Wizard quickly learn to perform interactive analysis tasks on the resulting Linked Data sets. In making Linked Data analysis effectively accessible to the general public, our tool has been integrated in a number of live services where people use it to analyse, discover and discuss facts with Linked Data.

## 1 Introduction

The already huge amount of valuable information available in the Linked Open Data (LOD) cloud keeps growing at increasing rate. Unfortunately, this wealth of openly available data is difficult to access and analyse. Without having in-depth knowledge on semantic technologies, such as SPARQL, this abundance of information remains inaccessible. The fact that Linked Data (LD) by definition exhibits a graph structure, even when it describes numeric facts, further complicates the situation. Graph structures, being inherently complex to evaluate and interpret, are not what the majority of users are accustomed working with.

Our goal is to empower users without semantic technology background to search, explore and analyse LD. We strive to make LD accessible to the general public, enabling them to utilise the knowledge stored therein. To do so, we developed tools and workflows designed to be as easy as possible to use. The complexities imposed by semantic technologies and by the LD format are hidden from the user, while at the same time we exploit the advantages arising from

P. Mika et al. (Eds.) ISWC 2014, Part I, LNCS 8796, pp. 309–324, 2014.

semantically rich data. Two web-based interfaces highlight our toolchain: the Query Wizard [6] and the Visualisation Wizard (Vis Wizard)[12]. Query Wizard makes searching in LD as simple as with standard web search engines, and provides a tabular interface supporting transformations on the retrieved data set (e.g., selecting/removing columns, filtering and aggregation). The Vis Wizard automatically derives visualisations of the created data sets and supports their interactive analysis using multiple coordinated visualisations.

A major novelty introduced by this paper is in realising integrated end-to-end workflows bringing extraction, search, transformation and interactive analysis of LD to "non-experts". While tools addressing each task separately have been previously described and evaluated in isolation, to our knowledge no single system or combination of tools has been reported enabling either experts or non-experts to accomplish these tasks in integrated workflows. We also present results of a formative usability evaluation focusing on visual analysis of LD, and discuss lessons learnt from deploying the workflows.

We draw the motivation and elicit requirements along two exemplary scenarios: i) discovery and analysis of LOD, and ii) analysis of research data embedded in scientific publications (described in Section 3). These scenarios drive the evolution of our tools, developed in the CODE[1] EU project, which went public and are live since late 2012. Design decisions and implementation are detailed in Section 4. Section 5, elaborates on the services that deploy our tools, and illustrates the scenarios (i) and (ii) in practical use cases. We present results of a formative usability evaluation (Section 6), and discuss benefits and lessons learnt along the design, development, and deployment of our tools.

## 2   Related Work

The problem of easy-to-use interfaces for accessing LD is still largely unsolved. The majority of current tools do not target regular web users. For example, Sindice [17], a major Semantic Web search engine, is practically useless for ordinary web users due to its complex user interface. Freebase Parallax [7] featured the ability to browse sets of related things, and was one of the few web-based tools that provided a table view for results. Both Freebase Parallax and the Falcons Explorer [3] featured a search box as the main entry point, a central idea in our prototype. Yet, in both cases the table view was not the central focus. OpenRefine[2] (formerly Google Refine) supports RDF and there are extensions such as LODRefine[3] that focus on LD. But its main goal is on cleaning tabular data and, although the interface is browser-based, it is not available as a web service. Our work has similarities with faceted search and navigation as described in [13] or [5], and used in OpenRefine, SIMILE Exhibit [8] or DBpedia's instance of Virtuoso's Faceted Search & Find feature[4]. Query Wizard further incorporates interactive elements and concepts from spreadsheet applications.

---

[1] CODE Project Website: http://code-research.eu
[2] http://openrefine.org
[3] http://code.zemanta.com/sparkica
[4] http://dbpedia.org/fct

Stolte et. al proposes a table-based interface for data in relational databases [16]. The system automatically suggests visualisations and coordinates the interaction between them. The mapping of data onto visual properties of a visualisation is not performed automatically, but has to be formulated by the user. Vispedia [2] is a web-based system to create visualisations for articles in Wikipedia. It is limited to Wikipedia data and requires users to choose one of the available visualisations and formulate the mappings manually. Many Eyes [18] is a public web site to upload, visualise and share visualisations. Its data model is a raw table similar to CSV (Comma-separated Values). It uses heuristics to determine whether a column is numeric or text, but it does not automate visualisation. CubeViz [14], similar to the Vis Wizard, enables visualisation and visual querying of statistical RDF Data Cubes. In contrast to our approach, it does not automatically suggest possible visualisations, neither does it support data cubes with multiple measures nor varying number of dimensions. The framework does not rely on semantic description of charts and offers a comparably restricted number of chart types. In [1] a method for automatic mapping of data attributes to visual attributes is described, but no automatic selection of visualisations for a given data set is supported. Marcello et. al[11] confirms the problem the semantic community is currently facing when trying to bring LOD search results in a way that users are comfortable with.

## 3   Scenarios

We begin by defining two usage scenarios, and then derive the central requirements for the proposed web-based toolchain.

**Scenario 1 – Search and Analysis of Linked Open Data** is our main scenario which focuses on the openly available information in the LOD cloud. A well-known example is open governmental data, such as made available by EU Open Data Portal[5], which provides a wide variety of statistical facts on our society. The capability to search for and analyse such data would benefit both the general public as well as professionals (e.g. data journalists). Therefore, our Scenario 1 shall consist of the following steps:

1. **Searching** for information in the LOD cloud.
2. **Transforming and preparing** the discovered data for analysis.
3. **Visualising and analysing** the resulting data set to generate new insights.

Using conventional means, the first two steps can be achieved by formulating and executing complex SPARQL queries against an endpoint. Obviously, users without knowledge of semantic technologies will need a simpler solution than that. Concerning the visualisation step, graph visualisation is usually employed because the information is provided as RDF. Instead, employing visualisations suitable for the particular type of information (e.g. statistical, temporal, geographical etc.) would significantly aid the interpretation of data.

---

[5] EU Open Data Portal: http://open-data.europa.eu

**Scenario 2 – Analysing Scientific Publication Data** addresses another source of hard to utilise, high-quality information: research data present in tables which are embedded in scientific publications in PDF format. In order to access and analyse such data one first needs to extract the tabular information from the PDF. The extracted tables, which typically contain numeric information, shall be semantically described in order to facilitate further analysis. Therefore, our Scenario 2 shall consists of the following steps:

1. **Extracting research data** present in tables embedded in PDF files.
2. **Visualisation and Analysis** of the extracted data set.

With common tools, the first step is achieved by copy-pasting from the PDF and transcribing the table back into the tabular form. Using a spreadsheet application users can correct the data and move it to the correct table cells, which is a laborious task. Visualisation is supported by spreadsheet applications, although users must manually select and configure the charts. Obviously, it would be beneficial for users if major parts of this process were automated.

### 3.1   Requirements

Taking into account the targeted user group and the defined scenarios, we derive a set of high-level requirements our toolchain needs to fulfil. In the following we differentiate between non-functional (NFR) and functional requirements (FR):

- **NFR1 - Ease of Use:** Tools targeting the general public should be as easy to use as possible. We shall, wherever possible, make use of UI concepts a typical user is already acquainted with.
- **NFR2 - Automation:** The tools should maximise automation and eliminate unnecessary steps which currently must be performed by the user.
- **NFR3 - Exploiting Semantics:** The system should exploit Semantic Web standards and the semantics of the data to the advantage of the user.
- **FR1 - LOD Search:** A search tool shall support retrieval in SPARQL endpoints.
- **FR2 - Data Transformation:** A tool shall support transforming and refining of the found/extracted data set.
- **FR3 - PDF Table Extraction:** A tool shall provide extraction of tabular data from scientific publications in PDF format.
- **FR4 - Data Triplification:** A triplification tool shall provide functionality for exporting of a data set as RDF.
- **FR5 - Interactive Visualisation:** A visualisation tool shall support visualisation and interactive analysis of Linked Data sets.

## 4   Proof of Concept

Driven by requirements NFR1 – NFR3, we present central design decisions for the tools introduced by FR1 – FR5. After that, as a proof of concept, we introduce workflows showing how these tools are employed to realise the scenarios defined in the previous section.

## 4.1  Design Decisions

Searching in LD shall come as close as possible to what users are accustomed with the major search engines (e.g. Google). The entry point to search shall be a search box that works as what is expected for standard (non-semantic) web search. After performing a full-text search the returned results shall be presented in the form of a table, where a row corresponds to a single subject, a column represents a predicate, and cells contain objects for the given subject and predicate. The rationale behind using tabular representation is that users are familiar with tables and are often proficient in using spreadsheet applications. Also, the tabular form is suitable for refining and transforming the retrieved data set. For example, with just a few clicks user shall be able to add and remove columns (i.e. predicates), filter the results (rows) depending on simple criteria, and aggregate (group by) columns. A tool supporting the described functionality, the **Query Wizard**, satisfies requirements NFR1, NFR3, FR1 and FR2.

Extracting tabular data from scientific publications and exporting it as RDF shall be the task of the **Data Extractor** tool. We choose the W3Cs RDF Data Cube Vocabulary[6] [4] which provides a semantic framework for expressing multi-dimensional data sets as Linked Data. The Data Extractor is composed of three components: i) an embedded **PDF Extractor** which takes a PDF file as input and returns extracted tables as output [10], ii) an (optional) user interface for correcting extraction errors and defining dimensions and measures of the data cube, and iii) a triplifier which exports a tabular data set as RDF Data Cube. Importantly, tabular data sets created by the Query Wizard already contain semantic information, which is utilised by the triplifier to create RDF Data Cubes in a fully automatic mode. The Data Extractor, with the embedded PDF Extractor, satisfies the requirements NFR2, NFR3, FR3 and FR4.

Semantic information present in the RDF Data Cubes shall be utilised to enable automated visualisation. Depending on semantic data characteristics, automatic visualisation suggests meaningful visual representations and disables those not suitable for the data. The automatism also includes configuring a visualisation, i.e. mapping different columns of the data set onto suitable visual properties (e.g. axes, colours etc.) of the visualisation. When multiple visualisations and configurations are possible, the user shall have the freedom to select only between the meaningful ones. Also, for complex multi-dimensional data, it should be possible to generate multiple visualisations (e.g. a geo- and a time-visualisation) in order to provide insights into different aspects of the data set. A tool supporting the described functionality, called the **Visualisation Wizard** (Vis Wizard for short), satisfies requirements NFR1, NFR2, NFR3, and FR5.

With this we have defined the design of a set of tools which satisfy the requirements derived in the previous section. Next, we briefly outline workflows specifying how these tools are employed to implement the scenarios.

---

[6] RDF Data Cube Vocabulary: http://w3.org/TR/vocab-data-cube

## 4.2 Workflows

Workflows shown in Figure 1 describe how the proposed tools are employed to realise the two scenarios.

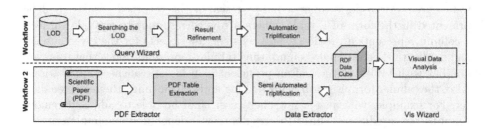

**Fig. 1.** Workflows using the proposed tools to implement the scenarios

**Workflow for Scenario 1** (up in the Figure 1) implements the process of searching the LOD, interactively transforming the data, automatically converting it into a data cube, and generating interactive visualisation of the data set. The Query Wizard, which accesses the Linked Open Data cloud, is used to execute full-text searches on an endpoint. Query Wizard is also employed for the next step: displaying the retrieved data in tabular form and manipulating it (e.g. selecting columns, filtering or aggregating). Following that, the data extractor automatically generates an RDF Data Cube relying on semantic information in the data. For the last step the Vis Wizard is used to automatically generate visualisations to support interactive analysis of the data.

**Workflow for Scenario 2** (bellow in the Figure 1) implements the process of extracting tabular data from publications, converting the data into an RDF data cube, and generating interactive visualisation of the data. In the first step the PDF Extractor analyses the structure of a scientific paper in PDF format and automatically extracts tables. In the next step, the extracted tabular data is passed to the Data Extractor which provides a user interface for semi-automatic triplification. Data Extractor analyses the data and suggests dimensions and measures of the cube. The user can perform corrections if the automatic data analysis produced errors. Following that an RDF Data Cube is generated and can be stored into a Linked Data endpoint. In the last step the user can analyse the data using the Vis Wizard. Optionally, before visualising, Query Wizard can be applied to display and transform the data set.

## 4.3 Selected Implementation Details

In this section we briefly describe the most relevant technical solutions behind our tools. For detailed reading the corresponding publications should be consulted.

**Query Wizard:** The Query Wizard [6] turns search terms entered by the user into a series of SPARQL queries, which are then sent to the endpoint chosen by the user. First, with the help of a full-text index, a search in all the rdfs:labels is performed, and the first 10 matching subjects are returned. Search results are shown as a table, where a row corresponds to a single subject and a column represents a predicate (by default the first row displays rdfs:label, the second rdf:type). Cells contain objects, i.e. any number of literals and/or entities, depending on the row and column. Using the SPARQL 1.1 COUNT feature the total number of matching results is also retrieved. Another query is generated to display all available predicates for the displayed subjects. When the user selects one of these predicates from the drop-down list, another query is performed to retrieve the respective data. When users set a filter on one of the displayed columns, a whole new set of SPARQL queries is generated and sent to the endpoint. With just a few interactions, the system can produce hundreds of lines of SPARQL code – all completely invisible to the user. Also, thanks to the aggregation features of SPARQL 1.1, tasks that usually involve a Pivot Table or specialised Data Warehousing software – such as calculating averages, sums, minima, maxima, or counts based on selected dimensions – can be performed by the Query Wizard with the help of a simple interface. The Query Wizard can also be used to explore available RDF Data Cubes which are publicly available through a SPARQL endpoint. The front page features automatically generated lists of RDF Data Cubes for endpoints such as EU Open Data[7] or Vienna Linked Open Data[8]). However, support for selecting endpoints based on available data is not included, representing an opportunity for future research.

**Data Extractor and PDF Extractor:** The Data Extractor [15] uses a semantically enriched HTML table produced by the Query Wizard to guess dimensions and measures of a data cube. The columns of the table are automatically classified as either dimensions (if the cell content is non-numeric), measures (for numeric cell content), or multi-value (if there are multiple values in at least one of the cells of the given column). For extracting tabular information from publications the embedded PDF extractor [10] analyses the structure of a PDF document using unsupervised machine learning techniques and heuristics. Contiguous text blocks and geometrical relations between them are extracted from the character stream. The blocks are categorised into different classes resulting in a logical structure of the document. Table extraction starts from a "table" caption, and then labels neighbouring sparse blocks recursively as table blocks, if their vertical distance is within a specific threshold.

**Visualisation Wizard:** To suggest appropriate visualisation for a data set in a RDF Data Cube, we developed visualisation vocabulary, which describes visualisations semantically in an OWL ontology. The vocabulary describes: (1) visualisations in terms of visual channels $va : hasVisualChannel(va : Chart, va : VisualChannel)$ (e.g., axes, colour, size), and (2) visual channels in terms of data types $va : hasDatatype(va : VisualChannel, va : DataType)$ (e.g., boolean, numeric). For a particular visualisation a visual channel may be optional, which is represented in $va : Occurrence$. The mapping algorithm identifies valid rela-

---

tions from $qb : dimensions$ to $va : VisualChannels$ in a $va : Chart$. The relation (mapping) between the RDF Data Cube is only valid, when the data types of the cube components and visual channels are compatible[12]. After analysing the data type compatibility the Vis Wizard automatically suggest any of the 10 currently available visualisations and valid mapping combinations.

The Vis Wizard offers interaction facilities to organise, refine and inspect the visualised data with coordinated brushing, mouse-over inspections, filtering and aggregation. Brushing and linking is a powerful interactive analysis technique, which combines different visualisations to overcome the shortcomings of single techniques [9]. Interactive changes made in one visualisation are automatically reflected in the other ones. Vis Wizard utilises semantic information (i.e. dimension URIs) to link different visualisations, which may be displaying different Data Cubes. These are created, for example, when data sets are aggregated.

## 5   CODE Tools in Use

During the development of the Query and Vis Wizards we followed the "release early, release often" principle. As soon as a new feature was complete and ready for testing, it immediately rolled out to our staging server and, if no major problems were found, a short time later it was publicly available at our production server. The prototypes have been online since November 2012 and have been under permanent scrutiny of fellow researchers and other interested colleagues for a year and a half now. Since then, the Query Wizard alone generated around 100.000 SPARQL queries that users did not have to formulate themselves, whereby this number comprises all queries generated within interactive exploration tasks. Both tools are available under:

- Query Wizard: http://code.know-center.tugraz.at/search
- Visualisation Wizard: http://code.know-center.tugraz.at/vis

**Integration with Other Platforms:** The Query Wizard and the Vis Wizard have been integrated into the 42-data[9]. 42-data is a data-centric question and answer platform, which focuses on discussions and answers backed by empirical facts in numerical LOD. Embedded Query Wizard tables and Vis Wizard visualisations facilitate exploration and analysis of LOD sets within the platform. Uptake of the 42-data social platform is steadily increasing usage of our tools. Another integration which benefits the usage rates of our tools is with the commercial MindMeister[10] mind mapping web platform. It enables the Query Wizard to export data sets in the form of mind maps, which can be shared and collaboratively edited by MindMeister users. Also, visualisations generated by the Vis Wizard can be added to mind maps as images which link back to the original interactive charts.

The following two use cases demonstrate the implementation of the scenarios.

---

[9]  42-data Platform: http://42-data.org

[10]  MindMeister Mind Mapping platform: http://www.mindmeister.com/

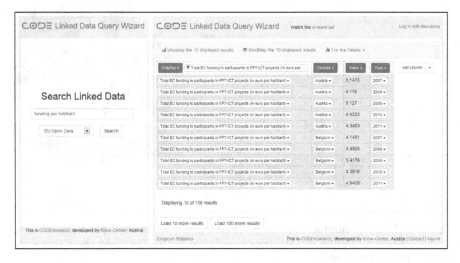

**Fig. 2.** Query Wizard: Searching (on left), tabular result representation (on right)

## 5.1 Use Case 1

Our first and primary use case implements Scenario 1 – Search and Analysis of Linked Open Data. Assume the user is interested in total EU project funding for different countries. Using the Query Wizard he selects an appropriate endpoint, in this case the EU Open Data endpoint, and search for "funding per habitant" (see Figure 2, on left). Search results, displayed in tabular form (Figure 2, on right), can be manipulated through filtering and adding/removing columns. Filtering by data value is performed by clicking on the specific value and selecting filtering in the drop-down list. Columns are added by using the "Add Column" button and selecting a predicate. Columns are removed by clicking on the column header and selecting "Remove column". In the shown data set we added the column "Dataset", filtered it by the value "Total EC funding to participants in FP7-ICT projects (in euro per habitant)", and added the columns "Country", "Year" and "Value" to obtain the data we are interested in. Before visualising we load the whole data set consisting of 158 entries using the "Load more results" buttons.

To visualise the data set we click on "Visualize the displayed results" link which loads the data into the Vis Wizard (see Figure 4). Six out of ten available visualisations are enabled for our data set ("Possible Charts" in the Figure 4). We select the scatterplot (left in the Figure 4) to visualise funding (y-axis) for countries (x-axis) in different years (colour coding). Next, we want to find out how the funding is spread over Europe. To achieve this we aggregate the data for countries by averaging over the years. A simple aggregation dialogue allows us to select "Country" and choose "average" as aggregation function. Aggregation generates a new data set which is visualised in a geo-chart (right chart in the 3), where colour coding is used to visualise the average funding (a deeper shade indicates higher funding). Finally, we want to discover which countries receive

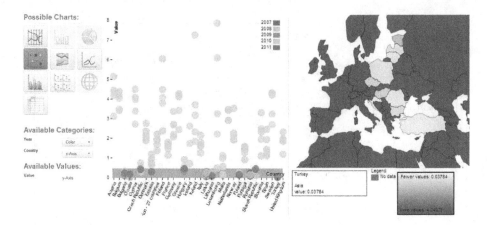

**Fig. 3.** Vis Wizard showing data on EC funding to participants, per habitant. The left chart displays funding for countries in different years. The right chart shows the average funding by country.

the lowest amounts of funding. Due to available semantic information Vis Wizard knows that "Country" has the same meaning in the original and aggregated data set. This allows us to apply a brush in the scatterplot (shown as grey rectangle) selecting the countries with lowest received amounts of funding. Brushing operation greys out all non-selected countries in both visualisations, which leads us to a new insight: in the geo-chart we can clearly observe that countries with the lowest amounts of funding are located in Eastern Europe. A screencast of the use case is available on YouTube[11].

## 5.2   Use Case 2

The second use case (schematically shown in Figure 4) briefly demonstrates the usage of our tools in Scenario 2 – Analysing Scientific Publication Data. Our user is interested in analysing research data available in a scientific paper. In particular, for the paper "Combined Regression and Ranking" from D. Sculley (2010) the user wishes to explore results found in "Table 1: RCV1 Experimental Results" (on left in the Figure 4). We start by uploading the PDF file into the Data Extractor which internally uses the PDF Extractor to extract the tables. Data Extractor guesses which rows and columns represent data cube dimensions and which cells contain observations. Next, the user selects the first table which is presented in an interface showing dimensions marked in blue and observation marked in green (in the middle of the Figure 4). The user has the opportunity to edit the table and, if necessary, correct extraction errors by: marking dimensions, removing columns and rows, modifying cell content etc. When ready, with a single click the table is converted into an RDF Data Cube and visualised in the Vis Wizard (parallel coordinates visualisation shown on right in the Figure 4).

---

[11] Use case 1 screencast: http://www.youtube.com/watch?v=mA_vilF7TSE

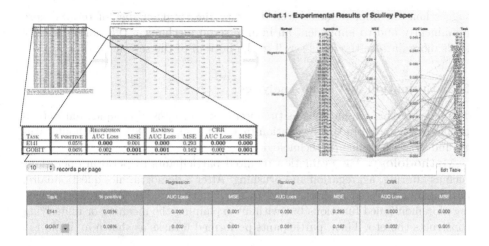

**Fig. 4.** Use Case 2 begins with a PDF document containing tables (on left), which are extracted and annotated with the RDF Data Cube Vocabulary using the Data Extractor (in the centre), and then visualised with the Vis Wizard (on right)

# 6   Formative Evaluations

This section presents formative usability evaluations performed with the precise goal to ascertain that users can: a) search, refine and transform LD, b) perform interactive analysis on complex data sets. The evaluations consisted of several tasks that required a conceptual understanding of different inherently complex operations on LD. In both cases we used the standard NASA Task Load Index (TLX) to measure workload in loosely time constrained tasks and followed the Thinking Aloud protocol to uncover usability issues. The time constrain was loosely maintained, meaning the moderator kept track of the timing but was not fully strict. No timer was shown to participants. This is a common way to introduce time pressure that participants need to keep track of mentally while performing the task. The time constrain combined with the Thinking Aloud adds up to effort and frustration when participants cannot progress as expected. Workload was computed with the simplified NASA R-TLX.

## 6.1   Evaluation 1: Search and Refinement

This section summarises a formative evaluation with eight participants focusing on search, refinement and transformation of LD, initially reported in [6]. The evaluation showed that people could perform these tasks using the provided abstractions (high Performance TLX), with little stress (Mental/Temporal Demand). Interestingly, people quickly learnt new features (mid-low Effort fluctuation). The Query Wizard was generally well received, both by users with and without a computer science background. The main point of critiques was a missing possibility to add URI filters through a menu in the table header. Additional suggestions for improvements were to show the total number of results more prominently and to implement an infinite scroll mechanism that automatically loads more data as the users scroll to the bottom of the screen.

## 6.2 Evaluation 2: Visual Analytics

The focus of this evaluation was the interactive analysis of complex datasets. 8 people participated in this evaluation (age in range[24 − 38]), all without background in LD or semantic technologies.

**Methodology.** The evaluation required participants to perform operations such as filtering, aggregation and brushing. After a demographics questionnaire, participants received a short guide to the Query and Vis Wizards, showcasing aforementioned functions but without explaining the meaning or underlying constructs thereto. Then, participants performed 6 tasks as shown in Table 1.

**Table 1.** Tasks. Summary of tasks and corresponding activities in the experiment.

| | |
|---|---|
| T1: Filtering in the Query Wizard | T4: Aggregation - Multiple Categories |
| T2: Filtering in the Vis Wizard | T5: Aggregating Multiple Values |
| T3: Aggregation | T6: Brushing in Multiple Views |

For example, the instruction for T1 was: *please show the data set in Query Wizard. We are interested only in the countries which have a CO2 Emission over 13 Tons per persons. After that, please visualise the results. You have 3 minutes to complete this task.* Upon finishing the task or when time-up was called, participants filled the NASA TLX and a subjective assessment questionnaire. An exit questionnaire was used to collect preferences and suggestions.

**Quantitative Subjective Workload.** From 54 tasks performed in total by 8 participants, 39 were successfully completed in time. Results on workload were positively below the $\frac{1}{3}^{rd}$ of the scale. T1 and T5 rated lowest on workload. T1 was the first task that we deemed less complex and received the lowest mental demand (MD) rating ($M = 12.5, Std = 10.35$) accordingly. MD remained stable in subsequent tasks. Temporal demand did not present major differences across tasks. The main visual analytics tasks T5 and T6 present high perceived performance ratings ($M = 91.25, Std = 11.25, M = 86.25, Std = 9.16$), accompanied by relatively low frustration (T5: $M = 6.25, Std = 10.60$).

**Qualitative Thinking Aloud.** Participants found it difficult to select the proper dataset in the first task (T1), but they clearly understood that they needed to use a filter, set the filter correctly and visualised the data without complications. Participants choose two general strategies to solve T2, either set a filter in the Query Wizard first and show the filtered data (6), or visualise the data and brush the parallel coordinates to filter (2). T3 was solved almost unanimously by visualising and then aggregating data. One participant aggregated the data first and then visualised it. Participants found T4 suddenly complex, mainly because the initially suggested visualisation was not the appropriate one to solve the task, but also by the need to group and aggregate data. Five participants grouped incorrectly at first, and after noting the error, had to redo it. Only two participants solved this task without issues. In T5, participants showed all the skills acquired throughout the experiment, three participants used parallel coordinates and two used scatterplot matrices to solve the task, two other participants used grouping and aggregation. Only one participant had difficulties with multiple aggregated values. In T6, two participants were confused by a usability issue of the brush in a scatterplot, but all could actually solve the task.

**Table 2.** Workload of Visual Analytics. Results on workload from the VA experiment. Green tones show positively lowest ratings, and red tones the opposite higher ratings.

| | T1 | | T2 | | T3 | | T4 | | T5 | | T6 | |
|---|---|---|---|---|---|---|---|---|---|---|---|---|
| **TLX** | M | STD | M | STD | M | STD | M | STD | M | STD | M | STD |
| Mental Demand | 12.5 | 10.35 | 33.75 | 18.46 | 28.75 | 26.42 | 35 | 26.18 | 31.25 | 22.32 | 30 | 27.25 |
| Physical Demand | 5 | 7.55 | 7.5 | 10.35 | 10 | 20.70 | 17.5 | 27.64 | 8.75 | 13.56 | 21.25 | 29.48 |
| Temporal Demand | 15 | 11.95 | 25 | 33.80 | 15 | 11.95 | 16.25 | 17.67 | 18.75 | 15.52 | 15 | 17.72 |
| Effort | 32.5 | 24.34 | 43.75 | 24.45 | 42.5 | 27.64 | 47.5 | 17.52 | 33.75 | 20.65 | 31.25 | 25.87 |
| Frustration | 15 | 22.67 | 25 | 25.63 | 16.25 | 26.15 | 17.5 | 25.49 | 6.25 | 10.60 | 16.25 | 24.45 |
| Performance | 83.75 | 15.97 | 66.25 | 34.20 | 77.5 | 8.86 | 68.75 | 25.31 | 91.25 | 11.25 | 86.25 | 9.16 |
| Workload | 16.04 | 11.01 | 28.125 | 21.01 | 22.5 | 15.88 | 27.5 | 18.89 | 17.91 | 10.71 | 21.25 | 20.50 |

**Preferences and Exit Questionnaires.** Users liked the workflow for data analysis, and were in general motivated to discover facts in the data through the provided functionality. They found it fast, simple and intuitive to use, and regarded the design highly. They appreciated the automated suggestion and mapping of visualisations. Still, participants rated the colours in the geo-chart really poor, and were at times confused by the brushing functionality. To the question, *what would you use this toolset for?*, participants answered: to visualise any kind of statistical data, server log analysis, project tracking and to quickly answer questions which involve data analysis. Finally, when asked if they could have solved the tasks with other tools of their choice, which ones they would have used, participants unanimously replied they would search with Google, and manually collect and copy the data into a spreadsheet application for analysis.

### 6.3 Discussion and Lessons Learnt

The study was designed as formative and not comparative in nature, to discover if people could actually perform otherwise complex analytics operations on LD. Thus instead of seeking statistical deviation from a baseline, we opted for finding correlation between observations, the Thinking Aloud, and TLX results. The formative evaluation sheds light on the expressive power of our toolset for interactive analysis of LD. Participants could apply complex operations with minimal effort on large datasets. The TLX provides interesting results. Although tasks were constrained in time, participants did not feel pressed to finish (TD

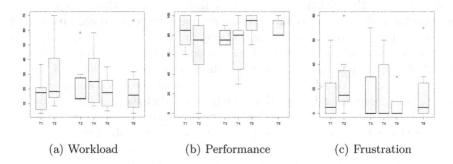

|  (a) Workload | (b) Performance | (c) Frustration |

**Fig. 5.** Workload from R-TLX computed inverse performance. Colours encode the type of task (filtering: pink, aggregation: blue, multiple views: yellow).

in table 2). They had more difficulties to solve T2 and T4, observable in the higher variance in results and confirmed in the Thinking Aloud. We hypothesise that this effect is due to confusing paths to the solution, either in the form of different strategies (T2) or because the Vis Wizard did not open the right tool for the task. Yet, people were confident solving tasks that involved more complex operations (performance in T5 and T6, Figure 5(a)). Indeed, participants expressed notably less effort and frustration to achieve higher performance in these tasks. One notable result was that people could convert narrative description of the task to a set of operations on the data without having to cope or knowing the complexity of the underlying implementation of these operations. In the following we summarise lessons learnt and directions for future work gained throughout the process of development, testing and deployment.

**Data Volume Ignored.** People seemed oblivious to the volumes of data they were actually handling. In the Query Wizard experiments people ignored the loaded number of records in the data set in several occasions, requiring time to realise that more records were available. Visualisations helped stress the issue, as visual abstractions may leave people without a clue as to the size of the data.

**Unrefined Suggestion of Visualisations.** Visualisations are suggested based on the characteristics of the data, whereby multiple visualisation may meaningfully represent a data set. However, many users were confused if the presented visualisation would not help solve the particular problem at hand. For them, selecting the right visualisation for a task is not trivial. Ranking of possible visualisations depending on data and context will improve suggestion quality.

**Navigating Paths to a Solution.** Most problems can be solved by combining operations in different ways. However, in cases when it became clear than an incorrect path to the solution was taken, participants often had to restart from the beginning. Backtracking in the operations applied to the data is not always supported, and clearly enough, people get frustrated by having to repeat steps.

**Analytics Workflow.** An exploratory process is one of hypothesis, experiment and discovery. To the experienced practitioner these stages are clear, but not so for novices. In this sense, although our tools let novices reach into the richness of LD, the analytics workflow is only implicitly supported. To facilitate the work of both novices and experts, our future tools need to include explicit representations of this workflow, so users can move back and forth along stages.

## 7 Conclusion

We have deployed a toolset that makes LD accessible to the general public. We used well-known metaphors to ensure a smooth learning of our tools, which hide the underlying technological complexities from users (NFR1), automate the analytical process (NFR2) through automated visualisation and Data Cube extraction, and leverage semantic technologies (NFR3) for both automation and interactive analysis. Our evaluations show that non-experts could pose complex queries and discover facts from LD using interactive visual analysis.

The CODE toolset has been online since well over a year and has been actively used for accessing and analysing Linked Open Data. Both tools are deployed as part of the 42-data Q&A platform, with the purpose of supporting data-centric discussions. Users of the MindMeister service benefit from the capability of our Wizards to generate mind maps from data sets and visualisations. The presented toolset opens a wealth of interesting avenues for research as well as for direct deployment in productive applications. It is our hope that these results will motivate other practitioners and scientists to try and incorporate described workflows and tools in their work, to design better solutions for LOD based on lessons exposed, to integrate end-points, enrich LOD with saved queries processed data to access and utilise LOD analysis in their daily work.

**Acknowledgements.** This work is funded by the EC 7th Framework project CODE (grant 296150). The Know-Center GmbH is funded by Austrian Federal Government within the Austrian COMET Program, managed by the Austrian Research Promotion Agency (FFG).

Query Wizard and Vis Wizard were developed by Know-Center's Knowledge Visualisation team. We thank our colleagues from the Knowledge Discovery team for providing the PDF Extractor, and our colleagues from the University of Passau for providing the Data Extractor.

## References

1. Cammarano, M. (Luna), D.X., Bryan, C., Jeff, K., Justin, T., Alon, H., Pat, H.: Visualization of heterogeneous data. IEEE Information Visualization (2007)
2. Chan, B., Wu, L., Talbot, J., Cammarano, M., Hanrahan, P.: Vispedia: Interactive visual exploration of wikipedia data via search-based integration. IEEE Trans. Visualization & Comp. Graphics, Proc. InfoVis (2008)
3. Cheng, G., Wu, H., Gong, S., Ge, W., Qu, Y.: Falcons Explorer: Tabular and Relational End-user Programming for the Web of Data. In: Semantic Web Challenge (2010)

4. Cyganiak, R., Reynolds, D.: The RDF Data Cube Vocabulary (2013)
5. Erling, O.: Faceted Views over Large-Scale Linked Data. Linked Data on the Web, LDOW (2009)
6. Hoefler, P., Granitzer, M., Veas, E., Seifert, C.: Linked Data Query Wizard: A Novel Interface for Accessing SPARQL Endpoints. In: Proceedings of Linked Data on the Web (LDOW) at WWW (2014)
7. Huynh, D., Karger, D.: Parallax and companion: Set-based browsing for the data web. WWW Conference (2009)
8. Huynh, D.F., Karger, D.R., Miller, R.C.: Exhibit: lightweight structured data publishing. In: Proc. of the 16th Int. Conf. on World Wide Web (2007)
9. Keim, D.A.: Information visualization and visual data mining. IEEE Transactions on Visualization and Computer Graphics 8(1), 1–8 (2002)
10. Klampfl, S., Kern, R.: An unsupervised machine learning approach to body text and table of contents extraction from digital scientific articles. In: Aalberg, T., Papatheodorou, C., Dobreva, M., Tsakonas, G., Farrugia, C.J. (eds.) TPDL 2013. LNCS, vol. 8092, pp. 144–155. Springer, Heidelberg (2013)
11. Leida, M., Afzal, A., Majeed, B.: Outlines for dynamic visualization of semantic web data. In: Meersman, R., Dillon, T., Herrero, P. (eds.) OTM 2010. LNCS, vol. 6428, pp. 170–179. Springer, Heidelberg (2010)
12. Mutlu, B., Höfler, P., Tschinkel, G., Veas, E.E., Sabol, V., Stegmaier, F., Granitzer, M.: Suggesting visualisations for published data. In: Proceedings of IVAPP 2014, pp. 267–275 (2014)
13. Oren, E., Delbru, R., Decker, S.: Extending faceted navigation for RDF data. In: Cruz, I., Decker, S., Allemang, D., Preist, C., Schwabe, D., Mika, P., Uschold, M., Aroyo, L.M. (eds.) ISWC 2006. LNCS, vol. 4273, pp. 559–572. Springer, Heidelberg (2006)
14. Salas, P.E., Martin, M., Da Mota, F.M., Breitman, K., Auer, S., Casanova, M.A.: Publishing statistical data on the web. In: 2012 Proceedings of 6th International IEEE Conference on Semantic Computing, pp. 285–292. IEEE (2012)
15. Seifert, C., Granitzer, M., Höfler, P., Mutlu, B., Sabol, V., Schlegel, K., Bayerl, S., Stegmaier, F., Zwicklbauer, S., Kern, R.: Crowdsourcing fact extraction from scientific literature. In: Holzinger, A., Pasi, G. (eds.) HCI-KDD 2013. LNCS, vol. 7947, pp. 160–172. Springer, Heidelberg (2013)
16. Stolte, C., Hanrahan, P.: Polaris: A system for query, analysis and visualization of multi-dimensional relational databases. IEEE Transactions on Visualization and Computer Graphics 8, 52–65 (2002)
17. Tummarello, G., Delbru, R., Oren, E.: Sindice.com: Weaving the open linked data. In: Aberer, K., Choi, K.-S., Noy, N., Allemang, D., Lee, K.-I., Nixon, L.J.B., Golbeck, J., Mika, P., Maynard, D., Mizoguchi, R., Schreiber, G., Cudré-Mauroux, P. (eds.) ASWC 2007 and ISWC 2007. LNCS, vol. 4825, pp. 552–565. Springer, Heidelberg (2007)
18. Viegas, F.B., Wattenberg, M., van Ham, F., Kriss, J., McKeon, M.: Manyeyes: a site for visualization at internet scale. IEEE Transactions on Visualization and Computer Graphics 13(6), 1121–1128 (2007)

# Col-Graph: Towards Writable and Scalable Linked Open Data

Luis-Daniel Ibáñez[1], Hala Skaf-Molli[1], Pascal Molli[1], and Olivier Corby[2]

[1] LINA, University of Nantes
{luis.ibanez,hala.skaf,pascal.molli}@univ-nantes.fr
[2] INRIA Sophia Antipolis-Méditerranée
olivier.corby@inria.fr

**Abstract.** Linked Open Data faces severe issues of scalability, availability and data quality. These issues are observed by data consumers performing federated queries; SPARQL endpoints do not respond and results can be wrong or out-of-date. If a data consumer finds an error, how can she fix it? This raises the issue of the *writability* of Linked Data. In this paper, we devise an extension of the federation of Linked Data to data consumers. A data consumer can make partial copies of different datasets and make them available through a SPARQL endpoint. A data consumer can update her local copy and share updates with data providers and consumers. Update sharing improves general data quality, and replicated data creates opportunities for federated query engines to improve availability. However, when updates occur in an uncontrolled way, consistency issues arise. In this paper, we define fragments as SPARQL CONSTRUCT federated queries and propose a correction criterion to maintain these fragments incrementally without reevaluating the query. We define a coordination free protocol based on the counting of triples derivations and provenance. We analyze the theoretical complexity of the protocol in time, space and traffic. Experimental results suggest the scalability of our approach to Linked Data.

## 1 Introduction

The Linked Open Data initiative (LOD) makes millions of RDF-triples available for querying through a federation of SPARQL endpoints. However, the LOD faces major challenges including availability, scalability [3] and quality of data [1].

These issues are observed by data consumers when they perform federated queries; SPARQL endpoints do not respond and results can be wrong or out-of-date. If a data consumer finds a mistake, how can she fix it? This raises the issue of the *writability* of Linked Data, as already pointed out by T. Berners-Lee [2].

We devise an extension of Linked Data with data replicated by Linked Data consumers. Consumers can perform intensive querying and improve data quality on their local replicas. We call replicated subsets of data, *fragments*. First, any participant creates fragments from different data providers and make them available to others through a regular SPARQL Endpoint. Local fragments are

P. Mika et al. (Eds.) ISWC 2014, Part I, LNCS 8796, pp. 325–340, 2014.
© Springer International Publishing Switzerland 2014

writable, allowing modifications to enhance data quality. Original data providers can be contacted to consume local changes in the spirit of *pull requests* in Distributed Version Control Systems (DVCS). Second, the union of local fragments creates an opportunistic replication scheme that can be used by federated query engines to improve data availability [13,17]. Finally, update propagation between fragments is powered by live feeds as in DBpedia Live [14] or sparqlPuSH [16].

Scientific issues arise concerning the consistency of these fragments. These questions have been extensively studied in Collaborative Data Sharing Systems (CDSS) [11], Linked Data with adaptations of DVCS [18,4] and replication techniques [10,25]. Existing approaches follow a total replication approach, *i.e.*, full datasets or their full histories are completely replicated at each participant or they require coordination to maintain consistency.

In this paper, we propose Col-Graph, a new approach to solve the availability, scalability and writability problems of Linked Data. In Col-Graph, we define fragments as SPARQL CONSTRUCT federated queries, creating a *collaboration network*, propose a consistency criterion and define a coordination-free protocol to maintain fragments incrementally without reevaluating the query on the data source. The protocol counts the derivations of triples for data synchronization and keeps provenance information to make decisions in case of a conflict.

We analyze the protocol's complexity and evaluate experimentally its efficiency. The main factors that affect Col-Graph performance are the number of concurrent insertions of the same data, the connectivity of the collaboration network and the overlapping between the fragments. Experimentations show that the overhead of storing counters is less than 6% of the fragment size, whenever there are up to 1,000 concurrent insertions or up to $10 \times 10^{16}$ simple paths between the source and the dataset. Synchronization is faster than fragment reevaluation up to when 30% of the triples are updated. We also report better performance on synthetically generated social networks than on random ones.

Section 2 describes Col-Graph general approach and defines the correction criterion. Section 3 formalizes Col-Graph protocol. Section 4 details the complexity analysis. Section 5 details experimentations. Section 6 summarizes related work. Finally, section 7 presents the conclusions and outlines future work.

## 2   Col-Graph Approach and Model

In Col-Graph, consumers create *fragments*, *i.e.*, partial copies of other datasets, based on simple federated CONSTRUCT queries, allowing them to perform intensive queries locally on the union of fragments and make updates to enhance data quality. In Figure 1, $Consumer\_1$ copies fragments from DBPedia and DrugBank, $Consumer\_2$ copies fragments from DBPedia and MusicBrainz and $Consumer\_3$ copies fragments from $Consumer\_2$ and $Consumer\_3$.

Consumers publish the updated dataset, allowing others to also copy fragments from them. They can also contact their data sources to ask them to incorporate their updates, in the spirit of DVCS pull requests. Updates at the fragment's source are propagated to consumers using protocols like

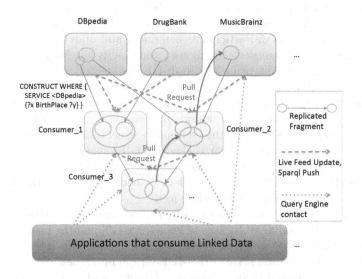

**Fig. 1.** Federation of Writable Linked Data

sparqlPuSH [16] or live feeds [14]. As replicated fragments could exist on several endpoints, adequate federated query engines could profit to improve general data availability and scalability [13,17]. Following this approach, data providers can share the query load and the data curation process with data consumers. Since data consumers become also data providers, they can gain knowledge of queries targeting their fragments.

We consider that each Linked Data participant holds one RDF-Graph and exposes a SPARQL endpoint. For simplicity, we use $P$ to refer to the RDF-Graph, the SPARQL endpoint or the name of a participant when is not confusing. An RDF-Graph is defined as a set of triples $(s, p, o)$, where $s$ is the subject, $p$ is the predicate and $o$ is the object. We suppose that a participant wants to copy *fragments* of data from other participants, *i.e.,* needs to copy a subset of their RDF-Graphs for a specific application [19] as in Figure 1.

**Definition 1 (Fragment).** *Let S be a SPARQL endpoint of a participant, a fragment of the RDF-Graph published by S, F[S], is a SPARQL CONSTRUCT federated query [22] where all graph patterns are contained in a single SERVICE block with S as the remote endpoint. We denote as eval(F[S]) the RDF-Graph result of the evaluation of F[S].*

A fragment $F[S]$ enables a participant $T$ to make a copy of the data of $S$ that answers the query. We denote the result of the evaluation of $F[S]$ materialized by a participant $T$ as $F[S]@T$, *i.e.*, a fragment of *source* $S$ materialized at *target* $T$. A fragment is partial if $F[S]@T \subset S$ or full if $F[S]@T = S$. The local data of a participant is composed of its own data union the fragments copied from other participants. We call the directed labeled graph where the nodes are the participants and the edges $(S; T)$ labeled with fragments a *Collaboration Network*, $CN$. A $CN$ defines how data are shared between participants and how updates are propagated. Participants can query and update the fragments they materialize, *e.g.*, $Consumer\_1$ in figure 1 can modify the fragments copied from DBPedia and DrugBank using SPARQL 1.1 Update [23]

When a source in a $CN$ updates its data, the materialized fragments may become outdated. Fragments could be re-evaluated at the data source, but if the data source has a popular knowledge base, *i.e.*, many other participants have defined fragments on it, the continuous execution of fragments would decrease the availability of the source's endpoint. To avoid this, a participant may synchronize its materialized fragment *incrementally* by using the updates published by the source. Some popular data providers such as DBpedia Live [14] and MusicBrainz[1] publish live update feeds.

To track updates done by a participant, we consider an RDF-triple as the smallest directly manageable piece of knowledge [15] and the insertion and deletion of an RDF-triple as the two basic types of updates. Each update is *globally uniquely identifiable* and it turns the RDF-Graph into a new state. SPARQL 1.1 updates are considered as an ordered set of deleted and/or inserted triples. Each time we refer to an update, we implicitly refer to the inserted/deleted triple. Blank nodes are considered to be skolemized, *i.e.*, also globally identifiable[2].

Incrementally synchronizing a materialized fragment using only the updates published by a data source and the locally materialized fragment without reevaluating the fragment on the data source requires to exclude join conditions from fragments [8], therefore, we restrict to *basic fragments* [21], *i.e.*, fragments where the query has only one triple pattern.

Figure 2 illustrates a $CN$ and how updates are propagated on it. $P1$ starts with data about the *nationality* and *KnownFor* properties of $M\_Perey$ (prefixes are omitted for readability). $P2$ materializes from $P1$ all triples with the *knownFor* property. With this information and its current data, $P2$ inserts the fact that $M\_Perey$ discovered Francium. On the other hand, $P3$ materializes from $P1$ all triples with the *nationality* property. $P3$ detects a mistake (nationality should be *French*, not *French\_People*) and promptly corrects it. $P4$ constructed a dataset materializing from $P2$ the fragment of triples with the property *discoverer* the fragment of triples with the property *nationality* from $P3$. $P1$ trusts $P4$ about data related to $M\_Perey$, so she materializes the relevant fragment, indirectly consuming updates done by $P2$ and $P3$.

Updates performed on materialized fragments are not necessarily integrated by the source, *e.g*, the deletion done by $P3$ did not reach $P1$, therefore, equivalence between source and materialized fragment cannot be used as consistency criterion for $CNs$. Intuitively, each materialized fragment must be equal to the evaluation of the fragment at the source after applying *local* updates, *i.e.*, the

---

[1] http://musicbrainz.org/doc/MusicBrainz_Database#Live_Data_Feed

[2] http://www.w3.org/TR/2014/REC-rdf11-concepts-20140225/
#section-skolemization

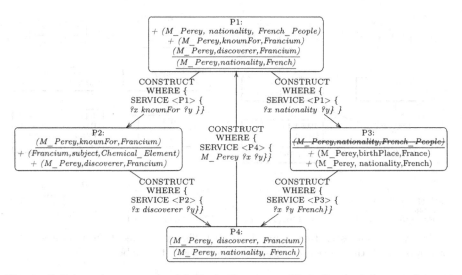

**Fig. 2.** Collaboration network with Basic Fragments. Underlined triples are the ones coming from fragments, triples preceded by a '+' are the ones locally inserted, struck-through triples are the ones locally deleted.

ones executed by the participant itself and the ones executed during synchronization with other fragments.

**Definition 2 (Consistency Criterion).** *Let $CN = (P, E)$ be a collaboration network. Assume each $P_i \in P$ maintains an ordered set of uniquely identified updates $\Delta_{P_i}$ with its local updates and the updates it has consumed from the sources of the fragments $F[P_j]@P_i$ it materializes. Given a $\Delta_P$, let $\Delta_P^{F[S]}$ be the ordered subset of $\Delta_P$ such that all updates concern $F[S]$, i.e., that match the graph pattern in $F[S]$. Let $apply(P_i, \Delta)$ be a function that applies an ordered set of updates $\Delta$ on $P_i$.*

*$CN$ is consistent iff when the system is idle, i.e., no participant executes local updates or fragment synchronization, then:*

$$(\forall P_i, P_j \in P : F[P_i]@P_j = apply(eval(F[P_i]), \Delta_{P_j}^{F[P_i]} \setminus \Delta_{P_i})$$

The $\Delta_{P_j}^{F[P_i]} \setminus \Delta_{P_i}$ term formalises the intuition that we need to consider only local updates when evaluating the consistency of each fragment, *i.e.*, from the updates concerning the fragment, remove the ones coming from the source.

Unfortunately, applying remote operations as they come does not always comply with Definition 2 as shown in Figure 3a: $P3$ synchronizes with $P1$, applying the updates identified as $P1\#1$ and $P1\#2$, then with $P2$, applying the updates identified as $P2\#1$ and $P2\#2$, however, the fragment materialized from $P2$ is not consistent. Notice that, had $P3$ synchronized with $P2$ before than with $P1$, its final state would be different $((s, p, o)$ would exist) and the fragment materialized from $P1$ would not be consistent.

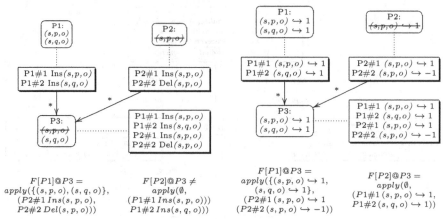

(a) Applying updates as they come does not comply with the correction criterion.

(b) The Annotated RDF-Graph enables a consistent Collaboration Network

**Fig. 3.** Illustration of the consistency criterion. Rounded boxes represent the graphs, and shaded boxes the sequences of updates. ∗ represents a full fragment.

## 3    A Protocol for Synchronization of Basic Fragments

To achieve consistency in every case, we propose, in the spirit of [7], to count the number of insertions and deletions of a triple, *i.e.*, we annotate each RDF-triple with positive or negative integers, positive values indicate insertions and negative values deletions. This allows a uniform representation of data and updates, yielding a simple way to synchronize fragments.

**Definition 3 (Annotated RDF-triple, Graph and Update)**

1. *Let $t$ an RDF-triple and $z \in \mathbb{Z}^*$. $t \hookrightarrow z$ is an annotated RDF-triple, with $t$ being the triple and $z$ the annotation.*
2. *An annotated RDF-Graph $G^A$ is a set of annotated RDF-triples such that $(\forall t, z | t \hookrightarrow z \in G^A : z > 0)$*
3. *An annotated update $u^A$ is represented by an annotated RDF-triple. More precisely, $t \hookrightarrow 1$ for insertion of $t$ and $t \hookrightarrow -1$ for deletion of $t$.*

Annotations in RDF-Graphs count the number of *derivations* of a triple. An annotation value higher than one indicates that the triple exists in more than one source or there are several paths in $CN$ leading from the source of the triple to the participant. Annotations in updates indicate, if positive, that $z$ derivations of $t$ were inserted; if negative, that $z$ derivations of $t$ were deleted. For example, an annotated RDF-triple $t_1 \hookrightarrow 2$ means that either $t_1$ has been inserted by two different sources or the same insert arrived through two different paths in the $CN$. The annotated update $t_2 \hookrightarrow -1$ means that $t_2$ was deleted at one source or by some participant in the path between the source and the target; $t_3 \hookrightarrow -2$ means that either $t_3$ was deleted by two sources or by some participant in the path between two sources and the target.

To apply annotated updates to annotated RDF-Graphs, we define an *Update Integration* function:

**Definition 4 (Update Integration).** *Let $A$ the set of all annotated RDF-Graphs and $B$ the set of all annotated updates. Assume updates arrive from source to target in FIFO order. The* Update Integration *function $\uplus : A \times B \to A$ takes an annotated RDF-Graph $G^A \in A$ and an annotated update $t \hookrightarrow z \in B$:*

$$G^A \uplus t \hookrightarrow z = \begin{cases} G^A \cup \{t \hookrightarrow z\} & if \, (\nexists w : t \hookrightarrow w \in G^A) \\ G^A \setminus \{t \hookrightarrow w\} & if \, t \hookrightarrow w \in G^A \wedge w + z \leq 0 \\ (G^A \setminus \{t \hookrightarrow w\}) \cup \{t \hookrightarrow w + z\} & if \, t \hookrightarrow w \in G^A \wedge w + z > 0 \end{cases}$$

The first piece of the Update Integration function handles incoming updates of triples that are not in the current state. As we are assuming FIFO in the update propagation from source to target, insertions always arrive before corresponding deletions, therefore, this case only handles insertions. The second piece handles deletions, only if the incoming deletion makes the annotation zero the triple is deleted from the current state. The third piece handles deletions that do not make the annotation zero and insertions of already existing triples by simply updating the annotation value.

We now consider each participant has an annotated RDF-Graph $G^A$ and an ordered set of annotated updates $U^A$. SPARQL queries are evaluated on the RDF-Graph $\{t \,|\, t \hookrightarrow z \in G^A\}$. SPARQL Updates are also evaluated this way, but their effect is translated to annotated RDF-Graphs as follows: the insertion of $t$ to the insertion of $t \hookrightarrow 1$ and the deletion of $t$ to the deletion of the annotated triple having $t$ as first coordinate. Specification 1.1 details the methods to insert/delete triples and synchronize materialized fragments. Figure 3b shows the fragment synchronization algorithm in action. A proof of correctness follows the same case-base analysis developed to prove [10].

## 3.1 Provenance for Conflict Resolution

In section 3 we solved the problem of consistent synchronization of basic fragments. However, our consistency criterion is based on the mere existence of triples, instead of on the possible conflicts between triples coming from different fragments and the ones locally inserted. Col-Graph's strategy in this case is that each participant is responsible for checking the semantic correctness of its dataset, as criteria often varies and what is semantically wrong for one participant, could be right for another. Participants can delete/insert triples to fix what they consider wrong. Participants that receive these updates can edit in turn if they do not agree with them.

In the event of two triples being semantically incompatible, the main criteria to choose which one of them delete is the *provenance* of the triples. With this information, the decision can be made based on the trust on its provenance. As in [11], we propose to substitute the integer annotations of the triple by

| Annotated Graph $G^A$,<br>Ordered Set $\Delta P_{ID}$ | IRI $P_{ID}$,<br>Annotated Graph $G^A$,<br>Ordered Set $\Delta P_{ID}$ |
|---|---|
| **void** *insert(t)*:<br>   **pre**: $t \notin \{t'\|t \hookrightarrow x \in G^A\}$<br>   $G^A := G^A \cup t \hookrightarrow 1$<br>   $Append(\Delta P_{ID}, t \hookrightarrow 1)$ | **void** *insert(t)*:<br>   **pre**: $t \notin \{t'\|t \hookrightarrow x \in G^A\}$<br>   $G^A := G^A \cup t \hookrightarrow P_{ID}$<br>   $Append(\Delta P_{ID}, t \hookrightarrow P_{ID})$ |
| **void** *delete(t)*:<br>   **pre**: $t \in \{t'\|t' \hookrightarrow x \in G^A\}$<br>   $G^A := G^A \uplus t \hookrightarrow -z$<br>   $Append(\Delta P_{ID}, t \hookrightarrow -z)$ | **void** *delete(t)*:<br>   **pre**: $t \in \{t'\|t' \hookrightarrow x \in G^A\}$<br>   $G^A := G^A \uplus t \hookrightarrow -m$<br>   $Append(\Delta P_{ID}, t \hookrightarrow -m)$ |
| **void** *sync(F[P_x], \Delta P_x)*:<br>   **for** $t \hookrightarrow z \in \Delta P_x$:<br>     **if** $t \hookrightarrow z \notin \Delta P_{ID}$:<br>       $G^A := G^A \uplus t \hookrightarrow z$<br>       $Append(\Delta P_{ID}, t \hookrightarrow z)$ | **void** *sync(F[P_x], \Delta P_x)*:<br>   **for** $t \hookrightarrow m \in \Delta P_x$:<br>     **if** $t \hookrightarrow m \notin \Delta P_{ID}$:<br>       $G^A := G^A \uplus t \hookrightarrow m$<br>       $Append(\Delta P_{ID}, t \hookrightarrow m)$ |

**Specification 1.1.** Class Participant when triples are annotated with elements of $Z$

**Specification 1.2.** Class Participant when triples are annotated with elements of the monoid M

an element of a commutative monoid that embeds $(Z, +, 0)$. We recall that a commutative monoid is an algebraic structure comprised by a set $K$, a binary, associative, commutative operation $\oplus$ and an identity element $0_K \in K$ such that $(\forall k \in K \| k \oplus 0_K = k$; a monoid $M = (K, \oplus, 0_K)$ embeds another monoid $M' = (K', \oslash, 0_{K'})$ iff there is a map $f : K \to K'$ such that $f(0_K) = f(0_{K'})$ and $(\forall a, b \in K : f(a \oplus b) = f(a) \oslash f(b))$. If we annotate with a monoid that embeds $(Z, +, 0)$, only a minor change is needed in our synchronization algorithm to achieve consistency. This monoid is used to encode extra provenance information.

**Definition 5.** *Assume each participant in the collaboration network has a unique ID, and let $X$ be the set of all of them. Let $M = (Z[X], \oplus, 0)$ be a monoid with:*

1. *The identity $0$.*
2. *The set $Z[X]$ of polynomials with coefficients in $Z$ and indeterminates in $X$.*
3. *The polynomial sum $\oplus$, for each monomial with the same indeterminate:*
   $aX \oplus bX = (a + b)X$
4. *$M$ embeds $(Z, +, 0)$ through the function $f(a_1 X_1 \oplus \cdots \oplus a_n X_n) = \sum_1^n a_i$*

Each time a participant inserts a triple, she annotates it with its ID with coefficient 1. The only change in definition 4 is the use of $\oplus$ instead of $+$. Specification 1.2 describes the algorithm to insert/delete triples and synchronize fragments with triples annotated with elements of $M$.

When annotating with $Z$, the only information encoded in triples is their number of derivations. $M$ adds (i) Which participant is the *author* of the triple.

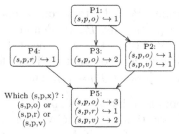

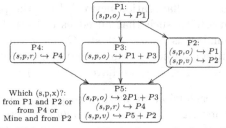

(a) Without provenance, P5 only information is the number of derivations. She does not know the author of the facts.

(b) With provenance, P5 also knows who inserted what and if it was concurrent, enabling trust based decisions to solve conflicts.

**Fig. 4.** Difference between annotating with $Z$ (4a) versus annotating with $M$ (4b). All fragments are full.

A triple stored by a participant $P$ with an annotation comprised by the sum of $n$ monomials indicates that the triple was inserted *concurrently* by $n$ participants from which there is a path in $CN$ to $P$. (ii) The number of paths in the Collaboration Network in which all edges concern the triple, starting from the author(s) of the triple to this participant, indicated by the coefficient of the author's ID.

Figure 4 compares annotations with $Z$ versus annotations with $M$. In the depicted collaboration network, the fact $(s,p,o)$ is inserted concurrently by P1 and P3, $(s,p,v)$ is inserted concurrently by P2 and P5 and $(s,p,r)$ inserted only by P4. When the synchronization is finished, P5 notices that it has three triples with $s$ and $p$ as subject and predicate but different object values. If P5 wants to keep only one of such triples based on trust, the $Z$ annotations (4a) do not give her enough information, while the $M$ annotations (4b) give more information for $P5$ to take the right decision. She can know that the triple $(s, p, o)$ was inserted by two participants $P1$ and $P3$, while $(s, p, r)$ was only inserted by $P4$ and that $(s, p, v)$ was inserted by $P2$ and herself.

## 4    Complexity Analysis

In this section, we analyze the complexity in time, space and traffic of RDF-Graphs annotated with $M$ and their synchronization, to answer the question: *how much does it cost to guarantee the correctness of a collaboration network?*.

Concerning time complexity, from specifications 1.1 and 1.2, we can see that for the insert and delete methods is constant. For the synchronization of a fragment $F[P_x]@P_y$, the complexity is $n(x_1 + x_2)$ where $n$ is the number of incoming updates, $x_1$ the complexity of checking if an update is in $\Delta P_y$ (which can be considered linear) and $x_2$ the complexity of the $\uplus$ function. For $Z$ annotations, $\uplus$ is constant, for $M$ is linear on the size of the largest polynomial.

Concerning space complexity, the overhead is the size of the annotations. For an annotated triple $t$ at a participant $P$, the relevant factors are: (i) the set of participants that concurrently inserted $t$ from which there is a path to $P$ such that all edges concern $t$, that we will denote $\beta_t$ (ii) the number of paths to $P$

in the collaboration network from the participants $P_1 \ldots P_n$ that concurrently inserted $t$ such that all edges concern $t$. For a participant $P_i$, we denote this number as $\rho_{t \leftarrow P_i}$. Let $sizeOf$ be a function that returns the space needed to store an object. Assume that the cost of storing ids is a constant $\omega$. Then, for $t \hookrightarrow z, z \in Z[x]$ we have $sizeOf(z) = |\beta_t|\omega + \sum\limits_{P_i \in \beta_t} sizeOf(\rho_{t \leftarrow P_i})$. Therefore, for each triple we need to keep a hash map from ids to integers of size $|\beta_t|$. The worst case for $|\beta_t|$ is a *strongly connected* Collaboration Network $CN$ where all participants insert $t$ concurrently, yielding an array of size $|CN|$ . The worst case for $\rho_{t \leftarrow P_i}$ is a *complete network*, as the number of different simple paths is maximal and in the order of $|CN|$!

The size of the log at a participant $P$ depends on two factors (i) the *dynamics* of $P$, *i.e.*, the number of local updates it does. (ii) the *dynamics* of the fragments materialized by $P$, i.e., the amount of updates at the sources that concern them.

In terms of the number of messages exchanged our solution is optimal, only one contact with the update log of each source is needed. In terms of message size, the overhead is in principle the same as the space complexity. However, many compression techniques could be applied.

The solution described so far uses an update log that is never purged. Having the full update history of a participant has benefits like enabling *historical queries* and *version control*. However, when space is limited and/or updates occur often, keeping such a log could not be possible. To adapt our solution to data feeds we need to solve two issues: (i) How participants materialize fragments for the first time? (ii) How to check if an incoming update has been already received?

To solve the first issue, an SPARQL extension that allows to query the annotated RDF-Graph and return the triples *and* their annotations is needed, for example the one implemented in [24]. To solve the second issue, we propose to add a second annotation to updates, containing a set of participant identifiers $\phi_u$ representing the participants that have already received and applied the update. When an update $u$ is created, $\phi_u$ is set to the singleton containing the ID of the author, when $u$ is pushed downstream, the receiving participant checks if his ID is in $\phi_u$, if yes, $u$ has already been received and is ignored, else, it is integrated, and before pushing it downstream it adds its ID to $\phi_u$. Of course, there is a price to pay in traffic, as the use of $\phi$ increases the size of the update. The length of $\phi_u$ is bounded by the length of the longest simple path in the Collaboration-Network, which in turn is bounded by the number of participants.

To summarize, the performance of our solution is mainly affected by the following properties of the CN: (i) The probability of concurrent insertion of the same data by many participants. The higher this probability, the number of terms of the polynomials is potentially higher. (ii) Its *connectivity*. The more connected, the more paths between the participants and the potential values of $\rho$ are higher. If the network is poorly connected, few updates will be consumed and the effects of concurrent insertion are minimized. (iii) The *overlapping* between the fragments. If all fragments are full, all incoming updates will be integrated by every participant, maximizing the effects of connectivity and concurrent insertion. If all fragments are disjoint, then all updates will be integrated only once and the effects of connectivity and concurrent insertion will be neutralized.

# 5  Experimentations

We implemented specification 1.2 on top of the SPARQL engine Corese[3] v3.1.1. The update log was implemented as a list of updates stored in the file system. We also implemented the $\phi$ annotation described in section 4 to check for double reception. We constructed a test dataset of 49999 triples by querying the DBpedia 3.9 public endpoint for all triples having as object the resource http://dbpedia.org/resource/France. Implementation, test dataset, and instructions to repeat the experiments are freely available[4].

Our first experiment studies the execution time of our synchronization algorithm. The goal is to confirm the linear complexity derived in section 4 and to check its cost w.r.t fragment re-evaluation. We defined a basic fragment with the triple pattern *?x :ontology/birthPlace ?z* (7972 triples 15% of the test dataset's size). We loaded the test dataset in a source, materialized the fragment in a target and measured the execution time when inserting and when deleting 1, 5, 10, 20, 30, 40 and 50% of triples concerning the fragment. As baseline, we set up the same datasets on two RDF-Graphs and measured the time of clearing the target and re-evaluating the fragment. Both source and target were hosted on the same machine to abstract from latency.

We used the Java MicroBenchmark Harness[5] v. 0.5.5 to measure the average time of 50 executions across 10 JVM forks with 50 warm-up rounds, for a total of 500 samples. Experiments were run on a server with 20 hyperthreaded cores with 128Gb of ram an Linux Debian Wheezy. Figure 5 shows a linear behaviour, consistent with the analysis in section 4. Synchronization is less expensive than re-evaluation up to approx. 30% of updates. We believe that a better implementation that takes full advantage of streaming, as Corese does by processing data in RDF/XML, could improve performance. Basic fragments are also very fast to evaluate, we expect than in future work, when we can support a broader class of fragments, update integration will be faster in most cases.

Our second experiment compares the impact on annotation's size produced by two of the factors analyzed in section 4: concurrent insertions and collaboration network connectivity, in order to determine which is more significant. We loaded the test dataset in: (i) An RDF-Graph. (ii) An annotated RDF-Graph, simulating $n$ concurrent insertions of all triples, at $n$ annotated RDF-Graphs with id http://participant.topdomain.org/$i$, with $i \in [0, n]$ (iii) An annotated RDF-Graph, simulating the insertion of all triples in other graph with id "http://www.example.org/participant", arriving to this one through $m$ different simple paths, and measured their size in memory on a Macbook Pro running

---

[3] http://wimmics.inria.fr/corese
[4] https://code.google.com/p/live-linked-data/wiki/ColGraphExperiments
[5] http://openjdk.java.net/projects/code-tools/jmh/

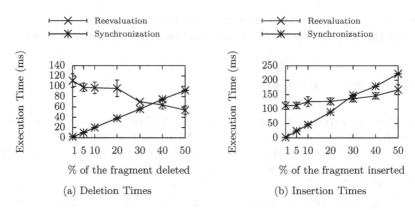

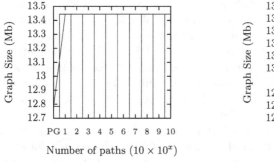 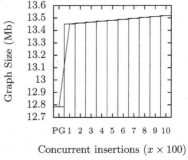

(a) Deletion Times

(b) Insertion Times

**Fig. 5.** Comparison of execution time (ms) between synchronization and fragment reevaluation. Error bars show the error at 95%.

(a) Simulation of one insertion arriving through multiple paths.

(b) Simulation of concurrent insertions arriving through one path.

**Fig. 6.** Space Overhead of the Annotated Graph w.r.t a plain graph (PG). Both Concurrency and Connectivity represent approx. 6% of overhead each.

MacOS Lion with java 1.7.0_10-ea-b13 and Java HotSpot(TM) 64-Bit Server VM (build 23.6-b04, mixed mode).

Figure 6 shows the results. Both cases represent nearly the same overhead, between 5 and 6 percent. Concurrency makes annotation's size grow sub-linearly. With respect to path number, annotation's size grows even slower , however, after $10 \times 10^{17}$ paths, the *long* type used in our implementation overflows, meaning that in scenarios with this level of connectivity, the implementation must use BigInt arithmetics. In conclusion, after paying the initial cost of putting annotations in place, Col-Graph can tolerate a high number of concurrent inserts and a high network connectivity.

The goal of our final experiment is to study the effect of network's topology on Col-Graph's annotation's size. We argue that the act of materializing fragments and sharing updates is socially-driven, therefore, we are interested in analyzing the behaviour of Col-Graph on social networks. We generated two sets of 40 networks with 50 participants each, all edges defining full fragments, one following the random Ërdos-Renyi model [5] and other following the social-network oriented Forest Fire model [12]. Each networkset is composed of 4 subsets of 10 networks with densities $\{0.025, 0.05, 0.075, 0.1\}$. Table 1 shows the average of the average node connectivity of each network set. Social networks in are less connected than random ones, thus, we expect to have better performance.

We loaded the networks on the Grid5000 platform (`https://www.grid5000.fr/`) and made each participant insert the same triple to introduce full concurrency, thus, fixing the overlapping and concurrency parameter in their worst case. Then, we let them synchronize repeatedly until quiescence with a 1 hour timeout. To detect termination, we implemented the most naive algorithm: a central overlord controls the execution of the whole network . We measured the maximum and average coefficient values and the maximum and average number of terms of annotations.

Figure 7 shows the results for Forest Fire networks. The gap between the average and maximum values indicates that topology has an important effect: only few triples hit high values. From the Ërdos-Renyi dataset, only networks with density 0.025 and finished before timeout without having a significant difference with their ForestFire counterparts. These results suggest that high connectivity affects the time the network takes to converge, and, as the number of rounds to converge is much higher, the coefficient values should also be much higher. We leave the study of convergence time and the implementation of a better termination detection strategy for future work.

**Table 1.** Average node connectivities of the experimental network sets

|              | 0.025  | 0.05   | 0.075  | 0.1    |
|--------------|--------|--------|--------|--------|
| Forest Fire  | 0.0863 | 0.2147 | 0.3887 | 0.5543 |
| Ërdos-Renyi  | 0.293  | 1.3808 | 2.5723 | 3.7378 |

## 6   Related Work

Linked Data Fragments (LDF) [21] proposes data fragmentation and replication as an alternative to SPARQL endpoints to improve availability. Instead of answering a complex query, the server publishes a set of fragments that corresponds to specific triple patterns in the query, offloading to the clients the responsibility of constructing the result from them. Col-Graph allows clients to define the fragments based on their needs, offloading also the fragmentation. Our proposal also solves the problem of *writability*, that is not considered by LDF.

[4,18] adapt the Distributed Version Control Systems Darcs and Git principles and functionality to RDF data. Their main goal is to provide versioning to Linked Data, they do not consider any correctness criterion when networks of collaborators copy fragments from each other, and they do not allow fragmentation, *i.e.*, the full repository needs to be copied each time.

[10,25] use *eventual consistency* as correctness criterion. However, this requires that all updates to be eventually delivered to all participants, which is

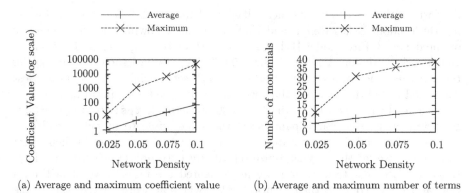

(a) Average and maximum coefficient value    (b) Average and maximum number of terms

**Fig. 7.** Performance of the synchronization algorithm when applied on networks generated with the Forest Fire model

not compatible with fragmentation nor with socially-generated collaboration network. [19] proposes a partial replication of RDF graph for mobile devices using the same principles of SVN with a limited lifetime of local replica checkout-commit cycle. Therefore, it is not possible to ensure synchronization of partial copies with the source since a data consumer has to checkout a new partial graph after committing changing to the data provider.

[9] formalizes an OWL-based syndication framework that uses description logic reasoning to match published information with subscription requests. Similar to us, they execute queries incrementally in response to changes in the published data. However, in their model consumers do not update data, and connection between consumers and publishers depends on *syndication brokers*.

Provenance models for Linked Data using annotations have been studied in [26,6] and efficiently implemented in [24], showing several advantages with respect to named graphs or reification. The model in [6] is based on provenance polynomials and is more general than the one we used, however, as basic fragments are a restricted class of queries, the $M$ monoid suffices.

Collaborative Data Sharing Systems (CDSS) like Orchestra [11] use Z-Relations and provenance to solve the data exchange problem in relational databases. CDSS have two requirements that we do not consider: support for full relational algebra in the fragment definition and strong consistency. However, the price to pay is limited scalability and the need of a global ordering on the synchronization operation, that becomes blocking [20]. Both drawbacks are not compatible with Linked Data requirements of scalability and participant's autonomy. Col-Graph uses the same tools to solve the different fragment synchronization problem, with an opposite trade-off: scalability and autonomy of participants in exchange of weaker consistency and limited expressiveness of fragment definitions.

# 7  Conclusions and Future Work

In this paper, we proposed to extend Linked Data federation to data consumers in order to improve its availability, scalability and data quality. Data consumers materialize fragments of data from data providers and put them at disposal of other consumers and clients. Adequate federated query engines can use these fragments to balance the query load among federation members. Fragments can be updated to fix errors, and these updates can be consumed by other members (including the original sources) to collaboratively improve data quality.

We defined a consistency criterion for networks of collaborators that copy fragments from each other and designed an algorithm based on annotated RDF-triples to synchronize them consistently. We analyzed the complexity of our algorithm in time, space and traffic, and determined that the main factors that affect performance are the probability of concurrent insertion, the connectivity of the collaboration network and the fragment overlapping.

We evaluated experimentally the incurred overhead using a 50k real dataset on our open source implementation, finding that in space, concurrency and connectivity represent approximately 6% of overhead each, and that it grows sublinearly; in time, our algorithm is faster than the reevaluation up to 30% of updated triples without taking in account latency. We also found that our algorithm performs better in socially generated networks than in random ones.

Future works include a large scale evaluation of Col-Graph focused on the effect of fragment overlapping, and using real dataset dynamics. We also plan to benchmark replication-aware federated query engines [13,17] on collaboration networks using Col-Graph to quantify the availability boost of our solution, and extend our model to handle dynamics on the fragment definitions themselves.

**Acknowledgements.** Some of the experiments presented in this paper were carried out using the Grid'5000 testbed, supported by a scientific interest group hosted by Inria and including CNRS, RENATER and several Universities as well as other organizations. This work is supported by the French National Research agency (ANR) through the KolFlow project (code: ANR-10-CONTINT-025).

# References

1. Acosta, M., Zaveri, A., Simperl, E., Kontokostas, D., Auer, S., Lehmann, J.: Crowdsourcing linked data quality assessment. In: Alani, H., et al. (eds.) ISWC 2013, Part II. LNCS, vol. 8219, pp. 260–276. Springer, Heidelberg (2013)
2. Berners-Lee, T., O'Hara, K.: The read-write linked data web. Philosophical Transactions of the Royal Society (2013)
3. Buil-Aranda, C., Hogan, A., Umbrich, J., Vandenbussche, P.-Y.: SPARQL web-querying infrastructure: Ready for action? In: Alani, H. (ed.) ISWC 2013, Part II. LNCS, vol. 8219, pp. 277–293. Springer, Heidelberg (2013)
4. Cassidy, S., Ballantine, J.: Version control for rdf triple stores. In: ICSOFT (2007)
5. Erdös, P., Rényi, A.: On the evolution of random graphs. Magyar Tud. Akad. Mat. Kutató Int. Közl 5 (1960)

6. Geerts, F., Karvounarakis, G., Christophides, V., Fundulaki, I.: Algebraic structures for capturing the provenance of sparql queries. In: ICDT (2013)
7. Green, T.J., Ives, Z.G., Tannen, V.: Reconcilable differences. Theory of Computer Systems 49(2) (2011)
8. Gupta, A., Jagadish, H., Mumick, I.S.: Data integration using self-maintainable views. In: Apers, P.M.G., Bouzeghoub, M., Gardarin, G. (eds.) EDBT 1996. LNCS, vol. 1057, pp. 140–144. Springer, Heidelberg (1996)
9. Halaschek-Wiener, C., Kolovski, V.: Syndication on the web using a description logic approach. J. Web Sem. 6(3) (2008)
10. Ibáñez, L.D., Skaf-Molli, H., Molli, P., Corby, O.: Live linked data: Synchronizing semantic stores with commutative replicated data types. International Journal of Metadata, Semantics and Ontologies 8(2) (2013)
11. Karvounarakis, G., Green, T.J., Ives, Z.G., Tannen, V.: Collaborative data sharing via update exchange and provenance. ACM TODS (August 2013)
12. Leskovec, J., Kleinberg, J., Faloutsos, C.: Graph evolution: Densification and shrinking diameters. ACM TKDD 1(1) (March 2007)
13. Montoya, G., Skaf-Molli, H., Molli, P., Vidal, M.E.: Fedra: Query Processing for SPARQL Federations with Divergence. Tech. rep., Université de Nantes (May 2014)
14. Morsey, M., Lehmann, J., Auer, S., Stadler, C., Hellmann, S.: Dbpedia and the live extraction of structured data from wikipedia. Program: Electronic Library and Information Systems 46(2), 157–181 (2012)
15. Ognyanov, D., Kiryakov, A.: Tracking changes in RDF(S) repositories. In: Gómez-Pérez, A., Benjamins, V.R. (eds.) EKAW 2002. LNCS (LNAI), vol. 2473, p. 373. Springer, Heidelberg (2002)
16. Passant, A., Mendes, P.N.: sparqlpush: Proactive notification of data updates in rdf stores using pubsubhubbub. In: Sixth Workshop on Scripting and Development for the Semantic Web, SFSW (2010)
17. Saleem, M., Ngonga Ngomo, A.-C., Xavier Parreira, J., Deus, H.F., Hauswirth, M.: DAW: Duplicate-aWare federated query processing over the web of data. In: Alani, H., et al. (eds.) ISWC 2013, Part I. LNCS, vol. 8218, pp. 574–590. Springer, Heidelberg (2013)
18. Sande, M.V., Colpaert, P., Verborgh, R., Coppens, S., Mannens, E., de Walle, R.V.: R&wbase:git for triples. In: LDOW (2013)
19. Schandl, B.: Replication and versioning of partial RDF graphs. In: Aroyo, L., Antoniou, G., Hyvönen, E., ten Teije, A., Stuckenschmidt, H., Cabral, L., Tudorache, T. (eds.) ESWC 2010, Part I. LNCS, vol. 6088, pp. 31–45. Springer, Heidelberg (2010)
20. Taylor, N.E., Ives, Z.G.: Reliable storage and querying for collaborative data sharing systems. In: ICDE (2010)
21. Verborgh, R., Sande, M.V., Colpaert, P., Coppens, S., Mannens, E., de Walle, R.V.: Web-scale querying through linked data fragments. In: LDOW (2014)
22. W3C: SPARQL 1.1 Federated Query (March 2013), http://www.w3.org/TR/sparql11-federated-query/
23. W3C: SPARQL 1.1 Update (March 2013), http://www.w3.org/TR/sparql11-update/
24. Wylot, M., Cudre-Mauroux, P., Groth, P.: Tripleprov: Efficient processing of lineage queries in a native rdf store. In: WWW (2014)
25. Zarzour, H., Sellami, M.: srce: a collaborative editing of scalable semantic stores on p2p networks. Int. J. of Computer Applications in Technology 48(1) (2013)
26. Zimmermann, A., Lopes, N., Polleres, A., Straccia, U.: A general framework for representing, reasoning and querying with annotated semantic web data. Web Semant 11 (March 2012)

# Transferring Semantic Categories with Vertex Kernels: Recommendations with SemanticSVD++

Matthew Rowe

School of Computing and Communications, Lancaster University, Lancaster, UK
m.rowe@lancaster.ac.uk

**Abstract.** Matrix Factorisation is a recommendation approach that tries to understand what factors interest a user, based on his past ratings for items (products, movies, songs), and then use this factor information to predict future item ratings. A central limitation of this approach however is that it cannot capture how a user's tastes have evolved beforehand; thereby ignoring if a user's preference for a factor is likely to change. One solution to this is to include users' preferences for semantic (i.e. linked data) categories, however this approach is limited should a user be presented with an item for which he has not rated the semantic categories previously; so called *cold-start categories*. In this paper we present a method to overcome this limitation by transferring rated semantic categories in place of unrated categories through the use of vertex kernels; and incorporate this into our prior $SemanticSVD^{++}$ model. We evaluated several vertex kernels and their effects on recommendation error, and empirically demonstrate the superior performance that we achieve over: (i) existing $SVD$ and $SVD^{++}$ models; and (ii) $SemanticSVD^{++}$ with no transferred semantic categories.

## 1 Introduction

Recommender systems have become a ubiquitous information filtering device that is prevalent across the web. At its core is the profiling of a user based on his prior behaviour to then forecast how he will behave in the future: i.e. how he will rate and consume items (movies, songs, products) thereafter. One of the most widespread approaches to recommending items to users is matrix factorisation; this method functions by *mining* a given user's affinity with a range of latent factors, in doing so allowing a user's rating for a given item to be predicted based on the dot-product ($\langle \mathbf{p}_u \mathbf{q}_i \rangle$) between the user's latent factor vector ($\mathbf{p}_u$) and the item's latent factor vector ($\mathbf{q}_i$). The problem with such approaches is that one cannot capture how a given user's tastes have *evolved* over time, given that the *mined* latent factors vary depending on the input - the *factor consistency problem*: where the latent factor vector indices of equivalent factors differ each time factorisation is performed. If we can capture information about how a user's tastes have changed then we can understand whether a user is likely to diverge in their preferences, or not, in the future and use this information to inform

P. Mika et al. (Eds.) ISWC 2014, Part I, LNCS 8796, pp. 341–356, 2014.

what recommendations to give. This prompts two research questions: *how can we capture the evolution of a user's tastes over time?* And *how can we include taste evolution information within a recommender system?*

In our recent prior work we presented a recommendation approach based on matrix factorisation called $SemanticSVD^{++}$ [9] - a modification of the existing $SVD^{++}$ model [4] - that captures a user's preferences for semantic categories of items, and how these preferences have *evolved* over time. One limitation of this approach, however, is the existence of *cold-start categories* where a user has not rated an item from a given category before. To overcome this limitation in this paper we present a technique to transfer existing, rated semantic categories via vertex kernels, thereby leveraging existing semantic category ratings into the $SemanticSVD^{++}$ model. Our contributions in this paper are as follows:

1. Identification and quantification of the *cold-start categories* problem, its implications on semantic recommendation approaches, and a method to *transfer* existing rated semantic categories via vertex kernels that function over the linked data graph - presenting four of such vertex kernels.
2. An extension of the $SemanticSVD^{++}$ recommendation approach that captures users' taste evolution, based on semantic categories, and transfers *rated* semantic categories to overcome the *cold-start categories* problem.
3. An empirical evaluation of our approach that demonstrates improved performance when transferring semantic categories over: (i) existing $SVD$ and $SVD++$ models; and (ii) not transferring rated semantic categories.

We have structured this paper as follows: section 2 presents the related work within the area of semantic recommender systems and how such existing approaches have functioned to date; section 3 explains the movie recommendation dataset that we used and the URI alignment procedure that we followed; section 4 explains the transferring of semantic categories to overcome the *cold-start category* problem; section 5 presents our approach for modelling users' taste profiles and how this enables the *evolution* of user's tastes to be captured; section 6 describes the $SemanticSVD^{++}$ model, the factors within the model, and the model learning procedure that we followed; section 7 presents our experimental evaluation of the model; section 8 discusses the limitations of this work and plans for future work; and section 9 draws the paper to a close with the conclusions gleaned from this work.

## 2   Related Work

There has been a flurry of recent work to combine recommender systems with the semantic web, and in particular linked data. Earlier work in this space was presented by Passant [8] to perform music recommendations by using the taste profile of a user's listening habits. The linked data graph could then be used to find the different pathways that connect two arbitrary nodes (e.g. resources of bands and artists) and how they can be linked together. These paths were then used to gauge how *close* artists are, and thus recommend similar bands to what the user had listened to. The linked data graph has also been used in recent work by Di Noia et al. [2] to extract movie features for a content-based recommender system in order to build user profiles. In this instance, features specific to movie items (e.g. actors, directors of movies) were extracted from linked data based on the surrounding context of the item. Work by Ostuni et al. [7] expanded on the work of Di Noia et al. [2] by mining path-based features that link the past ratings of users together; in doing so the authors were able to induce a top-*n* ranking function for recommendations. Such is the potential for linked data within recommender systems, that the Extended Semantic Web Conference 2014 has also held a recommendation challenge where participants must recommend books to users; where such books are aligned with their semantic web URIs on the web of linked data.[1]

Our recent work [9] combined semantic taste evolution information into a recommender system by modelling users' tastes at the semantic category level, thereby overcoming the *factor consistency problem* - i.e. where mined latent factor vector indices of equivalent factors differ each time factorisation is performed. However this approach is limited when presented with items assigned to *cold-start categories*; where a given user has not rated an item's categories beforehand. This paper extends our prior work by first explaining how the linked data graph can be harnessed to identify similar, previously rated semantic categories, for a given user, and transfer these into the recommendation approach - thereby overcoming the problem of *cold-start categories* - to do this we use vertex kernels. To aid reader comprehension, we provide a brief overview of how we model and track users' ratings for semantic categories, and how the $SemanticSVD^{++}$ model functions - for a more thorough overview please see our prior work [9].

## 3  Movie Recommendation Dataset and URI Alignment

For our experiments we used the MovieTweetings dataset,[2] obtained from the RecSys wiki page[3] after being provided with the data by Doom et al. [3]. This dataset was obtained by crawling Twitter for Tweets that contained Internet Movie DataBase (IMDB) links coupled with a rating (out of 10). To enable unbiased testing of our recommendation approach, we divided the dataset up as follows: we ordered the ratings by their creation time and maintained the first 80% as the training set, the next 10% for the validation set, and the final 10% as the test set. As the dataset covers a period of around 30-weeks (March 2013 to September 2013), this meant that the training set contained the first 24 weeks, with the subsequent 3 weeks' segments containing the validating and testing portions. In the following sections the training set is analysed for users' semantic taste evolution and used to train the recommendation model, we use

---

[1] http://2014.eswc-conferences.org/important-dates/call-RecSys

[2] This was the November 2013 version.

[3] http://recsyswiki.com/wiki/Movietweetings

the validation set for hyperparameter tuning, and the held-out test set for the final experiments.

Movie recommendation datasets provide numeric IDs for movie items, which users have rated, and assign metadata to these IDs: title, year, etc. As we shall explain below, the user profiling approach models users' affinity to semantic categories, therefore we need to *align* the numeric IDs of movie items to their semantic web URIs - to enable the semantic categories that the movie has been placed within to be extracted.[4]. In this work we use DBPedia SKOS categories as our semantic categories.

The URI alignment method functioned as follows: first, we used the SPARQL query from [7] to extract all films (instances of `dbpedia-owl:Film`) from DBPedia which contained a year within one of their categories.[5] Using the extracted mapping between the movie URI (`?movie`) and title (`?title`) we then identified the set of *candidate URIs* ($C$) by performing fuzzy matches between a given item's title and the extracted title from DBPedia - using the normalised reciprocal Levenshtein distance and setting the similarity threshold to 0.9. We used fuzzy matches here due to the different forms of the movie titles and abbreviations within the dataset and linked data labels. After deriving the set of candidate URIs, we then dereferenced each URI and looked up its year to see if it appears within an associated category (i.e. `?movie dcterms:subject ?category`). If the year of the movie item appears within a mapped category (`?category`) then we identified the given semantic URI as denoting the item. This *disambiguation* was needed here as multiple films can share the same title (i.e. film remakes). This approach achieved coverage (i.e. proportion of items mapped) of 69%: this reduced coverage is explained by the recency of the movies being reviewed and the lack of coverage of this on DBPedia at present. Table 1 presents the statistics of the dataset following URI alignment.

From this point on we use the following notations to aid comprehension: $u, v$ denote users, $i, j$ denote items, $r$ denotes a known rating value (where $r \in [1, 10]$), $\hat{r}$ denotes a predicted rating value, $c$ denotes a semantic category that an item has been mapped to, and $cats(i)$ is a convenience function that returns the set of semantic categories of item $i$.

**Table 1.** Statistics of the MovieTweetings dataset with the reduction from the original dataset shown in parentheses

| #Users | #Items | #Ratings | Ratings Period |
|---|---|---|---|
| 14,749 (-22.5%) | 7,913 (-30.8%) | 86,779 (-25.9%) | [28-03-2013,23-09-2013] |

---

[4] E.g. The 1979 Sci-Fi Horrow film Alien is placed within the semantic categories of `Alien_(franchise)_films` and `1979_horror_films`, by the `dcterms:subject` predicate.

[5] We used a local copy of DBPedia 3.9 for our experiments: `http://wiki.dbpedia.org/Downloads39`

## 4    Transferring Semantic Categories

A recommendation approach based upon semantic categories will assess how a user has rated items (books, movies, songs) beforehand, and associate those ratings with the items' categories to form a taste profile of the user. This taste profile, that captures the user's affinity for semantic categories, will then be used to predict how the user will rate a new item, given its semantic categories. A problem can arise here if the item's semantic categories have not been rated by the user: we define this as the *cold-start categories* problem. To demonstrate the extent of the problem, consider the plots shown in Fig. 1. In the left subfigure, the leftmost plot shows the association between the number of reviewed and unreviewed categories for each user when using the training dataset as background knowledge to form the profile of the user and the validation split to be the unseen data; while the rightmost figure shows the same association but with the training and validation splits as background data and the test split as the unseen data. In this instance we see that the more categories a user has rated, then the fewer categories they have missed. The right subfigure shows the relative frequency distribution of these missed categories, indicating a heavy-tailed distribution where a small number of categories are missed across many users. This indicates that cold-start categories hold additional information that a recommendation approach should consider.

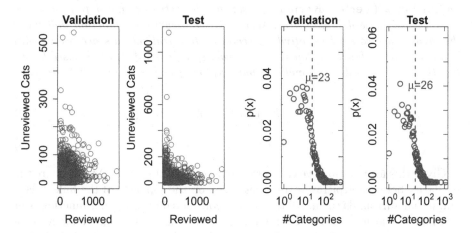

(a) Reviewed vs. Unreviewed Categories    (b) Distribution of Unreviewed Categories

**Fig. 1.** The left plot shows the association between the number of reviewed and un-reviewed categories for each user, and the right plot showing the relative frequency distribution of unreviewed categories within each split

### 4.1    Category Transfer Function and Vertex Kernels

To overcome the problem of cold-start categories we can include a user's preferences for *rated* semantic categories, where such categories are *similar* to the unreviewed categories. This is where the utility of the semantic web becomes evident: as the semantic categories are related to one another via SKOS relations (i.e. broader, narrower, related, etc.), we can identify semantic categories that are similar to the unreviewed categories by how they are related within the linked data graph - in a similar vein to prior work [8,2]:

**Definition 1 (Linked Data Graph).** *Let $G = \langle V, E, L \rangle$ denote a linked data graph, where $c \in V$ is the set of concept vertices within the graph (i.e. resources, classes), $e_{cd} \in E$ is an edge, or link, connecting $c, d \in V$ and $\sigma(e_{cd}) \in L$ denotes a label of the edge - i.e. the predicate associating $c$ with $d$.*

Now, let $C$ be the set of categories that a given user has rated previously, and $D$ be the set of categories that a given item has been mapped to, then we define the *Category Transfer function* as follows:

$$f(C, D) = \{\arg\max_{c \in C} k(c, d) : d \in D\} \qquad (1)$$

The codomain of the Category Transfer function is therefore a subset of the set of categories that the user has rated beforehand (i.e. $C' \subset C$). In the above function the vertex kernel $k$ computes the similarity between categories $c$ and $d$: this is often between the features vectors of the categories returned by the mapping function $\phi$:

**Definition 2 (Vertex Kernel).** *Given graph vertices $c$ and $d$ from a linked data graph $G'$, we define a vertex kernel ($k$) as a surjective function that maps the product of two vertices' attribute vectors into a real valued space, where $\phi(c)$ is a convenience function that returns kernel-specific attributes to be used by the function (i.e. an n-dimensional attribute vector of node $c$: $\phi(c) \in \mathbb{R}^n$). Hence:*

$$k : V \times V \to \mathbb{R} \qquad (2)$$

$$k(\phi(c), \phi(d)) \longmapsto x \qquad (3)$$

Given this formulation, we can vary the kernel function ($k(.,.)$) to measure the similarity between arbitrary categories based on the topology of the linked data graph that surrounds them. All the kernels considered in this paper function over two nodes' feature vectors. Therefore, to derive the feature vector for a given category node ($c$), we include information about the objects that $c$ is linked to within the linked data graph. Let `<c ?p ?o>` define a triple where $c$ appears within the subject position. We can then populate a vector ($\mathbf{x}$) based on the object concepts that $c$ links to over 1-hop: $\phi^1 \in \mathbb{R}^m$ - where $m$ denotes the dimensionality of the vector space. This can also be extended to $n$ hops away from $c$ by traversing edges away from $c$ and collecting the objects within the traversed triples. Each element in the vector is weighted by the out-degree of $c$, thereby capturing the probability of $c$ linking to a given category. Given the derivation of a *Triple-Object Vector*, using $\phi^n$, for each category node, we varied the vertex kernel between the four functions shown in Table 2.

**Table 2.** Vertex kernels used to measure concept node similarities

| Vertex Kernel | Function |
|---|---|
| Cosine | $k_{cos}^n(c,d) = \arccos \dfrac{\phi^n(c) \cdot \phi^n(d)}{\|\phi^n(c)\| \, \|\phi^n(d)\|}$ |
| Dice | $k_{dice}^n(c,d) = \dfrac{2\big(\phi^n(c) \cdot \phi^n(d)\big)}{\displaystyle\sum_{i=1}^{|\phi^n(c)|} \phi_i^n(c) + \sum_{i=1}^{|\phi^n(d)|} \phi_i^n(d)}$ |
| Squared Euclidean | $k_{se}^n(c,d) = \left( \displaystyle\sum_{i=1}^{|\phi^n(c)|} \big(\phi_i^n(c) - \phi_i^n(d)\big)^2 \right)^{-1}$ |
| Jensen-Shannon Divergence | $k_{js}^n(c,d) = \left( \dfrac{1}{2} \displaystyle\sum_{i=1}^{|\phi^n(c)|} \phi_i^n(c) \ln\left(\dfrac{2\phi_i^n(c)}{\phi_i^n(c) \times \phi_i^n(d)}\right) \right.$ $\left. + \dfrac{1}{2} \displaystyle\sum_{i=1}^{|\phi^n(d)|} \phi_i^n(d) \ln\left(\dfrac{2\phi_i^n(d)}{\phi_i^n(c) \times \phi_i^n(d)}\right) \right)^{-1}$ |

## 5   User Profiling: Semantic Categories

Semantic taste profiles describe a user's preferences for semantic categories at a given point in time, we are interested in understanding how these profiles change. Recent work [6] assessed user-specific evolution in the context of review platforms (e.g. BeerAdvocate and Beer Review) and found users to evolve based on their own 'personal clock'. If we were to segment a user's lifetime (i.e. time between first and last rating) in our recommendation dataset into discrete life-cycle periods where each period is the same width in time, then we will have certain periods with no activity in them: as the user may go away, and then return later. To counter this we divided user's lifecycle into 5 stages where each stage contained the same number of reviews - this was run for users with $\geq 10$ ratings within the training set. Prior work has used 20 lifecycle stages [6] to model user development, however we found this number to be too high as it dramatically reduced the number of users for whom we could mine taste evolution information - i.e. a greater number of stages requires more ratings.

To form a semantic taste profile for a given user we used the user's ratings distribution per semantic category within the allotted time window (provided by the lifecycle stage of the user as this denotes a closed interval - i.e. $s = [t, t'], t < t'$). We formed a discrete probability distribution for category $c$ at time period $s \in S$ (where $S$ is the set of 5 lifecycle stages) by *interpolating* the user's ratings within the distribution. We first defined two sets, the former $(D_{train}^{u,s,c})$ corresponding to the ratings by $u$ during period/stage $s$ for items from category $c$, and the latter $(D_{train}^{u,s})$ corresponding to ratings by $u$ during $s$, hence $D_{train}^{u,s,c} \subseteq D_{train}^{u,s}$, using the following construct:

$$D_{train}^{u,s,c} = \{(u,i,r,t) : (u,i,r,t) \in D_{train}, t \in s, c \in cats(i)\} \tag{4}$$

We then derived the discrete probability distribution of the user rating category $c$ favourably as follows, defining the set $C_{train}^{u,s}$ as containing all unique categories of items rated by $u$ in stage $s$:

$$Pr(c|D_{train}^{u,s}) = \frac{\frac{1}{|D_{train}^{u,s,c}|} \sum_{(u,i,r,t)\in D_{train}^{u,s,c}} r}{\sum_{c'\in C_{train}^{u,s}} \frac{1}{|D_{train}^{u,s,c'}|} \sum_{(u,i,r,t)\in D_{train}^{u,s,c'}} r} \tag{5}$$

We only consider the categories that item URIs are directly mapped to; i.e. categories connected to the URI by the dbterms:subject predicate.

## 5.1   Taste Evolution

We now turn to looking at the evolution of users' tastes over time in order to understand how their preferences change. Given our use of probability distributions to model the lifecycle stage specific taste profile of each user, we can apply information theoretic measures based on information entropy. We used conditional entropy to assess the information needed to describe the taste profile of a user at one time step $(Q)$ using his taste profile from the previous stage $(P)$. A reduction in conditional entropy indicates that the user's taste profile is similar to that of his previous stage's profile, while an increase indicates the converse:

$$H(Q|P) = \sum_{\substack{x\in P, \\ y\in Q}} p(x,y) \log \frac{p(x)}{p(x,y)} \tag{6}$$

Our second measure captures the influence that users *in general* have on the taste profiles of individual users - modelling user-specific (local) taste development and global development as two different processes. We used transfer entropy to assess how the taste profile $(P_s)$ of a user at one time step $(s)$ has been influenced by (his own) local profile $(P_{s-1})$ and global taste profile $(Q_{s-1})$ at the previous lifecycle stage $(s-1)$. For the latter taste profile $(Q_{s-1})$, we formed a global probability distribution (as above for a single user) using all users who posted ratings within the time interval of stage $s$. Now, assume that we have a random variable that describes the local categories that have been reviewed at the current stage $(Y_s)$, a random variable of local categories at the previous stage $(Y_{s-1})$. and a third random variable of global categories at the previous stage $(X_{s-1})$, we then define the transfer entropy of one lifecycle stage to another as [10]: $T_{X\to Y} = H(Y_s|Y_{s-1}) - H(Y_s|Y_{s-1},X_{s-1})$. Using the above probability distributions we can calculate the transfer entropy based on the joint and conditional probability distributions given the values of the random variables from $Y_s$, $Y_{s-1}$ and $X_{s-1}$:

$$T_{X\to Y} = \sum_{\substack{y\in Y_s, \\ y'\in Y_{s-1}, \\ x\in X_{s-1}}} p(y,y',x) \log \frac{p(y|y',x)}{p(y|y')} \tag{7}$$

We derived the conditional entropy and transfer entropy over the 5 lifecycle periods in a pairwise fashion, i.e. $H(P_2|P_1)$, for each user, and plotted the curve of the mean conditional and transfer entropy in Figure 2 using the training split - including the 95% confidence intervals. For conditional entropy, we find that users tend to diverge in their ratings and categories over time, given the increase in the mean curve towards later portions of the users' lifecycles. While for transfer entropy, we find that users' transfer entropy increases over time, indicating that users are less influenced by global taste preferences, and therefore the ratings of other users.

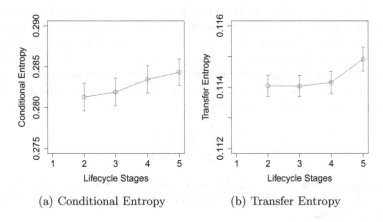

(a) Conditional Entropy                    (b) Transfer Entropy

**Fig. 2.** Taste evolution of users at the semantic category level: (i) comparing their divergence from prior semantic category ratings (2(a)); and (ii) comparing their influence of global semantic category taste trends (2(b))

## 6   SemanticSVD++

In this section we present a brief overview of $SemanticSVD^{++}$ [9], an extension of Koren et al.'s earlier matrix factorisation model: $SVD^{++}$ [4]. The predictive function of the model is shown in full in Eq. 8, we now explain each component.

$$\hat{r}_{ui} = \overbrace{\mu + b_i + b_u}^{\text{Static Biases}} + \overbrace{\alpha_i b_{i,cats(i)} + \alpha_u b_{u,cats(i)}}^{\text{Category Biases}}$$

$$+ \overbrace{\mathbf{q}_i^{\mathsf{T}}\left(\mathbf{p}_u + |R(u)|^{-\frac{1}{2}}\sum_{j \in R(u)} \mathbf{y}_j + |cats(R(u))|^{-\frac{1}{2}}\sum_{c \in cats(R(u))} \mathbf{z}_c\right)}^{\text{Personalisation Component}}$$

$$(8)$$

## 6.1   Static Biases

The static biases include the mean rating score ($\mu$) across all ratings within the training segment; the item bias ($b_i$), and the user bias ($b_u$). The item bias is the average deviation from the mean bias for the item $i$ within the training segment, while the user bias is the average deviation from the mean bias from the training segment's ratings by user $u$.

## 6.2   Item Biases Towards Categories

We model the biases that an item may have given the categories it has been linked to by capturing the proportional change in category ratings - i.e. in general over the provided training portion. Let $Q_s$ be the global taste profile (discrete probability distribution of all categories) in stage $s$, and $k$ be the number of stages *back* in the training segment from which either a monotonic increase or decrease in the probability of rating category $c$ began from, then the global taste development for $c$ is defined as follows:

$$\delta_c = \frac{1}{4-k} \sum_{s=k}^{4} \frac{Q_{s+1}(c) - Q_s(c)}{Q_s(c)} \qquad (9)$$

From this we then calculated the conditional probability of a given category being rated highly by accounting for the change rate of rating preference for the category as follows:

$$Pr(+|c) = \overbrace{Q_5(c)}^{\text{Prior Rating}} + \overbrace{\delta_c Q_5(c)}^{\text{Change Rate}} \qquad (10)$$

By averaging this over all categories for the item $i$ we can calculate the evolving item bias from the provided training segment:

$$b_{i,cats(i)} = \frac{1}{|cats(i)|} \sum_{c \in cats(i)} Pr(+|c) \qquad (11)$$

## 6.3   User Biases Towards Categories: Vertex Kernels

To capture the development of a user's preference for a category we derived the average change rate ($\delta_c^u$) over the $k$ lifecycle periods coming before the final lifecycle stage in the training set. The parameter $k$ is the number of stages *back* in the training segment from which either a monotonic increase or decrease in the probability of rating category $c$ highly began from:

$$\delta_c^u = \frac{1}{4-k} \sum_{s=k}^{4} \frac{P_{s+1}^u(c) - P_s^u(c)}{P_s^u(c)} \qquad (12)$$

We captured the change in transfer entropy for each user over time and modelled this as a *global influence factor* $\sigma^u$, based on measuring the proportional

change in transfer entropy starting from lifecycle period $k$ that produced a monotonic increase or decrease in transfer entropy:

$$\sigma^u = \frac{1}{4-k} \sum_{s=k}^{4} \frac{T_{Q \to P}^{s+1|s} - T_{Q \to P}^{s|s-1}}{T_{Q \to P}^{s|s-1}} \tag{13}$$

By combining the average change rate $(\delta_c^u)$ of the user highly rating a given
category $c$ with the global influence factor $(\sigma^u)$, we then derived the conditional
probability of a user rating a given category highly as follows, where $P_5^u$ denotes
the taste profile of the user observed for the final lifecycle stage (5):

$$Pr(+|c,u) = \overbrace{P_5^u(c)}^{\text{Prior Rating}} + \overbrace{\delta_c^u P_5^u(c)}^{\text{Change Rate}} + \overbrace{\sigma^u Q_5(c)}^{\text{Global Influence}} \tag{14}$$

We then took the average across all categories as the bias of the user given
the categories of the item:

$$b_{u,cats(i)} = \frac{1}{|cats(i)|} \sum_{c \in cats(i)} Pr(+|c,u) \tag{15}$$

Although the above summation will quantify the bias for categories linked
to item $i$ for which the user has provided a rating beforehand, the bias will
ignore any categories for which the user has yet to provide ratings - our so-called
*cold-start categories* - a limitation of the approach presented in our prior work
[9]. Therefore, to counteract this we used the Category Transfer Function for a
given vertex kernel to incorporate the most *similar* categories that the user $u$
has rated before. Let $C \equiv cats(D_{train}^u)$, then we define the bias of the user given
the categories of item $i$ as follows:

$$b_{u,cats(i)} = \left(\beta_k\right) \overbrace{\frac{1}{|C \cap cats(i)|} \sum_{c \in \{cats(i) \cap C\}} Pr(+|c,u)}^{\text{Prior Rated Categories}}$$

$$+ \left(1 - \beta_k\right) \overbrace{\frac{1}{|f_k(C, cats(i)/C)|} \sum_{c \in f_k(C, cats(i)/C)} Pr(+|c,u)}^{\text{Transferred Categories}} \tag{16}$$

Here we have $\beta_k$-weighted the influence of the transferred categories on the
bias in order assess the effects of the transferred categories on recommendation
accuracy. In essence, $\beta_k$ forms one of our hyperparameters that we optimise
when tuning the model over the validation set for a given vertex kernel $(k)$. As
$\beta_k \in [0,1]$ we can assess its effect: a larger $\beta_k$ places more emphasis on known
information, while a lower $\beta_k$ places more emphasis on transferred categories by
the given kernel $(k)$. As the category biases are, in essence, *static* features we

included two weights, one for each category bias, defined as $\alpha_i$ and $\alpha_u$ for the item biases to categories and the user biases to categories respectively - these weights are then learnt during the training phase of inducing the model.

### 6.4  Personalisation Component

The personalisation component of the $SemanticSVD^{++}$ model builds on the existing $SVD^{++}$ model by Koren et al. [4] by including four latent factor vectors: $\mathbf{q}_i \in \mathbb{R}^f$ denotes the $f$ latent factors associated with the item $i$; $\mathbf{p}_u \in \mathbb{R}^f$ denotes the $f$ latent factors associated with the user $u$; $\mathbf{y}_j \in \mathbb{R}^f$ denotes the $f$ latent factors for item $j$ from the set of rated items by user $u$: $R(u)$; and we have defined a new vector $\mathbf{z}_c \in \mathbb{R}^f$ which captures the latent factor vector, of $f$-dimensions, for a given semantic category $c$. This latter component captures the affinity of semantic categories with latent factors.

### 6.5  Model Learning

In order to learn our recommendation model (item and user biases, category bias weights, latent factor vectors) we sought to minimise the following objective function (including L2-regularisation of parameters):

$$\min_{b_*,\alpha_*,p_*,q_*} \sum_{(u,i,t,r)\in D} (r_{ui} - \hat{r}_{ui})^2 + \lambda(b_i^2 + b_u^2 + \alpha_i^2 + \alpha_u^2 + ||\mathbf{q}_i||_2^2 + ||\mathbf{p}_u||_2^2)$$

Stochastic Gradient Descent (SGD) [1] was used to learn the parameters by first shuffling the order of the ratings within the training set, and then running through the set of ratings one at a time. For each rating we calculated the predicted rating based on the user and item with the current model parameters, we then updated the model's parameters based on the error: $e_{ui} = r_{ui} - \hat{r}_{ui}$. We stopped the learning procedure once we converged on stable parameter vectors (i.e. the difference in parameters is less than $\epsilon = 10^{-7}$). The update rules for our model are shown in table 3. A single regularisation weight ($\lambda$) and learning rate ($\eta$) are used for all parameters in the model.

One situation that arises within the data is where the user has no prior rating information for a user within the training segment - i.e. *cold-start users*. In this instance we used the mean rating ($\mu$), the item static bias ($b_i$) and the category bias to the item ($i$) given the categories of the item ($b_{i,cats(i)}$): $\hat{r}_{ui}^{cold} = \mu + b_i + \alpha_i b_{i,cats(i)}$. This is an improvement of our prior approach [9] which did not address cold-start users.

## 7  Experiments

To test the efficacy of our recommendation model we used the existing $SVD$ and $SVD^{++}$ models as baselines, and tested two varieties of $SemanticSVD^{++}$: $SVD^{++}$ with Semantic Biases ($\Psi_{SB-SVD}$); and $SemanticSVD^{++}$ ($\Psi_{S-SVD}$),

**Table 3.** Update rules for each component within the $SemanticSVD^{++}$ model

| Model Parameter | Update Rule |
|---|---|
| Item bias | $b_i \leftarrow b_i + \eta(e_{ui} - \lambda b_i)$ |
| User bias | $b_u \leftarrow b_u + \eta(e_{ui} - \lambda b_u)$ |
| Item category bias weight | $\alpha_i \leftarrow \alpha_i + \eta(e_{ui} - \lambda \alpha_i)$ |
| User category bias weight | $\alpha_u \leftarrow \alpha_u + \eta(e_{ui} - \lambda \alpha_u)$ |
| Item vector | $\mathbf{q}_i \leftarrow \mathbf{q}_i + \eta\big(e_{ui}(\mathbf{p}_u + |R(u)|^{-\frac{1}{2}}\sum_{j \in R(u)} \mathbf{y}_j$ |
| | $\quad + |cats(R(u))|^{-\frac{1}{2}}\sum_{c \in cats(R(u))} \mathbf{z}_c) - \lambda \mathbf{q}_i\big)$ |
| User vector | $\mathbf{p}_u \leftarrow \mathbf{p}_u + \eta(e_{ui}\mathbf{q}_i - \lambda \mathbf{p}_u)$ |
| User items vector | $\forall j \in R(u):$ |
| | $\quad \mathbf{y}_j \leftarrow \mathbf{y}_j + \eta(e_{ui}|R(u)|^{-\frac{1}{2}}\mathbf{q}_i - \lambda \mathbf{y}_j)$ |
| User categories vector | $\forall c \in cats(R(u)):$ |
| | $\quad \mathbf{z}_c \leftarrow \mathbf{z}_c + \eta(e_{ui}|cats(R(u))|^{-\frac{1}{2}}\mathbf{q}_i - \lambda \mathbf{z}_c)$ |

which was the full model that we proposed earlier that includes latent factors for semantic categories. For these latter two models we tested the four vertex kernels and with the use of no kernel - to see how category transfer affected performance. We first performed model tuning, which we explain in more detail below, before then applying the best model, once hyperparameters had been selected. For model tuning, each recommendation model is trained using the training split and applied to the validation split, while for model testing each model is trained using both the training and validation split and applied to the test split. Our aim in both instances is to minimise the Root Mean Square Error (RMSE) over the respective test segment.

## 7.1 Model Tuning

In order to select the best model for application over the held-out test segment, we tuned the hyperparameters of each of the three models. For $SVD$ and $SVD^{++}$ we had three hyperparameter to tune: the regularisation weight ($\lambda$), the learning rate ($\eta$) and the number of factors ($f$). While for $SVD^{++}$ with semantic biases, and $SemanticSVD^{++}$ we have four kernels, each of which requires four hyperparameters to be tuned: the regularisation weight ($\lambda$), the learning rate ($\eta$), the number of factors ($f$), and the preference of transferred categories ($\beta_k$).[6] We varied these hyperparameters through the following settings, using an exhaustive grid search to find the combination that produced the lowest RMSE: $\lambda = \{10^{-9}, 10^{-8}, \dots, 10^0\}$; $\eta = \{10^{-7}, 10^{-6}, \dots, 10^{-1}\}$; $\mathbf{f} = \{5, 10, 20, 50, 100\}$; $\beta_k = \{0, 0.1, \dots, 1\}$. This was performed by searching the hyperparameter space using our parallel processing cluster (11 x AMD Quad Core machines each with 16Gb RAM and 2Tb disk space) - i.e. optimising the model's parameters with SGD given the hyperparameters and reporting the error over the validation split.

---

[6] We set $n = 1$ for each of the kernels therefore we are only forming feature vectors that are 1-top away from each category.

## 7.2  Results: Ratings Prediction Error

We now report on the results from forecasting the ratings within the test set based on the optimised models following hyperparmater tuning. Table 4 presents the RMSE values that we achieved. In order to assess for chance effects we performed significance testing using the Mann-Whitney test to assess for differences in location between the $SVD^{++}$ baseline model and each of the proposed models (with different kernels) - after randomly splitting the test segment into 25-folds and macro-averaging the RMSE.[7] We find that for all models we achieved a statistically significant reduction in RMSE over the baseline - with the significance probability levels indicated. The results also indicate that the inclusion of transferred categories reduces prediction error over the use of no vertex kernel, thereby suggesting that the use of prior rating information from related categories boosts performance.

We find that the Cosine kernel performs best over both $SVD^{++}$ with semantic biases, and $SemanticSVD^{++}$, in each case with a higher $\beta_k$ weighting. Under this weighting scheme, a higher $\beta_k$ places more emphasis on the item's categories that the user has previously rated, rather than transferring in ratings to cover the unreviewed categories. We find varying levels across the other kernels where, aside from the JS-Divergence kernel, the optimised $\beta_k$ places more emphasis on using rated semantic categories that the item is aligned to.

**Table 4.** Root Mean Square Error (RMSE) results with each model's best kernel is highlighted in bold with the p-value of the Mann-Whitney with the baseline marked

| Model | Kernel | Tuned Parameters | RMSE |
|---|---|---|---|
| $\Psi_{SVD}$ | - | $\lambda = 0.001$, $\eta = 0.1$, $f = 50$ | 1.786 |
| $\Psi_{SVD++}$ | - | $\lambda = 0.01$, $\eta = 0.05$, $f = 100$ | 1.591 |
| $\Psi_{SB-SVD++}$ | - | $\lambda = 10^{-5}$, $\eta = 0.05$, $f = 100$ | 1.590* |
| | Cosine | $\lambda = 10^{-5}$, $\eta = 0.05$, $f = 20$, $\beta_k = 0.9$ | **1.588*** |
| | Dice | $\lambda = 0.001$, $\eta = 0.05$, $f = 20$, $\beta_k = 0.7$ | 1.589** |
| | Squared-Euclidean | $\lambda = 10^{-5}$, $\eta = 0.05$, $f = 20$, $\beta_k = 0.6$ | 1.589** |
| | JS-Divergence | $\lambda = 0.01$, $\eta = 0.05$, $f = 50$, $\beta_k = 0.3$ | 1.590* |
| $\Psi_{S-SVD++}$ | - | $\lambda = 0.001$, $\eta = 0.05$, $f = 20$ | 1.590* |
| | Cosine | $\lambda = 0.01$, $\eta = 0.05$, $f = 5$, $\beta_k = 0.8$ | **1.588*** |
| | Dice | $\lambda = 0.001$, $\eta = 0.05$, $f = 20$, $\beta_k = 0.9$ | 1.590* |
| | Squared-Euclidean | $\lambda = 0.05$, $\eta = 0.05$, $f = 5$, $\beta_k = 0.7$ | 1.590* |
| | JS-Divergence | $\lambda = 10^{-4}$, $\eta = 0.05$, $f = 10$, $\beta_k = 0.8$ | 1.589** |

Significance codes: p-value < 0.001 *** 0.01 ** 0.05 * 0.1 .

## 8  Discussions and Future Work

The introduction of *semantic level* taste information allows for the evolution of a user's preferences to be captured and used within a recommendation approach.

---

[7] N.b. all tested models significantly outperformed $SVD$ at $p < 0.001$, so we do not report the different p-values here.

In this paper we have considered vertex kernels that transfer previously rated semantic categories by computing pairwise category similarity using triple-object vectors. One future direction of work will consider how the graph-space can be used, via traversal-based metrics, to compute the similarity between arbitrary pairs of category nodes. For instance, measures such as random walks hitting time and commute time, and the mixing rate of a random walk, measured over a subgraph of the linked data graph would be one future direction of work - forming the subgraph using the $n$-order egocentric network of the given category nodes.

Within this work we used a recent recommendation dataset derived from Twitter: MovieTweetings. Unlike existing movie recommendation datasets, such as MovieLens and NetFlix, this dataset suffers from a *recency* problem where the use of existing linked data datasets, such as DBPedia, are not timely enough to cover the items within the recommendation dataset - i.e. to provide URIs for those movie items. That said, we chose to use this single dataset as it presented a more recent resource to test our recommendation approach - as opposed to the heavily-subscribed MovieLens and Netflix datasets. Future work will examine the use of additional datasets, such as Freebase, for item to URI alignment that are more timely and could potentially lead to increased coverage of movie items and thus their alignment with semantic web URIs.

The objective function that we considered in this work, when optimising the presented recommendation approach, was the minimisation of the Root Mean Square Error. This objective has been criticised [5] as being unrealistic - i.e. in information filtering tasks limited screen-space renders a ranked list of items more appropriate. Therefore future work will focus on the adaptation of the approach to use a ranked-loss objective. Additionally, the optimisation procedure followed for identifying the best hyperparameters adopted an exhaustive grid-search approach, which is often intractable as the dimensionality of the dataset (i.e. number of items, and number of ratings) increases. Currently being explored is the use of Gaussian Processes in conjunction with Bayesian inference to estimate which portion of the hyperparameter space to examine next. This approach is necessary given the anticipated increased computational complexity that the graph-based kernels, mentioned above, will incur.

# 9   Conclusions

Recommender systems function by forming taste profiles of users, based on how they have rated items beforehand, and using those profiles to predict how the users will rate items in the future (e.g. movies, songs, products). One approach to forming such profiles is to capture how users have rated the semantic categories of items in the past, where such categories are linked to rated items. This approach is limited however in the presence of *cold-start categories*; semantic categories for which we have no prior rating information. In this paper we proposed a solution to this problem that uses the linked data graph space to identity similar categories that a user had previously rated, and transfer rating information from those categories to cover the unrated ones.. To demonstrate the efficacy of this solution, we extended our prior $SemanticSVD^{++}$ approach [9] to transfer semantic category ratings using a variety of vertex kernels. This new approach was evaluated using the MovieTweetings dataset, collected from users' movie review Tweets, against the existing $SVD$ and $SVD^{++}$ models. We significantly outperformed these baselines with the use of no kernel, thus using the standard $SemanticSVD^{++}$ approach, while using the the four tested kernel functions improved performance further; significantly outperforming the standard $SemanticSVD^{++}$ approach. Our results indicate that the use of vertex kernels is an effective means to leverage ratings from previously rated semantic categories and thus overcome the *cold-start categories* problem.

# References

1. Bottou, L., Bousquet, O.: The tradeoffs of large scale learning. In: NIPS, vol. 4, p. 2 (2007)
2. Di. Noia, T., Mirizzi, R., Ostuni, V.C., Romito, D., Zanker, M.: Linked open data to support content-based recommender systems. In: Proceedings of the 8th International Conference on Semantic Systems, pp. 1–8. ACM (2012)
3. Dooms, S., De Pessemier, T., Martens, L.: Movietweetings: a movie rating dataset collected from twitter. In: Workshop on Crowdsourcing and Human Computation for Recommender Systems, CrowdRec at RecSys, vol. 13 (2013)
4. Koren, Y.: Collaborative filtering with temporal dynamics. Communications of the ACM 53(4), 89–97 (2010)
5. Lee, J., Bengio, S., Kim, S., Lebanon, G., Singer, Y.: Local collaborative ranking. In: Proceedings of the 23rd International Conference on World Wide Web, International World Wide Web Conferences Steering Committee, pp. 85–96 (2014)
6. Julian McAuley and Jure Leskovec. From amateurs to connoisseurs: Modeling the evolution of user expertise through online reviews. In: Proceedings of World Wide Web Conference (2013)
7. Ostuni, V.C., Di Noia, T., Di Sciascio, E., Mirizzi, R.: Top-n recommendations from implicit feedback leveraging linked open data. In: 7th ACM Conference on Recommender Systems, RecSys 2013. ACM (2013)
8. Passant, A.: dbrec — music recommendations using dBpedia. In: Patel-Schneider, P.F., Pan, Y., Hitzler, P., Mika, P., Zhang, L., Pan, J.Z., Horrocks, I., Glimm, B. (eds.) ISWC 2010, Part II. LNCS, vol. 6497, pp. 209–224. Springer, Heidelberg (2010)
9. Rowe, M.: Semanticsvd++: Incorporating semantic taste evolution for predicting ratings. In: Web Intelligence Conference 2014 (2014)
10. Schreiber, T.: Measuring information transfer. Physical Review Letters 85(2), 461 (2000)

# Detecting Errors in Numerical Linked Data Using Cross-Checked Outlier Detection

Daniel Fleischhacker, Heiko Paulheim, Volha Bryl,
Johanna Völker*, and Christian Bizer

Research Group Data and Web Science, University of Mannheim, Germany
{daniel,heiko,volha,johanna,chris}@informatik.uni-mannheim.de

**Abstract.** Outlier detection used for identifying wrong values in data is typically applied to single datasets to search them for values of unexpected behavior. In this work, we instead propose an approach which combines the outcomes of two independent outlier detection runs to get a more reliable result and to also prevent problems arising from natural outliers which are exceptional values in the dataset but nevertheless correct. Linked Data is especially suited for the application of such an idea, since it provides large amounts of data enriched with hierarchical information and also contains explicit links between instances. In a first step, we apply outlier detection methods to the property values extracted from a single repository, using a novel approach for splitting the data into relevant subsets. For the second step, we exploit owl:sameAs links for the instances to get additional property values and perform a second outlier detection on these values. Doing so allows us to confirm or reject the assessment of a wrong value. Experiments on the DBpedia and NELL datasets demonstrate the feasibility of our approach.

**Keywords:** Linked Data, Data Debugging, Data Quality, Outlier Detection.

## 1 Introduction

The Linked Data Cloud is constantly growing, providing more and more information as structured data in the RDF format and interlinked between different repositories. Instead of being created and maintained manually, most data sources have their roots in unstructured or semi-structured information available throughout the Web. For example, data sources like DBpedia contain some data extracted from Wikipedia articles. However, though being a major reason for the large amount of Linked Data available, extracting data from unstructured or semi-structured information is error-prone. Even when extracting from semi-structured sources, representational variety (e.g., different thousands delimiters), can lead to problems in the parsing process and finally result in wrong Linked

---

* Johanna Völker is supported by a Margarete-von-Wrangell scholarship of the European Social Fund (ESF) and the Ministry of Science, Research and the Arts Baden-Württemberg.

P. Mika et al. (Eds.) ISWC 2014, Part I, LNCS 8796, pp. 357–372, 2014.

Data values. It is unrealistic to manually find errors due to the large amount of data in the repositories, thus automatic means for detecting errors are desirable.

In this paper, we introduce a method for detecting wrong numerical values in Linked Data. First, we determine outliers regarding a single data repository, e.g., on all values assigned by means of the `population` property. For this purpose, we present a way of discovering data subpopulations induced by classes and properties and apply outlier detection to these subpopulations. For example, on the full dataset, the populations of continents would be outliers for the `population` property values since their population values are larger than the predominant population values of cities or countries by several orders of magnitude.

Afterwards, as a second step, we exploit the `owl:sameAs` links of the instances (also called entities) for collecting values for the same property from other repositories. This is an especially important facet of our approach, since it actually uses the links that are a core concept of *Linked* Data which are rarely used in other works (see Sect. 3). If an outlier detected in the first step is only a natural outlier, it does not show up as an outlier in the second step which allows for mitigating the problem of falsely marking natural outliers as wrong values.

In the following, we describe this two-step approach in more detail. We first introduce the foundations of outlier detection in Sect. 2. Afterwards, we give an overview about other works on Linked Data error detection and Linked Data quality in general (Sect. 3). Then, in Sect. 4, we introduce our method for detecting erroneous numerical values in a Linked Data repository paying special attention to the choice of subpopulations of values and cross-checking by means of a second set of data. Afterwards, we evaluate the approach by an experiment on DBpedia and provide the first explorations on the NELL dataset in Sect. 5.

## 2    Preliminaries

Our approach presented in this paper is relying on the concept of *outlier detection* (sometimes also called *anomaly detection*). In this section, we give an overview of the most important notions used in our work. A more complete overview is given by Chandola et al. [5], where the outlier detection is defined as "finding patterns in data that do not conform to the expected normal behavior".

There can be different reasons for such deviations from the expected behavior. On the one hand, outliers can be caused by erroneous data where the error in the data leads to the actual deviation. On the other hand, there might also exist correct instances which deviate from those patterns, as in the example given above of the population of continents being outliers in the set of population values for cities, countries and continents. Such outliers are sometimes called *natural outliers*. Thus, when using outlier detection for finding errors in the data, special attention has to be paid on how to tell apart such natural outliers from outliers caused by actual data errors.

In all cases, the first step is the discovery of outliers. For this purpose, there are different categories of methods: supervised, semi-supervised, and unsupervised. Supervised and semi-supervised approaches require training data in which non-outlier values are labeled, and for the supervised approaches outlier values are also labeled. In contrast, unsupervised approaches are independent from such data. Since our approach should be able to work with many different data distributions (e.g., values for population, height, elevation etc.), the creation of training data would be rather expensive, so we only consider unsupervised outlier detection methods. In addition, the methods also differ in their output. Some methods return a binary decision whether a given value is an outlier while other methods provide an outlier score quantifying the degree of „outlierness". We only consider the latter group of approaches since they have the advantage that arbitrary thresholds can be chosen to address the trade-off between removing as many actual errors (true positives) vs. removing correct data points (false positives). There are also approaches which consider multiple dimensions of data at once (*multi-variate*) instead of just a single dimension (*univariate*) to improve the detection of outliers by considering values influencing each other. In this work, we only consider univariate approaches because multi-variate methods are more computationally expensive and require a way of determining which value combinations to consider.

In the literature, many different approaches are proposed for unsupervised outlier detection. Some methods assume there is an underlying distribution that generates the data. Values which are improbable according to this distribution, are qualified as outliers. One such approach is to assume an underlying Gaussian distribution of the values, compute mean $\mu$ and standard deviation $\sigma$ values and then mark all values as outliers that are not contained in the interval $[\mu - c\sigma, \mu + c\sigma]$ for a given $c$. For example, this assumption is backed by the Gaussian distribution's property that 99.7% of all values are within this interval for $c = 3$.

An alternative method for unsupervised outlier detection is the so-called *Local Outlier Factor* (LOF) proposed by Breunig et al. [2]. Compared to other globally working outlier detection approaches, LOF is trying to detect local outliers, i.e., values which deviate from their local neighbors. The idea is that real-world datasets contain data which might not be recognized as a global outlier but its deviation is only recognizable when considering its neighborhood. For this purpose, the LOF algorithm takes a parameter $k$ which defines the number of neighbors to look at. It then determines this number of neighbors and computes an outlier score based on the comparison of the distance of the neighbors to their nearest neighbors with the distance of the currently processed value.

## 3   Related Work

A number of automatic and semi-automatic approaches for correcting linked data have been proposed, which are either *internal*, i.e., they use only the data contained in the datasets at hand, or *external*, using either additional information sources (such as text corpora) or expert knowledge.

Recent *internal* approaches are mostly concerned with validating object-valued statements (in contrast, our approach targets at numeric literals). The approaches discussed in [9] and [16] first enrich the data source's schema by heuristically learned additional domain and range restrictions, as well as disjointness axioms, and then use the enhanced ontology for error detection by reasoning. Heuristic approaches for finding wrong dataset interlinks exist, which, for example, rely on finding inconsistent chains of `owl:sameAs` statements [13], or use outlier detection methods [14].

*External* approaches involve crowdsourcing [1], using platforms like Amazon Mechanical Turk which pay users for micro-tasks, such as the validation of a statement. Another possibility is using games with a purpose to spot inconsistencies as Waitelonis et al. [17] do. *DeFacto* [10] uses a pre-built pattern library of lexical forms for properties in DBpedia. Using those lexical patterns, DeFacto runs search engine requests for natural language representations of DBpedia statements. While it is designed to work on object properties, the approach is transferable to the problem of identifying errors in numerical data as well.

In this paper, we focus on *outlier detection* methods as a means to identify wrong numerical values. This approach is similar to our preliminary approach discussed in [18], but extends it in two respects. First, we identify meaningful subpopulations in a preprocessing step, which makes the outlier detection work more accurately. Second, most of the approaches discussed above do not use *dataset interlinks* at all, despite claiming to be data cleansing approaches for *linked* data. In contrast, we show in this paper that the explicit use of dataset interlinks improves the results of outlier detection, especially with respect to natural outliers.

## 4    Method

In the following, we describe our overall approach of detecting wrong values in a Linked Data dataset. First, we shortly describe how we determine the properties to check for wrong numerical values before we present the actual process of outlier detection. As discussed above, applying outlier detection to the full dataset might not result in good results since instances referring to different types of real world objects might be contained in the dataset. Thus, we also introduce our way of determining subsets of data to apply the outlier detection on. Finally, we describe the actual detection of erroneous values from the outlier detection results.

### 4.1    Dataset Inspection

Since we assume no prior knowledge about the dataset, we first have to gather some additional information about it. This step as well as the following steps are most easy to perform when the data is provided by a SPARQL endpoint.

First, we determine the number of instances contained in the repository as well as the names of all properties used in the data. Since we cannot assume to have an OWL vocabulary and its division between object and data type properties available in the dataset, we then determine how often each property is used with a numerical value[1] at the object position. Furthermore, we also determine how

---

[1] Numerical values are `xsd:int` and `xsd:float` as well as their subtypes.

many distinct numerical values are used with each property by means of the SPARQL query:

```
SELECT ?p, COUNT(DISTINCT ?o) AS ?cnt
WHERE {?s ?p ?o. FILTER (isNumeric(?o))} GROUP BY ?p
```

We then filter the properties to apply outlier detection and remove properties which were only used with a single distinct numerical value. All in all, this process results in a set of properties qualifying for the application of outlier detection.

## 4.2 Generation of Possible Constraints

Each property is now processed separately in several steps. It is important to note that the wrong value detection is always done for an instance-value pair and not only for an instance since an instance might have several values assigned by means of the same property, e.g., a city having different ZIP codes.

The first step here is to determine the set of constraints that are used to generate subpopulations from the full instance-value set on which a more fine-grained outlier detection is possible which in turn improves the detection of errors. The main motivation behind these constraints is that when always considering the full set of instances, some erroneous values could be *masked* by other values in the dataset while correct values could be erroneously highlighted as being wrong. Masking could for example occur when an instance of the type Country has an erroneous population count of 400. When considering the whole dataset, this population count would not arouse any suspicion since there are many instances of Village with similar population counts. However, when only considering instances of type Country, a population count of 400 would be suspicious because hardly any country has such a low population count. Erroneous highlighting of values could occur in the already provided case where instances of the class Continent having an actually correct population count are outliers in the dataset of all instances due to the low number of continents and their population counts being much higher than those of countries.

Thus, an important task is to define a way of generating subsets of the full instance set. In this work, we do this generation by applying constraints to the set of instances so that only those instances are retained which fulfill the constraints. We propose three different types of constraints:

- *Class constraints:* A class constraint on class $C$ applied to an instance set limits it to instances which belong to this class.
- *Property constraints:* A property constraint $p$ limits the instances to those connected to an arbitrary object (instance or data value) by means of $p$.
- *Property value constraints:* A property value constraint is defined by a property $p$ and a value $v$ which can be either an instance or a data value. It limits the instances to those which are connected to a value $v$ by means of $p$.

Class constraints as also applied by [18] are the most obvious way of utilizing the class structure already contained in the dataset. They allow capturing the masking for the population property described before.

In cases where the class structure is not detailed enough, the two additional constraint types can help to compensate these shortcomings. In real world datasets, property constraints can help to deduce statements about an instance's missing type [15]. For example, given a class Vehicle and a property maximumAltitude, this property can compensate for a missing class assertion to Aircraft and thus allow to detect, e.g., too high weight values for the instances that could otherwise be masked by other Vehicle instances such as ships. The choice of which properties to use as constraints is based on the number of usages in the current instance set. When even the property constraints are not able to provide a sufficiently fine-grained division into subpopulations, property-value constraints can be used. An example for such a constraint is the property locatedIn with the value UnitedArabEmirates (UAE). Since the average temperature in the UAE is higher than the temperature in most other countries, a too low averageTemperature assigned to a city in the UAE could be masked by cities from other countries. When only considering cities from the UAE, the low average temperature is suspicious and thus detectable as being erroneous.

Both property-based constraints share the problem that they might introduce a high number of constraints since the number of properties might be much higher than the number of classes used in the dataset. This can lead to higher computational effort for choosing the constraints. This effort is even higher for property-value constraints that do not only require to examine the used properties but also the values connected to instances by means of these properties.

## 4.3   Finding Subpopulations

Applying outlier detection to all of the potentially many subpopulations which can be defined on a dataset is impractical especially because the runtime of outlier detection algorithms heavily depends on the number of values they are applied on. Hence, we introduce an intermediate step for determining the most promising subpopulations to apply outlier detection on.

The exploration is organized in a lattice as shown in Fig. 1 similar to the one used by Melo et al. [12]. Each node of the lattice is assigned a set of constraints which determines the instances considered at this node. The root node has the empty constraint set assigned and thus represents all instances and corresponding values of the currently considered property. For this set of instances, we compute a histogram which represents the distribution of values in the subpopulation. Starting with the root node, our approach manages a queue of all not yet extended nodes and thus extends the lattice in a breadth-first-manner.

When processing a node from this queue, we create its child nodes, each having an additional constraint compared to the parent node. The additional constraints are those from the set of possible constraints which are not yet used in the parent node. If a node for the resulting set of constraints already exists in the lattice, we do not consider the new node further. Otherwise, we determine the instances which adhere to this new set of constraints and compute the histogram of the value distribution. Based on this value distribution, we enforce a set of pruning criteria to keep the search space clean which helps us to determine interesting

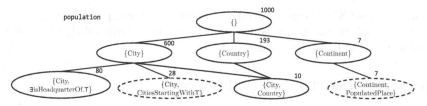

**Fig. 1.** Example for subpopulation lattice for property **population**. Numbers to the upper right of a node give the number of instances fulfilling the constraint set. Dashed nodes would be pruned, the left one for too low KL divergence, the right one for not reducing the instance set further.

subpopulations independently from any further knowledge about the constraints and their relation to each other. In particular, we prune subpopulations which only contain a low number of instances or maybe no instances at all since those are considered to be too specific.[2] As another criterion, we consider the instance reduction ratio, i.e., the change ratio in the number of instances of the new node compared to its parent node. If the additional constraint leads to a reduction of less than 1%, our approach prunes the node. For instance, this case could occur when adding a class constraint on **PopulatedPlace** to a constraint set which was previously also constrained on **Continent**.

Finally, we compute the Kullback-Leibler (KL) divergence [8] between the discrete value distributions represented by the histograms of the new node and the parent node. If the divergence is lower than a given threshold, we assume the additional constraint to be independent from the previously applied constraints, i.e., the actual distribution of values was not changed but only the number of instances. In these cases, an outlier detection run on the newly created set of instances would not yield additional insights and thus we prune those nodes. For example, this pruning could happen when adding a class constraint on the class **NamesStartingWithT** to a constraint set for a property representing the population count. Since each additional constraint leads to a smaller number of instances compared to the parent node, the sampling error might also influence the resulting KL divergence value. To address this effect in our considerations, we normalize the values using the number of instances of the resulting node leading to the formula

$$\text{divergence}(parent, child) = \left| \frac{|child|}{|parent|} \cdot \sum_{i=1}^{B} \ln \left( \frac{h_{\text{parent}}(i)}{h_{\text{child}}(i)} \right) h_{\text{parent}}(i) \right| \qquad (1)$$

where *parent* and *child* are the nodes of the lattice, $|n|$ the number of instances for a node $n$ and $h_{\text{parent}}$ as well as $h_{\text{child}}$ the histograms representing the respective value distribution which each have $B$ bins. Furthermore, we also apply Laplace smoothing to the histograms. We assume a higher divergence to show a more important change in the distribution of values and thus being more interesting for the further processing. Based on this assumption, we prioritize nodes

---

[2] In our experiments, a value of 5 was used.

having a higher KL divergence to their parents in later expansion steps, as well as in cases where too many nodes would have to be expanded, we limit the expansion to the highest ranked nodes.

## 4.4 Outlier Detection and Outlier Scores

After the lattice has been determined, we perform outlier detection on all un-pruned nodes of the lattice and store the resulting outlier scores together with the set of constraints which led to the corresponding instance set.

As soon as the outlier detection run is completed on the property, we have a list of instance-value combinations with a set of pairs, consisting of a constraint set and an outlier score. One advantage of having multiple outlier scores compared only a single outlier score for each instance-value combination is the possibility to apply different weighting schemas to the scores to combine them into a single assessment for each instance-value pair. At this point, it is also possible to further consider an ontology schema possibly contained in the dataset. For example, outlier scores for class constraints of more specific classes can be assumed to have more significance than those for constraints to more abstract classes and can thus be weighted higher. In particular, we explore a measure which assigns an instance-value combination with the outlier score of the constraint set containing the most specific constraint according to the hierarchy which performed best in our pre-studies in combination with the LOF outlier detection approach. It is noteworthy, that too specific constraint sets are already filtered during the creation of the subpopulation lattice which prevents us from choosing the outlier scores generated for such subpopulations. For determining the specificity of an entity in the hierarchy, we use property paths as introduced in SPARQL 1.1 like in the following query for a class specified by its IRI CLS

```
SELECT COUNT(DISTINCT ?i) AS ?cnt WHERE {<CLS> rdfs:subClassOf+ ?i}
```

This query provides us with the number of direct and indirect super classes of the given class which serves as an estimate for its specificness.

## 4.5 Cross-checking for Natural Outliers

As described in Section 2, values may not only be detected as outliers when they are wrong but also if they are natural outliers in the considered dataset. To prevent this false detection, we apply an additional cross-checking step to the results of the first outlier detection.

One of the unique selling points of Linked Data is the interlinking of datasets. Using URIs to point to resources in remote repositories, it is possible to specify for an instance which equivalent instances can be found in other repositories. Given that in the Linked Data and Semantic Web community the reuse and interlinking of schema vocabularies is encouraged, these equivalence assertions allow us to retrieve additional property values for the same instance. Even if the vocabulary is not reused, ontology matching techniques [7] can enable the re-trieval of additional property values by determining equivalent properties to the

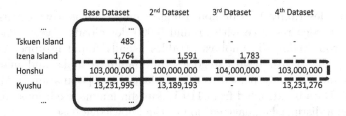

|  | Base Dataset | 2nd Dataset | 3rd Dataset | 4th Dataset |
|---|---|---|---|---|
| ... | ... | | | |
| Tskuen Island | 485 | - | - | - |
| Izena Island | 1,764 | 1,591 | 1,783 | - |
| Honshu | 103,000,000 | 100,000,000 | 104,000,000 | 103,000,000 |
| Kyushu | 13,231,995 | 13,189,193 | - | 13,231,276 |
| ... | ... | | | |

**Fig. 2.** Using two independent outlier approaches for the DBpedia property `populationTotal` and the instance "Honshu" to improve the detection result. Only considering the base dataset (vertical), the actually correct value is detected as an outlier. The detection run on the values from different sources (horizontal) confirms the value and thus prevents to mark the value as a wrong value.

currently relevant property. For the special case of DBpedia and its versions in several languages, inspections [3] revealed that the number of instances described in multiple datasets is relatively low. But even if the additional data is sparse, we assume that natural outliers are often more interesting for humans and hence more often described in several datasets (e.g., the highest mountain is probably described in more datasets than some arbitrary "non-special" mountain).

Using this feature of Linked Data, we have a way of compensating problems introduced by natural outliers. By gathering additional property values for an instance it is possible to test the value found in the current dataset for its "outlierness" in this second set of data. Since these values are expected to be the same if all values are fully correct, it is sufficient to assume a normal distribution for the values and check whether a value lies within a given number of standard deviations around the mean value (cf. Sect. 2). If the assessed value lies within the interval around the mean, the probability is high that the value is only a natural outlier and thus is not an erroneous value. We only consider values as wrong if they are outliers in both detections. This principle is depicted in the real-world example in Fig. 2 where an outlier detection based on the vertical axis would lead to a detection as a wrong value while the second outlier detection run on the horizontal axis confirms the population value in the base dataset.

## 5  Experiments

For testing the approach described in the previous section, we performed an evaluation on DBpedia[3] and its language versions which we present in detail in the following. Furthermore, we report on an evaluation on the NELL dataset in combination with cross-checking on several Linked Data sources.

### 5.1  DBpedia Experiment

The first experiment was performed on the DBpedia 3.9 dataset. DBpedia [11] is a large scale structured multi-lingual cross-domain knowledge base automatically extracted from Wikipedia. The current version of DBpedia contains 2.46

---

[3] http://dbpedia.org

billion facts describing 12.6 million unique things, and is a widely used high-impact knowledge resource with around 5,000 downloads a year. The data is extracted from Wikipedia infoboxes (tables usually found in upper right part of a Wikipedia page), page categories, interlanguage links and many more, which are automatically parsed to extract facts like "population of Mannheim is 314,931".Data is extracted from 119 Wikipedia language editions, and is represented as a distinct language edition of the knowledge base.

We let the approach run on the whole dataset, generating ranked lists of possibly wrong values for each property. As an outlier detection algorithm, we used the Local Outlier Factor in the implementation provided by the Rapidminer[4] Extension for Anomaly Detection.[5] The $k$ parameter of LOF was set to 10 resp. to the number of values if there were less than ten. Experiments using different number of bins for the histogram generation turned out that the single KL divergences between children and parent nodes had more variance for higher number of bins. This increased variance led to a more exact detection of similar distributions and thus more pruning in the lattice. However, increasing the number of bins further also increased the runtime of the lattice generation without leading to an adequate reduction of the outlier detection runtime and without clear improvements in the error detection. Thus, we used 100 bins as a compromise between exactness of pruning and runtime. The generation of subpopulations was done on the YAGO[6] classes assigned to the instances. The YAGO classes are very fine-grained (e.g., there is a class CitiesAndTownsInAbruzzo) which allows us to only work with class constraints in this experiment.

For the cross-checking of outliers by means of additional instance data, we used the multi-lingual data contained in the DBpedia dataset. This data is the result of different Wikipedia language versions describing the same things which leads to multiple DBpedia instances representing these things throughout the DBpedia language versions. Notably, the entity overlap across languages is not high: out of 2.7 million instances of the 17 most populated DBpedia ontology classes,[7] 60% are described (i.e., have at least one property) only in one language (predominantly English), and only around 23% of all entities are described in three or more languages. Note that we consider only those language editions for which infobox types and attributes are mapped to classes and properties of the DBpedia ontology. In DBpedia 3.9, mappings which were manually created by the DBpedia community for 24 languages were used for data extraction. In the datasets based on these mappings the same property URIs are used across languages: e.g., the DBpedia ontology property populationTotal is used for the population property of a populated place in, e.g., German or French editions even if the original Wikipedia infoboxes use language-specific attribute names.

To assess the performance of our approach for detecting wrong values, we chose the three DBpedia ontology properties: height, elevation and

---

[4] http://rapidminer.com

[5] https://code.google.com/p/rapidminer-anomalydetection/

[6] http://www.mpi-inf.mpg.de/yago

[7] http://wiki.dbpedia.org/Datasets39/CrossLanguageOverlapStatistics

**Table 1.** Inter annotator agreement observed for property samples and number of correct instance-value combinations according to majority of annotators

|                    | elevation | height | populationTotal |
|--------------------|-----------|--------|-----------------|
| Observed agreement | 0.987     | 0.960  | 0.960           |
| Fleiss' $\kappa$   | 0.968     | 0.916  | 0.917           |
| # correct          | 69        | 60     | 57              |

populationTotal. From each of the three ranked lists, we randomly sampled 100 instance-value combinations where we introduced a bias towards possibly wrong combinations by scaling the selection probability proportionally to the score determined by the outlier detection. The resulting values have been independently reviewed by three human annotators regarding the correctness of the values. For determining the correctness of a value, a typical process of the annotators was to first have a look at the current Wikipedia page describing the instance. Additionally, the Wikipedia page in its version as of the time of the extraction run was inspected. Using these two sources, it was possible in most cases to recognize errors in the values which stemmed from parsing errors or vandalism. If these inspections did not yet lead to the detection of an error, the most promising non-English Wikipedia articles about the instance were consulted, e.g., the article in the language most related to the instance. Finally, cited external sources were consulted or the annotators tried to find reliable information on the Web using search engines. If no proof for an error in the data was found, the instance-value combination was marked as correct, otherwise as wrong.

We computed the inter annotator agreement (IAA) between the three annotators on the evaluated lists by means of Fleiss' kappa.[8] The results of the IAA analysis are shown in Table 1. These values show a very high agreement for all three properties. From a short analysis of the few disagreements, we discovered that most of these were caused by an annotator not finding the relevant external information to assess the correctness of the value. Also the table shows the number of correct values in the datasets used for evaluation. It is important to note that, due to the way we sampled the example instances, these values are not able to provide an unbiased insight into the correctness of DBpedia but are overstating its incorrectness.

Furthermore, we plotted the distribution of the wrong instance-value combinations discovered during the manual evaluation and the actual value distribution not only over the sampled values but over all values in the dataset. These diagrams provide us with important knowledge about the erroneous values. For example, in Fig. 3b we see that there are two spikes of erroneous values. The first is located at the lower bound of the value range and mostly contains errors for entities of the class Person caused by using the wrong unit (1.98 cm instead of 1.98 m) and also values which are wrong but not directly recognizable as errors because they fit the usual height of people. The second spike is located around

---

[8] We used the tool at https://mlnl.net/jg/software/ira/ for computing IAA.

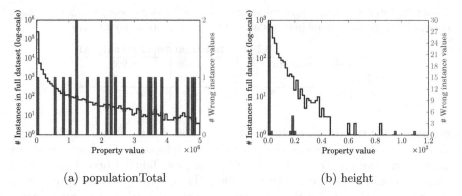

(a) populationTotal                    (b) height

**Fig. 3.** Distribution of all values in dataset (in log-scale) and erroneous values discovered in the manual evaluation for the different properties. Property value and all instance count scale restricted to the given ranges.

a value of 200 and again results from using the wrong unit in this case 198 m instead of 1.98 cm. This finding especially confirms the need for using subpopulations of the data instead of the full dataset since we see from the overall data that values close to 200 not directly point to data errors (e.g., for buildings this value is totally possible). The two other properties both show the erroneous values to be distributed relatively homogeneously as illustrated by Fig. 3a and not only found to be corner cases in the given ranges. These errors would not be recognizable without considering subpopulations of the data.

Based on these manually annotated value lists, we determined the performance of our approach with and without cross-checking as described in Section 4.5. For each evaluated property, we also provide two baseline values. The first baseline, which we identify by "Baseline", is computed by determining the median of all values and then computing the absolute difference between this median and the current instance's value. We use the resulting value as a score for the value being wrong. The second baseline (referred to as "Multi-lingual baseline") uses the multi-lingual data also employed by the cross-checking. For getting a score for an instance-value combination, we retrieve all values available for languages other than English. For two or more values, we compute the score for a value $v$ as $|v - \mu|/\sigma$ where $\mu$ is the mean of the non-English values and $\sigma$ their standard deviation. Assuming a normal distribution of the values, this means that approx. 95% of the values should have a score less or equal to 2. If we only retrieve zero or one value, we assign a score of 2. This fall-back value has been chosen since values for which not enough information is available in the multi-lingual dataset are more probable to be erroneous than values for which we find values which validate their correctness. In the cross-checking step, we consider all values with a score of at least 2 as outliers.

We plotted the receiver operating characteristic (ROC) curves for each property using the computed scores to rank the instance-value combinations. The results for the properties **height** and **populationTotal** are shown in Fig. 4a

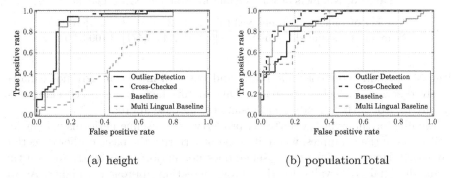

(a) height                          (b) populationTotal

**Fig. 4.** ROC curves for evaluated error detection methods

**Table 2.** Area under the curve determined for the given samples and approaches

| Approach | elevation | height | populationTotal |
|---|---|---|---|
| Outlier Detection | **0.872** | 0.888 | 0.876 |
| Cross-Checked Outlier Detection | 0.861 | **0.891** | **0.941** |
| Baseline | 0.745 | 0.847 | 0.847 |
| Multi-lingual Baseline | 0.669 | 0.509 | 0.860 |

and 4b, each containing the results for the raw detection approach, the filtered one and the two baselines. We also computed the area under the curve (AUC) for each property and each approach. The results are provided in Table 2.

First of all, we see that the AUC values of the cross-checked outlier detection approach are better than the baselines for all three properties. This approach is also superior to our non-cross-checked approach for `height` and `populationTotal`. Only for `elevation` it is slightly worse. Closer evaluation of this decrease showed that it was caused by a wrong value for elevation contained not only in the English dataset but also in the multi-lingual data. This duplication of wrong values could be caused by people copying values from one Wikipedia page to another one without checking the values. However, during the evaluation, this was not a frequent problem, and if it occurs more often for other datasets, a possible solution would be to employ copy-detection approaches [6].

For the property `height`, the difference between baseline methods and our methods is considerably smaller. This fact seems to be caused by a large number of persons in the example dataset. The median value used by the baseline is the height of one (correct) person instance. Since the `height` property for persons follows a normal distribution as also reported in [18], the median deviation works especially good and returns low scores for person instances. Although this behavior leads to high scores for the non-person instances, it gives a strong baseline for our dataset. Another interesting detail is that the multi-lingual baseline does not perform too well which is due to 86 instances not having enough multi-lingual data to assess their correctness. The greatest part of these instances is made up by the person class, especially by athletes of sports mostly famous in

**Table 3.** Numbers of values found for different NELL instances

| Number of values | 1 (only NELL) | 2 | 3 | 4 | 5 | Total |
|---|---|---|---|---|---|---|
| Number of instances | 6,187 | 5,043 | 3,144 | 6,471 | 13,100 | 33,946 |

English-speaking countries like rugby and baseball and seemingly not exhaustively described in other languages. Due to this fact, the cross-checking step hardly improves the already good results of the base approach.

Finally, for the `populationTotal` property, the baseline performs well in the first parts of the examples, where it even outperforms the basic outlier detection approach. However, since the baseline does not perform constantly well on the data, the final AUC value for the outlier detection approach is higher. As we can also derive from the multi-lingual baseline's comparably high AUC, there is more data available in the different language versions than for the other properties. Nevertheless, for 60 values there is not enough information for assessing the correctness. The higher availability of multi-lingual data also leads to a clear increase for the cross-checking method and makes it the clearly best performing approach on this dataset. Furthermore, it demonstrates the advantages of combining two orthogonal detections to reach a final correctness decision.

All in all, we see that the cross-checked method performs consistently well for all three properties. It always produces better results than the baseline approaches. Most of the time it is also better than the non-cross-checked approach showing that it indeed prevents natural outliers from being detected as errors.

## 5.2 NELL Experiment

For the second experiment, we let our approach run on the NELL dataset [4] in its RDF version [19]. The NELL dataset is produced by crawling the Web and extracting structured data out of the discovered unstructured information. Given this extraction method, we can assume that parsing errors and other difficulties result in some quality deficiencies in the data. We let our approach examine the latitude and longitude values contained in the RDF version of NELL and try to find wrong values in it. For getting data to cross-check the values, we used the Wikipedia links contained in the NELL data to the corresponding DBpedia instance. Besides the DBpedia values for longitude and latitude, we used the `owl:sameAs` links assigned to the DBpedia instances to find further instances in the Linked Data cloud which provided the desired values. We included the values we could retrieve from Freebase, GeoNames, YAGO and DBpedia. Statistics on the number of values we were able to find are shown in Table 3. These numbers demonstrate that it is possible to gather additional values from the Linked Data cloud to enable the cross-checking of detected outliers and to clean up the data.

However, during the actual run of the outlier detection only few values with a sufficiently high outlier score showed up. An inspection of the data from the other repositories, and for some instance values also an inspection using a web-based map service, showed that there is close to no deviation throughout the datasets. Almost all of the inspected values were correct possibly because of the highly standardized value format for latitude and longitude which leads to only few parsing errors. The small deviations of the values seem to be caused by subjective decisions, e.g., where to exactly position the longitude-latitude marker for the area of a county. Nevertheless, the latitude value with the highest outlier score which was not filtered by the cross-checking showed to be a data error. Being assigned to the NELL instance `http://nell-ld.telecom-st-etienne.fr/county_grey_county`, the latitude value was detected to be wrong also based on its outlierness for the population of the class `County`. An inspection of the Wikipedia page assigned by NELL showed that it should actually represent Grey County, Ontario, Canada[9] whereas the co-ordinates provided by NELL are in the area of Greymouth, New Zealand which belongs to the Grey District.[10] This hints to disambiguation problems. This result is in line with the findings of Paulheim [14] who also discovered that NELL has problems with homonyms when linking data. In this special case, the confusion could have been amplified by the near synonymy of district and county. All in all, though not finding greater amounts of data errors, we think this use case demonstrates the availability of data from different repositories and thus the applicability of cross-checking for improving wrong value detection.

## 6    Conclusion

In this work, we presented our approach for detecting wrong numerical values in Linked Data. The main contribution of our work is that we are especially taking advantage of the core concepts of Linked Data: links and vast amounts of data. By following `owl:sameAs` links for instances, we gather additional data for the same facts which we then use to cross-check the assessment of correctness gained during a first outlier detection run on a single repository. This procedure allows us to better handle natural outliers and thus reduce the false positive rate. In addition, we also presented a lattice-based method of detecting interesting subsets of values to apply outlier detection to. The performance of our approach was assessed on DBpedia and we also showed the applicability of cross-checking on more general repositories, here represented by the NELL dataset.

In future work, we will consider additional value types for checking correctness like dates. Furthermore, we will investigate the possibility of efficiently finding pairs of values on which multi-variate outlier detection can be applied. We also plan to gather human feedback on the validity of detected errors and use this feedback to investigate the possibilities of learning more promising combinations of different weighting schemes.

---

[9] http://en.wikipedia.org/wiki/Grey_County
[10] http://en.wikipedia.org/wiki/Grey_District

# References

1. Acosta, M., Zaveri, A., Simperl, E., Kontokostas, D., Auer, S., Lehmann, J.: Crowd-sourcing linked data quality assessment. In: Alani, H., et al. (eds.) ISWC 2013, Part II. LNCS, vol. 8219, pp. 260–276. Springer, Heidelberg (2013)
2. Breunig, M.M., Kriegel, H.-P., Ng, R.T., Sander, J.: LOF: Identifying density-based local outliers. SIGMOD Rec (2000)
3. Bryl, V., Bizer, C.: Learning conflict resolution strategies for cross-language Wikipedia data fusion. In: Proc. of the WebQuality Workshop at WWW 2014 (2014)
4. Carlson, A., Betteridge, J., Kisiel, B., Settles, B., Hruschka Jr., E.R., Mitchell, T.M.: Toward an architecture for never-ending language learning. In: Proc. of the 24th AAAI Conference on Artificial Intelligence (2010)
5. Chandola, V., Banerjee, A., Kumar, V.: Anomaly detection: A survey. ACM Comput. Surv (2009)
6. Dong, X.L., Berti-Equille, L., Srivastava, D.: Truth discovery and copying detection in a dynamic world. Proc. VLDB Endow (2009)
7. Euzenat, J., Shvaiko, P.: Ontology Matching, 2nd edn., pp. 1–511. Springer (2013)
8. Kullback, S., Leibler, R.A.: On information and sufficiency. The Annals of Mathematical Statistics 22(1), 79–86 (1951)
9. Lehmann, J., Bühmann, L.: ORE - A tool for repairing and enriching knowledge bases. In: Patel-Schneider, P.F., Pan, Y., Hitzler, P., Mika, P., Zhang, L., Pan, J.Z., Horrocks, I., Glimm, B. (eds.) ISWC 2010, Part II. LNCS, vol. 6497, pp. 177–193. Springer, Heidelberg (2010)
10. Lehmann, J., Gerber, D., Morsey, M., Ngonga Ngomo, A.-C.: DeFacto - deep fact validation. In: Cudré-Mauroux, P., et al. (eds.) ISWC 2012, Part I. LNCS, vol. 7649, pp. 312–327. Springer, Heidelberg (2012)
11. Lehmann, J., Isele, R., Jakob, M., Jentzsch, A., Kontokostas, D., Mendes, P.N., Hellmann, S., Morsey, M., van Kleef, P., Auer, S., Bizer, C.: DBpedia - a large-scale, multilingual knowledge base extracted from Wikipedia. Semantic Web Journal (2014)
12. Melo, A., Theobald, M., Völker, J.: Correlation-based refinement of rules with numerical attributes. In: Proc. of the 27th International Florida Artificial Intelligence Research Society Conference (2014)
13. de Melo, G.: Not quite the same: Identity constraints for the web of linked data. In: Proc. of the 27th AAAI Conference on Artificial Intelligence (2013)
14. Paulheim, H.: Identifying wrong links between datasets by multi-dimensional outlier detection. In: 3rd International Workshop on Debugging Ontologies and Ontology Mappings, WoDOOM (2014)
15. Paulheim, H., Bizer, C.: Type inference on noisy RDF data. In: Alani, H., et al. (eds.) ISWC 2013, Part I. LNCS, vol. 8218, pp. 510–525. Springer, Heidelberg (2013)
16. Töpper, G., Knuth, M., Sack, H.: DBpedia ontology enrichment for inconsistency detection. In: Proc. of the 8th International Conference on Semantic Systems (2012)
17. Waitelonis, J., Ludwig, N., Knuth, M., Sack, H.: Whoknows? evaluating linked data heuristics with a quiz that cleans up DBpedia. Interactive Technology and Smart Education (2011)
18. Wienand, D., Paulheim, H.: Detecting incorrect numerical data in dBpedia. In: Presutti, V., d'Amato, C., Gandon, F., d'Aquin, M., Staab, S., Tordai, A. (eds.) ESWC 2014. LNCS, vol. 8465, pp. 504–518. Springer, Heidelberg (2014)
19. Zimmermann, A., Gravier, C., Subercaze, J., Cruzille, Q.: Nell2RDF read the web, and turn it into RDF. In: Proc. of the 2nd International Workshop on Knowledge Discovery and Data Mining Meets Linked Open Data (2013)

# Noisy Type Assertion Detection in Semantic Datasets

Man Zhu, Zhiqiang Gao, and Zhibin Quan

School of Computer Science & Engineering, Southeast University, P.R. China
Key Laboratory of Computer Network and Information Integration,
Southeast University, Ministry of Education, P.R. China
{mzhu,zqgao,zbquan}@seu.edu.cn

**Abstract.** Semantic datasets provide support to automate many tasks such as decision-making and question answering. However, their performance is always decreased by the noises in the datasets, among which, noisy type assertions play an important role. This problem has been mainly studied in the domain of data mining but not in the semantic web community. In this paper, we study the problem of noisy type assertion detection in semantic web datasets by making use of concept disjointness relationships hidden in the datasets. We transform noisy type assertion detection into multiclass classification of pairs of type assertions which type an individual to two potential disjoint concepts. The multiclass classification is solved by Adaboost with C4.5 as the base classifier. Furthermore, we propose instance-concept compatability metrics based on instance-instance relationships and instance-concept assertions. We evaluate the approach on both synthetic datasets and DBpedia. Our approach effectively detect noisy type assertions in DBpedia with a high precision of 95%.

## 1 Introduction

Real world data is never as perfect as we would like it to be and can often suffer from corruptions that may impact interpretations of the data, models created from the data, and decisions made based on the data [1][2]. *Accuracy, relevancy, representational-consistency* and *interlinking* affect approximately 11.93% of DBpedia[1] resources. Among them, the detection of accuracy problem is the least to be automated [3]. We are interested in the factual errors (called noises in this paper) in the accuracy category. To be specific, we focus on the detection of noisy type assertions (asserting *Schubert's last sonatas* is of type *artist* for example), which is suggested to be more severe than noisy property assertions (asserting TV series *Wings*'s *opening theme* is *Schubert's last sonatas* for example) [4].

While there has been a lot of research on noise identification in data mining domain in the past two decades, the topic has not yet received sufficient attention from the Semantic Web community, especially the problem of noisy type detection. Zaveri et al. [3] analysed empirically the DBpedia dataset. They manually evaluated a part of indiviual resources, and semi-automatically evaluated the quality of schema axioms. Fürber and Hepp [5] summarized the important problems in semantic web data, including literal value problems and functional dependency violations, and correspondingly

---

[1] http://dbpedia.org

P. Mika et al. (Eds.) ISWC 2014, Part I, LNCS 8796, pp. 373–388, 2014.

developed SPARQL queries to identfy them. Yu et al. [6] focused on identifying noisy property assertions. They detected such assertions by using probabilistic rules learned from semantic web data and checked to what extent the rules agree with the context of assertions.

We find that noisy type assertions could be detected from knowledge hidden in real-world datasets.

**Example 1.** *If we execute the following SPARQL query in DBpedia*

```
select ?x where{?x a dbpedia-owl:Person.
              ?x a dbpedia-owl:Place.}
```

*which selects individuals belonging to both concept* Person *and* Place*, we get a list of individuals returned, such as* Pope[2]*. Because we, as human-beings, believe that concept* Person *and* Place *share no individuals, which is hidden in DBpedia because* Person *and* Place *share a very small number of individuals, it is reasonable to guess that the assertions typing the individuals to concept* Person *or* Place *are problematic.*

In this paper, we study the problem of noisy type assertion detection in semantic web datasets for the first time. Roughly speaking, our approach contains 2 steps: Firstly we cache the number of individuals belonging to a pair of concepts aiming at detecting abnormal data. We extract conflicts such as Pope belongs to both Person and Place. After that, we transform the detection of noisy type assertions into a multiclass classification problem, where a candidate conflict assertion can be labeled (1) none of them are noisy; (2) first assertion being noisy; (3) second assertion being noisy; (4) both of them are noisy. The conflicts are classified by Adaboost with decision tree algorithm C4.5 as the base classifier. In order to characterize the conflict assertions, we propose two kinds of features: First kind of features make use of type assertions. For example, the assertions "Pope is a Cleric" and "Cleric is subsumed by Person" increase the confidence of assertion "Pope is a Person" Another kind of feature utilizes role information, which we borrowed from [2]. For example, several individuals are linked with Pope by role beatifiedBy, and from the dataset, beatifiedBy is always connected with a Person, then "Pope is a Person" is more probable. To summarize, the main contributions of this paper are to:

- study the novel problem of noisy type assertion detection in semantic web datasets;
- formalize the noisy type assertion detection problem as a multiclass classification problem for the first time;
- propose various effective compatibility metrics that incorporate both concept and role relationships.

The rest of the paper is organized as follows. Section 2 describes decision tree (C4.5) and Adaboost classification algorithm. In Section 3, we motivate the approach in section 3.1 by analyzing the co-occurrence data in DBpedia, and then we formalize the research problem and introduce the framework. Section 4 details the approach focusing on the features. The experimental results are presented in section 5. Section 6 introduces related work, and section 7 concludes the paper and gives future works.

---

[2] In DBpedia 3.9 there are 17 individuals belonging to both Person and Place.

## 2   Decision Tree and Adaboost

We use Adaboost as the meta classifier with C4.5, a popular decision tree algorithm, as the base classifier. Decision tree (DT) is a set of if-then rules representing a mapping between data features and labels. Each internal node in a DT indicates a feature, and each leaf node represents a label. We adopt DT as the base classifier for the following reasons: (1) DT is a white-box model, which is easy to be understood and interpreted; (2) Rule is the suitable representation for the features proposed in this paper.

DTs can be inductively learned from training data. C4.5 is a popular DTs learning algorithm [7]. It builds decision trees from a set of training data using information entropy by divide-and-conquer. At each node of the tree, C4.5 chooses the attribute of the data that most effectively splits the examples into subsets by normalized information gain. The attribute with the highest normalized information gain is chosen. The initial tree is then pruned to avoid overfitting [8].

In order to improve the performance of classification algorithms, boosting iteratively learns a single strong learner from a set of base learners. There are many variations of boosting algorithms varying in their method for weighting training data and classifiers. Adaboost [9] uses an optimally weighted majority vote of meta classifiers. More concretely, the impact on the vote of base classifiers with small error rate is intensified by increasing their weights. The label of a data instance is predicted by the linear combination of meta classifiers, in our case, DTs, as follows:

$$T(x) = \sum_{m=1}^{M} \alpha_m T_m(x) \tag{1}$$

where $M$ DTs are learned, $\alpha_m$ is the weight of the $m$th DT, and $T_m(x)$ is the output of the $m$th DT.

## 3   Approach

In this section, we firstly motivate our approach by a co-occurrence analysis on DBpedia. Then we formalize the research problem and describe the framework.

### 3.1   Co-occurrence Analysis on DBpedia

Before we analyse the co-occurrence on DBpedia, we first give the definition of co-occurrence matrices as follows:

**Definition 1 (Co-occurrence Matirx).** *A co-occurrence matrix $M$ is a symmetric matrix defined over a semantic dataset $\mathcal{O}$. Mathematically, a co-occurrence matrix $M_{N \times N}$ is defined over $N$ concepts $\mathbf{C}$ in $\mathcal{O}$, where $M_{st} = |\{i|C_s(i) \in \mathcal{O} \text{ and } C_t(i) \in \mathcal{O}, C_s \in \mathbf{C}, C_t \in \mathbf{C}\}|$.*

We take 90 concepts in DBpedia containing at least 10,000 individuals, and sort them in descending order in terms of the number of individuals they have. The values in

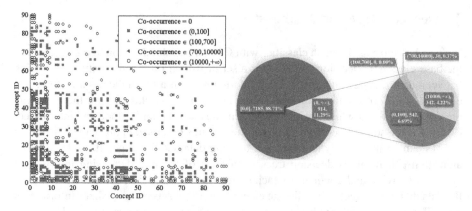

**Fig. 1.** Co-occurrence matrix of the top-90 concepts in terms of individuals they have in DBpedia. Left shows the co-occurrence values for each pair of concepts. The figure on the right represents the frequency of co-occurrence values in different scopes.

the co-occurrence matrix are retrieved by executing SPARQL queries as shown in Section 1.

The left in Fig. 1 shows directly the co-occurrence matrix. We can easily find from this figure red squares and black circles representing co-occurrence values below 100 and above 10,000. However, the numbers in between, represented by triangles, are quite rare. The numbers above 10,000 indicate highly overlapped concepts, while the numbers below 100, on the other hand, suggest abnormal data. The figure on the right shows the percentage of co-occurrence numbers varying scopes. Besides the largest amount of zero filling the co-occurrence matrix, more than half of the other numbers are below 100 (6.69% in 11.29%), which suggests that the amount of abnormal data can not be ignored and the noisy type assertions can be detected from them. If we take a closer look of the concept pairs sharing less than 100 individuals, we can find, for example, (Person Place), (Person Work), (Place Work), (Place Athlete) etc. These concepts, according to human knowledge, should share no individuals at all.

### 3.2  Problem Definition

We detect noisy type assertions through conflict in the semantic datasets, which is defined as follows:

**Definition 2 (Conflict Type Assertions).** *A pair of type assertions $A(i)$ and $B(i)$ is called conflict if $A \sqcap B \sqsubseteq \perp$, written as $< i, A, B >$, where $i$ is called the* target *individual. A conflict $< i, A, B >$ is called* full *noisy if $A(i)$ and $B(i)$ are both noisy;* 1-st half *noisy if only $A(i)$ is noisy; $< i, A, B >$ is called* 2-nd half *noisy if only $B(i)$ is noisy; It is called* fake *conflict if none of $A(i)$ and $B(i)$ are noisy.*

where $A \sqcap B \sqsubseteq \perp$ means concept $A$ and $B$ are disjoint. Explicitly asserting individuals to $A$ and $B$ will cause problems, if $A \sqcap B \sqsubseteq \perp$. We make use of $A \sqcap B \sqsubseteq \perp$ *hidden* in the datasets. Without ambiguity, conflict type assertions are called conflicts for short.

According to the definition of conflict type assertions, noisy type assertion detection from conflicts can be formalized as a multiclass classification problem.

**Definition 3 (Noisy Type Assertion Detection From Conflicts).** *Given a set of conflict type assertions* $\{< i, A, B >\}$, *the goal of noisy type assertion is to find a classifier* $\mathcal{M} :< i, A, B > \mapsto \{0, 1, 2, 3\}$ *such that* $\mathcal{M}$ *maps the full noisy conflict to class 0, 1-st half noisy to class 1, 2-nd half noisy to 2, and maps fake conflict to class 3.*

The multiclass classification problem can be solved by traditional machine learning algorithms, which require multidimensional features as the input. In noisy type assertion detection, we extract a feature vector for each conflict type assertion.

**Definition 4 (Feature Vector of Conflict Type Assertions).** *The n-dimensional feature vector v of a conflict type assertion* $< i, A, B >$ *consists of n various compatibility metrics of individual i with concepts A and B. Dimension* $v_i = d_i < i, A, B >$, *where* $d_i$ *is the ith compatibility metric function for* $< i, A, B >$.

The feature vector of a conflict type assertion indicates the compatibility of an individual $i$ and a pair of concepts, which are computed by several metric functions.

### 3.3 Framework

We observe that (1) due to the dataset enrichment mechanisms or data intrinsic statistics, when concepts share instances, they generally share a large portion of instances even compare to the number of instances they have themselves; (2) when two concepts share a small amount of instances (in another word, the concepts are suggested to be disjoint according to the data), there tend to be noises inside. Based on these observations, we propose to identify noisy types from conflict type assertions. The framework contains the following 5 steps (cf. Fig. 2):

(1) *Co-occurrence matrix construction.* In this step, we construct the co-occurrence matrix. The values in the co-occurrence matrix signify the relationship between the corresponding concept pair. For example, concepts `Person` and `Place` have 17 instances in common as shown in Fig. 2. Suppose the probability of concepts $A$ and $B$ being disjoint $P(A \sqcap B \sqsubseteq \bot)$ is $1 - P(A \sqcap B) = 1 - |\{a | A(a) \in \mathcal{O}, B(a) \in \mathcal{O}, \top(a) \in \mathcal{O}\}| / |\{a | \top(a) \in \mathcal{O}\}|$, $\mathcal{O}$ is the semantic dataset. If the cooccurrence is very small, the probability that the related concepts being disjoint is relatively large. If we are confident about them being disjoint, then the assertions of instances belonging to both concepts contain problems. The calculation of co-occurrence matrix includes executing $N \times N/2$ SPARQL queries, where $N$ is the number of concepts in the dataset.

(2) *Conflict type assertion generation.* Based on the cooccurrence matrix and by setting threshold, we generate disjoint concepts. By querying the dataset for list of instances belonging to each pair of disjoint concepts, the conflict type assertions are generated. For example, instances $I(A, B)$ belong to disjoint concepts $A$ and $B$, then $\forall i \in I(A, B)$, we add the triple $< i, A, B >$ to the conflict set.

(3) *Feature extraction.* We generate a feature vector for each conflict type assertion. The details of the compatibility metrics are described in Section 4. We cache all intermediate statistics required to calculate the metrics in a local relational database. Scan the relational database once will get the feature vectors.

(4) *Classification algorithm.* We use Adaboost with C4.5, a well-known classification algorithm, as the base learner to classify the conflicts.

(5) *Classification results.* From the classification results, which contain conflicts belonging to class 0, 1, 2, and 3, we output the final noisy type assertions by seperating conflict with class 0 into two noisy type assertions, output conflicts with class 1 or 2 into one noisy type assertion. To be specific, suppose the conflict is $< i, A, B >$, if its label is 0, $A(i)$ and $B(i)$ are added to the final results; if its label is 1, $A(i)$ is added, and similarly, if the label of the conflict is 2, $B(i)$ is added.

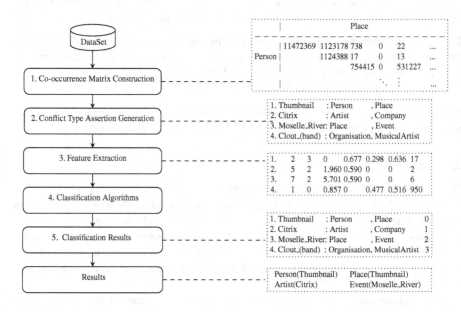

**Fig. 2.** Overview of the framework

# 4   Feature Extraction

The compatibility metrics in the feature vector of a conflict type assertion are based on the type assertions and property assertions of the target individual. In this section, we first introduce the weight functions of predicates. Then we describe the details of compatibility metrics in the feature vector.

## 4.1   Weighted Predicates

The importance of predicates (concepts or roles) playing in classifying conflicts may be different, especially in imbalanced datasets where the number of individuals belonging to different concepts are not approximately equally distributed. Paulheim and Bizer ([2]) defined weight of object properties. In this paper, we extend the weight to predicates defined as follows:

$$w_p := \sum_{\text{all concepts } C} (P(C) - P(C|p')) \qquad (2)$$

where

$$p' = \begin{cases} p & \text{if } p \text{ is a concept;} \\ \exists p. \top & \text{if } p \text{ is an object property.} \end{cases}$$

and $P(C) = |\{a|C(a) \in \mathcal{O}\}|/|\{a|\top(a) \in \mathcal{O}\}|$, $\mathcal{O}$ is the dataset. Additionally, the weight of concept $\exists p.\top$ is written as $w_p$, and the weight of $\exists p^-.\top$ is written as $w_{p^-}$.

## 4.2 Compatibility Metrics

We motivate the first kind of features by the following example.

**Example 1 Revisited.** Let us consider the conflict <Pope, Person, Place>. We want to use compatibility metrics to characterize individual Pope with respect to concept Person and Place. In the dataset, besides Person and Place, Pope also belongs to Agent. We know that Person is subsumed by Agent, and Place is not. Then we are more confident about "Pope is a Person". We simply compute the number of concepts of this kind, such as Agent, and call this feature *supSup* (super support), as shown in Table 1, where $A \sqsubseteq^+ A'$ means $A$ is indirectly subsumed by $A'$. Similarly, "Pope is a Cleric" and "Cleric is subsumed by Person also increases the confidence of "Pope is a Person". Based on the subsumed concepts, we define the feature *subSup* (subclass support). Another feature is calculated based on the equivalent concepts (equivSup), such as Pope is asserted to be of type a : Person, an equivalent class of Person. This kind of features is called plain concept related features. The calculation of the concept related features includes transitive subsumption relationships, which can be achieved for example from Virtuoso by:

```
SELECT count(?x) AS ?count WHERE{{
SELECT * WHERE {dbpedia:i      a                    ?x.
             {?x              rdf:type             ?y.} UNION
             {?x              owl:equivalentClass ?y.} UNION
             {?y              owl:equivalentClass ?x.}}}
OPTION (transitive, t_distinct, t_in (?x), t_out (?y)).
FILTER (?y=dbpedia-owl:A)}
```

However, the contributions of predicates can be different, as we discussed in Section 4.1. We propose two kinds of features to incorporate the differences. Firstly we simply compute the linear combination of all weights of the predicates related to the target individual by setting the coefficients to be 1. This kind is called *simple weighted concept related features*. Let us consider the following cases to motivate the second kind: Cleric is subsumed by Person and a : Person is equivalent with Person. If the individuals belonging to concept Person are always of type a : Person, the contribution of a : Person is lower than that of Cleric in classifying conflict <i, Person, Place>, if there are a lot of differences between individuals belonging

**Table 1.** Features used in the classification

| Plain concept related features | | |
|---|---|---|
| Name | Definition | Type |
| subSup(i, A) | $\lvert\{A'\mid A' \sqsubseteq^{+} A, \text{ and } A'(i) \in \mathcal{O}\}\rvert$ | numeric |
| supSup(i, A) | $\lvert\{A'\mid A \sqsubseteq^{+} A', A' \not\equiv \top, \text{ and } A'(i) \in \mathcal{O}\}\rvert$ | numeric |
| equivSup(i, A) | $\lvert\{A'\mid A' \equiv^{+} A, \text{ and } A'(i) \in \mathcal{O}\}\rvert$ | numeric |
| Simple weighted concept related features | | |
| Name | Definition | Type |
| simpleWSubSup(i, A) | $\sum_{A'\sqsubseteq^{+}A, A'(i)\in\mathcal{O}} w_{A'}$ | numeric |
| simpleWSupSup(i, A) | $\sum_{A\sqsubseteq^{+}A', A'\not\equiv\top, A'(i)\in\mathcal{O}} w_{A'}$ | numeric |
| simpleWEquivSup(i, A) | $\sum_{A\equiv^{+}A', A'(i)\in\mathcal{O}} w_{A'}$ | numeric |
| Weighted concept related features | | |
| Name | Definition | Type |
| wSubSup(i, A) | $\nu_1 \sum_{A'\sqsubseteq^{+}A, A'(i)\in\mathcal{O}} w_{A'}(1 - P(A'\mid A))$ $\nu_1 = 1/\sum_{A'\sqsubseteq^{+}A, A'(i)\in\mathcal{O}} w_{A'}$ | numeric |
| wSupSup(i, A) | $\nu_2 \sum_{A\sqsubseteq^{+}A', A'\not\equiv\top, A'(i)\in\mathcal{O}} w_{A'}(1 - P(A\mid A'))$ $\nu_2 = 1/\sum_{A\sqsubseteq^{+}A', A'\not\equiv\top, A'(i)\in\mathcal{O}} w_{A'}$ | numeric |
| Role related features | | |
| Name | Definition | Type |
| attrSup(i, A) (Paulheim and Bizer [2]) | $\nu_3 \cdot \sum_{\text{all roles r of i}} w_r \cdot P(A\mid\exists r.\top)$ $\nu_3 = 1/\sum_{\text{all roles r of i}} w_r$ | numeric |

to `Cleric` and that of `Person`'s. This is because the type assertion of `Pope` being a `a:Person` probably due to the mechanisms in constructing the dataset. For this reason, we propose to give weight to the subclass of concept $A$, $A'$, defined as $(1 - P(A'|A))$. Similarly the weight of the super class of concept $A$, $A'$, is defined as $(1 - P(A|A'))$. We use the compatibility metric of property assertions as defined in (Paulheim and Bizer [2]). There will be two numbers in the feature vector for each metric listed in Table 1. One calculates the compatibility metric of the first concept in the conflict, and the other one computes the metric of the second concept.

## 5   Experimental Evaluations

We conduct the evaluations on synthetic datasets and DBpedia. The questions we want to answer using synthetic datasets are: (1) How does the proposed approach work in the semantic web context? (2) What are the advantages and drawbacks of the proposed approach? By applying the proposed method on DBpedia, we show the effectiveness of the proposed method by manually checking the correctness of the detected triples.

### 5.1   Experimental Settings

For each experiment, we perform 10-fold cross-validation. We use the precision, recall, F1 scores defined as follows:

$$precision = \frac{\text{\# correctly detected noisy type assertions}}{\text{\# detected noisy type assertions}} \tag{3}$$

$$= \frac{2TP_0 + TP_1 + TP_2}{2TP_0 + 2FP_0 + TP_1 + FP_1 + TP_2 + FP_2} \tag{4}$$

$$recall = \frac{\text{\# correctly detected noisy type assertions}}{\text{\# noisy type assertions}} \tag{5}$$

$$= \frac{2TP_0 + TP_1 + TP_2}{2TP_0 + 2FN_0 + TP_1 + FN_1 + TP_2 + FN_2} \tag{6}$$

where $TP_0, TP_1, TP_2$ are the number of true positives of label 0, 1, and 2 respectively, $FP_0, FP_1, FP_2$ are the number of false positives of label 0, 1 and 2, and $FN_0, FN_1, FN_2$ are the number of false negatives of label 0, 1 and 2 respectively. F1 score is the harmonic mean of precision and recall, which is calculated by $2 \times \frac{precision \times recall}{precision + recall}$. In terms of the performance of the classifier, we use average accuracy as the final results. In terms of the classifier implementation, we use Adaboost and J48 - the Weka $3^3$ implementation of C4.5. We set the weight threshold of Adaboost to 100, and number of iterations to be 10. We also use resampling. All the experiments are carried out on a laptop computer with Ubuntu 12.04 64-bit with a i7 CPU, 8 GiB of memory.

**Feature Schemes.** We use different combinations of features described in this paper in the evaluations. The details of the compositions are as follows:

**CS:** use subSup, supSup, and equivSup features;
**WCS:** use wSubSup, wSupSup features;
**SWCS:** use simpleWSubSup, simpleWSupSup, and simpleWEquivSup as features;
**AS:** only use attrSup in the feature vector;
**ALL:** use all features.

## 5.2 Evaluations on Synthetic Datasets

In order to control the amount of noise in the synthetic dataset, we construct datasets containing noises based on LUBM [10] dataset, which is an automatically constructed dataset without any noises in the assertions. LUBM consists of 43 concepts, 25 object properties, 36 subClassOf axioms, 6 equivalentClass axioms, 1555 individuals. We use LUBM in order to get the full control on the noises, and we can also get a benchmark dataset.

**Noise Control Strategy.** A type assertion $A'(a)$ can be noisy in the following forms (suppose the correct assertion is $A(a)$): (1) $A'$ intersects with $A$, (2) $A'$ and $A$ share no individuals, and (3) $A'$ is subsumed by $A$. To simulate these possibilities, we adopt the following method: given a pair of classes (X, Y) and a noise level x, an instance with its label X has a $x \times 100\%$ chance to be corrupted and mislabeld as Y. We use this method

---

$^3$ http://www.cs.waikato.ac.nz/ml/weka/

because in realistic situations, only certain types of classes are likely to be mislabeled. Using this method, the percentage of the entire training set that is corrupted will be less than $x \times 100\%$ because only some pairs of classes are considered problematic. In the sections below, we construct the following 3 datasets based on LUBM:

**RATA:** To simulate the noisy type assertion of form (1), we corrupt the individuals of concept `TeachingAssistant` with concept `ResearchAssistant` according to the given noise levels.

**UGS:** To simulate the noisy type assertion of form (2), we corrupt the individuals of concept `GraduateStudent` with concept `University` according to the given noise levels.

**GCC:** To simulate the noisy type assertion of form (3), we corrupt the individuals of concept `Course` but not `GraduateCourse` with concept `GraduateCourse` according to the given noise levels.

**Data Partition Strategy.** Semantic web datasets differ from traditional datasets in the data linkage aspect, which makes data partition different from traditional data partition methods. We sketched the details of partition method used in this paper here, which prevented the training and testing set from containing uncontrolled amount of individuals. The datasets are partitioned by individuals. Given the original dataset, training and testing set individuals, we try to add all concept and property assertions related to the individuals in the corresponding training and testing datasets. Object property assertions can link individuals to others that are not in the individual set. We ignore these property assertions in order to maintain the size of the individual set. In each run, the dataset is randomly divided into a training set and a test set, and we corrupt the training and testing set by adding noise with the above method, and use the testing set to evaluate the system performance.

**Experimental Results.** Fig. 3 shows the evaluation results on the 4 datasets with noise level 10% - 50% using different feature schemes. From this figure, we find:

- As the noise level grows, we expect to see a decrease in the performance of classification in all evaluations. However, in many cases, we see an increase. This is because after we get more noises, the training data is more balanced to the 4 classes. This is the reason for the increase in the classification performance.
- We may expect the performance better on the disjoint concept pair, a.k.a. UGS. However, this might not be found from the evaluations. Actually, the evaluations on concept pair GCC seem to outperform others. Firstly, we corrupted Course individuals with GraduateCourse types under the condition that the individuals are not GraduateCourse themselves. Because otherwise we are not confident about the corruptions generated are really noises. In this way, the GCC pair is similar to pair UGS. Secondly, in the LUBM dataset, the individuals belonged to Course are less than that of GraduateStudent. Although the noise levels are the same, but the number of noisy type assertions in GCC is smaller than that in UGS.
- Applying the proposed approach with [ALL] gets the best results. Especially on dataset GCC. This indicates that relying solely on concept supports or role supports is not effective enough. Since in several cases, an individual possibly only has

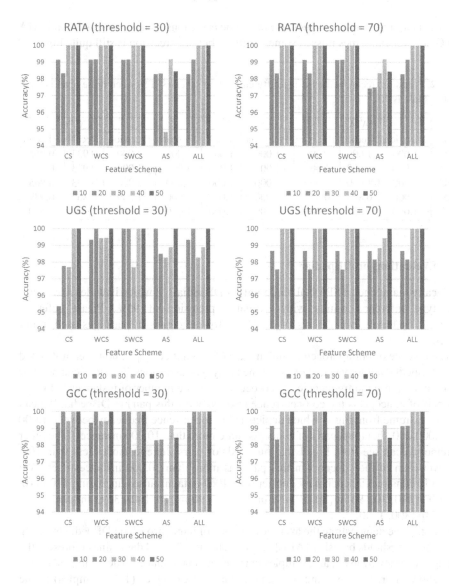

**Fig. 3.** The average accuracy using various feature schemes with different noise levels by setting thresholds to 30 and 70

concept labels, or only has role links, using one kind of features obviously cannot get enough information for classification.

– On RATA, the concept intersected pair, and GCC, the concept subsumption pair, the performance are also quite good.

In Table 2 we demonstrate the performance of the Adaboost with J48 when noise level is set to be 50%, and the threshold is 70. From this table, we find that in most cases, the proposed method is able to detect all noisy type assertions. When using [AS] on RATA and GCC, we sometimes missed some conflicts, but the precision is still quite high.

**Table 2.** Precision, recall, and F1 using different feature schemes (FS) when noise level is 50%, and threshold is 70

| FS | RATA | | | UGS | | | GCC | | |
|---|---|---|---|---|---|---|---|---|---|
| | Precision | Recall | F1 score | Precision | Recall | F1 score | Precision | Recall | F1 score |
| CS | 1.000 | 1.000 | 1.000 | 1.000 | 1.000 | 1.000 | 1.000 | 0.933 | 0.965 |
| WCS | 1.000 | 1.000 | 1.000 | 1.000 | 1.000 | 1.000 | 1.000 | 0.933 | 0.965 |
| SWCS | 1.000 | 1.000 | 1.000 | 1.000 | 1.000 | 1.000 | 1.000 | 0.933 | 0.965 |
| AS | 1.000 | 0.867 | 0.929 | 1.000 | 1.000 | 1.000 | 1.000 | 0.867 | 0.929 |
| ALL | 1.000 | 1.000 | 1.000 | 1.000 | 1.000 | 1.000 | 1.000 | 1.000 | 1.000 |

### 5.3   Evaluations on DBpedia

We locally maintained a SPARQL endpoint for DBpedia 3.9, which includes newly created type inference results with estimated precision of 95%. Please refer to http://github.com/fresheye/NoDe for the details of packages used in our server.

The essence of our approach is making use of disjoint concepts, however, not stated in the DBpedia ontology yet, to discover the noisy type assertions. This idea can be clear after we look into the frequencies of co-occurrence (the number of instances belonged to a pair of concepts is the co-occurrence frequency for this pair) in DBpedia. We can see one extreme from Fig. 1 which depicts the co-occurrence frequency between 1,000 and 1,000,000, that most pairs of concepts share more than 10,000 instances. The other extreme we can see from Fig. 1 that hundreds of pairs share instances less than 100, however each of the concepts in this pair has more than 10,000 instances itself. We manually construct a benchmark dataset with 4067 data instances, including 170 in (0, 10), 40 in [10, 30), 96 in [30, 50), 51 in [50, 70), 90 in [70, 100), 3673 in [100, 800), and 47 in [800, 1000]

In Fig. 4, we demonstrate the average accuracy of our approach on DBpedia by using difference thresholds by using [ALL] feature scheme. The "all data" lines represent the average accuracy by using all examples in the benchmark dataset. The "same data size" lines show the results of using the same number of examples (170 examples) in the experiment. From Fig. 4 we find:

- The accuracy grows with the threshold, especially when all data are used. This shows that more training examples bring us better model to classify the examples.
- The average accuracy of using J48 with Adaboost is normally better than J48 without Adaboost at approximately 3%.
- When we use same amount of examples in experiments, the accuracy also grows because when the size of the training set grows, the data are more balanced.

**Table 3.** Average precision (Prec.), recall (Rec.), and F1 score (F1) on DBpedia by setting threshold to 800

| Feature | J48 | | | J48(boost) | | |
|---|---|---|---|---|---|---|
| | Precision | Recall | F1-score | Precision | Recall | F1-score |
| CS | 0.837 | 0.831 | 0.832 | 0.785 | 0.782 | 0.783 |
| WCS | 0.768 | 0.768 | 0.768 | 0.844 | 0.845 | 0.844 |
| SWCS | 0.825 | 0.824 | 0.824 | 0.823 | 0.824 | 0.823 |
| AS | 0.812 | 0.761 | 0.729 | 0.812 | 0.761 | 0.729 |
| ALL | 0.936 | 0.936 | 0.936 | 0.956 | 0.956 | 0.956 |

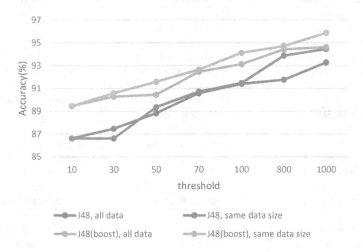

**Fig. 4.** Average accuracy by J48 and J48(boost) on all data and same size of data with [ALL] feature scheme. Thresholds are set to be 10, 30, 50, 70, 100, 800, and 1000.

We perform the evaluations setting concept disjoint threshold to 800. The evaluation results are shown in Table 3. From Table 3 we find conclusions similar to that in the synthetic evaluations. We expected [WCS] to give high level of statistics in terms of concept support, however the effect of them is limited. Using J48, the best features are [CS] and [SWCS]. Using Adaboost, [WCS] performs the best. Overall, the best features in classifying DBpedia are [SWCS] and [AS]. Combining all features together get the best average F1-score of 95.6%. Table 4 shows some examples of noisy type assertions can be found by our approach.

# 6  Related Work

Noise detection was mostly studied in the data mining community in the last decades. Zhu and Wu [4] presented a systematic evaluation on the impact of concept and role noises, with a focus on the latter. They concluded (1) Eliminating individuals containing concept noise will likely enhance the classification accuracy; (2) In comparison

**Table 4.** Examples of noises detected in DBpedia 3.9. The namespaces of the header (concepts) are all http://dbpedia.org/ontology/, and the namespaces of the content (instances) are all http://dbpedia.org/resource/.

| ID | Agent | Person | Place |
|---|---|---|---|
| 1 | Sponge | JSON | PHI |
| 2 | Kama | Xbox_Music | England_national_ field_hockey_team |
| 3 | SQL | Xbox_Video | American_Beaver |
| 4 | Free_State_Of_Saxony | Thumbnail | URS |
| 5 | Duero | Automobile_Craiova | Al-Qaeda |
| **ID** | **PopulatedPlace** | **Settlement** | **Work** |
| 1 | Eurovision_Song_ Contest_2007 | Anglican_Church_of_ Southern_Africa | Daugava |
| 2 | England_national_ field_hockey_team | Byzantine_Catholic_Metropolitan_ Church_of_Pittsburgh | North_Coast |
| 3 | American_Beaver | U.S._Highway_84_(Alabama) | New_York_State_Library |
| 4 | Catholics | River_Blackwater,_Northern_Ireland | Captain_Underpants |
| 5 | PHI | British_House_of_Commons | Goodman_School_of_Drama |
| **ID** | **Organization** | **MusicalWork** | **Artist** |
| 1 | Longfellow_(horse) | Mirage_Press | Citrix |
| 2 | Kama | South_African_War | Royal_Pharmaceutical_Society |
| 3 | U.S._Geological_Survey | Daugava | Argonne_National_Laboratory |
| 4 | Atlantic_ocean | North_Coast | PUC-Rio |
| 5 | Juris_Doctor | National_Broadcasting_Network | KOL |
| **ID** | **Broadcaster** | **RecordLabel** | **SportsTeam** |
| 1 | MHz | Kelin | DOS |
| 2 | Tate_Gallery | Velas | Coral_Springs |
| 3 | Louisiana_Tech | Central_Europe | Kama |
| 4 | TEENick_(block) | Catskills | FSO_Warszawa |
| 5 | List_of_Chinese-language _television_channels | Koliba | West_Point |

with concept noise, the role noise is usually less harmful. One technique often adopted is voting. Zhu et al. [11] inductively processed partitions of the original dataset; they evaluated the whole dataset using the selected good rules. They adopt majority and non-objection threshold schemes to find noises. Miranda et al. [12] used ML classifiers to make predictions on noisy examples in Bioinfomatics domain. They use majority voting and non-objection voting to filter out erroneous predictions. They concluded that non-objection voting was too conservative and majority voting identified low levels of noise. Kubica and Moore [1] identified corrupted fields, and used the remaining non-corrupted fields for subsequent modeling and analysis. They learned a probability model containing components for clean records, noise values, and the corruption process. Rebbapragada and Brodley [13] assigned a vector of class membership probabilities to each training instance, and proposed to use clustering to calculate a probability distribution over the class labels for each instance. Valizadegan and Tan [14] formulated mislabeled detection as an optimization problem and introduced a kernel-based approach for filtering the mislabeled examples.

Noise detection studies have just begun in the semantic web community. Fürber and Hepp [5] developed generic SPARQL queries to identify (1) missing datatype properties or literal values, (2) illegal values, and (3) functional dependency violations. Yu et al. [6] identified potential erroneous (the degree to which a triple deviates from similar triples can be an important heuristic for identifying "abnormal triples") relational descriptions between objects in triples by learning probabilistic rules from the reference data and checking to what extent these rules agree with the context of triples. Suominen and Mader [15] analysed the quality of SKOS vocabularies, and proposed heuristics to correct the problems in the vocabularies. The focus was mainly on syntax level, made the use of labels consistent for example.

Besides these works dealing with noises detection, type inference works are also related. Paulheim and Bizer [2] studied type inference on dataset like DBpedia. They use role links to infer types of individuals, but they do not detect noises. Gangemi et al. [16] automatically typed DBpedia entities by interpreting natural language definition of an entity. Lehmann et al. [17] validated facts by a deep fact validation algorithm, which provided excerpts of webpages to users who create and maintain knowledge bases. Fanizzi et al. [18] adopted a self-training strategy to iteratively predict instance labels. Fleischhacker and Völker [19] enriched learned or manually engineered ontologies with disjointness axioms. dAmato et al. [20] used inductive methods to handle noises in semantic search.

# 7 Conclusion and Future Work

In this paper, we study the problem of noisy type assertions, which plays an important role in the performance of semantic web applications. In large datasets, such as DBpedia, the numbers of type assertions are too large to be processed by most ML classifiers, we propose a novel approach that transforms the problem into multiclass classification of a pair of type assertions related to the same individual. We perform evaluations on both synthetic datasets and DBpedia. From the evaluations, we conclude that: (1) Our approach can be applicable to most situations where noises exist; (2) The feature composition that use both concept knowledge and role knowledge outperforms others by conducting evaluations using different feature compositions; (3) Our approach is effective in detecting noisy type assertions in DBpedia with the average precison of 95%.

In the future, we will try to explore the following issues: (1) We will study the impact of noisy types in other assertions in the dataset; (2) We will extend conflict type assertion extraction to the general type of disjointness, to be specific, the concept in the disjoint pair may not be atomic. (3) Currently the detected noises are recorded in a local DB. We will study how to correct them or remove them in the future.

**Acknowledgements.** This work is partially funded by the National Science Foundation of China under grant 61170165. Additionally, we thank Ying Xu's suggestions.

# References

1. Kubica, J., Moore, A.W.: Probabilistic noise identification and data cleaning. In: ICDM, Citeseer, pp. 131–138 (2003)

2. Paulheim, H., Bizer, C.: Type inference on noisy RDF data. In: Alani, H., et al. (eds.) ISWC 2013, Part I. LNCS, vol. 8218, pp. 510–525. Springer, Heidelberg (2013)
3. Zaveri, A., Kontokostas, D., Sherif, M.A., Bühmann, L., Morsey, M., Auer, S., Lehmann, J.: User-driven quality evaluation of DBpedia. In: Proceedings of the 9th International Conference on Semantic Systems, pp. 97–104. ACM (2013)
4. Zhu, X., Wu, X.: Class noise vs. attribute noise: A quantitative study. Artificial Intelligence Review 22, 177–210 (2004)
5. Fürber, C., Hepp, M.: Using semantic web resources for data quality management. In: Cimiano, P., Pinto, H.S. (eds.) EKAW 2010. LNCS, vol. 6317, pp. 211–225. Springer, Heidelberg (2010)
6. Yu, Y., Zhang, X., Heflin, J.: Learning to detect abnormal semantic web data. In: Proceedings of the Sixth International Conference on Knowledge Capture, pp. 177–178. ACM (2011)
7. Quinlan, J.R.: C4. 5: programs for machine learning, vol. 1. Morgan kaufmann (1993)
8. Wu, X., Kumar, V., Quinlan, J.R., Ghosh, J., Yang, Q., Motoda, H., McLachlan, G.J., Ng, A., Liu, B., Philip, S.Y., et al.: Top 10 algorithms in data mining. Knowledge and Information Systems 14, 1–37 (2008)
9. Freund, Y., Schapire, R.E.: Experiments with a new boosting algorithm. In: ICML, vol. 96, pp. 148–156 (1996)
10. Guo, Y., Pan, Z., Heflin, J.: LUBM: A benchmark for owl knowledge base systems. Web Semantics: Science. Services and Agents on the World Wide Web 3, 158–182 (2005)
11. Zhu, X., Wu, X., Chen, Q.: Eliminating class noise in large datasets. In: ICML, vol. 3, pp. 920–927 (2003)
12. Miranda, A.L.B., Garcia, L.P.F., Carvalho, A.C.P.L.F., Lorena, A.C.: Use of classification algorithms in noise detection and elimination. In: Corchado, E., Wu, X., Oja, E., Herrero, Á., Baruque, B. (eds.) HAIS 2009. LNCS, vol. 5572, pp. 417–424. Springer, Heidelberg (2009)
13. Rebbapragada, U., Brodley, C.E.: Class noise mitigation through instance weighting. In: Kok, J.N., Koronacki, J., Lopez de Mantaras, R., Matwin, S., Mladenič, D., Skowron, A. (eds.) ECML 2007. LNCS (LNAI), vol. 4701, pp. 708–715. Springer, Heidelberg (2007)
14. Valizadegan, H., Tan, P.N.: Kernel based detection of mislabeled training examples. In: SDM, SIAM (2007)
15. Suominen, O., Mader, C.: Assessing and improving the quality of skos vocabularies. Journal on Data Semantics, 1–27 (2013)
16. Gangemi, A., Nuzzolese, A.G., Presutti, V., Draicchio, F., Musetti, A., Ciancarini, P.: Automatic typing of dBpedia entities. In: Cudré-Mauroux, P., et al. (eds.) ISWC 2012, Part I. LNCS, vol. 7649, pp. 65–81. Springer, Heidelberg (2012)
17. Lehmann, J., Gerber, D., Morsey, M., Ngonga Ngomo, A.-C.: DeFacto - deep fact validation. In: Cudré-Mauroux, P., et al. (eds.) ISWC 2012, Part I. LNCS, vol. 7649, pp. 312–327. Springer, Heidelberg (2012)
18. Fanizzi, N.: Mining linked open data through semi-supervised learning methods based on self-training. In: 2012 IEEE Sixth International Conference on Semantic Computing (ICSC), pp. 277–284. IEEE (2012)
19. Fleischhacker, D., Völker, J.: Inductive learning of disjointness axioms. In: Meersman, R., et al. (eds.) OTM 2011, Part II. LNCS, vol. 7045, pp. 680–697. Springer, Heidelberg (2011)
20. Damato, C., Fanizzi, N., Fazzinga, B., Gottlob, G., Lukasiewicz, T.: Ontology-based semantic search on the web and its combination with the power of inductive reasoning. Annals of Mathematics and Artificial Intelligence 65, 83–121 (2012)

# A Cross-Platform Benchmark Framework for Mobile Semantic Web Reasoning Engines

William Van Woensel, Newres Al Haider, Ahmad Ahmad, and Syed S.R. Abidi

NICHE Research Group, Faculty of Computer Science,
Dalhousie University, Halifax, Canada
{william.van.woensel,newres.al.haider,ahmad.ahmad,raza.abidi}@dal.ca

**Abstract.** Semantic Web technologies are used in a variety of domains for their ability to facilitate data integration, as well as enabling expressive, standards-based reasoning. Deploying Semantic Web reasoning processes directly on mobile devices has a number of advantages, including robustness to connectivity loss, more timely results, and reduced infrastructure requirements. At the same time, a number of challenges arise as well, related to mobile platform heterogeneity and limited computing resources. To tackle these challenges, it should be possible to benchmark mobile reasoning performance across different mobile platforms, with rule- and datasets of varying scale and complexity and existing reasoning process flows. To deal with the current heterogeneity of rule formats, a uniform rule- and data-interface on top of mobile reasoning engines should be provided as well. In this paper, we present a cross-platform benchmark framework that supplies 1) a generic, standards-based Semantic Web layer on top of existing mobile reasoning engines; and 2) a benchmark engine to investigate and compare mobile reasoning performance.

**Keywords:** Semantic Web, benchmarks, software framework, rule-based reasoning, SPIN.

## 1 Introduction

By supplying a formal model to represent knowledge, Semantic Web technology facilitate data integration as well as expressive rule-based reasoning over Web data. For example, in the healthcare domain, the use of specialized, Semantic Web medical ontologies facilitate data integration between heterogeneous data sources [10], while Semantic Web reasoning processes are employed to realize Clinical Decision Support Systems (CDSS) [21,6].

Reflecting the importance of reasoning in the Semantic Web, a range of rule languages and reasoning engine implementations, using an assortment of reasoning techniques, are available. Such reasoners range from Description Logic (DL)-based reasoners relying on OWL ontology constraints [17] to general-purpose reasoners, supporting a variety of rule languages (e.g., RuleML [7],

P. Mika et al. (Eds.) ISWC 2014, Part I, LNCS 8796, pp. 389–408, 2014.

SWRL [20] and SPIN [24]) and relying on different technologies, including Prolog (e.g., XSB[1]), deductive databases (e.g., OntoBroker[2]) and triple stores (e.g., Jena[3]). In general, rule-based reasoning techniques, as for instance used in decision support systems, allow a clear separation between domain knowledge and application logic. Consequently, domain knowledge can be easily edited, updated and extended without the need to disrupt the underlying system.

Up until now, knowledge-centric reasoning systems are typically developed for deployment as desktop or server applications. With the emergence of mobile devices with increased memory and processing capabilities, a case can be made for mobile reasoning systems. In fact, mobile RDF stores and query engines are already available, including RDF On the Go [25], AndroJena[4], i-MoCo [32], and systems such as MobiSem [33]. As such, a logical next step is to deploy rule-based reasoning, an essential part of the Semantic Web, on mobile devices as well.

Deploying mobile reasoning processes, as opposed to relying on remote services, has a number of advantages. In particular, local reasoning support allows making timely inferences, even in cases where connectivity is lacking. This is especially important in domains such as healthcare, where non- (or too late) raised alerts can negatively impact the patient's health. Secondly, given the myriad of data that can be collected about mobile users, privacy issues can play a role. A mobile user could (rightly) be uncomfortable with sharing certain information outside of the mobile device, for instance in context-aware [29] and mobile health scenarios [2,19]. By deploying reasoning processes locally, no privacy-sensitive data needs to be wirelessly communicated, while the advantages of rule-based reasoning is still accessible to mobile apps.

Performing mobile reasoning gives rise to challenges as well, both related to mobile device and platform heterogeneity as well as limited device capabilities. Furthermore, it is clear that each system has its own particular requirements regarding reasoning [13], which determine the complexity and scale of the rule- and dataset, as well as the particular reasoning process flow. In light of mobile device limitations, this makes it paramount to supply developers with the tools to benchmark, under their particular reasoning setup, different mobile reasoning engines. This way, developers may accurately study the performance impact of mobile deployment, and identify the best reasoning engine for the job. For instance, this may inform architecture decisions where reasoning tasks are distributed across the server and mobile device based on their complexity [2]. In addition, considering the fragmented mobile platform market (with systems including Android, iOS, Windows Phone, BlackBerry OS, WebOS, Symbian, ..), it should be straightforward to execute the same benchmark setup across multiple mobile platforms.

Compounding the problem of mobile benchmarking, current freely and publicly available mobile reasoning solutions support a variety of different rule and

---

[1] http://xsb.sourceforge.net/

[2] http://www.semafora-systems.com/en/products/ontobroker/

[3] http://jena.sourceforge.net/

[4] http://code.google.com/p/androjena/

data formats. In fact, the heterogeneity of rule languages is a general problem among rule-based reasoners [26]. We also note that multiple Semantic Web rule standards are currently available as well (e.g., RuleML, SWRL, SPIN). To avoid developers having to re-write their rule- and dataset to suit each engine, a single rule and data interface should be available. For our purposes, the most interesting rule language is SPIN, a W3C Member Submission based on the SPARQL query language. SPARQL is well-known and understood by most Semantic Web developers, reducing the learning threshold compared to other alternatives.

In this paper, we present a cross-platform Benchmark Framework for mobile Semantic Web reasoning engines. As its main goal, this framework aims to empower developers to investigate and compare mobile reasoning performance in their particular reasoning setups, using their existing standards-based ruleset and dataset. This framework comprises two main components:

- A generic, standards-based **Semantic Web Layer** on top of mobile reasoning engines, supporting the SPIN rule language. Behind the scenes, the supplied ruleset (SPIN) and dataset (RDF) are converted to the custom rule and data formats of the various supported reasoning engines.

- A **Benchmark Engine** that allows the performance of the different reasoning engines to be studied and compared. In this comparison, any existing domain-specific rulesets and datasets of varying scale and complexity can be tested, as well as different reasoning process flows.

By realizing this framework as a *cross-platform* solution, the same benchmarks can be easily applied across different mobile platforms. The framework is implemented in JavaScript using the PhoneGap[5] development tool, which allows mobile web apps to be deployed as native apps on a multitude of platforms (e.g., Android, iOS) . As a result, our framework allows benchmarking both JavaScript and native systems. The framework further has an *extensible* architecture, allowing new rule/data converters, reasoning flows and engines to be easily plugged in. Finally, we present an *example benchmark* in an existing clinical decision support scenario, to serve as a proof-of-concept and to investigate mobile reasoning performance in a real-world scenario. Our **online documentation** [31], associated with the presented benchmark framework, links to the source code and contains detailed instructions on usage and extension as well (these docs are referenced throughout the paper).

This paper is structured as follows. In Section 2, we discuss relevant background. Section 3 elaborates on the Mobile Benchmark Framework architecture and its main components. We continue by summarizing the measurement criteria (Section 4) and how developers can use the framework (Section 5). Section 6 summarizes the results of the example benchmark. In Section 7, we present related work, and Section 8 presents conclusions and future work.

---

[5] http://phonegap.com/

## 2    Background

### 2.1    Semantic Web Reasoning

An important aspect of the Semantic Web is reasoning, whereby reasoners may exploit the assigned semantics of OWL data, as well as the added expressivity given by domain-specific rules and constraints. Current semantic rule standards include the Semantic Web Rule Language (SWRL) [20], Web Rule Language (WRL) [3], Rule Markup/Modeling Language (RuleML) [7] and SPARQL Inferencing Notation (SPIN) [24]. In addition, many reasoning engines also introduce custom rule languages (e.g., Apache Jena[6]). Clearly, this multitude of semantic rule languages prevent the direct re-use of a single ruleset when benchmarking. To tackle this problem, our benchmark framework supplies a generic Semantic Web layer across the supported rule engines, supporting SPIN as the input rule language.

SPIN (SPARQL Inferencing Notation) is a SPARQL-based rule- and constraint language. At its core, SPIN provides a natural, object-oriented way of dealing with constraints and rules associated with RDF(S)/OWL classes. In the object-oriented design paradigm, classes define the structure of objects (i.e., attributes) together with their behavior, including creating / changing objects and attributes (rules) as well as ensuring a consistent object state (constraints). Reflecting this paradigm, SPIN allows directly associating locally-scoped rules and constraints to their related RDF(S)/OWL classes.

To represent rules and constraints, SPIN relies on the SPARQL Protocol and RDF Query Language (SPARQL) [14]. SPARQL is a W3C standard with well-formed query semantics across RDF data, and has sufficient expressivity to represent both queries as well as general-purpose rules and constraints. Furthermore, SPARQL is supported by most RDF query engines and graph stores, and is well-known by Semantic Web developers. This results in a low learning curve for SPIN, and thus also facilitates the re-encoding of existing rulesets to serve as benchmark input. In order to associate SPARQL queries with class definitions, SPIN provides a vocabulary to encode queries as RDF triples, and supplies properties such as `spin:rule` and `spin:constraint` to link the RDF-encoded queries to concrete RDF(S)/OWL classes.

### 2.2    Reasoning Engines

Below, we elaborate on the reasoning engines currently plugged into the Mobile Benchmark Framework.

**AndroJena**[7] is an Android-ported version of the well-known Apache Jena[8] framework for working with Semantic Web data. In AndroJena, RDF data can be directly loaded from a local or remote source into an RDF store called a *Model*, supporting a range of RDF syntaxes.

---

[6] https://jena.apache.org/

[7] http://code.google.com/p/androjena/

[8] https://jena.apache.org/

Regarding reasoning, AndroJena supplies an RDFS, OWL and rule-based reasoner. The latter provides both forward and backward chaining, respectively based on the standard RETE algorithm [12] and Logic Programming (LP). In addition, the reasoning engine supports a hybrid execution model, where both mechanisms are employed in conjunction[9,10]. Rules are specified using a custom rule language (which resembles a SPARQL-like syntax), and are parsed and passed to a reasoner object that is applied on a populated Model, which creates an *InfModel* supplying query access to the inferred RDF statements. Afterwards, new facts can be added to this InfModel; after calling the `rebind` method, the reasoning step can be re-applied.

**RDFQuery**[11] is an RDF plugin for the well-known jQuery[12] JavaScript library. RDFQuery attempts to bridge the gap between the Semantic Web and the regular Web, by allowing developers to directly query RDF (e.g., injected via RDFa [18]) gleaned from the current HTML page. RDF datastores can also be populated directly with RDF triples.

In addition to querying, RDFQuery also supports rule-based reasoning. Conditions in these rules may contain triple patterns as well as general-purpose filters. These filters are represented as JavaScript functions, which are called for each currently matching data item; based on the function's return value, data items are kept or discarded. The reasoning algorithm is "naïve", meaning rule are executed in turn until no more new results occur[13].

**RDFStore-JS**[14] is a JavaScript RDF graph store supporting the SPARQL query language. This system can be either deployed in the browser or a Node.js[15] module, which is a server-side JavaScript environment.

Comparable to AndroJena (see Section 2.2), triples can be loaded into an RDF store from a local or remote data source, supporting multiple RDF syntaxes. Regarding querying, RDFStore-JS supports SPARQL 1.0 together with parts of the SPARQL 1.1 specification. However, RDFStore-JS does not natively support rule-based reasoning. To resolve this, we extended the system with a reasoning mechanism that accepts rules as SPARQL 1.1 INSERT queries, whereby the WHERE clause represents the rule condition and the INSERT clause the rule result. This mechanism is naïve, executing each rule in turn until no more new results are inferred (cfr. RDFQuery).

**Nools**[16] is a RETE-based rule engine, written in JavaScript. Like RDFStore-JS, this system can be deployed both on Node.js as well as in the browser.

---

[9] http://jena.apache.org/documentation/inference/#rules
[10] Currently, we rely on the default configuration settings, which uses the hybrid execution model.
[11] https://code.google.com/p/rdfquery/wiki/RdfPlugin
[12] http://jquery.com
[13] The engine had to be extended to automatically resolve variables in the rule result.
[14] http://github.com/antoniogarrote/rdfstore-js
[15] http://nodejs.org/
[16] https://github.com/C2FO/nools

In contrast to the two other evaluated JavaScript systems, Nools presents a fully-fledged reasoning engine, supporting a non-naïve reasoning algorithm (RETE). Also, as opposed to the other evaluated systems, Nools does not natively support RDF. The engine is also used differently when performing reasoning. In case of Nools, a developer first supplies the rules, formulated using their custom rule language, in the form of a *flow*. The supplied flow is afterwards compiled into an internal representation (whereby pre-compilation can be applied to avoid repeating the compilation step each time). A *session* is an instance of the flow, containing the RETE working memory in which new facts are asserted. After creating and compiling the rule flow, the dataset is asserted in the session, after which the asserted data is matched to the defined rules.

**Summary.** Despite the potential of mobile reasoning processes, we observe a current lack of freely and publicly available mobile solutions. The above mentioned JavaScript engines were developed for use on either the server-side (using an environment such as Node.js) or a desktop browser, which makes their performance on mobile platforms uncertain. And similarly, while AndroJena represents port to the mobile Android platform, it is unclear to what extent the reasoning engine was optimized for mobile devices.

At the same time, our example benchmark (see Section 6), conducted in a real-world clinical decision support scenario, shows that these reasoning engines already have acceptable performance for small rule- and datasets. Moreover, our Mobile Benchmark Framework empowers developers to cope with this uncertainty of mobile performance, by allowing them to investigate the feasibility of locally deploying particular reasoning tasks. We further note that, as mobile device capabilities improve and demand for mobile reasoning deployment increases, more mobile-optimized reasoning engines are likely to become available. Recent efforts from the literature to optimize mobile reasoning processes in certain domains (i.e., context-awareness) have been already observed [29].

# 3   Mobile Benchmark Framework

In this section, we give an architecture overview of the Mobile Benchmark Framework. The framework architecture comprises two main components: 1) a generic **Semantic Web layer**, supplying a uniform, standards-based rule- and dataset interface to mobile reasoning engines; and 2) a **Benchmark Engine**, to investigate and compare mobile reasoning performance. Figure 1 shows the framework architecture.

During benchmark execution, the particular benchmark rule- and dataset (encoded in SPIN and RDF, respectively) are first passed to the generic Semantic Web layer. In this layer, a local component (called Proxy) contacts an external Conversion Web service, to convert the given rules and data into the formats supported by the plugged-in reasoning engines. In this Web service, conversion is performed by custom converters, each of which supports a particular rule or data format. Afterwards, the conversion results are returned to the Proxy and passed on to the Benchmark Engine.

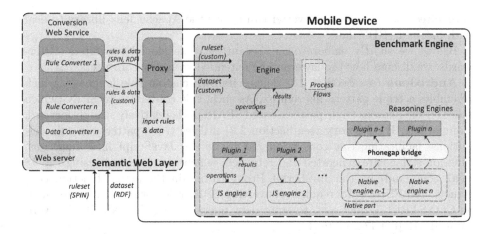

**Fig. 1.** Framework Architecture

In the Benchmark Engine, reasoning can be conducted using different process flows, to better align the benchmarks with actual, real-world reasoning systems (e.g., decision support). A particular reasoning flow is realized by invoking the uniform interface methods (e.g., load data, execute rules) of the benchmarked reasoning engine. Each mobile reasoning engine requires a plugin implementing this interface, which translates method invocations to the underlying reasoning engine. In case of native mobile reasoning engines, these plugins communicate with the native engine code over the PhoneGap communication bridge.

In the sections below, we elaborate on the two main architecture components.

### 3.1 Semantic Web Layer

This layer supplies a single, standards-based rule- and dataset interface for framework, allowing developers to cope with the heterogeneous rule- and dataset formats. Currently, the layer respectively supports SPIN[17] and RDF as input rule and data formats.

The conversion functionality is accessed via an intermediate JavaScript component called the Proxy, which comprises methods for rule and data conversion. Behind the scenes, the Proxy contacts a RESTful Conversion Web service (deployed on an external Web server) to perform the conversion tasks, thus introducing a layer of abstraction. We opted for a web service approach, since the only currently available SPIN API is developed for Java (by TopBraid [23]). The Conversion Web service utilizes the API to convert incoming SPIN rules into an Abstract Syntax Tree (AST). This AST is then analyzed by plugged-in converters, using the provided Visitor classes (Visitor design pattern), to convert the SPIN rules into equivalent rules[18] in other formats. In case data conversion

---

[17] The input SPIN rules do not need to be RDF-encoded.

[18] While only SPIN language features can be referenced in input rules, any (SPIN-encoded) core inferences should be mappable to a target IF-THEN rule format.

is required as well, a data converter can utilize the Apache Jena library to deal with incoming RDF data.

Below, we shortly elaborate on the currently developed converters. Afterwards, we discuss how the layer can be extended with new converters.

**AndroJena** (see Section 2.2) defines its own custom rule language, which resembles a triple pattern-like syntax. As such, rule conversion to SPIN (which relies on the likewise triple pattern-based SPARQL) is relatively straightforward. Comparably, **RDFQuery** (see Section 2.2) utilizes triple patterns in rule definitions, facilitating rule conversion. To create the JavaScript filter functions, function strings are generated and returned, which are evaluated (using the JS `eval` command) by the JavaScript Proxy to obtain the actual function constructs. **RDFStore-JS** requires converting SPIN rules, which are represented as CONSTRUCT queries[19], to equivalent queries using the INSERT keyword from SPARQL 1.1/Update [14].

As mentioned, **Nools** (see Section 2.2) is the only reasoning engine under consideration without built-in Semantic Web support. At the same time however, their generic rule language supports domain-specific extensions, by allowing rule definitions to include custom data types (e.g., data type `Message`). These data types can then be instantiated in the incoming dataset, and referenced in the defined rules. To add Semantic Web support, we include custom RDFStatement, RDFResource, RDFProperty and RDFLiteral data types into rule definitions, and convert incoming SPIN rules to Nools rules referencing these data types. The incoming RDF dataset is converted to instances of these custom data types, and asserted as facts in the *session*.

Currently, the converters support SPIN functions representing primitive comparators (greater, equal, ..), as well as logical connectors in FILTER clauses. Support for additional functions needs to be added to the respective converter classes. More advanced SPARQL query constructs, such as (not-)exists, optional, minus and union, are currently not supported, since it is difficult to convert them to all rule engine formats, and they have not been required up until now by our real-world test rule- and datasets (e.g., see example benchmark in Section 6).

**Extensibility.** To plugin a new data- or rule-format, developers create a new converter class. Each converter class implements a uniform rule- (or data-) conversion interface, which accepts the incoming SPIN rules / RDF data and returns Strings in the correct rule / data format. Each converter class also defines a unique identifier for the custom format, since conversion requests to the Web service specify the target format via its unique identifier.

New converter classes need to be listed (i.e., package and class name) in a configuration file, which is read by the Web service to dynamically load converter class definitions. As such, converters can be easily plugged in without requiring alterations to the web service code. Our online documentation [31] contains more detailed instructions on developing new converters.

---

[19] http://www.w3.org/Submission/2011/SUBM-spin-modeling-20110222/
#spin-rules-construct

## 3.2   Benchmark Engine

The Benchmark Engine performs benchmarks on mobile reasoning engines under particular reasoning setups, with the goal of investigating and comparing reasoning performances. Below, we first discuss currently supported reasoning setups; afterwards, we elaborate on the extensibility of this component.

Reasoning setups comprise the particular process flows via which reasoning may be executed. By supporting different setups (and allowing new ones to be plugged in), benchmarks can be better aligned to real-world reasoning systems. From our work in clinical decision support, we identified two general process flows:

*Frequent Reasoning:* In the first flow, the system stores all health measurements and observations (e.g., heart rate, symptoms), collectively called clinical facts, in a data store. To infer new clinical conclusions, frequent reasoning is applied to the entire datastore, comprising all collected clinical facts together with the patient's baseline clinical profile (e.g., including age, gender and ethnicity). Concretely, this entails loading a reasoning engine with the entire datastore each time a certain timespan has elapsed, and executing the relevant ruleset.

*Incremental Reasoning:* In the second flow, the system implements clinical decision support by applying reasoning each time a new clinical fact is entered. In this case, the reasoning engine is loaded with an initial baseline dataset, containing the patient's clinical profile and historical (e.g., previously entered) clinical facts. Afterwards, the engine is kept in memory, whereby new facts are dynamically added to the reasoning engine. After each add operation, reasoning is re-applied to infer new clinical conclusions[20].

It can be observed that the Frequent Reasoning process flow reduces responsiveness to new clinical facts, while also incurring a larger performance overhead since the dataset needs to be continuously re-loaded. Although the Incremental Reasoning flow improves upon responsiveness, it also incurs a larger consistent memory overhead, since the reasoning engine is continuously kept in memory. The most suitable flow depends on the requirements of the domain; for instance, Incremental Reasoning is a better choice for scenarios where timely (clinical) findings are essential. The Benchmark Engine enables developers to perform mobile reasoning benchmarking using process flows that are most suitable for their setting. We note that additional flows can be plugged in as well, as mentioned at the end of this Section.

In addition, the particular reasoning engine may dictate a particular process flow as well (see Section 2.2). For instance, in case of RDFQuery, RDFStore-JS and AndroJena, the data is first loaded into the engine and rules are subsequently executed (*LoadDataExecuteRules*). For Nools, rules are first loaded into the engine to compile the RETE network, after which the dataset is fed into the network and reasoning is performed (*LoadRulesDataExecute*).

---

[20] An algorithm is proposed in [16] to optimize this kind of reasoning, which is implemented by the reasoning engine presented in [29].

We note that the former type of process flow (i.e., Frequent and Incremental Reasoning) indicates the reasoning timing, and is chosen based on domain requirements; while the latter flow type defines the operation ordering, and is determined by the employed reasoning engine[21]. For a single benchmark, the *reasoning setup* thus comprises a combination of two flows of each type. Figures 2/A and B illustrate the possible setups for our current reasoning engines.

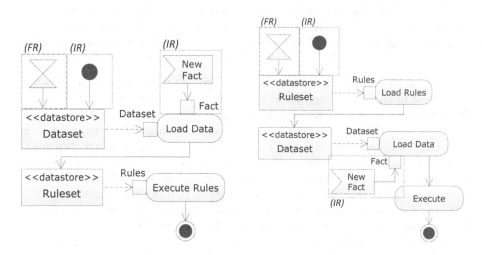

**Fig. 2.** (A) Frequent Reasoning and (B) Incremental Reasoning process flow (RDF-Query, RDFStore-JS, AndroJena)

Figure 2/A shows Frequent Reasoning (FR) and Incremental Reasoning (IR) for *LoadDataExecuteRules* (RDFQuery, RDFStore-JS and AndroJena), and Figure 2/B shows the same for *LoadDataRulesExecute* (Nools). For both diagrams, Frequent Reasoning entails going through the entire diagram each time a particular timespan has elapsed (time event). For Incremental reasoning, the system traverses the diagram from start to finish at startup time, and proceeds (from the indicated place) each time a new fact is received (receive signal event).

As mentioned, the Benchmark Engine is implemented in JavaScript and deployed as a native mobile app using the PhoneGap cross-platform development tool. We chose Android as the deployment platform since, to our knowledge, the only (publicly and freely available) native mobile reasoning engine (AndroJena, see Section 2.2) runs on that platform.

**Extensibility.** In the Benchmark Engine, each reasoning setup is represented by a JavaScript object. Its `runBenchmark` method invokes operations from the uniform reasoning engine interface (e.g., load data, execute rules) to realize its

---

[21] We also note that, for *LoadRulesDataExecute*, the Execute Rules step is separated into two steps.

particular process flows. The object is added to a folder called **setups** and listed in a **mapping.json** file, which maps combinations of process flows (e.g., *Frequentreasoning, LoadDataExecuteRules*) to their corresponding setup object.

A new mobile reasoning engine is plugged into the Benchmark Engine by writing a JavaScript "plugin" object. This object implements the uniform interface invoked by reasoning setups (see above) and translates method invocations to the underlying engine. In addition, each object specifies a unique engine ID, the rule- and dataformat accepted by the engine, as well as the process flow dictated by the engine (see Section 3.2). Each plugin object is put in a separate file and folder, both named after the reasoning engine id.

To insert *native* reasoning engines, developers implement the plugin on the native platform (e.g., Android), likewise implementing the uniform engine interface and specifying the aforementioned information. The Benchmark Engine comprises a native part (see Figure 1) to manage these plugins. In addition, developers add a dummy JavaScript plugin object for the engine, indicating the unique engine ID. Behind the scenes, the Benchmark Engine replaces this dummy object by a proxy component that implements communication with the native plugin. This setup is illustrated in the Benchmark Engine part of Figure 1.

More detailed instructions on developing Benchmark Engine extensions can be found in our online documentation [31].

## 4 Measurement Criteria

The Mobile Benchmark Framework allows studying and comparing the following metrics:

- *Data and rule loading times*: Time needed to load data and rules (if necessary) into the reasoning engine. Data loading time is commonly used in database benchmarks [9] as well as Semantic Web benchmarks [15,5]. Note that this time does not include converting the initial standards-based rule- and dataset to native formats.
- *Reasoning times*: Time needed to execute the rules on the dataset and infer new facts. Typically, database benchmarks capture the query response time as well, including Semantic Web benchmarks [15,4].

Ideally, and especially on mobile devices, these performance criteria would include memory consumption as well. However, it is currently not technically possible to automatically measure this criterium for all reasoning engines. Android Java heap dumps accurately measure the memory consumption of Android engines, but can only measure the entire memory size of the natively deployed web app (comprising the JavaScript reasoning engines). The Chrome DevTools remote debugging support[22] can only be employed to record heap allocations inside the mobile Chrome browser, and furthermore needs to be invoked manually. Other works also cite the accurate measuring of in-memory repository sizes as a difficult problem [15].

---

[22] https://developers.google.com/chrome-developer-tools/docs/
remote-debugging

Some related works also investigate completeness and soundness of inferencing [15]. This criterium was presented in the context of OWL constraint-based reasoning, which typically serves to enrich data access where incomplete inferences may already be acceptable. In rule-based systems (e.g., (clinical) decision support systems), inferencing completeness is often a hard requirement. That said, each reasoning engine plugin in our framework outputs any inferred facts, allowing developers to check inferencing completeness.

Other works focus on benchmarking performance for reasoning types such as large joins, Datalog recursion and default negation [26]. Although these benchmarks are certainly useful, the goal of the Mobile Benchmark Framework is not to measure performance for such specific reasoning types, but instead to facilitate mobile reasoning benchmarking given a particular existing reasoning setup; including rule- and datasets and reasoning process flows.

Finally, we do not measure rule- and dataset conversion performance. The goal of the Semantic Web layer is to provide a uniform rule- and data-interface to facilitate benchmarking; the layer will not be included in actual mobile reasoning deployments.

## 5    Usage

This section gives a birds-eye view of how developers can utilize the framework. More detailed deployment and usage instructions for the framework, including the Conversion Web service, are available in our online documentation [31].

To perform benchmarks, developers provide a configuration file that specifies the reasoning setup and engine to be used, the number of runs, as well as the benchmark dataset and ruleset. By performing multiple runs of the same benchmark and calculating average execution times, the impact of background OS processes is minimized. Below, we show the configuration for our example benchmark (see Section 6):

```
{
    processFlow : 'frequent_reasoning',
        // options: frequent_reasoning, incremental_reasoning
    engine : 'AndroJena',

    nrRuns : 20,

    ruleSet : {
        path : "res/rules/af/benchmark.spin-rules",
        format : 'SPIN' // options: SPIN, native
    },

    // in case of 'incremental reasoning': include 'baseline'
    // & 'single-item' config under dataSet
    dataSet : {
        path : "res/data/af/25/benchmark.nt",
```

```
    format : 'RDF', // options: RDF, native
    syntax : 'N-TRIPLE'
        // options: RDF/XML, N-TRIPLE, TURTLE, TTL, N3, RDF/XML-ABBREV
  }
}
```

This configuration indicates the process flow (`processFlow`) and reasoning engine (`engine`) to be used in the benchmark, as well as the number of benchmark runs (`nrRuns`). The ruleset and dataset can either be provided respectively in SPIN / RDF or native format (i.e., the engine's natively supported format). In the non-native case, the framework automatically contacts the Semantic Web layer on-the-fly for conversion to the engine's native format. Alternatively, a script is available to convert rules and data beforehand, ruling out the need for connecting to the Web service during benchmarking.

# 6  Example Benchmark

In this section, we present an example benchmark that serves as a proof-of-concept of our Mobile Benchmark Framework. As an added goal, this benchmark aims to indicate the performance of the presented mobile reasoning engines for a real-world reasoning task, namely an existing clinical decision support scenario. Importantly, we note that the goal of this section is not to exhaustively compare the performance of the plugged-in mobile reasoning engines[23].

Below, we shortly elaborate on the benchmark domain (including the data- and ruleset), and indicate the utilized hardware. Afterwards, we summarize the benchmarking results.

## 6.1  Benchmark Domain

The benchmark data and ruleset are taken from ongoing work on the Integrated Management Program Advancing Community Treatment of Atrial Fibrillation (IMPACT-AF) project [22]. IMPACT-AF aims to provide web- and mobile-based clinical decision support tools for primary care providers and patients, with the goal of better managing Atrial Fibrillation (AF). To improve the timeliness of clinical alerts and increase robustness to connectivity loss, this project includes outfitting a mobile app, used by patients to enter health measurements and observed symptoms, with local reasoning support.

The mobile **ruleset**, employed in this benchmark, represents part of the computerized guidelines for the treatment of Atrial Fibrillation, given by the Canadian Cardiovascular Society [8] and European Society of Cardiology [11]. The ruleset encompasses a total of 10 rules. An AF patient's **dataset** comprises health factors related to AF, including clinically relevant personal info (e.g., age, gender) and health measurements (e.g., blood pressure), as well as AF-specific symptoms and the International Normalized Ratio (INR). Collectively,

---

[23] A second paper, performing such a comparison for the same domain, is currently under review.

we refer to these data items as clinical facts. We generated benchmark datasets containing the above described clinical data, whereby clinical facts were created based on ranges encompassing both clinically normal values as well as abnormal ones. With the goal of investigating mobile reasoning scalability, our benchmarks consider a sequence of datasets, each containing an increasing amount of data. Each dataset triggers 40-50% of the rules.

The rule- and dataset of this benchmark, as well as instructions on how to run it, can be found in the online documentation [31] (for the latter, see the Usage part).

## 6.2  Hardware

The benchmarks were performed on a Samsung Galaxy SIII (model number GT-I9300), with a 1.4GHz quad-core processor, 1GB RAM and 16GB storage. The installed Android OS was version 4.3 (Jelly Bean) with API level 18.

## 6.3  Results

In Section 3.2, we described two main process flows to realize mobile reasoning, including Incremental Reasoning and Frequent Reasoning. Below, we separately summarize and discuss the results for each process flow.

**Frequent Reasoning.** Table 1 shows the average loading and reasoning times for each engine and for increasing dataset sizes. Each run of this flow involves loading the reasoning engine with the entire dataset (*load* column) and then executing the rules (*execute* column); the *total* column shows the total time of each run.

We note that for Nools, loading times also include loading the rules into the engine[24], in order to build the internal RETE network (data loading time is shown separately between parenthesis). For some engines, the reasoning step includes creating rule objects as well; since this rule creation step turned out to be trivial (never exceeding 50 ms), these times were added to the overall reasoning times.

**Incremental Reasoning.** In Table 2, we again summarize average loading and reasoning times for increasing sizes of the dataset. In this process flow, the reasoning engine is initially loaded with a baseline dataset (typically at startup time). As baseline dataset, we employed the dataset containing 25 clinical facts (1673 triples). A single run of this flow involves loading an additional fact into the engine (*load* column) and performing the execution step (*execute* column). The *total* column shows the total time of a single run. We refer to Table 1 for times on the initial loading of the baseline dataset.

---

[24] This time remains constant for increasing dataset sizes.

**Table 1.** Frequent Reasoning: Loading & Reasoning times for increasing dataset sizes (ms)

| #triples | RDFQuery | | | RDFStore-JS | | | Nools | | | AndroJena | | |
|---|---|---|---|---|---|---|---|---|---|---|---|---|
| | load | exec | total | load | exec | total | load | exec | total | load | exec | total |
| 137 | 95 | 154 | **249** | 196 | 985 | **1181** | 8411 (560) | 52 | **8463** | 94 | 104 | **198** |
| 393 | 230 | 506 | **736** | 750 | 1523 | **2273** | 9256 (1245) | 88 | **9344** | 160 | 138 | **298** |
| 713 | 362 | 1165 | **1527** | 1269 | 1479 | **2748** | 10061 (2521) | 78 | **10139** | 439 | 466 | **905** |
| 1673 | 673 | 6294 | **6967** | 2468 | 1606 | **4074** | 14707 (7399) | 58 | **14765** | 560 | 3205 | **3765** |
| 3273 | 1348 | 36603 | **37951** | 4269 | 2145 | **6414** | 25580 (18731) | 64 | **25644** | 1036 | 24921 | **25957** |
| 4873 | 1680 | 106212 | **107892** | 5592 | 2496 | **8088** | 49465 (41845) | 358 | **49823** | 1509 | 79699 | **81208** |

**Table 2.** Loading & Reasoning times for a single fact (ms)

| | RDFQuery | RDFStore-JS | Nools | AndroJena |
|---|---|---|---|---|
| load | 42 | 8 | 22 | 16 |
| execute | 5941 | 1677 | 19 | 3426 |
| **total** | **5983** | **1685** | **41** | **3442** |

## 6.4 Discussion

In this section, we shortly discuss the benchmark results summarized above for each reasoning process flow.

**Frequent Reasoning.** Table 1 shows the Nools data loading time is problematic for larger (> 713 triples) datasets (the rule loading time is constant and averages ca. 7-8s). Regarding loading times, especially RDFQuery and AndroJena perform well (< 1s) for medium datasets (< 3273 triples), whereby AndroJena has the best loading performance overall.

At the same time, we note that AndroJena and RDFQuery, while performing well for smaller datasets, have a very problematic reasoning performance for larger datasets (≥ 1673 triples). Nools has by far the best reasoning performance, only exceeding 100ms for the largest dataset. Reasoning performance for RDFStore-JS remains reasonable, rising steadily as the datasets increase in size.

From the total times, we observe that **RDFStore-JS** is the most scalable solution for this particular process flow, performing best for larger datasets (> 1673 triples). **AndroJena** is the better solution for smaller datasets (≤ 1673 triples).

It can be observed that the domain datasets are relatively small scale. Inside this limited scale however, the benchmark already identified clear differences in engine performance for increasing dataset sizes. For larger datasets, problematic mobile performance may for instance point the developer towards a distributed solution, combining local and server-side reasoning.

Also, we note the ruleset was not optimized to suit the employed reasoning mechanisms (e.g., RETE, Logic Programming) or dataset composition.

Investigating the effects of the various potential optimizations is beyond the scope of this paper, and will be considered in future work.

**Incremental Reasoning.** Table 2 shows that, as expected from the discussion above, Nools has by far the best performance in this reasoning step, with almost negligible reasoning times compared to the other engines. In contrast, reasoning times for the other three engines is comparable to their reasoning performance for this dataset size in the first process flow.

Consequently, we observe that, once the initial data and rule loading is out of the way, Nools has by far the best reasoning performance when incrementally adding facts in this process flow. As noted in the previous section, Nools data loading times for small datasets ($\leq 713$ triples) are still acceptable (while we note that rule loading time will also decrease with the ruleset size). Therefore, **Nools** is the best option for this flow in case of *small datasets and rulesets*, since the low reasoning time makes up for the increased initialization time. In case *scalability* is required, **RDFStore-JS** remains the best option.

**Conclusion.** The above results indicate that, as expected, the most suitable engine depends on the target reasoning process flow, as well as the dataset (and ruleset) scale. At the same time however, we observe that scalability represents a serious issue for most mobile engines. We also note that, although taken from an existing, real-world clinical decision support system, the utilized ruleset is relatively straightforward, with for instance no rule chaining. If that had been the case, naïve reasoning mechanisms (as employed by RDFStore-JS and RD-FQuery) would likely have a larger disadvantage compared to the fully-fledged AndroJena and Nools engines. If anything, this again indicates the importance of a Mobile Benchmark Framework that allows easily performing benchmarks with the particular rule- and dataset from the target use case.

# 7    Related Work

The Lehigh University Benchmark (LUBM) [15] supplies a set of test queries and a data generator to generate datasets, both referencing a university ontology. In addition, a test module is provided for carrying out data loading and query testing. This work aims to benchmark data loading and querying over large knowledge base systems featuring OWL / RDF(S) reasoning. The University Ontology Benchmark (UOBM) [27] builds upon this work, and extends it to support complete OWL-DL inferencing and improve scalability testing. Similarly, the Berlin SPARQL benchmark (BSBM) [5] supplies test queries, a data generator and test module for an e-commerce scenario. In this case, the goal is to compare performance of native RDF stores with SPARQL-to-SQL rewriters, and to put the results in relation with RDBMS.

The focus of the works presented above differs from our work, which is on the cross-platform benchmarking of mobile, rule-based Semantic Web reasoners; and facilitating such benchmarks by providing a uniform interface across different, natively supported rule- and data formats.

OpenRuleBench [26] is a suite of benchmarks for comparing and analyzing the performance of a wide variety of rule engines, spanning 5 different technologies and 11 systems in total. These benchmarks measure performance for types of reasoning such as large joins and Datalog recursion, targeting engines deployed on the desktop- and server-side. Instead, we focus on benchmarking Semantic Web reasoners deployed on mobile platforms. Additionally, we supply the tools for developers to benchmark their existing reasoning setup, including their rule- and dataset and particular reasoning flow.

The Intelligent Mobile Platform (IMP) supplies context-aware services to third-party mobile apps, and relies on the Delta Reasoner [29] to determine current context and identify appropriate actions. To cope with the particular requirements of context-aware settings, including the dynamicity of sensor data and the necessity of push-based access to context data, the Delta Reasoner implements features such as incremental reasoning and continuous query evaluation. However, this reasoner is currently not publicly available; and the integration of this reasoner into the mobile IMP still seems a work in progress.

## 8  Conclusions and Future Work

In this paper, we introduced a Mobile Benchmark Framework for the investigation and comparison of mobile Semantic Web reasoning engine performances. This framework was realized as a *cross-platform* solution, meaning a particular benchmark setup can be easily applied across mobile platforms. Furthermore, there is a strong focus on *extensibility*, allowing new rule- and data converters, reasoning process flows and engines to be plugged in. Throughout the paper, we indicated where and how extensions can be made by third-party developers.

An important goal of the framework is to empower developers to benchmark different reasoning engines, using their own particular reasoning setups and standards-based rule-and datasets. To that end, the framework comprises two main components:

- A generic, standards-based **Semantic Web Layer** on top of mobile reasoning engines, supporting the SPIN rule language. Given a standards-based ruleset (SPIN) and dataset (RDF), a conversion component returns this rule- and dataset transformed into the custom formats supported by the mobile reasoning engines.
- A **Benchmark Engine** that allows the performance of the different reasoning engines to be studied and compared. In this comparison, any domain-specific rule- and dataset with varying scale and complexity can be tested, as well as multiple reasoning process flows.

As a proof-of-concept, an example benchmark was performed using the framework, based on an existing clinical decision support system. Additionally, this benchmark aimed to measure the performance of mobile reasoning engines for such a real-world reasoning setup; and thus study the feasibility of locally deploying reasoning processes at this point in time. Although most benchmarked reasoning engines were not optimized for mobile use, the benchmark showed these engines already feature reasonable performance for limited rule- and datasets. At the same time, we note scalability is certainly an issue, with the most efficient overall execution times for Frequent Reasoning rising to ca. 8s for the largest dataset (comprising 4873 triples). To support larger-scale setups, it is clear that much more work is needed to optimize rule-based Semantic Web reasoners for mobile deployment. Interest in performing such optimization has been observed recently in the literature [29], and is likely to increase as demand for mobile reasoning processes increases (e.g., from domains such as health care [1,2,19]).

Future work includes benchmarking mobile reasoning engines with rulesets of increased complexity. Support for additional SPIN functions and more advanced SPARQL constructs should be added to the Semantic Web layer, as these will likely be needed by such complex rulesets. Moreover, different optimization techniques will be applied as well to systematically evaluate their impact on performance. A number of relevant techniques can be utilized for this purpose, for instance based on RETE [28] or borrowed from SPARQL query optimization [30].

Currently, we are employing one of the mobile reasoning engines in the IMPACT-AF mobile app (see Section 6.1), where it features sufficient performance for the current rule- and dataset. As requirements for local reasoning increase, it is possible we will investigate custom optimizations to these engines for mobile deployment.

**Acknowledgments.** This research project is funded by a research grant from Bayer Healthcare.

# References

1. Abidi, S.R., Abidi, S.S.R., Abusharek, A.: A Semantic Web Based Mobile Framework for Designing Personalized Patient Self-Management Interventions. In: Proceedings of the 1st Conference on Mobile and Information Technologies in Medicine, Prague, Czech Republic (2013)
2. Ambroise, N., Boussonnie, S., Eckmann, A.: A Smartphone Application for Chronic Disease Self-Management. In: Proceedings of the 1st Conference on Mobile and Information Technologies in Medicine, Prague, Czech Republic (2013)
3. Angele, J., Boley, H., De Bruijn, J., Fensel, D., Hitzler, P., Kifer, M., Krummenacher, R., Lausen, H., Polleres, A., Studer, R.: Web Rule Language (2005), http://www.w3.org/Submission/WRL/
4. Becker, C.: RDF Store Benchmarks with DBpedia comparing Virtuoso, SDB and Sesame (2008),
   http://wifo5-03.informatik.uni-mannheim.de/benchmarks-200801/
5. Bizer, C., Schultz, A.: The berlin sparql benchmark. International Journal on Semantic Web and Information Systems-Special Issue on Scalability and Performance of Semantic Web Systems (2009)
6. Blomqvist, E.: The use of semantic web technologies for decision support - a survey. Semantic Web 5(3), 177–201 (2014)

7. Boley, H., Tabet, S., Wagner, G.: Design rationale of RuleML: A markup language for semantic web rules. In: Cruz, I.F., Decker, S., Euzenat, J., McGuinness, D.L. (eds.) Proc. Semantic Web Working Symposium, pp. 381–402. Stanford University, California (2001)
8. Canadian Cardiovascular Society: Atrial Fibrillation Guidelines, http://www.ccsguidelineprograms.ca
9. Cattell, R.G.G.: An engineering database benchmark. In: The Benchmark Handbook, pp. 247–281 (1991), http://dblp.uni-trier.de/db/books/collections/gray91.html#Cattell91
10. Cheung, K.H., Prud'hommeaux, E., Wang, Y., Stephens, S.: Semantic web for health care and life sciences: a review of the state of the art. Briefings in Bioinformatics 10(2), 111–113 (2009)
11. European Society of Cardiology: Atrial Fibrillation Guidelines, http://www.escardio.org/guidelines-surveys/esc-guidelines/guidelinesdocuments/guidelines-afib-ft.pdf
12. Forgy, C.L.: Rete: A fast algorithm for the many patterns/many objects match problem. Artif. Intell. 19(1), 17–37 (1982)
13. Gray, J.: The Benchmark Handbook for Database and Transaction Systems. Morgan Kaufmann (1993)
14. Group, W.S.W.: SPARQL 1.1 Overview, W3C Recommendation (March 21, 2013), http://www.w3.org/TR/sparql11-overview/
15. Guo, Y., Pan, Z., Heflin, J.: Lubm: A benchmark for owl knowledge base systems. Web Semantics: Science, Services and Agents on the World Wide Web 3(2), 158–182 (2005)
16. Gupta, A., Mumick, I.S., Subrahmanian, V.S.: Maintaining views incrementally. In: Proceedings of the 1993 ACM SIGMOD International Conference on Management of Data, SIGMOD 1993, pp. 157–166. ACM, New York (1993), http://doi.acm.org/10.1145/170035.170066
17. Haarslev, V., Möller, R.: Description of the racer system and its applications. In: Goble, C.A., McGuinness, D.L., Möller, R., Patel-Schneider, P.F. (eds.) Description Logics. CEUR Workshop Proceedings, vol. 49 (2001)
18. Herman, I., Adida, B., Sporny, M., Birbeck, M.: RDFa 1.1 Primer, 2nd edn (2013), http://www.w3.org/TR/xhtml-rdfa-primer/
19. Hommersom, A., Lucas, P.J.F., Velikova, M., Dal, G., Bastos, J., Rodriguez, J., Germs, M., Schwietert, H.: Moshca - my mobile and smart health care assistant. In: 2013 IEEE 15th International Conference on e-Health Networking, Applications Services (Healthcom), pp. 188–192 (October 2013)
20. Horrocks, I., Patel-Schneider, P.F., Boley, H., Tabet, S., Grosof, B., Dean, M.: SWRL: A Semantic Web Rule Language Combining OWL and RuleML. W3C Member Submission (May 21, 2004), http://www.w3.org/Submission/SWRL/
21. Hussain, S., Raza Abidi, S., Raza Abidi, S.: Semantic web framework for knowledge-centric clinical decision support systems. In: Bellazzi, R., Abu-Hanna, A., Hunter, J. (eds.) AIME 2007. LNCS (LNAI), vol. 4594, pp. 451–455. Springer, Heidelberg (2007), http://dx.doi.org/10.1007/978-3-540-73599-1_60
22. Integrated Management Program Advancing Community Treatment of Atrial Fibrillation: Impact AF, http://impact-af.ca/
23. Knublauch, H.: The TopBraid SPIN API (2014), http://topbraid.org/spin/api/
24. Knublauch, H., Hendler, J.A., Idehen, K.: SPIN - Overview and Motivation (2011), http://www.w3.org/Submission/spin-overview/

25. Le-Phuoc, D., Parreira, J.X., Reynolds, V., Hauswirth, M.: RDF On the Go: An RDF Storage and Query Processor for Mobile Devices. In: 9th International Semantic Web Conference, ISWC 2010 (2010)
26. Liang, S., Fodor, P., Wan, H., Kifer, M.: Openrulebench: An analysis of the performance of rule engines. In: Proceedings of the 18th International Conference on World Wide Web, pp. 601–610. ACM, New York (2009), http://doi.acm.org/10.1145/1526709.1526790
27. Ma, L., Yang, Y., Qiu, Z., Xie, G., Pan, Y., Liu, S.: Towards a complete owl ontology benchmark. In: Sure, Y., Domingue, J. (eds.) ESWC 2006. LNCS, vol. 4011, pp. 125–139. Springer, Heidelberg (2006), http://dx.doi.org/10.1007/11762256_12
28. Matheus, C.J., Baclawski, K., Kokar, M.M.: Basevisor: A triples-based inference engine outfitted to process ruleml and r-entailment rules. In: Second International Conference on Rules and Rule Markup Languages for the Semantic Web, pp. 67–74 (November 2006)
29. Motik, B., Horrocks, I., Kim, S.M.: Delta-reasoner: A semantic web reasoner for an intelligent mobile platform. In: Proceedings of the 21st International Conference Companion on World Wide Web, WWW 2012 Companion, pp. 63–72. ACM, New York (2012), http://doi.acm.org/10.1145/2187980.2187988
30. Schmidt, M., Meier, M., Lausen, G.: Foundations of sparql query optimization. In: Proceedings of the 13th International Conference on Database Theory, ICDT 2010, pp. 4–33. ACM, New York (2010), http://doi.acm.org/10.1145/1804669.1804675
31. Van Woensel, W.: Benchmark Framework Online Documentation (2014), https://niche.cs.dal.ca/benchmark_framework/
32. Weiss, C., Bernstein, A., Boccuzzo, S.: I-MoCo: Mobile Conference Guide Storing and querying huge amounts of Semantic Web data on the iPhone-iPod Touch. In: Semantic Web Challenge 2008 (2008)
33. Zander, S., Schandl, B.: A framework for context-driven RDF data replication on mobile devices. In: Proceedings of the 6th International Conference on Semantic Systems, I-SEMANTICS 2010, pp. 22:1—22:5. ACM, New York (2010), http://doi.acm.org/10.1145/1839707.1839735

# A Power Consumption Benchmark
# for Reasoners on Mobile Devices

Evan W. Patton and Deborah L. McGuinness

Tetherless World Constellation
Rensselaer Polytechnic Institute
110 8th Street, Troy NY 12180 USA
{pattoe,dlm}@cs.rpi.edu
http://tw.rpi.edu/

**Abstract.** We introduce a new methodology for benchmarking the
performance per watt of semantic web reasoners and rule engines on
smartphones to provide developers with information critical for deploying semantic web tools on power-constrained devices. We validate our
methodology by applying it to three well-known reasoners and rule engines answering queries on two ontologies with expressivities in RDFS
and OWL DL. While this validation was conducted on smartphones running Google's Android operating system, our methodology is general
and may be applied to different hardware platforms, reasoners, ontologies, and entire applications to determine performance relevant to power
consumption. We discuss the implications of our findings for balancing
tradeoffs of local computation versus communication costs for semantic technologies on mobile platforms, sensor networks, the Internet of
Things, and other power-constrained environments.

**Keywords:** reasoner, rule engine, power, performance, mobile, OWL.

## 1 Introduction

The vision of the Semantic Web established by Berners-Lee, Hendler, and Lassila [4] has brought us a web with a variety of ontologies, interlinked datasets
[5], and efforts such as Schema.org to standardize terminology and encourage
webmasters to publish structured, machine-readable web content. Since 2001,
we have also seen the rise of the smartphone as a dominant platform for web
access. Smartphone use continues to grow. The International Telecommunica-
tions Union estimates that around 90% of the world's population has access to
cellular connectivity versus 44% with wired broadband to the home.[1] The ubiq-
uity of the mobile phone offers an opportunity to build previously impossible,
content-rich applications that benefit from semantic technologies.

One challenge that semantic technologies face when deployed on mobile platforms like smartphones is the amount of energy available for the device to compute and communicate with other semantic agents on the web. For example,

---

[1] http://www.itu.int/en/ITU-D/Statistics/Documents/facts/
ICTFactsFigures2014-e.pdf

P. Mika et al. (Eds.) ISWC 2014, Part I, LNCS 8796, pp. 409–424, 2014.
© Springer International Publishing Switzerland 2014

the Google Nexus One, one of the first Android smartphones, had a single core processor operating at 1 GHz and 512 MB of RAM. Samsung's latest offering, the Galaxy S5, has a quad core, 2.5 GHz processor and 2 GB of RAM, more than a 8-fold increase in processing power and 4-fold increase in capacity in 5 years. However, the battery capacity of the two phones are 1400 mAh and 2800 mAh, respectively, indicating that battery technology is progressing more slowly than processing technology, in a time period during which the complexity of applications has increased. We therefore need tools to help developers identify essential queries and to select ontologies of the appropriate expressivities for local reasoning or identify when off-device computation is a more practical use of devices' limited energy reserves.

Context awareness [29,14,18], ubiquitous computing [12], and other user-centric applications will benefit greatly by reasoning about different streams driven by smartphone sensors. However, rich data sources can pose new challenges. Access control [28] and privacy have always been critical topics to consider and are even more-so given revelations on weaknesses in various cryptography libraries, such as the OpenSSL Heartbleed attack.[2] Therefore, one scenario to consider is one where personal data are kept and used locally to perform computation rather than sending those data to an untrusted party. Alternatively, we may build applications that selectively expose context or perform computation in a context-sensitive way without sharing all inputs of those computations. Consider a scenario where a wine recommendation agent (e.g. [19]) wants to make a recommendation to a user, but only if the recommendation meets dietary, medical, or other restrictions available in a privileged document such as an electronic medical record. If a health agent were available to manage computation on the medical record, the wine agent would provide the recommendation to it. The health agent then responds affirmatively if the supplied recommendation is reasonable given the content of the medical record. The wine agent then makes its recommendation without ever having direct access to user's health information.

Democratization of application programming, accomplished via tools such as the MIT AppInventor, allows anyone to build mobile applications using predefined components. A linked data extension to AppInventor [21] allows users to take advantage of SPARQL on mobile devices. However, users are given no feedback about how their applications might affect the performance or battery life of their (or others') phones, where resources are relatively scarce. Therefore, a new set of tools are required to aid the AppInventor community to incorporate new technologies like those provided by the semantic web.

We introduce a methodology that we believe is broadly reusable and is specifically motivated by these different scenarios to evaluate the performance of semantic web technologies relative to the amount of energy consumed during operation. In particular, we are focusing on varying the reasoning engine but varying the query engine, ontologies, and datasets are all possible with our approach. Ultimately, these metrics will provide developers a deeper insight into power consumption and enable next-generation applications of semantic

---

[2] http://heartbleed.com/

technologies for power constrained devices. The remainder of this paper is organized as follows: Section 2 compares our contributions with related work on reasoner benchmarking; Section 3 describes our novel hardware and software configuration used for collecting performance data; Sections 4 & 5 discuss the ontologies, reasoners, and queries used for evaluating reasoner performance; Section 6 presents performance per watt findings using our approach; Section 7 discusses some unanticipated results and implications for mobile semantic web agents; and, Section 8 presents conclusions and opportunities for future research.

## 2  Related Work

While reasoner benchmarking is not new, performing benchmarks relative to system power consumption and the amount of inferred statements has not been previously explored to the best of our knowledge. We therefore look at a number of existing benchmarks related to processing time and memory consumption as well as evaluations performed by reasoner authors. We also consider some power related work done in other areas of computer engineering and computer science.

The Lehigh University Benchmark (LUBM) [8] and the extended University Ontology Benchmark (UOBM) [15] use an ontology written in OWL that models university concepts such as classes, departments, professors, and students. The goal of these benchmarks is to evaluate the scalability of inference systems using a controlled ontology and a random instance set generated based on statistical knowledge learned from real world data. We make use of LUBM as a portion of our power benchmark for reasoners that support OWL DL, but evaluate reasoners for memory and power consumption in addition to execution time.

The JustBench Framework [2] was developed to evaluate the performance of reasoners using the justifications of their entailments rather than by analyzing the reasoner's performance on the entirety of an ontology or a random subset. One of its goals is to aid ontology engineers in debugging performance of reasoners and ontologies. Bail et al. also highlighted five techniques for improving reasoning behavior: a) introduce further training for knowledge engineers; b) reduce expressivity to more tractable logics, such as the OWL 2 profiles; c) generate approximations in more tractable logics, e.g. OWL 2 EL approximation of a DL ontology; d) apply fixed rules of thumb during ontology design; e) and, apply analytical tools, such as profilers and benchmarks . They found that evaluating justifications was a good first step to understanding how reasoners performed over ontologies, but that such means are unable to test performance when no entailment exists. While this research is promising, the short amount of time required to generate a single justification is too small to be accurately detected by our hardware, making this method of evaluation infeasible for our purposes.

Seitz and Schönfelder [20] present an OWL reasoner for embedded devices based on CLIPS. The target device ran at 400 MHz with 64 MB of RAM. They evaluated the performance and memory use of the reasoner on OWL 2 RL ontologies and identified issues with existing reasoning systems on devices with limited resources. They benchmarked their reasoner using LUBM with 25,000 individuals. They found that runtime on the resource constrained platform runtime was

$O(n^2)$ with respect to triples in their knowledge base. Memory consumption was also observed as $O(n^2)$. Our benchmark includes a power metric to complement their means of measuring CPU time and memory consumption to provide a more holistic view of the resources a reasoner is consuming.

Henson, Thirunarayan, & Sheth [9] presented a novel bit vector algorithm for performing a subset of OWL inference on sensor data in a resource constrained device that showed performance on explanation and discrimination in a knowledge base $O(n)$ compared with Androjena, a variation of Jena designed to run on Google's Android operating system, at $O(n^3)$. Their evaluation introduced a benchmark that used completely orthogonal bipartite graph matching to generate worst-case complexity in each system. While their benchmark was aimed at resource constrained devices, it used a particularly limited subset of OWL that would not be expressive enough to cover the use cases discussed in Section 1.

Lim, Misra, and Mo [13] present an numeric analysis of energy efficiency of database query answering in a distributed environment. They approximate the amount of energy consumed by wireless transmission of data in a sensor platform using the theoretical power values for communications hardware set in the IEEE 802.11 and BlueTooth standards. Our work captures actual power use, which includes energy consumption of the CPU and real-world noise that may include energy consumed for checking for and retransmitting error packets, energy used responding to multicast/broadcast from other devices on the network, among others. We also provide figures for cellular radios not considered in that work.

The field of high-performance computing, in particular the area of fully-programmable gate array (FPGA) design, has looked at benchmarking custom hardware designs in a power-aware manner. Tinmaung et al. [26] present a power-aware mechanism for synthesizing FPGA logic. Jamieson et al. [10] present a method for benchmarking reconfigurable hardware architectures for applications in the mobile domain. While these works are oriented around power optimization, they are primarily interested in hardware design for specific highly parallelizable problems. Our benchmark focuses on establishing metrics for the semantic web community and in particular those looking to deploy semantic web technologies on off-the-shelf mobile hardware.

## 3  Power Consumption Measurement Methodology

Our methodology uses a physical device setup to capture power measurements. Benchmark evaluation is performed on the device, discussed in Section 3.2, and we also capture baseline measurements to provide an understanding of how reasoning performance compares to other basic operations, e.g. "screen on" for an extended period of time or data access via the device radios.

### 3.1  Power Monitor Setup

The goal of our work is to establish a metric for determining how much energy is consumed during reasoning tasks so developers can be aware of the effects of

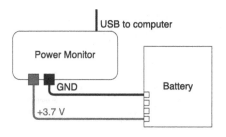

**Fig. 1.** Power bypass wiring for phone battery. Left, a conceptual diagram for bypassing the battery. Right, an example of the bypass implemented for the Google Nexus One.

semantic web tools on mobile device battery life. To this end, we need to provide a battery substitute that collects power samples during operation of the phone and use those data to compute the performance per watt of each reasoner.

We build our experimental framework around an external power supply sold by Monsoon Solutions[3] and use it as a battery substitute for Google Android smartphones. The power monitor captures voltage (2.1~4.5 Volts) and current (max. 3.0 Amperes) drawn by the phone at a frequency of 5 kHz.[4] Following the company's instructions, we bypassed the battery of the smartphone as demonstrated in Figure 1. The leads connected to the battery are 85 mm for the positive lead and 77 mm for the ground, exclusive of the manufacturer's leads.[5] The power monitor is connected to a laptop running Windows XP SP3 to collect data. We use Cygwin as a scripting environment for interacting with the test setup. Our test script sends a start command to the device via WiFi after which both systems wait for a period of 10 seconds to allow the WiFi radio to enter its idle state so that power draw is minimal. The script then starts the power monitor software set to begin recording when power increases above 750 mW and to stop recording when power falls below 60 mW. These threshold values were determined by pilot trials where the changes in power consumption were manually noted by the researchers. The complete code is released under the GNU General Public License and made available on GitHub.[6]

## 3.2   Experimental Platform

We execute each test three times per trial, with thirty trials executed per query. The first execution is run in order to warm up Android's Dalvik virtual machine (VM) so that classes are linked appropriately and that this linking operation does not penalize any particular implementation. The second run is used to determine performance as well as measure the amount of energy consumed during reasoning. The third run is performed using the Android Dalvik Debug Monitor

---

[3] http://www.msoon.com/LabEquipment/PowerMonitor/
[4] Power is voltage times amperage.
[5] Lead length affects the resistance between the power monitor and the phone, resulting in different power observations. We document the lengths here for reproducibility.
[6] https://github.com/ewpatton/muphro-test-framework

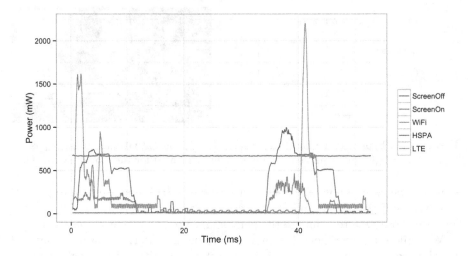

**Fig. 2.** Baseline power measurements for screen off (red), screen on (blue), data download over WiFi (green), HSPA+/3G (purple), and LTE/4G (orange). Note that the 4G/LTE radio consumes power at a rate of up to 2.5 times that of the 3G/HSPA+ radio, which in turn consumes power at a rate almost two to three times the WiFi radio. Thus, developers of distributed semantic web tools should carefully weigh the energy costs of WiFi vs 3G vs 4G for communication.

Server (DDMS), which collects memory consumption usage whenever the Dalvik VM collects garbage. Note that we collect memory usage separately due to the fact that DDMS works over the Android Debug Bridge that communicates with the device either by Universal Serial Bus (USB) or by WiFi. We cannot use USB with the power monitor because the phone attempts to "charge" the power monitor, resulting in bad data, and using WiFi to communicate with the device during the tests would skew the power measurements. We therefore save the DDMS-oriented execution for WiFi when power is not being measured to prevent interfering with the primary focus of our evaluation. Thus, we are able to collect and monitor time to completion, memory requirements, and performance per watt estimations for our benchmark.

We execute our benchmark on Samsung's Galaxy S4 running the stock Android 4.3 operating system. The S4 has a quad-core 1.9 GHz CPU, 2 GB of RAM, and a 2600 mAh battery. We note that the Dalvik VM limits process memory to 128 MB, so any task that requires more memory than this will fail.

### 3.3    Baseline Power Measurements

Since we are concerned with evaluating semantic web reasoner performance, we desire the ability to control for other phone components that may skew results. We took baseline measurements to understand the effects of different subsystems on power during common user actions or during normal system operation. We

**Table 1.** Summary of tested ontologies

| Ontology | Classes | Properties | Subclass | Subprops | Assertions |
|---|---|---|---|---|---|
| Schema.org | 582 | 778 | 580 | 1 | 171 |
| LUBM | 43 | 32 | 36 | 5 | 103074 |

measured screen off with all radios off, screen on with all radios off, and tested two scenarios where we downloaded a 1 MB SPARQL/XML resultset from a remote server with an artificial latency of 30 seconds between the request and the start of the transfer over the WiFi, 3G, and 4G radios. Figure 2 charts the outcome of these results. Important points to note are that the 3G radio during transmission and broadcast can draw 1.56 Watt of power, which would cause the battery to deplete in just over 5 hours. The same download over WiFi requires significantly less power. The 4G radio draws even more power, requiring a peak of 4.00 W.[7] Overall, the amount of energy consumed by the WiFi, 3G, and 4G radios is 4.82 kJ, 14.4 kJ, and 9.77 kJ, respectively.

## 4    Ontology Selection

We choose to use a selection of different ontologies for evaluation to mimic different types of workloads that may be seen in real applications of the results of this work. The ontologies we selected are in RDFS and OWL DL. Table 1 provides a summary of the class and property hierarchies for the different ontologies used.

We use schema.org as it is widely known and gaining rapid adoption due to search engines backing it. The schema.org ontology is primarily composed of subclass axioms on primitive classes. Given the broad domain coverage of schema.org, we anticipate easy repurposing for driving user interfaces for interacting with linked data, such as those presented in our previous work on a mobile wine recommendation agent [19].

We include the Lehigh University Benchmark (LUBM), as it has emerged as a popular benchmark for evaluating the query answering runtime performance of reasoning engines using 14 queries.[8] Due to the memory limitations of the platforms in question, we evaluated LUBM on a subset of the full A-Box, limiting our queries to the first 4 files produced by the LUBM data generator (~21 thousand triples). We intended to specify the knowledge base size explicitly, but the LUBM generator does not provide triple-level control over the output. The LUBM ontology is OWL DL, and thus we recognize that those reasoners that do not support OWL DL will potentially provide incomplete solutions.

---

[7] These peak times are taken directly from the raw data. The figure shown uses a moving average of one half second to smooth out excessive noise, which reduces the magnitude peak values in the visualization.

[8] http://swat.cse.lehigh.edu/projects/lubm/queries-sparql.txt

## 5   Reasoner Selection

We focus on Java-based reasoners to enable redeployment on mobile phones running the Android operating system.[9] We selected the reasoners based on their different algorithms (RETE networks, Tableaux, Hypertableaux) and supported expressivities in order to provide coverage of different techniques. Since we cannot evaluate all possible reasoners due to space constraints, most reasoners should be comparable to one of those identified here.

*Jena Rules.* The Jena Semantic Web Framework [6] provides an implementation of the RETE algorithm [7] along with rule sets for RDFS, OWL Lite, and a subset of OWL Full. We used a variant of Apache Jena 2.10.0 with references to the Java Management Interfaces removed since they are unavailable on Android.

*Pellet.* The Pellet reasoner [22] provides full support for OWL 2 DL, DL-safe SWRL, and uses the Tableaux algorithm. Due to this, its memory requirements often prohibit its use in memory-limited devices such as mobile phones.

*HermiT.* The HermiT reasoner [16] uses a novel hypertableaux resolution algorithm to provide complete support for OWL 2. Due to the nature of this algorithm, it can perform more operations in polynomial time and reduced space, making it useful in more scenarios than the tableaux algorithm.

We intended to include the reasoners $\mu$-OR [1], one of the first to be designed for OWL Lite inference on resource constrained devices, and COROR [24,25], a Jena variant that loads rules selectively based on class expressions, but we were unable to obtain source code or binaries from the original authors.

## 6   Results

We hypothesize that the amount of energy used for reasoning will be linearly related to the amount of time required to perform the reasoning, a common assumption that needs to be validated. We also hypothesize that the mean power will be similar between reasoners as they are primarily CPU bound.

We define *effective performance* of a semantic software stack as

$$\rho_e(q) = \frac{1}{n} \sum_{i=1}^{n} \frac{results_q}{time_{q,i}}$$

where $q$ is the query number, $n$ is the number of trials run, $results_q$ is the number of query results found by the reasoner for query $q$, and $time_{q,i}$ is the execution time for trial $i$. Mean power for a query is computed as:

---

[9] We recognize that Google provides a native development toolchain for cross-compiling existing C/C++ libraries for Android, but leave an evaluation of reasoners written in these languages as future work.

**Listing 1.** SPARQL queries used for evaluating RDFS inference on the Schema.org ontology

```
# query 1
SELECT ?cls (COUNT(?super) as ?supers) WHERE {
  ?cls rdfs:subClassOf ?super
} GROUP BY ?cls

# query 2
SELECT ?cls (COUNT(?property) as ?props) WHERE {
    ?cls rdfs:subClassOf schema:Organization .
    ?property schema:domainIncludes ?cls .
} GROUP BY ?cls

# query 3
SELECT ?property (COUNT(?cls) AS ?range) WHERE {
  ?property schema:rangeIncludes ?x .
  ?cls rdfs:subClassOf ?x .
} GROUP BY ?property
```

$$\bar{P}(q) = \frac{\sum\limits_{i=1}^{n} [\bar{P}_{q,i} time_{q,i}]}{\sum\limits_{i=1}^{n} time_{q,i}}$$

where $\bar{P}_{q,i}$ is the mean power reported by the power monitor for trial $i$.

## 6.1 Schema.org

Schema.org provides an upper ontology in RDFS for describing content in microdata on the web. Backed by four of the world's major search engines, it is poised to dramatically change how structured data are published and consumed on the web. In a recent interview,[10] RV Guha of Google shared that over 5 million websites are now publishing microdata using Schema.org. Understanding how consuming the schema provided by Schema.org affects power consumption on a mobile device will enable developers to determine when the local consumption of Schema.org content is useful versus performing that consumption in the cloud. We consider that the classes and relations defined by Schema.org are useful for driving user interfaces for mobile linked data publishing applications and being able to query the schema efficiently is paramount to making this vision a reality. Three key relationships within the schema that we wish to evaluate are subclass relationships (modeled using *rdfs:subClassOf*) and the *domainIncludes* and *rangeIncludes* properties. We provide three queries (Listing 1) to cover various common user interface needs: finding subtypes of the current type,

---

[10] http://semanticweb.com/schema-org-chat-googles-r-v-guha_b40607

418     E.W. Patton and D.L. McGuinness

**Table 2.** Summary of each reasoner on the three queries we designed for Schema.org's ontology. Left, the effective performance for each reasoner. Right, the performance per watt of each reasoner.

| Query | 1 | 2 | 3 |
|---|---|---|---|
| HermiT | 17.24 | N/A | N/A |
| Jena | 104.8 | 2.158 | 84.65 |

| Query | 1 | 2 | 3 |
|---|---|---|---|
| HermiT | 22.61 | N/A | N/A |
| Jena | 109.2 | 2.256 | 86.03 |

**Table 3.** Number of query answers for the subset of the 14 LUBM queries on which all reasoners returned results. Asterisks indicate those queries for which Jena's rule engine was unable to provide the complete result set found by HermiT and Pellet.

| Query | 1 | 3 | 4 | 5 | 6* | 7* | 8* | 9* | 14 |
|---|---|---|---|---|---|---|---|---|---|
| HermiT | 4 | 6 | 34 | 719 | 1682 | 67 | 1682 | 38 | 1319 |
| Pellet | 4 | 6 | 34 | 719 | 1682 | 67 | 1682 | 38 | 1319 |
| Jena | 4 | 6 | 34 | 719 | 1319 | 59 | 1319 | 15 | 1319 |

**Table 4.** Performance (results/sec) for the different reasoners on LUBM queries, measured as query answers per second. Larger values indicate better performance.

| Query | 1 | 3 | 4 | 5 | 6* | 7* | 8* | 9* | 14 |
|---|---|---|---|---|---|---|---|---|---|
| HermiT | 0.0419 | 0.0635 | 0.365 | 7.466 | 42.48 | 0.631 | 16.94 | 0.378 | 33.37 |
| Pellet | 0.1893 | 0.2793 | 1.592 | 32.57 | 74.46 | 2.541 | 65.84 | 1.562 | 60.43 |
| Jena | 0.4511 | 0.6297 | 3.927 | 59.99 | 150.0 | 4.574 | 99.56 | 1.408 | 151.2 |

identifying properties for which the current type is in the domain, and after selecting a property, finding valid range types, so an application can display relevant instances. We note that these queries are intended to stress how many and how quickly reasoners compute subclass and subproperty subsumptions.

Table 2 presents the reasoner evaluation results for the queries in Listing 1. We note that both HermiT and Pellet provide different challenges due to the fact that Schema.org's schema is not DL-compatible it lacks distinction between object and data properties. We were unable to execute queries 2 and 3 against HermiT using the OWL API due to this lack of delineation in the ontology and the API's inability to query at the level of rdf:Property. For all queries, Pellet used more than 128 MB of RAM, resulting in premature termination of the virtual machine so we exclude it from this analysis. A Mann-Whitney U test between HermiT and Jena's power measurements indicated no statistical difference (U = 158, p = 0.8177), thus the difference in performance per watt can be attributed entirely to the performance of each reasoner on the ontology.

**6.2   Lehigh University Benchmark**

Table 3 shows the number of query solutions found when all reasoners returned at least one answer. Due to their completeness, Pellet and Hermit generate the

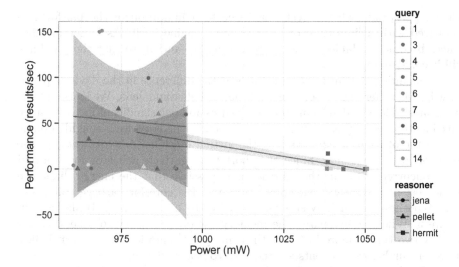

**Fig. 3.** Performance vs power for Jena, Pellet, and HermiT reasoners on LUBM queries. The shaded regions represent the standard error of the linear approximation of performance per watt.

same answer set. Jena fails to return a complete answer set in 4 queries (noted with asterisks) and finds no results in four of five others.[11] Table 4 shows the effective performance for each reasoner in the different query conditions.

A Kruskal-Wallis non-parametric one-way analysis of variance with mean power as a dependent variable and reasoner as the independent variable for each LUBM query presented in Table 3 showed significant difference in power drawn for all LUBM queries, with $p < 0.001$, with the exception of query 6 ($H = 3.08$, 2 d.f., $p = 0.214$). Pairwise Bonferroni-adjusted Mann-Whitney U comparisons on the differing queries indicated a statistically significant difference in the mean ranks of Hermit compared with Pellet and Jena. This finding is substantiated by Figure 3, which shows a tight clustering of HermiT's performance per watt measurements (except that for query 6) away from those of Jena and Pellet.

## 7  Discussion

Ali et al. [1] and Henson et al. [9] both demonstrated scalable, low expressivity reasoners for resource constrained devices, but also highlighted that traditional inference systems on resource constrained devices are either very costly (as with Jena, HermiT) or impossible (as with Pellet). We affirmed their difficulty with deploying traditional reasoners on resource-constrained devices and have noted

---

[11] No reasoner answered query 2 due to the subset of the dataset we are using. We assumed a uniform distribution in the types and quantity of triples generated by LUBM, but that assumption resulted in insufficient data to satisfy the patterns in query 2. Jena also found no results for queries 10-13.

where appropriate when a test failed due to a limitation of the platform as compared with a limitation of the reasoning engine itself. As larger memory spaces become available on mobile platforms, we anticipate that these failures will become fewer.

One unanticipated interesting result was the difference in the device's power draw between HermiT's operation and that of Pellet and Jena. We looked at the experimental logs to determine possible causes and one significant factor that we have identified is memory consumption. HermiT's memory use is roughly double that of the other reasoners, causing the virtual machine to invoke the garbage collector more frequently. Since the short term garbage collector for Android runs concurrently on another thread, it is possible that the energy difference is the cost of the system engaging a second CPU core for garbage collection. This hypothesis is partially substantiated by one outlier (query 6) observed in Figure 3. When we compared the memory use on this query to others, it was roughly two thirds, more in line with memory consumption observed in Pellet. However, further experiments are required to isolate this effect.

Lastly, the combination of reasoning time and power are critical to understanding how to deploy semantic technologies on mobile platforms. In the case of Jena, the total amount of energy consumed ranged anywhere from 4.5 kJ to 8.9 kJ, indicating that it takes less energy to reason about some of these ontologies than it would to request the results from an external source via the 3G or 4G radios. However, HermiT and Pellet exhibit much higher energy consumption due to the longer running time of their algorithms, suggesting that it is always a better use of energy to offload OWL DL reasoning to an external resource when completeness is required by the application.

## 7.1 Experiences

Our original intention was to use the library OWL-BGP [11] as a SPARQL interface to reasoners designed for the OWL API (e.g. HermiT). However, due to a limitation in the Android Dalvik byte-code format, we were unable to successfully compile the library. In its place, we reimplemented the SPARQL queries used in each of the different test conditions as Java classes that would accept the OWL API's `OWLReasoner` class and generate a SPARQL result set by performing an appropriate set of operations on the reasoner.

Memory consumption was another challenge we addressed in multiple ways. In all tests, we observed that reasoning under Jena's OWL profile was impossible as out-of-memory errors were thrown prior to completion and thus we limited our tests to the RDFS profile. This evaluation performed on a Mid 2013 Macbook Pro with a 2.8 GHz Intel Core i7 and 16 GB of RAM with a Java heap of 4 GB demonstrated that most reasoning operations would require at least 2.4 GB and in some instances, the Jena rules engine still exhausted the entire heap and failed to return results.

In order to execute the Jena reasoners, Hermit, and Pellet on the Android platform, we needed to make minor modifications to each library. While we will not explain details here, we note that all of the modified sources and binaries are made available under the appropriate source code license via our GitHub repository mentioned in Section 3.1.

The findings of this paper are subject to drastic changes in hardware design and power management that cannot be predicted from this work alone. For instance, advances in power management circuitry or power-efficient CPU architectures may have significant impact on power consumption that would improve the performance per watt observations that we have made (assuming such architectural changes do not negatively affect performance). Thus, we are making this software freely available under both the Apache 2.0 and GPL 3.0 licenses so that all of the tests performed herein can be repeated on alternative hardware as devices are made available.

## 8   Conclusions

We presented a novel, reusable, open-source methodology for evaluating semantic web reasoner performance on power-constrained hardware and evaluated three reasoners, Jena, Pellet, and HermiT, against standard benchmark ontologies and queries to establish the amount of power drawn during reasoning, information previously unknown in the field. The reusable methodology is one contribution and the use of the methodology to evaluate some best in class reasoners and standard benchmark ontologies is another contribution. We affirmed that single-threaded reasoners exhibit energy consumption linear in the amount of processing time and identified some discrepancies related to the effects of garbage collection on rate of energy consumption on an Android smartphone. We showed that incompleteness can greatly increase performance per watt if such incompleteness is acceptable in an application. Lastly, we demonstrated the effects of different smartphone features on power consumption to gain insights into the costs of communicating with external services to assist in making decisions about whether to perform processing on-device or off-device.

We found that for RDFS inference, the Jena RETE rule engine performed better than its complete OWL counterparts, a finding that is unsurprising given the overhead of the tableaux/hypertableaux algorithms. Another interesting finding is that while Jena was unable to perform OWL entailments on LUBM due to memory limitations, when executed with its RDFS transitivity rule set, it was able to answer some of the queries completely and others partially. This highlights how important it is for developers to identify essential queries and ontology expressivities to improve reasoning performance and reduce energy consumption.

Furthermore, we found a nearly linear relationship between energy required to complete an inference and the amount of computational time needed to perform the inference. This is due to the single-threaded nature of the design of the reasoners tested, but as our data show, there may be additional effects on power consumption outside of CPU runtime and we expect to see further differences as parallel and distributed techniques come to fruition.

## 8.1  Future Work

This benchmark lacks coverage for the complete OWL 2 semantics. Our examination focused on RDFS and OWL DL inference, primarily to exercise existing, well-known benchmarks used for evaluating reasoners in other contexts. A suite of different T-boxes and A-boxes providing coverage for all of the constructs in OWL 2 would allow us to more easily stress different parts of the reasoners and further research into parallelization techniques will enable us to gain a better understanding of the effects of communications on energy consumption.

We would also like to test parallel and distributed reasoning techniques such as those presented in [3,27,30,17,23]. Our findings in this work validate existing assumptions that power consumption for traditional RETE rule engines, tableaux, and hypertableaux reasoners will be linear in the compute time, but distributed algorithms will provide a richer execution strategy and power analysis that will benefit from the methodology we have outlined.

Due to the physical setup complexity and to ease adoption of power analysis of mobile semantic web applications, we intend to use a combination of factor analysis, clustering, and linear regression to build models that can consume power profiles of various devices, ontologies, and queries to generate expectations of energy consumption. This will eliminate the hardware barrier to entry by enabling an approximation of energy use. Furthermore, if the appropriate programming interfaces are available, we intend to build a reasoner that can take advantage of knowing the available energy remaining for computation to optimize its use of local versus remote resources.

Using the experiment metadata published by our framework, we intend to provide a portal of experimental conditions and evaluations with publicly accessible URIs. This portal will enable researchers to replicate results by providing a experiment URI to the benchmarking suite, which would download all the necessary resources and execute the experiment on a target device.

We plan to investigate more reasoners, such as those presented by [31], as well as those written in other languages, e.g. C or C++, to evaluate a wider breadth of technologies and to motivate extension of this work to other mobile platforms. In particular, we would like to provide a solution for phones without removable batteries, such as the Apple iPhone, so that practitioners can also assess performance characteristics of reasoners and ontologies for a greater breadth of devices. One possible approach may involve capturing battery level information from the operating system and running queries repeatedly and observing the reported drain. One challenge with this approach is the effective of battery degradation due to age.

**Acknowledgements.** Mr. Patton was funded by an NSF Graduate Research Fellowship and RPI. Prof. McGuinness and RPIs Tetherless World Constellation are supported in part by Fujitsu, Lockheed Martin, LGS, Microsoft Research, Qualcomm, in addition to sponsored research from DARPA, IARPA, NASA, NIST, NSF, and USGS. Our gratitude to Prof. Jim Hendler, Dr. Patrice Seyed, and Mr. Fuming Shih for their comments on early versions of this manuscript, and to the anonymous reviewers who provided detailed feedback to improve the manuscript.

# References

1. Ali, S., Kiefer, S.: μOR – A micro OWL DL reasoner for ambient intelligent devices. In: Abdennadher, N., Petcu, D. (eds.) GPC 2009. LNCS, vol. 5529, pp. 305–316. Springer, Heidelberg (2009)
2. Bail, S., Parsia, B., Sattler, U.: JustBench: A framework for OWL benchmarking. In: Patel-Schneider, P.F., Pan, Y., Hitzler, P., Mika, P., Zhang, L., Pan, J.Z., Horrocks, I., Glimm, B. (eds.) ISWC 2010, Part I. LNCS, vol. 6496, pp. 32–47. Springer, Heidelberg (2010)
3. Bergmann, F.W., Quantz, J.: Parallelizing description logics. In: Wachsmuth, I., Brauer, W., Rollinger, C.-R. (eds.) KI 1995. LNCS, vol. 981, pp. 137–148. Springer, Heidelberg (1995)
4. Berners-Lee, T., Hendler, J., Lassila, O.: The semantic web. Scientific American (May 2001)
5. Bizer, C., Heath, T., Berners-Lee, T.: Linked data - the story so far. International Journal on Semantic Web and Information Systems 5(3) (2009)
6. Carroll, J.J., Dickinson, I., Dollin, C., Reynolds, D., Seaborne, A., Wilkinson, K.: Jena: Implementing the semantic web recommendations. In: Proc. of the 13th Intl. World Wide Web Conference on Alternate Track Papers & Posters, pp. 74–83 (2004)
7. Forgy, C.: On the efficient implementation of production systems. Ph.D. thesis, Carnegie-Mellon University (1979)
8. Guo, Y., Pan, Z., Heflin, J.: LUBM: A benchmarking for OWL knowledge base systems. Web Semantics 3(2), 158–182 (2005)
9. Henson, C., Thirunarayan, K., Sheth, A.: An efficient bit vector approach to semantics-based machine perception in resource-constrained devices. In: Cudré-Mauroux, P., et al. (eds.) ISWC 2012, Part I. LNCS, vol. 7649, pp. 149–164. Springer, Heidelberg (2012)
10. Jamieson, P., Becker, T., Luk, W., Cheung, P.Y.K., Rissa, T., Pitkanen, T.: Benchmarking reconfigurable architectures in the mobile domain. In: IEEE Symposium on Field Programmable Custom Computing Machines, pp. 131–138 (2009)
11. Kollia, I., Glimm, B.: Optimizing SPARQL query answering over OWL ontologies. Journal of Artificial Intelligence Research 48, 253–303 (2013)
12. Lassila, O.: Using the semantic web in mobile and ubiquitous computing. In: Bramer, M., Terziyan, V. (eds.) Industrial Applications of Semantic Web. IFIP, vol. 188, pp. 19–25. Springer, Boston (2005)
13. Lim, L., Misra, A., Mo, T.: Adaptive data acquisition strategies for energy-efficient, smartphone-based, continuous processing of sensor streams. Distributed and Parallel Databases 31(2), 321–351 (2013)
14. Lukowicz, P., Nanda, S., Narayanan, V., Albelson, H., McGuinness, D.L., Jordan, M.I.: Qualcomm context-awareness symposium sets research agenda for context-aware smartphones. IEEE Pervasive Computing 11(1), 76–79 (2012)
15. Ma, L., Yang, Y., Qiu, Z., Xie, G.T., Pan, Y., Liu, S.: Towards a complete OWL ontology benchmark. In: Sure, Y., Domingue, J. (eds.) ESWC 2006. LNCS, vol. 4011, pp. 125–139. Springer, Heidelberg (2006)

16. Motik, B., Shearer, R., Horrocks, I.: Hypertableaux reasoning for description logics. Journal of Artificial Intelligence Research 36, 165–228 (2009)
17. Mutharaju, R., Maier, F., Hitzler, P.: A mapreduce algorithm for EL+. In: Proc. of the 23rd Intl. Workshop on Description Logics (DL 2010), pp. 464–474 (2010)
18. Narayanan, V., McGuinness, D.L.: Towards situation aware smartphones via semantics and reasoning. In: Semantic Technology & Business Conference (2012)
19. Patton, E.W., McGuinness, D.L.: The mobile wine agent: Pairing wine with the social semantic web. In: Proc. of the 2nd Social Data on the Web workshop (2009)
20. Seitz, C., Schönfelder, R.: Rule-based OWL reasoning for specific embedded devices. In: Aroyo, L., Welty, C., Alani, H., Taylor, J., Bernstein, A., Kagal, L., Noy, N., Blomqvist, E. (eds.) ISWC 2011, Part II. LNCS, vol. 7032, pp. 237–252. Springer, Heidelberg (2011)
21. Shih, F., Seneviratne, O., Miao, D., Licardi, I., Kagal, L., Patton, E.W., Castillo, C., Meier, P.: Democratizing mobile app development for disaster management. In: Proceedings of the 2nd Workshop on Semantic Cities (2013)
22. Sirin, E., Parsia, B., Cuenca-Grau, B., Kalyanpur, A., Katz, Y.: Pellet: A practical OWL-DL reasoner. Web Semantics: Science, Services and Agents on the World Wide Web 5(2), 51–53 (2007)
23. Soma, R., Prasanna, V.: Parallel inferencing for OWL knowledge bases. In: 37th International Conference on Parallel Processing, pp. 75–82 (September 2008)
24. Tai, W., Brennan, R., Keeney, J., O'Sullivan, D.: An automatically composable OWL reasoner for resource constrained devices. In: Proceedings of the IEEE International Conference on Semantic Computing, pp. 495–502 (2009)
25. Tai, W., Keeney, J., O'Sullivan, D.: COROR: A cOmposable rule-entailment owl reasoner for resource-constrained devices. In: Bassiliades, N., Governatori, G., Paschke, A. (eds.) RuleML 2011 - Europe. LNCS, vol. 6826, pp. 212–226. Springer, Heidelberg (2011)
26. Tinmaung, K.O., Howland, D., Tessier, R.: Power-aware FPGA logic synthesis using binary decision diagrams. In: Proc. of the 15th Intl. Symposium on Field Programmable Gate Arrays, New York, NY, USA, pp. 148–155 (2007)
27. Urbani, J., van Harmelen, F., Schlobach, S., Bal, H.: QueryPIE: Backward reasoning for OWL horst over very large knowledge bases. In: Aroyo, L., Welty, C., Alani, H., Taylor, J., Bernstein, A., Kagal, L., Noy, N., Blomqvist, E. (eds.) ISWC 2011, Part I. LNCS, vol. 7031, pp. 730–745. Springer, Heidelberg (2011)
28. Villata, S., Costabello, L., Delaforge, N., Gandon, F.: A social semantic web access control model. Journal on Data Semantics, 1–16 (2012)
29. Wang, X.H., Zhang, D.Q., Gu, T., Pung, H.K.: Ontology based context modeling and reasoning using OWL. In: Proceedings of the Second IEEE Annual Conference on Pervasive Computing and Communications Workshop. IEEE (March 2004)
30. Williams, G.T., Weaver, J., Atre, M., Hendler, J.A.: Scalable reduction of large datasets to interesting subsets. Web Semantics: Science, Services and Agents on the World Wide Web 8(4), 365–373 (2010)
31. Yus, R., Bobed, C., Esteban, G., Bobillo, F., Mena, E.: Android goes semantic: DL reasoners on smartphones. In: 2nd International Workshop on OWL Reasoner Evaluation (ORE 2013), pp. 46–52 (2013)

# Dynamic Provenance for SPARQL Updates

Harry Halpin and James Cheney

[1] World Wide Web Consortium/MIT, 32 Vassar Street Cambridge, MA 02139 USA
hhalpin@w3.org,
[2] University of Edinburgh, School of Informatics,
10 Crichton St.,
Edinburgh UK EH8 9AB

**Abstract.** While the Semantic Web currently can exhibit provenance information by using the W3C PROV standards, there is a "missing link" in connecting PROV to storing and querying for dynamic changes to RDF graphs using
SPARQL. Solving this problem would be required for such clear use-cases as the
creation of version control systems for RDF. While some provenance models and
annotation techniques for storing and querying provenance data originally developed with databases or workflows in mind transfer readily to RDF and SPARQL,
these techniques do not readily adapt to describing changes in dynamic RDF
datasets over time. In this paper we explore how to adapt the dynamic copy-
paste provenance model of Buneman et al. [2] to RDF datasets that change over
time in response to SPARQL updates, how to represent the resulting provenance
records themselves as RDF in a manner compatible with W3C PROV, and how
the provenance information can be defined by reinterpreting SPARQL updates.
The primary contribution of this paper is a semantic framework that enables the
semantics of SPARQL Update to be used as the basis for a 'cut-and-paste' provenance model in a principled manner.

**Keywords:** SPARQL Update, provenance, versioning, RDF, semantics.

## 1 Introduction

It is becoming increasingly common to publish scientific and governmental data on
the Web as RDF (the Resource Description Framework, a W3C standard for structured
data on the Web) and to attach provenance data to this information using the W3C
PROV standard. In doing so, it is crucial to track not only the provenance metadata,
but the changes to the graph itself, including both its derivation process and a history
of changes to the data over time. Being able to track changes to RDF graphs could, in
combination with the W3C PROV standards and SPARQL, provide the foundation for
addressing the important use-case of creating a Git-like version control system for RDF.

The term provenance is used in several different ways, often aligning with research
in two different communities, in particular the database community and the scientific
workflow community. We introduce some terminology to distinguish different uses of
the term. There is a difference between *static* provenance that describes data at a given
point in time versus *dynamic* provenance that describes how artifacts have evolved over
time. Second, there is a difference between provenance for *atomic* artifacts that expose

P. Mika et al. (Eds.) ISWC 2014, Part I, LNCS 8796, pp. 425–440, 2014.

no internal structure as part of the provenance record, versus provenance for *collections* or other structured artifacts. The workflow community has largely focused on static provenance for atomic artifacts, whereas much of the work on provenance in databases has focused on dynamic provenance for collections (e.g. tuples in relations). An example of static provenance would be attaching the name of an origin and time-stamp to a set of astronomical RDF data. Thus static provenance can often be considered metadata related to provenance. Currently the W3C PROV data model and vocabulary [15], provides a standard way to attach this provenance, and other work such as PROV-AQ [13] provides options for extracting this metadata by virtue of HTTP.

An example of *dynamic provenance* would be given by a single astronomical data-set that is updated over time, and then if some erroneous data was added at a particular time, the data-set could be queried for its state at a prior time before the erroneous data was added so the error could be corrected. Thus dynamic provenance can in some cases be reduced to issues of history and version control. Note that static and dynamic provenance are not orthogonal, as we can capture *static* provenance metadata at every step of recording dynamic provenance. The W3C Provenance Working Group has focused primarily on static provenance, but we believe a mutually beneficial relationship between the W3C PROV static provenance and SPARQL Update with an improved provenance-aware semantic model will allow dynamic provenance capabilities to be added to RDF. While fine-grained dynamic provenance imposes overhead that may make it unsuited to some applications, there are use-cases where knowing exactly when a graph was modified is necessary for reasons of accountability, including data-sets such as private financial and public scientific data.

## 1.1    Related Literature

The workflow community has largely focused on declaratively describing causality or derivation steps of processes to aid repeatability for scientific experiments, and these requirements have been a key motivation for the Open Provenance Model (OPM) [17,18], a vocabulary and data model for describing processes including (but certainly not limited to) runs of scientific workflows. OPM is important in its own right, and has become the foundation for the W3C PROV data model [19]. The formal semantics of PROV have been formalized, but do not address the relationship between the provenance and the semantics of the processes being described [7]. However, previous work on the semantics of OPM, PROV, and other provenance vocabularies focuses on temporal and validity constraints [14] and does not address the meaning of the processes being represented — one could in principle use them either to represent static provenance for processes that construct new data from existing artifacts or to represent dynamic provenance that represents how data change over time at each step, such as needed by version control systems. Most applications of OPM seem to have focused on static provenance, although PROV explicitly grapples with issues concerning representing the provenance of objects that may be changing over time, but does not provide a semantics for storing and querying changes over time. Our approach to dynamic provenance is complementary to work on OPM and PROV, as we show how any provenance metadata vocabulary such as the W3C PROV ontology [15] can be connected directly to query and update languages by presenting a semantics for a generalized provenance model and showing how this builds upon the formal semantics of the query and update languages.

Within database research, complex provenance is also becoming increasingly seen as necessary, although the work has taken a different turn than that of the workflow community. Foundational work on provenance for database queries distinguishes between *where-provenance*, which is the "locations in the source databases from which the data was extracted," and *why-provenance*, which is "the source data that had some influence on the existence of the data" [4]. Further, increasing importance is being placed on *how-provenance*, the operations used to produce the derived data and other annotations, such as who precisely produced the derived data and for what reasons. There is less work considering provenance for updates; previous work on provenance in databases has focused on simple atomic update operations: insertion, deletion, and copy [2]. A provenance-aware database should support queries that permit users to find the ultimate or proximate 'sources' of some data and apply data provenance techniques to understand why a given part of the data was inserted or deleted by a given update. There is considerable work on correct formalisms to enable provenance in databases [9]. This work on dynamic provenance is related to earlier work on version control in unstructured data, a classic and well-studied problem for information systems ranging from source code management systems to temporal databases and data archiving [23]. Version control systems such as CVS, Subversion, and Git have a solid track record of tracking versions and (coarse-grained) provenance for text (e.g. source code) over time and are well-understood in the form of temporal annotations and a log of changes.

On the Semantic Web, work on provenance has been quite diverse. There is widely implemented support for *named graphs*, where each graph $G$ is identified with a *name URI* [6], and as the new RDF Working Group has standardized the graph name in the semantics, the new standards have left the practical use of such a graph name underdefined; thus, the graph name could be used to store or denote provenance-related information such as time-stamps. Tackling directly the version control aspect of provenance are proposals such as Temporal RDF [10] for attaching temporal annotations and a generalized Annotated RDF for any partially-ordered sets already exist [25,16]. However, by confining provenance annotations to partially-ordered sets, these approaches do not allow for a (queryable) graph structure for more complex types of provenance that include work such as the PROV model. Static provenance techniques have been investigated for RDFS inferences [5,8,20] over RDF datasets. Some of this work considers updates, particularly Flouris et al. [8], who consider the problem of how to maintain provenance information for RDFS inferences when tuples are inserted or deleted using coherence semantics. Their solution uses 'colouring' (where the color is the URI of the source of each triple) and tracking implicit triples [8].

Understanding provenance for a language requires understanding the ordinary semantics of the language. Arenas et al. formalized the semantics of SPARQL [21,1], and the SPARQL Update recommendation proposes a formal model for updates [22]. Horne et al. [12] propose an operational semantics for SPARQL Updates, which however differs in some respects from the SPARQL 1.1 standard and does not deal with named graphs.

## 1.2   Overview

In this paper, we build on Arenas et al.'s semantics of SPARQL [21,1] and extend it to formalize SPARQL Update semantics (following a denotational approach similar to the SPARQL Update Formal Model [22]). Then, as our main contribution, we detail a provenance model for SPARQL queries and updates that provides a (queryable) record of how the raw data in a dataset has changed over time. This change history includes a way to insert static provenance metadata using a full-scale provenance ontology such as PROV-O [15].

Our hypothesis is that a simple vocabulary, composed of insert, delete, and copy operations as introduced by Buneman et al. [2], along with explicit identifiers for update steps, versioning relationships, and metadata about updates provides a flexible format for dynamic provenance on the Semantic Web. A primary advantage of our methodology is it keeps the changes to raw data separate from the changes in provenance metadata, so legacy applications will continue to work and the cost of storing and providing access to provenance can be isolated from that of the raw data. We will introduce the semantics of SPARQL queries, then our semantics for SPARQL updates, and finally describe our semantics for dynamic provenance-tracking for RDF graphs and SPARQL updates. To summarize, our contributions are an extension to the semantics of SPARQL Update that includes provenance semantics to handle dynamic semantics [21,1] and a vocabulary for representing changes to RDF graphs made by SPARQL updates, and a translation from ordinary SPARQL updates to provenance-aware updates that record provenance as they execute.

## 2   Background: Semantics of SPARQL Queries

We first review a simplified (due to space limits) version of Arenas et. al.'s formal semantics of SPARQL [21,1]. Note that this is not original work, but simply a necessary precursor to the semantics of SPARQL Update and our extension that adds provenance to SPARQL Update. The main simplification is that we disallow nesting other operations such as . , UNION, etc. inside GRAPH $A$ {...} patterns. This limitation is inessential.

Let Lit be a set of literals (e.g. strings), let Id be a set of resource identifiers, and let Var be a set of variables usually written $?X$. We write Atom $=$ Lit $\cup$ Id for the set of atomic values, that is literals or ids. The syntax of a core algebra for SPARQL discussed in [1] is as follows:

$$A ::= \ell \in \mathsf{Lit} \mid \iota \in \mathsf{Id} \mid ?X \in \mathsf{Var}$$
$$t ::= \langle A_1 \ A_2 \ A_3 \rangle$$
$$C ::= \{t_1, \ldots, t_n\} \mid \text{GRAPH } A \ \{t_1, \ldots, t_n\} \mid C \ C'$$
$$R ::= \text{BOUND}(?x) \mid A = B \mid R \wedge R' \mid R \vee R' \mid \neg R$$
$$P ::= C \mid P \ . \ P' \mid P \text{ UNION } P' \mid P \text{ OPT } P' \mid P \text{ FILTER } R$$
$$Q ::= \text{SELECT } ?\overline{X} \text{ WHERE } P \mid \text{CONSTRUCT } C \text{ WHERE } P$$

Here, $C$ denotes basic graph (or dataset) patterns that may contain variables; $R$ denotes conditions; $P$ denotes patterns, and $Q$ denotes queries. We do not distinguish between subject, predicate and object components of triples, so this is a mild generalization of [1], since SPARQL does not permit literals to appear in the subject or predicate position or as the name of a graph in the GRAPH $A$ $\{P\}$ pattern, although the formal semantics of RDF allows this and the syntax may be updated in forthcoming work on RDF. We also do not consider blank nodes, which pose complications especially when updates are concerned, and we instead consider them to be skolemized (or just replaced by generic identifiers), as this is how most implementations handle blank nodes. There has been previous work giving a detailed treatment of the problematic nature of blank nodes and why skolemization is necessary in real-world work.

The semantics of queries $Q$ or patterns $P$ is defined using functions from *graph stores* $\mathcal{D}$ to sets of *valuations* $\mu$. A graph store $\mathcal{D} = (G, \{g_i \mapsto G_1 \ldots, g_n \mapsto G_n\})$ consists of a default graph $G_0$ together with a mapping from names $g_i$ to graphs $G_i$. Each such graph is essentially just a set of ground triples. We often refer to graph stores as *datasets*, although this is a slight abuse of terminology.

We overload set operations for datasets, e.g. $\mathcal{D} \cup \mathcal{D}'$ or $\mathcal{D} \setminus \mathcal{D}'$ denotes the dataset obtained by unioning or respectively subtracting the default graphs and named graphs of $\mathcal{D}$ and $\mathcal{D}'$ pointwise. If a graph $g$ is defined in $\mathcal{D}$ and undefined in $\mathcal{D}'$, then $(\mathcal{D} \cup \mathcal{D}')(g) = \mathcal{D}(g)$ and similarly if $g$ is undefined in $\mathcal{D}$ and defined in $\mathcal{D}'$ then $(\mathcal{D} \cup \mathcal{D}')(g) = \mathcal{D}'(g)$; if $g$ is undefined in both datasets then it is undefined in their union. For set difference, if $g$ is defined in $\mathcal{D}$ and undefined in $\mathcal{D}'$ then $(\mathcal{D} \setminus \mathcal{D}')(g) = \mathcal{D}(g)$; if $g$ is undefined in $\mathcal{D}$ then it is undefined in $(\mathcal{D} \setminus \mathcal{D}')$. Likewise, we define $\mathcal{D} \subseteq \mathcal{D}'$ as $\mathcal{D}' = \mathcal{D} \cup \mathcal{D}'$.

A *valuation* is a partial function $\mu : \mathsf{Var} \rightharpoonup \mathsf{Lit} \cup \mathsf{Id}$. We lift valuations to functions $\mu : \mathsf{Atom} \cup \mathsf{Var} \to \mathsf{Atom}$ as follows:

$$\mu(?X) = \mu(X)$$
$$\mu(a) = a \qquad a \in \mathsf{Atom}$$

that is, if $A$ is a variable $?X$ then $\mu(A) = \mu(X)$ and otherwise if $A$ is an atom then $\mu(A) = A$. We thus consider all atoms to be implicitly part of the domain of $\mu$. Furthermore, we define $\mu$ applied to triple, graph or dataset patterns as follows:

$$\mu(\langle A_1\ A_2\ A_3 \rangle) = \langle \mu(A_1)\ \mu(A_2)\ \mu(A_3) \rangle$$
$$\mu(\{t_1, \ldots, t_n\}) = (\{\mu(t_1), \ldots, \mu(t_n)\}, \emptyset)$$
$$\mu(\text{GRAPH } A\ \{t_1, \ldots, t_n\}) = (\emptyset, \{\mu(A) \mapsto \{\mu(t_1), \ldots, \mu(t_n)\}\})$$
$$\mu(C\ C') = \mu(C) \cup \mu(C')$$

where, as elsewhere, we define $\mathcal{D} \cup \mathcal{D}'$ as pointwise union of datasets.

The conditions $R$ are interpreted as three-valued formulas over the lattice $L = \{\mathtt{true}, \mathtt{false}, \mathtt{error}\}$, where $\mathtt{false} \leq \mathtt{error} \leq \mathtt{true}$, and $\wedge$ and $\vee$ are minimum and maximum operations respectively, and $\neg\mathtt{true} = \mathtt{false}$, $\neg\mathtt{false} = \mathtt{true}$, and $\neg\mathtt{error} = \mathtt{error}$. The semantics of a condition is defined as follows:

$$[\![\text{BOUND}(?X)]\!]\mu = \begin{cases} \text{false if } ?X \notin \text{dom}(\mu) \\ \text{true} \;\; \text{if } ?X \in \text{dom}(\mu) \end{cases}$$

$$[\![A = B]\!]\mu = \begin{cases} \text{error if } \{A, B\} \not\subseteq \text{dom}(\mu) \\ \text{true} \;\; \text{if } \mu(A) = \mu(B) \text{ where } A, B \in \text{dom}(\mu) \\ \text{false if } \mu(A) \neq \mu(B) \text{ where } A, B \in \text{dom}(\mu) \end{cases}$$

$$[\![\neg R]\!]\mu = \neg [\![R]\!]\mu$$

$$[\![R \wedge R']\!]\mu = [\![R]\!]\mu \wedge [\![R']\!]\mu$$

$$[\![R \vee R']\!]\mu = [\![R]\!]\mu \vee [\![R']\!]\mu$$

We write $\mu \models R$ to indicate that $[\![R]\!] = \text{true}$.

We say that two valuations $\mu, \mu'$ are *compatible* (or write $\mu$ compat $\mu'$) if for all variables $x \in \text{dom}(\mu) \cap \text{dom}(\mu')$, we have $\mu(x) = \mu'(x)$. Then there is a unique valuation $\mu \cup \mu'$ that behaves like $\mu$ on $\text{dom}(\mu)$ and like $\mu'$ on $\text{dom}(\mu')$. We define the following operations on sets of valuations $\Omega$.

$$\Omega_1 \bowtie \Omega_2 = \{\mu_1 \cup \mu_2 \mid \mu_1 \in \Omega_1, \mu_2 \in \Omega_2, \mu_1 \text{ compat } \mu_2\}$$

$$\Omega_1 \cup \Omega_2 = \{\mu \mid \mu \in \Omega_1 \text{ or } \mu \in \Omega_2\}$$

$$\Omega_1 \setminus \Omega_2 = \{\mu \in \Omega_1 \mid \not\exists \mu' \in \Omega_2.\mu \text{ compat } \mu'\}$$

$$\Omega_1 \rtimes \Omega_2 = (\Omega_1 \bowtie \Omega_2) \cup (\Omega_1 \setminus \Omega_2)$$

Note that union is the same as ordinary set union, but difference is not, since $\Omega_1 \setminus \Omega_2$ only includes valuations that are incompatible with all those in in $\Omega_2$.

Now we can define the meaning of a pattern $P$ in a dataset $\mathcal{D}$ as a set of valuations $[\![P]\!]_{\mathcal{D}}$, as follows:

$$[\![C]\!]_{\mathcal{D}} = \{\mu \mid \text{dom}(\mu) = vars(C) \text{ and } \mu(C) \subseteq \mathcal{D}\}$$

$$[\![P_1 \; . \; P_2]\!]_{\mathcal{D}} = [\![P_1]\!]_{\mathcal{D}} \bowtie [\![P_2]\!]_{\mathcal{D}}$$

$$[\![P_1 \; \text{UNION} \; P_2]\!]_{\mathcal{D}} = [\![P_1]\!]_{\mathcal{D}} \cup [\![P_2]\!]_{\mathcal{D}}$$

$$[\![P_1 \; \text{OPT} \; P_2]\!]_{\mathcal{D}} = [\![P_1]\!]_{\mathcal{D}} \rtimes [\![P_2]\!]_{\mathcal{D}}$$

$$[\![P \; \text{FILTER} \; R]\!]_{\mathcal{D}} = \{\mu \in [\![P]\!]_{\mathcal{D}} \mid \mu \models R\}$$

Note that, in contrast to Arenas et al.'s semantics for SPARQL with named graphs [1], we do not handle GRAPH $A$ {...} patterns that contain other pattern operations such as . or UNION, and we do not keep track of the "current graph" $G$. Instead, since graph patterns can only occur in basic patterns, we can build the proper behavior of pattern matching into the definition of $\mu(C)$, and we select all matches $\mu$ such that $\mu(C) \subseteq \mathcal{D}$ in the case for $[\![C]\!]_{\mathcal{D}}$.

Finally, we consider the semantics of selection and construction queries. A selection query has the form SELECT $?\overline{X}$ WHERE $P$ where $?\overline{X}$ is a list of distinct variables. It simply returns the valuations obtained by $P$ and discards the bindings of variables not in $\overline{X}$. A construction query builds a new graph or dataset from these results. Note that in SPARQL such queries only construct anonymous graphs; here we generalize in order to use construction queries to build datasets that can be inserted or deleted.

$$[\![\text{SELECT } ?\overline{X} \text{ WHERE } P]\!]_\mathcal{D} = \{\mu|_{\overline{X}} \mid \mu \in [\![P]\!]_\mathcal{D}\}$$
$$[\![\text{CONSTRUCT } C \text{ WHERE } P]\!]_\mathcal{D} = \bigcup\{\mu(C) \mid \mu \in [\![P]\!]_\mathcal{D}\}$$

Here, note that $\mu|_{\overline{X}}$ stands for $\mu$ restricted to the variables in the list $\overline{X}$.

We omit discussion of the FROM components of queries (which are used to initialize the graph store by pulling data in from external sources) or of the other query forms ASK, and DESCRIBE, as they are described elsewhere [1] in a manner coherent with our approach.

## 3    The Semantics of SPARQL Update

We will describe the semantics of the core language for atomic updates, based upon [22]:

$U ::=$ INSERT $\{C\}$ WHERE $P$ | DELETE $\{C\}$ WHERE $P$
| DELETE $\{C\}$ INSERT $\{C'\}$ WHERE $P$ | LOAD $g$ INTO $g'$ | CLEAR $g$
| CREATE $g$ | DROP $g$ | COPY $g$ TO $g'$ | MOVE $g$ TO $g'$ | ADD $g$ TO $g'$

We omit the INSERT DATA and DELETE DATA forms since they are definable in terms of INSERT and DELETE.

SPARQL Update [22] specifies that transactions consisting of multiple updates should be applied atomically, but leaves some semantic questions unresolved, such as whether aborted transactions have to roll-back partial changes. It also does not specify whether updates in a transaction are applied sequentially (as in most imperative languages), or using a snapshot semantics (as in most database update languages). Both alternatives pose complications, so in this paper we focus on transactions consisting of single atomic updates.

We model a collection of named graphs as a dataset $\mathcal{D}$, as for SPARQL queries. We consider only a single graph in isolation here, and not the case of multiple named graphs that may be being updated concurrently. The semantics of an update operation $u$ on dataset $\mathcal{D}$ is defined as $[\![U]\!]_\mathcal{D}$.

The semantics of a SPARQL Update $U$ in dataset $\mathcal{D}$ is defined as follows:

$$[\![\text{DELETE } \{C\} \text{ WHERE } P]\!]_{\mathcal{D}} = \mathcal{D} \setminus [\![\text{CONSTRUCT } C \text{ WHERE } P]\!]_{\mathcal{D}}$$

$$[\![\text{INSERT } \{C\} \text{ WHERE } P]\!]_{\mathcal{D}} = \mathcal{D} \cup [\![\text{CONSTRUCT } C \text{ WHERE } P]\!]_{\mathcal{D}}$$

$$[\![\text{DELETE } \{C\} \text{ INSERT } \{C'\} \text{ WHERE } P]\!]_{\mathcal{D}} = (\mathcal{D} \setminus [\![\text{CONSTRUCT } C \text{ WHERE } P]\!]_{\mathcal{D}})$$
$$\cup [\![\text{CONSTRUCT } C' \text{ WHERE } P]\!]_{\mathcal{D}}$$

$$[\![\text{LOAD } g_1 \text{ INTO } g_2]\!]_{\mathcal{D}} = \mathcal{D}[g_2 := \mathcal{D}(g_1) \cup \mathcal{D}(g_2)]$$

$$[\![\text{CLEAR } g]\!]_{\mathcal{D}} = \mathcal{D}[g := \emptyset]$$

$$[\![\text{CREATE } g]\!]_{\mathcal{D}} = \mathcal{D} \uplus \{g \mapsto \emptyset\}$$

$$[\![\text{DROP } g]\!]_{\mathcal{D}} = \mathcal{D}[g := \bot]$$

$$[\![\text{COPY } g_1 \text{ TO } g_2]\!]_{\mathcal{D}} = \begin{cases} \mathcal{D}[g_2 := \mathcal{D}(g_1)] & \text{if } g_1 \neq g_2 \\ \mathcal{D} & \text{otherwise} \end{cases}$$

$$[\![\text{MOVE } g_1 \text{ TO } g_2]\!]_{\mathcal{D}} = \begin{cases} \mathcal{D}[g_2 := \mathcal{D}(g_1), g_1 := \bot] & \text{if } g_1 \neq g_2 \\ \mathcal{D} & \text{otherwise} \end{cases}$$

$$[\![\text{ADD } g_1 \text{ TO } g_2]\!]_{\mathcal{D}} = \mathcal{D}[g_2 := \mathcal{D}(g_1) \cup \mathcal{D}(g_2)]$$

Here, $\mathcal{D}[g := G]$ denotes $\mathcal{D}$ updated by setting the graph named $g$ to $G$, and $\mathcal{D}[g := \bot]$ denotes $\mathcal{D}$ updated by making $g$ undefined, and finally $\mathcal{D} \uplus [g := G]$ denotes $\mathcal{D}$ updated by adding a graph named $g$ with value $G$, where $g$ must not already be in the domain of $\mathcal{D}$. Set-theoretic notation is used for graphs, e.g. $G \cup G'$ is used for set union and $G \setminus G'$ for set difference, and $\emptyset$ stands for the empty graph. Note that the COPY $g$ TO $g'$ and MOVE $g$ TO $g'$ operations have no effect if $g = g'$. Also, observe that we do not model external URI dereferences, and the LOAD $g$ INTO $g'$ operation (which allows $g$ to be an external URI) behaves exactly as ADD $g$ TO $g'$ operation (which expects $g$ to be a local graph name).

## 4   Provenance Semantics

A single SPARQL update can read from and write to several named graphs (and possibly also the default graph). For simplicity, we restrict attention to the problem of tracking the provenance of updates to a single (possibly named) RDF graph. All operations may still use the default graph or other named graphs in the dataset as sources. The general case can be handled using the same ideas as for a single anonymous graph, only with more bureaucracy to account for versioning of all of the named graphs managed in a given dataset.

A graph that records all the updates of triples from a given graph $g$ is considered a *provenance graph* for $g$. For each operation, a *provenance record* is stored that track of the state of the graph at any given moment and their associated metadata. The general concept is that in a fully automated process one should be able to re-construct the state of the given graph at any time from its provenance graph by following the SPARQL queries and metadata given in the provenance records for each update operation tracked.

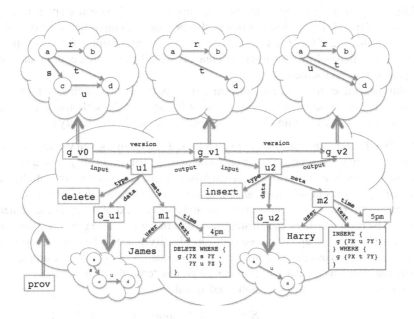

**Fig. 1.** Example provenance graph

We model the provenance of a single RDF graph $G$ that is updated over time as a set of history records, including the special provenance graph named *prov* which consists of indexed graphs for each operation such as G_v0,...,G_vn and G_u1...,G_um. These provenance records are immutable; that is, once they have been created and initialized, the implementation should fixed so that their content cannot be changed. The index of all provenance records then is also strictly linear and consistent (i.e. non-circular), although branching could be allowed. They can be stored as a special immutable type in the triple-store. Intuitively, G_vi is the named graph showing $G$'s state in version $i$ and G_ui is another named graph showing the triples inserted into or deleted from $G$ by update $i$. An example illustration is given in Figure 1.

The provenance graph of named graph G includes several kinds of nodes and edges:

- G_vi upd:version G_vi+1 edges that show the sequence of versions. Whenever a upd:version link is added between G_vi and G_vi+1, a backlink called upd:prevVersion between G_vi+1 and G_vi;
- nodes u1,...,un representing the updates that have been applied to $G$, along with a upd:type edge linking to one of upd:insert, upd:delete, upd:load, upd:clear, upd:create, or upd:drop.
- For all updates except create, an upd:input edge linking ui to G_vi.
- For all updates except drop, an upd:output edge linking ui to G_vi+1.
- For insert and delete updates, an edge ui upd:data G_ui where G_ui is a named graph containing the triples that were inserted or deleted by ui.

- Edges $\texttt{ui}$ $\texttt{upd:source}$ $\texttt{n}$ linking each update to each named graph $\texttt{n}$ that was consulted by $\texttt{ui}$. For an insert or delete, this includes all graphs that were consulted while evaluating $P$ (note that this may only be known at run time); for a load update, this is the name of the graph whose contents were loaded; create, drop and clear updates have no sources.
- Additional edges from $\texttt{ui}$ providing metadata for the update (such as author, commit time, log message, or the source text of the update); possibly using a standard vocabulary such as Dublin Core, or using OPM or PROV vocabulary terms.

Note that this representation does not directly link triples in a given version to places from which they were "copied" as it only contains the triples directly concerning the update in the history record. However, each history record in combination with the rest of the history records in the provenance graph does provide enough information to recover previous versions on request. As we store the source text of the update statements performed by each update in each history record of the provenance graph, we can trace backwards through the update sequence to to identify places where triples were inserted or copied into or deleted from the graph. For queries, we consider a simple form of provenance which calculates a set of named graphs "consulted" by the query. The set of sources of a pattern or query is computed as follows:

$$\mathcal{S}[\![C]\!]_\mathcal{D} = \bigcup \{\text{names}_\mu(C) \mid \mu \in [\![C]\!]_\mathcal{D}\}$$
$$\mathcal{S}[\![P_1 \, . \, P_2]\!]_\mathcal{D} = \mathcal{S}[\![P_1]\!]_\mathcal{D} \cup \mathcal{S}[\![P_2]\!]_\mathcal{D}$$
$$\mathcal{S}[\![P_1 \text{ UNION } P_2]\!]_\mathcal{D} = \mathcal{S}[\![P_1]\!]_\mathcal{D} \cup \mathcal{S}[\![P_2]\!]_\mathcal{D}$$
$$\mathcal{S}[\![P_1 \text{ OPT } P_2]\!]_\mathcal{D} = \mathcal{S}[\![P_1]\!]_\mathcal{D} \cup \mathcal{S}[\![P_2]\!]_\mathcal{D}$$
$$\mathcal{S}[\![P \text{ FILTER } R]\!]_\mathcal{D} = \mathcal{S}[\![P]\!]_\mathcal{D}$$
$$\mathcal{S}[\![\text{SELECT } ?\overline{X} \text{ WHERE } P]\!]_\mathcal{D} = \mathcal{S}[\![P]\!]_\mathcal{D}$$
$$\mathcal{S}[\![\text{CONSTRUCT } C \text{ WHERE } P]\!]_\mathcal{D} = \mathcal{S}[\![P]\!]_\mathcal{D}$$

where the auxiliary function $\text{names}_\mu(C)$ collects all of the graph names occurring in a ground basic graph pattern $C$:

$$\text{names}_\mu(\{t_1, \ldots, t_n\}) = \{\text{DEFAULT}\}$$
$$\text{names}_\mu(\text{GRAPH } A \, \{t_1, \ldots, t_n\}) = \{\mu(A)\}$$
$$\text{names}_\mu(C \, C') = \text{names}_\mu(C) \cup \text{names}_\mu(C')$$

Here, we use the special identifier DEFAULT as the name of the default graph; this can be replaced by its URI.

The $\mathcal{S}[\![P]\!]_\mathcal{D}$ function produces a set $S$ of graph identifiers such that replaying $[\![Q]\!]_{\mathcal{D}|_S} = [\![Q]\!]_\mathcal{D}$, where $\mathcal{D}|_S$ is $\mathcal{D}$ with all graphs not in $S$ set to $\emptyset$ (including the default graph if DEFAULT $\notin S$). Intuitively, $S$ identifies graphs that "witness" $Q$, analogous to why-provenance in databases [4]. This is not necessarily the *smallest* such set; it may be an overapproximation, particularly in the presence of $P_1$ OPT $P_2$ queries [24]. Alternative, more precise notions of source (for example involving triple-level annotations [8]) could also be used.

We define the provenance of an atomic update by translation to a sequence of updates that, in addition to performing the requested updates to a given named graph, also constructs some auxiliary named graphs and triples (provenance record) in a special named graph for provenance information called *prov* (the provenance graph). We apply this translation to each update posed by the user, and execute the resulting updates directly without further translation. We detail how provenance information should be attached to each SPARQL Update operation.

We consider simple forms of insert and delete operations that target a single, statically known, named graph $g$; full SPARQL Updates including simultaneous insert and delete operations can also be handled. In what follows, we write "(metadata)" as a placeholder where extra provenance metadata (e.g. time, author, etc. as in Dublin Core or further information given by the PROV vocabulary [15]) may be added. DROP commands simply end the provenance collection, but previous versions of the graph should still be available.

– A graph creation of a new graph CREATE $g$ is translated to

> CREATE $g$;
> CREATE $g\_v_0$;
> INSERT DATA {GRAPH *prov* {
>   $\langle g$ version $g\_v_0 \rangle$, $\langle g$ current $g\_v_0 \rangle$,
>   $\langle u_1$ type create$\rangle$, $\langle u_1$ output $g\_v_0 \rangle$,
>   $\langle u_1$ meta $m_i \rangle$, (metadata)
> }}

– A drop operation (deleting a graph) DROP $g$ is handled as follows, symmetrically to creation:

> DROP $g$;
> DELETE WHERE {GRAPH *prov* {$\langle g$ current $g\_v_i \rangle$}};
> INSERT DATA {GRAPH *prov* {
>   $\langle u_i$ type drop$\rangle$, $\langle u_i$ input $g\_v_i \rangle$,
>   $\langle u_i$ meta $m_i \rangle$, (metadata)
> }}

where $g\_v_i$ is the current version of $g$. Note that since this operation deletes $g$, after this step the URI $g$ no longer names a graph in the store; it is possible to create a new graph named $g$, which will result in a new sequence of versions being created for it. The old chain of versions will still be linked to $g$ via the version edges, but there will be a gap in the chain.

– A clear graph operation CLEAR $g$ is handled as follows:

> CLEAR $g$;
> DELETE WHERE {GRAPH *prov* {$\langle g$ current $g\_v_i \rangle$}};
> INSERT DATA {GRAPH *prov* {
>   $\langle g$ version $g\_v_{i+1} \rangle$, $\langle g$ current $g\_v_{i+1} \rangle$,
>   $\langle u_i$ type clear$\rangle$, $\langle u_i$ input $g\_v_i \rangle$,
>   $\langle u_i$ output $g\_v_{i+1} \rangle$, $\langle u_i$ meta $m_i \rangle$,
>   (metadata)
> }}

- A load graph operation LOAD $h$ INTO $g$ is handled as follows:

> LOAD $h$ INTO $g$;
> DELETE WHERE {GRAPH $prov$ {$\langle g$ current $g\_v_i \rangle$}};
> INSERT DATA {GRAPH $prov$ {
>    $\langle g$ version $g\_v_{i+1} \rangle$, $\langle g$ current $g\_v_{i+1} \rangle$,
>    $\langle u_i$ type load$\rangle$, $\langle u_i$ input $g\_v_i \rangle$,
>    $\langle u_i$ output $g\_v_{i+1} \rangle$, $\langle u_i$ source $h_j \rangle$,
>    $\langle u_i$ meta $m_i \rangle$, (metadata)
> }}

where $h_j$ is the current version of $h$. Note that a load will not create any new graphs because both the source and target should already exist. If no target exists, a new graph is created as outlined above with using the create operation.

- An insertion INSERT {GRAPH $g$ {$C$}} WHERE $P$ is translated to a sequence of updates that creates a new version and links it to URIs representing the update, as well as links to the source graphs identified by the query provenance semantics and a named graph containing the inserted triples:

> CREATE $g\_u_i$;
> INSERT {GRAPH $g\_u_i$ {$C$}} WHERE $P$;
> INSERT {GRAPH $g$ {$C$}} WHERE $P$;
> CREATE $g\_v_{i+1}$;
> LOAD $g$ INTO $g\_v_{i+1}$;
> DELETE DATA {GRAPH $prov$ {$\langle g$ current $g\_v_i \rangle$}};
> INSERT DATA {GRAPH $prov$ {
>    $\langle g$ version $g\_v_{i+1} \rangle$, $\langle g$ current $g\_v_{i+1} \rangle$,
>    $\langle u_i$ input $g\_v_i \rangle$, $\langle u_i$ output $g\_v_{i+1} \rangle$,
>    $\langle u_i$ type insert$\rangle$, $\langle u_i$ data $g\_u_i \rangle$
>    $\langle u_i$ source $s_1 \rangle$, ..., $\langle u_i$ source $s_m \rangle$,
>    $\langle u_i$ meta $m_i \rangle$, (metadata)}}

where $s_1, \ldots, s_m$ are the source graph names of $P$.

- A deletion DELETE {GRAPH $g$ {$C$}} WHERE $P$ is handled similarly to an insert, except for the update type annotation.

> CREATE $g\_u_i$;
> INSERT {GRAPH $g\_u_i$ {$C$}} WHERE $P$;
> DELETE {GRAPH $g$ {$C$}} WHERE $P$;
> CREATE $g\_v_{i+1}$;
> LOAD $g$ INTO $g\_v_{i+1}$;
> DELETE DATA {GRAPH $prov$ {$\langle g$ current $g\_v_i \rangle$}};
> INSERT DATA {GRAPH $prov$ {
>    $\langle g$ version $g\_v_{i+1} \rangle$, $\langle g$ current $g\_v_{i+1} \rangle$,
>    $\langle u_i$ input $g\_v_i \rangle$, $\langle u_i$ output $g\_v_{i+1} \rangle$,
>    $\langle u_i$ type delete$\rangle$, $\langle u_i$ data $g\_u_i \rangle$
>    $\langle u_i$ source $s_1 \rangle$, ..., $\langle u_i$ source $s_m \rangle$,
>    $\langle u_i$ meta $m_i \rangle$, (metadata)}}

Note that we still insert the deleted tuples into the $g\_u_i$.

- The DELETE $\{C\}$ INSERT $\{C'\}$ WHERE $P$ update can be handled as a delete followed by an insert, with the only difference being that both update steps are linked to the same metadata.
- The COPY $h$ TO $g$, MOVE $h$ TO $g$, and ADD $h$ TO $g$ commands can be handled similarly to LOAD $h$ INTO $g$; the only subtlety is that if $g = h$ then these operations have no visible effect, but the provenance record should still show that these operations were performed.

Our approach makes a design decision to treat DELETE $\{C\}$ INSERT $\{C'\}$ WHERE $P$ as a delete followed by an insert. In SPARQL Update, the effect of a combined delete–insert is not the same as doing the delete and insert separately, because both phases of a delete–insert are evaluated against the same data store before any changes are made. However, it is not clear that this distinction needs to be reflected in the provenance record; in particular, it is not needed to ensure correct reconstruction. Moreover, the connection between the delete and insert can be made explicit by linking both to the same metadata, as suggested above. Alternatively, the deletion and insertion can be treated as a single compound update, but this would collapse the distinction between the "sources" of the inserted and deleted data, which seems undesirable for use-cases such as version control.

Also note that our method does not formally take into account tracking the provenance of inferences. This is because of the complex interactions between SPARQL Update and the large number of possible (RDFS and the many varieties of OWL and OWL2) inference mechanisms and also because, unlike other research in the area [8], we do not consider it a requirement or even a desirable feature that inferences be preserved between updates. It is possible that an update will invalidate some inferences or that a new inference regime will be necessary. A simple solution would be that if the inferences produced by a reasoning procedure are necessary to be tracked with a particular graph, the triples resulting from this reasoning procedure should be materialized into the graph via an insert operation, with the history record's metadata specifying instead of a SPARQL Update statement the particular inference regime used. We also do not include a detailed treatment of blank nodes that takes their semantics as existential variables, as empirical research has in general shown that blank nodes are generally used as generic stable identifiers rather than existential variables, and thus can be treated as simply minting unique identifiers [11].

## 5   Update Provenance Vocabulary

For the provenance graph itself, we propose the following lightweight vocabulary called the "Update Provenance Vocabulary" (UPD) given in Table 2. Every time there is a change to a provenance-enabled graph by SPARQL Update, there is the addition of a provenance record to the provenance graph using the UPD vocabulary, including information such as an explicit time-stamp and the text of the SPARQL update itself. Every step in the transaction will have the option of recording metadata using W3C PROV vocabulary (or even some other provenance vocabulary like OPM) explicitly given by the "meta" link in our vocabulary and semantics, with UPD restricted to providing a record of the 'cut-and-paste' operations needed for applications of dynamic provenance like version control. We align the UPD vocabulary as a specialization of the W3C PROV vocabulary. A graph (upd:graph) is a subtype of prov:Entity and an update of a graph (upd:update) is a subtype of prov:Activity. For inverse properties, we use the inverse names recommended by PROV-O [15].

| Name | Description | PROV Subtype |
|---|---|---|
| upd:input | Link to provenance record from graph before an update | prov:wasUsedBy |
| upd:output | Link from provenance record to a graph after update | prov:generated |
| upd:data | Changed data in insert/delete operation | prov:wasUsedBy |
| upd:version | Sequential link forward in time between a version of a graph and an update | prov:hadRevision |
| upd:prevVersion | sequential link backwards in time between a version of a graph and an update | prov:wasRevisionOf |
| upd:type | Type of update operation (insert, delete, load, clear, create, or drop) | prov:type |
| upd:current | Link to most current state of graph | prov:hadRevision |
| upd:source | Any other graph that was consulted by the update | prov:wasUsedBy |
| upd:meta | Link to any metadata about the graph | rdfs:seeAlso |
| upd:user | User identifier (string or URI) | prov:wasAttributedTo |
| upd:text | Text of the SPARQL Update Query | prov:value |
| upd:time | Time of update to the graph | prov:atTime |

**Fig. 2.** Lightweight Update Provenance Vocabulary (UPD)

## 6  Implementation Considerations

So far we have formalized a logical model of the provenance of a graph as it evolves over time (which allow us to derive its intermediate versions), but we have not detailed how to store or query the intermediate versions of a graph efficiently. For any given graph one should likely store the most up-to-date graph so that queries on the graph in its present state can be run without reconstructing the entire graph. One could to simply store the graph G_vi resulting from each update operation in addition to the provenance record, but this would lead to an explosive growth in storage requirements. This would also be the case even for the provenance graph if the storage of an auxiliary graph G_ui in a provenance record involved many triples, although we allow this in the UPD vocabulary as it may be useful for some applications. For those operating over large graphs, the contents of the named graphs G_ui that store inserted or deleted triples can be represented more efficiently by just storing the original graph and the SPARQL Update statements themselves in each provenance record given by the upd:text property, and not storing the auxiliary named graphs given by upd:data.

Strategically, one can trade computational expense for storage in provenance, due to the immutability of the provenance information. A hybrid methodology to ameliorate the cost of reconstruction of the version of a graph would be to store the graph at various temporal intervals (i.e. "snapshots"). For small graphs where storage cost is low and processing cost is high, it would make more sense to store all provenance information for the entire graph. In situations where the cost of processing is high and storage cost is low, storing the SPARQL Updates and re-running them makes sense to reconstruct the graph. In this case, it also makes sense to store "snapshots" of the graph at various intervals to reduce processing cost. Simulation results for these scenarios are available.[1]

# 7 Conclusion

Provenance is a challenging problem for RDF. By extending SPARQL Update, we have provided a method to use W3C PROV (and other metadata vocabularies) to keep track of the changes to triple-stores. We formalized this approach by drawing on similar work in database archiving and copy-paste provenance, which allow us to use SPARQL Update provenance records to reconstruct graphs at arbitrary instances in time. This work is a first step in addressing the important issue of RDF version control. We hope this will contribute to discussion of how to standardize descriptions of changes to RDF datasets, and even provide a way to translate changes to underlying (e.g. relational or XML) databases to RDF representations, as the same underlying "cut-and-paste" model has already been well-explored in these kinds of databases [2]. Explorations to adapt this work to the Google Research-funded DatabaseWiki project, and implementation performance with real-world data-sets is a next step [3]. A number of areas for theoretical future work remain, including the subtle issue of combining it with RDFS inferences [8] or special-purpose SPARQL provenance queries [25,16].

**Acknowledgements.** This work was supported in part by EU FP7 project DIACHRON (grant number 601043). The authors, their organizations and project funding partners are authorized to reproduce and distribute reprints and on-line copies for their purposes notwithstanding any copyright annotation hereon.

# References

1. Arenas, M., Gutierrez, C., Perez, J.: On the semantics of SPARQL. In: Semantic Web Information Management: A Model Based Perspective, 1st edn. Springer (2009)
2. Buneman, P., Chapman, A., Cheney, J.: Provenance management in curated databases. In: Proceedings of the 2006 ACM SIGMOD International Conference on Management of Data, SIGMOD 2006, pp. 539–550. ACM, New York (2006)
3. Buneman, P., Cheney, J., Lindley, S., Müller, H.: DBWiki: a structured wiki for curated data and collaborative data management. In: Proceedings of the 2011 ACM SIGMOD International Conference on Management of Data, pp. 1335–1338. ACM (2011)
4. Buneman, P., Khanna, S., Tan, W.-C.: Why and where: A characterization of data provenance. In: Van den Bussche, J., Vianu, V. (eds.) ICDT 2001. LNCS, vol. 1973, pp. 316–330. Springer, Heidelberg (2000)
5. Buneman, P., Kostylev, E.: Annotation algebras for RDFS. In: SWPM (2010)
6. Carroll, J.J., Bizer, C., Hayes, P., Stickler, P.: Named graphs. Web Semant. 3, 247–267 (2005)
7. Cheney, J.: The semantics of the PROV data model. W3C Note (April 2013),
   http://www.w3.org/TR/2013/NOTE-prov-sem-20130430/

---

[1] *http://www.ibiblio.org/hhalpin/homepage/notes/dbprov-implementation.pdf*

8. Flouris, G., Fundulaki, I., Pediaditis, P., Theoharis, Y., Christophides, V.: Coloring RDF triples to capture provenance. In: Bernstein, A., Karger, D.R., Heath, T., Feigenbaum, L., Maynard, D., Motta, E., Thirunarayan, K. (eds.) ISWC 2009. LNCS, vol. 5823, pp. 196–212. Springer, Heidelberg (2009)

9. Green, T.J., Karvounarakis, G., Tannen, V.: Provenance semirings. In: Proceedings of the Twenty-Sixth ACM SIGMOD-SIGACT-SIGART Symposium on Principles of Database Systems, PODS 2007, pp. 31–40. ACM, New York (2007)

10. Gutierrez, C., Hurtado, C., Vaisman, A.: Temporal RDF. In: Gómez-Pérez, A., Euzenat, J. (eds.) ESWC 2005. LNCS, vol. 3532, pp. 93–107. Springer, Heidelberg (2005)

11. Halpin, H.: Is there anything worth finding on the semantic web? In: Proceedings of the 18th International Conference on World Wide Web, WWW 2009, pp. 1065–1066. ACM, New York (2009)

12. Horne, R., Sassone, V., Gibbins, N.: Operational semantics for SPARQL update. In: Pan, J.Z., Chen, H., Kim, H.-G., Li, J., Wu, Z., Horrocks, I., Mizoguchi, R., Wu, Z. (eds.) JIST 2011. LNCS, vol. 7185, pp. 242–257. Springer, Heidelberg (2012)

13. Klyne, G., Groth, P.: Provenance Access and Query. W3C Note (April 2013), http://www.w3.org/TR/2013/NOTE-prov-aq-20130430/

14. Kwasnikowska, N., Moreau, L., Van den Bussche, J.: A formal account of the Open Provenance Model (December 2010)

15. Lebo, T., Sahoo, S., McGuinness, D.: PROV-O: The PROV ontology. W3C Recommendation (April 2013), http://www.w3.org/TR/2013/REC-prov-o-20130430/

16. Lopes, N., Polleres, A., Straccia, U., Zimmermann, A.: AnQL: SPARQLing up annotated RDFS. In: Patel-Schneider, P.F., Pan, Y., Hitzler, P., Mika, P., Zhang, L., Pan, J.Z., Horrocks, I., Glimm, B. (eds.) ISWC 2010, Part I. LNCS, vol. 6496, pp. 518–533. Springer, Heidelberg (2010)

17. Moreau, L., Clifford, B., Freire, J., Futrelle, J., Gil, Y., Groth, P., Kwasnikowska, N., Miles, S., Missier, P., Myers, J., Plale, B., Simmhan, Y., Stephan, E., Van den Bussche, J.: The Open Provenance Model core specification (v1.1). Future Generation Computer Systems 27(6), 743–756 (2011)

18. Moreau, L.: Provenance-based reproducibility in the semantic web. J. Web Sem. 9(2), 202–221 (2011)

19. Moreau, L., Missier, P.: PROV-DM: The PROV data model. W3C Recommendation (August. 2013), http://www.w3.org/TR/2013/REC-prov-dm-20130430/

20. Papavassiliou, V., Flouris, G., Fundulaki, I., Kotzinos, D., Christophides, V.: On detecting high-level changes in RDF/S kBs. In: Bernstein, A., Karger, D.R., Heath, T., Feigenbaum, L., Maynard, D., Motta, E., Thirunarayan, K. (eds.) ISWC 2009. LNCS, vol. 5823, pp. 473–488. Springer, Heidelberg (2009)

21. Perèz, J., Arenas, M., Gutierrez, C.: Semantics and complexity of SPARQL. Transactions on Database Systems 34(3), A16 (2009)

22. Schenk, S., Gearon, P., Passant, A.: SPARQL 1.1 Update. W3C Recommendation (March 2013), http://www.w3.org/TR/2013/REC-sparql11-update-20130321/

23. Snodgrass, R.T.: Developing time-oriented database applications in SQL. Morgan Kaufmann Publishers Inc., San Francisco (2000)

24. Theoharis, Y., Fundulaki, I., Karvounarakis, G., Christophides, V.: On provenance of queries on semantic web data. IEEE Internet Computing 15(1), 31–39 (2011)

25. Udrea, O., Recupero, D.R., Subrahmanian, V.S.: Annotated RDF. ACM Trans. Comput. Logic 11, A10 (2010)

# Updating RDFS ABoxes and TBoxes in SPARQL

Albin Ahmeti[1], Diego Calvanese[2], and Axel Polleres[3]

[1] Vienna University of Technology, Favoritenstraße 9, 1040 Vienna, Austria
[2] Faculty of Computer Science, Free University of Bozen-Bolzano, Bolzano, Italy
[3] Vienna University of Economics and Business, Welthandelsplatz 1, 1020 Vienna, Austria

**Abstract.** Updates in RDF stores have recently been standardised in the SPARQL 1.1 Update specification. However, computing entailed answers by ontologies is usually treated orthogonally to updates in triple stores. Even the W3C SPARQL 1.1 Update and SPARQL 1.1 Entailment Regimes specifications explicitly exclude a standard behaviour for entailment regimes other than simple entailment in the context of updates. In this paper, we take a first step to close this gap. We define a fragment of SPARQL basic graph patterns corresponding to (the RDFS fragment of) *DL-Lite* and the corresponding SPARQL update language, dealing with updates both of ABox and of TBox statements. We discuss possible semantics along with potential strategies for implementing them. In particular, we treat both, (i) materialised RDF stores, which store all entailed triples explicitly, and (ii) reduced RDF Stores, that is, redundancy-free RDF stores that do not store any RDF triples (corresponding to *DL-Lite* ABox statements) entailed by others already. We have implemented all semantics prototypically on top of an off-the-shelf triple store and present some indications on practical feasibility.

## 1 Introduction

The availability of SPARQL as a standard for accessing structured Data on the Web may well be called one of the key factors to the success and increasing adoption of RDF and the Semantic Web. Still, in its first iteration the SPARQL [24] specification has neither defined how to treat ontological entailments with respect to RDF Schema (RDFS) and OWL ontologies, nor provided means how to update dynamic RDF data. Both these gaps have been addressed within the recent SPARQL 1.1 specification, which provides both means to define query answers under ontological entailments (SPARQL 1.1 Entailment Regimes [9]), and an update language to update RDF data stored in a triple store (SPARQL 1.1 Update [8]). Nonetheless, these specifications leave it open how SPARQL endpoints should treat entailment regimes other than simple entailment in the context of updates; the main issue here is how updates shall deal with implied statements:

- What does it mean if an implied triple is explicitly (re-)inserted (or deleted)?
- Which (if any) additional triples should be inserted, (or, resp., deleted) upon updates?

For the sake of this paper, we address such questions with the focus on a deliberately minimal ontology language, namely the minimal RDFS fragment of [19].[1] As it turns out, even in this confined setting, updates as defined in the SPARQL 1.1 Update

---

[1] We ignore issues like axiomatic triples [13], blank nodes [17], or, in the context of OWL, inconsistencies arising through updates [5]. Neither do we consider named graphs in SPARQL, which is why we talk about "triple stores" as opposed to "graph stores" [8].

P. Mika et al. (Eds.) ISWC 2014, Part I, LNCS 8796, pp. 441–456, 2014.

**Table 1.** *DL-Lite*$_{\text{RDFS}}$ assertions vs. RDF(S), where $A$, $A'$ denote concept (or, class) names, $P$, $P'$ denote role (or, property) names, $\Gamma$ is a set of constants, and $x, y \in \Gamma$. For RDF(S) vocabulary, we make use of similar abbreviations (sc, sp, dom, rng, a) introduced in [19].

| TBox | RDFS | TBox | RDFS | ABox | RDFS |
|---|---|---|---|---|---|
| 1 $A' \sqsubseteq A$ | $A'$ sc $A$. | 3 $\exists P \sqsubseteq A$ | $P$ dom $A$. | 5 $A(x)$ | $x$ a $A$. |
| 2 $P' \sqsubseteq P$ | $P'$ sp $P$. | 4 $\exists P^- \sqsubseteq A$ | $P$ rng $A$. | 6 $P(x,y)$ | $x$ P $y$. |

specification impose non-trivial challenges; in particular, specific issues arise through the interplay of INSERT, DELETE, and WHERE clauses within a single SPARQL update operation, which —to the best of our knowledge— have not yet been considered in this combination in previous literature on updates under entailment (such as for instance [5, 11]).

*Example 1.* As a running example, we assume a triple store $G$ with RDF (ABox) data and an RDFS ontology (TBox) $O_{fam}$ about family relationships (in Turtle syntax [2]), where :hasP, :hasM, and :hasF, resp., denote the parent, mother, and father relations.

```
ABox:   :joe :hasP :jack.      :joe :hasM :jane.
TBox:   :Father sc :Parent.     :Mother sc :Parent.
  :hasF sp :hasP.          :hasM sp :hasP.
  :hasF rng :Father; dom :Child. :hasM rng :Mother; dom :Child.
  :hasP rng :Parent; dom :Child.
```

The following query should return :jack and :jane as (RDFS entailed) answers:
```
SELECT ?Y WHERE { :joe :hasP ?Y. }
```
SPARQL engines supporting simple entailment would only return :jack, though.   ∎

The intended behaviour for the query in Ex. 1 is typically achieved by either *(i)* query rewriting techniques computing entailed answers at query run-time, or *(ii)* by materialising all implied triples in the store, normally at loading time. That is, on the one hand, borrowing from query rewriting techniques from *DL-Lite* (such as, e.g., *PerfectRef* [4][2]) one can reformulate such a query to return also implied answers. While the rewritten query is worst case exponential wrt. the length of the original query (and polynomial in the size of the TBox), for moderate size TBoxes and queries rewriting is quite feasible.

*Example 2 (cont'd).* The rewriting of the query in Ex. 1 according to *PerfectRef* [4] with respect to $O_{fam}$ as a DL TBox in SPARQL yields
```
SELECT ?Y WHERE { {:joe :hasP ?Y}
                  UNION {:joe :hasF ?Y}  UNION {:joe :hasM ?Y}}
```
Indeed, this query returns both :jane and :jack.   ∎

On the other hand, an alternative[3] is to materialise all inferences in the triple store, such that the original query can be used 'as is', for instance using the minimalistic inference rules for RDFS from [19][4] shown in Fig. 1.

---

[2] Alg. 1 in the Appendix shows a version of *PerfectRef* reduced to the essentials of RDFS.

[3] This alternative is viable for RDFS, but not necessarily for more expressive DLs.

[4] These rules correspond to rules 2), 3), 4) of [19]; they suffice since we ignore blank nodes.

*Example 3 (cont'd).* The materialised version of $G$ would contain the following triples—for conciseness we only show assertional implied triples here, that is triples from the four leftmost rules in Fig. 1.

```
:joe a :Child; :hasP :jack; :hasM :jane; :hasP :jane.
:jack a :Parent. :jane a :Mother, :Parent.
```

On a materialised triple store, the query from Ex. 1 would return the expected results.
∎

However, in the context of SPARQL 1.1 Update, things become less clear.

*Example 4 (cont'd).* The following operation tries to delete an implied triple and at the same time to (re-)insert another implied triple.
**DELETE** {?X a :Child} **INSERT** {?Y a :Mother} **WHERE** {?X :hasM ?Y} ∎

Existing triple stores offer different solutions to these problems, ranging from ignoring entailments in updates altogether, to keeping explicit and implicit (materialised) triples separate and re-materialising upon updates. In the former case (ignoring entailments) updates only refer to explicitly asserted triples, which may result in non-intuitive behaviours, whereas the latter case (re-materialisation) may be very costly, while still not eliminating all non-intuitive cases, as we will see. The problem is aggravated by no systematic approach to the question of which implied triples to store explicitly in a triple store and which not. In this paper we try to argue for a more systematic approach for dealing with updates in the context of RDFS entailments. More specifically, we will distinguish between two kinds of triple stores, that is *(i) materialised RDF stores*, which store all entailed ABox triples explicitly, and *(ii) reduced RDF Stores*, that is, redundancy-free RDF stores that do not store any assertional (ABox) triples already entailed by others. We propose alternative update semantics that preserve the respective types *(i)* and *(ii)* of triple stores, and discuss possible implementation strategies, partially inspired by query rewriting techniques from ontology-based data access (OBDA) [15] and *DL-Lite* [4]. As already shown in [11], erasure of ABox statements is deterministic in the context of RDFS, but insertion and particularly the interplay of DELETE/INSERT in SPARQL 1.1 Update has not been considered therein. Finally, we relax the initial assumption that terminological statements (using the RDFS vocabulary) are static, and discuss the issues that arise when also TBox statement are subject to updates.

The remainder of the paper continues with preliminaries (RDFS, SPARQL, *DL-Lite*, SPARQL update operations) in Sec. 2. We introduce alternative semantics for ABox updates in materialised and reduced triple stores in Sec. 3, and discuss them in Sec. 4 and Sec. 5, respectively. In Sec. 6, we present our results on TBox updates. After presenting in Sec. 7 an implementation on top of an off-the-shelf triple store along with experiments, followed in Sec. 8 by a discussion of future and related work, we conclude in Sec. 9.

$$\frac{?C \text{ sc } ?D. \quad ?S \text{ a } ?C.}{?S \text{ a } ?D.} \qquad \frac{?P \text{ dom } ?C. \quad ?S ?P ?O.}{?S \text{ a } ?C.} \qquad \frac{?C \text{ sc } ?D. \quad ?D \text{ sc } ?E.}{?C \text{ sc } ?E.}$$

$$\frac{?P \text{ sp } ?Q. \quad ?S ?P ?O.}{?S ?Q ?O.} \qquad \frac{?P \text{ rng } ?C. \quad ?S ?P ?O.}{?O \text{ a } ?C.} \qquad \frac{?P \text{ sp } ?Q. \quad ?Q \text{ sp } ?R.}{?P \text{ sp } ?R.}$$

**Fig. 1.** Minimal RDFS inference rules

## 2  Preliminaries

We introduce some basic notions about RDF graphs, RDFS ontologies, and SPARQL queries. Since we will draw from ideas coming from OBDA and *DL-Lite*, we introduce these notions in a way that is compatible with DLs.

**Definition 1 (RDFS ontology, ABox, TBox, triple store).** *We call a set $\mathcal{T}$ of inclusion assertions of the forms 1–4 in Table 1 an* RDFS ontology, *or* (RDFS) TBox, *a set $\mathcal{A}$ of assertions of the forms 5–6 in Table 1 an* (RDF) ABox, *and the union $G = \mathcal{T} \cup \mathcal{A}$ an* (RDFS) triple store.

In the context of RDF(S), the set $\Gamma$ of constants coincides with the set $I$ of IRIs. We assume the IRIs used for concepts, roles, and individuals to be disjoint from IRIs of the RDFS and OWL vocabularies.[5] In the following, we view RDF and DL notation interchangeably, i.e., we treat any RDF graph consisting of triples without non-standard RDFS vocabulary as a set of TBox and ABox assertions. To define the semantics of RDFS, we rely on the standard notions of (first-order logic) *interpretation*, satisfaction of assertions, and *model* (cf. e.g., [1, Def. 14]).

As for queries, we again treat the cases of SPARQL and DLs interchangeably. Let $\mathcal{V}$ be a countably infinite set of variables (written as '?'-prefixed alphanumeric strings).

**Definition 2 (BGP, CQ, UCQ).** *A* conjunctive query *(CQ) q, or* basic graph pattern *(BGP), is a set of atoms of the forms 5–6 from Table 1, where now $x, y \in \Gamma \cup \mathcal{V}$. A* union of conjunctive queries *(UCQ) Q, or* UNION *pattern, is a set of CQs. We denote with $\mathcal{V}(q)$ (or $\mathcal{V}(Q)$) the set of variables from $\mathcal{V}$ occurring in q (resp., Q).*

Notice that in this definition we are considering only CQs in which all variables are *distinguished* (i.e., are answer variables), and that such queries correspond to SPARQL basic graph patterns (BGPs). From the SPARQL perspective, we allow only for restricted forms of general SPARQL BGPs that correspond to standard CQs as formulated over a DL ontology; that is, we rule out on the one hand more complex patterns in SPARQL 1.1 [12] (such as OPTIONAL, NOT EXISTS, FILTER), and queries with variables in predicate positions, and on the other hand "terminological" queries, e.g., $\{?x \text{ sc } ?y.\}$. We will relax this latter restriction later (see Sec. 6). Also, we do not consider here blank nodes separately[6]. By these restrictions, we can treat query answering and BGP matching in SPARQL analogously and define it in terms of interpretations and models (as usual in DLs). Specifically, an *answer* (under RDFS Entailment) to a CQ $q$ over a triple store $G$ is a substitution $\theta$ of the variables in $\mathcal{V}(q)$ with constants in $\Gamma$ such that every model of $G$ satisfies all facts in $q\theta$. We denote the set of all such answers with $ans_{\text{rdfs}}(q, G)$ (or simply $ans(q, G)$). The set of answers to a UCQ $Q$ is $\bigcup_{q \in Q} ans(q, G)$.

From now on, let $rewrite(q, \mathcal{T})$ be the UCQ resulting from applying *PerfectRef* (or, equivalently, the down-stripped version Alg. 1) to a CQ $q$ and a triple store $G = \mathcal{T} \cup \mathcal{A}$,

---

[5] That is, we assume no "non-standard use" [23] of these vocabularies. While we could assume concept names, role names, and individual constants mutually disjoint, we rather distinguish implicitly between them "per use" (in the sense of "punning" [18]) based on their position in atoms or RDF triples.

[6] Blank nodes in a triple store may be considered as constants and we do not allow blank nodes in queries, which does not affect the expressivity of SPARQL.

and let $mat(G)$ be the triple store obtained from exhaustive application on $G$ of the inference rules in Fig. 1.

The next result follows immediately from, e.g., [4, 11, 19] and shows that query answering under RDF can be done by either query rewriting or materialisation.

**Proposition 1.** *Let* $G = \mathcal{T} \cup \mathcal{A}$ *be a triple store,* $q$ *a CQ, and* $\mathcal{A}'$ *the set of ABox assertions in* $mat(G)$. *Then,* $ans(q, G) = ans(rewrite(q, \mathcal{T}), \mathcal{A}) = ans(q, \mathcal{A}')$.

Various triple stores (e.g., BigOWLIM [3]) perform ABox materialisation directly upon loading data. However, such triple stores do not necessarily materialise the TBox: in order to correctly answer UCQs as defined above, a triple store actually does not need to consider the two rightmost rules in Fig. 1. Accordingly, we will call a triple store or (ABox) *materialised* if in each state it always guarantees $G \backslash \mathcal{T} = mat(G) \backslash mat(\mathcal{T})$. On the other extreme, we find triple stores that do not store *any* redundant ABox triples. By $red(G)$ we denote the hypothetical operator that produces the reduced "core" of $G$, and we call a triple store *(ABox) reduced* if $G = red(G)$. We note that this core is uniquely determined in our setting whenever $\mathcal{T}$ is acyclic (which is usually a safe assumption)[7]; it could be naïvely computed by exhaustively "marking" each triple that can be inferred from applying any of the four leftmost rules in Fig. 1, and subsequently removing all marked elements of $\mathcal{A}$. Lastly, we observe that, trivially, a triple store containing no ABox statements is both reduced and materialised.

Finally, we introduce the notion of a SPARQL update operation.

**Definition 3 (SPARQL update operation).** *Let* $P_d$ *and* $P_i$ *be BGPs, and* $P_w$ *a BGP or UNION pattern. Then an* update operation $u(P_d, P_i, P_w)$ *has the form*

**DELETE** $P_d$ **INSERT** $P_i$ **WHERE** $P_w$.

Intuitively, the semantics of executing $u(P_d, P_i, P_w)$ on $G$, denoted as $G_{u(P_d, P_i, P_w)}$ is defined by interpreting both $P_d$ and $P_i$ as "templates" to be instantiated with the solutions of $ans(P_w, G)$, resulting in sets of ABox statements $\mathcal{A}_d$ to be deleted from $G$, and $\mathcal{A}_i$ to be inserted into $G$. A naïve update semantics follows straightforwardly.

**Definition 4 (Naïve update semantics).** *Let* $G = \mathcal{T} \cup \mathcal{A}$ *be a triple store, and* $u(P_d, P_i, P_w)$ *an update operation. Then,* naive update of $G$ with $u(P_d, P_i, P_w)$, *denoted* $G_{u(P_d, P_i, P_w)}$, *is defined as* $(G \setminus \mathcal{A}_d) \cup \mathcal{A}_i$, *where* $\mathcal{A}_d = \bigcup_{\theta \in ans(P_w, G)} gr(P_d \theta)$, $\mathcal{A}_i = \bigcup_{\theta \in ans(P_w, G)} gr(P_i \theta)$, *and* $gr(P)$ *denotes the set of ground triples in pattern* $P$.

As easily seen, this naïve semantics neither preserves reduced nor materialised triple stores. Consider, e.g., the update from Ex. 4, respectively on the reduced triple store from Ex. 1 and on the materialised triple store from Ex. 3.

## 3 Defining Alternative Update Semantics

We investigate now alternative semantics for updates that preserve either materialised or reduced ABoxes, and discuss how these semantics can—similar to query answering—be implemented in off-the-shelf SPARQL 1.1 triple stores.

---

[7] We note that even in the case when the TBox is cyclic we could define a deterministic way to remove redundancies, e.g., by preserving within a cycle only the lexicographically smallest ABox statements. That is, given TBox $A \sqsubseteq B \sqsubseteq C \sqsubseteq A$ and ABox $A(x), C(x)$; we would delete $C(x)$ and retain $A(x)$ only, to preserve reducedness.

**Definition 5 (Mat-preserving and red-preserving semantics).** *Let* $G$ *and* $u(P_d, P_i, P_w)$ *be as in Def. 4. An update semantics Sem is called* mat-preserving, *if* $G^{Sem}_{u(P_d, P_i, P_w)} = mat(G^{Sem}_{u(P_d, P_i, P_w)})$, *and it is called* red-preserving, *if* $G^{Sem}_{u(P_d, P_i, P_w)} = red(G^{Sem}_{u(P_d, P_i, P_w)})$.

Specifically, we consider the following variants of materialised ABox preserving (or simply, *mat-preserving*) semantics and reduced ABox preserving (or simply, *red-preserving*) semantics, given an update $u(P_d, P_i, P_w)$:

$\mathbf{Sem}_0^{mat}$: As a baseline for a mat-preserving semantics, we apply the naïve semantics, followed by (re-)materialisation of the whole triple store.

$\mathbf{Sem}_1^{mat}$: An alternative approach for a mat-preserving semantics is to follow the so-called "delete and rederive" algorithm [10] for deletions, that is: *(i)* delete the instantiations of $P_d$ *plus "dangling" effects*, i.e., effects of deleted triples that after deletion are not implied any longer *by any non-deleted triples*; *(ii)* insert the instantiations of $P_i$ *plus all their effects*.

$\mathbf{Sem}_2^{mat}$: Another mat-preserving semantics could take a different viewpoint with respect to deletions, following the intention to: *(i)* delete the instantiations of $P_d$ *plus all their causes*; *(ii)* insert the instantiations of $P_i$ *plus all their effects*.

$\mathbf{Sem}_3^{mat}$: Finally, a mat-preserving semantics could combine $\mathbf{Sem}_1^{mat}$ and $\mathbf{Sem}_2^{mat}$, by deleting both causes of instantiations of $P_d$ and (recursively) "dangling" effects.[8]

$\mathbf{Sem}_0^{red}$: Again, the baseline for a red-preserving semantics would be to apply the naïve semantics, followed by (re-)reducing the triple store.

$\mathbf{Sem}_1^{red}$: This red-preserving semantics extends $\mathbf{Sem}_0^{red}$ by additionally deleting the causes of instantiations of $P_d$.

The definitions of semantics $\mathbf{Sem}_0^{mat}$ and $\mathbf{Sem}_0^{red}$ are straightforward.

**Definition 6 (Baseline mat-preserving and red-preserving update semantics).** *Let* $G$ *and* $u(P_d, P_i, P_w)$ *be as in Def. 4. Then, we define* $\mathbf{Sem}_0^{mat}$ *and* $\mathbf{Sem}_0^{red}$ *as follows:*

$$G^{\mathbf{Sem}_0^{mat}}_{u(P_d, P_i, P_w)} = mat(G_{u(P_d, P_i, P_w)}) \qquad G^{\mathbf{Sem}_0^{red}}_{u(P_d, P_i, P_w)} = red(G_{u(P_d, P_i, P_w)})$$

Let us proceed with a quick "reality-check" on these two baseline semantics by means of our running example.

*Example 5.* Consider the update from Ex. 4. It is easy to see that neither under $\mathbf{Sem}_0^{mat}$ executed on the materialised triple store of Ex. 3, nor under $\mathbf{Sem}_0^{red}$ executed on the reduced triple store of Ex. 1, it would have *any* effect. ∎

This behaviour is quite arguable. Hence, we proceed with discussing the implications of the proposed alternative update semantics, and how they could be implemented.

## 4   Alternative Mat-Preserving Semantics

We consider now in more detail the mat-preserving semantics. As for $\mathbf{Sem}_1^{mat}$, we rely on a well-known technique in the area of updates for deductive databases called "delete

---

[8] Note the difference to the basic "delete and rederive" approach. $\mathbf{Sem}_1^{mat}$ in combination with the intention of $\mathbf{Sem}_2^{mat}$ would also mean to recursively delete effects of causes, and so forth.

and rederive" (DRed) [6, 10, 16, 26, 27]. Informally translated to our setting, when given a logic program $\Pi$ and its materialisation $T_\Pi^\omega$, plus a set of facts $A_d$ to be deleted and a set of facts $A_i$ to be inserted, DRed *(i)* first deletes $A_d$ and all its effects (computed via semi-naive evaluation [25]) from $T_\Pi^\omega$, resulting in $(T_\Pi^\omega)'$, *(ii)* then, starting from $(T_\Pi^\omega)'$, re-materialises $(\Pi \setminus A_d) \cup A_i$ (again using semi-naive evaluation).

The basic intuition behind DRed of deleting effects of deleted triples and then re-materialising can be expressed in our notation as follows; as we will consider a variant of this semantics later on, we refer to this semantics as $\mathbf{Sem}_{1a}^{mat}$.

**Definition 7.** *Let $G = \mathcal{T} \cup \mathcal{A}$, $u(P_d, P_i, P_w)$, $A_d$, and $A_i$ be defined as in Def. 4. Then*
$$G_{u(P_d, P_i, P_w)}^{\mathbf{Sem}_{1a}^{mat}} = mat(\mathcal{T} \cup (\mathcal{A} \setminus mat(\mathcal{T} \cup A_d)) \cup A_i).$$

As opposed to the classic DRed algorithm, where Datalog distinguishes between view predicates (IDB) and extensional knowledge in the Database (EDB), in our setting we do not make this distinction, i.e., we do not distinguish between implicitly and explicitly inserted triples. This means that $\mathbf{Sem}_{1a}^{mat}$ would delete also those effects that had been inserted explicitly before.

We introduce now a different variant of this semantics, denoted $\mathbf{Sem}_{1b}^{mat}$, that makes a distinction between explicitly and implicitly inserted triples.

**Definition 8.** *Let $u(P_d, P_i, P_w)$ be an update operation, and $G = \mathcal{T} \cup \mathcal{A}_{expl} \cup \mathcal{A}_{impl}$ a triple store, where $\mathcal{A}_{expl}$ and $\mathcal{A}_{impl}$ respectively denote the explicit and implicit ABox triples. Then $G_{u(P_d, P_i, P_w)}^{\mathbf{Sem}_{1b}^{mat}} = \mathcal{T} \cup \mathcal{A}'_{expl} \cup \mathcal{A}'_{impl}$, where $\mathcal{A}_d$ and $\mathcal{A}_i$ are defined as in Def. 4, $\mathcal{A}'_{expl} = (\mathcal{A}_{expl} \setminus \mathcal{A}_d) \cup \mathcal{A}_i$, and $\mathcal{A}'_{impl} = mat(\mathcal{A}'_{expl} \cup \mathcal{T}) \setminus \mathcal{T}$.*

Note that in $\mathbf{Sem}_{1b}^{mat}$, as opposed to $\mathbf{Sem}_{1a}^{mat}$, we do not explicitly delete effects of $\mathcal{A}_d$ from the materialisation, since the definition just relies on re-materialisation from scratch from the explicit ABox $\mathcal{A}'_{expl}$. Nonetheless, the original DRed algorithm can still be used for computing $\mathbf{Sem}_{1b}^{mat}$ as shown by the following proposition.

**Proposition 2.** *Let us interpret the inference rules in Fig. 1 and triples in G respectively as rules and facts of a logic program $\Pi$; accordingly, we interpret $\mathcal{A}_d$ and $\mathcal{A}_i$ from Def. 8 as facts to be deleted from and inserted into $\Pi$, respectively. Then, the materialisation computed by DRed, as defined in [16], computes exactly $\mathcal{A}'_{impl}$.*

None of $\mathbf{Sem}_0^{mat}$, $\mathbf{Sem}_{1a}^{mat}$, and $\mathbf{Sem}_{1b}^{mat}$ are equivalent, as shown in Ex. 6 below.

*Example 6.* Given the triple store $G = \{:C \text{ sc } :D \text{ . } :D \text{ sc } :E\}$, on which we perform the operation INSERT$\{:x \text{ a } :C, :D, :E.\}$, *explicitly* adding three triples, and subsequently perform DELETE$\{:x \text{ a } :C, :E.\}$, we obtain, according to the three semantics discussed so far, the following ABoxes:

$\mathbf{Sem}_0^{mat}$: $\{:x \text{ a } :D. :x \text{ a } :E.\}$ $\quad$ $\mathbf{Sem}_{1a}^{mat}$: $\{\}$

$\mathbf{Sem}_{1b}^{mat}$: $\{:x \text{ a } :D. :x \text{ a } :E.\}$

While after this update $\mathbf{Sem}_0^{mat}$ and $\mathbf{Sem}_{1b}^{mat}$ deliver the same result, the difference between these two is shown by the subsequent update DELETE$\{:x \text{ a } :D.\}$

$\mathbf{Sem}_0^{mat}$: $\{:x \text{ a } :E.\}$ $\quad$ $\mathbf{Sem}_{1a}^{mat}$: $\{\}$ $\quad$ $\mathbf{Sem}_{1b}^{mat}$: $\{\}$ $\quad$ ∎

As for the subtle difference between $\mathbf{Sem}_{1a}^{mat}$ and $\mathbf{Sem}_{1b}^{mat}$, we point out that none of [16, 26], who both refer to using DRed in the course of RDF updates, make it clear whether explicit and implicit ABox triples are to be treated differently.

Further, continuing with Ex. 5, the update from Ex. 4 still would not have *any* effect, neither using $\mathbf{Sem}_{1a}^{mat}$, nor $\mathbf{Sem}_{1b}^{mat}$. That is, it is not possible in any of these update semantics to remove implicit information (without explicitly removing all its causes).

$\mathbf{Sem}_2^{mat}$ aims at addressing this problem concerning the deletion of implicit information. As it turns out, while the intention of $\mathbf{Sem}_2^{mat}$ to delete causes of deletions cannot be captured just with the $mat$ operator, it can be achieved fairly straightforwardly, building upon ideas similar to those used in query rewriting.

As we have seen, in the setting of RDFS we can use Alg. 1 *rewrite* to expand a CQ to a UCQ that incorporates all its "causes". A slight variation can be used to compute the set of all causes, that is, in the most naïve fashion by just "flattening" the set of sets returned by Alg. 1 to a simple set; we denote this flattening operation on a set $S$ of sets as $flatten(S)$. Likewise, we can easily define a modified version of $mat(G)$, applied to a BGP $P$ using a TBox $\mathcal{T}$[9]. Let us call the resulting algorithm $mat_{eff}(P, \mathcal{T})$[10]. Using these considerations, we can thus define both rewritings that consider all causes, and rewritings that consider all effects of a given (insert or delete) pattern $P$:

**Definition 9 (Cause/Effect rewriting).** *Given a BGP insert or delete template $P$ for an update operation over the triple store $G = \mathcal{T} \cup \mathcal{A}$, we define the* all-causes-rewriting *of $P$ as $P^{caus} = flatten(rewrite(P, \mathcal{T}))$; likewise, we define the* all-effects-rewriting *of $P$ as $P^{eff} = mat_{eff}(P, \mathcal{T})$.*

This leads (almost) straightforwardly to a rewriting-based definition of $\mathbf{Sem}_2^{mat}$.

**Definition 10.** *Let $u(P_d, P_i, P_w)$ be an update operation. Then*

$$G_{u(P_d, P_i, P_w)}^{\mathbf{Sem}_2^{mat}} = G_{u(P_d^{caus}, P_i^{eff}, \{P_w\}\{P_d^{fvars}\})},$$

*where $P_d^{fvars} = \{?v \text{ a rdfs:Resource.} \mid \text{for each } ?v \in Var(P_d^{caus}) \setminus Var(P_d)\}$.*

The only tricky part in this definition is the rewriting of the WHERE clause, where $P_w$ is joined[11] with a new pattern $P_d^{fvars}$ that binds "free" variables (i.e., the "fresh" variables denoted by '_' in Table 2, introduced by Alg. 1, cf. Appendix) in the rewritten DELETE clause, $P_d^{caus}$. Here, $?v$ a rdfs:Resource. is a shortcut for a pattern which binds $?v$ to any term occurring in $G$, cf. Sec. 7 below for details.

*Example 7.* Getting back to the materialised version of the triple store $G$ from Ex. 3, the update $u$ from Ex. 4 would, according to $\mathbf{Sem}_2^{mat}$, be rewritten to

---

[9] This could be viewed as simply applying the first four inference rules in Fig. 1 exhaustively to $P \cup \mathcal{T}$, and then removing $\mathcal{T}$.

[10] Note that it is not our intention to provide optimised algorithms here, but just to convey the feasibility of this rewriting.

[11] A sequence of '{ }'-delimited patterns in SPARQL corresponds to a join, where such joins can again be nested with UNIONs, with the obvious semantics, for details cf. [12].

```
DELETE  {?X a :Child. ?X :hasF ?x1. ?X :hasM ?x2. ?X :hasP ?x3.}
INSERT  {?Y a :Mother. ?Y a :Parent. }
WHERE   {{?X :hasM ?Y.}    {?x1 a rdfs:Resource.
          ?x2 a rdfs:Resource.   ?x3 a rdfs:Resource.}}
```

with $G_u^{\mathbf{Sem}_2^{mat}}$ containing :jane a :Mother, :Parent. :jack a :Parent.    ∎

It is easy to argue that $\mathbf{Sem}_2^{mat}$ is mat-preserving. However, this semantics might still result in potentially non-intuitive behaviours. For instance, subsequent calls of INSERTs and DELETEs might leave "traces", as shown by the following example.

*Example 8.* Assume $G = O_{fam}$ from Ex. 1 with an empty ABox. Under $\mathbf{Sem}_2^{mat}$, the following sequence of updates would leave as a trace —among others— the resulting triples as in Ex. 7, which would not be the case under the naïve semantics.

```
DELETE{} INSERT {:joe :hasM :jane; :hasF :jack} WHERE{};
DELETE {:joe :hasM :jane; :hasF :jack} INSERT{} WHERE{}
```
   ∎

$\mathbf{Sem}_3^{mat}$ tries to address the issue of such "traces", but can no longer be formulated by a relatively straightforward rewriting. For the present, preliminary paper we leave out a detailed definition/implementation capturing the intention of $\mathbf{Sem}_3^{mat}$; there are two possible starting points, namely combining $\mathbf{Sem}_{1a}^{mat} + \mathbf{Sem}_2^{mat}$, or $\mathbf{Sem}_{1b}^{mat} + \mathbf{Sem}_2^{mat}$, respectively. We emphasise though, that independently of this choice, a semantics that achieves the intention of $\mathbf{Sem}_3^{mat}$ would still potentially run into arguable cases, since it might run into removing seemingly "disconnected" implicit assertions, whenever removed assertions cause these, as shown by the following example.

*Example 9.* Assume a materialised triple store $G$ consisting only of the TBox triples :Father sc :Person, :Male . The behaviour of the following update sequence under a semantics implementing the intention of $\mathbf{Sem}_3^{mat}$ is arguable:

```
DELETE {} INSERT {:x a :Father.} WHERE {};
DELETE {:x a :Male.} INSERT {} WHERE {}
```
We leave it open for now whether "recursive deletion of dangling effects" is intuitive: in this case, should upon deletion of $x$ being Male, also be deleted that $x$ is a Person?    ∎

In a strict reading of $\mathbf{Sem}_3^{mat}$'s intention, :x a :Person. would count as a dangling effect of the cause for :x a :Male., since it is an effect of the inserted triple with no other causes in the store, and thus should be removed upon the delete operation.

Lastly, we point out that while implementations of (materialised) triple stores may make a distinction between implicit and explicitly inserted triples (e.g., by storing explicit and implicit triples separately, as sketched in $\mathbf{Sem}_{1b}^{mat}$ already), we consider the distinction between implicit triples and explicitly inserted ones non-trivial in the context of SPARQL 1.1 Update: for instance, is a triple inserted based upon implicit bindings in the WHERE clause of an INSERT statement to be considered "explicitly inserted" or not? We tend towards avoiding such distinction, but we have more in-depth discussions of such philosophical aspects of possible SPARQL update semantics on our agenda. For now, we turn our attention to the potential alternatives for red-preserving semantics.

A. Ahmeti, D. Calvanese, and A. Polleres

## 5   Alternative Red-Preserving Semantics

Again, similar to $\mathbf{Sem}_3^{mat}$, for both baseline semantics $\mathbf{Sem}_0^{red}$ and $\mathbf{Sem}_1^{red}$ we leave
it open whether they can be implemented by rewriting to SPARQL update operations
following the naïve semantics, i.e., without the need to apply $red(G)$ over the whole
triple store after each update; a strategy to avoid calling $red(G)$ would roughly include
the following steps:
- delete the instantiations $P_d$ *plus all the effects of instantiations* of $P_i$, which will be
  implied anyway upon the new insertion, thus preserving reduced;
- insert instantiations of $P_i$ only if they are *not implied*, that is, they are not already
  implied by the current state of $G$ or all their causes in $G$ were to be deleted.

We leave further investigation of whether these steps can be cast into update requests
directly by rewriting techniques to future work. Rather, we show that we can capture
the intention of $\mathbf{Sem}_1^{red}$ by a straightforward extension of the baseline semantics.

**Definition 11** ($\mathbf{Sem}_1^{red}$). *Let* $u(P_d, P_i, P_w)$ *be an update operation. Then*

$$G_{u(P_d,P_i,P_w)}^{\mathbf{Sem}_1^{red}} = red(G_{u(P_d^{caus},P_i,\{rewrite(P_w)\}\{P_d^{fvars}\})}),$$

*where* $P_d^{caus}$ *and* $P_d^{fvars}$ *are as before.*

*Example 10.* Getting back to the reduced version of the triple store $G$ from Ex. 1, the
update $u$ from Ex. 4 would, according to $\mathbf{Sem}_1^{red}$, be rewritten to
```
DELETE { ?X a :Child. ?X :hasFather ?x1.
         ?X :hasMother ?x2. ?X :hasParent ?x3. }
INSERT { ?Y a :Mother. }
WHERE  { { ?X :hasMother ?Y. }
         { ?x1 a rdfs:Resource.
           ?x2 a rdfs:Resource.
           ?x3 a rdfs:Resource.} }
```
with $G_u^{\mathbf{Sem}_1^{red}}$ containing the triple :jane a :Mother.. Observe here the deletion of
the triple :joe :hasParent :jack., which some might view as non-intuitive.  ■

In a reduced store effects of $P_d$ need not be deleted, which makes the considerations
that lead us to $\mathbf{Sem}_3^{mat}$ irrelevant for a red-preserving semantics, as shown next.

*Example 11.* Under $\mathbf{Sem}_1^{red}$, as opposed to $\mathbf{Sem}_2^{mat}$, the update sequence of Ex. 8
would leave no traces. However, the update sequence of Ex. 9 would likewise result
in an empty ABox, again losing idempotence of single triple insertion followed by
deletion.  ■

Note that, while the rewriting for $\mathbf{Sem}_1^{red}$ is similar to that for $\mathbf{Sem}_2^{mat}$, post-processing
for preserving reducedness is not available in off-the-shelf triple stores. Instead,
$\mathbf{Sem}_2^{mat}$ could be readily executed by rewriting on existing triple stores, preserving
materialisation.

# 6   TBox Updates

So far, we have considered the TBox as static. As already noted in [11], additionally allowing TBox updates considerably complicates issues and opens additional degrees of freedom for possible semantics. While it is out of the scope of this paper to explore all of these, we limit ourselves to sketch these different degrees of freedom and suggest one pragmatic approach to extend updates expressed in SPARQL to RDFS TBoxes.

In order to allow for TBox updates, we have to extend the update language: in the following, we will assume *general BGPs*, extending Def. 2.

**Definition 12 (general BGP).** *A general BGP is a set of triples of any of the forms from Table 1, where* $x, y, A, A', P, P' \in \Gamma \cup \mathcal{V}$.

We observe that with this relaxation for BGPs, updates as per Def. 3 can query TBox data, since they admit TBox triples in $P_w$. In order to address this issue we need to also generalise the definition of query answers.[12]

**Definition 13.** *Let* $Q$ *be a union of general BGPs and* $[\![Q]\!]_G$ *the simple SPARQL semantics as per [21], i.e., essentially the set of query answers obtained as the union of answers from simple pattern matching of the general BGPs in* $Q$ *over the graph* $G$. *Then we define* $ans_{RDFS}(Q, G) = [\![Q]\!]_{mat(G)}$.

In fact, Def. 13 does not affect ABox inferences, that is, the following corollary follows immediately from Prop. 1 for non-general UCQs as per Def. 2.

**Corollary 1.** *Let* $Q$ *be a UCQ as per Def. 2. Then* $ans_{RDFS}(Q, G) = ans_{rdfs}(Q, G)$.

As opposed to the setting discussed so far, where the last two rules in Fig. 1 used for TBox materialisation were ignored, we now focus on the discussion of terminological updates under the standard "intensional" semantics (essentially defined by the inference rules in Fig. 1) and attempt to define a reasonable (that means computable) semantics under this setting. Note that upon terminological queries, the RDFS semantics and DL semantics differ, since this "intensional" semantics does not cover all terminological inferences derivable in DL, cf. [7]; we leave the details of this aspect to future work.

*Observation 1.* TBox updates potentially affect both materialisation and reducedness of the ABox, that is, *(i)* upon TBox *insertions* a materialised ABox might need to be re-materialised in order to preserve materialisation, and, respectively, a reduced ABox might no longer be reduced; *(ii)* upon TBox *deletions* in a materialised setting, we have a similar issue to what we called "dangling" effects earlier, whereas in a reduced setting indirect deletions of implied triples could cause unintuitive behaviour.

*Observation 2.* Whereas deletions of implicit ABox triples can be achieved deterministically by deleting all single causes, TBox deletions involving sc  and sp  chains can be achieved in several distinct ways, as already observed by [11].

*Example 12.* Consider the graph $G = \{:A \text{ sc } :B. \ :B \text{ sc } :C. \ :B \text{ sc } :D.$ $:C \text{ sc } :E. \ :D \text{ sc } :E. \ :E \text{ sc } :F.\}$ with the update DELETE{:A sc :F.}

Independent of whether we assume a materialised TBox, we would have various choices here to remove triples, to delete all the causes for :A  sc  :F.            ∎

---

[12] As mentioned in Fn. 5, elements of $\Gamma$ may act as individuals, concept, or roles names in parallel.

In order to define a deterministic semantics for TBox updates, we need a canonical way to delete implicit and explicit TBox triples. Minimal cuts are suggested in [11] in the sc (or sp , resp.) graphs as candidates for deletions of sc (or sp , resp.) triples. However, as easily verified by Ex. 12, minimal multicuts are still ambiguous.

Here, we suggest two update semantics using rewritings to SPARQL 1.1 property path patterns [12] that yield canonical minimal cuts.

**Definition 14.** *Let* $u(P_d, P_i, P_w)$ *be an update operation where* $P_d, P_i, P_w$ *are general BGPs. Then*

$$G^{\mathbf{Sem}^{mat}_{outcut}}_{u(P_d,P_i,P_w)} = mat(G_{u(P'_d,P_i,P'_w)}),$$

*where each triple* $\{A_1 \; scp \; A_2\} \in P_d$ *such that* $scp \in \{\mathsf{sc}, \mathsf{sp}\}$ *is replaced within* $P'_d$ *by* $\{A_1 \; scp \; ?x.\}$, *and we add to* $P'_w$ *the property path pattern* $\{A_1 \; scp \; ?x. \; ?x \; scp^* \; A_2\}$. *Analogously,* $\mathbf{Sem}^{mat}_{incut}$ *is defined by replacing* $\{?x \; scp \; A_2\}$ *within* $P'_d$, *and adding* $\{A_1 \; scp^* \; ?x. \; ?x \; scp \; A_2\}$ *within* $P'_w$ *instead.*

Both $\mathbf{Sem}^{mat}_{outcut}$ and $\mathbf{Sem}^{mat}_{incut}$ may be viewed as straightforward extensions of $\mathbf{Sem}^{mat}_0$, i.e., both are mat-preserving and equivalent to the baseline semantics for non-general BGPs (i.e., on ABox updates):

**Proposition 3.** *Let* $u(P_d, P_i, P_w)$ *be an update operation, where* $P_d, P_i, P_w$ *are (non-general) BGPs. Then*

$$G^{\mathbf{Sem}^{mat}_{outcut}}_{u(P_d,P_i,P_w)} = G^{\mathbf{Sem}^{mat}_{incut}}_{u(P_d,P_i,P_w)} = G^{\mathbf{Sem}^{mat}_0}_{u(P_d,P_i,P_w)}.$$

The intuition behind the rewriting in $\mathbf{Sem}^{mat}_{outcut}$ is to delete for every deleted $A \; scp \; B$. triple, all directly outgoing $scp$ edges from $A$ that lead into paths to $B$, or, resp., in $\mathbf{Sem}^{mat}_{incut}$ all directly incoming edges to $B$. The intuition to choose these canonical minimal cuts is motivated by the following proposition.

**Proposition 4.** *Let* $u = \mathtt{DELETE} \; \{A \; scp \; B\}$, *and* $G$ *a triple store with materialised TBox* $\mathcal{T}$. *Then, the TBox statements deleted by* $G^{\mathbf{Sem}^{mat}_{outcut}}_{u(P_d,P_i,P_w)}$ *(or,* $G^{\mathbf{Sem}^{mat}_{incut}}_{u(P_d,P_i,P_w)}$, *resp.) form a minimal cut [11] of* $\mathcal{T}$ *disconnecting* $A$ *and* $B$.

*Proof (Sketch).* In a materialised TBox, one can reach $B$ from $A$ either directly or via $n$ direct neighbours $C_i \neq B$, which (in)directly connect to $B$. So, a minimal cut contains either the multicut between $A$ and the $C_i$s, or between the $C_i$s and $B$; the latter multicut requires at least the same amount of edges to be deleted as the former, which in turn corresponds to the outbound cut. This proves the claim for $\mathbf{Sem}^{mat}_{outcut}$. We can proceed analogously for $\mathbf{Sem}^{mat}_{incut}$. □

The following example illustrates that the generalisation of Prop. 4 to updates involving the deletion of several TBox statements at once does not hold.

*Example 13.* Assume the materialised triple store $G = \{ :\mathtt{A} \; scp \; :\mathtt{B}, :\mathtt{C}, :\mathtt{D}. \; :\mathtt{B} \; scp \; :\mathtt{C}, \; :\mathtt{D}. \}$ and $u = \mathtt{DELETE}\{:\mathtt{A} \; scp \; :\mathtt{C}. \; :\mathtt{A} \; scp \; :\mathtt{D}.\}$. Here, $\mathbf{Sem}^{mat}_{incut}$ does not yield a minimal *multicut* in $G$ wrt disconnecting $(:\mathtt{A}, :\mathtt{C})$ and $(:\mathtt{A}, :\mathtt{D})$.[13]   ∎

As the example shows, the extension of the baseline ABox update semantics to TBox updates already yields new degrees of freedom. We leave a more in-depth discussion of TBox updates also extending the other semantics from Sec. 3 for future work.

---

[13] We can give an analogous example where $\mathbf{Sem}^{mat}_{outcut}$ does not yield a minimal multicut.

# 7   Prototype and Experiments

We have implemented the different update semantics discussed above in Jena TDB[14] as a triple store that both implements the latest SPARQL 1.1 specification and supports rule based materialisation: our focus here was to use an existing store that allows us to implement the different semantics with its on-board features; that is, for computing $mat(G)$ we use the on-board, forward-chaining materialisation in Jena.[15]

We have implemented all the above-mentioned mat-preserving semantics, with two concrete variants of $P_d^{fvars}$. In the first variant, we replace $?v$ a rdfs:Resource by {{$?v$ $?v_p$ $?v_o$} UNION {$?v_s$ $?v$ $?v_o$} UNION {$?v_s$ $?v_p$ $?v$}}, to achieve a pattern that binds $?v$ to every possible term in $G$. This is not very efficient. In fact, note that $P_d^{fvars}$ is needed just to bind free variables $?v$ (corresponding to '_' in Table 2) in patterns $P_{?v}$ of the form $P(x, ?v)$ or $P(?v, x)$ in the rewritten DELETE clause. Thus, we can equally use $P_d^{fvars'} = \{\text{OPTIONAL}\{\bigcup_{?v \in Var(P_d^{caus}) \setminus Var(P_d)} P_{?v}\}$. We denote implementations using the latter variant $\mathbf{Sem}_{2'}^{mat}$ and $\mathbf{Sem}_{1'}^{red}$, respectively.

As for reduced semantics, remarkably, for the restricted set of ABox rules in Fig. 1 and assuming an acyclic TBox, we can actually compute $red(G)$ also by "on-board" means of SPARQL 1.1 compliant triple-stores, namely by using SPARQL 1.1 Update in combination with SPARQL 1.1 property paths [12, Section 9] with the following update:

```
DELETE  { ?S1 a ?D1. ?S2 a ?C2. ?S3 ?Q3 ?O3. ?O4 a ?C4. }
WHERE   {{ ?C1 sc+ ?D1. ?S1 a ?C1. }
  UNION { ?P2 dom/sc* ?C2. ?S2 ?P2 ?O2. }
  UNION { ?P3 sp+ ?Q3. ?S3 ?P3 ?O3. }
  UNION { ?P4 rng/sc* ?C4. ?S4 ?P4 ?O4. }}
```

We emphasise that performance results should be understood as providing a general indication of feasibility of implementing these semantics in existing stores rather than actual benchmarking: on the one hand, the different semantics are not comparable in terms of performance benchmarking, since they provide different results; on the other hand, for instance, we only use naive re-materialisation provided by the triple store in our prototype, instead of optimised versions of DRed, such as [26].

For initial experiments we have used data generated by the LUBM generator for 5, 10 and 15 Universities, which correspond to different ABox sizes merged together with an RDFS version of the LUBM ontology as TBox; this version of LUBM has no complex restrictions on roles, no transitive roles, no inverse roles, and no equality axioms, and axioms of type $A \sqsubseteq B \sqcap C$ are split into two axioms $A \sqsubseteq B$ and $A \sqsubseteq C$. Besides, we have designed a set of 7 different ABox updates in order to compare the proposed mat-preserving and red-preserving semantics. Both our prototype, as well as files containing the data, ontology, and the updates used for experiments are available on a dedicated Web page.[16]

We first compared, for each update semantics, the time elapsed for rewriting and executing the update. Secondly, in order to compare mat-preserving and red-preserving semantics, we also need to take into account that red-preserving semantics imply

---

[14] http://jena.apache.org/documentation/tdb/

[15] http://jena.apache.org/documentation/inference/

[16] http://dbai.tuwien.ac.at/user/ahmeti/sparqlupdate-rewriter/

additional effort on subsequent querying, since rewriting is required (cf. Prop. 1). In order to reflect this, we also measured the aggregated times for executing an update and subsequently processing the standard 14 LUBM benchmark queries in sequence.

Details of the results can be found on the above-mentioned Web page, we only provide a brief summary here: In general, among the mat-preserving semantics, the semantics implementable in terms of rewriting ($\mathbf{Sem}_2^{mat}$) perform better than those that need rematerialisation ($\mathbf{Sem}_{1a,b}^{mat}$), as could be expected. There might be potential for improvement here on the latter, when using tailored implementaions of DRed. Also, for both mat-preserving ($\mathbf{Sem}_{2'}^{mat}$) and red-preserving ($\mathbf{Sem}_{1'}^{red}$) semantics that rely on rewritings for deleting causes, the optimisation of using variant $P_d^{fvars'}$ instead of $P_d^{fvars}$ paid off for our queries. As for a comparison between mat-preserving vs. red-preserving, in our experiments re-reduction upon updates seems quite affordable, whereas the additionally needed query rewriting for subsequent query answering does not add dramatic costs. Thus, we believe that, depending on the use case, keeping reduced stores upon updates is a feasible and potentially useful strategy, particularly since – as shown above – $red(G)$ can be implemented with off-the-shelf feratures of SPARQL 1.1.

While further optimisations, and implementations in different triple stores remain on our agenda, the experiments confirm our expectations so far.

## 8    Further Related Work and Possible Future Directions

Previous work on updates in the context of tractable ontology languages such as RDFS [11] and *DL-Lite* [5] typically has treated DELETEs and INSERTs in isolation, but not both at the same time nor in combination with templates filled by WHERE clauses, as in SPARQL 1.1; that is, these approaches are not based on BGP matching but rather on a set of ABox assertions to be updated, known a priori. Pairing both DELETE and INSERT, as in our case, poses new challenges, which we tried to address here in the practically relevant context of both materialised and reduced triple stores. In the future, we plan to extend our work in the context of *DL-Lite*, where we could build upon thoroughly studied query rewriting techniques (not necessarily relying on materialisation), and at the same time benefit from a more expressive ontology language. Expanding beyond our simple minimal RDFS language towards more features of *DL-Lite* or coverage of unrestricted RDF graphs would impose new challenges: for instance, consistency checking and consistency-preserving updates (as those treated in [5]), which do not yet play a role in the setting of RDFS, would become relevant; extensions in these directions, as well as practically evaluating the proposed semantics on existing triple stores is on our agenda.

As for further related works, in the context of reduced stores, we refer to [22], where the cost of redundancy elimination under various (rule-based) entailment regimes, including RDFS, is discussed in detail. In the area of database theory, there has been a lot of work on updating logical databases: Winslett [28] distinguishes between model-based and formula-based updates. Our approach clearly falls in the latter category; more concretely, ABox updates could be viewed as sets of propositional knowledge base updates [14] generated by SPARQL instantiating DELETE/INSERT templates. Let us further note that in the more applied area of databases, there are obvious parallels between some of our considerations and CASCADE DELETEs in SQL (that is, deletions under foreign key constraints), in the sense that we trigger additional deletions of causes/effects in some of the proposed update semantics discussed herein.

# 9    Conclusions

We have presented possible semantics of SPARQL 1.1 Update in the context of RDFS. To the best of our knowledge, this is the first work to discuss how to combine RDFS with the new SPARQL 1.1 Update language. While we have been operating on a very restricted setting (only capturing minimal RDFS entailments, restricting BGPs to disallow non-standard use of the RDFS vocabulary), we could demonstrate that even in this setting the definition of a SPARQL 1.1 Update semantics under entailments is a non-trivial task. We proposed several possible semantics, neither of which might seem intuitive for all possible use cases; this suggests that there is no "one-size-fits-all" update semantics. Further, while ontologies should be "ready for evolution" [20], we believe that more work into semantics for updates of ontologies alongside with data (TBox & ABox) is still needed to ground research in *Ontology Evolution* into standards (SPARQL, RDF, RDFS, OWL), particularly in the light of the emerging importance of RDF and SPARQL in domains where data is continuously updated (dealing with dynamics in Linked Data, querying sensor data, or stream reasoning). We have taken a first step in this paper.

**Acknowledgments.** This work has been funded by WWTF (project ICT12-015), by the Vienna PhD School of Informatics, and by EU Project Optique (grant n. FP7-318338).

# References

1. Ahmeti, A., Calvanese, D., Polleres, A.: Updating RDFS ABoxes and TBoxes in SPARQL. CoRR Tech. Rep. arXiv:1403.7248 (2014), http://arxiv.org/abs/1403.7248
2. Beckett, D., Berners-Lee, T., Prud'hommeaux, E., Carothers, G.: RDF 1.1 Turtle – Terse RDF Triple Language. W3C Rec. (February 2014)
3. Bishop, B., Kiryakov, A., Ognyanoff, D., Peikov, I., Tashev, Z., Velkov, R.: OWLIM: A family of scalable semantic repositories. Semantic Web J. 2(1), 33–42 (2011)
4. Calvanese, D., De Giacomo, G., Lembo, D., Lenzerini, M., Rosati, R.: Tractable reasoning and efficient query answering in description logics: The *DL-Lite* family. J. of Automated Reasoning 39(3), 385–429 (2007)
5. Calvanese, D., Kharlamov, E., Nutt, W., Zheleznyakov, D.: Evolution of *DL-Lite* knowledge bases. In: Patel-Schneider, P.F., Pan, Y., Hitzler, P., Mika, P., Zhang, L., Pan, J.Z., Horrocks, I., Glimm, B. (eds.) ISWC 2010, Part I. LNCS, vol. 6496, pp. 112–128. Springer, Heidelberg (2010)
6. Ceri, S., Widom, J.: Deriving incremental production rules for deductive data. Information Systems 19(6), 467–490 (1994)
7. Franconi, E., Gutierrez, C., Mosca, A., Pirrò, G., Rosati, R.: The logic of extensional RDFS. In: Alani, H., et al. (eds.) ISWC 2013, Part I. LNCS, vol. 8218, pp. 101–116. Springer, Heidelberg (2013)
8. Gearon, P., Passant, A., Polleres, A.: SPARQL 1.1 Update. W3C Rec. (March 2013)
9. Glimm, B., Ogbuji, C.: SPARQL 1.1 Entailment Regimes. W3C Rec. (March 2013)
10. Gupta, A., Mumick, I.S., Subrahmanian, V.S.: Maintaining views incrementally. In: Proc. of ACM SIGMOD, pp. 157–166 (1993)
11. Gutierrez, C., Hurtado, C., Vaisman, A.: RDFS update: From theory to practice. In: Antoniou, G., Grobelnik, M., Simperl, E., Parsia, B., Plexousakis, D., De Leenheer, P., Pan, J. (eds.) ESWC 2011, Part II. LNCS, vol. 6644, pp. 93–107. Springer, Heidelberg (2011)
12. Harris, S., Seaborne, A.: SPARQL 1.1 Query Language. W3C Rec. (March 2013)
13. Hayes, P.: RDF Semantics. W3C Rec. (February 2004)
14. Katsuno, H., Mendelzon, A.O.: A unified view of propositional knowledge base updates. In: Proc. of IJCAI, pp. 1413–1419 (1989)

15. Kontchakov, R., Rodríguez-Muro, M., Zakharyaschev, M.: Ontology-based data access with databases: A short course. In: Rudolph, S., Gottlob, G., Horrocks, I., van Harmelen, F. (eds.) Reasoning Weg 2013. LNCS, vol. 8067, pp. 194–229. Springer, Heidelberg (2013)

16. Kotowski, J., Bry, F., Brodt, S.: Reasoning as axioms change - Incremental view maintenance reconsidered. In: Rudolph, S., Gutierrez, C. (eds.) RR 2011. LNCS, vol. 6902, pp. 139–154. Springer, Heidelberg (2011)

17. Mallea, A., Arenas, M., Hogan, A., Polleres, A.: On blank nodes. In: Aroyo, L., Welty, C., Alani, H., Taylor, J., Bernstein, A., Kagal, L., Noy, N., Blomqvist, E. (eds.) ISWC 2011, Part I. LNCS, vol. 7031, pp. 421–437. Springer, Heidelberg (2011)

18. Motik, B.: On the properties of metamodeling in OWL. J. of Logic and Computation 17(4), 617–637 (2007)

19. Muñoz, S., Pérez, J., Gutierrez, C.: Minimal deductive systems for RDF. In: Franconi, E., Kifer, M., May, W. (eds.) ESWC 2007. LNCS, vol. 4519, pp. 53–67. Springer, Heidelberg (2007)

20. Noy, N.F., Klein, M.C.A.: Ontology evolution: Not the same as schema evolution. Knowledge and Information Systems 6(4), 428–440 (2004)

21. Pérez, J., Arenas, M., Gutierrez, C.: Semantics and complexity of SPARQL. ACM Trans. on Database Systems 34(3), 16:1–16:45 (2009)

22. Pichler, R., Polleres, A., Skritek, S., Woltran, S.: Complexity of redundancy detection on RDF graphs in the presence of rules, constraints, and queries. Semantic Web J. 4(4) (2013)

23. Polleres, A., Hogan, A., Delbru, R., Umbrich, J.: RDFS and OWL reasoning for linked data. In: Rudolph, S., Gottlob, G., Horrocks, I., van Harmelen, F. (eds.) Reasoning Weg 2013. LNCS, vol. 8067, pp. 91–149. Springer, Heidelberg (2013)

24. Prud'hommeaux, E., Seaborne, A.: SPARQL Query Language for RDF. W3C Rec. (January 2008)

25. Ullman, J.D.: Principles of Database and Knowledge-Base Systems, vol. 1. Computer Science Press (1988)

26. Urbani, J., Margara, A., Jacobs, C., van Harmelen, F., Bal, H.: DynamiTE: Parallel materialization of dynamic RDF data. In: Alani, H., et al. (eds.) ISWC 2013, Part I. LNCS, vol. 8218, pp. 657–672. Springer, Heidelberg (2013)

27. Volz, R., Staab, S., Motik, B.: Incrementally maintaining materializations of ontologies stored in logic databases. In: Spaccapietra, S., Bertino, E., Jajodia, S., King, R., McLeod, D., Orlowska, M.E., Strous, L. (eds.) Journal on Data Semantics II. LNCS, vol. 3360, pp. 1–34. Springer, Heidelberg (2005)

28. Winslett, M.: Updating Logical Databases. Cambridge University Press (2005)

## Appendix

---

**Algorithm 1:** $rewrite(q, \mathcal{T})$

---

**Input**: Conjunctive query $q$, TBox $\mathcal{T}$
**Output**: Union (set) of conjunctive queries

```
1  P := {q}
2  repeat
3      P' := P
4      foreach q ∈ P' do
5          foreach g in q do    // expansion
6              foreach inclusion assertion I in T do
7                  if I is applicable to g then
8                      P := P ∪ {q[g/ gr(g, I)]}
9  until P' = P
10 return P
```

**Table 2.** Semantics of $\mathrm{gr}(g, I)$ in Alg.1

| $g$ | $I$ | $\mathrm{gr}(g/I)$ |
|---|---|---|
| $A(x)$ | $A' \sqsubseteq A$ | $A'(x)$ |
| $A(x)$ | $\exists P \sqsubseteq A$ | $P(x, \_)$ |
| $A(x)$ | $\exists P^- \sqsubseteq A$ | $P(\_, x)$ |
| $P_1(x, y)$ | $P_2 \sqsubseteq P_1$ | $P_2(x, y)$ |

Here, '$\_$' stands for a "fresh" variable.

# AGDISTIS - Graph-Based Disambiguation of Named Entities Using Linked Data

Ricardo Usbeck[1,2], Axel-Cyrille Ngonga Ngomo[1], Michael Röder[1,2],
Daniel Gerber[1], Sandro Athaide Coelho[3], Sören Auer[4], and Andreas Both[2]

[1] University of Leipzig, Germany
[2] R & D, Unister GmbH, Germany
[3] Federal University of Juiz de Fora, Brazil
[4] University of Bonn & Fraunhofer IAIS, Germany
{usbeck,ngonga}@informatik.uni-leipzig.de

**Abstract.** Over the last decades, several billion Web pages have been made available on the Web. The ongoing transition from the current Web of unstructured data to the Web of Data yet requires scalable and accurate approaches for the extraction of structured data in RDF (Resource Description Framework) from these websites. One of the key steps towards extracting RDF from text is the disambiguation of named entities. While several approaches aim to tackle this problem, they still achieve poor accuracy. We address this drawback by presenting AGDISTIS, a novel knowledge-base-agnostic approach for named entity disambiguation. Our approach combines the Hypertext-Induced Topic Search (HITS) algorithm with label expansion strategies and string similarity measures. Based on this combination, AGDISTIS can efficiently detect the correct URIs for a given set of named entities within an input text. We evaluate our approach on eight different datasets against state-of-the-art named entity disambiguation frameworks. Our results indicate that we outperform the state-of-the-art approach by up to 29% F-measure.

## 1 Introduction

The vision behind the Web of Data is to provide a new machine-readable layer to the Web where the content of Web pages is annotated with structured data (e.g., RDFa [1]). However, the Web in its current form is made up of at least 15 billion Web pages.[1] Most of these websites are unstructured in nature. Realizing the vision of a usable and up-to-date Web of Data thus requires scalable and accurate natural-language-processing approaches that allow extracting RDF from such unstructured data. Three tasks play a central role when extracting RDF from unstructured data: named entity recognition (NER), named entity disambiguation (NED), also known as entity linking [16], and relation extraction (RE). For the first sentence of Example 1, an accurate named entity recognition approach would return the strings Barack Obama and Washington,

---

[1] Data gathered from http://www.worldwidewebsize.com/ on January 4th, 2014.

P. Mika et al. (Eds.) ISWC 2014, Part I, LNCS 8796, pp. 457–471, 2014.

D.C.. A high-quality DBpedia-based named entity disambiguation (NED) approach would use these already recognized named entities and map the strings `Barack Obama` resp. `Washington, D.C.` to the resources `dbr:Barack_Obama` and `dbr:Washington,_D.C.`[2] [14].

---

**Example 1.** *Barack Obama arrived this afternoon in Washington, D.C.. President Obama's wife Michelle accompanied him.*

---

While NER has been explored extensively over the last decades [7], the disambiguation of named entities, i.e., the assignment of a resource's URI from an existing knowledge base to a string that was detected to label an entity remains a difficult task.

Current NED approaches suffer from two major drawbacks: First, they poorly perform on Web documents [20]. This is due to Web documents containing resources from different domains within a narrow context. An accurate processing of Web data has yet been shown to be paramount for the implementation of the Web of Data [8]. Well-know approaches such as *Spotlight* [15] and *TagMe 2* [6] have been designed to work on a particular knowledge base. However, Web data contains resources from many different domains. Hence, we argue that NED approaches have to be designed in such a way that they are agnostic of the underlying knowledge base. Second, most state-of-the-art approaches rely on exhaustive data mining methods [4,21] or algorithms with non-polynomial time complexity [11]. However, given the large number of entities that must be disambiguated when processing Web documents, scalable NED approaches are of central importance to realize the Semantic Web vision.

In this paper, we address these drawbacks by presenting AGDISTIS, a novel NED approach and framework. AGDISTIS achieves *higher F-measures* than the state of the art while remaining *polynomial in its time complexity*. AGDISTIS achieves these results by combining the HITS algorithm [12] with label expansion and string similarity measures. Overall, our contributions can be summed up as follows: (1) We present AGDISTIS, an accurate and scalable framework for disambiguating named entities that is agnostic to the underlying knowledge base (KB) and show that we are able to outperform the state of the art by up to 29% F-measure on these datasets. (2) We show that our approach has a quadratic time complexity. Thus, it scales well enough to be used even on large knowledge bases. (3) We evaluate AGDISTIS on eight *well-known and diverse open-source datasets.*[3]

The rest of this paper is organized as follows: We first give a brief overview of related work in Section 2. Then, we introduce the AGDISTIS approach in Section 3. After presenting the datasets, we evaluate our approach against the state of the art frameworks AIDA and TagMe 2 and the well-known DBpedia Spotlight. Furthermore, we measure the influence of using surface forms, i.e.,

---

[2] `dbr:` stands for `http://dbpedia.org/resource/`

[3] Further data, detailed experimental results and source code for this paper are publicly available on our project homepage `http://aksw.org/Projects/AGDISTIS`

synonymous label for a specific resource, in Section 4. We conclude in Section 5 by highlighting research questions that emerged from this work. A demo of our approach (integrated into the Named Entity Recognition framework FOX [25]) can be found at `http://fox.aksw.org`.

## 2   Related Work

AGDISTIS is related to the research area of Information Extraction [19] in general and to NED in particular. Several approaches have been developed to tackle NED. Cucerzan presents an approach based on extracted Wikipedia data towards disambiguation of named entities [4]. The author aims to maximize the agreement between contextual information of Wikipedia pages and the input text by using a local approach. *Epiphany* [2] identifies, disambiguates and annotates entities in a given HTML page with RDFa. Ratinov et al. [21] described an approach for disambiguating entities from Wikipedia KB. The authors argue that using Wikipedia or other ontologies can lead to better global approaches than using traditional local algorithms which disambiguate each mention separately using, e.g., text similarity. Kleb et al. [11,10] developed and improved an approach using ontologies to mainly identify geographical entities but also people and organizations in an extended version. These approaches use Wikipedia and other Linked Data KBs. LINDEN [23] is an entity linking framework that aims at linking identified named entities to a knowledge base. To achieve this goal, LINDEN collects a dictionary of the surface forms of entities from different Wikipedia sources, storing their count information.

Wikipedia Miner [17] is the oldest approach in the field of *wikification*. Based on different machine learning algorithms, the systems disambiguates w.r.t. prior probabilities, relatedness of concepts in a certain window and context quality. The authors evaluated their approach based on a Wikipedia as well as an AQUAINT subset. Unfortunately, the authors do not use the opportunities provided by Linked Data like DBpedia.

Using this data the approach constructs candidate lists and assigns link probabilities and global coherence for each resource candidate. The AIDA approach [9] for NED tasks is based on the YAGO2[4] knowledge base and relies on sophisticated graph algorithms. Specifically, this approach uses dense sub-graphs to identify coherent mentions using a greedy algorithm enabling Web scalability. Additionally, AIDA disambiguates w.r.t. similarity of contexts, prominence of entities and context windows.

Another approach is DBpedia Spotlight [15], a framework for annotating and disambiguating Linked Data Resources in arbitrary texts. In contrast to other tools, Spotlight is able to disambiguate against all classes of the DBpedia ontology. Furthermore, it is well-known in the Linked Data community and used in various projects showing its wide-spread adoption.[5] Based on a vector-space

---

[4] `http://www.mpi-inf.mpg.de/yago-naga/yago/`

[5] `https://github.com/dbpedia-spotlight/dbpedia-spotlight/wiki/Known-uses`

model and cosine similarity DBpedia Spotlight is publicly available via a web service[6].

In 2012, Ferragina et al. published a revised version of their disambiguation system called TagMe 2. The authors claim that it is tuned towards smaller texts, i.e., comprising around 30 terms. TagMe 2 is based on an anchor catolog (`<a>` tags on Wikipedia pages with a certain frequency), a page catalogue (comprising all original Wikipedia pages, i.e., no disambiguations, lists or redirects) and an in-link graph (all links to a certain page within Wikipedia). First, TagMe 2 identifies named entities by matching terms with the anchor catalog and second disambiguates the match using the in-link graph and the page catalog via a collective agreement of identified anchors. Last, the approach discards identified named entities considered as non-coherent to the rest of the named entities in the input text.

In 2014, Babelfy [18] has been presented to the community. Based on random walks and densest subgraph algorithms Babelfy tackles NED and is evaluated with six datasets, one of them the later here used AIDA dataset. In constrast to AGDISTIS, Babelfy differentiates between word sense disambiguation, i.e., resolution of polysemous lexicographic entities like *play*, and entity linking, i.e., matching strings or substrings to knowledge base resources. Due to its recent publication Babelfy is not evaluated in this paper.

Recently, Cornolti et al. [3] presented a benchmark for NED approaches. The authors compared six existing approaches, also using DBpedia Spotlight, AIDA and TagMe 2, against five well-known datasets. Furthermore, the authors defined different classes of named entity annotation task, e.g. *'D2W'*, that is the disambiguation to Wikipedia task which is the formal task AGDISITS tries to solve. We consider TagMe 2 as state of the art w.r.t. this benchmark although only one dataset has been considered for this specific task. We analyze the performance of DBpedia Spotlight, AIDA, TagMe 2 and our approach AGDISTIS on four of the corpora from this benchmark in Section 4.

# 3 The AGDISTIS Approach

## 3.1 Named Entity Disambiguation

The goal of AGDISTIS is to detect correct resources from a KB $K$ for a vector $N$ of $n$ a-priori determined named entities $N_1, \ldots, N_n$ extracted from a certain input text $T$. In general, several resources from a given knowledge base $K$ can be considered as candidate resources for a given entity $N_i$. For the sake of simplicity and without loss of generality, we will assume that each of the entities can be mapped to $m$ distinct candidate resources. Let $C$ be the matrix which contains all candidate-entity mappings for a given set of entities. The entry $C_{ij}$ stands for the $j^{th}$ candidate resource for the $i^{th}$ named entity. Let $\mu$ be a family of functions which maps each entity $N_i$ to exactly one candidate $C_{ij}$. We call such

---

[6] https://github.com/dbpedia-spotlight/dbpedia-spotlight/wiki/Web-service

functions *assignments*. The output of an assignment is a vector of resources of length $|N|$ that is such that the $i^{th}$ entry of the vector maps with $N_i$.

Let $\psi$ be a function which computes the similarity between an assignment $\mu(C, N)$ and the vector of named entities $N$. The *coherence* function $\phi$ calculates the similarity of the knowledge base $K$ and an assignment $\mu$, cf. Ratinov et al. [21], to ensure the topical consistency of $\mu$. The coherence function $\phi$ is implemented by the HITS algorithm, which calculates the most pertinent entities while the similarity function $\psi$ is, e.g., string similarity. Given this formal model, the goal is to find the assignment $\mu^\star$ with

$$\mu^\star = \arg\max_{\mu} \left( \psi(\mu(C, N), N) + \phi(\mu(C, N), K) \right).$$

The formulation of the problem given above has been proven to be NP-hard, cf. Cucerzan et al. [4]. Thus, for the sake of scalability, AGDISTIS computes an approximation $\mu^+$ by using HITS, a fast graph algorithm which runs with an upper bound of $\Theta(k \cdot |V|^2)$ with $k$ the number of iterations and $|V|$ the number of nodes in the graph. Furthermore, using HITS leverages 1) scalability, 2) well-researched behaviour and 3) the ability to explicate semantic authority.

### 3.2 Architecture

Our approach to NED thus consists of three main phases as depicted in Figure 1. Given an input text $T$ and a named entity recognition function (e.g., FOX [25]), we begin by retrieving all named entities from the input text. Thereafter, we aim to detect candidates for each of the detected named entities. To this end, we apply several heuristics and make use of known surface forms [15] for resources from the underlying KB. The set of candidates generated by the first step is used to generate a disambiguation graph. Here, we rely on a graph search algorithm which retrieves context information from the underlying KB. Finally, we employ the HITS algorithm to the context graph to find authoritative candidates for the discovered named entities. We assume that the resources with the highest authority values represent the correct candidates. All algorithms in AGDISTIS have a polynomial time complexity, leading to AGDISTIS also being polynomial in time complexity. Choosing candidates relates to the notion of $\phi$ while calculating the authority values confers to $\psi$. In the following, we present each of the steps of AGDISTIS in more detail.

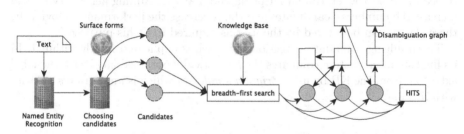

**Fig. 1.** Overview of AGDISTIS

## 3.3  Candidate Detection

In order to find the correct disambiguation for a certain set of named entities, we first need to detect candidate resources in the KB. We begin by creating an index comprising all labels of each resource. Our approach can be configured to use any set of properties as labeling properties (e.g., those in Ell et al. [5]). For our experiments, we only considered `rdfs:label` as labeling property. In addition, our approach can make use of known *surface forms* for each of the resources in case such knowledge is available [15]. These are simply strings that are used on the Web to refer to given resources. Surface forms are simply added to the set of available labels for each resource, cf. Section 4.1. In this paper, we do not consider abbreviations although these could be easily regarded by adding further labels into the KB (e.g., via WordNet[7]).

Next to searching the index we apply a *string normalization* approach and an *expansion policy* to the input text: The string normalization is based on eliminating plural and genitive forms, removing common affixes such as postfixes for enterprise labels and ignoring candidates with time information (years, dates, etc.) within their label. For example, the genitive `New York's` is transformed into `New York`, the postfix of `Microsoft Ltd.` is reduced to `Microsoft` and the time information of `London 2013` is ignored. Our *expansion policy* is a time-efficient approach to coreference resolution, which plays a central role when dealing with text from the Web, cf. Singh et al. [24]. In web and news documents, named entities are commonly mentioned in their full length the first time they appear, while the subsequent mentions only consist of a substring of the original mention due to the brevity of most news data. For example, a text mentioning Barack Obama's arrival in Washington D.C. will commonly contain `Barack Obama` in the first mention of the entity and use strings such as `Obama` or `Barack` later in the same text (see Example 1). We implement this insight by mapping each named entity label (e.g., `Obama`) which is a substring of another named entity label that was recognized previously (e.g., `Barack Obama`) to the same resource , i.e., `dbr:Barack_Obama`. If there are several possible expansions, we choose the shortest as a fast coreference resolution heuristic for web documents. Without the expansion policy AGDISTIS suffers from a loss of accuracy of ≈ 4%.

Additionally, AGDISTIS can be configured to fit named entities to certain domains to narrow the search space. Since our goal is to disambiguate persons, organizations and places, AGDISTIS only allows candidates of the types mentioned in Table 1 when run on DBpedia and YAGO2. Adding general types will increase the number of candidates and thus decrease the performance. Obviously, these classes can be altered by the user as required to fit his purposes.

The resulting candidate detection approach is explicated in Algorithm 1. In its final step, our system compares the heuristically obtained label with the label extracted from the KB by using *trigram similarity* which is an n-gram similarity with $n = 3$.

---

[7] http://wordnet.princeton.edu/

**Table 1.** DBpedia and YAGO2 classes used for disambiguation classes. Prefix dbo stands for `http://dbpedia.org/ontology/`, foaf for `http://xmlns.com/foaf/0.1/` and yago for `http://yago-knowledge.org/resource/`.

| Class | rdf:type |
|-------|----------|
| DBpedia Person | dbo:Person, foaf:Person |
| DBpedia Organization | dbo:Organization, dbo:WrittenWork (e.g., Journals) |
| DBpedia Place | dbo:Place, yago:YagoGeoEntity |
| YAGO2 Person | yago:yagoLegalActor |
| YAGO2 Organization | yago:yagoLegalActor, |
| | yago:wordnet_exchange_111409538 (e.g., NASDAQ) |
| YAGO2 Place | yago:YagoGeoEntity |

---

**Algorithm 1.** Searching candidates for a label.

---

**Data**: label of a certain named entity $N_i$, $\sigma$ trigram similarity threshold
**Result**: $C$ candidates found
$C \longleftarrow \emptyset$;
label $\longleftarrow$ **normalize**(label);
label $\longleftarrow$ **expand**(label);
$\bar{C} \longleftarrow$ **searchIndex**(label);
**for** c $\in \bar{C}$ **do**
    **if** $\neg$c .**matches**($[0\text{-}9]^+$) **then**
        **if** **trigramSimilarity**(c, label)$\geq \sigma$ **then**
            **if** **fitDomain**(c) **then**
                $C \longleftarrow C \cup$ c;

---

## 3.4 Computation of Optimal Assignment

Given a set of candidate nodes, we begin the computation of the optimal assignment by constructing a disambiguation graph $G_d$ with search depth $d$. To this end, we regard the input knowledge base as a directed graph $G_K = (V, E)$ where the vertices $V$ are resources of $K$, the edges $E$ are properties of $K$ and $x, y \in V, (x,y) \in E \Leftrightarrow \exists p : (x,p,y)$ is an RDF triple in $K$. Given the set of candidates $C$, we begin by building an initial graph $G_0 = (V_0, E_0)$ where $V_0$ is the set of all resources in $C$ and $E_0 = \emptyset$. Starting with $G_0$ we extend the graph in a breadth-first search manner. Therefore, we define the extension of a graph $G_i = (V_i, E_i)$ to a graph $\rho(G_i) = G_{i+1} = (V_{i+1}, E_{i+1})$ with $i = 0, \ldots, d$ as follows:

$$V_{i+1} = V_i \cup \{y : \exists x \in V_i \wedge (x,y) \in E\} \tag{1}$$

$$E_{i+1} = \{(x,y) \in E : x, y \in V_{i+1}\} \tag{2}$$

We iterate the $\rho$ operator $d$ times on the input graph $G_0$ to compute the initial disambiguation graph $G_d$.

After constructing the disambiguation graph $G_d$ we need to identify the correct candidate node for a given named entity. Using the graph-based HITS algorithm we calculate authoritative values $x_a, y_a$ and hub values $x_h, y_h$ for all $x, y \in V_d$. We initialize the authoritative and hub values (3) and afterwards iterate the equations (4) $k$ times as follows:

$$\forall x \in V_d, x_a = x_h = \frac{1}{|V_d|} \ (3) \text{ and } x_a \longleftarrow \sum_{(y,x)\in E_d} y_h, \quad y_h \longleftarrow \sum_{(y,x)\in E_d} x_a (4)$$

We choose $k$ according to Kleinberg [12], i.e., 20 iterations, which suffice to achieve convergence in general. Afterwards we identify the most authoritative candidate $C_{ij}$ among the set of candidates $C_i$ as correct disambiguation for a given named entity $N_i$. When using DBpedia as KB and $C_{ij}$ is a redirect AGDISTIS uses the target resource. AGDISTIS' whole procedure is presented in Algorithm 2. As can be seen, we calculate $\mu^+$ solely by using polynomial time complex algorithms.

---

**Algorithm 2.** Disambiguation Algorithm based on HITS and Linked Data.

---

**Data**: $N = \{N_1, N_2 \ldots N_n\}$ named entities, $\sigma$ trigram similarity threshold, $d$ depth, $k$ number of iterations
**Result**: $C = \{C_1, C_2 \ldots C_n\}$ identified candidates for named entities
$E \longleftarrow \emptyset$;
$V \longleftarrow$ **insertCandidates**$(N, \sigma)$;
$G \longleftarrow (V, E)$;
$G \longleftarrow$ **breadthFirstSearch**$(G, d)$;
**HITS**$(G(V, E), k)$;
**sortAccordingToAuthorityValue(V)**;
**for** $N_i \in N$ **do**
    **for** $v \in V$ **do**
        **if** $v$ **is a candidate for** $N_i$ **then**
            **store**$(N_i, v)$;
            **break**;

---

For our example, the graph depicted in Figure 2 shows an excerpt of the input graph for the HITS disambiguation algorithm when relying on DBpedia as knowledge base. The results can be seen in Table 2.

# 4   Evaluation

## 4.1   Experimental Setup

The aim of our evaluation was two-fold. First, we wanted to determine the F-measure achieved by our approach on different datasets. Several definitions of

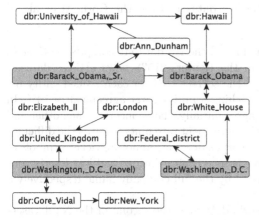

**Table 2.** Authority weights for example graph

| Node | $x_a$ |
|---|---|
| db:Barack_Obama | 0.273 |
| db:Barack_Obama,_Sr. | 0.089 |
| db:Washington,_D.C. | 0.093 |
| db:Washington,_D.C._(novel) | 0.000 |

**Fig. 2.** One possible graph for the example sentence, with candidate nodes in grey

F-measure have been used in previous work on NED. Cornolti et al. [3] define the micro F-measure (F1) w.r.t. a strong annotation match (i.e., a binary relation) and the possibility of assigning null to an entity. This F-measure, which we use throughout our evaluation, aggregates all true/false positives/negatives over all documents. Thus, it accounts for larger contexts in documents with more annotations, cf. Cornolti et al. [3].

Second, we wanted to know how AGDISTIS performs in comparison to other state-of-the-art NED approaches. Thus, we compare AGDISTIS with TagMe 2, the best approach according to [3] as well as with AIDA and DBpedia Spotlight because they are well-known in the Linked Data community. AGDISTIS is designed to be agnostic of the underlying knowledge base. Thus, we use the German and English DBpedia KB as well as the English YAGO 2 KB.

Within our experiments, we ran AGDISTIS with the following parameter settings: the threshold $\sigma$ for the trigram similarity was varied between 0 and 1 in steps of 0.01. Additionally, we evaluated our approach with $d = 1, 2, 3$ to measure the influence of the size of the disambiguation graph on AGDISTIS' F-measure. For our experiments, we fitted AGDISTIS to the domain of named entity recognition and only allow candidates of the types mentioned in Table 1. We report more details on the evaluation setup as well as complete results at the project homepage.

## 4.2 Datasets

Noisy and incorrect datasets can affect the performance of NED approaches which can be prevented by using well-known datasets. We carried out our evaluation on the following eight different, publicly available datasets, which consists of the three corpora from the benchmark dataset **N3** [22], the original AIDA evaluation corpus[8] and four of the five datasets from the Cornolti et al. [3] benchmark:

1. **Reuters-21578 Dataset.** The first of the N3 datasets comprises 145 news articles randomly sampled from the Reuters-21578 news articles dataset. Two domain experts determined the correct URI for each named entity using an online annotation tool reaching a initial voter agreement of 74%. In cases where the judges did not agree initially, they concerted each other and reached an agreement. This initial agreement rate hints towards the difficulty of the disambiguation task. The corpus does not annotate ticker symbols of companies (e.g., *GOOG* for Google Inc.), abbreviations and job descriptions because those are always preceded by the full company name respectively a person's name.

2. **news.de Dataset.** This real-world dataset is the second of the N3 datasets and was collected from 2009 to 2011 from the German web news portal **news.de** ensuring that each message contains the German word *Golf*. This word is a homonym that can semantically mean a geographical gulf, a car model or the sport discipline. This dataset contains 53 texts comprising over 600 named entities that were annotated manually by a domain expert. Although some meanings of Golf are not within the class range of our evaluation, they are kept for evaluation purposes.

3. **RSS-500 Dataset.** This corpus has been published in Gerber et al. [8] and is the third of the of the N3 datasets. It consists of data scrapped from 1,457 RSS feeds. The list includes all major worldwide newspapers and a wide range of topics, e.g., *World, U.S., Business, Science* etc. This list was crawled for 76 hours, which resulted in a corpus of about 11.7 million sentences. A subset of this corpus has been created by randomly selecting 1% of the contained sentences. Finally, domain experts annotated 500 sentences manually. Further information about the corpora and the datasets themselves can be found on the project homepage.[9]

4. **AIDA-YAGO2 Dataset.** This is the original dataset that was used while evaluating AIDA [9], stemming from the CoNLL 2003 shared task [26] and comprising 1,393 news articles which were annotated manually.

5. **AIDA/CO-NLL-TestB.** This dataset (like all the subsequent datasets) comes from the Cornolti et al. benchmarks and originates from the evaluation of AIDA [9]. As mentioned above, this dataset was derived from the CO-NLL 2003 shared task [26] and comprises 1,393 news articles which were annotated manually. Two students annotated each entity resolving conflicts by the authors of AIDA [9]. Cornolti et al.'s benchmark consists only of the second test part comprising 231 documents with 19.4 entities per document on average.

6. **AQUAINT.** In this dataset, only the first mention of an entity is annotated. The corpus consists of 50 documents which are on average longer than the

---

[8] https://www.mpi-inf.mpg.de/departments/databases-and-information-systems/research/yago-naga/aida/downloads/

[9] http://aksw.org/Projects/N3NERNEDNIF.html

**Table 3.** Test corpora specification including the number of documents (#Doc.) and the number of named entities (#Ent.) per dataset

| Corpus | Language | #Doc. | #Ent. | Ent./Doc. | Annotation |
|--------|----------|-------|-------|-----------|------------|
| AIDA/CO-NLL-TestB | English | 231 | 4458 | 19.40 | voter agreement |
| AQUAINT | English | 50 | 727 | 14.50 | voter agreement |
| IITB | English | 103 | 11,245 | 109.01 | domain expert |
| MSNBC | English | 20 | 658 | 31.90 | domain expert |
| Reuters-21578 | English | 145 | 769 | 5.30 | voter agreement |
| RSS 500 | English | 500 | 1,000 | 2.00 | domain expert |
| news.de | German | 53 | 627 | 11.83 | domain expert |
| AIDA-YAGO2 | English | 1,393 | 34,956 | 25.07 | voter agreement |

AIDA/CO-NLL-TestB documents. Each document contains 14.5 annotated elements on average The documents originate from different news services, e.g. Associated Press and have been annotated using voter agreement. The dataset was created by Milne et al. [17].

7. **IITB** The IITB corpus comprises 103 manually annotated documents. Each document contains 109.1 entities on average. This dataset displays the highest entity/document-density of all corpora. This corpus has been presented by Kulkarni et al. [13] in 2009.

8. **MSNBC** This corpus contains 20 news documents with 32.9 entities per document. This corpus was presented in 2007 by Cucerzan et al. [4].

We did not use the **Meij** dataset from Cornolti et al. since it comprises only tweets from twitter with 1.6 entities per document. The number of entities available in the datasets is shown in Table 3. All experiments were carried out on a MacBook Pro with a 2.7GHz Intel Core i7 processor and 4 GB 1333MHz DDR3 RAM using Mac OS 10.7.

## 4.3 Results

First, we evaluate AGDISTIS against AIDA and DBpedia Spotlight on three different knowledge bases using N3 corpora and the AIDA-YAGO2 corpus.

**Table 4.** Evaluation of AGDISTIS against AIDA and DBpedia Spotlight. Bold indicates best F-measure.

| Corpus | AGDISTIS | | | | | | AIDA | Spotlight |
|--------|----------|---|---|---|---|---|------|-----------|
| K | DBpedia | | | YAGO2 | | | YAGO2 | DBpedia |
| | F-measure | $\sigma$ | d | F-measure | $\sigma$ | d | F-measure | F-measure |
| Reuters-21578 | **0.78** | 0.87 | 2 | 0.60 | 0.29 | 3 | 0.62 | 0.56 |
| RSS-500 | **0.75** | 0.76 | 2 | 0.53 | 0.82 | 2 | 0.60 | 0.56 |
| news.de | **0.87** | 0.71 | 2 | — | — | — | — | 0.84 |
| AIDA-YAGO2 | 0.73 | 0.89 | 2 | 0.58 | 0.76 | 2 | **0.83** | 0.57 |

AGDISTIS performs best on the `news.de` corpus, achieving a maximal 0.87 F-measure for $\sigma = 0.71$ and $d = 2$ (see Table 4). Our approach also outperforms the state of the art on Reuters-21578 corpus (see Figure 3), where it reaches 0.78 F-measure for $\sigma = 0.87$ and $d = 2$. Considering the AIDA-YAGO2 dataset AGDISTIS achieves an F-measure of 0.73 for $\sigma = 0.89$ and $d = 2$. Our results suggest that $d = 2, \sigma = 0.82$ and using DBpedia as KB are a good setting for AGDISTIS and suffice to perform well. In the only case where $\sigma = 0.29$ leads to better results (Reuters-21578 corpus), the setting $0.7 < \sigma < 0.9$ is only outperformed by 0.03 F-measure using YAGO as KB for AGDISTIS.

**Table 5.** Performance of AGDISTIS, DBpedia Spotlight and TagMe 2 on four different datasets using micro F-measure (**F1**)

| Dataset | Approach | F1-measure | Precision | Recall |
|---|---|---|---|---|
| **AIDA/CO-NLL-TestB** | TagMe 2 | 0.565 | 0.58 | 0.551 |
| | DBpedia Spotlight | 0.341 | 0.308 | 0.384 |
| | AGDISTIS | **0.596** | **0.642** | **0.556** |
| **AQUAINT** | TagMe 2 | 0.457 | 0.412 | **0.514** |
| | DBpedia Spotlight | 0.26 | 0.178 | 0.48 |
| | AGDISTIS | **0.547** | **0.777** | 0.422 |
| **IITB** | TagMe 2 | 0.408 | 0.416 | 0.4 |
| | DBpedia Spotlight | **0.46** | 0.434 | **0.489** |
| | AGDISTIS | 0.31 | **0.646** | 0.204 |
| **MSNBC** | TagMe 2 | 0.466 | 0.431 | 0.508 |
| | DBpedia Spotlight | 0.331 | 0.317 | 0.347 |
| | AGDISTIS | **0.761** | **0.796** | **0.729** |

Second, we compared our approach with TagMe 2 and DBpedia using the datasets already implemented in the framework of Cornolti et al. AGDISTIS has been setup to use a breadth-first search depth $d = 2$ and a trigram similarity of $\sigma = 0.82$. All approaches used disambiguate w.r.t. the English DBpedia. AIDA was ommitted from this evaluation because it has been shown to be outperformed by TagMe 2 in [3] on the datasets we consider.

AGDISTIS achieves F-measures between 0.31 (IITB) and 0.76 (MSNBC) (see Table 5). We outperform the currently best disambiguation framework, TagMe 2, on three out of four datasets by up to 29.5% F-measure. Our poor performance on IITB is due to AGDISTIS not yet implementing a paragraph-wise disambiguation policy. By now, AGDISTIS performs disambiguation on full documents. The large number of resources in the IITB documents thus lead to our approach generating very large disambiguation graphs. The explosion of errors within these graphs results in an overall poor disambiguation. We will address this drawback in future work by fitting AGDISTIS with a preprocessor able to extract paragraphs from input texts. The local vector-space model used by Spotlight performs best in this setting.

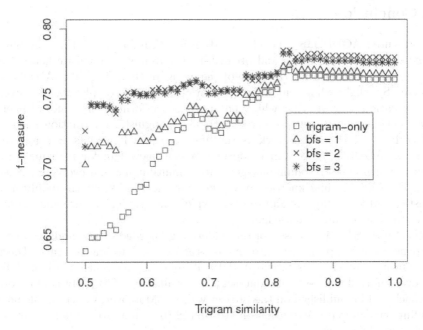

**Fig. 3.** F-measure on the **Reuters-21578** corpus using DBpedia as KB

Delving deeper into AGDISTIS' results lead to the following insights: (1) Varying the search depth $d$ does not significantly improve F-measure because within the underlying documents there are many similar named entities forming a shallow semantic background. However, using only string similarity measures ($d = 0$) results in lower F-measure (see Figure 3). (2) The expansion policy can have considerable knock-on effects: Either the first entity and its expansions are disambiguated correctly or the wrong disambiguation of the first entity leads to an avalanche of false results in a loss of $\approx 4\%$ accuracy. (3) We observed a significant enhancement of AGDISTIS when adding surface forms to the labels of resources as explained in Section 3.3. Employing additional labels (such as surface forms gathered from Wikipedia) increased the F-measure of AGDISTIS by up to 4%. (5) Using $n = 1, 2, 4$ as n-gram similarity has been proven to perform worse than using trigram similarity, i.e., $n = 3$. Our results suggest that $d = 2$ while using DBpedia as KB is a good setting for AGDISTIS and suffice to perform well. The iteration of $\sigma$ between 0.7 and 0.9 can lead to an improvement of up to 6% F-measure while $\sigma < 0.7$ and $\sigma > 0.9$ leads to a loss of F-measure.

Overall, our results suggest that $\sigma = 0.82$ and $d = 2$ is generally usable across datasets and knowledge bases leading to high quality results.[10]

---

[10] See    also    http://139.18.2.164/rusbeck/agdistis/supplementary.pdf    and
http://139.18.2.164/rusbeck/agdistis/appendix.pdf

## 5  Conclusion

We presented AGDISTIS a novel named entity disambiguation that combines the scalable HITS algorithm and breadth-first search with linguistic heuristics. Our approach outperforms the state-of-the-art algorithms TagMe 2, AIDA and DBpedia Spotlight while remaining quadratic in its time complexity. Moreover, our evaluation suggests that while the approach performs well in and of itself, it can benefit from being presented with more linguistic information such as surface forms. We see this work as the first step in a larger research agenda. Based on AGDISTIS, we aim to develop a new paradigm for realizing NLP services which employ community-generated, multilingual and evolving Linked Open Data background knowledge. Other than most work, which mainly uses statistics and heuristics, we aim to truly exploit the graph structure and semantics of the background knowledge.

Since AGDISTIS is agnostic of the underlying knowledge base and language-independent, it can profit from growing KBs as well as multilingual Linked Data. In the future, we will thus extend AGDISTIS by using different underlying KBs and even more domain-specific datasets. An evaluation of Babelfy against our approach will be published on the project website. Moreover, we will implement a sliding-window-based extension of AGDISTIS to account for large amounts of entities per document.

**Acknowledgments.** Parts of this work were supported by the ESF and the Free State of Saxony and the FP7 project Geo-Know (GA No. 318159).

## References

1. Adida, B., Herman, I., Sporny, M., Birbeck, M.: RDFa 1.1 Primer. Technical report, World Wide Web Consortium (June 2012),
   http://www.w3.org/TR/2012/NOTE-rdfa-primer-20120607/
2. Adrian, B., Hees, J., Herman, I., Sintek, M., Dengel, A.: Epiphany: Adaptable RDFa generation linking the web of documents to the web of data. In: Cimiano, P., Pinto, H.S. (eds.) EKAW 2010. LNCS, vol. 6317, pp. 178–192. Springer, Heidelberg (2010)
3. Cornolti, M., Ferragina, P., Ciaramita, M.: A framework for benchmarking entity-annotation systems. In: 22nd WWW, pp. 249–260 (2013)
4. Cucerzan, S.: Large-scale named entity disambiguation based on wikipedia data. In: EMNLP-CoNLL, pp. 708–716 (2007)
5. Ell, B., Vrandečić, D., Simperl, E.: Labels in the web of data. In: Aroyo, L., Welty, C., Alani, H., Taylor, J., Bernstein, A., Kagal, L., Noy, N., Blomqvist, E. (eds.) ISWC 2011, Part I. LNCS, vol. 7031, pp. 162–176. Springer, Heidelberg (2011)
6. Ferragina, P., Scaiella, U.: Fast and accurate annotation of short texts with wikipedia pages. IEEE Software 29(1) (2012)
7. Finkel, J.R., Grenager, T., Manning, C.: Incorporating non-local information into information extraction systems by gibbs sampling. In: ACL 2005, pp. 363–370. Association for Computational Linguistics, Stroudsburg (2005)

8. Gerber, D., Hellmann, S., Bühmann, L., Soru, T., Usbeck, R., Ngonga Ngomo, A.-C.: Real-time RDF extraction from unstructured data streams. In: Alani, H., et al. (eds.) ISWC 2013, Part I. LNCS, vol. 8218, pp. 135–150. Springer, Heidelberg (2013)
9. Hoffart, J., Yosef, M.A., Bordino, I., Fürstenau, H., Pinkal, M., Spaniol, M., Taneva, B., Thater, S., Weikum, G.: Robust Disambiguation of Named Entities in Text. In: Conference on Empirical Methods in Natural Language Processing, EMNLP 2011, Edinburgh, Scotland, pp. 782–792 (2011)
10. Kleb, J., Abecker, A.: Entity reference resolution via spreading activation on RDF-graphs. In: Aroyo, L., Antoniou, G., Hyvönen, E., ten Teije, A., Stuckenschmidt, H., Cabral, L., Tudorache, T. (eds.) ESWC 2010, Part I. LNCS, vol. 6088, pp. 152–166. Springer, Heidelberg (2010)
11. Kleb, J., Abecker, A.: Disambiguating entity references within an ontological model. In: WIMS, p. 22 (2011)
12. Kleinberg, J.M.: Authoritative sources in a hyperlinked environment. J. ACM 46(5), 604–632 (1999)
13. Kulkarni, S., Singh, A., Ramakrishnan, G., Chakrabarti, S.: Collective annotation of wikipedia entities in web text. In: 15th ACM SIGKDD, pp. 457–466 (2009)
14. Lehmann, J., Isele, R., Jakob, M., Jentzsch, A., Kontokostas, D., Mendes, P.N., Hellmann, S., Morsey, M., van Kleef, P., Auer, S., Bizer, C.: DBpedia - a large-scale, multilingual knowledge base extracted from wikipedia. SWJ (2014)
15. Mendes, P.N., Jakob, M., Garcia-Silva, A., Bizer, C.: Dbpedia spotlight: Shedding light on the web of documents. In: Proceedings of the 7th International Conference on Semantic Systems, I-Semantics (2011)
16. Mihalcea, R., Csomai, A.: Wikify!: linking documents to encyclopedic knowledge. In: 16th ACM Conference on Information and Knowledge Management, CIKM 2007, pp. 233–242. ACM, New York (2007)
17. Milne, D., Witten, I.H.: Learning to link with wikipedia. In: 17th ACM CIKM, pp. 509–518 (2008)
18. Moro, A., Raganato, A., Navigli, R.: Entity linking meets word sense disambiguation: A unified approach. TACL 2 (2014)
19. Nadeau, D., Sekine, S.: A survey of named entity recognition and classification. Lingvisticae Investigationes 30, 3–26 (2007)
20. Ratinov, L., Roth, D.: Design challenges and misconceptions in named entity recognition. In: CoNLL (June 2009)
21. Ratinov, L., Roth, D., Downey, D., Anderson, M.: Local and global algorithms for disambiguation to wikipedia. In: ACL (2011)
22. Röder, M., Usbeck, R., Hellmann, S., Gerber, D., Both, A.: N3 - a collection of datasets for named entity recognition and disambiguation in the nlp interchange format. In: 9th LREC (2014)
23. Shen, W., Wang, J., Luo, P., Wang, M.: Linden: linking named entities with knowledge base via semantic knowledge. In: 21st WWW, pp. 449–458 (2012)
24. Singh, S., Subramanya, A., Pereira, F., McCallum, A.: Large-scale cross-document coreference using distributed inference and hierarchical models. In: 49th ACL: Human Language Technologies, pp. 793–803 (2011)
25. Speck, R., Ngomo, A.-C.N.: Ensemble learning for named entity recognition. In: Mika, P., et al. (eds.) ISWC 2014. LNCS (LNAI), vol. 8796, pp. 511–526. Springer, Heidelberg (2001)
26. Sang, E.F.T.K., De Meulder, F.: Introduction to the conll-2003 shared task: Language-independent named entity recognition. In: Proceedings of CoNLL 2003, pp. 142–147 (2003)

# M-ATOLL: A Framework for the Lexicalization of Ontologies in Multiple Languages

Sebastian Walter, Christina Unger, and Philipp Cimiano

Semantic Computing Group, CITEC, Bielefeld University

**Abstract.** Many tasks in which a system needs to mediate between natural language expressions and elements of a vocabulary in an ontology or dataset require knowledge about how the elements of the vocabulary (i.e. classes, properties, and individuals) are expressed in natural language. In a multilingual setting, such knowledge is needed for each of the supported languages. In this paper we present M-ATOLL, a framework for automatically inducing ontology lexica in multiple languages on the basis of a multilingual corpus. The framework exploits a set of language-specific dependency patterns which are formalized as SPARQL queries and run over a parsed corpus. We have instantiated the system for two languages: German and English. We evaluate it in terms of precision, recall and F-measure for English and German by comparing an automatically induced lexicon to manually constructed ontology lexica for DBpedia. In particular, we investigate the contribution of each single dependency pattern and perform an analysis of the impact of different parameters.

## 1 Introduction

For many applications that need to mediate between natural language and elements of a formal vocabulary as defined by a given ontology or used in a given dataset, knowledge about how elements of the vocabulary are expressed in natural language is needed. This is the case, e.g., for question answering over linked data [23,20,10] and natural language generation from ontologies or RDF data [4]. Moreover, in case a system is supposed to handle different languages, this knowledge is needed in multiple languages. Take, for example, the following question from the Question Answering over Linked Data[1] (QALD-4) challenge, provided in seven languages:

1. English: Give me all Australian nonprofit organizations.
2. German: Gib mir alle gemeinnützigen Organisationen in Australien.
3. Spanish: Dame todas las organizaciones benéficas de Australia.
4. Italian: Dammi tutte le organizzazioni australiane non a scopo di lucro.
5. French: Donnes-moi toutes les associations australiennes à but non lucratif.
6. Dutch: Noem alle Australische organisaties zonder winstoogmerk.
7. Romanian: Dă-mi toate organizațiile non-profit din Australia.

---

[1] `www.sc.cit-ec.uni-bielefeld.de/qald/`

P. Mika et al. (Eds.) ISWC 2014, Part I, LNCS 8796, pp. 472–486, 2014.

All these questions can be interpreted as the same, language-independent query to the DBpedia dataset:

```
1  PREFIX dbo: <http://dbpedia.org/ontology/>
2  PREFIX res: <http://dbpedia.org/resource/>
3  SELECT DISTINCT ?uri
4  WHERE {
5          ?uri dbo:type res:Nonprofit_organization .
6          { ?uri dbo:locationCountry res:Australia . }
7          UNION
8          { ?uri dbo:location ?x .
9            ?x dbo:country res:Australia . }
10 }
```

In order to either map the natural language questions to the query or vice versa, a system needs to know how the individual Nonprofit_organization is verbalized in the above languages. In addition, it needs to know that the adjective Australian corresponds to the class of individuals that are related to the indivual Australia either directly via the property locationCountry or indirectly via the properties location and country. This goes beyond a simple matching of natural language expressions and vocabulary elements, and shows that the conceptual granularity of language often does not coincide with that of a particular dataset.

Such lexical knowledge is crucial for any system that interfaces between natural language and Semantic Web data. A number of models have been proposed to represent such lexical knowledge, realizing what has been called the *ontology-lexicon interface* [18], among them *lemon*[2] [12]. *lemon* is a model for the declarative specification of multilingual, machine-readable lexica in RDF that capture syntactic and semantic aspects of lexical items relative to some ontology. The meaning of a lexical item is given by reference to an ontology element, i.e. a class, property or individual, thereby ensuring a clean separation between the ontological and lexical layer.

We call the task of enriching an ontology with lexical information *ontology lexicalization*. In this paper we propose a semi-automatic approach, M-ATOLL, to ontology lexicalization which induces lexicalizations from a multilingual corpus. In order to find lexicalizations, M-ATOLL exploits a library of patterns that match substructures in dependency trees in a particular language. These patterns are expressed declaratively in SPARQL, so that customizing the system to another language essentially consists in exchanging the pattern library. As input, M-ATOLL takes a RDF dataset as well as a broad coverage corpus in the target language. We present an instantiation of the system using DBpedia as dataset and Wikipedia as corpus, considering English and German as languages to proof that our approach can be adapted to multiple languages. As output, M-ATOLL generates a lexicon in *lemon* format.

The paper is structured as follows: In the following section, we present the architecture of M-ATOLL and discuss its instantiation to both English and German, in particular describing the patterns used for each of these languages. In

---

[2] http://lemon-model.net

Section 3 we evaluate the system by comparing to existing manually constructed lexica for DBpedia. We discuss related work in Section 4, and provide a conclusion as well as an outlook on future work in Section 5.

## 2    Architecture

In this section we present the architecture behind M-ATOLL. The input is a RDF dataset with or without an underlying ontology as well as a parsed corpus for each of the languages into which the ontology is to be lexicalized; the output is an ontology lexicon in *lemon* format. M-ATOLL comprises two approaches: a *label-based approach* for extracting lexicalizations using ontology labels and additional information, such as synonyms, from external lexical resources, and a *dependency-based approach* for extracting lexicalizations of ontology properties from an available text corpus. We will present both approaches as instantiated for the DBpedia dataset and an English Wikipedia corpus, and then sketch how the system can be ported to other languages, in our case to German.

### 2.1    Dependency-Based Approach

Figure 1 presents an overview of the dependency-based approach. The main idea is to start from pairs of entities that are related by a given property, find occurrences of those entities in the text corpus, and generalize over the dependency paths that connect them. The assumption behind this is that a sentence containing both entities also contains a candidate lexicalization of the property in question.

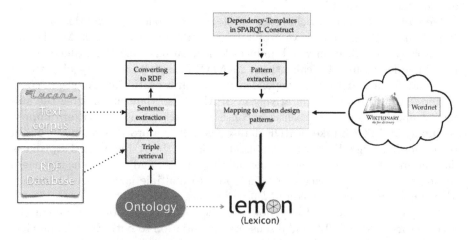

**Fig. 1.** Overview of the dependency-based approach

First, M-ATOLL expects an index of the available text corpus that stores the dependency parses of all sentences occuring in the corpus in CoNLL format[3]. Using such an index as input instead of raw text increases the flexibility for the adaptation to different languages, as the parsing of a text corpus with a specific dependency parser for the language is an external preparation step. In particular, relying only on an input in CoNLL format keeps the processing itself independent of a specific parser and tag set. In the following we describe all processing steps in detail.

**Triple Retrieval and Sentence Extraction.** Given a property, the first step of M-ATOLL consists in extracting all entities that are connected through the property from a given RDF knowledge base. For the DBpedia property `board`, for example, the following triples are returned (together with 873 other triples):[4]

```
<res:Woolf_Fisher, dbpedia:board, res:Auckland_Racing_Club>
<res:Ram_Shriram,  dbpedia:board, res:Google>
```

For those triples, all sentences that contain both the subject and object labels are retrieved from the text corpus. For example, for the second triple above, one of the retrieved sentences is `Kavitark Ram Shriram is a board member of Google and one of the first investors in Google`. The dependency parse of the sentence is displayed in Figure 2.

**Converting Parse Trees to RDF.** After extracting all dependency parses of the relevant sentences, they are converted into RDF using our own vocabulary (inspired by the CoNLL format) and stored using Apache Jena[5].

**Pattern Extraction.** After storing all parses in an RDF store, dependency patterns that capture candidate lexicalizations are extracted from the parses. In order to minimize noise, we define common, relevant dependency patterns that the extraction should consider. These patterns are implemented as SPARQL queries that can be executed over the RDF store. In this paper we consider the following six dependency patterns (given with an English and a German example each):

1. *Transitive verb*
   - Plato **influenced** Russell.
   - Plato **beeinflusste** Russel.
2. *Intransitive verb with prepositional object*
   - Lincoln **died in** Washington, D.C.
   - Lincold **starb in** Washington, D.C.
3. *Relational noun with prepositional object (appositive)*

---

[3] http://nextens.uvt.nl/depparse-wiki/DataFormat
[4] Throughout the paper, we use the prefix dbpedia for
   <http://dbpedia.org/ontology/> and res for <http://dbpedia.org/resource/>
[5] https://jena.apache.org/

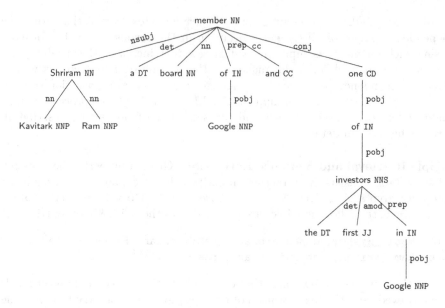

**Fig. 2.** Dependency tree for the sentence Kavitark Ram Shriram is a board member of Google and one of the first investors in Google

- Murdoch, **creator of** the Fox Broadcasting Company, retired.
- Murdoch, der **Gründer der** Fox Broadcasting Company, hat sich zur Ruhe gesetzt.

4. *Relational noun with prepositional object (copulative construction)*
   - Penelope is the **wife of** Odysseus.
   - Penelope is die **Ehefrau von** Odysseus.
5. *Relational adjective*
   - Portugese is **similar to** Spanish.
   - Portugiesisch ist **ähnlich zu** Spanisch.
6. *Relational adjective (verb participle)*
   - Audrey Hepburn was **born in** Belgium.
   - Audrey Hepburn wurde **in** Belgien **geboren**.

Note that these patterns cover relatively general grammatical structures and could be instantiated by several SPARQL queries. The appositive relational noun pattern, for example, is captured by two SPARQL queries that differ only in the direction of a particular dependency relation (both of which occur in the data, leading to the same kind of lexicalizations).

After extracting candidate lexicalizations using these patterns, the final step is to construct a lexical entry. To this end, we use WordNet [14] with the MIT Java Wordnet Interface [6] in order to determine the lemma of a word, e.g marry for the verb form marries, or member for the noun form members. Also, we determine the mapping between syntactic and semantic arguments. For example, in our example in 2, the subject of the property board (Ram_Shriram) corresponds to the subject of the sentence, while the object of the property (`Google`) corresponds to the prepositional object. The lexical entry created for the noun lexicalization board member then looks as follows:

```
RelationalNoun("board member",dbpedia:board,
     propSubj = CopulativeArg,
     propObj  = PrepositionalObject("of"))
```

This entry makes use of one of the macros for common lexicalization patterns defined in [13], a relational noun macro representing the prototypical syntactic frame $x$ is a board member of $y$. This entry is equivalent to the following RDF representation:

```
:boardMember a lemon:LexicalEntry;
  lexinfo:partOfSpeech lexinfo:noun;
  lemon:canonicalForm [ lemon:writtenRep "board member"@en ];
  lemon:sense [ lemon:reference dbpedia:board;
                lemon:subjOfProp :x;
                lemon:objOfProp  :y ] ;
  lexinfo:synBehavior [ a lexinfo:NounPPFrame;
                lexinfo:copulativeArg      :x;
                lexinfo:prepositionalObject :y ].

:y lemon:marker [ lemon:canonicalForm
                [ lemon:writtenRep "of"@en ]].
```

For each generated lexical entry we also store how often it was generated and with which SPARQL query it was retrieved.

## 2.2   Label-Based Approach

The label-based approach to the induction of lexical entries differs from the dependency-based approach described above in that it does not rely on a text corpus but only on the label of the ontology element in question (classes and properties) as well as on external lexical resources to find possible lexicalizations.

In particular, we use BabelNet [16] for finding synonyms. Currently we pick the first synset that is returned, but we plan to disambiguate the relevant synset by extending our approach to use Babelfy [15], using Wikipedia articles as disambiguation texts.

The label of the DBpedia class `Activity`, for example, is activity, for which we retrieve the synonym action from BabelNet. The following lexical entries are generated:

```
ClassNoun("activity",dbpedia:Activity)
ClassNoun("action",dbpedia:Activity)
```

The same processing is done for labels of properties, yielding, for example, the following entries for the property spouse:

```
RelationalNoun("spouse",dbpedia:spouse,
  propSubj = PossessiveAdjunct,
  propObj  = CopulativeArg)

RelationalNoun("partner",dbpedia:spouse,
  propSubj = PossessiveAdjunct,
  propObj  = CopulativeArg))

RelationalNoun("better half",dbpedia:spouse,
  propSubj = PossessiveAdjunct,
  propObj  = CopulativeArg)
```

## 2.3 Adaptation to Other Languages

This section gives an overview on how to adapt the dependency-based approach of M-ATOLL to other languages, in our case German, for which we present results in Section 3.

The adaptation of the label-based approach largely depends on the availability of external lexical resources, such as BabelNet, for the target language.

In order to adapt the dependency-based approach to German, we first parsed a corpus of around 175,000 sentences (sentences related to the QALD-3 lexicalization task) from the German Wikipedia, using the ParZu dependency parser [19], storing the resulting parses in CoNLL format in our corpus index. The ParZu parser has the advantage to also lemmatize the tokens of an input sentence, e.g. if the past tense verb form is heiratete, the parser also returns the infinitive verb form heiraten. Therefore no additional resources, such as WordNet, for retrieving the lemma of a word were needed. The next and final step for the adaptation is defining relevant dependency patterns as SPARQL queries in order to retrieve candidate lexicalizations, based on the part-of-speech tag set and dependency relations used by the parser. To this end, we transformed the SPARQL queries used for English into SPARQL queries that we can use for German. This mainly consisted in exchanging the part-of-speech tags and dependencies.

In general, the adaptation of queries to other languages might also involve changing the structure of the dependency patterns it queries for, but the patterns we currently employ are general enough to work well across languages that are structurally similar to English.

## 3 Evaluation

In this section we describe the evaluation measures and datasets, and then discuss results for English and German.

### 3.1 Methodology and Datasets

For English, we developed M-ATOLL using both training and test data of the ontology lexicalization task of the QALD-3 challenge [5] as development set, i.e. for creating the dependency patterns we query for. It comprises 20 DBpedia classes and 60 DBpedia properties that were randomly selected from different frequency ranges, i.e. including properties with a large amount of instances as well as properties with very few instances. M-ATOLL was then evaluated in terms of precison, recall and F-measure on the manually constructed English *lemon* lexicon for DBpedia[6] [21]. It comprises 1,217 lexicalizations of 326 classes and the 232 most frequent properties. From this dataset we removed all classes and properties used for development, in order to avoid any overlap, leaving a test dataset that is approximately 14 times bigger than the training dataset. As text corpus we use around 60 million parsed sentences from the English Wikipedia.

For German, we use the train/test split of the ontology lexicalization task of the QALD-3 challenge, and evaluate the approach with respect to a preliminary version of a manually constructed German *lemon* lexicon for DBpedia. This results in a training set of 28 properties and a test dataset of 27 properties (all those properties from the QALD-3 dataset that have lexicalizations in the gold standard lexicon). As text corpus, we use around 175,000 parsed sentences from the German Wikipedia.

## 3.2   Evaluation Measures

For each property and class, we evaluate the automatically generated lexical entries by comparing them to the manually created lexical entries in terms of lexical precision, lexical recall and lexical F-measure at the lemma level. To this end, we determine how many of the gold standard entries for a property are generated by our approach (recall), and how many of the automatically generated entries are among the gold standard entries (precision), where two entries count as the same lexicaliztation if their lemma, part of speech and sense coincide. Thus lexical precision $P_{lex}$ and recall $R_{lex}$ for a property $p$ are defined as follows:

$$P_{lex}(p) = \frac{|entries_{auto}(p) \cap entries_{gold}(p)|}{|entries_{auto}(p)|}$$

$$R_{lex}(p) = \frac{|entries_{auto}(p) \cap entries_{gold}(p)|}{|entries_{gold}(p)|}$$

Where $entries_{auto}(p)$ is the set of entries for the property $p$ in the automatically constructed lexicon, while $entries_{gold}(p)$ is the set of entries for the property $p$ in the manually constructed gold lexicon. The F-measure $F_{lex}(p)$ is then defined as the harmonic mean of $P_{lex}(p)$ and $R_{lex}(p)$, as usual.

All measures are computed for each property and then averaged for all properties. In the sections below, we will report only the average values.

As mentioned in Section 2, for each generated lexical entry we store how often it was generated. This frequency is now used to calculate a probability expressing how likely it is that this entry is used to lexicalize a particular property in question.

---

[6] https://github.com/cunger/lemon.dbpedia

480 S. Walter, C. Unger, and P. Cimiano

## 3.3 Results for English

Figure 3 shows results of the dependency-based approach on the training and test dataset in terms of precision, recall and F-measure, considering the top-$k$ generated lexical entries, with $k = 1, 5, 10, 15, 20$ as well as considering all generated entries. The best precision (0.47 on train and 0.44 on test) is reached with $k = 1$, while the best recall (0.29 on train and 0.32 on test) is reached when considering all candidate entries, which also yields the best F-measure (0.30 on train and 0.35 on test).

|          | Training | | | Test | | |
|----------|-----------|--------|-----------|-----------|--------|-----------|
|          | Precision | Recall | F-measure | Precision | Recall | F-measure |
| Top 1    | **0.47**  | 0.11   | 0.18      | **0.44**  | 0.06   | 0.11      |
| Top 5    | 0.37      | 0.20   | 0.26      | 0.42      | 0.19   | 0.26      |
| Top 10   | 0.33      | 0.22   | 0.27      | 0.40      | 0.24   | 0.30      |
| Top 15   | 0.32      | 0.24   | 0.27      | 0.40      | 0.27   | 0.32      |
| Top 20   | 0.31      | 0.26   | 0.28      | 0.39      | 0.27   | 0.31      |
| All      | 0.30      | **0.29** | **0.30** | 0.37      | **0.32** | **0.35** |

**Fig. 3.** Results of the dependency-based approach on the English dataset

Figure 4 presents the overall results on the English training and test set for the label-based approach, the dependency-based approach, and when combining both approaches. For performance reasons (especially for the test dataset) we limited the number of considered entity pairs per property to 2,500 pairs, although taking more entity pairs into account will increase the recall significantly, as preliminary tests showed.

Note that the label-based and the dependency-based approach complement each other in the sense that they find different lexicalizations, which leads to an increased recall when combining both.

|                   | Training | | | Test | | |
|-------------------|-----------|--------|-----------|-----------|--------|-----------|
|                   | Precision | Recall | F-measure | Precision | Recall | F-measure |
| Dependency-based  | 0.30      | 0.29   | 0.30      | 0.37      | 0.32   | 0.35      |
| Label-based       | **0.53**  | 0.24   | 0.33      | **0.56**  | 0.30   | 0.40      |
| Both              | 0.35      | **0.44** | **0.39** | 0.43      | **0.43** | **0.43** |

**Fig. 4.** Overall results on the English dataset, considering all generated entries

Finally, Figure 5 shows the contribution of each dependency pattern for English to the results over the training and test sets, when taking all generated entries into account.

| | Training | | | Test | | |
|---|---|---|---|---|---|---|
| | Precision | Recall | F-measure | Precision | Recall | F-measure |
| Transitive Verb | 0.48 | 0.06 | 0.10 | 0.47 | 0.07 | 0.13 |
| Intransitive Verb with prepositional object | 0.41 | 0.12 | 0.18 | 0.43 | 0.10 | 0.16 |
| Relational noun (appositive) with prepositional object | 0.42 | 0.04 | 0.07 | 0.44 | 0.07 | 0.12 |
| Relational noun (copulative) with prepositional object | 0.42 | 0.04 | 0.07 | 0.46 | 0.07 | 0.12 |
| Relational adjective | 0.79 | 0.04 | 0.07 | 0.70 | 0.02 | 0.04 |
| Relational adjective (verb participle) | 0.40 | 0.08 | 0.13 | 0.45 | 0.06 | 0.10 |

**Fig. 5.** Contribution of each dependency pattern for English to the results over training and test, taking all generated entries into account

### 3.4 Results for German

Figure 6 shows the results of the dependency-based approach on the training and test dataset for German. As for English, the highest precision is reached with the lowest $k$, while the highest recall and F-measure are achieved with higher $k$ or considering all candidate entries.

| | Training | | | Test | | |
|---|---|---|---|---|---|---|
| | Precision | Recall | F-measure | Precision | Recall | F-measure |
| Top 1 | **0.57** | 0.02 | 0.04 | **0.63** | 0.06 | 0.11 |
| Top 5 | 0.56 | 0.04 | 0.07 | 0.52 | 0.07 | 0.13 |
| Top 10 | 0.56 | 0.04 | 0.07 | 0.50 | **0.08** | **0.15** |
| Top 15 | 0.55 | 0.06 | 0.10 | 0.50 | **0.08** | **0.15** |
| Top 20 | 0.55 | **0.07** | 0.12 | 0.50 | **0.08** | **0.15** |
| All | 0.55 | **0.07** | **0.13** | 0.50 | **0.08** | **0.15** |

**Fig. 6.** Results of the dependency-based approach on the German dataset

The main reason for recall being so low is the rather small set of sentences contained in the text corpus sample. As a result, the approach finds candidate lexicalizations for a bit less than half of the properties. A manual inspection of the generated lexicalizations shows that the found candidates are indeed appropriate. For example, for the property spouse, our approach finds the lexicalizations heiraten (English to marry), Ehefrau von (English wife of), Gatte von (English husband of), leben mit (English to live with), among others, and for the property source (specifying the source of a river), our approach finds the lexicalizations entspringen in (English to originate from) and beginnen (English to begin), among others. We are therefore optimistic that moving to a larger corpus for German will yield results similar to the ones achieved for English.

## 3.5   Discussion of Results

Overall, the English results of the joining the label-based and the dependency-based approach over the test dataset is decent but still far from being able to be used in a fully automatic setting. Roughly, every second lexical entry that is generated is not appropriate. In fact, we rather envision our approach as the basis of a semi-automatic scenario, in which lexical entries are generated automatically and then are manually checked by a lexicon engineer and corrected if necessary. From this perspective, our approach has a clear potential to reduce the amount of manual work required to develop a high-quality lexicon.

The current lack in recall for English is mainly due to the limited number of defined dependency patterns. In addition, not all relevant lexicalizations occur in the available corpus. For example, for the property `birthDate` the gold standard lexicon contains three entries: born, birth date and date of birth, but only the first one occurs in the Wikipedia corpus in combination with one of our entity pairs from the given property. Capturing a wider variety of lexicalizations thus would require moving to a larger scale (and more diverse) corpus.

Also note that our approach only extracts verbalizations of classes and properties, not of property chains (e.g. grandchild as verbalization of `child ∘ cild`) or property-object pairs (e.g. Australian as verbalization of `country Australia`). Dealing with conceptual mismatches between ontological structures and natural language verbalizations will be subject of future work.

## 4   Related Work

An approach to extracting lexicalization patterns from corpora that is similar in spirit to our approach is *Wanderlust* [2], which relies on a dependency parser to find grammatical patterns in a given corpus—Wikipedia in their case as in ours. These patterns are generic and non-lexical and can be used to extract any semantic relation. However, *Wanderlust* also differs from our approach in one major aspect. We start from a given property and use instance data to find all different lexical variants of expressing one and the same property, while *Wanderlust* maps each dependency path to a different property (modulo some postprocessing to detect subrelations). They are therefore not able to find different variants of expressing one and the same property, thus not allowing for semantic normalization across lexicalization patterns.

Another related tool is DIRT [9] (*Discovery of Inference Rules from Text*), also very similar to *Snowball* [1], which is based on an unsupervised method for finding inferences in text, thereby for example establishing that $x$ is author of $y$ is a paraphrase of $x$ wrote $y$. DIRT relies on a similarity-based approach to group dependency paths, where two paths count as similar if they show a high degree of overlap in the nouns that appear at the argument positions of the paths. Such a similarity-based grouping of dependency paths could also be integrated into our approach, in order to find further paraphrases. The main difference to our approach is that DIRT does not rely on an existing knowledge base of instantiated triples to bootstrap the acquisition of patterns from textual data, thus being completely unsupervised. Given the fact that nowadays there are large knowledge bases such as Freebase and DBpedia, there is no reason why an approach should not exploit the available instances of a property or class to bootstrap the acquisition process.

A system that does rely on existing triples from a knowledge base, in particular DBpedia, is BOA [7]. BOA applies a recursive procedure, starting with extracting triples from linked data, then extracting natural language patterns from sentences and inserting this patterns as RDF data back into the Linked Data Cloud. The main difference to our approach is that BOA relies on simple string-based generalization techniques to find lexicalization patterns. This makes it difficult, for example, to discard optional modifiers and thus can generate a high amount of noise, which has been corroborated by initial experiments in our lab on inducing patterns from the string context between two entities.

*Espresso* [17] employs a minimally supervised bootstrapping algorithm which, based on only a few seed instances of a relation, learns patterns that can be used to extract more instances. *Espresso* is thus comparable to our approach in the sense that both rely on a set of seed sentences to induce patterns. In our case, these are derived from a knowledge base, while in the case of *Espresso* they are manually annotated. Besides a constrast in the overall task (relation extraction in the case of *Espresso* and ontology lexicalization in our case), one difference is that *Espresso* uses string-based patterns, while we rely on dependency paths, which constitutes a more principled approach to discarding modifiers and yielding more general patterns. A system that is similar to *Espresso* and uses dependency paths was proposed by Ittoo and Bouma [8]. A further difference is that *Espresso* leverages the web to find further occurrences of the seed instances. The corpus we use, Wikipedia, is bigger than the compared text corpora used in the evaluation by *Espresso*. But it would be bery interesting to extend our approach to work with web data in order to overcome data sparseness, e.g. as in [3], in case there is not enough instance data or there are not enough seed sentences available in a given corpus to bootstrap the pattern acquisition process.

The more recent approach by Mahenda et al. [11] also extracts lexicalizations of DBpedia properties on the basis of a Wikipedia corpus. In contrast to our approach, they do not consider the parse of a selected sentence, but the longest common substring between domain and range of the given property, normalizing it by means of DBpedia class labels, such as Person or Date.

Another multilingual system is *WRPA* [22], which extracts English and Spanish lexicalization patterns from the English and Spanish Wikipedia, respectively. Like other approaches, WRPA, considers only the textual pattern between two anchor texts from Wikipedia, no parse structure. WRPA is applied to four relations (date of birth, date of death, place of birth and authorship) on an English and Spanish corpus.

## 5   Conclusion and Future Work

We presented M-ATOLL as a first approach for the automatic lexicalization of ontologies in multiple languages and instantiated it for DBpedia in English and

German. It employs a combination of a dependency-based and a label-based approach, benefiting from the complementary lexicalizations they find. Furthermore, by extracting candidate lexicalizations by means of matching dependency parses with pre-defined dependency patterns, implemented as SPARQL queries, M-ATOLL offers much flexibility when adapting it to other languages.

However, M-ATOLL is still limited to a few dependency patterns, capturing the most basic grammatical structures. One main goal for future work thus is to increase recall by including more specialized structures. In order to minimize the manual effort in doing so, we intend to develop a procedure for automatically generating relevant patterns along the following lines: On the basis of already existing entries (either extracted by means of some general pre-defined patterns, or part of a gold standard lexicon), we will automatically generate SPARQL queries that retrieve the necessary parts from all sentences that contain the entity labels and the canonical form of the lexical entry. In a next step, these SPARQL queries will be generalized into commonly occurring patterns. This method can also reduce the cost of adapting M-ATOLL to other languages, as the process only needs a few basic patterns in order to bootstrap the pattern learning step would then provide the basis for the large-scale extraction of lexical entries.

Furthermore, we plan to improve the ranking of the generated lexical entries. Currently only the frequency of a certain entry is taken into account, whereas also the frequency of the underlying entity pair plays a role. For example, for properties that have an overlap in their entity pairs, the same verbalizations would be found. Confusing these lexicalizations could be avoided by ranking entries lower that were generated on the basis of entity pairs that also occur with other properties.

Moreover, we want to extend the evaluation of the German ontology lexicalization, running it on a much larger corpus. We plan to instantiate the approach also for Spanish, and finally intend to show that it can be adapted easily not only to other languages but also to other ontologies.

**Acknowledgment.** This work has been funded by the European Union's Seventh Framework Programme (FP7-ICT-2011-SME-DCL) under grant agreement number 296170 (PortDial).

# References

1. Agichtein, E., Gravano, L.: Snowball: Extracting relations from large plain-text collections. In: Proceedings of the Fifth ACM Conference on Digital Libraries, pp. 85–94. ACM (2000)
2. Akbik, A., Broß, J.: Wanderlust: Extracting semantic relations from natural language text using dependency grammar patterns. In: Proceedings of the Workshop on Semantic Search in Conjunction with the 18th Int. World Wide Web Conference (2009)

3. Blohm, S., Cimiano, P.: Using the web to reduce data sparseness in pattern-based information extraction. In: Kok, J.N., Koronacki, J., Lopez de Mantaras, R., Matwin, S., Mladenič, D., Skowron, A. (eds.) PKDD 2007. LNCS (LNAI), vol. 4702, pp. 18–29. Springer, Heidelberg (2007)
4. Bouayad-Agha, N., Casamayor, G., Wanner, L.: Natural language generation in the context of the semantic web. Semantic Web (2013)
5. Cimiano, P., Lopez, V., Unger, C., Cabrio, E., Ngonga Ngomo, A.-C., Walter, S.: Multilingual question answering over linked data (QALD-3): Lab overview. In: Forner, P., Müller, H., Paredes, R., Rosso, P., Stein, B. (eds.) CLEF 2013. LNCS, vol. 8138, pp. 321–332. Springer, Heidelberg (2013)
6. Finlayson, M.A.: Code for java libraries for accessing the princeton wordnet: Comparison and evaluation (2013)
7. Gerber, D., Ngomo, A.-C.N.N.: Bootstrapping the linked data web. In: 1st Workshop on Web Scale Knowledge Extraction ISWC (2011)
8. Ittoo, A., Bouma, G.: On learning subtypes of the part-whole relation: do not mix your seeds. In: Proceedings of the 48th Annual Meeting of the Association for Computational Linguistics, pp. 1328–1336 (2010)
9. Lin, D., Pantel, P.: DIRT - discovery of inference rules of text. In: Proceedings of the 7th ACM SIGKDD International Conference on Knowledge Discovery and Data Mining, pp. 323–328. ACM (2001)
10. Lopez, V., Fernández, M., Motta, E., Stieler, N.: Poweraqua: Supporting users in querying and exploring the semantic web. Semantic Web 3(3), 249–265 (2012)
11. Mahendra, R., Wanzare, L., Bernardi, R., Lavelli, A., Magnini, B.: Acquiring relational patterns from wikipedia: A case study. In: Proc. of the 5th Language and Technology Conference (2011)
12. McCrae, J., Spohr, D., Cimiano, P.: Linking lexical resources and ontologies on the semantic web with lemon. In: Antoniou, G., Grobelnik, M., Simperl, E., Parsia, B., Plexousakis, D., De Leenheer, P., Pan, J. (eds.) ESWC 2011, Part I. LNCS, vol. 6643, pp. 245–259. Springer, Heidelberg (2011)
13. McCrae, J., Unger, C.: Design patterns for engineering the ontology-lexicon interface. In: Buitelaar, P., Cimiano, P. (eds.) Towards the Multilingual Semantic Web. Springer (2014)
14. Miller, G., Fellbaum, C.: Wordnet: An electronic lexical database (1998)
15. Moro, A., Raganato, A., Navigli, R.: Entity linking meets word sense disambiguation: A unified approach. Proceedings of Transactions of the Association for Computational Linguistics, TACL (2014)
16. Navigli, R., Ponzetto, S.P.: Babelnet: The automatic construction, evaluation and application of a wide-coverage multilingual semantic network. Artificial Intelligence 193, 217–250 (2012)
17. Pantel, P., Pennacchiotti, M.: Espresso: Leveraging generic patterns for automatically harvesting semantic relations. In: Proceedings of the 21st International Conference on Computational Linguistics and the 44th Annual Meeting of the Association for Computational Linguistics, pp. 113–120 (2006)
18. Prévot, L., Huang, C.-R., Calzolari, N., Gangemi, A., Lenci, A., Oltramari, A.: Ontology and the lexicon: a multi-disciplinary perspective. In: Ontology and the Lexicon: A Natural Language Processing Perspective, pp. 3–24. Cambridge University Press (2010)
19. Sennrich, R., Schneider, G., Volk, M., Warin, M.: A new hybrid dependency parser for german. In: Proceedings of the German Society for Computational Linguistics and Language Technology, pp. 115–124 (2009)

20. Unger, C., Bühmann, L., Lehmann, J., Ngomo, A.-C.N., Gerber, D., Cimiano, P.: Template-based question answering over rdf data. In: Proceedings of the 21st International Conference on World Wide Web, pp. 639–648. ACM (2012)
21. Unger, C., McCrae, J., Walter, S., Winter, S., Cimiano, P.: A lemon lexicon for dbpedia. In: Proceedings of 1st International Workshop on NLP and DBpedia, Sydney, Australia, October 21-25 (2013)
22. Vila, M., Rodríguez, H., Martí, M.A.: Wrpa: A system for relational paraphrase acquisition from wikipedia. Procesamiento del Lenguaje Natural 45, 11–19 (2010)
23. Walter, S., Unger, C., Cimiano, P., Bär, D.: Evaluation of a layered approach to question answering over linked data. In: Cudré-Mauroux, P., et al. (eds.) ISWC 2012, Part II. LNCS, vol. 7650, pp. 362–374. Springer, Heidelberg (2012)

# Towards Efficient and Effective Semantic Table Interpretation

Ziqi Zhang

Department of Computer Science, University of Sheffield, UK
z.zhang@dcs.shef.ac.uk

**Abstract.** This paper describes TableMiner, the first semantic Table Interpretation method that adopts an incremental, mutually recursive and bootstrapping learning approach seeded by automatically selected 'partial' data from a table. TableMiner labels columns containing named entity mentions with semantic concepts that best describe data in columns, and disambiguates entity content cells in these columns. TableMiner is able to use various types of contextual information outside tables for Table Interpretation, including semantic markups (e.g., RDFa/microdata annotations) that to the best of our knowledge, have never been used in Natural Language Processing tasks. Evaluation on two datasets shows that compared to two baselines, TableMiner consistently obtains the best performance. In the classification task, it achieves significant improvements of between 0.08 and 0.38 F1 depending on different baseline methods; in the disambiguation task, it outperforms both baselines by between 0.19 and 0.37 in Precision on one dataset, and between 0.02 and 0.03 F1 on the other dataset. Observation also shows that the bootstrapping learning approach adopted by TableMiner can potentially deliver computational savings of between 24 and 60% against classic methods that 'exhaustively' processes the entire table content to build features for interpretation.

## 1 Introduction

Recovering semantics from tables on the Web is becoming a crucial task towards realizing the vision of Semantic Web. On the one hand, the amount of high-quality tables containing useful relational data is growing rapidly to hundreds of millions [5, 4]; on the other hand, classic search engines built for unstructured free-text perform poorly on such data as they ignore the underlying semantics in table structures at indexing time [12, 16]. Semantic **Table Interpretation** [12, 21–23, 16] aims to address this issue by solving three tasks: given a well-formed relational table[1] and a knowledge base defining a set of reference concepts and entities interlinked by relations, 1) recognize the semantic concept (or a property of a concept) that best describes the data in a column (i.e., classify columns); 2) identify the semantic relations between columns (i.e., relation enumeration); and 3) disambiguate content cells by linking them to existing (if any) entities in the knowledge base (i.e., entity disambiguation). Essentially, the knowledge

---

[1] Same as others, this work assumes availability of well-formed relational tables while methods of detecting them can be found in, e.g., [5]. A typical relational table is composed of regular rows and columns resembling those in traditional databases.

P. Mika et al. (Eds.) ISWC 2014, Part I, LNCS 8796, pp. 487–502, 2014.

base is a linked data set where resources are connected as triples. The outcome of semantic Table Interpretation is semantically annotated tabular data, which does not only enable effective indexing and search of the data, but ultimately can be transformed to new triples (e.g., new instances of concepts and relations) to populate the Linked Open Data (LOD) cloud.

The tasks resemble the classic Natural Language Processing tasks that have been extensively researched for decades, i.e., Named Entity Classification [18], Relation Extraction [19] and Named Entity Disambiguation [7]. However, classic approaches often fails at tabular data since they are trained for well-formed, unstructured sentences which are rare in table structures. Semantic Table Interpretation methods [12, 21–23, 16] typically depend on background knowledge bases to build features for learning. The typical workflow involves 1) retrieving candidates matching table components (e.g., a column header) from the knowledge base, 2) constructing features of candidates and model semantic interdependence between candidates and table components, and among various table components, and 3) applying inference to choose the best candidates.

This paper introduces TableMiner, designed to classify columns and disambiguate the contained cells in an unsupervised way that is both efficient and effective, addressing two limitations in existing works. First, existing methods have predominantly adopted an *exhaustive* strategy to build the candidate space for inference, e.g., column classification depends on candidate entities from *all* cells in the column [12, 16]. However, we argue this is unnecessary. Consider the table shown in Figure 1 as a snapshot of a rather large table containing over 50 rows of similar data. One does not need to read the entire table in order to label the three columns. Being able to make such inference using *partial* (as opposed to the entire table) data can improve the efficiency of Table Interpretation algorithms as the first two phases in the Table Interpretation workflow can cost up to 99% of computation time [12]. Second, inference algorithms of state-of-the-art are almost exclusively based on two types of features: those derived from background knowledge bases (in generic form, triples from certain linked data sets) and those derived from table components such as header text, and row content. This work notes that the document context that tables occur in (i.e., *around* and *outside* tables e.g., captions, page titles) offers equally useful clues for interpretation. In particular, another source of linked data - the pre-defined semantic markups within Webpages such as RDFa/microdata[2] annotations - provide important information about the Webpages and tables they contain. However such data have never been used in Table Interpretation tasks, even not in any NLP tasks in general.

TableMiner adopts a two-phase incremental, bootstrapping approach to interpret columns. A *forward-learning* phase uses an *incremental inference with stopping* algorithm (*I-inf*) that builds initial interpretation on an iterative row-by-row basis until TableMiner is 'sufficiently confident' (automatically determined by convergence) about the column classification result. Next, a *backward-update* phase begins by using initial results from the first phase (seeds) to constrain and guide interpretation of the remaining data. This can change the classification results on a column due to the newly disambiguated entity content cells. Therefore it is followed by a process to update classification and disambiguation results in the column in a mutually recursive pattern until

---

[2] E.g., with the schema.org vocabulary.

they become stabilized. In both tasks, TableMiner uses various types of table context (including pre-defined semantic markups within Webpages where available) to assist interpretation.

Evaluation on two datasets shows that TableMiner significantly outperforms two baselines in both classification (between 0.08 and 0.38 in F1) and disambiguation (between 0.19 and 0.37 Precision on one dataset based on manual inspection, and 0.02 to 0.03 F1 on another) tasks, and offers substantial potential to improve computational efficiency.

The remainder of this paper is organized as follows: Section 2 discusses related work, Section 3 introduces the methodology, Section 4 describes evaluation and discusses results, and Section 5 concludes this paper.

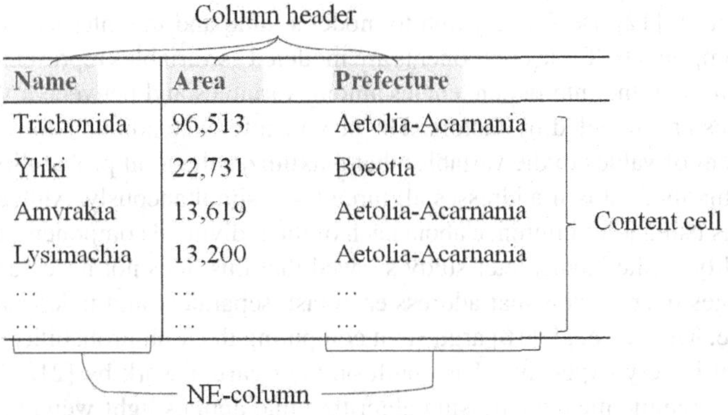

Column header

| Name | Area | Prefecture | |
|------|------|------------|---|
| Trichonida | 96,513 | Aetolia-Acarnania | |
| Yliki | 22,731 | Boeotia | |
| Amvrakia | 13,619 | Aetolia-Acarnania | Content cell |
| Lysimachia | 13,200 | Aetolia-Acarnania | |
| ... | ... | ... | |
| ... | ... | ... | |

NE-column

**Fig. 1.** Lakes in Central Greece (adapted from Wikipedia)

# 2    Related Work

This work belongs to the general domain of table information extraction covering a wide range of topics such as table structure understanding [25] that aims to uncover structural relations underlying table layout in complex tables; relational table identification that aims to separate tables containing relational data from noisy ones used for, e.g., page formatting, and then subsequently identifying table schema [5, 4, 1]; table schema matching and data integration that aims to merge tables describing similar data [2, 3, 13]; and semantic Table Interpretation, which is the focus of this work. It also belongs to the domain of (semi-)structured Information Extraction, where an extensive amount of literature is marginally related.

## 2.1    Semantic Table Interpretation

Venetis et al. [22] annotate columns in a table with semantic concepts and identify relations between the subject column (typically containing entities that the table is about) and other columns using a database mined with regular lexico-syntactic patterns such as the Hearst patterns [9]. The database records co-occurrence statistics for each pair of values extracted by such patterns. A maximum likelihood inference model is used to predict the best concepts and relations from candidates using these statistics.

Similarly, Wang et al. [23] first identify a subject column in the table, then based on subject entity mentions in the column and their corresponding values in other columns, associate a concept from the Probase knowledge base [24] that best describes the table schema (hence properties of the concept are used to label the columns). Essentially this classifies table columns and identifies relations between the subject column and other columns. Probase is a probabilistic database built in the similar way as that in Venetis et al. [22] and contains an inverted index that supports searching and ranking candidate concepts given a list of terms describing possible concept properties, or names describing possible instances. Interpretation heavily depends on these features and the probability statistics gathered in the database.

Limaye et al. [12] use factor graph to model a table and the interdependencies between its components. Table components are modeled as variables represented as nodes on the graph; then the interdependencies among variables and between a variable and its candidates are modeled by factors. The task of inference amounts to searching for an assignment of values to the variables that maximizes the joint probability. A unique feature of this method is it addresses all three tasks simultaneously. Although the key motivation is using joint inference about each of the individual components to boost the overall quality of the labels, later study showed that this does not necessarily guarantee advantages over models that address each task separately and independently [22]. Furthermore, Mulwad et al. [16] argue that computing the joint probability distribution in the model is very expensive. Thus built on their earlier work by [21, 17, 15], they introduce a semantic message passing algorithm that applies light-weight inference to the same kind of graphical model. TableMiner is similar in the way that the iterative *backward-update* phase could also be considered a semantic message passing process that involves fewer variables and factors, hence is faster to converge.

One limitation of the above methods is that the construction of candidate space and their feature representation is *exhaustive*, since they require evidence from all content cells of a column in order to classify that column. This can significantly damage the efficiency of semantic Table Interpretation algorithms as it is shown that constructing candidate space and their feature representations is the major bottleneck in Table Interpretation [12]. However, as illustrated before, human cognition does not necessarily follow the similar process but can be more efficient as we are able to infer on partial data.

Another issue with existing work is that many of them make use of non-generalizable, knowledge base specific features. For example, Venetis et al. [22] and Wang et al. [23] use statistics gathered during the construction of the knowledge bases, which is unavailable in resources such as Freebase[3] or DBpedia[4]. Syed et al. [21] and Mulwad et al. [17, 15, 16] use search relevance scores returned by the knowledge base that is also resource-specific and unavailable in, e.g., Freebase and DBpedia. TableMiner however, uses only generic features present in almost every knowledge base.

---

[3] http://www.freebase.com/
[4] http://dbpedia.org/

## 2.2   Information Extraction in General

The three subtasks tackled by semantic Table Interpretation are closely related to Named Entity Recognition (NER), Named Entity Disambiguation and Relation Extraction in the general Information Extraction domain. State-of-the-art methods [20, 10] however, are tailored to unstructured text content that is different from tabular data. The inter-dependency among the table components cannot be easily taken into account in such methods [14]. For NER and Relation Extraction, a learning process is typically required for each semantic label (i.e., class or relation) that must be known a-priori and training or seed data must be provided. In Table Interpretation however, semantic classes and relations are unknown a-priori. Further, due to the large candidate space, it is infeasible to create sufficient training or seed data in such tasks.

Wrapper induction [11, 8] automatically learns wrappers that can extract information from structured Webpages. It builds on the phenomenon that the same type of information are typically presented in similar structures in different Webpages and exploits such regularities to extract information. Technically, Wrapper induction can be adapted to partially address Table Interpretation by learning wrappers able to classify table columns. However, the candidate classes must be defined a-priori and training data are essential to build such wrappers. As discussed above, these are infeasible in the case of semantic Table Interpretation.

## 3   Methodology

This section describes TableMiner in details. $T$ denotes a regular, horizontal, relational table containing $i$ rows of content cells (excluding the row of table headers) and $j$ columns, $T_i$ denotes row $i$, $T_j$ denotes column $j$, $TH_j$ is the header of column $j$, and $T_{i,j}$ is a cell at row $T_i$ and column $T_j$. $X$ denotes different types of *context* used to support Table Interpretation. $C_j$ is a set of candidate concepts for column $j$. $E_{i,j}$ is a set of candidate entities for the cell $T_{i,j}$. Both $C_j$ and $E_{i,j}$ are derived from a reference knowledge base, details of which is to be described below. Function $l(o)$ returns the string content if $o$ is a table component (e.g., in Figure 1 $l(T_{2,1})$ ='Yliki'), or the label if $o$ is an annotation (i.e., any $c_j \in C_j$ or any $e_{i,j} \in E_{i,j}$). Unless otherwise stated, $bow(o)$ returns a bag-of-words (multiset) representation of $o$ by tokenizing $l(o)$, then normalizing each token by lemmatization and removing stop words. $bowset(o)$ is the de-duplicated set based on $bow(o)$. $w$ is a single token and $freq(w, o)$ counts the frequency of $w$ in $bow(o)$. $|\cdot|$ returns the size of a collection, either containing duplicates or de-duplicated.

TableMiner firstly identifies table columns that contain mostly ($> 50\%$ of non-empty rows) named entities (NE-columns). This is done by using regular expressions based on capitalization and number of tokens in each content cell. The goal is to distinguish such columns from others that are unlikely to contain named entities (e.g., columns containing numeric data, such as column 'Area' in Figure 1 and thus do not need classification). Then given an NE-column $T_j$, **column interpretation** proceeds in a two-phase bootstrapping manner, where each phase deals with both column classification and cell entity disambiguation. The first *forward-learning* phase builds initial interpretation based

**Table 1.** Table context elements

| Context | |
|---|---|
| Webpage title | out-table context |
| Table caption | |
| Semantic markups if any | |
| Surrounding paragraphs | |
| Column header | in-table context |
| Row content | |
| Column content | |

on partial data in the column, while the second *backward-update* phase interprets remaining cells and iteratively updates annotations (concept and entity) for the entire column until they are stablized.

### 3.1   Context

A list of the context types used for semantic Table Interpretation is shown in Table 1. A key innovation in TableMiner is using context *outside* tables, including **table captions**, **Webpage title**, **surrounding paragraphs**, and **semantic markups** inserted by certain websites.

Table captions and the title of the Webpage may mention key terms that are likely to be the focus concept in a table. Paragraphs surrounding tables may describe the content in the table, thus containing clue words indicating the concepts or descriptions of entities in the table. Furthermore, an increasing number of semantically annotated Webpages are becoming available under the heavily promoted usage of semantic markup vocabularies (e.g., microdata format at *schema.org*) by major search engines [6]. An example of this is IMDB.com, on which Webpages about movies contain microdata annotations such as movie titles, release year, directors and actors, which are currently used by Google Rich Snippet[5] to improve content access. Such data provides important clues on the 'aboutness' of a Webpage, and therefore tables (if any) within the Webpage.

### 3.2   The *forward-learning* Phase

Algorithm 1 shows the *incremental inference with stopping (I-inf)* algorithm used by *forward-learning*. Each iteration disambiguates a content cell $T_{i,j}$ by comparing candidate entities from $E_{i,j}$ against their context and choosing the highest scoring (i.e., winning) candidate (**Candidate search** and **Disambiguation**). Then the concepts associated with the entity are gathered to create $C_j$ the set of candidate concepts for column $T_j$, and each member $c_j \in C_j$ is scored based on its context and those already disambiguated entities (**Classification**). At the end of each iteration, $C_j$ from the current iteration is compared with the previous to check for convergence, by which 'satisfactory' initial annotations are created and *forward-learning* ends.

---

[5] http://www.google.com/webmasters/tools/richsnippets

---

**Algorithm 1.** Forward learning

---
1: Input: $T_j$; $C_j \leftarrow \emptyset$
2: **for all** cell $T_{i,j}$ in $T_j$ **do**
3:     $prevC_j \leftarrow C_j$
4:     $E_{i,j} \leftarrow$ disambiguate($T_{i,j}$)
5:     $C_j \leftarrow$ updateclass($C_j, E_{i,j}$)
6:     **if** convergence($C_j, prevC_j$) **then**
7:         break
8:     **end if**
9: **end for**

---

**Candidate Search.** In this step, the text content of a cell $l(T_{i,j})$ is searched in a knowledge base and entities whose labels $l(e_{i,j})$ overlaps with $l(T_{i,j})$ is chosen as candidates $(E_{i,j})$ for the cell (the number of overlapping words/tokens does not matter). For example, 'Trichonida' will retrieve candidate named entities 'Lake Trichonida' and 'Trichonida Province'. TableMiner does not use relevance-based rankings or scores returned by the knowledge base as features for inference, while others [21, 17, 15, 16] do.

**Disambiguation** ($disambiguate(T_{i,j})$). Each content cell $T_{i,j}$ is disambiguated by candidate entity's confidence score, which is based on two components: a *context* score $ctxe$ and a *name match* score $nm$.

The *context* score measures the similarity between each candidate entity and the context of $T_{i,j}$, denoted as $x_{i,j} \in X_{i,j}$. Firstly, a $bow(e_{i,j})$ representation for each $e_{i,j} \in E_{i,j}$ is created based on triples containing $e_{i,j}$ as subject. Let $<e_{i,j}, predicate, object>$ be the set of such triples retrieved from a knowledge base, then $bow(e_{i,j})$ simply concatenates $object$ from all triples, tokenizes the concatenated string, and normalizes the tokens by lemmatization and stop words removal. For each $x_{i,j}$, $bow(x_{i,j})$ converts the text content of the corresponding component into a bag-of-words representation following the standard definition introduced before. Finally, to compute the similarity between $e_{i,j}$ and $x_{i,j}$, two functions are used. For each type of out-table context shown in Table 1, the similarity is computed using a frequency weighted dice function:

$$dice(e_{i,j}, x_{i,j}) =$$
$$\frac{2 \times \sum_{w \in bowset(e_{i,j}) \cap bowset(x_{i,j})} (freq(w, e_{i,j}) + freq(w, x_{i,j}))}{|bow(e_{i,j})| + |bow(x_{i,j})|} \quad (1)$$

For in-table context, the similarity is computed by 'coverage':

$$coverage(e_{i,j}, x_{i,j}) = \frac{\sum_{w \in bowset(e_{i,j}) \cap bowset(x_{i,j})} freq(w, x_{i,j})}{|bow(x_{i,j})|}, \quad (2)$$

because the sizes of $bow(e_{i,j})$ and $bow(x_{i,j})$ can be often different orders of magnitude and Equation 1 may produce negligible values. Specifically, *row content* is the concatenation of $l(T_{i,j'})$ for all columns $j', j \neq j'$ (e.g., for the cell 'Yliki' in Figure 1 this includes 'Boeotia','22,731'). Intuitively, these are likely to be attribute data of the concerning entity. *Column content* is the concatenation of $l(T_{i',j})$ for all rows $i', i \neq i'$ (e.g., for the cell 'Yliki' in Figure 1 this includes 'Trichonida','Amvrakia', and 'Lysimachia'). Intuitively, these are names of entities that are semantically similar.

Therefore, the similarity score between $e_{i,j}$ and each $x_{i,j} \in X_{i,j}$ is computed as above and summed up to obtain the context score $ctxe(e_{i,j})$.

The *name match* score examines the overlap between the name of the entity and the cell content, to promote entities whose name matches exactly the content string:

$$nm(e_{i,j}, T_{i,j}) = \sqrt{\frac{2 \times |bowset(l(e_{i,j})) \cap bowset(T_{i,j})|}{|bowset(l(e_{i,j}))| + |bowset(T_{i,j})|}} \tag{3}$$

The final confidence score of a candidate entity, denoted by $fse(e_{i,j})$, is the product of $ctxe(e_{i,j})$ and $nm(e_{i,j}, T_{i,j})$.

**Classification ($updateclass(C_j)$).** In each iteration, the entity with the highest $fse(e_{i,j})$ score is selected for the current cell and its associated concepts are used to update the candidate set of concepts $C_j$ for the column. Each $c_j \in C_j$ is associated with a confidence score $fsc(c_j)$ also consisting of two elements: a *base* score $bs$ and a *context* score $ctxc$.

The *base* score is based on the *fse* scores of the winning entities from already disambiguated content cells by the current iteration. Let $disamb(c_j)$ be the sum of $fse(e_{i,j})$ where $e_{i,j}$ is a winning entity from a content cell and is associated with $c_j$, then $bs(c_j)$ is $disamb(c_j)$ divided by the number of rows in $T$. Note that as additional content cells are disambiguated in new iterations, new candidate concepts may be added to $C_j$; or for existing candidate concepts, their base scores can be updated if the winning entities from newly disambiguated content cell also select them.

The *context* score is based on the overlap between $l(c_j)$ and its context, and is computed in the similar way as the context score for candidate entities. Let $x_j \in X_j$ denotes various types of context for the column header $TH_j$. All types of context shown in Table 1 except row content is used. For each context $x_j \in X_j$, a similarity score is computed between $c_j$ and $x_j$ using the weighted dice function introduced before but replacing $e_{i,j}$ with $c_j$, and $x_{i,j}$ with $x_j$. $bow(c_j)$ and $bowset(c_j)$ is created following the standard definitions. Then the *sum* of the similarity scores becomes the context score $ctxc(c_j)$.

The final confidence score of a candidate concept $fsc(c_j)$ adds up $bs(c_j)$ and $ctxc(c_j)$ with equal weights.

**Convergence (convergence($C_j$, $prevC_j$)).** Results of the two above operations at each iteration may either create new concept candidates for the column, or resetting the scores of existing candidates, thus changing the 'state' of $C_j$. TableMiner does not exhaustively process every cell in a column. Instead, it automatically stops by detecting the convergence of 'entropy' of the state of $C_j$ at the end of an iteration as measured below. Convergence happens if the difference between the current and previous state's entropy is less than a threshold of $t$.

$$entropy(C_j) = - \sum_{c_j \in C_j} P(c_j) \log_2 P(c_j) \qquad (4)$$

$$P(c_j) = \frac{fsc(c_j)}{\sum_{c'_j \in C_j} fsc(c'_j)} \qquad (5)$$

The intuition is that when the entropy level stabilizes, the contribution by each $P(c_j)$ to the state is also expected to stabilize. In other words, the relative confidence score of $c_j$ to the collective sum (the denominator in Equation 5) changes little. As a result, the ranking of candidate concepts also stabilizes, and so winning candidates will surface.

### 3.3 The *backward-update* Phase

The *backward-update* phase begins (i.e., first iteration) by taking the classification outcome $C_j$ from the *forward* phase as constraints on the disambiguation of remaining cells in the same column. Let $C_j^+ \subset C_j$ be the set of highest scoring classes ('winning' concepts, multiple concepts with the same highest score is possible) for column $j$ computed by the *forward* phase. For each remaining cell in the column, disambiguation candidates are restricted to entities whose associated concepts overlap with $C_j^+$. Effectively, this reduces the number of candidates thus improving efficiency. **Disambiguation** follows the same procedure as in the *forward* phase, and its results may revise **classification** $C_j$ for the column, either adding new elements to $C_j$, or resetting scores of existing ones (due to changes of $fsc(c_j)$).

Thus after disambiguating the remaining cells, $C_j^+$ is re-selected. If the new $C_j^+$ is different from the previous, a new update operation is triggered. It repeats the disambiguation and classification operations on the entire column, while using the new $C_j^+$ as constraints to restrict candidate entity space. This procedure repeats until $C_j^+$ and the winning entity in each cell stabilizes (i.e., no change), completing interpretation.

In theory, starting from the second iteration, new candidate entities may be retrieved and processed due to the change in $C_j^+$. Empirically, it is found that 1) in most cases the update phase completes in one iteration; and 2) in cases where it doesn't, it converges fast and following iterations mostly re-selects from the pool of candidates that were already processed in the beginning of the update phase (first iteration), thus incurring little computational cost.

## 4 Evaluation

TableMiner is evaluated by the standard Precision, Recall and F1 metrics in the column classification and entity disambiguation tasks. It is compared against two baselines on two datasets (shown in Table 2). The knowledge base used in this experiment is Freebase. Freebase is currently the largest well-maintained knowledge base in the world, containing over 2.4 billion facts about over 43 million topics (e.g., entities, concepts), largely exceeding other popular knowledge bases such as DBpedia and YAGO.

## 4.1 Datasets

**Limaye112** contains a randomly selected 112 tables from the Limaye dataset [12]. The original dataset is annotated by Wikipedia article titles referring to named entities and YAGO concepts and relations. The dataset contains about 90% of Wikipedia article pages, while the other 10% are randomly crawled Webpages. Each Webpage contains a 'focus' relational table to be interpreted, together with the context such as page titles, table captions, and paragraphs around it. These Webpages do not have Microdata annotations. The dataset covers multiple domains, such as film, music, games, location, organization, events etc. These tables must be re-annotated due to the significant changes of such resources, also due to the usage of a different knowledge base in this work.

To create the ground truth for the classification task, the NE-columns in these tables are manually annotated following a similar process as Venetis et al. [22]. Specifically, TableMiner and the baselines (Section 4.2) are ran on these tables and the candidate concepts for all NE-columns are collected and presented to annotators. The annotators mark each label as *best*, *okay*, or *incorrect*. The basic principle is to prefer the most specific concept among all suitable candidates. For example, given a content cell 'Penrith Panthers', the concept 'Rugby Club' is the *best* candidate to label its parent column while 'Sports Team' and 'Organization' are *okay*. The annotators may also insert new labels if none of the candidates are suitable.

The top ranked prediction by TableMiner is checked against the classification ground truth. Each *best* label is awarded a score of 1 while each *okay* label is awarded 0.5. Further, if there are multiple top-ranked candidates, each candidate considered correct only receives a fraction of its score as $\frac{score}{\#topranked}$. For example, if a column containing film titles has two top-ranked concept candidates with the same score: 'Film' (best) and 'Book' (incorrect), this prediction receives a score of 0.5 instead of 1. This is to penalize the situation where the Table Interpretation system fails to discriminate false positives from true positives.

To create the ground truth for the disambiguation task, each Wikipedia article title in the original tables is automatically mapped to a Freebase topic (e.g., an entity or a concept) id by using the MediaWiki API[6] and the Freebase MQL[7] interface. As it will be discussed later, evaluation of entity disambiguation on this dataset reveals that the original dataset could be biased, possibly due to the older version of Wikipedia used in the original experiments. Therefore, a manual inspection of the output of TableMiner and the baselines evaluation is carried out to further evaluate the different systems.

**IMDB** contains 7,354 tables extracted from a random set of IMDB movie Webpages. They are annotated automatically to evaluate entity disambiguation. Each IMDB movie Webpage[8] contains a table listing a column of actors/actresses and a column of corresponding characters played. Cells in the actor/actress column are linked with an IMDB item ID, which, when searched in Freebase, returns a unique (if any) mapped Freebase topic. Thus these columns are annotated automatically in such a way. The 'character' column is not used since they are not mapped in Freebase.

---

[6] http://www.mediawiki.org/wiki/API:Main_page
[7] http://www.freebase.com/query
[8] e.g., http://www.imdb.com/title/tt0071562/

**Table 2.** Datasets for evaluation. The number in bracket shows the number of annotated columns for the corresponding 112 tables in the original Limaye dataset. The re-created dataset doubles the size of annotations.

|                       | Limaye112   | IMDB   |
|-----------------------|-------------|--------|
| Tables                | 112         | 7,354  |
| Annotated columns     | 254 (119)   | 7,354  |
| Annotated entity cells| 2,089       | 92,317 |

## 4.2  Configuration and Baseline

The convergence threshold in the *I-inf* algorithm is set to 0.01. Semantic markups are only available in the IMDB dataset. To use this type of context for semantic Table Interpretation, Any23[9] is used to extract the microdata format annotations as RDF triples and the *objects* of triples are concatenated as contextual text. Annotations within the HTML *<table>* tags are excluded.

Two **baselines** are created. Baseline 'first result' ($B_{first}$) firstly disambiguates every content cell in a column by choosing the top ranked named entity candidate in the Freebase search result. Freebase implements a ranking algorithm for its Search API to promote popular topics. TableMiner however, does not use such features. Then each disambiguated cell casts a vote to the set of concepts the winning named entity belongs to, and the concept that receives the majority vote is selected to label the column.

Baseline 'similarity based' ($B_{sim}$) uses both string similarity methods and a simple context-based similarity measure to disambiguate a content cell. Given a content cell and its candidate named entities, it computes a string similarity score between a candidate entity's name and the cell content using the Levenshtein metric. It then uses Equation 1 to compute a context overlap score between the bag-of-words representation of a candidate entity and the row context of its containing cell in the table. The two scores are added together as the final disambiguation score for a candidate named entity for the cell and the winning candidate is chosen for the cell. Candidate concepts for the column are derived from winning named entity for each content cell, then the score of a candidate concept is based on the fraction of cells that cast vote for that concept, plus the string similarity (Levenshtein) between the label of the concept and the column header text. Baseline $B_{sim}$ can be considered as an 'exhaustive' Table Interpretation method, which disambiguates every content cell before deriving column classification and uses features from in-table context that are commonly found in state-of-the-art [12, 21, 17, 15, 16].

Table 3 compares the three methods in terms of the contextual features used for learning.

## 4.3  Results and Discussion

**Effectiveness.** Table 4 shows disambiguation results obtained on the two datasets. TableMiner obtains the best F1 on both datasets. It also obtains the highest Precision

---

[9] https://any23.apache.org/

**Table 3.** Use of context features in the three methods for comparison

|                   | $B_{first}$ | $B_{sim}$ | TableMiner |
|-------------------|-------------|-----------|------------|
| In-table context  | No          | Yes       | Yes        |
| Out-table context | No          | No        | Yes        |

**Table 4.** Disambiguation results on the two datasets. The highest F1 on each dataset is marked in **bold**.

|             | Limaye112 | | | IMDB | | |
|-------------|-----------|--------|-------|-----------|--------|--------|
|             | Precision | Recall | F1    | Precision | Recall | F1     |
| $B_{first}$ | 0.927     | 0.918  | **0.922** | 0.927 | 0.922  | 0.925  |
| $B_{sim}$   | 0.907     | 0.898  | 0.902 | 0.937     | 0.932  | 0.935  |
| TableMiner  | 0.923     | 0.921  | **0.922** | 0.96  | 0.954  | **0.956** |

and Recall on the IMDB dataset, and the highest Recall on the Limaye112 dataset. It is surprising to note that even the most simplistic baseline $B_{first}$ obtains very good results: it achieves over 0.9 F1 on the IMDB dataset, while on the Limaye112 dataset it obtains results that betters $B_{sim}$ and equally compares to TableMiner. Note that the figures are significantly higher than those reported originally by Limaye et al (in the range of 0.8 and 0.85) [12].

The extremely well performance on the IMDB dataset could be attributed to the domain and the Freebase search API. As mentioned before, the Freebase search API assigns higher weights to popular topics. The result is that topics in the domains such as movie, book, pop music and politics are likely to be visited and edited more frequently, subsequently increasing their level of 'popularity'. Therefore, by selecting the top-ranked result, $B_{first}$ is very likely to make the correct prediction.

To uncover the contributing factors to its performance on the Limaye112 dataset, the ground truth is analyzed and it is found that, each of the 112 tables on average only 1.1 (minimum 1, maximum 2) columns that are annotated with entities, while TableMiner annotates on average 2.3 NE-columns. This suggests that the entity annotations in the ground truth are sparse. Moreover, the average length of entity names by number of tokens is 2.3, with the maximum being 12, and over 33% of entity names have 3 or more tokens while only 22% have a single-token name. This could possibly explain the extremely well performance by $B_{first}$ as typically, short names are much more ambiguous than longer names. By using a dataset that is biased toward entities with long names, the strategy by $B_{first}$ is very likely to succeed.

Hence to obtain a more balanced perspective, the results created by the three systems are manually inspected and re-annotated. To do so, for each method, the predicted entity annotations that are already covered by the automatically created ground truth are excluded. Then, in the remaining annotations, those that all three systems predict the same are removed. The remainder (932 entity annotations, of which 572 is predicted correctly by at least one system) are the ones that the three systems 'disagree' on, and are manually validated. Table 5 shows the analysis results. TableMiner significantly outperforms the two baseline. Manual inspection on 20% of the wrong annotations by all three methods reveals that it is largely (> 80%) because the knowledge base does

**Table 5.** Precision based on manual analysis of 932 entity annotations that the three systems disagree on

|            | Precision | Precision either-or |
|------------|-----------|---------------------|
| $B_{first}$ | 0.265     | 0.431               |
| $B_{sim}$   | 0.306     | 0.498               |
| TableMiner  | 0.491     | 0.801               |

**Table 6.** Classification result on the Limaye112 dataset. The highest F1 is marked in **bold**.

|            | *best* only |        |        | *best* or *ok* |        |        |
|------------|-------------|--------|--------|----------------|--------|--------|
|            | Precision   | Recall | F1     | Precision      | Recall | F1     |
| $B_{first}$ | 0.258       | 0.247  | 0.252  | 0.505          | 0.484  | 0.494  |
| $B_{sim}$   | 0.487       | 0.481  | 0.484  | 0.667          | 0.658  | 0.662  |
| TableMiner  | 0.646       | 0.618  | **0.632** | 0.761       | 0.729  | **0.745** |

not contain the correct candidate. When only annotations that are correct by any one method are considered (Precision either-or), TableMiner achieves a precision of 0.8 while $B_{first}$ 0.431 and $B_{sim}$ 0.498.

Table 6 shows the classification result on the Limaye112 dataset. TableMiner almost tripled the performance of $B_{first}$ and significantly outperforms $B_{sim}$. Again surprisingly, the superior performance by $B_{first}$ on the disambiguation task does not translate to equal performance on the classification task. Manual inspection shows that it is significantly penalized by predicting multiple top-ranked candidate concepts. In other words, it fails to discriminate true positives from false positives. It has been noted that the state-of-the-art methods often use a concept hierarchy defined within knowledge bases to solve such cases by giving higher weights to more specific concepts [12, 16]. However, concept hierarchies are not necessarily available in all knowledge bases. For example, Freebase has a rather loose concept network instead of a hierarchy. Nevertheless, TableMiner is able to predict a single best concept candidate in most cases without such knowledge. It also outperforms $B_{sim}$ by a substantial margin, suggesting the usage of various table context is very effective and that exhaustive approaches may not necessarily offer advantage but causes additional computation.

While not directly comparable due to the datasets and knowledge bases used, the classification results by TableMiner is higher than 0.56 in [12], 0.6-0.65 (*best* or *okay*) in [22], and 0.5-0.6 (*best* or *okay*) in [16].

**Efficiency.** The potential efficiency improvement by TableMiner can be assessed by observing the reduced number of candidate entities. As discussed earlier, candidate retrieval and feature space construction account the majority (>90%) of computation [12]. Experiments in this work show that retrieving candidate entities and their data (triples) from Freebase accounts for over 90% of CPU time, indeed a major bottleneck in semantic Table Interpretation.

TableMiner reduces the quantity of candidate entities to be processed by 1) generating initial interpretation (*forward-learning*) using *partial* instead of *complete* data as an exhaustive method would otherwise do; and 2) using the initial interpretation

**Table 7.** Number of iterations until convergence in the *forward learning* phase

|            | Max | Min | Mean |
|------------|-----|-----|------|
| Limaye112  | 42  | 2   | 9    |
| IMDB       | 15  | 2   | 8    |

outcome to constrain further learning (*backward-update*). Compared against $B_{sim}$ that exhaustively disambiguates every content cells in a table before classifying the columns, TableMiner reduces the total number of candidate entities to be considered by disambiguation operations by 32% in the Limaye112 and 24% in the IMDB datasets respectively. When only content cells processed in the *backward-update* phase are considered, the figures amount to 38% and 61%.

Furthermore, Table 7 shows the convergence speed in the *forward-learning* phase. Considering the column classification task only and using the Limaye112 dataset as an example, it suggests that on average only 9 rows are needed to create *initial* classification labels on NE-columns, as opposed to using all rows in a table (average of 27) by an exhaustive method. The slowest convergence happens in a table of 78 rows (converged at 46). The average fractions of rows that need not to be processed (i.e., savings) in the *forward* phase are 57% for Limaye112 and 43% for IMDB. Then In the *backward* phase, the number of columns that actually need iterative update is 10% of all columns in both datasets. The average number of iterations for those needing iterative update is 3 for both datasets. To summarize again using the Limaye112 dataset, TableMiner manages to produce 'stable' column classification for 90% of columns using only *forward-learning* with an average of 9 rows, resulting in a potential 57% of savings than an exhaustive method for this very specific task.

**Final Remark.** In summary, by using various types of in- and out-table context in semantic Table Interpretation, TableMiner obtains the best performance on both classification and disambiguation tasks. On the classification task, it delivers significant improvement by between 8 and 38% over the baselines, none of which uses features from out-table context. By adopting an incremental, bootstrapping pattern of learning, TableMiner can potentially deliver between 24 and 60% computational savings compared against exhaustive methods depending on tasks.

## 5    Conclusion

This paper introduced TableMiner, a Table Interpretation method that makes use of various types of context both within and outside tables for classifying table columns and disambiguating content cells, and learns in an incremental, bootstrapping, and mutually-recursive pattern. TableMiner contributes to the state-of-the-art by introducing 1) a generic Table Interpretation method able to be adapted to any knowledge bases; 2) a generic model of using various table context in such task, the first that uses semantic markups within Webpages as features; 3) an automatic method for determining sample data to bootstrap Table Interpretation.

TableMiner is evaluated on two datasets against two baselines, one of which represents an exhaustive method that only uses features from within-table context. TableMiner consistently obtains the best results on both tasks. It significantly outperforms both baselines in the classification task and on the re-annotated dataset (i.e., manual inspection and validation) in the disambiguation task.

One limitation of the current work is that the contribution of each type of out-table and in-table context in the task is not extensively evaluated. This will be addressed in future work. Further, future work will also focus on extending TableMiner to a full Table Interpretation method addressing all three subtasks. Other methods of sample selection will also be explored and compared.

**Acknowledgement.** Part of this research has been sponsored by the EPSRC funded project LODIE: Linked Open Data for Information Extraction, EP/J019488/1.

# References

1. Adelfio, M.D., Samet, H.: Schema extraction for tabular data on the web. Proc. VLDB Endow. 6(6), 421–432 (2013)
2. Ahmad, A., Eldad, L., Aline, S., Corentin, F., Raphaël, T., David, T.: Improving schema matching with linked data. In: First International Workshop on Open Data (2012)
3. Bhagavatula, C.S., Noraset, T., Downey, D.: Methods for exploring and mining tables on wikipedia. In: Proceedings of the ACM SIGKDD Interative Data Exploration and Analysis (IDEA), IDEA 2013 (2013)
4. Cafarella, M.J., Halevy, A., Madhavan, J.: Structured data on the web. Communications of the ACM 54(2), 72–79 (2011)
5. Cafarella, M.J., Halevy, A., Wang, D.Z., Wu, E., Zhang, Y.: Webtables: exploring the power of tables on the web. Proceedings of VLDB Endowment 1(1), 538–549 (2008)
6. Ciravegna, F., Gentile, A.L., Zhang, Z.: Lodie: Linked open data for web-scale information extraction. In: Maynard, D., van Erp, M., Davis, B. (eds.) SWAIE. CEUR Workshop Proceedings, vol. 925, pp. 11–22. CEUR-WS.org (2012)
7. Cucerzan, S.: Large-scale named entity disambiguation based on Wikipedia data. In: Proceedings of the 2007 Joint Conference on Empirical Methods in Natural Language Processing and Computational Natural Language Learning (EMNLP-CoNLL), pp. 708–716. Association for Computational Linguistics, Prague (2007)
8. Gentile, A.L., Zhang, Z., Augenstein, I., Ciravegna, F.: Unsupervised wrapper induction using linked data. In: Proceedings of the Seventh International Conference on Knowledge Capture, K-CAP 2013. ACM, New York (2013)
9. Hearst, M.A.: Automatic acquisition of hyponyms from large text corpora. In: Proceedings of the 14th Conference on Computational Linguistics, COLING 1992, vol. 2, pp. 539–545. Association for Computational Linguistics, Stroudsburg (1992)
10. Krishnan, V., Manning, C.D.: An effective two-stage model for exploiting non-local dependencies in named entity recognition. In: Proceedings of the 21st International Conference on Computational Linguistics and the 44th Annual Meeting of the Association for Computational Linguistics, pp. 1121–1128. ACL-44, Association for Computational Linguistics, Stroudsburg (2006)
11. Kushmerick, N., Weld, D.S., Doorenbos, R.: Wrapper induction for information extraction. In: Proc. IJCAI 1997 (1997)

12. Limaye, G., Sarawagi, S., Chakrabarti, S.: Annotating and searching web tables using entities, types and relationships. Proceedings of the VLDB Endowment 3(1-2), 1338–1347 (2010)

13. Ling, X., Halevy, A., Wu, F., Yu, C.: Synthesizing union tables from the web. In: Proceedings of the 23rd International Joint Conference on Artificial Intelligence, pp. 2677–2683 (2013)

14. Lu, C., Bing, L., Lam, W., Chan, K., Gu, Y.: Web entity detection for semi-structured text data records with unlabeled data. International Journal of Computational Linguistics and Applications (2013)

15. Mulwad, V., Finin, T., Joshi, A.: Automatically generating government linked data from tables. In: Working notes of AAAI Fall Symposium on Open Government Knowledge: AI Opportunities and Challenges (November 2011)

16. Mulwad, V., Finin, T., Joshi, A.: Semantic message passing for generating linked data from tables. In: Alani, H., et al. (eds.) ISWC 2013, Part I. LNCS, vol. 8218, pp. 363–378. Springer, Heidelberg (2013)

17. Mulwad, V., Finin, T., Syed, Z., Joshi, A.: T2ld: Interpreting and representing tables as linked data. In: Polleres, A., Chen, H. (eds.) ISWC Posters and Demos. CEUR Workshop Proceedings. CEUR-WS.org (2010)

18. Nadeau, D., Sekine, S.: A survey of named entity recognition and classification. Linguisticae Investigationes 30(1), 3–26 (2007), Publisher: John Benjamins Publishing Company

19. Sarawagi, S.: Information extraction. Found. Trends Databases 1(3), 261–377 (2008)

20. Sarawagi, S., Cohen, W.W.: Semi-markov conditional random fields for information extraction. In: Advances in Neural Information Processing Systems 17, pp. 1185–1192 (2004)

21. Syed, Z., Finin, T., Mulwad, V., Joshi, A.: Exploiting a web of semantic data for interpreting tables. In: Proceedings of the Second Web Science Conference (April 2010)

22. Venetis, P., Halevy, A., Madhavan, J., Paşca, M., Shen, W., Wu, F., Miao, G., Wu, C.: Recovering semantics of tables on the web. Proceedings of VLDB Endowment 4(9), 528–538 (2011)

23. Wang, J., Wang, H., Wang, Z., Zhu, K.Q.: Understanding tables on the web. In: Atzeni, P., Cheung, D., Ram, S. (eds.) ER 2012 Main Conference 2012. LNCS, vol. 7532, pp. 141–155. Springer, Heidelberg (2012)

24. Wu, W., Li, H., Wang, H., Zhu, K.Q.: Probase: a probabilistic taxonomy for text understanding. In: Proceedings of the 2012 ACM SIGMOD International Conference on Management of Data, SIGMOD 2012, pp. 481–492. ACM, New York (2012)

25. Zanibbi, R., Blostein, D., Cordy, J.: A survey of table recognition: Models, observations, transformations, and inferences. International Journal of Document Analysis and Recognition 7, 1–16 (2003)

# Semano: Semantic Annotation Framework for Natural Language Resources

David Berry[1] and Nadeschda Nikitina[2]

[1] QinetiQ, UK
[2] University of Oxford, UK

**Abstract.** In this paper, we present Semano — a generic framework for annotating natural language texts with entities of OWL 2 DL ontologies. Semano
generalizes the mechanism of JAPE transducers that has been introduced within
the General Architecture for Text Engineering (GATE) to enable modular development of annotation rule bases. The core of the Semano rule base model are
rule templates called *japelates* and their instantiations. While Semano is generic
and does not make assumptions about the document characteristics used within
japelates, it provides several generic japelates that can serve as a starting point.
Also, Semano provides a tool that can generate an initial rule base from an ontology. The generated rule base can be easily extended to meet the requirements of
the application in question. In addition to its Java API, Semano includes two GUI
components — a rule base editor and an annotation viewer. In combination with
the default japelates and the rule generator, these GUI components can be used by
domain experts that are not familiar with the technical details of the framework
to set up a domain-specific annotator. In this paper, we introduce the rule base
model of Semano, provide examples of adapting the rule base to meet particular
application requirements and report our experience with applying Semano within
the domain of nano technology.

## 1 Introduction

It is widely acknowledged that finding particular information within unstructured natural language documents is significantly harder than finding it within structured data
sets. Despite the impressive state of the art in the area of intelligent information infrastructure, accessing information enclosed within natural language documents remains a
big challenge. For instance, if we are looking for scientists married to politicians on the
Web using the Google search engine, we get back results that cover in detail the topic of
same-sex marriage. However, we do not get back a single document that mentions marriage between scientists and politicians. In contrast, if we look within documents that
contain the relevant information in form of *semantic annotations* — markup indicating
the meaning of document parts — we can find relevant results by means of structured
queries.

In recent years, semantic annotations have significantly gained in popularity due to
the Schema.org[1] initiative and semantic wikis such as Semantic MediaWiki [9]. Despite

---

[1] https://schema.org/

P. Mika et al. (Eds.) ISWC 2014, Part I, LNCS 8796, pp. 503–518, 2014.

the very recent introduction of Schema.org, around 30% of web pages crawled by Bing[2] early this year include semantic annotations [12].

While semantic annotations can be easily added to dynamically generated content on the Web, a considerable proportion of digital information is stored as natural language. For instance, PubMed – the online database of biomedical literature [20] – currently comprises over 23 million entries and continues growing at a rate of 1.5 publications per minute [18]. As a consequence, this information is inaccessible for a wide range of important applications.

In the recent years, considerable effort has been invested into research on extracting structured information from natural language resources. Numerous domain-specific and corpus-specific information extraction (*IE*) systems have been developed in the past to give rise to valuable, high-quality data sets such as Yago [17], DBpedia [4] and a large part of the Freebase [5] data set. These data sets are being intensively used by the community for a wide range of applications. For instance, the latter is being used by Google to enhance certain search results.

While those IE systems demonstrate that extracting high-quality structured data from unstructured or semi-structured corpora is possible in principle, the development of such systems involves a substantial amount of work. Recently, numerous tools have emerged facilitating the development of IE systems. Among them is *General Architecture for Text Engineering (GATE)* [6] – an open source framework for the development of IE systems. GATE has over 100,000 users[3] and around 70 plugable components. GATE supports the development of systems that *annotate* documents — recording specific characteristics of text within a document. The focus of this framework are *ontology-based semantic annotators* — systems that identify and record occurrences of ontology entities within documents.

At the core of the GATE framework are *JAPE transducers* — generic annotators that manipulate annotations within documents in accordance with a set of annotation rules provided by user. We refer to this set of rules as a *rule base*. While the mechanism of JAPE transducers can notably speed-up the development of annotators by reducing the amount of code that needs to be written, it still takes a considerable amount of work to develop a comprehensive rule base. The reason for this is the rule base model of JAPE transducers which does not support modularity. In particular in case of ontology-based annotators, JAPE rule bases tend to contain a significant amount of redundancy. As rules usually undergo numerous revisions, modifications are very common in rule base development. Thus, the lack of modularity results in substantial cost.

In this paper, we present Semano — a framework that can significantly reduce the effort of rule base development by enabling modularity. Semano is a modular rule store that has been designed to efficiently support the development of ontology-based annotators. The core of Semano are *Japelates* — JAPE-style rule templates — and *Japelate instantiations* — statements that define actual annotation rules by binding Japelate parameters to concrete values. As we will discuss in our paper, representing a rule base as Japelates and their instantiations significantly reduces redundancy within the rule base. For instance, the Semano representation of our example rule base *NanOn* is by an order

---

[2] https://www.bing.com/
[3] http://en.wikipedia.org/wiki/General_Architecture_for_Text_Engineering

of magnitude smaller due to the reduced amount of redundancy and is notably easier to update in comparison to its representation as a JAPE rule base. A further improvement is achieved in Semano by introducing *abstract instantiations* — japelate instantiations that bind only the values of certain parameters and can be reused in other instantiations — and variable number of arguments in analogy to `varargs` in programming languages such as Java.

Another important contribution of Semano to the community of GATE users is a module for accessing OWL 2 DL ontologies within GATE. Currently, GATE provides only a rudimentary support for ontology-based annotation. The built-in ontology module is based on OWLIM [3], which supports RDF(S) and a fragment of OWL Lite. This is a notable limitation as many domain-specific ontologies make use of more expressive ontology languages. Semano overcomes this limitation and introduces support for OWL 2 DL ontologies. Since many annotation rules rely on class hierarchies within ontologies, Semano can classify ontologies prior to document annotation. For this task, Semano has a choice of six different built-in reasoners. This is an important feature, as different reasoners work best for different fragments of the OWL 2 DL ontology language [2].

Further, Semano provides two GUI components — a rule base editor and an annotation viewer. They build on the GATE framework and enable an efficient use of a Semano rule base within GATE-based applications. The rule base editor provides a convenient way of exploring and extending the rule base. Its core features are assistance in creating japelate instantiations and flexible rule filters. The annotation viewer enables engineers to efficiently test a rule base on a particular document and update particular rules. In general, the annotation viewer can serve as a platform for evaluating the quality of generated annotations and building up a training corpus, which is otherwise significantly more work.

The paper is structured as follows. In Section 2, we discuss the impact of ontologies on the modularity of annotators and give a brief overview of Semano. In Section 3, we present the Semano rule base model and discuss its role in modular rule base development. In Section 4, we demonstrate how Semano's default features can be extended to meet application-specific requirements. Section 5 outlines the annotation of corpora with Semano and reports our experience of annotating a corpus with the NanOn rule base. In Section 6, we give an overview of the annotation viewer and the rule base editor before concluding in Section 7.

The Semano framework including example japelates and a test document is available at https://github.com/naditina/gate-semano. A demo video showing the main features of Semano is also available[4].

## 2  Supporting Ontology-Based Annotation with Semano

Semano has been developed within the context of a project called *NanOn*. The aim of NanOn was to annotate scientific literature within the domain of nano technology in order to make literature search more efficient. Over the course of the project, we found that ontologies bring certain important advantages for document annotation as opposed

---

[4] https://www.youtube.com/watch?v=nunxWXgWcBU&feature=youtu.be

to a simple set of semantic labels. In particular, we found the following benefits to be very prominent:

**Class Hierarchies:** We can use subsumption relationships between classes encoded within the ontology instead of repeating this information within annotation rules and annotated documents. If, for instance, the ontology includes the information that a `Scientist` is a `Person`, and we find an occurrence of a `Scientist` in a document, then we know that this is also an occurrence of `Person`. Thus, we do not need to include the second annotation into our annotated document. We also do not need to include rules for identifying occurrences of scientists into the set of rules for identifying occurrences of a person. Thus, systems that rely on class hierarchies within ontologies are more modular.

**Domain and Range Restrictions:** Detecting relations between entities within documents is a very difficult task. While classes often occur within a document as specific expressions, e.g., `Indium Tin Oxide` or ITO, the indication for a relation between entities is typically much more subtle and requires a detailed analysis of the corresponding document part. Among other things, the precision of relation annotation can be significantly improved by specifying which types of entities can be related to each other. In ontologies, this information can be modelled in an natural way as domain and range restrictions. In NanOn, we found the domain and range restrictions from the ontology to be indispensable indicators for the corresponding relations in documents. For example, the relation `materialProperyOf` within the expression *conductivity of ITO* is easy to detect, but only if we know that `conductivity` is a `MaterialPropery` and *ITO* is a `Material` and that `materialProperyOf` typically connects entities of type `MaterialPropery` and `Material`. In combination with class hierarchies, domain and range restrictions in ontologies allow us to significantly simplify the development of annotation rules and foster modularity of IE systems.

Within the NanOn project, an ontology specified in the Web Ontology Language OWL 2 DL[13] modelling the scientific domain of nano technology has been used to automatically annotate scientific publications. Within this context, the Semano framework has been developed to specifically address the needs of ontology-based annotation. We found that Semano has helped us to boost the productivity over the course of rule base development. The core functionality of Semano is accessible via a Java API as well as through a GUI application loadable within GATE and includes the following:

**Generating a Generic Rule Base from an Ontology:** To speed-up the development of a rule base, Semano can generate an initial rule base from an ontology that can serve as a starting point and can be refined into more specific annotation rules. For this purpose, we use the information within the ontology such as class names, labels as well as domain and range restrictions. This features can easily be customized or extended to be based on further information sources.

**Accessing and Manipulating a Rule Base:** The Semano Java API includes common manipulation operations for loading, exploring and updating a rule base. All these operations are also available within the Semano rule base editor. It is further possible to export a rule base in JAPE format for further processing in GATE.

**Loading and Classifying OWL 2 DL Ontologies:** To enable the use of OWL 2 DL ontologies in GATE-based applications, Semano provides a GATE module that is based on the OWL API [7] and supports numerous formats[5]. Semano enables the user to choose a reasoner for classifying a particular ontology. This is important as, depending on the ontology, the right choice of the reasoner has a notable impact on the overall performance. For instance, in order to use Snomed CT [16] as a basis for annotation, Snorocket [10] or ELK [8] have to be selected as other reasoners fail to classify it. However, for ontologies making use of further OWL 2 DL features, these reasoners might miss some subsumption relationships as they have not been designed to deal with the entire set of OWL 2 DL features. Currently, Semano provides access to six reasoners that can be used for document annotation including HermiT [14], FacT++ [19], Pellet [15], MoRe [1], Snorocket [10] and ELK [8]. In general, Semano can be easily extended to include further reasoners that implement the corresponding Reasoner interface in OWL API.

**Annotating Corpora with a Rule Base:** Semano can be used to annotate documents or entire corpora with given a rule base and an OWL ontology. Semano builds on JAPE transducers. It translates the rule base into a JAPE rule base before instantiating a JAPE transducer. Per default, Semano saves annotated documents in GATE format. However, it can also export annotations as ontology instances, triples or quads.

**GUI Components:** Semano includes two GUI components — a rule base editor and an annotation viewer. The former provides convenient means of accessing and updating the rule base, while the annotation viewer is designed to efficiently support an evaluation of generated annotations in documents.

In the subsequent sections, we elaborate on selected features of Semano. In particular, we discuss the modularity of Semano rule bases, the two GUI components and demonstrate how Semano can be used to implement rules that meet application-specific requirements.

## 3 Achieving Modularity with the Semano Rule Base Model

The rule base model of Semano builds on the framework of *JAPE transducers* and provides an abstraction layer to add support for modularity. Like JAPE rules, Semano rules operate on annotations enclosed within documents and their characteristics called *features*. The richer the information provided within these annotations, the more information can be accessed within Semano rules. In our examples within this section, we assume that documents have been pre-processed using an English tokenizer, a sentence splitter, a part of speech (POS) tagger and an orthoMatcher, which are all included within the standard GATE application *ANNIE*. Our examples refer to annotations of type Token, Sentence and Mention. The former annotate distinctive words within the document with certain characteristics, from which we use *category* — the POS category of the token, e.g., NN for noun and JJ for adjective, and *string* — the actual value of

---

[5] http://owlapi.sourceforge.net/index.html

```
1   Phase: metaPropertyOf
2   Input: Mention
3   Options: control = appelt debug = true
4
5   Rule: rule113
6   (
7        ({Mention.class=="Meta_property"}):domain
8        ({Mention.class=="Material_property"}):range
9   ):binding
10  -->
11  {   ... 40 more lines of Java code
12          to create an annotation ...
13  }
```

**Fig. 1.** JAPE rule for the ontology relation *metaPropertyOf*

the token within the document. Annotations of type Mention are generated by Semano and include arbitrary features set by annotation rules. We use the feature *class*, which refers to the ontology entity occurring in the annotated document part.

We now discuss the differences within the rule base model of JAPE transducers and Semano. To this end, we briefly introduce the former before elaborating on the latter. Annotation rules passed to JAPE transducers are defined within scripts written in a language specifically introduced for programming JAPE transducers, and Java. An example of a JAPE script is given in Fig. 1. A JAPE script typically consists of a header (lines 1-3) and a set of rule definitions (line 5 onwards). In this example, we have only one rule — rule113 — that annotates documents with the ontology relation metaPropertyOf. Each such rule definition in turn consists of a rule *body* (lines 6-9) — a JAPE-style regular expression over an annotation set — and a *head* (line 11 onwards) — code that will be executed when the rule body matches a certain part of the document. In Fig. 1, the rule body matches two consecutive annotations of type Mention that record an occurrence of the ontology classes Meta_property and Material_property, respectively. The rule head is Java code that creates an annotation of type Mention and sets its features.

While the mechanism of JAPE transducers enables a development of sophisticated annotation rules, it is not suitable as a basis for large rule bases. The reason for this is the poor support for modularity, which makes the development of annotation rules unnecessarily cumbersome. For instance, if we consider the JAPE script given in Fig. 1 and examine other rules developed for NanOn, we notice that 18 rule definitions within the NanOn rule base are identical except for the values in blue. The most frequently shared rule structure is used in NanOn in over 16,000 different rules. An even larger number of rules share a large proportion of the code within the rule head. Thus, while the functionality provided by transducers is highly valuable for the development of IE applications, the mechanism of JAPE scripts in its current form leads to a significant amount of redundancy in rule specifications. Since extension and modification of rule specifications are rather common in IE development, the problem needs to be addressed in order to avoid a substantial overhead. In the following, we discuss the mechanisms developed within Semano to achieve higher modularity.

## 3.1  Introducing Parameters

The first step taken in Semano to increase modularity of rule bases is introducing parameters for rules analogously to parameters of methods which are typical in programming languages. Semano introduces *japelates* — rule templates that define the basic structure of an annotation rule based on a set of parameters. At a later point, a japelate can be *instantiated* to form a concrete rule by specifying actual values for the parameters declared within the japelate. For instance, the JAPE script given in Fig. 1 can be transformed into a japelate `consecutiveDomainRangeMatcher` that accepts parameters for the values in blue, i.e., the rule name and two class IRIs. Additionally, we introduce parameters for the ontology IRI and the relation IRI, which are used within the rule header. The japelate `consecutiveDomainRangeMatcher` is shown in Fig.2. Based on this japelate, can then obtain a definition of `rule113` by instantiating it as follows:

```
 1   JAPELATE PARAMETERS:
 2   0: LITERAL, Rule ID
 3   1: LITERAL, Ontology IRI
 4   2: ENTITY,  Relation IRI
 5   3: ENTITY,  Domain class IRI
 6   4: ENTITY,  Range class IRI
 7
 8
 9   JAPELATE BODY:
10   Rule: $0$
11   (
12        ({Mention.class=="$3$"}):domain
13        ({Mention.class=="$4$"}):range
14   ):binding
15   -->
16   { ... Java code referring to $1$ and $2$ ... }
```

**Fig. 2.** Japelate `consecutiveDomainRangeMatcher`

**rule113**: domainRangeBased ( http ://www. nanon . de/ ontology / ,
metaPropertyOf , Meta_property , Material_property )

Within the NanOn rule base, the separation into japelates and rules was very effective for increasing modularity. Overall, over 17,000 rules instantiated from in total seven japelates encode the entire NanOn rule base, which otherwise would be represented by the same number of relatively long JAPE rules. As a result, the NanOn rule base is not only significantly smaller, but also notably easier to update. For instance, renaming an annotation feature that is being set within the Java code in the rule head (lines 11-13, Fig.1) will affect over 1,000 JAPE rules. In contrast, within a Semano rule base it affects only a few japelates and no rules.

## 3.2   Variable Number of Arguments

While introducing parameters is already a big step towards modular rule base development, the result can be further improved as demonstrated by the following example. We consider the rule head of the japelate nonINMatcher, which is a simplified version of the corresponding japelate within the NanOn rule base:

```
Rule: $0$
(
        {Token. string ==~"$3$($4$)", Token. category !=IN}
): binding
```

This japelate can be instantiated, for instance, by setting $3$ to *(?i)* and setting $4$ to *absorbed|absorption*. This will match all annotations of type Token that are not a preposition (ensured by Token.category!=IN) and whose string value contains either *absorbed* or *absorption* ignoring the case. While this japelate can be used for all terms consisting of a single word that is not a preposition, we need a new japelate for terms consisting of *n* such words. For instance, if we would like to match the term *Tin oxide*, we would need a japelate for *n* = 2. Such a japelate can look as follows:

```
Rule: $0$
(
        {Token. string ==~"$3$($4$)", Token. category !=IN}
        {Token. string ==~"$5$($6$)", Token. category !=IN}
): binding
```

Clearly, these two japelates share a large proportion of code and will need to be updated in case of a change within the rule head. This problem has been addressed in the Java programming language by introducing the possibility of methods accepting a variable number of arguments of the same type. We transfer this notion to japelates as follows:

```
Rule: $0$
(
        ${Token. string ==~"$3$($4$)", Token. category !=IN}$
): binding
```

This version of the nonINMatcher japelate accepts a variable number of arguments and repeats the expression enclosed by ${ and }$ while using a different value for parameter 4 in each line. Within NanOn, this construct has been excessively used to match annotations against ontology classes whose names consist of more than one word.

### 3.3  Abstract Instantiations

The introduction of parameters and variable number of arguments help to reduce the amount of JAPE code within a rule base. However, it should be observed that there is a trade-off between the redundancy within japelates and the redundancy within the actual rules: by introducing an additional parameter, we might be able to reduce the number of japelates and the redundancy within those, but we also increase the number of arguments that need to be passed within each japelate instantiation. For instance, we could generalize two japelates that are identical apart from one single expression (A and B in Fig.3) into a single japelate by introducing a parameter within this expression (expression C in Fig.3).

$${Token.string==~"$3$($4$)", Token.category=~NN}$ \hspace{2cm} (A)$$

$${Token.string==~"$3$($4$)", Token.category=~JJ}$ \hspace{2cm} (B)$$

$${Token.string==~"$3$($5$)", Token.category=~$4$}$ \hspace{2cm} (C)$$

**Fig. 3.** Expressions accepting sequences of strings with certain POS tags

If we have a considerable number of rules that have the same value for parameter 5, the overall redundancy within the rule base will increase. We now have to provide an additional value for every instantiation of the japelate in question. Moreover, sometimes it is convenient to be able to update certain values for parameter 5 all at once, e.g. in order to change the value *JJ* to *JJS* in all rules. In order to overcome the problem of redundancy within japelate instantiations and to provide more flexibility for reusing rule definitions, Semano introduces *abstract instantiations* — instantiations that do not bind all parameters to certain values and in turn need to be instantiated before being used for document annotation. Fig.4 shows an abstract instantiation seqWithPOS that includes expression C from Fig.3.

Overall, the Semano representation of the NanOn annotation rules is by an order of magnitude smaller than its JAPE representation due to the reduced amount of redundancy. It should be noted that the above difference is uninfluenced by the fact that the JAPE grammar provides the construct *MACRO* which can be applied to reuse identical parts within rule bodies. For instance, if the expression in line 7, Fig. 1 occurs several times within the rule body, we can introduce a MACRO and use it instead of the above expression. While this construct can be useful in large rule bodies, within the NanOn rule base we did not encounter a single rule body with two or more identical parts.

## 4  Extendability of Annotation Features

To maximize the recall and precision achieved by an ontology-based annotator, it is usually necessary to optimize the rule base for a particular corpus, ontology and the

```
1   JAPELATE HEADER:
2   0:  LITERAL,  Rule ID
3   1:  LITERAL,  Ontology IRI
4   2:  ENTITY,   Class IRI
5   3:  LITERAL,  Case insensitivity expression (?i) or empty
6   4:  ENTITY,   Main expression
7
8
9   ABSTRACT JAPELATE BODY:
10  $0$:    seqWithPOS($1$,$2$,$3$,NN,$4$)
```

**Fig. 4.** Abstract japelate instantiation `seqWithPOS` with a concrete value for parameter 4

particular application requirements in question. Consequently, the concrete characteristics of the generated annotations can vary significantly from application to application. Semano is a generic framework and accounts for the diversity of application requirements. In particular, it does not make any assumptions about application-specific annotation features, which can be used in japelates in the same way as the default features. In this section, we discuss how japelates can be extended to implement application-specific annotation rules.

Semano provides a selection of generic default japelates that can serve as a starting point for developing a rule base and can be extended into application-specific ones. In our example, we are using the default japelate `domainRangeMatcher` shown in Fig. 5. This japelate finds sentences enclosing an occurrence of a domain and a range class for a particular ontology relation.

Fig. 5 shows how a selection of default features are set in annotations of type *Mention* (lines 19-26). In addition to the ontology IRI (line 19) and the IRI of the ontology relation (line 23), which are set from the parameters 1 and 2, the japelate sets the references to the two entities connected to each other by this relation (lines 21-22). It also sets some meta information that is interpreted by the Semano annotation viewer presented in Section 6. For instance, it records that this annotation has been created by Semano (as opposed to annotations created manually by an engineer) and which rule and japelate have been used.

We now demonstrate how we can add a confidence value to annotations by extending `domainRangeMatcher`. In NanOn, we found it useful to be able to assign confidence values to annotation rules. Along other things, this enabled us to divide the entire rule base into *precise* and *recall-boosting* annotation rules. The former aim at identifying only candidates with a high chance of being correct and tend to be very specific. In contrast, the latter rules aim at identifying as many potential candidates as possible and are deliberately vague. We found recall-boosting rules to be very helpful at an early stage of rule base development to identify candidates for precise annotation rules. In fact, many precise annotation rules within the NanOn rule base that aim at identifying ontology relations are concretizations of recall-boosting rules.

One way to add a confidence feature to an annotation would be to set a particular value within the japelate, for instance, by adding the following line after line 26, Fig. 5:

```
 1   JAPELATE PARAMETERS:
 2   0:  LITERAL,  Rule  ID
 3   1:  LITERAL,  Ontology  IRI
 4   2:  ENTITY,   Relation  IRI
 5   3:  ENTITY,   Domain  class  IRI
 6   4:  ENTITY,   Range  class  IRI
 7
 8   JAPELATE  BODY:
 9   Rule:  $0$
10   ({
11         Sentence  contains  {Mention.class=="$3$"},
12         Sentence  contains  {Mention.class=="$4$"}
13   }):binding
14   -->
15   {
16         ...  Java  code  to  initialize  some  annotation  features  ...
17
18         gate.FeatureMap  features  =  Factory.newFeatureMap();
19         features.put("ontology",  "$1$");
20         features.put("autoannotation",  "true");
21         features.put("domain",  domainAnnotation.getId());
22         features.put("range",  rangeAnnotation.getId());
23         features.put("relation","$2$");
24         features.put("language",  "en");
25         features.put("rule",  "$0$");
26         features.put("japelate",  "domainRangeMatcher");
27
28         ...  Java  code  creating  the  annotation  ...
29   }
```

**Fig. 5.** Japelate domainRangeMatcher with confidence values

```
features.put("confidence","0.2");
```

This would be sufficient if all rules instantiating this japelate have the same confidence. However, later, we might notice that the confidence varies depending on the ontology relation in question. For instance, this japelate might yield good results for materialPropertyOf, but rather poor results for hasFabricationProcess as the latter relation has the same domain and range as another relation inputMaterialOf. To make it possible to set the confidence value in a rule rather than a japelate, we can add a parameter for confidence value after line 6, Fig. 5:

```
5:  LITERAL,  Confidence  value
```

and then set the confidence of the annotation to parameter 5 as follows after line 26, Fig. 5:

```
features.put("confidence",  "$5$");
```

As we expect this japelate to serve as a basis for recall-boosting rules rather then precise ones, we might find it cumbersome to repeat a low confidence value in numerous rules. In that case, we can add an abstract instantiation, e.g., `domainRangeMatcherLowConf`, which fixes confidence to some low value as shown in Fig. 6.

```
1   JAPELATE HEADER:
2   0: LITERAL, Rule ID
3   1: LITERAL, Ontology IRI
4   2: ENTITY,  Relation IRI
5   3: ENTITY,  Domain class IRI
6   4: ENTITY,  Range class IRI
7
8   ABSTRACT JAPELATE BODY:
9   $0$:   domainRangeMatcher($1$,$2$,$3$,$4$,0.2)
```

**Fig. 6.** Abstract japelate instantiation `domainRangeMatcherLowConf`

Thus, we can use the more flexible japelate `domainRangeMatcher` for rules with a low confidence value, while not having to repeat frequently occurring confidence values in other rules.

## 5  Semano in Action

We used Semano to annotate all volumes (1-12) of the *Journal of Applied Physics* from 2009 with the NanOn rule base. In total, the corpus consists of 3,358 articles. We pre-annotated the corpus with the standard GATE application *ANNIE*. On average, after this step each article contained around 8,000 annotations. Subsequently, we annotated the corpus with the NanOn rule base, which included 17,292 rules. On average, each rule within the rule base had 7 arguments.

The default workflow of corpus annotation is shown in Fig. 7. First, rules and japelates are compiled into JAPE files. Then, a set of transducers is initialized with a classified OWL ontology and the JAPE files produced in the previous step. Subsequently, they are run on the document corpus. During the initialization of transducers, GATE compiles JAPE scripts into binary Java code, which can take some time for a large rule base. Annotated documents are saved as XML files in GATE format and can be viewed and evaluated with the Semano annotation viewer as described in Section 6.

The annotation has been carried out on a MacBook Pro notebook with 16 GB of memory and 2.3 GHz Intel Core processor and yielded around 1000 ontology annotations per document, which corresponds to one ontology annotation for every four words within a document. The compilation of japelates and rules into JAPE files took in total 24 seconds for the entire rule base. The initialisation of transducers took in total 215 seconds. Thus, the additional time required for compiling japelates and rules into JAPE files is small in comparison to the overall initialization time. In our evaluation, we used a parallelized version of Semano, which has internally initialized four JAPE transducers. The annotation of the corpus with this parallelized version took on average 19 seconds

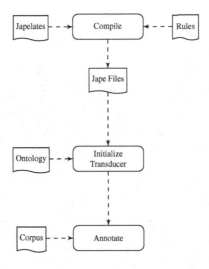

**Fig. 7.** Annotating a corpus with Semano

per document, which was 2.8 times faster than a single JAPE transducer that has been initialized in a usual way through GATE (54 seconds). We conclude that, on a machine with multiple cores, it is worthwhile parallelizing the annotation with Semano in order to speed up the annotation of large corpora.

## 6  GUI Components

In this section, we give an overview of the two GUI components within Semano — the annotation viewer and the rule base editor.

### 6.1  Annotation Viewer

Evaluating generated annotations is a crucial task in IE development. Appropriate software support is essential as it can take up a significant proportion of the overall project budget. Semano includes an annotation viewer that has been developed to make this process as efficient as possible. Fig.8 shows its general User Interface.

Supporting the evaluation of generated annotations is the key purpose of the annotation viewer. Given a GATE document, an ontology and a rule base, Semano annotation viewer highlights the relevant annotations within the current document and enables the engineer to record his/her feedback about their correctness. It provides a flexible way to filter the highlighted annotations within the document. For instance, it is possible to de-highlight annotations for particular japelates, rules and ontology entities.

Often it is during the evaluation of annotations that errors in rules or examples for further annotation rules are encountered. To support an efficient update of the rule base, the annotation viewer enables editing rules used within generated annotations or adding a new rule to the rule base and applying it to the current document. In this way, the new

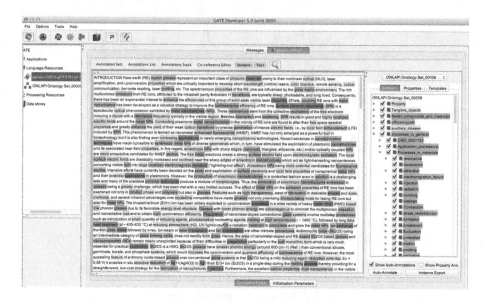

**Fig. 8.** Semano Annotation Viewer

rule can be tested immediately after its creation. A rule-wise document annotation is also significantly faster than the annotation with the entire rule base.

In addition to the above features, the annotation viewer provides a shortcut for annotating the current document with the entire rule base and ontology and exporting the annotations as ontology entities.

## 6.2 Rule Base Editor

In case of large rule bases, finding a particular rule becomes difficult. The Semano rule base editor provides flexible filters that enable an engineer to explore a particular part of the rule base. Further, it provides a convenient way of updating, adding and deleting rules from the rule base. Among other things, it assists the user in instantiating a particular japelate, for instance, by auto-completing the entity names for parameters of type ENTITY based on the available entities within the ontology.

## 7   Summary and Future Work

In this paper, we have discussed the role of ontologies within IE systems and presented Semano, which is a generic framework for ontology-based annotation. We have discussed various features of Semano such as its module for accessing OWL 2 DL ontologies within the GATE framework and access to services of various reasoners. We have presented Semano's rule base model and have discussed its role in modular rule base development. We have also discussed the generality of Semano and have shown an example of how this model can be used to implement rules given particular requirements.

We have further outlined the features of the two GUI components — a rule base editor and an annotation viewer — that provide a convenient access to a Semano rule base and Semano-generated annotations within documents, respectively. Overall, we can conclude that various features of Semano, in particular the modular rule base model, can help to significantly reduce the budget required for developing ontology-based annotators. In case of our example rule base NanOn, we have observed a significant increase in modularity: NanOn was by an order of magnitude smaller and significantly easier to update than its representation as a JAPE rule base, which is the original GATE rule base model.

As for any software framework, there are numerous features that could be added to Semano. One such feature is a more flexible type system for japelate parameters, which could be used to assist the engineer in creating japelate instantiations. Another direction for extending the functionality of Semano is to enable import of declarative ontology lexica such as lemon lexica [11].

# References

1. Armas Romero, A., Cuenca Grau, B., Horrocks, I.: MORe: Modular combination of OWL reasoners for ontology classification. In: Cudré-Mauroux, P., et al. (eds.) ISWC 2012, Part I. LNCS, vol. 7649, pp. 1–16. Springer, Heidelberg (2012)
2. Bail, S., Glimm, B., Gonçalves, R.S., Jiménez-Ruiz, E., Kazakov, Y., Matentzoglu, N., Parsia, B. (eds.): Informal Proceedings of the 2nd International Workshop on OWL Reasoner Evaluation (ORE 2013), Ulm, Germany, July 22. CEUR Workshop Proceedings, vol. 1015. CEUR-WS.org (2013)
3. Bishop, B., Kiryakov, A., Ognyanoff, D., Peikov, I., Tashev, Z., Velkov, R.: Owlim: A family of scalable semantic repositories. Semant. Web 2(1), 33–42 (2011), http://dl.acm.org/citation.cfm?id=2019470.2019472
4. Bizer, C., Lehmann, J., Kobilarov, G., Auer, S., Becker, C., Cyganiak, R., Hellmann, S.: Dbpedia - a crystallization point for the web of data. Web Semant. 7(3), 154–165 (2009), http://dx.doi.org/10.1016/j.websem.2009.07.002
5. Bollacker, K., Evans, C., Paritosh, P., Sturge, T., Taylor, J.: Freebase: A collaboratively created graph database for structuring human knowledge. In: Proceedings of the 2008 ACM SIGMOD International Conference on Management of Data, SIGMOD 2008, pp. 1247–1250. ACM, New York (2008), http://doi.acm.org/10.1145/1376616.1376746
6. Cunningham, H., Maynard, D., Bontcheva, K., Tablan, V., Aswani, N., Roberts, I., Gorrell, G., Funk, A., Roberts, A., Damljanovic, D., Heitz, T., Greenwood, M.A., Saggion, H., Petrak, J., Li, Y., Peters, W.: Text Processing with GATE, Version 6 (2011), http://tinyurl.com/gatebook
7. Horridge, M., Bechhofer, S.: The owl api: A java api for working with owl 2 ontologies. In: Hoekstra, R., Patel-Schneider, P.F. (eds.) OWLED. CEUR Workshop Proceedings, vol. 529. CEUR-WS.org (2009)
8. Kazakov, Y., Krötzsch, M., Simančík, F.: ELK: a reasoner for OWL EL ontologies. System description, University of Oxford (2012), http://code.google.com/p/elk-reasoner/wiki/Publications
9. Krötzsch, M., Vrandecic, D.: Semantic mediawiki. In: Foundations for the Web of Information and Services, pp. 311–326. Springer (2011)

10. Lawley, M.J., Bousquet, C.: Fast classification in Protégé: Snorocket as an OWL 2 EL rea-soner. In: Meyer, T., Orgun, M.A., Taylor, K. (eds.) Australasian Ontology Workshop 2010 (AOW 2010): Advances in Ontologies. CRPIT, vol. 122, pp. 45–50. ACS, Adelaide (2010); Winner of Payne-Scott Best Paper Award

11. McCrae, J., Spohr, D., Cimiano, P.: Linking lexical resources and ontologies on the semantic web with lemon. In: Antoniou, G., Grobelnik, M., Simperl, E., Parsia, B., Plexousakis, D., De Leenheer, P., Pan, J. (eds.) ESWC 2011, Part I. LNCS, vol. 6643, pp. 245–259. Springer, Heidelberg (2011)

12. Mika, P., Potter, T.: Metadata statistics for a large web corpus. In: Bizer, C., Heath, T., Berners-Lee, T., Hausenblas, M. (eds.) LDOW. CEUR Workshop Proceedings, vol. 937. CEUR-WS.org (2012)

13. OWL Working Group, W.: OWL 2 Web Ontology Language: Document Overview. W3C Recommendation (October 27, 2009), http://www.w3.org/TR/owl2-overview/

14. Shearer, R., Motik, B., Horrocks, I.: HermiT: A Highly-Efficient OWL Reasoner. In: Pro-ceedings of the 5th International Workshop on OWL: Experiences and Directions, OWLED 2008 (2008)

15. Sirin, E., Parsia, B., Cuenca Grau, B., Kalyanpur, A., Katz, Y.: Pellet: A practical OWL-DL reasoner. Web Semantics: Science, Services and Agents on the World Wide Web 5(2), 51–53 (2007), http://dx.doi.org/10.1016/j.websem.2007.03.004

16. Spackman, K.A., Campbell, K.E., Cote, R.A.: SNOMED RT: A reference terminology for health care. In: Proceedings of the AIMA Fall Symposium, pp. 640–644 (1997)

17. Suchanek, F.M., Kasneci, G., Weikum, G.: YAGO: A Large Ontology from Wikipedia and WordNet. Web Semantics: Science, Services and Agents on the World Wide Web 6, 203–217 (2008)

18. Tipney, H., Hunter, L.: Knowledge-Driven Approaches to Genome-Scale Analysis. John Wi-ley & Sons, Ltd. (2010), http://onlinelibrary.wiley.com/doi/10.1002/9780470669716.ch2/summary

19. Tsarkov, D., Horrocks, I.: FaCT++ Description Logic Reasoner: System Description. In: Fur-bach, U., Shankar, N. (eds.) IJCAR 2006. LNCS (LNAI), vol. 4130, pp. 292–297. Springer, Heidelberg (2006)

20. Wheeler, D.L., Chappey, C., Lash, A.E., Leipe, D.D., Madden, T.L., Schuler, G.D., Tatusova, T.A., Rapp, B.A.: Database resources of the National Center for Biotechnology Information. Nucleic Acids Research 28(1), 10–14 (2000), http://dx.doi.org/10.1093/nar/28.1.10

# Ensemble Learning for Named Entity Recognition

René Speck and Axel-Cyrille Ngonga Ngomo

AKSW, Department of Computer Science, University of Leipzig, Germany
{speck,ngonga}@informatik.uni-leipzig.de

**Abstract.** A considerable portion of the information on the Web is still only available in unstructured form. Implementing the vision of the Semantic Web thus requires transforming this unstructured data into structured data. One key step during this process is the recognition of named entities. Previous works suggest that ensemble learning can be used to improve the performance of named entity recognition tools. However, no comparison of the performance of existing supervised machine learning approaches on this task has been presented so far. We address this research gap by presenting a thorough evaluation of named entity recognition based on ensemble learning. To this end, we combine four different state-of-the approaches by using 15 different algorithms for ensemble learning and evaluate their performace on five different datasets. Our results suggest that ensemble learning can reduce the error rate of state-of-the-art named entity recognition systems by 40%, thereby leading to over 95% f-score in our best run.

**Keywords:** Named Entity Recognition, Ensemble Learning, Semantic Web.

## 1 Introduction

One of the first research papers in the field of named entity recognition (NER) was presented in 1991 [32]. Today, more than two decades later, this research field is still highly relevant for manifold communities including Semantic Web Community, where the need to capture and to translate the content of natural language (NL) with the help of NER tools arises in manifold semantic applications [15, 19, 20, 24, 34]. The NER tools that resulted from more than 2 decades of research now implement a diversity of algorithms that rely on a large number of heterogeneous formalisms. Consequently, these algorithms have diverse strengths and weaknesses.

Currently, several services and frameworks that consume NL to generate semi-structured or even structured data rely on solely one of the formalisms developed for NER or simply merging the results of several tools (e.g., by using simple voting). By doing so, current approaches fail to make use of the diversity of current NER algorithms. On the other hand, it is a well-known fact that algorithms with diverse strengths and weaknesses can be aggregated in various ways to create a system that outperforms the best individual algorithms within the system [44]. This learning paradigm is known as *ensemble learning*. While previous works have already suggested that ensemble learning can be used to improve NER [34], no comparison of the performance of existing supervised machine-learning approaches for ensemble learning on the NER task has been presented so far.

P. Mika et al. (Eds.) ISWC 2014, Part I, LNCS 8796, pp. 519–534, 2014.

We address this research gap by presenting and evaluating an open-source framework for NER that makes use on ensemble learning. In this evaluation, we use four state-of-the-art NER algorithms, fifteen different machine learning algorithms and five datasets. The statistical significance our results is ensured by using Wilcoxon signed-rank tests.

The goal of our evaluation is to answer the following questions:

1. Does NER based on ensemble learning achieve higher f-scores than the best NER tool within the system?
2. Does NER based on ensemble learning achieve higher f-scores than simple voting based on the results of the NER tools?
3. Which ensemble learning approach achieves the best f-score for the NER task?

The rest of this paper is structured as follows. After reviewing related work in Section 2, we give an overview of our approach in Section 3. Especially, we present the theoretical framework that underlies our approach. Subsequently, in Section 4, we present our evaluation pipeline and its setup. Thereafter, in Section 5, we present the results of a series of experiments in which we compare several machine learning algorithms with state-of-the-art NER tools. We conclude by discussing our results and elaborating on some future work in Section 6. The results of this paper were integrated into the open-source NER framework FOX.[1] Our framework provides a free-to-use RESTful web service for the community. A documentation of the framework as well as a specification of the RESTful web service can be found at FOX's project page.

## 2    Related Work

NER tools and frameworks implement a broad spectrum of approaches, which can be subdivided into three main categories: dictionary-based, rule-based and machine-learning approaches [31]. The first systems for NER implemented dictionary-based approaches, which relied on a list of named entities (NEs) and tried to identify these in text [2,43]. Following work then showed that these approaches did not perform well for NER tasks such as recognizing proper names [39]. Thus, rule-based approaches were introduced. These approaches rely on hand-crafted rules [8,42] to recognize NEs. Most rule-based approaches combine dictionary and rule-based algorithms to extend the list of known entities. Nowadays, hand-crafted rules for recognizing NEs are usually implemented when no training examples are available for the domain or language to process [32]. When training examples are available, the methods of choice are borrowed from supervised machine learning. Approaches such as Hidden Markov Models [46], Maximum Entropy Models [10] and Conditional Random Fields [14] have been applied to the NER task. Due to scarcity of large training corpora as necessitated by supervised machine learning approaches, the semi-supervised [31,35] and unsupervised machine learning paradigms [13,33] have also been used for extracting NER from text. In [44], a system was presented that combines with stacking and voting classifiers which were trained with several languages, for language-independent NER. [31] gives an exhaustive overview of approaches for the NER task.

---

[1] Project page:http://fox.aksw.org. Source code, evaluation data and evaluation results:http://github.com/AKSW/FOX

Over the last years, several benchmarks for NER have been proposed. For example, [9] presents a benchmark for NER and entity linking approaches. Especially, the authors define the named entity annotation task. Other benchmark datasets include the manually annotated datasets presented in [38]. Here, the authors present annotated datasets extracted from RSS feeds as well as datasets retrieved from news platforms. Other authors designed datasets to evaluate their own systems. For example, the Web dataset (which we use in our evaluation) is a particularly noisy dataset designed to evaluate the system presented in [37]. The dataset Reuters, which we also use, consists annotated documents chosen out of the Reuters-215788 corpus and was used in [4].

## 3 Overview

### 3.1 Named Entity Recognition

NER encompasses two main tasks: (1) The identification of names[2] such as "Germany", "University of Leipzig" and "G. W. Leibniz" in a given unstructured text and (2) the classification of these names into predefined entity types[3], such as Location, Organization and Person. In general the NER task can be viewed as the sequential prediction problem of estimating the probabilities $P(y_i|x_{i-k}...x_{i+l}, y_{i-m}...y_{i-1})$, where $\mathbf{x} = (x_1, .., x_n)$ is an input sequence (i.e., the preprocessed input text) and $\mathbf{y} = (y_1, ..., y_n)$ the output sequence (i.e., the entity types) [37].

### 3.2 Ensemble Learning

The goal of an ensemble learning algorithm $\mathcal{S}$ is to generate a classifier $\mathcal{F}$ with a high predictive performance by combining the predictions of a set of $m$ basic classifiers $\mathcal{C}_1, ..., \mathcal{C}_m$ [12]. One central observation in this respect, is that combining $\mathcal{C}_1, ..., \mathcal{C}_m$ can only lead to a high predictive performance when these classifiers are *accurate* and *diverse* [45]. Several approaches have been developed to allow an efficient combination of basic classifiers. The simplest strategy is voting, where each input token is classified as belonging to the class that was predicted by the largest number of basic classifiers [12]. Voting can be extended to weighted voting, where each of the basic classifiers is assigned a weight and $\mathcal{S}$ returns the class with the highest total prediction weight. More elaborate methods try to ensure the diversity of the classifiers. Approaches that aim to achieve this goal include drawing random samples (with replacement) from the training data (e.g., bagging, [5]) or generating sequences of classifiers of high diversity that are trained to recognized each other's mistakes (e.g., boosting, [40]). The results of all classifiers are finally combined via weighted voting.

Here, we consider ensemble learning for NER. Thanks to the long research tradition on the NER topic, the *diversity* and *accuracy* of the tools is already available and can be regarded as given. However, classical ensemble learning approaches present the disadvantage of relying on some form of weighted vote on the output of the classifiers.

---

[2] Also referred as instances.

[3] Also referred as classes.

Thus, if all classifiers $C_i$ return wrong results, classical ensemble learning approaches are bound to make the same mistake [12]. In addition, voting does not take the different levels of accuracy of classifiers for different entity types into consideration. Rather, it assigns a global weight to each classifier that describes its overall accuracy. Based on these observations, we decided to apply ensemble learning for NER based at entity-type level. The main advantage of this ensemble-learning setting is that we can now assign different weights to each tool-type pair.

Formally, we model the ensemble learning task at hand as follows: Let the matrix $M^{mt \times n}$ (Equation 1) illustrate the input data for $S$, where $\mathcal{P}^m_{n,t}$ are predictions of the $m$-th NER tool that the $n$-th token is of the $t$-th type.

$$\begin{pmatrix} \mathcal{P}^1_{1,1} & \cdots & \mathcal{P}^1_{1,t} & \mathcal{P}^2_{1,1} & \cdots & \mathcal{P}^2_{1,t} & \cdots & \mathcal{P}^m_{1,1} & \cdots & \mathcal{P}^m_{1,t} \\ \vdots & \ddots & \vdots & \vdots & \ddots & \vdots & & \vdots & \ddots & \vdots \\ \mathcal{P}^1_{n,1} & \cdots & \mathcal{P}^1_{n,t} & \mathcal{P}^2_{n,1} & \cdots & \mathcal{P}^2_{n,t} & \cdots & \mathcal{P}^m_{n,1} & \cdots & \mathcal{P}^m_{n,t} \end{pmatrix} \quad (1)$$

The goal of ensemble learning for NER is to detect a classifier that leads to a correct classification of each of the $n$ tokens into one of the types $t$.

## 4 Evaluation

We performed a thorough evaluation of ensemble learning approaches by using five different datasets and running a 10-fold cross-validation for 15 algorithms. In this section, we present the pipeline and the setup for our evaluation as well as our results.

### 4.1 Pipeline

Figure 1 shows the workflow chart of our evaluation pipeline. In the first step of our evaluation pipeline, we preprocessed our reference dataset to extract the input text for the NER tools as well as the correct NEs, which we used to create training and testing data. In the second step, we made use of all NER tools with this input text to calculate the predictions of all entity types for each token in this input. At this point, we represented the output of the tools as matrix (see Equation 1). Thereafter, the matrix was randomly split into 10 disjoint sets as preparation for a 10-fold cross-validation. We

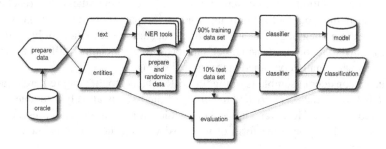

**Fig. 1.** Workflow chart of the evaluation pipeline

trained the different classifiers at hand (i.e., $S$) with the training dataset (i.e., with 9 of 10 sets) and tested the trained classifier with the testing dataset (i.e., with the leftover set). To use each of the 10 sets as testing set once, we repeated training and testing of the classifiers 10 times and used the disjoint sets accordingly. Furthermore, the pipeline was repeated 10 times to deal with non-deterministic classifiers. In the last step, we compared the classification of the 10 testing datasets with the oracle dataset to calculate measures for the evaluation.

We ran our pipeline on 15 ensemble learning algorithms. We carried out both a token-based evaluation and an entity-based evaluation. In the *token-based evaluation*, we regarded partial matches of multi-word units as being partially correct. For example, our gold standard considered "Federal Republic of Germany" as being an instance of Location. If a tool generated "Germany" as being a location and omitted "Federal Republic of", it was assigned 1 true positive and 3 false negatives. The *entity-based evaluation* only regarded exact matches as correct. In the example above, the entity was simply considered to be incorrect. To provide transparent results, we only used open-source libraries in our evaluation. Given that some of these tools at hand do not allow accessing their confidence score without any major alteration of their code, we considered the output of the tools to be binary (i.e., either 1 or 0).

We integrated four NER tools so far: the Stanford Named Entity Recognizer[4] (Stanford) [14], the Illinois Named Entity Tagger[5] (Illinois) [37], the Ottawa Baseline Information Extraction[6] (Balie) [30] and the Apache OpenNLP Name Finder[7] (OpenNLP) [3]. We only considered the performance of these tools on the classes Location, Organization and Person. To this end, we mapped the entity types of each of the NER tools to these three classes. We utilized the Waikato Environment for Knowledge Analysis (Weka) [21] and the implemented classifiers with default parameters: AdaBoostM1 (ABM1) [16] and Bagging (BG) [5] with J48 [36] as base classifier, Decision Table (DT) [26], Functional Trees (FT) [18, 27], J48 [36], Logistic Model Trees (LMT) [27, 41], Logistic Regression (Log) [28], Additive Logistic Regression (LogB) [17], Multilayer Perceptron (MLP), Naïve Bayes (NB) [23], Random Forest (RF) [6], Support Vector Machine (SVM) [7] and Sequential Minimal Optimization (SMO) [22]. In addition, we used voting at class level (CVote) and a simple voting (Vote) approach [44] with equal weights for all NER tools. CVote selects the NER tool with the highest prediction performance for each type according to the evaluation and uses that particular tool for the given class. Vote as naive approach combines the results of the NER tools with the Majority Vote Rule [25] and was the baseline ensemble learning technique in our evaluation.

## 4.2  Experimental Setup

We used five datasets and five measures for our evaluation. We used the recommended Wilcoxon signed-rank test to measure the statistical significance of our results [11]. For

---

[4] http://nlp.stanford.edu/software/CRF-NER.shtml (version 3.2.0).

[5] http://cogcomp.cs.illinois.edu/page/software_view/NETagger (version 2.4.0).

[6] http://balie.sourceforge.net (version 1.8.1).

[7] http://opennlp.apache.org/index.html (version 1.5.3).

this purpose, we applied each measurement of the ten 10-fold cross-validation runs for the underlying distribution and we set up a 95% confidence interval.

**Datasets.** An overview of the datasets is shown in Table 1. The Web dataset consists of 20 annotated Web sites as described in [37] and contains the most noise compared to the other datasets. The dataset Reuters consists of 50 documents randomly chosen out of the Reuters-215788 corpus[8] [4]. News* is a small subset of the dataset News that consists of text from newspaper articles and was re-annotated manually by the authors to ensure high data quality. Likewise, Reuters was extracted and annotated manually by the authors. The last dataset, All, consists of the datasets mentioned before merged into one and allows for measuring how well the ensemble learning approaches perform when presented with data from heterogenous sources.

**Table 1.** Number of entities separated according entity types and in total

| Class | News | News* | Web | Reuters | All |
|---|---|---|---|---|---|
| Location | 5117 | 341 | 114 | 146 | 5472 |
| Organization | 6899 | 434 | 257 | 208 | 7467 |
| Person | 3899 | 254 | 396 | 91 | 4549 |
| Total | 15915 | 1029 | 767 | 445 | 17488 |

**Measures.** To assess the performance of the different algorithms, we computed the following values on the test datasets: The number of true positives $TP_t$, the number of true negatives $TN_t$, the number of false positives $FP_t$ and the number of false negatives $FN_t$. These numbers were collected for each entity type $t$ and averaged over the ten runs of the 10-fold cross-validations. Then, we applied the one-against-all approach [1] to convert the multi-class confusion matrix of each dataset into a binary confusion matrix.

Subsequently, we determined with macro-averaging the classical measures recall ($rec$), precision ($pre$) and f-score ($F_1$) as follows:

$$rec = \frac{\sum_{t\in T} \frac{TP_t}{(TP_t+FN_t)}}{|T|}, pre = \frac{\sum_{t\in T} \frac{TP_t}{TP_t+FP_t}}{|T|}, F_1 = \frac{\sum_{t\in T} \frac{2pre_t rec_t}{pre_t+rec_t}}{|T|}. \quad (2)$$

For the sake of completeness, we averaged the error rate ($error$) (Equation 3) and the Matthews correlation coefficient ($MCC$) [29] (Equation 4) similarly.

$$error = \frac{\sum_{t\in T} \frac{FP_t+FN_t}{TP_t+TN_t+FP_t+FN_t}}{|T|} \quad (3)$$

$$MCC = \frac{\sum_{t\in T} \frac{TP_t TN_t - FP_t FN_t}{\sqrt{(TP_t+FP_t)(TP_t+FN_t)(TN_t+FP_t)(TN_t+FN_t)}}}{|T|} \quad (4)$$

---

[8] The Reuters-215788 corpus is available at: http://kdd.ics.uci.edu/databases/reuters21578/reuters21578.html

The error rate monitors the fraction of positive and negative classifications for that the classifier failed. The Matthews correlation coefficient considers both the true positives and the true negatives as successful classification and is rather unaffected by sampling biases. Higher values indicating better classifications.

## 5 Results

Table 2–Table 11 show the results of our evaluation for the 15 classifiers we used within our pipeline and the four NER tools we integrated so far. The best results are marked bold and the NER tools are underlined. Figure 2–Figure 4 depict the f-scores separated according classes of the four NER tools, the simple voting approach Vote and the best classifier for the depicted dataset.

**Table 2.** News* token-based

| $S$ | $rec$ | $pre$ | $F_1$ | $error$ | $MCC$ |
|---|---|---|---|---|---|
| MLP | **95.19** | **95.28** | **95.23** | **0.32** | **0.951** |
| RF | 95.15 | **95.28** | 95.21 | **0.32** | **0.951** |
| ABM1 | 94.82 | 95.18 | 95.00 | 0.33 | 0.948 |
| SVM | 94.86 | 95.09 | 94.97 | 0.33 | 0.948 |
| J48 | 94.78 | 94.98 | 94.88 | 0.34 | 0.947 |
| BG | 94.76 | 94.93 | 94.84 | 0.34 | 0.947 |
| LMT | 94.68 | 94.95 | 94.82 | 0.34 | 0.946 |
| DT | 94.63 | 94.95 | 94.79 | 0.34 | 0.946 |
| FT | 94.30 | 95.15 | 94.72 | 0.35 | 0.945 |
| LogB | 93.54 | 95.37 | 94.44 | 0.37 | 0.943 |
| Log | 94.05 | 94.75 | 94.40 | 0.37 | 0.942 |
| SMO | 94.01 | 94.37 | 94.19 | 0.39 | 0.940 |
| NB | 94.61 | 92.64 | 93.60 | 0.42 | 0.934 |
| Stanford | 92.36 | 91.01 | 91.68 | 0.53 | 0.914 |
| CVote | 92.02 | 90.84 | 91.42 | 0.54 | 0.911 |
| Vote | 89.98 | 82.97 | 85.92 | 0.94 | 0.857 |
| Illinois | 82.79 | 87.35 | 84.95 | 0.92 | 0.845 |
| Balie | 77.68 | 82.05 | 79.80 | 1.21 | 0.792 |
| OpenNLP | 71.42 | 90.47 | 79.57 | 1.13 | 0.797 |

**Table 3.** News* entity-based

| $S$ | $rec$ | $pre$ | $F_1$ | $error$ | $MCC$ |
|---|---|---|---|---|---|
| FT | 93.95 | **92.27** | **93.10** | **0.30** | **0.930** |
| MLP | **94.10** | 92.13 | 93.09 | **0.30** | 0.929 |
| LMT | 94.08 | 91.91 | 92.97 | 0.31 | 0.928 |
| RF | 93.76 | 92.07 | 92.90 | 0.31 | 0.928 |
| BG | 93.51 | 92.18 | 92.83 | 0.31 | 0.927 |
| SVM | 93.85 | 91.46 | 92.62 | 0.32 | 0.925 |
| ABM1 | 93.30 | 91.65 | 92.47 | 0.33 | 0.923 |
| J48 | 93.30 | 91.65 | 92.47 | 0.33 | 0.923 |
| Log | 93.42 | 91.39 | 92.37 | 0.33 | 0.922 |
| LogB | 92.89 | 91.68 | 92.27 | 0.33 | 0.921 |
| SMO | 92.55 | 91.26 | 91.90 | 0.36 | 0.917 |
| DT | 92.44 | 91.29 | 91.86 | 0.34 | 0.917 |
| NB | 94.08 | 88.26 | 91.01 | 0.40 | 0.909 |
| Stanford | 92.00 | 87.58 | 89.72 | 0.45 | 0.895 |
| CVote | 91.43 | 86.94 | 89.10 | 0.47 | 0.889 |
| Illinois | 82.07 | 84.84 | 83.34 | 0.67 | 0.831 |
| Vote | 91.42 | 76.52 | 82.67 | 0.83 | 0.829 |
| Balie | 81.54 | 79.66 | 80.48 | 0.79 | 0.801 |
| OpenNLP | 69.36 | 85.02 | 75.78 | 0.88 | 0.760 |

We reached the highest f-scores on the News* dataset (Table 2 and Table 3) for both the token-based and the entity-based evaluation. In the token-based evaluation, the MLP and RF classifiers perform best for precision (95.28%), error rate (0.32%) and Matthews correlation coefficient (0.951). MLP performs best for f-score (95.23%) with 0.04% more recall than RF. The baseline classifier (i.e., simple voting) is clearly outperformed by MLP by up to +5.21% recall, +12.31% precision, +9.31% f-score, -0.62% error rate and +0.094 MCC. Furthermore, the best single approach is Stanford and outperformed by up to +2.83% recall, +4.27% precision, +3.55% f-score, -0.21% error rate (that is a reduction by 40%) and +0.037 MCC. Slightly poorer results are achieved in the entity-based evaluation, where MLP is second to FT with 0.01% less f-score.

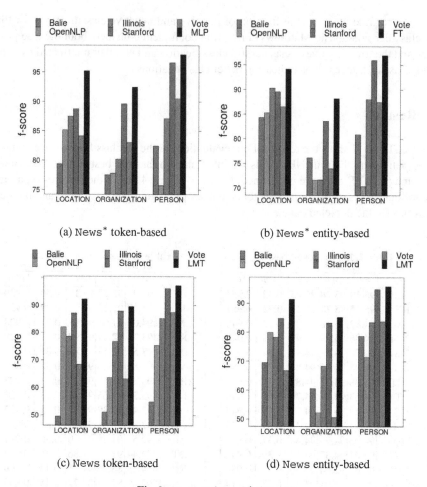

(a) News* token-based

(b) News* entity-based

(c) News token-based

(d) News entity-based

**Fig. 2.** News and News* dataset

On the News dataset (Table 4-Table 5), which was the largest homogenous dataset in our evaluation, we repeatedly achieved high f-scores. The best approach w.r.t. the token-based evaluation is LMT with an f-score of 92.94%. Random Forest follows the best approach with respect to f-score again. Moreover, the best single tool Stanford and the baseline classifier Vote are repeatedly outperformed by up to +2.6% resp. +19.91% f-score. Once again, the entity-based results are approximately 2% poorer, with LMT leading the table like in the token-based evaluation.

On the Web dataset (Table 6-Table 7), which is the worst-case dataset for NER tools as it contains several incomplete sentences, the different classifiers reached their lowest values. For the token-based evaluation, AdaBoostM1 with J48 achieves the best f-score (69.04%) and Matthews correlation coefficient (0.675) and is followed by Random Forest again with respect to f-score. Naïve Bayes performs best for recall (96.64%), Logistic Regression for precision (77.89%) and MLP and RF for the error rate (3.33%). Simple voting is outperformed by ABM1 by up to +3.5% recall, +20.08% precision,

**Table 4.** News token-based

| $S$ | rec | pre | $F_1$ | error | $MCC$ |
|---|---|---|---|---|---|
| LMT | **93.73** | 92.16 | **92.94** | **0.51** | **0.927** |
| RF | 93.56 | 92.19 | 92.87 | **0.51** | 0.926 |
| DT | 93.64 | 92.10 | 92.86 | **0.51** | 0.926 |
| J48 | 93.50 | 92.20 | 92.84 | 0.52 | 0.926 |
| ABM1 | 93.49 | 92.17 | 92.83 | 0.52 | 0.926 |
| BG | 93.11 | **92.49** | 92.79 | 0.52 | 0.925 |
| FT | 93.44 | 92.15 | 92.79 | 0.52 | 0.925 |
| MLP | 93.22 | 92.26 | 92.73 | 0.52 | 0.925 |
| SVM | 92.19 | **92.49** | 92.31 | 0.54 | 0.920 |
| SMO | 92.15 | 91.90 | 92.01 | 0.57 | 0.917 |
| Log | 91.38 | 91.36 | 91.35 | 0.63 | 0.910 |
| LogB | 91.42 | 91.32 | 91.34 | 0.62 | 0.910 |
| Stanford | 92.70 | 88.09 | 90.34 | 0.68 | 0.900 |
| CVote | 92.70 | 88.09 | 90.34 | 0.68 | 0.900 |
| NB | 93.36 | 86.17 | 89.58 | 0.77 | 0.893 |
| Illinois | 82.43 | 78.11 | 80.20 | 1.37 | 0.795 |
| OpenNLP | 75.21 | 74.41 | 73.71 | 2.06 | 0.732 |
| Vote | 83.13 | 69.14 | 73.03 | 2.36 | 0.735 |
| Balie | 70.81 | 72.86 | 71.54 | 1.90 | 0.707 |

**Table 5.** News entity-based

| $S$ | rec | pre | $F_1$ | error | $MCC$ |
|---|---|---|---|---|---|
| LMT | **92.95** | 88.84 | **90.84** | **0.44** | **0.906** |
| BG | 92.82 | 88.95 | 90.83 | **0.44** | **0.906** |
| DT | 92.89 | 88.88 | 90.83 | **0.44** | **0.906** |
| ABM1 | 92.87 | 88.82 | 90.79 | **0.44** | **0.906** |
| J48 | 92.87 | 88.82 | 90.79 | **0.44** | **0.906** |
| FT | 92.90 | 88.78 | 90.78 | **0.44** | **0.906** |
| RF | 92.84 | 88.77 | 90.74 | **0.44** | **0.906** |
| MLP | 92.83 | 88.69 | 90.70 | **0.44** | 0.905 |
| SVM | 91.56 | **89.22** | 90.33 | 0.45 | 0.901 |
| SMO | 91.13 | 88.36 | 89.69 | 0.49 | 0.895 |
| Log | 90.62 | 88.09 | 89.29 | 0.51 | 0.891 |
| LogB | 90.76 | 87.83 | 89.22 | 0.51 | 0.890 |
| Stanford | 91.78 | 83.92 | 87.66 | 0.58 | 0.875 |
| CVote | 91.78 | 83.92 | 87.66 | 0.58 | 0.875 |
| NB | 92.54 | 81.16 | 86.34 | 0.69 | 0.863 |
| Illinois | 81.66 | 72.50 | 76.71 | 1.11 | 0.763 |
| Balie | 71.58 | 68.67 | 69.66 | 1.42 | 0.692 |
| OpenNLP | 72.71 | 67.29 | 67.89 | 1.80 | 0.681 |
| Vote | 82.71 | 61.30 | 67.10 | 2.19 | 0.686 |

**Table 6.** Web token-based

| $S$ | rec | pre | $F_1$ | error | $MCC$ |
|---|---|---|---|---|---|
| ABM1 | 64.40 | 74.83 | **69.04** | 3.38 | **0.675** |
| RF | 64.36 | 74.57 | 68.93 | 3.38 | 0.674 |
| MLP | 63.86 | 75.11 | 68.81 | **3.33** | 0.674 |
| FT | 62.98 | 75.47 | 68.25 | **3.33** | 0.670 |
| LMT | 63.39 | 74.24 | 68.04 | 3.43 | 0.666 |
| DT | 62.80 | 74.18 | 67.85 | 3.43 | 0.664 |
| CVote | 63.16 | 73.54 | 67.66 | 3.49 | 0.662 |
| SVM | 62.94 | 73.45 | 67.60 | 3.49 | 0.661 |
| LogB | 60.47 | 77.48 | 67.57 | 3.40 | 0.665 |
| Log | 60.31 | **77.89** | 67.50 | 3.39 | 0.666 |
| SMO | 63.47 | 72.45 | 67.49 | 3.57 | 0.659 |
| BG | 61.06 | 76.19 | 67.46 | 3.34 | 0.663 |
| J48 | 62.21 | 73.78 | 67.21 | 3.49 | 0.658 |
| NB | **71.19** | 63.42 | 66.88 | 4.42 | 0.647 |
| Stanford | 60.57 | 72.19 | 65.81 | 3.51 | 0.643 |
| Illinois | 69.64 | 60.56 | 64.44 | 5.09 | 0.621 |
| Vote | 66.90 | 54.75 | 58.59 | 6.02 | 0.567 |
| OpenNLP | 45.71 | 58.81 | 49.18 | 5.93 | 0.477 |
| Balie | 38.63 | 43.83 | 40.15 | 7.02 | 0.371 |

**Table 7.** Web entity-based

| $S$ | rec | pre | $F_1$ | error | $MCC$ |
|---|---|---|---|---|---|
| MLP | 64.95 | 61.86 | **63.36** | 1.99 | **0.624** |
| Stanford | 64.80 | 61.31 | 62.83 | 1.95 | 0.619 |
| LogB | 61.25 | **64.10** | 62.60 | **1.94** | 0.616 |
| FT | 63.67 | 61.10 | 62.21 | 2.09 | 0.612 |
| ABM1 | 63.49 | 61.01 | 62.17 | 2.08 | 0.611 |
| Log | 60.43 | 63.62 | 61.95 | 1.99 | 0.610 |
| CVote | 65.69 | 59.54 | 61.82 | 2.05 | 0.612 |
| J48 | 63.21 | 59.72 | 61.39 | 2.12 | 0.603 |
| BG | 64.04 | 59.10 | 61.30 | 2.13 | 0.603 |
| RF | 64.15 | 55.88 | 59.69 | 2.27 | 0.587 |
| SVM | 62.36 | 57.26 | 59.57 | 2.15 | 0.586 |
| DT | 61.92 | 57.05 | 59.34 | 2.17 | 0.583 |
| LMT | 61.25 | 56.89 | 58.96 | 2.19 | 0.579 |
| SMO | 62.44 | 56.01 | 58.83 | 2.21 | 0.579 |
| NB | **74.18** | 49.20 | 58.55 | 3.17 | 0.586 |
| Illinois | 69.31 | 45.85 | 54.25 | 3.82 | 0.541 |
| Vote | 67.42 | 37.77 | 47.12 | 4.84 | 0.477 |
| OpenNLP | 46.94 | 46.78 | 43.99 | 3.71 | 0.437 |
| Balie | 38.07 | 32.92 | 35.07 | 3.63 | 0.334 |

528    R. Speck and A.-C. Ngonga Ngomo

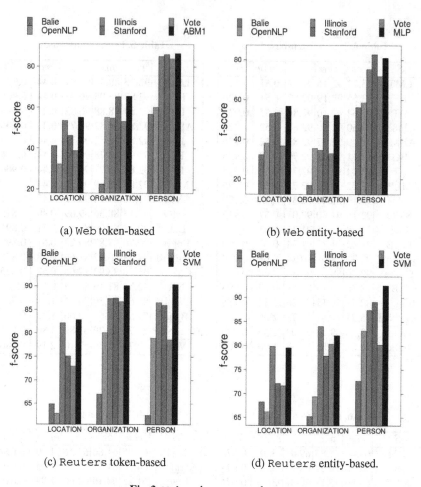

(a) Web token-based

(b) Web entity-based

(c) Reuters token-based

(d) Reuters entity-based.

**Fig. 3.** Web and Reuters dataset

+10.45% f-score, -2.64% error rate and +0.108 MCC, while Stanford (the best tool for this dataset) is outperformed by up to +3.83% recall, +2.64% precision, +3.21% f-score, -0.13% error rate and +0.032 MCC. Similar insights can be won from the entity-based evaluation, with some classifiers like RF being approximately 10% poorer that at token level.

On the Reuters dataset (Table 8-Table 9), which was the smallest dataset in our evaluation, Support Vector Machine performs best. In the token-based evaluation, SVM achieves an f-score of 87.78%, an error rate of 0.89% and a Matthews correlation coefficient of 0.875%. They are followed by Random Forest with respect to f-score once again. Naïve Bayes performs best for recall (86.54%). In comparison, ensemble learning outperforms Vote with SVM by up to +4.46% recall, +3.48% precision, +2.43% f-score, -0.54% error rate and +0.082 MCC. Moreover, the best NER tool for this dataset, Illinois, is outperformed by up to +0.83% recall, +3.48% precision, +2.43% f-score, -0.20% error rate and +0.024 MCC. In Figure 3a, we barely see a learning effect as

**Table 8.** Reuters token-based

| $\mathcal{S}$ | rec | pre | $F_1$ | error | MCC |
|---|---|---|---|---|---|
| SVM | 84.57 | **91.75** | **87.78** | **0.89** | **0.875** |
| RF | 86.11 | 89.24 | 87.58 | 0.90 | 0.872 |
| MLP | 85.89 | 89.46 | 87.55 | 0.90 | 0.871 |
| LMT | 84.41 | 91.08 | 87.43 | **0.89** | 0.871 |
| J48 | 84.64 | 90.70 | 87.33 | 0.93 | 0.870 |
| Log | 84.33 | 90.85 | 87.27 | **0.89** | 0.870 |
| LogB | 84.22 | 91.01 | 87.22 | 0.90 | 0.870 |
| ABM1 | 84.51 | 90.47 | 87.15 | 0.93 | 0.868 |
| BG | 84.70 | 90.16 | 87.14 | 0.94 | 0.868 |
| FT | 85.25 | 88.75 | 86.87 | 0.95 | 0.864 |
| DT | 84.41 | 89.00 | 86.43 | 0.99 | 0.861 |
| SMO | 84.45 | 88.49 | 86.28 | 0.98 | 0.859 |
| Illinois | 83.74 | 88.27 | 85.35 | 1.09 | 0.851 |
| NB | **86.54** | 83.18 | 84.77 | 1.10 | 0.842 |
| CVote | 81.96 | 88.66 | 84.64 | 1.14 | 0.844 |
| Stanford | 81.57 | 84.85 | 82.85 | 1.20 | 0.824 |
| Vote | 80.11 | 81.15 | 79.41 | 1.43 | 0.793 |
| OpenNLP | 67.94 | 82.08 | 73.96 | 1.76 | 0.736 |
| Balie | 64.92 | 68.61 | 64.78 | 2.62 | 0.645 |

**Table 9.** Reuters entity-based

| $\mathcal{S}$ | rec | pre | $F_1$ | error | MCC |
|---|---|---|---|---|---|
| SVM | 81.37 | **88.85** | **84.71** | **0.69** | **0.846** |
| ABM1 | 80.60 | 88.72 | 84.15 | 0.73 | 0.840 |
| LMT | 80.80 | 87.92 | 83.96 | 0.73 | 0.838 |
| J48 | 80.41 | 88.50 | 83.95 | 0.73 | 0.838 |
| BG | 80.55 | 87.70 | 83.75 | 0.75 | 0.836 |
| Illinois | 82.77 | 85.73 | 83.74 | 0.72 | 0.836 |
| LogB | 80.70 | 86.23 | 83.32 | 0.75 | 0.830 |
| DT | 81.11 | 85.20 | 82.95 | 0.79 | 0.827 |
| RF | 80.08 | 86.11 | 82.86 | 0.78 | 0.826 |
| Log | 80.01 | 85.51 | 82.62 | 0.78 | 0.823 |
| MLP | 80.27 | 84.09 | 81.98 | 0.83 | 0.817 |
| SMO | 79.62 | 83.21 | 81.36 | 0.88 | 0.809 |
| FT | 80.00 | 82.71 | 81.32 | 0.85 | 0.809 |
| CVote | 77.86 | 85.42 | 81.00 | 0.85 | 0.809 |
| NB | **83.80** | 77.68 | 80.61 | 0.92 | 0.802 |
| Stanford | 77.56 | 82.38 | 79.68 | 0.90 | 0.794 |
| Vote | 80.35 | 76.25 | 77.37 | 1.03 | 0.773 |
| OpenNLP | 66.85 | 80.33 | 72.89 | 1.18 | 0.726 |
| Balie | 68.90 | 70.14 | 68.71 | 1.39 | 0.684 |

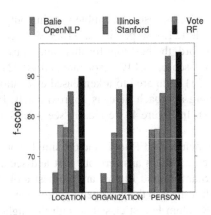

(a) All token-based.

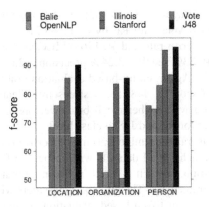

(b) All entity-based.

**Fig. 4.** All dataset

ABM1 is almost equal to one of the integrated NER tools assessed at class level especially for the class Organization on the Web dataset but in Figure 3c on the Reuters dataset we clearly see a learning effect for the class Organization and Person with the SVM approach.

On the All dataset for token-based evaluation (Table 10), the Random Forest approach performs best for f-score (91.27%), error rate (0.64%) and Matthews correlation coefficient (0.909). Support Vector Machine achieves the best precision (91.24%) and

**Table 10.** All token-based

| $S$ | rec | pre | $F_1$ | error | $MCC$ |
|---|---|---|---|---|---|
| RF | 91.58 | 90.97 | **91.27** | **0.64** | **0.909** |
| LMT | 91.67 | 90.86 | 91.26 | **0.64** | **0.909** |
| ABM1 | 91.49 | 90.99 | 91.24 | **0.64** | **0.909** |
| J48 | 91.46 | 90.98 | 91.22 | **0.64** | **0.909** |
| DT | 91.59 | 90.84 | 91.21 | **0.64** | **0.909** |
| FT | 91.49 | 90.82 | 91.16 | 0.65 | 0.908 |
| BG | 91.25 | 91.00 | 91.12 | 0.65 | 0.908 |
| MLP | 90.94 | 91.05 | 90.99 | 0.66 | 0.907 |
| SVM | 90.15 | **91.24** | 90.67 | 0.67 | 0.903 |
| SMO | 90.13 | 90.48 | 90.27 | 0.71 | 0.899 |
| Log | 88.69 | 90.57 | 89.59 | 0.76 | 0.892 |
| LogB | 88.92 | 90.21 | 89.53 | 0.76 | 0.892 |
| Stanford | 90.75 | 87.73 | 89.21 | 0.78 | 0.888 |
| CVote | 90.75 | 87.73 | 89.21 | 0.78 | 0.888 |
| NB | **92.00** | 85.27 | 88.46 | 0.89 | 0.881 |
| Illinois | 81.66 | 77.61 | 79.54 | 1.48 | 0.788 |
| Vote | 81.85 | 69.96 | 72.90 | 2.44 | 0.733 |
| OpenNLP | 72.63 | 75.60 | 72.65 | 2.19 | 0.723 |
| Balie | 67.75 | 71.65 | 69.40 | 2.09 | 0.685 |

**Table 11.** All entity-based

| $S$ | rec | pre | $F_1$ | error | $MCC$ |
|---|---|---|---|---|---|
| J48 | 92.68 | 88.62 | **90.59** | **0.44** | **0.904** |
| ABM1 | 92.66 | 88.59 | 90.56 | **0.44** | **0.904** |
| LMT | 92.59 | 88.50 | 90.48 | 0.45 | 0.903 |
| DT | 92.56 | 88.44 | 90.44 | 0.45 | 0.902 |
| RF | 92.51 | 88.33 | 90.35 | 0.45 | 0.902 |
| FT | 92.47 | 88.37 | 90.35 | 0.45 | 0.902 |
| BG | 92.17 | 88.55 | 90.31 | 0.45 | 0.901 |
| MLP | 92.07 | 88.60 | 90.28 | 0.45 | 0.901 |
| SVM | 90.91 | **88.97** | 89.88 | 0.46 | 0.897 |
| SMO | 90.94 | 87.31 | 89.00 | 0.52 | 0.888 |
| Log | 89.49 | 88.10 | 88.70 | 0.53 | 0.885 |
| LogB | 89.21 | 87.68 | 88.36 | 0.54 | 0.881 |
| Stanford | 92.00 | 84.48 | 88.05 | 0.56 | 0.879 |
| CVote | 92.00 | 84.48 | 88.05 | 0.56 | 0.879 |
| NB | **92.69** | 80.59 | 86.04 | 0.71 | 0.860 |
| Illinois | 81.43 | 71.82 | 76.25 | 1.12 | 0.759 |
| Balie | 69.27 | 67.47 | 67.82 | 1.48 | 0.674 |
| OpenNLP | 71.29 | 69.44 | 67.66 | 1.80 | 0.682 |
| Vote | 81.97 | 62.17 | 67.27 | 2.17 | 0.687 |

Naïve Bayes the best recall (91.00%) again. In comparison, ensemble learning outperformed Vote with RF by up to +9.71% recall, +21.01% precision, +18.37% f-score, -1.8% error rate and +0.176% MCC and Stanford, the best tool for this dataset, by up to +0.83% recall, +3.24% precision, +2.06% f-score, -0.14% error rate and +0.021% MCC. Again, entity-based evaluation (Table 11) compared to token-based evaluation, the f-score of J48, the best ensemble learning approach here, is approximately 1% poorer with higher recall but lower precision. In Figure 4, we clearly see a learning effect for RF and J48 at class level.

Overall, ensemble learning outperform all included NER tools and the simple voting approach for all datasets with respect to f-score, which answers our first and second question. Here, it is worth mentioning that Stanford and Illinois are the best tools in our framework. The three best classifiers with respect to the averaged f-scores over our datasets for token-based evaluation are the Random Forest classifier with the highest value, closely followed by Multilayer Perceptron and AdaBoostM1 with J48 and for entity-based evaluation AdaBoostM1 with J48 with the highest value, closely followed by MLP and J48. We cannot observe a significant difference between these.

In Table 12 and Table 13, we depict the f-scores of these three classifiers at class level for our datasets. The statistically significant differences are marked in bold. Note that two out of three scores being marked bold for the same setting in a column means that the corresponding approaches are significantly better than the third one yet not significantly better than each other. In the token-based evaluation, the Multilayer Perceptron and Random Forest classifier surpass the AdaBoostM1 with J48 on the News* and Web datasets. On the News* dataset, MLP surpasses RF for Location but RF surpasses MLP for Person. On the Web dataset, RF is better than MLP for Location but not

Table 12. F-score of the best 3 classifiers on class level token-based

| $S$ | Class | News | News* | Web | Reuters | All |
|---|---|---|---|---|---|---|
| RF | Location | **92.12** | 94.96 | **54.58** | **82.25** | **89.98** |
| RF | Organization | **89.45** | **92.44** | **65.60** | **90.53** | **87.93** |
| RF | Person | 97.02 | **98.25** | **86.61** | 89.95 | **95.91** |
| MLP | Location | 91.79 | **95.22** | 53.78 | **82.13** | 89.62 |
| MLP | Organization | 89.34 | **92.45** | **65.72** | **90.38** | 87.63 |
| MLP | Person | **97.07** | 98.04 | **86.94** | 90.14 | 95.73 |
| ABM1 | Location | 91.75 | 95.10 | 55.11 | 81.19 | 89.90 |
| ABM1 | Organization | **89.49** | 92.00 | 65.47 | 89.91 | **87.96** |
| ABM1 | Person | **97.12** | 97.89 | 86.53 | 90.37 | 95.87 |

Table 13. F-score of the best 3 classifiers on class level entity-based

| $S$ | Class | News | News* | Web | Reuters | All |
|---|---|---|---|---|---|---|
| ABM1 | Location | 91.26 | 95.71 | **58.21** | **78.99** | 90.05 |
| ABM1 | Organization | **85.19** | 85.87 | 50.66 | **80.45** | 85.43 |
| ABM1 | Person | **95.91** | 95.81 | 77.63 | **93.02** | 96.21 |
| MLP | Location | 91.14 | 95.35 | 56.72 | 76.32 | 89.63 |
| MLP | Organization | 85.17 | **87.30** | **52.29** | 78.74 | 85.38 |
| MLP | Person | 95.79 | 96.61 | **81.09** | 90.88 | 95.83 |
| J48 | Location | 91.27 | 95.71 | 56.53 | **78.99** | **90.08** |
| J48 | Organization | 85.18 | 85.87 | 50.56 | **80.49** | 85.44 |
| J48 | Person | **95.91** | 95.81 | 77.10 | 92.36 | **96.23** |

significantly different from one another for `Person`. Also, for the `Organization` class, no significant difference could be determined on both datasets. On the `Reuters` dataset, MLP and RF are better than ABM1 for `Location` and `Organization`, but do not differ one another. For the class `Person`, no significant difference could be determined for all three classifiers. On the `News` and `All` dataset, Random Forest is significantly best for `Location`. Random Forest and AdaBoostM1 with J48 surpass the Multilayer Perceptron for `Organization` but are not significantly different. For the class `Person`, ABM1 is significantly best on the `News` dataset and RF is best on the `All` dataset. The entity-level results also suggest shifts amongst the best systems depending on the datasets. Interestingly, MLP and ABM1 are the only two classes of algorithm that appear as top algorithms in both evaluation schemes.

Consequently, our results suggest that while the four approaches RF, MLP, ABM1 and J48 perform best over the datasets at hand, MLP and ABM1 are to be favored. Note that significant differences can be observed across the different datasets and that all four paradigms RF, MLP, ABM1 and J48 should be considered when applying ensemble learning to NER. This answers the last and most important question of this evaluation.

# 6 Conclusion and Future Work

In this paper, we evaluated named entity recognition based on ensemble learning, an approach to increase the performance of state-of-the-art named entity recognition tools.

On all datasets, we showed that ensemble learning achieves higher f-scores than the best named entity recognition tool integrated in our system and higher f-scores compared with a simple voting on the outcome of the integrated tools. Our results suggest that Multilayer Perceptron and AdaBoostM1 with J48 as base classifier work best for the task at hand. We have now integrated the results of this evaluation into the FOX framework, which can be found at `http://fox.aksw.org`. The main advantages of our framework are that it is not limited to the integration of named entity recognition tools or ensemble learning algorithms and can be easily extended. Moreover, it provides additional features like linked data and a RESTful web service to use by the community.

## References

1. Allwein, E.L., Schapire, R.E., Singer, Y.: Reducing multiclass to binary: A unifying approach for margin classifiers. J. Mach. Learn. Res. 1, 113–141 (2001)
2. Amsler, R.: Research towards the development of a lexical knowledge base for natural language processing. SIGIR Forum 23, 1–2 (1989)
3. Baldridge, J.: The opennlp project (2005)
4. Bay, S.D., Hettich, S.: The UCI KDD Archive (1999), `http://kdd.ics.uci.edu`
5. Breiman, L.: Bagging predictors. Machine Learning 24(2), 123–140 (1996)
6. Breiman, L.: Random forests. Machine Learning 45(1), 5–32 (2001)
7. Chang, C.-C., Lin, C.-J.: LIBSVM - a library for support vector machines. The Weka classifier works with version 2.82 of LIBSVM (2001)
8. Coates-Stephens, S.: The analysis and acquisition of proper names for the understanding of free text. Computers and the Humanities 26, 441–456 (1992), doi:10.1007/BF00136985
9. Cornolti, M., Ferragina, P., Ciaramita, M.: A framework for benchmarking entity-annotation systems. In: Proceedings of the 22nd International Conference on World Wide Web, pp. 249–260. International World Wide Web Conferences Steering Committee (2013)
10. Curran, J.R., Clark, S.: Language independent ner using a maximum entropy tagger. In: Proceedings of the Seventh Conference on Natural Language Learning at HLT-NAACL 2003, vol. 4, pp. 164–167 (2003)
11. Demšar, J.: Statistical comparisons of classifiers over multiple data sets. J. Mach. Learn. Res. 7, 1–30 (2006)
12. Dietterich, T.G.: Ensemble methods in machine learning. In: Kittler, J., Roli, F. (eds.) MCS 2000. LNCS, vol. 1857, pp. 1–15. Springer, Heidelberg (2000)
13. Etzioni, O., Cafarella, M., Downey, D., Popescu, A.-M., Shaked, T., Soderland, S., Weld, D.S., Yates, A.: Unsupervised named-entity extraction from the web: an experimental study. Artif. Intell. 165, 91–134 (2005)
14. Finkel, J.R., Grenager, T., Manning, C.: Incorporating non-local information into information extraction systems by gibbs sampling. In: ACL, pp. 363–370 (2005)
15. Freire, N., Borbinha, J., Calado, P.: An approach for named entity recognition in poorly structured data. In: Simperl, E., Cimiano, P., Polleres, A., Corcho, O., Presutti, V. (eds.) ESWC 2012. LNCS, vol. 7295, pp. 718–732. Springer, Heidelberg (2012)
16. Freund, Y., Schapire, R.E.: Experiments with a New Boosting Algorithm. In: International Conference on Machine Learning, pp. 148–156 (1996)
17. Friedman, J., Hastie, T., Tibshirani, R.: Additive logistic regression: a statistical view of boosting. Technical report, Stanford University (1998)
18. Gama, J.: Functional trees 55(3), 219–250 (2004)

19. Gangemi, A.: A comparison of knowledge extraction tools for the semantic web. In: Cimiano, P., Corcho, O., Presutti, V., Hollink, L., Rudolph, S. (eds.) ESWC 2013. LNCS, vol. 7882, pp. 351–366. Springer, Heidelberg (2013)

20. Hakimov, S., Oto, S.A., Dogdu, E.: Named entity recognition and disambiguation using linked data and graph-based centrality scoring. In: Proceedings of the 4th International Workshop on Semantic Web Information Management, SWIM 2012, pp. 4:1–4:7. ACM, New York (2012)

21. Hall, M., Frank, E., Holmes, G., Pfahringer, B., Reutemann, P., Witten, I.H.: The weka data mining software: An update. SIGKDD Explor. Newsl. 11(1), 10–18 (2009)

22. Hastie, T., Tibshirani, R.: Classification by pairwise coupling. In: Jordan, M.I., Kearns, M.J., Solla, S.A. (eds.) Advances in Neural Information Processing Systems, vol. 10. MIT Press (1998)

23. John, G.H., Langley, P.: Estimating continuous distributions in bayesian classifiers. In: Eleventh Conference on Uncertainty in Artificial Intelligence, pp. 338–345. Morgan Kaufmann, San Mateo (1995)

24. Khalili, A., Auer, S.: Rdface: The rdfa content editor. In: ISWC 2011 Demo Track (2011)

25. Kittler, J., Hatef, M., Duin, R.W., Matas, J.: On combining classifiers. IEEE Transactions on Pattern Analysis and Machine Intelligence 20(3), 226–239 (1998)

26. Kohavi, R.: The power of decision tables. In: Lavrač, N., Wrobel, S. (eds.) ECML 1995. LNCS, vol. 912, pp. 174–189. Springer, Heidelberg (1995)

27. Landwehr, N., Hall, M., Frank, E.: Logistic model trees. Machine Learning 95(1-2), 161–205 (2005)

28. le Cessie, S., van Houwelingen, J.C.: Ridge estimators in logistic regression. Applied Statistics 41(1), 191–201 (1992)

29. Matthews, B.W.: Comparison of the predicted and observed secondary structure of T4 phage lysozyme. Biochim. Biophys. Acta 405, 442–451 (1975)

30. Nadeau, D.: Balie—baseline information extraction: Multilingual information extraction from text with machine learning and natural language techniques. Technical report, University of Ottawa (2005)

31. Nadeau, D.: Semi-supervised Named Entity Recognition: Learning to Recognize 100 Entity Types with Little Supervision. PhD thesis, Ottawa, Ont., Canada, Canada, AAINR49385 (2007)

32. Nadeau, D., Sekine, S.: A survey of named entity recognition and classification. Linguisticae Investigationes 30(1), 3–26 (2007)

33. Nadeau, D., Turney, P., Matwin, S.: Unsupervised named-entity recognition: Generating gazetteers and resolving ambiguity, pp. 266–277 (2006)

34. Ngonga Ngomo, A.-C., Heino, N., Lyko, K., Speck, R., Kaltenböck, M.: SCMS – Semantifying Content Management Systems. In: Aroyo, L., Welty, C., Alani, H., Taylor, J., Bernstein, A., Kagal, L., Noy, N., Blomqvist, E. (eds.) ISWC 2011, Part II. LNCS, vol. 7032, pp. 189–204. Springer, Heidelberg (2011)

35. Pasca, M., Lin, D., Bigham, J., Lifchits, A., Jain, A.: Organizing and searching the world wide web of facts - step one: the one-million fact extraction challenge. In: Proceedings of the 21st National Conference on Artificial Intelligence, vol. 2, pp. 1400–1405. AAAI Press (2006)

36. Ross Quinlan, J.: C4.5: Programs for Machine Learning. Morgan Kaufmann Publishers Inc., San Francisco (1993)

37. Ratinov, L., Roth, D.: Design challenges and misconceptions in named entity recognition. In: Proceedings of the Thirteenth Conference on Computational Natural Language Learning, CoNLL 2009, pp. 147–155. Association for Computational Linguistics, Stroudsburg (2009)

38. Röder, M., Usbeck, R., Hellmann, S., Gerber, D., Both, A.: $N^3$ - A Collection of Datasets for Named Entity Recognition and Disambiguation in the NLP Interchange Format. In: Proceedings of LREC 2014 (2014)
39. Sampson, G.: How fully does a machine-usable dictionary cover english text. Literary and Linguistic Computing 4(1) (1989)
40. Schapire, R.E.: The strength of weak learnability. Mach. Learn. 5, 197–227 (1990)
41. Sumner, M., Frank, E., Hall, M.: Speeding up logistic model tree induction. In: Jorge, A.M., Torgo, L., Brazdil, P.B., Camacho, R., Gama, J. (eds.) PKDD 2005. LNCS (LNAI), vol. 3721, pp. 675–683. Springer, Heidelberg (2005)
42. Thielen, C.: An approach to proper name tagging for german. In: Proceedings of the EACL 1995 SIGDAT Workshop (1995)
43. Walker, D., Amsler, R.: The use of machine-readable dictionaries in sublanguage analysis. In: Analysing Language in Restricted Domains (1986)
44. Wu, D., Ngai, G., Carpuat, M.: A stacked, voted, stacked model for named entity recognition. In: Proceedings of the Seventh Conference on Natural Language Learning at HLT-NAACL 2003, CONLL 2003, vol. 4, pp. 200–203. Association for Computational Linguistics, Stroudsburg (2003)
45. Yang, P., Yang, Y.H., Zhou, B.B., Zomaya, A.Y.: A review of ensemble methods in bioinformatics. Current Bioinformatics 5(4), 296–308 (2010)
46. Zhou, G., Su, J.: Named entity recognition using an hmm-based chunk tagger. In: Proceedings of ACL, pp. 473–480 (2002)

# OBDA: Query Rewriting or Materialization? In Practice, Both!

Juan F. Sequeda[1], Marcelo Arenas[2], and Daniel P. Miranker[1]

[1] Department of Computer Science, The University of Texas at Austin
[2] Department of Computer Science, PUC Chile

**Abstract.** Given a source relational database, a target OWL ontology and a mapping from the source database to the target ontology, Ontology-Based Data Access (OBDA) concerns answering queries over the target ontology using these three components. This paper presents the development of Ultrawrap$^{OBDA}$, an OBDA system comprising bidirectional evaluation; that is, a hybridization of query rewriting and materialization. We observe that by compiling the ontological entailments as mappings, implementing the mappings as SQL views and materializing a subset of the views, the underlying SQL optimizer is able to reduce the execution time of a SPARQL query by rewriting the query in terms of the views specified by the mappings. To the best of our knowledge, this is the first OBDA system supporting ontologies with transitivity by using SQL recursion. Our contributions include: (1) an efficient algorithm to compile ontological entailments as mappings; (2) a proof that every SPARQL query can be rewritten into a SQL query in the context of mappings; (3) a cost model to determine which views to materialize to attain the fastest execution time; and (4) an empirical evaluation comparing with a state-of-the-art OBDA system, which validates the cost model and demonstrates favorable execution times.

## 1 Introduction

Given a source relational database, a target OWL ontology and a mapping from the relational database to the ontology, Ontology-Based Data Access (OBDA) concerns answering queries over the target ontology using these three components. Commonly, researchers have taken two approaches to developing OBDA systems: materialization or rewriting. In the materialization approach, the input relational database $D$, target ontology $\mathcal{O}$ and mapping $\mathcal{M}$ (from $D$ to $\mathcal{O}$) are used to derive new facts that are stored in a database $D_o$, which is the materialization of the data in $D$ given $\mathcal{M}$ and $\mathcal{O}$. Then the answer to a query $Q$ over the target ontology is computed by directly posing $Q$ over $D_o$ [3]. In the rewriting approach, three steps are executed. First, a new query $Q_o$ is generated from the query $Q$ and the ontology $\mathcal{O}$: the rewriting of $Q$ w.r.t to $\mathcal{O}$. The majority of the OBDA literature focuses on this step [19]. Second, the mapping $\mathcal{M}$ is used to compile $Q_o$ to a SQL query $Q_{\text{sql}}$ over $D$ [21,22]. Finally, $Q_{\text{sql}}$ is evaluated on the database $D$, which gives us the answer to the initial query $Q$.

We develop an OBDA system, Ultrawrap$^{OBDA}$, which combines materialization and query rewriting. Our objective is to effect optimizations by pushing processing into the Relational Databases Management Systems (RDBMS) and closer to the stored data,

P. Mika et al. (Eds.) ISWC 2014, Part I, LNCS 8796, pp. 535–551, 2014.

hence making maximal use of existing SQL infrastructure. We distinguish two phases: a compile and runtime phase. In the compile phase, the inputs are a relational database $D$, an ontology $\mathcal{O}$ and a mapping $\mathcal{M}$ from $D$ to $\mathcal{O}$. The first step is to embed in $\mathcal{M}$ the ontological entailments of $\mathcal{O}$, which gives rise to a new mapping $\mathcal{M}^\star$, the *saturation* of $\mathcal{M}$ w.r.t. $\mathcal{O}$. The mapping $\mathcal{M}^\star$ is implemented using SQL views. In order to improve query performance, an important issue is to decide which views should be materialized. This is the last step of the compilation phase. In the runtime phase, the input is a query $Q$ over the target ontology $\mathcal{O}$, which is written in the RDF query language SPARQL, and the problem is to answer this query by rewriting it into some SQL queries over the views. A key observation at this point is that some existing SQL optimizers are able to perform rewritings in order to execute queries against materialized views.

To the best of our knowledge, we present the first OBDA system which supports ontologies with transitivity by using SQL recursion. More specifically, our contributions are the following. (1) We present an efficient algorithm to generate saturated mappings. (2) We provide a proof that every SPARQL query over a target ontology can be rewritten into a SQL query in our context, where mappings play a fundamental role. It is important to mention that such a result is a minimal requirement for a query-rewriting OBDA system relying on relational database technology. (3) We present a cost model that help us to determine which views to materialize to attain the fastest execution time. And (4) we present an empirical evaluation using (i) Oracle, (ii) two benchmarks including an extension of the Berlin SPARQL Benchmark, and (iii) six different scenarios. This evaluation includes a comparison against a state-of-the-art OBDA system, and its results validate the cost model and demonstrate favorable execution times for Ultrawrap$^{\text{OBDA}}$.

**Related Work.** This research builds upon the work of Rodriguez-Muro et. al. implemented in Ontop [24,25] and our previous work on Ultrawrap [27]. Rodriguez-Muro et. al. uses the tree-witness rewriting algorithm and introduced the idea of compiling ontological entailments as mappings, which they named $\mathcal{T}$-Mappings. There are three key differences between Rodriguez-Muro et. al. and our work in this paper: (1) we have extended the work of Rodriguez-Muro et. al. to support more than hierarchy of classes and properties, including transitivity; (2) we introduce an efficient algorithm that generates saturated mappings while Rodriguez-Muro et. al. has not presented an algorithm before; and (3) we represent the mappings as SQL views and study when the views should be materialized. Ultrawrap is a system that encodes a fix mapping, the direct mapping [4,26], of the database as RDF. These mappings are implemented using unmaterialized SQL views. The approach presented in this paper extends Ultrawrap in three important aspects: (1) supports a customized mapping language; (2) supports reasoning through saturated mappings; and (3) considers materializing views for query optimization. Another related work is the combined approach [16], which materializes entailments as data, without considering mappings, and uses a limited form of query rewriting. The main objective of this approach is to deal with the case of infinite materialization, which cannot occur for the type of ontologies considered in this paper.

## 2 Preliminaries

**Relational Databases.** Assume, a countably infinite domain $\mathbf{D}$. A *schema* $\mathbf{R}$ is a finite set of relation names, where for each $R \in \mathbf{R}$, $att(R)$ denotes the nonempty finite set of attributes names associated to $R$ and $arity(R)$ is the arity of $R$ (that is, $arity(R)$ is the number of elements of the set $att(R)$). An instance $I$ of $\mathbf{R}$ assigns to each relation symbol $R \in \mathbf{R}$ a finite set $R^I = \{t_1, \ldots, t_\ell\}$ of tuples, where each tuple $t_j$ ($1 \leq j \leq \ell$) is a function that assigns to each attribute in $att(R)$ a value from $\mathbf{D}$. We use notation $t.A$ to refer to the value of a tuple $t$ in an attribute $A$. Moreover, we say that $R(t)$ is a fact in $I$ if $t \in R^I$, and we use notation $R(t) \in I$ in this case (that is, we also view instances as sets of facts).

*Example 1. We use a relational database for an organization as a running example. The schema of this database consists of the table* EMP *with* $att(\mathtt{EMP}) = \{\mathtt{SID}, \mathtt{NAME}, \mathtt{JOB}\}$, *and the following is an instance of this schema:* $I = \{\mathtt{EMP}(1, \mathtt{Alice}, \mathtt{CEO}),$ $\mathtt{EMP}(2, \mathtt{Bob}, \mathtt{JavaProgrammer}), \mathtt{EMP}(3, \mathtt{John}, \mathtt{SysAdmin})\}$.

In what follows, we assume some familiarity with the syntax and semantics of first-order logic. In particular, we assume that a formula over a relational schema $\mathbf{R}$ is constructed by using the relation names in $\mathbf{R}$, the equality predicate $=$ and the elements (also referred as constants) in $\mathbf{D}$. Moreover, a tuple of variables is denoted by $\bar{x}$ and a tuple of elements from $\mathbf{D}$ is denoted by $\bar{c}$, notation $\varphi(\bar{x})$ is used to indicate that the free variables of $\varphi$ are exactly the variables in $\bar{x}$, and $\varphi(\bar{c})$ is the formula obtained from $\varphi(\bar{x})$ by replacing every variable in $\bar{x}$ by the corresponding element in $\bar{c}$. Finally, given an instance $I$ over a relational schema $\mathbf{R}$ and a set $\Sigma$ of first-order formulae over $\mathbf{R}$, notation $I \models \psi$ is used to indicate that a first-order formula $\psi$ over $\mathbf{R}$ holds in $I$, while notation $\Sigma \models \psi$ is used to indicate that $\psi$ is implied by $\Sigma$.

**RDF and Ontologies.** Assume there are disjoint countably infinite sets $\mathbf{U}$ (URIs) and $\mathbf{L}$ (literals). A tuple $(s, p, o) \in \mathbf{U} \times \mathbf{U} \times (\mathbf{U} \cup \mathbf{L})$ is called an RDF triple,[1] where $s$ is the subject, $p$ is the predicate and $o$ is the object. A finite set of RDF triples is called an RDF graph.

In order to define the notion of ontology, define $\mathbf{O}$ as the following set of reserved keywords: $\{\mathtt{subClass}, \mathtt{subProp}, \mathtt{dom}, \mathtt{range}, \mathtt{type}, \mathtt{equivClass}, \mathtt{equivProp},$ $\mathtt{inverse}, \mathtt{symProp}, \mathtt{transProp}\}$, and assume that $\mathbf{O} \subseteq \mathbf{U}$. Moreover, following [28] say that an RDF triple $(a, b, c)$ is ontological if : (1) $a \in (\mathbf{U} \smallsetminus \mathbf{O})$, and (2) either $b \in (\mathbf{O} \smallsetminus \{\mathtt{type}\})$ and $c \in (\mathbf{U} \smallsetminus \mathbf{O})$, or $b = \mathtt{type}$ and $c$ is either $\mathtt{symProp}$ or $\mathtt{transProp}$. Additionally, say that an RDF triple $(a, b, c)$ is assertional if $(a, b, c)$ is not ontological. Then an ontology $\mathcal{O}$ is simply defined as a finite set of ontological triples. The semantics of an ontology $\mathcal{O}$ is usually defined by representing it as a set of description logic axioms, and then relying on the semantics of this logic [5] (which, in turn, is inherited from the semantics of first-order logic). For our purpose, it is more convenient to directly define a set $\Sigma_{\mathcal{O}}$ of first-order formulae encoding the ontology $\mathcal{O}$. More precisely, assume that $\mathtt{triple}$ is a ternary predicate that is used to store RDF graphs in

---

[1] For simplicity, we do not consider blank nodes as a skolemization process can be used to replace them by URIs.

the obvious way: every triple $(a, b, c) \in G$ is stored as $\texttt{triple}(a, b, c)$. Then for every triple $t \in \mathcal{O}$, define a first-order formula $\varphi_t$ over $\texttt{triple}$ as follows:

$$\varphi_{(a,\texttt{subClass},b)} = \forall x \, (\texttt{triple}(x, \texttt{type}, a) \rightarrow \texttt{triple}(x, \texttt{type}, b))$$

$$\varphi_{(a,\texttt{subProp},b)} = \forall x \forall y \, (\texttt{triple}(x, a, y) \rightarrow \texttt{triple}(x, b, y))$$

$$\varphi_{(a,\texttt{dom},b)} = \forall x \forall y \, (\texttt{triple}(x, a, y) \rightarrow \texttt{triple}(x, \texttt{type}, b))$$

$$\varphi_{(a,\texttt{range},b)} = \forall x \forall y \, (\texttt{triple}(x, a, y) \rightarrow \texttt{triple}(y, \texttt{type}, b))$$

$$\varphi_{(a,\texttt{equivClass},b)} = \forall x \, (\texttt{triple}(x, \texttt{type}, a) \leftrightarrow \texttt{triple}(x, \texttt{type}, b))$$

$$\varphi_{(a,\texttt{equivProp},b)} = \forall x \forall y \, (\texttt{triple}(x, a, y) \leftrightarrow \texttt{triple}(x, b, y))$$

$$\varphi_{(a,\texttt{inverse},b)} = \forall x \forall y \, (\texttt{triple}(x, a, y) \leftrightarrow \texttt{triple}(y, b, x))$$

$$\varphi_{(a,\texttt{type},\texttt{symProp})} = \forall x \forall y \, (\texttt{triple}(x, a, y) \rightarrow \texttt{triple}(y, a, x))$$

$$\varphi_{(a,\texttt{type},\texttt{transProp})} = \forall x \forall y \forall z \, (\texttt{triple}(x, a, y) \wedge \texttt{triple}(y, a, z) \rightarrow \texttt{triple}(x, a, z)),$$

and define $\Sigma_{\mathcal{O}}$ as $\{\varphi_t \mid t \in \mathcal{O}\}$.

Note that $\texttt{subClass}, \texttt{subProp}, \texttt{dom}, \texttt{range}, \texttt{type}, \texttt{equivClass}, \texttt{equivProp}$ are in RDFS [7], $\texttt{inverse}, \texttt{symProp}$ are in OWL 2 QL but not in OWL 2 EL and $\texttt{transProp}$ is in OWL 2 EL but not in OWL 2 QL [17]. Actually, the ontologies we consider are in the non-standard profiles known as RDFS-Plus [1], OWL-LD[2] and RDFS 3.0[3].

In an OBDA system, we need to map relational databases into RDF graphs, which forces us to transform every constant from **D** into either a URI or a literal. This process is usually carried over by using some built-in transformation functions [4,26]. For the sake of simplicity, we assume that $\mathbf{D} = (\mathbf{U} \smallsetminus \mathbf{O}) \cup \mathbf{L}$, which allows us to use the constants in a relational database directly as URIs or literals in an RDF graph, and which also allows us to view a set of facts of the form $\texttt{triple}(a, b, c)$ as an instance over the relational schema $\{\texttt{triple}\}$. Notice that the keywords in **O** are not allowed in **D**, as these as reserved for the specification of ontologies.

## 3   Mapping Relational Databases to RDF for OBDA

We describe how mappings are handled in our approach. We start by defining the mappings from relational databases to RDF, which are called RDB2RDF mappings, and then introduce the notion of saturation of an RDB2RDF mapping w.r.t. an ontology, which plays a fundamental role in our approach. We provide an efficient algorithm to compute it for ontologies not containing transitive predicates, and then show how our results can be extended to deal with transitive predicates. Finally, we show how RDB2RDF mappings are implemented in our system.

### 3.1   Relational Databases to RDF Mappings

We introduce the notion of mapping from a relation database to RDF, which is denoted as an RDB2RDF mapping. Two proposals to standardize this notion can be found in [4,11]. However, we follow here an alternative approach that has been widely used in

---

[2] http://semanticweb.org/OWLLD/
[3] http://www.w3.org/2009/12/rdf-ws/papers/ws31

the data exchange [3] and data integration areas [15], and which is based on the use of first-order logic and its semantics to define mappings. More precisely, given a relational schema $\mathbf{R}$ such that $\texttt{triple} \notin \mathbf{R}$, a class RDB2RDF-rule $\rho$ over $\mathbf{R}$ is a first-order formula of the form:

$$\forall s \forall p \forall o \forall \bar{x} \; \alpha(s, \bar{x}) \wedge p = \texttt{type} \wedge o = c \rightarrow \texttt{triple}(s, p, o), \tag{1}$$

where $\alpha(s, \bar{x})$ is a domain-independent first-order formula over $\mathbf{R}$ and $c \in \mathbf{D}$. Moreover, a predicate RDB2RDF-rule $\rho$ over $\mathbf{R}$ is a first-order formula of the form:

$$\forall s \forall p \forall o \forall \bar{x} \; \beta(s, o, \bar{x}) \wedge p = c \rightarrow \texttt{triple}(s, p, o), \tag{2}$$

where $\beta(s, o, \bar{x})$ is a domain-independent first-order formula over $\mathbf{R}$ and $c \in \mathbf{D}$. Finally, an RDB2RDF-rule over $\mathbf{R}$ is either a class or a predicate RDB2RDF-rule over $\mathbf{R}$. In what follows, we omit the universal quantifiers $\forall s \forall p \forall o \forall \bar{x}$ from RDB2RDF rules, and we implicitly assume that these variables are universally quantify.

*Example 2. Consider the relational database from Example 1. Then the following RDB2RDF rule maps all the instances of the* EMP *table as instances of the* Employee *class:* $\texttt{EMP}(s, x_1, x_2) \wedge p = \texttt{type} \wedge o = \texttt{Employee} \rightarrow \texttt{triple}(s, p, o)$.

Let $\mathbf{R}$ be a relational schema. An RDB2RDF mapping $\mathcal{M}$ over $\mathbf{R}$ is a finite set of RDB2RDF rules over $\mathbf{R}$. Given an RDB2RDF mapping $\mathcal{M}$ and an instance $I$ over $\mathbf{R}$, the result of applying $\mathcal{M}$ over $I$, denoted by $[\![\mathcal{M}]\!]_I$, is an instance over the schema $\{\texttt{triple}\}$ that is defined as the result of the following process. For every RDB2RDF rule of the form (1) and value $c_1 \in \mathbf{D}$, if there exists a tuple of values $\bar{d}$ from $\mathbf{D}$ such that $I \models \alpha(c_1, \bar{d})$,[4] then $\texttt{triple}(c_1, \texttt{type}, c)$ is included as a fact of $[\![\mathcal{M}]\!]_I$, and likewise for every RDB2RDF rule of the form (2). Notice that this definition coincides with the notion of canonical universal solution in the context of data exchange [3]. Besides, notice that $[\![\mathcal{M}]\!]_I$ represents an RDF graph and, thus, mapping $\mathcal{M}$ can be considered as a mapping from relational databases into RDF graphs.

*Example 3. Consider the relational database from our running example, and let $\mathcal{M}$ be an RDB2RDF mapping consisting of the rule in Example 2 and the following rule:*

$$\texttt{EMP}(s, x_1, \texttt{CEO}) \wedge p = \texttt{type} \wedge o = \texttt{Executive} \rightarrow \texttt{triple}(s, p, o). \tag{3}$$

*If $I$ is the instance from Example 1, then $[\![\mathcal{M}]\!]_I$ consists of the following facts:*

$$\texttt{triple}(1, \texttt{type}, \texttt{Employee}), \; \texttt{triple}(2, \texttt{type}, \texttt{Employee}),$$

$$\texttt{triple}(3, \texttt{type}, \texttt{Employee}), \; \texttt{triple}(1, \texttt{type}, \texttt{Executive}).$$

### 3.2 Saturation of RDB2RDF Mappings

As mentioned in Section 1, being able to modify an RDB2RDF mapping to embed a given ontology is a fundamental step in our approach. This process is formalized by means of the notion of saturated mapping.

---

[4] Given that $\alpha(s, \bar{x})$ is domain-independent, there exists a finite number of tuples $(c_1, \bar{d})$ such that $I \models \alpha(c_1, \bar{d})$.

**Table 1.** Inference rules to compute saturated mappings

$$(\text{A}, \text{subClass}, \text{B}) : \frac{\alpha(s, \bar{x}) \wedge p = \text{type} \wedge o = \text{A} \rightarrow \text{triple}(s, p, o)}{\alpha(s, \bar{x}) \wedge p = \text{type} \wedge o = \text{B} \rightarrow \text{triple}(s, p, o)}$$

$$(\text{A}, \text{subProp}, \text{B}) : \frac{\beta(s, o, \bar{x}) \wedge p = \text{A} \rightarrow \text{triple}(s, p, o)}{\beta(s, o, \bar{x}) \wedge p = \text{B} \rightarrow \text{triple}(s, p, o)}$$

$$(\text{A}, \text{dom}, \text{B}) : \frac{\beta(s, o, \bar{x}) \wedge p = \text{A} \rightarrow \text{triple}(s, p, o)}{\beta(s, y, \bar{x}) \wedge p = \text{type} \wedge o = \text{B} \rightarrow \text{triple}(s, p, o)}$$

$$(\text{A}, \text{range}, \text{B}) : \frac{\beta(s, o, \bar{x}) \wedge p = \text{A} \rightarrow \text{triple}(s, p, o)}{\beta(y, s, \bar{x}) \wedge p = \text{type} \wedge o = \text{B} \rightarrow \text{triple}(s, p, o)}$$

$$\begin{array}{c}(\text{A}, \text{equivClass}, \text{B}) \\ \text{or } (\text{B}, \text{equivClass}, \text{A})\end{array} : \frac{\alpha(s, \bar{x}) \wedge p = \text{type} \wedge o = \text{A} \rightarrow \text{triple}(s, p, o)}{\alpha(s, \bar{x}) \wedge p = \text{type} \wedge o = \text{B} \rightarrow \text{triple}(s, p, o)}$$

$$\begin{array}{c}(\text{A}, \text{equivProp}, \text{B}) \\ \text{or } (\text{B}, \text{equivProp}, \text{A})\end{array} : \frac{\beta(s, o, \bar{x}) \wedge p = \text{A} \rightarrow \text{triple}(s, p, o)}{\beta(s, o, \bar{x}) \wedge p = \text{B} \rightarrow \text{triple}(s, p, o)}$$

$$\begin{array}{c}(\text{A}, \text{inverse}, \text{B}) \\ \text{or } (\text{B}, \text{inverse}, \text{A})\end{array} : \frac{\beta(s, o, \bar{x}) \wedge p = \text{A} \rightarrow \text{triple}(s, p, o)}{\beta(o, s, \bar{x}) \wedge p = \text{B} \rightarrow \text{triple}(s, p, o)}$$

$$(\text{A}, \text{type}, \text{symProp}) : \frac{\beta(s, o, \bar{x}) \wedge p = \text{A} \rightarrow \text{triple}(s, p, o)}{\beta(o, s, \bar{x}) \wedge p = \text{A} \rightarrow \text{triple}(s, p, o)}$$

**Definition 1 (Saturated mapping).** *Let $\mathcal{M}$ and $\mathcal{M}^\star$ be RDB2RDF mappings over a relational schema $\mathbf{R}$ and $\mathcal{O}$ an ontology. Then $\mathcal{M}^\star$ is a saturation of $\mathcal{M}$ w.r.t. $\mathcal{O}$ if for every instance $I$ over $\mathbf{R}$ and assertional RDF-triple $(a, b, c)$:*

$$[\![\mathcal{M}]\!]_I \cup \Sigma_\mathcal{O} \models \text{triple}(a, b, c) \quad \textit{iff} \quad \text{triple}(a, b, c) \in [\![\mathcal{M}^\star]\!]_I.$$

In this section, we study the problem of computing a saturated mapping from a given mapping and ontology. In particular, we focus on the case of ontologies not mentioning any triple of the form $(a, \text{type}, \text{transProp})$, which we denote by non-transitive ontologies. In Section 3.3, we extend these results to the case of arbitrary ontologies.

In our system, the saturation step is performed by exhaustively applying the inference rules in Table 1, which allow us to infer new RDB2RDF rules from the existing ones and the input ontology. More precisely, given an inference rule $t: \frac{\rho_1}{\rho_2}$ from Table 1, where $t$ is a triple and $\rho_1, \rho_2$ are RDB2RDF rules, and given an RDB2RDF mapping $\mathcal{M}$ and an ontology $\mathcal{O}$, we need to do the following to apply $t: \frac{\rho_1}{\rho_2}$ over $\mathcal{M}$ and $\mathcal{O}$. First, we have to replace the letters A and B in $t$ with actual URIs, say $a \in \mathbf{U}$ and $b \in \mathbf{U}$, respectively.[5] Second, we need to check whether the triple obtained from $t$ by replacing A by $a$ and B by $b$ belongs to $\mathcal{O}$, and whether the RDB2RDF rule obtained from $\rho_1$ by replacing A by $a$ belongs to $\mathcal{M}$. If both conditions hold, then the inference rule can be applied, and the result is an RDB2RDF mapping $\mathcal{M}'$ consisting of the rules in $\mathcal{M}$ and the rule obtained from $\rho_2$ by replacing A by $a$ and B by $b$.

---

[5] If $t = (\text{A}, \text{type}, \text{symProp})$, then we only need to replace A by $a$.

*Example 4.  Consider the RDB2RDF rule* (3) *from Example 3, and assume that we are given an ontology $\mathcal{O}$ containing the triple* (Executive, subClass, Employee). *Then by applying the first inference rule in Table 1, we infer the following RDB2RDF rule:*
$\text{EMP}(s, x_1, \text{CEO}) \wedge p = \text{type} \wedge o = \text{Employee} \rightarrow \text{triple}(s, p, o)$.

Given an RDB2RDF mapping $\mathcal{M}$ and an ontology $\mathcal{O}$, we denote by $\text{SAT}(\mathcal{M}, \mathcal{O})$ the RDB2RDF mapping obtained from $\mathcal{M}$ and $\mathcal{O}$ by successively applying the inference rules in Table 1 until the mapping does not change. The following theorem shows that $\text{SAT}(\mathcal{M}, \mathcal{O})$ is a saturation of $\mathcal{M}$ w.r.t. $\mathcal{O}$, which justifies its use in our system.

**Theorem 1.** *For every RDB2RDF mapping $\mathcal{M}$ and ontology $\mathcal{O}$ in RDFS, it holds that $\text{SAT}(\mathcal{M}, \mathcal{O})$ is a saturation of $\mathcal{M}$ w.r.t. $\mathcal{O}$.*

Theorem 1 is a corollary of the fact that the first six rules in Table 1 encode the rules to infer assertional triples from an inference system for RDFS given in [18]. A natural question at this point is whether $\text{SAT}(\mathcal{M}, \mathcal{O})$ can be computed efficiently. In our setting, the approach based on exhaustively applying the inference rules in Table 1 can be easily transformed into a polynomial time algorithm for this problem. However, if this transformation is done in a naïve way, then the resulting algorithm is not really efficient. For this reason, we present here an efficient algorithm to compute $\text{SAT}(\mathcal{M}, \mathcal{O})$ that is linear in the size of the input RDB2RDF mapping $\mathcal{M}$ and ontology $\mathcal{O}$, which are denoted by $\|\mathcal{M}\|$ and $\|\mathcal{O}\|$, respectively.

**Theorem 2.** *There exists an algorithm that, given an RDB2RDF mapping $\mathcal{M}$ and a non-transitive ontology $\mathcal{O}$, computes $\text{SAT}(\mathcal{M}, \mathcal{O})$ in time $O(\|\mathcal{M}\| \cdot \|\mathcal{O}\|)$.*

We now give the main ingredients of the algorithm mentioned in Theorem 2. Fix a mapping $\mathcal{M}$ and an ontology $\mathcal{O}$. In the first place, the algorithm transforms $\mathcal{O}$ into an instance $I_{\mathcal{O}}$ over the relational schema {triple}, which satisfies that for every $(a, b, c) \in \mathcal{O}$: (1) if $b \in$ {subClass, subProp, dom, range, type}, then triple$(a, b, c) \in I_{\mathcal{O}}$; (2) if $b =$ equivClass, then triple$(a, \text{subClass}, c) \in I_{\mathcal{O}}$ and triple$(c, \text{subClass}, a) \in I_{\mathcal{O}}$; (3) if $b =$ equivProp, then triple$(a, \text{subProp}, c) \in I_{\mathcal{O}}$ and triple$(c, \text{subProp}, a) \in I_{\mathcal{O}}$; and (4) if $b =$ inverse, then triple$(a, \text{inverse}, c) \in I_{\mathcal{O}}$ and triple$(c, \text{inverse}, a) \in I_{\mathcal{O}}$. Obviously, $I_{\mathcal{O}}$ can be computed in time $O(\|\mathcal{O}\|)$.

In the second place, the algorithm transforms as follows $\mathcal{M}$ into an instance $I_{\mathcal{M}}$ over a relational schema consisting of binary predicates $\text{F}_{\text{class}}$ $\text{F}_{\text{pred}}$, $\text{Ch}$, $\text{R}_s$ and $\text{R}_o$. First, for every class RDB2RDF-rule in $\mathcal{M}$ of the form (1), a fresh natural number $m$ is assigned as an identifier of formula $\alpha(s, \bar{x})$, and then fact $\text{F}_{\text{class}}(m, c)$ is included in $I_{\mathcal{M}}$ (thus, $\text{F}_{\text{class}}$ is used to store the class RDB2RDF-rules in $\mathcal{M}$). Second, for every predicate RDB2RDF-rule in $\mathcal{M}$ of the form (2), a fresh natural number $n$ is assigned as an identifier of formula $\beta(s, o, \bar{x})$, and then fact $\text{F}_{\text{pred}}(n, c)$ is included in $I_{\mathcal{M}}$ (thus, $\text{F}_{\text{pred}}$ is used to store the predicate RDB2RDF-rules in $\mathcal{M}$). Moreover, in this case fresh natural numbers $k_1$, $k_2$ and $k_3$ are assigned as identifiers of formulae $\beta(o, s, \bar{x})$, $\beta(s, y, \bar{x})$ and $\beta(y, s, \bar{x})$ (where $y$ is a fresh variable), respectively, and then the facts $\text{Ch}(n, k_1)$, $\text{Ch}(k_1, n)$, $\text{R}_s(n, k_2)$ and $\text{R}_o(n, k_3)$ are included in $I_{\mathcal{M}}$ (thus, these predicates are used to store some syntactic modifications of formulae that are needed in the inference rules in Table 1). Finally, in this case fresh natural numbers $\ell_1$ are $\ell_2$ are assigned as identifiers of formulae $\beta(o, z, \bar{x})$ and $\beta(z, o, \bar{x})$ (where $z$ is a fresh variable), respectively, and then the facts $R_s(k_1, \ell_1)$ and $R_o(k_1, \ell_2)$ are included in $I_{\mathcal{M}}$. It is easy to see that $I_{\mathcal{M}}$ can be computed in time $O(\|\mathcal{M}\|)$.

With all the previous terminology, the problem of computing $\text{SAT}(\mathcal{M}, \mathcal{O})$ can be reduced to the problem of computing the minimal model of a Datalog program $\Pi_{\mathcal{M}, \mathcal{O}}$, which consists of the facts in $(I_{\mathcal{O}} \cup I_{\mathcal{M}})$ together with the following set $\Delta$ of rules representing the inference rules in Table 1:

$$\text{triple}(X, \text{subClass}, Y), F_{\text{class}}(U, X) \rightarrow F_{\text{class}}(U, Y)$$
$$\text{triple}(X, \text{subProp}, Y), F_{\text{pred}}(U, X) \rightarrow F_{\text{pred}}(U, Y)$$
$$\text{triple}(X, \text{dom}, Y), F_{\text{pred}}(U, X), R_s(U, V) \rightarrow F_{\text{class}}(V, Y)$$
$$\text{triple}(X, \text{range}, Y), F_{\text{pred}}(U, X), R_o(U, V) \rightarrow F_{\text{class}}(V, Y)$$
$$\text{triple}(X, \text{inverse}, Y), F_{\text{pred}}(U, X), Ch(U, V) \rightarrow F_{\text{pred}}(V, Y)$$
$$\text{triple}(X, \text{type}, \text{symProp}), F_{\text{pred}}(U, X), Ch(U, V) \rightarrow F_{\text{pred}}(V, X),$$

where $X$, $Y$, $U$ and $V$ are variables. Notice that $\Delta$ is a fixed set of rules (it depends neither on $\mathcal{M}$ nor on $\mathcal{O}$), and also that $\Delta$ does not include rules for the keywords equivClass and equivProp, as these are represented in $I_{\mathcal{O}}$ by using the keywords subClass and subProp, respectively.

In order to compute the minimal model of $\Pi_{\mathcal{M}, \mathcal{O}}$, we instantiate the variables in the above rules to generate a ground Datalog program $\Pi'_{\mathcal{M}, \mathcal{O}}$ having the same minimal model as $\Pi_{\mathcal{M}, \mathcal{O}}$. The key observation here is that $\Pi'_{\mathcal{M}, \mathcal{O}}$ can be computed in time $O(\|\mathcal{M}\| \cdot \|\mathcal{O}\|)$, which proves Theorem 2 as the minimal model of a ground Datalog program can be computed in linear time [10] and the time needed to compute $(I_{\mathcal{O}} \cup I_{\mathcal{M}})$ is $O(\|\mathcal{M}\| + \|\mathcal{O}\|)$. More precisely, $\Pi'_{\mathcal{M}, \mathcal{O}}$ is defined as $(I_{\mathcal{O}} \cup I_{\mathcal{M}}) \cup \Delta'$, where $\Delta'$ is generated from $\Delta$ as follows. For every fact $\text{triple}(a, b, c) \in I_{\mathcal{O}}$, we look for the only rule in $\Delta$ where this fact can be applied, and we replace this rule by a new one where $X$ is replaced by $a$ and $Y$ is replaced by $c$ (or just $X$ is replaced by $a$ if $b = \text{type}$ and $c = \text{symProp}$). For example, if we consider a triple $\text{triple}(a, \text{subClass}, c)$, then we generate the rule $\text{triple}(a, \text{subClass}, b), F_{\text{class}}(U, a) \rightarrow F_{\text{class}}(U, b)$. Let $\Delta_1$ be the result of this process. Given that the set of rules $\Delta$ is fixed, we have that $\Delta_1$ can be computed in time $O(\|\mathcal{O}\|)$. Now for every rule $\rho$ in $\Delta_1$, we do the following to transform $\rho$ into a ground rule. We first replace the variable $U$ in $\rho$ by a value $n$ in $I_{\mathcal{M}}$. If $\rho$ also contains a variable $V$, then we notice that there exists at most one value $m$ in $I_{\mathcal{M}}$ for which the antecedent of the rule could hold, as there exists at most one value $m$ such that $R_s(n, m)$ holds, and likewise for predicates $R_o$ and $Ch$. Thus, in this case we replace variable $V$ in $\rho$ for such a value $m$ to generate a ground Datalog rule, and we conclude that the resulting set $\Delta'$ of ground Datalog rules is computed in time $O(\|\mathcal{M}\| \cdot \|\mathcal{O}\|)$ (given that the size of $\Delta_1$ is $O(\|\mathcal{O}\|)$). This concludes the sketch of the proof of Theorem 2.

### 3.3 Dealing with Transitive Predicates

We show here how the approach presented in the previous section can be extended with recursive predicates. This functionality is of particular interest as the current work on

OBDA does not consider transitivity, mainly because the query language considered in that work is SQL without recursion [8]. From now on, given a first-order formula $\varphi(x, y)$, we use $\mathrm{TC}_\varphi(x, y)$ to denote the transitive closure of $\varphi(x, y)$. This formula can be written in many different formalisms. For example, if $\varphi(x, y)$ is a conjunction of relational atoms, then $\mathrm{TC}_\varphi(x, y)$ can be written as follows in Datalog:

$$\varphi(x, y) \rightarrow \mathrm{TC}_\varphi(x, y), \qquad \varphi(x, z), \mathrm{TC}_\varphi(z, y) \rightarrow \mathrm{TC}_\varphi(x, y).$$

In our system, $\mathrm{TC}_\varphi(x, y)$ is written as an SQL query with recursion. Then to deal with an ontology $\mathcal{O}$ containing transitive predicates, the set of inference rules in Table 1 is extended with the following inference rule:

$$(\mathtt{A}, \mathtt{type}, \mathtt{transProp}) : \frac{\{\beta_i(s, o, \bar{x}_i) \wedge p = \mathtt{A} \rightarrow \mathtt{triple}(s, p, o)\}_{i=1}^k}{\mathrm{TC}_{[\bigvee_{i=1}^k \exists \bar{x}_i \beta_i]}(s, o) \wedge p = \mathtt{A} \rightarrow \mathtt{triple}(s, p, o)}.$$

This rule tell us that given a transitive predicate A, we can take any number $k$ of RDB2RDF rules $\beta_i(s, o, \bar{x}_i) \wedge p = \mathtt{A} \rightarrow \mathtt{triple}(s, p, o)$ for this predicate, and we can generate a new RDB2RDF rule for A by putting together the conditions $\beta_i(s, o, \bar{x}_i)$ in a formula $\gamma(s, o) = \bigvee_i \exists \bar{x}_i \beta_i(s, o, \bar{x}_i)$, and then using the transitive closure $\mathrm{TC}_\gamma(s, o)$ of $\gamma$ in an RDB2RDF rule $\mathrm{TC}_\gamma(s, o) \wedge p = \mathtt{A} \rightarrow \mathtt{triple}(s, p, o)$. In order for this approach to work, notice that we need to extend the syntax of RDB2RDF rules (1) and (2), so that formulae $\alpha$ and $\beta$ in them can be arbitrary formulae in a more expressive formalism such as (recursive) Datalog.

## 3.4 Implementing RDB2RDF Mappings as Views

We conclude this section by showing how RDB2RDF mappings are implemented in our system. Inspired by our previous work on Ultrawrap [27], every RDB2RDF rule is implemented as a triple-query, that is, as a SQL query which outputs triples. For example, the RDB2RDF rules:

$$\mathtt{EMP}(s, x_1, \mathtt{CEO}) \wedge p = \mathtt{type} \wedge o = \mathtt{Employee} \rightarrow \mathtt{triple}(s, p, o)$$

$$\mathtt{EMP}(s, x_1, \mathtt{SysAdmin}) \wedge p = \mathtt{type} \wedge o = \mathtt{Employee} \rightarrow \mathtt{triple}(s, p, o)$$

give rise to the following triple-queries:

SELECT SID as S, "type" as P, "Employee" as O FROM EMP WHERE JOB = "CEO"

SELECT SID as S, "type" as P, "Employee" as O FROM EMP WHERE JOB = "SysAdmin"

In practice, the triple-queries may include additional projections in order to support indexes, URI templates, datatypes and languages. However, for readability, we will consider here this simple version of these queries (we refer the reader to [27] for specific details). Then to implement an RDB2RDF mapping, all the class (resp. predicate) RDB2RDF-rules for the same class (resp. predicate) are grouped together to generate a triple-view, that is, a SQL view comprised of the union of the triple-queries for this class (resp. predicate). For instance, in our previous example the following is the triple-view for the class Employee:

```
CREATE VIEW EmployeeView AS
SELECT SID as S, "type" as P, "Employee" as O FROM EMP WHERE JOB = "CEO"   UNION ALL
SELECT SID as S, "type" as P, "Employee" as O FROM EMP WHERE JOB = "SysAdmin"
```

## 4  Executing SPARQL Queries

In this section, we describe how SPARQL queries are executed and optimized over the RDBMS through a cost model that determines which views should be materialized.

### 4.1  SPARQL Rewriting

The runtime phase executes SPARQL queries on the RDBMS. We reuse Ultrawrap's approach of translating SPARQL queries to SQL queries in terms of the views defined for every class and property, which are denoted as triple-views in our system (see Section 3.4). Thus, we make maximal use of existing query optimization tools in commercial RDBMS, such as Oracle, to do the SPARQL query execution and rewriting [27].

Continuing with the example in Section 3.4, consider now a SPARQL query which asks for all the Employees: SELECT ?x WHERE {?x type Employee}. It is clear that this query needs to be rewritten to ask for the CEO and SysAdmin. The EmployeeView triple-view in Section 3.4 implements the mappings to the Employee class which consists of two triple-queries, one each for CEO and SysAdmin. Therefore, it is sufficient to generate a SQL query in terms of the EmployeeView. Given that a triple-view models a table with three columns, a SPARQL query is syntactically translated to a SQL query in terms of the triple-view. The resulting SQL query is SELECT t1.s AS x FROM EmployeeView t1.

A natural question at this point is whether every SPARQL query has an equivalent SQL query in our context, where RDB2RDF mappings play a fundamental role. In what follows we give a positive answer to this question, but before we introduce some terminology. Due to the lack of space, we do not formally present the syntax and semantics of SPARQL. Instead, we refer the reader to [23,20] for this definition, and we just point out here that $[\![P]\!]_G$ denotes the answer to a SPARQL query $P$ over an RDF graph $G$, which consists of a set of solution mappings, that is, a set of functions that assign a value to each selected variable in $P$. For example, if $P$ is the SPARQL query SELECT ?x WHERE {?x type ?y}, and $G$ is an RDF graph consisting of the triples $(1, \text{type}, \text{Employee})$ and $(2, \text{type}, \text{Employee})$, then $[\![P]\!]_G = \{\mu_1, \mu_2\}$, where $\mu_1$ and $\mu_2$ are functions with domain $\{?x\}$ such that $\mu_1(?x) = 1$ and $\mu_2(?x) = 2$. Moreover, given a SQL query $Q$ (that may use recursion) over a relational schema $\mathbf{R}$ and an instance $I$ of $\mathbf{R}$, we use notation $[\![Q]\!]_I$ to represent the answer of $Q$ over $I$, which consists of a set of tuples in this case. Finally, to compare the answer of a SQL query with the answer of a SPARQL query, we make use of a function $tr$ to transform a tuple into a solution mapping (this function is defined in the obvious way, see [26]). Then given an RDB2RDF mapping $\mathcal{M}$ over a relational schema $\mathbf{R}$ and a SPARQL query $P$, an SQL query $Q$ over $\mathbf{R}$ is said to be a SQL-rewriting of $P$ under $\mathcal{M}$ if for every instance $I$ of $\mathbf{R}$, it holds that $[\![P]\!]_{[\![\mathcal{M}]\!]_I} = tr([\![Q]\!]_I)$. Moreover, $P$ is said to be SQL-rewritable under $\mathcal{M}$ if there exists a rewriting of $P$ under $\mathcal{M}$.

**Theorem 3.** *Given an RDB2RDF mapping $\mathcal{M}$, every SPARQL query is SQL-rewritable under $\mathcal{M}$.*

The proof that the previous condition holds is by induction on the structure of a SPARQL query $P$ and, thus, it gives us a (naïve) bottom-up algorithm for translating $P$ into an equivalent SQL query $Q$ (given the mapping $\mathcal{M}$). More precisely, in the base case we are given a triple pattern $t = \{s\ p\ o\}$, where each one of its component is either a URI or a literal or a variable. This triple pattern is first translated into a SPARQL query $P_t$, where each position in $t$ storing a URI or a literal is replaced by a fresh variable, a filter condition is added to ensure that these fresh variables are assigned the corresponding URIs or literals, and a SELECT clause is added to ensure that the output variables of $t$ and $P_t$ are the same. For example, if $t = \{?x\ \text{type}\ \text{Employee}\}$, then $P_t$ is the following SPARQL query: SELECT ?x WHERE $\{?x\ ?y\ ?z\}$ FILTER ($?y = \text{type}\ \&\&\ ?z = \text{Employee}$). Then a SQL-rewriting of $P_t$ under $\mathcal{M}$ is computed just by replacing a triple pattern of the form $\{?s\ ?p\ ?o\}$ by a union of all the triple-queries representing the RDB2RDF rules in $\mathcal{M}$, and also replacing the SPARQL filter condition in $P_t$ by a filter condition in SQL.

In the inductive step, we assume that the theorem holds for two SPARQL queries $P_1$ and $P_2$. The proof then continues by presenting rewritings for the SPARQL queries constructed by combining $P_1$ and $P_2$ through the operators SELECT, AND (or '.' operator), OPTIONAL, FILTER and UNION, which is done by using existing approaches to translate SPARQL to SQL [2,9].

### 4.2 Cost Model for View Materialization

A common approach for query optimization is to use materialized views [13]. Given that we are implementing RDB2RDF mappings as views, it is a natural to pursue this option. There are three implementation alternatives: (1) Materialize all the views: This approach gives the best query response time. However, it consumes the most space. (2) Materialize nothing: In this approach, every query needs to go to the raw data. However, no extra space is needed. (3) Materialize a subset of the views: Try to find a trade-off between the best query response time and the amount of space required.

In this section, we present a cost model for these three alternatives. First we must introduce some terminology. We consider ontologies consisting of hierarchy of classes which form a tree with a unique root, where a root class of an ontology is a class that has no superclasses. Then a leaf class of an ontology is a class that has no subclasses, and the depth of a class is the number of subclass relationships from the class to the root class (notice that there is a unique path from a class to the root class). Moreover, the depth of an ontology is the maximum depth of all classes present in the ontology.

First, we consider the cost of answering a query $Q$ is equal to the number of rows present in the relation used to construct Q. For example, if a relation $R$ has 100 rows, then the cost of the query SELECT $*$ FROM R is 100. Second, assume we have a single relation $R$ and that mappings are from a query on the relation $R$ with a selection on an attribute $A$, to a class in the ontology. In Example 3, the relation $R$ is EMP, the attribute $A$ is JOB and the mapping is to the class Executive. Finally, we consider a query workload of queries asking for the instances of a class in the ontology, i.e. SELECT ?x WHERE $\{?x\ \text{type}\ \text{C}\}$, which can be translated into the triple-view implementing the mapping to the class C.

Our cost model is the following: If all the views implementing mappings are materialized, the query cost is $n \times N_R \times S(A, R)$ where $n$ is the number of leaf classes underneath the class that is being queried for, $N_R$ is the number of tuples of the relation $R$ in the mapping, and $S(A, R)$ is the selectivity of the attribute $A$ of the relation $R$ in the mapping. The space cost is $N_R + (N_R \times d)$ where $d$ is the depth of the ontology. The reason for this cost is because the number of rows in a materialized view depends on the selectivity of the attribute and the number of leaf classes. Additionally, the sum of all the rows of each triple-view representing the mapping to classes in a particular depth $d$ of an ontology, is equivalent at most to the number of rows of the relation. If no views are materialized, then the query cost is $n \times N_R$, assuming there are no indices. The space cost is simply $N_R$. The reason for this cost is because to answer a query, the entire relation needs to be accessed $n$ times because there are no indices[6].

The question now is: How can we achieve the query cost of materializing all the views while keeping space to a minimum? Our hypothesis is the following: If a RDBMS rewrites queries in terms of materialized views, then by only materializing the views representing mappings to the leaf classes, the query cost would be $n \times N_R \times S(A, R)$, the same as if we materialized all the views, and the space cost would only be $2 \times N_R$. The rationale is the following: A triple-view representing a mapping to a class, can be rewritten into the union of triple-views representing the mapping to the child classes. Subsequently, a triple-view representing the mapping to any class in the ontology can be rewritten into a union of triple-views representing the mappings to leaf classes of an ontology. Finally, given a set of triple-views representing mappings from a relation to each leaf class of an ontology, the sum of all the rows in the set of triple-views is equivalent to the number of rows in the relation.

Given the extensive research of answering queries using views [14] and the fact that Oracle implements query rewriting on materialized views[7], we strongly suspect that our hypothesis will hold. The following evaluation section provides empirical results supporting our hypothesis.

## 5 Experimental Evaluation

**Benchmarks:** The evaluation requires benchmarks consisting of a relational database schema and data, ontologies, mappings from the database to ontologies and a query workload. Thus, we created a synthetic benchmark, the *Texas Benchmark*, inspired by the Wisconsin Benchmark [12] and extended the Berlin SPARQL Benchmark (BSBM) Explore Use Case [6]. More precisely, the Texas Benchmark is composed of a single relation with 1 million rows. The relation has a first attribute which serves as a primary key, a set of additional filler attributes in order to take up space and then a set of six different integer-valued attributes which are non-unique. The main purpose of these attributes is to provide a systematic way to model a wide range of selectivity factors. Each attribute is named after the range of values the attribute assumes: TWO, FIVE, TEN, TWENTY, FIFTY and HUNDRED. For example, the attribute FIVE assumes a range of values from 1 to 5. Thus, the selection FIVE $= 1$ will have a 20% selectivity. In addition to the data, we created five different ontologies, consisting of a depth between 2-5. The branching factor is uniform and the number of leaves is 100 for each ontology.

---

[6] In the evaluation, we also consider the case when indices are present.

[7] http://docs.oracle.com/cd/B28359_01/server.111/
b28313/qrbasic.htm

The query workload consists of asking for an instance of a class at each depth of the ontology. On the other hand, the extension of BSBM replicates the query workload of an e-commerce website. Products have a type that is part of a ProductType ontology. Every product is mapped to one leaf class of the ProductType ontology. In our experiments, we created a dataset consisting of 1 million products with the benchmark driver, hence the product table has 1 million rows. The resulting ProductType ontology has a depth of 4 and consists of 3949 classes from which 3072 are leaf-level classes. The selectivity of the attribute in the mappings to ProductTypes is approximately 0.1%. In order to replicate the results of the Texas Benchmark, the query workload also consists of asking for an instance of a class at each depth of the ontology. In order to evaluate queries with transitivity, we use the child-parent relationship in the ProductType table which models the subclass relationship. The query workload for the transitivity part consists of asking for Products of a particular ProductType including the label and a numeric property of the Products, therefore including joins. More details about the benchmarks can be found at http://obda-benchmark.org

| | ontop | or index | or leaves | union index | union leaves | all mat |
|---|---|---|---|---|---|---|
| D6_100 | 7.31 | 7.37 | 7.44 | 5.28 | 5.42 | 4.80 |
| D6_50 | 7.44 | 7.55 | 7.54 | 5.14 | 5.76 | 4.92 |
| D6_20 | 9.76 | 9.88 | 9.88 | 6.28 | 5.71 | 5.26 |
| D6_10 | 10.51 | 10.74 | 10.43 | 7.20 | 6.90 | 6.37 |
| D6_5 | 17.24 | 17.26 | 10.97 | 19.75 | 13.42 | 9.09 |
| D6_2 | 22.54 | 22.88 | 20.36 | 23.21 | 21.17 | 20.18 |
| D5_100 | 5.38 | 5.39 | 5.42 | 4.97 | 4.38 | 3.85 |
| D5_50 | 5.56 | 5.84 | 5.61 | 4.92 | 4.52 | 4.02 |
| D5_20 | 9.01 | 8.52 | 8.41 | 6.16 | 5.47 | 5.05 |
| D5_10 | 9.86 | 9.30 | 9.04 | 7.20 | 6.52 | 6.13 |
| D5_5 | 17.32 | 17.80 | 9.71 | 20.24 | 10.98 | 9.32 |
| D5_2 | 21.80 | 25.28 | 19.33 | 23.27 | 19.67 | 20.13 |
| D4_100 | 5.63 | 5.88 | 5.81 | 4.92 | 4.59 | 3.96 |
| D4_50 | 5.83 | 6.08 | 6.25 | 5.10 | 4.82 | 4.18 |
| D4_20 | 6.28 | 6.56 | 6.46 | 5.51 | 5.34 | 5.00 |
| D4_10 | 7.43 | 7.76 | 7.52 | 6.47 | 6.10 | 5.80 |
| D4_5 | 17.54 | 17.60 | 10.84 | 20.96 | 11.89 | 9.74 |
| D4_2 | 22.33 | 23.30 | 20.25 | 23.40 | 19.96 | 19.88 |
| D3_100 | 6.21 | 7.36 | 6.48 | 3.80 | 3.92 | 3.53 |
| D3_50 | 6.40 | 6.64 | 10.15 | 4.09 | 3.76 | 3.54 |
| D3_20 | 6.93 | 7.15 | 6.94 | 4.41 | 4.25 | 3.90 |
| D3_10 | 8.30 | 8.47 | 8.08 | 5.91 | 5.38 | 5.14 |
| D3_5 | 16.55 | 16.93 | 7.85 | 16.80 | 7.61 | 7.58 |
| D3_2 | 23.61 | 23.43 | 19.91 | 22.78 | 20.09 | 19.98 |
| D2_100 | 1.13 | 1.28 | 1.24 | 1.23 | 1.10 | 1.05 |
| D2_50 | 1.41 | 1.50 | 1.48 | 1.45 | 1.28 | 1.30 |
| D2_20 | 2.23 | 2.40 | 2.20 | 2.23 | 1.99 | 1.99 |
| D2_10 | 4.22 | 4.42 | 3.99 | 4.26 | 3.91 | 3.81 |
| D2_5 | 16.39 | 16.98 | 10.47 | 16.77 | 7.67 | 8.14 |
| D2_2 | 23.43 | 23.19 | 20.24 | 22.66 | 19.59 | 20.18 |
| Average | 10.85 | 11.16 | 9.34 | 10.21 | 8.11 | 7.59 |

**Fig. 1.** Results of Texas Benchmark (sec)

**Measurements and Scenarios:** The objective of our experiments is to observe the behavior of a commercial relational database, namely Oracle, and its capabilities of supporting subclass and transitivity reasoning under our proposed approach. Therefore, the evaluation compares execution time and queries plans of SPARQL queries. With the Texas Benchmark, we compare w.r.t. two dimensions: depth of an ontology and selectivity of the attribute that is being mapped. In BSBM, because we are using a fixed 1 million product dataset, the depth of the hierarchy and selectivity is also fixed. We ran each query ten times and averaged the execution time, hence the experiments ran on a warm cache. In the evaluation we considered six scenarios: (**all-mat**) all the views are materialized; (**union-leaves**) only views representing mappings to the leaf classes are materialized, implemented with UNION; (**or-leaves**) same as in the previous scenario but with the views implemented with OR instead of UNION, (**union-index**) none of the views, implemented with UNION, are materialized, instead an index on the respective attributes have been added, (**or-index**) same as in the previous scenario but with the views implemented with OR; and (**ontop**) we compare against Ontop, a state of the art OBDA system [25]. We only compare against Ontop because to the best of our knowledge, this is the only OBDA system that supports RDB2RDF mappings and SPARQL. The experiments were conducted on Oracle 11g R2 EE installed on a Sun Fire X4150 with a four core Intel Xeon X7460 2.66 GHz processor and 16 GB of RAM, running Microsoft Windows Server 2008 R2 Standard on top of VMWare ESX 4.0.

**Results:** An initial assessment suggests the following four expected observations: (1) The fastest execution time is *all-mat*; (2) our hypothesis should hold, meaning that the execution time of *union-leaves* should be comparable, if not equal, to the execution time of *all-mat*; (3) given that the Ontop system generates SQL queries with OR instead of UNION [25], the execution time of *ontop* and *or-index* should be comparable if not equal; (4) with transitivity, the fastest execution time is when the views are materialized.

Figure 1 shows the results of the Texas Benchmark in a form of a heat map, which evaluates subclass reasoning. The darker colors corresponds to the fastest query execution time. The x-axis consists of the six scenarios. In the y-axis, D6_100 means Depth 6 on Selectivity of 100. The values are the average execution time of the query workload. Notice that the expected observations (1), (2) and (3) hold. The fastest execution time corresponds to *all-mat*. The execution time of *union-leaves* is comparable, if not equal, to the execution time of *all-mat*, because Oracle was able to rewrite queries in terms of the materialized views. The number of rows examined is equivalent to the number of rows in the views where everything was materialized. This result provides evidence supporting our hypothesis and validates our cost model. Finally the execution time of *ontop* and *or-index* are comparable.

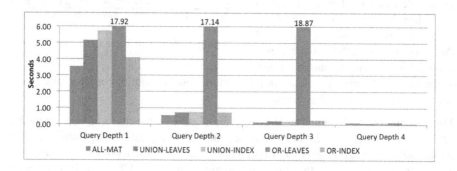

**Fig. 2.** Results of Subclass reasoning on BSBM

Figure 2 shows the results of the BSBM Benchmark for subclass reasoning. Our expected observations also hold in this case. Note that we do not report results for Ontop because the setup of the SPARQL endpoint timed-out after 2 hours.[8] Given that the selectivity is much lower compared to the selectivities in the Texas Benchmark, we observe that for queries asking for instances of classes that are in depth 1 (child of the root Class), the or-index outperforms union-leaves. We speculate that there is a slight

---

[8] We have reported the issue to the Ontop developers.

overhead when rewriting queries over a large amount of views. However, for the rest of the queries, the overhead diminishes. We observe that the execution time of or-leaves is the worst because the database is not able to rewrite the query into the materialized views when the views are implemented with OR. Finally, throughout both benchmarks, we observe that *or-index* is competitive w.r.t *union-leaves*.

Figure 3 shows the results of the transitivity experiments on the BSBM Benchmark. Notice that the expected observations (4) holds. Given that Ontop does not support transitivity, we cannot compare with them. Therefore we only compare between materialized and non-materialized views. The Simple query requests all the ancestors of the given ProductType. The Join query requests all ancestors of the given ProductType and its corresponding Products. Therefore there is a join between ProductType and Product. The More Join query is similar to Join query, however it requests the name and a numeric property of the products, hence there are more joins. It is clear that materializing the view outperforms the non-materialized view for the following reasons: when the view is materialized, the size of the view is known beforehand and the optimizer is able to do a range scan with the index. However, when the view is not materialized, the size is not known therefore the optimizer does a full scan of the table. Detailed results can be found at http://ribs.csres.utexas.edu/ultrawrap.

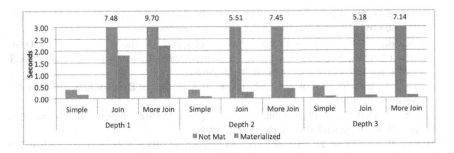

**Fig. 3.** Results of Transitivity reasoning on BSBM

# 6 Concluding Remarks

We presented Ultrawrap$^{OBDA}$, which to the best of our knowledge, is the first OBDA system supporting ontologies with transitivity by using SQL recursion. Ultrawrap$^{OBDA}$ is able to push processing into the RDBMS by implementing mappings using materialized views and taking advantage of existing query rewriting techniques.

Per related work, existing OBDA approaches only exploit the relational algebra capabilities of RDBMS. Our experimental results provide evidence that existing advanced capabilities implemented in RDBMS, such as recursion and query rewriting using materialized views, can be utilized for OBDA. We are not saying that we should rely exclusively on RDBMS technology to do the heavy lifting. RDBMS such as MySQL lack these advanced optimizations. However, we strongly suggest that the OBDA community should exploit the advanced optimizations in existing RDBMS.

Several open questions remain unanswered: What is the cost of maintaining views when the underlying data is updated? What is the state of the art of other RDBMS's optimizers in order to support OBDA? How does this approach respond to complex query workload? What is the trade-off between reasoning over relational databases with mappings and using native RDF databases supporting reasoning? We believe that these questions can be answered by developing systematic and real-world benchmark consisting of relational database schemas, data, ontologies and mappings and evaluating beyond just query rewriting. The Texas Benchmark and OBDA-Benchmark.org is a first step in this process and we invite the community to contribute. As future work, we plan to evaluate Ultrawrap$^{OBDA}$on other RDBMSs and compare against additional OBDA systems and native RDF databases that support reasoning.

**Acknowledgments.** Sequeda and Miranker were supported by NSF Grant IIS 1018554. Arenas was supported by the Millennium Nucleus Center for Semantic Web Research under Grant NC120004 and Fondecyt grant 1131049. We thank the anonymous referees for many helpful comments.

# References

1. Allemang, D., Hendler, J.: Semantic Web for the Working Ontologist: Effective Modeling in RDFS and OWL. Morgan Kaufmann Publishers Inc. (2008)
2. Angles, R., Gutierrez, C.: The expressive power of sparql. In: Sheth, A.P., Staab, S., Dean, M., Paolucci, M., Maynard, D., Finin, T., Thirunarayan, K. (eds.) ISWC 2008. LNCS, vol. 5318, pp. 114–129. Springer, Heidelberg (2008)
3. Arenas, M., Barceló, P., Libkin, L., Murlak, F.: Foundations of Data Exchange. Cambridge University Press (2014)
4. Arenas, M., Bertails, A., Prud'hommeaux, E., Sequeda, J.: Direct mapping of relational data to RDF. W3C Recomendation (September 27, 2012)
5. Baader, F., Calvanese, D., McGuinness, D.L., Nardi, D., Patel-Schneider, P.F. (eds.): The Description Logic Handbook. Cambridge University Press (2003)
6. Bizer, C., Schultz, A.: The berlin sparql benchmark. Int. J. Semantic Web Inf. Syst. 5(2), 1–24 (2009)
7. Brickley, D., Guha, R.: RDF vocabulary description language 1.0: RDF schema. W3C recommendation (February 2004)
8. Calvanese, D., De Giacomo, G., Lembo, D., Lenzerini, M., Rosati, R.: Data complexity of query answering in description logics. Artif. Intell. 195, 335–360 (2013)
9. Chebotko, A., Lu, S., Fotouhi, F.: Semantics preserving sparql-to-sql translation. Data Knowl. Eng. 68(10), 973–1000 (2009)
10. Dantsin, E., Eiter, T., Gottlob, G., Voronkov, A.: Complexity and expressive power of logic programming. ACM Comput. Surv. 33(3), 374–425 (2001)
11. Das, S., Sundara, S., Cyganiak, R.: R2RML: RDB to RDF mapping language. W3C Recomendation (September 27, 2012)
12. DeWitt, D.J.: The wisconsin benchmark: Past, present, and future. In: The Benchmark Handbook, pp. 119–165 (1991)
13. Gupta, A., Mumick, I.S.: Materialized Views: Techniques, Implementations, and Applications. MIT Press (1999)
14. Halevy, A.Y.: Answering queries using views: A survey. VLDB J. 10(4), 270–294 (2001)
15. Lenzerini, M.: Data integration: A theoretical perspective. In: PODS, pp. 233–246 (2002)

16. Lutz, C., Seylan, İ., Toman, D., Wolter, F.: The combined approach to OBDA: Taming role hierarchies using filters. In: Alani, H., et al. (eds.) ISWC 2013, Part I. LNCS, vol. 8218, pp. 314–330. Springer, Heidelberg (2013)
17. Motik, B., Grau, B.C., Horrocks, I., Wu, Z., amd Carsten Lutz, A.F.: OWL 2 web ontology language profiles, 2nd edn. W3C recommendation (December 2012)
18. Muñoz, S., Pérez, J., Gutierrez, C.: Simple and efficient minimal RDFS. J. Web Sem. 7(3), 220–234 (2009)
19. Ortiz, M., Šimkus, M.: Reasoning and query answering in description logics. In: Eiter, T., Krennwallner, T. (eds.) Reasoning Web 2012. LNCS, vol. 7487, pp. 1–53. Springer, Heidelberg (2012)
20. Pérez, J., Arenas, M., Gutierrez, C.: Semantics and complexity of SPARQL. ACM Trans. Database Syst. 34(3) (2009)
21. Pinto, F.D., Lembo, D., Lenzerini, M., Mancini, R., Poggi, A., Rosati, R., Ruzzi, M., Savo, D.F.: Optimizing query rewriting in ontology-based data access. In: EDBT (2013)
22. Poggi, A., Lembo, D., Calvanese, D., Giacomo, G.D., Lenzerini, M., Rosati, R.: Linking data to ontologies. J. Data Semantics 10, 133–173 (2008)
23. Prud'hommeaux, E., Seaborne, A.: SPARQL query language for RDF. W3C Recommendation (January 15, 2008), http://www.w3.org/TR/rdf-sparql-query/
24. Rodríguez-Muro, M., Calvanese, D.: Dependencies: Making ontology based data access work in practice. In: AMW (2011)
25. Rodríguez-Muro, M., Kontchakov, R., Zakharyaschev, M.: Ontology-based data access: Ontop of databases. In: Alani, H., et al. (eds.) ISWC 2013, Part I. LNCS, vol. 8218, pp. 558–573. Springer, Heidelberg (2013)
26. Sequeda, J.F., Arenas, M., Miranker, D.P.: On directly mapping relational databases to RDF and OWL. In: WWW, pp. 649–658 (2012)
27. Sequeda, J.F., Miranker, D.P.: Ultrawrap: Sparql execution on relational data. J. Web Sem. 22, 19–39 (2013)
28. Weaver, J., Hendler, J.A.: Parallel materialization of the finite rdfs closure for hundreds of millions of triples. In: Bernstein, A., Karger, D.R., Heath, T., Feigenbaum, L., Maynard, D., Motta, E., Thirunarayan, K. (eds.) ISWC 2009. LNCS, vol. 5823, pp. 682–697. Springer, Heidelberg (2009)

# Answering SPARQL Queries over Databases under OWL 2 QL Entailment Regime

Roman Kontchakov[1], Martin Rezk[2], Mariano Rodríguez-Muro[3],
Guohui Xiao[2], and Michael Zakharyaschev[1]

[1] Department of Computer Science and Information Systems,
Birkbeck, University of London, U.K.
[2] Faculty of Computer Science, Free University of Bozen-Bolzano, Italy
[3] IBM T.J. Watson Research Center, Yorktown Heights, NY, USA

**Abstract.** We present an extension of the ontology-based data access platform *Ontop* that supports answering SPARQL queries under the OWL 2 QL direct semantics entailment regime for data instances stored in relational databases. On the theoretical side, we show how any input SPARQL query, OWL 2 QL ontology and R2RML mappings can be rewritten to an equivalent SQL query solely over the data. On the practical side, we present initial experimental results demonstrating that by applying the *Ontop* technologies—the tree-witness query rewriting, $\mathcal{T}$-mappings compiling R2RML mappings with ontology hierarchies, and $\mathcal{T}$-mapping optimisations using SQL expressivity and database integrity constraints—the system produces scalable SQL queries.

## 1 Introduction

Ontology-based data access and management (OBDA) is a popular paradigm of organising access to various types of data sources that has been developed since the mid 2000s [11,17,24]. In a nutshell, OBDA separates the user from the data sources (relational databases, triple stores, etc.) by means of an ontology which provides the user with a convenient query vocabulary, hides the structure of the data sources, and can enrich incomplete data with background knowledge. About a dozen OBDA systems have been implemented in both academia and industry; e.g., [27,30,24,4,23,15,12,8,20,22]. Most of them support conjunctive queries and the OWL 2 QL profile of OWL 2 as the ontology language (or its generalisations to existential datalog rules). Thus, the OBDA platform *Ontop* [29] was designed to query data instances stored in relational databases, with the vocabularies of the data and OWL 2 QL ontologies linked by means of global-as-view (GAV) mappings. Given a conjunctive query in the vocabulary of such an ontology, *Ontop* rewrites it to an SQL query in the vocabulary of the data, optimises the rewriting and delegates its evaluation to the database system.

One of the main aims behind the newly designed query language SPARQL 1.1—a W3C recommendation since 2013—has been to support various entailment regimes, which can be regarded as variants of OBDA. Thus, the OWL 2 direct semantics entailment regime allows SPARQL queries over OWL 2 DL ontologies and RDF graphs (which can be thought of as 3-column database tables). SPARQL queries are in many aspects more expressive than conjunctive queries as they offer more complex query

P. Mika et al. (Eds.) ISWC 2014, Part I, LNCS 8796, pp. 552–567, 2014.

constructs and can retrieve not only domain elements but also class and property names using second-order variables. (Note, however, that SPARQL 1.1 does not cover all conjunctive queries.) OWL 2 DL is also vastly superior to OWL 2 QL, but this makes query answering under the OWL 2 direct semantics entailment regime intractable (CONP-hard for data complexity). For example, the query evaluation algorithm of [19] calls an OWL 2 DL reasoner for each possible assignment to the variables in a given query, and therefore cannot cope with large data instances.

In this paper, we investigate answering SPARQL queries under a less expressive entailment regime, which corresponds to OWL 2 QL, assuming that data is stored in relational databases. It is to be noted that the W3C specification[1] of SPARQL 1.1 defines entailment regimes for the profiles of OWL 2 by restricting the general definition to the profile constructs that can be used in the queries. However, in the case of OWL 2 QL, this generic approach leads to a sub-optimal, almost trivial query language, which is essentially subsumed by the OWL 2 RL entailment regime.

The first aim of this paper is to give an optimal definition of the OWL 2 QL direct semantics entailment regime and prove that—similarly to OBDA with OWL 2 QL and conjunctive queries—answering SPARQL queries under this regime is reducible to answering queries under *simple entailment*. More precisely, in Theorem 4 we construct a rewriting $\cdot^{\dagger}$ of any given SPARQL query and ontology under the OWL 2 QL entailment regime to a SPARQL query that can be evaluated on any dataset directly.

In a typical *Ontop* scenario, data is stored in a relational database whose schema is linked to the vocabulary of the given OWL 2 QL ontology via a GAV mapping in the language R2RML. The mapping allows one to transform the relational data instance into an RDF representation, called the virtual RDF graph (which is not materialised in our scenario). The rewriting $\cdot^{\dagger}$ constructs a SPARQL query over this virtual graph.

Our second aim is to show how such a SPARQL query can be translated to an equivalent SQL query over a relational representation of the virtual RDF graph as a 3-column table (translation $\tau$ in Theorem 7). The third aim is to show that the resulting SQL query can be unfolded, using a given R2RML mapping $\mathcal{M}$, to an SQL query over the original database ($\mathrm{tr}_{\mathcal{M}}$ in Theorem 12), which is evaluated by the database system.

$$\begin{array}{ccccccc}
\text{SPARQL query} & \xrightarrow{\ \dagger\ } & \text{SPARQL query} & \xrightarrow{\ \tau\ } & \text{SQL query} & \xrightarrow{\ \mathrm{tr}_{\mathcal{M}}\ } & \text{SQL query} \\
\text{\& ontology} & & \text{simple } \downarrow \text{ entailment} & & \text{evaluation } \downarrow & & \text{evaluation } \downarrow \\
\text{entailment} & & & & & & \\
\text{regime} & \searrow\ \longrightarrow & \text{virtual RDF graph} & \underset{\approx}{\longleftarrow} & \text{triple-database} & \underset{\text{mapping } \mathcal{M}}{\longleftarrow} & \text{database}
\end{array}$$

Unfortunately, each of these three transformations may involve an exponential blowup. We tackle this problem in *Ontop* using the following optimisation techniques. (*i*) The mapping is compiled with the ontology into a $\mathcal{T}$-mapping [29] and optimised by database dependencies (e.g., primary, candidate and foreign keys) and SQL disjunctions. (*ii*) The SPARQL-to-SQL translation is optimised using null join elimination (Theorem 8). (*iii*) The unfolding is optimised by eliminating joins with mismatching R2RML IRI templates, de-IRIing the join conditions (Section 3.3) and using database dependencies.

Our contributions (Theorems 4, 7, 8 and 12 and optimisations in Section 3.3) make *Ontop* the first system to support the W3C recommendations OWL 2 QL, R2RML, SPARQL and the OWL 2 QL direct semantics entailment regime; its architecture is

---

[1] http://www.w3.org/TR/sparql11-entailment

outlined in Section 4. We evaluate the performance of *Ontop* using the LUBM Benchmark [16] extended with queries containing class and property variables, and compare it with two other systems that support the OWL 2 entailment regime by calling OWL DL reasoners (Section 5). Our experiments show that *Ontop* outperforms the reasoner-based systems for most of the queries over small datasets; over larger datasets the difference becomes dramatic, with *Ontop* demonstrating a solid performance even on 69 million triples in LUBM$_{500}$. Finally, we note that, although Ontop was designed to work with existing relational databases, it is also applicable in the context of RDF triple stores, in which case approaches such as the one from [3] can be used to generate suitable relational schemas. Omitted proofs and evaluation details can be found in the full version at http://www.dcs.bbk.ac.uk/~michael/ISWC-14-v2.pdf.

## 2   SPARQL Queries under OWL 2 QL Entailment Regime

SPARQL is a W3C standard language designed to query RDF graphs. Its vocabulary contains four pairwise disjoint and countably infinite sets of symbols: I for *IRIs*, B for *blank nodes*, L for *RDF literals*, and V for *variables*. The elements of $C = I \cup B \cup L$ are called *RDF terms*. A *triple pattern* is an element of $(C \cup V) \times (I \cup V) \times (C \cup V)$. A *basic graph pattern (BGP)* is a finite set of triple patterns. Finally, a *graph pattern*, $P$, is an expression defined by the grammar

$$P ::= \text{BGP} \mid \text{FILTER}(P, F) \mid \text{BIND}(P, v, c) \mid \text{UNION}(P_1, P_2) \mid$$
$$\text{JOIN}(P_1, P_2) \mid \text{OPT}(P_1, P_2, F),$$

where $F$, a *filter*, is a formula constructed from atoms of the form *bound*$(v)$, $(v = c)$, $(v = v')$, for $v, v' \in V$, $c \in C$, and possibly other built-in predicates using the logical connectives $\wedge$ and $\neg$. The set of variables in $P$ is denoted by $var(P)$.

A *SPARQL query* is a graph pattern $P$ with a *solution modifier*, which specifies the *answer variables*—the variables in $P$ whose values we are interested in—and the form of the output (we ignore other solution modifiers for simplicity). The values to variables are given by *solution mappings*, which are *partial* maps $s \colon V \to C$ with (possibly empty) domain *dom*$(s)$. In this paper, we use the set-based (rather than bag-based, as in the specification) semantics for SPARQL. For sets $S_1$ and $S_2$ of solution mappings, a filter $F$, a variable $v \in V$ and a term $c \in C$, let

- FILTER$(S, F) = \{s \in S \mid F^s = \top\}$;
- BIND$(S, v, c) = \{s \oplus \{v \mapsto c\} \mid s \in S\}$ (provided that $v \notin dom(s)$, for $s \in S$);
- UNION$(S_1, S_2) = \{s \mid s \in S_1 \text{ or } s \in S_2\}$;
- JOIN$(S_1, S_2) = \{s_1 \oplus s_2 \mid s_1 \in S_1 \text{ and } s_2 \in S_2 \text{ are compatible}\}$;
- OPT$(S_1, S_2, F) = \text{FILTER}(\text{JOIN}(S_1, S_2), F) \cup \{s_1 \in S_1 \mid \text{for all } s_2 \in S_2,$
  either $s_1, s_2$ are incompatible or $F^{s_1 \oplus s_2} \neq \top\}$.

Here, $s_1$ and $s_2$ are *compatible* if $s_1(v) = s_2(v)$, for any $v \in dom(s_1) \cap dom(s_2)$, in which case $s_1 \oplus s_2$ is a solution mapping with $s_1 \oplus s_2 \colon v \mapsto s_1(v)$, for $v \in dom(s_1)$, $s_1 \oplus s_2 \colon v \mapsto s_2(v)$, for $v \in dom(s_2)$, and domain $dom(s_1) \cup dom(s_2)$. The *truth-value* $F^s \in \{\top, \bot, \varepsilon\}$ *of a filter* $F$ *under a solution mapping* $s$ *is defined inductively*:

- $(bound(v))^s$ is $\top$ if $v \in dom(s)$ and $\bot$ otherwise;
- $(v = c)^s = \varepsilon$ if $v \notin dom(s)$; otherwise, $(v = c)^s$ is the classical truth-value of the predicate $s(v) = c$; similarly, $(v = v')^s = \varepsilon$ if either $v$ or $v' \notin dom(s)$; otherwise, $(v = v')^s$ is the classical truth-value of the predicate $s(v) = s(v')$;
- $(\neg F)^s = \begin{cases} \varepsilon, & \text{if } F^s = \varepsilon, \\ \neg F^s, & \text{otherwise,} \end{cases}$ and $(F_1 \wedge F_2)^s = \begin{cases} \bot, & \text{if } F_1^s = \bot \text{ or } F_2^s = \bot, \\ \top, & \text{if } F_1^s = F_2^s = \top, \\ \varepsilon, & \text{otherwise.} \end{cases}$

Finally, given an RDF graph $G$, the *answer to a graph pattern $P$ over $G$* is the set $\llbracket P \rrbracket_G$ of solution mappings defined by induction using the operations above and starting from the following base case: for a basic graph pattern $B$,

$$\llbracket B \rrbracket_G = \{s \colon var(B) \to \mathsf{C} \mid s(B) \subseteq G\}, \tag{1}$$

where $s(B)$ is the set of triples resulting from substituting each variable $u$ in $B$ by $s(u)$. This semantics is known as *simple entailment*.

*Remark 1.* The condition '$F^{s_1 \oplus s_2}$ *is not true*' in the definition of OPT is different from '$F^{s_1 \oplus s_2}$ has an effective Boolean value of false' given by the W3C specification:[2] the effective Boolean value can be undefined (type error) if a variable in $F$ is not bound by $s_1 \oplus s_2$. As we shall see in Section 3.1, our reading corresponds to LEFT JOIN in SQL. (Note also that the informal explanation of OPT in the W3C specification is inconsistent with the definition of DIFF; see the full version for details.)

Under the *OWL 2 QL direct semantics entailment regime*, one can query an RDF graph $G$ that consist of two parts: an *extensional* sub-graph $\mathcal{A}$ representing the *data* as OWL 2 QL class and property assertions, and the *intensional* sub-graph $\mathcal{T}$ representing the background *knowledge* as OWL 2 QL class and property axioms. We write $(\mathcal{T}, \mathcal{A})$ in place of $G$ to emphasise the partitioning. To illustrate, we give a simple example.

*Example 2.* Consider the following two axioms from the LUBM ontology $(\mathcal{T}, \mathcal{A})$ (see Section 5), which are given here in the functional-style syntax (FSS):

SubClassOf(ub:UGStudent, ub:Student),  SubClassOf(ub:GradStudent, ub:Student).

Under the entailment regime, we can write a query that retrieves all named *subclasses* of students in $(\mathcal{T}, \mathcal{A})$ and all *instances* of each of these subclasses (cf. $q_9'$ in Section 5):

SELECT ?x ?C WHERE { ?C rdfs:subClassOf ub:Student. ?x rdf:type ?C. }.

Here ?C ranges over the class names (IRIs) in $(\mathcal{T}, \mathcal{A})$ and ?x over the IRIs of individuals. If, for example, $\mathcal{A}$ consists of the two assertions on the left-hand side, then the answer to the query over $(\mathcal{T}, \mathcal{A})$ is on the right-hand side:

| $\mathcal{A}$ | ?x | ?C |
|---|---|---|
| ClassAssertion(ub:UGStudent, ub:jim) | ub:jim | ub:UGStudent |
| ClassAssertion(ub:Student, ub:bob) | ub:jim | ub:Student |
|  | ub:bob | ub:Student |

---

[2] http://www.w3.org/TR/sparql11-query/#sparqlAlgebra

To formally define SPARQL queries that can be used under the OWL 2 QL direct semantics entailment regime, we assume that the set I of IRIs is partitioned into disjoint and countably infinite sets of *class names* $I_C$, *object property names* $I_R$ and *individual names* $I_I$. Similarly, the variables V are also assumed to be a disjoint union of countably infinite sets $V_C$, $V_R$, $V_I$. Now, we define an *OWL 2 QL BGP* as a finite set of triple patterns representing OWL 2 QL axiom and assertion templates in the FSS such as:[3]

SubClassOf($SubC, SuperC$),                  DisjointClasses($SubC_1, \ldots, SubC_n$),
ObjectPropertyDomain($OP, SuperC$),    ObjectPropertyRange($OP, SuperC$),
SubObjectPropertyOf($OP, OP$),              DisjointObjectProperties($OP_1, \ldots, OP_n$),
ClassAssertion($SuperC, I$),                      ObjectPropertyAssertion($OP, I, I$),

where $I \in I_I \cup V_I$ and *OP*, *SubC* and *SuperC* are defined by the following grammar with $C \in I_C \cup V_C$ and $R \in I_R \cup V_R$:

$$OP \ ::= \ R \ | \ \text{ObjectInverseOf}(R),$$
$$SubC \ ::= \ C \ | \ \text{ObjectSomeValuesFrom}(OP, \text{owl:Thing}),$$
$$SuperC \ ::= \ C \ | \ \text{ObjectIntersectionOf}(SuperC_1, \ldots, SuperC_n) \ |$$
$$\text{ObjectSomeValuesFrom}(OP, SuperC).$$

*OWL 2 QL graph patterns* are constructed from OWL 2 QL BGPs using the SPARQL operators. Finally, an *OWL 2 QL query* is a pair $(P, V)$, where $P$ is an OWL 2 QL graph pattern and $V \subseteq var(P)$. To define the answer to such a query $(P, V)$ over an RDF graph $(\mathcal{T}, \mathcal{A})$, we fix a *finite* vocabulary $I_{\mathcal{T}, \mathcal{A}} \subseteq I$ that includes all names (IRIs) in $\mathcal{T}$ and $\mathcal{A}$ as well as the required finite part of the OWL 2 RDF-based vocabulary (e.g., owl:Thing but not the infinite number of the rdf:_n). To ensure finiteness of the answers and proper typing of variables, in the following definition we only consider solution mappings $s: var(P) \to I_{\mathcal{T}, \mathcal{A}}$ such that $s^{-1}(I_\alpha) \subseteq V_\alpha$, for $\alpha \in \{C, R, I\}$. For each BGP $B$, we define the *answer* $[\![B]\!]_{\mathcal{T}, \mathcal{A}}$ to $B$ over $(\mathcal{T}, \mathcal{A})$ by taking

$$[\![B]\!]_{\mathcal{T}, \mathcal{A}} = \{s: var(B) \to I_{\mathcal{T}, \mathcal{A}} \mid (\mathcal{T}, \mathcal{A}) \models s(B)\},$$

where $\models$ is the entailment relation given by the OWL 2 direct semantics. Starting from the $[\![B]\!]_{\mathcal{T}, \mathcal{A}}$ and applying the SPARQL operators in $P$, we compute the set $[\![P]\!]_{\mathcal{T}, \mathcal{A}}$ of *solution mappings*. The *answer* to $(P, V)$ over $(\mathcal{T}, \mathcal{A})$ is the restriction $[\![P]\!]_{\mathcal{T}, \mathcal{A}}|_V$ of the solution mappings in $[\![P]\!]_{\mathcal{T}, \mathcal{A}}$ to the variables in $V$.

*Example 3.* Suppose $\mathcal{T}$ contains

SubClassOf(:A, ObjectSomeValuesFrom(:P, owl:Thing)),
SubObjectPropertyOf(:P, :R),    SubObjectPropertyOf(:P, ObjectInverseOf(:S)).

Consider the following OWL 2 QL BGP $B$:

ClassAssertion(ObjectSomeValuesFrom(:R, ObjectSomeValuesFrom(:S,
                           ObjectSomeValuesFrom(:T, owl:Thing))), ?x).

---

[3] The official specification of legal queries under the OWL 2 QL entailment regime only allows ClassAssertion($C, I$) rather than ClassAssertion($SuperC, I$), which makes the OWL 2 QL entailment regime trivial and essentially subsumed by the OWL 2 RL entailment regime.

Assuming that $\mathcal{A} = \{$ClassAssertion(:A, :a), ObjectPropertyAssertion(:T, :a, :b)$\}$, it is not hard to see that $[\![B]\!]_{\mathcal{T},\mathcal{A}} = \{?x \mapsto$ :a$\}$. Indeed, by the first assertion of $\mathcal{A}$ and the first two axioms of $\mathcal{T}$, any model of $(\mathcal{T}, \mathcal{A})$ contains a domain element $w$ (not necessarily among the individuals in $\mathcal{A}$) such that ObjectPropertyAssertion(:R, :a, $w$) holds. In addition, the third axiom of $\mathcal{T}$ implies ObjectPropertyAssertion(:S, $w$, :a), which together with the second assertion of $\mathcal{A}$ mean that $\{?x \mapsto$ :a$\}$ is an answer.

The following theorem shows that answering OWL 2 QL queries under the direct semantics entailment regime can be reduced to answering OWL 2 QL queries under simple entailment, which are evaluated only on the extensional part of the RDF graph:

**Theorem 4.** *Given any intensional graph $\mathcal{T}$ and OWL 2 QL query $(P, V)$, one can construct an OWL 2 QL query $(P^\dagger, V)$ such that, for any extensional graph $\mathcal{A}$ (in some fixed finite vocabulary), $[\![P]\!]_{\mathcal{T},\mathcal{A}}|_V = [\![P^\dagger]\!]_{\mathcal{A}}|_V$.*

*Proof sketch.* By the definition of the entailment regime, it suffices to construct $B^\dagger$, for any *BGP* $B$; the rewriting $P^\dagger$ is obtained then by replacing each BGP $B$ in $P$ with $B^\dagger$. First, we instantiate the class and property variables in $B$ by all possible class and property names in the given vocabulary and add the respective BIND operations. In each of the resulting BGPs, we remove the class and property axioms if they are entailed by $\mathcal{T}$; otherwise we replace the BGP with an empty one. The obtained BGPs are (SPARQL representations of) conjunctive queries (with non-distinguished variables in complex concepts *SuperC* of the assertions ClassAssertion(*SuperC, I*)). The second step is to rewrite these conjunctive queries together with $\mathcal{T}$ into unions of conjunctive queries (BGPs) that can be evaluated over any extensional graph $\mathcal{A}$ [5,21]. (We emphasise that the SPARQL algebra operations, including difference and OPT, are applied to BGPs and do not interact with the two steps of our rewriting.)    □

We illustrate the proof of Theorem 4 using the queries from Examples 2 and 3.

*Example 5.* The class variable $?C$ in the query from Example 2 can be instantiated, using BIND, by all possible values from $I_C \cap I_{\mathcal{T},\mathcal{A}}$, which gives the rewriting

```
SELECT ?x ?C WHERE {
        { ?x rdf:type ub:Student. BIND(ub:Student as ?C) } UNION
        { ?x rdf:type ub:GradStudent. BIND(ub:GradStudent as ?C) } UNION
        { ?x rdf:type ub:UGStudent. BIND(ub:UGStudent as ?C) } }.
```

The query from Example 3 is equivalent to a (tree-shaped) conjunctive query with three non-distinguished and one answer variable, which can be rewritten to

```
SELECT ?x WHERE { { ?x :R ?y. ?y :S ?z. ?z :T ?u. } UNION
                  { ?x rdf:type :A. ?x :T ?u. } }.
```

## 3  Translating SPARQL under Simple Entailment to SQL

A number of translations of SPARQL queries (under simple entailment) to SQL queries have already been suggested in the literature; see, e.g., [9,13,7,32,27]. However, none of them is suitable for our aims because they do not take into account the three-valued logic used in the OPTIONAL and BOUND constructs of the current SPARQL 1.1 (the semantics of OPTIONAL was not compositional in SPARQL 1.0). Note also that SPARQL has been translated to Datalog [25,2,26].

We begin by recapping the basics of relational algebra and SQL (see e.g., [1]). Let $U$ be a finite (possibly empty) set of *attributes*. A *tuple over $U$* is a map $t: U \to \Delta$, where $\Delta$ is the underlying domain, which always contains a distinguished element *null*. A ($|U|$-*ary*) *relation over $U$* is a finite set of tuples over $U$ (again, we use the set-based rather than bag-based semantics). A *filter $F$ over $U$* is a formula constructed from atoms $isNull(U')$, $(u = c)$ and $(u = u')$, where $U' \subseteq U$, $u, u' \in U$ and $c \in \Delta$, using the connectives $\wedge$ and $\neg$. Let $F$ be a filter with variables $U$ and let $t$ be a tuple over $U$. The *truth-value $F^t \in \{\top, \bot, \varepsilon\}$ of $F$ over $t$* is defined inductively:

- $(isNull(U'))^t$ is $\top$ if $t(u)$ is *null*, for all $u \in U'$, and $\bot$ otherwise;
- $(u = c)^t = \varepsilon$ if $t(u)$ is *null*; otherwise, $(u = c)^t$ is the classical truth-value of the predicate $t(u) = c$; similarly, $(u = u')^t = \varepsilon$ if either $t(u)$ or $t(u')$ is *null*; otherwise, $(u = u')^t$ is the classical truth-value of the predicate $t(u) = t(u')$;

$$ (\neg F)^t = \begin{cases} \varepsilon, & \text{if } F^t = \varepsilon, \\ \neg F^t, & \text{otherwise,} \end{cases} \quad \text{and} \quad (F_1 \wedge F_2)^t = \begin{cases} \bot, & \text{if } F_1^t = \bot \text{ or } F_2^t = \bot, \\ \top, & \text{if } F_1^t = F_2^t = \top, \\ \varepsilon, & \text{otherwise.} \end{cases} $$

(Note that $\neg$ and $\wedge$ are interpreted in the same three-valued logic as in SPARQL.) We use standard relational algebra operations such as union, difference, projection, selection, renaming and natural (inner) join. Let $R_i$ be a relation over $U_i$, $i = 1, 2$.

- If $U_1 = U_2$ then the standard $R_1 \cup R_2$ and $R_1 \setminus R_2$ are relations over $U_1$.
- If $U \subseteq U_1$ then $\pi_U R_1 = R_1|_U$ is a relation over $U$.
- If $F$ is a filter over $U_1$ then $\sigma_F R_1 = \{t \in R_1 \mid F^t = \top\}$ is a relation over $U_1$.
- If $v \notin U_1$ and $u \in U_1$ then $\rho_{v/u} R_1 = \{t_{v/u} \mid t \in R_1\}$, where $t_{v/u}: v \mapsto t(u)$ and $t_{v/u}: u' \mapsto t(u')$, for $u' \in U_1 \setminus \{u\}$, is a relation over $(U_1 \setminus \{u\}) \cup \{v\}$.
- $R_1 \bowtie R_2 = \{t_1 \oplus t_2 \mid t_1 \in R_1 \text{ and } t_2 \in R_2 \text{ are compatible}\}$ is a relation over $U_1 \cup U_2$. Here, $t_1$ and $t_2$ are *compatible* if $t_1(u) = t_2(u) \neq null$, for all $u \in U_1 \cap U_2$, in which case a tuple $t_1 \oplus t_2$ over $U_1 \cup U_2$ is defined by taking $t_1 \oplus t_2: u \mapsto t_1(u)$, for $u \in U_1$, and $t_1 \oplus t_2: u \mapsto t_2(u)$, for $u \in U_2$ (note that if $u$ is *null* in either of the tuples then they are incompatible).

To bridge the gap between partial functions (solution mappings) in SPARQL and total mappings (on attributes) in SQL, we require one more operation (expressible in SQL):

- If $U \cap U_1 = \emptyset$ then the *padding* $\mu_U R_1$ is $R_1 \bowtie null^U$, where $null^U$ is the relation consisting of a single tuple $t$ over $U$ with $t: u \mapsto null$, for all $u \in U$.

By an *SQL query, $Q$*, we understand any expression constructed from relation symbols (each over a fixed set of attributes) and filters using the relational algebra operations given above (and complying with all restrictions on the structure). Suppose $Q$ is an SQL query and $D$ a data instance which, for any relation symbol in the schema under consideration, gives a concrete relation over the corresponding set of attributes. The *answer to Q over D* is a relation $\|Q\|_D$ defined inductively in the obvious way starting from the base case: for a relation symbol $Q$, $\|Q\|_D$ is the corresponding relation in $D$.

We now define a translation, $\tau$, which, given a graph pattern $P$, returns an SQL query $\tau(P)$ with the same answers as $P$. More formally, for a set of variables $V$, let $ext_V$ be a function transforming any solution mapping $s$ with $dom(s) \subseteq V$ to a tuple over $V$ by padding it with *nulls*:

$$ext_V(s) = \{v \mapsto s(v) \mid v \in dom(s)\} \cup \{v \mapsto null \mid v \in V \setminus dom(s)\}.$$

The *relational answer to $P$ over $G$* is $\|P\|_G = \{ext_{var(P)}(s) \mid s \in [\![P]\!]_G\}$. The SQL query $\tau(P)$ will be such that, for any RDF graph $G$, the relational answer to $P$ over $G$ coincides with the answer to $\tau(P)$ over *triple*$(G)$, the database instance storing $G$ as a ternary relation *triple* with the attributes *subj*, *pred*, *obj*. First, we define the translation of a SPARQL filter $F$ by taking $\tau(F)$ to be the SQL filter obtained by replacing each *bound*$(v)$ with $\neg isNull(v)$ (other built-in predicates can be handled similarly).

**Proposition 6.** *Let $F$ be a SPARQL filter and let $V$ be the set of variables in $F$. Then $F^s = (\tau(F))^{ext_V(s)}$, for any solution mapping $s$ with $dom(s) \subseteq V$.*

The definition of $\tau$ proceeds by induction on the construction of $P$. Note that we can always assume that graph patterns *under simple entailment* do not contain blank nodes because they can be replaced by fresh variables. It follows that a BGP $\{tp_1, \ldots, tp_n\}$ is equivalent to $\mathrm{JOIN}(\{tp_1\}, \mathrm{JOIN}(\{tp_2\}, \ldots))$. So, for the basis of induction we set

$$\tau(\{\langle s, p, o\rangle\}) = \begin{cases} \pi_\emptyset \sigma_{(subj=s)\wedge(pred=p)\wedge(obj=o)} \; triple, & \text{if } s, p, o \in \mathsf{I}\cup\mathsf{L}, \\ \pi_s \rho_{s/subj} \, \sigma_{(pred=p)\wedge(obj=o)} \; triple, & \text{if } s \in \mathsf{V} \text{ and } p, o \in \mathsf{I}\cup\mathsf{L}, \\ \pi_{s,o} \rho_{s/subj} \, \rho_{o/obj} \, \sigma_{pred=p} \; triple, & \text{if } s, o \in \mathsf{V}, s \neq o, p \in \mathsf{I}\cup\mathsf{L}, \\ \pi_s \rho_{s/subj} \, \sigma_{(pred=p)\wedge(subj=obj)} \; triple, & \text{if } s, o \in \mathsf{V}, s = o, p \in \mathsf{I}\cup\mathsf{L}, \\ \ldots \end{cases}$$

(the remaining cases are similar). Now, if $P_1$ and $P_2$ are graph patterns and $F_1$ and $F$ are filters containing only variables in $var(P_1)$ and $var(P_1)\cup var(P_2)$, respectively, then we set $U_i = var(P_i)$, $i = 1, 2$, and

$$\tau(\mathrm{FILTER}(P_1, F_1)) = \sigma_{\tau(F_1)}\tau(P_1),$$
$$\tau(\mathrm{BIND}(P_1, v, c)) = \tau(P_1) \bowtie \{v \mapsto c\},$$
$$\tau(\mathrm{UNION}(P_1, P_2)) = \mu_{U_2\setminus U_1}\tau(P_1) \cup \mu_{U_1\setminus U_2}\tau(P_2),$$
$$\tau(\mathrm{JOIN}(P_1, P_2)) = \bigcup_{\substack{V_1, V_2 \subseteq U_1 \cap U_2 \\ V_1 \cap V_2 = \emptyset}} \mu_{V_1 \cup V_2}\left[(\pi_{U_1\setminus V_1}\sigma_{isNull(V_1)}\tau(P_1))\bowtie(\pi_{U_2\setminus V_2}\sigma_{isNull(V_2)}\tau(P_2))\right],$$
$$\tau(\mathrm{OPT}(P_1, P_2, F)) = \sigma_{\tau(F)}(\tau(\mathrm{JOIN}(P_1, P_2))) \cup$$
$$\mu_{U_2\setminus U_1}\left(\tau(P_1) \setminus \pi_{U_1}\sigma_{\tau(F)}(\tau(\mathrm{JOIN}(P_1, P_2)))\right).$$

It is readily seen that any $\tau(P)$ is a valid SQL query and defines a relation over $var(P)$.

**Theorem 7.** *For any RDF graph $G$ and any graph pattern $P$, $\|P\|_G = \|\tau(P)\|_{triple(G)}$.*

*Proof.* The proof is by induction on the structure of $P$. Here we only consider the induction step for $P = \text{JOIN}(P_1, P_2)$. Let $U_i = var(P_i)$, $i = 1, 2$, and $U = U_1 \cap U_2$.

If $t \in \|\text{JOIN}(P_1, P_2)\|_G$ then there is a solution mapping $s \in [\![\text{JOIN}(P_1, P_2)]\!]_G$ with $ext_{U_1 \cup U_2}(s) = t$, and so there are $s_i \in [\![P_i]\!]_G$ such that $s_1$ and $s_2$ are compatible and $s_1 \oplus s_2 = s$. Since, $ext_{U_i}(s_i) \in \|P_i\|_G$, by IH, $ext_{U_i}(s_i) \in \|\tau(P_i)\|_{triple(G)}$. Let $V = dom(s_1) \cap dom(s_2)$ and $V_i = U \setminus dom(s_i)$. Then $V_1$, $V_2$ and $V$ are disjoint and partition $U$. By definition, $ext_{U_i}(s_i): v \mapsto null$, for each $v \in V_i$, and therefore $ext_{U_i}(s_i)$ is in $\|\sigma_{isNull(V_i)}\tau(P_i)\|_{triple(G)}$. Let $t_i = ext_{U_i \setminus V_i}(s_i)$ and $Q_i = \pi_{U_i \setminus V_i}(\sigma_{isNull(V_i)}\tau(P_i))$. We have $t_i \in \|Q_i\|_{triple(G)}$, and since $s_1$ and $s_2$ are compatible and $V$ are the common non-null attributes of $t_1$ and $t_2$, we obtain $t_1 \oplus t_2 \in \|Q_1 \bowtie Q_2\|_{triple(G)}$. As $t$ extends $t_1 \oplus t_2$ to $V_1 \cup V_2$ by *null*s, we have $t \in \|\tau(\text{JOIN}(P_1, P_2))\|_{triple(G)}$.

If $t \in \|\tau(\text{JOIN}(P_1, P_2))\|_{triple(G)}$ then there are disjoint $V_1, V_2 \subseteq U$ and compatible tuples $t_1$ and $t_2$ such that $t_i \in \|\pi_{U_i \setminus V_i}(\sigma_{isNull(V_i)}\tau(P_i))\|_{triple(G)}$ and $t$ extends $t_1 \oplus t_2$ to $V_1 \cup V_2$ by *null*s. Let $s_i = \{v \mapsto t(v) \mid v \in U_i$ and $t(v)$ is not $null\}$. Then $s_1$ and $s_2$ are compatible and $ext_{U_i}(s_i) \in \|\tau(P_i)\|_{triple(G)}$. By IH, $ext_{U_i}(s_i) \in \|P_i\|_G$ and $s_i \in [\![P_i]\!]_G$. So, $s_1 \oplus s_2 \in [\![\text{JOIN}(P_1, P_2)]\!]_G$ and $ext_{U_1 \cup U_2}(s_1 \oplus s_2) = t \in \|\text{JOIN}(P_1, P_2)\|_G$.     □

## 3.1   Optimising SPARQL JOIN and OPT

By definition, $\tau(\text{JOIN}(P_1, P_2))$ is a union of exponentially many natural joins ($\bowtie$). Observe, however, that for any BGP $B = \{tp_1, \ldots, tp_n\}$, none of the attributes in the $\tau(tp_i)$ can be *null*. So, we can drastically simplify the definition of $\tau(B)$ by taking

$$\tau(\{tp_1, \ldots, tp_n\}) = \tau(tp_1) \bowtie \cdots \bowtie \tau(tp_n).$$

Moreover, this observation can be generalised. First, we identify the variables in graph patterns that are not necessarily bound in solution mappings:

$$\nu(B) = \emptyset, \qquad B \text{ is a BGP},$$
$$\nu(\text{FILTER}(P_1, F)) = \nu(P_1) \setminus \{v \mid bound(v) \text{ is a conjunct of } F\},$$
$$\nu(\text{BIND}(P_1, v, c)) = \nu(P_1),$$
$$\nu(\text{UNION}(P_1, P_2)) = (var(P_1) \setminus var(P_2)) \cup (var(P_2) \setminus var(P_1)) \cup \nu(P_1) \cup \nu(P_2),$$
$$\nu(\text{JOIN}(P_1, P_2)) = \nu(P_1) \cup \nu(P_2),$$
$$\nu(\text{OPT}(P_1, P_2, F)) = \nu(P_1) \cup var(P_2).$$

Thus, if a variable $v$ in $P$ does not belong to $\nu(P)$, then $v \in dom(s)$, for any solution mapping $s \in [\![P]\!]_G$ and RDF graph $G$ (but not the other way round). Now, we observe that the union in the definition of $\tau(\text{JOIN}(P_1, P_2))$ can be taken over those subsets of $var(P_1) \cap var(P_2)$ that only contain variables from $\nu(P_1) \cup \nu(P_2)$. This gives us:

**Theorem 8.** *If* $var(P_1) \cap var(P_2) \cap (\nu(P_1) \cup \nu(P_2)) = \emptyset$ *then we can define*

$$\tau(\text{JOIN}(P_1, P_2)) = \tau(P_1) \bowtie \tau(P_2), \qquad \tau(\text{OPT}(P_1, P_2, F)) = \tau(P_1) \bowtie_{\tau(F)} \tau(P_2),$$

*where* $R_1 \bowtie_F R_2 = \sigma_F(R_1 \bowtie R_2) \cup \mu_{U_2 \setminus U_1}(R_1 \setminus \pi_{U_1}(\sigma_F(R_1 \bowtie R_2)))$, *for* $R_i$ *over* $U_i$.

(Note that the relational operation $\bowtie_F$ corresponds to LEFT JOIN in SQL with the condition $F$ placed in its ON clause.)

*Example 9.* Consider the following BGP $B$ taken from the official SPARQL specification ('find the names of people who do not know anyone'):

$$\text{FILTER}(\text{OPT}(\{\ ?x\ \text{foaf:givenName}\ ?n\ \},\ \{\ ?x\ \text{foaf:knows}\ ?w\ \},\ \top),\neg bound(?w)).$$

By Theorem 8, $\tau(B)$ is defined as $\sigma_{isNull(w)}(\pi_{x,n}Q_1 \bowtie \pi_{x,w}Q_2)$, where $Q_1$ and $Q_2$ are $\sigma_{pred=\text{foaf:givenName}}\rho_{x/subj}\rho_{n/obj}$ *triple* and $\sigma_{pred=\text{foaf:knows}}\rho_{x/subj}\rho_{w/obj}$ *triple*, respectively (we note in passing that the projection on $x$ is equivalent to $\pi_x Q_1 \setminus \pi_x Q_2$).

## 3.2 R2RML Mappings

The SQL translation of a SPARQL query constructed above has to be evaluated over the ternary relation *triple*$(G)$ representing the virtual RDF graph $G$. Our aim now is to transform it to an SQL query over the actual database, which is related to $G$ by means of an R2RML mapping [10]. A variant of such a transformation has been suggested in [27]. Here we develop the idea first presented in [28]. We begin with a simple example.

*Example 10.* The following R2RML mapping (in the Turtle syntax) populates an object property ub:UGDegreeFrom from a relational table students, whose attributes id and degreeuniid identify graduate students and their universities:

```
_:m1 a rr:TripleMap;
        rr:logicalTable [ rr:sqlQuery "SELECT * FROM students WHERE stype=1" ];
        rr:subjectMap [ rr:template "/GradStudent{id}" ] ;
        rr:predicateObjectMap [ rr:predicate ub:UGDegreeFrom ;
                        rr:objectMap [ rr:template "/Uni{degreeuniid}" ] ]
```

More specifically, for each tuple in the query, an R2RML processor generates an RDF triple with the predicate ub:UGDegreeFrom and the subject and object constructed from attributes id and degreeuniid, respectively, using IRI templates.

Our aim now is as follows: given an R2RML mapping $\mathcal{M}$, we are going to define an SQL query $\text{tr}_{\mathcal{M}}(triple)$ that constructs the relational representation $triple(G_{D,\mathcal{M}})$ of the virtual RDF graph $G_{D,\mathcal{M}}$ obtained by $\mathcal{M}$ from any given data instance $D$. Without loss of generality and to simplify presentation, we assume that each triple map has

- one logical table (rr:sqlQuery),
- one subject map (rr:subjectMap), which does not have resource typing (rr:class),
- and one predicate-object map with one rr:predicateMap and one rr:objectMap.

This normal form can be achieved by introducing predicate-object maps with rdf:type and splitting any triple map into a number of triple maps with the same logical table and subject. We also assume that triple maps contain no referencing object maps (rr:parentTriplesMap, etc.) since they can be eliminated using joint SQL queries [10]. Finally, we assume that the term maps (i.e., subject, predicate and object maps) contain no constant shortcuts and are of the form [rr:column $v$], [rr:constant $c$] or [rr:template $s$].

Given a triple map $m$ with a logical table (SQL query) $R$, we construct a selection $\sigma_{\neg isNull(v_1)}\cdots\sigma_{\neg isNull(v_k)}R$, where $v_1,\ldots,v_k$ are the *referenced columns* of $m$ (attributes of $R$ in the term maps in $m$)—this is done to exclude tuples that contain *null* [10]. To construct $\text{tr}_m$, the selection filter is prefixed with projection $\pi_{subj,pred,obj}$

and, for each of the three term maps, either with renaming (e.g., with $\rho_{obj/v}$ if the object map is of the form [rr:column $v$]) or with value creation (if the term map is of the form [rr:constant $c$] or [rr:template $s$]; in the latter case, we use the built-in string concatenation function ∥). For instance, the mapping _:m1 from Example 10 is converted to the SQL query

    SELECT ('/GradStudent' ∥ id) AS subj, 'ub:UGDegreeFrom' AS pred,
            ('/Uni' ∥ degreeuniid) AS obj FROM students
    WHERE (id IS NOT NULL) AND (degreeuniid IS NOT NULL) AND (stype=1).

Given an R2RML mapping $\mathcal{M}$, we set $\text{tr}_{\mathcal{M}}(\textit{triple}) = \bigcup_{m \in \mathcal{M}} \text{tr}_m$.

**Proposition 11.** *For any R2RML mapping $\mathcal{M}$ and data instance $D$, $t \in \|\text{tr}_{\mathcal{M}}(\textit{triple})\|_D$ if and only if $t \in \textit{triple}(G_{D,\mathcal{M}})$.*

Finally, given a graph pattern $P$ and an R2RML mapping $\mathcal{M}$, we define $\text{tr}_{\mathcal{M}}(\tau(P))$ to be the result of replacing every occurrence of the relation *triple* in the query $\tau(P)$, constructed in Section 3, with $\text{tr}_{\mathcal{M}}(\textit{triple})$. By Theorem 7 and Proposition 11, we obtain:

**Theorem 12.** *For any graph pattern $P$, R2RML mapping $\mathcal{M}$ and data instance $D$, $\|P\|_{G_{D,\mathcal{M}}} = \|\text{tr}_{\mathcal{M}}(\tau(P))\|_D$.*

### 3.3 Optimising SQL Translation

The straightforward application of $\text{tr}_{\mathcal{M}}$ to $\tau(P)$ can result in a very complex SQL query. We now show that such queries can be optimised by the following techniques:

– choosing matching $\text{tr}_m$ from $\text{tr}_{\mathcal{M}}(\textit{triple})$, for each occurrence of *triple* in $\tau(P)$;
– using the distributivity of ⋈ over ∪ and removing sub-queries with *incompatible IRI templates* and *de-IRIing* join conditions;
– functional dependencies (e.g., primary keys) for self-join elimination [6,18,29,30].

To illustrate, suppose we are given a mapping $\mathcal{M}$ containing _:m1 from Example 10 and the following triple maps (which are a simplified version of those in Section 5):

    _:m2 a rr:TripleMap;
        rr:logicalTable [ rr:sqlQuery "SELECT * FROM students WHERE stype=0" ];
        rr:subjectMap [ rr:template "/UGStudent{id}"; rr:class ub:Student ].
    _:m3 a rr:TripleMap;
        rr:logicalTable [ rr:sqlQuery "SELECT * FROM students WHERE stype=1" ];
        rr:subjectMap [ rr:template "/GradStudent{id}"; rr:class ub:Student ].

which generate undergraduate and graduate students (both are instances of ub:Student, but their IRIs are constructed using different templates [16]). Consider the following query (a fragment of $q_2^{obg}$ from Section 5):

    SELECT ?x ?y WHERE { ?x rdf:type ub:Student. ?x ub:UGDegreeFrom ?y }.

The translation $\tau$ of its BGP (after the SPARQL JOIN optimisation of Section 3.1) is

$$\left(\pi_x \rho_{x/subj}\sigma_{(pred=\text{rdf:type}) \wedge (obj=\text{ub:Student})}\, \textit{triple}\right) \bowtie$$
$$\left(\pi_{x,y} \rho_{x/subj} \rho_{y/obj}\sigma_{pred=\text{ub:UGDegreeFrom}}\, \textit{triple}\right)$$

First, since *triple* always occurs in the scope of some selection operation $\sigma_F$, we can choose only those elements in $\bigcup_{m \in \mathcal{M}} \text{tr}_m$ that have matching values of *pred* and/or *obj*. In our example, the first occurrence of *triple* is replaced by tr_:m2 ∪ tr_:m3, and the second one by tr_:m1. This results in the natural join of the following union, denoted A:

    (SELECT DISTINCT '/UGStudent' || id AS x FROM students
     WHERE (id IS NOT NULL) AND (stype=0))
    UNION (SELECT DISTINCT '/GradStudent' || id AS x FROM students
           WHERE (id IS NOT NULL) AND (stype=1))

and of the following query, denoted B:

    SELECT DISTINCT '/GradStudent' || id AS x, '/Uni' || degreeuniid AS y FROM students
    WHERE (id IS NOT NULL) AND (degreeuniid IS NOT NULL) AND (stype=1)

Second, observe that the IRI template in B is compatible only with the second component of A. Moreover, since the two compatible templates coincide, we can *de-IRI* the join, namely, replace the join over the constructed strings (A.x = B.x) by the join over the numerical attributes (A.id = B.id), which results in a more efficient query:

    SELECT DISTINCT A.x, B.y FROM
        (SELECT id, '/GradStudent' || id AS x FROM students
         WHERE (id IS NOT NULL) AND (stype=1)) A
        JOIN
        (SELECT id, '/GradStudent' || id AS x, '/Uni' || degreeuniid AS y FROM students
            WHERE (id IS NOT NULL) AND (degreeuniid IS NOT NULL) AND (stype=1)) B
        ON A.id = B.id

Finally, by using self-join elimination and the fact that id and stype are the composite primary key in students, we obtain the query (without DISTINCT as x is unique)

    SELECT '/GradStudent' || id AS x, '/Uni' || degreeuniid AS y FROM students
    WHERE (degreeuniid IS NOT NULL) AND (stype=1)

## 4   Putting It All Together

The techniques introduced above suggest the following architecture to support answering SPARQL queries under the OWL 2 QL entailment regime with data instances stored in a database. Suppose we are given an ontology with an intensional part $\mathcal{T}$ and an extensional part stored in a database, $D$, over a schema $\Sigma$. Suppose also that the languages of $\Sigma$ and $\mathcal{T}$ are connected by an R2RML mapping $\mathcal{M}$. The process of answering a given OWL 2 QL query $(P, V)$ involves two stages, off-line and on-line.

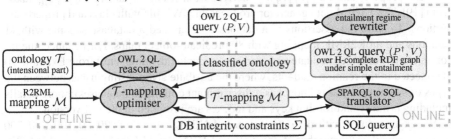

The *off-line* stage takes $\mathcal{T}$, $\mathcal{M}$ and $\Sigma$ and proceeds via the following steps:

❶ An OWL 2 QL reasoner is used to obtain a complete class / property hierarchy in $\mathcal{T}$.

❷ The composition $\mathcal{M}^{\mathcal{T}}$ of $\mathcal{M}$ with the class and property hierarchy in $\mathcal{T}$ is taken as an initial $\mathcal{T}$-mapping. Recall [29] that a mapping $\mathcal{M}'$ is a $\mathcal{T}$-*mapping over* $\Sigma$ if, for any data instance $D$ satisfying $\Sigma$, the *virtual* (not materialised) RDF graph $G_{D,\mathcal{M}'}$ obtained by applying $\mathcal{M}'$ to $D$ contains all class and property assertions $\alpha$ with $(\mathcal{T}, G_{D,\mathcal{M}'}) \models \alpha$. As a result, $G_{D,\mathcal{M}'}$ is complete with respect to the class and property hierarchy in $\mathcal{T}$ (or H-complete), which allows us to avoid reasoning about class and property inclusions (in particular, inferences that involve property domains and ranges) at the query rewriting step ❹ and drastically simplify rewritings (see [29] for details).

❸ The initial $\mathcal{T}$-mapping $\mathcal{M}^{\mathcal{T}}$ is then optimised by (*i*) eliminating redundant triple maps detected by query containment with inclusion dependencies in $\Sigma$, (*ii*) eliminating redundant joins in logical tables using the functional dependencies in $\Sigma$, and (*iii*) merging sets of triple maps by means of interval expressions or disjunctions in logical tables (see [29] for details). Let $\mathcal{M}'$ be the resulting $\mathcal{T}$-mapping over $\Sigma$.

The *on-line* stage takes an OWL 2 QL query $(P, V)$ as an input and proceeds as follows:

❹ The graph pattern $P$ and $\mathcal{T}$ are rewritten to the OWL 2 QL graph pattern $P^{\dagger}$ over the H-complete virtual RDF graph $G_{D,\mathcal{M}'}$ *under simple entailment* by applying the classified ontology of step ❶ to instantiate class and property variables and then using a query rewriting algorithm (e.g., the tree-witness rewriter of [29]); see Theorem 4.

❺ The graph pattern $P^{\dagger}$ is transformed to the SQL query $\tau(P^{\dagger})$ over the 3-column representation *triple* of the RDF graph (Theorem 7). Next, the query $\tau(P^{\dagger})$ is unfolded into the SQL query $\mathrm{tr}_{\mathcal{M}'}(\tau(P^{\dagger}))$ over the original database $D$ (Theorem 12). The unfolded query is optimised using the techniques similar to the ones employed in step ❸.

❻ The optimised query is executed by the database.

As follows from Theorems 4, 7 and 12, the resulting query gives us all correct answers to the original OWL 2 QL query $(P, V)$ over $\mathcal{T}$ and $D$ with the R2RML mapping $\mathcal{M}$.

## 5   Evaluation

The architecture described above has been implemented in the open-source OBDA system *Ontop*[4]. We evaluated its performance using the OWL 2 QL version of the Lehigh University Benchmark LUBM [16]. The ontology contains 43 classes, 32 object and data properties and 243 axioms. The benchmark also includes a data generator and a set of 14 queries $q_1$–$q_{14}$. We added 7 queries with second-order variables ranging over class and property names: $q_4'$, $q_4''$, $q_9'$, $q_9''$ derived from $q_4$ and $q_9$, and $q_2^{obg}$, $q_4^{obg}$, $q_{10}^{obg}$ taken from [19]. The LUBM data generator produces an OWL file with class and property assertions. To store the assertions in a database, we created a database schema with 11 relations and an R2RML mapping with 89 predicate-object maps. For instance, the information about undergraduate and graduate students (id, name, etc.) from Example 10 is collected in the relation **students**, where the attribute **stype** distinguishes between the types of students (**stype** is known as a discriminant column in databases); more details including primary and foreign keys and indexes are provided in the full version.

We experimented with the data instances $\mathrm{LUBM}_n$, $n = 1, 9, 20, 50, 100, 200, 500$ (where $n$ specifies the number of universities; $\mathrm{LUBM}_1$ and $\mathrm{LUBM}_9$ were used in [19]).

---

[4] http://ontop.inf.unibz.it

**Table 1.** Start up time, data loading time (in s) and query execution time (in ms): O is *Ontop*, $OB_H$ and $OB_P$ are OWL-BGP with Hermit and Pellet, respectively, and P is standalone Pellet

| Q | LUBM$_1$ | | | | LUBM$_9$ | | | LUBM$_{100}$ | | LUBM$_{200}$ | LUBM$_{500}$ |
|---|---|---|---|---|---|---|---|---|---|---|---|
| | O | OB$_H$ | OB$_P$ | P | O | OB$_H$ | P | O | P | O | O |
| $q_1$ | 2 | 8 | 29 | 1 | 3 | 97 | 1 | 3 | 1 | 3 | 2 |
| $q_2$ | 2 | 25 | 11 137 | 19 | 3 | 2 531 | 256 | 16 | 30 593 | 36 | 88 |
| $q_3$ | 1 | 6 | 86 | 9 | 2 | 78 | 158 | 2 | 2 087 | 63 | 12 |
| $q_4$ | 13 | 7 | 19 | 14 | 15 | 44 | 164 | 27 | 2 093 | 24 | 22 |
| $q_5$ | 16 | 12 | 4 451 | 10 | 22 | 98 | 158 | 32 | 2 182 | 28 | 23 |
| $q_6$ | 455 | 27 | 32 | 21 | 5 076 | 411 | 317 | 58 968 | 10 781 | 123 578 | 434 349 |
| $q_7$ | 5 | 21 | 34 005 | 10 | 6 | 429 | 157 | 8 | 2 171 | 8 | 9 |
| $q_8$ | 726 | 195 | 95 875 | 80 | 760 | 917 | 192 | 796 | 2 131 | 820 | 855 |
| $q_9$ | 60 | 972 | 168 978 | 78 | 668 | 189 126 | 857 | 7 466 | 12 125 | 15 227 | 44 598 |
| $q_{10}$ | 2 | 6 | 126 | 9 | 3 | 97 | 158 | 2 | 2 134 | 3 | 2 |
| $q_{11}$ | 4 | 5 | 58 | 10 | 6 | 43 | 160 | 11 | 2 093 | 18 | 44 |
| $q_{12}$ | 3 | 4 | 19 | 15 | 4 | 70 | 236 | 3 | 2 114 | 5 | 5 |
| $q_{13}$ | 6 | 4 | 67 | 8 | 7 | 40 | 157 | 14 | 2 657 | 38 | 58 |
| $q_{14}$ | 91 | 20 | 24 | 15 | 1 168 | 329 | 287 | 13 524 | 4 457 | 29 512 | 92 376 |
| $q'_4$ | 93 | 58 | 190 | 46 | 99 | 98 | 767 | 92 | 4 422 | 95 | 107 |
| $q''_4$ | 108 | 21 | 35 | 63 | 122 | 72 | 719 | 115 | 9 179 | 108 | 127 |
| $q'_9$ | 257 | 716 | 91 855 | 174 | 4 686 | 40 575 | 1 385 | 54 092 | 19 945 | 115 110 | 295 228 |
| $q''_9$ | 557 | 951 | 65 916 | 102 | 6 093 | 178 401 | 1 214 | 67 123 | 19 705 | 151 376 | 356 176 |
| $q_2^{obg}$ | 150 | 30 | 57 141 | 29 | 9 992 | 520 | 348 | 39 477 | 5 411 | 79 351 | 206 061 |
| $q_4^{obg}$ | 6 | 7 | 241 | 25 | 31 | 40 | 273 | 7 | 3 969 | 7 | 494 |
| $q_{10}^{obg}$ | 641 | 760 | 31 269 | 253 | 6 998 | 149 191 | 2 258 | 163 308 | 17 929 | 174 362 | 459 669 |
| start up | 3.1s | 13.6s | 7.7s | 3.6s | 3.1s | 80m33s | 18s | 3.1s | 3m23s | 3.1s | 3.1s |
| data load | 10s | n/a | n/a | n/a | 15s | n/a | n/a | 1m56s | n/a | 3m35s | 10m17s |

Here we only show the results for $n = 1, 9, 100, 200, 500$ containing 103k, 1.2M, 14M, 28M and 69M triples, respectively; the complete table can be found in the full version. All the materials required for the experiments are available online[5]. We compared *Ontop* with two other systems, OWL-BGP r123 [19] and Pellet 2.3.1 [31] (Stardog and OWLIM are incomplete for the OWL 2 QL entailment regime). OWL-BGP requires an OWL 2 reasoner as a backend; as in [19], we employed HermiT 1.3.8 [14] and Pellet 2.3.1. The hardware was an HP Proliant Linux server with 144 cores @3.47GHz, 106GB of RAM and a 1TB 15k RPM HD. Each system used a single core and was given 20 GB of Java 7 heap memory. *Ontop* used MySQL 5.6 database engine.

The evaluation results are given in Table 1. OWL-BGP and Pellet used significantly more time to start up (last but one row) because they do not rely on query rewriting and require costly pre-computations. OWL-BGP failed to start on LUBM$_9$ with Pellet and on LUBM$_{20}$ with HermiT; Pellet ran out of memory after 10hrs loading LUBM$_{200}$. For *Ontop*, the start up is the off-line stage described in Section 4; it does not include the time of loading the data into MySQL, which is specified in the last row of Table 1 (note that the data is loaded only once, not every time *Ontop* starts; moreover, this could be improved with CSV loading and delayed indexing rather than SQL dumps we used).

On queries $q_1$–$q_{14}$, *Ontop* generally outperforms OWL-BGP and Pellet. Due to the optimisations, the SQL queries generated by *Ontop* are very simple, and MySQL is able to execute them efficiently. This is also the case for large datasets, where *Ontop* is able to maintain almost constant times for many of the queries. Notable exceptions are $q_6$, $q_8$ and $q_{14}$ that return a very large number (hundreds of thousands) of results (low selectivity). A closer inspection reveals that execution time is mostly spent on fetching the results from disk. On the queries with second-order variables, the picture is mixed.

---

[5] https://github.com/ontop/iswc2014-benchmark

While indeed these queries are not the strongest point of *Ontop* at the moment, we see that in general the performance is good. Although Pellet outperforms *Ontop* on small datasets, only *Ontop* is able to provide answers for very large datasets. For second-order queries with high selectivity (e.g., $q_4'$ and $q_4''$) and large datasets, the performance of *Ontop* is very good while the other systems fail to return answers.

## 6   Conclusions

In this paper, we gave both a theoretical background and a practical implementation of a procedure for answering SPARQL 1.1 queries under the OWL 2 QL direct semantics entailment regime in the scenario where data instances are stored in a relational database whose schema is connected to the language of the given OWL 2 QL ontology via an R2RML mapping. Our main contributions can be summarised as follows:

- We defined an entailment regime for SPARQL 1.1 corresponding to the OWL 2 QL profile of OWL 2 (which was specifically designed for ontology-based data access).
- We proved that answering SPARQL queries under this regime is reducible to answering SPARQL queries under simple entailment (where no reasoning is involved).
- We showed how to transform such SPARQL queries to equivalent SQL queries over an RDF representation of the data, and then unfold them, using R2RML mappings, into SQL queries over the original relational data.
- We developed optimisation techniques to substantially reduce the size and improve the quality of the resulting SQL queries.
- We implemented these rewriting and optimisation techniques in the OBDA system *Ontop*. Our initial experiments showed that *Ontop* generally outperforms reasoner-based systems, especially on large data instances.

Some aspects of SPARQL 1.1 (such as RDF types, property paths, aggregates) were not discussed here and are left for future work.

**Acknowledgements.** Our work was supported by EU project Optique. We thank S. Komla-Ebri for help with the experiments, and I. Kollia and B. Glimm for discussions.

## References

1. Abiteboul, S., Hull, R., Vianu, V.: Foundations of Databases. Addison-Wesley (1995)
2. Angles, R., Gutierrez, C.: The expressive power of SPARQL. In: Sheth, A.P., Staab, S., Dean, M., Paolucci, M., Maynard, D., Finin, T., Thirunarayan, K. (eds.) ISWC 2008. LNCS, vol. 5318, pp. 114–129. Springer, Heidelberg (2008)
3. Bornea, M., Dolby, J., Kementsietsidis, A., Srinivas, K., Dantressangle, P., Udrea, O., Bhattacharjee, B.: Building an efficient RDF store over a relational database. In: Proc. of SIGMOD 2013, pp. 121–132. ACM (2013)
4. Calvanese, D., De Giacomo, G., Lembo, D., Lenzerini, M., Poggi, A., Rodriguez-Muro, M., Rosati, R., Ruzzi, M., Savo, D.F.: The MASTRO system for ontology-based data access. Semantic Web 2(1), 43–53 (2011)
5. Calvanese, D., De Giacomo, G., Lembo, D., Lenzerini, M., Rosati, R.: Tractable reasoning and efficient query answering in description logics: The DL-Lite family. J. of Automated Reasoning 39(3), 385–429 (2007)
6. Chakravarthy, U.S., Grant, J., Minker, J.: Logic-based approach to semantic query optimization. ACM Transactions on Database Systems 15(2), 162–207 (1990)
7. Chebotko, A., Lu, S., Fotouhi, F.: Semantics preserving SPARQL-to-SQL translation. Data Knowl. Eng. 68(10), 973–1000 (2009)

8. Chortaras, A., Trivela, D., Stamou, G.: Optimized query rewriting for OWL 2 QL. In: Bjørner, N., Sofronie-Stokkermans, V. (eds.) CADE 2011. LNCS, vol. 6803, pp. 192–206. Springer, Heidelberg (2011)
9. Cyganiak, R.: A relational algebra for SPARQL. Tech. Rep. HPL-2005-170, HP Labs (2005)
10. Das, S., Sundara, S., Cyganiak, R.: R2RML: RDB to RDF Mapping Language (September 2012), http://www.w3.org/TR/r2rml
11. Dolby, J., Fokoue, A., Kalyanpur, A., Ma, L., Schonberg, E., Srinivas, K., Sun, X.: Scalable grounded conjunctive query evaluation over large and expressive knowledge bases. In: Sheth, A.P., Staab, S., Dean, M., Paolucci, M., Maynard, D., Finin, T., Thirunarayan, K. (eds.) ISWC 2008. LNCS, vol. 5318, pp. 403–418. Springer, Heidelberg (2008)
12. Eiter, T., Ortiz, M., Šimkus, M., Tran, T.K., Xiao, G.: Query rewriting for Horn-SHIQ plus rules. In: Proc. of AAAI. AAAI Press (2012)
13. Elliott, B., Cheng, E., Thomas-Ogbuji, C., Özsoyoglu, Z.M.: A complete translation from SPARQL into efficient SQL. In: Proc. of IDEAS, pp. 31–42. ACM (2009)
14. Glimm, B., Horrocks, I., Motik, B., Stoilos, G.: Optimising ontology classification. In: Patel-Schneider, P.F., Pan, Y., Hitzler, P., Mika, P., Zhang, L., Pan, J.Z., Horrocks, I., Glimm, B. (eds.) ISWC 2010, Part I. LNCS, vol. 6496, pp. 225–240. Springer, Heidelberg (2010)
15. Gottlob, G., Orsi, G., Pieris, A.: Ontological queries: Rewriting and optimization. In: Proc. of ICDE, pp. 2–13. IEEE Computer Society (2011)
16. Guo, Y., Pan, Z., Heflin, J.: LUBM: A benchmark for OWL knowledge base systems. J. of Web Semantics 3(2-3), 158–182 (2005)
17. Heymans, S., et al.: Ontology reasoning with large data repositories. In: Ontology Management, Semantic Web, Semantic Web Services, and Business Applications. Springer (2008)
18. King, J.J.: Query Optimization by Semantic Reasoning. Ph.D. thesis, Stanford, USA (1981)
19. Kollia, I., Glimm, B.: Optimizing SPARQL query answering over OWL ontologies. J. of Artificial Intelligence Research 48, 253–303 (2013)
20. König, M., Leclère, M., Mugnier, M.-L., Thomazo, M.: On the exploration of the query rewriting space with existential rules. In: Faber, W., Lembo, D. (eds.) RR 2013. LNCS, vol. 7994, pp. 123–137. Springer, Heidelberg (2013)
21. Kontchakov, R., Rodríguez-Muro, M., Zakharyaschev, M.: Ontology-based data access with databases: A short course. In: Rudolph, S., Gottlob, G., Horrocks, I., van Harmelen, F. (eds.) Reasoning Weg 2013. LNCS, vol. 8067, pp. 194–229. Springer, Heidelberg (2013)
22. Lutz, C., Seylan, İ., Toman, D., Wolter, F.: The combined approach to OBDA: Taming role hierarchies using filters. In: Alani, H., et al. (eds.) ISWC 2013, Part I. LNCS, vol. 8218, pp. 314–330. Springer, Heidelberg (2013)
23. Pérez-Urbina, H., Rodríguez-Díaz, E., Grove, M., Konstantinidis, G., Sirin, E.: Evaluation of query rewriting approaches for OWL 2. In: SSWS+HPCSW. CEUR-WS, vol. 943 (2012)
24. Poggi, A., Lembo, D., Calvanese, D., De Giacomo, G., Lenzerini, M., Rosati, R.: Linking data to ontologies. J. on Data Semantics X, 133–173 (2008)
25. Polleres, A.: From SPARQL to rules (and back). In: Proc. WWW, pp. 787–796. ACM (2007)
26. Polleres, A., Wallner, J.P.: On the relation between SPARQL 1.1 and Answer Set Programming. J. of Applied Non-Classical Logics 23(1-2), 159–212 (2013)
27. Priyatna, F., Corcho, O., Sequeda, J.: Formalisation and experiences of R2RML-based SPARQL to SQL query translation using Morph. In: Proc. of WWW, pp. 479–490 (2014)
28. Rodríguez-Muro, M., Hardi, J., Calvanese, D.: Quest: Efficient SPARQL-to-SQL for RDF and OWL. In: Proc. of the ISWC 2012 P&D Track, vol. 914. CEUR-WS.org (2012)
29. Rodríguez-Muro, M., Kontchakov, R., Zakharyaschev, M.: Ontology-based data access: Ontop of databases. In: Alani, H., et al. (eds.) ISWC 2013, Part I. LNCS, vol. 8218, pp. 558–573. Springer, Heidelberg (2013)
30. Sequeda, J.F., Miranker, D.P.: Ultrawrap: SPARQL execution on relational data. J. of Web Semantics 22, 19–39 (2013)
31. Sirin, E., Parsia, B., Cuenca Grau, B., Kalyanpur, A., Katz, Y.: Pellet: A practical OWL-DL Reasoner. J. of Web Semantics 5(2), 51–53 (2007)
32. Zemke, F.: Converting SPARQL to SQL. Tech. rep., Oracle Corp. (2006)

# kyrie2: Query Rewriting under Extensional Constraints in $\mathcal{ELHIO}$

Jose Mora[1,2], Riccardo Rosati[1], and Oscar Corcho[2]

[1] Dipartimento di Ingegneria Informatica, Automatica e Gestionale Antonio Ruberti Sapienza
Università di Roma, Italy
`lastname@dis.uniroma1.it`
[2] Ontology Engineering Group, Departamento de Inteligencia Artificial,
Facultad de Informática,Universidad Politécnica de Madrid, Spain
`{jmora,ocorcho}@fi.upm.es`

**Abstract.** In this paper we study query answering and rewriting in ontology-based data access. Specifically, we present an algorithm for computing a perfect rewriting of unions of conjunctive queries posed over ontologies expressed in the description logic $\mathcal{ELHIO}$, which covers the OWL 2 QL and OWL 2 EL profiles. The novelty of our algorithm is the use of a set of ABox dependencies, which are compiled into a so-called EBox, to limit the expansion of the rewriting. So far, EBoxes have only been used in query rewriting in the case of DL-Lite, which is less expressive than $\mathcal{ELHIO}$. We have extensively evaluated our new query rewriting technique, and in this paper we discuss the tradeoff between the reduction of the size of the rewriting and the computational cost of our approach.

**Keywords:** Ontology-Based Data Access, Query Rewriting, Reasoning, EBox.

## 1 Introduction

In Ontology Based Data Access (OBDA) [1], *ontologies* are used to superimpose a conceptual layer as a view to an underlying *data source*, which is usually a relational database. The conceptual layer consists of a TBox, i.e. a set of axioms expressed in a Description Logic (DL). This layer abstracts away from how that information is maintained in the data layer and may provide inference capabilities. The conceptual layer and the data source layer are connected through *mappings* that specify the semantic relationship between the database schema terms and the terms in the TBox.

Query rewriting is currently the most important reasoning technique for OBDA. It consists in transforming a query posed in ontological terms into another query expressed over the underlying database schema. The rewritten query allows for obtaining the *certain answers* to the original query, i.e. results explicitly stated for the query in the database and those that are entailed by the TBox. To do so, the rewritten query "encodes" the intensional knowledge expressed by the TBox and the mappings [1].

Recently, some approaches [2,3,4] have proposed the use of *ABox dependencies*, or *extensional constraints*, to optimise query rewriting in OBDA. An extensional constraint is an axiom (in the TBox language) that the data are known to satisfy. As such, it can be viewed as an integrity constraint for the OBDA system. Such constraints can

P. Mika et al. (Eds.) ISWC 2014, Part I, LNCS 8796, pp. 568–583, 2014.

be automatically derived from OBDA specifications, in particular, they can be deduced from the mappings and from the integrity constraints in the source database [4]. Following [3], we call *EBox* a set of extensional constraints. For ontologies expressed in the logic DL-Lite$_A$, EBoxes can be used to optimise reasoning and query rewriting in OBDA [2,3]. In fact, since extensional constraints express forms of completeness of the data, they can be used during query rewriting in a complementary way with respect to the usual TBox axioms, allowing for significant simplifications of the rewritten query.

In this paper we explore the application of an EBox to the rewriting process performed by kyrie [5], which deals with the expressive DL $\mathcal{ELHIO}$ by performing resolution in several stages with some optimisations.

The contributions of the paper are the following:

1. *Extension of the kyrie algorithm.* We define a new query rewriting algorithm for $\mathcal{ELHIO}$. The algorithm is based on kyrie, and takes into account, besides the TBox, the presence of an $\mathcal{ELHIO}$ EBox. This extension is inspired by Prexto [3], a query rewriting algorithm for DL-Lite$_R$: however, such an extension is technically challenging, due to the expressiveness of $\mathcal{ELHIO}$.

2. *Extension of a query rewriting benchmark.* We extend an existing benchmark for the evaluation of query rewriting in OBDA [6], considering EBoxes in addition to TBoxes, so as to experimentally evaluate the use of EBoxes in $\mathcal{ELHIO}$ ontologies.

3. *Implementation and experimental evaluation.* We perform an experimental analysis of the new query rewriting algorithm. Our results show the effectiveness of using EBoxes in the optimisation of query rewriting, and highlight some interesting properties of the similarity between TBox and EBox.

This paper is structured as follows. In Section 2 we briefly recall the DL $\mathcal{ELHIO}$ and extensional constraints and the state of the art is briefly summarized. In Section 3 we present the kyrie2 query rewriting algorithm for $\mathcal{ELHIO}$. The operations performed by the algorithm are formalised as a set of propositions in Section 4. Finally, Section 5 and Section 6 contain, respectively, the evaluation of our proposal and some conclusions drawn from it[1].

## 2   Preliminaries

We briefly recall Horn clauses, $\mathcal{ELHIO}$, OBDA systems and extensional constraints.

**Horn Clauses.** Following [7,5], our technique makes use of a representation of DL axioms as Horn clauses. A Horn clause (or Horn rule) is an expression of the form $\beta_0 \leftarrow \beta_1, \ldots, \beta_n$, with $n \geq 0$ and where each term appearing in each of the atoms $\beta_0, \beta_1, \ldots, \beta_n$ may be a constant $c$ from an alphabet of constant symbols, a variable $x$ from an alphabet of variable symbols, or a unary Skolem function $f(x)$ (where $f$ is from an alphabet of function symbols) whose argument is a variable. Clauses are safe, i.e., all variables occurring in $\beta_0$ (which is called the clause head) also occur in $\beta_1, \ldots, \beta_n$ (which is called the clause body). The arity of the clause is the number of arguments of

---

[1] Due to space constraints, proofs of theorems are available at
http://j.mp/kyrieproofebox

its head atom. A clause is Boolean if it has no variables in its head. We say that an atom $\beta_a$ subsumes another atom $\beta_b$ ($\beta_a \succeq_s \beta_b$) if there is some unification of its variables $\mu$ such that $\mu\beta_a = \beta_b$. A Horn clause subsumes another Horn clause if after some variable renaming both of their heads are equal and there is some unification such that all the atoms in the body of the subsuming clause unify with some atom in the body of the subsumed clause, i.e. $\forall\gamma_a, \gamma_b.(head(\gamma_a) = head(\gamma_b) \land \exists\mu.\forall\beta_i \in body(\gamma_a).\exists\beta_j \in body(\gamma_b).\mu\beta_i = \beta_j) \rightarrow \gamma_a \succeq_s \gamma_b$.

Let $R$ be the Horn clause $\beta_0 \leftarrow \beta_1, \ldots, \beta_n$ and let $x$ be the variables occurring in $R$. We define $FO(R)$ as the first-order sentence $\forall x(\beta_0 \lor \neg\beta_1 \lor \ldots \lor \neg\beta_n)$. Moreover, given a set of Horn clauses $\Sigma$, we define $FO(\Sigma)$ as $\bigcup_{R \in \Sigma} FO(R)$.

**OBDA Systems.**    An OBDA system [1] allows for accessing a set of data sources $\mathcal{D}$ using an ontology composed of TBox and ABox $\mathcal{O} = \langle \mathcal{T}, \mathcal{A} \rangle$ as a view for the data in $\mathcal{D}$. To do this, a set of mappings $\mathcal{M}$ is normally used to map the information in $\mathcal{D}$ to the elements in the TBox $\mathcal{T}$ [8].

In $\mathcal{ELHIO}$, concept ($C$) and role ($R$) expressions are formed according to the following syntax (where $A$ denotes a concept name, $P$ denotes a role name, and $a$ denotes an individual name):

$$C ::= A \mid C_1 \sqcap C_2 \mid \exists R.C \mid \{a\}$$
$$R ::= P \mid P^-$$

An $\mathcal{ELHIO}$ axiom is an expression of the form $C_1 \sqsubseteq C_2, C \sqsubseteq \bot, R_1 \sqsubseteq R_2$ or $R \sqsubseteq \bot$ where $C_1, C_2$ are concept expressions and $R_1, R_2$ are role expressions (as usual, $\bot$ denotes the empty concept). An $\mathcal{ELHIO}$ TBox $\mathcal{T}$ is a set of $\mathcal{ELHIO}$ axioms.

An OBDA system is a pair $\mathcal{O} = \langle \mathcal{T}, \mathcal{A} \rangle$, where $\mathcal{T}$ is an $\mathcal{ELHIO}$ TBox, and $\mathcal{A}$ is an ABox, i.e., a set of ground atoms, representing the pair $\langle \mathcal{M}, \mathcal{A} \rangle$.

Notably, each $\mathcal{ELHIO}$ axiom corresponds to a set of Horn clauses [7,5]. We can thus define the semantics of OBDA systems by using the clause translation of an $\mathcal{ELHIO}$ TBox into a set of clauses. More precisely, given an $\mathcal{ELHIO}$ axiom $\psi$, we denote by $\tau_c(\psi)$ the set of clauses corresponding to $\psi$, and given a TBox $\mathcal{T}$, we denote by $\tau_c(\mathcal{T})$ the set of clauses corresponding to $\mathcal{T}$. Then, the set of models of an OBDA system $\langle \mathcal{T}, \mathcal{A} \rangle$ is the set of models of the first-order theory $FO(\tau_c(\mathcal{T})) \cup \mathcal{A}$.

We refer the reader to [5] for more details on the translation of $\mathcal{ELHIO}$ axioms into Horn clauses. From now on, we assume that the OBDA system $\langle \mathcal{T}, \mathcal{A} \rangle$ is consistent, i.e., has at least one model. The extension of our results to possibly inconsistent OBDA systems is trivial.

The OBDA system allows for accessing the data by posing queries and returning the *certain answers* to these queries. As usual in OBDA, we consider unions of conjunctive queries. A conjunctive query (CQ) is a function-free Horn clause. As usual, we assume that the head predicate $q$ of the CQ does not occur in $\langle \mathcal{T}, \mathcal{A} \rangle$. For ease of exposition, we assume that constants may not occur in the head of a CQ. A union of conjunctive queries (UCQ) is a finite, non-empty set of CQs having the same head predicate $q$ and the same arity.

The set of *certain answers* for a UCQ $q$ posed to a system $\langle \mathcal{T}, \mathcal{A} \rangle$, denoted by $\Phi^q_{\langle \mathcal{T}, \mathcal{A} \rangle}$, is the set of tuples of constants $t_1, \ldots, t_n$ such that the atom $q(t_1, \ldots, t_n)$ holds in all models of $FO(\Sigma \cup q) \cup \mathcal{A}$, where $\Sigma = \tau_c(\mathcal{T})$.

**Query Rewriting in OBDA.** The main approaches to query answering in OBDA are based on query rewriting techniques whose goal is to compute so-called perfect rewritings. A *perfect rewriting* for a UCQ $q$ and a TBox $\mathcal{T}$ is a query $q'$ such that, for every ABox $\mathcal{A}$, $\varPhi^q_{\langle \mathcal{T}, \mathcal{A} \rangle} = \varPhi^{q'}_{\langle \emptyset, \mathcal{A} \rangle}$ (i.e., the TBox is "encoded" by the rewritten query).

In OBDA, special attention has been paid in these systems to ontology languages that are *first-order (FO) rewritable* [9,10], i.e. such that UCQs always admit a perfect rewriting expressed in first-order logic. $\mathcal{ELHIO}$ falls out of this expressiveness, since recursive Datalog is sometimes needed to express perfect rewritings of UCQs, i.e., it is *Datalog-rewritable*.

**Related Systems.** Several systems have been implemented to perform query rewriting, these systems and their main characteristics including the expressiveness for the aforementioned $\Sigma$ are summarised in Table 1. A more detailed description of these systems and the logics they handle can be found in [6]. The interest in this kind of systems is shown by commercial applications like Stardog[2], which can perform query answering with several reasoning levels (RDFS, QL, RL, $\mathcal{EL}$ and DL).

**Table 1.** Main systems for OBDA query rewriting in the state of the art

| System | Input | Output | Year | Reference |
|---|---|---|---|---|
| Quonto | DL-Lite$_R$ | UCQ | 2007 | Calvanese et al. [9] |
| REQUIEM | $\mathcal{ELHIO}^{\neg}$ | Datalog or UCQ | 2009 | Pérez-Urbina et al. [7] |
| Presto | DL-Lite$_R$ | Datalog | 2010 | Rosati and Almatelli [11] |
| Rapid | DL-Lite$_R$[3] | Datalog or UCQ | 2011 | Chortaras et al. [12] |
| Nyaya | Datalog$^{\pm}$ | UCQ | 2011 | Gottlob et al. [10] |
| Venetis' | DL-Lite$_R$ | UCQ | 2013 | Venetis et al. [13] |
| Prexto | DL-Lite$_R$ and EBox | Datalog or UCQ | 2012 | Rosati [3] |
| Clipper | Horn-$\mathcal{SHIQ}$ | Datalog | 2012 | Eiter et al. [14] |
| kyrie | $\mathcal{ELHIO}^{\neg}$ | Datalog or UCQ | 2013 | Mora and Corcho [5] |

**EBoxes and Query Rewriting.** Description logic (DL) ontologies are usually decomposed into ABox (assertional box) and TBox (terminological box). The former includes the assertions or facts, corresponding to the individuals, constants or values (i.e. the extension) of some predicates. The latter is a set of DL axioms that describe the concepts and predicates in the ontology and how they are related. These DL axioms can be converted to rules or implications (or data dependencies) in first order logic (more expressive) and to some extent in Datalog (adding Skolem functions when needed).

*Extensional constraints*, also known as *ABox dependencies*, are assertions that restrict the syntactic form of allowed or admissible ABoxes in an OBDA system. These assertions have the form of the usual TBox axioms and are interpreted as integrity constraints over the ABox, i.e. under a closed-world assumption instead of the usual open-world assumption of DLs. For example, for an ABox $\mathcal{A}$ that satisfies some EBox $\mathcal{E}$ and expressions $C_1$, $C_2$ in $\mathcal{A}$; if $\mathcal{E} \vDash C_1 \sqsubseteq C_2$ then $\{x_1 \mid C_1(x_1) \in \mathcal{A}\} \subseteq \{x_2 \mid C_2(x_2) \in \mathcal{A}\}$. A set of such assertions is called an extensional constraint box (EBox) [4].

---

[2] http://docs.stardog.com/owl2/
[3] Close to OWL2 QL, $B_1 \sqsubseteq \exists R.B_2$ axioms are supported.

As shown in [3], extensional constraints can be used to simplify the perfect rewriting of a query, because such constraints may imply that some parts of the query are actually redundant. We can see this more easily with an example. For example we may have the following TBox:

$$UndergradStudent \sqsubseteq Student \qquad MasterStudent \sqsubseteq GradStudent$$
$$PhDStudent \sqsubseteq GradStudent \qquad IndustryMasterStudent \sqsubseteq MasterStudent$$
$$GradStudent \sqsubseteq Student \qquad ResearchMasterStudent \sqsubseteq MasterStudent$$
$$BachelorStudent \sqsubseteq UndergradStudent$$

And the following EBox:

$$IndustryMasterStudent \sqsubseteq GradStudent \qquad Student \sqsubseteq \bot$$
$$ResearchMasterStudent \sqsubseteq GradStudent \qquad BachelorStudent \sqsubseteq \bot$$
$$PhDStudent \sqsubseteq GradStudent \qquad MasterStudent \sqsubseteq \bot$$

And we may want to retrieve a list of all the students.

We can consider an ABox that satisfies the previous EBox, for example an ABox with the following individuals:

- $UndergradStudent$: Al
- $GradStudent$: Ben, Don, Ed
- $ResearchMasterStudent$: Ben
- $IndustryMasterStudent$: Cal
- $PhdStudent$: Don

Querying for the most general concept ($Student$) would yield no results. Querying for the most specific concepts ($BachelorStudent$, $ResearchMasterStudent$, $IndustryMasterStudent$ and $PhdStudent$) requires four queries and yields an incomplete answer, missing Ed and Al in the example. Finally querying for all concepts would provide all answers, but that implies eight queries (one for each concept) and retrieving some duplicates. In this case the duplicates are Ben and Don. Duplicated answers have no impact on the correctness of the answer set, but they are a big burden in the efficiency of the process when considering more complex queries and ontologies. In particular, in the example we only need three queries (as opposed to eight) to retrieve all answers, querying respectively for instances of $UndergradStudent$, $GradStudent$ and $IndustryMasterStudent$, since the EBox states that the ABox extension of every other concept is either empty or contained in $GradStudent$. There are therefore six queries that are only a waste of computational resources in the query answering.

A naïve algorithm could generate the perfect rewriting and then reduce it by checking for subsumption with the EBox. However, such a naïve algorithm could have a prohibitive cost for large rewritings and would only be applicable over non-recursive rewritings. In the following sections we will show that it is possible to face more complex scenarios and handle them better than with such a naïve algorithm.

This example illustrates that the combination of ABoxes that are already (partially) complete and a complete query rewriting on the TBox causes redundancy in the results, which is a burden for efficiency. Hence, the characterization of ABox completeness as a set of dependencies can serve to optimise TBoxes, and create ABox repositories that appear to be complete [2]. Additional optimisations can be done with the Datalog query before unfolding it into a UCQ, and finally with the UCQ, reducing redundancy at every step. For instance, in our example we have in the EBox that $PhDStudent \sqsubseteq GradStudent$ just like in the TBox. Therefore, we do not need to consider this axiom in the TBox when retrieving students: the ABox is complete in that sense and no *GradStudent* needs to be obtained from *PhDStudent*.

Using the EBox, the perfect rewriting can be reduced along with the inference required for its generation. We can redefine the perfect rewriting in the presence of EBoxes as follows [3]: a perfect rewriting for a UCQ $q$ and a TBox $\mathcal{T}$ under an EBox $\mathcal{E}$ is a query $q'$ such that, for every ABox $\mathcal{A}$ that satisfies $\mathcal{E}$, $\Phi^q_{\langle \mathcal{T}, \mathcal{A} \rangle} = \Phi^{q'}_{\langle \emptyset, \mathcal{A} \rangle}$.

## 3   Using Extensional Constraints in Query Rewriting

In this section we present the kyrie2 algorithm, providing an overview of the previous kyrie algorithm and detailing the use of extensional constraints. Extensional constraints can be used both in the preprocessing stage, performed before queries are posed to the system, and in the main algorithm for the rewriting of queries when they are available. We conclude this section with the algorithm that prunes a Datalog program (or a UCQ as a specific case of Datalog program) using the available extensional constraints.

**Overview of the Technique.**   kyrie2 extends the earlier kyrie algorithm [5] to handle EBoxes. The original kyrie algorithm obtains a set of clauses $\Sigma$ from the TBox $\mathcal{T}$ and a query $q$ and performs resolution on this set of clauses.

The usual operations performed in these algorithms are equal to those in kyrie. Here we briefly describe them, a more detailed description can be found in [5]:

- *Saturate* performs a saturation of a set of clauses using a selection function to guide the atoms that should be unified in the resolution. The selection function may be:
  - *sfRQR* is the selection function used in REQUIEM, it avoids the unification of unary predicates with no function symbols to produce a Datalog program.
  - *sfAux* selects auxiliary predicates to perform the inferences in which these predicates may participate and remove them if possible.
  - *sfSel(p)* selects the predicate p.
  - *sfNoRec(P)* selects all predicates except those that included in the set of predicates P (used to avoid infinite resolution on recursive predicates).

  Additionally, the saturation algorithm has a parameter (p, s or u):
  - *p* preserves the clauses that have been used in the resolution, contrarily other modes do not preserve these clauses, e.g. clauses with functional symbols are removed to obtain a Datalog program.
  - *s* separates the clauses that are obtained anew from the old ones, returning only those that are new, e.g. when saturating the query with the clauses derived from the TBox all produced clauses will be query clauses.
  - *u* for unfolding, this method does not skip the cleaning stage and does not separate the results.
- *Condensate* is used to condensate clauses, i.e. remove redundant atoms.
- *RemoveSubsumed* removes clauses that are subsumed in a set of clauses.

There are three main stages in which resolution is performed:

- *Preprocessing* is performed once for the $\mathcal{ELHIO}$ TBox ($\mathcal{T}$), before any query is posed to the system. In this stage some inferences are materialised to save time later and the set of clauses $\Sigma$ is generated according to the TBox.

- *Saturation* is performed when the query arrives: the query is added to $\Sigma$, then functional symbols are removed from $\Sigma$, reducing $\Sigma$ to a Datalog program (i.e., a function-free set of Horn clauses).
- *Unfolding* is performed partially or completely, depending on the respective presence or absence of recursive predicates in the Datalog rewriting.

In kyrie2, we add a further operation in each of these stages, highlighted in the corresponding algorithms. In this paper, we focus of this new and additional operation, referring the reader to [5] for details on the other aspects of the algorithm. The new operation makes use of the EBox to infer extensional subsumption between atoms and between clauses. Atom subsumption in a conjunction of atoms means that the values for one are a subset of the values for another (the most general atom is eliminated from the conjunction). Clause subsumption in a disjunction of clauses means that the values provided by a clause for a predicate are a subset of the values provided by some other clause (the most specific clause is eliminated from the disjunction). In other words, the new operation detects extensional redundancy in the set of clauses, thus allowing for reducing the size of the initial set of clauses, the subsequent Datalog program, and the final UCQ. Since, for technical reasons, the EBox is represented in two different ways in the algorithm (both as a set of standard DL axioms and as a set of clauses), this operation is defined and executed on both representations.

Before introducing the algorithms, we give two preliminary and analogous definitions of graphs relative to an $\mathcal{ELHIO}$ TBox and to a set of Horn clauses, respectively.

**Definition 1.** *We define* $dlgraph(\mathcal{T})$, *the* axiom graph *for an $\mathcal{ELHIO}$ TBox $\mathcal{T}$, as the directed graph $(V, W)$ such that: (i) for each axiom $\psi \in \mathcal{T}$, $\psi \in V$; and (ii) for each pair $(\psi_a, \psi_b)$ such that $\psi_a, \psi_b \in \mathcal{T}$ if there is a predicate $p$ such that $p \in RHS(\psi_b)$ and $p \in LHS(\psi_a)$ then $(\psi_a, \psi_b) \in W$. Where LHS and RHS are respectively the left and the right hand sides of the axiom.*

**Definition 2.** *We define* $cgraph(\Sigma)$, *the* clause graph *for a set of clauses $\Sigma$, as the directed graph $(V, W)$ such that: (i) for each clause $\gamma \in \Sigma$ then $\gamma \in V$; and (ii) for each pair $(\gamma_a, \gamma_b)$ such that $\gamma_a, \gamma_b \in \Sigma$ and $\exists p.p \in body(\gamma_b) \wedge p \in head(\gamma_a)$ then $(\gamma_a, \gamma_b) \in W$.*

Both graph notions are equivalent for our purposes, the syntactical differences are due to the stages in the algorithm where each of these notions will be used.

Our algorithms will use both the DL and the clause representation of TBoxes and EBoxes (obtained from the DL syntax through the function $\tau_c$). Therefore, from now on we will use the terms TBox, EBox and OBDA system for both kinds of representations, and will use the symbols $\Sigma$, $E$ and $\Gamma$ to denote, respectively, a TBox, an EBox, and an OBDA system in the Horn clause representation.

**Preprocessing.** Algorithm 1 constitutes a preprocessing stage on the TBox and the EBox before any query is available. The algorithm removes, through the function delEBoxSCC, the strongly connected components (SCCs) of the TBox graph that are implied by the EBox and do not receive incoming connections, i.e. for all axioms $\psi_b$ in the SCC there is no $\psi_a$ in the TBox such that $(\psi_a, \psi_b)$ is in the set of edges of

---

**Algorithm 1.** kyrie2 preprocess algorithm

---

**Input**: $\mathcal{ELHIO}$ TBox $\mathcal{T}$, $\mathcal{ELHIO}$ EBox $\mathcal{E}$
**Output**: TBox $\Sigma$, EBox $E$, minimal sets of recursive predicates $R_\Sigma$ and $R_E$
1 $T' = \texttt{delEBoxSCC}(\mathcal{T}, \mathcal{E})$
2 $\Sigma = \tau_c(T')$
3 $E = saturate(\texttt{p}, sfNonRec(R_E), \tau_c(\mathcal{E}), \emptyset)$
4 $\langle R_\Sigma, R_E \rangle = \texttt{reducedRecursiveSets}(\Sigma, E)$
5 $\Sigma = saturate(\texttt{p}, sfRQR, \Sigma, \emptyset)$
6 $\Sigma = saturate(\texttt{s}, sfAux, \Sigma, \emptyset)$
7 $\Sigma = removeSubsumed(condensate(\Sigma))$
8 **return** $\langle \Sigma, E, R_\Sigma, R_E \rangle$

---

**Algorithm 2.** Remove extensionally implied strongly connected components (SCCs) of axioms: $\texttt{delEBoxSCC}$

---

**Input**: $\mathcal{ELHIO}$ TBox $\mathcal{T}$, $\mathcal{ELHIO}$ EBox $\mathcal{E}$
**Output**: $\mathcal{ELHIO}$ TBox $\mathcal{T}$ without extensionally implied SCCs
1 **repeat**
2     **forall the** $(C : component) \in SCCs(dlgraph(\mathcal{T}))$ **do**
3         **if** $incomingConnections(C) = 0 \wedge \forall \psi \in C.\mathcal{E} \models \psi$ **then**
4             $\mathcal{T} = \mathcal{T} \backslash C$
5 **until** *Fixpoint*
6 **return** $\mathcal{T}$

---

$dlgraph(\mathcal{T})$. We formalise in Section 4 (Proposition 1) the principles on which we remove this type of SCCs.

Then, through the function *saturate* [5], Algorithm 1 computes a deductive closure of the EBox, except for recursive predicates: a reduced set of recursive predicates is excluded from the inference to make the saturation process finite. This reduced set is computed by Algorithm 4, where $count(p, \Lambda) = card(\{\lambda \in \Lambda \mid p \in \lambda\})$ and $LoopsIn(\Gamma)$ finds the loops of clauses in the given set of clauses that produce infinite property paths. Excluding some predicates from the inference limits the effect of the EBox in the reduction of the rewritten queries and the possible unfolding of these queries. This limited effect of the EBox means some redundant answers can be produced, which has obviously no effect on the correctness of the answers.

**General Algorithm.** The result of the preprocessing stage is then used by the general kyrie2 algorithm (Algorithm 3). This algorithm preserves the same stages and optimisations of kyrie to obtain the Datalog program and the unfolding. The main difference with kyrie is the call to the function $\texttt{useEBox}$ (Algorithm 5).

**Pruning the Rewriting with the EBox.** The $\texttt{useEBox}$ function, defined by Algorithm 5, uses the EBox to reduce a Datalog program. This can be done by removing clauses or by replacing some of the clauses with other shorter ones. This algorithm performs a set of stages iteratively to reduce the Datalog program considered, until a fixpoint is reached. These stages are:

- Predicates with no extension ($p \sqsubseteq \bot$ in the EBox) are removed, if possible, after saturating the inferences where they participate. A reduced set of recursive

**Algorithm 3.** General kyrie2 algorithm

**Input**: TBox $\Sigma$, EBox $E$, recursive predicates in $\Sigma$ ($R_\Sigma$), recursive predicates in $E$ ($R_E$), UCQ $q$, working mode $mode \in \{\texttt{Datalog}, \texttt{UCQ}\}$
**Output**: Rewritten query $q_\Sigma$

1  $q = removeSubsumed(condensate(q))$
2  $\Sigma_r = reachable(\Sigma, q)$
3  $\Sigma_q = saturate(\texttt{s}, sfRQR, q, \Sigma_r)$
4  $\Sigma_q = \texttt{useEBox}(\Sigma_q, E, R_\Sigma, R_E)$
5  **if** $mode = \texttt{Datalog}$ **then return** $\Sigma_q$  $\Sigma_q = \{q_i \in \Sigma_q \mid head(q_i) \neq head(q)\}$
6  $\Sigma_q = \{q_i \in \Sigma_q \mid head(q_i) = head(q)\}$
7  $\Sigma_q = saturate(\texttt{u}, sfNonRec(R_\Sigma), \Sigma_q, \Sigma_q)$
8  $\Sigma_q = \texttt{useEBox}(\Sigma_q, E, R_\Sigma, R_E)$
9  **return** $\Sigma_q$

---

**Algorithm 4.** Find reduced sets of recursive predicates: reducedRecursiveSet

**Input**: Datalog program $\Sigma_q$, EBox $E$
**Output**: Recursive predicates in $\Sigma_q$ ($R_{\Sigma_q}$), recursive predicates in $E$ ($R_E$)

1  $\Lambda_{\Sigma_q} = \texttt{loopsIn}(\Sigma_q)$
2  $\Lambda_E = \texttt{loopsIn}(E)$
3  $R_{\Sigma_q} = \emptyset$
4  $R_E = \emptyset$
5  **while** $\Lambda_{\Sigma_q} \neq \emptyset \wedge \Lambda_E \neq \emptyset$ **do**
6  $\quad$ **if** $\Lambda_{\Sigma_q} \cap \Lambda_E \neq \emptyset$ **then**
7  $\quad\quad$ $p = p_i \in \Lambda_{\Sigma_q} \cap \Lambda_E / count(p_i, \Lambda_{\Sigma_q}) + count(p_i, \Lambda_E) = max(count(p_j, \Lambda_{\Sigma_q}) + count(p_j, \Lambda_E)) \forall p_j \in \Lambda_{\Sigma_q} \cap \Lambda_E$
8  $\quad\quad$ $R_{\Sigma_q} = R_{\Sigma_q} \cup \{p\}$
9  $\quad\quad$ $R_E = R_E \cup \{p\}$
10 $\quad\quad$ $\Lambda_{\Sigma_q} = \Lambda_{\Sigma_q} \backslash \{\lambda \in \Lambda_{\Sigma_q} \mid p \in \lambda\}$
11 $\quad\quad$ $\Lambda_E = \Lambda_E \backslash \{\lambda \in \Lambda_E \mid p \in \lambda\}$
12 $\quad$ **else**
13 $\quad\quad$ **if** $\Lambda_{\Sigma_q} \neq \emptyset$ **then**
14 $\quad\quad\quad$ $p = p_i \in \Lambda_{\Sigma_q} / count(p_i, \Lambda_{\Sigma_q}) = max(count(p_j, \Lambda_{\Sigma_q})) \forall p_j \in \Lambda_{\Sigma_q}$
15 $\quad\quad\quad$ $R_{\Sigma_q} = R_{\Sigma_q} \cup \{p\}$
16 $\quad\quad\quad$ $\Lambda_{\Sigma_q} = \Lambda_{\Sigma_q} \backslash \{\lambda \in \Lambda_{\Sigma_q} \mid p \in \lambda\}$
17 $\quad\quad$ **if** $\Lambda_E \neq \emptyset$ **then**
18 $\quad\quad\quad$ $p = p_i \in \Lambda_E / count(p_i, \Lambda_E) = max(count(p_j, \Lambda_E)) \forall p_j \in \Lambda_E$
19 $\quad\quad\quad$ $R_E = R_E \cup \{p\}$
20 $\quad\quad\quad$ $\Lambda_E = \Lambda_E \backslash \{\lambda \in \Lambda_E \mid p \in \lambda\}$
21 **return** $\langle R_{\Sigma_q}, R_E \rangle$

---

predicates (selected according to Algorithm 4) needs to be kept. We formalise the conditions for removal in Proposition 4.

- Clauses whose answers are subsumed by other clauses are removed. The subsumption of the answers according to the algorithm is formalised in Proposition 5 and therefore they are redundant, as Proposition 6 states.

**Algorithm 5.** Prune Datalog program $\Sigma_q$: useEBox

> **Input**: EBox $E$, TBox $\Sigma_q$, recursive predicates in $E$ ($R_E$), recursive predicates in $\Sigma_q$ ($R_{\Sigma_q}$)
> **Output**: Pruned TBox program $\Sigma_q$

1 **repeat**
2 $\quad P_e = \{p_i \mid p_i \in predicates(\Sigma_q) \wedge (p_i \sqsubseteq \bot) \in E \wedge p_i \notin R_{\Sigma_q}\}$
3 $\quad \Sigma_q = saturate(\mathtt{u}, \mathtt{sfSel}(P_e), \Sigma_q, \emptyset)$
4 $\quad E_e = \{\gamma_i \in E \mid \forall p \in \gamma_i.\forall \gamma_j \in \Sigma_q.p \notin head(\gamma_j)\}$
5 $\quad E_{\Sigma_q} = \emptyset$
6 $\quad$ **forall the** *clauses* $\gamma_1 \in \Sigma_q \cup E_{\Sigma_q}$ **do**
7 $\quad\quad$ **forall the** *clauses* $\gamma_2 \in E_e$ **do**
8 $\quad\quad\quad \Gamma = \mathtt{resolve}(\gamma_1, \gamma_2, \mathtt{sfNoRec}(R_E))$
9 $\quad\quad\quad$ **forall the** $\gamma_i \in \Gamma, \gamma_i \neq \gamma_1$ **do**
10 $\quad\quad\quad\quad$ **forall the** $\gamma_j \in \Sigma_q$ **do**
11 $\quad\quad\quad\quad\quad$ **if** $subsumes(\gamma_i, \gamma_j)$ **then**
12 $\quad\quad\quad\quad\quad\quad \Sigma_q = \Sigma_q \backslash \{\gamma_j\}$
13 $\quad\quad\quad\quad\quad\quad$ **if** $\neg subsumes(\gamma_j, \gamma_i)$ **then**
14 $\quad\quad\quad\quad\quad\quad\quad \Sigma_q = \Sigma_q \cup \{\gamma_i\}$
15 $\quad\quad\quad E_{\Sigma_q} = E_{\Sigma_q} \cup \Gamma$
16 $\quad$ **forall the** $C \in stronglyConnectedComponents(cgraph(\Sigma_q))$ **do**
17 $\quad\quad$ **if** $(incomingConnections(C) = 0 \wedge \forall \gamma \in C.\gamma \in E_e$ **then**
18 $\quad\quad\quad \Sigma_q = \Sigma_q \backslash C$
19 $\quad \Sigma_q = reachable(\Sigma_q)$
20 **until** *Fixpoint*
21 **return** $\Sigma_q$

- Clauses where an atom subsumes another atom are condensed. We use resolution to find the condensed version of the clause, which subsumes the original clause. Due to propositions 2 and 7 we know that we can keep any of both clauses. We keep the condensed version, the subsuming clause, since this clause will more likely subsume some other clauses.
- SCCs that are implied by the EBox and receive no connections are removed. This is done again according to Proposition 3.

## 4 Formalisation

In this section we provide a formalisation for the operations of our algorithms. In particular, we formalise the optimisations of the original kyrie algorithm presented in Section 3. For an easier explanation we introduce two definitions: the contributions of a clause ($\varphi_\Gamma(\gamma)$) and the values for a predicate ($\upsilon_\Gamma(p)$). We recall we denote $\gamma_a$ subsumes $\gamma_b$ with $\gamma_a \succeq_s \gamma_b$.

**Definition 3.** $\varphi_\Gamma(\gamma)$ *Contributions of a clause* $\gamma$ *in a OBDA system* $\Gamma = \langle \Sigma, \mathcal{A} \rangle$. *Let $p$ be the predicate in the head of $\gamma$, we define the contributions of $\gamma$ on $\Gamma$ as the set $\varphi_\Gamma(\gamma) = \{t_1, \ldots, t_n \mid \exists \mu.(\Gamma \models \mu \ body(\gamma)) \wedge (\mu \ head(\gamma) = p(t_1, \ldots, t_n))\}$ where $\mu$ is a substitution of the variables in $\gamma$ with the constants $t_1, \ldots, t_n$. Please note that*

$\Gamma \models \mu \, body(\gamma)$ *means that* $\Sigma \cup \mathcal{A} \models \mu \, body(\gamma)$, *i.e. the values for the contribution may be implied by other clauses in* $\Sigma$.

**Definition 4.** $v_\Gamma(p)$ ***Values for a predicate*** $p$ ***on*** $\Gamma$. *For a given OBDA system* $\langle \Sigma, \mathcal{A} \rangle = \Gamma$, *we define as the values for a predicate* $p \in \Gamma$ *the set* $v_\Gamma(p) = \{t_1, \ldots, t_n \mid \Gamma \models p(t_1, \ldots, t_n)\}$.

*Moreover, the values for a predicate* $p$ *on* $\Gamma$, $v_\Gamma(p)$ *are divided into the extensional values* $(v_\Gamma^e(p))$ *and the intensional values* $(v_\Gamma^i(p))$, *so that* $v_\Gamma(p) = v_\Gamma^e(p) \cup v_\Gamma^i(p)$ *where* $v_\Gamma^e(p) = \{t_1, \ldots, t_n \mid \mathcal{A} \models p(t_1, \ldots, t_n)\}$ *and* $v_\Gamma^i(p) = \{t_1, \ldots, t_n \mid \exists \gamma, \mu . \gamma \in \Gamma \wedge \mu \, head(\gamma) = p(t_1, \ldots, t_n) \wedge t_1, \ldots, t_n \in \varphi_\Gamma(\gamma)\}$ *where* $\mu$ *is the most general unifier (MGU) applied to* $head(\gamma)$, *from the variables in* $\gamma$ *to the constants in* $t_1, \ldots, t_n$.

Informally, the intensional values for a predicate $p$ are the contributions of the clauses where $p$ is in the head, while the contributions of a clause are a projection and selection of the values for the predicates in its body.

For instance, consider the example in Section 2 and more specifically two of the clauses that can be extracted from its axioms:

$\gamma_1$: GradStudent(x) :- MasterStudent(x) and

$\gamma_2$: GradStudent(x) :- PhDStudent(x)

We keep the ABox as in the example in Section 2. In this example, the extensional values for GradStudent on our system $\Gamma$ ($v_\Gamma^e(GradStudent)$) are Ben, Don and Ed. The intensional values for GradStudent on our system $\Gamma$ ($v_\Gamma^i(GradStudent)$) are Ben, Cal and Ed. The values for the predicate $p$ are therefore the union of both sets: Ben, Cal, Don and Ed. The contributions from clause $\gamma_1$ ($\varphi_\Gamma(\gamma_1)$) are Ben and Cal. The contributions from clause $\gamma_2$ ($\varphi_\Gamma(\gamma_2)$) are just Don.

**Proposition 1.** *Let* $\mathcal{A}$ *be an ABox,* $\Sigma$ *and* $\Sigma'$ *be two sets of Datalog clauses such that* $\Sigma' = \Sigma \cup \{\gamma_r\}$ *with* $p_r$ *as the predicate in the head of* $\gamma_r$. *For the two corresponding OBDA systems* $\Gamma \equiv \langle \Sigma, \mathcal{A} \rangle$ *and* $\Gamma' \equiv \langle \Sigma', \mathcal{A} \rangle$ *if* $\varphi_{\Gamma'}(\gamma_r) \subseteq v_\Gamma(p_r)$ *then* $v_\Gamma(p) = v_{\Gamma'}(p)$ *for every predicate* $p$ *in* $\Sigma$.

**Proposition 2.** *Let* $\Gamma = \langle \Sigma, \mathcal{A} \rangle$ *be a OBDA system and let* $\gamma_a, \gamma_b$ *be two clauses in* $\Sigma$ *such that* $\gamma_a \succeq_s \gamma_b$. *Then,* $\varphi_\Gamma(\gamma_b) \subseteq \varphi_\Gamma(\gamma_a)$. *For* $\Gamma' = \Gamma \setminus \{\gamma_b\}$ *holds that* $\Phi_\Gamma^q = \Phi_{\Gamma'}^q$.

We also know that clauses $\gamma_r$ in the previous context such that $\varphi_{\Gamma \cup \{\gamma_r\}}(\gamma_r) \subseteq v_{\Gamma \setminus \{\gamma_r\}}(p_r)$ can be added or removed safely from the OBDA system $\Gamma$

**Proposition 3.** *Let* $\Gamma = \langle \Sigma, \mathcal{A} \rangle$ *be an OBDA system, let* $E$ *be an EBox satisfied by* $\mathcal{A}$ *and* $cgraph(\Sigma) = \{V_\Sigma, W_\Sigma\}$. *Let* $C$ *be a set of clauses in* $\Sigma$ *such that* $cgraph(C)$ *is a SCC in* $cgraph(\Sigma)$ *that receives no connections from other SCCs* $(\forall (\gamma_a, \gamma_b) \in W . \gamma_b \in cgraph(C) \to \gamma_a \in cgraph(C))$, *and* $\forall \gamma \in V . E \models \gamma$. *Then,* $\Phi_{\langle \Sigma, \mathcal{A} \rangle}^q = \Phi_{\langle \Sigma \setminus C, \mathcal{A} \rangle}^q$.

The removal of SCCs for $dlgraph(\mathcal{T})$ is analogous to the previously described removal of SCCs for $cgraph(\Sigma)$.

**Proposition 4.** *Let* $\Gamma = \langle \Sigma, \mathcal{A} \rangle$ *be an OBDA system where* $\Sigma$ *is a set of Datalog clauses, let* $q$ *be a query, let* $\Gamma_q = q \cup \Gamma$ *be a Datalog program and let* $P$ *be a set of non-recursive predicates in* $\Gamma_q$ *that have no extensional values, i.e.* $\forall p \in P . v_{\Gamma_q}^e(p) = \emptyset$

and no $p \in P$ is the query predicate. Let $\Gamma_b$ be the set of clauses in $\Gamma_q$ such that $\forall \gamma \in \Gamma_q.\exists p \in P.p \in body(\gamma)$ and let $\Gamma_h$ be the set of clauses in $\Gamma_q$ such that $\forall \gamma \in \Gamma_q.\exists p \in P.p \in head(\gamma)$. Let $\Gamma_r$ be the set of clauses that do not contain $p$ and are generated through resolution from $\Gamma_b$ and $\Gamma_h$ with a selection function that selects the predicates $p \in P$. Let $\Gamma_s$ be the set of clauses $\{\gamma \in \Gamma_q \cup \Gamma_r \mid \gamma \notin \Gamma_h \cup \Gamma_b\}$. Then, $\Phi_\Gamma^q = \Phi_{\Gamma_q \cup \Gamma_r}^q = \Phi_{\Gamma_s}^q$.

**Proposition 5.** *Let* $\Gamma = \langle \Sigma, \mathcal{A} \rangle$ *be an OBDA system, let* $E$ *be an EBox such that* $\mathcal{A}$ *satisfies* $E$ *and let* $E_e$ *the part of the EBox* $E$ *that contains only predicates with no intensional definition in* $\Sigma$. *For every pair* $\gamma, \gamma_r$ *such that* $\gamma \in \Sigma$ *and* $E_e \cup \gamma \vdash \gamma_r$ *then* $\varphi_\Gamma(\gamma_r) \subseteq \varphi_\Gamma(\gamma)$.

**Proposition 6.** *Let* $\Gamma = \langle \Sigma, \mathcal{A} \rangle$, $E$ *and* $E_e$ *be defined as in Proposition 5. Then, for every pair* $\gamma, \gamma_r$ *such that* $\gamma \in \Sigma$ *and* $E_e \cup \gamma \vdash \gamma_r$, *and for every query* $q$, $\Phi_\Gamma^q = \Phi_{\Gamma'}^q$, *where* $\Gamma' = \Gamma \backslash \{\gamma_r\}$.

**Proposition 7.** *Let* $\Gamma = \langle \Sigma, \mathcal{A} \rangle$, $E$ *and* $E_e$ *be defined as in Proposition 5. Then, for every triple* $\gamma, \gamma_r, \gamma_s$ *such that* $(\gamma, \gamma_s \in \Sigma) \wedge (E_e \cup \gamma \vdash \gamma_r) \wedge (\gamma_r \succeq_s \gamma_s)$, *and for every query* $q$, $\Phi_\Gamma^q = \Phi_{\Gamma'}^q$, *where* $\Gamma' = (\{\gamma_r\} \cup \Gamma) \backslash \{\gamma_s\}$.

# 5 Evaluation

Having formalised the proposal, we have performed an empirical evaluation to check our query rewriting optimisations. There is no benchmark in the state of the art to test query rewriting with EBoxes, therefore we have decided to use some of the most widely used ontologies for the evaluation of query rewriting systems [6], in particular we used: Several real world ontologies used in independent projects like Adolena (A), Vicodi (V) and StockExchange (S). Benchmark ontologies, like a DL-Lite$_R$ version of LUBM (U). Artificial ontologies to test the impact of property paths, path1 and path5 (P1, P5). Previous ontologies with auxiliary predicates for DL-Lite compliance [9] (UX, P5X). Additionally, we consider the extension of previous ontologies with axioms in $\mathcal{ELHIO}$ and beyond DL-Lite (UXE, P5XE).

We have have expanded previous assets with a set of synthetically-generated EBoxes, using a randomized and parametrised algorithm, with parameters:

**size:** the size of the EBox relative to the size of the TBox: zero is an empty EBox, and one is an EBox with as many axioms as the TBox.

**cover:** how much of the TBox is covered by the EBox: zero means that all the axioms in the EBox will be randomly generated, one means that all the axioms in the EBox will come from the TBox.

**reverse:** how many of the axioms obtained from the TBox (cover) are reversed in the EBox (the reverse of $A \sqsubseteq B$ being $B \sqsubseteq A$) wrt the original form in the TBox: zero means that no axioms are reversed, one means that all the axioms are reversed. The reversed axioms belong to the cover, i.e. if the cover is zero this number has no effect.

**Table 2.** Results for ontology V (original size 222 clauses) with EBoxes I, II, III and IV

| Query independent information | | | | query | Datalog time(ms) | | | | Datalog size | | | | UCQ time(ms) | | | | UCQ size | | | |
|---|---|---|---|---|---|---|---|---|---|---|---|---|---|---|---|---|---|---|---|---|
| EBox | I | II | III | IV | | I | II | III | IV | I | II | III | IV | I | II | III | IV | I | II | III | IV |
| PT | 109 | 2047 | 24266 | 2859 | 1 | 0 | 0 | 157 | 235 | 15 | 13 | 14 | 9 | 0 | 0 | 516 | 672 | 15 | 13 | 14 | 9 |
| PS | 222 | 195 | 171 | 111 | 2 | 16 | 16 | 157 | 234 | 10 | 10 | 10 | 10 | 16 | 16 | 500 | 656 | 10 | 10 | 10 | 10 |
| size | 0.0 | 0.2 | 0.8 | 0.8 | 3 | 0 | 0 | 125 | 235 | 35 | 30 | 28 | 15 | 31 | 15 | 485 | 813 | 72 | 57 | 54 | 15 |
| cover | 0.0 | 0.8 | 0.2 | 0.8 | 4 | 0 | 16 | 219 | 188 | 41 | 38 | 22 | 16 | 63 | 94 | 735 | 719 | 185 | 170 | 3 | 42 |
| rev | 0.0 | 0.0 | 0.0 | 0.0 | 5 | 16 | 16 | 172 | 250 | 8 | 5 | 7 | 1 | 32 | 31 | 609 | 719 | 30 | 9 | 15 | 1 |
| PT: preprocess time (ms) | | | | 6 | 0 | 15 | 234 | 188 | 18 | 14 | 14 | 11 | 0 | 15 | 578 | 641 | 18 | 14 | 14 | 11 |
| PS: preprocessed size | | | | 7 | 0 | 0 | 125 | 172 | 27 | 23 | 23 | 20 | 94 | 125 | 1359 | 1359 | 180 | 140 | 140 | 110 |

All these parameters can be any real number between zero and one, except for size, which can be greater than one (e.g. a size of two means the EBox is twice the size of the TBox). Of course, the latter parameters are only significant when previous ones are greater than zero. If the cover is less than one then axioms up to one are generated by selecting randomly the LHS or RHS of other rules, adding an axiom $A_1 \sqsubseteq A_2$ for each pair $A_1, A_2$ found this way. For the $A_i$ that are classes, nothing else is done. If some of them is a property $P$ then the axiom $\exists P$ is added and with a probability of $1/2$ some other LHS or RHS $A_3$ of some other rule is selected. If $A_3$ is selected then $\exists P$ is expanded into $\exists P.A_3$. This is repeated recursively until (1) a class is selected or (2) a property is selected and not expanded (expansion probability: $1/2$).

The "size" is the main parameter. It is meant to help to evaluate the impact of the EBox on the results. The "cover" specifies how much of the EBox is related to the TBox and how much is random. It is meant to help to evaluate how the relation between EBox and TBox impacts on the results. The "reverse" specifies how many of the EBox axioms that are obtained from the TBox remain unaltered and how many are reversed. If the axiom is unaltered then the subconcepts are redundant, otherwise the superconcept is redundant. This parameter helps to evaluate the impact of redundancy in these cases.

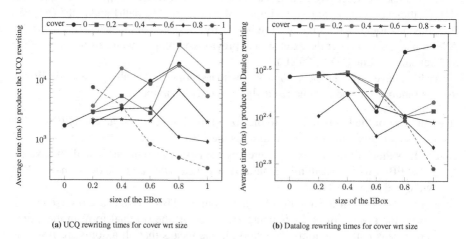

(a) UCQ rewriting times for cover wrt size                    (b) Datalog rewriting times for cover wrt size

**Fig. 1.** Average rewriting times relating size and cover. All queries and ontologies considered. "Reverse" is zero in all cases.

We have run the tests with a set of EBoxes, selecting the values 0.0, 0.2, 0.4, 0.6, 0.8 and 1.0 for each of the parameters described above. When the size is zero all the other parameters are zero, and when cover is zero reverse is zero as well. This involves a total of $1 + 5 * (1 + 5 * 6) = 156$ EBoxes, for each ontology, used for all queries. Due to space limitations, we present a small excerpt of the results for a single ontology in Table 2: the full results for all the ontologies and the EBoxes can be found online[4].

The results have been obtained on cold runs, by restarting the application after every query (passed in the application invocation parameters). The consistency of the results regardless of how the system is run has been ensured by measuring the query rewriting time and discarding operations done before and after it. The hardware used in the evaluation is a Intel®Core™2 6300 @1.86GHz with 2GB of RAM, Windows® XP and Java™version 1.6.0_33, with default settings for the Java Virtual Machine.

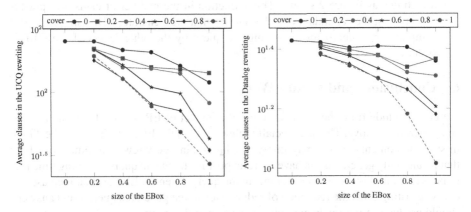

(a) number of clauses in the UCQ rewriting for cover wrt size    (b) number of clauses in the Datalog rewriting for cover wrt size

**Fig. 2.** Average rewriting sizes relating size and cover. All queries and ontologies considered. "Reverse" is zero in all cases.

With the evaluation results we can observe that:

- In the computation of Datalog rewritings, *using the EBox allows for obtaining equal or smaller Datalog programs for all queries, with negligible effects on the query rewriting time.*
- For UCQ rewritings, our results show that, in general, *the number of clauses is reduced as the EBox increases in size and similarity ("cover") with the TBox.* This reduction in the number of clauses usually implies a reduction in the time required for the query rewriting process, as we can see in Figure 1. This figure shows the average time to produce a UCQ or a Datalog rewriting and how EBoxes with different sizes and TBox coverage influence this time. More precisely:
  - We can notice that EBoxes with both a high value for cover and size tend to reduce the query rewriting time when compared with other EBoxes or no EBox.

---

[4] http://purl.org/net/jmora/extensionalqueryrewriting

○ When the EBox involves more random axioms (e.g. EBox III in Table 2 with 0.8 for "size" and 0.2 for "cover") the results are less predictable. More specifically, we can see that for UCQ size the EBox III behaves better than EBox IV in query 4 and it behaves worse than EBox II in query 5. This variation depends on the query, the EBox may contain axioms that imply the subsumption of atoms in the query. If these axioms are in the TBox, their presence in the EBox has no impact in the results (EBox IV). However, if these axioms are not in the TBox, this can lead to further clause condensation, with the elimination of subsumed clauses and the ones generated from these. This elimination of clauses means a potentially strong reduction in the size of the results and the time required to produce them.

• Even *in the cases where the query rewriting times are higher*, we can see *an important reduction in the number of clauses generated*, in the Datalog and UCQ rewritings, as Figure 2 shows. This reduction in the number of clauses implies a reduction in the redundancy of the queries that are generated. This simplifies the computation required for answering the query by the other layers of the OBDA system.

# 6    Conclusions and Future Work

We can conclude from the evaluation that the impact of EBoxes is clearly noticeable and generally positive. This is especially relevant when the EBox is similar to the TBox in size and contents, which may imply a reduction in query rewriting time. An EBox that is randomly generated can have a strong positive impact in query rewriting time if it implies subsumption between the atoms in the query. Even for EBoxes that increase the query rewriting time, the reduction of redundancy in the generated queries and answers should produce an improvement in the execution of these queries.

Among the possibilities for future work we consider the extension to Datalog± [15]. The Datalog± family of languages provides interesting opportunities to explore the expressiveness that can be achieved while dealing with recursion [16].

Another line to explore in the future is considering only the part of the EBox that is similar to the TBox, which is guaranteed to have a positive impact. For example, the axioms or clauses in the EBox that are not related with the TBox could be discarded during the preprocessing. By doing this, the results would be more predictable and the impact of a large EBox not related with a TBox would be the same as for a small EBox that is very related to the TBox.

We also consider exploring whether it is possible to extend the input and output query language to SPARQL. The expressiveness of SPARQL 1.1 allows for a limited recursion, e.g., property paths. The possibility of using subqueries is also interesting to limit the combinatorial explosion implied by the unfolding.

Finally, we plan to experiment our technique on some real-world use cases [17], which would provide information about the relation between the TBox and the corresponding ABox and EBox. This would allow further optimisations that would address specific characteristics of the EBoxes that are more usual in the use cases. With populated ABoxes, obtaining the answers to the queries would allow a better quantification and evaluation of the impact in the whole query answering process.

**Acknowledgements.** The work presented in this paper has been funded by a PIF grant (Personal Investigador en Formación) from UPM (RR01/2008) and by the EU FP7 project Optique – Scalable End-user Access to Big Data (grant n. FP7-318338).

# References

1. Poggi, A., Lembo, D., Calvanese, D., De Giacomo, G., Lenzerini, M., Rosati, R.: Linking data to ontologies. In: Spaccapietra, S. (ed.) Journal on Data Semantics X. LNCS, vol. 4900, pp. 133–173. Springer, Heidelberg (2008)
2. Rodríguez-Muro, M., Calvanese, D.: Dependencies: Making ontology based data access work in practice. In: Alberto Mendelzon Workshop on Foundations of Data Management (2011)
3. Rosati, R.: Prexto: Query rewriting under extensional constraints in DL – *lite*. In: Simperl, E., Cimiano, P., Polleres, A., Corcho, O., Presutti, V. (eds.) ESWC 2012. LNCS, vol. 7295, pp. 360–374. Springer, Heidelberg (2012)
4. Console, M., Lenzerini, M., Mancini, R., Rosati, R., Ruzzi, M.: Synthesizing extensional constraints in ontology-based data access. In: Description Logics, pp. 628–639 (2013)
5. Mora, J., Corcho, O.: Engineering optimisations in query rewriting for OBDA. In: I-SEMANTICS 2013, Austria, pp. 41–48. ACM (2013)
6. Mora, J., Corcho, O.: Towards a systematic benchmarking of ontology-based query rewriting systems. In: Alani, H., et al. (eds.) ISWC 2013, Part II. LNCS, vol. 8219, pp. 376–391. Springer, Heidelberg (2013)
7. Pérez-Urbina, H., Motik, B., Horrocks, I.: Tractable query answering and rewriting under description logic constraints. Journal of Applied Logic, 186–209 (2010)
8. Calvanese, D., Lembo, D., Lenzerini, M., Poggi, A., Rosati, R.: Ontology-based database access. Technical report, CiteSeerX (2007)
9. Calvanese, D., De Giacomo, G., Lembo, D., Lenzerini, M., Rosati, R.: Tractable reasoning and efficient query answering in description logics: The DL-Lite family. Journal of Automated Reasoning 39(3), 385–429 (2007)
10. Gottlob, G., Orsi, G., Pieris, A.: Ontological queries: Rewriting and optimization (extended version). arXiv:1112.0343 (December 2011)
11. Rosati, R., Almatelli, A.: Improving query answering over DL-Lite ontologies. In: Principles of Knowledge Representation and Reasoning. AAAI Press (2010)
12. Chortaras, A., Trivela, D., Stamou, G.: Optimized query rewriting for OWL 2 QL. In: Bjørner, N., Sofronie-Stokkermans, V. (eds.) CADE 2011. LNCS, vol. 6803, pp. 192–206. Springer, Heidelberg (2011)
13. Venetis, T., Stoilos, G., Stamou, G.: Query extensions and incremental query rewriting for OWL 2 QL ontologies. Journal on Data Semantics (2013)
14. Eiter, T., Ortiz, M., Simkus, M., Tran, T.K., Xiao, G.: Query rewriting for Horn-SHIQ plus rules. In: 26th AAAI Conference on Artificial Intelligence (2012)
15. Calì, A., Gottlob, G., Lukasiewicz, T.: A general datalog-based framework for tractable query answering over ontologies. Journal of Web Semantics (2012)
16. Cadoli, M., Palopoli, L., Lenzerini, M.: Datalog and description logics: Expressive power. In: Cluet, S., Hull, R. (eds.) DBPL 1997. LNCS, vol. 1369, pp. 281–298. Springer, Heidelberg (1998)
17. Priyatna, F., Corcho, O., Sequeda, J.F.: Formalisation and experiences of R2RML-based SPARQL to SQL query translation using Morph. In: International World Wide Web Conference, International World Wide Web Conferences Steering Committee (2014)

# Schema-Agnostic Query Rewriting in SPARQL 1.1

Stefan Bischof[1], Markus Krötzsch[2], Axel Polleres[3], and Sebastian Rudolph[2]

[1] Vienna University of Technology, Austria and Siemens AG Österreich, Austria
[2] Technische Universität Dresden, Germany
[3] Vienna University of Economics and Business, Austria

**Abstract.** SPARQL 1.1 supports the use of ontologies to enrich query results with logical entailments, and OWL 2 provides a dedicated fragment OWL QL for this purpose. Typical implementations use the OWL QL schema to rewrite a conjunctive query into an equivalent set of queries, to be answered against the non-schema part of the data. With the adoption of the recent SPARQL 1.1 standard, however, RDF databases are capable of answering much more expressive queries directly, and we ask how this can be exploited in query rewriting. We find that SPARQL 1.1 is powerful enough to "implement" a full-fledged OWL QL reasoner in a single query. Using additional SPARQL 1.1 features, we develop a new method of schema-agnostic query rewriting, where arbitrary conjunctive queries over OWL QL are rewritten into equivalent SPARQL 1.1 queries in a way that is fully independent of the actual schema. This allows us to query RDF data under OWL QL entailment without extracting or preprocessing OWL axioms.

## 1 Introduction

SPARQL 1.1, the recent revision of the W3C SPARQL standard, introduces significant extensions to the capabilities of the popular RDF query language [10]. Even at the very core of the query language, we can find many notable new features, including *property paths*, *value creation* (BIND), inline data (VALUES), negation, and extended filtering capabilities. In addition, SPARQL 1.1 now supports query answering over OWL ontologies, taking full advantage of ontological information in the data [8].

Query answering in the presence of ontologies is known as *ontology-based data access* (OBDA), and has long been an important topic in applied and foundational research. Even before SPARQL provided support for this feature, several projects have used ontologies to integrate disparate data sources or to provide views over legacy databases, e.g. [5,15,16,6,11]. The W3C OWL 2 Web Ontology Language includes the OWL QL language profile, which was specifically designed for this application [12]. With the arrival of SPARQL 1.1, every aspect of OBDA is thus supported by tailor-made W3C technologies.

In practice, however, SPARQL and OWL QL are rarely integrated. Most works on OBDA address the problem of answering *conjunctive queries* (CQs), which correspond to SELECT-PROJECT-JOIN queries in SQL, and (to some degree) to Basic Graph Patterns in SPARQL. The most common approach for OBDA is *query rewriting*, where a given CQ is rewritten into a (set of) CQs that fully incorporate the schema information of the ontology. The answers to the rewritten queries (obtained without considering the

P. Mika et al. (Eds.) ISWC 2014, Part I, LNCS 8796, pp. 584–600, 2014.

ontology) are guaranteed to agree with the answers of the original queries (over the ontology). This approach separates the ontology (used for query rewriting) from the rest of the data (used for query answering), and it is typical that the latter is stored in a relational database. Correspondingly, the rewritten queries are often transformed into SQL for query answering. SPARQL and RDF do not play a role in this.

In this paper, we thus take a fresh look on the problem of OBDA query rewriting with SPARQL 1.1 as our target query language. The additional expressive power of SPARQL 1.1 allows us to introduce a new paradigm of *schema-agnostic query rewriting*, where the ontological schema is not needed for rewriting queries. Rather, the ontology is stored *together with the data* in a single RDF database. This is how many ontologies are managed today, and it corresponds to the W3C view on OWL and RDF, which does not distinguish schema and data components. The fact that today's OBDA approaches separate both parts testifies to their focus on relational databases. Our work, somewhat ironically, widens the scope of OWL QL to RDF-based applications, which have hitherto focused on OWL RL as their ontology language of choice.

Another practical advantage of schema-agnostic query rewriting is that it supports frequent updates of both data and schema. The rewriting system does not need any information on the content of the database under query, while the SPARQL processor that executes the query does not need any support for OWL. This is particularly interesting if a database can only be accessed through a restricted SPARQL query interface that does not support reasoning. For example, we have used our approach to check the consistency of DBpedia under OWL semantics, using only the public Live DBpedia SPARQL endpoint[1] (it is inconsistent: every library is inferred to belong to the mutually disjoint classes "Place" and "Agent").

Our main contributions are as follows:

- We express the standard reasoning tasks for OWL QL, including consistency checking, classification, and instance retrieval, in *single, fixed* SPARQL 1.1 queries that are independent of the ontology. For this, we use SPARQL 1.1 property paths, which support a simple form of recursion that is powerful enough for OWL QL reasoning.
- We show how to rewrite arbitrary SPARQL Basic Graph Patterns (BGPs) into single SPARQL 1.1 queries of polynomial size. This task is simplified by the fact that SPARQL does not support "non-distinguished" variables as used in general CQs.
- We present a schema-agnostic rewriting of general CQs in SPARQL 1.1, again into single queries of polynomial size. This rewriting is more involved, and we use two additional features: inline data (VALUES) and (in)equality checks in filters.
- We show the limits of schema-agnostic rewriting in SPARQL 1.1 by proving that many other OWL features cannot be supported in this way. This includes even the most basic features OWL EL and OWL RL, and mild extensions of OWL QL.

Worst-case reasoning complexity remains the same in all cases, yet our approach is much more practical in the case of standard reasoning and BGP rewriting. For general CQs, the rewritten queries are usually too complex for today's RDF databases to handle. Nevertheless, we think that our "SPARQL 1.1 implementation" of OWL QL query answering is a valuable contribution, since it reduces the problem of supporting OWL QL

---

[1] http://live.dbpedia.org/sparql

in an RDF database to the task of optimizing a single (type of) query. Since OWL QL subsumes RDFS, one can also apply our insights to implement query answering under RDFS ontologies, which again leads to much simpler queries.

In Section 2, we start by giving a compact introduction to the parts of SPARQL 1.1 that we require. Thereafter, in Section 3, we introduce OWL QL and relate its semantics to a *chase* procedure. In Section 4, we develop queries for implementing basic QL reasoning in SPARQL 1.1, and in Section 5, we extend this into a schema-agnostic query rewriting procedure for conjunctive queries. Finally, we investigate the limits of schema-agnostic query rewriting, and present several negative results in Section 6. We close with a short discussion and outlook in Section 7. Omitted proofs can be found in the accompanying technical report [3].

## 2   Preliminaries: RDF and SPARQL 1.1

We consider RDF documents based on the set **IRI** of IRIs and **BN** of blank node identifiers; we do not consider literals, since they would complicate our exposition without adding technical insights (they can mostly be treated like named individuals in OWL QL). We use Turtle syntax for denoting RDF throughout this paper.

In addition to IRIs and blank nodes, SPARQL 1.1 queries use variables as constituents, which are indicated by a preceding question mark. For compatibility with the entailment regimes, we will consider SPARQL 1.1 under the set semantics, i.e., multiplicities of solutions will be ignored, as indicated by the DISTINCT keyword. Next, we introduce syntax and semantics of the SPARQL 1.1 fragment employed in this paper.

*Path expressions* are defined inductively as follows: (i) Every IRI is a property path. (ii) For $p$ and $q$ property paths, the following expressions are property paths as well: $(\hat{\ }p)$ for inverse, $(p \mathbin{/} q)$ for sequence, $(p \mid q)$ for alternative, $(p^*)$ for Kleene star. As usual, parentheses can be omitted if there is no danger of confusion. *Triple expressions* are of the form $s\ p\ o$ where $s$ and $o$ are IRIs, blank nodes, or variables, whereas $p$ is an IRI, a variable, or a path expression. *Basic graph patterns* are defined as finite sequences of triple expressions separated by a period. *Values blocks* for inline data have the shape VALUES $(?x_1 \ldots ?x_n)\{(v_{1,1} \ldots v_{1,n}) \ldots (v_{k,1} \ldots v_{k,n})\}$ for natural numbers $n$ and $k$ with $v_{i,j} \in$ **IRI** $\cup$ **BN**. *Filter expressions* are of the form FILTER(*boolexp*) where *boolexp* is an algebraic expression encoding the application of filter functions to variables resulting in a Boolean value (for more details see [10]). *Graph patterns* are defined inductively: (i) any basic graph pattern is a graph pattern (ii) if $gp_1$ and $gp_2$ are graph patterns then $\{gp_1\}$ UNION $\{gp_2\}$ is a graph pattern (iii) any sequence of graph patterns, values blocks and filter expressions is again a graph pattern. A SELECT-DISTINCT *query* is a SPARQL 1.1 query of the shape SELECT DISTINCT *varlist* WHERE $\{gp\}$, where $gp$ is a graph pattern and *varlist* is a list of variables occurring in $gp$.

We now define the sematics of SPARQL 1.1 queries, without taking reasoning into account; this is known as *simple entailment* (as opposed to OWL DL entailment, where the OWL axioms are evaluated under OWL Direct Semantics [8]). We define the *evaluation* of path expressions w.r.t. $G$ as a binary relation over **IRI** $\cup$ **BN** in an inductive way: $eval_G(p) = \{(u_1, u_2) \mid u_1\ p\ u_2 \in G)\}$ for $p \in$ **IRI**, inverse $eval_G(\hat{\ }p) = \{(u_2, u_1) \mid (u_1, u_2) \in eval_G(p)\}$, sequence $eval_G(p \mathbin{/} q) = \{(u_1, u_3) \mid$

$(u_1, u_2) \in eval_G(p)$, $(u_2, u_3) \in eval_G(q)$}, alternative $eval_G(p \mid q) = eval_G(p) \cup eval_G(q)$, Kleene star $eval_G(p^*) = \bigcup_{n \geq 0} eval_G(p^n)$ where $eval_G(p^0) = \{(u, u) \mid u \in \mathbf{IRI} \cup \mathbf{BN}$ occurs in $G\}$ and $eval_G(p^{n+1}) = eval_G(p^n) \circ eval_G(p)$. The *evaluation* $eval_G(bgp)$ of a basic graph pattern $bgp$ w.r.t. some RDF graph $G$ is the set of all partial mappings $\mu$ from variables in $bgp$ to IRIs or blank nodes of $G$, such that there exists some mapping $\sigma$ from all blank nodes in $bgp$ to terms of $G$ for which $\mu(\sigma(bgp)) \in G$. Moreover, $eval_G(\mathsf{VALUES} \ (?x_1 \ldots ?x_n)\{(v_{1,1} \ldots v_{1,n}) \ldots (v_{k,1} \ldots v_{k,n})\}) = \{\{?x_1 \mapsto v_{1,1}, \ldots, ?x_n \mapsto v_{1,n}\}, \ldots \{?x_1 \mapsto v_{k,1}, \ldots, ?x_n \mapsto v_{k,n}\}\}$ and $eval_G(\{gp_1\} \ \mathsf{UNION} \ \{gp_2\}) = eval_G(gp_1) \cup eval_G(gp_2)$. For graph patterns $gp$ that are sequences of graph patterns, values blocks and filter expressions $\mathsf{FILTER}(boolexp_1), \ldots, \mathsf{FILTER}(boolexp_\ell)$ we let $eval_G(gp) = \{\mu \mid \mu \in J \wedge \mu(boolexp_1) = true \wedge \ldots \wedge \mu(boolexp_\ell) = true\}$ where $J$ is the join over all $eval_G(block)$ where $block$ ranges over all graph patterns and values blocks of the sequence. We say a graph pattern $gp$ has a *match* into a graph $G$ if $eval_G(gp) \neq \emptyset$. Finally, the set of *answers* of a SELECT-DISTINCT query SELECT DISTINCT *varlist* WHERE $\{gp\}$ is the set obtained by restricting every partial function $\mu \in eval_G(gp)$ to the variables contained in *varlist*.

## 3  OWL QL: RDF Syntax and Rule-Based Semantics

OWL QL is one of the OWL 2 profiles, which restrict the OWL 2 DL ontology language to ensure that reasoning is tractable [12]. To ensure compatibility with SPARQL, we work only with the RDF representation of OWL QL here [13]. Like OWL 2 DL, OWL QL requires "standard use" of RDFS and OWL vocabulary, i.e., special vocabulary that is used to encode ontology axioms in RDF is strictly distinct from the ontology's vocabulary, and can only occur in specific triple patterns. Only a few special IRIs, such as owl:Thing, can also be used like ontology vocabulary in axioms.

OWL classes, properties, and individuals are represented by RDF elements, where complex class and property expressions are represented by blank nodes. Whether an expression is represented by an IRI or a blank node does not have an impact on ontological entailment, so we ignore this distinction in most cases. OWL 2 DL allows us to use a single IRI to represent an individual, a class, and a property in the same ontology; owing to the restrictions of standard use, it is always clear which meaning applies in a particular case. Hence we will also work with one single set of IRIs.

Next, we define the constrains that an RDF graph has to satisfy to represent an OWL QL ontology. To this end, consider a fixed RDF graph $G$. A *property expression in $G$* is an IRI or a blank node _:b that occurs in a pattern {_:b owl:inverseOf $P$} with $P \in \mathbf{IRI}$. We use $\mathbf{PRP}$ for the set of all property elements in a given RDF graph. OWL QL further distinguishes two types of class expressions with different syntactic constraints. The set $\mathbf{SBC}$ of *subclasses in $G$* consists of all IRIs and all blank nodes _:b that occur in a pattern {_:b owl:onProperty $P$; owl:someValuesFrom owl:Thing}, where $P \in \mathbf{PRP}$. The set $\mathbf{SPC}$ of *superclasses in $G$* is defined recursively as follows. An element $x$ is in $\mathbf{SPC}$ if it is in $\mathbf{IRI}$, or if it is in $\mathbf{BN}$ and $G$ contains one of the following patterns:

- {$x$ owl:onProperty $\mathbf{PRP}$; owl:someValuesFrom $y$} where $y \in \mathbf{SPC}$;
- {$x$ owl:intersectionOf $(y_1, \ldots, y_n)$} where $y_1, \ldots, y_n \in \mathbf{SPC}$;
- {$x$ owl:complementOf $y$} where $y \in \mathbf{SBC}$.

$G$ is an *OWL QL ontology* may use the following triple patterns to encode *axioms*:

- {IRI PRP IRI}
- {IRI rdf:type SPC}
- {SBC rdfs:subClassOf SPC}
- {SBC owl:equivalentClass SBC}
- {SBC owl:disjointWith SBC}
- {PRP rdfs:range SPC}

- {PRP rdfs:domain SPC}
- {PRP rdfs:subPropertyOf PRP}
- {PRP owl:equivalentProperty PRP}
- {PRP owl:inverseOf PRP}
- {PRP owl:propertyDisjointWith PRP}
- {IRI owl:differentFrom IRI}

- {BN rdf:type owl:AllDisjointClasses; owl:members (SBC, . . . , SBC)}

- {BN rdf:type owl:AllDisjointProperties; owl:members (PRP, . . . , PRP)}

- {BN rdf:type owl:AllDifferent; owl:members (IRI, . . . , IRI)}

$G$ is an OWL QL ontology if every triple in $G$ is part of a unique axiom or a unique complex class or property definition used in such axioms. For simplicity, we ignore triples used in annotations or ontology headers. Moreover, we do not consider the OWL QL property characteristics symmetry, asymmetry, and global reflexivity. Asymmetry and reflexivity are not a problem, but their explicit treatment would inflate our presentation considerably. Symmetry, in contrast, cannot be supported with SPARQL 1.1, as we will show in Section 6. This is no major limitation of our approach, since symmetry can be expressed using inverses. This shows that rewritability of an ontology language does not depend on ontological expressiveness alone.

The semantics of OWL QL is inherited from OWL DL, but it can also be described by defining a *universal model*, i.e., a structure that realizes precisely the entailments of an ontology. Such a "least model" exactly captures the semantics of an ontology. To define a universal model for OWL QL, we define a set of RDF-based inference rules, similar to the rules given for OWL RL in the standard [12]. In contrast to OWL RL, however, the application of rules can introduce new elements to an RDF graph, and the universal model that is obtained in the limit is not finite in general. Indeed, our goal is not to give a practical reasoning algorithm, but to define the semantics of OWL QL in a way that is useful for analyzing the correctness of the rewriting algorithms we introduce.

The main rules for reasoning in OWL QL are defined in Table 1. A rule is *applicable* if the premise on the left matches the current RDF graph and the conclusion on the right does not match the current graph; in this case, the conclusion is added to the graph. In case of rule (2), this requires us to create a fresh blank node. In all other cases, we only add new triples among existing elements. Rules like (3) are actually schemas for an infinite number of rules for lists of any length $n$ and any index $i \in \{1, \ldots, n\}$. Rules (15)–(16) cover owl:Thing and owl:topObjectProperty, which lead to conclusions that are true for "all" individuals. To ensure standard use, we cannot simply assert $x$ rdf:type owl:Thing for *every* IRI $x$, and we restrict instead to IRIs that are used as individuals in the ontology. We define INDIVIDUAL($x$) to be the SPARQL pattern {$x$ rdf:type owl:NamedIndividual} UNION {$x$ rdf:type ?C . ?C rdf:type owl:Class} UNION {$x$ ?P ?Y . ?P rdf:type owl:ObjectProperty} UNION {?Y ?P $x$ . ?P rdf:type owl:ObjectProperty}. Note that this also covers any newly introduced individuals.

**Table 1.** RDF inference rules for OWL QL

$$\rightarrow \text{[] rdf:type owl:Thing} \quad (1)$$

$$\text{?X rdf:type [owl:onProperty ?P; owl:someValuesFrom ?C]} \rightarrow \text{?X ?P [rdf:type ?C]} \quad (2)$$

$$\text{?X rdf:type [owl:intersectionOf (?C1,\ldots,?C}i\text{,\ldots,?C}n\text{)]} \rightarrow \text{?X rdf:type ?C}i \quad (3)$$

$$\text{?X rdf:type ?C . ?C rdfs:subClassOf ?D} \rightarrow \text{?X rdf:type ?D} \quad (4)$$

$$\text{?X rdf:type ?C . ?C owl:equivalentClass ?D} \rightarrow \text{?X rdf:type ?D} \quad (5)$$

$$\text{?X rdf:type ?C . ?D owl:equivalentClass ?C} \rightarrow \text{?X rdf:type ?D} \quad (6)$$

$$\text{?X ?P ?Y .}$$

$$\text{?C owl:onProperty ?P; owl:someValuesFrom owl:Thing} \rightarrow \text{?X rdf:type ?C} \quad (7)$$

$$\text{?X ?P ?Y . ?P rdfs:domain ?C} \rightarrow \text{?X rdf:type ?C} \quad (8)$$

$$\text{?X ?P ?Y . ?P rdfs:range ?C} \rightarrow \text{?Y rdf:type ?C} \quad (9)$$

$$\text{?X ?P ?Y . ?P owl:inverseOf ?Q} \rightarrow \text{?Y ?Q ?X} \quad (10)$$

$$\text{?X ?P ?Y . ?Q owl:inverseOf ?P} \rightarrow \text{?Y ?Q ?X} \quad (11)$$

$$\text{?X ?P ?Y . ?P rdfs:subPropertyOf ?Q} \rightarrow \text{?X ?Q ?Y} \quad (12)$$

$$\text{?X ?P ?Y . ?P owl:equivalentProperty ?Q} \rightarrow \text{?X ?Q ?Y} \quad (13)$$

$$\text{?X ?P ?Y . ?Q owl:equivalentProperty ?P} \rightarrow \text{?X ?Q ?Y} \quad (14)$$

$$\text{INDIVIDUAL(?X)} \rightarrow \text{?X rdf:type owl:Thing} \quad (15)$$

$$\text{?X rdf:type owl:Thing . ?Y rdf:type owl:Thing} \rightarrow \text{?X owl:topObjectProperty ?Y} \quad (16)$$

**Definition 1.** *The chase $G'$ of an OWL QL ontology $G$ is a possibly infinite RDF graph obtained from $G$ by fair application of the rules of Tables 1, meaning that every rule that is applicable has eventually been applied.*

Finally, some features of OWL QL can only make the ontology inconsistent, but not introduce any other kinds of positive entailments. According patterns are shown in Table 2. If any of these match, the ontology is inconsistent, every OWL axiom is a logical consequence, and there is no universal model.

**Theorem 1.** *Consider an OWL QL ontology $G$ with chase $G'$, and a basic graph pattern $P$. A variable mapping $\mu$ is a solution for $P$ over $G$ under the OWL DL entailment regime if and only if either (1) $\mu$ is a solution for $P$ over $G'$ under simple entailment, or (2) one of the patterns of Table 2 matches $G'$.*

## 4 QL Reasoning with SPARQL Property Expressions

Next, we define SPARQL 1.1 queries to solve standard reasoning tasks of OWL QL. We start with simple cases and then consider increasingly complex reasoning problems.

We first focus on the property hierarchy. An axiom of the form $p$ rdfs:subPropertyOf $q$ is entailed by an ontology $G$ if, for newly introduced individuals $a$ and $b$, $G \cup \{a \ p \ b\}$ entails $\{a \ q \ b\}$. By Theorem 1, the rules of Section 3 represent all possibilities for deriving this information. In this particular case, we can see that only rules (10)–(14) in Table 1 can derive a triple of the form $a \ q \ b$, where q is a regular property. The case $q =$owl:topObjectProperty is easy to handle, since $p$ rdfs:subPropertyOf

**Table 2.** RDF inference patterns for inconsistency in OWL QL

$$?X \; \text{owl:bottomObjectProperty} \; ?Y \qquad (17)$$

$$?X \; \text{rdf:type owl:Nothing} \qquad (18)$$

$$?X \; \text{rdf:type} \; ?C \; . \; ?X \; \text{rdf:type [owl:complementOf} \; ?C] \qquad (19)$$

$$?X \; \text{rdf:type} \; ?C \; . \; ?X \; \text{rdf:type} \; ?D \; . \; ?C \; \text{owl:disjointWith} \; ?D \qquad (20)$$

$$?X \; \text{rdf:type} \; ?Ci \; . \; ?X \; \text{rdf:type} \; ?Cj.$$
$$\_{:}b \; \text{rdf:type owl:AllDisjointClasses; owl:members} \; (?C1, \ldots, ?Ci, \ldots, ?Cj, \ldots, ?Cn) \qquad (21)$$

$$?X \; ?P \; ?Y \; . \; ?X \; ?Q \; ?Y \; . \; ?P \; \text{owl:propertyDisjointWith} \; ?Q \qquad (22)$$

$$?X \; ?Pi \; ?Y \; . \; ?X \; ?Pj \; ?Y.$$
$$\_{:}b \; \text{rdf:type owl:AllDisjointProperties; owl:members} \; (?P1, \ldots, ?Pi, \ldots, ?Pj, \ldots, ?Pn) \qquad (23)$$

$$?X \; \text{owl:differentFrom} \; ?X \qquad (24)$$

$$\_{:}b \; \text{rdf:type owl:AllDifferent; owl:members} \; (?I1, \ldots, ?X, \ldots, ?X, \ldots, ?In) \qquad (25)$$

owl:topObjectProperty is always true (which is also shown by rules (15) and (16)). In addition, it might be that $G \cup \{a \; p \; b\}$ is inconsistent, implied by rules of Table 2; we will ignore this case for now, since it requires more powerful reasoning.

**Definition 2.** *We introduce* sPO, invOf, *and* eqP *as abbreviations for* rdfs:subPropertyOf, owl:inverseOf, *and* owl:equivalentProperty, *respectively, and define the following composite property path expressions* SPOEQP := (sPO | eqP | ^eqP), INV := (invOf | ^invOf), SUBPROPERTYOF := (SPOEQP | (INV / SPOEQP* / INV))*, *as well as* SUBINVPROPERTYOF := SPOEQP* / INV / SUBPROPERTYOF. *Moreover, for an arbitrary term* $x$, *let* UNIVPROPERTY[$x$] *be the pattern* {owl:topObjectProperty (SPOEQP | INV)* $x$}.

The pattern SUBPROPERTYOF does not check for property subsumption that is caused by the inconsistency rules in Table 2, but it can be used to check for subsumptions related to owl:topObjectProperty. The corresponding correctness result is as follows:

**Proposition 1.** *Consider an OWL QL ontology $G$ with properties $p, q \in$ **PRP** such that $G \cup \{\_{:}a \; p \; \_{:}b\}$ is consistent. Then $G$ entails $p$ rdfs:subPropertyOf $q$ iff the pattern $\{p$ SUBPROPERTYOF $q\}$ UNION UNIVPROPERTY[$q$] matches $G$.*

We will extend this to cover the inconsistent case in Theorem 2 below. First, however, we look at entailments of class subsumptions. In this case, the main rules are (2)–(9). However, several of these rules also depend on property triples derived by rules (10)–(14), and we apply our results on property subsumption to take this into account.

**Definition 3.** *Let* eqC *and* sCO *abbreviate* owl:equivalentClass *and* rdfs:subClassOf, *respectively. We define property path expressions*

- INTLISTMEMBER := (owl:intersectionOf / rdf:rest* / rdf:first),
- SOMEPROP := (owl:onProperty / SUBPROPERTYOF / (^owl:onProperty | rdfs:domain)),
- SOMEPROPINV := (owl:onProperty / SUBINVPROPERTYOF / rdfs:range),
- SUBCLASSOF := (sCO | eqC | ^eqC | INTLISTMEMBER | SOMEPROP | SOMEPROPINV)*.

**Table 3.** Pattern EMPTYCLASS[$x$] for detecting empty classes

$x$ (sCO | eqC | ^eqC | INTLISTMEMBER | owl:someValuesFrom |
  (owl:onProperty / (INV | SPOEQP)* / (^owl:onProperty | rdfs:domain | rdfs:range))* ?C . {
  {?C SUBCLASSOF owl:Nothing} UNION
  {?C SUBCLASSOF ?D1 {{?C SUBCLASSOF ?D2} UNION UNIVCLASS[?D2]} {
    {?D1 DISJOINTCLASSES ?D2} UNION
    {?V rdf:type owl:AllDisjointClasses . TWOMEMBERS[?V, ?D1, ?D2]}
  }} UNION
  {?C (owl:onProperty / (INV | SPOEQP)*) ?P . {
    {?P SUBPROPERTYOF owl:bottomObjectProperty} UNION
    {?P SUBPROPERTYOF ?Q1 {{?P SUBPROPERTYOF ?Q2} UNION UNIVPROPERTY[?Q2]} {
      {?Q1 (owl:propertyDisjointWith | ^owl:propertyDisjointWith) ?Q2} UNION
      {?V rdf:type owl:AllDisjointProperties . TWOMEMBERS[?V, ?Q1, ?Q2]}
    }
  }}
}

*Moreover, we let* UNIVCLASS[$x$] *denote the pattern* {owl:Thing SUBCLASSOF $x$} UNION
{owl:topObjectProperty ((SPOEQP | INV)* / (^owl:onProperty | rdfs:domain | rdfs:range)/
SUBCLASSOF) $x$}

**Proposition 2.** *Consider an OWL QL ontology G with classes $c \in$* **SPC** *and $d \in$* **SBC**
*such that $G \cup \{\_$:a rdf:type $c\}$ is consistent. Then G entails $c$ rdfs:subClassOf $d$ iff the*
*pattern* {$c$ SUBCLASSOF $d$} UNION UNIVCLASS[$d$] *matches G.*

It remains to identify classes that are incoherent, i.e., for which $c$ rdfs:subClassOf
owl:Nothing is entailed. To do this, we need to consider the patterns of Table 2.

**Definition 4.** *For arbitrary terms $x$, $y$, and $z$, let* TWOMEMBERS[$x, y, z$] *be the pattern*
{$x$ (owl:members / rdf:rest*) ?W . ?W rdf:first $y$ . ?W (rdf:rest$^+$ / rdf:first) $z$}, *and let*
DISJOINTCLASSES *be the property path expression* (owl:disjointWith | ^owl:disjointWith |
owl:complementOf | ^owl:complementOf). *The query pattern* EMPTYCLASS[$x$] *is defined*
*as in Table 3, and the query pattern* EMPTYPROPERTY[$x$] *is defined as in Table 4.*

We can now completely express OWL QL schema reasoning in SPARQL 1.1:

**Theorem 2.** *An OWL QL ontology G is inconsistent iff it has a match for the pattern*

{?X rdf:type ?C . EMPTYCLASS[?C]} UNION {?X ?P ?Y . EMPTYPROPERTY[?P]} UNION
{?X owl:differentFrom ?X} UNION
{?V rdf:type owl:AllDifferent . TWOMEMBERS[?V, ?X, ?X]}.     (26)

*G entails $c$ rdfs:subClassOf $d$ for $c \in$* **SPC** *and $d \in$* **SBC** *iff G is either inconsistent or*
*has a match for the pattern*

{$c$ SUBCLASSOF $d$} UNION UNIVCLASS[$d$] UNION EMPTYCLASS[$c$].     (27)

**Table 4.** Pattern EMPTYPROPERTY[*x*] for detecting empty properties

*x* (INV | SPOEQP | (^owl:onProperty /
   (sCO | eqC | ^eqC | INTLISTMEMBER | owl:someValuesFrom)* / owl:onProperty))* ?P . {
   {?P SUBPROPERTYOF owl:bottomObjectProperty} UNION
   {?P SUBPROPERTYOF ?Q1 {{?P SUBPROPERTYOF ?Q2} UNION UNIVPROPERTY[?Q2]} {
      {?Q1 (owl:propertyDisjointWith | ^owl:propertyDisjointWith) ?Q2} UNION
      {?V rdf:type owl:AllDisjointProperties . TWOMEMBERS[?V, ?Q1, ?Q2]}
   }} UNION
   {?P ((^owl:onProperty | rdfs:domain | rdfs:range) / SUBCLASSOF) ?C . {
      {?C SUBCLASSOF owl:Nothing} UNION
      {?C SUBCLASSOF ?D1 {{?C SUBCLASSOF ?D2} UNION UNIVCLASS[?D2]} {
         {?D1 DISJOINTCLASSES ?D2} UNION
         {?V rdf:type owl:AllDisjointClasses . TWOMEMBERS[?V, ?D1, ?D2]}
      }
   }}
}

*G entails x* rdf:type *c iff G is either inconsistent or has a match for the pattern*

{{*x* (rdf:type / SUBCLASSOF) *c*} UNION

   {*x* ?P ?Y . ?P (SUBPROPERTYOF / (^owl:onProperty | rdfs:domain) / SUBCLASSOF) *c*} UNION

   {?Y ?P *x* . ?P (SUBPROPERTYOF / rdfs:range / SUBCLASSOF) *c*}

   } UNION UNIVCLASS[*c*]                                                                      (28)

*G entails p* rdfs:subPropertyOf *q for p, q ∈* **PRP** *iff G is either inconsistent or has a match for the pattern*

{*p* SUBPROPERTYOF *q*} UNION UNIVPROPERTY[*q*] UNION EMPTYPROPERTY[*p*].          (29)

*G entails x p y iff G is either inconsistent or has a match for the pattern*

{*x* ?R *y* . ?R SUBPROPERTYOF *p*} UNION {*y* ?R *x* . ?R SUBINVPROPERTYOF *p*}

UNION UNIVPROPERTY[*p*].                                                              (30)

# 5   OWL QL Query Rewriting with SPARQL 1.1

We now turn towards query answering over OWL QL ontologies using SPARQL 1.1. Research in OWL QL query answering typically considers the problem of answering *conjunctive queries* (CQs), which are conjunctions of OWL property and class assertions that use variables only in the place of individuals, not in the place of properties or classes. Conjunction can easily be represented by a Basic Graph Pattern in SPARQL, yet CQs are not a subset of SPARQL, since they also support existential quantification of variables. Normal query variables are called *distinguished* while existentially quantified variables are called *non-distinguished*. Distinguished variables can only bind to elements of the ontology, whereas for non-distinguished variables it suffices if the ontology implies that some binding must exist.

*Example 1.* Consider an OWL ontology with the assertion :peter rdf:type :Person and the axiom :Person rdfs:subClassOf [owl:onProperty :father; owl:someValuesFrom :Person]. This implies that :peter has some :father but the ontology may not contain any element of which we know that it plays this role. In this case, the SPARQL pattern {?X :father ?Y} would not have a match with ?X = :peter under OWL DL entailment. In contrast, if the variable ?Y were non-distinguished, the query would match with ?X = :peter (and ?Y would not receive any binding).

SPARQL can only express CQs where all variables are distinguished. To define this fragment of SPARQL, recall that the OWL DL entailment regime of SPARQL 1.1 requires every variable to be *declared* for a certain type (individual, object property, datatype property, or class) [8]. This requirement is the analogue of "standard use" on the level of query patterns, and it allows us to focus on instance retrieval here. We thus call a Basic Graph Pattern $P$ *CQ-pattern* if: (1) $P$ does not contain any OWL, RDF, or RDFS URIs other than rdf:type in property positions, (2) all variables in $P$ are declared as required by the OWL DL entailment regime, (3) property variables occur only in predicate positions, and (4) class variables occur only in object positions of triples with predicate rdf:type. Rewriting CQ-patterns is an easy application of Theorem 2:

**Definition 5.** *For a triple pattern e* rdf:type *c, the rewriting* $[\![x$ rdf:type $c]\!]$ *is the graph pattern* (28) *as in Theorem 2; for a triple pattern x p y, the rewriting* $[\![x\ p\ y]\!]$ *is the graph pattern* (30). *The rewriting* $[\![P]\!]$ *of a CQ-pattern P is obtained by replacing every triple pattern s p o in P by* $\{[\![s\ p\ o]\!]\}$.

**Theorem 3.** *If G is the RDF graph of a consistent OWL QL ontology, then the matches of a CQ-pattern P on G under OWL DL entailment are exactly the matches of* $[\![P]\!]$ *on G under simple entailment.*

## 5.1 Rewriting General Conjunctive Queries

We now explain the additional aspects that we need to take into account for computing answers to CQs with non-distinguished variables, and give an intuitive overview of our rewriting approach. A general challenge that we have to address is that classical query rewriting for OWL QL may lead to exponentially many queries, owing to the fact that many non-deterministic choices have to be made to find a query match. Some of these choices depend on the ontology, e.g., on the depth of the class hierarchy, and are naturally represented in (small) SPARQL 1.1 queries in our approach. Other choices, however, depend on the query, e.g., the decision which variables should be identified (query factorization). It is not immediately clear how to represent these choices in a polynomial query, even when using path expressions. Our solution depends on the creative use of the VALUES feature of SPARQL 1.1.

As explained before, non-distinguished variables can be matched to inferred individuals that are not named in the ontology. The chase introduced in Section 3 still captures this more general notion of query answering. The only rule to infer new individuals is (2), which introduces fresh bnodes that we call *anonymous individuals*. The elements of the original ontology (bnode or not) are *named individuals*. It is well known that a

QL ontology $G$ entails a CQ $q$ if and only if there is a match from $q$ to the (possibly infinite) chase of $G$ such that all distinguished variables are mapped to named individuals. Non-distinguished variables can be mapped to either named or anonymous individuals.

To represent the match of a query variable $x$ in the rewritten query, we introduce a SPARQL variable ?Mx. For named individuals, ?Mx can bind to the individual in the RDF graph. However, if $x$ is non-distinguished, then it could match to anonymous individuals, which are not represented by any individual in RDF. In this case, we bind ?Mx to the bnode _:b representing the OWL property restriction _:b owl:onProperty ?P; owl:someValuesFrom ?C that was used in rule (2) to generate the anonymous individual. Indeed, all class and property assertions that are derived for the anonymous individual can be deduced from ?P and ?C only, so this binding allows us to check query conditions.

However, the bnode _:b does not determine the identity of the anonymous individual, since infinitely many anonymous individuals can be generated from the same OWL property restriction. Example 1 illustrates this: every person has another person as is its father, *ad infinitum*. Nevertheless, the query :peter :father ?Z . ?Z :father ?Z should not have a match, even if ?Z is non-distinguished. Disregarding universal property assertions that follow from rule (16), anonymous individuals can only be related to their parent individual (represented by ?X in rule (2)) or to their children (which have the anonymous element as their parent). Therefore, to check if a triple pattern ?X $p$ ?Y can match, we may need to know if ?X is the parent of ?Y. We capture this with auxiliary variables ?Pxy which we bind to one of two possible values (interpreted as *true* and *false*).

We thus introduce variables ?Pxy for every pair of CQ variables $x$ and $y$ where $y$ is non-distinguished. This completely specifies the parenthood of the matches. Together with the generating OWL restriction represented by ?Mx, this gives us enough information to verify property assertions. To find all matches of a CQ, one has to allow for the possibility that several query variables represent the same element of the chase. To capture this, we introduce variables ?Exy that tell us if the values of $x$ and $y$ are equal; again we use two possible values to represent *true* and *false*. Additional conditions in our query will ensure that there are no cycles in the parenthood relation, and that equal values are indeed equal. Many of these can be encoded in propositional logic, as explained next.

### 5.2 Expressing Propositional Logic in SPARQL 1.1

Our intuitive explanation above uses "Boolean" variables like ?Pxy and ?Exy, which can have one of two values. Moreover, the bindings of these variables should obey further constraints. For example, if $x$ is the parent of $y$ and $y$ is identified with $z$, then $x$ is the parent of $z$. This corresponds to a propositional logic implication ?Pxz $\land$ ?Eyz $\rightarrow$ ?Pxz.

We express this using the VALUES feature of SPARQL 1.1, which allows us to assign a fixed set of bindings to a list of variables. For example, the pattern VALUES (?Pxy){(<http://example.org/true>)(<http://example.org/false>)} has exactly two solutions, binding ?Pxy to one of the given URIs. The URIs used here are irrelevant, and it does not even matter if they occur in the data; we thus use the abbreviations T and F to denote two distinct URIs that we use to represent Boolean values. Propositional logic formulae can now be represented by encoding their truth table using VALUES. For example, the implication $?Pxz \land ?Eyz \rightarrow ?Pxz$ can be expressed as:

$$VALUES\ (?Pxy\ ?Eyz\ ?Pxz)\{(F\ F\ F)(T\ F\ F)(F\ T\ F)(F\ F\ T)(T\ F\ T)(F\ T\ T)(T\ T\ T)\}. \quad (31)$$

We denote this pattern as $[\![?Pxz \land ?Eyz \rightarrow ?Pxz]\!]$, and similarly for any other propositional logic formula over SPARQL variables. The solutions to (31) are exactly the truth assignments under which the implication holds. In particular, every solution requires each of the three variables to be bound to T or F (and thus to never be undefined).

## 5.3 A Schema-Agnostic Rewriting for Conjunctive Queries

We now specify the complete rewriting of CQs in SPARQL 1.1, which consists of rewritings for the individual triple patterns and several additional patterns to ensure that the bindings of all (auxiliary) variables are as intended. Consider a CQ $q$ with variables $Var(q)$, partitioned into the set $Var_d(q)$ of distinguished variables and $Var_n(q)$ of non-distinguished variables. Our encoding uses the following sets of SPARQL variables:

- for every $x \in Var(q)$, a variable $?Mx$ (encoding the "match for $x$").

In addition, we use the following propositional SPARQL variables:

- for every $x \in Var(q)$, a variable $?Nx$ ("$x$ is a named individual").
- for every pair $x, y \in Var(q)$, a variable $?Exy$ ("$x$ is equal to $y$");
- for every pair $x \in Var(q)$ and $y \in Var_n(q)$, a variable $?Pxy$ ("$x$ is the parent of $y$");
- for every pair $x, y \in Var_n(q)$, a variable $?Axy$ ("$x$ is an ancestor of $y$");

The variables $?Axy$ are used to encode the transitive closure over the parent relations on non-distinguished variables; this is necessary to preclude cyclic ancestries. We use PROPCONSTRAINTS($q$) to denote the SPARQL encoding of all of the following implications (for every possible combination of the above variables, if no other condition is given):

$$for\ x \in Var_d(q)\colon T \rightarrow ?Nx$$

| | | |
|---|---|---|
| $?Exy \rightarrow ?Eyx$ | $?Exy \land ?Nx \rightarrow ?Ny$ | $?Pxy \rightarrow ?Axy$ |
| $?Exy \land ?Eyz \rightarrow ?Exz$ | $?Exy \land ?Pxz \rightarrow ?Pyz$ | $?Axy \land ?Ayz \rightarrow ?Axz$ |
| $?Pxz \land ?Pyz \rightarrow ?Exy$ | $?Exy \land ?Pzx \rightarrow ?Pzy$ | $?Axx \rightarrow F$ |

The previous conditions do not ensure yet that the bindings for $?Mx$ and $?My$ are the same whenever $?Exy$ is true. This cannot be encoded using VALUES. Instead, we define EQUALITYFILTER($q$) to be the condition of the following filter conditions:

$$FILTER(?Exy = F\ ||\ ?Mx = ?My) \qquad x, y \in Var(q)$$

We can now define the rewriting of the actual query conditions. For readability, we use $[\![?V := u]\!]$ to abbreviate VALUES $(?V)\{(u)\}$. The triple pattern $x$ rdf:type $c$ is rewritten into the following pattern, denoted REWRITE($x$ rdf:type $c$):

{⟦?Nx := T⟧ . ⟦?Mx rdf:type *c*⟧}

UNION {univClass[*c*]}

UNION {⟦?Nx := F⟧ . ?E subClassOf *c*

   {{?Mx owl:someValuesFrom ?E} UNION

   {?Mx (owl:onProperty / subPropertyOf / rdfs:range) ?E} UNION

   {?Mx (owl:onProperty / subInvPropertyOf / (^owl:onProperty | rdfs:domain)) ?E}}

A triple pattern $x\ p\ y$ is rewritten into the following pattern, denoted Rewrite($x\ p\ y$):

{⟦?Nx := T⟧ . ⟦?Ny := T⟧ . ⟦?Mx *p* ?My⟧}

UNION {univProperty[*p*]}

UNION {⟦?Ny := F⟧ . ⟦?Pxy := T⟧ . ?My (owl:onProperty / subPropertyOf) *p*

   {Rewrite(*x* rdf:type ?My)}

UNION {⟦?Nx := F⟧ . ⟦?Pyx := T⟧ . ?Mx (owl:onProperty / subInvPropertyOf) *p*

   {Rewrite(*y* rdf:type ?Mx)}

Note that the parenthood relationship ?Pyx is only relevant for checking certain triple patterns. In each of these cases, we verify that the parent element is really capable of creating the required child. This ensures that all assumed parenthoods that are relevant to prove the query are really derived. In addition, we still need to check that all anonymous elements are really derived (from some original ancestor element in the ontology).

*Example 2.* Consider an OWL ontology with the assertion :peter rdf:type :Person and the axiom :Person rdfs:subClassOf [owl:onProperty :mother; owl:someValuesFrom :Woman]. Then the query {?X rdf:type :Woman} with ?X non-distinguished has a match. However, if we remove the triple :peter rdf:type :Person, then the query does not have a match. In contrast, our pattern Rewrite($x$ rdf:type :Mother) could match in either case.

To fix this, we introduce, for every non-distinguished variable $x$, an additional pattern MatchExists($x$) that verifies that an element of the assumed type is actually derived. This pattern also ensures that named individuals are always bound to individuals. Anonymous individuals may be inferred from our assumption that the domain is not empty, or they must be derived from a named individual, which we represent by a bnode:

{⟦?Nx := T⟧ . individual(?Mx)}

UNION {⟦?Nx := F⟧ . ⟦?Mx := owl:Thing⟧}

UNION {⟦?Nx := F⟧ . ⟦_:b rdf:type ?E⟧ . ?E (rdfs:subClassOf | intListMember |

   (owl:onProperty / (Inv | SpoEqp)* / (^owl:onProperty | rdfs:domain | rdfs:range)) |

   ^owl:equivalentClass | owl:equivalentClass | owl:someValuesFrom)* ?Mx}

We do not need to check that this derivation agrees with the guessed parenthood relations, since the check is only relevant for the elements that do not have a parent represented by a query variable.

**Definition 6.** *The rewriting* REWRITE($q$) *a CQ $q$ with distinguished variables $x_1, \ldots, x_n$ is the following SPARQL 1.1 query:*

> SELECT DISTINCT ?M$x$1, ..., ?M$xn$ WHERE {
> PROPCONSTRAINTS($q$)
> REWRITE($x$ rdf:type $c$) *for each condition $x$* rdf:type $c$ *in $q$*
> REWRITE($x$ $p$ $y$) *for each condition $x$ $p$ $y$ in $q$*
> MATCHEXISTS($x$) *for each variable $x$ in $q$*
> EQUALITYFILTER($q$)
> }

**Theorem 4.** *The answers of a conjunctive query $q$ over an OWL QL ontology $G$ are exactly the answers of the SPARQL 1.1 query* REWRITE($q$) *over $G$ under simple entailment.*

# 6   Limits of Schema-Agnostic Query Rewriting

We have seen that schema-agnostic query rewriting works for (almost) all of OWL QL, so it is natural to ask how far this approach can be extended. In this section, we outline the natural limits of SPARQL 1.1 as a query rewriting language, point out extensions to overcome these limits.

In Section 3, we excluded owl:SymmetricProperty from our considerations. Indeed, schema-agnostic SPARQL 1.1 queries cannot support this feature. This might be surprising, given that one can write $p$ rdf:type owl:SymmetricProperty as $p$ rdfs:subPropertyOf [owl:inverseOf $p$]. To see why this problem occurs, consider the following ontology:

:c rdfs:subClassOf [rdf:type owl:Restriction; owl:onProperty :p; owl:someValuesFrom owl:Thing] .

[] rdf:type owl:Restriction; owl:onProperty [owl:inverseOf :p]; owl:someValuesFrom owl:Thing;

   rdfs:subClassOf :d .

:p rdf:type owl:SymmetricProperty .

This ontology states: every :c has an outgoing :p property; everything with an incoming :p property is a :d; and :p is symmetric. Clearly, this implies that :c is a subclass of :d. We call this ontology $G$(:c, :p, :d). Now assume that we have a chain of such ontologies $G_n := G(\text{:c1, :p1, :c2}), \ldots, G(\text{:c}n, \text{:p}n, \text{:d})$. Clearly, $G_n$ implies that :c1 rdfs:subClassOf :d, but there is no SPARQL 1.1 graph pattern with property paths that recognizes this triple structure in an ontology. The intuitive explanation is that $G_n$ contains a property path of length $4n$ that matches the following expression:

(rdfs:subClassOf / owl:onProperty / ^owl:onProperty / rdfs:subClassOf)*

A SPARQL query that matches $G_n$ for any $n$ needs to use such a path expression; no other feature in SPARQL 1.1 can navigate arbitrary distances. However, it is impossible to verify that each :p$i$ on this path is of type owl:SymmetricProperty. For the formal proof, we analyze general properties of the graphs that a SPARQL 1.1 query matches [3]. The essence of our argument is that property paths, being linear, cannot reliably detect an arbitrary number of individuals with more than two neighbors, as found in $G_n$.

While this limitation is hardly more than a syntactic inconvenience, one might ask if there are query languages that can deal with this type of encoding. Indeed, one possible approach is nSPARQL, which has been proposed as an extension of SPARQL 1.0 with a form of path expressions that can test for the presence of certain side branches in property paths [14]. Similar test expressions have been considered in OBDA recently [2]. These query languages can handle the RDF encoding of symmetric properties.

Besides such "syntactic" limitations, schema-agnostic query rewriting is also restricted by complexity theoretic arguments. Simply put, the reasoning task solved in this way can not be harder (computationally speaking) than the data complexity of the underlying query language. The data complexity of the subset of SPARQL used in this paper is NLogSpace: SPARQL 1.1 patters are a variant of positive regular path queries [7], which have NLogSpace data complexity (by translation to linear Datalog [9]); inline data (VALUES) does not affect data complexity; and final filtering with equality checks can clearly be implemented in logarithmic space. Since P is widely assumed to be strictly harder than NLogSpace (though no proof has been given yet), we can exclude many lightweight ontology languages:

**Theorem 5.** *If* P *is strictly harder than* NLogSpace, *then reasoning for the following ontology languages cannot be expressed in SPARQL 1.1 using property paths,* UNION, VALUES *and (in)equality filters:*

- *any subset of OWL with* owl:intersectionOf *in subclass positions, especially OWL EL and OWL RL;*
- *any subset of OWL with unrestricted* owl:someValuesFrom *in subclasses and superclasses (not limited to* owl:Thing*);*
- *the extension of OWL QL with regular property chain axioms.*

These complexity-theoretic limitations can only be overcome by using a more complex query language. Many query languages with P-complete data complexity can be found in the Datalog family of languages, which are supported by RDF databases like OWLIM and Oracle 11g that include rule engines.

## 7    Conclusions and Outlook

To the best of our knowledge, our work is the first to present a query rewriting approach for ontology-based data access in OWL QL that is completely independent of the ontology. The underlying paradigm of schema-agnostic query rewriting appears to be a promising approach that can be applied in many other settings. Indeed, two previous works, nSPARQL [14] and PSPARQL [1], independently proposed query-based mechanisms for reasoning in RDFS. While these works have not considered SPARQL 1.1, OWL QL, or arbitrary conjunctive queries, they still share important underlying ideas. We think that a common name is very useful to denote this approach to query rewriting.

In this paper, we have focused on laying the foundations for this new reasoning procedure. An important next step is to study its practical implementation and optimization. Considering the size of some of the queries we obtain, one would expect them to be challenging for RDF stores. We have started to implement our approach in a prototype system [3], and initial experiments confirm this expectation. Encouragingly, however, executing rewritten queries seems to be feasible, even in the raw, unoptimized form they have in this paper. Future work will be concerned with developing further optimizations that can be used in practical evaluations.

Indeed, while the queries we obtain might be challenging for current RDF stores, large parts of the queries are fixed and can be optimized for. Our work thus reduces the problem of adding OWL QL reasoning support to RDF stores to a query optimization problem. This can also guide future work in stores, such as OWLIM, which implement reasoning with inference rules: rather than trying to materialize (part of) an infinite OWL QL chase [4], they could materialize (sub)query results to obtain a sound and complete procedure. This provides completely new perspectives on the use of OWL QL in areas that have hitherto been reserved to OWL RL and RDFS.

Finally, our work also points into several interesting directions for foundational research, as mentioned in Section 6. Promising approaches include development of schema-agnostic rewriting procedures for languages like OWL EL that cannot be captured by SPARQL 1.1, and the development of query languages that suit this task [17].

**Acknowledgements.** This work has been funded by the Vienna Science and Technology Fund (WWTF, project ICT12-015), and by the DFG in project DIAMOND (Emmy Noether grant KR 4381/1-1).

# References

1. Alkhateeb, F.: Querying RDF(S) with Regular Expressions. Ph.D. thesis, Université Joseph Fourier – Grenoble 1 (2008)
2. Bienvenu, M., Calvanese, D., Ortiz, M., Šimkus, M.: Nested regular path queries in description logics. CoRR abs/1402.7122 (2014)
3. Bischof, S., Krötzsch, M., Polleres, A., Rudolph, S.: Schema-agnostic query rewriting in SPARQL 1.1: Technical report (2014),
   http://stefanbischof.at/publications/iswc14/
4. Bishop, B., Bojanov, S.: Implementing OWL 2 RL and OWL 2 QL rule-sets for OWLIM. In: Dumontier, M., Courtot, M. (eds.) Proc. 8th Int. Workshop on OWL: Experiences and Directions (OWLED 2011). CEUR Workshop Proceedings, vol. 796. CEUR-WS.org (2011)
5. Calvanese, D., Giacomo, G.D., Lembo, D., Lenzerini, M., Rosati, R.: Tractable reasoning and efficient query answering in description logics: The DL-Lite family. J. Automated Reasoning 39(3), 385–429 (2007)
6. Di Pinto, F., Lembo, D., Lenzerini, M., Mancini, R., Poggi, A., Rosati, R., Ruzzi, M., Savo, D.F.: Optimizing query rewriting in ontology-based data access. In: Proceedings of the 16th International Conference on Extending Database Technology, pp. 561–572. ACM (2013)
7. Florescu, D., Levy, A., Suciu, D.: Query containment for conjunctive queries with regular expressions. In: Mendelzon, A.O., Paredaens, J. (eds.) Proc. 17th Symposium on Principles of Database Systems (PODS 1998), pp. 139–148. ACM (1998)
8. Glimm, B., Ogbuji, C. (eds.): SPARQL 1.1 Entailment Regimes. W3C Recommendation (March 21, 2013), http://www.w3.org/TR/sparql11-entailment/
9. Gottlob, G., Papadimitriou, C.H.: On the complexity of single-rule datalog queries. Inf. Comput. 183(1), 104–122 (2003)

10. Harris, S., Seaborne, A. (eds.): SPARQL 1.1 Query Language. W3C Recommendation (March 21, 2013), http://www.w3.org/TR/sparql11-query/
11. Kontchakov, R., Rodríguez-Muro, M., Zakharyaschev, M.: Ontology-based data access with databases: A short course. In: Rudolph, S., Gottlob, G., Horrocks, I., van Harmelen, F. (eds.) Reasoning Weg 2013. LNCS, vol. 8067, pp. 194–229. Springer, Heidelberg (2013)
12. Motik, B., Cuenca Grau, B., Horrocks, I., Wu, Z., Fokoue, A., Lutz, C. (eds.): OWL 2 Web Ontology Language: Profiles. W3C Recommendation (October 27, 2009), http://www.w3.org/TR/owl2-profiles/
13. Patel-Schneider, P.F., Motik, B. (eds.): OWL 2 Web Ontology Language: Mapping to RDF Graphs. W3C Recommendation (October 27, 2009), http://www.w3.org/TR/owl2-mapping-to-rdf/
14. Pérez, J., Arenas, M., Gutierrez, C.: nSPARQL: A navigational language for RDF. J. Web Semantics 8, 255–270 (2010)
15. Pérez-Urbina, H., Motik, B., Horrocks, I.: Tractable query answering and rewriting under description logic constraints. J. Applied Logic 8(2), 186–209 (2010)
16. Rodríguez-Muro, M., Kontchakov, R., Zakharyaschev, M.: Ontology-based data access: Ontop of databases. In: Alani, H., et al. (eds.) ISWC 2013, Part I. LNCS, vol. 8218, pp. 558–573. Springer, Heidelberg (2013)
17. Rudolph, S., Krötzsch, M.: Flag & check: Data access with monadically defined queries. In: Hull, R., Fan, W. (eds.) Proc. 32nd Symposium on Principles of Database Systems (PODS 2013), pp. 151–162. ACM (2013)

# How Semantic Technologies Can Enhance Data Access at Siemens Energy*

Evgeny Kharlamov[1,**], Nina Solomakhina[2], Özgür Lütfü Özçep[3],
Dmitriy Zheleznyakov[1], Thomas Hubauer[2], Steffen Lamparter[2],
Mikhail Roshchin[2], Ahmet Soylu[4], and Stuart Watson[5]

[1] University of Oxford, UK
evgeny.kharlamov@cs.ox.ac.uk
[2] Siemens Corporate Technology, Germany
[3] Hamburg University of Technology, Germany
[4] University of Oslo, Norway
[5] Siemens Energy, UK

**Abstract.** We present a description and analysis of the data access challenge in the Siemens Energy. We advocate for Ontology Based Data Access (OBDA) as a suitable Semantic Web driven technology to address the challenge. We derive requirements for applying OBDA in Siemens, review existing OBDA systems and discuss their limitations with respect to the Siemens requirements. We then introduce the Optique platform as a suitable OBDA solution for Siemens. Finally, we describe our preliminary installation and evaluation of the platform in Siemens.

## 1 Introduction

The growth of available information in enterprises requires new efficient methods for data access by domain experts whose ability to analyse data is at the core of making business decisions. Current centralised approaches, where an IT expert translates the requirements of domain experts into Extract-Transform-Load (ETL) processes to integrate the data and to apply predefined analytical reporting tools, are too heavy-weight and inflexible [1]. In order to support interactive data exploration, domain experts therefore want to access and analyse available data sources *directly*, without IT experts being involved.

This direct data access is particularly important for Siemens Energy[1] that runs several service centres for power plants. The main task of a service centre is remote monitoring and diagnostics of many thousands appliances, such as gas and steam turbines, generators, and compressors installed in plants. Monitoring and diagnostics are performed by service engineers and are typically conducted in four steps: *(i)* engineers receive a notification about a potential or detected issue with an appliance, *(ii)* they gather data relevant to the case, *(iii)* analyse the data, and finally *(iv)* report about ways to address the issue to the appliance owner. Currently, Step (ii) of the process is the bottleneck consuming up to 80% of the overall time needed by the engineer to accomplish the task. The main reason for this time consumption is the indirect data access, i.e., in many cases the engineers have to access data via IT experts. Involvement of IT experts in the

---

* The research was supported by the FP7 grant Optique (n. 318338).
** Corresponding author.
[1] http://www.energy.siemens.com/

process slows it down dramatically due to reasons including the overload of IT experts and miscommunication between them and the engineers.

Enabling direct data access for engineers in Siemens is a challenging task primarily due to the Big Data dimensions as well as the conceptual mismatch between the language and structures that the engineers use to describe the data, and the way the data is actually described and structured in databases. Regarding the Big Data dimensions, the data accessible from Siemens service centres naturally reflects the variety, volume, and velocity dimensions of Big Data: it is stored in several thousands databases where many have different schemata, its size is in the order of hundreds of terabytes, and it currently grows with the average rate of 30 GB per day. Regarding the conceptual mismatch, it occurs because industrial schemata are often integrated from autonomously evolving databases that have been adapted over years to the purposes of the applications they underlay, and not to the purpose of being intuitive for domain experts. Only IT experts fully understand this evolving structure of databases and thus currently only they can write queries over these databases in order to extract information relevant for engineers.

*Ontology Based Data Access* (OBDA) [2] has been recently proposed as a means to enhance end-user direct data access. The key idea behind OBDA is to use *ontologies*, i.e., semantically rich conceptual domain models, to mediate between users and data. Ontologies describe the domain of interest on a higher level of abstraction and in terms that are clear for domain experts. Ontologies have become a common and successful mechanism to describe application domains in, e.g., biology, medicine, and the (Semantic) Web [3]. This success is partially due to a number of available formal languages for describing ontologies, including the Web Ontology Language (OWL) standardised by W3C. In OBDA users formulate their information needs as queries using terms defined in the ontology, and ontological queries are then translated into SQL or some other database query languages and executed over the data automatically, without an IT expert's intervention. To this end a set of *mappings* is maintained that describes the relationship between the ontological vocabulary and the schema of the data.

The goal of this paper is to argue that OBDA has a good potential in improving direct access by engineers to the data at Siemens Energy. To this end, in Section 2 we analyse reactive and predictive diagnostics at Siemens and derive five Siemens direct data access requirements. In Section 3 we introduce OBDA, show that it conceptually satisfies the Siemens requirements, and argue that existing OBDA systems are not mature enough to fulfill the requirements. In Section 4 we give a brief overview of the Optique platform, a novel OBDA platform developed within the Optique project [4, 5, 6], and focus on our advances in the development of the platform for Siemens. More precisely, we present a diagnostic dashboard that integrates tools for query formulation together with tools for visualisation of query answers, and our advances in processing timestamped static and streaming data. In Section 5 we present our preliminary deployment of the Optique platform over Siemens data and a preliminary user evaluation. In Section 6 we conclude and discuss the lessons we learned as well as future work.

## 2  Siemens Monitoring and Diagnostic Service

Siemens produces a variety of rotating appliances, including gas and steam turbines, generators, and compressors. These appliances are complex machines and typically

**Fig. 1.** High-level view on the turbine service process

used in different critical processes including power generation where each hour of downtime may cost thousands of euros. Thus, these appliances should be under a constant monitoring that requires an in-depth knowledge about their components and setup. Siemens provides such monitoring via service centres and operates over fifty such centres worldwide, where each centre is responsible for several thousands appliances. Typical monitoring tasks of a service centre include *(i) reactive and preventive diagnostics* of turbines which is about offline data analysis applied after a malfunction or an abnormal behaviour such as vibration, temperature or pressure increase, unexpected events, or even unexpected shutdowns, of a unit is detected; *(ii) predictive analysis* of turbine conditions which is about real-time data analyses of data streams received from appliances. We now discuss these monitoring tasks in detail and present requirements to enhance these tasks.

## 2.1 Reactive and Preventive Diagnostics

Reactive diagnostics is usually applied after a malfunction of a unit has occurred, e.g., a turbine abnormal shutdown. Complementarily, the preventive diagnostic task is performed before a malfunction of a unit, when its abnormal behaviour is detected, e.g., high vibration or temperature increase. Both diagnostic tasks are triggered either when a customer sends a service ticket claiming assistance or an automated diagnostic system creates such a ticket. Figure 1 depicts a general process triggered when a service ticket arrives. We now discuss each step of the process in detail.

*Arrival of a service ticket.* A service ticket typically contains information on when a problem occurred and its frequency. In some cases the ticket isolates the location of the problem in the appliance and its cause, but often it has no or few details.

*Example 1.* An example of a reactive monitoring request from a customer is:

> *Figure out why the turbine failed to start during the last five hours, with the goal of checking that there will be no fault of the turbine.*

A typical preventive monitoring request could be

> *Will there be a failure of the turbine after the observed temperature increase?* ∎

*Data acquisition.* Service engineers gather relevant data by querying databases that are updated every hour and on demand and contain sensor and event data. In order to support data gathering, Siemens equips service centres with more than 4,000 predefined queries and query patterns of different complexity. Engineers use the queries by setting parameters such as time periods, names of events or sensors, sensor types, etc.

*Example 2.* Based on the service ticket of Example 1, the engineer formulates the following information need and has to find appropriate queries to cover it:

> *Return the most frequent start failure and warning messages of the gas turbine T01 during the last week. Moreover, find analogous cases of failures for turbines of the same type as T01 in the last three months.*    ∎

*Query results visualisation.* Sensor data is visualised with the use of standard diagrams, and event messages are presented as a list, i.e., as an Excel spreadsheet, with timestamps and additional attributes.

*Data preprocessing.* The queried data is preprocessed using generic procedures such as sensor check (i.e., whether sensor data quality is appropriate), threshold and trend analysis. Independent from the concrete ticket, these preprocessing steps are done manually, e.g., over the visualised Excel spreadsheets, or using specialised analytic tools.

*Data analysis.* The engineer uses sophisticated diagnostic models and tools for complex analysis, e.g., Principal Component Analysis or other statistical methods, to detect and isolate the given problem based on the preprocessed data. Typically, analysis tasks are executed individually for each ticket. The gathering and analysis steps are often carried out iteratively, i.e., the results from one iteration are used to pose additional queries.

*Report preparation.* This process terminates when an explanation for the problem in the service ticket is established. In this case the engineer provides the customer with a report aggregating the result of the analysis and describing possible further actions.

## 2.2   Predictive Analysis

In predictive analysis, in contrast to the diagnostic process described above, appliances are continuously monitored, i.e., without prior service tickets, using online processing of the incoming sensor data. The other process steps of predictive analysis are similar to the ones described in the previous section, but have to be applied online to streaming data with minimal user intervention. The purpose here is to analyse the current condition of an appliance by combining operating information, system data, specifications of concrete product lines, and temporal phases of operating regimes. This information allows to predict whether some parts of an appliance should be repaired soon, assess risks related to the use of this parts, and adjust maintenance intervals for each part by automatically integrating this information into service scheduling, thus, minimizing maintenance cost.

*Example 3.* For predictive analysis of turbines, the diagnostic engineer may want to be automatically notified when a turbine shows repetitive start failures combined with increased vibration values during its operating time. This can be formulated as follows:

> *Notify me if a turbine that had more than three start failures in the last two weeks additionally shows abnormal vibration values in operative phases.*    ∎

## 2.3   Siemens Requirements

The main bottleneck for diagnostics is the data gathering part, which takes up to 80% of the overall diagnostic time. The main reason is that finding the *right* data for analytics is very hard due to limitations of predefined queries, complexity of data, complexity of query formulation, and limitation to explicitly stated information. We now derive concrete requirements that a system for supporting diagnostic process should fulfill.

**R1: Integrated Data Access.** Siemens data over which the queries are formulated naturally reflects the variety, volume, and velocity dimensions of Big Data. The data is stored in so-called data centres, each responsible for several thousand of appliances such as turbines, where a typical turbine has about 2,000 sensors constantly producing measurements. This data can be roughly grouped into three categories: *(i)* sensor and event data from appliances, *(ii)* analytical data obtained as results of monitoring tasks conducted by service centres for the last several years, and *(iii)* miscellaneous data, typically stored in XML, contains technical description of appliances, types of configurations for appliances, indicates in which databases information from sensors is stored, history of whether forecasts, etc. All in all the data is stored in several thousand databases having a large of different schemata. The size of the data in the order of hundreds of terabytes, e.g., there is about 15 GB of data associated to a single turbine, and it currently grows with the average rate of 30 GB per day. At the moment there is no unified access point to the Siemens data and it is required.

**R2: Flexible Definition of Queries.** Existing predefined queries in the Siemens query catalogue, about 4,000 queries, are often not sufficient to cover information needs as they are often either too general, thus yielding an overload of irrelevant information, or too specific, thus not providing enough relevant data. For gathering relevant data, service engineers often have to use several queries and combine their results. When this is not sufficient, existing queries have to be modified or new queries should be created. To this end the engineer contacts an IT expert and this leads to a complex and time-consuming interaction that takes up to weeks. The reason why it takes so long is miscommunication, high workload of IT personnel, complexity of query formulation, and long query execution times. In average up to 35 queries require modification every month, and up to 10% of queries are changed throughout a year. Moreover, several new queries are developed monthly. Therefore, flexible modification and definition of queries is one of the strong requirements for the improvement of the diagnostic process.

**R3: Utilising Implicit Information.** In databases it is typically assumed that only explicit data matters, i.e., the data which is stored in the system. From a formal perspective, they adopt the so-called *closed-world* semantics, meaning that exactly the information stated is true, and anything not stated is false. While this perspective may be valid in the context of controlled systems, completeness of data is hardly ever the case in practical industry applications such as the ones in Siemens. Here, the fact that we do not have a measurement tuple for a certain time point does not mean there is no

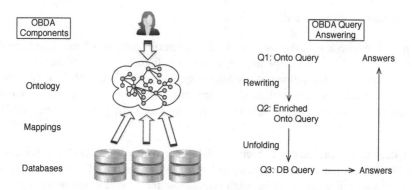

**Fig. 2.** OBDA: components and a general idea of query processing

measurement. This could be reflected by the so-called *open-world* semantics, that allows to derive *implicit information* from the data stated explicitly, typically using some forms of background knowledge. This implicit information logically follows from what is stated explicitly, and its use can greatly increase the practical benefit of a diagnostic system.

**R4: Stream Data Processing.** Predictive analysis requires the use of both static information from the past and streaming information on the current status of appliances. Access to data from the past allows to detect, for instance, seasonal patterns. Continuous monitoring of the streaming data provides prognoses for key performance indicators and countermeasures before a system shutdown occurs. Currently, service engineers do not have a direct access to streaming data. However, engineers often need to access event and sensor data from several appliances, and as of now it requires downloading streaming data for each related turbine. One of the requirements for the predictive analysis is the possibility to integrate sensor and event streaming data from several turbines and diagnostic centres and provide the use of continuous queries on data streams.

Summing up on the requirements above, Siemens needs a solution that naturally integrates the existing databases, allows for flexible query definition, exploits both explicit and implicit data, and allows for processing (multiple) data streams. The last technical requirement for a desired solution naturally arises from practical considerations:

**R5: System Deployment and Maintenance Support.** The cost of the deployment and maintenance of the proposed solution should not exceed the benefits from the use of the system. In particular, the solution should support semi-automatic deployment over Siemens databases.

In the next section we present an approach that addresses these requirements.

## 3   Ontology Based Data Access

Ontology Based Data Access (OBDA) is a prominent approach for end-user oriented access to databases. OBDA relies on Semantic Web technologies and it has been heavily studied by the Semantic Web community [2, 7].

The main idea behind OBDA is to provide a user with access to the data via an *ontology* that is specific to the user's domain. The ontology can be written in some ontology language, e.g., in the Web Ontology Language OWL 2 standardised by W3C. This ontology hides from the user technical details about the database schemata while it exhibits to the user a domain specific vocabulary of classes and properties i.e., unary and binary predicates, that the user is familiar with. This vocabulary is related to the database schemata via *mappings*, which are declarative specifications, similar to view definitions in databases. There are several mapping languages available, e.g., R2RML standardised by W3C. Figure 2 presents a general conceptual diagram illustrating OBDA: its main components and the workflow of query answering in OBDA systems.

The user formulates queries over ontologies in terms of the classes and properties. The standard query language for ontologies is SPARQL 1.1 standardised by W3C. An ontological query $Q_1$ is evaluated over databases in three steps. First, $Q_1$ is expanded with relevant information from the ontology in order to retrieve both explicit and implicit answers from the databases. This is accomplished by *query rewriting*, which takes the query $Q_1$ and the ontology, and produces the query $Q_2$. Note that $Q_2$ is logically equivalent to $Q_1$ with respect to the ontology while it "absorbs" a fragment of the ontology necessary for retrieving all answers relevant to $Q_1$. We refer the reader to, e.g., [8], for details on query rewriting techniques. OBDA systems typically do rewriting of so-called *conjunctive queries* with ontologies that fall in the OWL 2 QL profile of OWL 2. This profile is specifically tailored for data access and allows for efficient query processing [8]. As the second step, the query $Q_2$ is translated using mappings into a query $Q_3$ over the database schemata, e.g., into SQL when the data is relational. This step is referred to as *unfolding*. Finally, $Q_3$ is executed over the data by a DBMS and the answers are returned to the user.

We now illustrate OBDA on the following example which is based on the ontology and mappings that we developed for the Siemens use case. Note that, for the sake of clarity, the example is based on simplified versions of these ontology and mappings.

*Example 4.* The ontology in Figure 3 says that turbines can be either gas or diesel. A gas turbine may have the following parts: *(i)* a control system that in turn has a control unit of types ART or ART2, *(ii)* inner turbine, *(iii)* lube-oil system that may have several sensors for measuring pressure, and *(iv)* gearbox. Moreover, a gas turbine can be located in a place such as a desert, or a frost, etc. For the sake of simplicity, we assume that diesel turbines are modelled in the same way as the gas ones.

The query in Figure 3 asks: *"Return the pressure measured by sensors of lube oil systems in turbines."* This is an ontological query which corresponds to $Q_1$ in Figure 2. This query can be written in SPARQL as follows:

```
SELECT ?Measurement
WHERE {?X rdf:type siemens:Turbine. ?X siemens:hasPart ?Y.
       ?Y rdf:type siemens:LubeOilSystem.
       ?Y siemens:hasSensor ?Z. ?Z rdf:type siemens:Sensor.
       ?Z siemens:hasPressure ?Measurement.}
```

Query rewriting techniques applied to this query and the turbine ontology produce two more queries that have the same structure, as $Q_1$, but the first query has Gas Turbine and the second one has Diesel Turbine in the place of Turbine. The query $Q_2$ is the

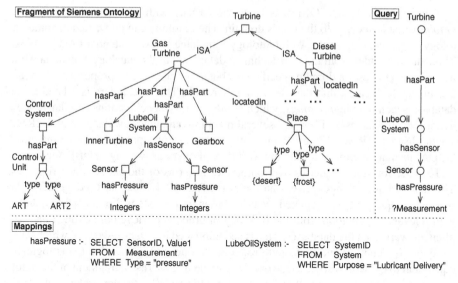

**Fig. 3.** Simplified Siemens ontology and mappings, example query

union of $Q_1$ with these two queries. In terms of SPARQL, $Q_2$ can be obtained from $Q_1$ by substituting the first triple of its WHERE clause with the following expression:

```
{ ?X rdf:type siemens:Turbine } UNION
{ ?X rdf:type siemens:GasTurbine } UNION
{ ?X rdf:type siemens:DieselTurbine }
```

There are two mappings in Figure 3. The left one says how to "populate" the property hasPressure: one has to project tuples of the table Measurement, where the value of the attribute Type is "pressure". The projection on the attribute SensorID gives the subject and on the attribute Value1 gives the object of hasPressure. The right mapping says how to "populate" the class LubeOilSystem: one has to project tuples of the table System where the Purpose is "Lubricant Delivery" on the SystemID attribute. These mappings can be used to unfold the SPARQL query $Q_2$ into an SQL query $Q_3$. We do not give $Q_3$ here due to space limit since this would require to introduce six more mappings. ■

### 3.1   How OBDA Can Help in Improving Data Access in Siemens

In Section 2.3, we presented five Siemens data access requirements. We will discuss now how OBDA naturally addresses all of them and thus we believe that OBDA has a potential in improving data access in Siemens.

OBDA naturally addresses Requirement R1 on integrated data access since one ontology can mediate the user and several databases with different formats via mappings. Regarding Requirement R2 on flexible definition of queries, since ontologies describe the domain of end users, formulation of queries over ontologies is conceptually much easier than over databases. Thus, by relying on intuitive query formulation tools, users can combine existing queries and write new queries without any knowledge of the schemata of multiple databases residing behind the ontology. Regarding Requirement R3 on utilising implicit information, OBDA naturally does so via logical reasoning during the query rewriting process. Regarding Requirement R4 on stream data processing, OBDA is powerful enough in addressing this, e.g., by employing temporal ontologies, mappings, and queries involving temporal operators. Regarding Requirement R5 on system installation support, there is a body of work on semi-automatic ontology and mapping discovery as well as bootstrapping techniques that allow to extract ontologies and mappings from relational schemata.

Thus, what we need for Siemens is an OBDA system that *(i)* supports distributed data processing, *(ii)* provides a flexible intuitive query formulation and visualisation support, *(iii)* relies on logical reasoning to obtain both explicit and implicit answers, *(iv)* accommodates temporal and data steams, and *(v)* allows to bootstrap, edit, and reuse ontologies and mappings. As we see next, no such OBDA system exists.

### 3.2 Existing OBDA Systems and Their Limitations

We now show that, despite the recent advances in OBDA systems, they are currently not mature enough to be applied off-the-shelf in Siemens and both theoretical and practical developments are required. There are several academic and industrial systems for OBDA or that are very similar to OBDA in spirit. Mastro [9], morph-RDB [10], and Ontop [11] support ontology reasoning and thus address Requirement R3, while D2RQ [12], OntoQF [13], Virtuoso[2], Spyder[3], and Ultrawrap [14] do not support reasoning and thus fail Requirement R3. Moreover, all these systems fail Requirement R2: Ultrawrap, Ontop, Mastro, and morph-RDB lack user-oriented query formulation interfaces and query visualisation; they provide SPARQL end-points and predefined queries; OntoQF considers ontology queries as OWL statements and has no visual query formulation support. To the best of our knowledge, there are no OBDA systems that support streaming queries of Requirement R4 and address distributed query processing of Requirement R1. Ontop and Mastro support a limited form of data federation, which is not sufficient to allow for data integration of R1. Ontop provides a restricted deployment support in the form of bootstrapping, while OntoQF, Mastro, and morph-RDB lack it. Ultrawrap extended with QODI system [15] allows for so-called query-driven ontology alignment that can allow to import existing ontologies and thus facilitate installation of OBDA systems. Virtuoso, Spyder, and D2RQ provide a limited installation support via direct mapping bootstrappers and simple user interfaces for navigating the data graph. However, no advanced mapping management of Requirement R5 is supported.

In the following section we will overview the Optique platform [4, 5], that addresses the limitations of existing systems discussed above, and is adopted for Siemens.

## 4   Enhancing OBDA Technology for Siemens

The Optique platform is an end-to-end OBDA solution, i.e., it supports the whole OBDA cycle from deployment to query answer visualisation. Optique platform integrates a number of existing systems and provides several new components. It was tested

---

[2] http://virtuoso.openlinksw.com/

[3] http://www.revelytix.com/content/spyder

with various use cases, including Norwegian Petroleum Directorate Fact Pages [16], and demonstrated in [17].[4] We now give an overview of the platform. Details on the architecture and the individual components of the platform cab be found in [17, 5] and by following the references given below.

## 4.1  Optique Platform

The system is currently under development and it allows to: *(a)* create and edit mappings, *(b)* create, edit, and import ontologies, *(c)* integrate several relational databases and data streams, *(d)* formulate and visualise one time and continuous queries, and *(e)* browse query results. Thus, the Optique platform satisfies all the Siemens system Requirements R1-R5. Note that the current version provides only a limited support of distributed query processing and a limited treatment of temporal and streaming data.

We now discuss the workflow of the system. For the system deployment, one can bootstrap ontologies and mappings from the underlying relational data sources, incorporate external ontologies into the system, and edit ontologies and mappings [18]. This heavily relies on logical reasoning, for which we use the HermiT ontology reasoner [19]. After the system is deployed, the underlying data sources can be queried via our query formulation tools. They allow to compose queries by navigation over the system's ontology, by writing natural language queries, and rely on ontology reasoning (with HermiT). The formulated queries are internally translated into SPARQL queries and sent to the query transformation engine for processing: rewriting against the ontology and further unfolding into SQL queries with the mappings [20]. For rewriting and unfolding, we rely on the Ontop query transformation engine [11]. SQL queries are executed over the data sources underlying the system by the DBMSs of the sources. For distributed query planning [21] and processing of temporal queries [22], we rely on the ADP system [23], which is a system for large scale elastic data processing on the cloud, which, in particular, is needed to cope with the huge data sets provided by Siemens. Both Ontop and ADP are integral components of the Optique platform. Resulting query answers are visualised using templates and widgets such as tables, timelines, maps, charts, etc., depending on the data modalities. The Optique platform implementation is based on the Information Workbench (IWB) [24], a generic and extensible platform for semantic data management which provides a rich infrastructure for platform.

We now consider two aspects of the platform specific for Siemens in detail: its diagnostics dashboard for query formulation and answer visualisation, and temporal and streaming processing part.

## 4.2  Diagnostics Dashboard

In order to address diverse needs of end users in query formulation and answer visualisation we developed a flexible wiki-based *Diagnostic Dashboard* that can be easily customised by end users themselves. In Figure 4 we illustrate the engineer's work cycle with the platform through the dashboard. Engineers can define and refine queries via

---

[4] Optique demo video: www.youtube.com/user/optiqueproject/playlists

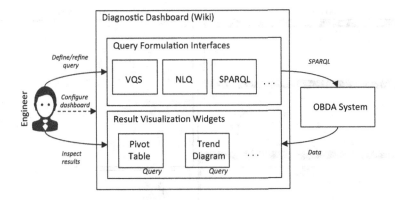

**Fig. 4.** Components of Diagnostic Dashboard

several query formulation tools, that include *(i)* Visual Query System (VQS), *(ii)* Natural Language Query (NLQ) interface, and *(iii)* SPARQL query editor. In the upper part of Figure 5 we present screenshots of our VQS, SPARQL editor embedded in it, as well as our NLQ interface. VQS depicts the domain of interest and queries using a graph based representation paradigm, so end users can directly manipulate visual objects and construct queries. VQL combines query-by-navigation and faceted search techniques over an underlying ontology graph (see [25, 26] for more details). NLQ allows users to specify a query by means of a controlled natural language. Sentences written by engineers are parsed and mapped to concepts, properties, and individuals of the underlying ontology, taking into account ontological axioms. Then, based on additional rules, the the result of the mapping is translated into a SPARQL query (see [27] for more details).

Result visualisation widgets allow to visualise query answers, inspect query results, do incremental query refinement, and export of relevant result fragments to external diagnostic tools. Moreover, the widgets allow to perform monitoring of incoming data streams and query answers for continuos queries over these streams. In the lower part of Figure 5 we present four examples of our visualisation widgets. Depending on the type of data (e.g., time series data, appliance structure), a suitable visualisation paradigm has to be selected (e.g., pivot table, trend diagram, histogram). The diagnostic dashboard can also choose the representation paradigm for query answers automatically by analysing the corresponding SPARQL query.

## 4.3 Temporalised and Streamified OBDA

Recent efforts on temporalised [28, 29] and streamified [30, 31, 32] OBDA systems provide first steps towards handling temporal and streaming data in industrial applications. However, none of these approaches satisfies the requirements of the Siemens use case: either there is no implemented engine or it is still not fully developed (see the benchmark tests in [33]). Besides, in all cases some aspects of query processing in temporalised and streamified OBDA are not addressed, e.g., unfolding with mappings, ontology reasoning.

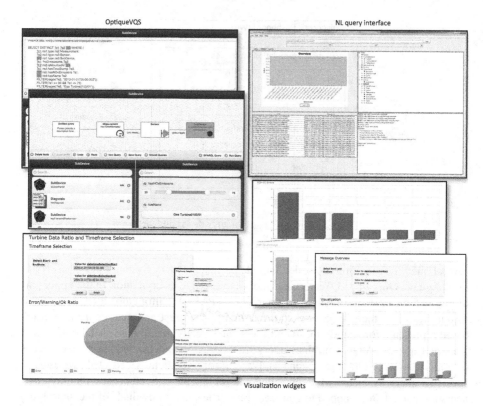

**Fig. 5.** Query formulation and data visualisation interfaces provided by the software demonstrator

Streaming and Temporal ontology Access with a Reasoning-based Query Language (*STARQL*) [34, 35] offers a query framework allowing to deal with streams of time-stamped RDF triples on the background of mappings and an ontology. The development of STARQL was inspired by the Siemens use case requirements. The STARQL query language framework and the prototype streaming engine enjoy the following features:

*Expressivity.* STARQL allows to express typical mathematical, statistical, and event pattern features needed in real-time monitoring scenarios. In spite of its expressivity, answering STARQL queries is still efficient since they can be transformed into relational stream queries.

*Neat Semantics.* STARQL comes with a formal syntax and semantics. The latter one uses certain answer semantics [7] and on top of it, first-order logic semantics as in model checking, thereby combining open and closed-world reasoning. A snapshot semantics for window operators [36] is extended with a sequencing semantics that can handle integrity constraints such as functionality assertions.

*Orthogonality.* Both inputs and outputs of STARQL queries are timestamped RDF triples. Therefore, triples, coming from the result of one query, can be used as input when constructing another query.

*Scope Locality.* While producing a SPARQL query, one can select an ontology and streams over which the query will be evaluated. This feature can be important in different cases, e.g., in the case of failure testing, where one is interested in querying only the streams stemming from sensors which are (or are not) suspected to be broken.

*Library Functions.* Often-used query patterns can be stored in the special library and re-used during query construction.

Now we illustrate the STARQL framework by example.

*Example 5.* Consider the preventive monitoring request from Example 1. To fulfill it, the following sub-task should be performed: *"Detect a monotonic increase from the temperature sensor"*. We now see how this detection can be done within the STARQL framework.

First, assume that the data stream S_Msmt is being received from the sensor; its sub-stream that contains data received during the first five seconds is as follows:

$$\{\{\text{s0} : \text{val } 90\}<0\text{s}>, \{\text{s0} : \text{val } 93\}<1\text{s}>, \{\text{s0} : \text{val } 94\}<2\text{s}>,$$
$$\{\text{s0} : \text{val } 92\}<3\text{s}>, \{\text{s0} : \text{val } 93\}<4\text{s}> , \{\text{s0} : \text{val } 95\}<5\text{s}>\}. \quad (1)$$

This data is in the form of timestamped RDF triples. For example, the first triple $\{\text{s0} : \text{val } 90\}<0\text{s}>$ says that at the time point "0s" the sensor s0 sent the value 90.

Consider the following STARQL query fulfilling the task:

```
CREATE      STREAM S_out_1 AS
SELECT      {s0 rdf:type RMInc}<NOW>
FROM        S_Msmt [NOW-2s, NOW] -> 1s
SEQUENCE    BY StdSeq AS SEQ
HAVING      FORALL i < j IN SEQ, ?x, ?y:
            IF {s0 :val ?x}<i> AND {s0 :val ?y}<j> THEN ?x <= ?y
```

Intuitively, the structure of the query is as follows:

- The HAVING clause specifies that the sensor's value should monotonically increase.
- The FROM clause tells that the query performs its check every second, considering only the data from the stream S_Msmt in the last two seconds.
- The SEQUENCE BY clause groups the output triples using some standard method StdSeq.
- The CREATE clause declares the query's output stream S_out_1.
- The SELECT clause determines the format of the timestamped RDF triples in the output stream. For instance, the output stream corresponding to the input data stream from Equation (1) is

$$\{\{\text{s0 rdf:type RMInc}\}<0\text{s}>, \{\text{s0 rdf:type RMInc}\}<1\text{s}>,$$
$$\{\text{s0 rdf:type RMInc}\}<2\text{s}>, \{\text{s0 rdf:type RMInc}\}<5\text{s}>\},$$

where RMInc stands for Resent Monotonic Increase, so the timestamped RDF triple $\{\text{s0 rdf:type RMInc}\}<2\text{s}>$ designates that the sensor s0 has been experiencing a monotonic increase for the last two seconds, from 0s to 2s.

Under the OBDA approach, data is stored in databases, and not in RDF format. Hence, the STARQL engine operates on a virtual stream induced by mappings from the stream S_Msmt. In Optique, we are going to use a stream extended version of ADP [23].    ∎

## 5    Demonstrating Capabilities of Extended OBDA at Siemens

In order to demonstrate the potential of OBDA in enhancing data access in Siemens we did a preliminary deployment of the Optique OBDA platform over Siemens data and conducted a preliminary user study. We now give details of our experience.

### 5.1    Demonstration System

We customised the Optique platform for Siemens and extended it with several components. The demonstration runs on a server with four 8-core Intel64 processors, 512 GB RAM, and 7 TB of internal and 24 TB of external storage.

*Data for the demonstration.* We installed the platform over databases with 3 TB of historical sensor and event data about 200 gas and steam turbines (15 GB per turbine) gathered between 2002 and 2011. We also developed a data stream generator that simulates the original sensor measurements and events streaming from these turbines.

*Demonstration ontology.* Although there are ontologies describing machinery with sensors, e.g., the Semantic Sensor Network (SSN) ontology [37], we could not use them: for our use case, they are too generic and overloaded with irrelevant terms, moreover, they miss required terms. Therefore, we constructed our ontologies being guided by the best practices of the SSN ontology. Our ontologies characterize Siemens database schemata of sensor and event data and abstract away from representations varying across data sources. Moreover, our ontologies are manually enriched with the domain information encoded in multiple semiformal and informal models available at Siemens. We developed three ontologies: *(i)* the turbine, *(ii)* sensor, and *(iii)* diagnostic ontology.

The *turbine ontology* describes the internal structure of a turbine, i.e., it lists all its parts, functional units, and their hierarchy. For example, it models that every Turbine must have a ControlSystem and a Generator, and that LiquidFuelPump is a part of a LubOilSystem. The ontology contains 60 classes and 15 object and data properties. There are three central classes in this ontology: *(i)* Turbine class for modeling product families of appliances, *(ii)* Component for modeling a hierarchy of subclasses defining the types of components that turbines are constructed of, using relations such as hasPart and hasDirectPart, *(iii)* FunctionalUnit for defining functional interrelation of components, i.e., important blocks of an appliance, such as GasPath, FuelSystem and others, as well as components belonging to these functional units.

The *sensor ontology* lists and categorizes types of sensors and measuring devices mounted in a turbine as well as their deployment, measurements properties, such as accuracy and precision, and other related information. For example, it models that each sensor is mounted at some turbine's component or functional unit, or that a sensor of a specific type does only produce observations of a given type. The ontology contains 40 classes and 20 properties. The main class `Sensor` covers all types of measuring devices, e.g., `GasDetector`, `TemperatureSensor`. Further branching on classes gives more detailed characteristics information on them, e.g., temperature sensors could measure: `BurnerTipTemperature`, `InletTemperature`, `CompressorExitTemperature`, etc.

The *diagnostics ontology* formalizes relationships between measurements and events generated in by turbine's sensors and control units as well as typical symptoms of faults in turbines. For example, it models that each diagnosis has to be assigned to a turbine or its component, and must be supported by some symptoms. The ontology contains 30 classes and 10 properties. The core classes are `Observation` and `Diagnosis` connected with a relation `indicatesAt` for listing symptoms for each diagnosis.

Each of the three ontologies can be used independently and we also developed an ontology that integrates the three. The turbine and sensor ontologies are expressed in OWL 2 QL, a tractable profile of the OWL 2 ontology language and therefore can be used straightforwardly in our OBDA setting. The diagnostics ontology must be represented in a richer ontology language: OWL 2 DL. An example of a diagnostic axiom that cannot be expressed in OWL 2 QL is: "If `Turbine` has `Failure` F1, then there must be a `Symptom` S1 in `Turbine Component` C1". To support answering diagnostic queries using OBDA, we provided an approximation of the ontology into OWL 2 QL.

### 5.2 Preliminary Evaluation at Siemens

We used a two-fold approach to assess the system capabilities at Siemens: *(i)* a query catalog constructed based on the functionality requirements, *(ii)* a user workshop conducted with service engineers to get a feedback from the end users.

*Query catalogue.* Based on interviews of service engineers and their needs on data acquisitions, we constructed a query catalogue with 27 query patterns from reactive and preventive diagnostics of turbines. This catalogue served as a basis for the development of the temporal query language STARQL (see Section 4.3). There are two types of query patterns: *(i)* on events and measurements, and *(ii)* on diagnostics that requires the usage of semantic knowledge. Query patterns of Type (i) allow to aggregate available sensor values and/or events, generate statistics and visualise results as bar charts and graphical models. An example of such query is "Return the TOP 10 errors and warnings for turbines of product family X". Moreover, some of the query patterns require the usage of temporal operators, e.g., "List sensor values and events within a specific time interval, before an event X occurred". Patterns of Type (ii) reveal interdependency and correlations between *(a)* the occurrence of events, *(b)* sensor measurements, and *(c)* occurrence of events and presence of specific sensor values. An example of a diagnostics query is "Which events frequently occur before the specific point in time?".

We analysed the coverage of the query catalog by the STARQL query language. Though within the development of the STARQL query language the focus was on handling streaming data, it also supports purely temporal reasoning on historical data—which is needed for reactive diagnostics. This can be achieved by considering the time window as a static time filter for the relevant time interval (thereby setting the slide to 0) and then to express the needed patterns in the HAVING clause. With this approach, currently, approximately 70% of the query patterns in the catalog can be expressed within STARQL, although some of the queries have to rely on calls to external functions from the ADP system, which provides statistical and mathematical functions.

*User workshop.* We demonstrated the customised Optique platform at the Siemens service centre in Lincoln, UK, and conducted a preliminary evaluation of the system with IT experts and service engineers. The goal of the evaluation was to obtain an initial feedback from the end users which reinforced and guided our further development of the platform. In particular, the end users were asked to assess the system with respect to the requirements of Section 2. We now summarize the feedback.

The users gave a positive feedback on how the proposed solution addressed Requirement R1 on the integrated data access: information from different source is integrated and can be accessed through one ontology and visualised in the diagnostics dashboard. The users provided also a very positive feedback to the query formulation components of Requirement R2 and highlighted that these facilities may greatly simplify and accelerate the process of query construction. In particular, by using the VQS and the NLQ interface the users were able to specify even complex queries from the query catalogue in a very intuitive way, which currently requires extensive SQL know-how as well as in-depth knowledge about the database schemata. Additionally, component suggestions on refinements and/or generalisations of the terms used in the query, additional terms and constraints helped the users in understanding the querying capabilities of the platform and in constructing queries, which was highly valued by the users. Likewise, we received good comments on the possibility to derive implicit information using the logical reasoning—thereby satisfying Requirement R3. The streaming support defined in Requirement R4 which is addressed by introducing STARQL query framework was highly welcomed as an important feature for realizing predictive maintenance in future. The ontology and mapping deployment and management support of Requirement R5 was evaluated by the users as crucial to keep the diagnostic knowledge up-to-date.

# 6   Conclusion and Future Work

In this paper we presented OBDA, a promising paradigm to provide a direct end-user access to data, and how OBDA could enhance this access in Siemens. We derived five requirements that an OBDA solution should fulfill in order to be deployed in Siemens and showed that, while the previous research and system development established the theoretical basis and demonstrated viability of OBDA, a number of limitations have to be solved before industrial deployment of such systems. We then presented an OBDA solution developed within the Optique project that satisfies the five Siemens requirements. We focused on two aspects of the platform specific for Siemens: *(i)* visualisation dashboard and *(ii)* the support of temporal and streaming queries. We also presented preliminary evaluation of the solution at Siemens where we got a positive feedback.

During the evaluation we determined several items to address on our ongoing work on the platform. One of the core questions is the ontology development: The diagnostics ontology is expressed in OWL 2 DL which is not natively supported by the system. Therefore, ontology approximation techniques are strongly required in order to extensively use the knowledge provided by the domain. Also, current ontologies were constructed manually based on formal as well as informal models of the domain. However, bootstrapping information from database schemata, previously executed queries, and already existing formal models and ontology has to be used to reduce manual efforts. Additionally, a possibility to import existing ontologies is strongly needed to support integration of existing ontologies with the ones manually developed.

Another direction of system improvement is the diagnostics dashboard. During the evaluation at Siemens the users pointed out two functionalities that were missing in the demonstrated system: *(i)* reports that incorporate marketing or business intelligence queries, e.g., "Return all gas turbine of a particular product line sold after 2006", and *(ii)* query interface feature with provenance of query answers and suggestions on possible query repairs. E.g., if a query returns an empty answer, then the users would like to know why the answer set is empty and how the query can be reformulated to obtain answers. Furthermore, to reach 100% coverage of query catalogue we plan to extend functionality of STARQL. We also work on improving the support of temporal and streaming queries.

Integrating the platform into the Siemens IT environment is another important challenge we have to address during future work. The solution has to be adapted in order to be used with the existing Siemens systems for monitoring and analytics. Also, scaling up the solution for the usage in Siemens monitoring environment leads to the integration of multiple streams and databases. Thus, there is a need for distributed query processing and there is an active work within the Optique project in this direction.

# References

1. Doan, A., Halevy, A.Y., Ives, Z.G.: Principles of Data Integration. Morgan Kaufmann (2012)
2. Kogalovsky, M.R.: Ontology-Based Data Access Systems. Programming and Computer Software 38(4) (2012)
3. Horrocks, I.: What are ontologies good for? In: Evolution of Semantic Systems, pp. 175–188. Springer (2013)
4. Giese, M., Calvanese, D., Horrocks, I., Ioannidis, Y., Klappi, H., Koubarakis, M., Lenzerini, M., Moller, R., Ozcep, O., Rodriguez Muro, M., Rosati, R., Schlatte, R., Soylu, A., Waaler, A.: Scalable end-user access to big data. In: Big Data Computing, Chapman and Hall/CRC (2013)
5. Kharlamov, E., et al.: Optique: Towards OBDA Systems for Industry. In: Cimiano, P., Fernández, M., Lopez, V., Schlobach, S., Völker, J. (eds.) ESWC 2013. LNCS, vol. 7955, pp. 125–140. Springer, Heidelberg (2013)
6. Calvanese, D., et al.: Optique: OBDA solution for big data. In: Cimiano, P., Fernández, M., Lopez, V., Schlobach, S., Völker, J. (eds.) ESWC 2013. LNCS, vol. 7955, pp. 293–295. Springer, Heidelberg (2013)
7. Poggi, A., Lembo, D., Calvanese, D., De Giacomo, G., Lenzerini, M., Rosati, R.: Linking Data to Ontologies. J. Data Semantics 10, 133–173 (2008)

8. Calvanese, D., De Giacomo, G., Lembo, D., Lenzerini, M., Rosati, R.: Tractable reasoning and efficient query answering in Description Logics: The DL-Lite family. J. of Automated Reasoning 39(3), 385–429 (2007)

9. Calvanese, D., De Giacomo, G., Lembo, D., Lenzerini, M., Poggi, A., Rodriguez-Muro, M., Rosati, R., Ruzzi, M., Savo, D.F.: The mastro system for ontology-based data access. Semantic Web 2(1), 43–53 (2011)

10. Priyatna, F., Corcho, O., Sequeda, J.: Formalisation and Experiences of R2RML-based SPARQL to SQL Query Translation Using Morph. In: WWW (2014)

11. Rodriguez-Muro, M., Kontchakov, R., Zakharyaschev, M.: Obda with ontop. In: ORE, pp. 101–106 (2013)

12. Bizer, C., Seaborne, A.: D2RQ-Treating non-RDF Databases as Virtual RDF Graphs. In: ISWC (2004)

13. Munir, K., Odeh, M., McClatchey, R.: Ontology-driven relational query formulation using the semantic and assertional capabilities of owl-dl. Knowl.-Based Syst. 35, 144–159 (2012)

14. Sequeda, J.F., Miranker, D.P.: Ultrawrap: SPARQL execution on relational data. J. of Web Sem. 22 (2013)

15. Tian, A., Sequeda, J.F., Miranker, D.P.: QODI: Query as Context in Automatic Data Integration. In: Alani, H., et al. (eds.) ISWC 2013, Part I. LNCS, vol. 8218, pp. 624–639. Springer, Heidelberg (2013)

16. Skjæveland, M.G., Lian, E.H., Horrocks, I.: Publishing the Norwegian Petroleum Directorate's FactPages as Semantic Web Data. In: Alani, H., et al. (eds.) ISWC 2013, Part II. LNCS, vol. 8219, pp. 162–177. Springer, Heidelberg (2013)

17. Kharlamov, E., Giese, M., Jiménez-Ruiz, E., Skjæveland, M.G., Soylu, A., Zheleznyakov, D., Bagosi, T., Console, M., Haase, P., Horrocks, I., Marciuska, S., Pinkel, C., Rodriguez-Muro, M., Ruzzi, M., Santarelli, V., Savo, D.F., Sengupta, K., Schmidt, M., Thorstensen, E., Trame, J., Waaler, A.: Optique 1.0: Semantic Access to Big Data: The Case of Norwegian Petroleum Directorate's FactPages. In: ISWC (Posters & Demos) (2013)

18. Haase, P., Horrocks, I., Hovland, D., Hubauer, T., Jiménez-Ruiz, E., Kharlamov, E., Klüwer, J.W., Pinkel, C., Rosati, R., Santarelli, V., Soylu, A., Zheleznyakov, D.: Optique system: towards ontology and mapping management in obda solutions. In: WoDOOM, pp. 21–32 (2013)

19. Glimm, B., Horrocks, I., Motik, B., Stoilos, G.: Optimising Ontology Classification. In: Patel-Schneider, P.F., Pan, Y., Hitzler, P., Mika, P., Zhang, L., Pan, J.Z., Horrocks, I., Glimm, B. (eds.) ISWC 2010, Part I. LNCS, vol. 6496, pp. 225–240. Springer, Heidelberg (2010)

20. Calvanese, D., Horrocks, I., Jiménez-Ruiz, E., Kharlamov, E., Meier, M., Rodriguez-Muro, M., Zheleznyakov, D.: On rewriting, answering queries in obda systems for big data. In: OWLED (2013)

21. Kllapi, H., Bilidas, D., Horrocks, I., Ioannidis, Y.E., Jiménez-Ruiz, E., Kharlamov, E., Koubarakis, M., Zheleznyakov, D.: Distributed query processing on the cloud: the optique point of view. In: OWLED (2013)

22. Horrocks, I., Hubauer, T., Jiménez-Ruiz, E., Kharlamov, E., Koubarakis, M., Möller, R., Bereta, K., Neuenstadt, C., Özçep, Ö.L., Roshchin, M., Smeros, P., Zheleznyakov, D.: Addressing streaming and historical data in obda systems: Optique's approach. In: KNOW@LOD, pp. 33–40 (2013)

23. Tsangaris, M.M., Kakaletris, G., Kllapi, H., Papanikos, G., Pentaris, F., Polydoras, P., Sitaridi, E., Stoumpos, V., Ioannidis, Y.E.: Dataflow processing and optimization on grid and cloud infrastructures. IEEE Data Eng. Bull. 32(1), 67–74 (2009)

24. Haase, P., Hütter, C., Schmidt, M., Schwarte, A.: The Information Workbench as a Self-Service Platform for Linked Data Applications. In: WWW (2012)

25. Soylu, A., Giese, M., Jimenez-Ruiz, E., Kharlamov, E., Zheleznyakov, D., Horrocks, I.: OptiqueVQS – Towards an Ontology-Based Visual Query System for Big Data. In: MEDES (2013)
26. Soylu, A., Skjæveland, M.G., Giese, M., Horrocks, I., Jimenez-Ruiz, E., Kharlamov, E., Zheleznyakov, D.: A preliminary approach on ontology-based visual query formulation for big data. In: Garoufallou, E., Greenberg, J. (eds.) MTSR 2013. Communications in Computer and Information Science, vol. 390, pp. 201–212. Springer, Heidelberg (2013)
27. Waltinger, U., Tecuci, D., Olteanu, M., Mocanu, V., Sullivan, S.: Natural language access to enterprise data. AI Magazine 35(1), 38–52 (2014)
28. Artale, A., Kontchakov, R., Wolter, F., Zakharyaschev, M.: Temporal description logic for ontology-based data access. In: IJCAI 2013, pp. 711–717 (2013)
29. Borgwardt, S., Lippmann, M., Thost, V.: Temporal query answering in the description logic DL-lite. In: Fontaine, P., Ringeissen, C., Schmidt, R.A. (eds.) FroCoS 2013. LNCS, vol. 8152, pp. 165–180. Springer, Heidelberg (2013)
30. Barbieri, D.F., Braga, D., Ceri, S., Valle, E.D., Grossniklaus, M.: C-sparql: a continuous query language for rdf data streams. Int. J. Semantic Computing 4(1), 3–25 (2010)
31. Calbimonte, J.P., Corcho, O., Gray, A.J.G.: Enabling Ontology-Based Access to Streaming Data Sources. In: Patel-Schneider, P.F., Pan, Y., Hitzler, P., Mika, P., Zhang, L., Pan, J.Z., Horrocks, I., Glimm, B. (eds.) ISWC 2010, Part I. LNCS, vol. 6496, pp. 96–111. Springer, Heidelberg (2010)
32. Le-Phuoc, D., Dao-Tran, M., Xavier Parreira, J., Hauswirth, M.: A native and adaptive approach for unified processing of linked streams and linked data. In: Aroyo, L., Welty, C., Alani, H., Taylor, J., Bernstein, A., Kagal, L., Noy, N., Blomqvist, E. (eds.) ISWC 2011, Part I. LNCS, vol. 7031, pp. 370–388. Springer, Heidelberg (2011)
33. Zhang, Y., Duc, P.M., Corcho, O., Calbimonte, J.-P.: SRBench: A Streaming RDF/SPARQL Benchmark. In: Cudré-Mauroux, P., et al. (eds.) ISWC 2012, Part I. LNCS, vol. 7649, pp. 641–657. Springer, Heidelberg (2012)
34. Özçep, Ö.L., Möller, R., Neuenstadt, C., Zheleznyakov, D., Kharlamov, E.: Deliverable D5.1 – a semantics for temporal and stream-based query answering in an OBDA context. In: Deliverable FP7-318338, EU (2013)
35. Özçep, Ö.L., Möller, R., Neuenstadt, C.: Obda stream access combined with safe first-order temporal reasoning. Technical report, Hamburg University of Technology (2014)
36. Arasu, A., Babu, S., Widom, J.: The CQL Continuous Query Language: Semantic Foundations and Query Execution. The VLDB Journal 15(2), 121–142 (2006), doi:10.1007/s00778-004-0147-z
37. Compton, M., Barnaghi, P.M., Bermudez, L., Garcia-Castro, R., Corcho, Ó., Cox, S., Graybeal, J., Hauswirth, M., Henson, C.A., Herzog, A., Huang, V.A., Janowicz, K., Kelsey, W.D., Phuoc, D.L., Lefort, L., Leggieri, M., Neuhaus, H., Nikolov, A., Page, K.R., Passant, A., Sheth, A.P., Taylor, K.: The SSN Ontology of the W3C Semantic Sensor Network Incubator Group. J. Web Sem. 17, 25–32 (2012)

# Author Index